Inside dBASE 5 for Windows

Virginia Andersen
Chris Bolte
Kenneth Chan
Keith Chuvala
Jay Parsons
Richard Wagner
Jim Wetzel

NRP
NEW RIDERS
PUBLISHING
New Riders Publishing, Indianapolis, Indiana

Inside dBASE 5 for Windows

By Virginia Andersen, Chris Bolte, Kenneth Chan, Keith Chuvala, Jay Parsons, Jim Wetzel, Richard Wagner

Published by:
New Riders Publishing
201 West 103rd Street
Indianapolis, IN 46032 USA

Printed in the United States of America 1 2 3 4 5 6 7 8 9 0

Library of Congress Cataloging-in-Publication Data

```
Inside dBASE 5 for Windows / Virginia Andersen ... [et al.]
        p.      cm.
    Includes index.
    ISBN 1-56205-241-1 : $39.99
    1. Data base management. 2. dBASE for Windows. I. Andersen,
Virginia T.
QA76.9.D3I54572  1994
005.75'65--dc20                                          94-27228
                                                          CIP
```


Warning and Disclaimer

This book is designed to provide information about the dBASE computer program. Every effort has been made to make this book as complete and as accurate as possible, but no warranty or fitness is implied.

The information is provided on an "as is" basis. The author and New Riders Publishing shall have neither liability nor responsibility to any person or entity with respect to any loss or damages arising from the information contained in this book or from the use of the disks or programs that may accompany it.

Publisher	Lloyd J. Short
Associate Publisher	Tim Huddleston
Product Development Manager	Rob Tidrow
Marketing Manager	Ray Robinson
Director of Special Projects	Cheri Robinson
Managing Editor	Matthew Morrill

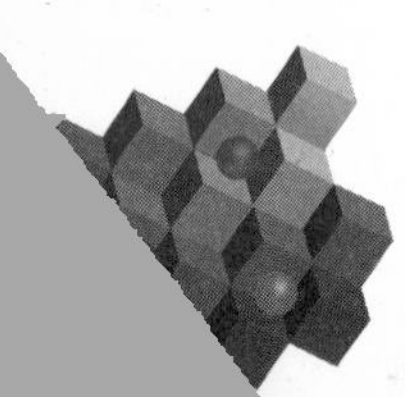

The text in this book is printed on recycled paper.

About the Authors

Virginia Andersen has taught at the university level for fifteen years, teaching at undergraduate and graduate levels in the field of mathematics, computer science, software engineering, and systems analysis. She has been a technical writer for computer science applications for 25 years, and has been an author for several computer books, including several books, including *Inside WordPerfect 6 for Windows* and *Inside 1-2-3 Release 4 for Windows* by New Riders Publishing. She has an M.S. in Systems Management and an M.S. in Computer Science from the University of Southern California, and a B.S. in Mathematics from Stanford University.

Chris Bolte is a computer consultant with Bolte Enterprises in Arcadia, Indiana. He received a B.S. in CS/EE from Rose-Hulman Institute of Technology in 1978. After four years of active duty with the U.S. Army Corps of Engineers, he joined Science Applications International Corporation. He has designed, coded, and documented systems from embedded microprocessors to mainframes.

Kenneth Chan has been programming with dBASE for eight years and answering technical questions for four. A member of Team Borland, he volunteers to answer user questions on CompuServe. He also is the author of several add-on products for dBASE, including LUCTRL, a proportional font engine for LaserJet and PostScript printers, and YAME, a programmer's memo editor. He can be found every month at the meeting of the Database SIG of PIBMUG, the Pasadena IBM User Group.

Keith G. Chuvala is an instructor in computer science at Southwestern College in Winfield, Kansas. He also offers programming and consulting services through his company, KeyStrokes Computer Works. An avid dBASE user and developer, Keith has been a member of Team Borland since 1992. His love of personal computers stems from being rescued from the clutches of a Royal typewriter by an Apple][+ in college, and has carried him from there to computer retailing to programming to consulting and teaching. Keith is a closet musician and songwriter ("People prefer for me to sing in the closet"), holds a degree in Biblical and Ecclesiastical languages, and spends most of his time away from the keyboard with his wife and four sons.

Jay Parsons is a lawyer practicing in Bernardsville, New Jersey, primarily in the fields of taxation, estates and trust. He holds degrees from Princeton University, Harvard University Law School, the Graduate School of Law at New York University, and Fairleigh Dickinson University. He taught himself assembler programming in 1979 and has been programming in dBASE since the early days of dBASE II. He also programs in C, C++, and BASIC and has written numerous ".bin" programs extending the functionality of dBASE, as well as functions and procedures for the dBASE Forum library on CompuServe. He lives with his wife of 31 years in Bernardsville, New Jersey, and has four grown children and two grandchildren. He is a member of the Bars of New York and New Jersey, and of the Tax Court of the United States.

Richard Wagner is a specialist in Windows database management, applications integration, and applications development. He is author of *Inside Microsoft Access, Integrating Windows Applications* and *Inside CompuServe,* all from New Riders Publishing. Besides writing, Richard performs consulting services assisting companies and non-profit organizations to develop customized Windows solutions to their business problems. He also serves as a member of Team Borland, a group of volunteers who provide technical support on the Borland forums on CompuServe. Richard did his undergraduate work at Taylor University in Upland, Indiana and completed graduate studies at The American University in Washington, D.C. He lives in Muncie, Indiana, with his wife and two sons.

Jim Wetzel is an MIS professional, consultant, and shareware author. He lives near Baltimore, Maryland, and is an active member of Team Borland—a group of volunteers that provide assistance to users of Borland products on CompuServe and GEnie. When not on CompuServe or working full time in the MIS department of a large east-coast utility, Jim is active marketing his shareware programs or spending time with his wife, Debbie and his two sons, Paul and Doug. Jim's CompuServe ID is: 75300,2531.

Trademark Acknowledgments

Product Director
Mike Groh

Acquisitions Editor
Alicia Krakovitz

Senior Editor
Tad Ringo

Production Editor
Patrice Hartmann

Editors
Amy Bezak
Kelly Currie
Laura Frey
Cliff Shubs
John Sleeva
Phil Worthington

Technical Editors
Pat Kennedy
Todd Miller
Sal San Phillipo
Bill Valaski

Acquisitions Coordinator
Stacey Beheler

Editorial Assistant
Karen Opal

Publisher's Assistant
Melissa Lynch

Cover Designer
Jean Bisesi

Book Designer
Roger S. Morgan

Production Imprint Manager
Juli Cook

Production Imprint Team Leader
Katy Bodenmiller

Graphics Image Specialists
Tim Montgomery
Dennis Sheehan
Susan VandeWalle

Production Analysts
Dennis Clay Hager
Mary Beth Wakefield

Production Team
Nick Anderson
Jo Anna Arnott
Mona Brown
Elaine Brush
Cheryl Cameron
Mary Ann Cosby
Elaine Crabtree
David Dean
Rob Falco
Angela P. Judy
Greg Kemp
Ayanna Lacey
Jamie Milazzo
Stephanie J. McComb
Shelly Palma
Kim Scott
Susan Shepard
Tonya R. Simpson
Kevin Spear
SA Springer
Dennis Wesner
Michelle Worthington

Indexer
Jeanne Clark

Contents at a Glance

Table of Contents

Introduction

In the summer of 1994, Borland International announced the availability of dBASE for Windows: their long-awaited Windows database product. Combining the best features of the standard Windows interface, the extremely popular dBASE language, and a powerful relational database engine, dBASE for Windows promises to be a major contender in the database market for quite some time.

Borland enjoys the majority share of the DOS database market, and dBASE for Windows adds to the Borland's juggernaut. Unlike many competitors, dBASE for Windows is a true Windows application and was not simply ported from DOS or another operating system. Although dBASE for DOS and dBASE for Windows share certain features, dBASE for Windows was developed explicitly for Windows users. Therefore, the behavior of dBASE for Windows, the dBASE language dialect used in dBASE for Windows, and the menu selections are exactly what you expect from any Windows application. As an experienced Windows user, you will find it very easy to learn the basics of dBASE for Windows.

Like most advanced Windows applications, dBASE for Windows is a complex, sophisticated software product. Although dBASE for Windows features a friendly graphical user interface, the rich feature set and many layers of complexity required to deliver the feature set make learning dBASE for Windows a daunting proposition for even the most skilled developer.

As you read through this section of the book, please keep in mind that the term "dBASE" specifically refers to Borland's dBASE for Windows. Please do not confuse "dBASE" in this context to mean the dBASE for DOS product also available from Borland.

Throughout this introduction and the rest of this book, the expression "Windows" refers to Microsoft Windows 3.1. Although much of the information presented in *Inside dBASE 5 for Windows* applies equally to this product when used under Windows 3.0 or future versions of Windows, this book was designed and written with the Windows 3.1 user in mind.

How This Book Is Different

Inside dBASE 5 for Windows was written to aid the database professional in understanding dBASE principles. Most books about dBASE for Windows dive right into the heart of this exciting application, teaching you how to use dBASE without first making sure you understand why the dBASE for Windows feature set and objects are important to successful database implementation.

Other books treat dBASE at a very superficial level. You simply cannot "learn dBASE for Windows in a day." A "10-minute guide" to dBASE for Windows cannot teach you very much about this complex and sophisticated software product.

Inside dBASE 5 for Windows is an ambitious book. Within these pages, you not only learn to use dBASE for Windows, you also discover what you need to know about the differences between developing dBASE applications under DOS and Windows.

Inside dBASE 5 for Windows Understands Your Database Needs

Database management systems such as dBASE for Windows are strategic applications. You spend a great deal of time and energy designing and implementing your database applications. Furthermore, your data (a very valuable asset) is handled (or mishandled) by the database application you design. It is imperative that your applications be designed with safety, convenience, and efficiency in mind throughout the development process.

Furthermore, advanced applications such as dBASE contain many features that ease the burden of designing and maintaining database applications. You, as the database designer or administrator, need a book that teaches you more than just the mechanics of creating databases with dBASE for Windows. *Inside dBASE 5 for Windows* serves as your guide to the advanced features and capabilities of this database product.

The Authors are dBASE Experts

New Riders Publishing was very fortunate to acquire the select group of authors who wrote *Inside dBASE 5 for Windows.* Every author was an active member of the dBASE beta testing team and has months and months of intensive, practical experience with dBASE for Windows. Each author is a professional database developer who uses dBASE on a daily basis.

How dBASE for Windows Is Different

Many database management systems compete for attention in the PC software market. dBASE for Windows stands out above the crowd for several important reasons.

dBASE Accommodates Both End Users and Database Experts

dBASE was designed from the ground up to address the needs of both the professional database developer and the casual user. Powerful and useful dBASE for Windows databases can be built with a minimum of programming. The Query-By-Example engine built into dBASE for Windows provides an excellent environment for *ad hoc* database queries.

Furthermore, the object-oriented extensions of the dBASE programming language provide a robust platform for developing high-quality database applications. The professional database developer will be pleased with the wealth of functions and features built into the dBASE language and the extendibility of this powerful language.

dBASE for Windows Provides Powerful Design Tools

As you learn in *Inside dBASE 5 for Windows,* many tasks required to produce tables, forms, queries, and reports have been automated in dBASE for Windows. The forms you can create using this database product include common Windows controls such as selection lists, combo boxes, and command buttons. When you need to build a script to automate a task, you will find it very easy to invoke the dBASE edit window to build and debug scripts attached to your form objects.

dBASE for Windows Is a Powerful Relational Database System

dBASE for Windows addresses the demanding needs of the most ambitious database applications. Many thousands of successful databases have already been built using the

DOS version of dBASE. By following the principles and concepts presented in *Inside dBASE 5 for Windows* for just a few short weeks, you will begin building sophisticated database applications that exceed your wildest expectations.

Help Is Always Available

dBASE for Windows features the excellent on-line help system for which all Borland applications are famous. Context-sensitive help quickly guides you to the solutions to your questions, greatly simplifying the process of building database applications.

dBASE for Windows Is a Native Windows Product

Borland International has invested considerable resources in the development of dBASE. dBASE for Windows is a 100-percent Borland product and was written specifically for the Windows environment, rather than being ported to Windows from an existing DOS application. Several years of very hard work were required to produce dBASE for Windows and give it the extensive set of features you will use when building and maintaining your databases. Borland is clearly committed to dBASE for Windows and will continue working to ensure its success.

Applications are often rewritten to run on an operating system or environment other than the system or environment for which it was originally designed. When an application is rewritten to work on another system, it is said to have been "ported" from the first system to the second.

Who Should Read This Book

New Riders Publishing developed and produced *Inside dBASE 5 for Windows* with a number of different readers in mind. The only assumption we have made is that the reader of this book is an experienced Windows user who normally uses one or more other Windows applications on a daily or weekly basis.

The New Database User

Inside dBASE 5 for Windows is the perfect companion for the experienced Windows user embarking on database projects for the first time. Much of the material in *Inside dBASE 5 for Windows* is devoted to describing how to design and implement successful databases. Other portions of this book explain in detail how to exploit the many features and short-cuts available in dBASE for Windows.

No experience with dBASE is assumed in *Inside dBASE 5 for Windows.* A significant portion of this book describes how to use the dBASE for Windows environment to produce efficient databases without hopelessly complicating the underlying database structure. This information provides you with the background material necessary to confidently approach most any dBASE for Windows database project.

The User of Another Windows or DOS Database System

If you have tried to build database applications using another Windows or DOS database management system and were not happy with the results, *Inside dBASE 5 for Windows* provides all of the background necessary to avoid the many pitfalls of database design.

Many Windows database management systems currently available were ported from existing Windows applications. Although you can develop perfectly valid and powerful database systems through a DOS-to-Windows port, not all such porting efforts are successful. Typically, not all Windows features are incorporated into DOS-to-Windows ports—eliminating the advantages of a Windows application.

Sometimes an application that was optimized to run under DOS performs very poorly in the Windows environment, because it does not effectively work with the facilities provided by Windows.

For all of these reasons (and many others as well), you might be unhappy with your current database system. *Inside dBASE 5 for Windows* provides you with the information necessary for a successful database implementation with dBASE for Windows.

The User Migrating from dBASE for DOS

It is entirely possible that you are a serious database professional migrating to dBASE for Windows from dBASE for DOS. If this is the case, *Inside dBASE 5 for Windows* provides you with the information necessary to help you as you migrate your database applications to dBASE for Windows.

You'll be happy to find that dBASE for Windows contains the best features of earlier versions of dBASE. Essentially all of your hard-earned dBASE language learning will transfer directly into your Windows applications. *Inside dBASE 5 for Windows* shortens the time required to become proficient with the rich feature set of dBASE for Windows and aids in your adoption of this exciting application.

Conventions Used in This Book

Throughout this book, certain conventions are used to help you distinguish the various elements of Windows, DOS, their system files, and sample data. Before you look ahead, you should spend a moment examining these conventions:

- ✔ Shortcut keys are normally found in the text where appropriate. In most applications, for example, Shift+Ins is the shortcut key for the **P**aste command.
- ✔ Key combinations appear in the following formats:

  Key1+Key2. When you see a plus sign (+) between key names, you should hold down the first key while you press the second key. Then release both keys. If you see "Press Ctrl+F2," for example, hold down the Ctrl key, press the F2 function key once, then release both keys.

  Key1,Key2. When a comma (,) appears between key names, you should press and release the first key, then press and release the second key. "Alt,S" means press the Alt key once and then press S once.

  Hot Keys. On the screen, Windows underlines the letters on some menu names, file names, and option names. For example, the File menu is displayed on-screen as <u>F</u>ile. This underlined letter is the letter you can type to choose that command or option when it appears on the screen. (In this book, however, such letters are displayed in bold, underlined type: **<u>F</u>**ile.)
- ✔ Information you type is in **boldface**. This applies to individual letters and numbers as well as to text strings. This convention, however, does not apply to special keys, such as Enter, Tab, Esc, or Ctrl.
- ✔ New terms appear in *italics.*
- ✔ Text that is displayed on-screen, but which is not part of Windows or a Windows application—such as DOS prompts and messages—appears in a `special typeface`.

Special Text Used in This Book

Throughout this book, you find examples of special text. These passages have been given special treatment so that you can instantly recognize their significance and so that you can easily find them for future reference.

Notes, Tips, and Stops

Inside dBASE 5 for Windows features many special sidebars, which are set apart from the normal text by icons. This book includes three distinct types of sidebars: "Notes," "Tips," and "Stops."

A note includes "extra" information that you should find useful, but which complements the discussion at hand instead of being a direct part of it. A note might describe special situations that can arise when you use Windows under certain circumstances, and might tell you what steps to take when such situations arise.

A tip provides quick instructions for getting the most from your Windows system as you follow the steps outlined in the general discussion. A tip might show you how to conserve memory, how to speed up a procedure, or how to perform one of many timesaving and system-enhancing techniques. Tips also might tell you how to avoid problems with your software and hardware.

A stop tells you when a procedure might be dangerous—that is, when you run the risk of losing data, locking your system, or even damaging your hardware. Stops generally tell you how to avoid such losses or describe the steps you can take to remedy them.

New Riders Publishing

The staff of New Riders Publishing is committed to bringing you the very best in computer reference material. Each New Riders book is the result of months of work by the authors and staff, who research and refine the information contained within its covers.

As part of this commitment to you, the NRP reader, New Riders invites your input. Please let us know if you enjoy this book, if you have trouble with the information and examples presented, or if you have a suggestion for the next edition.

Please note, however, that the New Riders staff cannot serve as a technical resource for dBASE or dBASE application-related questions, including hardware- or software-related problems. Refer to the documentation that accompanies your dBASE or dBASE application package for help with specific problems.

If you have a question or comment about any New Riders book, please write to NRP at the following address. We will respond to as many readers as we can. Your name, address, or phone number will never become part of a mailing list or be used for any other purpose than to help us continue to bring you the best books possible.

New Riders Publishing
Macmillan Computer Publishing
Attn: Associate Publisher
201 W. 103rd St.
Indianapolis, IN 46290

If you prefer, you can fax New Riders Publishing at (317) 581-4670. We also welcome your CompuServe electronic mail; our CompuServe ID is MHS:DATABASE@NEWRIDER.

Thank you for selecting *Inside dBASE 5 for Windows.*

Part I

Getting Started with dBASE for Windows

Chapter Snapshot

In this chapter, you learn how to get started with dBASE 5.0 for Windows and how to perform essential dBASE tasks. You learn about:

If you are a new user of Windows and need help with the essentials of Windows use and navigation, see Appendix F, "Windows Basics for First-Time Users."

Quick Start with dBASE for Windows

By Jay Parsons

This chapter provides a tour of the essentials of dBASE 5.0 for Windows. You should read the chapter after you install dBASE, and if possible while at your computer, so you can follow the examples and perform the exercises. If you have difficulty installing dBASE on your system, see Appendix E, "Installing dBASE for Windows."

The first part of this chapter gives you a start with dBASE for Windows quickly. Later sections of the chapter contain background information you may want if you are moving up from dBASE III+ or dBASE IV, or if you are new to database management.

Getting Started with dBASE for Windows

From Windows Program Manager, double-click on the dBASE program group icon. A window opens showing the icons for the seven items in the group. If you did not read the README file at installation, you might want to double-click its icon to read it now. Double-click the dBASE icon and you should see the Borland splash screen with its copyright notice, followed by the dBASE for Windows desktop either as shown in figure 1.1 or with the right portion of the desktop empty.

The term "double-click" and the essentials of navigating in Windows are explained in Appendix F, " Windows Basics for First-Time Users."

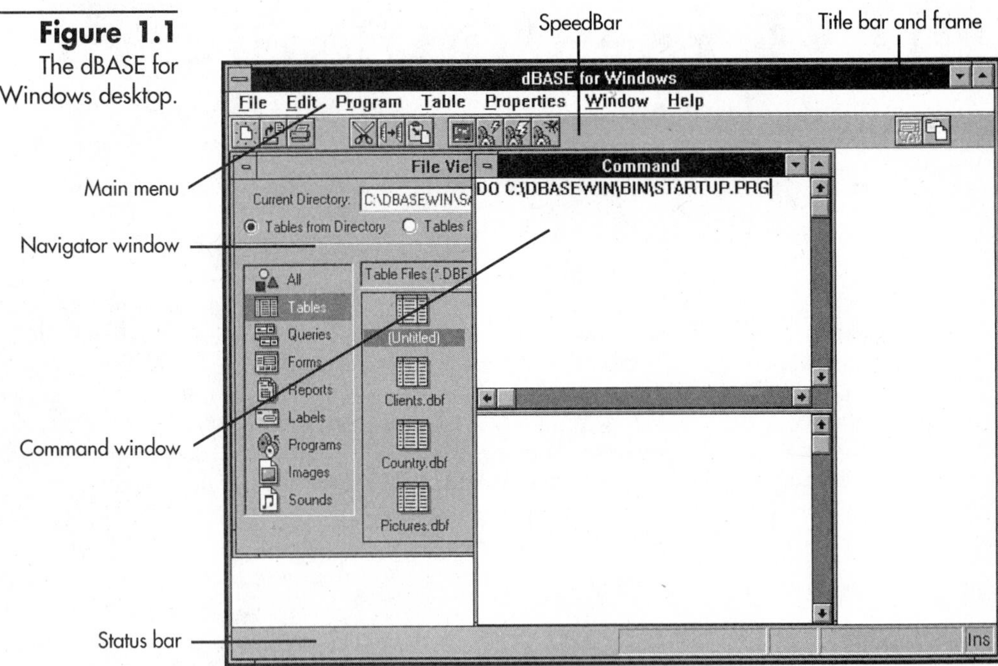

Figure 1.1 The dBASE for Windows desktop.

If the right portion of your desktop is empty, your Command window is minimized. You may never need the Command window, but you learn later in the chapter how to use it.

Using the dBASE for Windows Desktop

The desktop has several parts: the title bar and frame, the main menu, the SpeedBar, the Navigator—which fills most of the left of the screen—and the Command window, which (if not minimized) fills most of the right of the screen. At the bottom of the main window, a status bar displays messages and information about the current menu or SpeedBar item. At its right end, the status bar displays other information that depends on the context. If the Command window is open, the status bar displays `Ins`—if the Ins key has been pressed, which causes typed characters to be inserted instead of overwriting text. If a table is open, the status bar displays the name numbers of its current and last records.

The Title Bar

The desktop has a title bar at the top and a frame around the entire window. The *title bar* identifies the dBASE application and contains three additional controls. A *control* is any object that is part of the user interface. Many controls, such as the dBASE EntryFields, checkboxes and pushbuttons, respond to user input. Other controls, such as text, images, and bitmaps, only show their contents.

The controls on the title bar are square pushbuttons, one at the left end and two at the right. The appearance of the desktop title bar, the use of these controls, and the methods of moving and resizing the desktop by its frame are standard for all Windows applications. You can find an explanation of how to use these controls and how to move and resize the desktop in Appendix F.

The color of the desktop title bar background contrasts with the window background. The contrasting and highly visible background of the title bar identifies dBASE as the current foreground application—the one with which the user is interacting. In Windows parlance, dBASE is the application with the focus. The same contrasting color is used to identify which of the applications child windows has the focus. The *child windows* are the windows belonging to the application, of which the Navigator and perhaps the Command window are initially open. If the Command window is open, you can shift the focus between it and the Navigator. A click on either window gives that window the focus. Thereafter, any keystrokes you type go to the window with the focus.

The Main Menu and Help

Directly below the title bar is the main menu. You can click on any word of the menu to open menus for other tasks. Alternatively, you can press the Alt key, and then the underlined letter of any menu item, to do the same thing. Keystrokes and keystroke combinations that provide shortcut ways to do things are called called shortcut keys, hot keys, or accelerator keys. For purposes of this book, those keys will be called hot keys.

Click on the Help menu to open the dBASE help system and give it the focus. The Help menu enables you to seek help by major topics, by tasks and by keyword. To get help by keyword, click on Search. The Help window changes to appear as shown in figure 1.2.

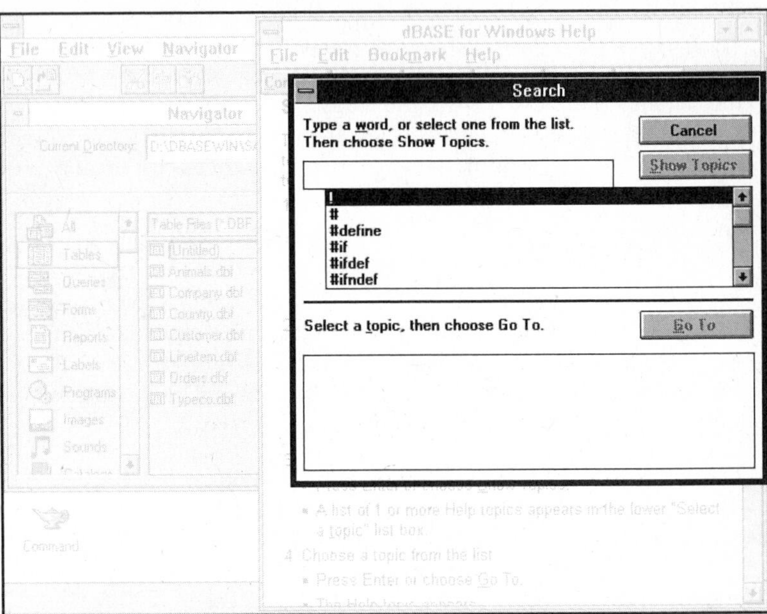

Figure 1.2 The Help Search window.

You can scroll through all the listed keywords, or type your own selection into the small upper window (an *EntryField* control). As you type a selection, the keywords shown in the upper list box *control* (a *list box* is a window showing a list of possible selections from which you can select one and sometimes more) change to those starting with the characters you have typed. You can finish typing or click on a choice from the list box. Click on Show Topics to see the help topics using the keyword. Click on a selection from the lower list box, and then click on Go To to see the help screen for the topic. Familiarize yourself with the Help system; close the Help window when you are ready.

The SpeedBar

The *SpeedBar* is the row of icons underneath the main menu. You can click on the SpeedBar icons to perform common tasks. The contents of the SpeedBar change with the context. The icons on the opening desktop (see fig. 1.3) fall into four groups:

- ✔ The two icons on the left relate to files. They enable you to create a new file or to open an existing file.
- ✔ Next (and familiar to experienced Windows users) are the three icons you can use to cut, copy, and paste. You use these icons to copy and move text and objects when editing forms, programs or memos and to exchange data between dBASE and the Windows Clipboard.
- ✔ The third group, initially of three icons, varies with the context. If the Navigator has the focus, its three icons permit you, from left to right, to run, design or delete a file. If the Command window has the focus, the three icons, again from left to right, permit you to execute a command or currently selected block of commands, to run a program or to debug a program.
- ✔ Finally, four icons at the right represent the Navigator and Command windows, the Form Expert and the Tutor. The Navigator has a ship's steering wheel as its icon. The Command window has Aladdin's lamp ("Your wish is my command," said the genie). You may restore the Navigator or Command window if it is minimized, or give it the focus, by clicking on its icon. The Form Expert has a lightbulb icon and assists you in creating forms, the main vehicle for interaction with the user in dBASE for Windows. The Tutor icon is the head of a graduate wearing a mortarboard. Clicking on it launches the dBASE tutorial.

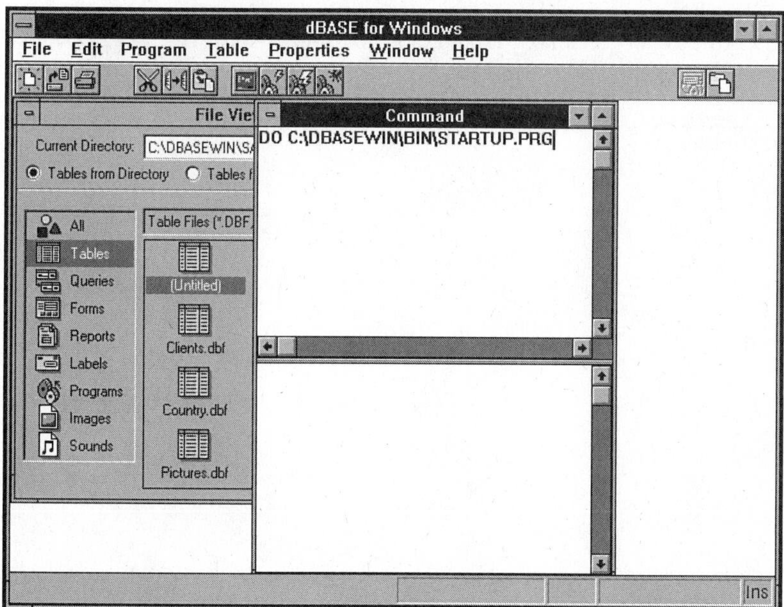

Figure 1.3
The SpeedBar of the opening desktop.

The Command Window

You might never need the Command window. It is designed to accommodate the typing in of commands and for seeing their results dBASE-IV style. If you do not write programs, or if you write programs using forms as dBASE 5.0 for Windows encourages you to do, you might be able to do everything you want to without ever opening the Control window.

The Command window, if not minimized, occupies much of the right side of the default desktop. It has two panes. The top pane, the Command pane, is for input and accepts and displays the commands you enter. The bottom half, the Results pane, displays the output of your commands. You can move and resize the two panes only as a unit, but you can move the boundary between the panes to alter their shares of their combined space.

If you are accustomed to working from the dot prompt of dBASE III+ or dBASE IV, you can use the Command window in the same manner. Click on the Command window or its icon to give it the focus. You should see a blinking vertical line within the Command window. This is the text cursor. It indicates that anything you type at the keyboard will appear in the Command window at the cursor.

Next, type your commands at the cursor. Start by typing a question mark, a space, and **"Hello"** (including the quotation marks), and then press Enter. The Results window should now contain `Hello` on the second line, the result of your typing **? "Hello"** into the Command window as shown in figure 1.4. **?** is the command to print in dBASE; you have directed dBASE to print the word Hello, which it did. To remove the `Hello`, type **`CLEAR`** in the Command window, and then press Enter.

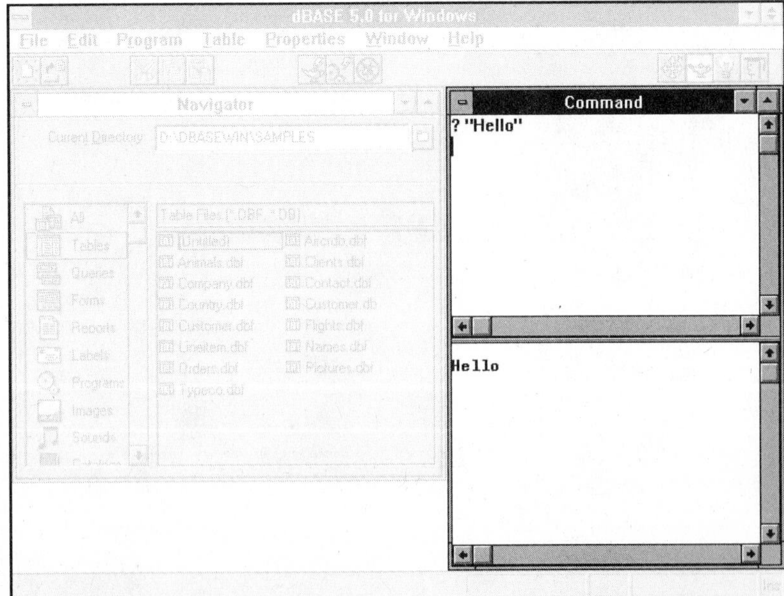

Figure 1.4 Using the Command window.

You must press Enter to end any dBASE command you type into the Command window. You must also press Enter to complete any selection you make by typing in an EntryField. This book might omit mention of pressing Enter because the requirement is invariable. If you type something and nothing happens, press Enter.

dBASE provides numerous ways to accomplish similar tasks. You can use the menus, mouse or accelerator keys, or enter commands into the Command window. When a task invoked by a menu selection, mouse click, or accelerator key is equivalent to issuing a dBASE command, the Command window displays that command. Displaying commands in the Command window helps you by confirming that dBASE is doing what you intend. If you do not know the language, the display of the command should help you learn it.

When a program runs, the Command pane of the Command window is unnecessary. It yields its space to the Results pane so that more of the results of the program shows on the screen. This is particularly helpful when you are running programs written for dBASE for DOS that use the entire screen for display.

When you are running programs, set TALK off by typing `SET TALK OFF` into the Command window or by using the Programming tab of Desktop on the Properties menu. Setting TALK off prevents the display of the results of intermediate commands executed within the program. Suppressing intermediate results enables the program to display its final results in the Results window without displaying a confusing clutter of other numbers and values as well.

The Navigator

On the left half of the opening screen is the most interesting of the dBASE windows: the Navigator. The *Navigator* contains icons for the files in the selected directory or database. DBASEWIN\SAMPLES is the default directory, and the Navigator shows all tables in that directory.

Tables, which contain your data such as names, addresses, and more, are one type of dBASE-related file. A dBASE table can have indexes and a memo file associated with it. The Navigator does not show these files because they relate to the table and are opened and closed automatically. You do not need to consider them separately.

A dBASE application normally consists of a number of related tables, programs, forms, indexes, labels, and reports contained in separate files. You can select a type of files other than Tables using the file types pane at the left of the Navigator display and selecting files of types other than tables.

The files relating to a single application will usually be contained in a single directory—and often in a single catalog. If you select a catalog in the Navigator, icons for only the files in that catalog will be displayed.

You use the sample files that come with dBASE in the following exercises. You might want to first copy them to a disk or to an empty directory on your hard disk drive, to simplify restoring them if you change one of them by mistake. You can copy them in a group by using the Windows File Manager or by typing **RUN COPY *.* A:** into the Command window, substituting the appropriate drive or directory for drive A. To create a temporary directory below the Samples directory on your hard disk drive, assuming that you are in the Samples directory, type **MKDIR Temp** into the Command window. Then type **RUN COPY *.* Temp** to copy all the Samples files to the new directory for temporary safe-keeping.

Click on the Navigator to give it the focus. Giving the Navigator the focus makes it the top window so that the Command window does not overlap and hide some of its contents. Click on the All icon in the left panel of the Navigator to see all dBASE-related files. Not all the icons for the sample files will fit in the visible portion of the Navigator.

Next, scroll the Navigator window up and down to see the icons for the rest of the sample files. Click the maximize button in the Navigator title bar to see all the icons at once. Then, click the maximize button again—it should now have an up and down arrow—to restore the Navigator. Then click the Tables icon in the column to the left of the file icons to remove the icons for file types other than tables from view.

You can change the spacing of the icons used in the Navigator using the Navigator item of the Properties menu, for either large or small icons. To switch the display in the Navigator from large icons to small or vice versa, you must use the View menu.

Table is the dBASE for Windows term for a DBF or DB file containing your data. Older versions of dBASE called a DBF file a database. Borland has changed its terminology to conform to the standard terms used by others. dBASE for Windows uses *database* to refer to a set of one or more tables that together contain the data relevant to an application, often on an SQL data server, and *table* to refer to a single DBF or DB file of the set.

Find the icon for CUSTOMER.DB as shown in figure 1.5 and double-click on it with the left mouse button. The Common User Access (CUA) standard used by Windows 3.1, which uses only the left mouse button, has been extended by Borland. The extended standard used in dBASE provides consistent ways for you to manage each type of object with the mouse. The acronym *SWIM* may help you remember them.

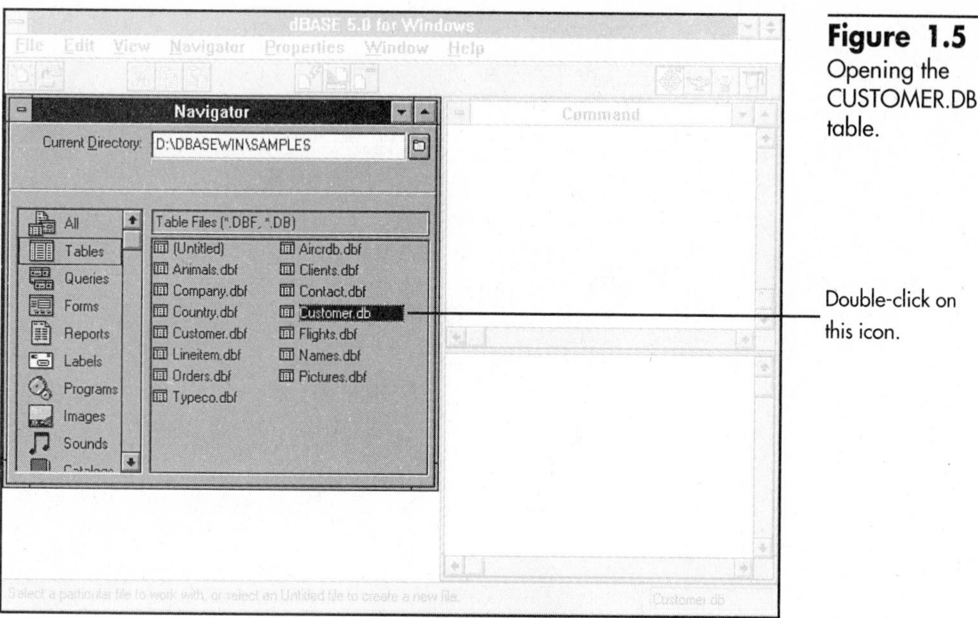

Figure 1.5 Opening the CUSTOMER.DB table.

- ✔ **Select**. A click with the left mouse button selects the object. In the case of many menu items and some controls, clicking the left mouse button may pull down the same menu as clicking the right mouse button.
- ✔ **Work**. A double-click with the left mouse button causes the object to work, run, or do whatever it is capable of doing.
- ✔ **Inquire**. A single right-click opens a menu showing what actions you can do with or to the object.
- ✔ **Modify**. A right double-click enables you to modify the design of the object.

In the case of a table, its purpose is to hold data and enable it to be edited. The double-click selects the table and displays its data in a window as shown in figure 1.6. Borland calls this view of the table *run mode*, distinguishing it from the *design mode* view you can bring up with a right double-click to modify the design of the table. The run mode of a data table is also known as a "browse" window. You can create the browse window by issuing the BROWSE command. If you create a browse window with your mouse, dBASE shows you the equivalent commands in the Command window.

You can use the browse view of the table created by a double-click on its icon to examine the various fields and records of the table, and to change or delete the contents of particular fields. Move around through the window, either with the mouse or by using the key strokes listed in table 1.1. You can make changes, but will probably want to restore the original data to maintain the sample file unchanged before leaving the browse window.

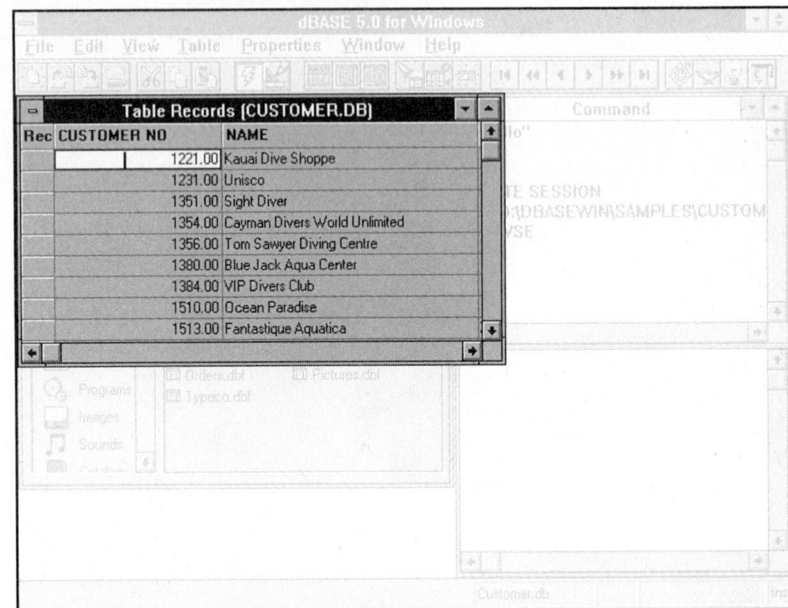

Figure 1.6 Browsing the CUSTOMER.DB table.

Table 1.1
Browse Window Navigation Keys

Keys	Effect
Tab or Shift+Tab	Moves right or left one field, respectively. A Tab from the last field of a record moves to the first field of the next record. A Shift+Tab from the first field of a record moves to the last field of the preceding record.
Up or Down arrow	Moves up or down one record.
PgUp or PgDn	Moves up or down as many records as show in the window, less one. This leaves the record that was at the top or bottom remaining visible at the opposite edge of the window to give you a reference.
Right arrow	Moves forward one character, moving as needed to the next field or record.

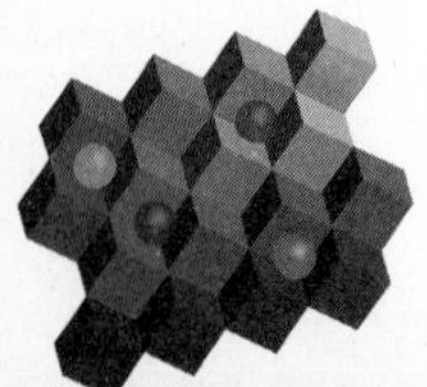

Keys	Effect
Left arrow	Moves back within a field one character to the first character of the field. From the first character of a field, moves back to the first character of the preceding field, if any, otherwise to the first character of the preceding record.
Home or End	Moves to the first or last character of the current field.
Ctrl+right arrow Ctrl+left arrow	Same as left or right arrow but jumps to the first character of the next or preceding word in the field.
Ctrl+Home	Moves to the first character of the first field of the current record.
Ctrl+End	Moves to the first character of the last field of the current record.
Ctrl+PgUp Ctrl+PgDn	Moves to the first character of the or corresponding field of the first or last record

To terminate browsing, click on the Close option from the windows Control menu, or double-click on the Control menu button. If you use either of these methods to terminate the browse, all changes you made to any field of any record, or any marks you made to delete records, are saved.

You also can terminate browsing by pressing Esc. This closes the browse window without saving changes you made to the record that was current when you pressed Esc. dBASE saves changes you made to other records. If you changed a record, moved to another record, came back to the first record and pressed Esc, the changes you made to the first record on the first edit are saved.

CUSTOMER.DB is a Paradox table. Paradox tables use the DB extension by default whereas native dBASE tables, such as ANIMALS.DBF, use DBF. You can browse either type of table the same way.

Double-click ANIMALS.DBF to browse it. Be sure to double-click on the BMP field of at least one record of ANIMALS.DBF to see what happens. When you have finished browsing through the ANIMALS table, press Esc or double-click on the browse windows system menu button to end the browse.

Records in dBASE tables can be marked for deletion without deleting them irrevocably. By default, when you browse a table, you do not see records marked for deletion. You see them if you enter **SET DELETED OFF** in the Command window or uncheck the Deleted checkbox on the Table tab of the Desktop item of the Properties menu. If you enable display of records marked for deletion, a column of checkboxes headed "Del" appears between the record numbers and the first field of the table when you browse it. You can check or uncheck the DELETED() state of any record to mark it or unmark it for deletion.

Closing a browse window does not close the table. To close the table, issue the USE command, choose Close from the table icons control menu or select a different table.

Right double-click on the icon for the ANIMALS.DBF table and you will see the table in Design Mode as shown in figure 1.7.

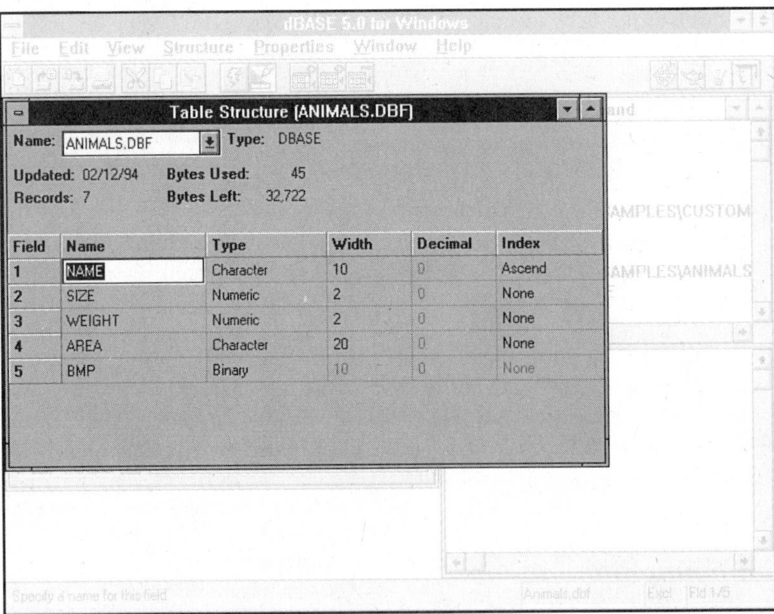

Figure 1.7
Modifying the design of ANIMALS.DBF.

You can also open this window by issuing the MODIFY STRUCTURE command. You can use this window to add or subtract fields or to resize or redesign them, although there is no good reason to do so with ANIMALS.DBF. Close the structure-design window by pressing Esc, and then right-click the ANIMALS.DBF icon and select Close to close the table.

The Navigator Icons

The next seven Navigator icons restrict the files shown to Queries, Forms, Reports, Labels, Programs, Images, and Sounds, respectively. In each case, a right double-click on a file icon brings up a tool appropriate to design that type of file. Two other Navigator icons select Catalogs and custom file types.

A Query expresses the relationship among data tables and their fields and indexes. The Query Designer, about which you will learn in Chapter 8, "Querying Your Data," enables you to specify which fields of each table will be visible, in what order the records of each will appear, and the links between the tables. A link might connect, for example, a transaction from a table of transactions to the record in the Customer table of the appropriate customer.

Forms are the screens and windows you design for user interaction with your programs and data. The Forms Designer enables you to design forms visually, using primarily your mouse to select the size, color, placement, and behavior of the forms and the controls you place on them. You learn about the Forms Designer in Chapter 6, "Developing Forms."

Reports is the dBASE term for printed output in general, lists and summaries of your data, and your calculations upon it. Labels are in a sense a special case of reports, but have their own structure and design system to facilitate the creation of mailing labels of the many standard and nonstandard sizes and types. You will learn about each of these in Chapter 9, "Developing Reports and Labels."

Programs are text files containing sequences of dBASE commands; dBASE compiles them, and then executes the specified commands to perform complex actions. You may need the dBASE Debugger to run your programs, stopping as you direct and displaying intermediate results, in order to fine tune them to do what you intend. Programs and the Debugger are the subject of Parts IV through VI of this book, starting with Chapter 10, "Understanding the dBASE Language."

Click on the Programs icon in the column at the left of the Navigator. This limits the display of files in the Navigator to program, PRG files. Find the icon for EVENT.PRG.

In the case of a program, its purpose is to run. Double-click on the EVENT.PRG icon to run the program. When you have finished with it, right double-click the EVENT.PRG icon. The right double-click directs a modification or change of design. The way you change the design of a program is to change the code, so this brings up the code of the program in a text editor window. Scroll around in the editor window to see the code. Edit any lines of it you want.

dBASE provides its own design systems for Queries, Forms, Reports, Labels, and Programs, also calling upon the program editor to edit memo fields. It calls upon the Windows utilities Paintbrush and Sound Recorder to create and modify image and sound files. You can explore any of these by a right double-click on an icon of the appropriate type.

The built-in dBASE editor is adequate to most needs, but you may have a favorite text editor you would prefer to use to edit program files or memo fields. You may even prefer different custom editors for programs and for memos. You can set up your own editors for either or both of these purposes using the Files tabcard of the Desktop item of the Properties menu, or by editing the DBASEWIN.INI file—which is analogous to the CONFIG.DB file used in dBASE for DOS. dBASE then runs your editors when required instead of its own. You can similarly substitute different painting or sound editors by changing the DBASEWIN.INI.

When you have finished examining or editing the ANIMALS.PRG file, double-click its windows control menu box to end the edit. If you have made changes in the code of a program while editing, a window will pop up asking whether you want to save the changes before closing the file. In this case, you probably do not want to save the changes; if this window appears, click on the No button.

If you want to save your changes but to a different file, click on Cancel to return to edit mode. Click the **F**ile item of the dBASE for Windows main menu and choose Save **A**s to save the edited version under a new name. Then close the edit window without saving the changes to preserve the original version.

You may have noticed that each Navigator window displays Untitled as the first file of each type. dBASE for DOS had two almost identical commands, CREATE and MODIFY, to modify files. If the file you wanted to change did not exist, you would use CREATE, otherwise MODIFY. dBASE continues to support both commands, but you do not have to use either one. To modify an existing file, right double-click its icon. To create a new file and modify it, right double-click the Untitled icon. When you finish your modifications of Untitled and try to save them, dBASE prompts you for the name of the new file.

Images are files in either of two standard formats, BMP and PCX.; sounds are WAV files containing sounds. Chapter 23, "Working with Graphical and Multimedia Data," discusses both of these capabilities.

The Catalogs icon of the Navigator displays your catalogs. If you double-click on an icon of a catalog, a slightly smaller Navigator window appears. It contains icons for the files of that catalog, organized by file type as in the regular Navigator window. You may create catalogs and organize your files into the catalogs to make it easier for you to see which files work together for a particular application.

The Custom icon of the Navigator displays nothing by default. Select it, and then use the **C**ustom Files text box at the top of the main pane of the Navigator to enter a list of skeletons—file names with the DOS asterisk and question mark wild card characters replacing characters you do not care about. Separate the skeletons with commas. For

example, you might create the Custom Files list "*.DLL, *.EXE" to see two types of files that the Navigator does not ordinarily display. There are no files of these types in the Samples directory, but if you change to the DBASEWIN\BIN directory you will see several listed.

The Directory Window

At the top of the Navigator is a small window showing the full specification, path and name of the current directory. By default, the directory is C:\DBASEWIN\SAMPLES. dBASE typically provides several ways to do the same thing, and changing the directory displayed in the Navigator is no exception. There are at least five ways to change the directory within dBASE, in addition to the possibilities of using the RUN command or the Windows File Manager, as described in the following exercise.

Five Ways of Changing a Directory

To use the dBASE IV for DOS method, type **SET DIRECTORY TO <directory name>** into the Command window (after clicking on that window to select it)	Changes the directory
If you prefer the standard DOS method, type **CD <directory name>** into the Command window after selecting the Command window. CD is now a dBASE command that does just what the DOS CD command does	Changes the directory
You can use the text box way; Click on the Current Directory directory text box within the Navigator	Gives Navigator the focus

You will see the vertical-line text cursor within the text box. This indicates that what you type appears at the cursor within the text box. You can type in or edit the contents of the Current Directory text box to the name of the desired directory, as shown in figure 1.8.

You can use the Current Directory text box on the Files tabcard of the Desktop item of the Properties menu to change a directory. You can type in the directory name, or click on the Tool Button to open the Choose Directory dialog box. You might prefer the mouse way.

continues

continued

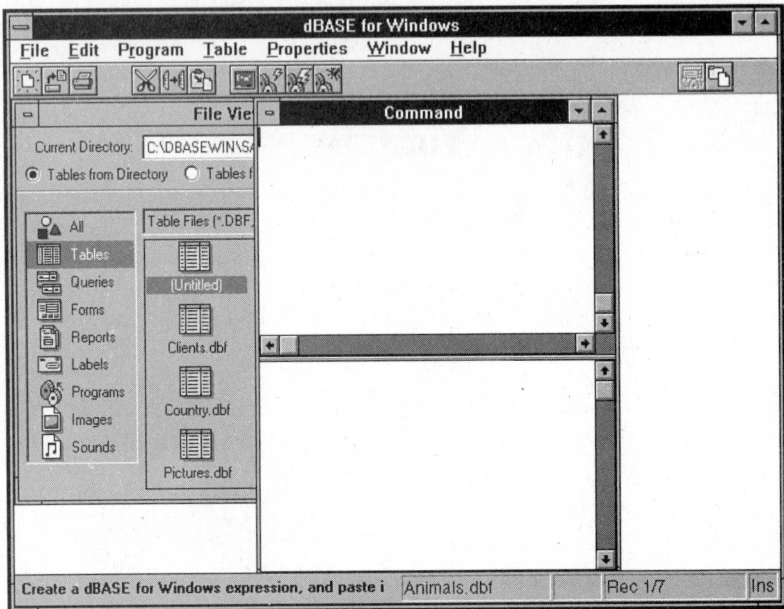

Figure 1.8
The Current Directory text box.

Click on the small icon of a file folder just to the right of the Current Directory text box	This opens up a window with icons for the directories of the current level and above, and for any subdirectories immediately below the current directory as shown in figure 1.9
Click on the desired directory. If the desired directory does not show, click on the directory that is in its path and click on the Show Subdirectories button	Shows you subdirectories of the chosen directory
Click on OK	Completes the selection

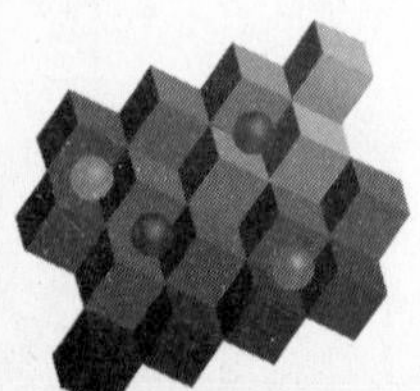

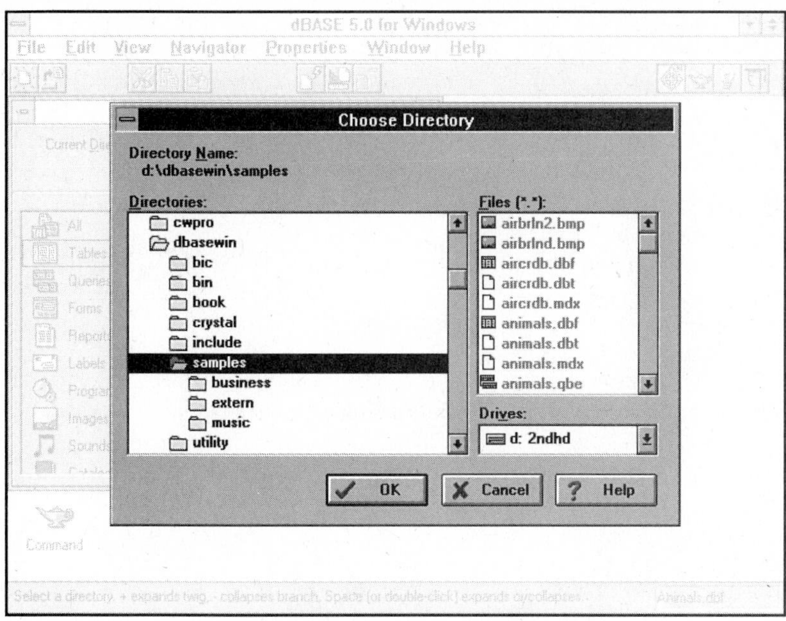

Figure 1.9
The Choose Directory dialog box.

The Properties Dialog Boxes

The Properties pull-down menu of the dBASE for Windows main menu enables you to change the properties of the desktop or the windows. When the Navigator has the focus, the pull-down menu contains a Navigator item. Selecting the Navigator item opens a dialog box that enables you to change the spacing of the icons in the Navigator and to direct that the Navigator displays and makes use of a supplemental search path for files.

When the Command window is open, the Properties pull-down menu contains a Command Window item. Selecting it opens a dialog box that enables you to change the relative positions of the panes of the Command window and to change the fonts it uses. To change a font, click on the Tool Button with the wrench icon to the right of the text box for the pane you want to change, or enter the hot key letter for the Input or Results pane. dBASE opens a dialog box enabling you to select among your installed Windows fonts.

The Properties pull-down menu always contains a Desktop item. Selecting the Desktop opens the Desktop Properties inspector with six tab cards. These do not affect the appearance of the desktop as you might expect, but the way dBASE works.

The first tab card, Country, contains settings related to the currency symbols and date formats in use in different countries. You will not need them if you and your work are within the United States and Canada. It also contains a Century setting that controls whether the year portion of a date is displayed in two digits or four, an issue that is increasing in importance as the century nears its end.

You use the second tab card, Table, to set the default type for tables you create or use, either dBASE or Paradox type. This tab card also contains multiuser settings, settings for the block sizes of index and memo files, which advanced users may change to improve performance, and five important settings grouped as Other settings. These include Autosave, Deleted, Exact, Near and Language Driver Check.

Autosave is normally off with its box unchecked. If you check its box, dBASE will write your tables to disk every time a record changes, increasing safety at some cost in speed.

Deleted is normally on, checked, and hides records in dBASE tables that you have marked for deletion. If you uncheck it, you will see the marked records and dBASE commands will process them.

Exact and Near control how dBASE searches for character data. Both are normally off and unchecked. Setting Exact on requires that a character string must match the one you specify exactly to be a match. Normally, if you tell dBASE to search a name field for "S" it will return the first field with a name that starts with "S." Setting Near on tells dBASE to stop at the next record if it finds no exact match in an indexed table, rather than going to the end of the table.

Setting Language Driver Check on—it is normally off—causes dBASE to check that each table you open was created using the language driver dBASE is using. It is useful if you use tables created by people speaking different languages.

The third tab card, Data Entry, enables you to change (or determine) the following:

- ✔ The sound of the bell
- ✔ The size of the type ahead buffer
- ✔ Determine whether dBASE asks for confirmation of data entered
- ✔ Determine how the Esc key and Enter key act
- ✔ Determine what delimiters, if any, dBASE uses for data fields

The fourth tab card, Files,is where you specify custom editors for program files and memo fields and the supplemental search path dBASE and the Navigator use to find and display files. You can also do the following:

- ✔ Change the directory
- ✔ Specify what file types appear in the Navigator
- ✔ Specify whether dBASE uses the full path by default
- ✔ Specify whether dBASE will prompt you for a description when adding a file to a catalog
- ✔ Determine the display mode used to add records or browse tables
- ✔ Specify whether dBASE opens separate sessions with their own settings and work areas for forms

The fifth tab card, Application, concerns the position of the SpeedBar, the Status Bar font, how the Forms Inspector displays properties and how many Most Recently Used files are listed at the bottom of the File pull-down menu.

The sixth tab card, Programming, appears in figure 1.10. You use it to set the number of decimal places in which dBASE displays numbers, the number of digits it uses internally for calculations and the left margin for printed output. It also contains several options normally on and one normally off, Coverage, which programmers can turn on to generate coverage files to assist in testing code.

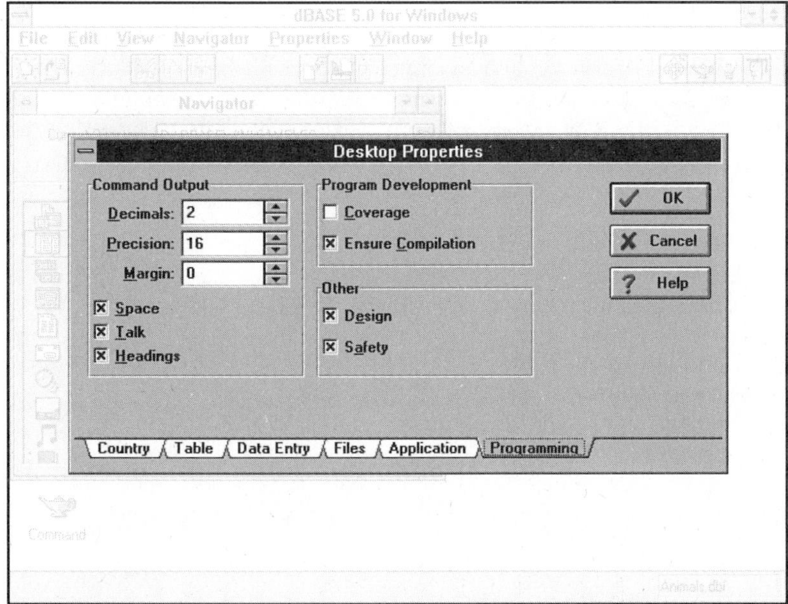

Figure 1.10 The Programming tabcard of the Desktop Properties inspector.

The remaining options in one group are Space, which inserts a single space between each two expressions in a list when printing them, Talk, which causes display in the Results pane of the effect of many commands, and Headings, which places the field names in the output of the AVERAGE, DISPLAY, and LIST commands. Ensure Compilation recompiles programs whenever changed. Design provides, for compatibility with earlier versions of dBASE, a limited form of restricting users from making undesirable changes to data. Safety causes dBASE to prompt you for confirmation before enabling you to overwrite a file with other data.

The Expression Builder

The last stop on this chapters tour of dBASE is the Expression Builder. You will use *expressions* to tell dBASE the conditions under which it should include or exclude data from some operation, when it should branch to some other section of code and how to calculate and format values. An expression is any combination of constants, fields, variables, operators, and functions that dBASE can resolve to a value. For example, the following expression:

```
trim(First_Name)+" "+iif(" "=Initial,"",Initial +". ")+Last_Name
```

contains four constants, character strings consisting of a single space twice, an empty string and a period followed by a space. It contains references to three fields or variables holding the parts of a name. It calls two functions, TRIM() and IIF(), and uses the (,), + and = operators. It resolves to a character value, the name formatted for printing.

The Expression Builder enables you to build an expression from elements of all types. It tells you what the various elements do and what syntax they require, as shown in figure 1.11. As you paste elements of the various sorts into your expression in its main window, it checks your syntax and advises you of any problems. Its Safety Net setting enables you to choose between two levels of help according to your needs.

You can access the Expression Builder by giving the focus to the Command window. After you have done so, either press Ctrl+E or select Build Expression from the Edit pull-down menu.

You may also call up the Expression Builder by inserting the function GETEXPR() into your code wherever an expression is needed. When GETEXPR() is executed, the Expression Builder pops up, enabling you to complete your code by pasting in the expression you need. In addition to checking your syntax, the Expression Builder lists the purposes of the functions built in to the dBASE language by category. This enables you to choose the function you need from a short list of the functions most likely to be applicable.

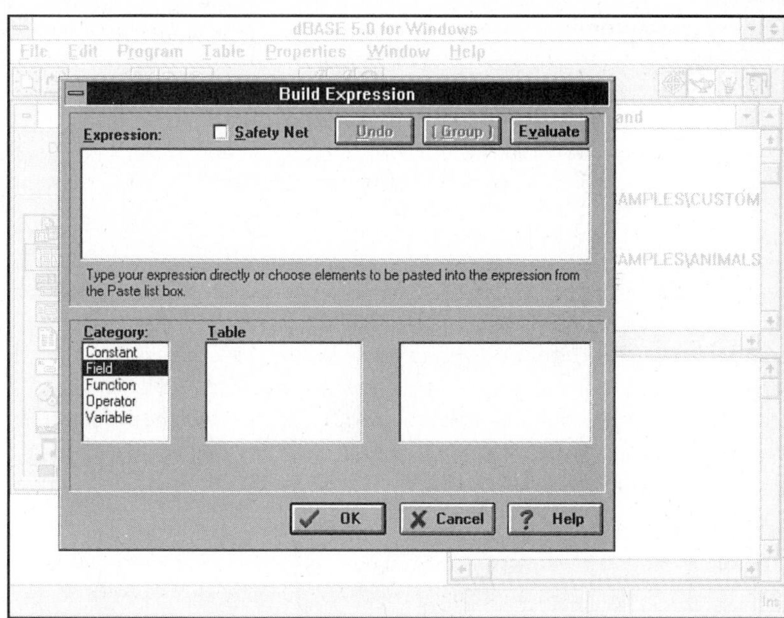

Figure 1.11
The Build Expression dialog box.

If you use numerous user-defined functions and external functions in your code, add them to the Expression Builder. The function database for the Expression Builder is the file DBASEWIN.FNF found in the DBASEWIN\BIN subdirectory. It is a standard DBF table in spite of its FNF extension. You can add to it what you want. Add functions in alphabetical order using INSERT, because it is not indexed, and ignore the last, ID field. The ID field enables dBASE quick access to built-in functions but has no application to user-defined or external functions.

Learning dBASE for Windows

You have now gotten a quick start with dBASE. You have explored the parts of its desktop, have examined its Help and File Directory systems and have learned how to browse, create, and modify tables and how to create and modify files of the other Navigator types. If you feel ready, move on to the later chapters of this book to learn the full power of dBASE.

For basic information about dBASE and database management, continue to read this chapter, or the parts that interest you. If you have had trouble installing dBASE, read Appendix E, "Installing dBASE for Windows."

If you are finished with dBASE for now, click on the control menu box at the upper left of its main-window title bar to bring up the system menu, and then click Close. Or, click on its File menu and select Close, or double-click the dBASE control menu box, or type **QUIT** into the Command window, or press Alt+F4. Any of these executes the dBASE QUIT command. These actions instruct dBASE to close its files, enable Windows to close the dBASE windows, end the dBASE session, and return control to the Windows Program Manager.

Do not terminate dBASE, any other Windows application or Windows itself, by simply turning off power to the computer. Doing so is the primary cause of data corruption, which can cost you or your clients large sums of money and large amounts of time. Form the habit—and train your users—to terminate each application by closing its main window. This gives dBASE or the other application the opportunity to run its exit code, flush any file buffers to disk, close its files, and clean up after itself.

In theory, you may skip this step and terminate Windows by closing the Program Manager. Windows will request each application including dBASE to terminate properly. However, if you leave dBASE running while you are doing other Windows tasks, you run the risk that some problem occurring in another application might crash the system while dBASE remains open. For maximum safety, close dBASE when you have finished with it, as well as making frequent backups of your data.

If You Are Upgrading from dBASE for DOS

There is a great deal to learn about dBASE even for the experienced dBASE user or programmer. The dBASE for DOS Control Center is missing in dBASE and the look and feel of the Windows environment are very different from DOS. These differences need not cause you any difficulties in making immediate use of dBASE.

Using Your Existing Code and Data

dBASE is fully compatible with dBASE for DOS. Your table (DBF), memo (DBT), index (NDX and MDX), memory (MEM), and catalog (CAT) data files retain the same format as under dBASE IV, so you can use them unchanged under dBASE. You may still use the data backup file types DBK, MBK, and TBK to recover lost data by renaming them as DBF, MDX, or DBT type respectively.

You can also use your format (FMT, FRG, FRM for dBASE III only), program (PRG), print form (PRF), query (QBE, QRY for dBASE III+ only, UPD) label (LBG, LBL for dBASE III only) and view (VUE) files. If you have created a window definition file (WIN) for dBASE IV, you may use it unchanged.

Some differences do exist. dBASE does not read compiled program files and the like (DBO, FMO, FRO, LBO, QPO, UPO) or the application (APP) files created by dBASE IV. It can, however, read and compile all types of source files created for dBASE III+ or dBASE IV. If you need to use a dBASE III+ LBL file in dBASE, you will have to use the dBASE IV label designer to generate LBG files from them. Similarly, you cannot use dBASE IV screen (SCR) or report design (FRM) files but can use the FRG and FMT files generated from them.

dBASE does not read a CONFIG.DB file. Some of its settings, such as the default colors and default formatting for times, dates, and currency, come from Windows. You may set these on a global basis using the Windows Control Panel. You may make settings local to dBASE in DBASEWIN.INI, by using the Desktop Properties inspector or by including appropriate SET commands in your programs.

You must use dBASE IV to decrypt any encrypted tables before using them in dBASE. To decrypt your tables, you will need privileges to update, delete, and extend them and full field access to all fields you need. From the dBASE IV dot prompt, type:

```
SET ENCRYPTION OFF, USE <the name of the table to decrypt>
```

Then type:

```
COPY TO <newfilename> WITH PRODUCTION
```

You will have to change any programs calling on binary (.BIN) code files using the LOAD and CALL|call() syntax. dBASE does not support such files or syntax. You can continue to call code written in other languages, but the method is different and more flexible, as explained in Chapter 25, “Linking dBASE Applications with DLLs.”

Printer driver names are different under Windows. Any of your programs that set the _pdriver variable to one of the dBASE IV printer driver (PR2) files will have to change the driver name to the corresponding Windows printer driver. You need not change other system variables.

Windows reserves a few key combinations. See table F.1 in Appendix G for a list of key combinations reserved by Windows. If your programs use any of these combinations with ON KEY or otherwise you should change your code to use different keys.

Finally, dBASE has changed some of the error numbers from those dBASE IV used. If your programs use ERROR() to obtain the error number and act on it, check to be sure that the error number remains the one the programs expect.

The full command set of dBASE IV Version 2.0 is carried into dBASE, so if you are accustomed to working at the dot prompt you can continue to work in the same fashion. Type the same commands into the Command window that you used to type at the dot prompt. dBASE for DOS programs will run with no or minimal changes in the maximized Command window. Just double-click the programs Navigator icon or type **DO <programname>** in the Command window, and then click on the maximize button of the Command window so that the full screen is available to your program.

Finding New Ways To Do Familiar Tasks

You will, sooner than you may think, want to learn the new ways dBASE provides to do the tasks you are familiar with in dBASE III+ or IV for DOS. Clicking the mouse is easier than typing lengthy commands. The Navigator provides an easily understood way to see what files are available and which are in use. The Query Designer makes setting relations between tables natural and the visibility of their fields apparent. The Forms Designer provides a visual and intuitive way to design screen forms.

Thus, the variety and power of the controls you may place on your forms eliminates most of the coding and drudgery often associated with programming the user interface in dBASE IV for DOS. In addition, controls placed on a form may be tested at once. The familiar wait for code to be regenerated before being able to run it, modify it, and regenerate again is no more.

You learn the object-oriented features of dBASE in Chapter 11, "Understanding the Object-Oriented Language Extension." The forms, windows, controls, and the like you create under dBASE are *objects,* and objects have *properties.* How many and what the properties are depends on the type of object, but in all cases you can change one or more of the properties to suit your needs. You can do this using the Forms Designer or, if the change is simple (like changing the color or size of a line of text), by typing it into the Command window.

The object-oriented extensions to dBASE in dBASE go much farther than properties. Those extensions enable you to create new classes of windows, forms, and controls. Each new class inherits the properties of the class from which it is derived, but you can change the properties or add to them. The dBASE object-oriented extensions enable you to think in terms of events, mouse actions, and key presses, and how your objects will react to them. This gives you broad control over how the objects act and interact with very little coding and almost no risk of inadvertently affecting the behavior of unrelated objects.

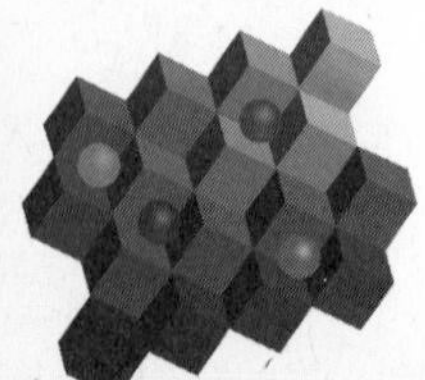

If You Are New to dBASE

dBASE is the Windows version of the database-management program originally published as dBASE II. It was followed by dBASE III, which became the still-popular dBASE III+, and by dBASE IV. dBASE IV has two versions in general use, 1.5 and 2.0, and still claims many users of version 1.1. If you are unfamiliar with database management, see the next section.

All versions of dBASE contain at root a set of specifications for the storage of data as files on disk. All versions contain and support the commands every user needs to access and manipulate the data easily. Finally, all versions define and support the additional commands programmers need to combine a series of commands into a program. Because dBASE began with its programming language as one of its primary features, it continues to include and support an extremely powerful programming language.

dBASE makes its share of improvements in all areas. Among the most noticeable and perhaps most important are in making use of Windows to support user-interface elements and controls that are much more powerful and easier to use than in any DOS version.

In order to help users move up from the DOS versions, dBASE lists (in the Command window) the dBase language commands executed. These may at first mean little to you, but they will become familiar.

Learning What Files dBASE Uses

dBASE creates and uses files of the major types shown in table 1.2 below. In each case, the table gives the default DOS file name extension given by dBASE to that type of file. You can override or change the extension, but it is rarely useful to do so and likely to confuse other users if not yourself. The table does not contain the temporary and other files dBASE creates for its own uses or that are not normally accessible to users, including the files it creates by generating or compiling other types. Neither does it contain files of types created by dBASE IV that it can read but does not write.

Table 1.2
Major dBASE File Types

File type	Extension	Contents
Data table	DBF	Your data in fields and records of defined type and length

continues

Table 1.2, Continued
Major dBASE File Types

File type	Extension	Contents
Memo table	DBT	The character, image, or sound data, which may be of any length, for each memo or binary field in the associated data table
Index file	NDX	The index information required to present the records of a data table in the order specified by a single key field or expression
Multiple index file	MDX	Up to 47 indexes for a single data table
Catalog file	CAT	Names and descriptions of the tables relating to a particular application
Memory	MEM	Saved memory variables
Program file	PRG	Source text of programs in the dBASE language
Windows form	WFM	dBASE screen forms
Bitmap file	BMP	Graphics in bitmapped format
Picture file	PCX	Graphics in picture format
Query file	QBE	Relations and visibility of tables and fields
Label file	LBG	Source code for labels
Report file	RPG	Source code for reports
Sound file	WAV	Digitized sound

Understanding How dBASE Works

It is natural and convenient to store data in files that contain one *record* for each individual, with *fields* in the record for the various items of information about that individual. This structure of records and fields is what you saw by double-clicking on the icons for the Customer and Animals tables earlier in the chapter.

It is essential to dBASE that the fields of each record are of fixed lengths. dBASE reads the field lengths, the record length, and the length of the header itself from the file header and does a quick calculation to determine where in the file to find the desired data.

dBASE cannot ignore data that vary in length from record to record. A field for Resume in an Employee table is an example. The resume of one employee may run several pages. Other employees may not have submitted a resume at all. For this kind of data, and now in dBASE for special data, such as objects linked from other applications, images and sound, dBASE provides the binary, *memo*, and OLE types of field. In the data table, a binary memo or OLE field occupies a fixed length and contains a number. The number identifies the block of the associated DBT file in which the text or other data of that field begins. In the DBT file, the data can occupy as much space as it needs. Table 1.3 lists the types of fields dBASE enables in tables.

Table 1.3
dBASE field types

Field type	Usage
CHARACTER	Holds character data, such as a name, address, or number not used for calculations, such as a ZIP code
NUMERIC	Holds a number used in financial and general calculations
MEMO	Holds the block address in .DBT file of memo text
LOGICAL	Holds logical true (.T.) or false (.F.)
DATE	Holds a date
FLOAT	Holds a number used in scientific calculations
BINARY	Holds the block address in DBT file of image, sound, or binary data
OLE	Holds reference to a linked object

If there are numerous records in a table, it is slow to move everyone from Baldwin to Zabriskie down a record in order to add Arnold. dBASE solves this by allowing additions to be made at the physical end of the table. *Indexes* enable you to view the table in alphabetical or other order without physically rearranging the records in the file.

dBASE does much more than this. It enables you to create forms for you or your clients to enter new data in a way that makes sense to them. It enables you to build in verifications of the data entered to prevent duplicate entries or entry of nonsense dates or amounts. It enables you to create mailing labels in standard or custom sizes from your data, reports listing and summarizing the data or parts of it as you want and programs manipulating the data in countless ways. You will learn all about these in later chapters.

If You Are New to Database Management

If you have never used a database manager such as dBASE, you may wonder what it does that can help you.

Appreciating the Uses of a Database Manager

If your only need is to keep a list of your friends, it is easier to keep such a list in a pocket address book. You are more likely to have the book than your computer with you when you want to telephone a friend. Or, you could use a spreadsheet program to list your friends, one per line, and it will even permit you to add new ones and delete obsolete entries quickly and sort them into order. Finally, you could use a word processor to enter whatever you wanted about each friend. The word processor might also permit you to create labels or address envelopes for your friends and to print out whatever lists you could want.

What you do need a database manager for is to manage data that requires multiple tables due to one-to-many relationships or many-to-many relationships. You learn more about these in Chapter 4, "Designing and Creating Relational Databases." You will also find a database manager unequaled to manage data in a situation where the ways the data may be used are numerous or not completely known at first.

Either a spreadsheet or a word processor can keep a list in only one way at a time. Suppose that you set up a list of your friends in alphabetical order by last name. If you then decide you need to find all the ones in Chicago, you will have to do at least some work to extract the ones you want in the order you want. With dBASE, you may create a filter on the City field by a single command, and only the friends in Chicago will be visible. To speed performance, you may create an index on City by another single command. You then select the order you want. dBASE does the rest for you. If you decide to change the index keys, add a new index, or perhaps delete one, a single command does it.

The example files you will see later in this book suppose a more complicated application, the operation of a real estate agency. It has customers with varying needs and homes for sale of varying sizes, locations, and amenities.

It would be extremely difficult to use a spreadsheet or word processor to keep any single list that would satisfy all these needs. dBASE, as a *relational database manager,* permits the data to be kept in several tables, one for customers, one for homes, and so forth. These are related to each other to provide instant views of all combinations of data from each that may be useful.

Treating the Data with Reverence

If you keep a list of friends in a spreadsheet program or with a word processor, it is easy to add a friend or change his or her address. It is also easy to add a friend who is already on the list, to delete a friend by mistake, and make other errors that cause the list to be incorrect. It takes some effort to use the list for different purposes. It may be tricky to use the same list for mailing labels, and for printing a list of those friends in Massachusetts with their telephone numbers but without the addresses. There may be a risk that in the process of doing any of these, you will wipe out or corrupt some of the entries in the list.

A database manager treats the data, the membership of the list, as being very important quite apart from what you may be doing with it. It provides ways for you to test the data you are adding, or your users are adding, to prevent errors. It enables programmers to restrict less-sophisticated users to operations that cannot scramble the data. Most of all, a database manager keeps the data apart from, and independent of, any particular program or operation done with it. This safeguards the data and allows it to be used simultaneously or later for other programs and operations.

Meeting the Relational Model

A *relational* database manager, such as dBASE, enables you to keep information in separate tables structured logically for what they contain. You then relate the tables to each other in ways that reflect the situation the database models.

An application for a school will naturally have a table of students. Each student is a "thing" in common sense—each one is an individual with his or her own goals, talents, achievements, and problems. Each requires a record in the Students file, probably with a field for a unique ID, such as a Social Security Number or student number. Other fields in the Students file might include the student's name, birth date, credit hours achieved, and cumulative GPA.

Each student takes many courses, and each section has many students. Each teacher teaches many sections, too. The relational model says that a course is a thing, as is a teacher and a section. Each should have its own table. You will soon find it second nature to know what information should go in which table. The Teachers table should have, for each teacher, his or her ID, name, department, address, hire date, and degrees or other accomplishments affecting his or her rank and salary.

The Courses table has fields for the course ID, title, department, level, description, credit hours, prerequisites, and the like. The Sections table has fields for its ID, the teacher ID (linking it to the Teachers file), the course ID (linking it to the Courses file), and probably the room number and time of its meetings.

A school will also need a Grades table, with fields for the Student ID (linking it to Students), the Section ID (linking it to Sections), and the interim and final grades achieved by the student in the section. This table has one record for each student for each section in which he or she is enrolled.

dBASE, with a little help from you, can use these tables and the links they provide from one to the other to organize and present whatever information is needed.

The typical school situation outlined above is complex, although many businesses are much more complex. You need not concern yourself with the details. dBASE can model the components of any complex situation and their relationships to each other. By doing so, dBASE assists you to achieve your goal of efficiently maintaining, manipulating, and presenting the information you or your clients need.

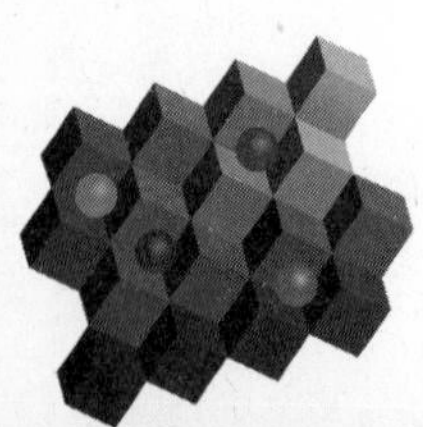

Chapter Snapshot

With dBASE running in the new interactive Windows environment, you are likely to find that creating tables, designing forms and reports, and writing programs are much easier and more intuitive than they ever were before. In this chapter, you learn about the following:

This chapter describes the new dBASE interactive design tools and discusses migration considerations and how to make the transition as smooth as possible.

Migrating from dBASE for DOS

By Virginia Andersen

You will find that moving from the dBASE for DOS Control Center environment to the new interactive dBASE for Windows environment is easily done. Most of the DOS files are usable in Windows, and most of your programs work just as well as before. New design surfaces provide powerful tools for creating forms, queries, and other objects.

dBASE for Windows normally conforms to the standard Windows Multiple Document Interface (MDI). With MDI, you can open multiple documents or multiple views of the same document within the same application window. Each view appears in a separate window that you can freely resize, move, maximize or minimize. The document window menu also replaces the application menu in the menu bar. The document window is a *child window* inside the parent (application) window. Refer to your Windows documentation for more information about MDI.

Introducing the Powerful New Interactive Environment

In the previous chapter, you learned about components that make up the new dBASE desktop. You can do everything you used to do at the Control Center but now you work with menu selections and catalog windows on the desktop. Catalogs are still used to group related files, but the relationships are shown with graphics images in the Catalog window.

Table, form, query, and other files are selected through the Navigator. You even can tell the Navigator you want to create a new table, form, or other file, and you immediately receive access to the new interactive design tools. These tools create the code you used to have to enter at the dot prompt. The code created by the design tool appears in the Command window as you build the design. The code can then be reviewed, edited, and selectively rerun.

The paragraphs that follow briefly describe each of these design tools. To see more detailed information and instructions for using the tools, refer to chapters later in this book.

dBASE for Windows User Assistance

dBASE for Windows provides online interactive user assistance in the form of two tutorials and a context-sensitive online Help feature. The Interactive Tutor takes you through basic features of dBASE and helps you to create tables, queries, and reports using data from the SAMPLES files or your own data. Choose **H**elp, Interactive **T**utors to begin the tutorial (see fig. 2.1).

The Crystal Report generator Personal Trainer is a separate step-by-step tutorial focused on creating dBASE reports. To start the personal trainer, you must begin to create a new report. When you open Personal Trainer, the program remains active while you work and continues to coach you as requested. Figure 2.2 shows the opening screen of Personal Trainer.

The online Help feature provides information relating to the current activity or enables you to search for specific topics. You can access and use dBASE Help the way you would a typical Windows help feature—from the Help menu. After viewing the topic information, you can print the topic, annotate the text, place a bookmark, move to related information, or jump to a specific definition. Figure 2.3 shows a typical Help topic within the Help menu.

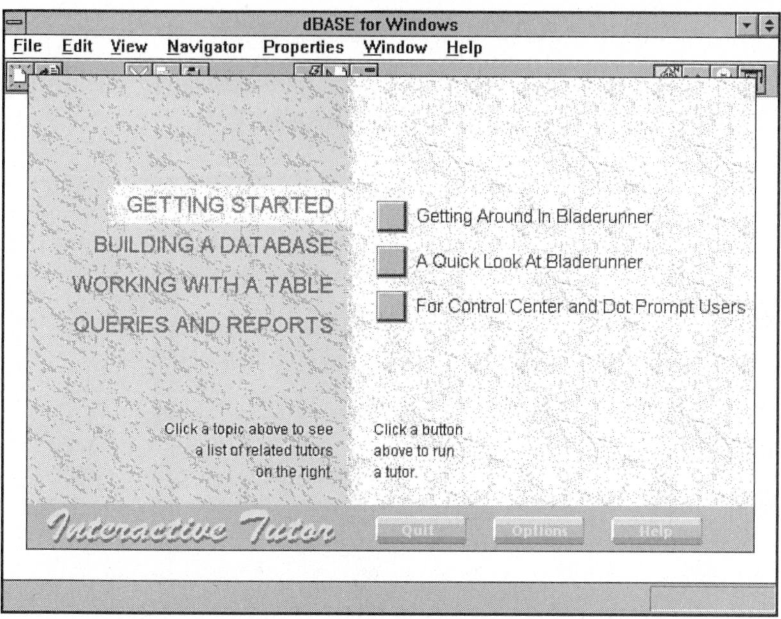

Figure 2.1 Beginning the dBASE for Windows Interactive Tutor.

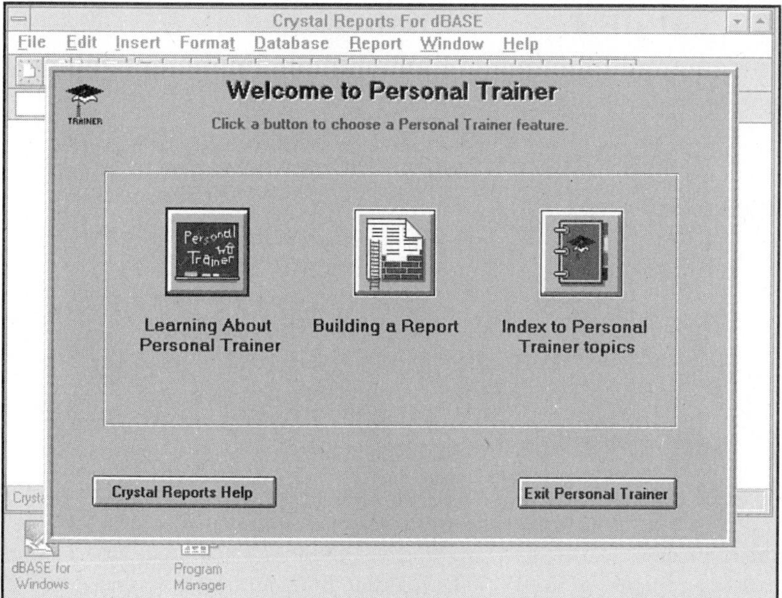

Figure 2.2 Beginning the Crystal Report generator Personal Trainer.

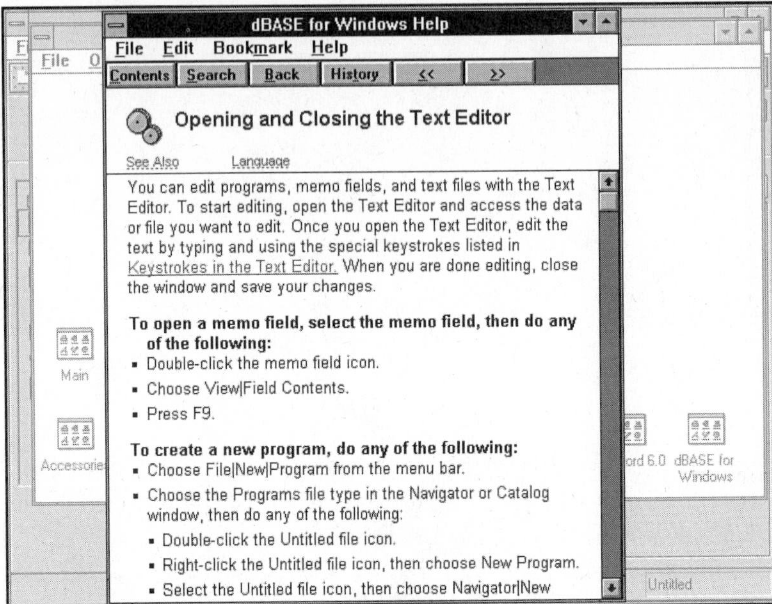

Figure 2.3
A typical dBASE Help topic.

The Table Designer

The Table Designer Table Structure dialog box shown in figure 2.4 contains the complete table structure, including the following:

- ✔ Table Name
- ✔ Table Type (dBASE or Paradox)
- ✔ Date of last table update
- ✔ Number of bytes used in field definitions
- ✔ Number of bytes remaining of the maximum 32,767 bytes allowed.
- ✔ The individual field definitions

The field structure includes the field number, name, type, width, number of decimal places, and an index specification. You can move around the field structure area with the mouse or with the keyboard. Chapter 4, "Designing and Creating Relational Databases," contains information on the use of the Table Designer to build and modify table structures.

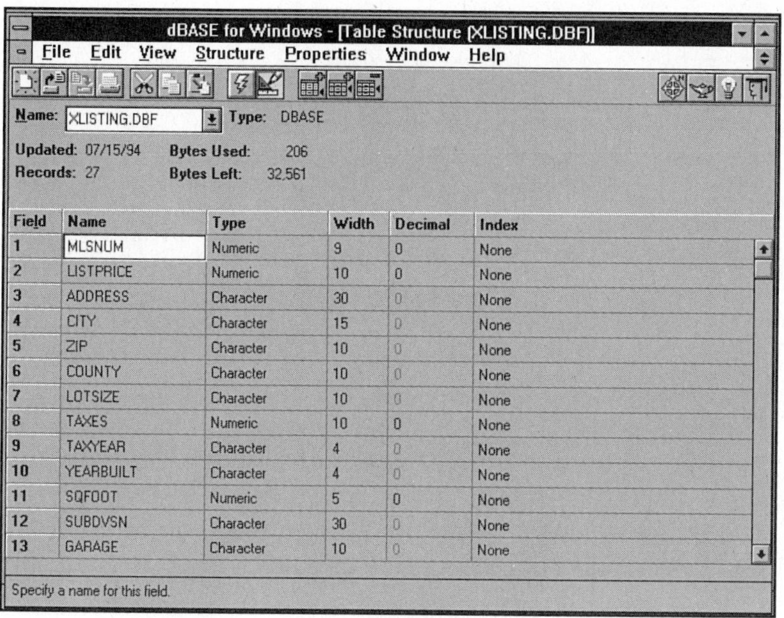

Figure 2.4
The Table Designer Table Structure dialog box.

The dBASE for Windows Form Designer

You use the interactive Form Designer tool to lay out a form, add elements to the form, and specify its appearance and behavior. The front-end Form Expert offers choices of table, fields, layout style, and appearance before arriving at the actual form design surface. While creating a form, you can change from the design view to the run view and see how the data in the current record looks in the form window.

Figure 2.5 shows the design surface for a form used to enter or edit agent records. The Form Designer includes a Controls palette of standard control object tools such as text, entry fields, push buttons, edit boxes, and spin boxes. Click on any object and move it to the design surface to add it to your form design. A second, tabbed page, located in the Controls palette, contains many customized control objects such as an OK push-button and a Cancel push-button.

After adding controls to the form design surface, you can change the object properties with the Object Inspector tool. The specific properties depend on the type of object selected. You can also attach events such as a mouse click to an object and attach a method (a segment of code) to be executed when the specified event occurs.

A Procedure Editor tool is available in the Forms Designer to help you write code to define the behavior of the form's objects.

The Form Designer has special menu options and SpeedBar buttons. See Chapter 6, "Developing Forms," for more information on using the Form Designer.

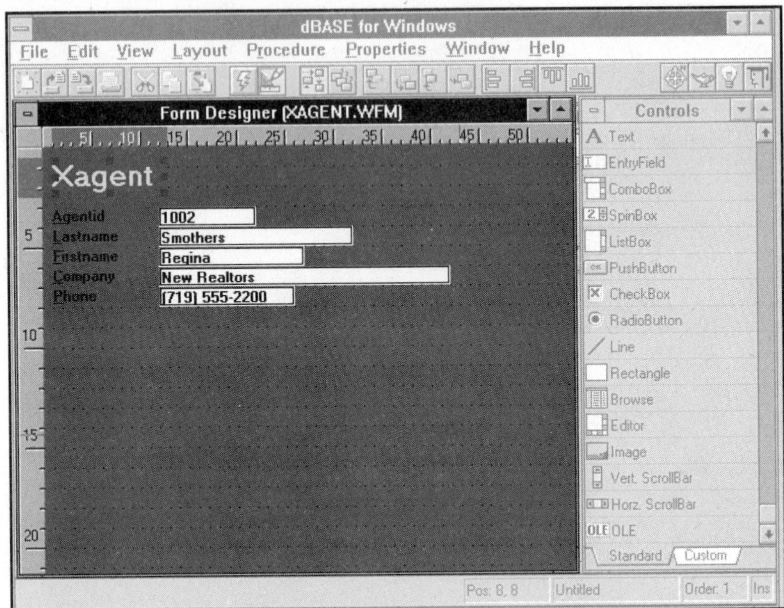

Figure 2.5 The Form Designer, ready to begin creating a form.

The Query Designer

The Query Designer displays a table skeleton in which you can select and arrange the fields to include in the query. You can link two or more tables in the design and have access to field data from all of them. The record order also can be specified in the query design, and filter conditions can limit the records in the resulting view.

Figure 2.6 shows a table skeleton in the Query Designer. Notice the menu options and SpeedBar buttons. See Chapter 8, "Querying Your Data," for more details about building and running queries.

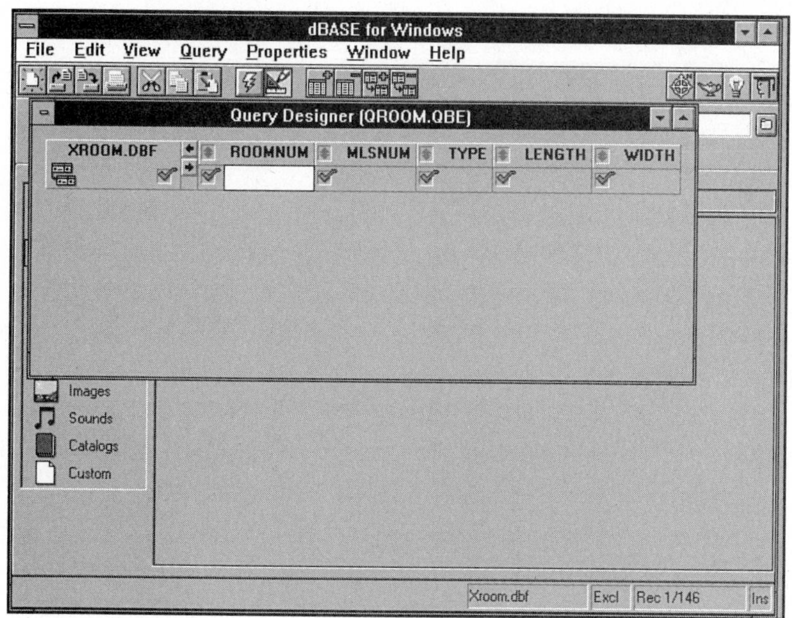

Figure 2.6
The Query Designer with a table skeleton.

The Crystal Report Designer

The Crystal Report Designer is a separate program used to create customized reports, form letters, and mailing labels using existing dBASE table data. The Report Designer contains tools to manipulate data in many ways. It can perform mathematical calculations, compare values, convert data, and merge text with other text or with data.

You can use it to prepare many types of report segments including lists, cross-tabs, data analyses, pre-specified forms, graphs, and charts.

In addition to SpeedBar buttons, the Report Designer displays a Format Bar containing formatting options such as font type and size, line spacing, and alignment.

The report design window shown in figure 2.7 contains an edit box where you build the report. The edit box is divided into horizontal sections such as page header and footer, and a details section. When you design a report, specify what text and objects are to appear in each section of the report. As you create the report, you can add other sections representing summaries and grouped data.

See Chapter 9, "Developing Reports and Labels," for more information on using the Report Designer.

Figure 2.7
The Crystal Report Designer report window.

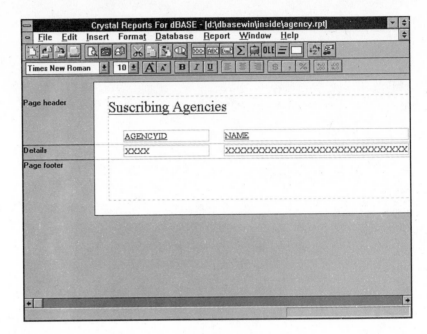

The Menu Designer

The Menu Designer is a tool available through the Form Designer and is used to design horizontal bar menus and pull-down menus for an application. The Menu Designer is reached through the To̲ols option of the L̲ayout menu. You can specify menu options, set properties, and write procedures to attach to the menu options. The Menu Designer writes the code to implement the menu system you design.

The Menu Designer runs from within the Form Designer but it has a different menu bar and different SpeedBar buttons, as shown in figure 2.8. See Chapter 13, "Creating the User Interface," for more details on creating your own menu system using the Menu Designer.

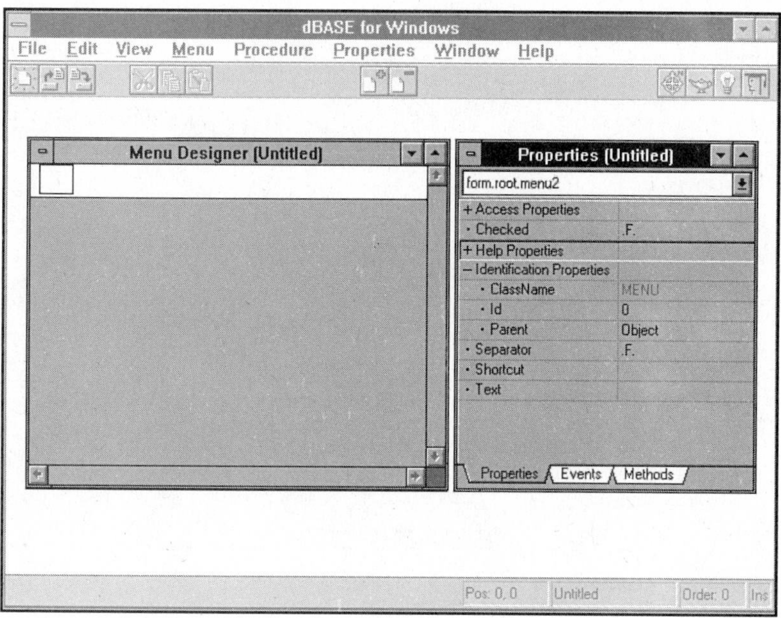

Figure 2.8
The Menu Designer runs from within the Form Designer.

The Expression Builder

The Expression Builder is an interactive tool that helps you create a valid dBASE expression and paste it into the current window or dialog box. An *expression* is a combination of one or more dBASE elements that results in a single value. You use an expression when you build a condition that tests the value in a field in order to filter the records. The records are included in the query or index only if the expression evaluates to be true.

The Expression Builder displays a dialog box (see fig. 2.9) in which you create the expression either manually or with the help of the builder itself. Helpful information is displayed as you work, and the Expression Builder does not paste the expression to the window or dialog box until it is valid and error-free.

See Chapter 7, "Indexing, Sorting, and Locating Your Data," for more information on using the Expression Builder.

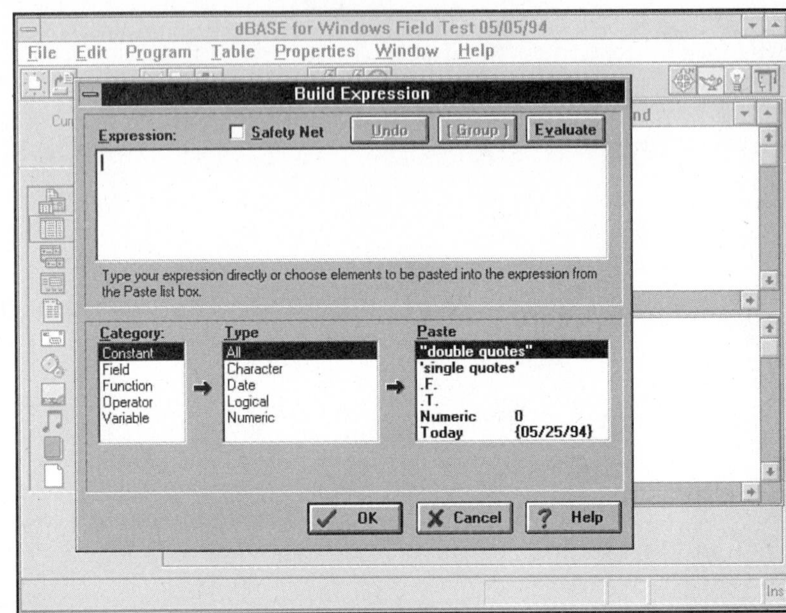

Figure 2.9
The Expression Builder dialog box.

The Editors

dBASE provides two editors—one for editing text (in correspondence) and in memo fields, and another editor for editing program files. If you have an external text editor that you prefer to use, you can specify it in place of either or both dBASE editors.

Editors can be active in more than one window at a time. Therefore, you can edit several files at once, or edit different parts of the same file by moving from one window to another. If you are editing the same file in more than one window, whatever changes you make in one window automatically show up in the other.

Refer to Chapter 10, "Understanding the dBASE Language," for more information on using the Program Editor and Chapter 12, "Understanding the Event-Driven Programming," for the Text Editor.

Three-Dimensional Dialog Boxes

A few of the dBASE dialog boxes are actually three-dimensional with multiple pages. Each page contains a different category of options from which to choose. To reach another page, click the page tab at the bottom edge of the dialog box.

For example, the Desktop Properties dialog box shown in figure 2.10 has six pages containing properties relating to Country, Table, Data Entry, Files, Application, and Programming. Most of the options in the six pages replace the SET commands used in earlier versions of dBASE.

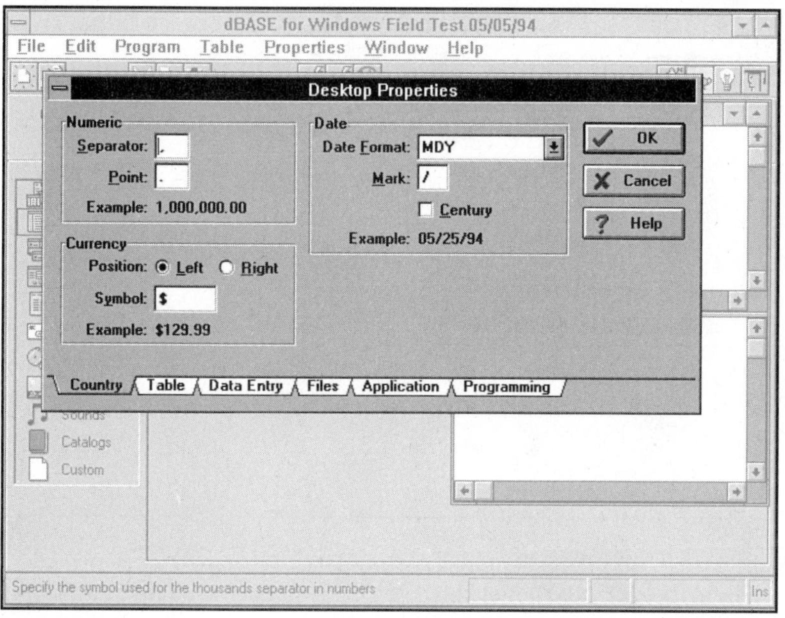

Figure 2.10
The Desktop Properties dialog box has six pages.

Taking a Look at Migration Considerations

Most of the dBASE IV features are retained and new ones have been added in dBASE for Windows. However, many of the commands have been replaced by dialog box options and menu selections. For example, the six pages of the Desktop Properties dialog box contain most of the environmental SET command features. Additional functions have been created that can replace some user-defined functions.

Most programs run without changes. Any commands that no longer apply are simply ignored. The Results pane of the Command window displays what used to appear in the DOS full-screen.

The following sections describe in more detail some of the changes you should consider when migrating from dBASE for DOS to Windows.

Files

Your dBASE for DOS files fall into one of three categories: files that can be used as is, files that must be converted before opening, and files that no longer apply.

The files that dBASE for Windows supports with no changes are listed in table 2.1.

Table 2.1
Files supported by dBASE for Windows.

File Type	File Extensions
Catalog	CAT
Data	DBF, DBT, MDX, NDX
Forms	FMT
Labels	LBG, LBL for dBASE III
Programs	PRG, MEM
Queries	QBE, VUE, QRY for dBASE III
Reports	FRG, FRM for dBASE III

Files that cannot be used in dBASE for Windows are any data and memo files (DBF and DBT) and index files (MDX and NDX) that have been encrypted. If you want to use the encrypted files in dBASE for Windows, you must first decrypt them in dBASE IV with the SET ENCRYPTION OFF command.

The files that do not apply in dBASE for Windows include all compiled object and temporary files generated by dBASE IV. Template language, multiuser, and application generator files are also not supported. Refer to your dBASE User's Guide for a complete list of unsupported file types.

dBASE enables you to create and use Paradox and SQL files. The table structure dialog box gives you the option of creating a Paradox table with the specific field name and type criteria. You also can create primary and secondary indexes for Paradox tables. To access SQL tables, you need to install the Borland SQL Link software that translates commands into syntax understood by SQL.

To use existing files, copy or move the files into the directories you are using in dBASE. Update the directory path, if necessary. The file names then appear in the Navigator window and are accessible.

Tables

dBASE for Windows no longer refers to collections of records as database files. The current terminology used is *tables,* although *database* refers to a collection of tables and related files used for a common purpose. For example, the tables, reports, and forms used by a company to maintain contact with their sales representatives' activities and progress would constitute a database.

Two new field types have been added to dBASE: binary, and object linking and embedding (OLE). *Binary* fields provide multimedia capabilities to dBASE by containing data stored in binary form such as bitmap images or sound data. The binary fields can contain BMP or PCX image files or WAV sound files. The binary field data is stored in the DBT file with the memo text and is updated right along with the other field data.

OLE fields contain objects that have been imported from other Windows applications. OLE field data is also stored in the DBT file.

Table data can now be viewed in three different layouts, instead of only two. You have a choice of the familiar browse or columnar layouts, or the new form layout. The form layout displays a single record like the columnar layout, but with the fields arranged horizontally in the window. Figures 2.11–2.13 compare the three ways you can view table data.

You no longer have to choose a menu option to clear the data from a field. You simply choose the field and press the Del or backspace keys or just type new data over it.

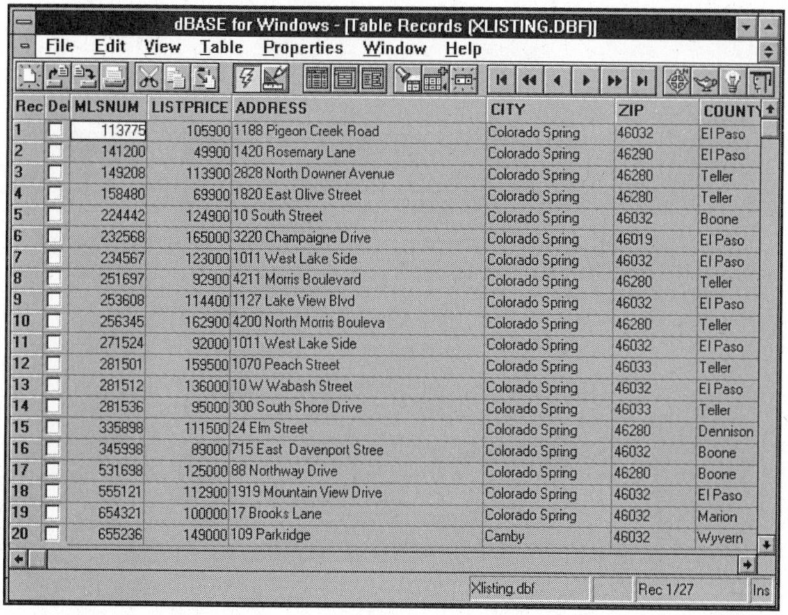

dBASE for Windows - [Table Records (XLISTING.DBF)]

File Edit View Table Properties Window Help

Rec	Del	MLSNUM	LISTPRICE	ADDRESS	CITY	ZIP	COUNTY
1		113775	105900	1188 Pigeon Creek Road	Colorado Spring	46032	El Paso
2		141200	49900	1420 Rosemary Lane	Colorado Spring	46290	El Paso
3		149208	113900	2828 North Downer Avenue	Colorado Spring	46280	Teller
4		158480	69900	1820 East Olive Street	Colorado Spring	46280	Teller
5		224442	124900	10 South Street	Colorado Spring	46032	Boone
6		232568	165000	3220 Champaigne Drive	Colorado Spring	46019	El Paso
7		234567	123000	1011 West Lake Side	Colorado Spring	46032	El Paso
8		251697	92900	4211 Morris Boulevard	Colorado Spring	46280	Teller
9		253608	114400	1127 Lake View Blvd	Colorado Spring	46032	El Paso
10		256345	162900	4200 North Morris Bouleva	Colorado Spring	46280	Teller
11		271524	92000	1011 West Lake Side	Colorado Spring	46032	El Paso
12		281501	159500	1070 Peach Street	Colorado Spring	46033	Teller
13		281512	136000	10 W Wabash Street	Colorado Spring	46032	El Paso
14		281536	95000	300 South Shore Drive	Colorado Spring	46033	Teller
15		335898	111500	24 Elm Street	Colorado Spring	46280	Dennison
16		345998	89000	715 East Davenport Stree	Colorado Spring	46032	Boone
17		531698	125000	88 Northway Drive	Colorado Spring	46280	Boone
18		555121	112900	1919 Mountain View Drive	Colorado Spring	46032	El Paso
19		654321	100000	17 Brooks Lane	Colorado Spring	46032	Marion
20		655236	149000	109 Parkridge	Camby	46032	Wyvern

Xlisting.dbf Rec 1/27 Ins

Figure 2.11
The browse layout.

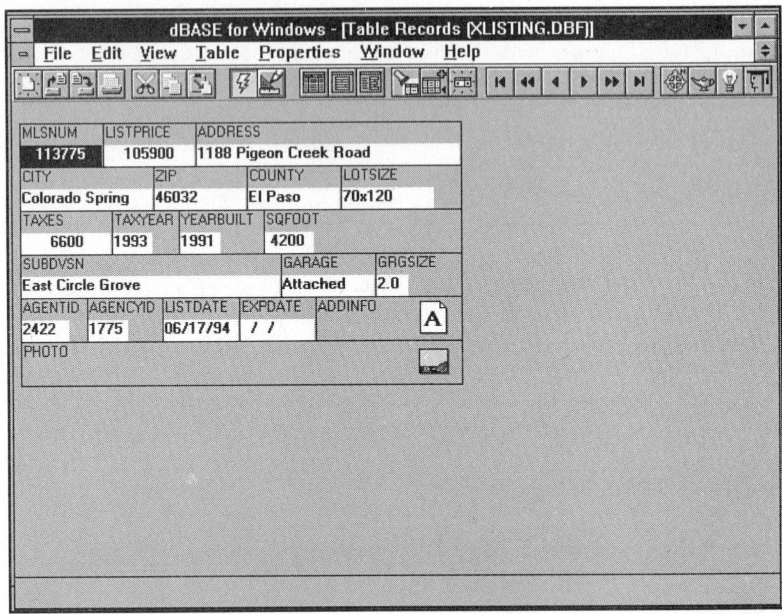

Figure 2.12 The columnar layout.

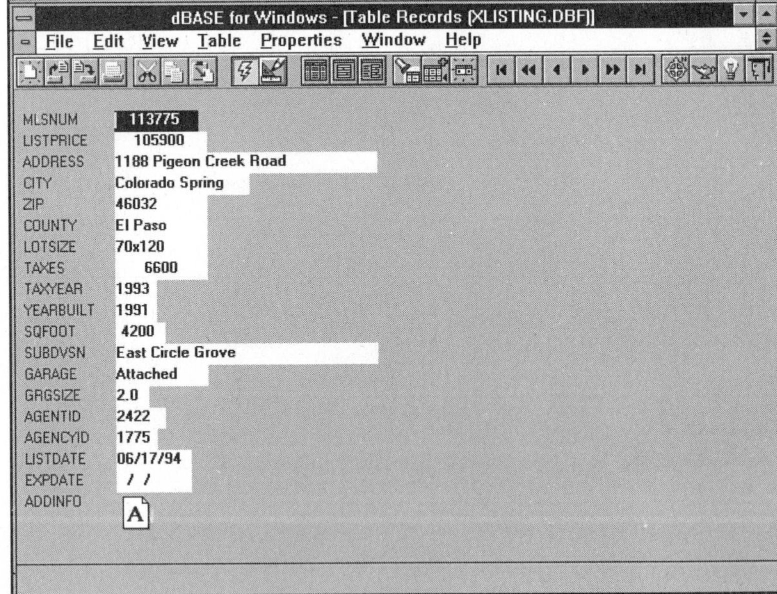

Figure 2.13 The form layout.

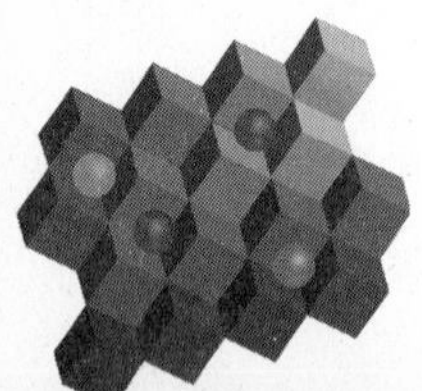

Indexes

dBASE uses MDX files to store indexes and recognizes MDX files created by earlier versions of dBASE. The Manage Indexes dialog box provides most of the capabilities of the Data menu of the Control Center.

You can use NDX single index files in dBASE, but you have to open them with a dBASE command through the Command window or in a program. NDX files are not included in the Manage Indexes feature, so it is a good idea to convert the NDX indexes to tags in an MDX file with the COPY INDEXES command.

You can also index Paradox tables through dBASE for Windows. See Chapter 7, "Indexing, Sorting, and Locating Your Data," for more information on creating and using indexes.

Forms

dBASE enables you to use the Forms designer to modify WFM files. You also can use the Form Designer to modify PRG files containing a code that creates a form—if the Form Designer can understand the commands in the program. See Chapter 6, "Developing Forms," for more information on using the Form Designer to modify dBASE for DOS form files.

Queries

You can run VUE and QRY files from previous versions of dBASE, but you can't modify them. If you do change one and save it from dBASE for Windows, it is saved as QBE file. Some of the query elements such as GROUP BY and the AGGREGATE operators do not appear when you open a query in dBASE for Windows. In addition, the update query types, such as the Find, Replace, Delete, Undelete, and Append queries, are replaced by Table menu selections.

The condition boxes you used to create the query with dBASE IV might not display, but the conditions they imposed do appear in the skeleton. Any AND operator is replaced by a comma in the skeleton. The condition boxes in dBASE for Windows treat separate lines differently from dBASE IV. Separate lines now indicate an OR condition instead of AND. This will be discussed more in the upcoming section about cautions in this chapter.

Programs

Most programs run with no changes. Some commands and functions used in dBASE IV are no longer supported or are not appropriate for a Windows application environment and are simply ignored. Some are no longer necessary and have been removed. Others, though, have been replaced by new commands and functions or by dialog box options.

Programs run inside the Command window instead of in the full DOS screen. The results of the commands appear in the Results pane of the Command window. Online help is available to provide information about any error messages.

You should enhance your applications to take advantage of the new dBASE for Windows object-oriented programming features. Use the conversion utility program, the Component Builder, to convert DOS files to Windows equivalents:

- ✔ DOS screens (FMT) to dBASE for Windows forms (WFM)
- ✔ Code that creates menus to code in a dBASE for Windows MNU file.
- ✔ DOS report forms (FRM) to Crystal reports (RPT)
- ✔ DOS label forms (LBL) to Crystal label files (RPL)

Take precautions when converting programs or other code segments. After you make sure the code runs the way you want it to, print out the existing code and capture a screen shot so you have some documentation. Then you should create text objects for the @ . . . SAY commands, entry field objects for the GET commands, and push button objects for menu options and the OK and Cancel buttons.

Finally, assign event handlers, such as OnClick, to the buttons and attach a segment of code to each one. The code is called a *method*, which tells dBASE what is supposed to happen when the event occurs.

Many of the SET commands are replaced by properties. For example, the SET BORDER command has been replaced by the Border property.

A new interactive tool has been created to help you debug new programs. Part Four, "Developing for the Windows Environment," of this book contains complete information on object-oriented dBASE for Windows programming.

Menus

The menu definitions created in dBASE IV are retained and usable in dBASE for Windows. However, there also is some new terminology. The row of menu options across the top of the window is now called the menu bar instead of the horizontal menu. The pop-up menu has become a pull-down menu, and a menu that results from making a selection from a pull-down menu is called a cascading menu.

You can use the Component Builder utility program to convert existing menus into code for the updated version of the menu system. The new menu definition file has the same name as the host PRG file but has a MNU extension.

Reports and Labels

You can use your old report and label files as is, but if you want to modify them, they get converted to the new RPT and RPL file formats. The conversion is done by the Crystal Report generator as described more fully in Chapter 9, "Developing Reports and Labels."

Understanding Compatibility Concerns

A few inconsistencies can cause trouble if you aren't aware of them. Those inconsistencies include reserved key combinations, the renumbering of some error messages, a lack of backward compatibility, and a significant difference in creating conditions with a Condition box.

The next paragraphs discuss these and some other, more minor differences that might cause incompatibility.

Reserved Key Combinations

Because dBASE now runs in a Windows environment, Windows reserves certain key combinations as shortcuts to commands. If you have assigned a procedure or user-defined function to any of the key combinations listed in table 2.2, you should change the assignment to another combination.

Table 2.2
Reserved Key Combinations

Key Combination	Windows Action
Ctrl+Esc	Displays list of running applications.
Alt+Esc	Switches to next application.
Alt+Tab	Switches to previous application.
Shift+Alt+Tab	Cycles through task list (hold Shift+Alt while you press Tab).
Alt+Spacebar	Opens Control menu of the application window.
Alt+Hyphen	Opens Control menu of the document window.
Alt+Spacebar	Opens Control menu of a non-Windows application.
Print Screen	Copies an image on the screen to the Clipboard (non-Windows applications must be in Text mode).

continues

Table 2.2, Continued
Reserved Key Combinations

Key Combination	Windows Action
Alt+Print Screen	Copies image of the active window to the Clipboard.
Alt+F4	Quits an application or closes a window.
Ctrl+F4	Closes active group or document window.
Ctrl+F6	Cycles among open windows.

Error Message Numbers

Many of the error messages have different numbers than previously. If you have used an error-trapping routine in your application, before you try to run it, check to see that the error numbers you want to trap are still the same.

File Formats

If you modify a DBF or DBT file in dBASE and add one of the new field types, binary or OLE, you might not use the file in the previous version of dBASE. Files with the new field types are not backward compatible.

User-Defined Functions

dBASE for Windows includes many new functions. You might have created some user-defined functions for use in applications that are now implemented as dBASE functions. Your functions work, but you must make sure none have the same name as one of the new dBASE functions.

Queries

In addition to replacing several of the update query types with menu options, dBASE has reversed the meaning of multiple lines in the Condition box. When you create a query and add filter conditions under the field name, two lines create an OR condition. Similarly, two lines in the Condition box also create an OR condition in dBASE for Windows. dBASE IV treated the second line in the Condition box as an AND condition. Check out your queries carefully before accepting the results as correct.

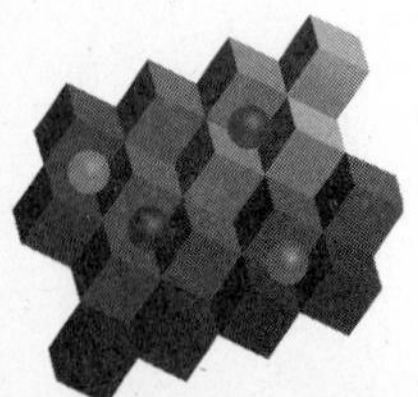

Part II

Organizing and Finding Data

Chapter Snapshot

dBASE for Windows offers you a totally new way to interact with dBASE. The dBASE for DOS dot prompt and the Control Center have been replaced with a highly interactive and intuitive environment. In this chapter you learn to:

The first place to begin is with the opening screen in dBASE for Windows.

Working in dBASE Interactive Environment Databases

By Jim Wetzel

You might have used dBASE for DOS and are now migrating to the Windows environment. Or you might be a Windows user who just needs to know about the special options of dBASE in the Windows desktop environment.

Either way, this chapter helps you by pointing out integral options and tools that you can use as you make your way through the workings of dBASE for Windows. You learn, for instance, how to work with the menu bar to perform commands. You also learn about SpeedBar shortcuts and learn to set your desktop and dBASE environment preferences. After reading this chapter, you should have a more thorough background of the dBASE for Windows user interface.

Understanding the dBASE Development Environment

After you start up dBASE, you see a screen that looks similar to figure 3.1.

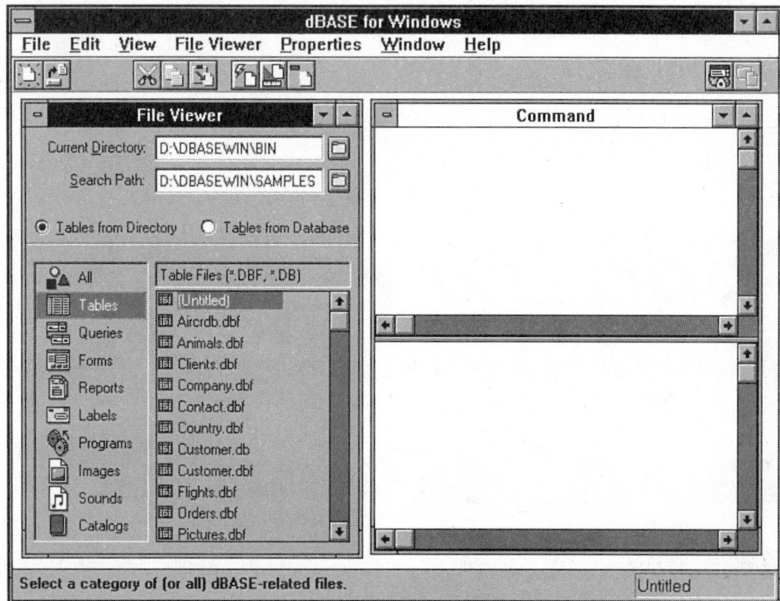

Figure 3.1
The standard view of dBASE at start-up.

The menus represent standard Windows menus with the File, Edit, Window, and Help items. dBASE offers a key difference, however, in that the menu bar is dynamic and changes as the Navigator and Command windows gain focus.

Click on the Navigator and Command windows in succession and watch the items on the menu bar change. Note that the File, Edit, Properties, Window, and Help items remain constant and that the two items following Edit change between View and Navigator, and Program and Table. These items change to present you with the operations and commands you are most likely to use while that window has focus.

The *SpeedBar* is a group of buttons that represent common operations that you need often and instantaneously, such as create file, open file, copy, cut, and paste. The *Navigator window* presents you with quick access to all of the common dBASE file types, such as Tables, Queries, Forms, Labels, Reports, Programs, and Catalogs. Additionally, the Navigator supports views for images and sounds that are new to dBASE.

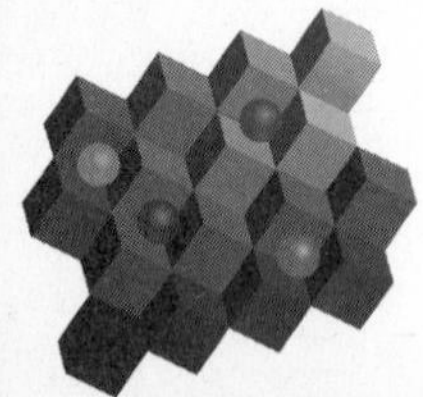

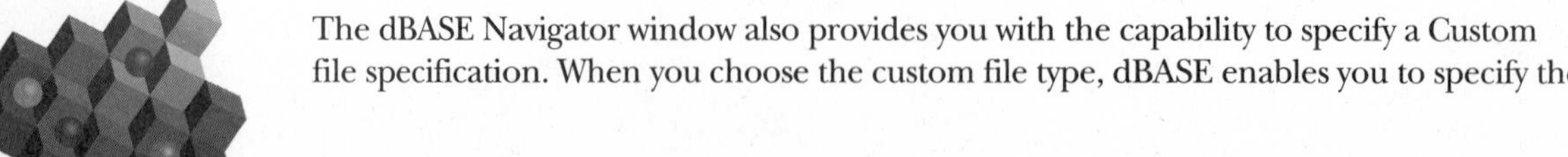

The dBASE Navigator window also provides you with the capability to specify a Custom file specification. When you choose the custom file type, dBASE enables you to specify the type of files you want shown (see fig. 3.2). You can specify *.?DX to show all dBASE index files or *.??K to show all dBASE created backup files.

The *Command window* is a two-paned window for standard keyboard input of commands and the display for command results. The input portion is the equivalent of the dBASE for DOS dot (.) prompt where you can type in any dBASE command.

Most dBASE commands you issue from the menu bar or SpeedBar will be entered in the Command window for you.

The *results* portion of the window is where the results or output of the commands issued in the input pane are displayed. To see a quick illustration of this, click on the Command window to give it focus, type **? "Hello World"** in the input pane, and press Enter. See the results in the lower portion? The *status bar* at the bottom of the screen gives you a text description with additional information about the highlighted menu item or object.

Displaying the status bar is affected by the SET STATUS command and by the status bar settings on the Application page of the Desktop Properties. The Desktop Properties, described later in this chapter, give you control over many of the elements affecting the look and actions of the dBASE desktop.

Windows Control Menu

dBASE uses the standard Windows controls, such as move, size, maximize, and close, for all of its windows. Prior to looking at the other elements of the dBASE environment, this is a good time to briefly review some of those controls so that you will be able to manipulate the windows later.

Changing the Placement of a Window

You can change the placement of any of dBASE windows simply by moving your mouse to the title bar of the window, clicking and holding down the left mouse button, and dragging the window to its new position.

Alternatively, you can click on the Windows Control menu to drop down the menu of choices and click on the **M**ove option. At this point a crossed arrow appears, indicating that you can move the window using any one of the four arrow keys. When the window is in the place you want it, press Enter to accept the move. If you change your mind at any time, press Esc and the operation will be abandoned.

Changing the Size of a Window

Similar to moving the dBASE windows around, you might also want to resize one or more of the windows. This can be especially helpful if you are running Windows on a high resolution monitor that supports video resolution of 800×600 or above. To resize any one of your windows, all you need to do is move your mouse pointer to any one of the window edges, wait for the pointer to change into a double-headed arrow, and then click and hold down the left mouse button and drag the edge the direction you want to expand or contract the window. You can also move your mouse to one of the corners and stretch the top and a side or the bottom and a side at the same time.

As with the **M**ove command, you can also use the keyboard to resize windows by using the Windows Control menu.

At 1024×768 display resolution you have more than enough room to have the Navigator and Command windows open simultaneously. This also gives you the ability to have the equivalent of a DOS text screen 80×25 for the command results portion. This is a great aid if you are migrating your dBASE for DOS applications.

Minimizing, Maximizing, and Closing a Window

In dBASE it is often helpful to focus on a particular window, or remove a window that you are not presently using. If you find yourself working in the Command window most of the time, you might want to consider minimizing the Navigator window. An alternative to minimizing the Navigator window is to maximize the Command window. Either one of these options provides more screen on which to work and removes items that might be distracting. Similarly, if you use only the menus and the Navigator window, there may be no need to have the Command window displayed. Again, this provides more screen display area without the distraction of unused windows.

As with other standard windows, the Minimize and Maximize options in the Control menu control each of the main windows in dBASE. To completely close and remove a window, double-click the left mouse button on the Windows Control menu. You can also click on the minimize or maximize Windows controls to achieve the same results.

The Command window continues to record commands even after you close it.

Cascading and Tiling Windows

As indicated in the preceding section, the default arrangement of dBASE may not always be well-suited to the way you work. Although you can take the time to move the windows to suit your specific needs, you can also let Windows do the work for you. The Window item on the menu bar offers you three options for positioning your windows: Cascade, Tile Horizontally, and Tile Vertically. These three options arrange your windows similar to figures 3.2 through 3.4.

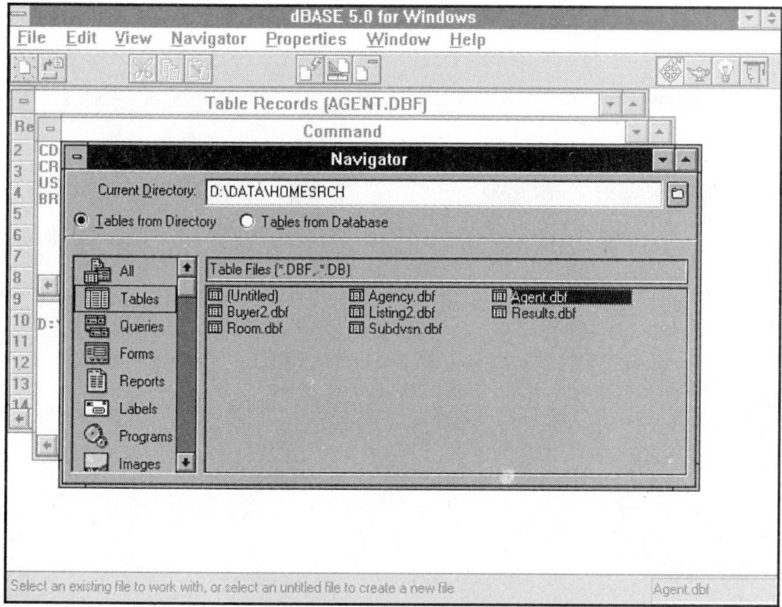

Figure 3.2
The Navigator, Command, and Listing table in a cascaded view.

You may have noticed that the Cascade and Tile Vertically options each have a speed or accelerator key associated with them (Shift+F5 and Shift+F4, respectively). As you will see later, many of the menu items have accelerator keys associated with them to provide you another way of issuing the same command action.

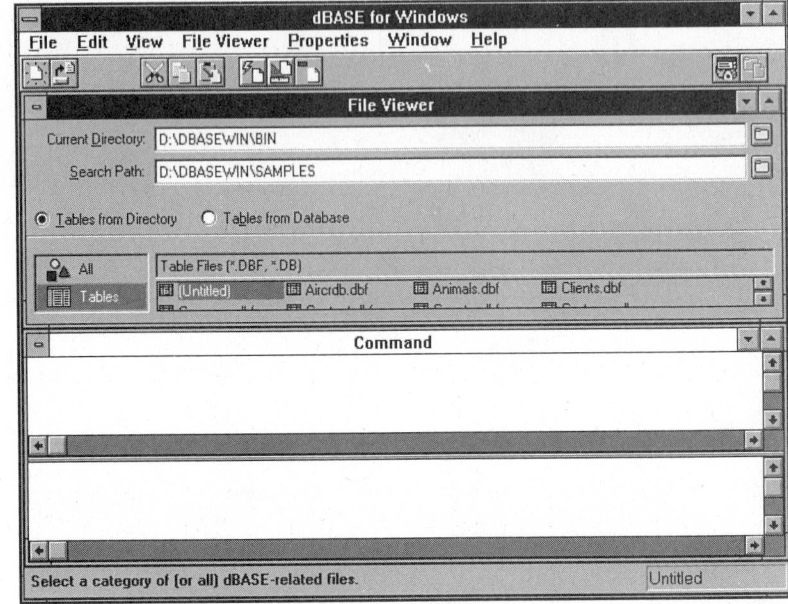

Figure 3.3 The Navigator, Command, and Listing table in a horizontal tiled view.

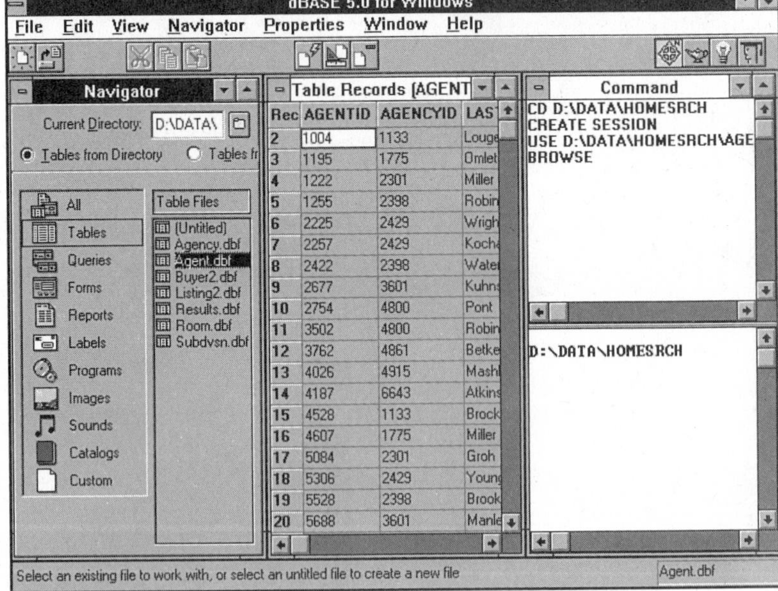

Figure 3.4 The Navigator, Command, and Listing table in a vertical tiled view.

Setting Command Window Properties

In addition to the standard Windows tiling options, the Command window has some special tiling features of its own. If you right-click anywhere in the input pane of the Command window, a property inspector for that window appears. The first option in the property inspector is the Command **W**indow Properties. Clicking on this option opens the Command Window Properties dialog box (see fig. 3.5).

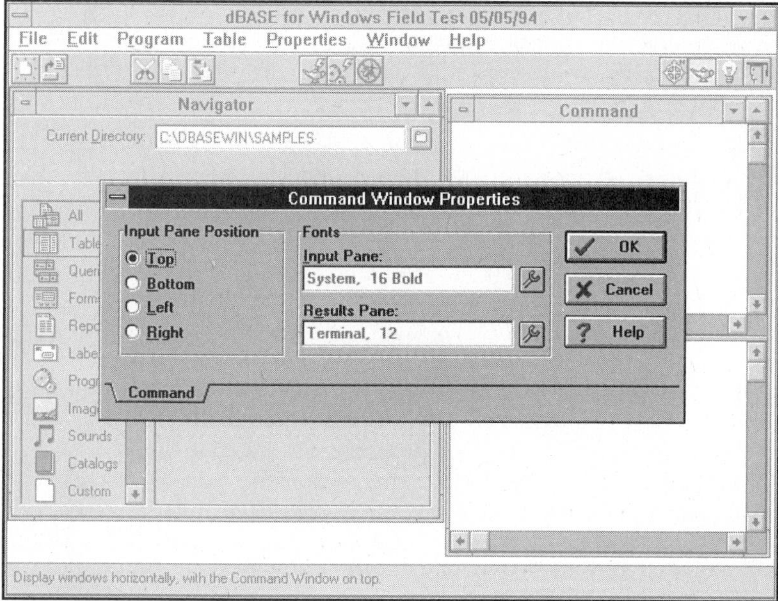

Figure 3.5
The Command Window Properties dialog box.

The Command Window Properties dialog box can also be opened by selecting the **C**ommand Window option in the **P**roperties menu.

The Command Window Properties dialog box enables you to change the orientation of the input pane of the Command window relative to the results pane. The options in the Input Pane Position area of the Command Window Properties dialog box enable you to have the input pane on the **T**op, **B**ottom, **L**eft, or **R**ight side of the Command window. These and other properties of the Command window are covered later in this chapter.

Object Inspection

The Object Inspector is a powerful feature of dBASE that uses the right mouse button to bring up local menus for actions that can be performed on the current object. You can click the right mouse button at almost any place in the dBASE environment to bring up a local option menu specific to the closest object. These menus provide most of the commonly needed functions for the currently highlighted or pointed to item. Some of the options are copy, cut, and paste, as well as menu items for modifying or viewing the objects' properties. Object inspection is just one of the many productivity advances brought to you by the interactive environment of dBASE.

Properties

While working in the dBASE environment, you have a great deal of control over the appearance of the environment as well as the standard settings. The following sections describe the various options you can set.

Desktop

The Desktop option of the Properties menu item enables you to control just about every aspect of the dBASE interactive environment. For dBASE for DOS users, this option replaces the DBSETUP program, which enabled you to set options in the DOS CONFIG.DB file. The options set in the Desktop properties are stored in the DBASEWIN.INI file. The six categories in the following sections are available in the Desktop Options of the Properties menu item. An overview of each item is presented.

The Desktop Option of the Properties menu item displays a notebook metaphor, with each category being represented by an index tab.

Country

As you make changes to each of the fields on the Country page, there is a visual representation of how the date, number, or currency value will appear, as shown in figure 3.6.

For numbers, you can specify the character you want to use for the thousands separator and decimal point. For dollar values, you can use the Currency options to specify the currency symbol and its position to the right or left of the dollar value. The Date area gives you the flexibility to specify the date separator mark, whether the year includes the century, and the format in which the date is presented. The format of the date can be one of the following:

Option	Format
AMERICAN	MM/DD/YY
ANSI	YY.MM.DD
BRITISH	DD/MM/YY

Option	Format
FRENCH	DD/MM/YY
GERMAN	DD.MM.YY
ITALIAN	DD-MM-YY
JAPAN	YY/MM/DD
USA	MM-DD-YY
MDY	MM/DD/YY
DMY	DD/MM/YY
YMD	YY/MM/DD

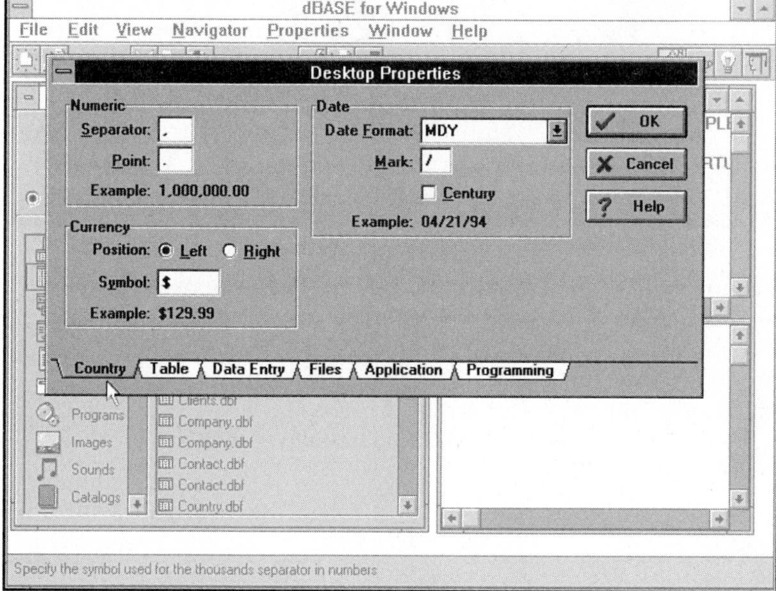

Figure 3.6
The Country page of the Desktop Properties dialog box enables you to change how numbers, dates, and currency are displayed.

The default value for each of these fields is set by the International option of the Windows Control Panel

Table

The Table page of Desktop Properties enables you to specify options that dBASE uses when operating in a multiuser environment, default data base types (dBASE or Paradox), block sizes for Index and Memo Blocks, and various other table-related properties (see fig. 3.7)

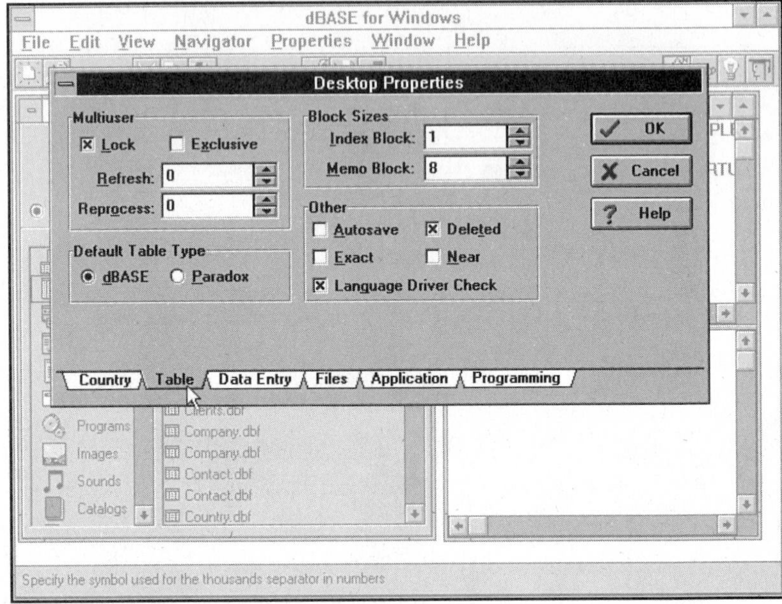

Figure 3.7 The Table page of the Desktop Properties dialog box controls Multiuser and other Table options.

The multiuser properties enable you to specify whether you want to lock table records while reading data and how many times you want dBASE to attempt to lock the file if another user has control. You also can specify whether or not you want to open tables for your exclusive use, or if you want to open them for sharing with others. Also, if you are operating in a shared environment, you can specify the refresh rate for your screen to tell dBASE how often to update your display with current table information that may have been altered or added by others.

The Multiuser options are for the advanced dBASE user and should not be altered unless you are familiar with your networking environment. Please consult your LAN Administrator prior to making any changes to these settings.

Some of the other important settings on the Tables page include the following:

- ✔ **Autosave.** Determines whether records are written to disk each time they are changed or added.
- ✔ **Deleted.** Controls whether deleted records are displayed in table views and used when processing certain dBASE commands.

✔ **Near.** Tells dBASE to place the record pointer to the closest match when a SEEK or FIND operation is unsuccessful at finding an exact match. If unchecked, dBASE places the record pointer at the end of file when a successful match is not found.

Data Entry

The entries on the Data Entry page enable you to control three main areas. The first is how the keyboard reacts to the Enter and Esc keys as well as the size of the type ahead buffer. The second is the sound of the bell when dBASE detects an error or that you have completed data entry for a field. The last area specifies whether delimiters are used to mark the beginning and end of a data entry field, and, if used, what character will serve as the delimiter. See figure 3.8 for an example of the Data Entry page.

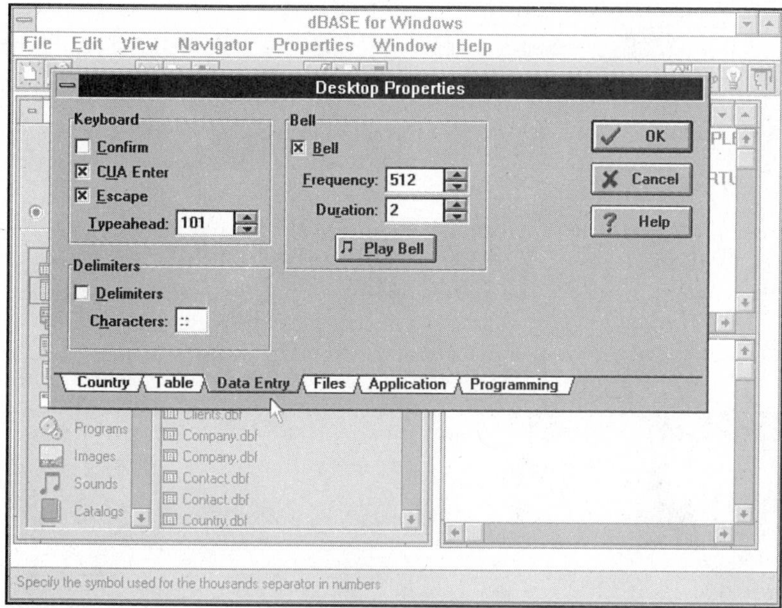

Figure 3.8
The Data Entry page of the Desktop Properties dialog box controls the keyboard, bell, and delimiters.

Files

The Files page of the Desktop Properties enables you to tell dBASE the location of the default search path and set the default current directory at startup. The search path operates similarly to the DOS PATH command in that it enables dBASE to look beyond the current directory for the files and programs it needs (see fig. 3.9).

Figure 3.9
The Files page of the Desktop Properties specifies file locations and edit and add data formats.

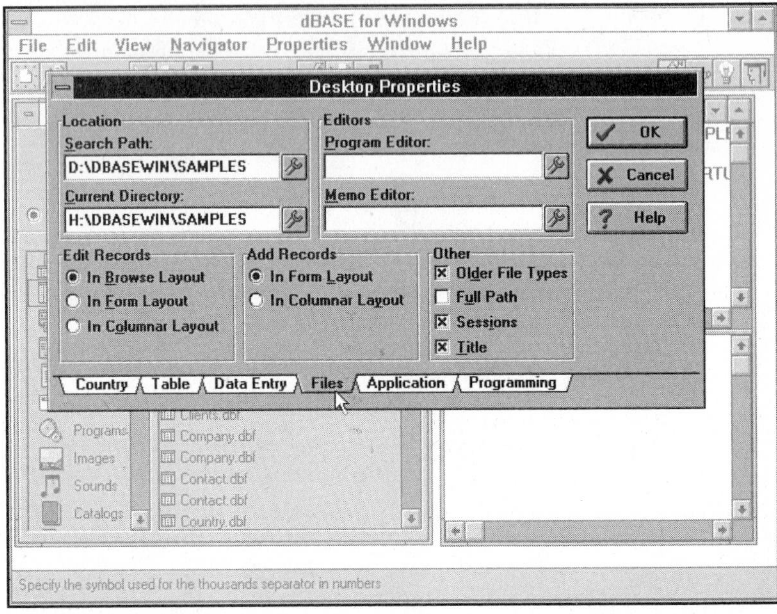

There also is an area to specify an optional external editor to use when modifying dBASE programs and editing dBASE memo fields. Also in the Files section are areas where you can tell dBASE what mode you want to use as a default for adding and editing records. You can edit records in Browse, Form, or Columnar layouts (see figs. 3.10 through 3.13). Adding records is restricted to the Form and Columnar layouts.

Figure 3.10
Editing records in Browse view.

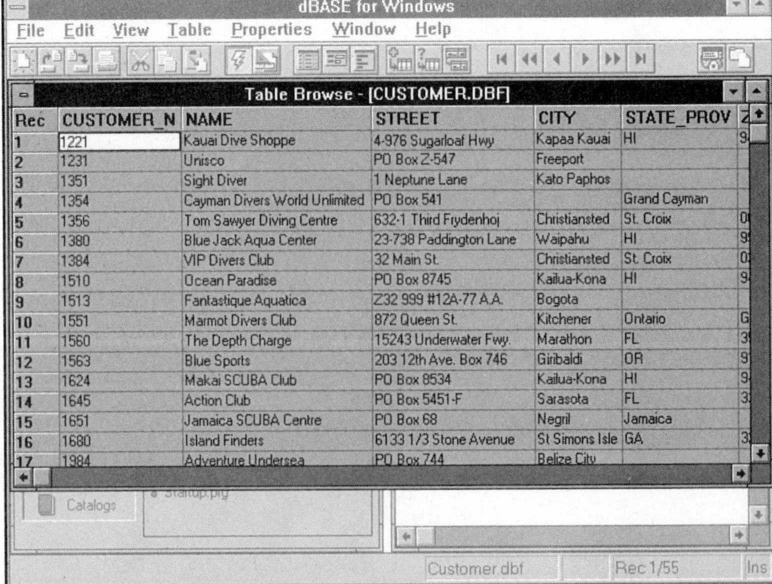

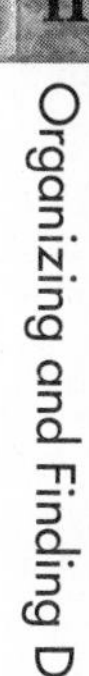

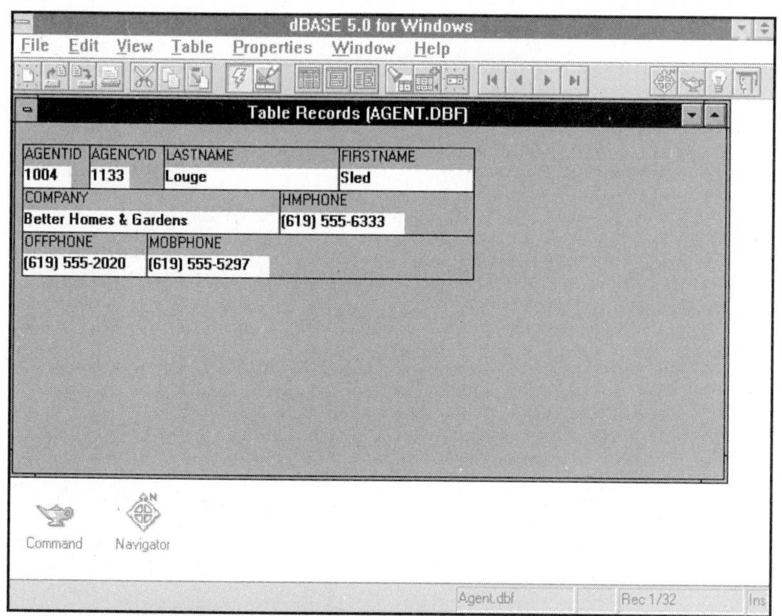

Figure 3.11 Editing records in Form view.

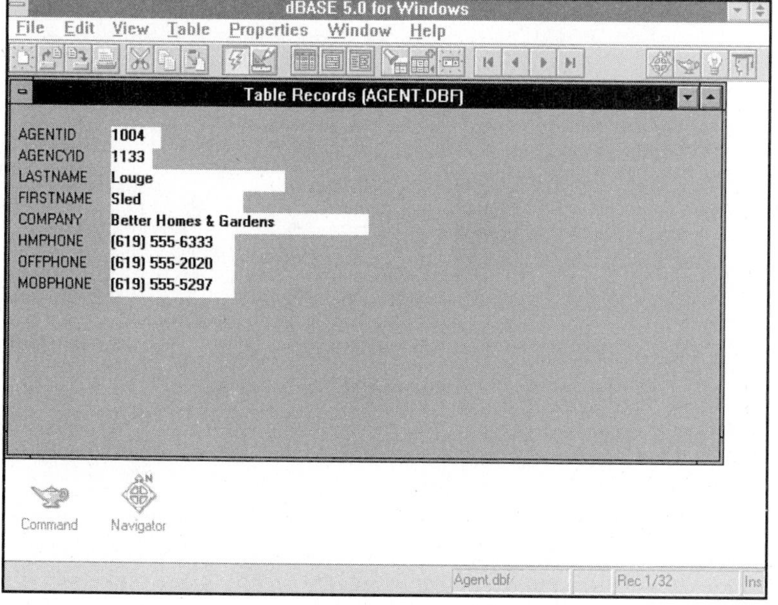

Figure 3.12 Editing records in Columnar view.

Although you cannot add records in Browse mode by default, you can switch to Browse mode from Form or Columnar mode by pressing F2 to cycle through the display modes.

The Other available settings enable you to specify whether dBASE returns a full path name for files in use and whether you are prompted to enter a title when new files are created while a catalog is open.

Application

The Application page of the Desktop Properties options has settings for the SpeedBar Position, Status Bar Settings, and a setting for the Most Recently Used files list (see fig. 3.13).

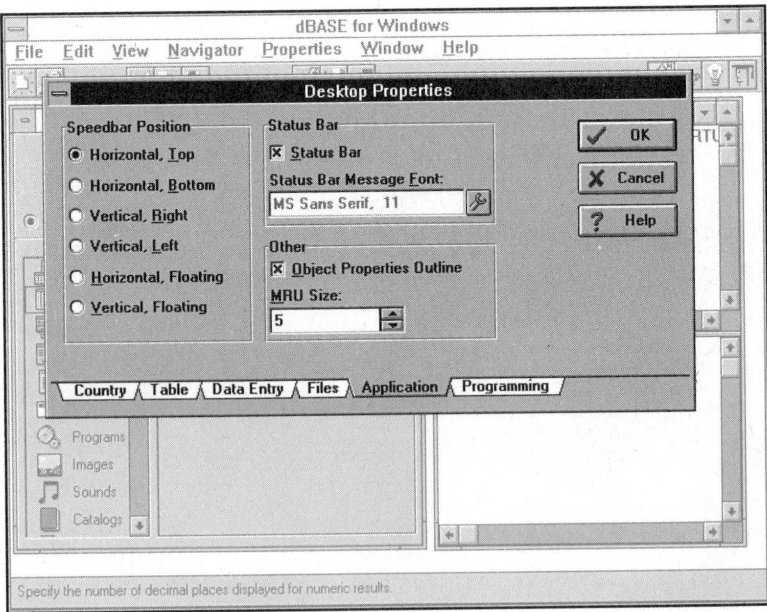

Figure 3.13
The Application page controls some of the general dBASE application controls.

The SpeedBar Position option gives you control over the orientation of the SpeedBar, horizontal or vertical as well as the placement of the SpeedBar. The options for placement include all four sides of the screen as well as letting the SpeedBar float or be placed in a specific screen position.

The Status Bar setting enables you to control whether or not you want to have a status bar at the bottom of the screen, and what font you want to use to display the status messages.

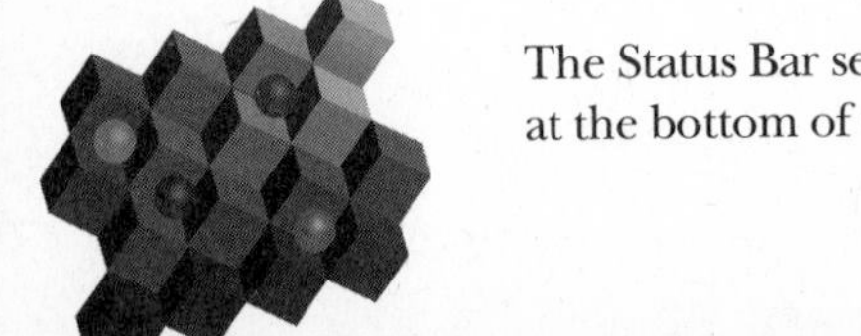

The MRU setting determines how many file names are displayed at the bottom of the File menu item.

Programming

The Programming page of the Desktop Properties options gives you control over some of the basic programming aspects of the dBASE environment. There are settings for Command Output, Program Development, and Other fields that help you protect users of your programs (see fig. 3.14).

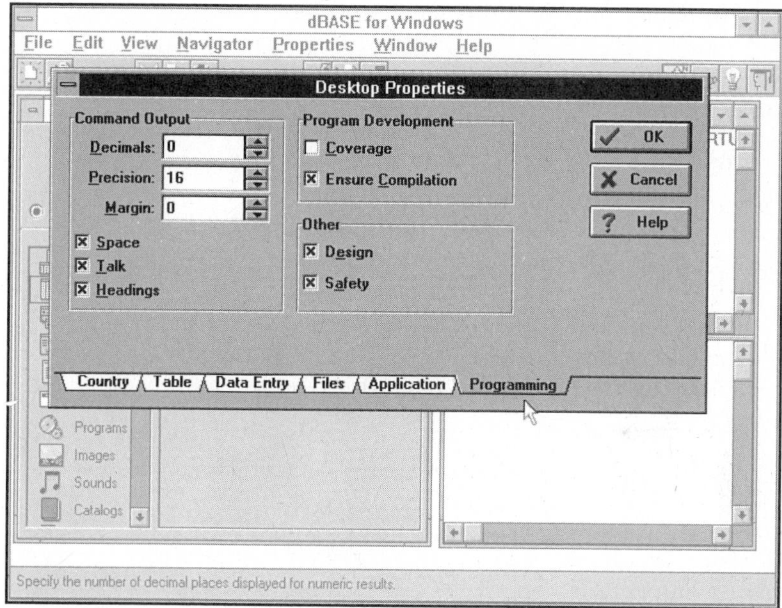

Figure 3.14
The Programming page controls command output and some of the programming development environment.

Under Command Output, you can control how numbers are presented by altering the number of decimal place shown and the precision that dBASE uses in doing calculations and storing its numeric data.

The Precision field, which defaults to 16, can be set to any value between 10 and 20. The Precision field affects only numeric data, however. Float numbers are always handled with a precision of 15.

Other Command Output options enable you to specify whether you want a space between fields when using the ? or ?? commands to evaluate and print expressions, have headings appear over output fields of the Display and List results, and have status information displayed on the dBASE status line.

The Command Output options also enable you to specify the column number of the left margin.

There also are controls for Program Development in the Programming page of the Desktop Properties. The Coverage control tells dBASE whether to create/update a coverage (COV) or trace file for program execution. The Ensure Compilation option tells dBASE to compare program source files (PRG) with the compiled program files (PRO) prior to execution and, if the source file is newer, to recompile the program.

For additional information, see the SET commands for_COVERAGE and DEVELOPMENT. In addition, each of the SET options are covered in more depth in the programming sections of this book.

The final two options, DESIGN and SAFETY, are for protection of data and programs, reports, and forms that you have created. When set off, the DESIGN option does not enable you to modify any tables, reports, forms, or other files using the CREATE or MODIFY commands.

When set on, the SAFETY option protects you from accidentally overwriting files or removing records from files by requesting confirmation before the action is taken. Some of the commands protected by the SAFETY option are COPY, COPY, FILE, COPY, TO . . . STRUCTURE EXTENDED, CREATE/MODIFY, INDEX, JOIN, SAVE, SET ALTERNATE TO, SORT, TOTAL, UPDATE, and ZAP.

Navigator

The Navigator option of the Properties menu is visible if the Navigator window is active. This option enables you to set various properties that control the appearance of the Navigator. In addition to being able to control the horizontal and vertical spacing of the Navigator Icons and Details, you can also specify whether you want dBASE to use a Supplemental Search Path.

A shortcut to bringing up the Navigator property inspector is to right-click with the mouse anywhere in the upper portion or left side of the Navigator window

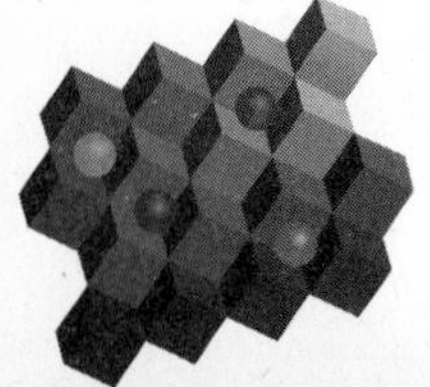

Command Window

Like the Navigator option, the Command Window option is visible only if the Command window has focus. The options available enable you to alter the position and orientation of the Input and Results portion of the Command window and specify the display fonts for both portions of the window.

Understanding the Navigator

In this section, you learn your way around the Navigator window and some of the many functions that can be accomplished with it. Beginning with dBASE IV, the Assist menu from dBASE III was replaced by a new user interface: the Control Center. dBASE takes the concept of the Control Center one step further as it moves dBASE into the GUI environment of Windows.

The Navigator (see fig. 3.15) gives you quick and easy access to all of your dBASE files.

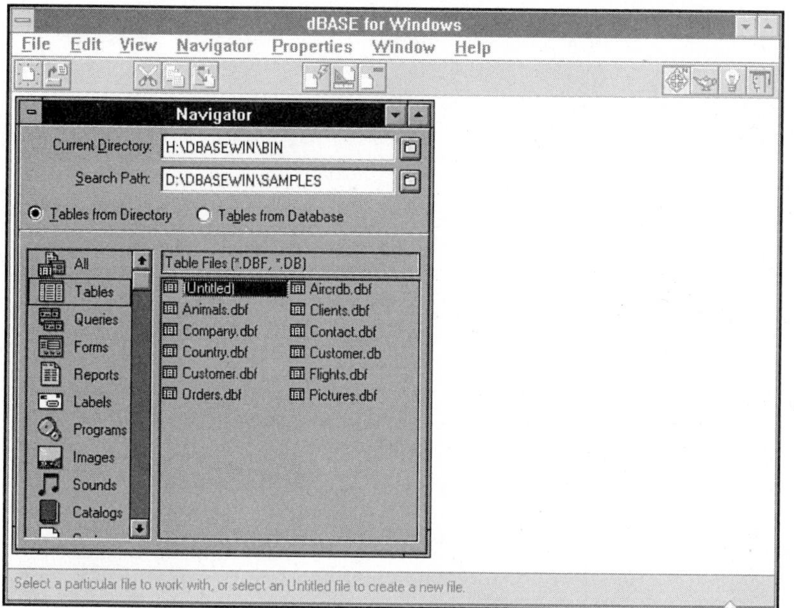

Figure 3.15
The Navigator window has three areas for displaying directory, file type, and file list information.

The first area of the Navigator is the Directory area. Here you can specify and select the Current Directory and supplemental Search Path. Each of these options can be entered manually, or you can click on the folder icon to invoke a Choose Directory dialog box (see fig. 3.16). From the Choose Directory dialog box, you click on the directory you want to highlight it and then click on the OK button to select it for your Current Directory or Search Path.

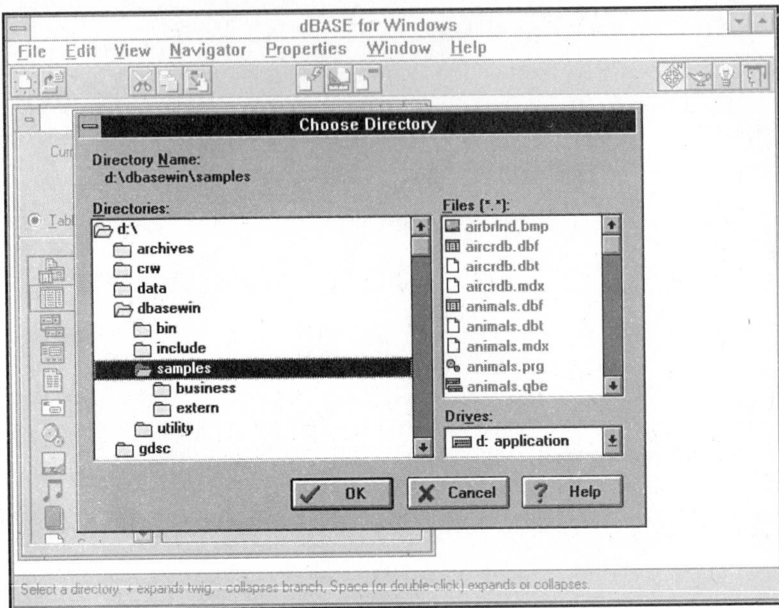

Figure 3.16 The Choose Directory dialog box.

The Navigator menu also provides the capability to use tables from other databases instead of the tables from the current directory. This option is primarily used when accessing remote databases such as Oracle, SYBASE, and DB2.

The File Type area of the Navigator window enables you to specify the types of files with which you want to work. You can think of it as a filtered view of your directory of files.

The File Types available are Tables, Queries, Forms, Reports, Labels, Programs, Images, Sounds, Catalogs, Custom, and ALL. Because the File Type area and File List area are so tightly integrated, each area is discussed as a unit.

The Navigator menu provides you with quick access to the most common commands for each of the dBASE objects. For database files, the Navigator options enable you to add records, edit records, modify the current structure, or to delete the currently selected database. When working with Queries, Forms, and Reports, the Navigator presents you with options to **R**un or Design the selected object type. When a program (PRG) file is highlighted, the Navigator drop/down menu includes options to invoke the dBASE debugger as well as options to run, design, or edit the program.

The **N**avigator menu item is visible only visible when the Navigator window is the active window. **N**avigator is one of dBASE's dynamic menu items that is changed depending on the commands or functions necessary for the active window. You also can display the same options by right-clicking on the dBASE object with your mouse.

The Navigator's View Menu

When the Navigator has the focus, the View menu provides an alternate way of highlighting or selecting file types in the Navigator and also gives you additional control over the appearance and order of the items in the Navigator window.

In addition to providing an alternative way of selecting objects that you want to have appear in the Navigator window, the View menu provides several other options.

Sort

While the Navigator has the focus, the Sort option has a submenu that gives you the ability to display dBASE objects in one of four ways:

- ✔ **By Name**. All dBASE file objects sorted by name regardless of type
- ✔ **By Type and Extension**. All dBASE file objects sorted by name within type (tables, queries, forms, and so forth)
- ✔ **By Size**. All dBASE objects sorted by file size
- ✔ **By Date and Time**. All dBASE objects sorted by the date and time stamp of the file

Icons and Details

In addition to the Sort options, you can also specify the size of the dBASE objects icons. The default is small icons, but you also can have dBASE display large icons. Displaying the large icons is easier on your eyes, but take up extra screen space that could be used for other purposes. Selecting the large icons also causes dBASE to use a slightly larger font for the file names and make identification a bit easier when using higher display resolutions. The last option of the View menu, Details, enables you to display the file details (size, date, and time) along with the small file type icon. The Details option is not available with large icons.

Tables

When you click on the Tables icon, the files list displays all files in the current directory that have either a DBF (dBASE) or a DB (Paradox) extension.

The local table menu gives you the same options that are available from the Navigator menu item discussed earlier. In addition, you also can access a dialog box containing the Tables Properties. These properties provide you with additional information about the table, such as number of records, date and time last changed, size in bytes, and the settings of the Read Only and Archive status.

Figure 3.17
A local table menu.

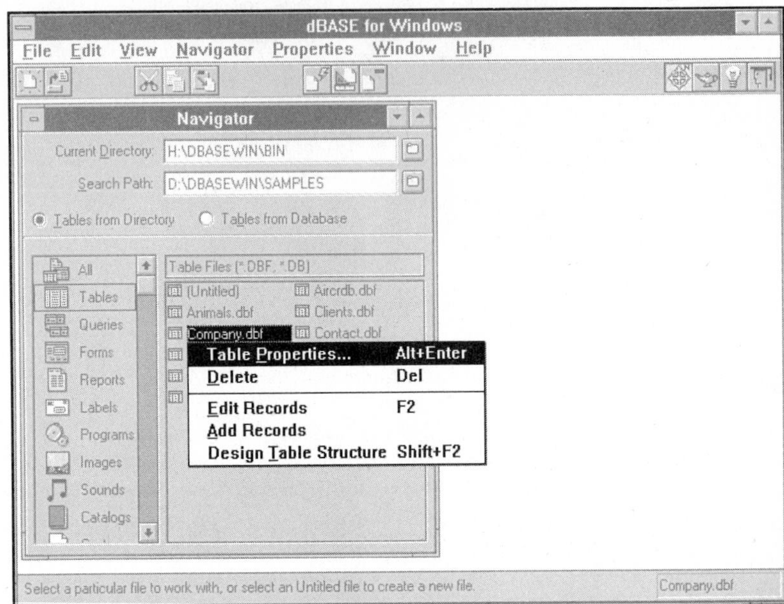

Most of the Table options also have shortcut keys associated with them. Table Properties (Alt+Enter), Delete (Ctrl+D), Edit Records (F2), Design Table Structure (Shift+F2).

Queries

Like the Tables icon, clicking on the Queries icon displays all dBASE query file types in the files list portion of the window. These files include files with the extensions QBE, VUE, and QRY.

Right-clicking on a query file in the Files List portion brings up a local menu to enable you to view the query file's properties, delete the query file, or design or run the query file.

If the DBW files' only option is checked on the Files page of the Desktop Properties option, only the QBE file extensions will be shown.

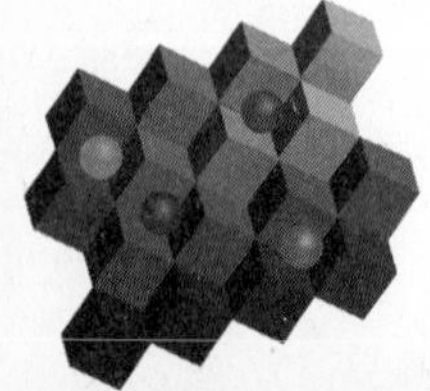

Forms, Reports, and Other File Icons

As in the previous two examples, each of the remaining File Type icons displays a list of files that pertain to the currently highlighted icon. Double-clicking on the icon invokes the New or Create function for the respective file type. Right-clicking on a specific file in the list brings up a local menu that enables you to run, design, delete, or otherwise act on the particular items. Each of the actions that can be performed are explored elsewhere in detail.

Using the Command Window

The best way to think of the Command window is as a direct replacement for the DOS version of dBASE's DOT prompt screen. The Command window is divided into an input pane and a results pane and enables you to enter dBASE commands directly. Although this is a primary benefit to users migrating from the DOS environment, it also is the only way to enter some dBASE commands, specifically some with more advanced options.

The minimized icon and SpeedBar button for the Command window is a replica of a magic lamp. In dBASE, your wish is its command.

One of the many advantages you have over the DOS environment is that you can have both the input and results portion displayed simultaneously. You also can control the placement and orientation of the panes as well as the fonts used to display the input commands and output results.

The Command Window's Program Menu

The Program menu item is a dynamic menu that appears when the Command window has the focus. Earlier it was mentioned that the Command window is much like the dBASE for DOS dot prompt. To assist you in working with programs, the Program menu item provides you with quick access to the DO, COMPILE, DEBUG, and DISPLAY COVERAGE commands.

To run a program from the Command window, you can either type in the full DO command or select the Program menu item and click on the DO option. In the later case, a Execute Program dialog box is displayed that enables you to search easily through the various drives and directories on your disk to run the desired program (see fig. 3.18). In this case, dBASE considers all programs (PRG and PRO) and forms (WFM) as candidates for execution.

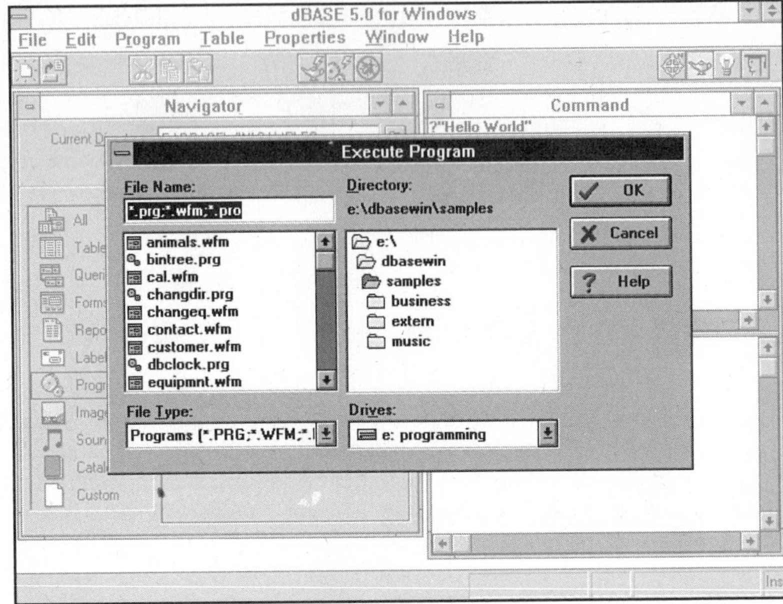

Figure 3.18
The DO option of the Program menu displays an Execute Program dialog box.

Table

The Table menu item provides you with most of the commands you need to access and manipulate tables in the interactive dBASE environment. This menu appears when the Command window is active and when a Table Browse or Table Edit window is active (see fig. 3.19).

If there is no table in use and you select one of the options under the Table menu, dBASE prompts you to open a table. Prior to delving into all the options available in the Table menu item, a little additional background is necessary.

The Dot Prompt

The input portion of the Command window is a direct replacement for the DOT prompt from dBASE for DOS. From the input pane, you can enter any dBASE command and the results are displayed in the window below.

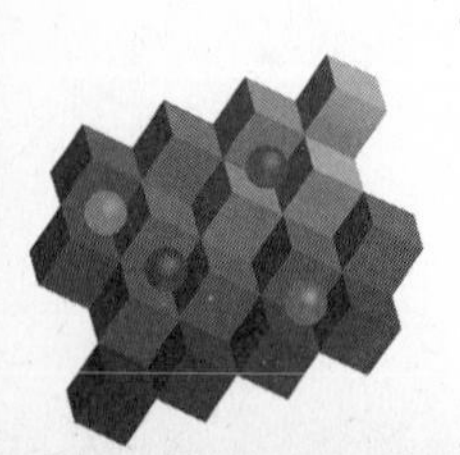

Some commands that calculate results, such as Average, Minimum, Maximum, Sum, and so forth, also generate a Window to display the results.

Also, the displaying of results in the results pane depends on the status of the SET TALK option. SET TALK ON displays the results in the results window and creates a separate window. With SET TALK OFF, only the supplemental window is displayed and there is no output in the results pane.

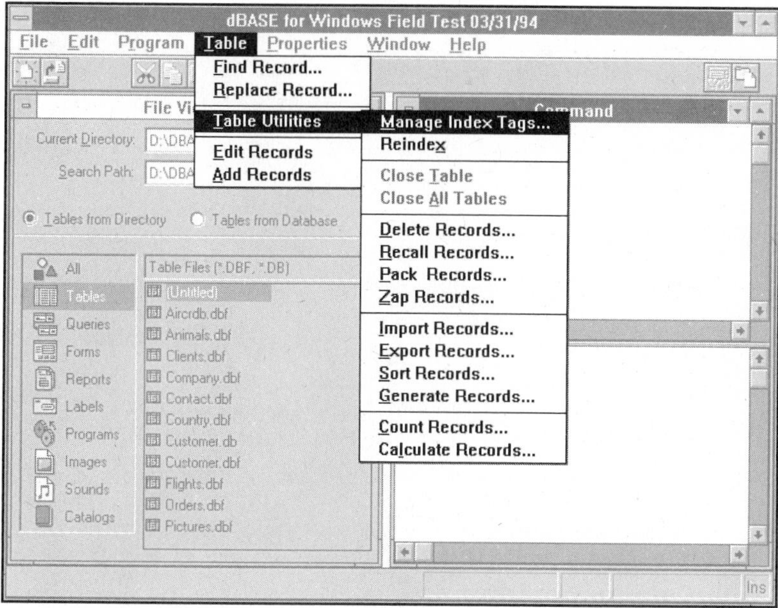

Figure 3.19
The **Table** menu provides a complete array of table manipulation options.

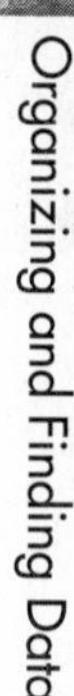

After commands are entered into the input pane of Command window, they can be run over again simply by clicking anywhere on that command and pressing Enter. Another option for rerunning commands is to highlight the entire command line(s) and right-click on the highlighted selection. This displays a local menu that enables you to Execute Selection. This is a quick and convenient way to rerun a list of commands you may be testing.

Other options in the pop-up local menu include the capability to cut and paste from the any of the items displayed in the input pane of the Command window. With the combination of cut and paste and the capability to highlight and execute selected commands, the dBASE environment saves you time during your interactive sessions.

Understanding the Menu Bar

Now that you are familiar with the various dBASE windows, it is time to learn a little more about the dBASE menu selection. The dBASE menu bar provides a dynamic set of commands that give you complete control over your dBASE environment and application. You have access to a majority of the dBASE operations as well as the standard windows/related operations, such as File, Window, and Help. As you learn all of the operations available to you through the menu bar, you see that for a majority of dBASE tasks there is little if any reason to use the Command window for issuing dBASE commands.

File Menu

The File pull-down menu offers you all the standard Windows options.

- ✔ New, which creates new files
- ✔ Open, which opens existing files
- ✔ Import, which imports a spreadsheet file
- ✔ Close, which closes the active window or view
- ✔ Exit, which exits or quits dBASE

Most of these options are found in every Windows application and are not discussed in great detail here. There are a few options that have been enhanced for the dBASE environment.

In addition to the preceding standard items, dBASE has a list of the last five files used or referenced. You can use this most recently used file list to quickly open a file that you have recently referenced.

The number of files in the file list can be changed on the Application page of the Desktop Properties window. You can specify from 0 to 9 in the Most Recently Used files (MRU) input area.

Also, like other dBASE menus, the File menu is dynamic in that its contents change depending on the window that has the focus. These variations are discussed along with the features where they appear.

New

As shown in figure 3.20, when you click on the File menu item you will notice that the New option has an arrow (>) out to the right. This arrow indicates an additional pull-down menu. The pull-down menu for the New option further defines the type of file or object you want to create. The options are Table, Query, Form, Report, Cross-Tab, Labels, Program, and Catalog.

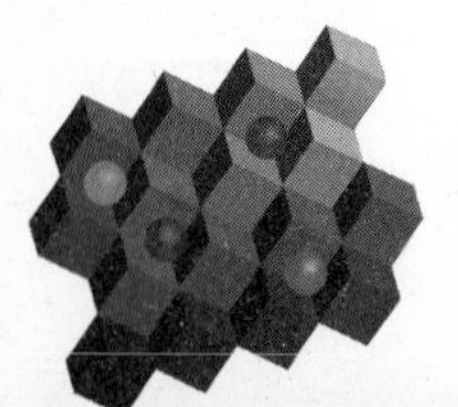

Throughout this book are specific references to dBASE file types. At times it is necessary to reference all dBASE file types as a single entity or object. In these cases, the items as a group are referred to as a dBASE object.

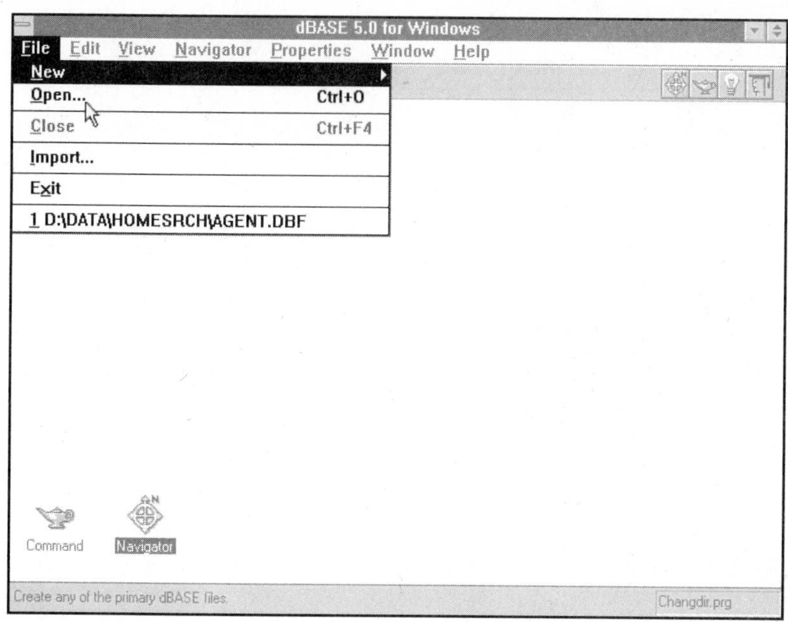

Figure 3.20 The additional options and dialog boxes available in the **F**ile menu.

Open

When you click on the **O**pen option of the **F**ile menu, you are presented with the Open File dialog box. This dialog box enables you to select the type of file you want to open and work with.

You can open a file in one of two modes: run mode or design/edit mode. Generally, the run mode is selected by default. You can open a dBASE object in design/edit mode by clicking on the Design **P**rogram in the lower right corner of the Open File dialog box (see fig. 3.21).

Run mode and design mode are used as generic terms here to reference the two options available with dBASE objects. Table 3.1 helps clarify the options for the basic dBASE file types.

Table 3.1
dBASE File Types

File Type	Run Mode	Design Mode
Tables	Display Table	Modify Structure
Queries	Run Query	Design Query
Forms	Run Form	Design Form
Reports	Run Report	Design Report
Labels	Run Labels	Design Labels
Programs	Do	Design Program
Images	Display Image	Design Image
Sounds	Play Sound	Design Sound
Catalogs	Open Catalog	

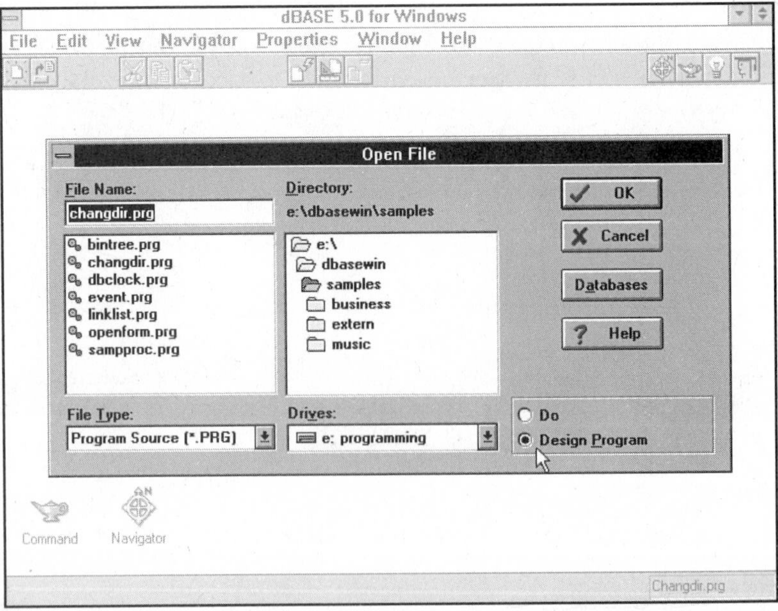

Figure 3.21 Opening of PRG files defaults to Design Program (MODIFY COMMAND) mode.

If you click on the Design Program, the files are opened in their natural edit or change mode. For instance, programs are opened by the dBASE editor, and tables are opened for editing in either browse, columnar, or form mode. For program files, this is the equivalent of the dBASE MODIFY COMMAND command.

The Open option of the File menu provides two options for table (DBF) files: open as Table Records, which is the equivalent of the USE command followed by a BROWSE command, and open as Design Table Structure, which issues the USE and MODIFY STRUCTURE commands in sequence.

As you read through this section, several of the menu items are explained in terms of their dBASE command equivalents. Although these are recognizable to the experienced dBASE user, new users to dBASE can find additional information about these commands in Appendix A. In either case, most of these commands are discussed in depth in later chapters.

Import

The Import option enables you to import Quattro Pro (WB1) or Lotus (WK1) spreadsheets into a dBASE table. Spreadsheet have always been popular tools for building small databases. dBASE enables you to preserve that data and import it into a dBASE table as your application grows.

Close

The Close option of the File menu minimizes the Navigator or Command window from the screen, depending on which is active. For all other windows, the Close option removes the window from display.

Exit

The Exit option of the File menu closes your dBASE application. All active windows are closed and pending table modifications are completed. If you have made an unsaved change to a form or a program, you are prompted to save your changes.

Recently Used Files List

The File menu also maintains a list of the most recently used files (see fig. 3.22). This list of files enables you to quickly open a dBASE object. To open one of the most recently used files, click on it with the mouse and dBASE opens the file in edit mode.

The number of files can be changed on the Application page of the Desktop Properties window. See the item MRU (Most Recently Used) Size earlier in this chapter.

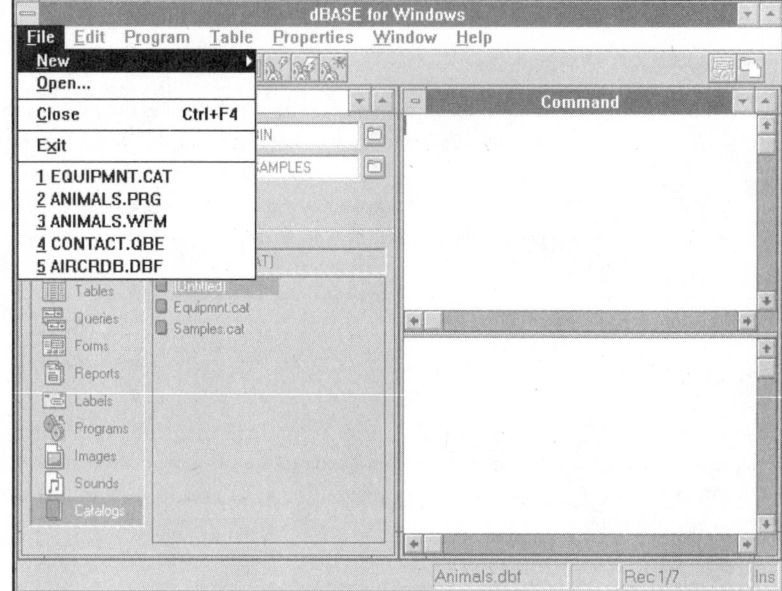

Figure 3.22 The recently used files list enables you to quickly access files from your last dBASE session.

Edit Menu

The dBASE Edit menu, shown in figure 3.23, is another menu that changes dynamically based on the active window.

Undo

The Undo option of the Edit menu generally enables you to restore information that you might have inadvertently erased (for instance if you were trying to copy a company name from one place in a table to another and accidentally erased the name with a cut action when you had really intended to copy it). The Undo command enables you to restore the original contents to the field. The Undo option is generally shaded or inactive when just the Navigator and Command window are active.

The Undo command can undo only the most recent action. If you issue an additional command or action, the undo buffer is erased or overlaid.

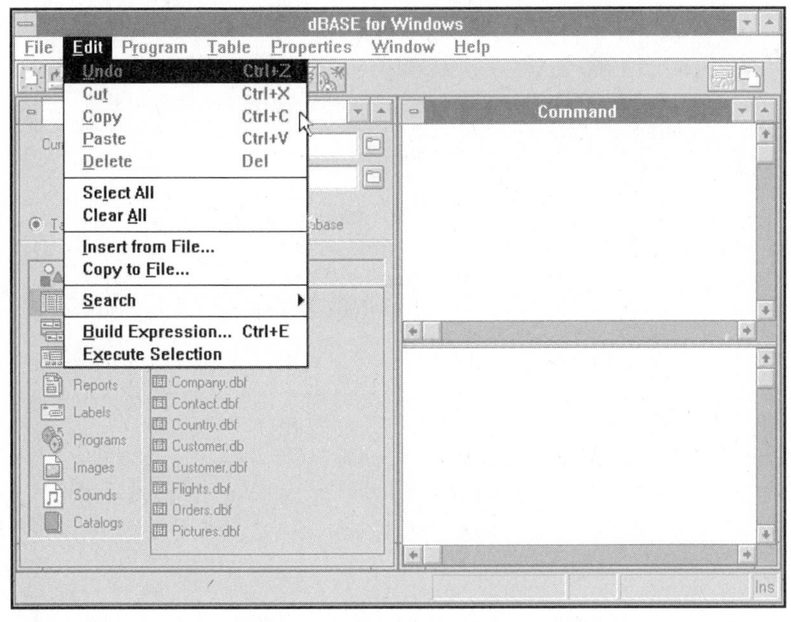

Figure 3.23
Most options of the Edit menu have a shortcut key listed on the right when the Navigator has focus.

Cut

The Cut option of the Edit menu enables you to highlight a portion of text or graphic object from the active window and place the highlighted information into the Windows Clipboard buffer. The information is removed from the original area.

Copy

Like the Cut command, the Copy command enables you to highlight a portion of text or graphic object from the active window and copy that information into the Clipboard. Unlike the Cut command, the information is not removed from the original area.

Paste

The Paste option takes the contents of the Clipboard and inserts it into the active window at the point indicated by the Windows cursor. You can use the Paste option to insert one or more commands into the Command window, add data to a field in a table, or insert code into a dBASE program.

Delete

The Delete option removes the highlighted text or graphic from the active window. The removed item is not saved to the Clipboard and can be recovered only by immediately using the Undo command.

Select All

The Select All option is a quick way to select all of the text or graphic items in the active window. Select All is often used in conjunction with Copy (to Windows clipboard) or Copy to File to save the contents of the active window. The Copy to File option is available as an option of the Edit menu.

One way to use this combination is to establish a particular command sequence that you want to issue on a regular basis from the command window. Next, you can use Select All from the Edit menu to highlight the commands. Then use Copy to File to copy the commands to a dBASE program (PRG) file. This saves the sequence as a program that can be run later using the DO command.

Once a code segment has been saved to a file you can use the dBASE program editor to remove unwanted segments or make any other desired changes.

Clear Results

The Clear Results option, which is available only when the Command window has focus, clears all information from the results portion of the window.

Insert from File

The Insert from File option from the Edit menu enables you to insert a file from some other storage location into the active window at the current insertion point.

Insert from File is frequently used when programming in dBASE and using the internal program editor. After saving common portions of code as files, you can insert those files (code segments) into other programs that are being developed.

Copy to File

The Copy to File option on the Edit menu is similar to the Insert from File option. Copy to File enables you to copy selected portions of a text file to a new file. You must select or highlight the information you want to copy.

The Select All command from the Edit menu is one way to select text. You also can select a subset of the text by clicking on the beginning of the text you want to select with the mouse, and then draging the mouse to the end of the desired text. After you release the mouse button, you can invoke the Copy to File option to copy only the portion of the text you specified.

Search

Selecting the Search option, which appears when the Command window or Program Editor windows have focus, produces an additional menu that has three options: Find Text, Find Next Text, and Replace Text. The Find Text and Replace Text options each bring up a dialog box to specify additional information about the search. The Replace Text dialog box is an enhanced version of the Find Text dialog box.

The Command window maintains an extensive list of the most recently used commands. Using the Find and Find Next options, you can quickly search back through the Command window to locate commands you have previously issued. This can be handy if you want to look up the format of a command that dBASE has entered for you or if there is a set of commands that you want to return to and re-execute. To search for a recently used command, you can select Search from the Edit menu while the Command window has focus and pick the Find Text option.

After the Find Text dialog box is displayed, you can enter the text information you want to search for. The important thing to note is where you are in the Command window. More than likely you will be at the end of the command list, so you will want to select Up for the search direction. In the event you are at the top of the command list, you can let the search direction default to the Down direction.

After the text has been specified and the direction has been selected, you can click on the Find button to execute the search.

The Find Text option also has some additional capabilities to fine tune your searches. These options are Match Whole Words and Match Case. With the standard find, dBASE looks for information that has the same contents of the Find What field. If you entered "the" in the Find What field, dBASE finds any data that has any combination of "the". (For example, this finds "**the**," "**The**," "**The**re," and "toge**the**r."

Selecting Match Whole Words only finds "**the**" and "**The**." Further refining the selection with Match Case only finds "**the**." If you select Match Case without Match Whole Word, dBASE locates both "**the**" and "toge**the**r."

The Search options have the following accelerator keys associated with them:

Find Text	Ctrl+F
Find Next Text	Ctrl+L
Replace Text	Ctrl+R

As shown in figure 3.24, dBASE gives you similar options for the replace text operation. You can specify the direction of the search (**U**p or **D**own) from the current insertion point, whether you want to match whole or partial words, and whether the search should be case sensitive. Match **W**hole Words finds only text that has a blank on both sides. Match **C**ase finds only text that matches exactly, letter for letter, including upper- and lowercase.

Figure 3.24
The Replace Text dialog box.

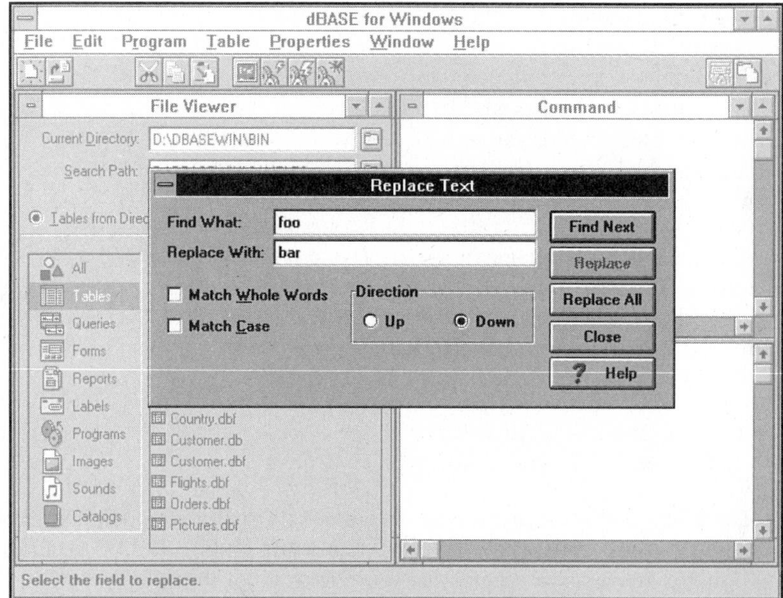

If you highlight a portion of text prior to selecting the **S**earch option, the highlighted text automatically appears in the F**i**nd What portion of the Find Text or Replace Text dialog boxes.

In addition to the standard find text options, dBASE provides an area to enter replacement text and two additional buttons to control the text replacement. After you have keyed in your replacement text, you can either click on the **F**ind button to find the first occurrence of the text or click on the Replace **A**ll button to automatically replace all occurrences of the F**i**nd What text with the **R**eplace With text.

If you choose the first option of finding the text, dBASE searches for the first occurrence of the text string and activates the **R**eplace button. At this point, you can either choose to replace the text or find the next occurrence. If you choose to replace the text, dBASE automatically performs the find next function for you.

While working with text files, such as programs (PRG) and forms (WFM), the actual changes are not permanent until the file is closed and saved. Therefore, you might want to consider saving your changes more frequently so that if you make a mistake some of your changes will have been saved and you will not have to restart from the beginning.

Although the Search options are available within the Command window, they provide much more value when you are developing dBASE application programs. The find and replace options are used extensively to make sure that variables are named consistently and for finding instances of commands and code segments.

Build Expression

The Build Expression option is a tremendous aid for learning the dBASE programming language. Whether you are programming from the command line or writing a program in the editor, the Build Expression dialog box helps you painlessly learn the entire dBASE language, providing you with all the prompts for putting together dBASE commands.

Window

The first three Window options, Cascade, Tile Horizontal, and Tile Vertical are covered at the beginning of this chapter. The Arrange Icons option straightens up the icons of any windows you may have minimized. Figure 3.25 and 3.26 show the before and after effects of the Arrange Icon option.

The next two options, Navigator and Command, open the respective window if is closed or restore it to its normal size if it has been minimized.

The next section in this menu represents all the known windows. The items appear on this list whether they are in normal view, hidden behind some other window, or minimized. Selecting an item from this area gives the selected window focus and restores it to its original position if it has been minimized.

Help

The Help menu item invokes the standard Windows help system. In dBASE, you have documentation for almost the entire product on-line. This documentation is fully searchable and you can look up most dBASE topics.

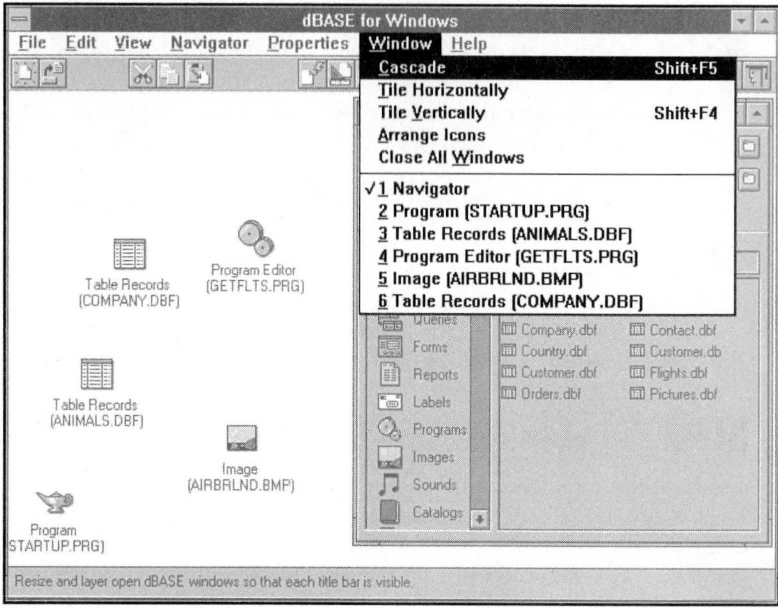

Figure 3.25 The Window menu item.

Figure 3.26 The Arrange Icons selection straightens up your desktop.

Chapter Snapshot

The key to designing and creating good relational databases is understanding what database systems are, the different structure or organizational forms they can accept, and the relationships that exist between the various database elements. In this chapter you learn the following:

A database is a powerful tool that you can use to help organize the vast amounts of data you are exposed to each day. Like the human mind, a database needs to be able to identify, categorize, and store this data for later recall. To use a database effectively, you need to be familiar with the concepts and definitions provided throughout this chapter.

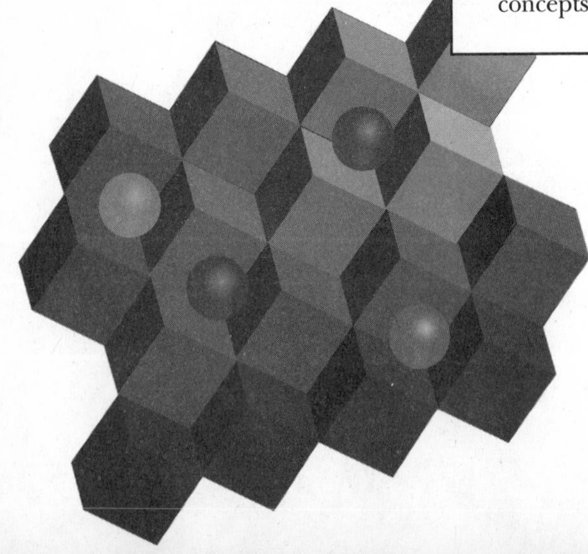

Designing and Creating Relational Databases

By Jim Wetzel

For many years, people have collected, stored, organized, and retrieved data. Most businesses, schools, churches, and government agencies need to collect and process data to function. You probably even collect data for use in everyday household activities. The list of potential database uses is endless, and includes the following:

- ✔ The local video store maintains an inventory of films and knows what films are on-hand and available for checkout. The store maintains a customer list so that it knows the name, address, and phone number of each person who has checked out one of the these films.
- ✔ A school needs to keep track of every student's address and grades. They also need to keep track of attendance to insure all state and federal regulations are followed.
- ✔ A church might store contribution data from all of its congregation so it can keep track of donations people make and the amount of income the church is receiving.

- The Internal Revenue Service, because it keeps track of the income and taxes paid by every United States citizen, has literally millions of pieces of financial data to organize.
- Members of a household collect many pieces of data as they track investments, expenditures, baseball cards, or the recipes used to prepare meals.

A *database* is a collection of logically related data in a group of one or more files.

The preceding examples demonstrate the vast amount of data you can accumulate in your home, business, or organization. The challenge is knowing how to store that data so that you can find it quickly. With personal computers, this challenge is achieved by placing or storing the data in electronic files.

After storing the data, your next task is to organize it. This task is simplified with the Data Base Management System (DBMS). A *DBMS* is simply a program or set of programs used to collect, store, and retrieve data. A DBMS adds structure to the data, and provides the underlying relationship to the individual items or entities. Although this book concentrates on the dBASE for Windows DBMS, many other DBMSs are available, including Paradox for the desktop or PC, Interbase and Oracle for the mid-range or minicomputer, and IBMs IMS and DB2 for the mainframe environment.

Defining Database Terminology

Before delving further into database structures and relationships, you should understand some of the terms that are typically used when referring to various parts of a database. These terms describe the basic components of a database: the table, columns, rows, and fields.

Defining Tables

In its simplest form, a database consists of a collection of related files or *tables.* Perhaps the easiest way to visualize a table is to think in terms of a spreadsheet or a series of horizontal rows and vertical columns.

Defining Columns

Columns represent a particular set of fields within the database. In figure 4.2, the Last Name column is highlighted. The other columns are First Name, Street, City, State, Zip and Phone.

Quattro Pro for Windows - CUSTOMER.WB1

File Edit Block Data Tools Graph Property Window Help

	A	B	C	D	E	F	G
1	Last name	First name	Street	City	State	Zip	Phone
2	Getz	Steve	Rt. 4 Box 349	Athens	WA	94903	(415) 555-8608
3	Harrison	Bimal	RD2 N Tyner Rd	Bernardsville	WA	49442	(410) 555-9385
4	Holmen	Brigitte	P.O. Box 926	Bonsall	VA	92129	(619) 555-2269
5	Holton	Dan	P.O. Box 5899	Carrollton	VA	94043	(415) 555-2838
6	Hui	Miles	9932 Kika Ct. #3217	Cary	UT	21175	(416) 555-5465
7	Schnur	Andrew	95-39 112th Street	Chamblee	TX	84084	(801) 555-2031
8	Flemming	Ed	820 Bundaberg Lane	Doraville	TX	07712	(908) 555-3190
9	Smith	Paul	788 Martin Ct. West	Easthampton	TX	95018	(408) 555-9341
10	Todd	Ken	78 Rockaway Ave	Edmond	RI	11419	(718) 555-5196
11	Wagner	Richard	72 Knapp Ave.	Felton	PR	55411	(612) 555-2776
12	Walker	Patrick	4388 Diane Dr. NW	Mountain View	NC	94609	(510) 555-1889
13	Wetzel	Bill	40 Miller Ranch Ct.	Muskegon	MN	75007	(214) 555-6069
14	Wilden	Rachel	2106 Cameron Drive	San Antonio	CA	94530	(510) 555-5879
15	Withnell	Brian	1150 Arcade Blvd	Tuscon	CA	27511	(919) 555-4668
16	Zink	William	0404 Massachusetts	Worth	AL	95134	(408) 555-1066
17							
18							
19							
20							
21							
22							
23							
24							
25							

A B C D E F G H I J K L G

Figure 4.1
List of names and addresses in a spreadsheet format.

Quattro Pro for Windows - CUSTOMER.WB1

File Edit Block Data Tools Graph Property Window Help

	A	B	C	D	E	F	G
1	Last name	First name	Street	City	State	Zip	Phone
2	Getz	Steve	Rt. 4 Box 349	Athens	WA	94903	(415) 555-8608
3	Harrison	Bimal	RD2 N Tyner Rd	Bernardsville	WA	49442	(410) 555-9385
4	Holmen	Brigitte	P.O. Box 926	Bonsall	VA	92129	(619) 555-2269
5	Holton	Dan	P.O. Box 5899	Carrollton	VA	94043	(415) 555-2838
6	Hui	Miles	9932 Kika Ct. #3217	Cary	UT	21175	(416) 555-5465
7	Schnur	Andrew	95-39 112th Street	Chamblee	TX	84084	(801) 555-2031
8	Flemming	Ed	820 Bundaberg Lane	Doraville	TX	07712	(908) 555-3190
9	Smith	Paul	788 Martin Ct. West	Easthampton	TX	95018	(408) 555-9341
10	Todd	Ken	78 Rockaway Ave	Edmond	RI	11419	(718) 555-5196
11	Wagner	Richard	72 Knapp Ave.	Felton	PR	55411	(612) 555-2776
12	Walker	Patrick	4388 Diane Dr. NW	Mountain View	NC	94609	(510) 555-1889
13	Wetzel	Bill	40 Miller Ranch Ct.	Muskegon	MN	75007	(214) 555-6069
14	Wilden	Rachel	2106 Cameron Drive	San Antonio	CA	94530	(510) 555-5879
15	Withnell	Brian	1150 Arcade Blvd	Tuscon	CA	27511	(919) 555-4668
16	Zink	William	0404 Massachusetts	Worth	AL	95134	(408) 555-1066
17							
18							
19							
20							
21							
22							
23							
24							
25							

A B C D E F G H I J K L G

Figure 4.2
A Column is a vertical view of a group of fields within a table.

Defining Rows

Rows are the horizontal collection of columns. As highlighted in figure 4.3, this collection of data comprises a single record.

Figure 4.3
A row represents a collection of fields that represent a single record.

Quattro Pro for Windows - CUSTOMER.WB1

File Edit Block Data Tools Graph Property Window Help

	A	B	C	D	E	F	G
1	Last name	First name	Street	City	State	Zip	Phone
2	Getz	Steve	Rt. 4 Box 349	Athens	WA	94903	(415) 555-8608
3	Harrison	Bimal	RD2 N Tyner Rd	Bernardsville	WA	49442	(410) 555-9385
4	Holmen	Brigitte	P.O. Box 926	Bonsall	VA	92129	(619) 555-2269
5	Holton	Dan	P.O. Box 5899	Carrollton	VA	94043	(415) 555-2838
6	Hui	Miles	9932 Kika Ct. #3217	Cary	UT	21175	(416) 555-5465
7	Schnur	Andrew	95-39 112th Street	Chamblee	TX	84084	(801) 555-2031
8	Flemming	Ed	820 Bundaberg Lane	Doraville	TX	07712	(908) 555-3190
9	Smith	Paul	788 Martin Ct. West	Easthampton	TX	95018	(408) 555-9341
10	Todd	Ken	78 Rockaway Ave	Edmond	RI	11419	(718) 555-5196
11	Wagner	Richard	72 Knapp Ave.	Felton	PR	55411	(612) 555-2776
12	Walker	Patrick	4388 Diane Dr. NW	Mountain View	NC	94609	(510) 555-1889
13	Wetzel	Bill	40 Miller Ranch Ct.	Muskegon	MN	75007	(214) 555-6069
14	Wilden	Rachel	2106 Cameron Drive	San Antonio	CA	94530	(510) 555-5879
15	Withnell	Brian	1150 Arcade Blvd	Tuscon	CA	27511	(919) 555-4668
16	Zink	William	0404 Massachusetts	Worth	AL	95134	(408) 555-1066
17							
18							
19							
20							
21							
22							
23							
24							
25							

A B C D E F G H I J K L

Defining Fields

A *field* is the intersection of a row and a column (see fig. 4.4) and is the location in the database where a particular piece of information is stored. The field has a single attribute or type of data, and usually has a value.

Quattro Pro for Windows - CUSTOMER.WB1

File Edit Block Data Tools Graph Property Window Help

	A	B	C	D	E	F	G
1	Last name	First name	Street	City	State	Zip	Phone
2	Getz	Steve	Rt. 4 Box 349	Athens	WA	94903	(415) 555-8608
3	Harrison	Bimal	RD2 N Tyner Rd	Bernardsville	WA	49442	(410) 555-9385
4	Holmen	Brigitte	P.O. Box 926	Bonsall	VA	92129	(619) 555-2269
5	Holton	Dan	P.O. Box 5899	Carrollton	VA	94043	(415) 555-2838
6	Hui	Miles	9932 Kika Ct. #3217	Cary	UT	21175	(416) 555-5465
7	Schnur	Andrew	95-39 112th Street	Chamblee	TX	84084	(801) 555-2031
8	Flemming	Ed	820 Bundaberg Lane	Doraville	TX	07712	(908) 555-3190
9	Smith	Paul	788 Martin Ct. West	Easthampton	TX	95018	(408) 555-9341
10	Todd	Ken	78 Rockaway Ave	Edmond	RI	11419	(718) 555-5196
11	Wagner	Richard	72 Knapp Ave.	Felton	PR	55411	(612) 555-2776
12	Walker	Patrick	4388 Diane Dr. NW	Mountain View	NC	94609	(510) 555-1889
13	Wetzel	Bill	40 Miller Ranch Ct.	Muskegon	MN	75007	(214) 555-6069
14	Wilden	Rachel	2106 Cameron Drive	San Antonio	CA	94530	(510) 555-5879
15	Withnell	Brian	1150 Arcade Blvd	Tuscon	CA	27511	(919) 555-4668
16	Zink	William	0404 Massachusetts	Worth	AL	95134	(408) 555-1066
17							
18							
19							
20							
21							
22							
23							
24							
25							

A B C D E F G H I J K L G

Figure 4.4
A field is where a records column and row intersect.

Introducing Database Models

Over the years, various database structures have been used, and each one has its own particular strengths and weaknesses. Although this book concentrates on the relational data structure, the other structures are briefly discussed for more complete understanding.

Exploring Flat-File Data Structures

The flat-file structure is one of the first and most popular database structures. The *flat-file* structure is a single file or table that represents a collection of logically related data. Typically, the flat-file stands on its own because it has no relationships to other data. An example of a flat-file database would be a simple name and address file, such as the one shown in figure 4.5.

Think of the check register as a flat-file database that contains the check number, date written, payee, and amount. Just like the name and address table, the check register contains no check "hierarchy." You easily can find a particular check because the register is arranged by check number. Similarly, most people organize their name and address file by last name.

Figure 4.5
A check register—one example of a flat-file database.

Microsoft Money - MSMONEY.MNY - [Account Book]

File Edit List Report Options Window Help

Account: EQ Checking View: All (by Date)

Num	Date	Payee / Memo / Category	C	Payment	Deposit	Balance
3012	2/9/93	BJ's Wholesale Club Split	R	45.86		634.06
	2/10/93	Transfer from Savings Transfer From : EQ Money Market	R		1,400.00	2,034.06
3013	2/10/93	Sunpaper Brian Ferry Misc. Debbie	R	13.60		2,020.46
3014	2/10/93	North Arundel CATV Household	R	22.15		1,998.31
3015	2/10/93	C&P Telephone Utility : C&P Telephone	R	29.71		1,968.60
3166	2/10/93	US Sprint Split	R	30.78		1,937.82
3167	2/10/93	VOID	R		0.00	**VOID**

Ending Balance: 137.80

Press Enter to edit the transaction.

Before the early database programs such as dBASE II, many people used spreadsheet programs to enter and store data instead of specialized database programs. As was shown in figure 5.1, the spreadsheet arrangement of rows and columns formed a natural flat-file database structure.

A Note from the Author

The practice of using a spreadsheet to store database information is still widely used. Although dBASE might be the largest selling DBMS for the personal computer, spreadsheets such as Quattro Pro, Excel, and Lotus 1-2-3 are the most widely used database programs.

The simplicity of the flat-file structure creates certain limitations. If the name and address file is organized by the people's last names, you will encounter difficulty when registering all of the people who live in a single state. Similarly, if your check register is organized by check number, you might take a while to list or find any checks that you've written out to your local food store. To solve this problem, many people file their canceled checks by *payee* after the bank returns them (see fig. 4.6). This arrangement can also make it easy to find last December's house payment or your last three car payments.

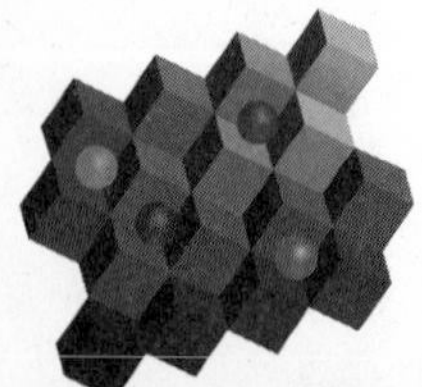

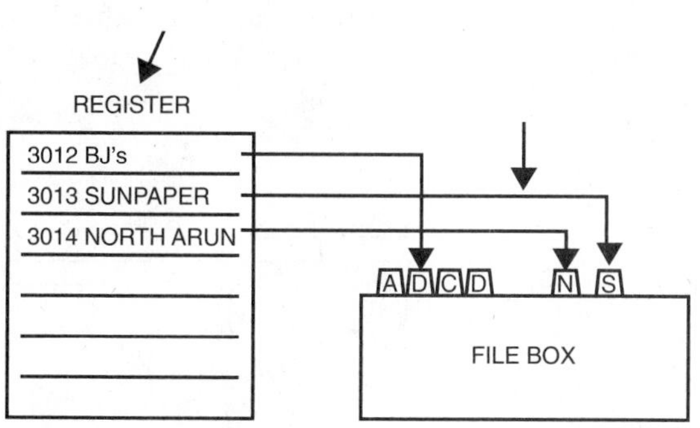

Figure 4.6
Returned checks are often filed alphabetically rather than by check number.

In filing the checks by payee, a new database concept is introduced—indexing. Indexing is a technique used to speed up database searches. Organized by check number, the check register becomes an index or pointer to the check file organized by check recipient. The check file may contain thousands of checks, but given a check number or a payee, you can now find a check (such as last month's mortgage payment) easily.

Indexing is explored further in Chapter 7, "Indexing, Sorting, and Locating Your Data."

When designing databases, consider how you will want to access your data and then plan accordingly. During its life span, a well-planned database will need to fulfill many different roles and be accessed in a variety of ways.

Exploring Hierarchical Data Structures

The *hierarchical* model is perhaps one of the easiest and most fundamental of all the database structures, because you deal with hierarchies on a daily basis.

In the school system, you have a principal at the top of the structure with many teachers under the principal's responsibility. The teachers, in turn, have responsibility for many students.

In the business world, most organizations are built around the hierarchical model with a president at the top of the organization and a number of vice-presidents reporting to him. Each vice-president, in turn, has a number of managers reporting to him, followed by a number of supervisors reporting to each manager. Finally, you get down to the worker (where the real work is performed), who reports to the supervisor.

Data or information is also often arranged in a hierarchical form, with a main category or grouping at the top of the pyramid, with more detailed information toward the bottom of the pyramid—much like an organization chart (see fig. 4.7).

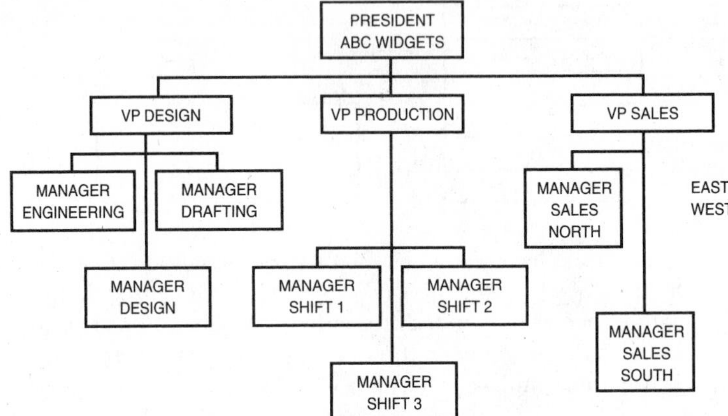

Figure 4.7
An Organization chart is a good representation of the hierarchical model.

Although this structure has its advantages in that there is a fixed structured relationship and responsibility, you can imagine how difficult it might be to find information while traversing up and down each part of the organization. All of the product design information is located within one area, but to find information on production or shipping, you need to go up the chain of command and over to the next level and back down.

A practical example is a hospital and its need to store various types of information; a hospital database needs to store information about both patients and surgeons. The patient database would likely contain a patient ID number, name, and address at the top level of the pyramid, possibly followed on lower levels by surgery or prescription data. Similarly, the surgeon database would perhaps contain a list of surgeries below a surgeon ID number, name, and address data level. As demonstrated in figure 4.8, finding information about an individual surgeon or patient would be a relatively easy task. Starting with the ID number shown on the top level, you find related information by working down through the levels held beneath it.

Consider a question, however, such as the following: Which patients have received prescription medication *X* from particular surgeon *Y*? Here you see the difficulties a hierarchical database structure creates. As long as you search only a single structure for information, the task is relatively straightforward. When a task requires a cross-reference between two structures, it suddenly becomes much more difficult.

Simplicity and the capability to find directly related data in a straightforward manner is the hierarchical structure's strength. Its main weakness is exposed when you have to group or organize data across two dissimilar structures. Traversing multiple branches of a hierarchy to find something that may or may not be present can be an inefficient method of retrieving data.

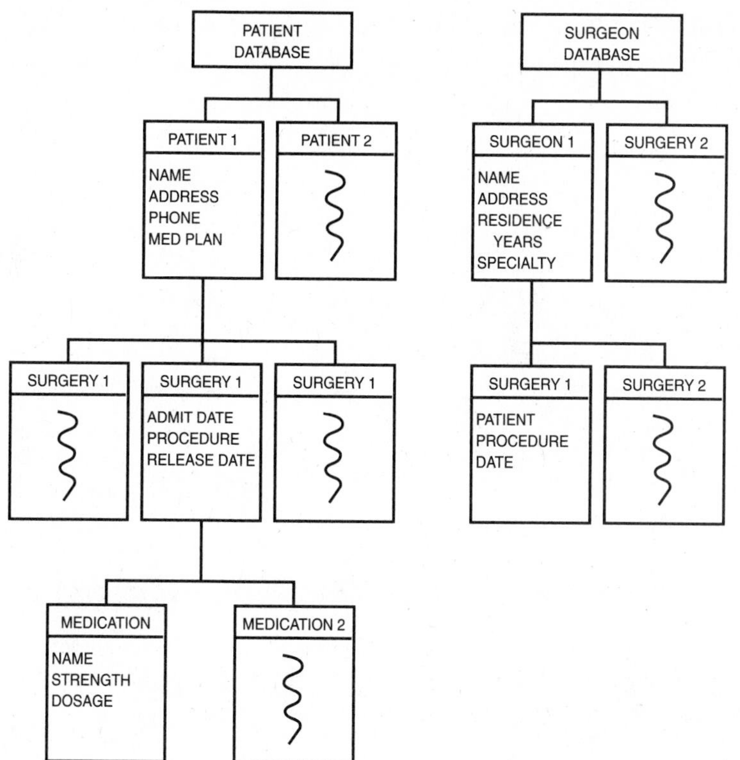

Figure 4.8 Patient and surgeon information are examples of a hierarchical structure.

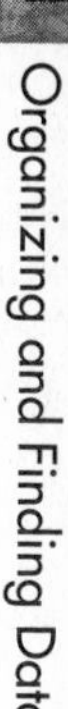

Exploring Relational Data Structures

The most popular database structure in use today is the relational structure. The *relational database* extends the concept that a file is a collection of related data; database tables are collections of logically related data organized into groups of one or more files. With the relational data structure, you begin to see the real power and potential database management systems possess. Although relational database theory is rooted according to well-established abstract mathematical principles, for the purposes of this book, the discussion of relational structures will stay at a more practical level.

To clearly understand the relational structure, examine the name and address table defined earlier. In a typical business, this has most of the basic elements of a typical customer database record. A business will typically sell a product or service to a customer. Using the flat-file structure discussed earlier (refer back to fig. 4.1), you can see that in order to track sales or invoices for the customer, you would need to add additional columns or rows to the flat-file structure for each sale or invoice to that customer (see fig. 4.9).

The first option of adding invoice columns will cause problems if you have more sales for one customer than another because all records need to be expanded equally (see fig. 4.10).

Figure 4.9 Additional columns are needed to track invoices.

Quattro Pro for Windows - CUSTOMER.WB1

File Edit Block Data Tools Graph Property Window Help

	A	B	C	H	I	J	K
1	Last name	First name	Street	Invoice #1	Invoice #2	Invoice #3	
2	Getz	Steve	Rt. 4 Box 349	23259	33234		
3	Harrison	Bimal	RD2 N Tyner Rd	23276			
4	Holmen	Brigitte	P.O. Box 926	23293	33251	43234	
5	Holton	Dan	P.O. Box 5899	23310			
6	Hui	Miles	9932 Kika Ct. #3217	23327	33268		
7	Schnur	Andrew	95-39 112th Street	23344			
8	Flemming	Ed	820 Bundaberg Lane	23361			
9	Smith	Paul	788 Martin Ct. West	23378	33285	43251	
10	Todd	Ken	78 Rockaway Ave	23395			
11	Wagner	Richard	72 Knapp Ave.	23412			
12	Walker	Patrick	4388 Diane Dr. NW	23429	33302		
13	Wetzel	Bill	40 Miller Ranch Ct.	23446			
14	Wilden	Rachel	2106 Cameron Drive	23463	33319	43268	
15	Withnell	Brian	1150 Arcade Blvd	23480			
16	Zink	William	0404 Massachusetts	23497	33336		

Figure 4.10 Adding rows creates duplicate data.

Quattro Pro for Windows - CUSTOMER.WB1

File Edit Block Data Tools Graph Property Window Help

	A	B	C	D	E	H	I
1	Last name	First name	Street	City	State	Invoice	
2	Getz	Steve	Rt. 4 Box 349	Athens	WA	23259	
3	Getz	Steve	Rt. 4 Box 349	Athens	WA	23260	
4	Getz	Steve	Rt. 4 Box 349	Athens	WA	23261	
5	Getz	Steve	Rt. 4 Box 349	Athens	WA	23262	
6	Harrison	Bimal	RD2 N Tyner Rd	Bernardsville	WA	23276	
7	Holmen	Brigitte	P.O. Box 926	Bonsall	VA	23293	
8	Holmen	Brigitte	P.O. Box 926	Bonsall	VA	23294	
9	Holmen	Brigitte	P.O. Box 926	Bonsall	VA	23295	
10	Holton	Dan	P.O. Box 5899	Carrollton	VA	23310	
11	Hui	Miles	9932 Kika Ct. #3217	Cary	UT	23327	
12	Schnur	Andrew	95-39 112th Street	Chamblee	TX	23344	
13	Schnur	Andrew	95-39 112th Street	Chamblee	TX	23345	
14	Flemming	Ed	820 Bundaberg Lane	Doraville	TX	23361	
15	Smith	Paul	788 Martin Ct. West	Easthampton	TX	23378	
16	Todd	Ken	78 Rockaway Ave	Edmond	RI	23395	
17	Wagner	Richard	72 Knapp Ave.	Felton	PR	23412	
18	Walker	Patrick	4388 Diane Dr. NW	Mountain View	NC	23429	
19	Wetzel	Bill	40 Miller Ranch Ct.	Muskegon	MN	23446	
20	Wilden	Rachel	2106 Cameron Drive	San Antonio	CA	23463	
21	Withnell	Brian	1150 Arcade Blvd	Tuscon	CA	23480	
22	Zink	William	0404 Massachusetts	Worth	AL	23497	

You can also add rows to accomplish the same thing. In this instance, customers Getz, Holmen, and Schnur have multiple invoices. Again several columns have been hidden for display purposes.

This second option multiplies the customer's data many times within the database, causing a huge amount of duplicate data.

With the flat-file example, you begin to see more of its limitations as a database. The prior figure only showed adding an invoice number to the rows, but you would likely want to add such information as sales date, products or services sold, and dollar amount.

Now use a relational approach to this problem. Using the same customer file add an account or customer number. This number becomes a key or link to other tables related to this customer.

Now, if you want to create a sales record, simply create another table with all the sales information you want to track. Some columns or fields you want are: the customer to whom the goods were sold, the sale date, a description of items sold, and the quantify and price of the items sold. The important goal here is that you establish a *relationship* or *link* between the two tables.

Having a detailed description of every item sold in each customers invoice would lead to unnecessary duplication of data, higher storage costs, and slower response time to inquires. This process of breaking down tables to their simplest form is called *normalization.* Normalization is a process of refining your database until you have a set of tables that represent your data precisely with little or no duplication.

Relational database design offers many features not available in some of the other structures presented. Some of these advantages include:

- ✔ **Simplicity.** The relational model builds upon the simplicity of the flat-file model and, through the process of normalization, supports tables that clearly represent data in its simplest, non-redundant form.
- ✔ **Flexibility.** By storing data in a normalized table, you can add more relationships and change data in a single place and have that change replicated throughout the database. For instance, if the phone number of a customer changed, you would only need to reflect that change in one row of one table. From that point on, all records and reports about that customer would reflect the new number.
- ✔ **Power.** Using the relational structure, you have the ability to group, find, and report on your data in a greater variety of ways. As you will see in the next section, a number of relationships can be defined using the relational model—relationships that are just not possible by using the flat-file or hierarchical approach.
- ✔ **Manageability.** Based on the simplicity described above, your tables are typically smaller and contain less data. These attributes lead to a more manageable database.

Now that you have a good foundation in database structures, the next section explores the various types of relationships that can be present between tables within a relational database.

Understanding Data Relationships

As was illustrated earlier, the key to the relational structure is the linking of tables using a common element or column value. You saw that certain relationships began to emerge as the data became more and more normalized. Those relationships are explored in more detail in the following sections.

Introducing One-to-One Relationships

The *one-to-one* relationship, denoted as 1:1, is the simplest of all relationships between two tables, yet it might also be one of the rarest. The typical customer record, which commonly holds basic information such as name, address, and phone number, makes a good example. Depending on the business you are in, you might need to keep additional data about a customer, including information that might need to be confidential, such as annual income, credit rating, age, or sex.

In this case, there might be a number of employees who need to access the basic data so they can place phone calls and mail correspondence, yet there might only be a few authorized to see the confidential portions of the data. This is a good situation in which two tables need to be created with a one-to-one relationship (see fig. 4.11).

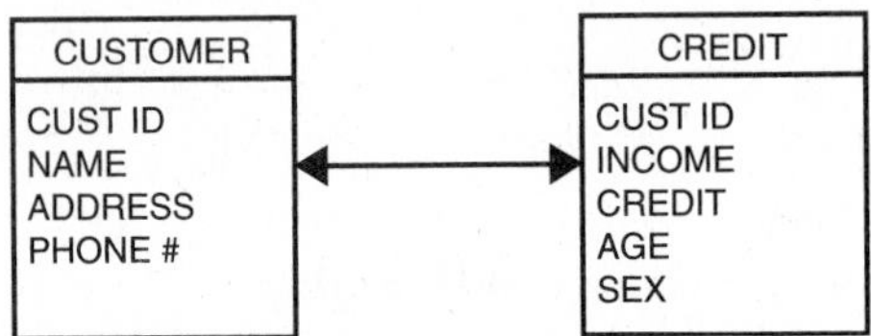

Figure 4.11 There is one and only one credit record for each customer record.

You can join two customer information tables by the customer account number, yet the data can be accessed separately if necessary. Note that only one customer record exists for each credit record and only one credit record for each customer record. This is the basis for the one-to-one relationship.

Some database management systems enable you to place security on individual fields and restrict user access to that field. This might eliminate the need to create tables with one-to-one relationships.

Introducing One-to-Many Relationships

The most common relationship in a relational database is the *one-to-many* relationship, denoted 1:M. In a one-to-many relationship, each record in the primary table has one or more records in another table related to it. To understand this concept, switch your focus to the operation of your neighborhood video store.

Again, the foundation of the relational database used in the video store is the customer record. Each time a customer comes into the store, he is likely to check out one or more videos. This could be illustrated as shown in figure 4.12.

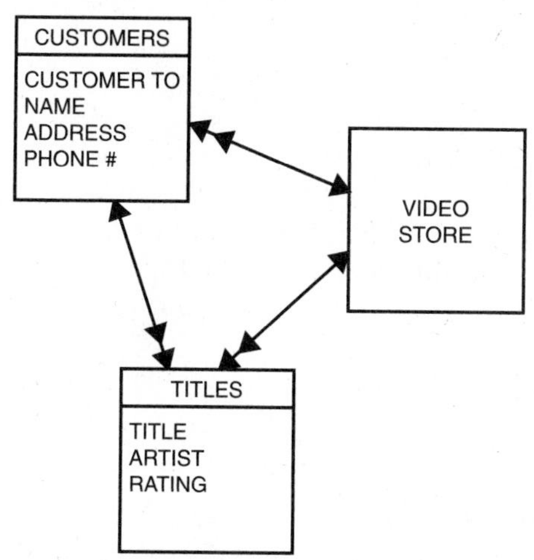

Figure 4.12 The Customer may check out one or more videos.

In the preceding figure, the customer leaves the store with a 1:M relationship to the videos he checked out, however, the videos he has can only be attributed to one customer at a time. Clearly, the same physical video cannot be checked out by more than one customer at a time.

Introducing Many-to-Many Relationships

With the hospital model, you see an example of a *many to many* relationship denoted m:m. When you stay at a hospital for any length of time, you see many nurses as the care for you continues around the clock. At the same time, each nurse in the hospital is not dedicated solely to your care. Each patient can have many nurses caring for them, and each nurse can care for many patients. This creates the many-to-many relationship as shown in figure 4.13.

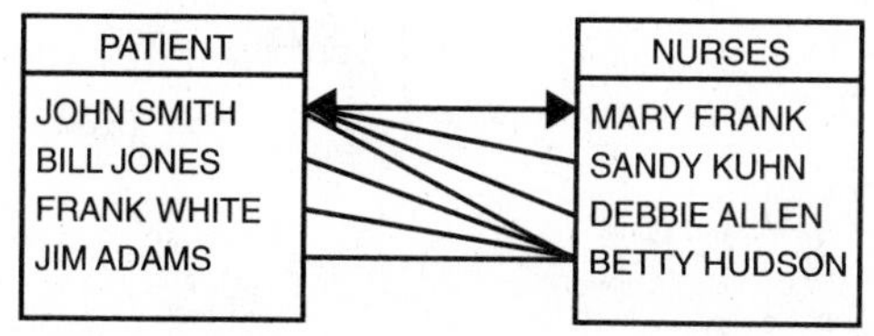

Figure 4.13 Each nurse cares for many patients, and each patient has many nurses.

In comparing the video store to the hospital example, you can see that (assuming multiple copies of the film title are available) one film title can be checked out by many customers, and that one customer can also check out many films, including duplicate copies of the same film if desired.

Understanding Data Types

You have so far read about various structures, relationships, and how a database is defined. This section delves into the various types of data that are available and some of their characteristics.

As you travel to work each day, you notice many forms of transportation. Some people walk; some people ride in a bus or car; still others ride a bicycle. The common element is that all of these people are doing the same thing: transporting themselves from one place to another. However, each person has chosen a different mode by which to do this. A similar analogy can be made for data. All data has the ability to communicate or convey information, yet each piece of data does it with slightly different attributes and characteristics.

The following sections explore the characteristics or attributes of the different data types available to dBASE for Windows.

Defining Character Fields

Character fields are the most common field type because you can use them to store a wide variety of data. *Character fields* are often called Alphanumeric fields because they can store all the characters of the *Alpha*bet (A–Z, a–z) as well as *Numeric* data such as 0 through 9. However, the Character field is really more diverse than that because it can store any value from the ASCII character set.

Using the ASCII chart, you can see that the ability to use some of the other ASCII characters in a database opens many possibilities for enhancing your data. In dBASE, the maximum size of a character field is 254 bytes or characters. If you need to store more information in a single field, you need to use the dBASE memo field described later.

Although you can store almost all data in a character field, you should still take care to choose the most appropriate field type for the data—based on how you are going to use it. For instance, the numbers 1 through 100 sort differently when stored as characters than as a numeric or floating point value. You might get the sequence 1, 10, 100, 11, 12, 13, 14 rather than the 1, 10, 11, 12, 13, 14, 100 you expect. Similarly, fields containing dates can be manipulated much easier when stored in a date field, even though you could store it in a character field.

Defining Date Fields

dBASE *date* fields always occupy eight characters or positions within a dBASE table. Internally, dates are stored in the format YYYYMMDD, which stands for the four-digit year, two-digit month, and two-digit day. For instance, the date July 23, 1994 would be stored as 19940723. This storage method makes it easy for dBASE to sort dates chronologically and to mathematically evaluate dates.

You can control the external presentation of a dBASE date field by many methods. The default for the DATE display format is controlled by the International option of the Windows Control Panel. This default can be overridden by changing the DATE setting parameter in DBASEWIN.INI (all of the options available in the DBASEWIN.INI file are described in detail in Appendix A). This default can be temporarily overridden with the SET DATE command. Some of the common formats are described in the following table. Using the SET DATE command overrides the default. dBASE can display dates in a number of formats shown below. If the user does nothing, the date is displayed in American format.

Table 4.1
Date Formats

Setting	Format
AMERICAN	MM/DD/YY
ANSI	YY.MM.DD
BRITISH	DD/MM/YY
USA	MM-DD-YY
MDY	MM/DD/YY
DMY	DD/MM/YY
YMD	YY/MM/DD

Depending on the option selected, note that the order of the month, day, and year might change, as well as the delimiters "/", "-", and ".".

Defining Numeric Fields

Numeric fields come in two varieties in dBASE for Windows. The first is the standard Numeric type or binary coded decimal (BCD), and the second is the floating-point type described in the next section. Numeric fields are the most accurate when performing financial or business calculations. By default, dBASE performs its internal calculations using 16 decimal places, but the SET PRECISION command varies the precision from 10 to 20 places. This value affects the way dBASE stores the numbers for calculations, not the way they are displayed. To alter the way the values are displayed, use the SET DECIMAL command.

If the Numeric number grows to be very large or very small, it displays as a floating point number.

Defining Floating-Point Fields

Floating-point fields are more applicable for numbers that are very small or vary large. These numbers are typically used in scientific calculations. These calculations are not quite as precise as calculations using BCD numbers and the sum of a column of floating point numbers might not add up to exactly the number you would expect. This occurs because numbers far to the right of the decimal point must be rounded or truncated to be shown on the field. Therefore, floating-point numbers are vulnerable to rounding and truncation errors.

The reason for the minor inaccuracy seen in floating-point calculations is deeply rooted in the binary number system the computer system uses to calculate numbers. Generally, numeric (BCD) data is not subject to this error in precision because the application program typically goes through extra conversion processes to insure the accuracy of the data. Extra conversion also is the reason why calculations involving numeric data take longer than calculations involving floating-point data.

The SET PRECISION has no affect on floating-point type numbers. Floating-point numbers have a precision of 15 regardless of the SET PRECISION. Calculations involving both numeric and float numbers always yield a float value for the result.

When planning your reports and forms, take into account all the characters comprising a floating-point number. For instance, the number 1.6E+21 will require a minimum of eight positions on a form or report. (There is an implied sign either "+" or "-" in front of the "1.6").

Defining Logical Fields

Logical fields are by far the least complex of all the dBASE field types and have only two values: *true* (.T.) or *false* (.F.). The logical field takes up one byte or character position in the database. When entering logical values into your database, the following values are all accepted as TRUE; .T., .t., .Y., .y.. Likewise, the values .F., .f., .N., .n. are all accepted as FALSE. As will be explained later in the programming section of this book, logical values are extremely efficient for testing an ON/OFF or YES/NO state, such as the end-of-file when reading a database sequentially.

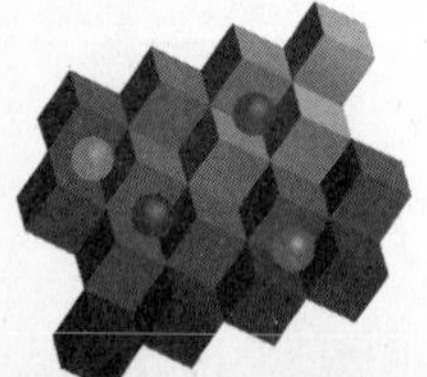

Defining Memo Fields

A *Memo* field has a variety of uses and special properties within dBASE. As mentioned earlier, the size of a Character field (254 characters) is sometimes too limiting for your application. In the video store example, you might want to store a detailed synopsis of a film within your database. A person deciding on a film to check out needs to see more information on the story line or a list of the stars appearing in it. This is a good use for Memo fields.

A Memo field is comprised of two separate parts: a 10-character pointer or place holder that is part of your main dBASE for Windows database (a DBF file); and the memo data itself, which is physically stored in a special file. This special file has the same basic name as your database file except that the file extension is DBT rather than DBF. The size of the Memo field varies in each record in the database because the Memo field size is only as large as it needs to be to store the data. However, the primary portion or pointer field in the main DBF file always consumes the full 10 bytes of data.

Sometimes you will find it advantageous to store data in a Memo field when that data could easily fit into a character field. The advantage comes when you have a high degree of variability in the amount of data needed for each record. Take, for example, a survey form on which numeric scores are listed, as well as space for optional comments. Experience shows that most surveyors complete the numeric scores without entering any comments in the area provided. The comments that are submitted often vary widely in terms of length and content. Rather than defining one or more Character fields for the survey comments, you can create a separate Memo field for comments. This enables you not only to store all of the comments entered but also to save a great deal of disk space.

Within the past several years, new data types have begun to appear in some of the more sophisticated database management packages. The next section explores two new field types introduced in dBASE.

Promote Binary Data Types

One of the most exciting new features in dBASE for Windows is the ability to store graphics and sound data directly in the database. dBASE supports many of the popular sound and graphics file formats such as BMP, PCX, and WAV files.

These new data types open a whole new world of information and effects you can add to your applications. Imagine a video store where you could go in, search for a title using a computer database, click on a special icon, and hear a sound clip from the movie or see a still-shot segment.

The concept of graphics and sound data in a database introduces the potential of more applications such as photo ID systems, as well as applications where sound and possibly voice recognition play a key role.

OLE Data Types

Another data type new to dBASE is OLE (object linking and embedding). OLE is a Windows feature you can use to store or reference a document from one application inside of a dBASE table. For example, you could store a company logo, a sales graph, or a word-processing document inside a dBASE OLE field.

While OLE and Binary fields appear very similar, they do have some distinct differences. With binary fields, you can store any type of binary data. There does not have to be an associated application. OLE data, on the other hand, draws its strength from the fact that it is linked to an application permitting you to edit or view the information by opening the embedded application.

As alluded to above, OLE files can either be embedded directly into the dBASE table or they can be linked to the table. Linking to the OLE file can save you disk space by not creating multiple copies of the data.

Chapter 24 "Integrating dBASE Applications with OLE and DDE" provides additional detail on OLE integration.

Creating a Simple Table

Now that you are familiar with each of dBASE for Windows many data types, it is time to create a table for the application we will be working on throughout this book: HomeGuide, the real estate and housing information system.

Planning Your Tables

The importance of carefully planning your database is one task that cannot be overstated. Although dBASE for Windows makes it simple and relatively painless to add elements at a later date, time spent planning at the outset more than pays for itself later. Before you start creating your table with the dBASE for Windows Table Designer, it is a good idea to plan your work first on a sheet of paper.

The following are some things for which you should plan:

- ✔ **Fields.** What data do you want to store?

- ✔ **Field names.** What are you going to call each piece of data so that you understand its use?
- ✔ **Field types.** What is the most appropriate data type to use to store your data?
- ✔ **Field size.** What is the largest piece of information you need to store in each field?
- ✔ **Organization and layout.** What data do you want together in a single table, and what data belongs in separate tables?

The sample application you build throughout this book is a small replica of an application that a national real estate agency might use. If you think about the application, you realize that there are three major elements to the real estate business: homes for sale, buyers looking for homes, and agents trying to bring the buyers and homes together.

Before you begin creating tables with the dBASE Table Designer, you need to understand a little bit more about this application, the tables involved, and the contents of the tables. This is where the planning portion of your application comes in.

The first major element mentioned above was homes. You will need to create a Listing table that contains all of the key information about the homes listed by the real estate agency. This table will contain vital information about the home, including the address, list price, age, and tax information. In addition, it will be handy to have a unique ID number associated with each home, so that you can link other information to it, if necessary, and search for it quickly as your table sizes grow.

The second element needed in the application is agents. An Agent table should contain information on the agents within the agency that either listed the homes or show the homes to perspective customers. An Agent table, for this application, could be as simple as the agent's name, address, phone number, and agency name.

The final major table needed is one for buyers. A Buyer table should contain information about people looking for a home, such as the buyers name, address, phone number, price range desired, and the area in which the home should be located.

In addition to these major tables, the HomeGuide application also might need a number of tables for supporting information. There should be a Room table to list a number of specific details about each major room within a home. This ties back to the one-to-many (1:M) discussion in which a house can have one or more rooms associated with it. There could also be an Agency table to provide additional information about the agency each real estate agent works for. The following relationships exist:

- ✔ An agency has agents
- ✔ Each home has one or more rooms
- ✔ The home is linked to the agent and agency through codes in the table

Using the Table Designer

The easiest way to become familiar with the dBASE Table Designer is to work with it. The Listing table is probably the one that is most familiar to you and presents some basic table elements that can be used in many other tables. The remainder of this chapter assumes you have dBASE loaded on your machine and are following along and doing the steps as described.

To create the Listing table, open the Table Designer in dBASE by clicking on the tables icon in the Navigator window. The Navigator bar and the Tables item on the left side of the Navigator window are highlighted. Note the list box (on the right side of the Navigator window) of one or more tables with the one in the upper left corner called Untitled. This Untitled table is the starting point for creating all of your new dBASE for Windows tables.

As you right-click on the Untitled table in the Navigator window, a menu appears with New Table highlighted (see fig. 4.14).

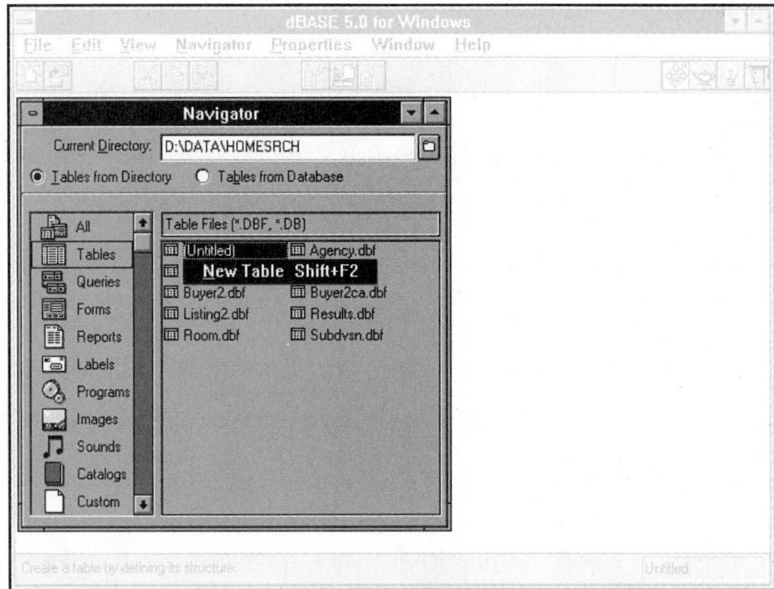

Figure 4.14
Standard initial configuration for dBase for Windows when you first start the program.

Although most of the dBASE operations presented in this and subsequent chapters can be accomplished from the command line in the Command window, they are demonstrated using the equivalent mouse actions as often as possible.

You can quickly bring up the Table Designer dialog box by double-clicking on the Untitled table. dBase is programmed to anticipate the most likely action you would want to take with the highlighted object, and executes that action when the object is selected (see fig. 4.15).

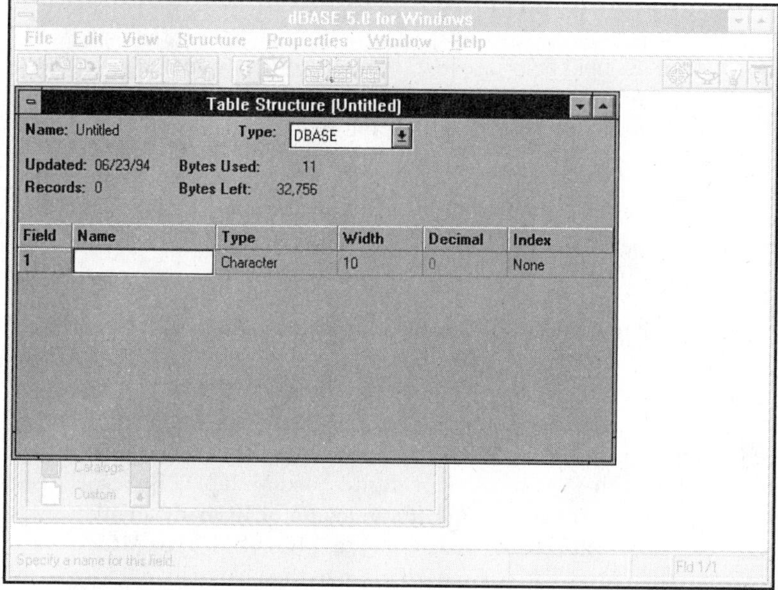

Figure 4.15
Annotated Table Designer dialog box.

Parts of the Table Designer Window

Following are the various text boxes in the dBASE Table Designer window, with a brief explanation and a description of the valid values each box can hold.

- ✔ **Name.** The name of your dBASE table. This remains Untitled until you have saved it with a valid file name.

- ✔ **Type.** The type of database you are creating or using. dBASE supports dBASE and Paradox type tables.

- ✔ **Updated.** The date the table was last modified.

- ✔ **Records.** The number of records currently in the table

- ✔ **Bytes Used.** The number of bytes used by each record.

- ✔ **Bytes Left.** The number of bytes that can be used for defining additional fields in the table. A dBASE record can hold a maximum of 32,767 bytes.

- **Field.** The number of the field being created or modified.
- **Name.** The name of the field being created or modified. The name can be from 1 to 10 characters long and consist of digits (0–9), letters (A–Z), and underscores (_).
- **Type.** The type of field being created or modified, whether it is **C**haracter, **N**umeric, **M**emo, **L**ogical, **D**ate, **F**loat, **O**LE, or **B**inary.
- **Width.** The size of the field being created or modified. The values in parentheses indicate the maximum size of the field. The width of a Numeric field should include a position for the decimal point. Also, for Memo, Binary, and OLE field types the width field is grayed out and defaults to 10 bytes that are used for pointer information. You cannot modify fields when they are grayed out.
- **Decimal.** The number of the digits to the right of the decimal point in the field being created or modified.
- **Index.** The order of the index (None, Ascending, or Descending) if this field is to be used to organize the table in a specific order.

Your cursor should now be located at the beginning of the Name area for Field 1. For each home in the Listing table, there needs to be a code or number that uniquely identifies the home. The code that will be used for this is called Multiple List Service Number. Because dBASE field names have a maximum length of 10 characters (letters, digits, and underscores) you can abbreviate this number as MLSNUM. Type **MLSNUM** into the Name area, and then press Tab or Enter to move to the next field.

Clicking on the next field definition with the mouse is another method to move from field to field. This action requires you to remove your hand from the keyboard and then return it; although the mouse is a valuable tool in the graphical user interface (GUI), it is not always the most efficient.

However you select it, the type area is highlighted. Notice that once this area is selected, a down arrow appears indicating that a list box became available (see fig. 4.16). At this point, click on this down arrow to see the list of field choices available or simply press the first character of the desired field type (**C**haracter, **N**umeric, **M**emo, **L**ogical, **D**ate, **F**loat, **O**LE, or **B**inary). After the correct field type is displayed, press Enter to accept your choice. For the MLSNUM, choose **C**haracter, and then press Enter.

After you choose the type of field you want, the cursor advances to the width column. For MLSNUM, enter eight and press Enter. This time, when you press Enter, the cursor does not stop at the Decimal column, but goes directly to the Index column. Because you are defining a Character field, there cannot be a decimal portion, so dBASE for Windows automatically skips that column.

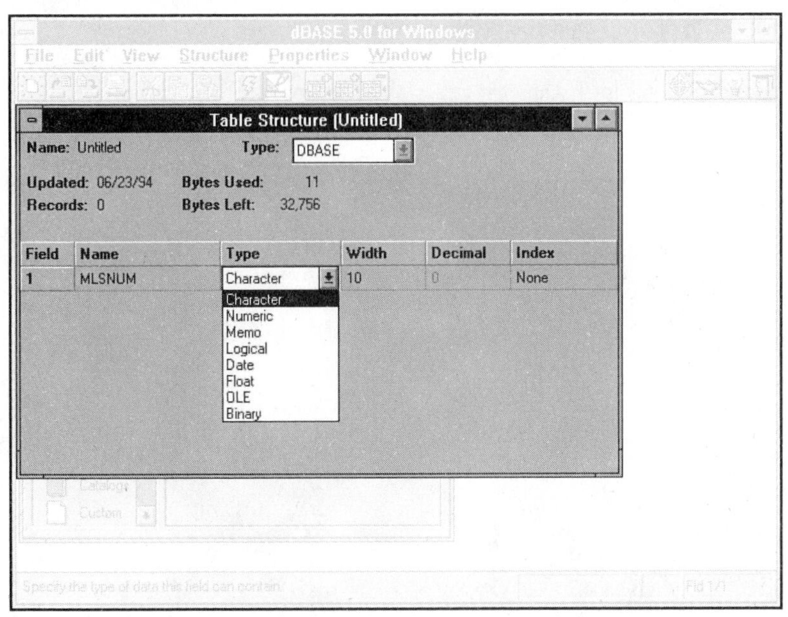

Figure 4.16
The Field list box offers eight data types from which to choose.

The Index column is similar to the Type column, in that it has a pull-down list box for the choices **N**one, **A**scend, and **D**escend. Because MLSNUM will later be used as an index to link other tables in the application and searching for specific homes, it should be an Indexed field. At this point, click on the down arrow to see the list of field choices available. You can either click on the Ascend or simply press the first character A to choose **A**scend.

For the most part, Indexed fields are commonly used in ascending order, but there are a few exceptions—such as when you are organizing fields by date and want the most recent first. In such a case, you would index by descending order.

With the first field of your table defined, your screen should now look like the one shown in figure 4.17.

The bytes field in the Table Designer should show 19. dBASE has summed the MLSNUM field and anticipated the default 10 characters of the field you are about to define. But where does the other byte come from? dBASE for Windows, like its DOS counterpart, maintains a one-character field at the beginning of each record to keep track of whether or not the record has been

continues

deleted. In dBase, when you delete a record, the record is not physically deleted but merely marked for deletion at a later time. This concept is discussed more thoroughly later when the topics of delete, recall, and pack are introduced.

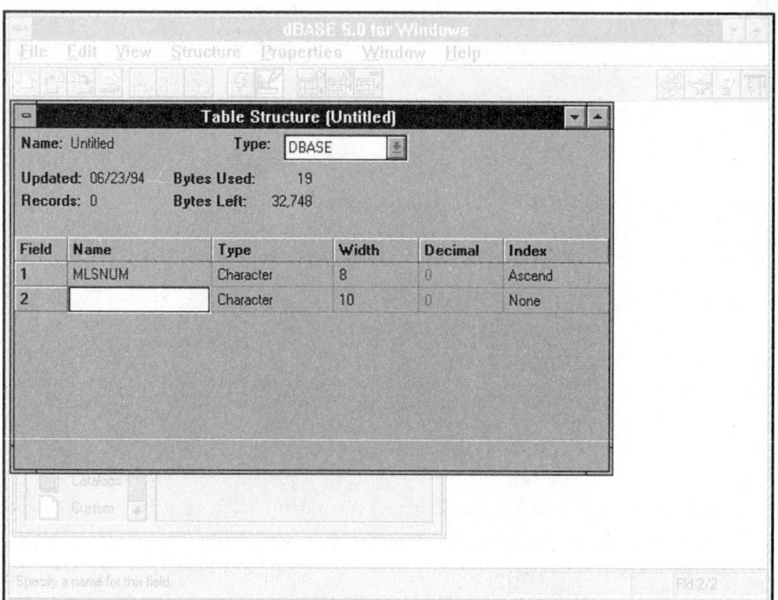

Figure 4.17
The MLSNUM field is the first field defined.

The next field to create is for the homes list price. This field provides one of the key pieces of information to prospective buyers and will also be a key part of any search criteria that will be used later in the application.

Enter **LISTPRICE** into the second fields Name column and press Enter. Next, instead of selecting the default Character, press **N** to define a Numeric field or click on the selection arrow to display the field types and choose Numeric. After you have selected Numeric in the Type column, press either Enter or Tab to advance to the width field and enter **10**. Next press either Enter or Tab again to advance to the Decimal field. Because most homes are sold in whole dollars, you should enter **0** for this field or just press Enter to accept 0 as the default.

Because you will probably not want to do any special table organizing or linking using the list price, this field will not be indexed.

Now it is time to create the rest of the listing table structure. You can either enter the rest of the fields as indicated in the following table, or use the tables supplied with the *Inside dBASE for Windows Bonus Disk.*

Field	Field Name	Type	Length	Dec	Index
1	MLSNUM	Character	8		Y
2	LISTPRICE	Numeric	10		N
3	ADDRESS	Character	25		N
4	MAIL	Character	20		N
5	TAX	Character	20		N
6	ZIP	Character	10		N
7	COUNTY	Character	10		N
8	LOTSIZE	Character	10		N
9	TAXES	Numeric	10		N
10	TAXYEAR	Character	4		N
11	TAXKEY	Character	8		N
12	YEARBUILT	Character	4		N
13	SQFOOT	Numeric	5		N
14	SUBDVSN	Character	30		N
15	GARAGE	Character	10		N
16	GRGSIZE	Numeric	3	1	N
17	AGENTID	Character	5		N
18	LISTDATE	Date	8		N
19	EXPDATE	Date	8		N
20	ADDINFO	Memo	10		N
21	PHOTO	Binary	10		N

Some of the fields defined in the preceding table might need further explanation. The lot size (LOTSIZE) field is defined as Character instead of Numeric. This field is used to store the relative dimensions of the lot such as 70×120 instead of the actual size in acres or square feet. Total square feet can be found in the SQFOOT field found later in the table.

Similarly, the garage size field (GRGSIZE) is a Numeric field to indicate the relative number of vehicles that can be parked in the garage.

The agent field (AGENT) was also highlighted earlier as an important field in the listing table. This will be the main link that enables you to link a listed home back to the responsible agent from the agent table.

The ZIP code field is created large enough to handle the newer nine digit ZIP codes with a dash to separate the ZIP+4, and it is designated as a Character field so that it can accommodate non-numeric codes such as those used in Canada. Although the real estate application starts out small, there is great potential for growth, and you don't want to set too many limits on your listing territory.

The ADDINFO field is the Notes field for the listing table. This area is useful to store additional information about the home that might highlight some significant selling points or other pieces of information. This field also could provide additional contact information on the seller, or just generally talk about the neighborhood and surrounding schools and churches.

The last field of special interest is the PHOTO field. Using dBASE's advanced capabilities, you can actually store a photograph of the home right in the table. This enables you to show potential buyers an actual photograph of the home side by side with all pertinent sales information.

After entering all of the table structure information, you will need to save the structure so that you can begin using it to enter and retrieve data. To save your structure, click on the File menu item and select the Save option. Clicking on this option displays a Save Table dialog box, which enables you to specify a file name for your table (see fig. 4.18).

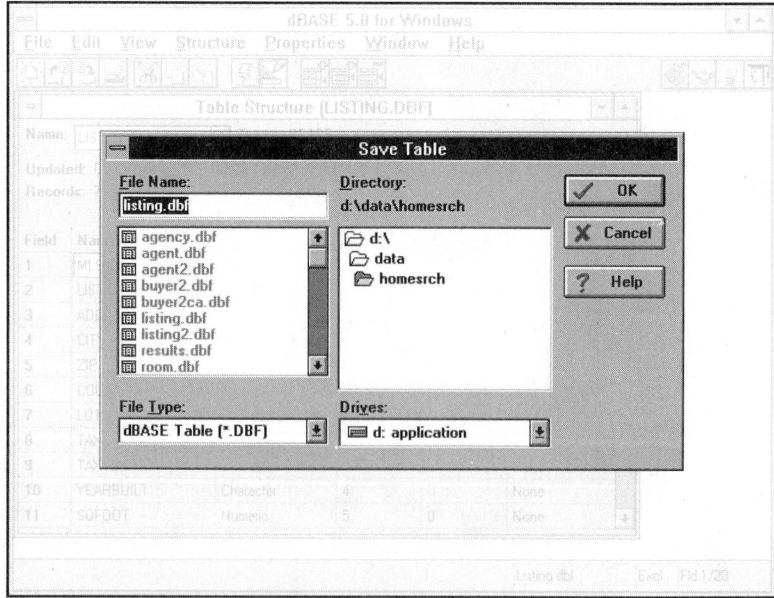

Figure 4.18 The Save Table dialog box enables you to specify a name for your table.

Displaying Your Structure

Before entering data into your new table, do another visual inspection of the table to ensure that all the fields are defined and have the proper attributes or characteristics. If you entered the data using the Table Designer, you probably noticed that there was never more than eight fields on the screen at one time, yet the Listing table has twenty-one fields defined. You can use the DISPLAY STRUCTURE command to display the complete structure of your table.

To run the DISPLAY STRUCTURE command, activate the Command window by left-clicking on it, and then ensure that the table whose structure you want to display is in use by issuing the USE LISTING command.

You can have multiple tables in use at one time by using dBASE work areas. Only one work area is technically active and available to you at a time, however. Work areas are discussed in more detail in Chapter 5, "Using dBASE for Windows Databases."

Because the structure display is likely to need more room than is currently in the Command window, click the upper right hand corner of the window to expand it to full size. Next, enter the DISPLAY STRUCTURE command in the Command window. The Command window should look similar to figure 4.19.

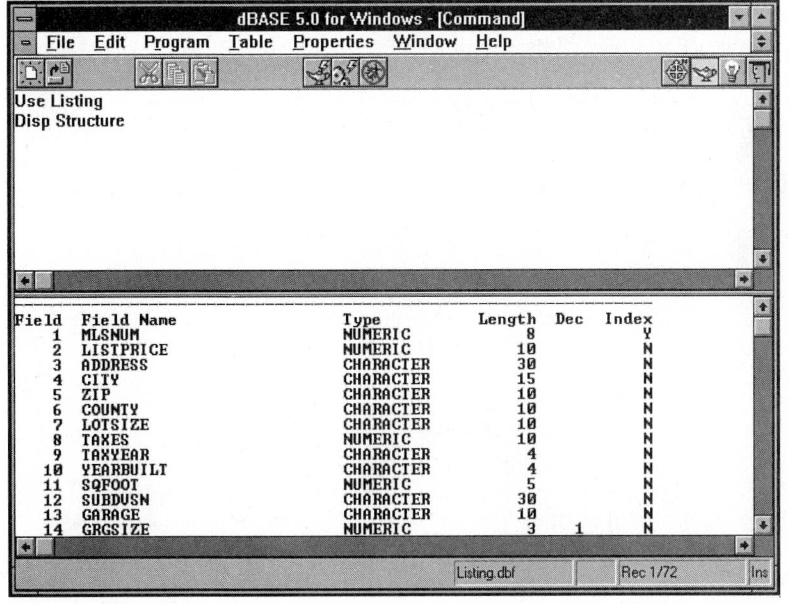

Figure 4.19
The Command window shows the command and the results of the display structure of the table you just created.

The DISPLAY STRUCTURE command has additional parameters that enable you to route the output of your structure to the printer or to a file. The format of these commands are as follows:

- ✔ **DISPLAY STRUCTURE to PRINTER.** This command directs the output to the printer and the Command Results window.
- ✔ **DISPLAY STRUCTURE to FILE <filename> | ?.** This command directs the output to the text file named filename and the Command Results window. You don't need to specify an extension because, by default, dBASE assigns a TXT extension to filename and saves the file in the current directory. If you want to save the output somewhere else on your disk, specify the ? parameter. The ? option opens the Create File dialog box and enables you specify the name of the target file and the directory in which to save it.

After verifying that the new table structure is correct, define the rest of your tables or begin adding data to them. The rest of the tables (Agent, Buyer, Room, and Listing) have been created for you and are included on the book disk.

Using Previously Created Structures

As mentioned earlier in this chapter, the Listing table can serve as the basis for a number of other tables that you might want to create to run outside the realm of the real estate application. Although it was easy to create the Listing table, you will find it much easier to simply copy the structure of the existing Listing table if you were to need a similar table.

To copy the structure of a dBASE table, you must first ensure that it is in use. To do this, right-click on the Command window to make it active, and then type **USE LISTING**.

Now issue the COPY STRUCTURE command from the command Window. Type the following:

```
COPY STRUCTURE to NEWLIST WITH PRODUCTION
```

If you activate the Navigator window at this point, you should see that it is updated to reflect that there is now a Newlist table available for use.

There are many command line options available to the COPY STRUCTURE command. The command line COPY STRUCTURE to NEWLIST WITH PRODUCTION represents the minimum needed to make an exact copy of the Customer table. The WITH PRODUCTION option is used to ensure that Index fields are copied with their index setting (ASCEND or DESCEND). There are other options available to create different database types and to restrict the fields that are copied. To learn more about the additional options, see Appendix A at the end of this book.

Understanding Table Limits

Throughout this chapter, most of the limits that apply to the various tables have been described. When planning your database, however, be aware of the maximum number of records your database can hold, as well as the size of each individual record.

Chapter Snapshot

In the last chapter, you learned many of the fundamentals of database technology and how to create your first dBASE for Windows database. This chapter builds on that knowledge and teaches you some of the basic functions and operations you can perform on your newly created table. Some of the more important functions include:

With the information in this chapter, you can make changes and enhancements to your tables.

Using dBASE for Windows Databases

By Jim Wetzel

In the last chapter, you created your first dBASE for Windows database. Now you will enter data so that you will be able to use the rest of dBASE for Windows' many features. dBASE for Windows gives you a number of alternatives for entering data into a table.

Understanding the basic concepts of tables is the key to getting the most from this book. Spend some time here working with the table menu item (see fig. 5.1) and the examples in this chapter so that you will be familiar with manipulating data in tables.

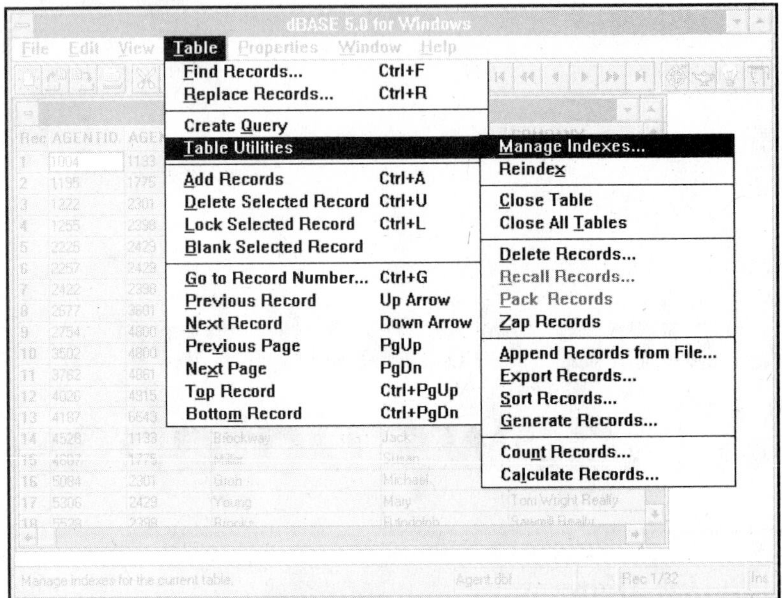

Figure 5.1
The table menu item contains many of the functions and features described in this chapter.

Adding Data to a Table

The easiest way to add data to your tables is to right-click on the table you want to work with in the Navigator window to highlight it, and then select the Add Records option from the local menu.

If the file you want to work with is already highlighted, you can also start adding records by selecting the Add Records option from the Navigator menu option. Either of these methods opens the table to a blank record—ready for you to start keying in data.

Using the Different Views When Adding Data

dBASE for Windows provides you with a number of different formats to use when you add data to your tables (see fig. 5.2). Chapter 4, "Designing and Creating Relational Databases," covered changing the default view to either Form Layout or Columnar Layout using the Files option of the Desktop Properties menu. Another view you can use—Browse Layout view—is in the View menu. Figures 5.2 through 5.4 show you Form, Columnar, and Browse layout views.

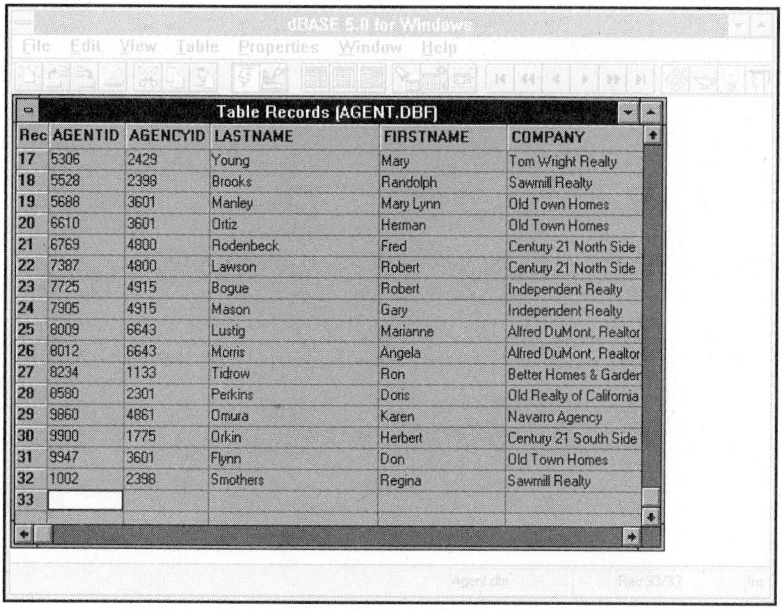

dBASE 5.0 for Windows

File Edit View Table Properties Window Help

Table Records (AGENT.DBF)

Rec	AGENTID	AGENCYID	LASTNAME	FIRSTNAME	COMPANY
17	5306	2429	Young	Mary	Tom Wright Realty
18	5528	2398	Brooks	Randolph	Sawmill Realty
19	5688	3601	Manley	Mary Lynn	Old Town Homes
20	6610	3601	Ortiz	Herman	Old Town Homes
21	6769	4800	Rodenbeck	Fred	Century 21 North Side
22	7387	4800	Lawson	Robert	Century 21 North Side
23	7725	4915	Bogue	Robert	Independent Realty
24	7905	4915	Mason	Gary	Independent Realty
25	8009	6643	Lustig	Marianne	Alfred DuMont, Realtor
26	8012	6643	Morris	Angela	Alfred DuMont, Realtor
27	8234	1133	Tidrow	Ron	Better Homes & Garden
28	8580	2301	Perkins	Doris	Old Realty of California
29	9860	4861	Omura	Karen	Navarro Agency
30	9900	1775	Orkin	Herbert	Century 21 South Side
31	9947	3601	Flynn	Don	Old Town Homes
32	1002	2398	Smothers	Regina	Sawmill Realty
33					

Figure 5.2
Form layout view.

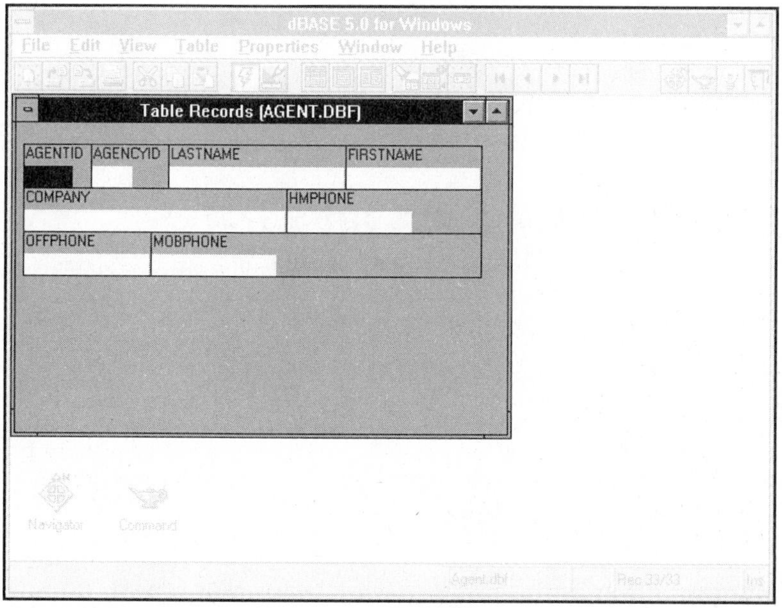

dBASE 5.0 for Windows

File Edit View Table Properties Window Help

Table Records (AGENT.DBF)

AGENTID AGENCYID LASTNAME FIRSTNAME

COMPANY HMPHONE

OFFPHONE MOBPHONE

Figure 5.3
Columnar layout view.

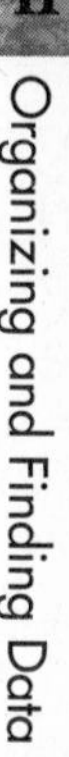

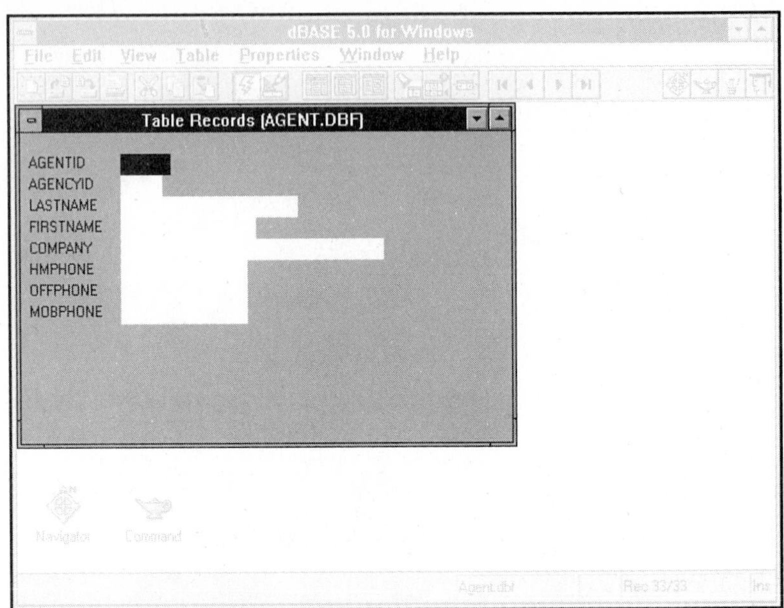

Figure 5.4
Browse layout view.

Press F2 to toggle between the three views.

Understanding Special Data Entry Cases

For the most part, data entry in dBASE involves simply typing the information you want into the desired field. A few special features exist, however, that you should be aware of when entering data.

Automatic Field Advance

By default, dBASE will advance to the next field when you do any one of three actions; press Enter, press Tab, or completely fill in the field (that is, type five characters into a field defined as Type - Character with a Width of 5).

Automatic advance is an option you can set to occur whenever a field is completely filled in. You can turn off this option by selecting Keyboard Confirm option from the Data Entry page of the Desktop Properties menu, or by issuing the SET CONFIRM OFF command in the Command window.

Date Entry

Another feature you should be aware of is data entry into a dBASE Date type field. Date fields only need to have the digits entered. dBASE will automatically supply the forward slash "/" date delimiters.

The "/" is the default date delimiter. You can change this by typing a different separator mark in the Country page of the Desktop Properties menu or by issuing a SET MARK TO command in the Command window.

Text Memo

Entering data into a memo field is a two-step process. The first step is to double-click on the Memo icon to open a memo text window (see fig. 5.5). After the memo text window is open, you can type any Alphanumeric data of almost an unlimited length. The second step is to close the text editor window after you have entered your text by double-clicking on the windows control panel, or by selecting File, Close.

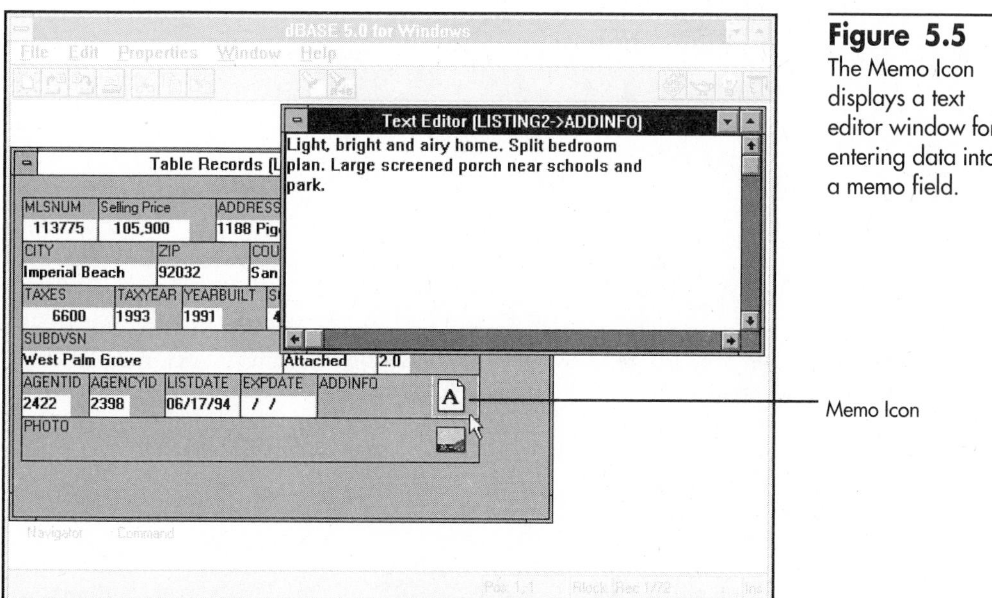

Figure 5.5
The Memo Icon displays a text editor window for entering data into a memo field.

Memo fields that contain data will display an A in the paper Icon.

Binary Fields

Binary fields are new to dBASE and are a special case in terms of data entry. Binary fields are used to store graphic or sound data such as BMP, PCX, and WAV files.

The process of adding binary data to a dBASE file is similar to that of Memo fields. The first step is to double click on the Binary Field. If the Binary field is empty an Empty Binary Field dialog box appears, as shown in figure 5.6.

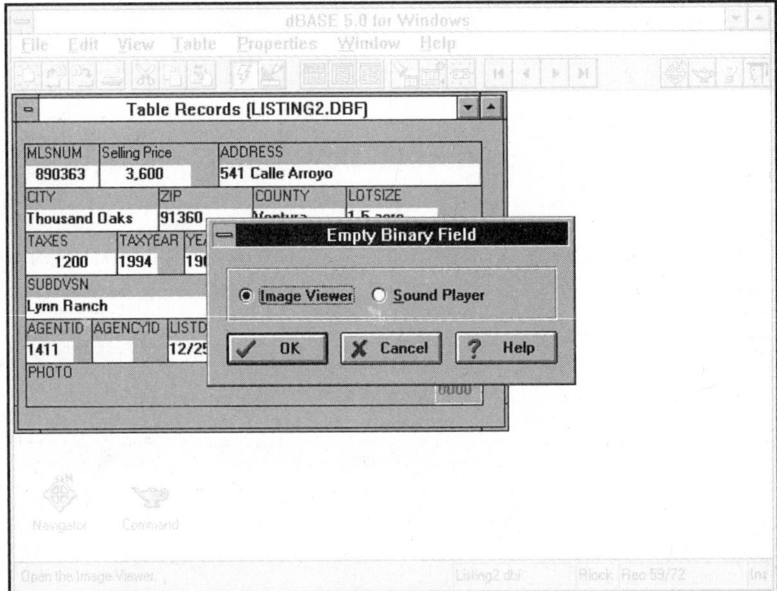

Figure 5.6 Use the Empty Binary Field dialog box to select the dBASE Image Viewer or Sound Player.

Select one of the binary field options from the Empty Binary Field dialog box, and select OK to display either the Image Viewer Window or Sound Player Window. When either of these windows is active, you can use the Insert from File option from the File menu to insert a file into these fields.

If the Binary field already has data in it, then the Empty Binary Field dialog box does not appear. The Image Viewer or Sound Player window displays directly, depending on the type of data in the field.

If you prefer, you can also use the REPLACE BINARY command in the command window to add or replace data in a Binary field. The format of the command is as follows:

```
REPLACE BINARY <binary field name> FROM <file name> ¦ ? [TYPE <binary
type user number>]
```

In this case, the binary field name is the binary field in the table you want to change and the FROM <*file name*> is the name of the file you want to insert into the dBASE binary field.

The use of the question mark (?) for the FROM option of the REPLACE BINARY command invokes a dialog box that will let you search your disk drives and directories and pick the binary file you want to insert into the binary field.

The last part of the REPLACE BINARY command enables you to specify the type of binary data you are inserting into the dBASE field. dBASE has a number of predefined types:

Binary Types	Description
1 to 32767	User-defined file types
32768	WAV files
32769	BMP & PCX files

These type codes can be interrogated by the program to determine what type of data is in the field.

OLE Fields

Like the Binary Field type, the OLE field type is new to dBASE. You can add OLE objects to your database with the REPLACE OLE command. The syntax for this command is as follows:

```
REPLACE OLE <OLE field name> FROM <file name> ¦ ? [LINK [CLASS <class
name>]]
```

The *OLE field name* is any OLE field defined in your database and the *FROM file name* represents the OLE document you want to insert into your database. The key difference is the LINK clause. Without specifying the LINK option, dBASE will actually store the OLE object in your database. If you specify the LINK option, only a pointer to the OLE object is stored. The class identifies the application used to create, modify, or display the OLE object.

OLE data can also be inserted into the OLE field using the Paste option of the Edit Menu. To add or insert data into an OLE field you need to follow these steps:

1. Double-click on the OLE Field to open the OLE Viewer Window.

2. Minimize dBASE and open or switch to the application containing the OLE object you want to use in the link.

3. Select or highlight the data in the external application and use the copy option in the application to copy the data to the Windows Clipboard.

4. Return to the dBASE OLE Viewer Window and select the **P**aste option from the **E**dit menu.

Importing Data from Other Applications

Occasionally, you might want to import spreadsheet or text files from other programs into dBASE. dBASE provides a consistent format for you to store, manipulate, and report on your data. In dBASE there are two ways to import data into your data table.

The first method is the **I**mport option from the **F**ile Menu. With this option, you can import Quattro Pro (WB1) or Lotus (WK1) spreadsheets into a dBASE table (see fig. 5.7). The Spreadsheet has always been a popular tool for building small databases. dBASE allows you to preserve that data and import it into a dBASE table as your application grows.

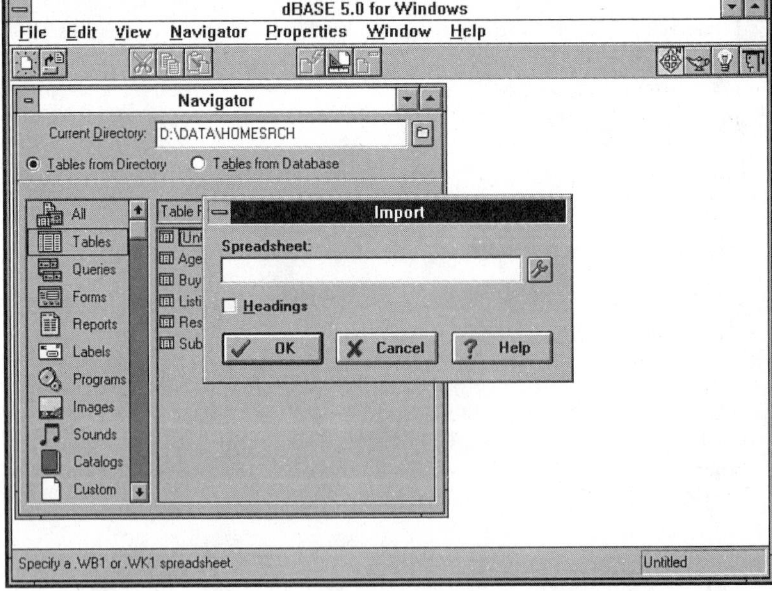

Figure 5.7
The **I**mport option of the **F**ile Menu allows you to Import Quattro Pro spreadsheets.

If you check the Heading option of the Import dialog box, dBASE will use the first row of the imported columns as the field name. Otherwise, you have to modify the field names in the structure manually.

You can also use the IMPORT command in the command window to import files into dBASE. The format of the command is as follows:

```
IMPORT FROM <file name> ¦ ? [[TYPE] WK1 ¦ WB1] [HEADING]
```

The second method you can use to import data is the Append From option of the Table Utilities located in the Table menu (see fig. 5.8). For this option to work, you must have an open table for dBASE to append records.

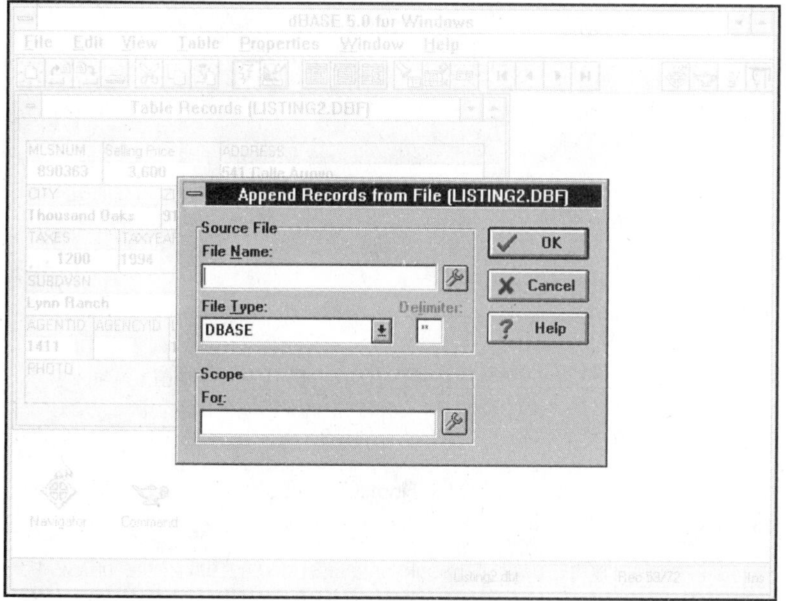

Figure 5.8
The Append Records From File dialog box is available from the Table Utilities option of the Table Menu.

The Append Records from file dialog box gives you options that enable you to search for and select the table you want to append from, specify the format of the data in the table you are appending, and specify the scope of the data to be appended.

The Scope section of this dialog box is an extremely powerful tool. You can either specify an expression directly in the For field or click on the tool button to invoke the dBASE expression builder. The dBASE expression builder enables you to build an expression to limit the range of the appended records.

One use of this option would be if you wanted to build a subset of a database. Suppose, for example, you want to extract all the buyers from California in the HomeGuide BUYER2 table and put those buyers into a new BUYER2CA table? You could specify the selection criteria as shown in figure 5.9.

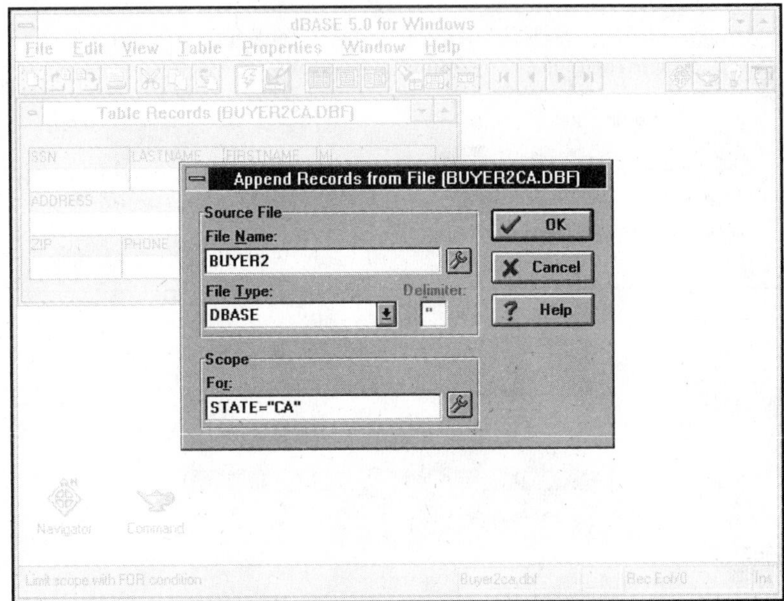

Figure 5.9 The Scope statement of the Append Records dialog box only selects records that have STATE equal to "CA".

This would select the five records from the BUYER2 table and append them to the BUYER2CA table.

You could also create a subset of the HomeGuide BUYER2 table by using the following command in the command window:

```
APPEND FROM D:\DATA\DBWBOOK\SAMPLES\BUYER2.DBF TYPE DBASE FOR
BUYER2CO->STATE="CA"
```

The full syntax of the APPEND FROM command is as follows:

```
APPEND FROM <file name> ¦ ? ¦ <filename skeleton> [FOR
<condition>] [[TYPE] SDF ¦ WB1 ¦ DBMEMO3 ¦ PARADOX ¦ DBASE ¦
DELIMITED [WITH <char> ¦ BLANK] ] [POSITION] [REINDEX]
```

Generating Test Data

Occasionally, you might need some data in a table so that you can test an application. Applications that run well with 10 or 20 records in a database can have performance problems when the number of records exceed 100 or 1000. Manually entering data to test this can be a real chore but fortunately dBASE has a quick method to fill a table with test data.

The Generate Records selection on the Table Utilities option of the Table menu enables you to effortlessly create tables full of data. Figure 5.10 illustrates this helpful feature.

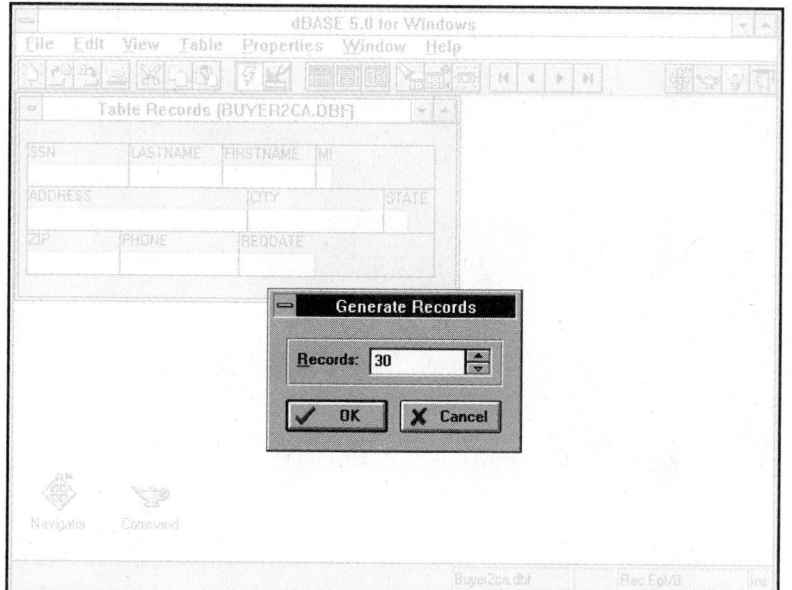

Figure 5.10
The Generate Records dialog box creates records with random information.

When generating records, you need to be aware that dBASE does not use any intelligence. As you can see in figure 5.10, dBASE fills the field with random data of the specified type. There is no attempt to verify that valid 2 digit codes go in the STATE field and the ZIP field will not resemble valid ZIP codes because the field was defined as Character instead of Numeric.

Browsing and Editing a Table

After you have your tables populated with usable data (rather than the random data described earlier) you will want to browse through your data looking for specific information and on occasion change data that has been previously entered.

Using the Table Browse Window

Browsing a table is as simple as double-clicking on the table in the Navigator window (see fig. 5.11) or clicking on the table in the Navigator window and pressing F2. In either case, dBASE displays your table and enables you to edit your data.

Figure 5.11
Double Clicking on the AGENT.DBF displays the Agent Table.

dBASE 5.0 for Windows

File Edit View Table Properties Window Help

Table Records (AGENT.DBF)

Rec	AGENTID	AGENCYID	LASTNAME	FIRSTNAME	COMPANY
1	1004	1133	Louge	Sled	Better Homes & Gardens
2	1195	1775	Omlet	Peggy	Century 21 South Side
3	1222	2301	Miller	Sandra	Old Realty of California
4	1255	2398	Robinson	Jack	Sawmill Realty
5	2225	2429	Wright	Tom	Tom Wright Realty
6	2257	2429	Kochanek	Diane	Tom Wright Realty
7	2422	2398	Waters	Sam	Sawmill Realty
8	2677	3601	Kuhns	Peter	Old Town Homes
9	2754	4800	Pont	John	Century 21 North Side
10	3502	4800	Robinson	Cheri	Century 21 North Side
11	3762	4861	Betker	Rosie	Navarro Agency
12	4026	4915	Mashburn	Roy	Independent Realty
13	4187	6643	Atkinson	Jane	Alfred DuMont, Realtor
14	4528	1133	Brockway	Jack	Better Homes & Gardens
15	4607	1775	Miller	Susan	Century 21 South Side
16	5084	2301	Groh	Michael	Old Realty of California

The table shown in figure 5.11 is displayed in the Browse Layout setting. This format is helpful because it can display multiple rows of information simultaneously on-screen.

The Browse Layout format also provides a great deal of flexibility in the order in which columns are displayed and the width of each column. Figure 5.12 shows one example of these custom settings.

To change the position of a column, place the mouse pointer on the column name. When the mouse pointer turns into a hand you can drag the column to its new position. The next step is to press and hold down the left mouse button and drag the column to its new position. As soon as you press the mouse button, the column will be displayed with a dotted outline around it. As you move the column, dBASE dynamically shows you how the table looks with the new column position.

In addition to controlling the placement of the columns, you can also adjust column size by making it wider or narrower (see fig. 5.13). To adjust the size of a column you need to move the mouse pointer to the right edge of the columns border. At this point, the mouse pointer turns into a double arrow cross mark that indicates it is in column mode.

The next step is to press and hold down the left mouse button and drag the column border to the right to enlarge it or to the left to shrink its size.

dBASE 5.0 for Windows

Table Records (AGENT.DBF)

Rec	AGENTID	AGENCYID	FIRSTNAME	LASTNAME	COMPANY
1	1004	1133	Sled	Louge	Better Homes & Gardens
2	1195	1775	Peggy	Omlet	Century 21 South Side
3	1222	2301	Sandra	Miller	Old Realty of California
4	1255	2398	Jack	Robinson	Sawmill Realty
5	2225	2429	Tom	Wright	Tom Wright Realty
6	2257	2429	Diane	Kochanek	Tom Wright Realty
7	2422	2398	Sam	Waters	Sawmill Realty
8	2677	3601	Peter	Kuhns	Old Town Homes
9	2754	4800	John	Pont	Century 21 North Side
10	3502	4800	Cheri	Robinson	Century 21 North Side
11	3762	4861	Rosie	Betker	Navarro Agency
12	4026	4915	Roy	Mashburn	Independent Realty
13	4187	6643	Jane	Atkinson	Alfred DuMont, Realtor
14	4528	1133	Jack	Brockway	Better Homes & Gardens
15	4607	1775	Susan	Miller	Century 21 South Side
16	5084	2301	Michael	Groh	Old Realty of California

Figure 5.12
You can change the position of a column while in Browse Layout mode.

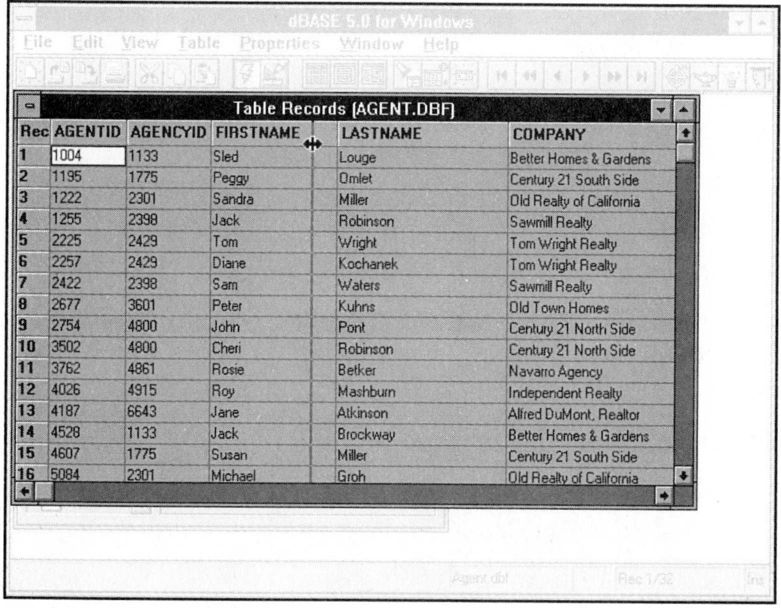

dBASE 5.0 for Windows

Table Records (AGENT.DBF)

Rec	AGENTID	AGENCYID	FIRSTNAME	LASTNAME	COMPANY
1	1004	1133	Sled	Louge	Better Homes & Gardens
2	1195	1775	Peggy	Omlet	Century 21 South Side
3	1222	2301	Sandra	Miller	Old Realty of California
4	1255	2398	Jack	Robinson	Sawmill Realty
5	2225	2429	Tom	Wright	Tom Wright Realty
6	2257	2429	Diane	Kochanek	Tom Wright Realty
7	2422	2398	Sam	Waters	Sawmill Realty
8	2677	3601	Peter	Kuhns	Old Town Homes
9	2754	4800	John	Pont	Century 21 North Side
10	3502	4800	Cheri	Robinson	Century 21 North Side
11	3762	4861	Rosie	Betker	Navarro Agency
12	4026	4915	Roy	Mashburn	Independent Realty
13	4187	6643	Jane	Atkinson	Alfred DuMont, Realtor
14	4528	1133	Jack	Brockway	Better Homes & Gardens
15	4607	1775	Susan	Miller	Century 21 South Side
16	5084	2301	Michael	Groh	Old Realty of California

Figure 5.13
You can display more columns on-screen by adjusting the column width.

You cannot adjust the size of the "Rec" or "Del" columns.

The format of the browse window is controlled by the Edit Records setting on the Files page of Desktop Properties, shown in figure 5.14. If there are a lot of fields in each record, however, it is unlikely you will be able to display all of them on one page using the In Browse Layout setting.

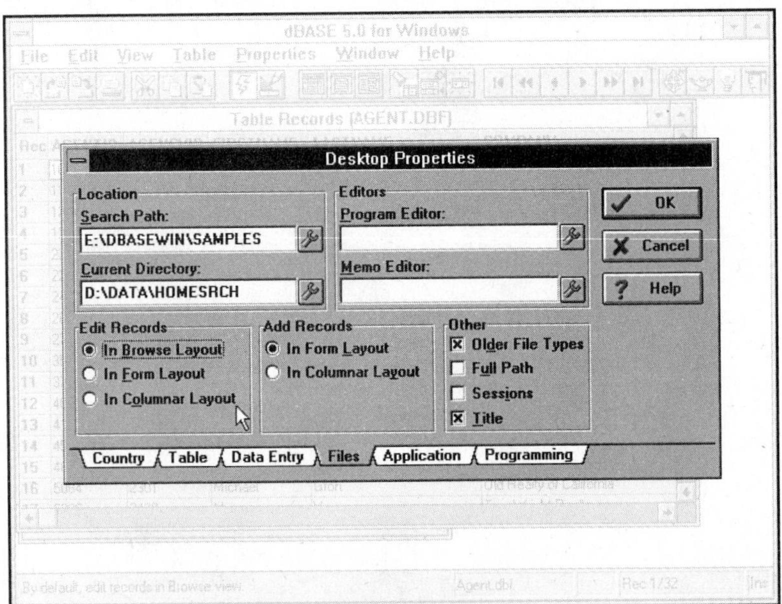

Figure 5.14 The Edit Records setting on the Files page of Desktop Properties controls the Browse/Edit format.

Using the Table Edit Window

The three default views discussed in this chapter provide a different format for editing your data. As you can see in figures 5.15 and 5.16, you can press F2 to toggle between these two views and the Browse Layout format discussed earlier. In Form Layout and Columnar Layout, only a single record is displayed—but much more information (columns) is available for editing.

You can edit a specific field by clicking on it with the mouse, or you can press the Tab key to move forward through the record or Shift+Tab to move backward through the record. When you tab past the last field or press Shift+Tab until you move past the first field, you move to the next or previous record in the table.

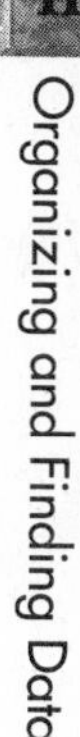

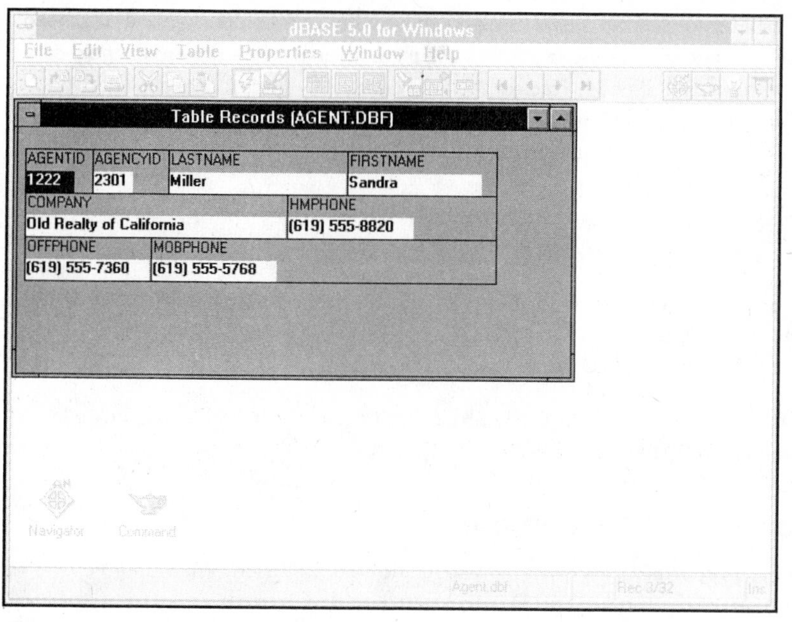

Figure 5.15 Pressing F2 will switch you from the default Browse View to the Form and Columnar Views.

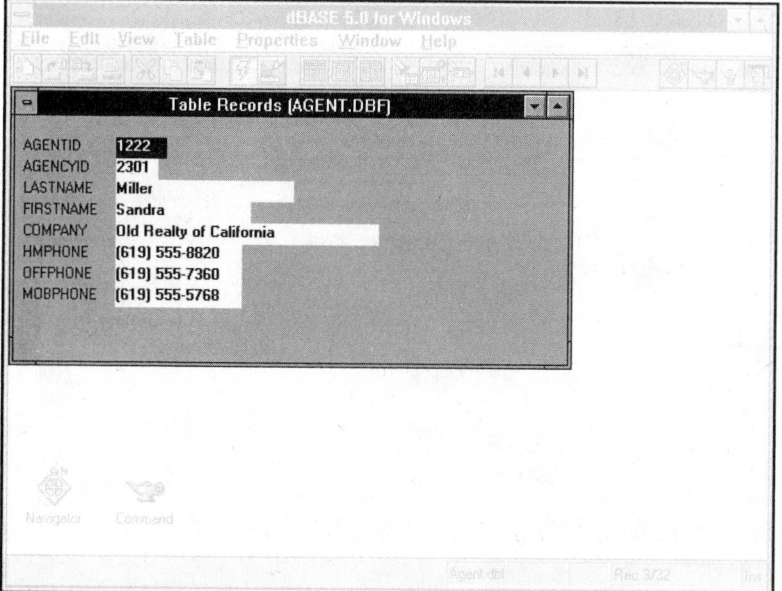

Figure 5.16 Pressing F2 will switch you from the default Browse View to the Form and Columnar Views.

When you click on a field to begin editing, the insertion pointer will be placed where you clicked. Data you key will either overwrite the data in the field or be inserted at that point. To clear the field completely, just double-click and the whole field is highlighted. The next character typed will clear the field and be placed at the beginning of the field.

Moving Around In the Database

Now that you know how to display your data, the next step is to learn how to move around to different parts of the table. As you have seen in other areas of dBASE a number of different ways are available for accomplishing the same task.

Most of the movement possible within a database can be accomplished using the SpeedBar—a bar of icons that serve different purposes.

Record to Record Movement

Movement between records varies with the display mode being used. When a table is displayed in Browse mode, the Up and Down arrows enable you to move forward and backward in the table. If the table is displayed in Form or Columnar mode the PgUp and PgDn keys move from record to record (see fig. 5.17).

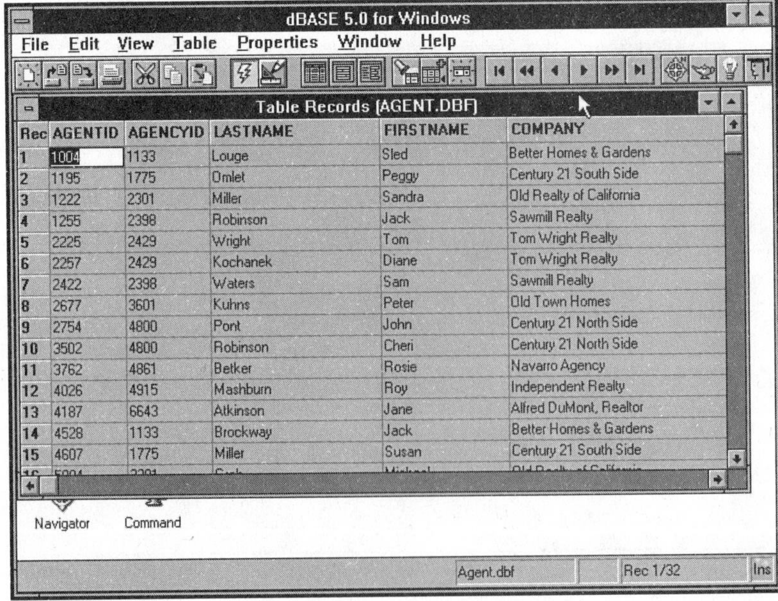

Figure 5.17 The SpeedBar provides a quick way to move between records using the mouse.

The Table Menu Item also provides you with a Next Record and Previous Record selection.

Page to Page Movement

A table displayed in Browse mode enables you to work with a number of records at one time. By using the PgUp and PgDn keys, you can advance the display a page at a time. Displaying the AGENT table in Browse mode shows the first page of 17 records. By pressing the PgUp key or selecting the Next Page option from the Table menu, the display will be advanced to show the next page of 15 records. The last record displayed on one page will always be the first one displayed on the next page. dBASE does this to provide you with some continuity as you page through your table (see fig. 5.18).

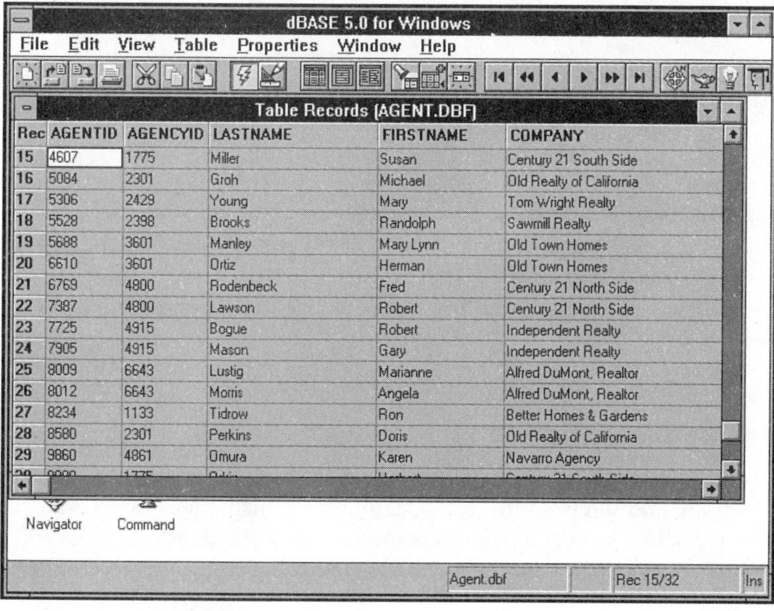

Rec	AGENTID	AGENCYID	LASTNAME	FIRSTNAME	COMPANY
15	4607	1775	Miller	Susan	Century 21 South Side
16	5084	2301	Groh	Michael	Old Realty of California
17	5306	2429	Young	Mary	Tom Wright Realty
18	5528	2398	Brooks	Randolph	Sawmill Realty
19	5688	3601	Manley	Mary Lynn	Old Town Homes
20	6610	3601	Ortiz	Herman	Old Town Homes
21	6769	4800	Rodenbeck	Fred	Century 21 North Side
22	7387	4800	Lawson	Robert	Century 21 North Side
23	7725	4915	Bogue	Robert	Independent Realty
24	7905	4915	Mason	Gary	Independent Realty
25	8009	6643	Lustig	Marianne	Alfred DuMont, Realtor
26	8012	6643	Morris	Angela	Alfred DuMont, Realtor
27	8234	1133	Tidrow	Ron	Better Homes & Gardens
28	8580	2301	Perkins	Doris	Old Realty of California
29	9860	4861	Omura	Karen	Navarro Agency

Figure 5.18
The SpeedBar gives you the ability to move between pages using the mouse.

Top to Bottom

You can use the Ctrl+PgUp and Ctrl+PgDn keys to jump to the top or bottom of the table (see fig. 5.19). Think of the Ctrl key as accelerating the page-up or page-down movement. This is equivalent to selecting the Top Record or Bottom Record from the Table menu item.

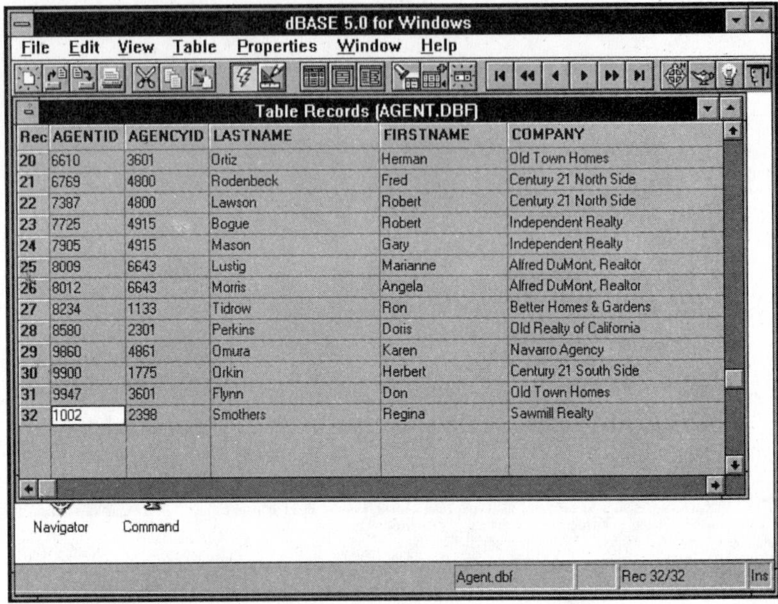

Rec	AGENTID	AGENCYID	LASTNAME	FIRSTNAME	COMPANY
20	6610	3601	Ortiz	Herman	Old Town Homes
21	6769	4800	Rodenbeck	Fred	Century 21 North Side
22	7387	4800	Lawson	Robert	Century 21 North Side
23	7725	4915	Bogue	Robert	Independent Realty
24	7905	4915	Mason	Gary	Independent Realty
25	8009	6643	Lustig	Marianne	Alfred DuMont, Realtor
26	8012	6643	Morris	Angela	Alfred DuMont, Realtor
27	8234	1133	Tidrow	Ron	Better Homes & Gardens
28	8580	2301	Perkins	Doris	Old Realty of California
29	9860	4861	Omura	Karen	Navarro Agency
30	9900	1775	Orkin	Herbert	Century 21 South Side
31	9947	3601	Flynn	Don	Old Town Homes
32	1002	2398	Smothers	Regina	Sawmill Realty

Figure 5.19
The SpeedBar also enables you to move to the top or bottom of the table using the mouse.

If you are at the end of a table and you try to advance to the next record, dBASE assumes you want to add additional records to your table. dBASE displays a dialog box asking you if that is what you really intended. To stop this query from occurring and not allow records to be appended, you can uncheck the Append box in the Edit Options of the Table Records Properties Records page.

Moving to a Specific Record

Often you might want to move to or find a specific record in your table. dBASE provides the Go to Record Number option from the Table Menu item, which quickly locates a specific row in a dBASE table (see fig. 5.20). Select this option or use the shortcut Ctrl+G to display a Go To Record dialog box in which you can specify the record number of the row you want.

The Go To Record Number feature is only available for dBASE tables.

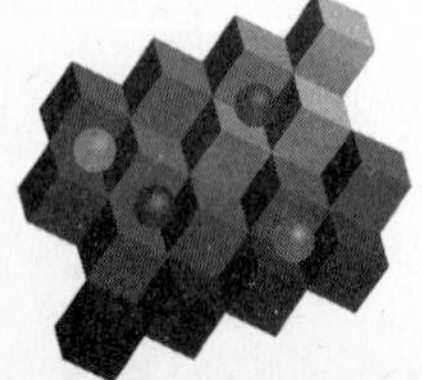

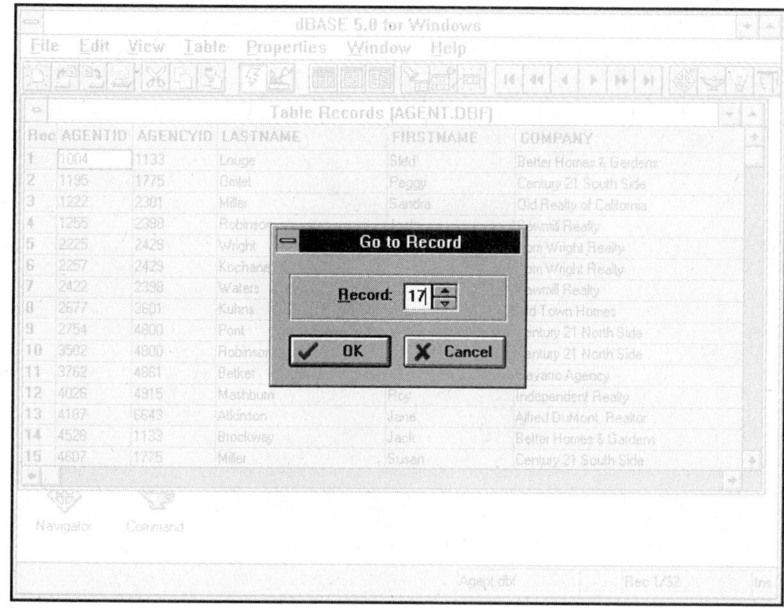

Figure 5.20
dBASE ensures the record number you enter is valid.

Finding Specific Information

Often you don't know the record number of the record you want to go to, but you have some idea of its contents. dBASE provides the Find Records option from the Table Menu—shown in figure 5.21—for finding a specific record. This option is more powerful because it searches any field in your table for specific contents, and it works with dBASE and Paradox tables. Figure 5.22 shows you an example of the Advanced button.

Suppose, for example, you want to find all the property in the City of Imperial Beach in the Listing table. To do this you first select the Find Records option from the Table menu, press Ctrl+F, or click on the Find Record icon in the Find Records dialog box (see fig. 5.23).

Either one of these options displays the Find Records dialog box. In this example you will notice that dBASE has the City item in the Located in Field section highlighted. dBASE automatically highlights whatever column was selected at the time the Find Record option was invoked.

At this point, all you need to do is click in the "Find What" field, key in **Imperial Beach**, without the quotes, and click on the Find key. dBASE finds and highlights the next record in the table with Imperial Beach in the City field (see fig. 5.24).

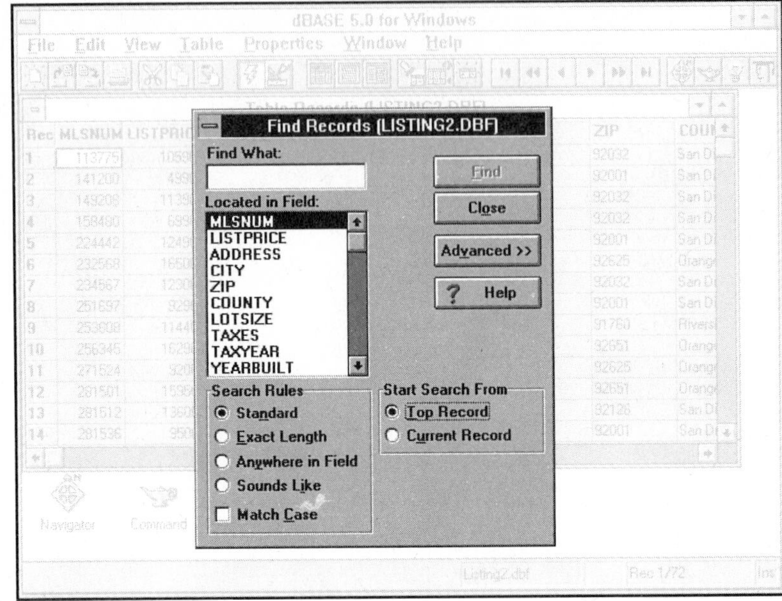

Figure 5.21 The primary Find Record dialog box enables you to specify the contents and the field you want to search.

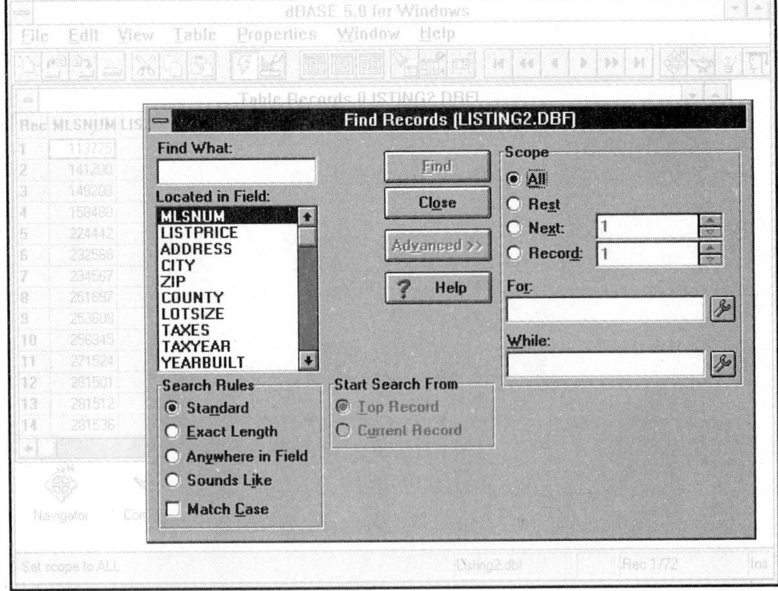

Figure 5.22 Clicking on the Advanced button will display an enlarged window to narrow the search criteria.

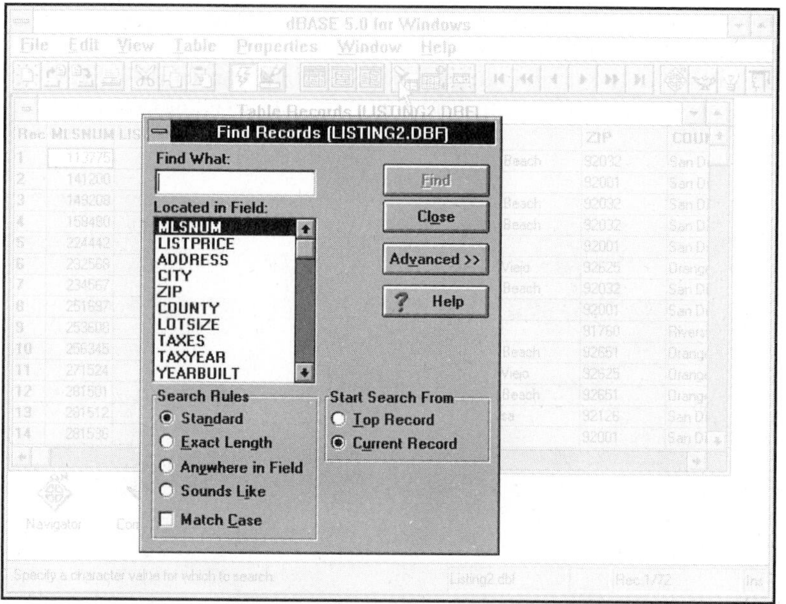

Figure 5.23
Find Record Icon.

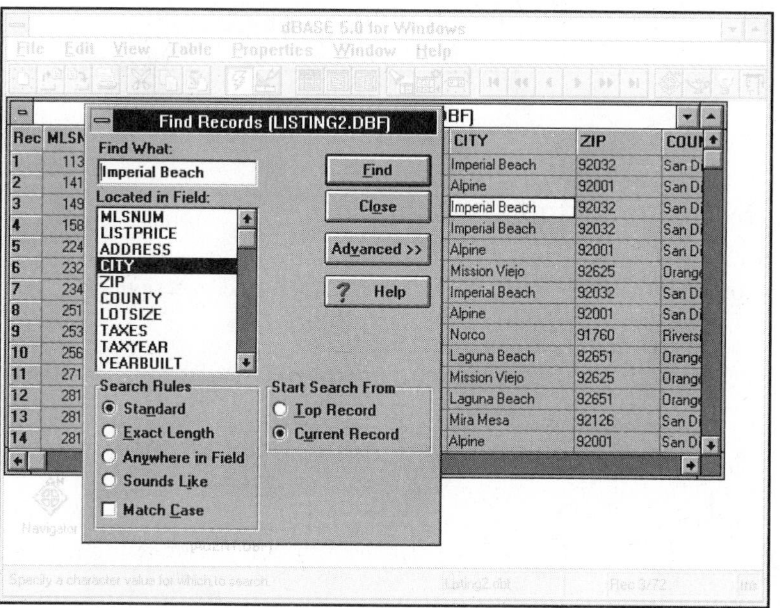

Figure 5.24
dBASE finds the next record meeting the condition specified.

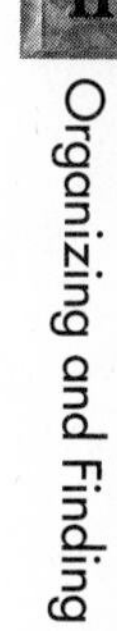

Now suppose you want to limit your search to just those homes in Imperial Beach with a list price of under $110,000 (see fig. 5.25). This process is the same, except that prior to clicking on the Find key you click on the Advanced key, select the For field by clicking in it and then key in the expression: **LISTPRICE<110000**. Now you are ready to click on the Find key to have dBASE search the table.

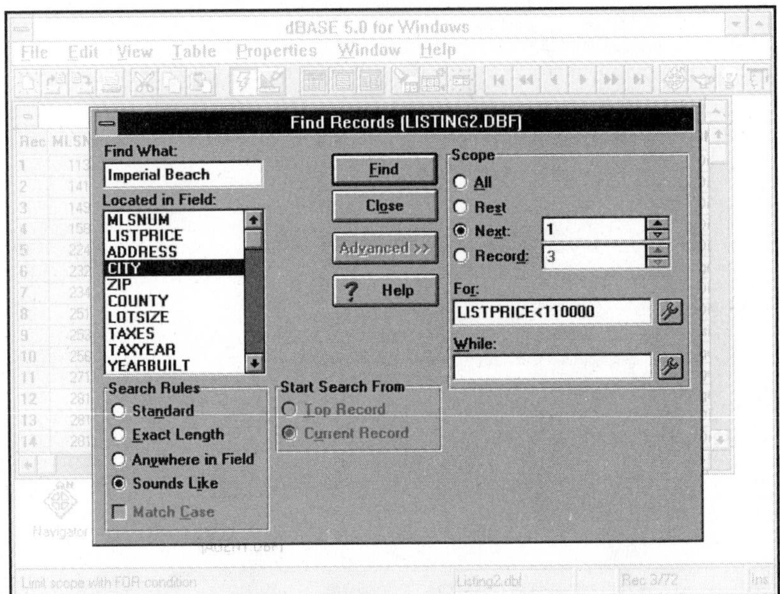

Figure 5.25
With another qualifier of $110,000 dBASE selects a smaller subset of records.

Exploring Standard Find Options

A number of other options appear in the Find Records dialog box. The easiest way to understand these options is to experiment with each of them. A brief description is included here.

The primary Find Records dialog box enables you to specify search rules and a starting point for the search. The search rules are as follows:

- ✓ **Standard.** This option looks for columns in your table that begin with the contents of the Find What field or match the contents of the Find What field. If you entered "the" in the Find What field, dBASE would find columns that began with "the" and any other combination beginning with "the". As an example Standard would find "the," "The," "There," and "thesis."

- ✓ **Exact Length.** This option enables you to ensure that the Find What contents and the data in the matching column are the same length. Exact Length would find "the" and "The" but not "There" and "thesis" because the latter two have more than three characters.

- **Anywhere in Field.** The previous two options assume that the data in the Find What field is at the beginning of the column being searched. The Anywhere in Field option tells dBASE to look anywhere in the column for the Find What data. In the HomeGuide example you might want to search for any City that contains the word "beach." If you checked the Anywhere in Field option you would find records with "Laguna Beach" and "Imperial Beach" in the city column.

- **Sounds Like.** This option is used when you are not sure of the specific spelling of the item you are looking for. dBASE will try to do a phonetic search of the column for the Find What data.

- **Match Case.** This option is an additional condition that can be placed on the first three search rules described earlier. With this option checked a search for "The" would not find a match on "the" or "THE."

Each of these options is only available for dBASE character and memo fields, and Paradox alpha, memo, and formatted memo fields. For other fields, such as numeric, float, and date, the options will be grayed out and unavailable.

The other option, Start Search From, enables you to specify whether you want to start your search from the current record or you want to search from the start of the table. Generally you will want to begin searches from the top of the table. You may want to modify or further define the item you are searching for and pick up from the current position. When you hit the last record dBASE will NOT automatically wrap around and resume searching from the first record.

Exploring Advanced Find Options

The Advanced button in the Find Records dialog box reveals additional options to help narrow your search. The Scope portion of the advanced page includes:

- **All.** Look through every record in the table.

- **Rest.** Look at the remaining records in the table from the current row forward.

- **Next.** Look at the next specific number of records.

- **Record.** Specify the record in which you want to search. This option is helpful when you put in a specific value in either the first record or last record to indicate a specific action or condition. Occasionally you might want to know when you are at the end of a dBASE table before dBASE triggers the end of file condition.

  Like other functions that depend on specific record numbers this option is only available for dBASE formatted tables.

- **For.** Only look at records that meet a specific condition. All other records are skipped. An example would be to limit a search of homes to a specific ZIP code.

- ✓ **While.** Continue the search only while a condition is true. Once the while condition is met the search stops. As an example, if your table were sorted in ascending order by price you might only want to look at homes less than $110,000.

Each of these options extend the dBASE search capabilities so that you can narrow your search to specific records of interest.

Changing the Tables Field Properties

In addition to changing the view between Browse mode, Form mode, and Columnar mode, dBASE also enables you to customize the way records are displayed by using the pages of the Table Record Properties window. The Table Records Properties page is invoked by right-clicking anywhere in the Table Records window, or by selecting the Table Records Window from the Properties menu option.

In this section, you learn how to use all the features included in the Table Records Properties window, and learn shortcuts and other important information that will help you organize the appearance of records in your database tables.

Selecting Columns to Display

Occasionally, you might want to display a subset of the columns for a table or change the appearance of the columns. dBASE enables you to change the view using the Fields page of the Tables Records Properties menu, shown in figure 5.26. This function is available from the Properties menu or by right-clicking anywhere in the Table Records Window.

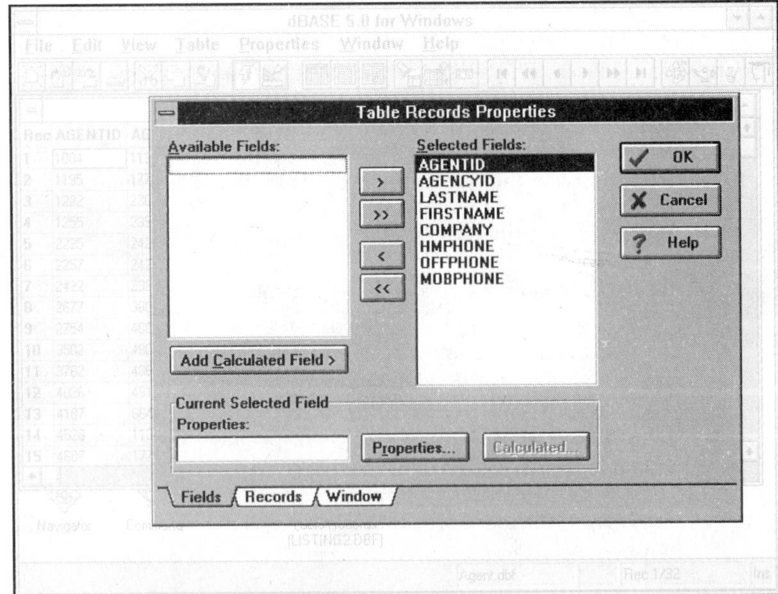

Figure 5.26 The Fields page enables you to select the columns you want displayed.

On the right of the Fields page is a list of the fields selected for display. By default dBASE selects all fields. To remove a field from the display click on the field and then click on the Remove Field button designated by the less than arrow "<".

If you need to remove a large number of fields, use the Remove All button. This will place all the fields in the Available Fields box, parallel to the selected fields box. From here they can be added back one by one in the order you want them displayed.

When you want to take a field from the available field column and display it again, the process is reversed. Click on the field in the Available Fields box that you want to add back to the display, click on the field in the Selected Fields box that will precede the field you are about to add (see fig. 5.27), then click on the Add Calculated Field button.

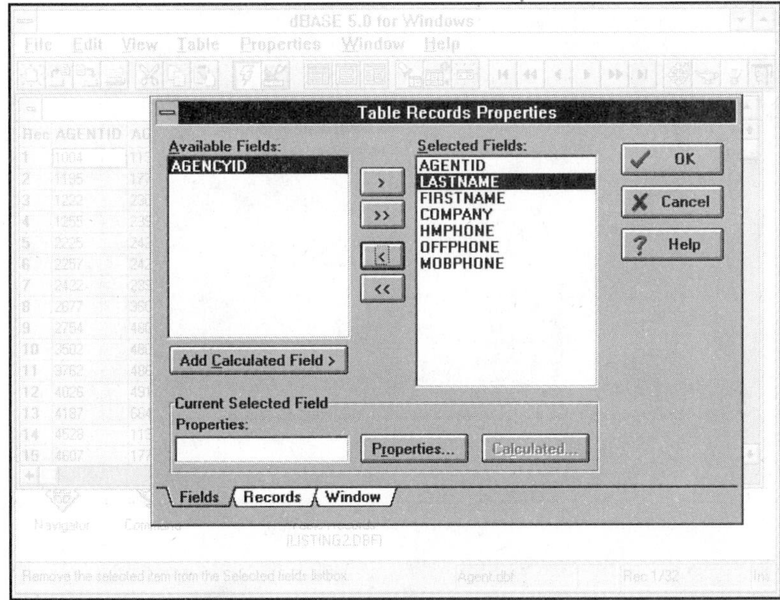

Figure 5.27 Fields are inserted after the highlighted field in the selected column.

To move a field to the top of the list—the first field displayed—the process is a bit more complicated. You must first insert the available field after the first field in the selected field box, then remove the first field from the selected field box, then re-add the field you just removed so that it follows the new first field. Fortunately, there is an easier way.

The easiest way to place a new field at the beginning of a table is to return to viewing the table in browse mode and use the mouse to move the fields around. With this process you can move fields, but you cannot remove them from the display.

Adding Calculated Fields

The Fields page of the Table Records Properties window also enables you to add calculated data to the display. *Calculated data* is data derived arithmetically and is displayed, although it is not really part of the table structure. One use for this in the HomeGuide application would be for the display of area with the Room table.

To create a calculated field, you first click on the Add Calculated Field button to bring up the local Calculated Field dialog box (see fig. 5.28).

Figure 5.28
Click on Add Calculated Field, then create the calculated field.

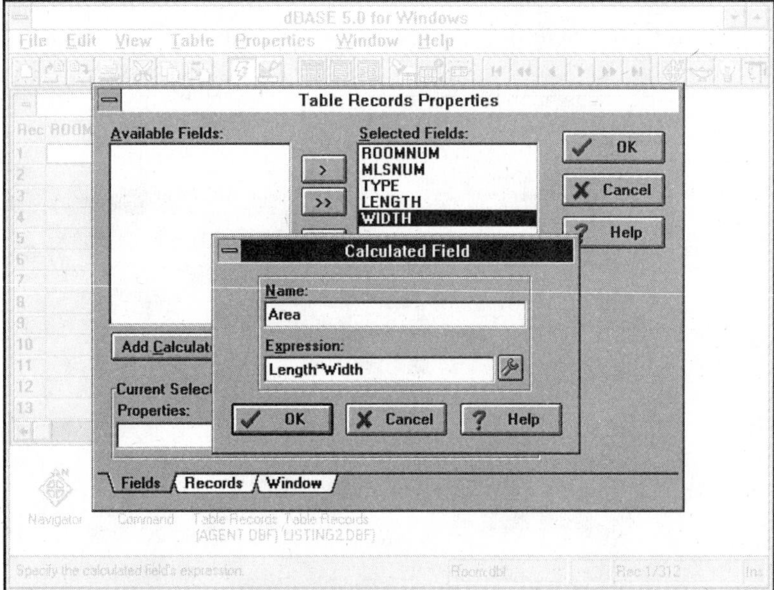

The next step is to enter the name you wanted to call the calculated field; in this case it is Area. After the name is entered you can tab to the Expression Area and type: **Length*Width**. This expression tells dBASE to take the Length field, multiple it by the contents of the Width field and store the result is a temporary field named Area.

Click on OK to add the field to the Selected Fields list (see fig. 5.29). Note that the field is inserted after the field highlighted in the selected fields column. Make sure you know the order in which you want you data displayed or the order of fields because the calculated field is always added after the currently highlighted field. You will want to click on the field to highlight it prior to creating the calculated field.

dBASE 5.0 for Windows

File Edit View Table Properties Window Help

Table Records (ROOM.DBF)

Rec	ROOMNUM	MLSNUM	TYPE	LENGTH	WIDTH	AREA
1	1	232568	Bedroom, Master	20	14	280
2	1	113775	Bedroom, Master	15	11	165
3	1	141200	Living Room	11	17	187
4	1	149208	Bathroom	10	10	100
5	1	158480	Bedroom, Master	13	17	221
6	1	224442	Bathroom	15	12	180
7	1	234567	Bathroom	3	5	15
8	1	251697	Bedroom, Master	15	11	165
9	1	253608	Bathroom	12	10	120
10	1	256345	Bedroom, Master	16	14	224
11	1	271524	Bedroom, Master	15	12	180
12	1	281501	Bedroom, Master	14	12	168
13	1	281512	Bathroom	8	8	64
14	1	281536	Bedroom, Master	13	13	169

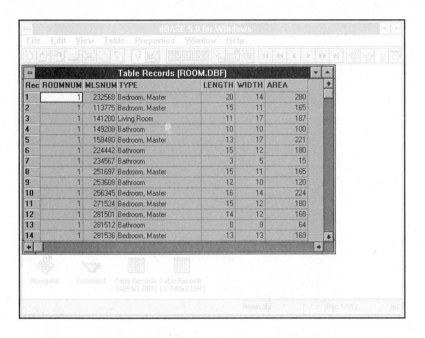

Figure 5.29
The Room Table now shows Area in the display.

There is no way to delete a calculated field directly. To remove a calculated field from the Selected and Available lists, you must first move the calculated field to the available fields list, then click on OK to close the Table Records Properties dialog box. The next time you display the Table Records dialog box the calculated field will be gone.

Changing Column Properties

In addition to adding calculated fields and other fields to the table display and choosing their order, dBASE also enables you to define the properties of the displayed data. The Properties dialog window includes options that do the following:

- ✔ Specify a field Heading to give your column heading a more descriptive title.
- ✔ Specify a field Width to control the maximum number of characters to be displayed. You can add spacing to the display by making the width wider than the field will be or you can compress the amount of characters displayed by specifying only the first *n* number of characters of the field.
- ✔ Specify a field Template to add special formatting to the field without actually storing the formatting in the database. This option is helpful when you need to add commas to numeric fields or format phone numbers.
- ✔ Specify a When condition to designate when this field can be edited or modified.

- ✔ Specify an Expression that determines when the data being entered into the field is valid.
- ✔ Specify an Error Message that displays if the expression evaluated is not satisfied.
- ✔ Specify if the Validity check is Required even if the field is not changed.
- ✔ Specify a Lower and Upper Limit for the data being entered into the field.
- ✔ Specify if the Validity check is Required even if the field is not changed.

To change the property of a field, first select the field you want to work with and then click on the Properties button. This will bring up the Field Properties dialog box shown in figure 5.30.

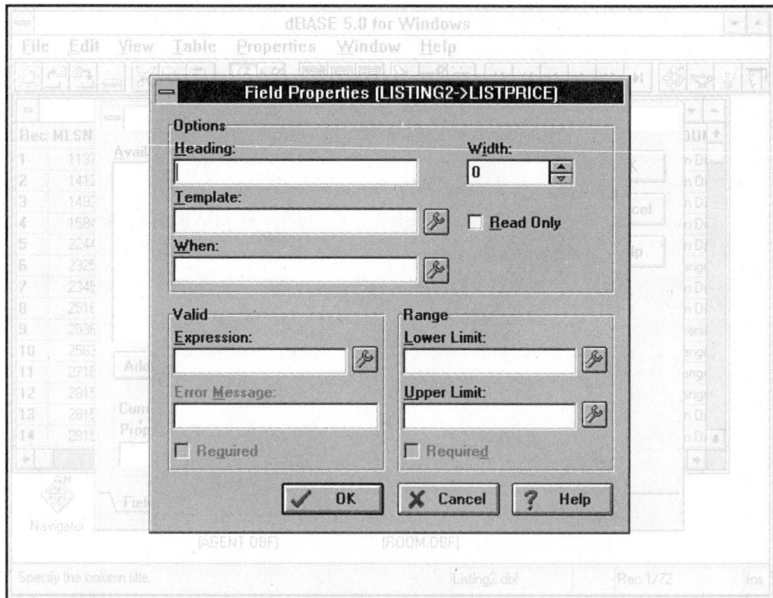

Figure 5.30
The Properties Button enables you to control the display attributes of the specific field.

In the HomeGuide application included with this book, there are a number of tables you might want to display and work with within the Navigator Window. Double click on the LISTING2.DBF icon to display the table shown in figure 5.31.

This display provides a clean arrangement of your data, but you may want to customize it a bit further.

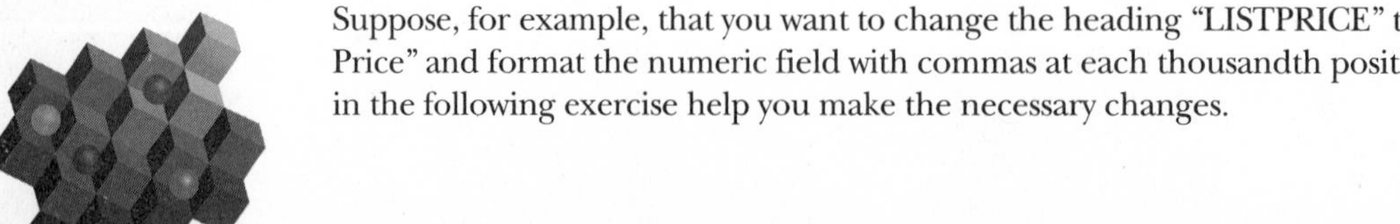

Suppose, for example, that you want to change the heading "LISTPRICE" to "Selling Price" and format the numeric field with commas at each thousandth position. The steps in the following exercise help you make the necessary changes.

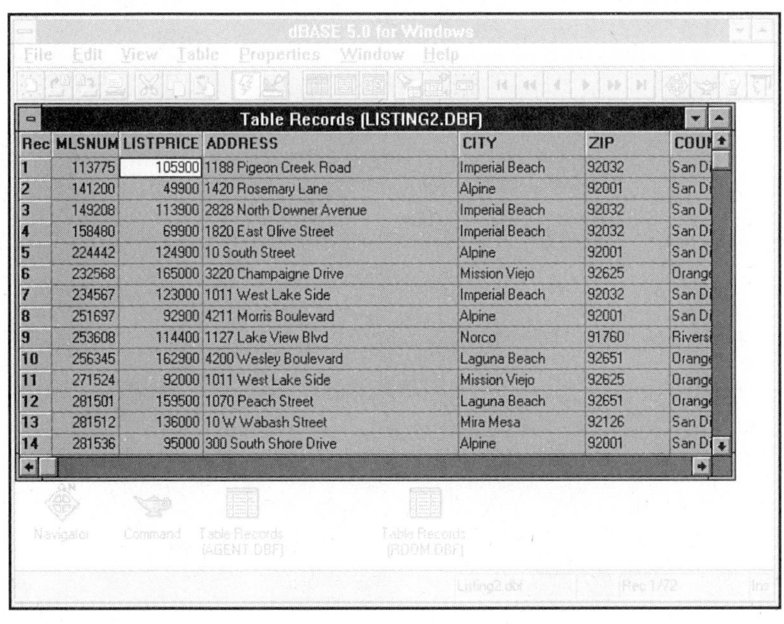

Rec	MLSNUM	LISTPRICE	ADDRESS	CITY	ZIP	COU
1	113775	105900	1188 Pigeon Creek Road	Imperial Beach	92032	San D
2	141200	49900	1420 Rosemary Lane	Alpine	92001	San D
3	149208	113900	2828 North Downer Avenue	Imperial Beach	92032	San D
4	158480	69900	1820 East Olive Street	Imperial Beach	92032	San D
5	224442	124900	10 South Street	Alpine	92001	San D
6	232568	165000	3220 Champaigne Drive	Mission Viejo	92625	Orang
7	234567	123000	1011 West Lake Side	Imperial Beach	92032	San D
8	251697	92900	4211 Morris Boulevard	Alpine	92001	San D
9	253608	114400	1127 Lake View Blvd	Norco	91760	Rivers
10	256345	162900	4200 Wesley Boulevard	Laguna Beach	92651	Orang
11	271524	92000	1011 West Lake Side	Mission Viejo	92625	Orang
12	281501	159500	1070 Peach Street	Laguna Beach	92651	Orang
13	281512	136000	10 W Wabash Street	Mira Mesa	92126	San D
14	281536	95000	300 South Shore Drive	Alpine	92001	San D

Figure 5.31
The default display for the LISTING2.DBF.

Customizing Your Data

Right click anywhere in the Table Records window, then click on the Table Records Window Properties in the local property menu	The Table Records Window Properties appear
Select LISTPRICE by clicking on it and then click on the Properties button	The Field Properties dialog box appears
In the Field Properties window (see fig. 5.32) select the Heading input area if the insertion pointer is not already there, and type "**Selling Price**" without the quotes	The heading is changed
Tab to the Template Field (or click on it with the mouse) and enter **"99,999,999"** without the quotes.	Enters the field
Click on OK to accept the property definitions	

This is also a good time to enter a range check to make sure the selling price is valid.

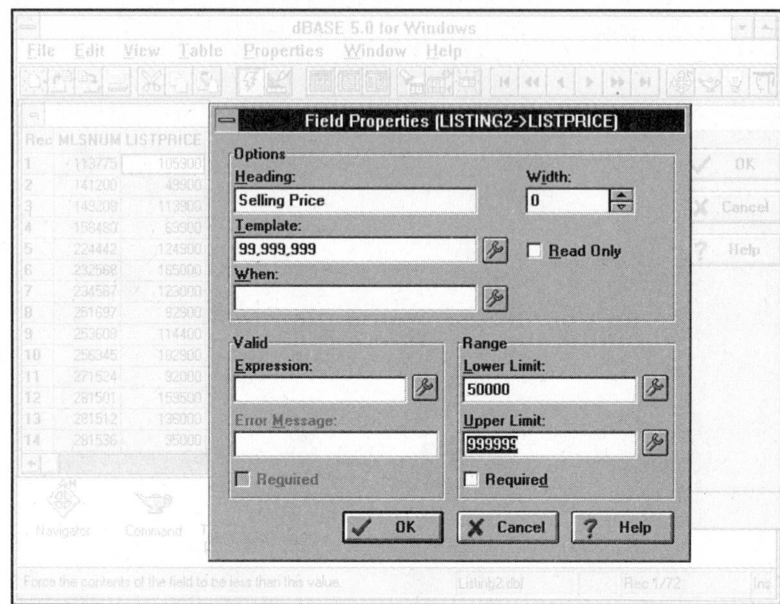

Figure 5.32 Specify Heading, Templates, Input Ranges, and other attributes in the Field Properties page.

For the following exercise, suppose the selling prices were always higher than $50,000 and less than $1,000,000. To enter this range, you would perform the following steps:

Changing the Price Range

Tab to the Lower Limit range field or click on it with the mouse, then type **50000**	Entering a field range
Tab to the Upper Limit field and enter **999999**	Your Field Properties Window should look similar to figure 5.30
Click on OK	You are returned to the Table Records Properties page
Click on OK again to return to the Table Records window	Figure 5.33 shows the results of these limits and the changes made earlier in this section

As a final check on the property modifications you made click on any Selling Price field and try to enter the value 45000. When you press Enter or try to leave the field in any other way you should receive an error message like the one displayed in figure 5.34.

dBASE 5.0 for Windows

File Edit View Table Properties Window Help

Table Records (LISTING2.DBF)

Rec	MLSNUM	Selling Price	ADDRESS	CITY	ZIP	COU
1	113775	105,900	1188 Pigeon Creek Road	Imperial Beach	92032	San
2	141200	49,900	1420 Rosemary Lane	Alpine	92001	San
3	149208	113,900	2828 North Downer Avenue	Imperial Beach	92032	San
4	158480	69,900	1820 East Olive Street	Imperial Beach	92032	San
5	224442	124,900	10 South Street	Alpine	92001	San
6	232568	165,000	3220 Champaigne Drive	Mission Viejo	92625	Oran
7	234567	123,000	1011 West Lake Side	Imperial Beach	92032	San
8	251697	92,900	4211 Morris Boulevard	Alpine	92001	San
9	253608	114,400	1127 Lake View Blvd	Norco	91760	River
10	256345	162,900	4200 Wesley Boulevard	Laguna Beach	92651	Oran
11	271524	92,000	1011 West Lake Side	Mission Viejo	92625	Oran
12	281501	159,500	1070 Peach Street	Laguna Beach	92651	Oran
13	281512	136,000	10 W Wabash Street	Mira Mesa	92126	San
14	281536	95,000	300 South Shore Drive	Alpine	92001	San

Navigator Command Table Records (AGENT.DBF) Table Records (ROOM.DBF)

Listing2.dbf Rec 1/72 Ins

Figure 5.33 The Table Records window reflects the Heading change and comma formatting.

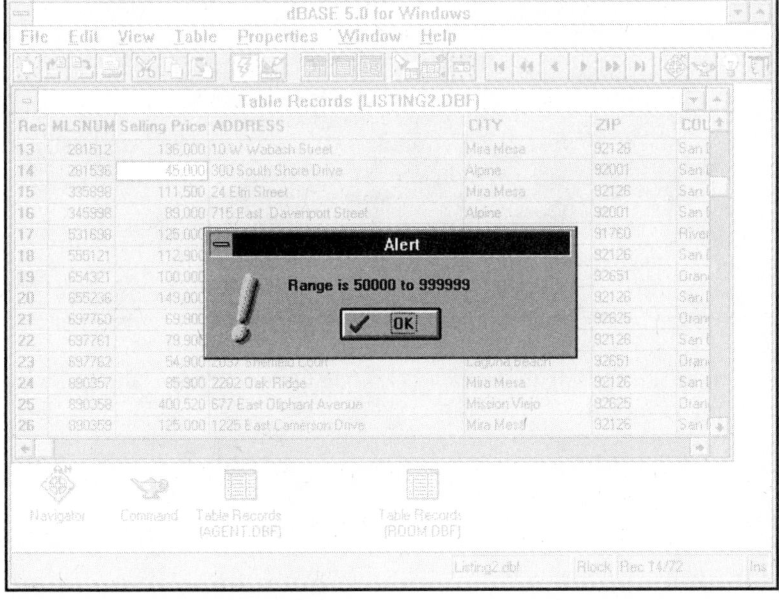

Figure 5.34 dBASE supplies a range check error message when the value entered is outside the valid range.

Next to the Template Field on the Field Properties dialog box is a wrench icon. Click on this icon to access a Template dialog box for entering valid masks for the data. The Template box has separate pages for formatting Character, Numeric, and Data type data.

Changing a Tables Record Properties

In addition to columns, you can also change record properties from the Table Record Properties dialog box. The Records page, shown in figure 5.35, of the Table Record Properties dialog box enables you to control the editing of records within your table.

Figure 5.35 The Records page.

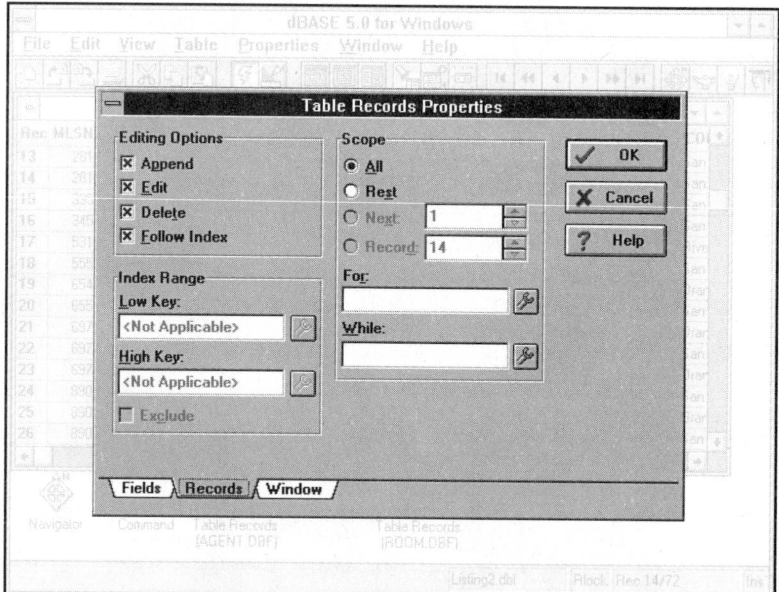

The Records page can be used to fine-tune a table's Editing Options, Scope, and Index Range The editing options include:

- ✔ **Append.** Control the addition of records to the selected table.
- ✔ **Edit.** Allow editing of entire records or rows in the table.
- ✔ **Delete.** Control the deletion of records from the table.
- ✔ **Follow Index.** Tell dBASE to follow records to their new location in a table if you modify an index value.

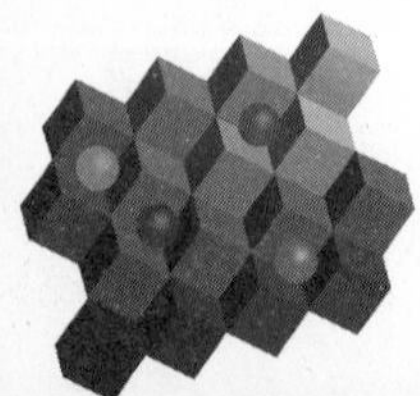

The Records page also can be used to limit the scope of records that display by using the For and While expressions. These scope functions work the same as the For and While scope functions used with Tables.

The For/While scope selection in the Records page also includes an Index Range option. If your table is indexed you can limit the scope of records shown by specifying a minimum display value, maximum display value, or both.

If you specify only the Low Key value, all records with an index value equal to or greater than the value specified will be displayed. If you specify only a High Key value, all records with an index value equal to or less than the index value specified will be displayed.

Specify the Low Key and High Key values to display all values between and including the specified values (see fig. 5.36 for an example).

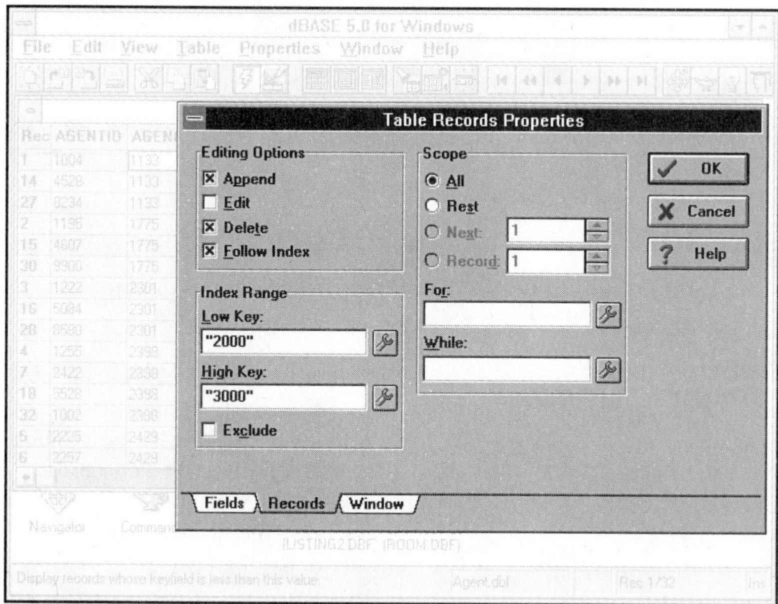

Figure 5.36
Specifying the Low key and High key values.

The Exclude check box enables you to exclude records from the display. In this case, specifying a high or low Index value excludes that particular key. Specifying a high and low value will exclude the entire range (see fig. 5.37 for an example).

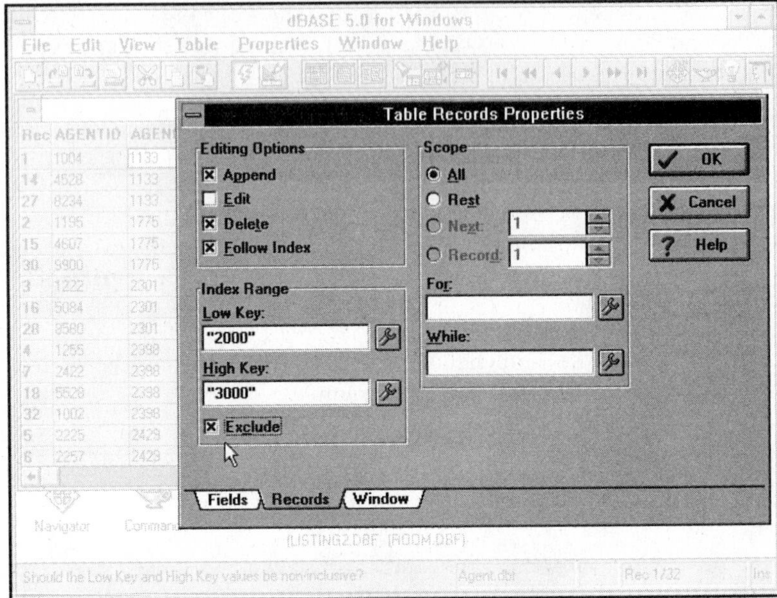

Figure 5.37
Note the effect of the same Index Range with the Exclude box checked.

Changing a Tables Window Properties

Another page of the Table Record Properties dialog box controls various display attributes of the Table Record page.

Changing Display Options

The first display option on the Table Record page is the Title of the Table Records dialog box (see fig. 5.38). You can change the title to something different than Table Records (TABLE.DBF). To do this, all you need to do is right click anywhere on the Table Records window, select Table Records Properties from the local menu, and click on the Window Page tab. Next, type the Title you want to display, then click on OK.

The Window page enables you to remove the Horizontal and Vertical Grids when displaying records in Browse mode. Click on the grid options to clear the fields and remove the grids or toggle the grids on and off with the Alt+H and Alt+V key combinations.

When the remaining option, Toggle Layout, is checked, you can toggle among the Browse, Form, and Columnar display modes using the F2 key. Clear this option to freeze the display in the current format and eliminate the use of F2 or the View menu to toggle between modes.

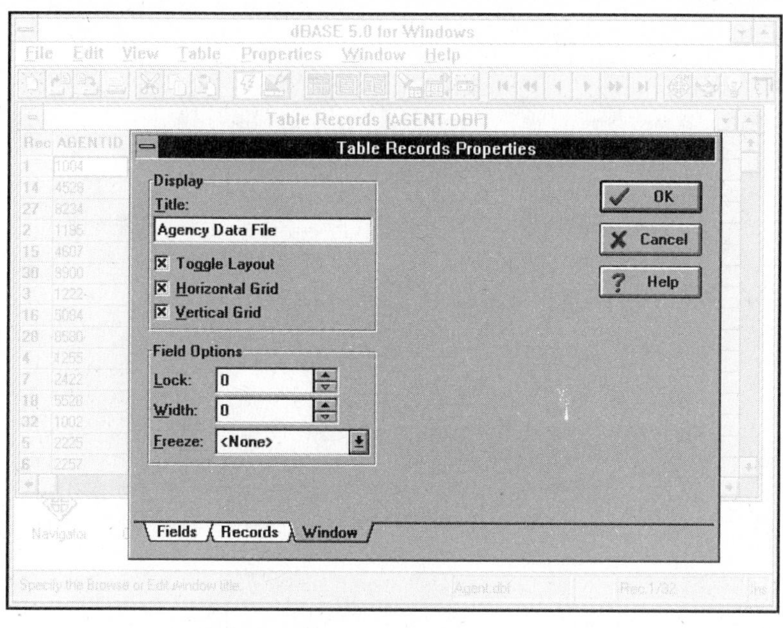

Figure 5.38 Changing the Table Records caption.

Using Field Options

The field Options on the Window page of the Table Records Properties dialog box enables you to do the following:

- ✔ Use the Lock Option to fix the number of columns that always display for a record.
- ✔ Set a consistent Width for all character fields.
- ✔ Freeze the cursor in a single field while editing records or moving through the table.

The Lock option enables you to specify the number of fields, beginning on the left, that permanently display as you scroll to the right in Browse Layout mode. As an example, if you set this field to 3 for the Agency Table in the HomeGuide application, the AGENTID, AGENCYID, and LASTNAME fields would always display (see fig. 5.39). The use of this option enables you to scroll or move the cursor over to the Office Phone Number field—OFFPHONE—and still be able to see the agent's name.

The Lock option always works on fields formatted from left to right in a table. You can use a combination of Column Movement and Locking to ensure specific fields are always displayed. The lock and column movement only affect the display, not the order the data appears in the table.

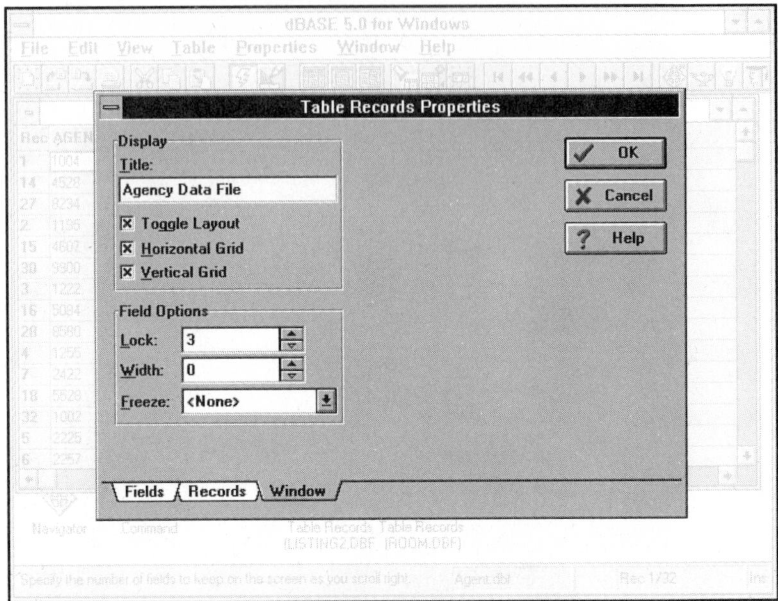

Figure 5.39
Locks allows you to see both the beginning and end of the table at the same time.

The **W**idth option can be used to specify a maximum display width for all character data appearing in Browse mode (see fig. 5.40). This is helpful when you need a quick view of many columns that, because of their width, usually do not appear on-screen.

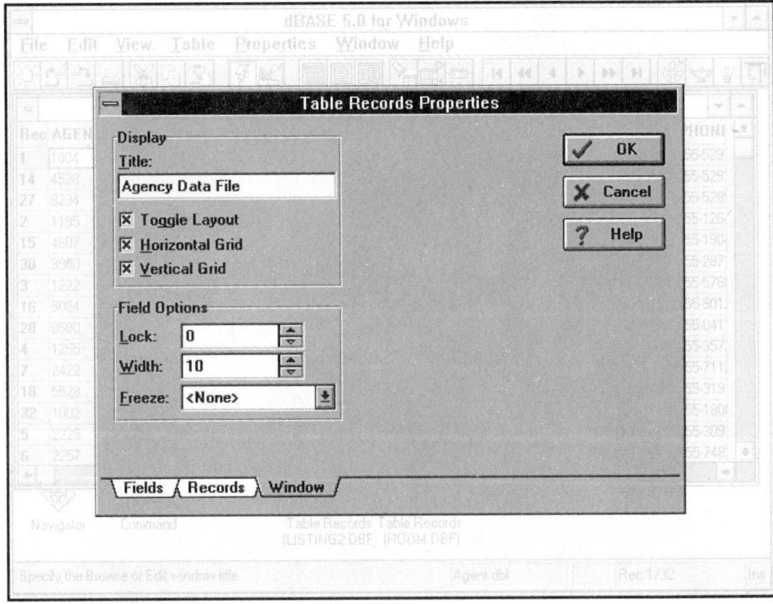

Figure 5.40
Setting the width to 10 shows more records on the display.

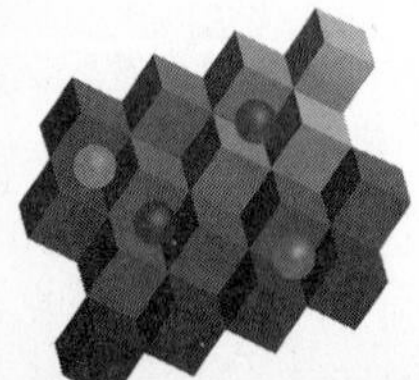

The last option, Freeze, controls the field the cursor will move in while editing or navigating the table (see fig. 5.41). This is helpful for data entry when you want to stay in a single column.

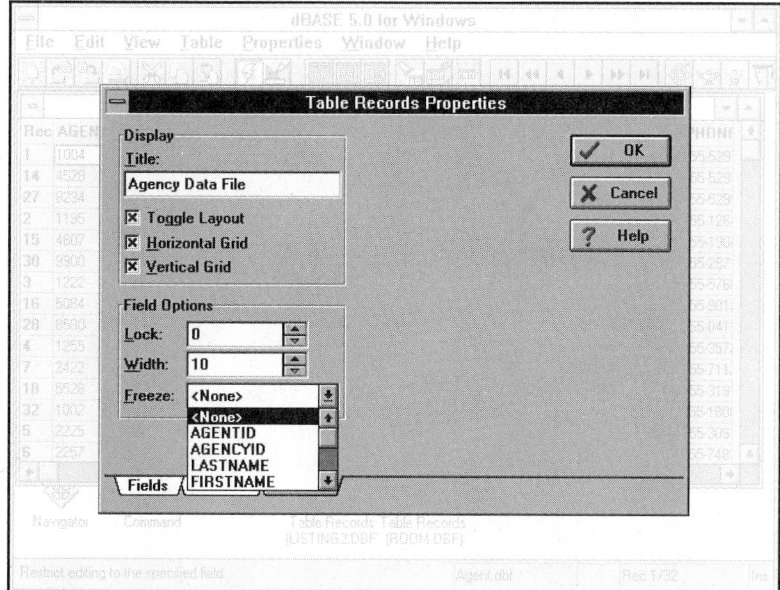

Figure 5.41
The Freeze option has a pull-down menu of the available fields in the table.

Listing Your Data

Occasionally you will want to print some or all of your table records for verification or for other record keeping purposes. dBASE provides you with two methods of printing the records in your table. One method, the Crystal Report Writer, is for specifically formatted data and is discussed later in this book. The second method, the use of dBASEs internal printer capabilities, is discussed here.

Accessing the Print Records Dialog Box

The Print Records dialog box can be accessed in one of three ways: clicking on the Printer Icon on the dBASE toolbar (see fig. 5.42), selecting the Print option from the File menu, or pressing Ctrl+P.

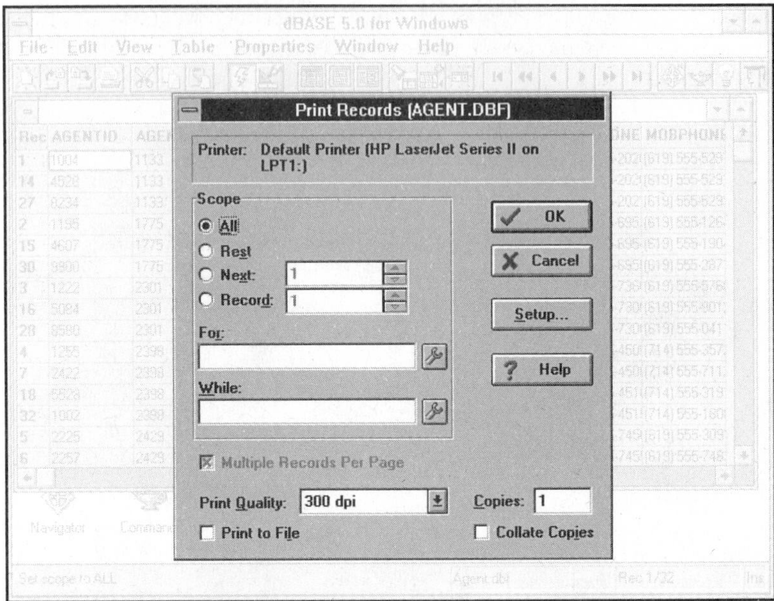

Figure 5.42
The Printer Icon displays the Print Records dialog box.

Limiting the Scope

As you can see in figure 5.42, dBASE again presents you with the capability to limit the scope of your printed output. By using the **A**ll, Re**s**t, Ne**x**t, and Recor**d** options you can select the number of records you want to print. In addition, the now familiar For and While boxes give you additional selection criteria.

Other Print Options

In addition to the scope possibilities of All, Rest, Next, and Record, dBASE also includes options you can use to specify:

- ✔ **Multiple Records Per Page.** Print up to three records per page when in Form or Columnar Layout. This option will cut down on the number of printed pages. This option is the default while in Browse mode and is therefore grayed out.

- ✔ **Print Quality.** Specifies the quality and resolution of the printed output. The available setting here will depend on the type of printer you have and the resolutions supported by your Window's printer driver.

- ✔ **Print to File.** Direct output to the file you will specify in the Print to File dialog box. This option is sometimes used to export dBASE data or save a report for later printing if you are on the road with a laptop PC and no printer.

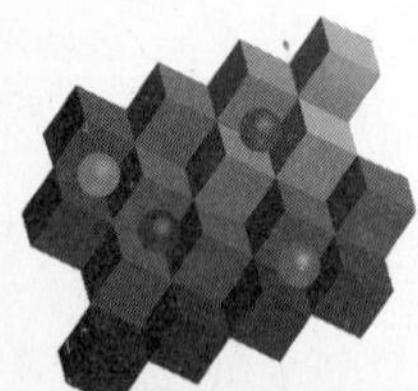

- **Copies.** Specifies the number of copies of the table or selected records to print. The default is one copy and the maximum is 99,999.
- **Collate Copies.** Prints all the records of the table as a set rather than a single page of data multiple times, based on Copies, before moving to the next page of records.

Evaluate the Collate Copies option carefully. Some printers, such as Laser printers, will store a whole page of data in memory before printing it out. The printer retains the page information in memory so that it can print multiple copies of the same page without having to force the computer to read additional data and transfer it to the printer. The collate function forces dBASE to reread the entire scope of the printed output for each copy of the report.

- **Setup.** Invokes the Print Setup dialog box, in which you can specify a number of additional printer options, such as the printer, paper source, and orientation. The process of clicking on the Setup Button is the same as picking the Print Setup option from the File menu.

Print Formats

Output from the dBASE print function resembles closely the display in the Table Records window. Form and Columnar reports mimic the displayed records. Each record appears on a single page unless the multiple records per page option in the Print Setup dialog box is checked. In Browse mode, records are printed as straight text. Because of this, the browse format prints each record on a single line and uses as many pages across as necessary to complete the record. This may require you to tape several pages side by side to see an entire record.

Use the Width option from the Table Records Properties dialog box to reduce the size of some of the columns. This helps minimize the number of pages you need to see an entire record (see fig. 5.43).

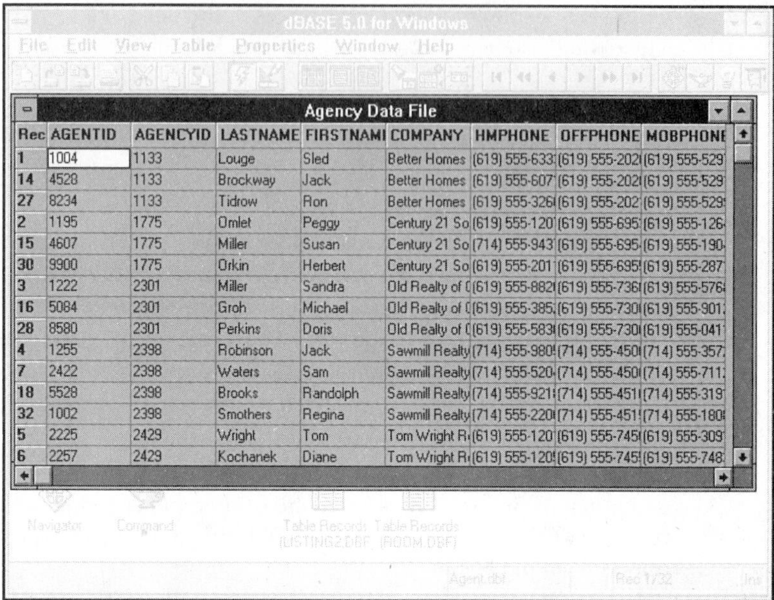

Figure 5.43 A width of 10 allows the entire Agent table to be displayed on a single page.

Deleting Data

Occasionally, there will be records in your tables that you no longer need. In the HomeGuide application, an agent may leave an agency, a house could be sold and deleted from the table, or a buyer could decide he or she was no longer interested in looking. dBASE gives you several alternatives for removing data for your tables.

Blanking Selected Records

One method of deleting data from a record is to simply clear it or blank it out. To blank out a specific record, all you need to do is open a table in one of the edit views by double clicking on it in the Navigator window. It doesn't matter if the table is in Browse, Form, or Columnar View. The next step is to go to the specific record you want to clear by using one of the record movement keys, or by using the GOTO command if you know the specific record number.

When the record is selected, you can blank it by choosing the Blank Selected Record option from the Table Menu. This option clears all columns of the table and leaves the cursor ready to enter more data. This option can be handy if you have a limited size table that cannot exceed a certain size, for example a roster of a sports team that had twenty-five positions. One player may leave the team and another may join. You could blank the former player's position and enter the new player's information.

If you accidentally blank a record, you can still recover the data as long as you don't move the cursor and make another record the active record. Just press the escape key and the table will be closed without updating (blanking) the last record. When you reopen the table you will see the last blanked record intact.

Deleting Selected Records

Deleting specific records is a lot like blanking records. To remove the record from the display, select a specific record and then choose the Delete Selected Record option from the Table menu. If you have Ignore Deleted Records unchecked on the Table page in the Desktop Properties dialog box, you will see a red "X" appear in the Del column (see fig. 5.44). The "X" indicates that the record has been deleted from the table or is no longer active.

dBASE 5.0 for Windows

File Edit View Table Properties Window Help

Agency Data File

Rec	Del	AGENTID	AGENCYID	LASTNAME	FIRSTNAMI	COMPANY	HMPHONE	OFFPHONE	MOBPHOI
2	☐	1195	1775	Omlet	Peggy	Century 21 So	(619) 555-120	(619) 555-695	(619) 555-12
3	☐	1222	2301	Miller	Sandra	Old Realty of (	(619) 555-882	(619) 555-736	(619) 555-57
4	☒	1255	2398	Robinson	Jack	Sawmill Realty	(714) 555-980	(714) 555-450	(714) 555-35
5	☐	2225	2429	Wright	Tom	Tom Wright R	(619) 555-120	(619) 555-745	(619) 555-30
6	☐	2257	2429	Kochanek	Diane	Tom Wright R	(619) 555-120	(619) 555-745	(619) 555-74
7	☐	2422	2398	Waters	Sam	Sawmill Realty	(714) 555-520	(714) 555-450	(714) 555-71
8	☐	2677	3601	Kuhns	Peter	Old Town Hon	(818) 555-202	(818) 555-901	(818) 555-43
9	☐	2754	4800	Pont	John	Century 21 No	(619) 555-223	(619) 555-711	(619) 555-55
10	☐	3502	4800	Robinson	Cheri	Century 21 No	(619) 555-202	(619) 555-711	(619) 555-32
11	☐	3762	4861	Betker	Rosie	Navarro Agen	(619) 555-583	(619) 555-575	(619) 555-12
12	☐	4026	4915	Mashburn	Roy	Independent F	(619) 555-231	(619) 555-375	(619) 555-68
13	☐	4187	6643	Atkinson	Jane	Alfred DuMont	(714) 555-790	(714) 555-131	(714) 555-55
14	☐	4528	1133	Brockway	Jack	Better Homes	(619) 555-607	(619) 555-202	(619) 555-52
15	☐	4607	1775	Miller	Susan	Century 21 So	(714) 555-943	(619) 555-695	(619) 555-19
16	☐	5084	2301	Groh	Michael	Old Realty of (	(619) 555-385	(619) 555-730	(619) 555-90

Figure 5.44 Two views of the Agent table showing deleted records.

As you can see dBASE really doesn't delete the records exactly when you tell it to. The actual record is just marked inactive. Later in this section you will see how to completely remove records from your tables.

The Delete Selected Record menu item is also available on the local table menu that you access by right-clicking anywhere in the Table Records window. Or you can use the short-cut key Ctrl+U.

Deleting Multiple Records

Deleting a range of records is a simple task in dBASE. To delete a range of records, all you need to do is open a table in browse or edit mode and select Delete Records from the Table Utilities submenu of the Table menu item. When you choose this option, the Delete Records dialog box appears and displays the now familiar scope statements you use to define the range you want to delete (see fig. 5.45).

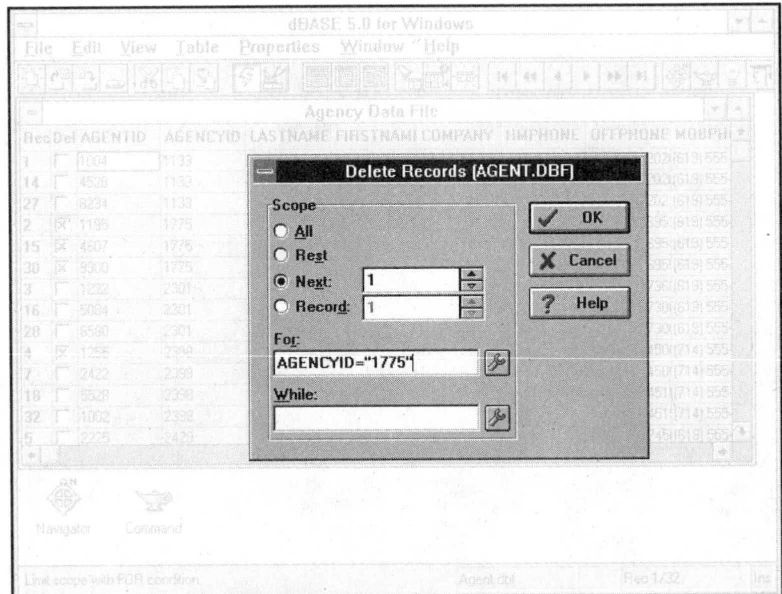

Figure 5.45
The scope statement deletes all Agencies with an AGENCYID 1175.

To delete selected records and multiple records issue the DELETE command from the command window. See Appendix A for additional information on the Delete command.

Recalling Records

When records are deleted from a table, they are not physically removed but simply flagged for removal at a later time. This flagging process provides you with an opportunity to recall records that may have been deleted accidentally or recall records that need to become active again.

Two methods are available for recalling records back into view. The first is selecting Recall Records from the Table Utilities submenu of the Table menu item (see fig. 5.46).

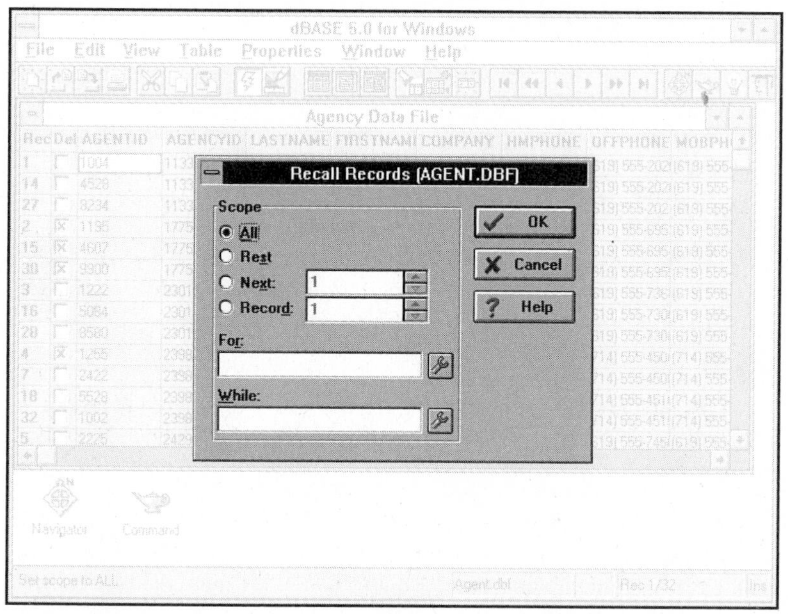

Figure 5.46
The Recall Records dialog box has the same options as the Delete Records dialog box.

To recall deleted records, you specify the scope of the records to be recalled and click on OK. The second method of recalling or undeleting records is to just click on the red "X" in the DEL column of the Table Record window (see fig. 5.47).

dBASE 5.0 for Windows

File Edit View Table Properties Window Help

Agency Data File

Rec	Del	AGENTID	AGENCYID	LASTNAME	FIRSTNAMI	COMPANY	HMPHONE	OFFPHONE	MOBPH
1		1004	1133	Louge	Sled	Better Homes	(619) 555-633	(619) 555-202	(619) 555-
14		4528	1133	Brockway	Jack	Better Homes	(619) 555-607	(619) 555-202	(619) 555-
27		8234	1133	Tidrow	Ron	Better Homes	(619) 555-326	(619) 555-202	(619) 555-
2		1195	1775	Omlet	Peggy	Century 21 So	(619) 555-120	(619) 555-695	(619) 555-
15	X	4607	1775	Miller	Susan	Century 21 So	(714) 555-943	(619) 555-695	(619) 555-
30	X	9900	1775	Orkin	Herbert	Century 21 So	(619) 555-201	(619) 555-695	(619) 555-
3		1222	2301	Miller	Sandra	Old Realty of (	(619) 555-882	(619) 555-736	(619) 555-
16		5084	2301	Groh	Michael	Old Realty of (	(619) 555-385	(619) 555-730	(619) 555-
28		8580	2301	Perkins	Doris	Old Realty of (	(619) 555-583	(619) 555-730	(619) 555-
4	X	1255	2398	Robinson	Jack	Sawmill Realty	(714) 555-980	(714) 555-450	(714) 555-
7		2422	2398	Waters	Sam	Sawmill Realty	(714) 555-520	(714) 555-450	(714) 555-
18		5528	2398	Brooks	Randolph	Sawmill Realty	(714) 555-921	(714) 555-451	(714) 555-
32		1002	2398	Smothers	Regina	Sawmill Realty	(714) 555-220	(714) 555-451	(714) 555-
5		2225	2429	Wright	Tom	Tom Wright R	(619) 555-120	(619) 555-745	(619) 555-

Navigator Command

Agent.dbf Rec 1/32 Ins

Figure 5.47
Click on the red "X" in the DEL column to recall deleted records.

See Appendix A for additional information on using the RECALL command from the command window.

Packing your Database

At some point in the life of your database table, you might want to remove the records you have deleted. The reasons for doing this may range from improving performance to simply housecleaning. The process of actually removing data is called *packing* the database.

You can perform the packing operation by selecting the Pack Records option from the Table Utilities submenu. Selecting this option will physically remove all deleted records from the database and reuse the space previously taken by the deleted records.

When you are attempting to pack a table or remove the deleted records, dBASE requires that you have exclusive use of the table. This is to prevent you from deleting records and reorganizing the data while someone else is accessing it. If dBASE needs exclusive access and you have not opened the table with the exclusive option you will be prompted with the message displayed in figure 5.48.

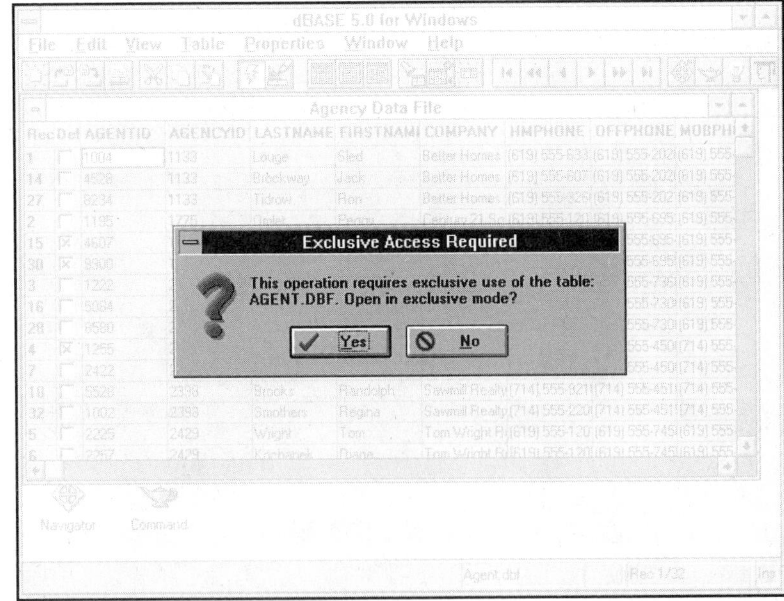

Figure 5.48
The Packing operation requires exclusive use of the table. Select Yes to open the table.

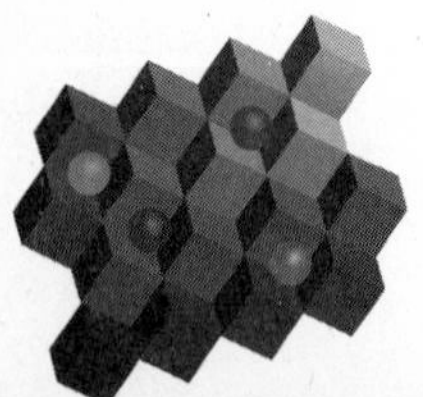

Two things happen when you pack a table. First, all deleted records are removed. This is a permanent deletion and the data CANNOT be recovered. The next step is a table reorganization; dBASE reuses the space taken up by the previously deleted records.

Note that all record numbers after the first deleted record will be changed. Each record's number will be reduced by the number of deleted records that preceded it. If you depend on specific record numbers for specific data, use the pack option with extreme caution.

Deleting All Records

At times you may want to clean out or erase an entire table and begin data entry all over again. dBASE provides you with a feature to do this. This process is called *ZAPing* your database. The ZAP Records option, available in the Table Utilities submenu, removes all records from your table.

Like the packing process, ZAP checks to ensure you have exclusive use of the table. In addition, dBASE queries you after you select the Zap Records option to make sure you really want to Zap the table (see fig. 5.49).

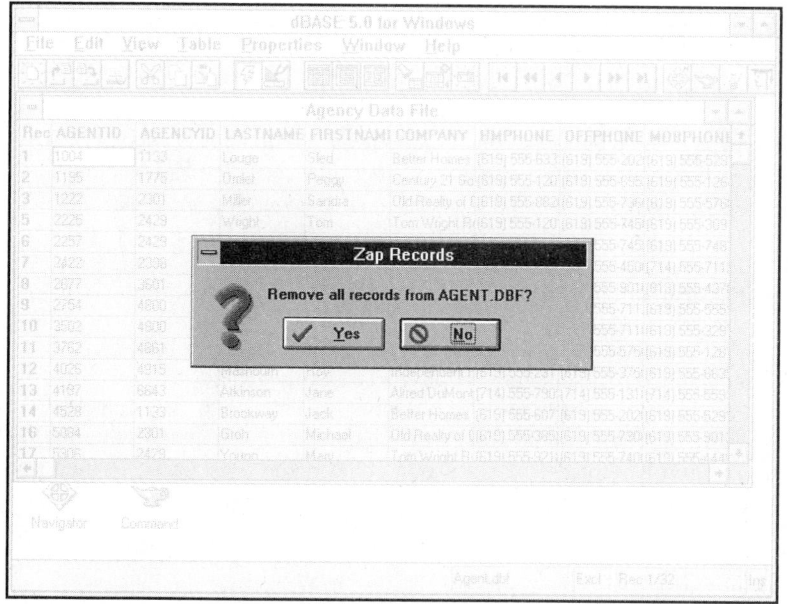

Figure 5.49 dBASE double-checks with you before ZAPing a table.

See Appendix A for additional information on using the ZAP command from the command window.

Maintaining Your Database

Previous sections in this chapter introduced you to many common tasks for routine database manipulation. This section introduces some other options you will find handy while developing and using your dBASE tables.

Changing the Structure

Rarely does a database remain the same. Over time, you probably will need to add an additional column, change the format or length of a column, or maybe even change the name of a column to give it a different meaning.

dBASE enables you to modify the *structure* of the table. To change one of the characteristics of a table you need to open the structure instead of the table of data itself. The easiest way to do this is to click on an existing table in the Navigator Window and press Shift+F2. This will open the structure for modification; the use of F2 by itself opens the table of data.

The Design Table Structure option is also available from the Navigator Menu option and the local Navigator menu. The local menu is invoked by right-clicking in the Navigator Window while a table is selected or highlighted.

After the design table structure function is invoked, the Table Structure window appears (see fig. 5.50).

From this point, you can make the changes required. To change a field name, simply click in the field name box you want to change and type the new name. To change the size of a field you click in the Width field and enter the new width. To insert a column click on the column that will be placed after the new column and press Ctrl+N. When you have completed the changes required you can double-click on the window control box or press Alt+4 to close the structure and make the changes.

When dBASE makes a structure change for you, it goes through a two-step process. The first step is to make a backup copy of your data to allow you a chance to recover if the restructuring doesn't work as expected (see fig. 5.51). To do this, dBASE renames your Table (DBF) file with a DBK extension. Thus, AGENT.DBF becomes AGENT.DBK. If a

memo file were associated with the table, it would get a TBK extension to replace the standard DBT. The second step is to create the new structure and copy over all the existing data with the specified changes being made as the copy progresses.

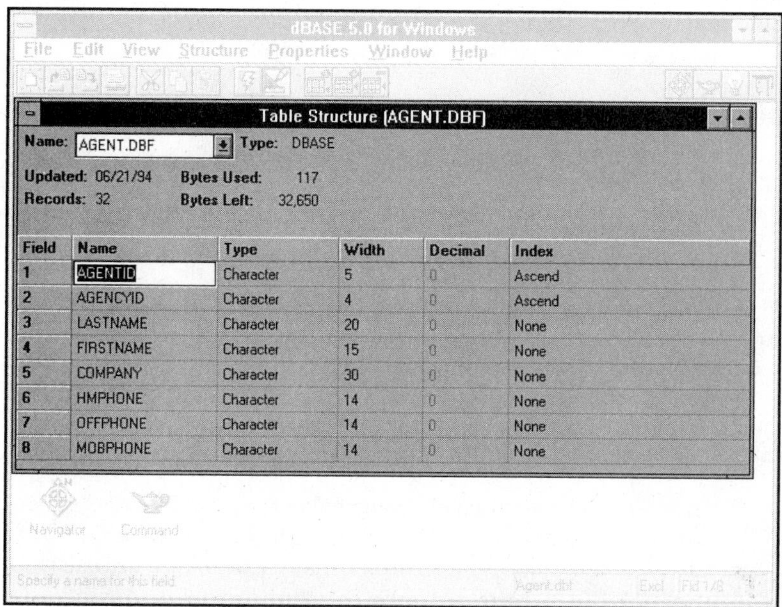

Figure 5.50
The Table Structure window is used for initial design as well as table modifications.

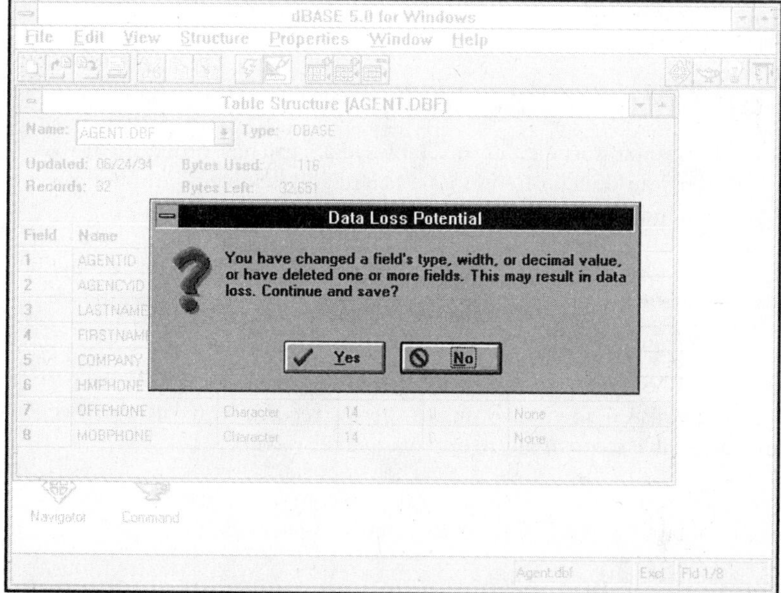

Figure 5.51
dBASE gives you one last opportunity to cancel the changes.

Because of the way the modify structure process works, you will need to ensure that enough disk space exists on your system to hold the temporary tables—as well as any working storage area that dBASE may need to perform the operation. Free space equaling two times the original table size should be more than sufficient.

Special Considerations

When making structure modifications, dBASE will make every attempt to copy and convert the table correctly. However, there are a few modifications that deserve special caution.

- ✔ Never change a column name and its type or width at the same time. dBASE is unable to understand the matching and may not be able to copy the data successfully. If you need to change both parameters change the name first, save the changes, and then come back and change the width or type.
- ✔ Never change a column name and insert or delete columns in the same session. dBASE will lose some of its matching logic and you may lose data.
- ✔ Some care also needs to be taken when changing field types. Numeric to Character always works, but the reverse can cause problems if the field contains non-numeric data. Likewise, you cannot change from Numeric to Logical or Date type formats. See the dBASE Help screen for Modify Structure for more information.

dBASE makes every attempt to convert the data correctly, but the conversion must make logical sense to come out accurate.

Creating and Managing Indexes

Although dBASE enables you to sort data in your tables in a particular order, the use of indexes to alter the order your data is often more efficient and flexible. A number of key differences exist between indexing and sorting your tables:

- ✔ Indexing creates a file of pointers to a table that describe how the table should be logically ordered. Sorting will create a copy of the table and change its physical order.
- ✔ Indexing helps dBASE perform certain functions, such as searching for data faster, by allowing dBASE to go directly to a specific record. With sorting, dBASE still has to read a table sequentially to get to a specific record.
- ✔ Indexing enables you to order tables according to complex functions derived from data in the table. Sorting can only be done on specific fields.

- ✔ Records added to an indexed table are automatically inserted in their correct logical position. Records added to a sorted table are added to the end and may need to be resorted.

Creating Standard Indexes

dBASE will automatically create an index for you if you specify Ascend or Descend in the index field during the creation of the table structure. Occasionally, you may want to go back after the table has been created to create additional or complex indexes.

To create an index for a database you must first open the table you want to build the index for by double clicking on the table icon in the Navigator window. With the table open choose the Table Utilities option from the Table menu and then select Manage Indexes from the submenu. Try this with the LISTING2 table supplied with the HomeGuide application and your display should look something like figure 5.52.

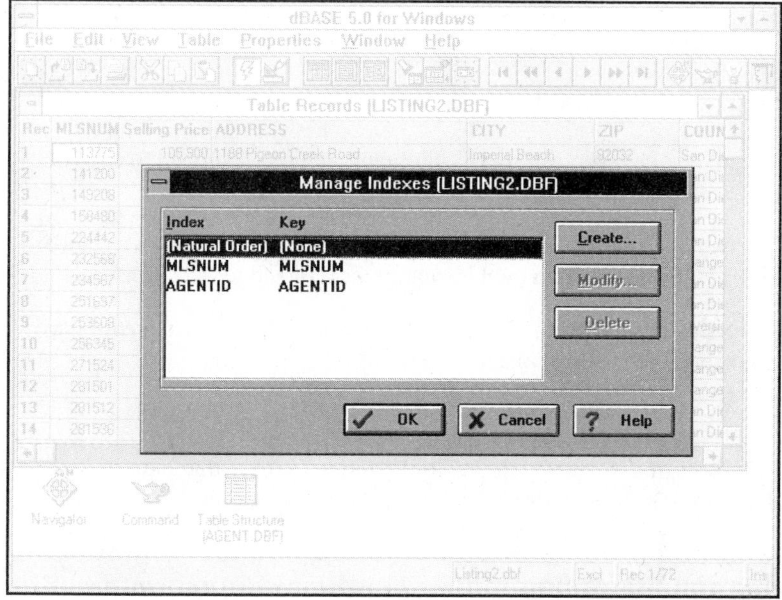

Figure 5.52
The Listing table is indexed on MLSNUM and AGENTID.

The existing indexes shown in figure 5.42 are those that are created when you specify Ascend or Descend in the index field during the creation of the table structure.

There might be times you would like to view the Listing table in order by location or ZIP Code. You have a choice of sorting the table in that order or simply creating a new index on the ZIP code. The best choice in this case is creating a new index. To do so, click on the Create button (see fig. 5.53).

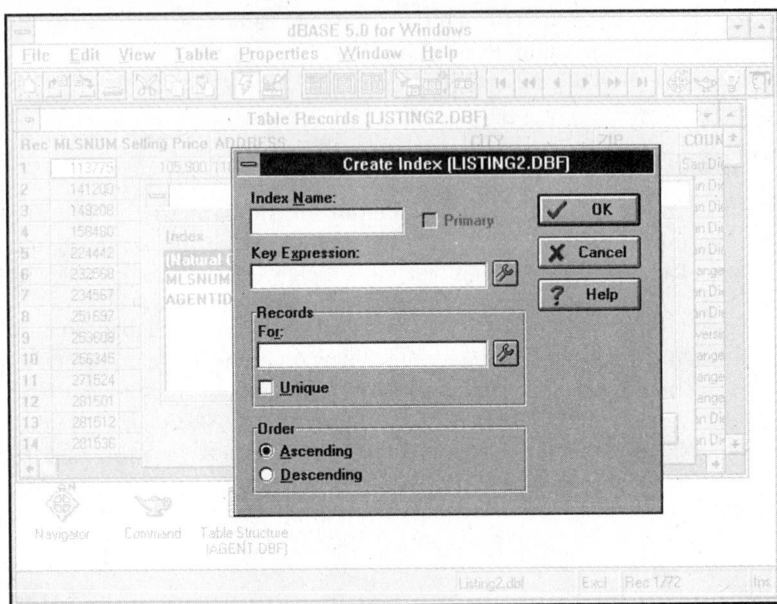

Figure 5.53
The Create Index dialog box.

In the Create Index dialog box, you can specify all the parameters you need to create a new index. The parameters include:

- **Index Name:** Specifies the name you want to call your index. This is a standard 10 character dBASE name. This field is sometimes referred to as a *Tag.*
- **Key Expression:** Tells dBASE the field you want to index on or the expression you want to use to create a complex expression.
- **For:** Limits the scope of the indexed records to a portion of the database.
- **Unique:** Restricts the records included in the index to those that have unique index values. If multiple records have the same index value only the first one in the natural order (lowest record number) will be included in the index.
- **Ascending and Descending.** Specifies the order in which you want the records to appear.

To create an index for ZIP codes, you would first enter ZIPCODE into the Index Name Field, followed by entering the field name ZIP in the Key Expression Field. Next, click on OK to return to the Manage Indexes dialog box, and then click on OK again to return to the Table Records window. The index will be created and the table should now appear in ZIP code order similar to figure 5.54.

dBASE 5.0 for Windows

Table Records (LISTING2.DBF)

Rec	MLSNUM	Selling Price	ADDRESS	CITY	ZIP	COUN
59	890363	3,600	541 Calle Arroyo	Thousand Oaks	91360	Ventura
9	253608	114,400	1127 Lake View Blvd	Norco	91760	Riversi
17	531698	125,000	88 Northway Drive	Norco	91760	Riversi
27	890360	139,900	4509 West Gramercy Way	Norco	91760	Riversi
2	141200	49,900	1420 Rosemary Lane	Alpine	92001	San Di
5	224442	124,900	10 South Street	Alpine	92001	San Di
8	251697	92,900	4211 Morris Boulevard	Alpine	92001	San Di
14	281536	95,000	300 South Shore Drive	Alpine	92001	San Di
16	345998	89,000	715 East Davenport Street	Alpine	92001	San Di
1	113775	105,900	1188 Pigeon Creek Road	Imperial Beach	92032	San Di
3	149208	113,900	2828 North Downer Avenue	Imperial Beach	92032	San Di
4	158480	69,900	1820 East Olive Street	Imperial Beach	92032	San Di
7	234567	123,000	1011 West Lake Side	Imperial Beach	92032	San Di
13	281512	136,000	10 W Wabash Street	Mira Mesa	92126	San Di

Figure 5.54
Indexing on the ZIP code field displays the table in ZIP Code order.

Creating Complex Indexes

Complex indexes are indexes that contain more than a single field value or are a combination of a field and an external expression. These indexes are created in the same manner as the standard indexes, but the expression used for them is generally a bit more complicated.

To continue with the ZIP code index, you can further refine this index and see the table ordered by List Price within ZIP code (see fig. 5.55).

Instead of creating a totally new index, you can take the existing index ZIPCODE and change it by first clicking on it in the Manage Indexes dialog box and then clicking on the Modify button. With the Modify Index dialog box, you can change the index name and expression as shown in figure 5.53. Click on OK several times to back out to the records display window, create the new index, and display the data in the new order.

Because ZIP is a character field and LISTPRICE is a numeric field, the two must be converted to the same field type to be used in an index expression. In this case, the LISTPRICE was converted to character using the STR function, but you could get the same result by converting the ZIP to numeric using the VAL function.

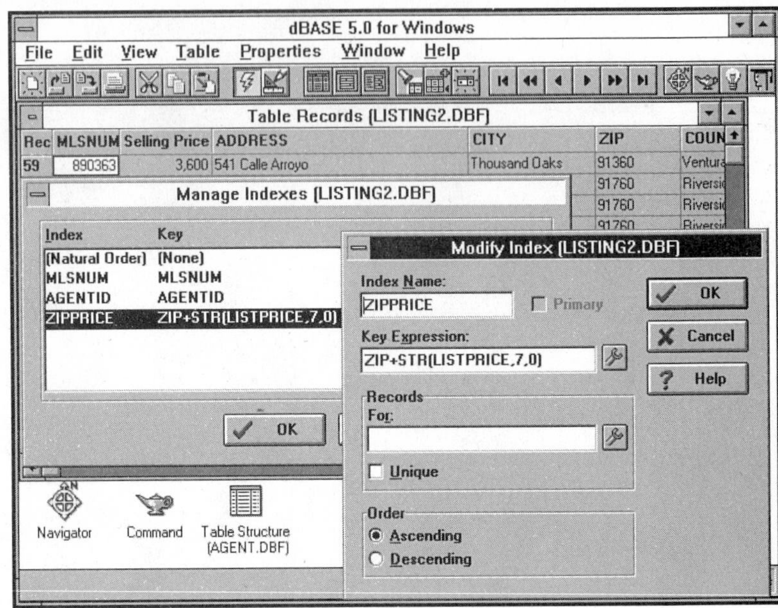

Figure 5.55 The Key Expression shows that the ZIP Code and List Price are both part of the index expression.

As you can see dBASE has a number of options to give you a great deal of flexibility when displaying and processing your data. For more information on Indexes, see the INDEX command in Appendix A.

Re-Indexing Tables

As long as the index file is open dBASE will automatically keep the index up-to-date. There may be a time when you have updated a table without its index file(s) being open. One example of this would be if you restored a copy of a database from a backup without restoring the corresponding index file(s). This would cause the current index to be out of sync with the current copy of the table.

To re-synchronize the tables and indexes, all you need to do is select Re-index from the Table Utilities submenu. dBASE will then regenerate and update the indexes.

In the interactive environment, dBASE finds all of the index files in the current directory to update. If you have open the file from the command line you must either specify the index file in the USE statement or issue a SET INDEX command to open the appropriate index files.

Removing Indexes

The more indexes you have, the more work dBASE has to go through to keep them maintained. If performance begins to be a problem or if you realize you just don't need an index expression it is a good idea to remove or delete the index. To delete an index use the Manage Indexes dialog box. Click on the index you want to delete and then click on the delete button; the index will be removed.

Sorting Records

In the last section, you learned some of the advantages of indexing tables. While working within the dBASE environment, indexing is generally the preferred method for ordering your records. However, there are times when you will want to have the data physically ordered in a specific sequence. One use of a sorted table would be if you wanted to export data to another application.

To sort a table, it first must be open. The next step is to select Sort Records from the Table Utilities submenu of the Table menu item (see fig. 5.56).

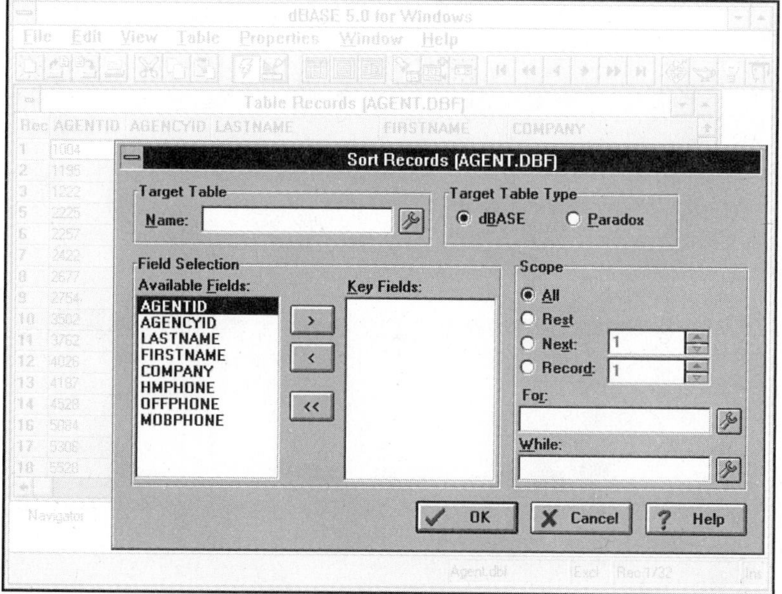

Figure 5.56
The Sort Records dialog box enables you to specify the target table and key fields.

The Sort Records dialog box provides several fields you use to specify the parameters necessary to perform the sort:

- ✔ **Target Table Name.** The output from the sort function is always a new table. dBASE enables you to specify an existing table and overwrite it but it is recommended that you create a completely separate table.

- ✔ **Target Table Type.** Enables you to select either a dBASE format or Paradox format table for the sorted results.

- **Field Selection.** Shows you a list of Available Fields and lets you select the Key Fields you want to use in the sort and order of the fields selected.
- **Scope.** Enables you to limit the selection of the records to be sorted.

In the HomeGuide application, the Agent table has indexes that enable you to view it by Agent ID or Agency ID. Suppose you want to sort the table by Agent ID within Agency? The steps to do this would be as follows:

Sorting the Table by Agent ID

Open the Agent table from the Navigator window by double-clicking on it	The Agent table opens
Click on the Table Menu item and select Table Utilities	The Table Utilities submenu appears
Click on the Sort Records option of the Table Utilities submenu	The Sort Records dialog box appears (see fig. 5.57)

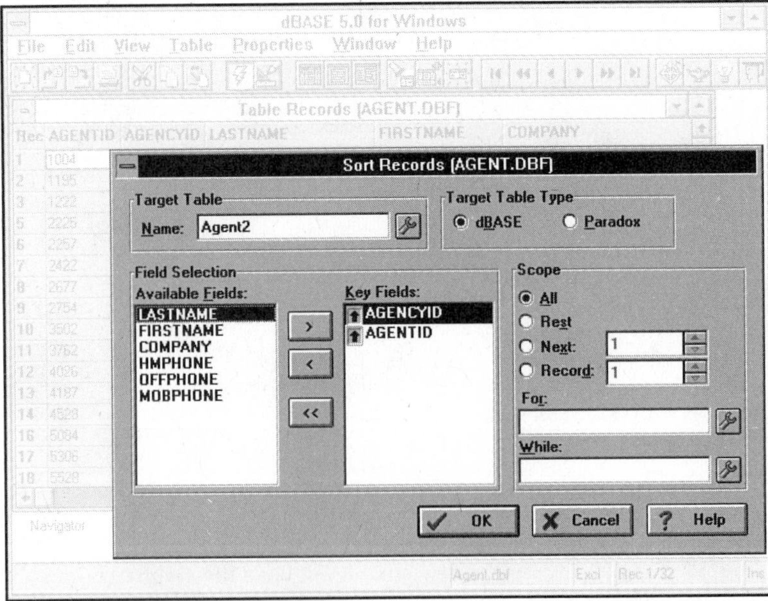

Figure 5.57 The Sort Records dialog box shows available and selected fields for sorting.

Click in the Name field and type **AGENT2**	Specifies the sort by name

Click on AGENCYID, the second field in the available fields box, to select it, then click on the > to select AGENCYID as a Key Field	Selects the fields you want
Repeat the process in the preceding step for the AGENTID field	

Next to each field in the Key Fields box is a drop-down list box for selecting the sort order. The available choices are Ascending and Descending and the option to ignore case in either direction. In this example, the default Ascending order is the desired order.

Click on OK	The sorting process is carried out

If you activate the Navigator window you will now see an AGENT2.DBF file. Double click on the table icon to open the table in browse mode and you will see that the table is now sorted to your specifications (see fig. 5.58).

dBASE 5.0 for Windows

File Edit View Table Properties Window Help

Table Records (AGENT2.DBF)

Rec	AGENTID	AGENCYID	LASTNAME	FIRSTNAME	COMPANY
1	1004	1133	Louge	Sled	Better Homes & Gardens
2	4528	1133	Brockway	Jack	Better Homes & Gardens
3	8234	1133	Tidrow	Ron	Better Homes & Gardens
4	1195	1775	Omlet	Peggy	Century 21 South Side
5	1222	2301	Miller	Sandra	Old Realty of California
6	5084	2301	Groh	Michael	Old Realty of California
7	8580	2301	Perkins	Doris	Old Realty of California
8	1002	2398	Smothers	Regina	Sawmill Realty
9	2422	2398	Waters	Sam	Sawmill Realty
10	5528	2398	Brooks	Randolph	Sawmill Realty
11	2225	2429	Wright	Tom	Tom Wright Realty
12	2257	2429	Kochanek	Diane	Tom Wright Realty
13	5306	2429	Young	Mary	Tom Wright Realty
14	2677	3601	Kuhns	Peter	Old Town Homes

Navigator Command Table Records (AGENT.DBF) Table Records (LISTING2.DBF)

Agent2.dbf Rec 1/29 Ins

Figure 5.58
Agent2 table is sorted by Agency ID and Agent ID.

Other Database Functions

In addition to the standard database functions to modify, order, and print portions of the database, dBASE has functions for quick calculations and counts of specific data items.

Counting Records

dBASE has a number of quick functions for querying the contents of your table. One of these functions is COUNT.

Suppose you want to know the number of homes that have a list price below $125,000 in the HomeGuide application. One way to find this information would be to index the records by list price and manually count the ones less than $125,000. The more expedient way would be to use the Count Records function (see fig. 5.59).

Figure 5.59
The Count Records dialog box enables you to count the number of records that match the specified scope or criteria.

If you have the Listing table open select the Count Records option from the Table Utilities submenu to display the Count Records dialog box as shown in figure 5.56. Next, click on the "For" field and type **LISTPRICE<125000**, then click on OK to tell dBASE to perform the work. Shortly after that, you should see a Counted Records window similar to the one in figure 5.60. The count operation can be performed on any field type.

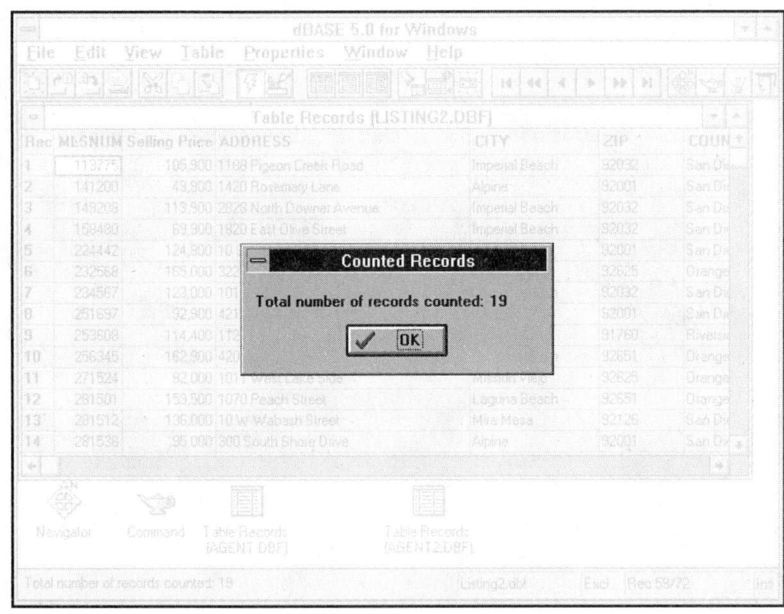

Figure 5.60
dBASE displays a Counted Records window to display the results of its count operation.

Quick Record Calculations

In addition to the standard count operation dBASE also supports a number of other arithmetic calculations. These functions are generally performed on any numeric field within the table.

The Calculate Records dialog box shown in figure 5.61 is also invoked from a selection on the Table Utilities submenu.

As shown in the preceding figure, the Calculate Records function supports the basic mathematical functions of Average, Minimum, Maximum, Standard Deviation, Sum, and Variance. Note for all but the Minimum and Maximum function only the numeric fields are displayed for selection.

In the last example, you counted the number of records with a list price of less than $125,000. In this example you will find the average list price for all of the homes listed in the table.

The first step in using the Calculate Records function is to specify the calculation to be performed. In this case, you want to click on Average if it is not already selected or you can also use the Alt+G shortcut key. The next step is to select the field you want to perform the calculation on by clicking on it. Choose LISTPRICE for this. In this case, you don't want to limit the scope in any way, so the final step is to click on OK. After clicking on OK, dBASE then calculates the Average list price and displays the results in a Calculation Results window. Your results should resemble the list price shown in figure 5.62.

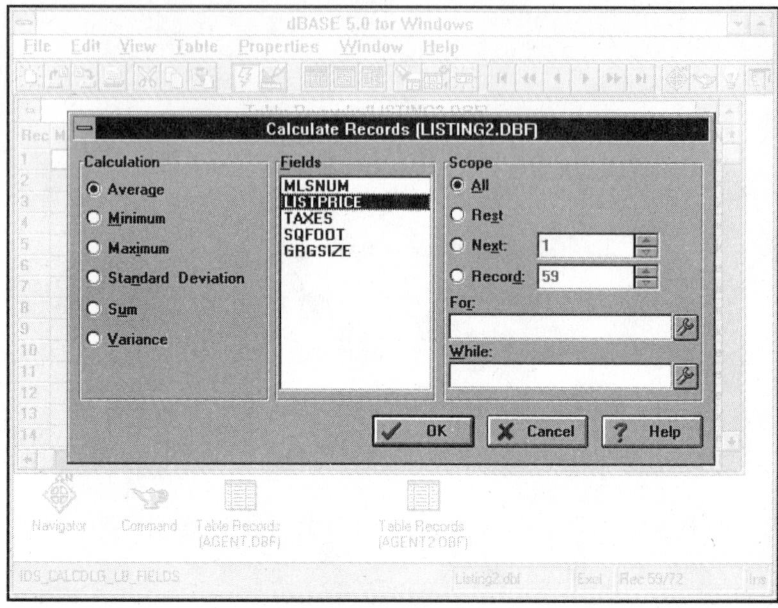

Figure 5.61 The Calculate Records dialog box displays the valid numeric fields in a table.

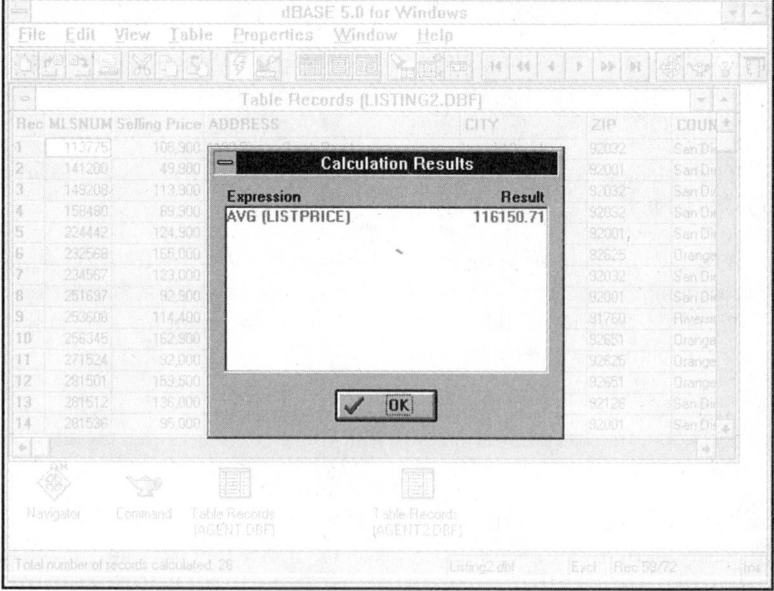

Figure 5.62 dBASE calculates the Average list price of all records in the table.

All of the other calculations work in a similar manner. In addition to changing the calculations you can also restrict the scope of the data that dBASE takes into account when performing the calculation.

Chapter Snapshot

Now that you have created your data table, you need to have a way to enter data and display it. You can use the default Edit screen or the Browse table, but neither of these methods provides information on the required contents of a field. A better choice is to create a form. In this chapter, you learn the following:

After completing this chapter, you will have several methods of entering and displaying information in a data table.

Developing Forms

By Chris Bolte

In dBASE for Windows, each form is a window on your screen. Because dBASE is object-oriented, all forms also are objects. Objects have specific properties, based on the type of object, that determine how the object acts. Form windows themselves contain various other objects, such as control buttons, entry fields, or lists.

You can create forms to provide information or menus, or to get user input for the data table. Forms can be associated with a view of a data table, and thus be used for data entry or display; or they can be independent of a data table, and thus be used for menus and information display.

Understanding the Form Tool

You can create a form by setting up a blank window, setting its properties, and then adding the appropriate objects.

The dBASE Form Designer provides you with a graphical user interface that enables you to see your form as you are designing it. Starting with a blank form, the Form Designer enables you to select from a list of graphical objects and place them where you want them to appear.

When you save the completed form, dBASE generates the code required to display the form you designed and store it in a text file with a WFM file extension. Creating and editing forms with the command editor is discussed in Chapter 13, "Creating the User Interface." In this section, you learn how to start the Form Designer and customize it for your own design session.

Starting the Form Designer

From the Windows desktop, double-click on the dBASE for Windows icon to start dBASE. Depending upon how the last session ended, the Navigator and Command windows might be open or shown as icons on the dBASE desktop. You can start the Form Designer in several different ways, depending upon which window is currently active. You can change the active window using the Command or Navigator buttons on the SpeedBar. dBASE for Windows starts with the Command window menu active. The following methods are available on either the Command window menu or the Navigator window menu:

- ✔ Select File, New, Form
- ✔ Select the Expert button from the SpeedBar as shown in figure 6.1 and select Form Expert

From the Navigator menu, you also have three additional choices:

- ✔ Select Navigator, New Form
- ✔ Press the key combination Shift+F2
- ✔ Single-click on the Forms icon in the Navigator window and double-click on *Untitled* in the Form Files list that is displayed.

In the Command window, you also can type either of two commands to start the Form Designer:

- ✔ CREATE FORM EXPERT
- ✔ CREATE SCREEN EXPERT

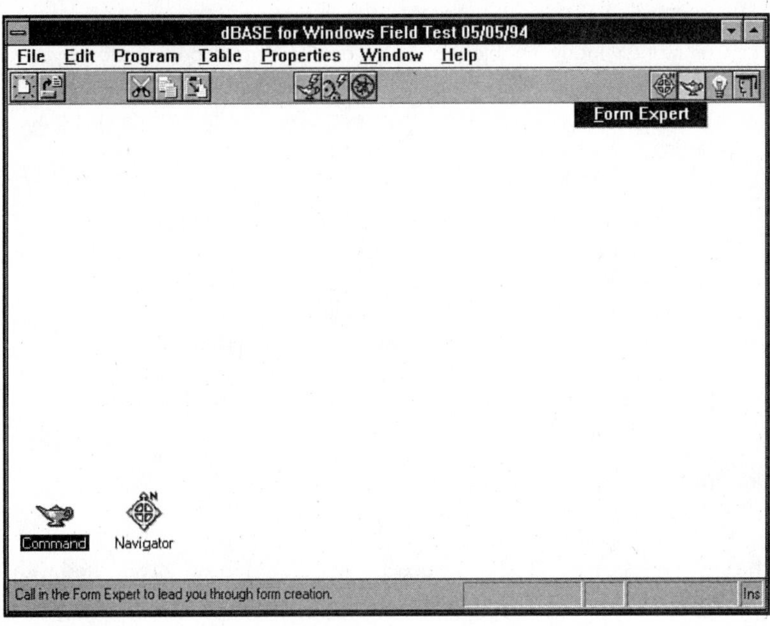

Figure 6.1
The Expert speed button on the dBASE for Windows desktop.

By default, all these methods open the Form Expert window (see fig. 6.2). The Form Expert window enables you to decide whether to let the Form Expert help you design the form or to start with a blank form. Click on Blank Form and then select Create to open the Form Designer on a blank form.

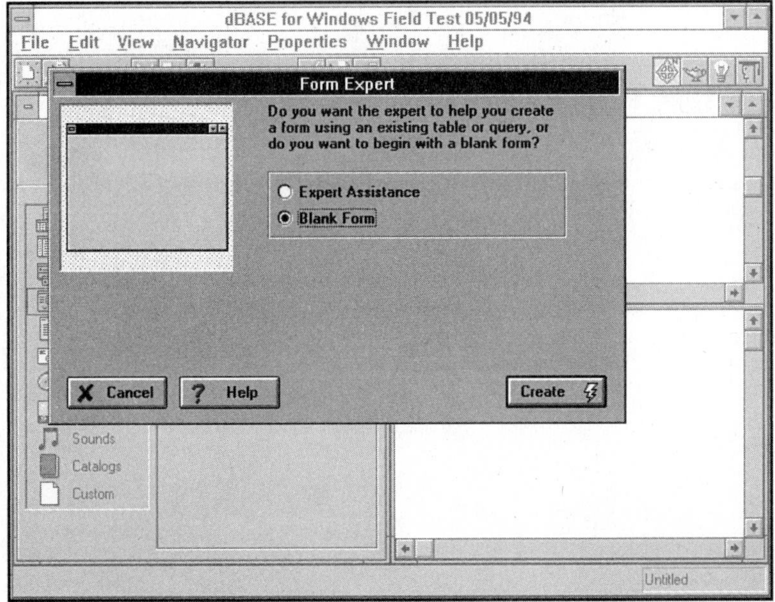

Figure 6.2
The Form Expert window enables selection of blank form.

The Command window enables you to bypass the Form Expert window by leaving off the word EXPERT on the command line. You can bypass the Form Expert in the other methods (except the Expert SpeedBar button) by changing the selection in the Form Designer Properties for creating new forms.

The Form Designer has four windows associated with it—any or all of which can be opened when the Form Designer starts. When you start the Form Designer, at least the Form Designer window is displayed. Other windows are open if they were left that way when the Form Designer was closed on the previous form edit session. Each window is a different tool that can be used while you are designing your form.

- ✔ **Form Designer**. The design surface for the form, which provides a visual picture of what the form looks like on the screen.
- ✔ **Controls**. Displays the Control Palette, a list of the objects that can be added to the form. These are divided into two tabs, Standard and Custom.
- ✔ **Properties**. Provides three lists, Properties, Events, and Methods, associated with the currently selected object. Each list appears on a separate tab in the window.
- ✔ **Procedures**. Provides access to the Procedure Editor to modify procedures associated with the selected object.

Figure 6.3 shows all four windows for the Form Designer and the associated tools. If you are designing a menu, the Form Designer has an additional tool, the Menu Designer, which also has its own window. Activating the Menu Designer closes the Controls window, because controls are not used in the menu design.

Setting Up the Forms Environment

Several selections can determine how the Form Designer appears on the screen and how it functions. You can change these selections to customize the Forms Designer to work the way you normally do. Some of these choices are available on the Menu. Under the View choice, you can check which tool windows you want to have displayed when you start the Form Designer. These choices also are available on the Form Designer SpeedMenu (see fig. 6.4), which pops up when you click the right mouse button. Other choices are available on the Form Designer Properties dialog box.

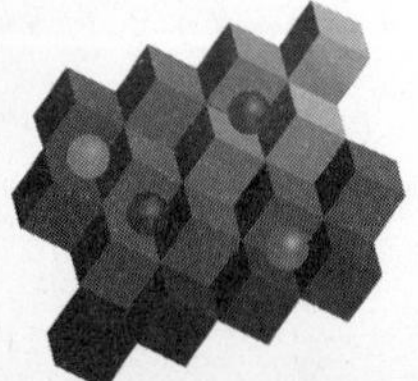

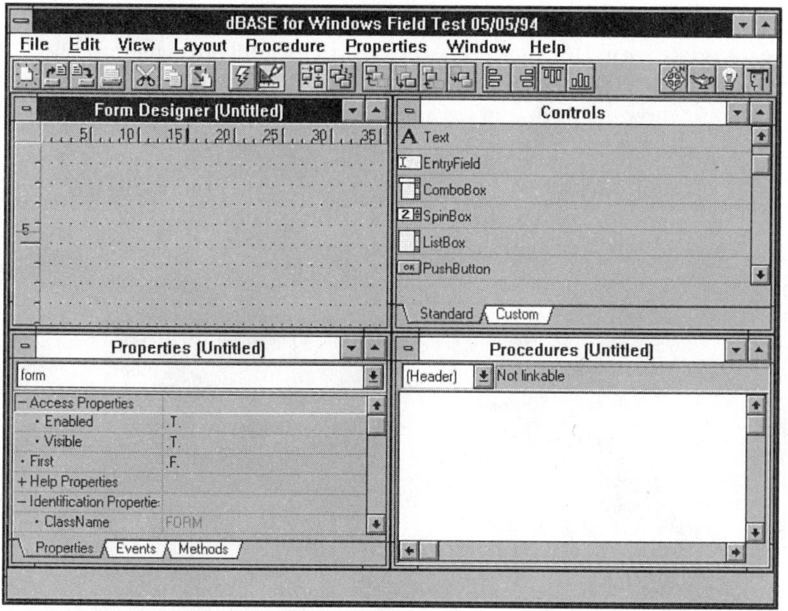

Figure 6.3
The Form Designer and tool windows.

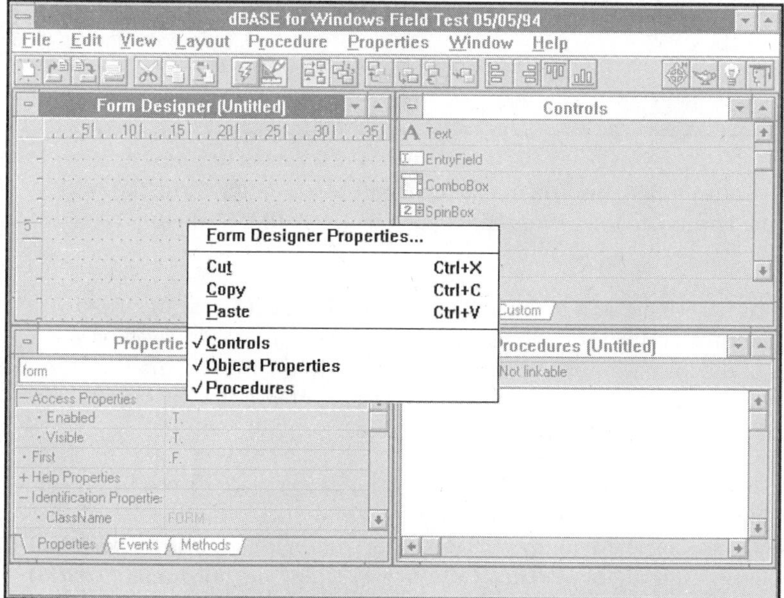

Figure 6.4
The Form Designer SpeedMenu.

With the Form Designer open, right-click anywhere on the form. From the pop-up window that appears, select Form Designer Properties (from the pull-down menus, select Properties, Form). The Form Designer Properties dialog box shown in figure 6.5 appears. These controls determine how the form window appears while you are designing the form.

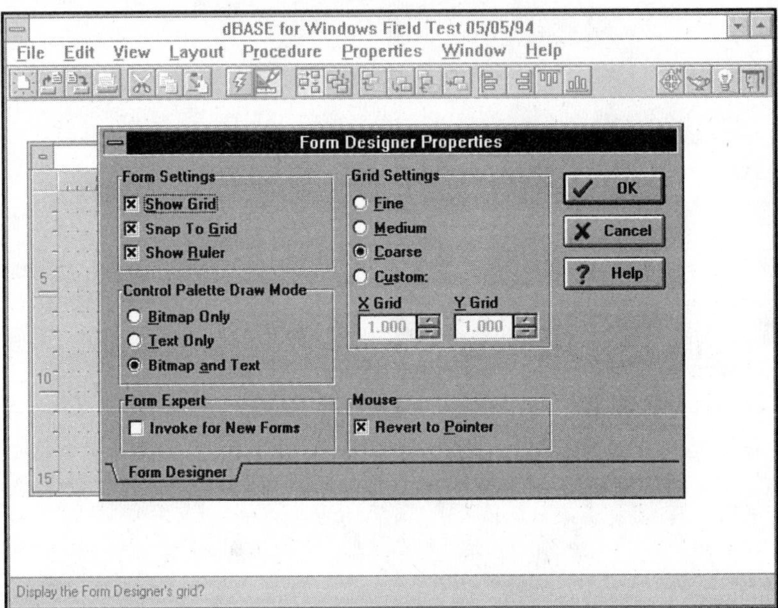

Figure 6.5
The Form Designer Properties dialog box.

dBASE offers two features that assist you in placing your objects on the form: the ruler and the grid. In the Forms Designer Properties dialog box, tell dBASE whether you want to use them or not.

The *ruler* measures character spaces in the default font pitch and line spacing. If you select to display the ruler (using the Visible Ruler option), the ruler is displayed on the top and left sides of the form window. Displaying the ruler during the design process helps you place your objects precisely. When you are placing objects, markers on the top and left rulers indicate the current location of the cursor.

The *grid* is the equivalent of electronic graph paper. It helps you place objects by providing a framework in which you can position the objects. Three standard grid intervals are provided: Coarse (1 character), Medium (2/3 character), and Fine (1/3 character). You also can input your own interval by selecting Custom and setting the horizontal (X Grid) and vertical (Y Grid) intervals. The intervals are defined in terms of character width and height for the form font.

If you want all your objects aligned horizontally and vertically, you can turn on Snap To Grid. When this option is enabled, each object anchors itself to the nearest intersection in the grid when the object is placed. Clicking on Show Grid puts a dot at each intersection in the grid. Some developers find the dots too distracting during the design process. You can use Snap To Grid whether or not the grid is displayed.

For the most accurate placement of objects, select Snap To Grid, select Custom, enter 0.1 in the X Grid and Y Grid text boxes, and select Show Grid to turn off the grid display.

If you want the Form Expert started for all new form design sessions, check the Invoke for New Forms box in the Form Expert rectangle. Leaving this box unchecked starts the Form Designer without the Form Expert window.

The Control Palette Draw Mode rectangle enables you to change how the controls displayed in the Control window appear. By default, both the picture and the text name for the controls are shown in the window. This selection is made by checking the Bitmap and Text box. To display only the pictures for the controls, check the Bitmap only box. To display only the name of the control, check the Text only box.

When you select a control from the Control Palette, the mouse pointer is used to place the control on the design surface. By default, the mouse pointer returns to being a pointer after placing the control. This enables you to move or resize the control. This behavior is selected by checking the Revert to Pointer box in the Mouse rectangle. If you are placing several of the same kind of control, you can change this action. If you turn off the Revert to Pointer box, after a control is placed the mouse remains attached to that control type. You are able to move the mouse and add another control to the form without returning to the Control Palette. Select the pointer object from the Control Palette to return the mouse to a pointer.

Saving the Forms Environment

Save the options by clicking on OK in the Forms Designer Properties dialog box. The options that you have selected remain in effect for all future dBASE sessions until you reset them. They are stored in the dBASE initialization file (DBASEWIN.INI) that is read each time dBASE is started.

Creating a Quick Form

The easiest way to create a form is to use the Form Expert. Although the available formats might not exactly match what you want, they give you a good starting point that you can modify.

The Form Expert enables you to select fields from an existing table or view and place them into a form. Several different templates for field placement are provided, and you can choose the one that best matches your application. After you have chosen the fields and format, select Create and the Form Expert places all the objects on the form for you. The steps you follow are detailed in the following exercise.

Using the Form Expert to Select Fields

Click on the Expert button	A list of available experts is provided
Select the Form Expert	The Form Expert dialog box (see fig. 6.6) is displayed

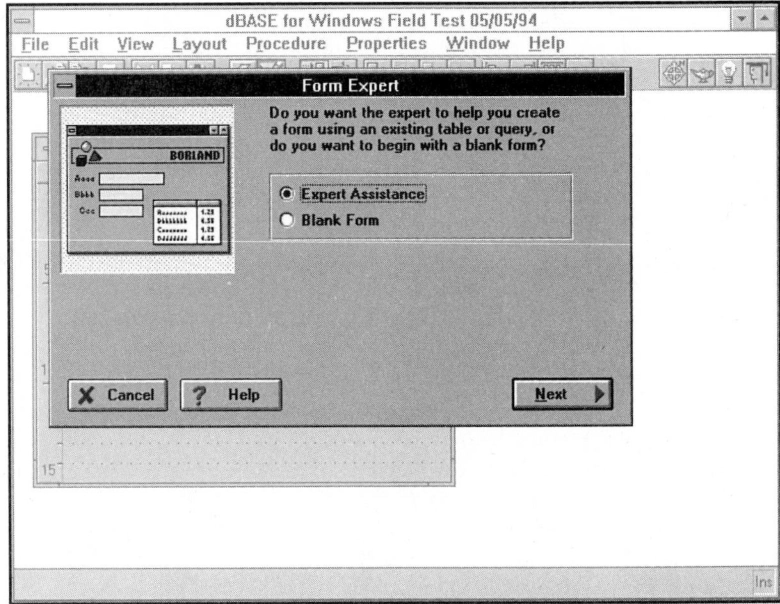

Figure 6.6
The Form Expert with Expert Assistance selected.

Select Expert Assistance and click Next	The Form Expert displays a file selection list box (see fig 6.7)

All tables and views in the default directory are shown in the Available Files list. To select from a different directory, you can click on the Tool button beside the selected file field.

Click on the Tool button	The Choose View dialog box (see fig. 6.8) is displayed

You can change disks or directories using the Dri**v**e and **D**irectory lists. The types of files displayed are shown in the File **T**ypes field. You can select from QBE, DBF, or VUE file extensions. You can also enter a specific file name in the **F**ile Name field.

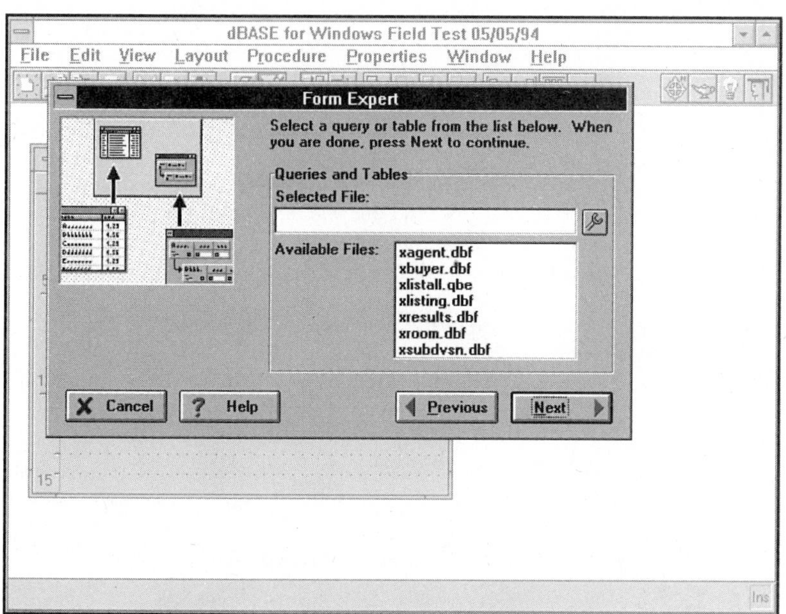

Figure 6.7
The file selection list box in the Form Expert.

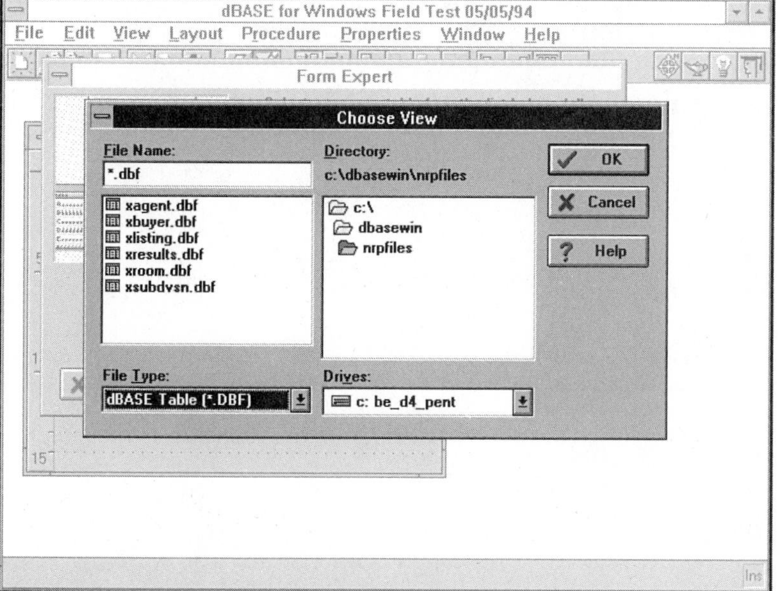

Figure 6.8
The Choose View dialog box.

continues

continued

Double-click on a file name	The Choose View window closes, and the selected file appears in the File Name field on the file selection window
Click on Next	The field selection window (see fig. 6.9) is displayed; (the available fields are shown in the left list the fields that have been selected are shown in the right list)

Fields can be selected by clicking on a field name in the Available Fields list and clicking the '>' button. To select all the fields, use the '>>' button. To deselect a field, click on the field name in the Selected Fields list and click the '<' button. All fields can be deselected by clicking on the '<<' button.

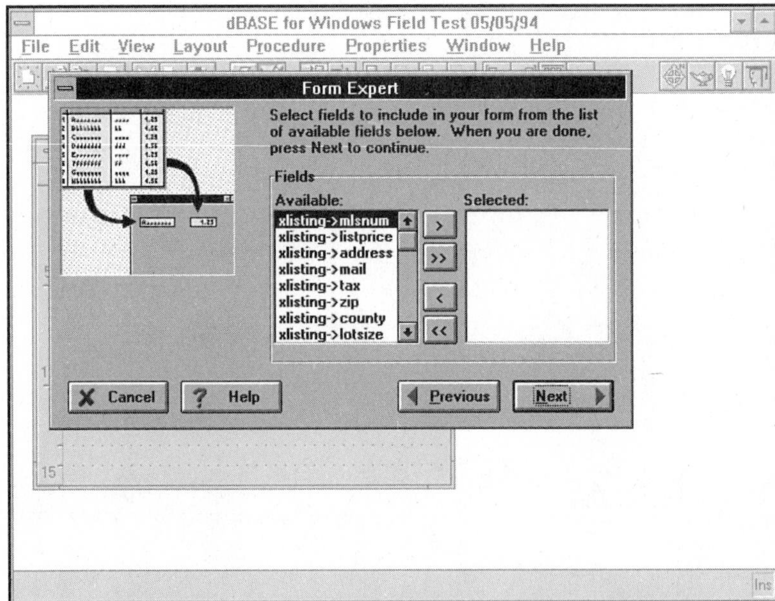

Figure 6.9 The field selection list box in the Form Expert.

Click on the '<<' button	All fields in the Available Fields list are moved to the Selected Fields list
Click on Next	The layout scheme window (see fig. 6.10) is shown

Four choices of layout are provided: Columnar, Form, Browse, and One to Many. As each choice is selected, the matching picture is highlighted in the upper left rectangle.

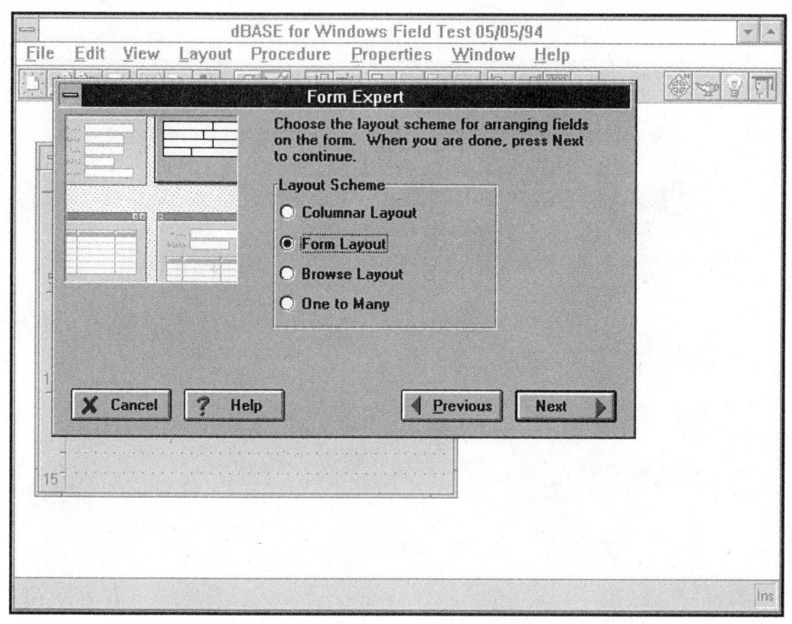

Figure 6.10
The layout scheme window in the Form Expert.

Select Form Layout	The Form Layout is highlighted in the window
Click on Next	The display properties window (see fig. 6.11) is displayed; this window enables you to select the fonts and colors that are used on your form

You can select different fonts and foreground colors for the title, text, and field entries. You can select different background colors for the form and the entry fields. You can also decide whether or not to place a border around your entry fields.

Click on the Title tool button	The Font window (see fig. 6.12) is displayed; you can choose from any of the fonts, styles, and sizes available in Windows. (This same window is displayed for the Text and Entry choices on the display properties window)
Select the font and click on OK	The selected font is inserted into the Title field
Click Entry Borders	The X disappears from the Entry Borders box and the borders disappear from the sample display in the upper left corner
Click Create	The Form Expert window disappears and is replaced by the Form Designer window with your form displayed (see fig. 6.13)

continues

continued

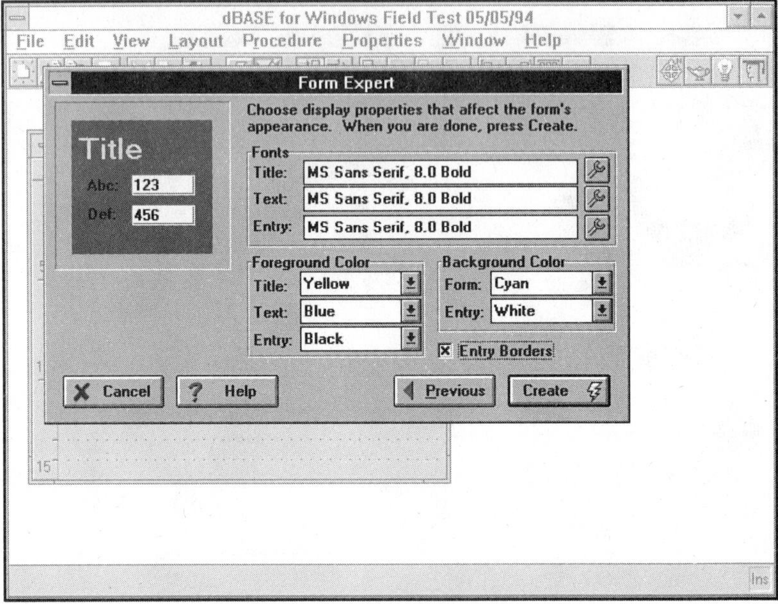

Figure 6.11 The display properties window in the Form Expert.

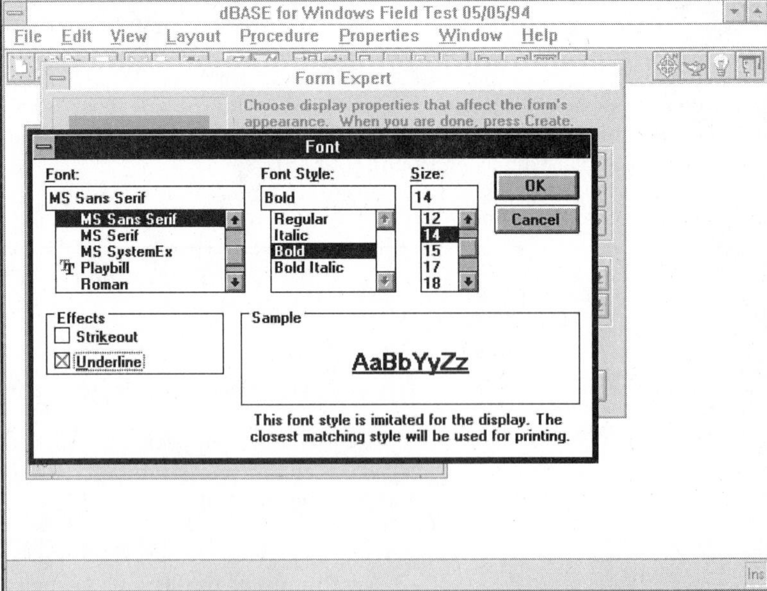

Figure 6.12 The font dialog box window in the Form Expert.

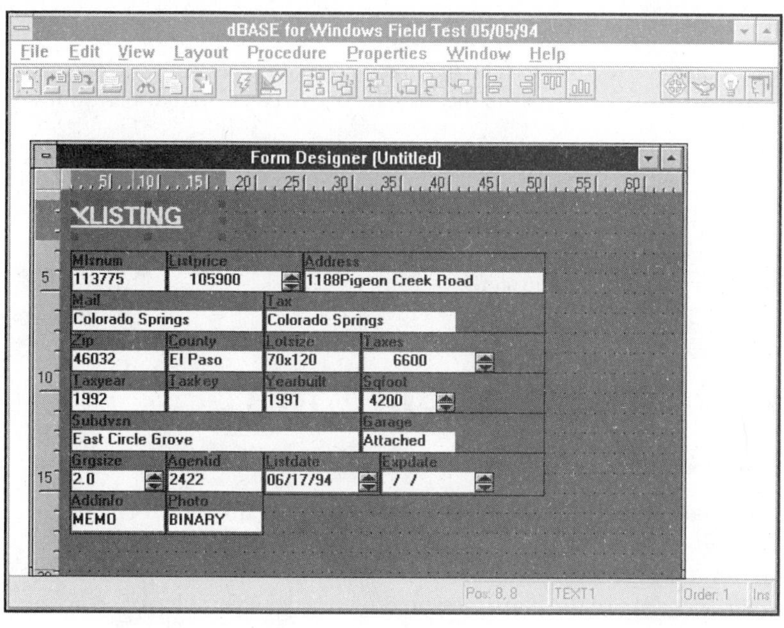

Figure 6.13
The form created by Form Expert.

Click **F**ile, **S**ave

The Create file window (see fig. 6.14) is displayed to enable you to name the file and save it to disk; the default extension is WFM, for **W**indows **F**or**M**

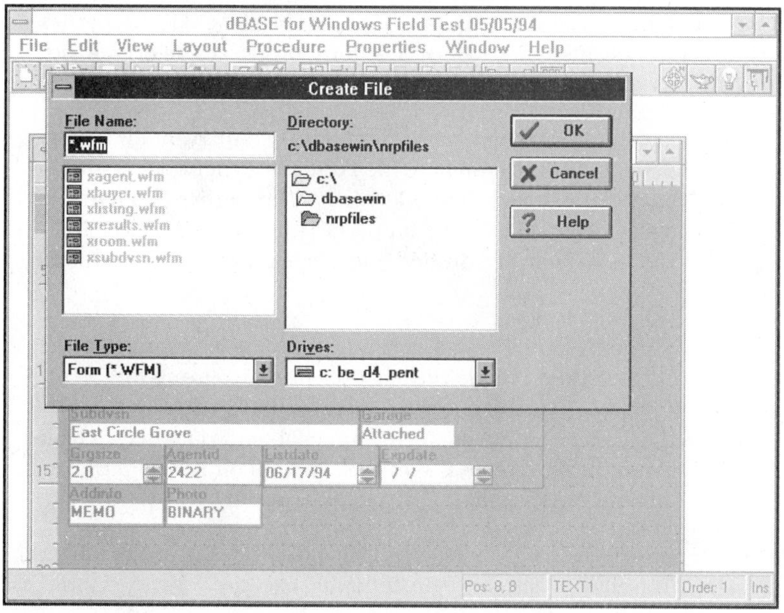

Figure 6.14
Save your file from the Create file window.

continues

continued

Type in a name and click on OK	The file that is created is a text file that contains all the dBASE code to create and display your form

The only additional step required to make this form completely usable is to add control buttons where you want them. See the section "Adding Buttons to Forms" later in this chapter for a description of the required steps.

Designing Forms by Using the Form Designer

You are now ready to start modifying your form—whether it is a blank form, one generated by the Form Designer, or an existing form. Using the Form Designer, you set the properties for your form, add and size objects, and associate data tables and queries. This section describes how you can use the Form Designer to make your form look and act exactly the way you want.

Using the Object Inspector Tool

The Object Inspector tool in the Form Designer enables you to change the properties associated with a form and the objects in the form. dBASE divides the object properties into three groups: Properties, Events and Methods. The form properties determine how the form appears to the user and functions during data input or display.

The Object Inspector is accessed through the Properties window. If this window is not currently open, you can open it now. After you have the Forms Designer open, right-click anywhere on the form. From the pop-up window, select Object Properties (from pull-down menus, select View, Object Properties). The Properties window (see fig. 16.15) displays all the properties of the form object, divided into a Properties tab, an Events tab, and a Methods tab.

Several of the lines in the Properties window show a (+) or (–) in the left margin. These indicate property groups or categories. Double-clicking on a property group with a (+) beside it opens a list of the properties in the group for modification or display. Double-clicking on the (–) closes the list, shortening the menu and enabling you to see all major properties and property groups on the screen. You can expand or contract all the groups by pressing Ctrl and the + or – on the keypad.

You can eliminate the groups entirely and change the listing of properties to alphabetical order using the Desktop Properties, as shown in the following exercise.

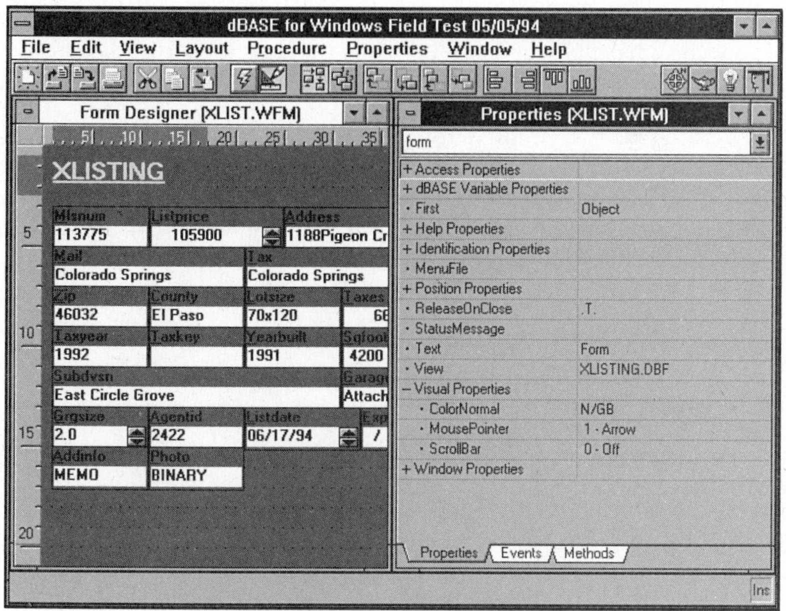

Figure 6.15
The Properties window lists the form properties.

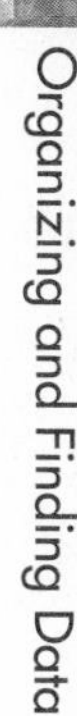

Using Desktop Properties to Change Property Listings

Double-click on Properties close bar	Close the Properties window
Select **P**roperties, **D**esktop Form Designer menu	The Desktop from the Properties window is displayed
Click on the Object Properties Outline checkbox	The check is cleared
Click on OK	The Desktop Properties window closes
Select View, Object Properties	The Properties window is opened with all the properties now shown in alphabetical order

Executing the same steps again turns the Object Properties Outline back on and resorts the properties into their groups.

Setting Form Properties

The properties of the form shown on the Properties tab include the position of the form window, what objects it contains, and how it acts in the Windows environment. These form properties are listed in table 6.1. Properties that are not in a property group are shown with (None) as a group name. Most of the properties can be modified to change the way the form appears or functions, except for the Identification Properties that are internal flags used by dBASE to track the form.

To ensure that you make a valid entry, most of the properties provide a list or selection window as indicated in table 6.1. If you type an invalid value in the Logical fields, dBASE sets the value to FALSE (.F.). If you try to type characters into the numeric fields, dBASE does not accept the input until numbers are typed. If you type an invalid number in the list fields, the error message "Value out of range" is displayed in an error window.

Table 6.1
Form Properties.

Group Property	Values
Access Properties	
Enabled	Logical. True if form is enabled. Option list available.
Visible	Logical. True if form is visible. Option list available.
dBASE Variable Properties	
objectname	Object. All named objects that have been placed on the form. Tool button moves the cursor to that object on the form and displays its properties in the Properties window.
(None)	
First	Object. First object on form. Selecting this moves the cursor to the first object and displays its properties in the Properties window.
Help Properties	
HelpFile	Fileid. Name of the HLP file containing Windows help text. Text entry with no validation.
HelpId	Text. The keyword searched for in the help text. Text entry with no validation.
Identification Properties	
ClassName	Text. Name of object. Unmodifiable.
hWnd	Number. Internal object identifier. Unmodifiable.

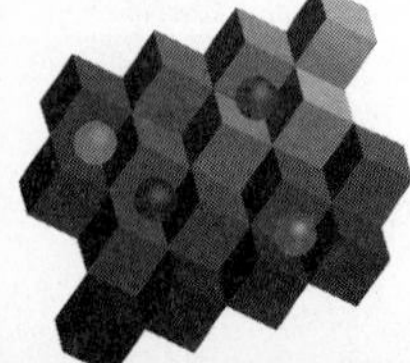

Group Property	Values
(None)	
MenuFile	FileId. Name of the file containing the menu. Tool button opens the Menu file dialog box.
Position	
Height	Number. Height in characters of the form. Scroll bar increments or decrements.
Left	Number. Characters from left of screen of the form. Scroll bar increments or decrements.
Top	Number. Characters from top of screen. Scroll bar increments or decrements.
Width	Number. Width in characters. Scroll bar increments or decrements.
(None)	
ReleaseOnClose	Logical. True to release the form on window close. Option list available.
StatusMessage	Text. Message for status line.
Text	Text. This is the title of the window that appears when the form is executed.
View	FileID. Indicates which view or table is used by the object. Tool button activates the select view/design query window.
Visual Properties	
ColorNormal	Foreground/background colors. Dialog box available from tool button. Validated against dBASE colors.
MousePointer	List. Shape of the mouse pointer. Option list available.
ScrollBar	List. Determines whether the scroll bars appears. Option list available.
Window Properties	
AutoSize	Logical. Whether window automatically sizes to contain the information. Option list available.

continues

Table 6.1, Continued
Form Properties

Group Property	Values
EscExit	Logical. Whether escape exits the window. Option list available.
Maximize	Logical. Whether the form has a maximize button in the upper right corner of the window. Option list available.
MDI	Logical. Whether the object meets Windows Multiple Document Interface specification. Option list available.
Minimize	Logical. Whether the window has a minimize button in the upper right corner of the window. Option list available.
Moveable	Logical. Whether the window is moveable. Option list available.
ScaleFontName	Text. Name of the font. Dialog box available from tool button. No validation.
ScaleFontSize	Number. Decimal font size in points. Scroll bar increments or decrements number.
Sizable	Logical. Whether the window can be resized using the mouse. Option list available.
SysMenu	Logical. Whether the window control menu is accessible from the button in the upper left corner of the window. Option list available.
WindowState	List. Whether the window is minimized, maximized, or normal. Option list available.

Some of these properties require a little more explanation. The Position group shows the position of the top left corner of the form in characters from the Desktop top left corner. The form size is then given by the height and width. Changing the values of these properties immediately is reflected in the position and size of the Form Designer window.

The View property enables you to associate your form to an existing query, view, or data table. By default, the value of the View property is the data table or view that was used to create the form. Entering a value in this field, or picking from the selection window, enables you access to any of the fields in the selected view or table. You can add these fields into your form later.

The MDI property determines whether a form meets the Windows Multiple Document Interface specification. This specification enables multiple child windows to run inside a parent window. If MDI is set to true (.T.), the properties for Moveable and Sizeable are ignored, because they must be true to meet the specification. Setting MDI makes your form a child of the dBASE application window. If you want your form to be independent of dBASE's application window, set this to false (.F.); otherwise, leave it true. Setting the MDI property to false makes your form *modal*, which means that it must be closed before any other window can be accessed. This state is normally used for dialog boxes in which the user must make a selection for the program to be able to continue.

The Moveable, Sizable, and SysMenu properties are required to be true for MDI forms. For a simple dialog box with an OK button, you can to set them to false. Currently the Form Designer does not allow these properties to be set to false, but you can modify the code that is generated by the Form Designer to change the values of these properties.

Select the Menu choice to associate a menu with your form. Click on the tool button to open the Choose Menu dialog box or type in the name of the menu to be used. This menu replaces the default dBASE form menu when the form is executed. If a menu name is already in the field, the Modify Menu Property window is displayed. This enables you to modify the current menu by starting the Menu Designer, or to open the Choose Menu dialog box to select a menu file.

Identifying Form Events

Click on the Events tab to display the list of events that can be used with the form (see fig. 6.16). Events detail how a form acts when various actions are performed. These actions include opening the form, moving from field to field, clicking, and closing the form. Each action that might occur in the form is listed, and the procedure to call when that action occurs is shown in the form.

By default, all procedure names are null, and the events are ignored by the form. If you want to have a global procedure for handling an event in the form, enter the procedure name in the event field for the form properties.

To create a global procedure for an event in your form, or for any event associated with any object in the form, use the Procedure Editor. Assuming the Properties window is already displayed with the Events tab selected, the following exercise adds an event handling procedure, or *event handler*, to the form.

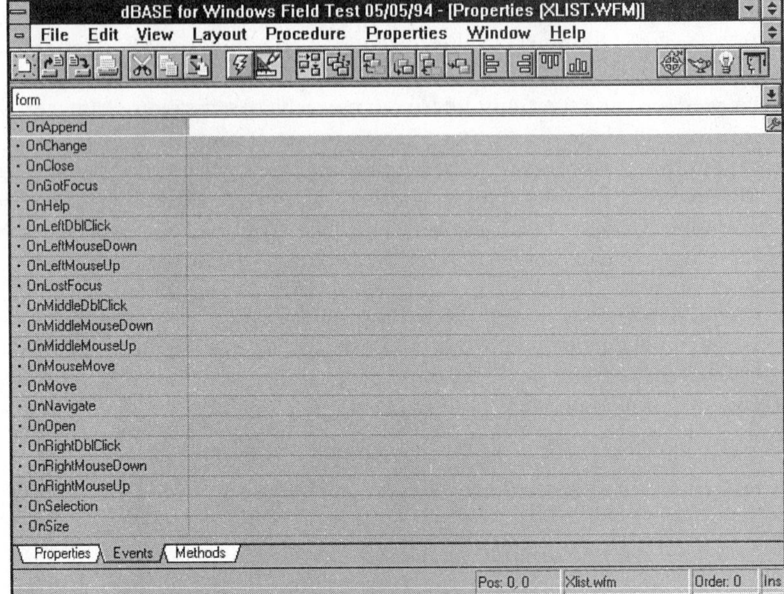

Figure 6.16 The Events tab in the Properties window.

Adding an Event Handling Procedure to a Form

Click on the form in the Form Designer window	This makes the form active and displays the events for the form
Click on OnHelp	The field opens with a tool button on the right
Click on the tool button	The Procedure Editor opens in the Procedure window (The default name for the event handler for OnHelp is in the window; the Procedure title is already entered)
Type in code	Form.StatusMessage = No Help Available
	Return
Click on the close bar	The Procedure window closes and the procedure name appears in the field OnHelp
Select <u>F</u>ile, <u>S</u>ave	Saves the form changes

Any executable dBASE commands can be placed in an event handler procedure. The above procedure displays a message on the status line when the F1 button is pressed that tells you no help is available. Using the Form.StatusMessage variable enables the procedure to be used on any form.

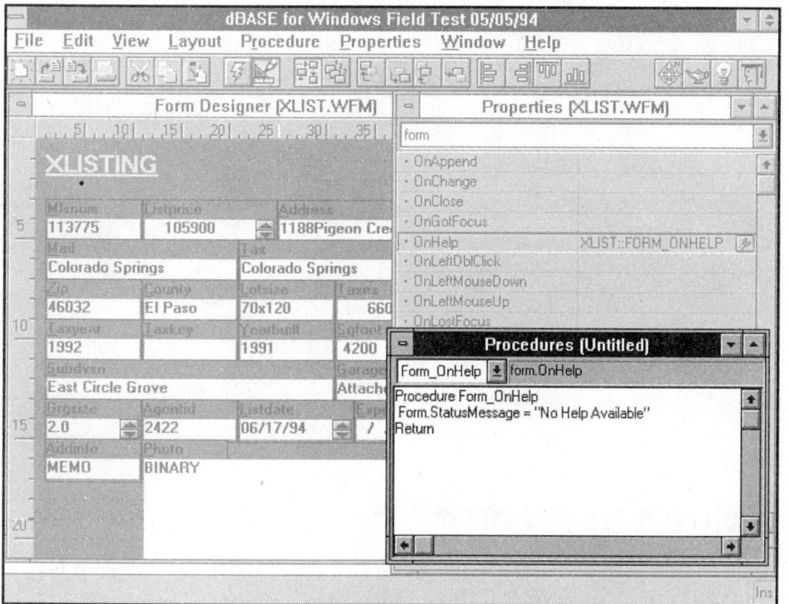

Figure 6.17
Writing an Event Handler in the Procedure window.

Identifying Form Methods

Select the Methods tab in the Properties window to display the methods associated with the form (see fig. 6.18). This tab is a reference page and is not directly modifiable by the user. Methods are procedures or functions that act on the properties defined in an object. The procedure or function can be defined in the object, or can be an external routine that is assigned to a property in the object. The methods listed include all the normal procedures that would enable the form to behave in a windows environment and that are required for a form. These include procedures to move, print, and close the window, and the procedures to move from field to field within the form. In addition, the procedures that were associated with events are shown on this tab under the dBASE Variables group.

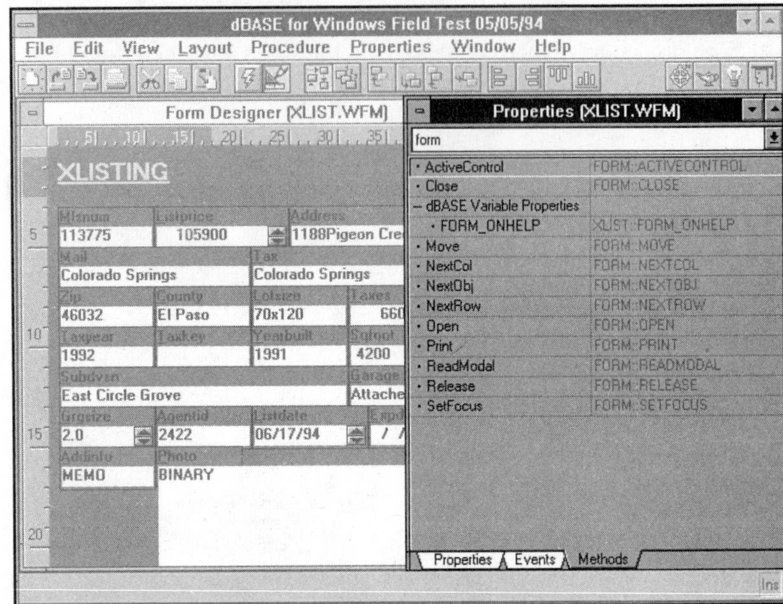

Figure 6.18 The Methods tab in the Properties window.

Adding Objects to a Form

After you have defined the form level properties for your form, you can add objects for data display, input, and action. You can add these objects to a new form, a form created by the Form Expert, or an existing form. The basic method of adding and placing objects is the same for all object types. Each object has certain properties you can set based on the data type of the object. From the Form Designer Speed Menu, click on Controls (or select View, Controls). This opens the Controls window with the standard controls shown as in figure 6.19. Additional controls are available on the custom tab as shown in figure 6.20.

Adding Controls

Controls are any of the field, text, and graphic objects that can be added to your form. Standard controls provide the basic text, field, and graphic objects. These controls are listed in table 6.2.

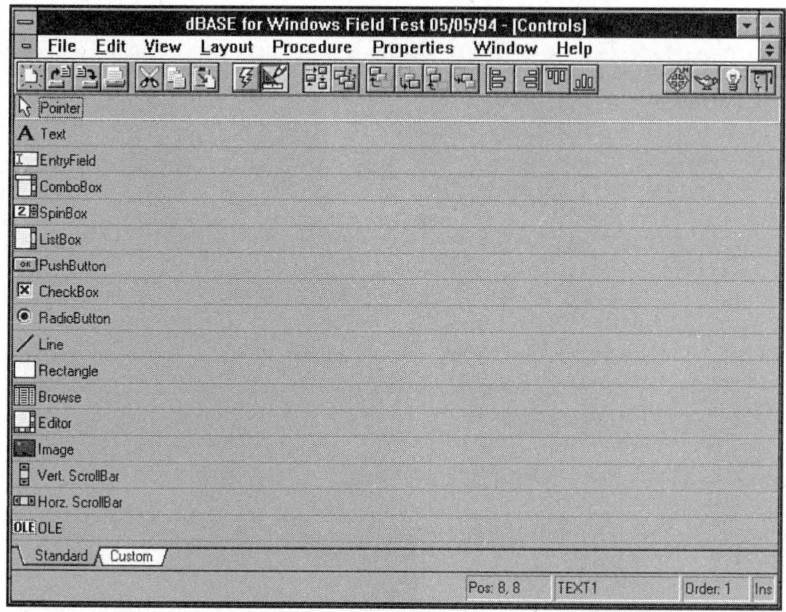

Figure 6.19
Standard objects available in the Controls window.

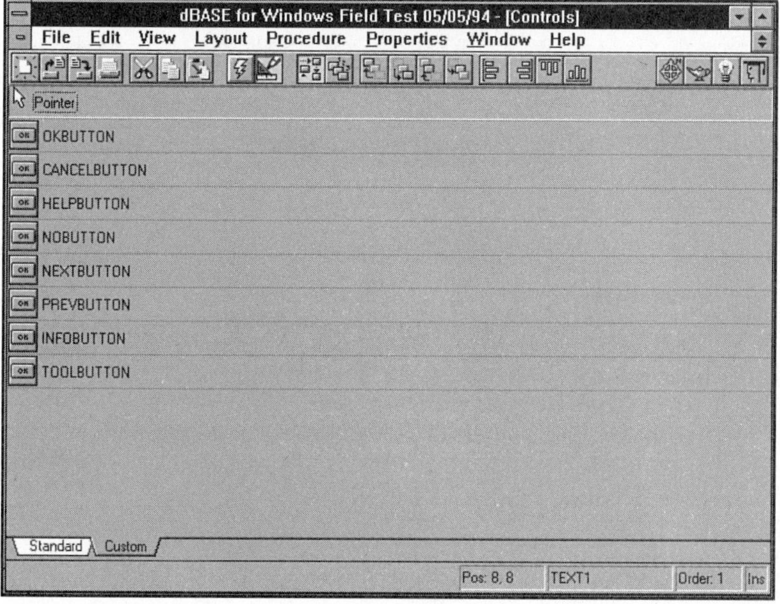

Figure 6.20
Custom objects available in the Controls window.

Table 6.2
Controls You Can Add to a Form

Control	Description
Text	Labels and information.
EntryField	A data field.
ComboBox	A data field with a selection list.
SpinBox	An increment/decrement data field.
ListBox	A selection list.
PushButton	A click selection button.
CheckBox	An on/off selection box.
RadioButton	A locking selection button.
Line	A line.
Rectangle	A rectangle for highlights.
Browse	A data browser box.
Editor	A file editor box.
Image	A bitmap image field.
VertScrollBar	A vertical scroll bar.
HorzScrollBar	A horizontal scroll bar.
OLE	An object linking and embedding reference field.

The Custom controls provide buttons that can be used to enhance the functionality of your form. Each of these buttons is shown as a raised rectangle when placed on the form, and each is completely resizable. The Custom tab provides the following buttons in table 6.3.

Table 6.3
Custom Control buttons

Control	Description
OKBUTTON	A button with OK and a check mark.
CANCELBUTTON	A button with CANCEL and an X.

Control	Description
HELPBUTTON	A button with HELP and a question mark.
NOBUTTON	A button with NO and a slashed circle.
NEXTBUTTON	A button with NEXT and a right arrow.
PREVBUTTON	A button with PREV and a left arrow.
INFOBUTTON	A button with INFO and an i in a circle.
TOOLBUTTON	A button with a wrench.

Additional custom controls can be added to the tab using the File, Set Custom Control choice from the menu. Custom controls can be either dBASE, dBX, controls stored as .CC files, or Visual Basic 1.0 controls stored as VBX files. To add a control to your palette, use the steps in the following exercise.

Adding a Control to Your Palette

Select File,Set Custom Controls	The Choose Custom Control dialog box is displayed
Select a file	The file name is inserted into the File Name field
Click OK	The dialog box closes and the control appears on the Custom tab in the Controls window

Any of the controls from the Standard or Custom tab can be added to your form. The basic procedure is the same for all the controls; use the following exercise to add the controls.

Adding Controls from the Standard or Custom Tab

Click on the Custom tab	The Custom control palette is displayed
Click on the OKBUTTON	The control shows as depressed on the control palette; you can also double-click and have the control immediately placed on the form
Move the cursor to the Form window	Cross hairs appear extending back to the rulers to enable exact placement of the control

continues

continued

Click where you want the button	The button is placed on the form with six active handles
Click and drag a handle	The button resizes to the size you want
Click and hold in the middle of the button	The cursor changes to a small hand enabling you to reposition the button
Drag the button and release	The button moves to the new position; repeat for each object; figure 6.21 shows a form with all the buttons and identifying text placed on it

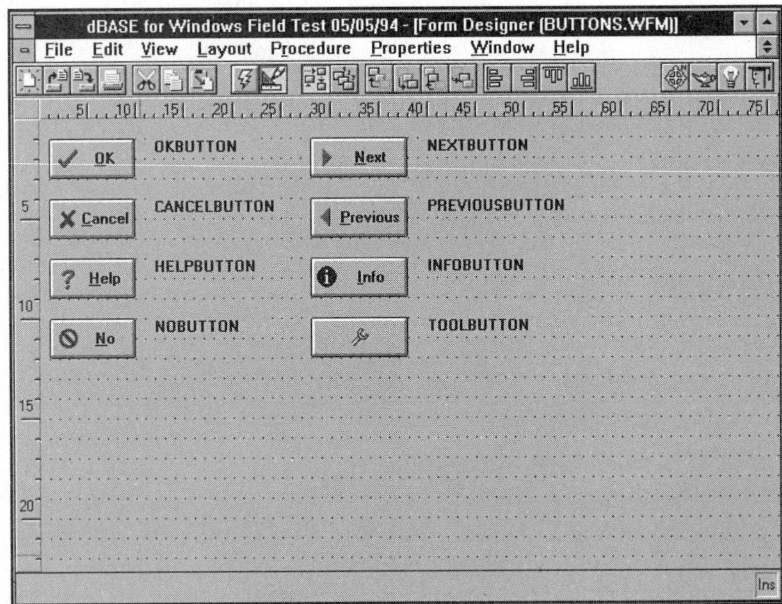

Figure 6.21 Form containing all the custom buttons.

After an object is placed on the form, you can select it by clicking on the object. The object is selected when the handles appear around it. As the active object, it can now be moved or the properties can be modified in the Properties window. If the Properties window was not left open, you can open it from Object Properties on the SpeedMenu or by selecting View, Object Properties. If the window was left open, but is not visible, you can select Windows, Properties to make it the active window.

Placing Text

To place text on your form, select the Text object from the Object Selector window. Follow the steps outlined in the preceding section, "Adding Controls," to place the text box on the form. The text box is added to the form with six handles shown. To size the box, move the mouse cursor to any of the handles, hold down the left button, and drag the mouse cursor. An outline box shows what the finished size is when you release the mouse button.

To modify the contents, you must change the properties of the text box. Activating the Properties window as detailed in the previous section enables you to modify the properties of the text box. Click on the Properties tab to display all the properties.

The default content of a text box is the name of the box, such as Text1. To change the contents of the box, use the Properties tab in the Properties window. The Text field shows the contents of the text box on the form. Click on the Text line to open the field for edit. Type in the text as you want it to appear on the form. The field contents do not wrap, and you cannot use carriage returns. As you type the text into the Text Property, the text appears on the form.

It is possible to type in more text than fits into your text box. The box on the form only displays as much text as will fit. Click on the text box on the form to select it. Drag the right handle until the box is long enough for all of your text to appear. The text does not appear until you release the mouse button.

The default font of the text box is the font selected for the form. To change the font, follow these steps:

Changing the Font

If the Font Properties group is not expanded, double-click on it to expand it.	The list of font properties expands, showing the font name, size, and styles (bold, italic, strikeout, underline)
Click on the FontName	The field is opened, and a tool button appears on the line
Click on the tool button	The Font Selection dialog box opens
Select the Font	The selected font name appears in the Font field, and the Sample changes to display the font
Select the Style	The selected style appears in the Font Style field and the Sample changes
Select the Effects	The Strikeout and Underline boxes are checked or unchecked and the Sample changes
Select the Size	The selected size appears in the Size field and the Sample changes

continues

continued

Click OK	The dialog box closes and all of the font properties are adjusted to match the selections made in the dialog box. The text box on the form displays the text in the selected font

Adding Other Fields to Forms

If you chose not to use the Form Expert, or you decide to add more fields from the data table after creating the form, you can select any of several data entry and display controls on the standard tab in the Controls window:

- ✔ The EntryField enables text entry into a fixed field.
- ✔ The ComboBox enables text entry into a fixed field with a selection list attached to the field.
- ✔ The SpinBox is usually used for the increment or decrement of values in the field.
- ✔ The ListBox is a fixed list of values that is always on the form.

An example of how this might be used can be seen in the form generated earlier with the Form Expert. The data table had a binary field that the Form Expert inserted into the form as a text EntryField. The following exercise starts with the Form Designer window, the Controls window, and the Properties window all open. To correct this problem, use the steps in the following exercise.

Adding More Fields to the Table Form

On the Form window, select the EntryField below the word Photo	Two error windows appear as dBASE tries to resolve the discrepancy between binary data and a text field
Click OK twice	The handles appear around EntryField15; the Properties window displays the properties of the field
Press Delete	EntryField15 is deleted from the form
Select Window, Controls	The Controls window is brought to the front
Select Image	The Image field is depressed to show that it is selected
Move the cursor to the Form window just below the word Photo	Crosshairs appear on the rulers to indicate placement

Click and drag until the outline is 35 characters wide and 5 characters high	The outline shows the size the box has on the form
Release the mouse	A blank box is placed on the form
Select Window, Properties	The Properties window is brought to front
Select Properties tab	The Properties of the field are listed
Select DataSource	The field opens and a tool button appears in the field
Click the tool button	The Choose Bitmap dialog box appears; you have a choice of Resources, Filename, or Binary for the Location
Click on the Location scroll bar and select Binary	The selection list closes and Binary is placed in the Location field
Click on the tool button beside Bitmap	The Choose Field dialog box appears
Double-click on the field name	The dialog box closes and the field name appears in the Bitmap field
Click OK	The data table field name is entered into the DataSource property; the image box on the form contains the bitmap from the data table
Select File, Save	Saves your changes

Adding Custom Controls

Every form normally requires at least one button for the user to acknowledge that he or she has read the screen. For a simple text box, the OK button is sufficient. For error boxes, an OK and a Cancel button might be required.

Adding custom control buttons was demonstrated as the generic example. Follow those steps to add any button.

If you prefer, you can resize the button by using any of the handles around the button, or drag the button to any location on the form. Click on the form outside the button to turn off the handles.

The buttons on the Custom tab are preprogrammed to act as expected for data-entry forms. OK accepts the changes into the data table. Cancel exits the form. Previous and Next move up and down the table one record at a time. You can modify the actions by changing the events associated with each button on the Events tab, the same way you do for the form. The info button has no predefined function and must be defined using event procedures if you want to use it.

Linking Form Objects to Data Table Fields

Your form now contains objects for displaying information from your data tables and views. Using the Properties window, you can assign specific fields from your data tables to objects on your form. The Data Linkage properties group provides information such as the field name or names associated with the object on the form. Depending on the object, the Data Linkage Properties group might or might not be shown. Certain objects only have one property from the group, and therefore the group is not provided. The Data Linkage Properties include the following:

- ✔ DataLink — The field name associated with a single value object: EntryField, SpinBox, ComboBox, Editor, and OLE.
- ✔ DataSource — The field name associated with a list object: ComboBox, ListBox, Image.
- ✔ Alias — The table name used in a Browse box.
- ✔ Fields — The fields displayed in a Browse box.
- ✔ Sorted — True if the entries in a ListBox or ComboBox should be sorted.
- ✔ Multiple — True enables the user to select more than one choice from a ListBox.

To assign a field from your data tables to a ComboBox object, use the following exercise.

Assigning a Field to a ComboBox Object

Click on a ComboBox on your Form	The handles appear indicating the object has been selected
Select <u>W</u>indow, Properties	The Properties window becomes active
Click on the Properties tab	The field properties are displayed
Click on DataSource	The property opens and a tool button appears in the field
Click on the tool button	The Choose Data Source dialog box appears
Click on the <u>T</u>ype scroll bar	You are provided a choice of source types: Array, Field, File, Structure, or Table

Click on Field	The list closes and Field is entered in the type field
Click on the tool button beside Data Source	If you have already assigned a view to this form, the Choose Field dialog box appears with the list of data tables and fields; otherwise the View Selection dialog box appears to let you chose a view or table
Double-click a field	This is the field that is used as the list of possible values for the field you associate with the DataLink property; the Choose Field dialog box closes and the field name is placed in the Choose Data Source dialog box
Click OK	The Choose Data Source dialog box closes and the field name is placed in the DataSource property
Click on DataLink	The property opens and a tool button appears in the field
Click on the tool button	The Choose Field dialog box appears
Double-click a field	The Choose Field dialog box closes and the field name is placed in the DataLink property

Linking Tables to Form Objects

Linking the table to the form is similar to linking the fields to the objects. The View property of the Form determines what data table or view is used for all the field names associated to objects on the form. If this property is not set before the Data Linkage Properties, you are prompted for a view to use to access field names. A selection made while setting Data Linkage Properties is not stored in the View property. To set the View property, use the following steps.

Setting the View Property

Click on the Form	Makes the form the active object
Select Window, Properties	Makes the Properties window active
Click on View	The property opens and a tool button appears in the field
Click on the tool button	The Choose View dialog box appears. You can select the disk and directory to search. You are given a choice of listing files of type VUE, QBE, DB or DBF

continues

continued

Select the disk, directory, and file type	The list of available files appears
Double-click on the file name	The dialog box closes and the view or table name is entered into the View property

Tying Tables Together on a Form

If you select a view or a query rather than a single data table for your field, you can have objects on the form reference any field in the view. You cannot have multiple tables referenced on the form unless a view has been created that includes those fields.

Using Your New Form

Forms are saved on the disk as WFM files. These files are listed in the Navigator window when the Forms icon is selected.

Running Your Form

To run your form, double-click on the form name in the Navigator window. Your form is opened in the default view.

Using Your Form with Other Tables

By opening the Form Designer on your form, you can modify any of the properties of the form. Use the Object Inspector tool in the Properties window. Select the View property, and press the tool button. You then can select a different view or table from the Choose View dialog box.

Make sure the chosen view or table has all the fields that you are referencing on your form. Otherwise, you generate an error.

Printing Your Form

While your form is running, select the Print icon from the menu bar. A print dialog box is displayed. You can change the printer and select whether to print all of the table or only a range of pages. Click on OK to print.

Part III

Using the dBASE for Windows Development Environment

Chapter Snapshot

Storing information in a database is useless unless you can retrieve the information when you need it and arrange it in some meaningful order. In this chapter, you learn about the following:

This chapter shows you how to create and manage table indexes and how to locate specific data. The next chapter shows you how you can use indexing to extract specific information through queries.

Indexing, Sorting, and Locating Your Data

By Virginia Andersen

You usually enter data into a database as you acquire that data, rather than entering the data in any particular order. Sometimes, however, the information you enter must appear in some logical arrangement, such as in alphabetic, numeric, or chronological order.

dBASE helps you organize your data. With dBASE, you have two methods for arranging table records: indexing and sorting. Indexing is faster and more efficient than sorting. It is also more versatile because it enables you to use complex key expressions based on combinations of fields, functions, and operators. Sorting simply copies the records to a new table in a new order—based on one or more field values.

If you want just to locate a specific record or range of records—rather than create a new table order with an index—you can use the dBASE basic search features. You can find records by record number, by record position, or by the value in a field. When dBASE finds the record, the record pointer is moved to it, and that record becomes the current record.

The exercises in this chapter use the exercise files on your *Inside dBASE for Windows Bonus Disk*. Follow the directions given in Appendix G to install and use the files on the bonus disk.

Exploring Ordering Techniques

When you open a table in dBASE, the records are displayed in *natural order*, which is by record number—reflecting the sequence in which they were entered into the table. The records are physically stored in the natural order. If you want to see them in a different order, you must rearrange them before you begin your application.

Ordering records in a table is a process of arranging the data in a meaningful way according to values found in a specified field or combination of fields. You have two methods of arranging records in numerical, alphabetical, or chronological order: by sorting or by indexing.

Sorting a table changes the physical order of the records (usually to a new table), but *indexing* changes only the logical order and leaves the records in their original sequence. An *index* is a separate file that contains the value of the key field and a pointer (usually the record number) to the position of the corresponding record in the table. You can liken a database table index to the index in the back of this book, which lists subjects and the page numbers where you can find information about the subjects. The information itself is not in the index.

Figures 7.1 through 7.3 show the results of sorting a table and indexing the same table.

The Deleted option in the Desktop Table Properties dialog box has been set off so you see the Deleted indicator boxes next to the record numbers and view records marked for deletion.

You have several advantages when indexing (rather than sorting) a table, including the following:

- ✔ Indexing is faster and more efficient than sorting because indexing creates a small index file, and sorting creates a complete new table file.
- ✔ Indexing requires less hard disk space.
- ✔ An open table index is automatically updated when you change table data, but you need to re-sort a sorted table to include any changes.

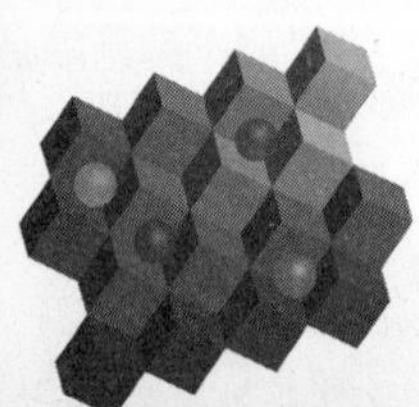

dBASE for Windows

File Edit View Table Properties Window Help

Table Records (XAGENT.DBF)

Rec	Del	AGENTID	LASTNAME	FIRSTNAME	COMPANY	PHONE
1		1002	Smothers	Regina	New Realtors	(719) 555-2200
2		1004	Louge	Sled	Better Homes & Gardens	(303) 555-6333
3		1195	Omlet	Peggy	Colorado Springs Realty	(719) 555-1207
4		1222	Miller	Sandra	Old Realty of Colorado	(719) 555-8820
5		1255	Robinson	Jack	Sell Em Realty	(719) 555-9805
6		2225	Wright	Tom	Century 21	(719) 555-1201
7		2257	Kochanek	Diane	Sell Em Realty	(719) 555-1205
8		2422	Waters	Sam	Colorado Springs Realty	(719) 555-5204
9		2677	Kuhns	Peter	Colorado Springs Realty	(317) 555-2020
10		2754	Pont	John	Century 21	(317) 555-2233
11		3502	Robinson	Cheri	Sell Em Realty	(317) 555-2020
12		3762	Betker	Rosie	Colorado Springs Realty	(317) 555-5830
13		4026	Mashburn	Roy	Sell Em Realty	(317) 555-2340
14		4187	Atkinson	Jane	Century 21	(317) 555-7909
15		4528	Brockway	Jack	Colorado Springs Realty	(317) 555-6071

Xagent.dbf Excl Rec 1/32 Ins

Figure 7.1
An example of a natural order table.

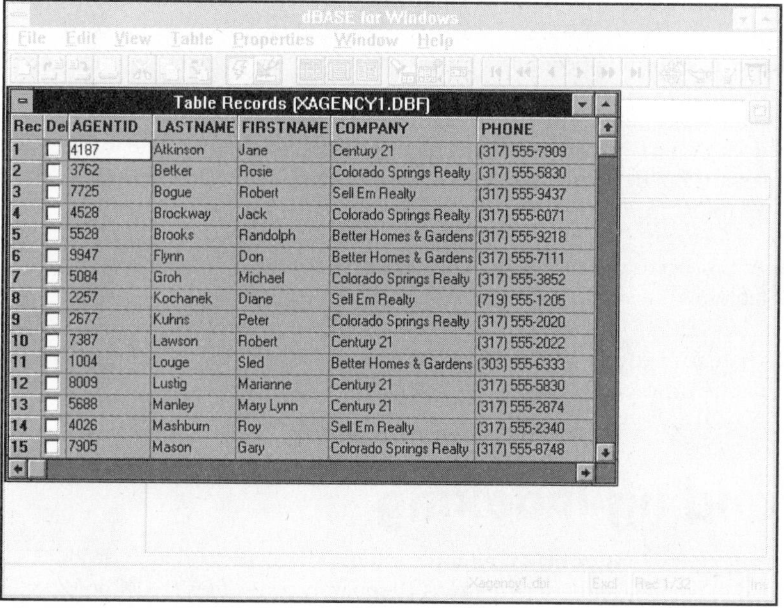

dBASE for Windows

File Edit View Table Properties Window Help

Table Records (XAGENCY1.DBF)

Rec	Del	AGENTID	LASTNAME	FIRSTNAME	COMPANY	PHONE
1		4187	Atkinson	Jane	Century 21	(317) 555-7909
2		3762	Betker	Rosie	Colorado Springs Realty	(317) 555-5830
3		7725	Bogue	Robert	Sell Em Realty	(317) 555-9437
4		4528	Brockway	Jack	Colorado Springs Realty	(317) 555-6071
5		5528	Brooks	Randolph	Better Homes & Gardens	(317) 555-9218
6		9947	Flynn	Don	Better Homes & Gardens	(317) 555-7111
7		5084	Groh	Michael	Colorado Springs Realty	(317) 555-3852
8		2257	Kochanek	Diane	Sell Em Realty	(719) 555-1205
9		2677	Kuhns	Peter	Colorado Springs Realty	(317) 555-2020
10		7387	Lawson	Robert	Century 21	(317) 555-2022
11		1004	Louge	Sled	Better Homes & Gardens	(303) 555-6333
12		8009	Lustig	Marianne	Century 21	(317) 555-5830
13		5688	Manley	Mary Lynn	Century 21	(317) 555-2874
14		4026	Mashburn	Roy	Sell Em Realty	(317) 555-2340
15		7905	Mason	Gary	Colorado Springs Realty	(317) 555-8748

Xagency1.dbf Excl Rec 1/32 Ins

Figure 7.2
An example of a table indexed by last name.

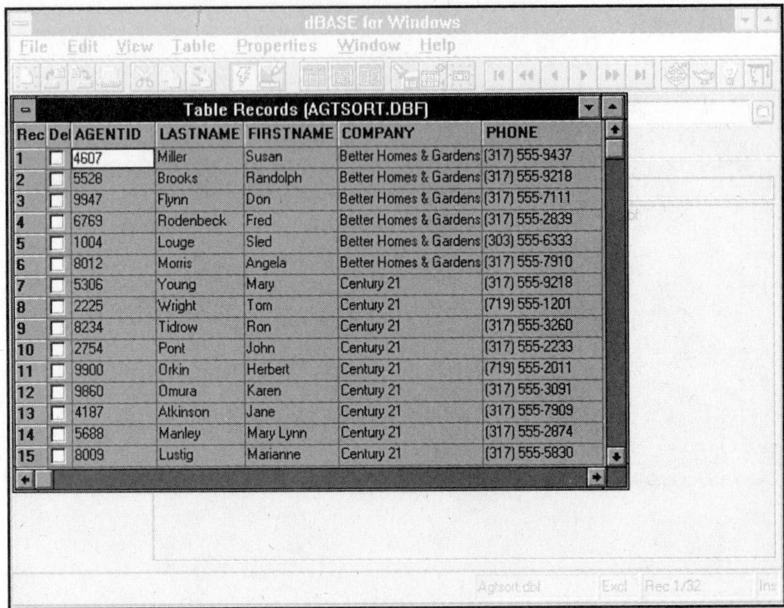

Rec	Del	AGENTID	LASTNAME	FIRSTNAME	COMPANY	PHONE
1		4607	Miller	Susan	Better Homes & Gardens	(317) 555-9437
2		5528	Brooks	Randolph	Better Homes & Gardens	(317) 555-9218
3		9947	Flynn	Don	Better Homes & Gardens	(317) 555-7111
4		6769	Rodenbeck	Fred	Better Homes & Gardens	(317) 555-2839
5		1004	Louge	Sled	Better Homes & Gardens	(303) 555-6333
6		8012	Morris	Angela	Better Homes & Gardens	(317) 555-7910
7		5306	Young	Mary	Century 21	(317) 555-9218
8		2225	Wright	Tom	Century 21	(719) 555-1201
9		8234	Tidrow	Ron	Century 21	(317) 555-3260
10		2754	Pont	John	Century 21	(317) 555-2233
11		9900	Orkin	Herbert	Century 21	(719) 555-2011
12		9860	Omura	Karen	Century 21	(317) 555-3091
13		4187	Atkinson	Jane	Century 21	(317) 555-7909
14		5688	Manley	Mary Lynn	Century 21	(317) 555-2874
15		8009	Lustig	Marianne	Century 21	(317) 555-5830

Figure 7.3 An example of a table sorted by company.

- ✔ When you add records to an indexed table, the new records automatically fall into their appropriate places. If you add records to a sorted table, you must re-sort before the new records appear in the proper positions.
- ✔ An index can order data on a single field or on an expression composed of fields combined with operators and functions, but sorting relies only on field values. The Expression Builder, discussed later in this chapter, helps you construct valid expressions to use in your indexes.
- ✔ Some dBASE procedures such as searches, queries, and table linking require indexed tables.

Sorting is appropriate for exporting tables to another application or for creating temporary tables for separate processing.

Understanding Indexing

dBASE supports two types of index files: a multiple index (MDX) file and an individual index (NDX) file. Each table can have as many as 10 separate index files (NDX or MDX) open at one time. Each MDX index file can contain up to 47 separate index orders, each of which represents an arrangement of records.

A special MDX file is the *production index,* which opens automatically when you open the table and is maintained as you make changes in the data. The production index file bears the same name as the table. You must assign names to the other MDX files. You also must name the NDX files when you create them.

The index orders that are included in a multiple index file are called *tags*—each of which represents a record order and has a meaningful name. Only one index, called the *controlling* or *master index*, can be in control at a time. The other indexes can be active—that is, they can be open and are updated automatically as changes are made in the record data; only one index, however, can determine the logical order of records in the table. You can change the order of records in the table by changing the controlling index as often as you like during a session. An index can order records in ascending or descending order.

An NDX index contains a single sorting order. The NDX index file capability is maintained primarily to provide compatibility with earlier versions of dBASE. If you have an application from a previous version of dBASE, you can convert the NDX files to tags in an MDX file or keep them as separate single indexes. But then you must remember to open each one when you begin a session; otherwise, they are not kept current.

Planning the Table Indexing Scheme

Although you can modify, add, or delete indexes at any time, the best approach is to plan ahead and try to identify the indexes you will need and create them when you structure the table. You might need one or more indexes to do the following:

- ✔ Enter or edit data
- ✔ Look up data
- ✔ Run queries
- ✔ Print reports
- ✔ Relate multiple tables

Deciding the types of indexes you need depends not only on what you want to do, but also on what you know already. You might, for example, want to change the phone number for customer #123. You already know the customer number, and if the table is indexed on that field, you can go right to it and change the phone number. If you expect to be modifying a key field, you should not set a master index until you have finished editing the table. After you have set the corresponding index as the master index, the record is immediately repositioned and seems to disappear each time you change a value in the key expression. That situation gets confusing.

You might want to index on the results of a calculation. Suppose, for example, that you want a list of contributors to your charity who have not sent any donations for 90 days. In that case, you should index on an expression that calculates the number of days between the date of the last contribution and the current date. Then add the conditional indexing option FOR to limit the list of donors to those with a key expression value equal to or greater than 90.

If you plan to create queries for the table, try to anticipate what types of questions will be asked. A query might ask, for example, for the addresses of all contributors in California, in order by ZIP code. A simple index on the ZIP code field used as the controlling index is useful.

Look at the reports that the user expects to print from the table data, and find out in what order the records should appear and what calculations are needed to summarize the information. If the quarterly report of sales needs to be grouped by sales district, for example, you need an index to arrange that order.

A Note from the Author

In my experience, you think you have gleaned from all possible requirements for printed reports. Every sort order, every aggregation and summary has been defined. Then, when you present the finished product, the user is inspired to imagine additional arrangements and formats. Luckily, dBASE is so flexible that it is easy to do and once more you become a hero.

You might want to create a list of records with only one record for each of the key values. Suppose, for example, that you want a list of unique part numbers for a certain aircraft subassembly. Choose the Unique option when you create an index on the part number field to display only one occurrence of each value.

If the application requires two or more tables to be related by common fields, you need to know which fields are the common fields and then construct indexes using those fields as keys. In a one-to-many relationship, for example, the child table (the table on the many side) must be indexed on the common field.

You might want to include in the production index all the frequently used indexes, and then group the less-used indexes in another MDX file according to the associated application. Updating indexes takes time, especially when your tables get large and you have many indexes. You can use infrequently used record orders, for example, in the preparation of the company's annual report or an income tax summary. You must open and update the nonproduction MDX and the NDX files before using them, because they are not automatically kept current as you work with the table data.

You also can create a temporary index to use for infrequent tasks. No maintenance is involved if you create it just before you need it, and then erase it when the task is completed. You can save time and disk space with temporary indexes.

Creating and Using Multiple Index Files (MDX)

You have two ways to create a new index: from the Table Designer or through the Create Index dialog box—depending on the complexity of the index. If you plan a simple index based on a field value, the Table Designer is easier, but you can use the Create Index dialog box if you want to create several indexes for the same table at the same time. If the index is to involve multiple fields or include an operator or function in the key expression, you must use the Index Designer.

If you need to create a new single index (NDX) file, use the command window and the INDEX ON command. NDX files are discussed later in this chapter (see "Creating and Using Single Index Files (NDX)").

Adding a Simple Index in the Table Structure

A simple index is defined by a single key field that you can specify in the table structure. To add a simple index to your table, open the Table Designer, and change the structure to include the index field. You can add a simple index to the XLISTING.DBF table on your bonus disk. Follow the steps in the following exercise.

Adding an Index to the XLISTING.DBF

Make sure that you are in the exercise working directory; then click on the Tables icon in the Navigator window	A list of the available tables is displayed
Double-click on the XLISTING.DBF table icon and choose Design Table Structure from the Table Space Menu (alternatively, select the table name in the Navigator, then click the table design button, which is shown in figure 7.4)	The XLISTING.DBF table is displayed
Move to the MLSNUM field (Multiple Listing Service Number), click on the word None in the Index column shown in Figure 7.4, then click on the down arrow	The pull-down menu of options is displayed: None, Ascend, and Descend
Select Ascend from the list of index options and then click on the View Table button	You are returned to the browse screen
Choose Yes when asked whether you want to save the changes	The new structure is saved

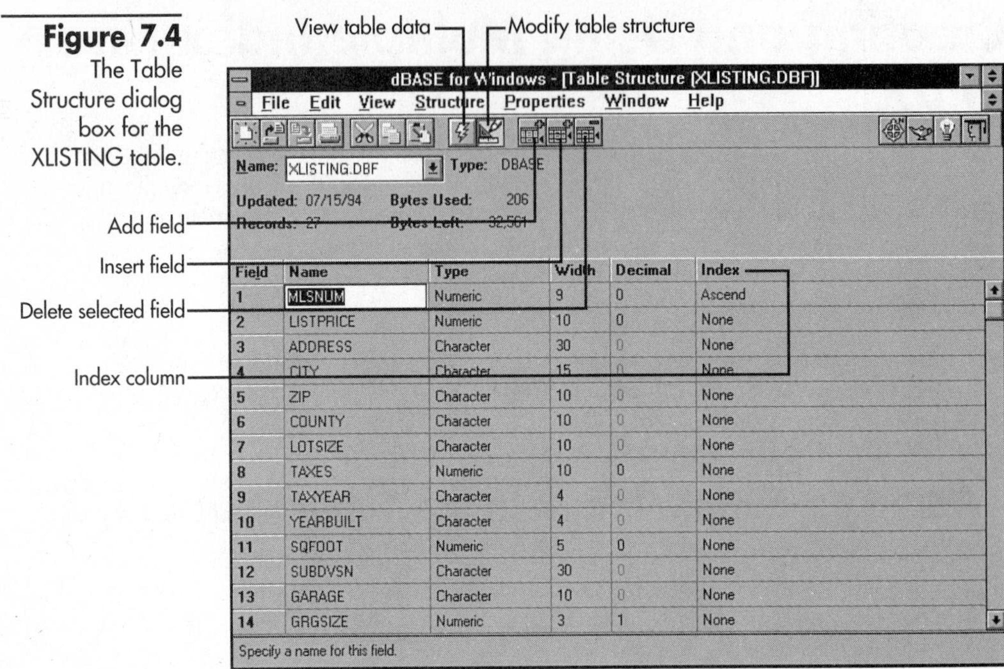

Figure 7.4 The Table Structure dialog box for the XLISTING table.

The records are still in their natural order. To change to the index order you just created, you must set it as the master index. Follow these steps:

Changing the Index Order

Select Table, Table Utilities, Manage Indexes	The Manage Indexes dialog box appears, see figure 7.5
Select MLSNUM and choose OK	The browse screen is refreshed with the records in the new order, ascending by MLSNUM, as shown in figure 7.6 (The columns have been resized to get more fields in the display window)

Keep the XLISTING table open for the next exercise.

If some of the records seem to disappear, they might be repositioned above the current record and not be visible on-screen. Scroll up to see the hidden records.

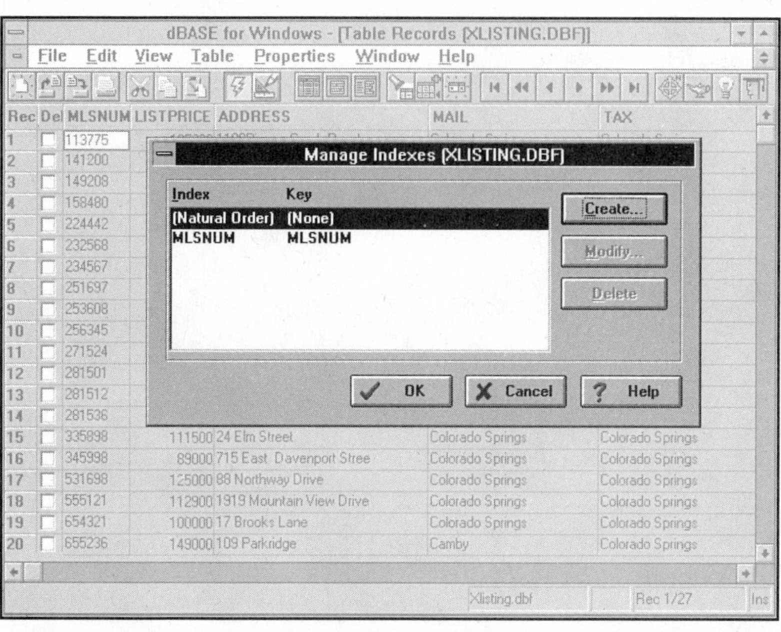

Figure 7.5
Use the Manage Indexes dialog box to set the master index.

dBASE for Windows - [Table Records (XLISTING.DBF)]

File Edit View Table Properties Window Help

Rec	Del	MLSNUM	LISTPRICE	ADDRESS	CITY	ZIP	COUNTY
1	☐	113775	105900	1188 Pigeon Creek Road	Colorado Spring	46032	El Paso
2	☐	141200	49900	1420 Rosemary Lane	Colorado Spring	46290	El Paso
3	☐	149208	113900	2828 North Downer Avenue	Colorado Spring	46280	Teller
4	☐	158480	69900	1820 East Olive Street	Colorado Spring	46280	Teller
5	☐	224442	124900	10 South Street	Colorado Spring	46032	Boone
6	☐	232568	165000	3220 Champaigne Drive	Colorado Spring	46019	El Paso
7	☐	234567	123000	1011 West Lake Side	Colorado Spring	46032	El Paso
8	☐	251697	92900	4211 Morris Boulevard	Colorado Spring	46280	Teller
9	☐	253608	114400	1127 Lake View Blvd	Colorado Spring	46032	El Paso
10	☐	256345	162900	4200 North Morris Bouleva	Colorado Spring	46280	Teller
11	☐	271524	92000	1011 West Lake Side	Colorado Spring	46032	El Paso
12	☐	281501	159500	1070 Peach Street	Colorado Spring	46033	Teller
13	☐	281512	136000	10 W Wabash Street	Colorado Spring	46032	El Paso
14	☐	281536	95000	300 South Shore Drive	Colorado Spring	46033	Teller
15	☐	335898	111500	24 Elm Street	Colorado Spring	46280	Dennison
16	☐	345998	89000	715 East Davenport Stree	Colorado Spring	46032	Boone
17	☐	531698	125000	88 Northway Drive	Colorado Spring	46280	Boone
18	☐	555121	112900	1919 Mountain View Drive	Colorado Spring	46032	El Paso
19	☐	654321	100000	17 Brooks Lane	Colorado Spring	46032	Marion
20	☐	655236	149000	109 Parkridge	Camby	46032	Wyvern

Xlisting.dbf Rec 1/27 Ins

Figure 7.6
This screen shows the XLISTING table records in the MLSNUM order.

The index is given the name of the key field and is included in the production index, unless you create the index (instead of specifying the key field in the table structure) and give it a different name. Remember that when you close the table file, the records remain in the natural (record number) order.

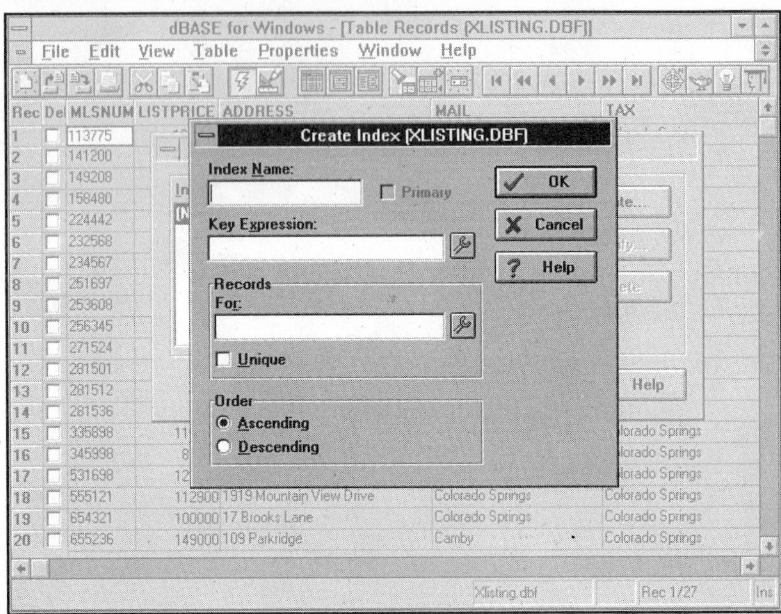

Figure 7.7
The Create Index dialog box.

Adding a Complex Index with the Index Designer

When a simple, single field index is insufficient to give you the record order you want, you can create a complex index. A complex index can include multiple fields and expressions.

You use the Create Index dialog box shown in figure 7.7 to build the table index. Creating a complex index for your table involves four basic steps:

1. Name the index
2. Specify the key expression
3. Add a filter to limit the records in the index, if desired
4. Specify the sort order—ascending or descending

Details of each of the preceding steps are presented in the following sections.

Understanding dBASE Expressions

An *expression* is a combination of one or more dBASE elements such as fields, functions, operators, constants, memory variables, and array elements that evaluates to a single value in a single data type. The expression value might be a character, date, logical, or numeric data type. The expression evaluates to a logical value if it is used with an IFF conditional command. You can use several data types within the expression, but you must convert them to the same type for evaluation, usually character.

Specific rules apply to constructing an index key expression:

- ✔ The expression must be a valid dBASE expression with proper syntax.
- ✔ The expression must contain at least one field name.
- ✔ If you use more than one field name, you must concatenate them with a plus (+) or minus (–) sign.
- ✔ Concatenated fields must be of the same data type. If they are not, you must convert them to the same type before connecting them in the expression.
- ✔ The expression can contain as many as 220 characters, but the key itself (the value returned by the expression) can contain no more that 100 characters.

The following examples are valid single-element expressions:

YEARBUILT evaluates to the value in that field.

The date {01/01/95} evaluates to itself.

"IN" evaluates to the character string *IN*.

You can use dBASE functions in the key expression. The key expression is case-sensitive, so if you are using character fields in the index, convert the text format with the UPPER() function so that all values are in uppercase. The SUBSTR() function enables you to index on a portion of an otherwise long character field. Usually only the first few characters are required to differentiate among records anyway.

The following examples use functions and operators in expressions:

- ✔ The expression CMONTH(12/01/94) evaluates to December.
- ✔ The expression 1500*1.05+10 evaluates to 1585.
- ✔ The expressions UPPER(SUBDVSN)+", "+UPPER(AGENTID)+", "+DTOS(LISTDATE) might evaluate to Cheyenne Mountain, 1002, November 30, 1994, depending on the values in the current record.
- ✔ The expression SUBSTR(LASTNAME,1,3) evaluates to the first three characters in the LastName field.
- ✔ The expression STR(PRICE) converts the numeric value in the Price field to a character string.

When you index on a numeric or float field, you also can choose to use only part of the field. Use the INT() function, for example, to limit the comparison to the integer portion of the number.

✔ The expression INT(15.764) evaluates to 15.

When indexing on a date field, be sure to convert the date to a chronological format that puts the year first, YYYY/MM/DD or YY/MM/DD. If you index on the month, be sure to use the numeric value function MONTH() rather than the character function CMONTH() because the months do not occur in alphabetic order.

Creating the Key Expression

To begin creating a complex index, you open the Manage Indexes dialog box shown earlier in figure 7.5. From there, you create a new index tag.

In the following exercise, you create an index that orders records in the XLISTING table by subdivision and MLS number. Follow these steps:

Indexing by Subdivision and MLS Number

If you are currently in the Table Editor, select Table, Table Utilities, Manage Indexes — The Manage Indexes dialog box is displayed, as shown in figure 7.5

Choose Create — The Create Index dialog box appears, as shown earlier in figure 7.7

Enter **SUBDVSN** in the Index Name text box and click in the Key Expression text box — The Key Expression box is where you enter the expression that will form the index

Enter the following expression:

UPPER(SUBDVSN)+STR(MLSNUM)

Leave the For condition blank for now, and accept the default unchecked Unique option and Ascending order — Your screen should now look something like figure 7.8

Choose OK to save the index structure — The new tag appears in the Manage Indexes dialog box

dBASE builds the index after you choose OK, so the process might take some time if your table is large or the key expression is complex.

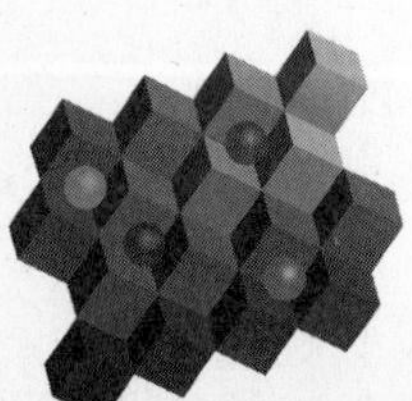

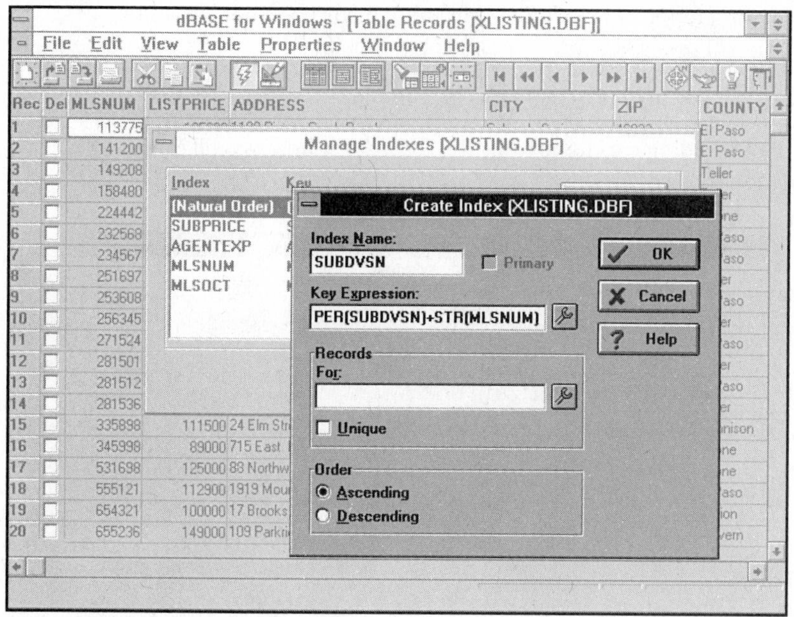

Figure 7.8
The Create Index dialog box, all filled out.

Select the new index in the Manage Indexes dialog box, and choose OK	Your XLISTING table should appear in the new index order first by subdivision, then by MLS number within the subdivision group, as shown in figure 7.9 (the subdivision field was moved so that you could see it on the screen with the MASNUM field)

Limiting the Records in the Index

You usually want to include all the records in the index, but you do have the option of including only a specific set of records. Limiting the index to a subset of records improves the efficiency of the index. Use the For condition option in the Create Index Tag dialog box to set up the filter for records that are scattered throughout the table.

A *For condition* is an expression that specifies which records are to be processed. dBASE examines each record and compares the evaluated expression to the condition expression; it then decides whether to include the record in the index. A For condition always starts at the top of the table and considers all the records. Suppose, for example, that you want information for a report that includes only those records for homes built in 1993 and 1994. Enter the following condition in the For text box:

YEARBUILT="1993" .OR. YEARBUILT="1994"

After entering the preceding condition, only the records for homes built in those two years are included in the index.

Figure 7.9 The XLISTING table in the SUBDVSN (tag name) order.

dBASE for Windows - [Table Records (XLISTING.DBF)]

File Edit View Table Properties Window Help

Rec	Del	MLSNUM	LISTPRICE	SUBDVSN	ADDRESS	CITY	ZIP
9	☐	253608	114400	Broadmoor Circle	1127 Lake View Blvd	Colorado Spring	46032
17	☐	531698	125000	Broadmoor Circle	88 Northway Drive	Colorado Spring	46280
27	☐	890360	139900	Broadmoor Circle	4509 West Gramercy Way	Colorado Spring	46032
2	☐	141200	49900	Cheyenne Mountain	1420 Rosemary Lane	Colorado Spring	46290
5	☐	224442	124900	Cheyenne Mountain	10 South Street	Colorado Spring	46032
8	☐	251697	92900	Cheyenne Mountain	4211 Morris Boulevard	Colorado Spring	46280
11	☐	271524	92000	Cheyenne Mountain	1011 West Lake Side	Colorado Spring	46032
14	☐	281536	95000	Cheyenne Mountain	300 South Shore Drive	Colorado Spring	46033
16	☐	345998	89000	Cheyenne Mountain	715 East Davenport Stree	Colorado Spring	46032
1	☐	113775	105900	East Circle Grove	1188 Pigeon Creek Road	Colorado Spring	46032
3	☐	149208	113900	East Circle Grove	2828 North Downer Avenue	Colorado Spring	46280
4	☐	158480	69900	East Circle Grove	1820 East Olive Street	Colorado Spring	46280
7	☐	234567	123000	East Circle Grove	1011 West Lake Side	Colorado Spring	46032
10	☐	256345	162900	Garden of the Gods Highlands	4200 North Morris Bouleva	Colorado Spring	46280
12	☐	281501	159500	Garden of the Gods Highlands	1070 Peach Street	Colorado Spring	46033
19	☐	654321	100000	Garden of the Gods Highlands	17 Brooks Lane	Colorado Spring	46032
22	☐	697762	54900	Garden of the Gods Highlands	2037 Sheffield Court	Security	80229
6	☐	232568	165000	Mountain Shadows	3220 Champaigne Drive	Colorado Spring	46019
13	☐	281512	136000	Mountain Shadows	10 W Wabash Street	Colorado Spring	46032
15	☐	335898	111500	Mountain Shadows	24 Elm Street	Colorado Spring	46280

A Note from the Author

I have found that using conditional indexes saves a lot of time when you are creating reports based on a small amount of records in a large table. When I design the report format, I base it on the indexed table.

In the following exercise, you create a conditional index that limits the records indexed to only the homes listed before October. Follow these steps:

Creating a Conditional Index

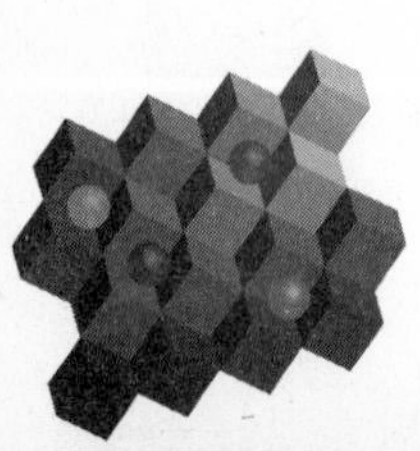

With the XLISTING table open, select Table, Table Utilities, Manage Indexes	The Manage Indexes dialog box reopens

Select Create	The Create Index dialog box opens
Enter **MLSOCT** in the Index Name text box and enter **MLSOCT** in the Key Expression text box	The Create Index dialog box also can specify filtering conditions
Click in the For text box, and enter **MONTH(LISTDATE)<10** as the condition	The dialog box now looks like figure 7.10

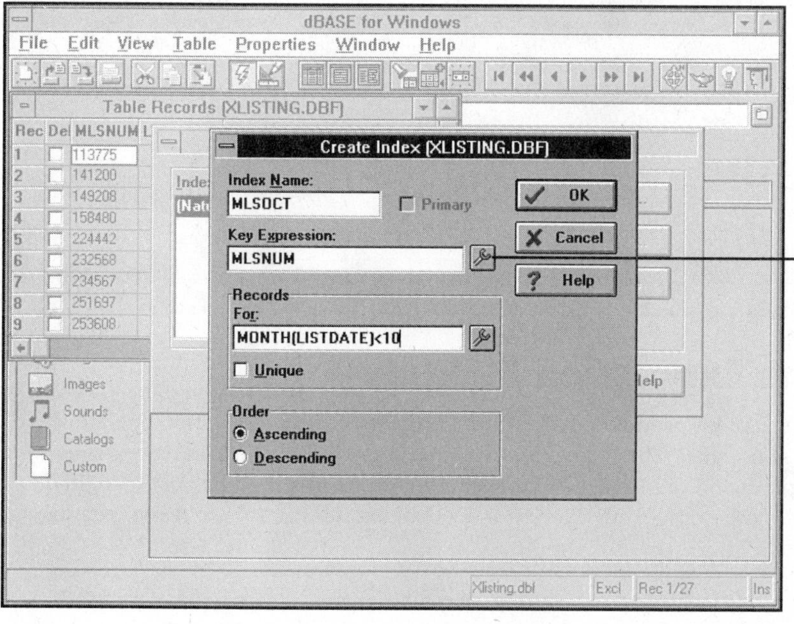

Figure 7.10 The completed MLSOCT tag in the Create Indexes dialog box.

Choose OK	You are returned to the Manage Indexes dialog box
Select the new tag, MLSOCT, to highlight it, then choose OK	

The screen now shows, in MLS number order, only those listings that were made prior to October (see fig. 7.11). The LISTDATE field has been moved left so that you can see it with the MLSNUM field. (Keep the table open for the next exercise.)

If you are unfamiliar with entering expressions, you can click on the Expression Builder tool button (shown in figure 7.8) and get help with building an expression for the For clause.

Figure 7.11
Viewing records for properties listed before October.

dBASE for Windows - [Table Records (XLISTING.DBF)]

File Edit View Table Properties Window Help

Rec	Del	MLSNUM	LISTPRICE	LISTDATE	ADDRESS	CITY	ZIP	COUN
1		113775	105900	06/17/94	1188 Pigeon Creek Road	Colorado Spring	46032	El Paso
3		149208	113900	09/24/94	2828 North Downer Avenue	Colorado Spring	46280	Teller
6		232568	165000	01/13/94	3220 Champaigne Drive	Colorado Spring	46019	El Paso
7		234567	123000	08/12/94	1011 West Lake Side	Colorado Spring	46032	El Paso
9		253608	114400	07/31/94	1127 Lake View Blvd	Colorado Spring	46032	El Paso
10		256345	162900	08/12/94	4200 North Morris Bouleva	Colorado Spring	46280	Teller
11		271524	92000	07/31/94	1011 West Lake Side	Colorado Spring	46032	El Paso
13		281512	136000	09/23/94	10 W Wabash Street	Colorado Spring	46032	El Paso
15		335898	111500	08/15/94	24 Elm Street	Colorado Spring	46280	Dennisc
16		345998	89000	09/12/94	715 East Davenport Stree	Colorado Spring	46032	Boone
17		531698	125000	03/14/94	88 Northway Drive	Colorado Spring	46280	Boone
18		555121	112900	08/23/94	1919 Mountain View Drive	Colorado Spring	46032	El Paso
20		655236	149000	07/15/94	109 Parkridge	Camby	46032	Wyvern
25		890358	400520	09/25/94	677 East Oliphant Avenue	Woodland Park	80962	Teller

Using the Expression Builder

The Expression Builder provides a handy tool for those of you who are not familiar with dBASE expression syntax. The Expression Builder helps you assemble an expression out of dBASE elements and validates the expression before pasting it in the current field or window. You can use this tool anywhere you need an expression, such as when creating an index or a query.

You can type the expression directly into the Expression box, or select parts of the expression from a list and paste them into the expression as you build it. The Safety Net feature of the Expression Builder keeps you from creating an invalid expression. The Evaluate option enables you to test an expression and compute the results based on values in the current record.

The basic steps in creating a key expression, using the Expression Builder tool, include the following:

1. Open the Expression Builder from the Create Index dialog box.
2. Set the Safety Net on or off, as you prefer. The Safety Net will help prevent you from creating an invalid expression.
3. Select elements from the Category, Type, and Paste list boxes and paste the elements into the Expression box, or type them directly into the Expression box.

4. Replace any placeholders with valid expressions, values, or operators, and edit the constant elements.

5. Group the elements to set the precedence of evaluation, as necessary.

6. Evaluate the expression, if you prefer.

A For condition always evaluates to either True or False because it decides whether to include a record in the index or query.

7. Paste the expression in the Create Indexes dialog box.

The Safety Net feature helps inexperienced users build an expression with all the required elements in the proper syntax. When the Safety Net is turned on, the Expression box turns gray, and you cannot type the expression directly into it. You must paste all elements from the Paste list box.

With the Safety Net turned off, the Expression box turns white, and you can type elements in as well as paste from the list box. You also can cut, copy, and paste from the Clipboard.

Decide whether you want the **S**afety Net on or off before you begin to build the expression. You can't turn it on or off later unless the **E**xpression box is empty or contains a valid, complete expression.

To activate the Expression Builder, click on the Tool button next to the Key Expression text box in the Create Index dialog box. The resulting Build Expression dialog box (shown in fig. 7.12) contains three lists in boxes beneath the window where you create the expression. The boxes are progressively more specific as you move left to right. The leftmost box, the Category box, always contains the list of major dBASE element categories: Constant, Field, Function, Operator, and Variable. The other two lists vary in content, depending on choices made in the previous boxes.

A Note from the Author

In addition to creating valid expressions for indexes, I found that the Expression Builder is a great help in debugging an expression I want to use in a program. I don't have to wait for the compiler to give me an error message. I can debug my expression syntax in the Build Expression dialog box.

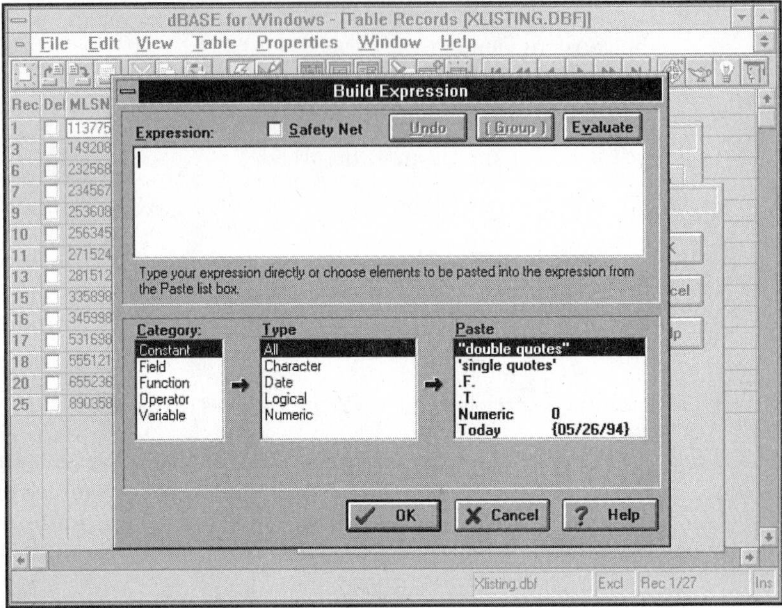

Figure 7.12 The Build Expression dialog box of the Expression Builder.

Selecting Elements

When you make a selection from the Category list, the second subcategory list displays a list of more specific element classes. If you click on the Constant category in the first list, for example, the second box is titled Type and contains a list of constant types: Character, Date, Logical, and Numeric.

When you select the type of constant you want, the Paste box contains specific elements in that category. If you choose Date as the constant type, for example, the Paste list includes LastWeek, NextWeek, Today, Tomorrow, and Yesterday—all with the actual date relative to the current system date, as shown in figure 7.11. The two information panels at the bottom of both halves of the dialog box show prompts and information about the element currently highlighted in the Paste box or the expression in the window. In figure 7.13, the upper information panel is instructing you to type an expression or choose elements form the Paste list box.

If you click on the Field category in the Category list, the second box is labeled Table and contains a list of all tables open in the work areas. When you click on a table name, the Paste box contains the names of the fields in that table.

When you select the Function category, the Type box contains a long list of function types, such as Data type conversion, Colors/fonts, and Date/time data. After you select a function type, the Paste list contains all the dBASE functions of that type. Several functions have more than one syntax, a fact that is indicated by dots following the function name. Each additional variation has one more dot. In the Fields/records function type, for example, the BOF function occurs in two variations:

- **BOF** represents BOF(), which tests for the beginning of the file in the current work area.

- **BOF.** (with one dot) represents BOF(*alias*), which tests for the beginning of the file in a specified work area.

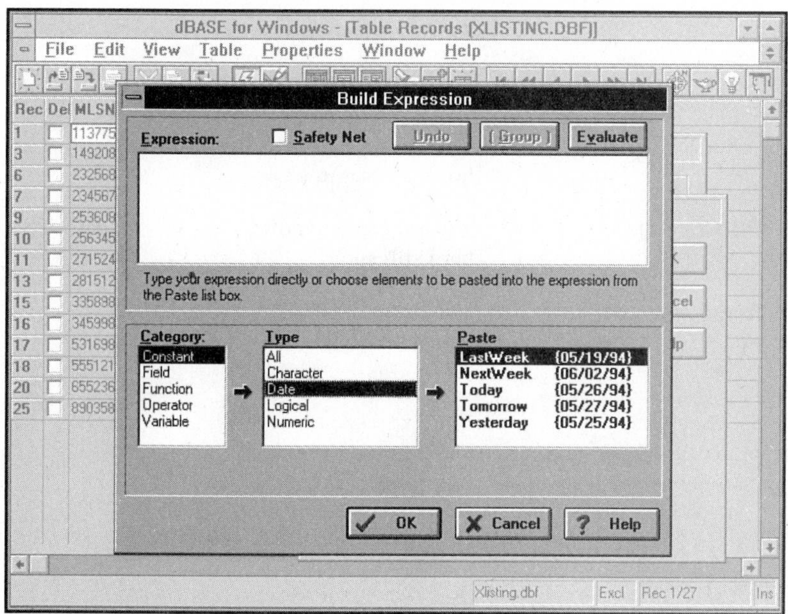

Figure 7.13
Date elements available for pasting into the expression.

Operator elements are grouped in four types: string (+ and -), logical (.AND., .OR., <>, and =), numeric (*, +, -, /, ^), and relational ($, <, <=, <>, =, >, >=).

The variable elements you can insert into an expression include the dBASE system variables and any user-defined variables you have created.

To paste an element from the Paste box into the expression, double-click on the element or select it and then press the spacebar. You also can click and drag the element into the Expression box. dBASE pastes the element at the current position of the insertion point, whether it is at the end of the expression or between two adjacent elements. The element might also replace a selected sequence of characters already in the expression.

To remove an element from the expression, select the characters and press Del, or simply select the element and type new text over it (if the Safety Net is turned off). To delete all the characters between two spaces, double-click anywhere in the sequence of characters, and then press Del. At any time, click on the Undo button to reverse the preceding operation.

As an exercise, open the Expression Builder, and paste elements into a complex index expression to use as an index for the XLISTING table. Use the steps in the following exercise.

Creating an Index for the XLISTING Table

With the XLISTING table open, select Table, Table Utilities, Manage Indexes	The Manage Indexes dialog box opens
Choose Create in the Manage Indexes dialog box	The Create Index dialog box is displayed
Enter the name **SUBPRICE** in the Index Name text box	You are ready to enter a key expression
Click on the Tool button next to the Key Expression text box	The Build Expression dialog box (see fig.7.12) appears
Uncheck the Safety Net checkbox so that you can type an expression directly into the Expression box	The Expression box shows a white background, indicating that the Safety Net is set off
Enter the expression **SUBDVSN+STR(LISTPRICE)**	LISTPRICE is a numeric field that you must convert before concatenating with the SUBDVSN field
Click on the Evaluate button	Figure 7.14 shows the completed expression in the Build Expression dialog box. Using the fields in the current record, the expression evaluates to East Circle Grove 105900, the values in the first record of the table
Choose OK	The expression is pasted into the Key Expression text box of the Create Index dialog box (see fig. 7.15)

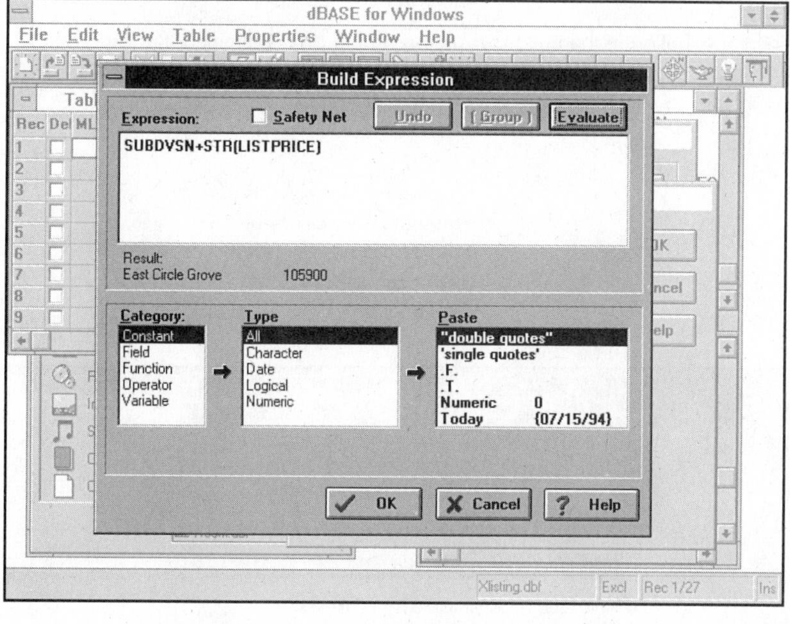

Figure 7.14
The completed expression in the Build Expression dialog box.

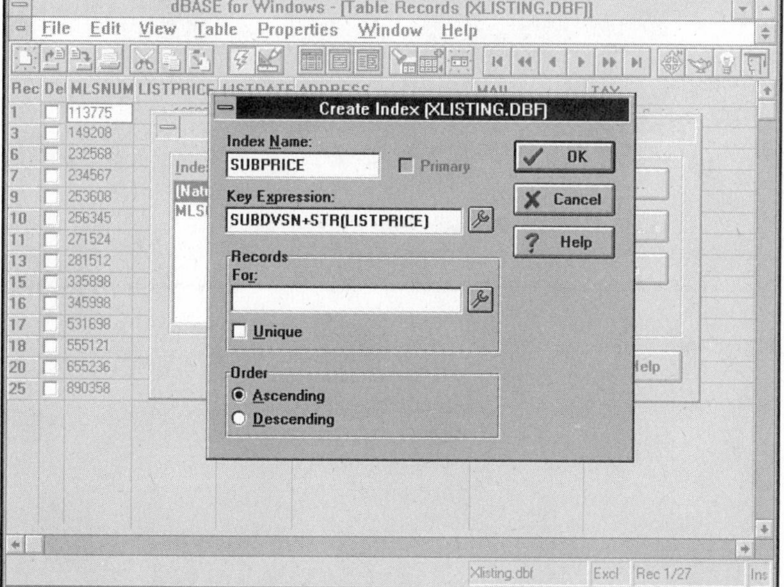

Figure 7.15
The new expression appears in the Create Index dialog box.

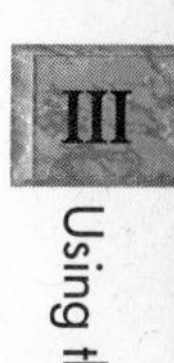

If the OK button in the Build Expression dialog box is dimmed, the expression is not valid; you cannot leave the Expression Builder until you correct the problem or cancel the operation.

Choose OK — You are returned to the Manage Indexes dialog box. The new tag appears in the list, as shown in figure 7.16

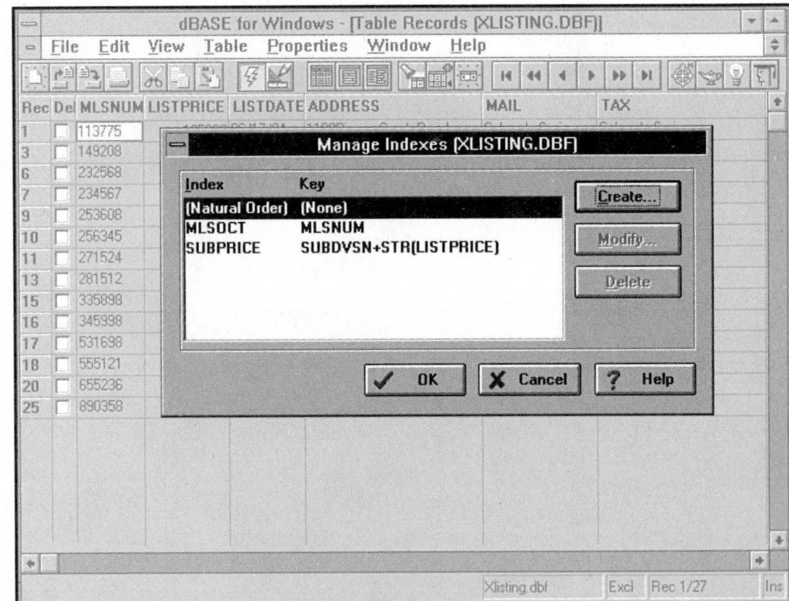

Figure 7.16
The Manage Indexes dialog box showing the new SUBPRICE tag.

Highlight the SUBPRICE index and choose OK — The XLISTING records now appear in ascending alphabetic order of subdivision and in ascending order of list price within the subdivison (see fig. 7.17)

Keep the XLISTING table open for the next exercises.

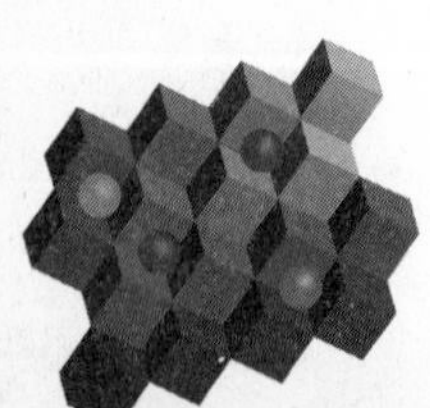

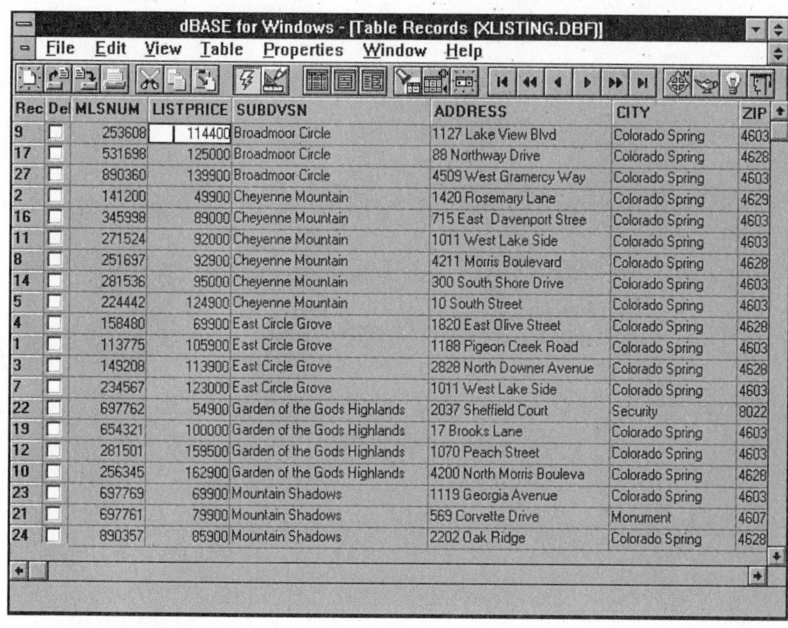

Rec	Del	MLSNUM	LISTPRICE	SUBDVSN	ADDRESS	CITY	ZIP
9		253608	114400	Broadmoor Circle	1127 Lake View Blvd	Colorado Spring	4603
17		531698	125000	Broadmoor Circle	88 Northway Drive	Colorado Spring	4628
27		890360	139900	Broadmoor Circle	4509 West Gramercy Way	Colorado Spring	4603
2		141200	49900	Cheyenne Mountain	1420 Rosemary Lane	Colorado Spring	4629
16		345998	89000	Cheyenne Mountain	715 East Davenport Stree	Colorado Spring	4603
11		271524	92000	Cheyenne Mountain	1011 West Lake Side	Colorado Spring	4603
8		251697	92900	Cheyenne Mountain	4211 Morris Boulevard	Colorado Spring	4628
14		281536	95000	Cheyenne Mountain	300 South Shore Drive	Colorado Spring	4603
5		224442	124900	Cheyenne Mountain	10 South Street	Colorado Spring	4603
4		158480	69900	East Circle Grove	1820 East Olive Street	Colorado Spring	4628
1		113775	105900	East Circle Grove	1188 Pigeon Creek Road	Colorado Spring	4603
3		149208	113900	East Circle Grove	2828 North Downer Avenue	Colorado Spring	4628
7		234567	123000	East Circle Grove	1011 West Lake Side	Colorado Spring	4603
22		697762	54900	Garden of the Gods Highlands	2037 Sheffield Court	Security	8022
19		654321	100000	Garden of the Gods Highlands	17 Brooks Lane	Colorado Spring	4603
12		281501	159500	Garden of the Gods Highlands	1070 Peach Street	Colorado Spring	4603
10		256345	162900	Garden of the Gods Highlands	4200 North Morris Bouleva	Colorado Spring	4628
23		697769	69900	Mountain Shadows	1119 Georgia Avenue	Colorado Spring	4603
21		697761	79900	Mountain Shadows	569 Corvette Drive	Monument	4607
24		890357	85900	Mountain Shadows	2202 Oak Ridge	Colorado Spring	4628

Figure 7.17
The XLISTING records ordered by subdivision and list price.

Pasting Elements from the List Box

In the next exercise, you use the Expression Builder to paste elements into the Expression box to create a tag indexing the XLISTING table by agent ID and the expiration date of the listing. You also add a FOR clause to limit the index to those records that contain an expiration date.

To create a new index tag using the Expression Builder and the paste method, follow these steps:

Creating a New Index Tag

If you have closed the XLISTING table, reopen it in the browse mode	The records appear in natural order
Select Table, Table Utilities, Manage Indexes, and then choose Create in the Manage Indexes dialog box	The Create Index dialog box appears

continues

continued

Enter **AGENTEXP** as the index Name in the Create Index Tag dialog box, and then click on the Expression Builder Tool button next to the Key Expression text box	The Build Expression dialog box opens
Check that the Safety Net is on, then select Field in the Category list	The Table list is displayed in the middle left box
If more than one table is open, select XLISTING in the Table list	A list of the XLISTING field names is displayed in the Paste list box
Double-click on AGENTID	The AGENTID name is placed in the Expression box
Select Operator in the Category list and String in the Type list.	Two concatenation operators appear in the Paste list box.
Double-click on the plus sign (+) in the Paste list.	The plus sign is added to the expression.
Select Function in the Category list and Data type conversion in the Type list.	The list of data type conversion functions appears in the Paste list box.
Scroll down the Paste list, and double-click on STR.	The function appears in the Expression box with an expression placeholder.

Click inside the function parentheses, and select Date/time data in the Type box; then double-click on the MONTH function in the Paste list.

The Build Expression dialog box should look like figure 7.18. Notice that the information panel reminds you that you have one placeholder to fill in. The <expD> placeholder is displayed in a different color from the rest of the expression.

Replacing Placeholders and Editing Constants

Placeholders are characters inserted into an expression to indicate where you must enter values before the expression is completed. The characters used in the placeholder show you what type of value is expected (see the following list):

Placeholder	Value Expected
<expC>	Character between delimiters
<expD>	Date
<expL> or <condition>	Logical
<expN>	Numeric
<exp>	Any type
Op	Operator

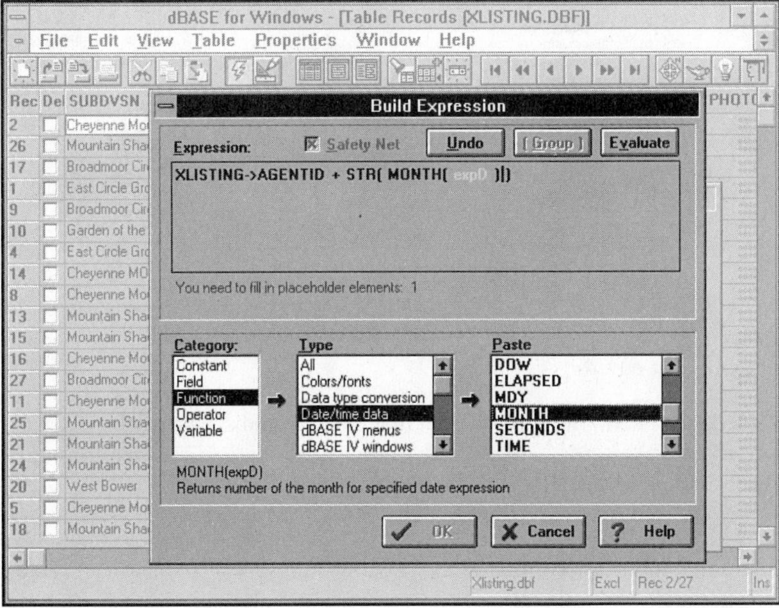

Figure 7.18 The Build Expression dialog box with the beginnings of the AGENTEXP key expression.

The placeholders appear in color (expression placeholders in yellow and operator placeholders in white) when the Safety Net is on. The number of placeholders yet to replace is also displayed in the information panel.

With the Safety Net off, replace a placeholder by selecting it and typing the appropriate constant or expression. You also can select and paste an expression from the Paste list. Be sure to replace the placeholder with the indicated data type. With the Safety Net on, you are limited to pasting a constant or building another expression with the list boxes.

Figure 7.19 shows an expression in the Build Expression dialog box that contains several placeholders, both expression and operator types. Notice that the lower information panel shows the syntax and a description of the highlighted function.

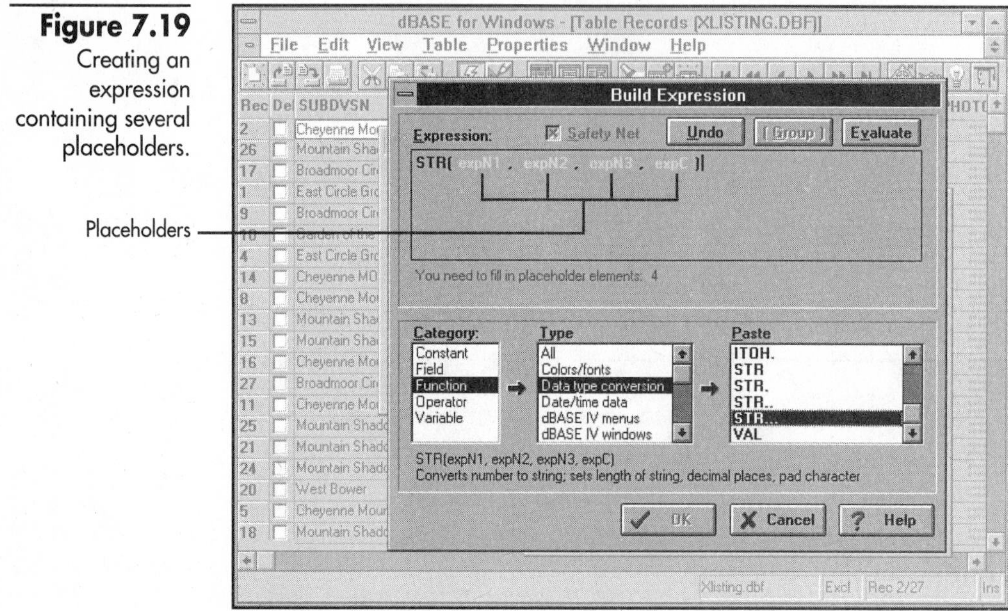

Figure 7.19 Creating an expression containing several placeholders.

When you replace a placeholder by pasting a constant in its place, dBASE inserts a default constant. For example, the default constant for a numeric placeholder is 0. If you want a different number, you must edit the constant.

When you replace a date placeholder, you have a choice of constants: Last week, Next week, Today, Tomorrow, or Yesterday—all relative to the system date. Character constants are simply the string delimiters and a logical constant can be either .T. or .F.

To edit a constant with the safety net off, double-click on the constant then type the new value. You may lose a delimiter or a comma in the process which you must replace.

If the Safety Net is on, right-click on the constant to display an entry box below the constant. Delete the default constant, if any, from the box and type in the desired value. The Safety Net will make sure all the delimiters are included. Right-clicking on a logical constant does not open an entry box. The value simply toggles between T and F.

You now have the information necessary to replace the placeholders left in the expression in the last exercise. Follow these steps:

Replacing the Placeholders

Click to the right of the <expD> placeholder

The insertion point moves inside the parentheses with the placeholder, expD

Select Field in the Category list, and double-click on EXPDATE in the Paste list

XLISTING EXPDATE replaces the placeholder

Click on the Evaluate button to see what value the expression returns using the current record (see figure 7.20)

You can see the results in the information panel

Remember you used the month number instead of name so the index would appear in chronological order

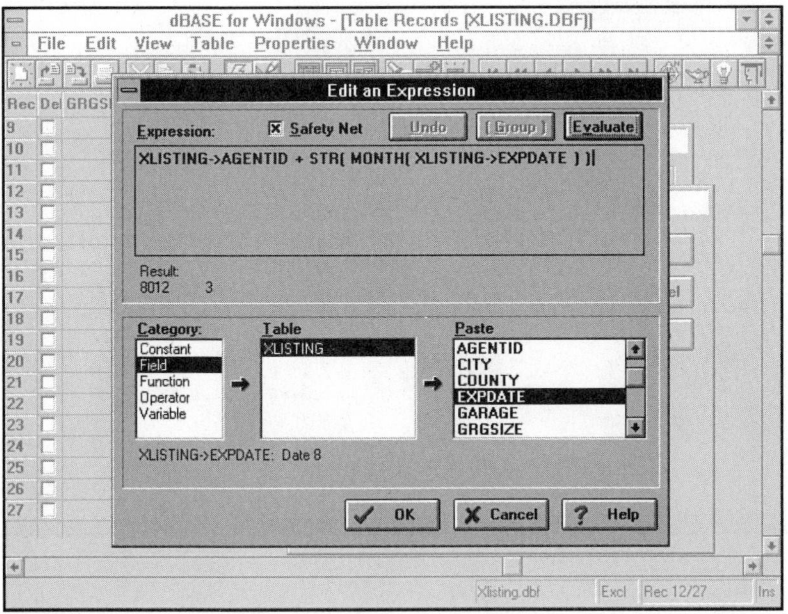

Figure 7.20 The completed expression evaluated with the current record.

Choose OK to paste the expression into the Create Index Tag dialog box

The Expression Builder will disappear, and you will be returned to the Create Index dialog box

continues

continued

Move to the For text box, and enter the following condition: **EXPDATE<>{}**	This condition excludes records whose ExpDate field is blank
Choose OK	You are returned to the Manage Indexes dialog box
Highlight the AGENTID tag. Choose OK.	Figure 7.21 shows the table records in the new AGENTEXP order
	Notice that only those records with an expiration date are included in the indexed table

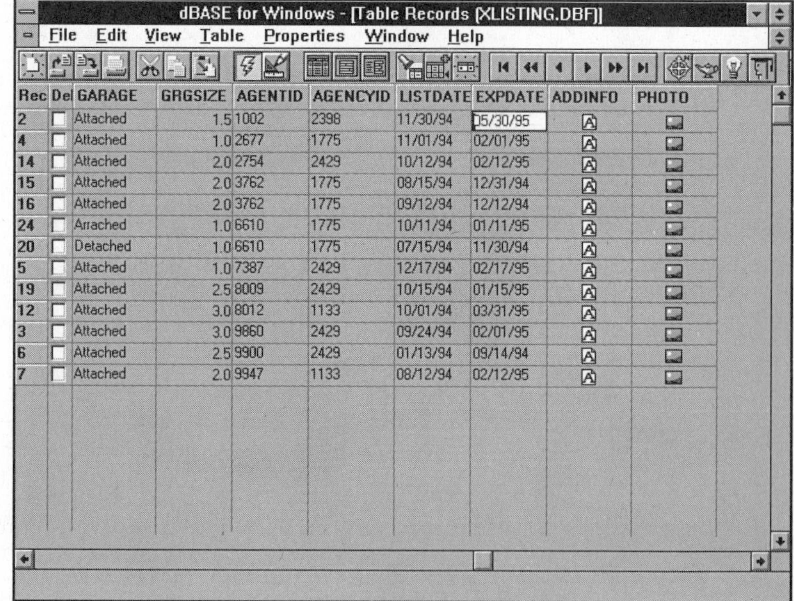

Rec	Del	GARAGE	GRGSIZE	AGENTID	AGENCYID	LISTDATE	EXPDATE	ADDINFO	PHOTO
2		Attached	1.5	1002	2398	11/30/94	05/30/95		
4		Attached	1.0	2677	1775	11/01/94	02/01/95		
14		Attached	2.0	2754	2429	10/12/94	02/12/95		
15		Attached	2.0	3762	1775	08/15/94	12/31/94		
16		Attached	2.0	3762	1775	09/12/94	12/12/94		
24		Arrached	1.0	6610	1775	10/11/94	01/11/95		
20		Detached	1.0	6610	1775	07/15/94	11/30/94		
5		Attached	1.0	7387	2429	12/17/94	02/17/95		
19		Attached	2.5	8009	2429	10/15/94	01/15/95		
12		Attached	3.0	8012	1133	10/01/94	03/31/95		
3		Attached	3.0	9860	2429	09/24/94	02/01/95		
6		Attached	2.5	9900	2429	01/13/94	09/14/94		
7		Attached	2.0	9947	1133	08/12/94	02/12/95		

Figure 7.21 The XLISTING records with expiration dates, ordered by agent ID number and expiration date.

You now can close all files

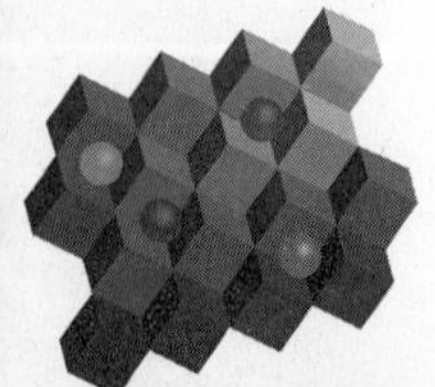

Grouping Elements

As you might recall from high school algebra, if you want to change the natural precedence of operations in an expression, you can add parentheses. Grouping is usually used in numerical expressions. The expression 5*2+5 evaluates to 15, for example, but the expression 5*(2+5) evaluates to 35.

If the Safety Net is on, select the part of the expression that you want inside the parentheses, and click on the Group button. dBASE places parentheses around the selected elements.

If the Safety Net is off, click in the expression where you want the group to start, and type the opening parenthesis. Then click where you want the group to end, and type the closing parenthesis.

Grouping elements is not so important in creating an index expression because the expression usually just concatenates field values. A For condition expression evaluates to true or false, depending on whether the record meets the criteria for being included in the index.

Evaluating an Expression

When you evaluate an expression, you perform all the indicated calculations and comparisons. Although the new key expression might be valid, it still might not give you the result you want. If the Safety Net is set on, you can click on the Evaluate button, as you did in earlier exercises, and see the result of a valid expression in the information panel beneath the Expression box.

The values used are those found in the current record of the underlying table. If the expression is invalid, a diagnostic message is displayed in the information panel instead, and the OK button is dimmed. You must go back to the expression and correct the problem before you can paste the expression to the dialog box called the Expression Builder. If you give up altogether, choose Cancel.

In the following exercise, you create an expression that is not used in an index but serves simply as another example of using the Expression Builder. Follow these steps:

Creating an Expression with the Expression Builder

Click in the command window then select Edit, Build Expression	The Build Expression dialog box opens
Set the Safety Net on by clicking on the Safety Net checkbox, (if not already on) then select Function in the Category list and select Data type conversion in the Type list	A list of data type conversion functions appears in the Paste list box
Double-click on the fourth variation of the STR function, (STR . . .)	Fig. 7.17 above shows the STR function in the Expression box with four placeholders: three numeric values and one character value.
To begin replacing the expression placeholders, click near <expN1>	The insertion point appears at one end of the placeholder
Select Constant in the Category list and Numeric in the Type list; then double-click on 0 in the Paste list	The placeholder is replaced by a 0
Right-click the 0 in the expression to open	An edit box containing 0 opens just below the expression
Enter **5678.952** and press Enter	See figure 7.22
Repeat steps 6 through 9 to replace <expN2> with **10** and <expN3> with **2**	The next two placeholders are replaced by constants, then by values

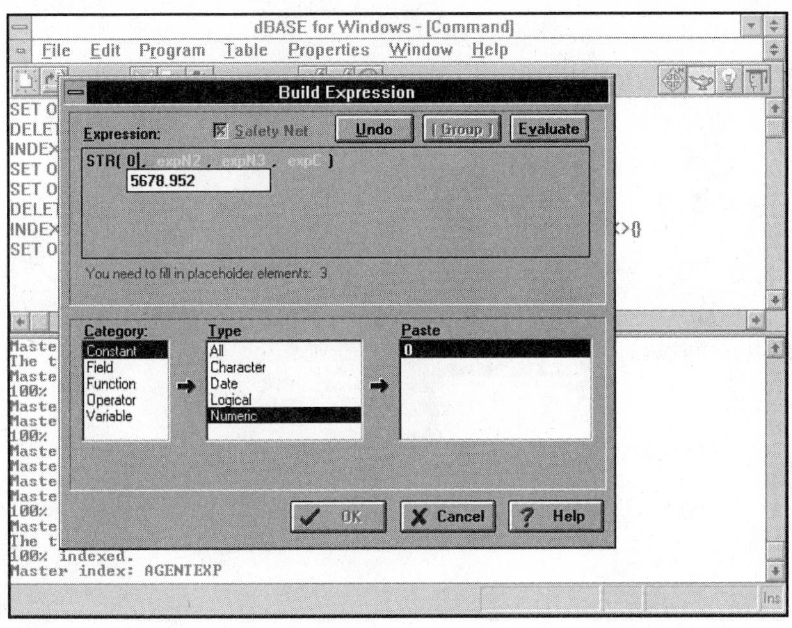

Figure 7.22
Replacing the first numeric placeholder.

Click near the <expC> placeholder, and select Constant in the Category list and Character in the Type list; then double-click on "double quotes"

A pair of double quotation marks replace the fourth placeholder

Right-click the double quotes in the expression, and enter **$** in the edit box. Press Enter

A dollar sign appears between the quotation marks in the expression

Click on Evaluate

Figure 7.23 shows the Expression Builder with the returned value displayed in the information panel

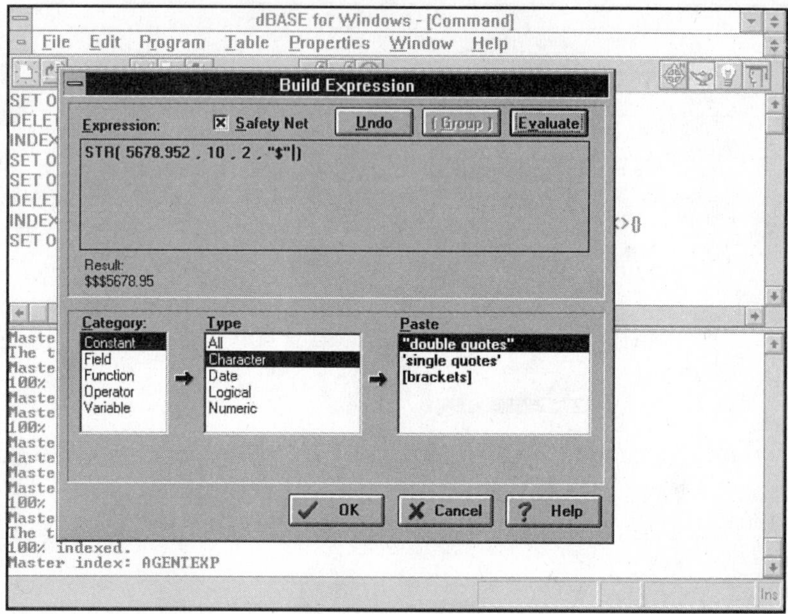

Figure 7.23 The evaluated STR expression in the Expression Builder.

An operator indicates how the two objects on either side of it relate to each other. For example, if you put two numeric concatenates in your expression, you need to tell dBASE whether you want the numbers added, subtracted, or whatever!

When you concatenate two character strings, you must insert an operator between them. You add another string constant to the end of the expression. Follow these steps:

Concatenating Two Character Strings

With the insertion point at the end of the expression, select Constant from the **C**ategory list and Character from the **T**ype list. Then double-click on "double quotes"	Figure 7.24 shows the new operator placeholder between the two character elements
Click near the Op placeholder; select Operator from the **C**ategory list and Character from the **T**ype list; then double-click on the plus sign (+) in the **P**aste list	The Op placeholder is replaced by the concatenation symbol +

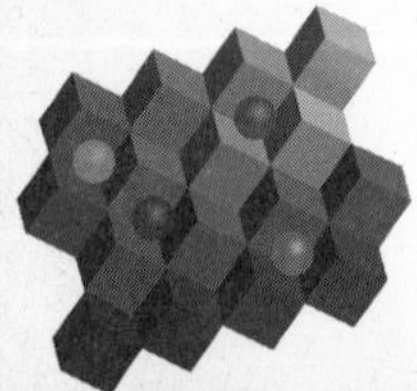

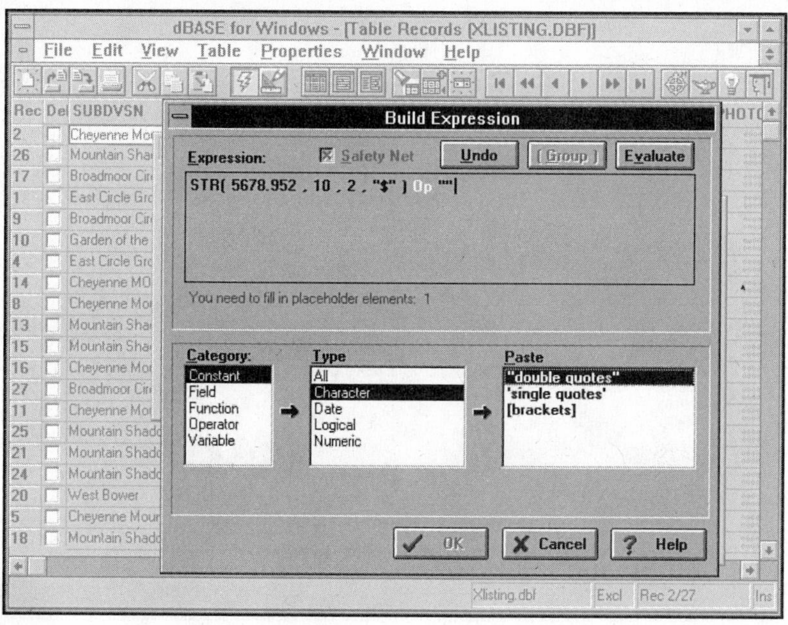

Figure 7.24
The expression with an operator placeholder.

Right-click near the double quotes	The edit box opens below the quotation marks
Finally, enter the second character string	
Press the spacebar, then enter **is the total amount.**, and press Enter	The space is to separate the STR expression from the remaining text
Click on Evaluate	The results of the expression, as shown in figure 7.25

Modifying an Index

You use the same procedures and similar dialog boxes for modifying a tag as you did for creating a new one. As an exercise, modify one of the indexes you created earlier.

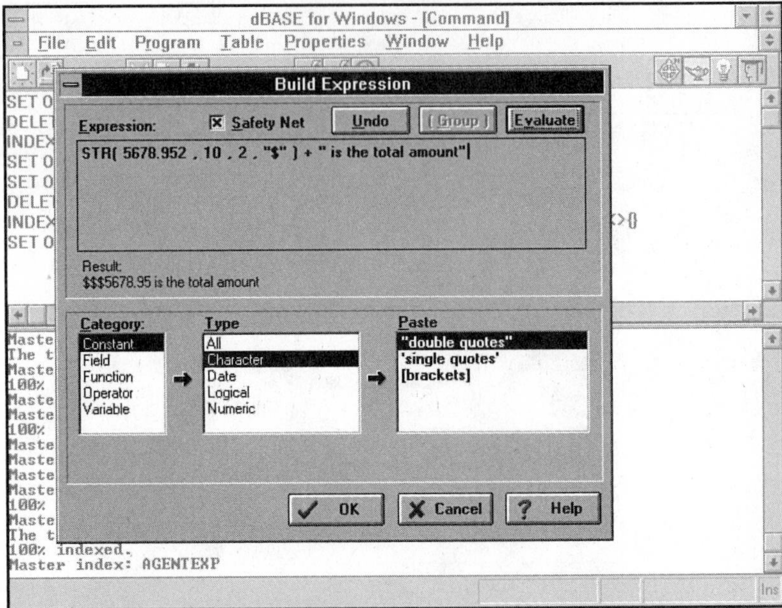

Figure 7.25 The final results of the new expression.

Modify the MLSOCT tag so that it indexes records for homes that were listed before September (rather than October). Follow these steps:

Modifying the MLSOCT Tag

Open the XLISTING table in the browse mode	The XLISTING records appear in natural order
Select Table, Table Utilities, Manage Indexes	The Manage Indexes dialog box opens
Select the MLSOCT index and choose Modify	The modify Index dialog box opens with the tag specifications in the text boxes
Change the index Name to MLSSEP then Move to the For text box, and change 10 to 9. Choose OK	The new MLSSEP index appears in the Manage Indexes dialog box list of indexes

Select MLSSEP in the Manage Indexes dialog box, or Choose OK	You are returned to the table view where the records for all homes listed before September are arranged in MLS number order

Creating and Using Single Index Files (NDX)

One MDX (multiple index) file may contain only one or as many as 47 separate indexes. An NDX index on the other hand, is a single index order with one key expression. An NDX file is comparable to one of the index orders in a MDX file. The capability is maintained primarily for compatibility with dBASE III PLUS.

To create an NDX index file, you open the table from the command window (not the Navigator) then use the INDEX ON command. To create a single index named ZIPORDER on the ZIP field of the XLISTING table, for example, enter the following command:

```
USE XLISTING
INDEX ON ZIP TO ZIPORDER
```

To create a slightly more complex single index on the SUBDVSN and AGENTID fields, you can enter the following commands:

```
USE XLISTING
INDEX ON SUBDVSN + AGENTID TO SUBAGENT
```

As soon as you create the NDX index, dBASE rearranges the table in that order. The index name appears with the full path, including the drive designator (C:) in the list of indexes in the Manage Indexes dialog box. The index name is also highlighted, indicating that it is currently the master index. Although the index name is included in the list, you can't set it as the master from the Manage Indexes dialog box. If you try, you get an error message objecting to the back slash (\) in the path designator. If you choose Modify, the Create Index dialog box is displayed rather than the Modify Index dialog box with the index expression showing. Give the index a name and choose OK. This converts the NDX file into an index in the production MDX file.

To use the NDX index, you must open the file and include the INDEX clause with the USE command or the SET INDEX TO command after the table is opened. To open the two indexes ZIPORDER and SUBAGENT with the XLISTING table, for example, enter

USE XLISTING INDEX ZIPORDER, SUBAGENT

or

USE XLISTING

SET INDEX TO ZIPORDER, SUBAGENT

The first index name in the list, ZIPORDER in this example, becomes the master index.

To close all the index files, use the SET INDEX TO command with no file name, as in

SET INDEX TO

The DELETE FILE command deletes an NDX file. The file must be closed before you can delete it. You also can use the ERASE file utility command to delete the file.

Moving Between Single and Multiple Indexes

You can convert NDX files into MDX indexes or break out MDX indexes into individual single indexes. When you are upgrading from an earlier version of dBASE, it is a good idea to convert the NDX files you use often to tags in the production index using the COPY INDEXES command. If, for example, you want to convert the ZIPORDER and SUBAGENT indexes, use this command:

COPY INDEXES ZIPORDER, SUBAGENT

The new indexes appear in the Manage Index dialog box along with the NDX index references. After copying the NDX file to the MDX file, close all files and delete the NDX files with the DELETE FILE or ERASE command. You may not delete them by choosing Delete in the Manage Indexes dialog box.

If you want to copy the indexes to a multiple index file other than the production index, add a TO clause with the name of the file, as in the following:

COPY INDEXES ZIPORDER, SUBAGENT TO MULT2

The new indexes keep the assigned index names and appear in the index list in the Manage Indexes dialog box.

To reverse the process and copy a multiple index tag into an NDX file, use the COPY TAG command as follows:

COPY TAG ZIPORDER TO ZIPORDER

COPY TAG SUBAGENT TO SUBAGENT

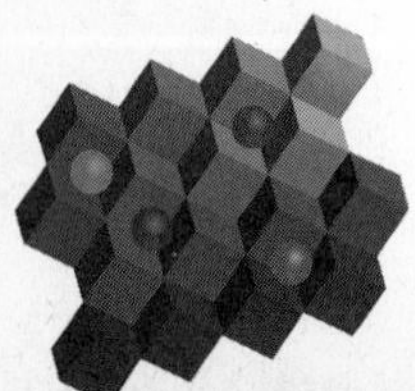

If the tags are not in the production index, use the OF clause and add the name of the multiple index:

```
COPY TAG ZIPORDER OF MULT2 TO ZIPORDER
```

Then delete the tag from the Manage Indexes list or use the DELETE TAG command. You must convert the tags to single indexes one at a time, but you can convert many NDX files to tags in one command.

A Note from the Author

With the new dBASE for Windows indexing capabilities, I have found no reason not to convert all my NDX files in earlier dBASE applications into MDX indexes. I put the ones that are referenced most frequently in the production index then create one or two more production MDX files for special purpose indexes. MDX indexes seem more robust than the earlier NDX files and you don't have to remember to open each one to keep them current.

Maintaining Your Indexes

dBASE automatically keeps all open indexes current as you edit table data. Through the Index Designer, you can add, modify, and delete index tags as you have seen in earlier exercises. You should keep all indexes up-to-date and review the index list occasionally for relevance and then delete the ones you no longer need.

Reindexing the Table

All indexes in the production index are automatically maintained as you work with the table. Other multiple indexes—as well as the NDX indexes—that are not kept open during a session need to be updated before you put them in control. Indexes also occasionally become damaged or corrupted and need to be rebuilt.

To rebuild an index, open the table and all the indexes you want to update, and then select Table, Table Utilities, Reindex. If you have many indexes or your table is large, the process might take some time.

Saving an Index

No special steps are required to save a new or modified index. When you choose OK in the Create Index dialog box, dBASE automatically saves the index if no errors occur in the expression. If an error exists, an alert box is displayed with a short error message.

When you respond to the alert by clicking OK, you are returned to the Create Index dialog box where you must correct the error or cancel the operation.

Deleting Indexes and Tags

As your application grows and adds more capabilities, so does the list of indexes. Deleting indexes that you no longer need speeds up processing and frees up disk space. Deleting an index has no effect on the records in the table, but just removes the index file and the index name.

Create a new index, then delete it to see the effects on record order.

Deleting an Index to Check Record Order

Open the XAGENT table	The records appear in natural order
Choose Table, Table Utilities, Manage Indexes	The Manage Indexes dialog box appears
Choose Create	The Create Index dialog box is displayed
Create a new index named TRYIT using AGENCYID as the key expression; choose OK	The new index appears in the Manage Indexes dialog box list of indexes
Highlight the TRYIT index and choose OK	The records now appear reordered by agency ID number
Choose Table, Table Utilities, Manage Indexes again	The TRYIT index name is still highlighted
Choose Delete then OK	You are returned to the table view and the XAGENT records are back in natural order

If you delete the currently controlling index tag (MDX or NDX), the table reverts to its natural order.

When you choose **D**elete, the index disappears at once. If you have made a mistake, choose **C**ancel rather than OK to close the dialog box. When you open it again, the index is back.

Creating Indexes for Paradox Tables

dBASE for Windows handles Paradox for DOS and for Windows tables in their native formats without converting any of the features to dBASE. This includes the Paradox indexing scheme which differs from dBASE. Paradox uses primary and secondary indexes both of which you can create and modify with the Manage Indexes dialog box.

The *primary index* of a Paradox table is the main index and is based on one or more consecutive fields in the table structure, beginning with the first field. The primary index is stored in a file with the same name as the table but with a PX extension.

Secondary indexes can be added only if the table already has a primary index. There are two types of secondary indexes: maintained and non-maintained. The *maintained* secondary indexes are analogous to the indexes in the dBASE production MDX file. The *non-maintained* indexes are similar to NDX indexes and are not automatically opened and maintained as you update the table. You may not create non-maintained secondary indexes for Paradox tables in dBASE.

All Paradox indexes are case-sensitive and specify only ascending order. A *single-field index* is based on the value in one field while a *composite index* (similar to the dBASE complex index) combines the values in multiple fields. Since Paradox insists on unique key values for all indexes, you may have to combine several fields to obtain a unique composite value.

The first index you create for a Paradox table is automatically defined as the primary index and must contain the first field in the table structure. The index is named Primary in the index list. Subsequent indexes are given the name of the key field.

If the Paradox table has a primary index, the records appear in that order when you open the table. dBASE tables always open in the natural order.

Your *Inside dBASE for Windows Bonus Disk* contains a Paradox table named PLISTING.DB with the same data as the XLISTING dBASE table but in Paradox format. In the following exercise, you create the primary index based on the MLSNUM field then a secondary index based on the ADDRESS field.

Creating Primary and Secondary Indexes

Double-click on the PLISTING.DB icon in the Navigator panel

The PLISTING table opens in the browse mode

Choose Table, Table Utilities, Manage Indexes

The Manage Indexes dialog box opens

Choose Create

The Create Index dialog box opens with many of the options dimmed as shown in figure 7.26

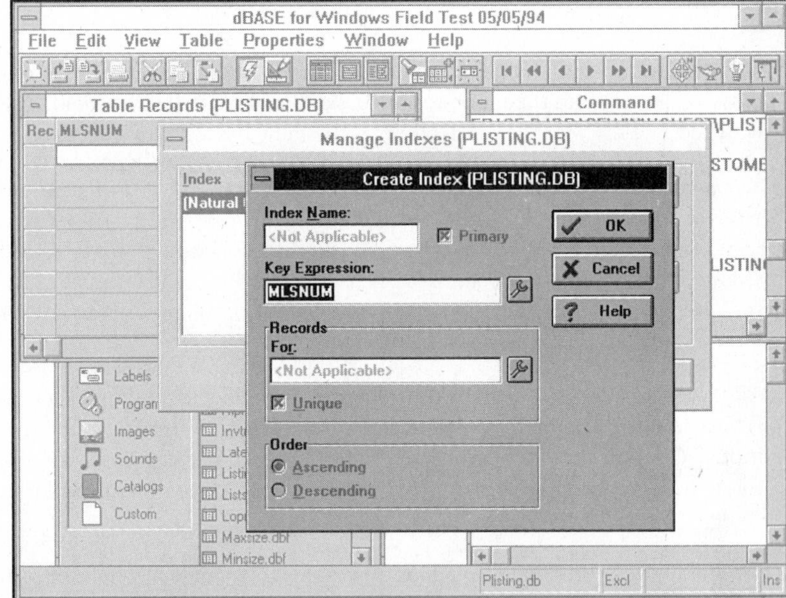

Figure 7.26
The Create Index dialog box for a Paradox table.

When you open the Create Index dialog box to create the first index for a Paradox table, the Primary option is automatically checked and the name of the first field in the table is entered into the Key Expression box. Notice also that you are not prompted to enter an index name, Paradox names indexes after the key fields. In addition, there is no capability to filter the index with a For condition and Paradox indexes are only in ascending order.

Action	Result
Choose OK	MLSNUM appears in the Manage Indexes list as the primary index as shown in figure 7.27

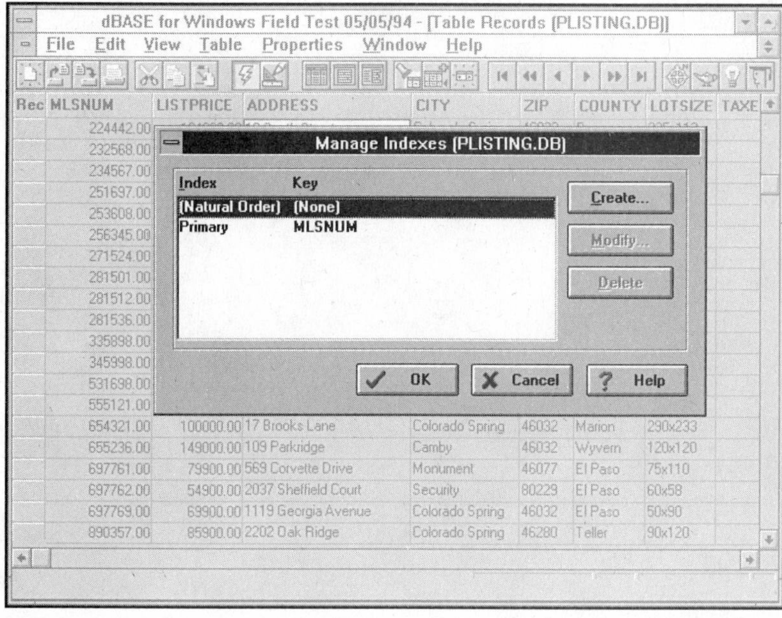

Figure 7.27
The Manage Indexes dialog box showing the new MLSNUM primary index.

Action	Result
Highlight the Primary index and choose OK	The table records are ordered in primary index order
Choose **T**able, **T**able Utilities, **M**anage Indexes again to create a secondary index for the PLISTING table	The Manage Indexes dialog box reopens
Choose **C**reate and enter ADDRESS in the Key Expression box then press OK	The ADDRESS secondary index appears in the Manage Indexes list
Highlight the ADDRESS index name and choose OK	The PLISTING records appears reordered by the ADDRESS field value (see fig. 7.28)

continues

continued

Figure 7.28 PLISTING records reordered by ADDRESS.

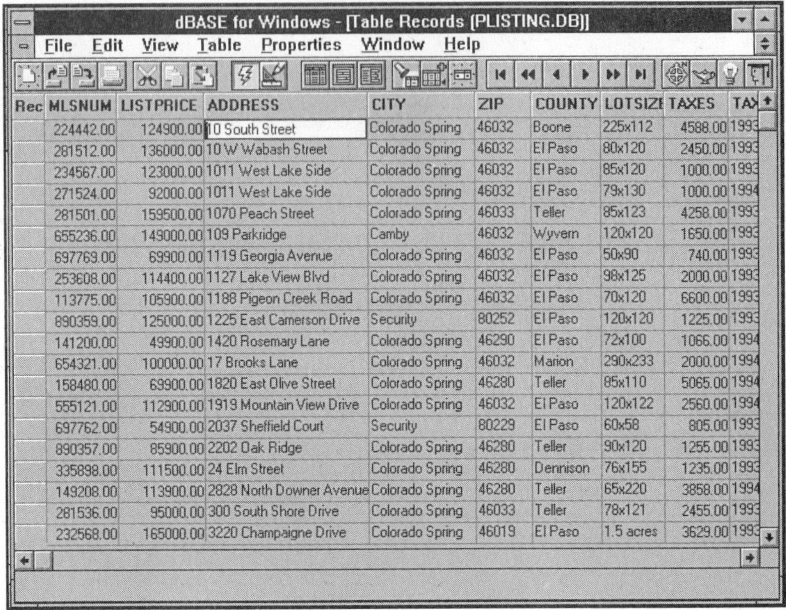

Rec	MLSNUM	LISTPRICE	ADDRESS	CITY	ZIP	COUNTY	LOTSIZI	TAXES	TA
	224442.00	124900.00	10 South Street	Colorado Spring	46032	Boone	225x112	4588.00	199
	281512.00	136000.00	10 W Wabash Street	Colorado Spring	46032	El Paso	80x120	2450.00	199
	234567.00	123000.00	1011 West Lake Side	Colorado Spring	46032	El Paso	85x120	1000.00	199
	271524.00	92000.00	1011 West Lake Side	Colorado Spring	46032	El Paso	79x130	1000.00	1994
	281501.00	159500.00	1070 Peach Street	Colorado Spring	46033	Teller	85x123	4258.00	199
	655236.00	149000.00	109 Parkridge	Camby	46032	Wyvern	120x120	1650.00	199
	697769.00	69900.00	1119 Georgia Avenue	Colorado Spring	46032	El Paso	50x90	740.00	199
	253608.00	114400.00	1127 Lake View Blvd	Colorado Spring	46032	El Paso	98x125	2000.00	199
	113775.00	105900.00	1188 Pigeon Creek Road	Colorado Spring	46032	El Paso	70x120	6600.00	199
	890359.00	125000.00	1225 East Camerson Drive	Security	80252	El Paso	120x120	1225.00	199
	141200.00	49900.00	1420 Rosemary Lane	Colorado Spring	46290	El Paso	72x100	1066.00	1994
	654321.00	100000.00	17 Brooks Lane	Colorado Spring	46032	Marion	290x233	2000.00	1994
	158480.00	69900.00	1820 East Olive Street	Colorado Spring	46280	Teller	85x110	5065.00	1994
	555121.00	112900.00	1919 Mountain View Drive	Colorado Spring	46032	El Paso	120x122	2560.00	1994
	697762.00	54900.00	2037 Sheffield Court	Security	80229	El Paso	60x58	805.00	199
	890357.00	85900.00	2202 Oak Ridge	Colorado Spring	46280	Teller	90x120	1255.00	199
	335898.00	111500.00	24 Elm Street	Colorado Spring	46280	Dennison	76x155	1235.00	199
	149208.00	113900.00	2828 North Downer Avenue	Colorado Spring	46280	Teller	65x220	3858.00	1994
	281536.00	95000.00	300 South Shore Drive	Colorado Spring	46033	Teller	78x121	2455.00	199
	232568.00	165000.00	3220 Champaigne Drive	Colorado Spring	46019	El Paso	1.5 acres	3629.00	199

Close the PLISTING table	You are returned to the dBASE desktop

You can also create composite indexes for a Paradox table with dBASE by entering the expression in the Key Expression text box of the Create Index dialog box. The expression must be such that there is no possibility of duplicate key values in the Paradox table.

Sorting a dBASE Table

Sorting is used mostly to create files for exporting to other applications or for creating a temporary file for a special report. When you sort a table in dBASE, you copy the records to an entirely new table with a different name, in the specified sort order. The name must be a valid DOS file name. The original table is called the *source table*, and the new table, the *target table*. The source table is not changed by the sort operation.

Several options are available when you're sorting a table. In addition to specifying the order in which the records appear in the target table, you can limit the records by indicating a scope or by adding FOR and WHILE conditions. The target table can be either a dBASE or a Paradox table.

The record order is determined by the fields you select as the sort fields. The first field in the list represents the primary sort, the second field, the secondary sort, and so forth. To sort a long list of names that might contain more than one person with the same last name, for example, you could sort first by the last name, then by the first name within the last name.

In addition, you specify either ascending or descending order for each field and whether dBASE is to consider case when sorting. You need not assign the same order to all fields in the Sort Fields list. The sort orders include the following:

Ascending sorts records in ascending order: A to Z, 1 to 9, past to future, and false to true. Uppercase letters are sorted first, then lowercase letters: A,B,C... then a,b,c....

Ascending/No Case is similar to Ascending except that it ignores case: a,A,b,B,c,C....

Descending sorts records in the reverse of ascending: Z to A, 9 to 1, future to past, and true to false. Lowercase letters are sorted first, then uppercase: ...c,b,a...C,B,A.

Descending/No Case ignores the case of alphabetic characters in the descending order: ...C,c,B,b,A,a.

All fields are included in the resulting table, in the original field order within the record. The sorted table is read-only, so you cannot edit or append any records.

The steps involved in sorting a table include:

1. Name the target table
2. Choose the target table type: dBASE or Paradox
3. Select the sort fields and specify ascending or descending order
4. Specify the scope of the sort

As an exercise, sort the XLISTING table by subdivision and list price to a new table named LISTSORT. First, open the XLISTING table in the browse mode, then follow these steps:

Creating a New Table Named LISTSORT

Select Table, Table Utilities, Sort as shown in figure 7.29	The Sort Records dialog Records box appears (if no file is open, the Open File dialog box appears first so that you can select a table)

continues

continued

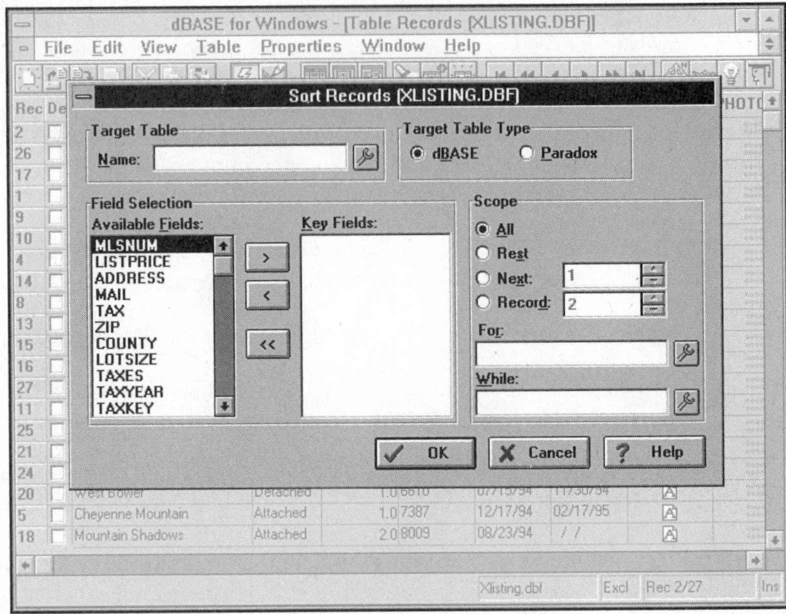

Figure 7.29 The Sort Records dialog box.

Enter **LISTSORT** as the name of the target table and check dBASE as the table type, if it is not already checked	If you click on the Tool button, the Save dialog box appears, where you can choose a file complete with path name
Highlight the LISTPRICE field name in the available Fields list, and click the right-pointing arrow	LISTPRICE is added to the Sort Fields list
Highlight the SUBDVSN field name	SUBDVSN is added to the bottom of the list
You want to change the order and sort first by the subdivision name, so select SUBDVSN in the Sort Fields list, and click the left-pointing arrow	SUBDIVSN is removed from the list
Highlight SUBDVSN again, and click the right-pointing arrow	SUBDVSN is inserted at top of list

The right-pointing arrow inserts the new field into the list above the currently highlighted key field name. Double-clicking places the new field at the bottom of the list.

Click on the up arrow displayed next to LISTPRICE in the Sort Fields list (see fig. 7.30), and select the down arrow	The LISTPRICE sort order is changed to descending

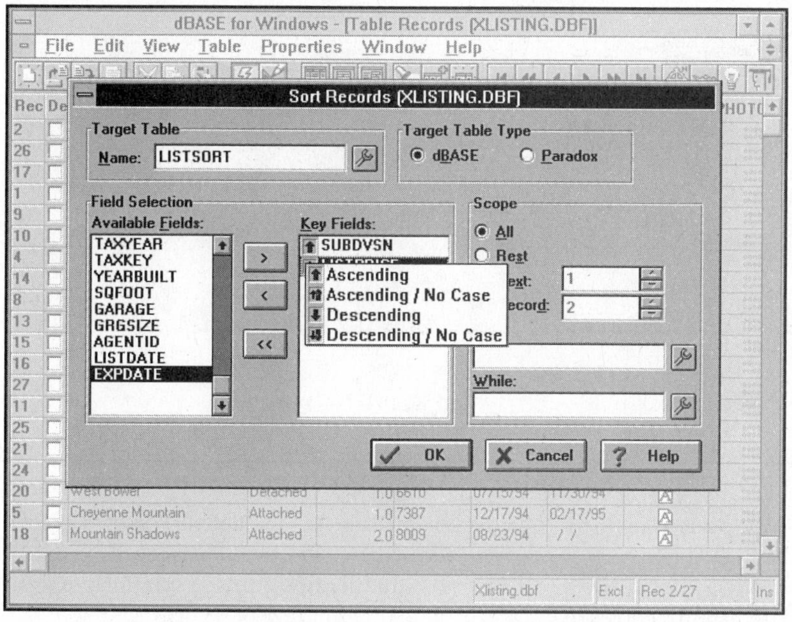

Figure 7.30
You can change the sort order individually for each field in the Key Fields list.

Select <u>A</u>ll as the scope, and leave the Fo<u>r</u> and <u>W</u>hile condition boxes blank then choose OK. (If the table already exists, you are asked whether you want to overwrite it)	The LISTSORT target table has been created but it is not in view
Open the LISTSORT table, and view the records in the new order	The XLISTING records appear in a new order in the LISTSORT table and the record numbers are requested in the new order (see fig. 7.31)

continues

continued

Figure 7.31 The LISTSORT table sorts records in subdivision and list price order.

dBASE for Windows - [Table Records (LISTSORT.DBF)]

File Edit View Table Properties Window Help

Rec	Del	MLSNUM	LISTPRICE	ADDRESS	SUBDVSN	CITY	ZIP
1	☐	890360	139900	4509 West Gramercy Way	Broadmoor Circle	Colorado Spring	46032
2	☐	531698	125000	88 Northway Drive	Broadmoor Circle	Colorado Spring	46280
3	☐	253608	114400	1127 Lake View Blvd	Broadmoor Circle	Colorado Spring	46032
4	☐	224442	124900	10 South Street	Cheyenne Mountain	Colorado Spring	46032
5	☐	281536	95000	300 South Shore Drive	Cheyenne Mountain	Colorado Spring	46033
6	☐	251697	92900	4211 Morris Boulevard	Cheyenne Mountain	Colorado Spring	46280
7	☐	271524	92000	1011 West Lake Side	Cheyenne Mountain	Colorado Spring	46032
8	☐	345998	89000	715 East Davenport Stree	Cheyenne Mountain	Colorado Spring	46032
9	☐	141200	49900	1420 Rosemary Lane	Cheyenne Mountain	Colorado Spring	46290
10	☐	234567	123000	1011 West Lake Side	East Circle Grove	Colorado Spring	46032
11	☐	149208	113900	2828 North Downer Avenue	East Circle Grove	Colorado Spring	46280
12	☐	113775	105900	1188 Pigeon Creek Road	East Circle Grove	Colorado Spring	46032
13	☐	158480	69900	1820 East Olive Street	East Circle Grove	Colorado Spring	46280
14	☐	256345	162900	4200 North Morris Bouleva	Garden of the Gods Highlands	Colorado Spring	46280
15	☐	281501	159500	1070 Peach Street	Garden of the Gods Highlands	Colorado Spring	46033
16	☐	654321	100000	17 Brooks Lane	Garden of the Gods Highlands	Colorado Spring	46032
17	☐	697762	54900	2037 Sheffield Court	Garden of the Gods Highlands	Security	80229
18	☐	890358	400520	677 East Oliphant Avenue	Mountain Shadows	Woodland Park	80962
19	☐	232568	165000	3220 Champaigne Drive	Mountain Shadows	Colorado Spring	46019
20	☐	281512	136000	10 W Wabash Street	Mountain Shadows	Colorado Spring	46032

(Close LISTSORT but keep the XLISTING table open for the next exercise)	The LISTSORT table closes and XLISTING remains in the window

Note that the scope options in the Sort dialog box include **A**ll (the default), Re**s**t, Ne**x**t, and Recor**d**. The Re**s**t option sorts the current record and all subsequent records to the target table. When you choose Ne**x**t, you enter the number of records to sort, including the current record. dBASE copies to the target table that number of records (or fewer, if end-of-file is reached before the specified number of records is copied). The Recor**d** option is meaningless in a sort operation because it specifies a single record by record number.

The Tool buttons in the Sort dialog box provide help in constructing expressions and naming the target table. Clicking on the Tool button next to the Target Table text box opens the Save File dialog box. The Tool buttons associated with the scope options in the Records panel open the Build Expression dialog box.

In this exercise, you specify a slightly more complex sort operation. You sort the XLISTING table in descending order by listing date and limit the records to those properties whose taxes exceed 6 percent of the list price. Follow these steps to complete the sort:

Sorting the XLISTING Table

With the XLISTING table open on the desktop, choose Table, Table Utilities, Sort Records

The Sort dialog box dBASE opens

Enter **TAXSORT** as the name for the target table then double-click LISTDATE in the Available Fields list

MSTDATE is the first name in the Day Fields list

Accept the All scope, and Enter **TAXES/LISTPRICE >.06** in the For text box

The For filter will limit records to those whose Tax rate exceeds 6 percent of list price

Click on the arrow next to the LISTDATE field in the Key Fields list, and select Descending from the pull-down menu

The Sort Records dialog box should look like figure 7.32

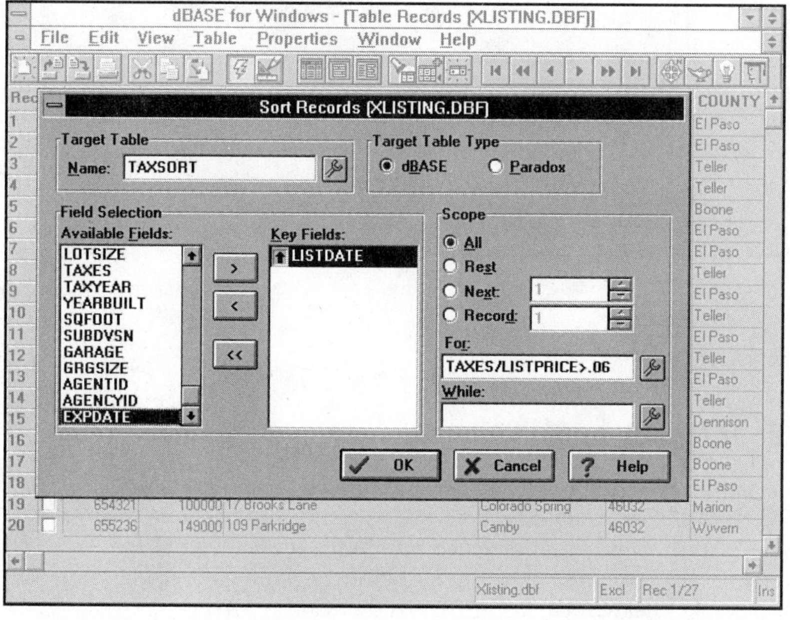

Figure 7.32 The completed TAXSORT specifications in the Sort Records dialog box.

Choose OK

The TAXSORT table has been created

continues

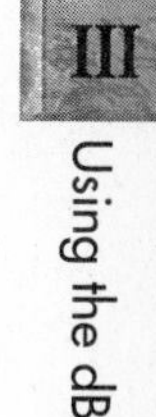

continued

Open the new TAXSORT table	The three records that meet the For condition sorted by LISTDATE appear as shown in fig. 7.33

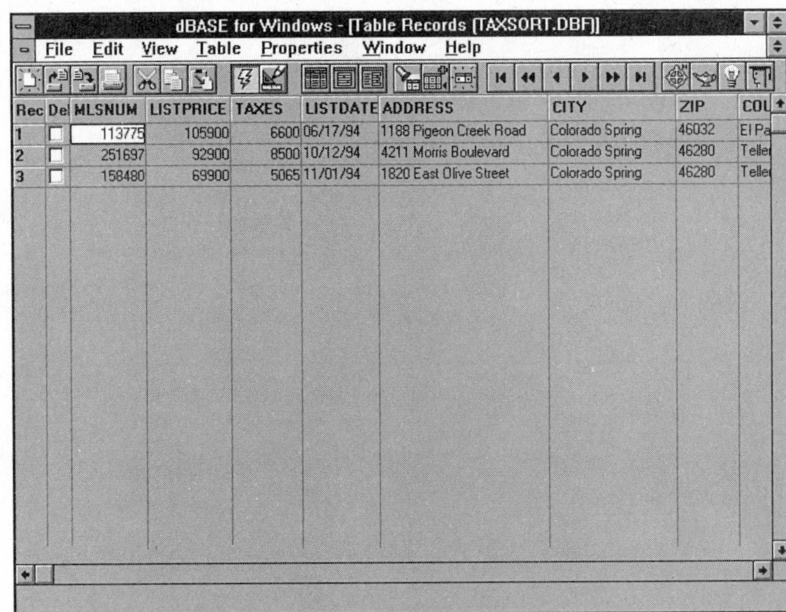

Figure 7.33 The TAXSORT table lists properties whose taxes exceed 6 percent of the list price.

You now can close all the files.

Locating Table Data

In addition to being able to scroll through the records on-screen and move to particular records with the navigation keys, you can locate a record based on the contents of a field. If the field you want to search is an index key field, the search goes faster if you set that index as the master index before beginning the search. You can, however, use non-key fields, including memo fields, to locate records.

When dBASE locates a record that matches the search criterion, the record pointer moves to that record, and it becomes current. You then can view the information or edit or delete the record. (If you want to replace located information with specific values, use the Replace feature rather than Find described a little later in this chapter.)

When you search a table, you specify the field to examine and the value for which you are looking. You can search all or part of the field for exact or partial matches. You can limit the search to a range of records by using much the same scope and condition options that are available when you're indexing tables.

A Note from the Author

I use the Find operation only for viewing the data in the located record since I cannot return to the table to edit the record without closing the Find dialog box. I usually have to drag the dialog box out of the way to see all the relevant data in the record. I use Find mostly as a quick lookup.

By default, dBASE begins the search at the current record and locates the next occurrence of the specified value. If you want to search the entire table, be sure to go to the top record before beginning the search. After finding the first record that matches, you can choose to locate the next occurrence or stop looking. The records are not extracted from or moved within the table, the record pointer just moves down the table.

If you are searching on the key field in an indexed table, when you find the first occurrence of the value, you are at the first of a group of records—all of which have the same key value. You then can close the Find dialog box and proceed to edit the records in succession, as necessary.

The major steps in locating records with a specific value in a field include the following:

1. Open the table
2. Enter the value for which you are looking
3. Select the field to search
4. Specify the type of match
5. Limit the search, if you prefer
6. Conduct the search

You can conduct all these steps interactively with the Find Records dialog box or manually with commands in the command window. The next sections describe the process of locating records by value.

Setting Up the Search Criteria

After you have selected the field to search, you need to enter the value you want to find in that field. If the field you are searching is in a character or memo type, dBASE does a character-by-character comparison, beginning at the leftmost character in the field. You do not have to provide a search string as long as the field itself—a partial string is usually enough. To locate the first listing of property in the Cheyenne Mountain subdivision, for example, the string *Che* is sufficient.

You don't need to enclose a character string in double quotation marks or a date value in curly brackets. dBASE assumes that the value you enter is a character or date if the field you selected is of that data type.

You can specify match options for character and memo fields. These options include the following:

- ✔ **Standard,** which applies a standard ruler for matching
- ✔ **Exact Length,** which requires the field value length match the length of the search string
- ✔ **Anywhere in Field,** which does not limit the string to the first characters but looks for the string throughout the field
- ✔ **Sounds Like,** which matches values that sound like the specified character string and have the same number of syllables
- ✔ **Match Case,** which is case-sensitive

Use the Anywhere in Field option to search a memo field for a word or expression. You could find all listings that refer to the garage in the AddInfo field, for example, by entering **garage** as the Find What string and specifying the Anywhere in Field search option.

Numeric and date values must be complete, and dBASE always looks for an exact match. No options are available for numeric or date field searches. Wild cards are not valid in the Find What value, but you can use them in the FOR and WHILE clauses to limit the records to search.

As an exercise, search the XLISTING table for all listings entered by Agent #6610. Follow these steps:

Searching the XLISTING Table

Open the XLISTING table

The XLISTING records appear in natural order

Select <u>T</u>able, <u>F</u>ind Records

The Find Records dialog box appears, as shown in figure 7.34

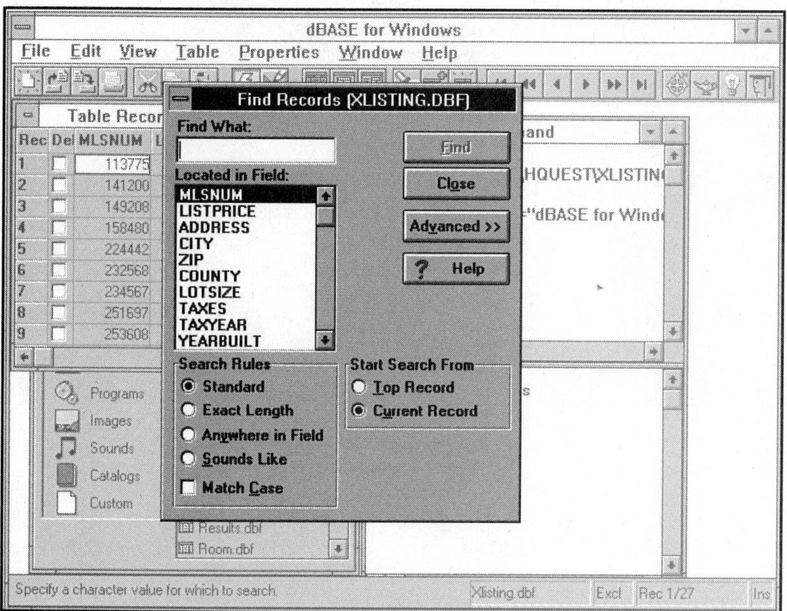

Figure 7.34
The Find Records dialog box.

Enter **6610** in the Find What text box then scroll down the Located in Field list and select AGENTID

You have specified the value you want to find and told dBASE what field to look in

Accept the default Standard Search Rule option and choose <u>T</u>op Record in the Start Search From group and choose <u>F</u>ind

The record pointer moves to the first field of the first record with 6610 in the AGENTID field (see fig. 7.35). Drag the dialog box aside to see the record data if necessary

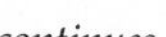
continues

continued

Figure 7.35
The first record for a listing entered by Agent 6610.

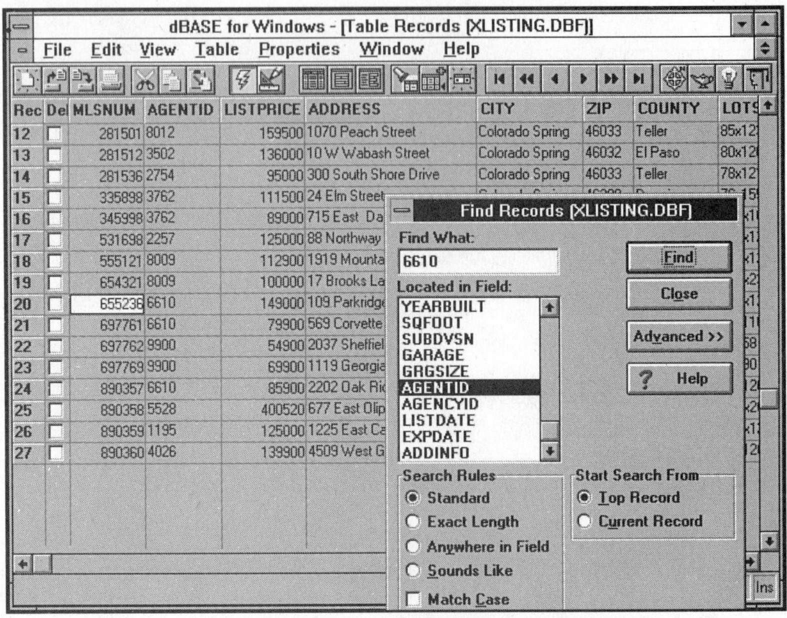

Choose <u>F</u>ind again	The record pointer moves to the next listing for Agent 6610
When you're finished viewing the records, choose <u>C</u>lose	The Find Records dialog box closes

(Leave the XLISTING table open for the next exercise.)

If dBASE finds no record that matches the Find What value when you choose Find, the program displays an alert box saying that the value was not found.

Limiting the Records To Search

Selecting the records to search saves time, especially if you are searching a non-key field. By expanding the Find Records dialog box to include Advanced features, you can limit the scope of records to search (see fig. 7.36.) The same record range options are available for the search as for indexing: **<u>A</u>**ll, Re<u>s</u>t, Ne<u>x</u>t *n* records, or Recor**<u>d</u>**. If you do not set a range of records, dBASE defaults to Re<u>s</u>t and searches from the current record to the end of the table.

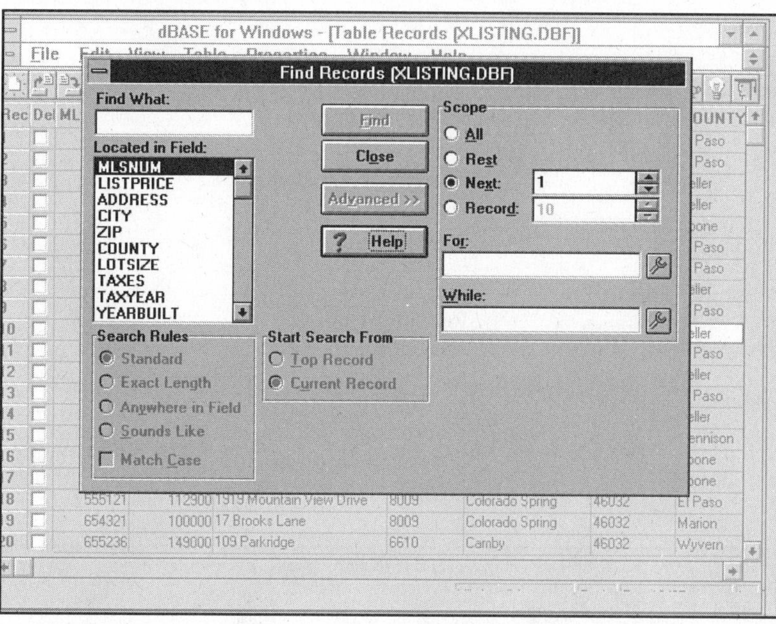

Figure 7.36
The Find Records dialog box expanded to include the Scope panel.

In addition, you can specify For and While conditions to limit the records to be searched to only those meeting specified criteria. The For condition searches for all records that meet the criteria, beginning at the top of the table. The While condition also searches for all records that meet the criteria but starts with the current record and continues sequentially until a record fails to meet the criteria.

You set the range of records to search before you choose Find the first time. Choose Advanced from the Find Records dialog box to open the dialog box to the Scope panel, which is where you specify the search range.

This time, search the XLISTING table for all the listings in the Cheyenne Mountain subdivision among the first 10 records in the table that have a list price of more than $80,000. Follow these steps:

Searching the Cheyenne Mountain Subdivision

Select Table, Find Record	The Find Records dialog box opens
Enter **Che** in the Find What text box, and accept the Standard option	dBASE will look for records that have the characters Che in the subdivision field (first 3 characters)

continues

continued

Choose Start Search From **T**op Record	dBASE will begin the search at the top of the table
Choose Advanced	The Scope panel appears with scope and filter options
Choose Ne**x**t, and enter **10** in the edit box	You have asked dBASE to look in the next 10 records for the value
Enter **LISTPRICE >80000** in the For tent box	You are filtering the records by specifying a list price of more than $80,000 (see fig. 7.37)

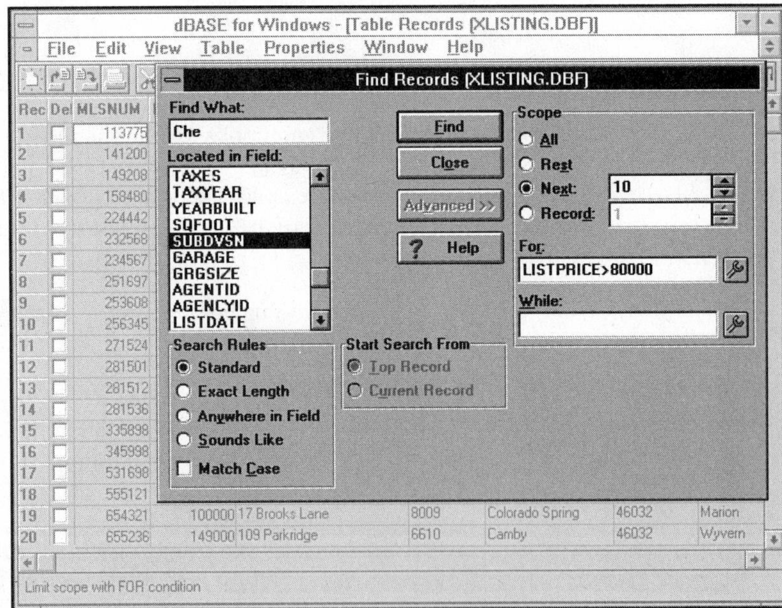

Figure 7.37
The completed Find Records dialog box.

Choose **F**ind	The record pointer moves to record #5, the first listing for more than $80,000 in the Cheyenne Mountain Subdivision

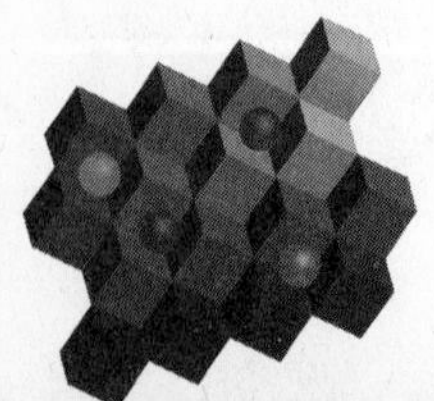

Choose Find again.	The record pointer moves to record #8
Repeat the preceding steps until you have reached record #10	The search stops because you limited the search to the first 10 records
Choose Close and close the XLISTING table file	The Find Records dialog box closes and you are returned to the dBASE desktop

Replacing Field Data

The Replace feature takes the Find feature one step further and enables you to replace data in the records that are found. You can replace the value in one or all fields that match the search criteria. The user interface looks very much like Find, with many of the same options in a similar dialog box.

You search for a value in one field and replace a value in that field or another field in the same record. You can replace the value of any type of field. Changes you make appear immediately in the table view window.

When you choose Table, Replace Records, the Replace Records dialog box opens as shown in figure 7.38. The only difference between this and the Find Records dialog box is the Replace With panel in which you specify the value you want entered into that field.

If you are replacing the value in a memo field, the replacement must be a character data type. For non-memo fields, the replacement must be of the same data type as the field you are replacing. An additional constraint on numeric and float fields is that the replacement value must not exceed the field width as defined in the table structure. If it does, you will see a string of asterisks in the field. Character data that is wider than field width is simply truncated.

All the Search Rules, Start Search From, and Scope options are the same as for Find Records. When you have specified the replacement text, choose Find to locate the first occurrence of the Find What value. Then choose Replace to replace that value and find the next occurrence or choose Find to skip that one and go on to the next. If you are sure you want to replace all the values, you can choose Replace All at first instead of Find.

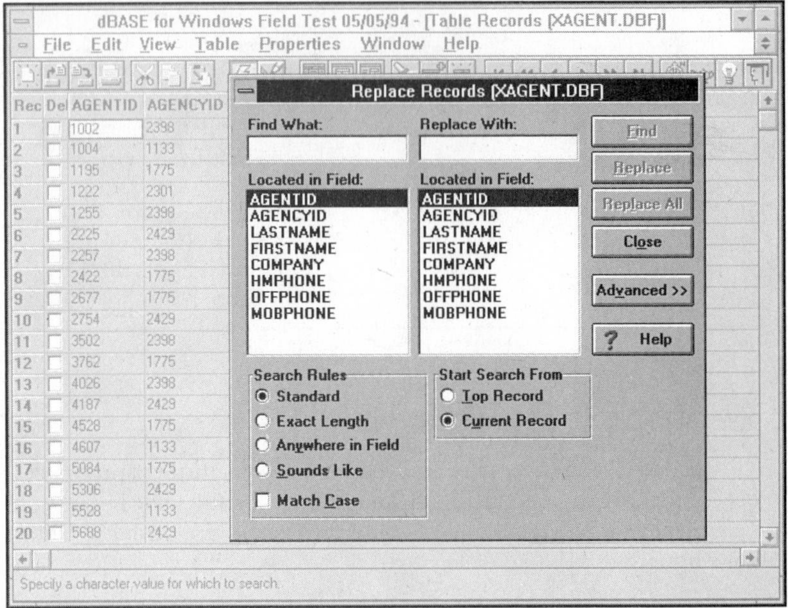

Figure 7.38
The Replace Records dialog box.

Watch out replacing values in a key field in the production index. When you change a key value in the master index, the record pops to a new position in the table, according to the new key value, and takes the record pointer with it. The next record is now a different one than before. You can get unpredictable results, including orphaned child records if you change a parent key field value.

In the next exercise, one of the agents has changed agencies and taken the listings along. You need to change the agent's record in the XAGENT table and update XLISTING table with the new AGENCYID for those listings.

Updating the Table Records

In the Navigator window, double-click on the XAGENT table icon	The XAGENT table opens in the browse mode
Choose Table, Replace Records	The Replace Records dialog box opens
Enter **2422** in the Find What text box and select AGENTID as the field to search in	You ask dBASE to find records with the value 2422 in the AGENTID field

Enter **2398** in the Replace With text box and select the AGENCYID as the Located in Field name

You have specified the new value for the AGENCYID field

Choose Start Search From <u>T</u>op Record and choose <u>F</u>ind

The screen now looks like figure 7.39

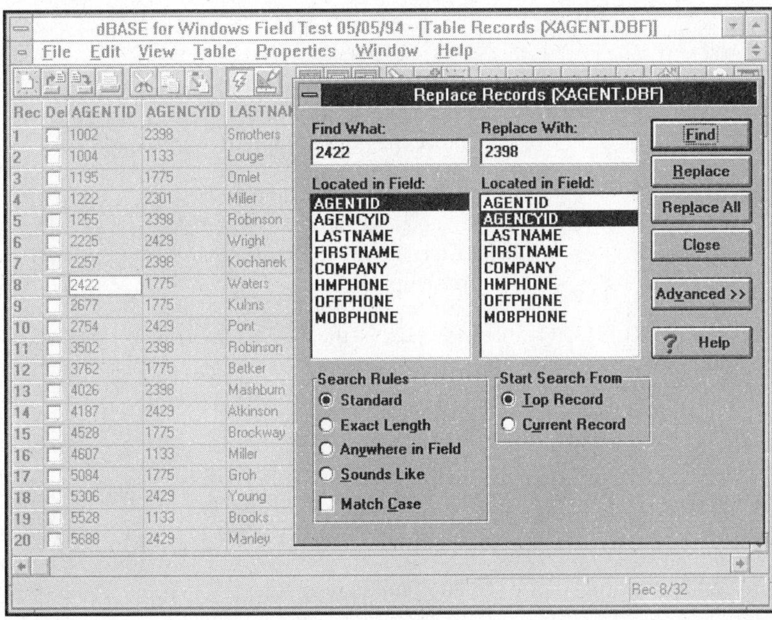

Figure 7.39
dBASE has found the first record for agent 2422.

Choose <u>R</u>eplace

dBASE automatically replaces 1775 in the AGENCYID field with 2398 and looks for the next record for agent 2422. Since there was only one, no more matches are found

Choose OK

The message box closes

Because the COMPANY field in the XAGENT table contains the name of the agency, you need to replace it with the new agency name: Sell Em Realty.

continues

continued

Leave the AGENTID value in the Find What panel of the dialog box and enter **Sell Em Realty** in the Replace With text box. Then select the field COMPANY as the field value to replace

You have specified a change in the COMPANY field in the agent 2422 record

Choose Find, then Replace

The new value for AGENCYID is entered into one record and the Alert box again says that no more matches are found

Choose OK, then Close. Close the XAGENT table

The message box and dialog box close and you are returned to the dBASE desktop

Next find all the listings in the XLISTING table with 2422 in the AGENTID field and replace the AGENCYID value with 2398, the new employer

Open the XLISTING table and choose Table, Replace Records

The Replace Records dialog box opens as before with the XLISTING fields listed in the Located in Field panels

Enter **2422** in the Find What box and select AGENTID in the field list. Then enter **2398** in the Replace With box and select AGENCYID in the field list

The find and replace specifications are complete

Choose the Start Search from Top Record option then choose Replace All

A question box appears indicating the number of records that meet the search criteria and ask for confirmation that you want to change them all (see fig. 7.40)

Choose Yes

All changes are made and the record pointer appears at the bottom record in the table

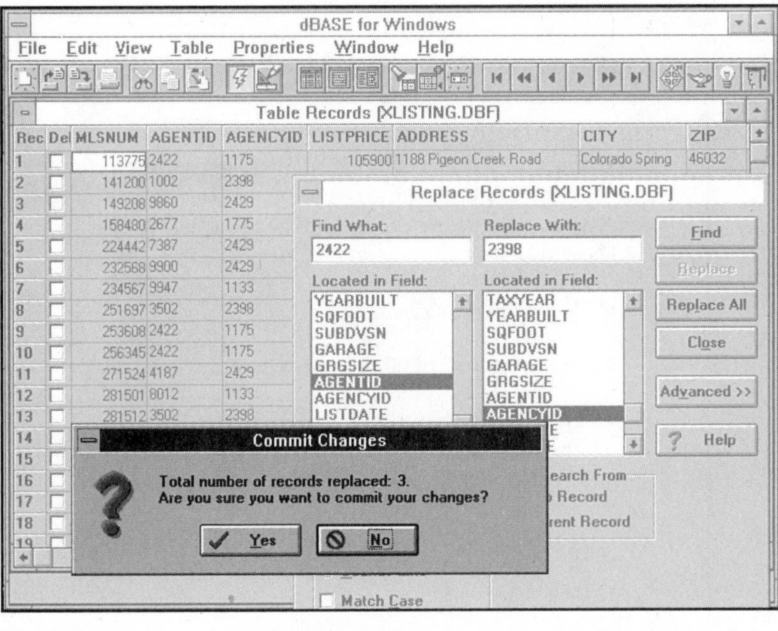

Figure 7.40
You are asked for confirmation before changing the records.

Choose Cl<u>o</u>se and scroll up the table	The dialog box closes and you can see all the agent 2422 records (#s 1, 9, and 10) have a new AGENCYID value
Close the XLISTING table	You are returned to the dBASE desktop

In many cases, a query is more useful for finding records that meet search criteria. A query extracts the records for further processing, including editing and using in reports. The next chapter discusses creating and using queries with dBASE tables.

Chapter Snapshot

The dBASE Query Designer provides a flexible tool for extracting selected data from a single table or from multiple tables. Once you have extracted the data, you can use it much as you would any other table data. In this chapter, you will learn about:

This chapter includes exercises which call for you to use tables on your *Inside dBASE for Windows Bonus Disk* and which will give you experience in creating and running queries. The next chapter will call for you to use some of these queries as a basis for customized reports.

Querying Your Data

By Virginia Andersen

A *query* is a question for which your database should be able to provide you an answer. For example, you might decide that you want to find the names and addresses of the agents who listed the most properties during the summer months, so you can send a congratulatory letter to them and to their agencies. A complex search such as that is easy when you use the dBASE Query Designer.

You can use queries to link two or more tables and establish a relationship between them. You can use the resulting view in turn as the basis for a report or form. You also can edit the table that is the result of running the query, and the changes are automatically passed on to the underlying tables.

The dBASE Query Designer enables you to create complex queries for extracting the specific data you need with ease.

Understanding the Query Designer

The Query Designer presents a graphical user interface that has special SpeedBar buttons and menu options. The query design window includes table skeletons that have all the field names displayed. Figure 8.1 shows a typical new query window, in which the XLISTING table skeleton is visible.

Figure 8.1
The Query Designer window with the XLISTING table skeleton.

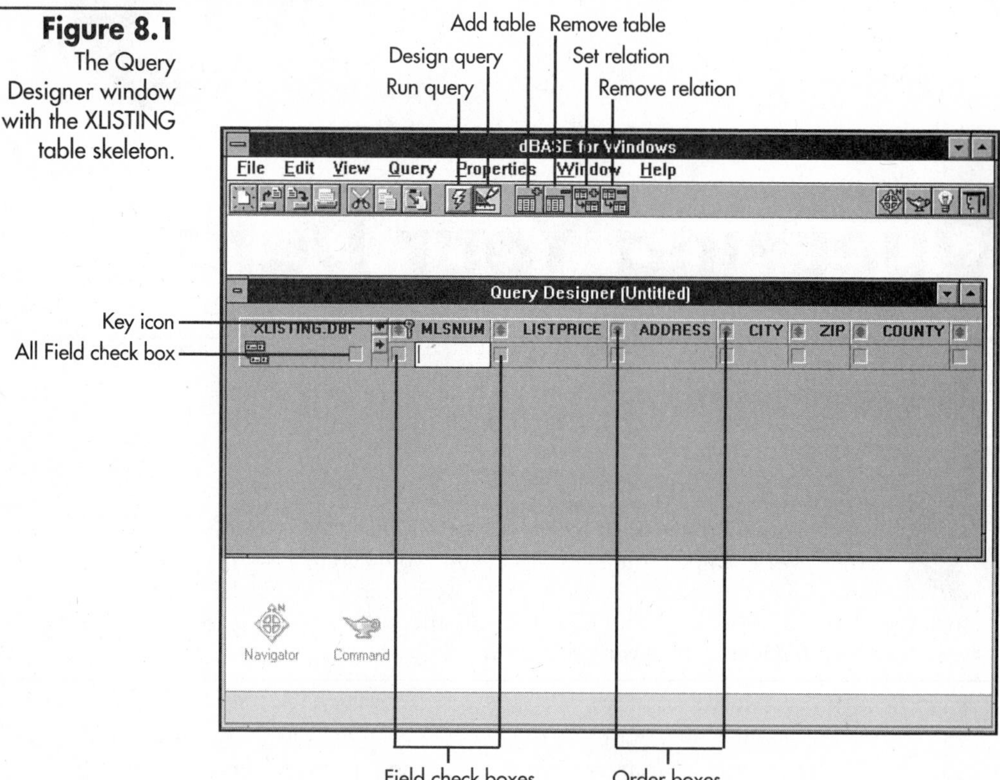

What a Query Can Do for You

The result of a query is a table that contains the answer to the question posed in the query design. This Results table is called a view. The *view* is a window that has the information you requested, ordered, screened, and focused according to your special purpose. It can serve as the basis for a data-entry form or a report. After you link the query to the form or report, any time you display the form or print the report, the query is run beforehand—ensuring that you get the most current version of the underlying table data.

The view can also serve as an editing or deletion tool, in that you can use it to single out the field and records you want to change. You can also screen sensitive information by using the view to exclude particular fields from the resulting table.

The Query Designer generates dBASE commands as you create the query. Then when you run a query, you can see the commands in the command window as dBASE executes them—which can serve as an excellent learning tool if you want to write your own programs. The query is saved as a QBE command file which you can edit in the dBASE text editor by entering the command, MODIFY COMMAND followed by the complete query file name, including the QBE extension.

Things the Query Designer Needs To Know

Having glimpsed the new design window and tools, you might want to look at what information the Query Designer requires before it can extract the information you want. The query environment requires some specific information before it can generate an answer.

First, you must specify the table or tables from which you want to extract data and, if more than one table is involved, you must identify the field that links the tables. After you provide these specifications, you can choose to include in the view all of the fields or only some of the fields. Chances are, you will not need all the fields—especially in a multitable query—because the object is to extract certain specific related information, not all the data.

After you decide which fields to include, you specify the order in which you want the records to appear. You can use one of the key fields, a complex index, or any field in the table to determine the sort order.

Next, you set any filter conditions that are necessary to limit the results to your desired subset of the available records. You used a FOR condition in the preceding chapter to limit the records to be included in an index. You can use other types of filter conditions with queries as well. For example, you can combine fields from more than one table into a complex condition, using AND and OR relational operators.

Finally, you can add calculated fields which you can in turn include in the view. For example, you could calculate the number of days a property has been listed (but not sold) and extract those records that have a list date in excess of 90 days. The elapsed time is a calculated field which you can (but do not have to) include in the view. The exercises in this chapter give you the opportunity to practice all these techniques.

Extracting Data from a Table

Indexes give you a logical view of table data while the records remain in their natural order in the table. When you run a query, however, dBASE may actually physically copy to a new table the data that forms the basis of the answer to your question. The trick is to design the query so that you get a complete set of the data you need, but nothing extra.

The simplest query is based on a single table and contains most of the fields from the table.

Building a Single-Table Query

To begin a new query, open the Query Designer by selecting Query from the File, New menu or right-clicking on the <Untitled> icon in the Query group of the Navigator window (see fig. 8.2) and choosing New Query. Select the table that you want to use as the basis for the query from the dialog box that appears. If you are already browsing the table you want to query, you can open the Query Designer by clicking on the Create a New Query button (see fig. 8.3), or selecting Create Query from the Table menu.

If a warning box appears when you try to create a new query for the table you are currently browsing, announcing that the file is being used by another, just choose OK and the Query Designer will open as usual.

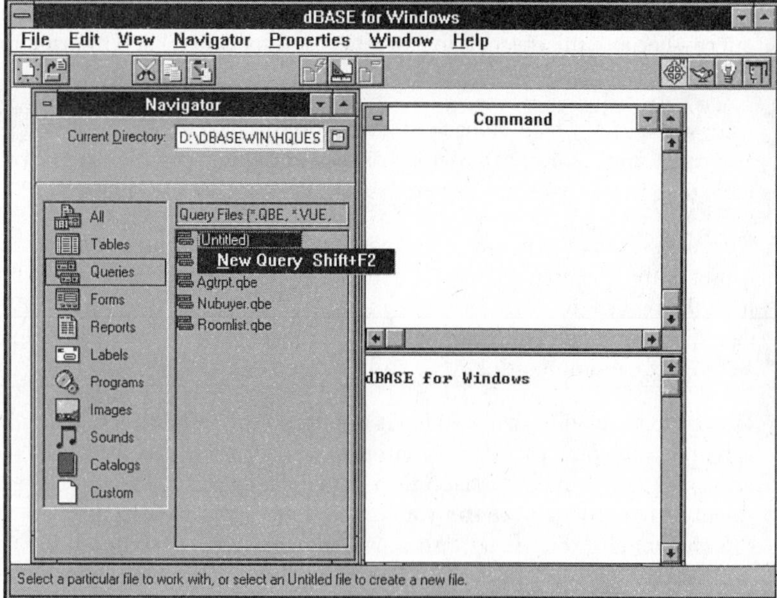

Figure 8.2
The Query group in the Navigator window.

In many of the figures in this chapter, some of the columns have been moved or resized for better illustration. Your screen might have a somewhat different appearance.

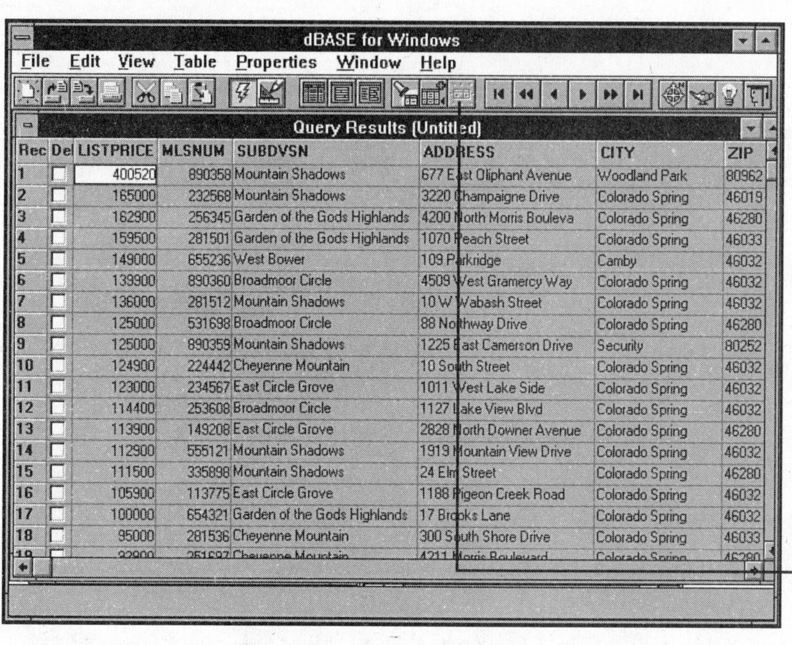

Figure 8.3
The Create a New Query SpeedBar button in a table view.

To begin to learn about the Query Designer, create a simple query based on the XLISTING table you used in previous chapters.

Using the Query Designer to Create a Query

Select File, New, Query	The Open Table Required dialog box appears
Select XLISTING from the list and choose OK	The Query Designer window opens with the XLISTING table skeleton, as shown earlier in figure 8.1

If the table you want to query is a Paradox table, select File Type in the Open Table Required dialog box and choose Paradox (*.DB) from the drop-down list. Then select the file name from the list of Paradox tables in the current directory or change directories. Everything is the same from there on.

Use the following keys to move around the Query Designer:

Key	Action
Tab	Moves to next field in the table skeleton
Shift+Tab	Moves to previous field

continues

continued

Key	Action
Shift+F2	Return from query results to query design
Ctrl+Home	Moves to the beginning field
Ctrl+End	Moves to the last field
F2	View results
F3	Moves to next table (multitable query)
F4	Moves to previous table (multitable query)
F5	Toggles field checkbox

You can also change the order of the fields in the skeleton by clicking and dragging them to a new position.

Click on the small square under the table name (the All Field checkbox)

All the fields are checked, indicating they will be included in the query

If you don't check any fields, or simply forget, dBASE includes them all. If you forget to check any fields while you are creating a multitable query, only the fields of the parent table are included—none of the child table fields.

Press Tab or click the right-pointing arrow several times until you reach the last fields

The highlight moves to other fields. The last fields are the indexes you created in the previous chapter (notice the key icons that indicate index fields and existing complex indexes)

Move back to the TAXES field and click the check mark

The TAXES field is unchecked

Repeat the last step to uncheck the TAXYEAR, ADDINFO, PHOTO fields and all the indexes

The check marks disappear from those fields and from the All Fields check box; see figure 8.4

Click on the Run Query button or choose View, Query Results

The Results table shows all the records in the XLISTING table, arranged in their natural order

Keep the query Results table open for the next exercise.

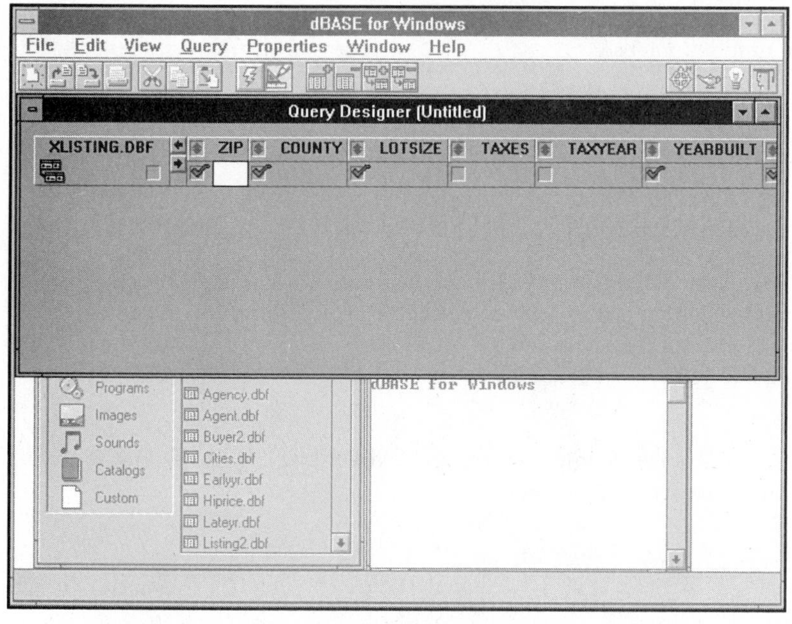

Figure 8.4
The first query design.

I find that if I need only a few of the fields, I just check them one at a time. But if I need all *but* a few, I find it is quicker to check them all first, then uncheck the ones I don't need.

Setting the Record Order

You do not have to arrange the records in the view in the same record order as the original table. You can sort the records based on any of the fields in the table or on an index. All fields have a small order box next to their field names in the skeleton. A key icon appears between the order box and the field name of fields that are already designated as index fields. You use the order box to specify the record order based on the value found in that field. You are not required to include in the view the field you use as the sort order.

You can usually edit and append records to a results table. Sometimes, however, the view is read-only because it is based on a sorted, rather than indexed, copy of the table. dBASE orders the records in the view according to a set of rules, as follows:

- ✔ If you do not specify a field or index as the sort order, the records appear in natural order in the view.

- ✔ If you indicate a single field or complex index, the resulting record order matches the field or index you use.
- ✔ If you specify a single, non-key field and the table is a DBF table, dBASE creates a temporary index to use as the sort order.
- ✔ If you have specified none of the above, dBASE creates a sorted copy of the table which results in a read-only view. Check the status bar for the read-only restriction.

Different field types have different sort order options. Numeric and date fields are limited to ascending and descending orders. Character fields can be ordered ascending or descending with or without consideration for case. Memo and binary fields have no order boxes, indicating that you cannot order the records by values for memo and binary field types.

To ensure a view that is not read-only, select only one order box and use the ASCII (case-sensitive) order or create a complex index.

If you specify a sort—which is not case-sensitive—on a character field, the resulting view is read-only. To get around this and to create an editable view, create an index on that field using the UPPER() function index of UPPER(<FLD>) TAG(TAGNAME). Select this index. This converts all values in the field to uppercase, thereby eliminating the need for a case-insensitive sort.

When you click on an order box, a drop-down list appears, as shown in figure 8.5. To choose a sort order, drag the highlight down to the order you want to select and release the mouse button.

If you have an existing complex index that represents the record order you want, just select that index. The indexes appear as fields at the right end of the table skeleton. To select the index, check the order box (you get only one option). Do not check any other order box or the results will be read-only.

A query window by default includes the complex indexes in the table skeleton. You can change this property. To suppress the display of the complex indexes, select Properties, Query Window in the Query Designer window. Then uncheck the Display Complex Indexes option in the Query Window Properties dialog box. You can also right-click in the Query window and click on the properties menu header bar (on the three dots) to open the Query Windows Properties dialog box and deselect the option.

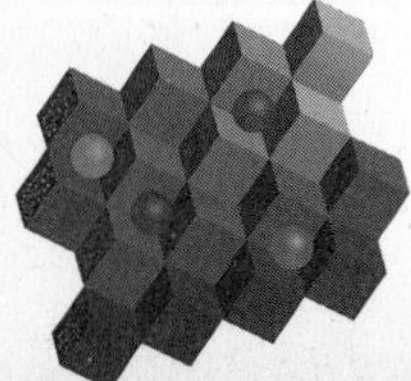

In the following exercise, you continue to build the query for the XLISTING table by rearranging the field order and changing the record order.

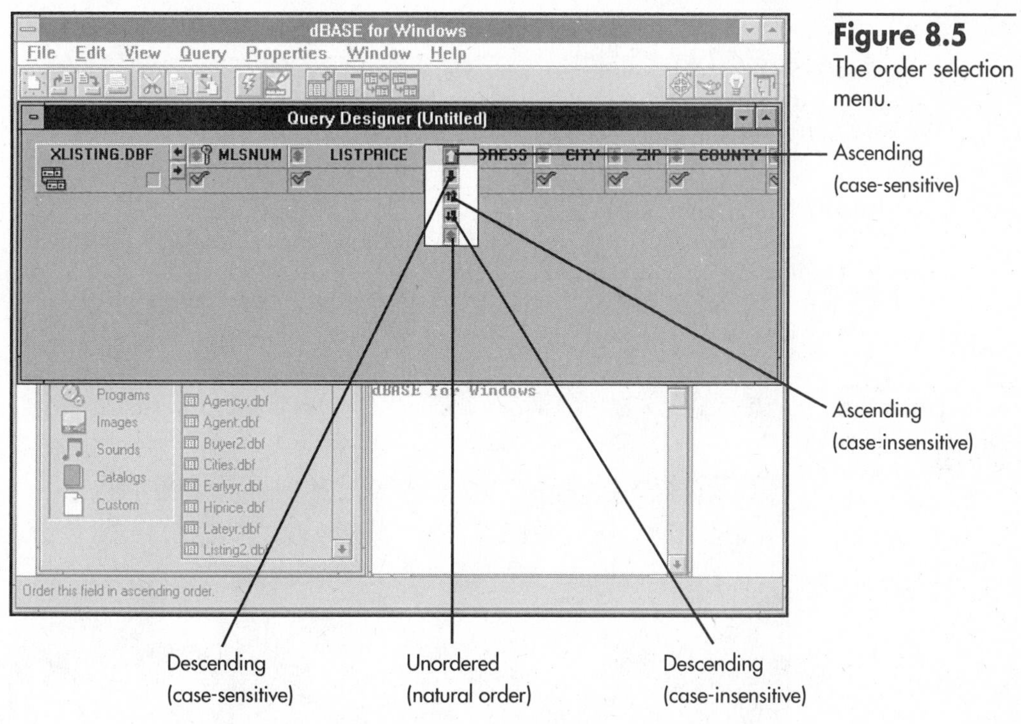

Figure 8.5
The order selection menu.

Building the Query for the XLISTING Table

Click on the Design button or choose View, Query Design	You are returned to the Query Designer window
Click on the MLSNUM field name and drag the field right one position	The mouse pointer changes to a hand when you move it over a field name. The MLSNUM field is repositioned
Move to the SUBDVSN field, click on the order button and drag down the order list to highlight Ascending order (case-insensitive), then release the mouse button	Watch the status bar for a description of the selections; an up arrow is displayed next to the SUBDVSN field name

You can also change the order option by clicking on the order box and pressing F6. Pressing F6 allows you to move through the other options in the drop-down list, one at a time, and the order arrow changes shape.

continues

continued

Drag the SUBDVSN field to the third field position in the skeleton (it will take you a few steps to get all the way across the skeleton)

The SUBDVSN field now appears next to the MLSNUM field

Move to the LISTPRICE field (now in the first field position) and set the order to Descending

A down arrow appears next to the LISTPRICE field name (notice that you have only two choices in this numeric field); the query design now looks like figure 8.6

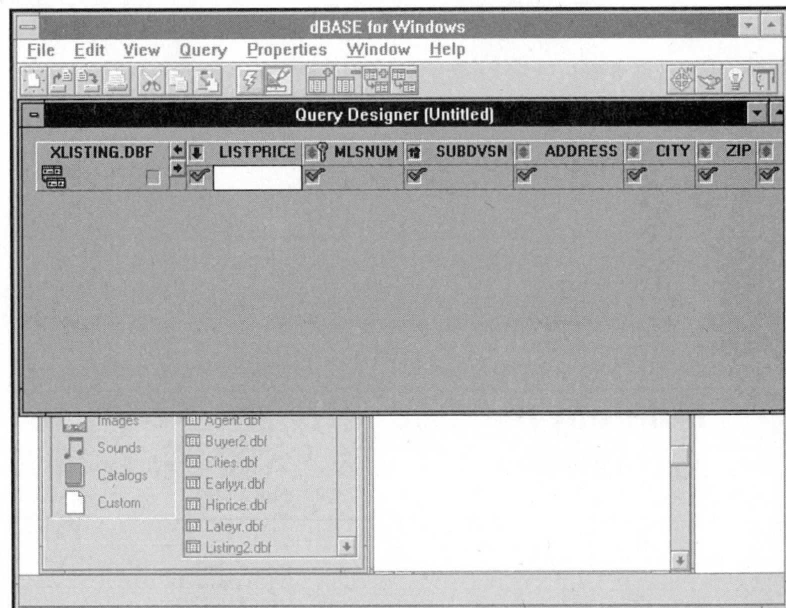

Figure 8.6
The query design with the record order changed.

Select **V**iew, Query **R**esults or click on the Run Query button

The Results table appears, as shown in figure 8.7

The table would make more sense ordered first by subdivision, then by list price within the subdivision. The priority of sort orders is from left to right in the table skeleton. To sort first on the SUBDVSN field, it must be moved to the left of the LISTPRICE field in the skeleton. You can rearrange the fields in the view if they are not arranged how you want them to appear.

Click on the Query Design button

You are returned to the Query Designer window

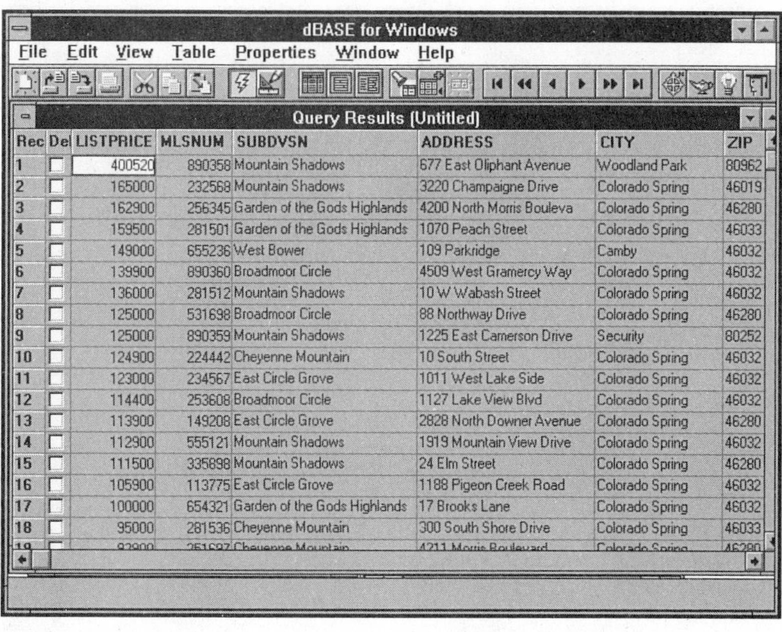

Rec	Del	LISTPRICE	MLSNUM	SUBDVSN	ADDRESS	CITY	ZIP
1		400520	890358	Mountain Shadows	677 East Oliphant Avenue	Woodland Park	80962
2		165000	232568	Mountain Shadows	3220 Champaigne Drive	Colorado Spring	46019
3		162900	256345	Garden of the Gods Highlands	4200 North Morris Bouleva	Colorado Spring	46280
4		159500	281501	Garden of the Gods Highlands	1070 Peach Street	Colorado Spring	46033
5		149000	655236	West Bower	109 Parkridge	Camby	46032
6		139900	890360	Broadmoor Circle	4509 West Gramercy Way	Colorado Spring	46032
7		136000	281512	Mountain Shadows	10 W Wabash Street	Colorado Spring	46032
8		125000	531698	Broadmoor Circle	88 Northway Drive	Colorado Spring	46280
9		125000	890359	Mountain Shadows	1225 East Cameron Drive	Security	80252
10		124900	224442	Cheyenne Mountain	10 South Street	Colorado Spring	46032
11		123000	234567	East Circle Grove	1011 West Lake Side	Colorado Spring	46032
12		114400	253608	Broadmoor Circle	1127 Lake View Blvd	Colorado Spring	46032
13		113900	149208	East Circle Grove	2828 North Downer Avenue	Colorado Spring	46280
14		112900	555121	Mountain Shadows	1919 Mountain View Drive	Colorado Spring	46032
15		111500	335898	Mountain Shadows	24 Elm Street	Colorado Spring	46280
16		105900	113775	East Circle Grove	1188 Pigeon Creek Road	Colorado Spring	46032
17		100000	654321	Garden of the Gods Highlands	17 Brooks Lane	Colorado Spring	46032
18		95000	281536	Cheyenne Mountain	300 South Shore Drive	Colorado Spring	46033

Figure 8.7
The Results table ordered by LISTPRICE and SUBDVSN.

Drag the SUBDVSN field to the first field position	The SUBDVSN field is the left-most field
Uncheck the following fields: ADDRESS, ZIP, COUNTY, YEARBUILT, GARAGE, GRGSZE, and AGENCYID	Only SUBDVSN, LISTPRICE, MLSNUM, CITY, LOTSIZE, SQFOOT, AGENTID, LISTDATE, and EXPDATE are still checked in the table skeleton
Click on the Run Query button	The finished query design is shown in figure 8.8. See figure 8.9 for the resulting view; notice the 8-digit file name and the Rdnly (Read-only) indicator in the status bar

Keep the view on the screen so you can save the query in the next exercise.

A Note from the Author

When I am designing a new query, I find that it really helps to view the data often during the process. It is so quick and easy to switch back and forth between the Query Designer window and the Results view. I build a little at a time, view the results, then return to the designer for more improvements.

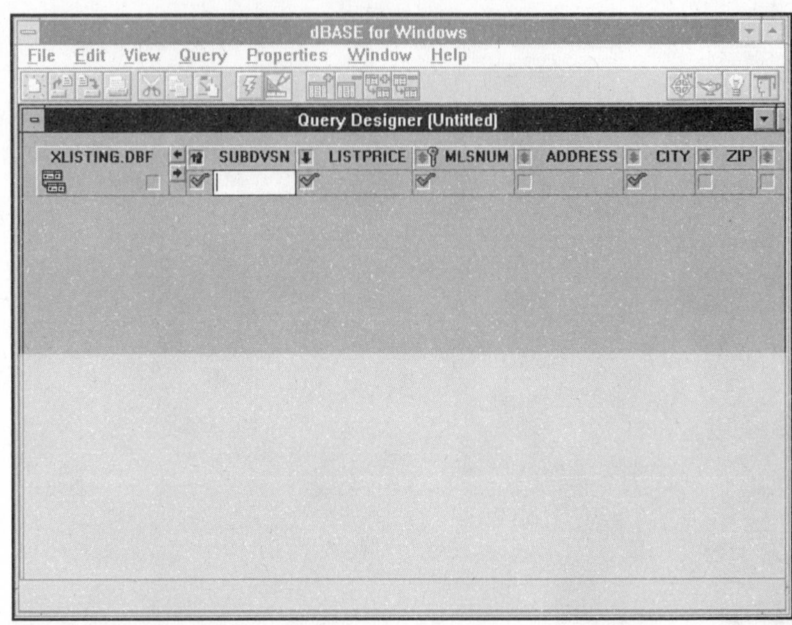

Figure 8.8 The completed Subdivision and List Price query.

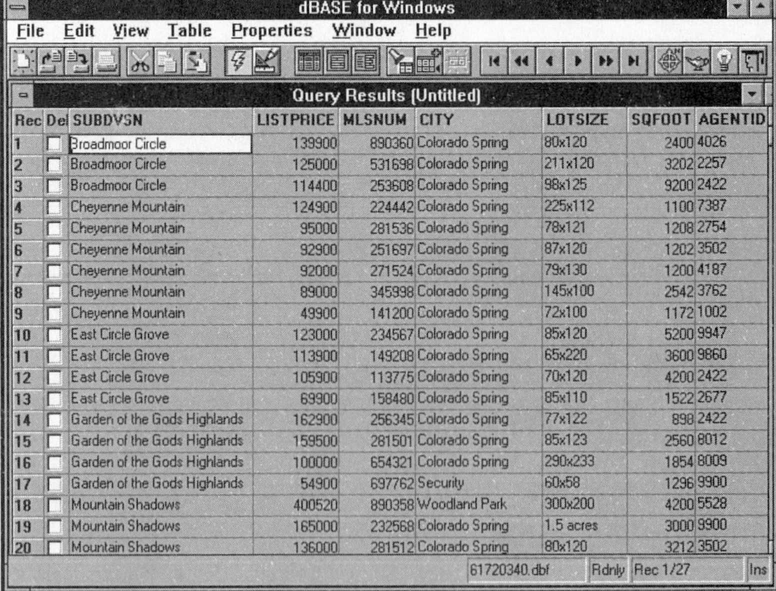

Rec	Del	SUBDVSN	LISTPRICE	MLSNUM	CITY	LOTSIZE	SQFOOT	AGENTID
1		Broadmoor Circle	139900	890360	Colorado Spring	80x120	2400	4026
2		Broadmoor Circle	125000	531698	Colorado Spring	211x120	3202	2257
3		Broadmoor Circle	114400	253608	Colorado Spring	98x125	9200	2422
4		Cheyenne Mountain	124900	224442	Colorado Spring	225x112	1100	7387
5		Cheyenne Mountain	95000	281536	Colorado Spring	78x121	1208	2754
6		Cheyenne Mountain	92900	251697	Colorado Spring	87x120	1202	3502
7		Cheyenne Mountain	92000	271524	Colorado Spring	79x130	1200	4187
8		Cheyenne Mountain	89000	345998	Colorado Spring	145x100	2542	3762
9		Cheyenne Mountain	49900	141200	Colorado Spring	72x100	1172	1002
10		East Circle Grove	123000	234567	Colorado Spring	85x120	5200	9947
11		East Circle Grove	113900	149208	Colorado Spring	65x220	3600	9860
12		East Circle Grove	105900	113775	Colorado Spring	70x120	4200	2422
13		East Circle Grove	69900	158480	Colorado Spring	85x110	1522	2677
14		Garden of the Gods Highlands	162900	256345	Colorado Spring	77x122	898	2422
15		Garden of the Gods Highlands	159500	281501	Colorado Spring	85x123	2560	8012
16		Garden of the Gods Highlands	100000	654321	Colorado Spring	290x233	1854	8009
17		Garden of the Gods Highlands	54900	697762	Security	60x58	1296	9900
18		Mountain Shadows	400520	890358	Woodland Park	300x200	4200	5528
19		Mountain Shadows	165000	232568	Colorado Spring	1.5 acres	3000	9900
20		Mountain Shadows	136000	281512	Colorado Spring	80x120	3212	3502

Figure 8.9 The view extracted by the Subdivision and List Price query.

Saving the Query

After you finish a query that you know you will want to use again, you can save it in a file with a QBE file extension. The QBE file contains all the commands that are executed when you run the query, but it does not contain any data. You can save the results of the query in a DBF file as well, but any changes you make to the underlying tables are not reflected in the view. It is safer to save the query and run it again with a freshly updated data table.

Before you can save a query, you must be in the design window. You can save only the results table from the view window. You save the query file just like any other file—by selecting File, Save (or Save As), or by pressing Ctrl+W—and then giving it a name. If you try to leave the Query Designer after you create or change a query without first saving it, you are asked if you want to save it. Save your new query with the name SUBPRICE.

Saving Your Query

Choose View, Query Design or click on the Design Query button	You are returned to the Query Designer window
Choose File, Save As	The Save File dialog box appears with the specified QBE file type
Enter the name, **SUBPRICE**, in the File Name text box and choose OK	The query command file is saved as SUBPRICE.QBE
Choose File, Close	The Query Designer window closes
Move to the Navigator window and click on the Query file type icon	Your new query name appears in the list of query files in the current directory

If you have run your query at least once, dBASE has compiled the commands into a QBO file. After you delete a query that you don't need anymore, dBASE removes the QBE file from the Navigator window and the corresponding QBO file name appears in its place. You must delete it also.

Adding Filter Conditions

If you do not want all the records to appear in the view, you can add filter conditions to the query. A *filter* is an expression that examines the value found in a field and returns either true or false. If it evaluates to true, the record is included in the view; if it returns false, the record is not included.

A filter can refer to a field value, a range of field values, or a combination of field values. For example, you can use a filter to screen all records except those from El Paso county, or except those that have a list price of more than $100,000. Another filter might combine two conditions— for example, records of homes in El Paso county that were listed by a specific agency.

You can enter filters in two ways: by entering a value or expression in the space beneath the field name in the skeleton, or by using the Condition box to enter a more complex filter. In the next exercise, you will enter simple conditions in the skeleton, and in the next section you will use the Condition box for a more complex filter.

You enter the filter value in the space below the field name in the skeleton. To limit the records to those with a specific value in a field, enter that value. For example, if you want records only for agent 6610, enter "**6610**" in the space under the name AGENTID. Note that AGENTID is a character field with numbers stored in it. Unless you are doing math with numbers, you should store fields such as ZIP codes in character field format. Do not use quotes if the field is numeric.

Many of the filters include a relational operator that specifies the type of condition, such as "LISTPRICE greater than $100,000." The relational operator symbols are explained in table 8.1. If you do not include an operator, dBASE assumes you mean "equal to."

Table 8.1
The Relational Operators Used in Queries

Operator	Meaning
<	Less than
=	Equal to
>= or =>	Greater than or equal to
<= or =<	Less than or equal to
<> or #	Not equal to
$	Contains (or is contained in)
LIKE	Pattern match

The following are examples of using these relational operators in query filters:

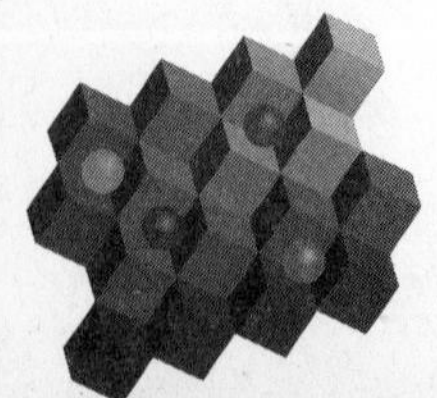

Example	Interpretation
>="G"	Matches all values in the character field that begin with "G" or with any letter higher in the alphabet; case-sensitive.
<>"ABC"	Matches records that do not equal "ABC."
<{01/01/95}	Matches records with dates before January 1, 1995.
$ "garage"	Matches records with the word "garage" somewhere in the field.
LIKE *Realty	Matches any record that ends with the word "Realty."
>123 $"TEXT" .T.	ND quotes for numeric field For memo field Logistical field

The LIKE operator uses wild cards to search for a pattern of characters in a field. dBASE uses the standard wild-card characters: an asterisk (*) to represent any number of characters (or none), and a question mark (?) to represent a single character. Enter the wild cards in the character string you use for filtering. You must enclose the search string, including the wild cards, in quotation marks. For example, the filter expression, LIKE "(619)*" in the PHONE field includes all phone numbers that have a 619 prefix. The expression LIKE "S???h" includes all values such as Smith and Scoth but not Smithe or Such.

Rules for Using Filters

Certain rules apply to using filter conditions with different data types. To add a filter to a character data type, you must enclose the value in a set of delimiters: double quotation marks (""), single quotation marks (''), or square brackets ([]). For example, to find all records for the Cheyenne Mountain subdivision, type **"Cheyenne Mountain"** in the space under the SUBDVSN field name. If you are testing for blank character fields, use the delimiters with no text between them: **""**. To test for fields that are not blank, use **<>""** (not equal to blank).

To filter on a numeric field, enter the value in the space below the field name just the way it is stored in the table. You can use a decimal point, commas, and a negative sign.

When you enter a value for a date field, you must enclose the value in curly brackets ({}). Again, to find all fields with blank dates use the delimiters with no date. To find all records that are not blank in the date field, use **<>{}**.

To query on a logical field, enter one of the logical expressions in the space under the field name: **.t.**, **.T.**, **.y.**, or **.Y.** for "true" and **.f.**, **.F.**, **.n.**, or **.N.** for "false."

To search a memo field for a value, use the $ operator, which means that the specified character string occurs somewhere in the memo text.

If you make an error when you enter the filter condition expression, it is highlighted when you try to run the query and an error message appears in the status bar.

In the next exercise, you will modify the query you saved earlier and add some filters that limit the records to those for listings made before January 1, 1995 and with list prices greater than $100,000.

You can open an existing query in several ways from the Navigator window:

- ✔ Right-click the Query icon and choose **R**un Query or Design **Q**uery from the Query SpeedMenu shown in figure 8.10

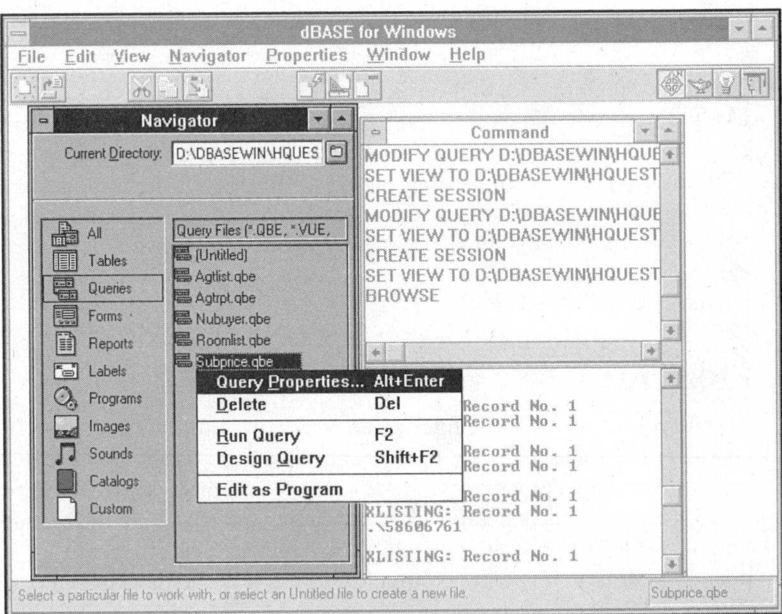

Figure 8.10
The Query SpeedMenu.

- ✔ Click the Query icon, then click the Run Query or Design Query button
- ✔ Double-click the Query icon to run the query
- ✔ Double-right-click the Query icon to open the Query Designer window

You can also open the query by selecting **F**ile, **O**pen, **Q**uery or by clicking the Open File button. Then select the query file name from the list in the Open File dialog box and choose **R**un Query or Design **Q**uery.

A Note from the Author

When I choose **F**ile, **N**ew, sometimes I get a list of data tables (DBF files) and sometimes a list of queries or reports. I discovered that the type of file listed in the Open File dialog box is the one currently highlighted in the Navigator file type panel.

The quickest way to open a saved query in the design mode is through the Navigator. Use the steps in the following exercise.

Opening a Query in Design Mode

Click the Query file type icon in the Navigator	A list of saved QBE files appears
Right-click on the SUBPRICE file name	The Query SpeedMenu appears
Choose Design **Q**uery	The Query Designer window opens with the saved structure
Move to the LISTPRICE field and enter **>100000**	You have added the condition that the view will include only those records with more than $100,000 in the LISTPRICE field
Move to the EXPDATE field and enter **<={01/01/95}**	You have set a filter to include records with expiration dates before Jan. 1, 1995 (see fig. 8.11); the EXPDATE field was moved to be in sight
Click the Run Query button	The resulting view is shown in figure 8.12
Click the Design button	You are returned to the Query Designer window

continues

continued

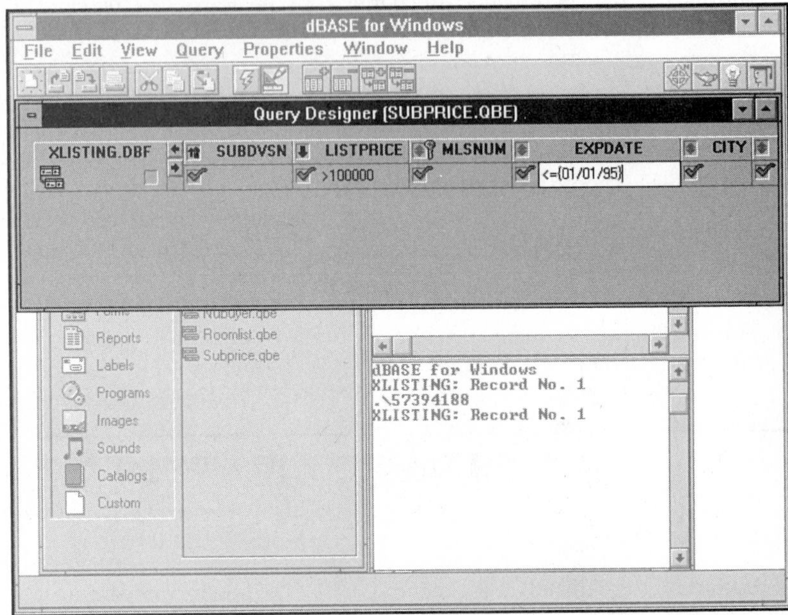

Figure 8.11 The query design with a filter set on the EXPDATE field.

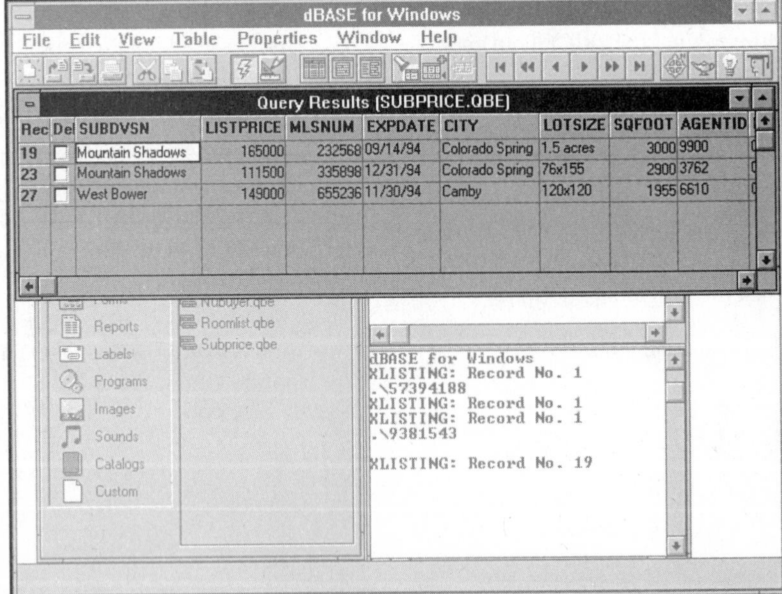

Figure 8.12 The revised SUBPRICE view containing three records that met the filter conditions.

Close the file, saving the changes	You are returned to the dBASE desktop

A Note from the Author

When I returned to the saved SUBPRICE query, the fields were not in the same sequence in the skeleton as when I left it. The fields were, however, all correctly checked and arranged in the same relative positions so that the ordering sequence was not disturbed.

Combining Filter Conditions

If you include two or more filter conditions, you must specify whether they must all be met for the record to be included in the view or just any one of them. The two conditions you entered into the query design in the previous exercise limited the records to those that meet *both* the conditions and is called an AND relationship. If meeting *any one* of the conditions will allow the record to be included, it is an OR relationship.

If you want to include two or more filters in the same field with an AND relationship, enter all the conditions in the space below the field name and separate them with commas. For example, the filter >={01/01/94}, <={12/31/94} will include all records with dates in the year 1994. If the conditions apply to different fields, enter each condition in the appropriate field space.

If you want to include two or more filters with an OR relationship in the same field or different fields, place the conditions on separate lines in the query structure. To add a line to the query, press the down arrow. For example, if you want records for Mr. Smith and Ms. Jones, enter **"Smith"** on one line, press the down arrow and enter **"Jones"** on the second line (don't forget the quotation marks).

In the next exercise you will see how to create an OR relationship in which either condition will qualify the record for inclusion in the view.

Creating an OR Relationship

Double-click the Untitled icon in the Navigator Query file panel	The Open File Required dialog box appears
Select the XLISTING table file and choose OK	The XLISTING table skeleton appears in the Query Designer window as before
Check the following fields: MLSNUM, LISTPRICE, ADDRESS, COUNTY, SUBDVSN, and LISTDATE	The six fields appear with check marks

continues

continued

Click and drag the fields so they are all next to each other in the skeleton but do not change their relative order	All six checked fields now show on the screen at once
Create an OR condition in the same field:	
Move to the COUNTY field and enter **"El Paso"** (be sure to include the quotation marks) then press the down arrow	A second line is added to the query skeleton, as shown in figure 8.13
Enter **"Boone"** in the second line under the COUNTY field name	You have created a condition that will extract records with either El Paso or Boone in the COUNTY field
Run the query	

Figure 8.14 shows the records that appear in the new view.

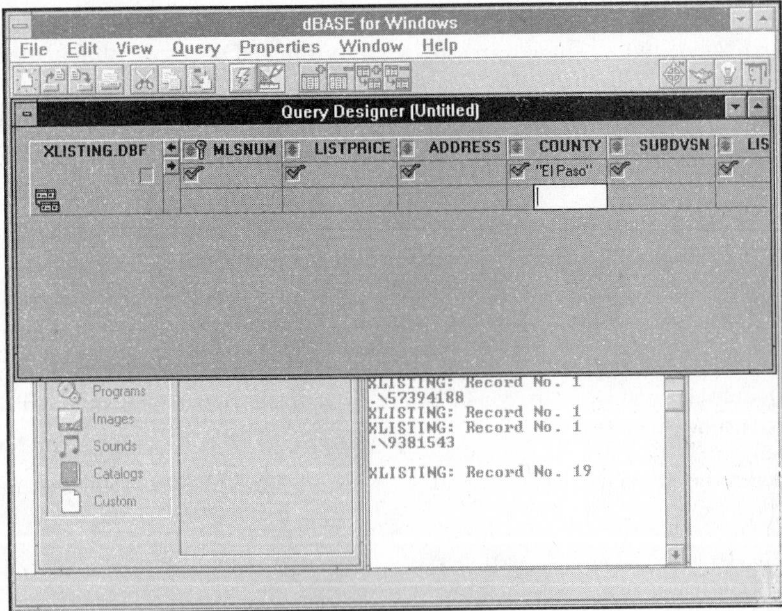

Figure 8.13 The query design with a second line added.

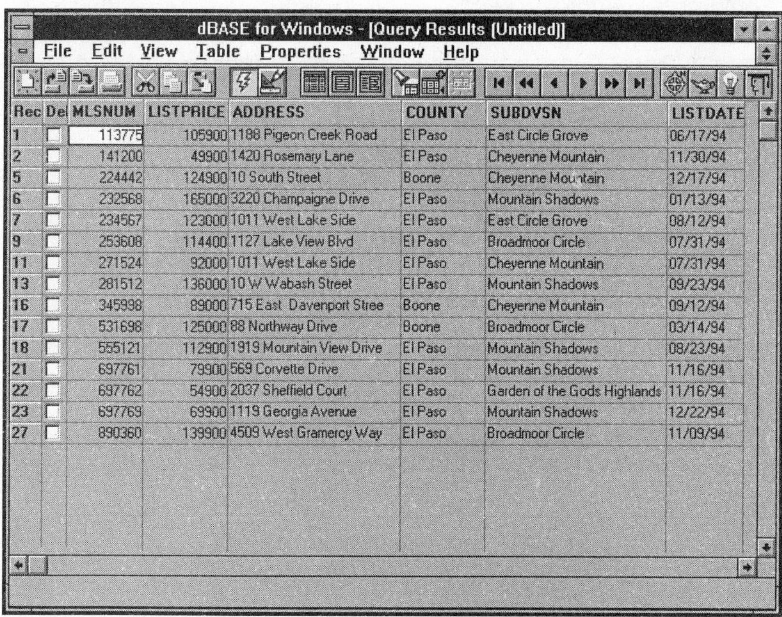

Rec	Del	MLSNUM	LISTPRICE	ADDRESS	COUNTY	SUBDVSN	LISTDATE
1		113775	105900	1188 Pigeon Creek Road	El Paso	East Circle Grove	06/17/94
2		141200	49900	1420 Rosemary Lane	El Paso	Cheyenne Mountain	11/30/94
5		224442	124900	10 South Street	Boone	Cheyenne Mountain	12/17/94
6		232568	165000	3220 Champaigne Drive	El Paso	Mountain Shadows	01/13/94
7		234567	123000	1011 West Lake Side	El Paso	East Circle Grove	08/12/94
9		253608	114400	1127 Lake View Blvd	El Paso	Broadmoor Circle	07/31/94
11		271524	92000	1011 West Lake Side	El Paso	Cheyenne Mountain	07/31/94
13		281512	136000	10 W Wabash Street	El Paso	Mountain Shadows	09/23/94
16		345938	89000	715 East Davenport Stree	Boone	Cheyenne Mountain	09/12/94
17		531698	125000	88 Northway Drive	Boone	Broadmoor Circle	03/14/94
18		555121	112900	1919 Mountain View Drive	El Paso	Mountain Shadows	08/23/94
21		697761	79900	569 Corvette Drive	El Paso	Mountain Shadows	11/16/94
22		697762	54900	2037 Sheffield Court	El Paso	Garden of the Gods Highlands	11/16/94
23		697763	69900	1119 Georgia Avenue	El Paso	Mountain Shadows	12/22/94
27		890360	139900	4509 West Gramercy Way	El Paso	Broadmoor Circle	11/09/94

Figure 8.14
The view containing listings in El Paso and Boone counties.

When you want to extract records from El Paso and Boone counties, you must create an OR relationship even though when you speak the condition, you say "and." A home obviously could not be in both counties at once, so if you asked for records that had both El Paso and Boone in the same field, you would get an empty view.

Next, create an OR condition using two different fields by limiting the records to those for homes in the Mountain Shadows subdivision or with a list price of less than or equal to $100,000.

Creating an OR Condition Using Two Different Fields

Choose View, Query Design	You are returned to the Query Designer window
Delete the "Boone" entry in the second line and press the up arrow	The second line is removed

continues

continued

Delete the "El Paso" entry in the COUNTY field and move to the SUBDVSN and enter **Mountain Shadows**, then press the down arrow	A second line is added to the field skeleton again
Move to the LISTPRICE field, press the down arrow, and enter **<=100000** on the second line; run the query	The Results table contains records of all the homes in the Mountain Shadows subdivision plus all the homes with list prices less than or equal to $100,000

In the next set of steps, you will build an AND condition with both requirements relating to the same field, the LISTDATE field. You want to extract records for all listings made during the months of July, August and September.

Click the Design Query button	You are returned to the Query Designer window
Delete both the conditions you added in the preceding steps and remove the second line by pressing the up arrow	The design returns to the original state with no filter conditions
Move to the LISTDATE field and enter **>={07/01/94}, <={09/30/94};** (be sure to separate the two conditions with a comma and enclose the dates in curly brackets)	The field width expands to include all the characters of the compound filter condition, as shown in figure 8.15

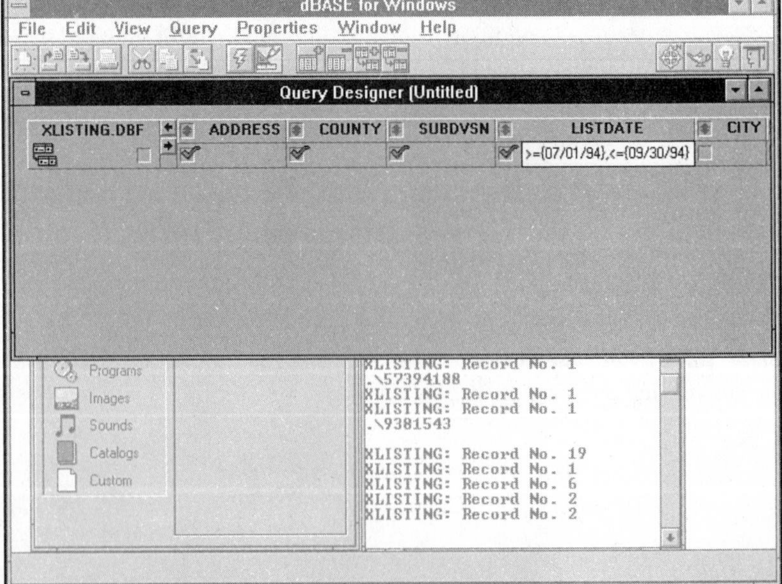

Figure 8.15
The query design with an AND filter on a single field.

Run the query	The results of the query are shown in figure 8.16

dBASE for Windows - [Query Results (Untitled)]

File Edit View Table Properties Window Help

Rec	Del	MLSNUM	LISTPRICE	ADDRESS	COUNTY	SUBDVSN	LISTDATE
3		149208	113900	2828 North Downer Avenue	Teller	East Circle Grove	09/24/94
7		234567	123000	1011 West Lake Side	El Paso	East Circle Grove	08/12/94
9		253608	114400	1127 Lake View Blvd	El Paso	Broadmoor Circle	07/31/94
10		256345	162900	4200 North Morris Bouleva	Teller	Garden of the Gods Highlands	08/12/94
11		271524	92000	1011 West Lake Side	El Paso	Cheyenne Mountain	07/31/94
13		281512	136000	10 W Wabash Street	El Paso	Mountain Shadows	09/23/94
15		335898	111500	24 Elm Street	Dennison	Mountain Shadows	08/15/94
16		345998	89000	715 East Davenport Stree	Boone	Cheyenne Mountain	09/12/94
18		555121	112900	1919 Mountain View Drive	El Paso	Mountain Shadows	08/23/94
20		655236	149000	109 Parkridge	Wyvern	West Bower	07/15/94
25		890358	400520	677 East Oliphant Avenue	Teller	Mountain Shadows	09/25/94

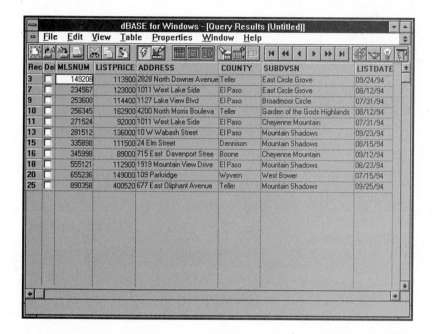

Figure 8.16
The records extracted by the date range filter.

Choose **F**ile, **C**lose without saving	You are returned to the dBASE desktop

Using the Condition Box

Another way to add filter conditions to your query is to enter them in the Condition box. The Condition box enables you to combine several conditions into a single expression. The expression also allows use of dBASE functions you normally wouldn't have in the condition field. You can also build filters based on comparisons of field values from two or more related tables. The filter statement generated from the condition must contain less than 4KB characters. You are not likely to exceed this limit in normal operations. When you place filter conditions in the condition box, you must include the relevant field name.

All the relational operators are used the same in the Condition box as in the field areas, except the $ operator. In the field, the $ means "contains." For example, **$ "garage"** placed in the ADDINFO field filter means "contains the word 'garage' somewhere in the field." In the Condition box, the syntax becomes: **"garage" $ ADDINFO** (the word 'garage' is contained somewhere in the ADDINFO field).

In the next exercise you will create a query to extract records that meet the prospective buyer's list of requirements from the XLISTING table. You will enter all the criteria in one condition statement in the Condition box.

In that exercise, your prospective buyer is looking for a home in a price range between $80,000 and $150,000, between 1,000 and 3,000 square feet in size, and built between 1985 and 1992. All conditions must be met before the home will be considered.

Creating a Query to Extract Records

Choose File, New, Query	The Open File Required dialog box appears
Select XLISTING from the file list	The Query Designer window appears, containing the XLISTING table skeleton
Click the order box in the MLSNUM field and choose ascending	The view will be ordered by ascending MLSNUM
Check the following fields: MLSNUM, LISTPRICE, ADDRESS, YEARBUILT, SQFOOT, AGENTID	Only those fields are to be included in the resulting view
Choose Query, Add Conditions	An empty Condition box opens below the query
Enter the following conditions *all on one line* in the Condition box (don't forget the commas):	The Condition box looks like figure 8.17

LISTPRICE>80000,LISTPRICE<150000,SQFOOT>1000,

SQFOOT<3000,YEARBUILT>="1985",YEARBUILT<="1992"

You can add lines to the Condition box, but each additional line represents an OR condition. In the preceding case, you want an AND condition (all conditions must be met), so you must enter the entire statement in one line. If it becomes too long for the width of the window, dBASE scrolls the text out of sight.

Click the Run Query button	The resulting view is shown in figure 8.18; eight records were extracted
Return to the design window and save the query as BUYREQ, then choose File; close without saving.	You are returned to the dBASE desktop

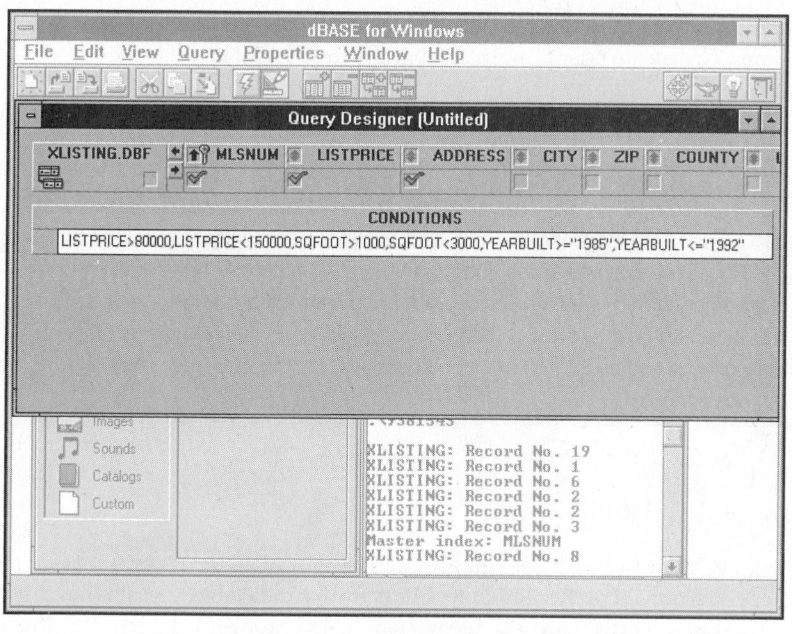

Figure 8.17
The Condition box containing the compound condition.

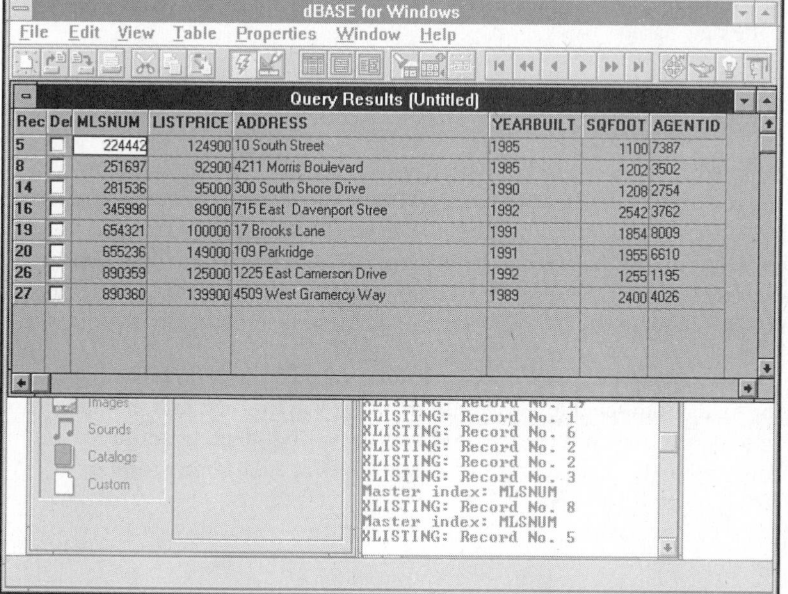

Figure 8.18
The view containing listings matching the buyer's requirements.

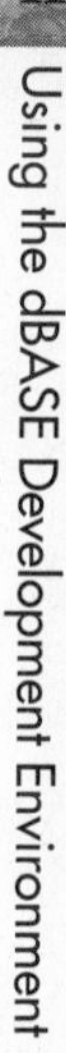

Reopen the Query Designer for the BUYREQ query you just saved and move through the table skeleton	The Condition box is no longer displayed and the filters have been added to the appropriate fields

To delete conditions placed in the Condition box, click in the box and select **Q**uery, Remove Conditions. To remove conditions placed in the field areas, highlight the expression and press Delete.

A Note from the Author

When I built a filter using the Condition box and saved the query, then reopened the designer, the Condition box was gone. I thought the entire filter had been erased, but when I looked at the table skeleton, I discovered that the conditions I had specified in the Condition box had been moved to their proper positions in the field areas. So if the conditions can be expressed in terms of field values, dBASE puts them there when you save the query design.

Using the Results Table

When you run a query, the result is a table that contains a copy of all the records that met the specified filter conditions. The Results table differs from a data table in that it is a temporary file. dBASE saves a view as a DBF file with an 8-digit number for a name. If you want to use the view in a later session, you should copy the records to a new file that has a more meaningful name and save it. To copy the view, select **Q**uery, Copy Results to New Table and enter the new name.

You cannot use the new table to update the original file because it is no longer coupled to the original file by the query.

You can treat the Results table as you would treat any other table. You can scroll up and down through the records, resize the columns, rearrange the fields, switch view layouts, edit the data, make calculations, print the view, create new indexes, and so forth. The only restriction is that if dBASE has used a sorted copy of the original table, the Results table is read-only and you cannot edit records in it or append more records. The conditions under which dBASE must create a sorted table are described earlier in this chapter.

The advantage of using queries is that you can combine data from several related tables and select specific fields from specific records. In that way, you can view and update across the related tables and ensure data accuracy and integrity among them. In addition, you can be sure to have updated information from all the tables in a data-entry form or a printed report that is based on a query.

You can apply the data-controlling features of the Table Records Properties dialog box to the Results table, but if you are planning to use the query as a basis for a data-entry form it is better to have the form itself perform the data validation operations. The view is a temporary file and the controls are not saved. The controls added to the form design, on the other hand, are saved permanently and are imposed on any data you enter into it, including data from a query.

Extracting Data from Multiple Tables

If you want to create a view that contains data that is stored in two or more tables, you can add all the tables to a query and establish relationships among them. You can add up to 255 tables (the maximum number of work areas) to one query. The first table selected for the query becomes the parent table and all subsequent tables are subordinate (child tables) to the first.

You must index the child table on the field that provides the link to the parent. When you set the relation in the Query Designer, you can create a new temporary index for the child table just for the link.

See Chapter 4, "Designing and Creating Relational Databases," for more information on parent-child table relations and how to establish them.

Creating a Two-Table Query

During the creation of a multitable query design, you can add or remove the tables and modify or remove relations in the following three ways:

- ✔ Right-click in the Query Design window and select an object from the Query Designer Properties menu shown in figure 8.19
- ✔ Choose from the Query menu
- ✔ Click a Query Designer SpeedBar button (refer back to fig. 8.1)

In the following exercise, you will build a query that extracts data from both the XAGENT and XLISTING tables. The relationship between them is *one-to-many*, because one agent can have several listings—but a single listing refers to only one agent. When you build a query, select the parent table first and then add the subordinate tables.

In the following exercise, you want to find the listings that are not in El Paso county and that are listed for more than $100,000. You also want to limit the fields to the relevant agent and listing information.

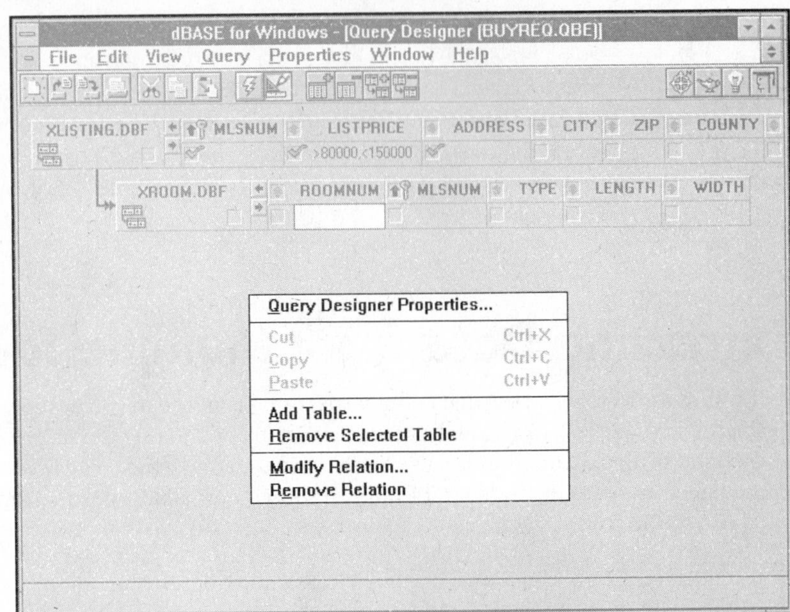

Figure 8.19
The Query Designer Properties menu.

Limiting Your Search Listings

Click on the Query file type icon in the Navigator window	The list of available query files appears
Double-click on the Untitled icon	The Open Table Required dialog box appears
Choose XAGENT from the file name list	The XAGENT table skeleton appears in the Query Designer window
Click the Add Table button or choose Query, Add Table	The Open Table Required dialog box appears
Select XLISTING from the list and choose OK	The XLISTING skeleton is added to the query design as shown in figure 8.20

Next join the two tables by the common AGENTID field.

Click on the XAGENT table icon and drag the Create Link pointer to the XLISTING table icon	Figure 8.21 shows the Create Link pointer linking the XAGENT and XLISTING tables

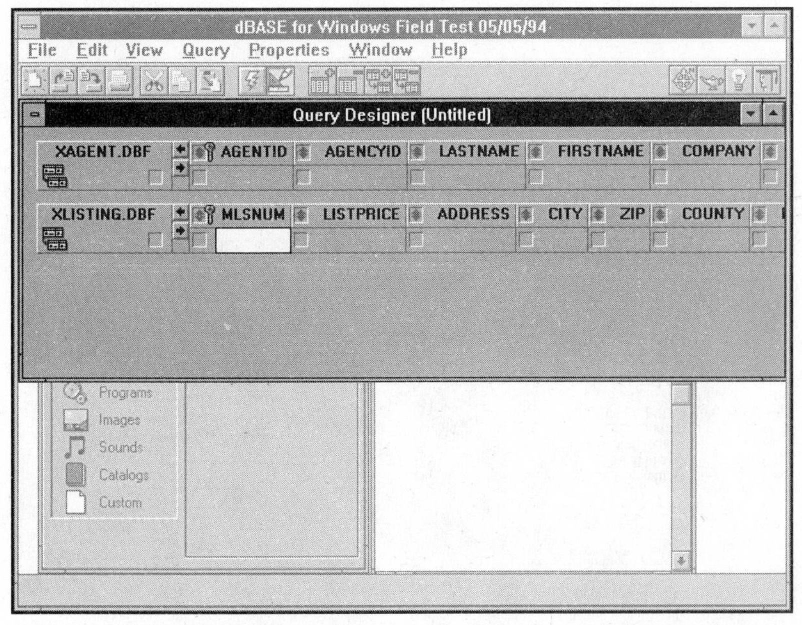

Figure 8.20
The query design with two tables.

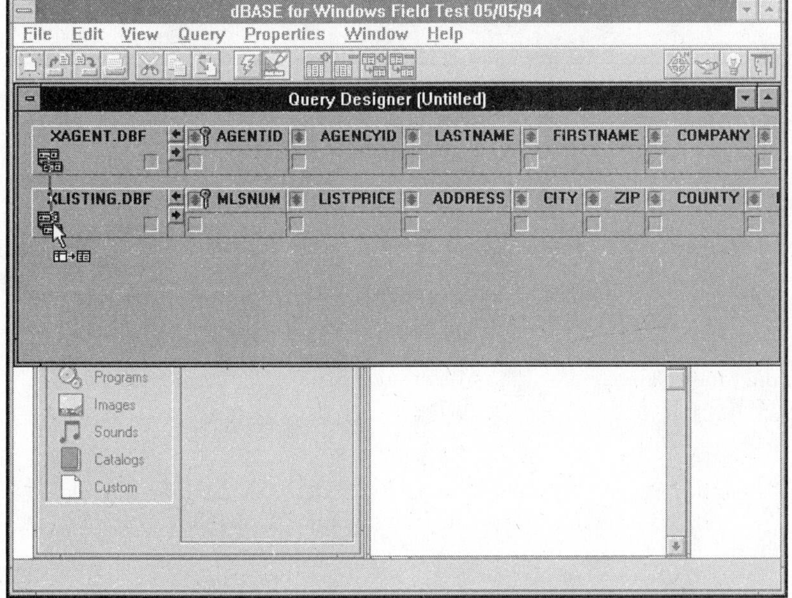

Figure 8.21
Dragging the Create Link pointer to link two tables.

continues

continued

Release the mouse button

The Define Relation dialog box appears, as shown in figure 8.22

Figure 8.22
The Define Relation dialog box.

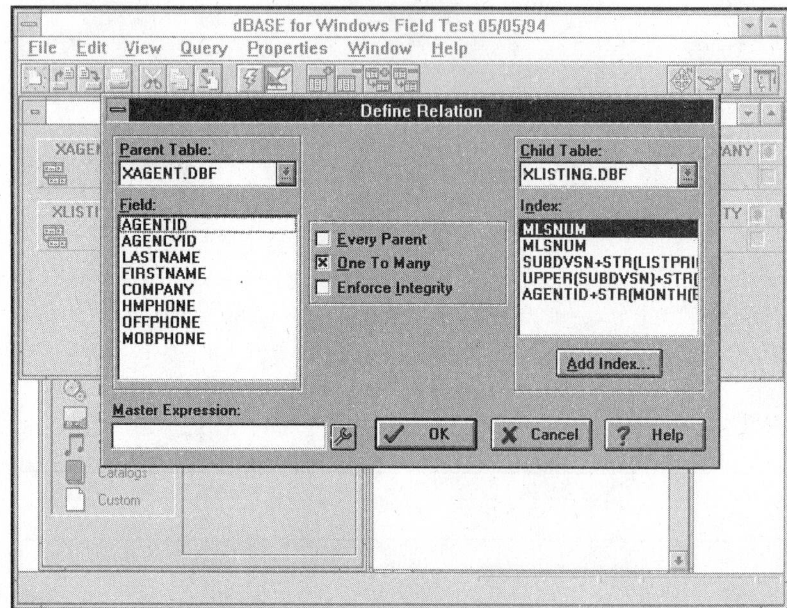

Choose AGENTID from the Parent Table Field list

No index in the child table (XLISTING) is equivalent to the AGENTID key field of the parent table

Choose Add Index in the Child Table panel

The Create Index dialog box appears; refer to Chapter 7, "Indexing, Sorting and Locating Your Data," for details on creating a simple index

Enter LISTAGT in the Index Name text box and enter AGENTID as the key expression; choose OK

You are returned to the Define Relation dialog box

Select AGENTID as the Index for the Child Table

You have completed establishing the relation; the dialog box now looks like figure 8.23

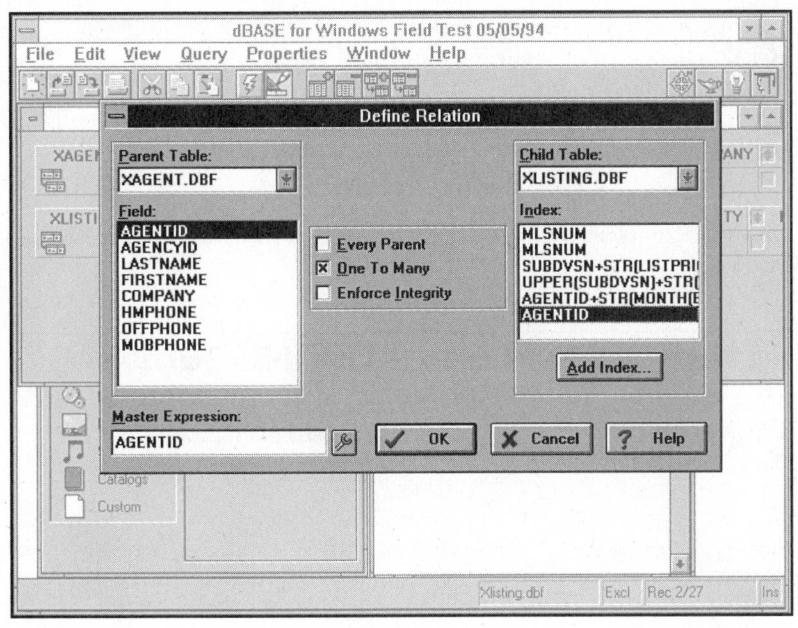

Figure 8.23
The completed Define Relation dialog box.

Accept the One to Many link option and choose OK

You are returned to the Query Designer window; the double-headed arrow that connects the two tables indicates that the relation is one-to-many

Keep the window open for the next exercise.

When you relate two tables, you can choose from among the following link options:

- ✔ **Every Parent.** Specifies that every record in the parent table appears in the view, regardless of whether it matches any child records. If you do not check this option, only records in the parent table that match one or more records in the child table appear in the view.

- ✔ **One-to-Many.** Specifies that all the child records that match a parent record appear in the view. If you leave this option unchecked, only the first child record that matches the parent record appears.

- ✔ **Enforce Integrity.** Determines what happens if you try to do something to interfere with the referential integrity between the parent and child table. For example, if this option is checked and you try to delete a parent record that has matching child records, you are asked if you want to cancel the deletion or delete the child records as well. If this option is not checked, you can delete the parent record and not affect any child records.

To change the link option in a query design, click once in the child table and select Query, Modify Relation to open the Define Relation dialog box, where you can select a different option. To delete the relation, click in the child table and select Query, Remove Relation. These two options are also available in the Query Designer Properties menu, which you can reach by selecting a child table skeleton and right-clicking within the Query Designer window.

In the next exercise, you complete the query you started earlier—linking the XAGENT and XLISTING tables.

Linking the XAGENT and XLISTING Tables

In the XAGENT table skeleton, select the following fields: AGENTID, AGENCYID, LASTNAME, and OFFPHONE. Click the AGENTID order box and select Ascending Order (case-sensitive)

Check marks appear in the field areas and the AGENTID field shows an up arrow in the order box

In the XLISTING table skeleton, select the following fields: MLSNUM, LISTPRICE, and ADDRESS

You do not need to check the AGENTID field in both tables; if you do, you will get two of them

Move to the LISTPRICE field and enter **>=100000** under the field name as the filter

The query design looks like figure 8.24

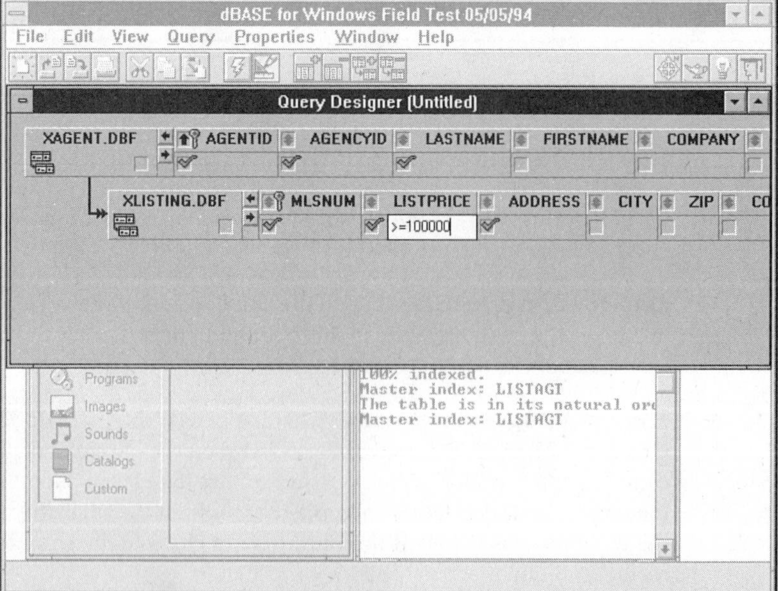

Figure 8.24
The completed query design.

Run the query	The Results table is shown in figure 8.25

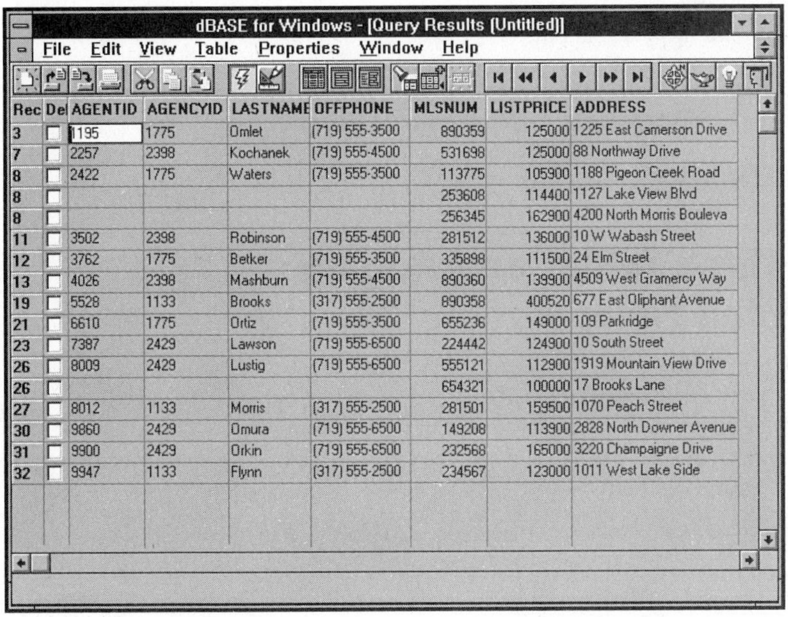

dBASE for Windows - [Query Results (Untitled)]

File Edit View Table Properties Window Help

Rec	Del	AGENTID	AGENCYID	LASTNAME	OFFPHONE	MLSNUM	LISTPRICE	ADDRESS
3		1195	1775	Omlet	(719) 555-3500	890359	125000	1225 East Camerson Drive
7		2257	2398	Kochanek	(719) 555-4500	531698	125000	88 Northway Drive
8		2422	1775	Waters	(719) 555-3500	113775	105900	1188 Pigeon Creek Road
8						253608	114400	1127 Lake View Blvd
8						256345	162900	4200 North Morris Bouleva
11		3502	2398	Robinson	(719) 555-4500	281512	136000	10 W Wabash Street
12		3762	1775	Betker	(719) 555-3500	335898	111500	24 Elm Street
13		4026	2398	Mashburn	(719) 555-4500	890360	139900	4509 West Gramercy Way
19		5528	1133	Brooks	(317) 555-2500	890358	400520	677 East Oliphant Avenue
21		6610	1775	Ortiz	(719) 555-3500	655236	149000	109 Parkridge
23		7387	2429	Lawson	(719) 555-6500	224442	124900	10 South Street
26		8009	2429	Lustig	(719) 555-6500	555121	112900	1919 Mountain View Drive
26						654321	100000	17 Brooks Lane
27		8012	1133	Morris	(317) 555-2500	281501	159500	1070 Peach Street
30		9860	2429	Omura	(719) 555-6500	149208	113900	2828 North Downer Avenue
31		9900	2429	Orkin	(719) 555-6500	232568	165000	3220 Champaigne Drive
32		9947	1133	Flynn	(317) 555-2500	234567	123000	1011 West Lake Side

Figure 8.25
The view resulting from the query joining the XAGENT and XLISTING tables.

Choose <u>V</u>iew, Query <u>D</u>esign	You are returned to the Query Designer window
Move to the COUNTY field in the XLISTING skeleton and enter the condition, **<>"El Paso"** (meaning not in El Paso County)	The field does not need to be checked to be used in a filter condition
Run the query again	There are fewer records in the view
Return to the design window and delete the filter on the COUNTY field; move to the OFFPHONE field in the XAGENT skeleton and enter the condition, **LIKE "(317)*"** and run the query	The view contains records for the three listings for agents whose office telephone number bears the (317) prefix
Choose <u>F</u>ile, <u>C</u>lose without saving	You are returned to the dBASE desktop

To remove a table from the query design, click in the table skeleton you want to delete and do one of the following:

- ✔ Click on the Remove Table button
- ✔ Right-click in the Query Designer window and choose **R**emove Selected Table from the Query Designer Properties menu
- ✔ Choose **Q**uery, **R**emove Selected Table

Linking Three Tables and Adding a Calculated Field

When you add more tables to the query design, you have more data from which to choose. Each table must be linked to a table already in the design with a valid dBASE relationship. You can get more information out of the resulting view by combining fields and performing calculations. Use a calculated field on field data to compute such values as commission fees and discounts.

Calculated fields need not be exclusively numeric. You can combine character fields with the concatenation operators to create a new field. For example, the expression

```
LASTNAME-", "+FIRSTNAME
```

uses the trim operator (-) to strip off the trailing blanks from the LASTNAME field before adding a comma and a space. Then the regular concatenation operator (+) adds the FIRSTNAME.

The calculated field appears as the last fields in the Results table, but you can reposition them later. To include the field in the view, check the field box just as you would any other field. You can also add a filter condition to limit the records in the view based on the result of the calculation. Calculated fields are always read-only.

dBASE names the calculated fields sequentially as they are defined: CALC01, CALC02, and so forth. You can rename them by clicking on the field name and typing in a new name. If you are going to include the field in the view, you probably want to use more useful names.

In the next exercise, you will link three tables in one query, XAGENCY, XAGENT and XLISTING with XAGENCY as the parent table. Fields from each table will be included in the view table and the records will be ordered in ascending order of AGENCYID. You will add a calculated field that shows the number of days since the home was first listed. Because this is a calculated field and results in a read-only field in the view, it can be used as a secondary index to order the child records within the parent record group.

Linking Three Tables in One Query

Action	Result
Click on the Query file type icon in the Navigator window and double-click on the Untitled icon	The Open Table in Required dialog box appears
Select the XAGENCY table name and choose OK	The XAGENCY table skeleton appears in the Query Designer window
Right-click in the query window and choose Add Table from the Query Designer Properties menu	The Open Table Required dialog box appears, as before
Select XAGENT from the list of table names and choose OK	The XAGENT skeleton is added to the query design
Repeat step 3 and select XLISTING from the list of table names and choose OK	Three tables are included in the query design as shown in figure 8.26

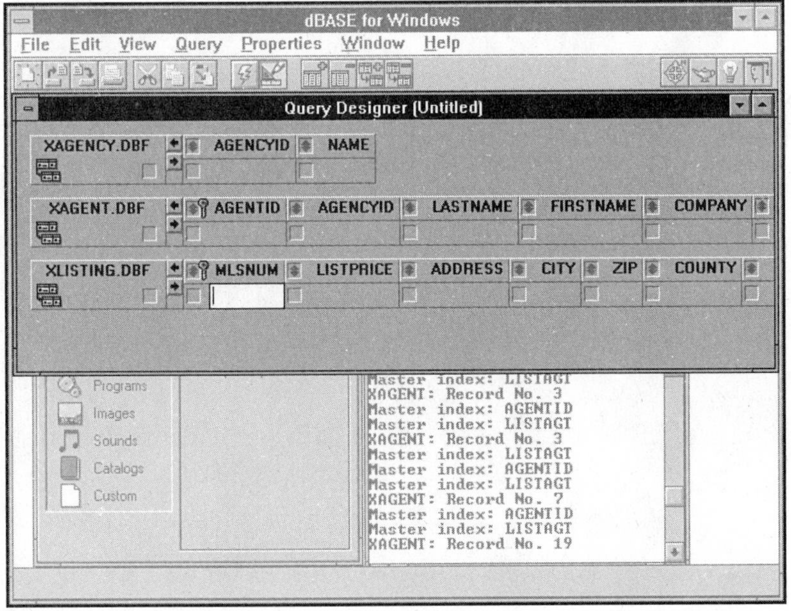

Figure 8.26
The query design containing three tables.

Action	Result
Click the XAGENCY table icon and drag the Create Link pointer to the XAGENT icon	The Set Relation dialog box appears

continues

continued

Choose AGENCYID as the Parent Table linking field	AGENCYID appears in the Master Expression text box
Choose Add Index in the child table panel	The Create Index dialog box appears
Enter AGYCO as the index name and AGENCYID as the Master Expression. Choose OK	You are returned to the Set Relation dialog box
Select the new AGENCYID Index in the Child Table panel, accept the One to Many link option and choose OK	You are returned to the Query Designer window
Choose Query, Set Relation	The Set Relation dialog box appears
Select AGENTID in both Field and Index lists, accept the One to Many relation, and choose OK	You are returned to the Query Designer window showing the three tables are linked with one-to-many relations, as shown in figure 8.27

Figure 8.27 The query design with three linked tables.

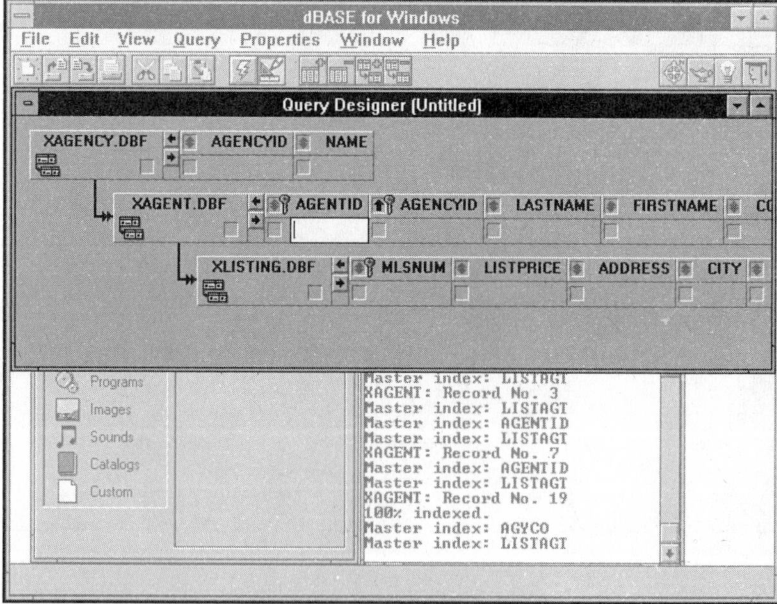

Run the query with no fields checked	The view contains both fields in the parent table (XAGENCY) but none from the child tables, even though there are blank records representing records from both child tables

Click the Design Query button and select the fields to include in the view: from the XAGENCY table, select NAME; from the XAGENT table, select AGENTID, LASTNAME, and HMPHONE; from the XLISTING table, select MLSNUM, LISTPRICE, and ADDRESS	The query design shows check marks in the selected fields
Run the query	The resulting view is shown in figure 8.28; you can see that several agents work for each agency and that a few of the agents have more than one current listing

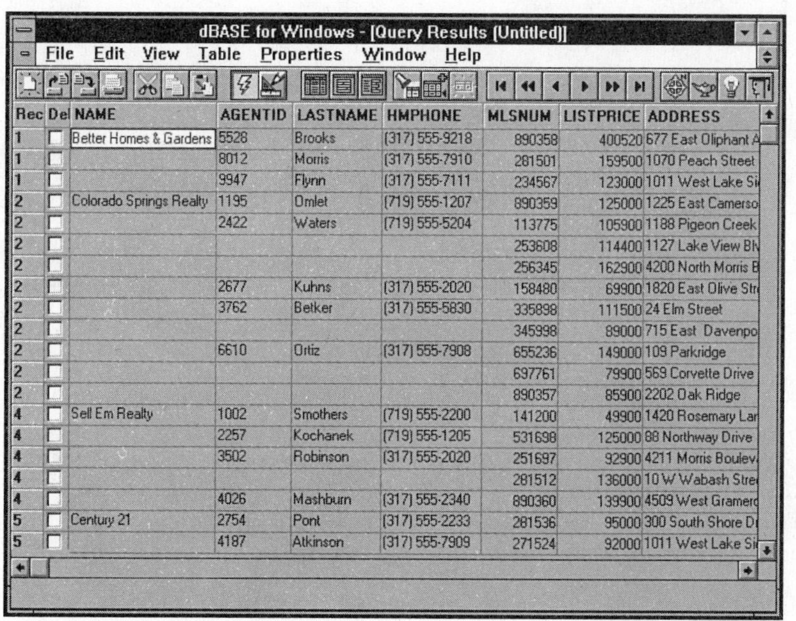

Rec	Del	NAME	AGENTID	LASTNAME	HMPHONE	MLSNUM	LISTPRICE	ADDRESS
1		Better Homes & Gardens	5528	Brooks	(317) 555-9218	890358	400520	677 East Oliphant A
1			8012	Morris	(317) 555-7910	281501	159500	1070 Peach Street
1			9947	Flynn	(317) 555-7111	234567	123000	1011 West Lake Si
2		Colorado Springs Realty	1195	Omlet	(719) 555-1207	890359	125000	1225 East Camerso
2			2422	Waters	(719) 555-5204	113775	105900	1188 Pigeon Creek
2						253608	114400	1127 Lake View Bl
2						256345	162900	4200 North Morris B
2			2677	Kuhns	(317) 555-2020	158480	69900	1820 East Olive Str
2			3762	Betker	(317) 555-5830	335898	111500	24 Elm Street
2						345998	89000	715 East Davenpo
2			6610	Ortiz	(317) 555-7908	655236	149000	109 Parkridge
2						697761	79900	569 Corvette Drive
2						890357	85900	2202 Oak Ridge
4		Sell Em Realty	1002	Smothers	(719) 555-2200	141200	49900	1420 Rosemary Lar
4			2257	Kochanek	(719) 555-1205	531698	125000	88 Northway Drive
4			3502	Robinson	(317) 555-2020	251697	92900	4211 Morris Boulev
4						281512	136000	10 W Wabash Stre
4			4026	Mashburn	(317) 555-2340	890360	139900	4509 West Gramerc
5		Century 21	2754	Pont	(317) 555-2233	281536	95000	300 South Shore D
5			4187	Atkinson	(317) 555-7909	271524	92000	1011 West Lake Si

Figure 8.28
The view showing listings by agency and agent.

Return to the design window and choose Query, Create Calculated Field	A small box labeled CALC01 appears in the design window below the table skeletons as shown in figure 8.29
Delete the name CALC01 and enter a new field name for the calculated field **LISTTIME**; enter the formula, **DATE()-LISTDATE**, in the area below the field name after the equal sign, then press Enter	The calculated name field box is renamed and contains the formula needed to calculated the number of days since the property was listed

continues

continued

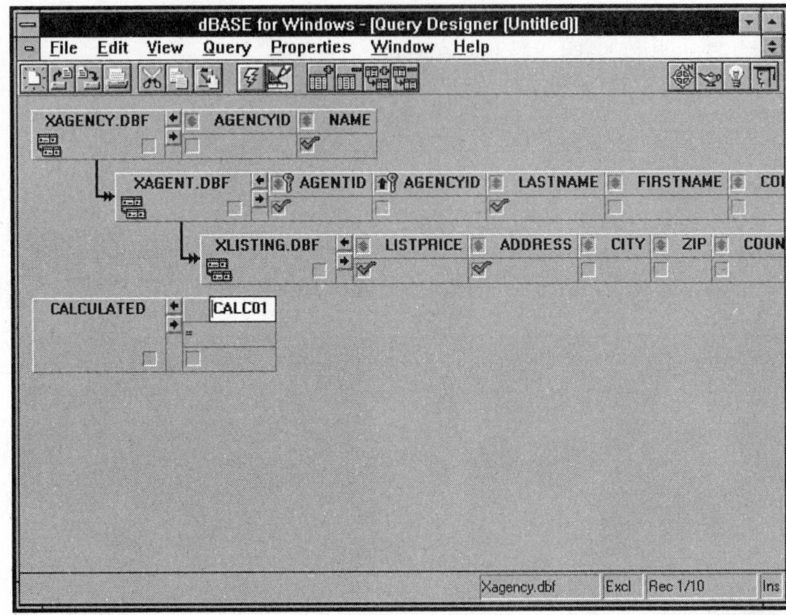

Figure 8.29 The calculated field box.

Check the calculated field so it will be included in the view

The calculated field box shows a check mark

Choose **Q**uery, Create Calculated **F**ield again and add a second calculated field named **TAXPCNT** using the formula **(TAXES/LISTPRICE)*100**, then press Enter; run the query

The query design is shown in figure 8.30; the resulting view is shown in figure 8.31; the calculated fields were moved in the view so they would appear in the figure

If the calculated field does not appear in the view, you might have forgotten to check it. Return to the design window and make sure it is checked.

Return to the query design window and add a filter condition

The Query Designer window appears with the calculated field box still in view

Move to the EXPDATE field, check the field and add the condition: **<>{},<{02/01/95}** (include all records whose EXPDATE field is not blank and the expiration date is before February 1, 1995); then press Enter and run the query

The result of the modified query looks like figure 8.32

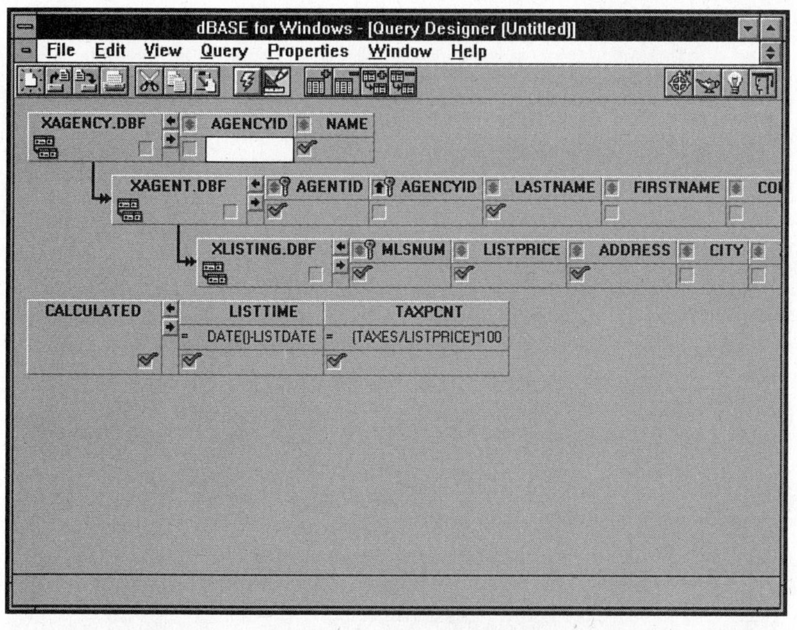

Figure 8.30
The query design that links three tables and includes calculated fields.

dBASE for Windows - [Query Results (Untitled)]

File Edit View Table Properties Window Help

Rec	Del	NAME	AGENTID	LASTNAME	HMPHONE	LISTTIME	TAXPCNT	MLSNUM	LISTP
1	☐	Better Homes & Gardens	5528	Brooks	(317) 555-9218	55	5.99	890358	
1	☐		8012	Morris	(317) 555-7910	49	2.67	281501	
1	☐		9947	Flynn	(317) 555-7111	99	0.81	234567	
2	☐	Colorado Springs Realty	1195	Omlet	(719) 555-1207	10	0.98	890359	
2	☐		2422	Waters	(719) 555-5204	155	6.23	113775	
2	☐					111	1.75	253608	
2	☐					99	2.78	256345	
2	☐		2677	Kuhns	(317) 555-2020	18	7.25	158480	
2	☐		3762	Betker	(317) 555-5830	96	1.11	335898	
2	☐					68	5.39	345998	
2	☐		6610	Ortiz	(317) 555-7908	127	1.11	655236	
2	☐					3	0.87	697761	
2	☐					39	1.46	890357	
4	☐	Sell Em Realty	1002	Smothers	(719) 555-2200	-11	2.14	141200	
4	☐		2257	Kochanek	(719) 555-1205	250	3.40	531698	
4	☐		3502	Robinson	(317) 555-2020	38	9.15	251697	
4	☐					57	1.80	281512	
4	☐		4026	Mashburn	(317) 555-2340	10	0.86	890360	
5	☐	Century 21	2754	Pont	(317) 555-2233	38	2.58	281536	
5	☐		4187	Atkinson	(317) 555-7909	111	1.09	271524	

Figure 8.31
The view linking three tables and including two calculated fields.

continues

continued

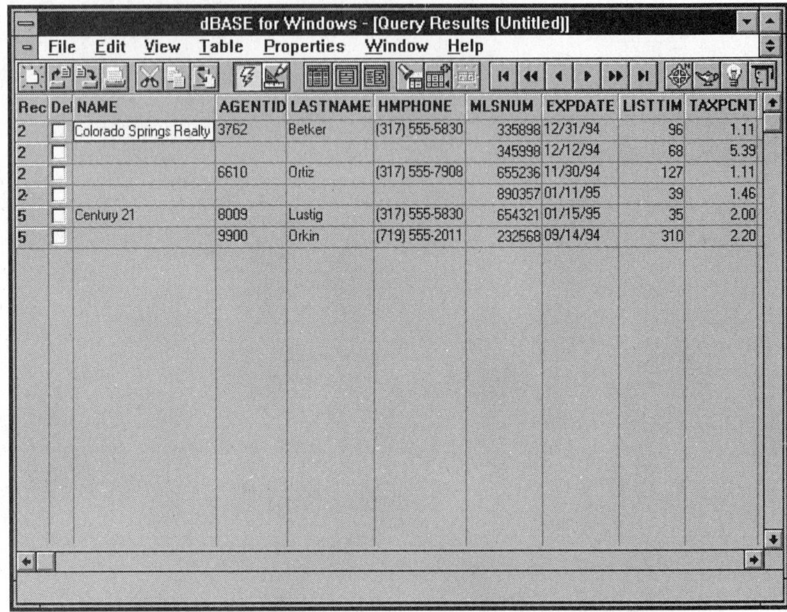

dBASE for Windows - [Query Results (Untitled)]
File Edit View Table Properties Window Help
Rec Del NAME AGENTID LASTNAME HMPHONE MLSNUM EXPDATE LISTTIM TAXPCNT
2 Colorado Springs Realty 3762 Betker (317) 555-5830 335898 12/31/94 96 1.11
2 345998 12/12/94 68 5.39
2 6610 Ortiz (317) 555-7908 655236 11/30/94 127 1.11
2 890357 01/11/95 39 1.46
5 Century 21 8009 Lustig (317) 555-5830 654321 01/15/95 35 2.00
5 9900 Orkin (719) 555-2011 232568 09/14/94 310 2.20

Figure 8.32 The Results table showing listings that will expire before February 1, 1995, arranged by agency and agent.

Choose File, Close without saving the query	You are returned to the dBASE desktop

If you change your mind and want to delete the calculated field from the query design, select the calculated field name and choose Query, Delete Selected Calculated Field.

Running Queries from Earlier dBASE Versions

dBASE for Windows can run VUE and QRY files from earlier versions of dBASE, but if you modify one of those and save it, dBASE automatically converts it to a QBE file.

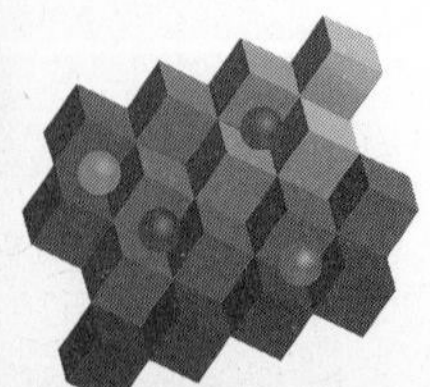

dBASE no longer provides update and aggregate queries. These operations have been replaced by menu commands, as follows:

Query Type	Use Instead
Find	Table, Find Records
Replace	Table, Replace Records
Delete	Table, Table Utilities, Delete Records
Undelete	Table, Table Utilities, Recall Records
Append	Table, Add Records

The GROUP BY and AGGREGATE operators do not appear when you open the dBASE IV query in dBASE for Windows. To perform those aggregating functions in dBASE for Windows, run the query, then use Table, Table Utilities, Count Records (or Calculate Records).

You can use any MDX index to set the sort order of the view, but if you need to use an NDX index, you must open it with the USE or the SET INDEX TO command before you can create the query. The query then can recognize the index when it is run. If you plan to use the query often, you might want to convert the NDX index file to a tag in the production MDX file. See Chapter 7, "Indexing, Sorting and Locating Your Data," for information on index conversion.

The Condition box in dBASE for Windows treats separate lines as OR conditions, whereas in dBASE IV separate lines are considered as AND conditions. If queries you built in dBASE IV do not produce expected results, check to see if you have switched OR for AND. In addition, if you create a complex condition in a Condition box in dBASE IV, then run the query in dBASE for Windows, dBASE might convert the Condition box contents to field-related conditions and move them to the corresponding fields in the skeleton.

Chapter Snapshot

The dBASE default report printer offers a quick way to put table data into hard-copy form, from which you can examine the data. If you want customized reports, use the integrated report generator, Crystal Reports for dBASE. This chapter explains how to perform the following tasks:

This chapter includes exercises based on the tables on your *Inside dBASE for Windows Bonus Disk.* These exercises introduce you to the field of report design and printing.

Developing Reports and Labels

By Virginia Andersen

Reports are a very important part of database design. A properly designed report can present information quickly and concisely with emphasis on the conclusions that can be drawn from the underlying data.

Using the dBASE report generator, you can print data from your database in almost limitless ways. You can develop reports to present information in any arrangement and appearance. You can select just the data you want to show and include summaries that interpret and give additional meaning to the supporting data. dBASE reports are not limited to fields from a single table—you can link two or more tables and access data from all the tables for your report.

Creating a Quick Report

dBASE uses standard Windows printing and printer setup software and drivers to print Quick Reports from table data. You can print your table data from any of the editing views: browse, form, or columnar layout. Or, you can print from the Query Results. A standard header and footer are included in the Quick Report; you cannot customize these. The header contains the table or window name, and the footer contains the page number.

The Print menu option and Print SpeedBar button are not available when you are in the Navigator, Command, or Catalog window.

To begin a Quick Report, choose **F**ile, **P**rint or click on the Print SpeedBar button. The Print Records dialog box appears, as shown in figure 9.1.

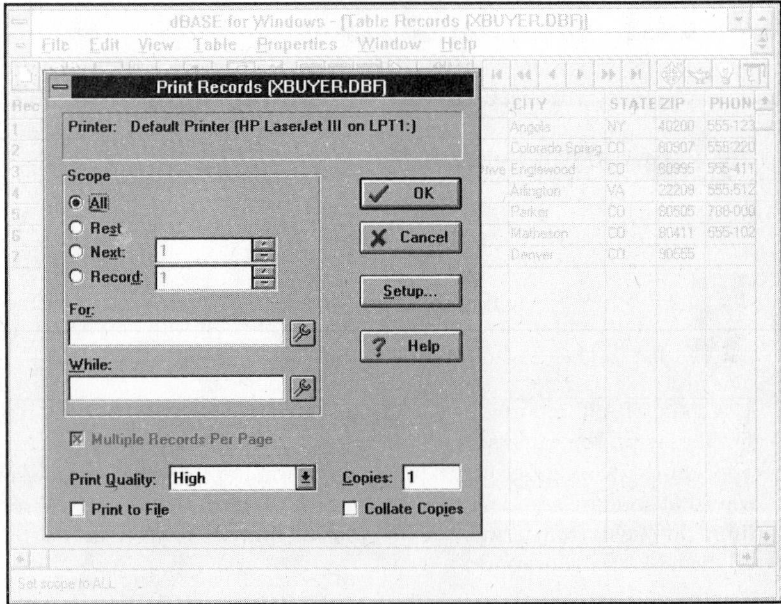

Figure 9.1
The Print Records dialog box.

Choosing the Data to Print

In the Print Records dialog box, you have a choice of printing all records or limiting the scope to some of the records in the table. In addition, you have some options for controlling the print process itself.

The Scope options follow:

- ✔ All, which prints all records in the table.
- ✔ Rest, which prints records from the current record to the end of the table.
- ✔ Next, in which you specify how many records to print, beginning with the current record.
- ✔ Record, in which you enter the record number of the record you want to print.

You also can filter the records to print with a For or While condition. Enter a filter condition in the text box or click on the Tool icon to open the Expression Builder. See Chapter 7, "Indexing, Sorting, and Locating Your Data," for information on creating expressions and using the Expression Builder.

If you are printing from a form or columnar layout, the printed report looks like the report on-screen. By default, dBASE prints one record per page unless you specify to print multiple records per page. You also have the standard options of printing multiple copies, setting the print quality, and collating multiple copies. The final option is to print the report to a disk file instead of sending the report to the printer.

The Quick Report feature is useful for accessing table data if you just want to check some information in your table, and you don't care how the table looks.

Print some of the Buyer records from the XBUYER.DBF file on the bonus disk. Use the steps in the following exercise

Printing Records from the XBUYER.DBF File

Open the Xbuyer table in Browse mode

Click on the Print SpeedBar button	The Print Records dialog box appears
Accept the default options and choose OK	The report prints as shown in figure 9.2; Notice that it took two pages to print all fields in the records because the record was wider than the page

continues

continued

Figure 9.2 The Xbuyer records printed with the default Quick Report options.

SSN	LASTNAME	FIRSTNAME	MI	ADDRESS	CITY	STATE
255-55-855	Pentz	George	P	2929 List Drive	Angola	NY
305-88-925	Polog	Tracy	P	90 West Fillmore	Colorado Sprin	CO
308-55-555	Graves	Robert	K	677 East Liverdale Drive	Englewood	CO
505-55-850	Smith	Ken	Y	21520 East 77th	Arlington	VA
555-22-025	Farmer	Holly	O	45 Mercury Avenue	Parker	CO
555-55-202	Anderson	James	S	RR 1 Box 222	Matheson	CO
696-55-880	Baylor	Madison	K	212 East 21st Street	Denver	CO

ZIP	PHONE	REQDATE
40200	555-1233	/ /
80907	555-2202	/ /
80995	555-4111	/ /
22209	555-5122	/ /
80505	788-0005	/ /
80411	555-1022	/ /
90555		/ /

Change the view layout to Form by clicking on the Form View SpeedBar button (or by pressing F2) and choose File, Print

The Print Records dialog box opens, but this time the Multiple Records per Page option is available and checked

Choose Next and enter 2 in the text box

Click on OK to print the report as shown in figure 9.3 one record when

dBASE prints the entire view window as you are viewing the table in form or columnar layout. Choosing Multiple Records per Page prints at least two records on a standard page; keep the Xbuyer table open for the next exercise

Choosing Printer Options

When you want a different printer setup, you use the standard Windows Print Setup dialog box, as shown in figure 9.4. The options include the choice of printer, the print orientation, and the paper size and source.

The Orientation setting is useful when printing a Quick Report such as the tabular Xbuyer report in the preceding exercise. Use that setting now to print the report again:

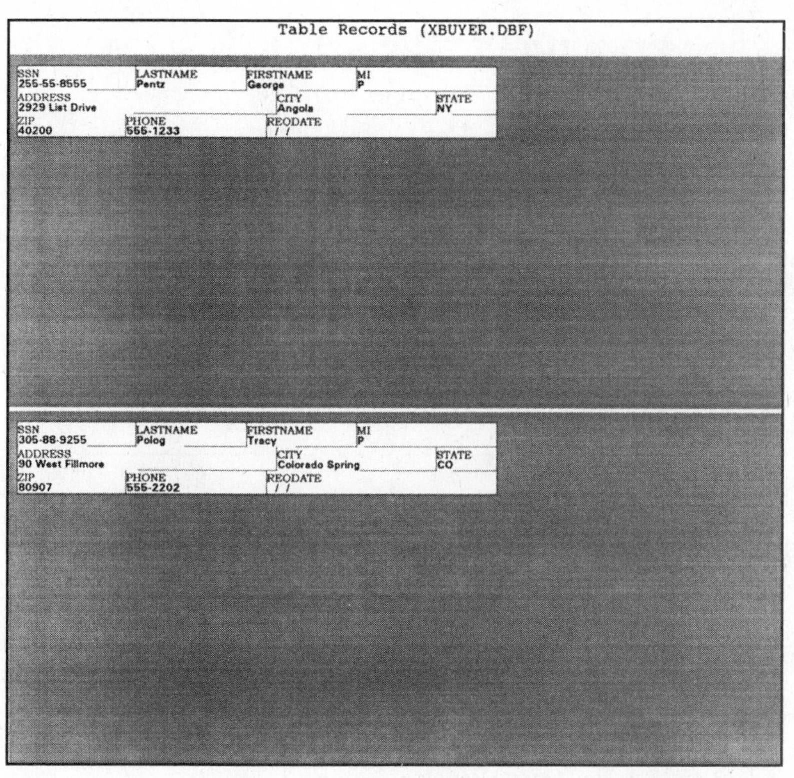

Figure 9.3 Two Xbuyer records printed from the form layout view.

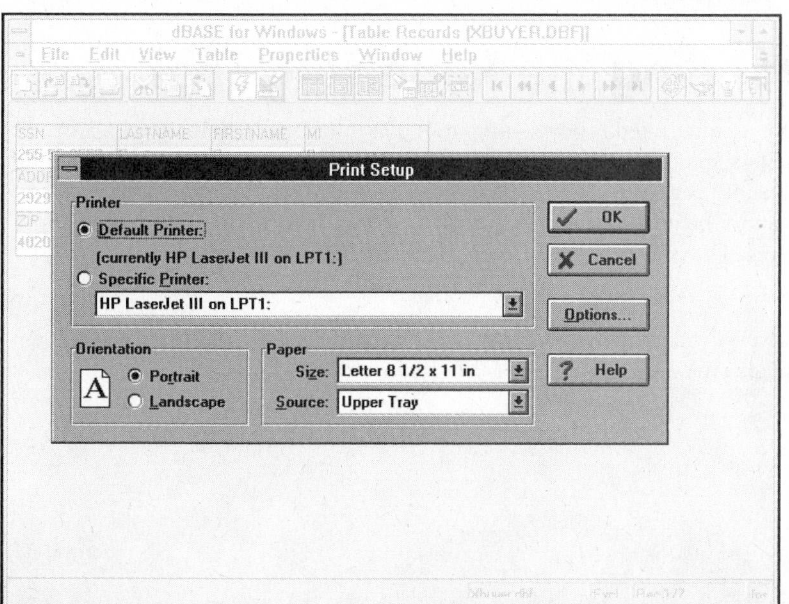

Figure 9.4 The Print Setup dialog box.

Printing the Report

Choose File, Printer Setup	The Print Setup dialog box appears
Select Landscape and then choose OK	The Print Setup dialog button box closes; Notice that the sample page now shows the paper in the new orientation
Click on the Tabular Layout SpeedBar	You are returned to table view
Click on the Print button and accept the default options; Choose OK	The Quick Report is printed in landscape orientation, as shown in figure 9.5
Choose Window, Close All to end this exercise	

Table Records (XBUYER.DBF)

SSN	LASTNAME	FIRSTNAME	MI	ADDRESS	CITY	STATE	ZIP	PHONE	REQDATE
255-55-855	Pentz	George	P	2929 List Drive	Angola	NY	4020	555-1233	/ /
305-88-925	Polog	Tracy	P	90 West Fillmore	Colorado S	CO	8090	555-2202	/ /
308-55-555	Graves	Robert	K	677 East Liverda	Englewood	CO	8099	555-4111	/ /
505-55-850	Smith	Ken	Y	21520 East 77th	Arlington	VA	2220	555-5122	/ /
555-22-025	Farmer	Holly	O	45 Mercury Avenu	Parker	CO	8050	788-0005	/ /
555-55-202	Anderson	James	S	RR 1 Box 222	Matheson	CO	8041	555-1022	/ /
696-55-880	Baylor	Madison	K	212 East 21st St	Denver	CO	9055		/ /

Figure 9.5
The Xbuyer records printed in landscape orientation.

When your reporting needs exceed the capabilities of the Quick Report, dBASE passes you to another program: Crystal Reports. The remainder of this chapter shows you how to create several kinds of reports using Crystal Reports.

Understanding the Reporting Tool

Crystal Reports is an integrated report-writing tool that interactively helps you create reports, form letters, mailing labels, envelopes, cross tabs, and any type of data formatting for inserting data into preprinted forms. The capabilities of Crystal Reports are very extensive and cannot be encompassed in a single chapter. This chapter introduces you to the major features of Crystal and gives you enough information to experiment on your own.

Crystal Reports works with all types of dBASE table data, including graphics, and can base a report on a single table, related tables, or the results of a query.

When preparing a report using Crystal, you can do the following:

- ✔ Include calculations and summaries
- ✔ Group records and summarize by group
- ✔ Filter the records to include only a subset of the total table
- ✔ Convert data types
- ✔ Change the report appearance with font varieties and sizes
- ✔ Merge data fields into text
- ✔ Compare field values

The Crystal Reports design window contains all the tools you need to create a custom report. As you are designing the report, you can preview the data in the report format and quickly make changes.

When the report is finished, you have the choice of sending the report to the printer, printing it to a disk file, or distributing the report electronically via electronic mail.

If you have an existing report created in Crystal, you can run it from dBASE by selecting the report title in the report pane of the Navigator window and clicking the right mouse button. Then choose Run Report from the SpeedMenu. To modify an existing report or to create a new report, you must use the Crystal Reports program.

The next section takes you on a tour of the Crystal Reports design window.

Understanding the Crystal Reports Design Window

The Crystal Reports design window contains the standard Windows application work space with minimize/maximize buttons, a Control menu button, a title bar, a menu bar, a SpeedBar, a format bar, and a status bar (see fig. 9.6).

The minimize/maximize and Control menu buttons operate the same as in any Windows application, and the title bar contains the name of the program running in the window. Click on the title bar to activate the window, double-click on the title bar to maximize the window, and click on the title bar and drag it to move the window.

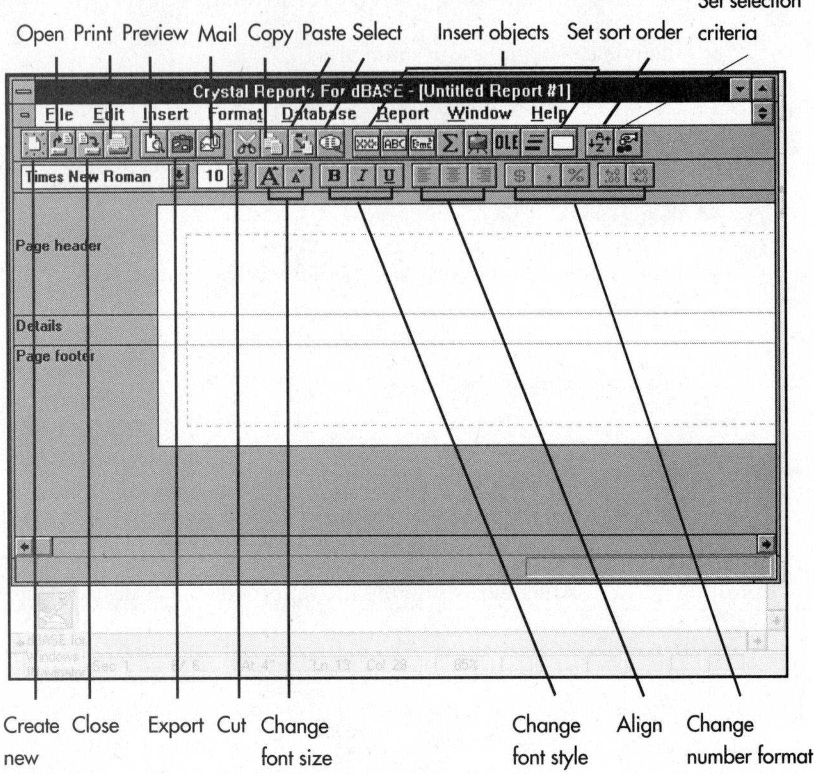

Figure 9.6 The Crystal Reports design window.

The Menu Bar

The menu bar contains many options familiar to Windows users, and some options unique to Crystal:

- ✔ The File menu contains the customary options to create new files, to open existing files, to save files, to close the application, and to exit the application. In addition, the Print option enables you to preview the report and to make last-minute adjustments before sending the report to the printer, to a file, or to e-mail. You also can change the printer settings and adjust the page margins through the File menu. Finally, the Options selection presents a means of changing the default options for Crystal. These options are discussed in more detail later in this chapter.

- ✔ The Edit menu contains all the options you need to modify the report design. In addition to the usual cut, copy, and paste options, other options are available so that you can edit formulas, text, and summary fields; examine the table data that appears in the field; show field names in the report; hide or delete sections; and perform group selection (called *lasso* in Crystal).

- ✔ The Insert menu is the main report design menu that gives you the options of inserting all the objects that will appear in your report. This menu consists of commands that insert fields containing data, formulas, or text; compute various summaries (count, average, min/max, and so on) in the group sections; include page, record, or group numbers, and date; and insert static elements such as lines, boxes, graphics, and OLE objects.

- ✔ The Format menu includes options to change the appearance of all objects in the report design, including changing the font and editing the report title; formatting data fields, sections, graphics, lines, and boxes; and adding borders, background color, and drop shadows to the report design.

- ✔ The Database menu contains an option you can use to tell Crystal to look in another location for tables to use in the report. This menu also has two verification options that control the behavior of the report design when minor changes are made to the underlying table structure.

- ✔ The Report menu includes options that help you create filter expressions for limiting the records or groups that appear in the report and specify the sort order (by group or by record). Other options enable you to save the data with the report design and then refresh the report with any changes to the data before running it. You also can specify a report date other than the current system date.

- ✔ The Window menu includes the standard Windows options for arranging windows and icons on the desktop and closing all windows at once.

- ✔ The Help menu contains Crystal Reports' on-line Help index and search options. This menu also enables you to look at product information and to choose other options. One option activates the Personal Trainer, Crystal Reports' interactive tutorial program. The Personal Trainer is discussed in a later section in this chapter.

The SpeedBar

The Crystal Reports SpeedBar contains buttons that activate many of the commonly used menu options. These buttons provide one-click access to report-design functions.

The first four buttons on the SpeedBar create a new report, open an existing report, save the current report, and print the report (refer to fig. 9.6). The next three buttons preview the report, export the report file to another application, and mail the report to an electronic distribution. The next three buttons provide the standard cut, copy to the clipboard, and paste to the design functions.

The next button shows a lasso icon and enables you to group-select multiple objects in the design window so that you can work with all the objects at once. Click on the lasso button and drag the mouse pointer (now a crosshair cursor) over the fields you want to select.

The next eight buttons are design tools that insert various elements into the design. In order of appearance from left to right, they insert a database field, text field, formula, summary, graphic image, OLE object, line, or box.

The next-to-last button enables you to set the record sort order for the report. The final button helps you establish a selection criterion to limit the records in the report.

The Format Bar

The format bar contains text and number-formatting options. You can select the font and font size from the two pull-down menus on the left side of the bar. You use the two buttons that follow those menus to increase or decrease the font size by one point with each click on the button. You can use the next three buttons to change the font style to bold, italic, or underline. Those buttons are followed by three alignment buttons: left, center, and right alignment.

You use the last five buttons to format number field data. The first button places a currency symbol with the selected number, the second button adds a thousands separator, and the third button adds a percent sign. The last two buttons add or subtract a decimal place to or from the number. Clicking once on the last button, for example, removes the far right of the decimal point. The decimal point is not moved, and the resulting number is not rounded off. If the number 456.6789 appears in a field, for example, and you click on the last button, that number then appears as 456.678.

The Status Bar

The Crystal Reports status bar includes information pertaining to the current activity. As you pass the mouse pointer over a SpeedBar button or highlight a menu option, a brief description appears in the status bar. When you select an object in the report design, the name of the object is displayed. If the object is a text field, the contents are displayed. If the selected object is a graphic object, its file name is displayed, along with the coordinates of its position in the design.

The Design Window

There are at least three sections in the report design window (refer to fig. 9.6 again): the page header contains any objects that should print above the table data, the Details section contains all the data, and the Page Footer contains the information that prints at the bottom of the page. In addition, as you create a report, you can add other group sections that divide the data into groups based on field value or other criteria.

Generally, the page header and footer allow for three lines of text each (the actual space depends on the default font size for the section). If you need more room for text in these sections, you can place the insertion point in the section and press Enter once for each additional line of text. You also can move the mouse pointer to the section boundary, and when it changes shape to a vertical, double-pointed arrow, click and drag the boundary to the size you want.

You can place objects in the edit box (the white area) of any section of the report and increase or decrease the size of the sections. In the section "Creating a Single Table-Report," scroll bars are available for you to move to parts of the design that are off the screen. Later in this chapter, you learn how to insert objects into the report design and how to increase the page header to include a title.

Using the Right Mouse Button

Many of the options you can select from the menu bar are available quickly in the Crystal Reports SpeedMenus. These menus are element-specific and contain only those options that relate to the selected object. To open a SpeedMenu, click the right mouse button on an object in the design window.

Figure 9.7 shows a typical SpeedMenu. This menu was opened by right-clicking on a string field named Address in a report design.

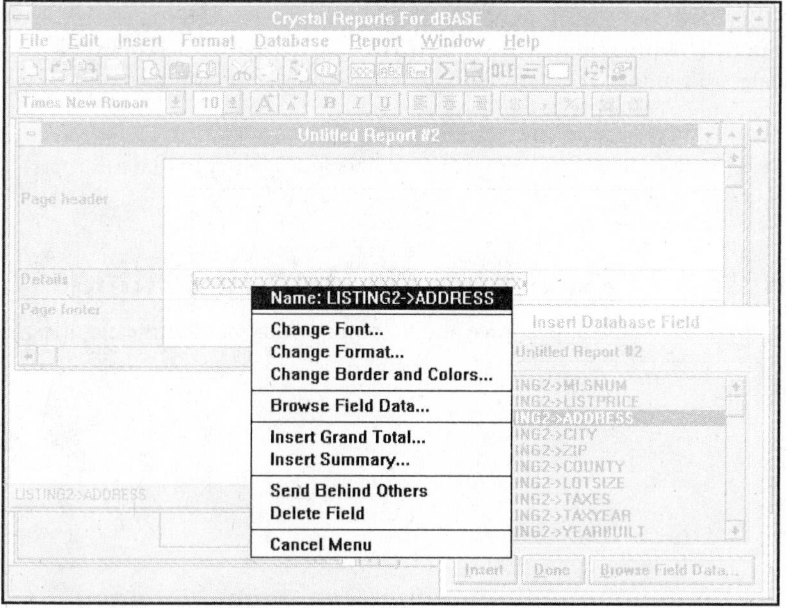

Figure 9.7
A SpeedMenu, activated by right-clicking on a string field.

The name of the field appears at the top of the menu, followed by three options that change the appearance of the object. If you want to see what data is in the Address field, choose Browse Field Data. The next two options help you insert report grand totals and group-section summaries.

The last three options appear in almost every SpeedMenu. Send Behind Others is used by advanced users who are working with stacked objects to move the object to the bottom of the stack. Delete Field removes the field from the design, and Cancel Menu closes the SpeedMenu.

The SpeedMenus differ somewhat—depending on the type of object that is selected—but they all offer ways to change the object's appearance or format. Many of the SpeedMenu options lead you to the same dialog box that would result from choosing comparable options from the menu bar.

Moving between dBASE and Crystal Reports

You can keep the dBASE and Crystal Reports programs active at the same time. Because they are different programs, you need to use the Windows Alt+Tab command to switch between the programs. Hold down Alt while you press Tab until the icon of the program you want appears in the gray box in the center of the window. Then release the Alt key to open the program. If you have several programs open, you might need to press Tab several times before you reach the program you want.

Using the Personal Trainer

The Personal Trainer is a context-sensitive Help program that works with you when you are creating a report. This program stays on-screen as a long narrow window down the right side of the design window. The Personal Trainer also uses larger windows with graphics to explain major concepts as you request.

You also can access the normal Help system from the Personal Trainer to find information on other topics.

Changing the Crystal Reports Default Settings

Crystal Reports groups its default appearance and behavior options into four categories:

- ✔ General
- ✔ Database
- ✔ Format
- ✔ Fonts

You can set these default options by choosing File, Options to open the General Options dialog box (see fig. 9.8). The first six check boxes in this dialog box modify the design window display. You can use these options to display the three window bars (button, format, and status), to abbreviate the section names in the report design window (including the field names), or to add field titles to the details section.

Two other options enable you to update the data from the table or query every time you print and save the table data with the report design when you close the file. The last two options in the General Options dialog box enable you to set the directory where you want to store the report (you also have access to the Browser to find and change to another directory) and to select an e-mail destination.

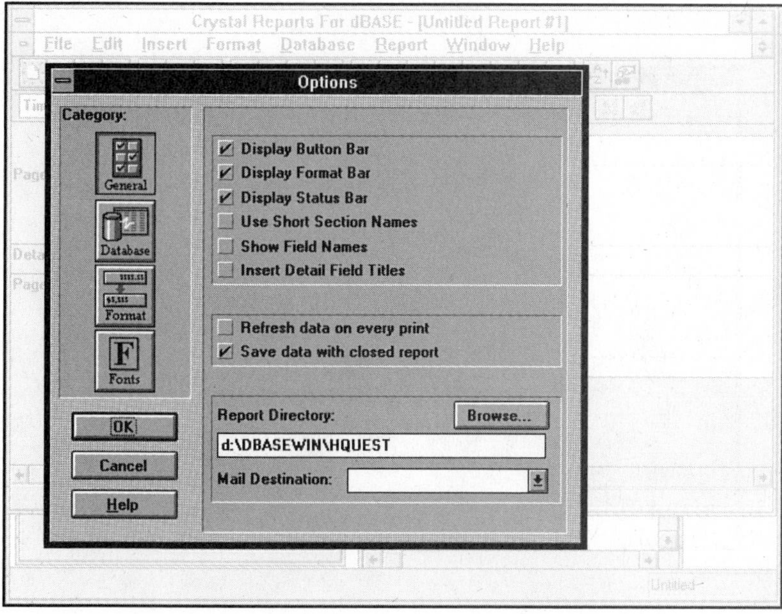

Figure 9.8 The General Options dialog box.

If you click on the Database category button, the Database Options dialog box opens, as shown in figure 9.9. With the selections in this dialog box, you can specify the directory where Crystal finds the data to use in the report, the specific database to use, and the controlling index. Three check boxes enable you to access the data in index order and to translate DOS strings and memos. You also have access to the Browser if you need to look up a different directory.

If you click on the Format category button, the Format Options dialog box appears, with a set of five buttons that lead you to the Format dialog box for that field type: string, number, currency, date, or Boolean (see fig. 9.10). You make the changes you want in the Format dialog boxes, and they are saved as the new default formats. You see many of these dialog boxes as you work through the exercises in this chapter.

Changes to the default format settings affect only those fields you insert after you make the changes. The fields already in the report design are not changed to the new default settings.

The final category button in the Options dialog box is Fonts. In the Fonts Options dialog box, you select the default font appearance for the field data and text inserted in every section of your report (see fig. 9.11). Choosing any of the font options opens the same Font dialog box, where you choose the font face, style, size, and color (see fig. 9.12).

Using these options, you can create exactly the report design environment you need.

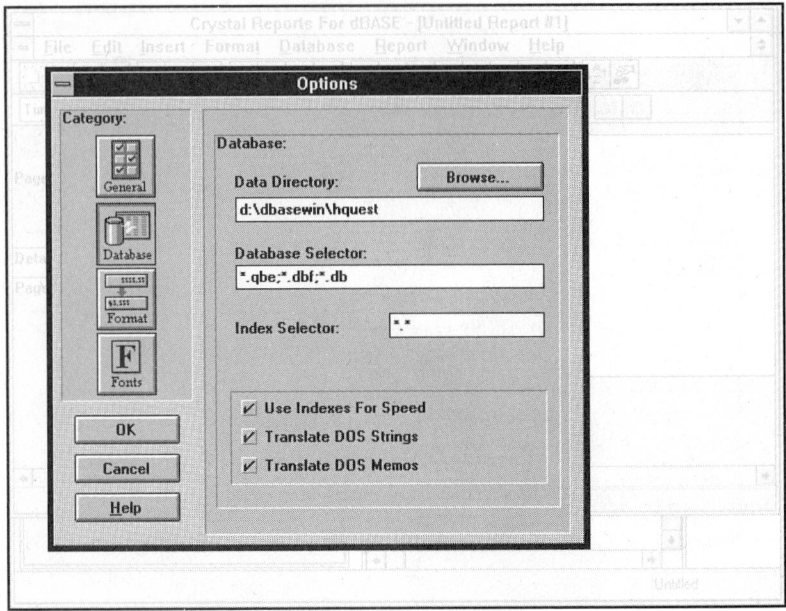

Figure 9.9 The Database Options dialog box.

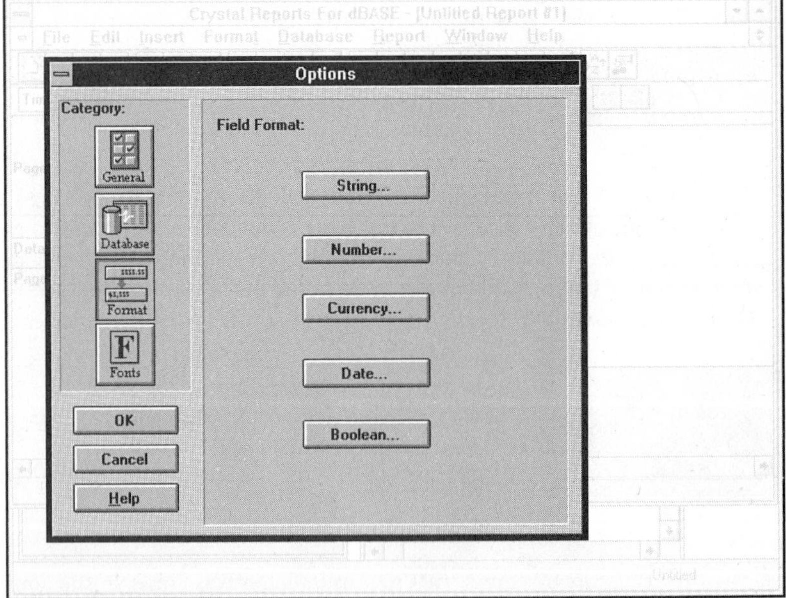

Figure 9.10 The Format Options dialog box.

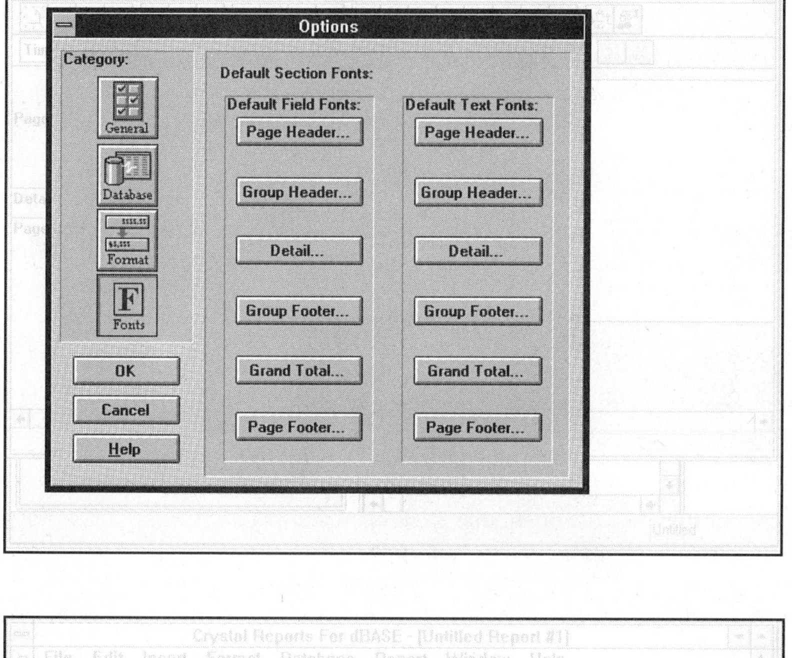

Figure 9.11
The Fonts Options dialog box.

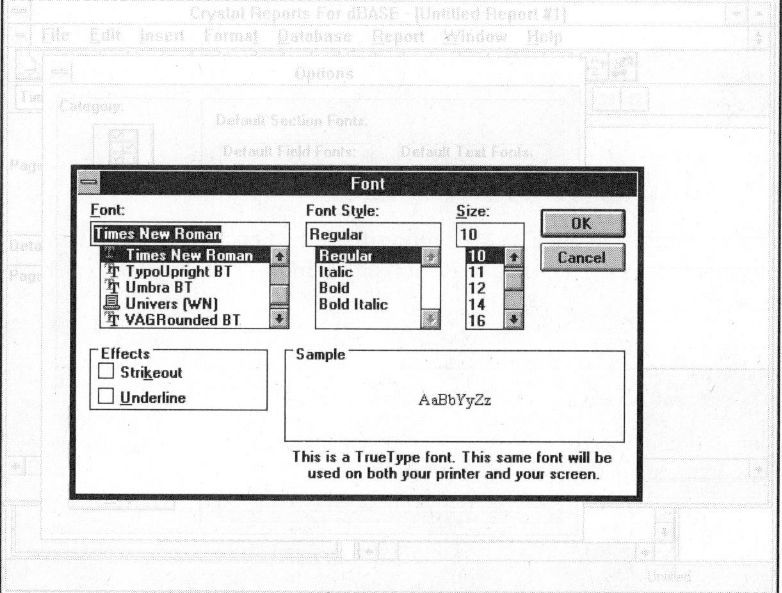

Figure 9.12
The Font dialog box.

Delving into the Reporting Capabilities

Now that you know your way around the Crystal Report design window, you can begin to create a report. The first step is to start the Crystal Report program from dBASE. You might have a data file open at this time—it does not matter. To start Crystal, perform one of the following actions:

- ✔ Choose File, New, Report from the menu bar.
- ✔ Click on the Reports icon in the Navigator window and choose Navigator, New Report from the menu bar.
- ✔ Click on the Reports icon in the Navigator window. Then double-click on the <Untitled> icon.
- ✔ Click on the New SpeedBar button and choose Report.
- ✔ Click in the Command window and type **CREATE REPORT**.

If you have a table or other data file open, that file is open automatically in Crystal. If no file is open, the Open Table Required dialog box appears so that you can select a file name from the list. You can use one of several file types as the basis for a Crystal report: DBF, DB, QBE, and so on.

The next step is to select the fields you want to include in the report and to place the fields in the design. Add group sections as you want, and then add a title or other text to complete the report.

Creating a Single-Table Report

Use the Xagent table to create a better looking report than the Quick Report you created for the Xbuyer data in "Choosing the Data to Print," earlier in this chapter. To create the report, follow these steps:

Using the Xagent Table to Create a Report

Step	Result
Start Crystal using one of the methods described earlier, with no table open in dBASE	The Open Table Required dialog box appears
Select Xagent from the File Name list and choose OK	The report design window appears with the Insert Database Field dialog box open, as shown in figure 9.13

The Insert Database Field dialog box stays on-screen for you to select the fields you want in the report. When you have finished, choose Done to close the dialog box.

Select the AGENTID field and choose Insert

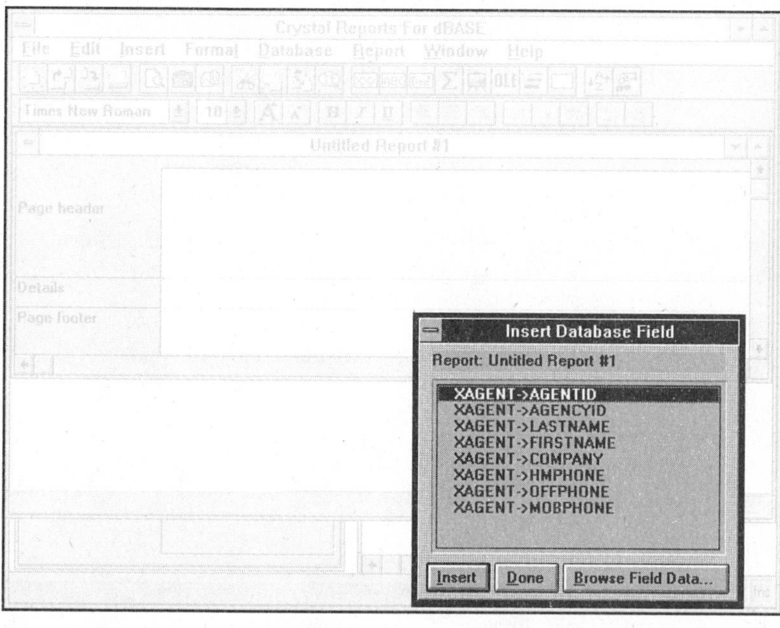

Figure 9.13 The Insert Database Field dialog box, with the report design window in the background.

Move the mouse pointer to the Details section of the report design, as shown in figure 9.14, then click the mouse

The object is placed at the left end of the Details section

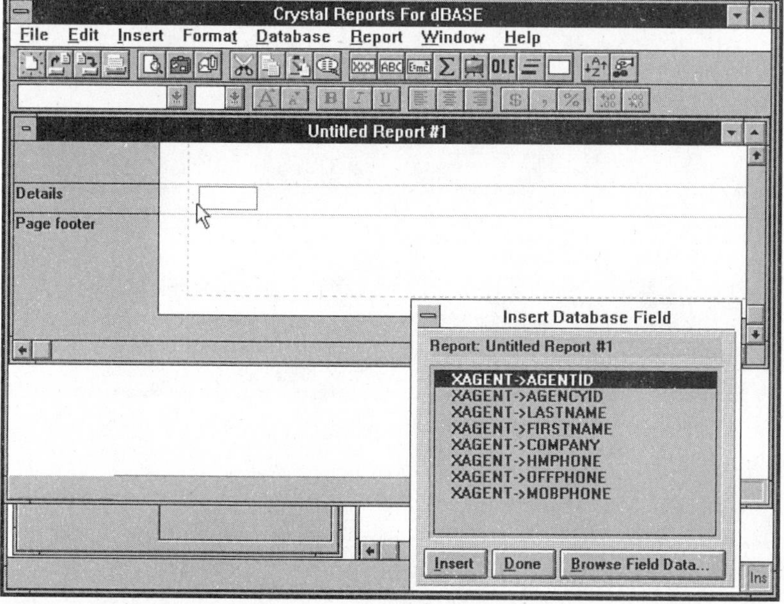

Figure 9.14 Placing a field object in the Details section.

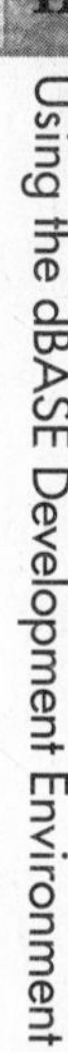

continues

continued

Select the following fields, one by one, from the Insert Database Field list and place the fields next to each other in the Details section of the report design: LastName, Company, and OffPhone	Places the fields

Notice that the field widths are indicated by a series of Xs, indicating that these are all string fields. Number fields are represented by a series of 5s, and a date field is represented by 12/31/99.

Click on **D**one	The Insert Database Field dialog box closes
Click on the Preview button (move the mouse pointer over the SpeedBar and watch the status bar to find the Preview button)	You can see how the report looks so far (see fig. 9.15)

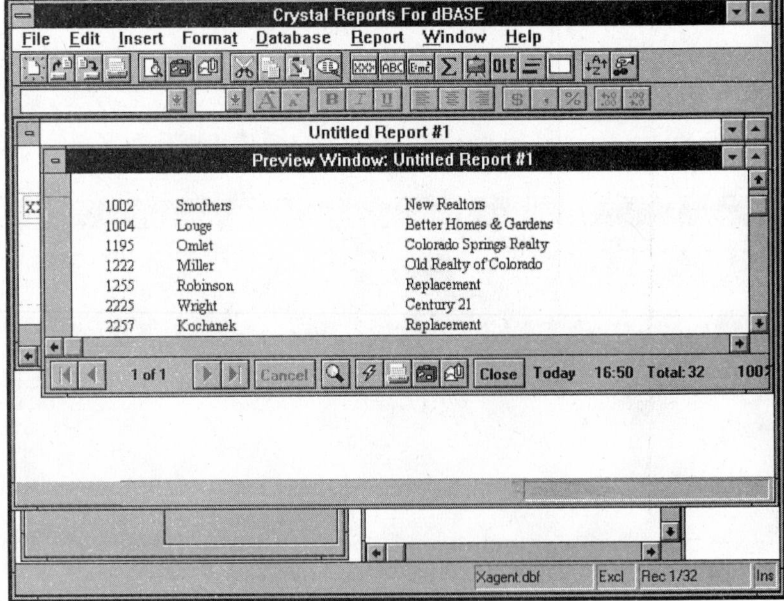

Figure 9.15
The new report in the Preview window.

Click on Close to return to the design window	
Click on the Page Header section, and click on the Text tool button	The Edit Text Field dialog box opens

In Crystal, you type the text first, and then place it in the design.

Type **HomeGuide Agents** in the text box (see fig. 9.16)

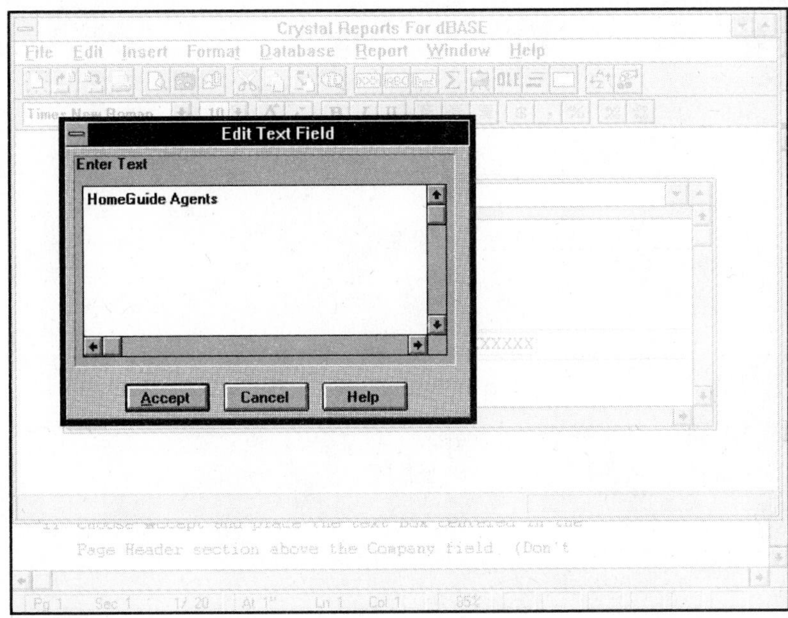

Figure 9.16
The Edit Text Field dialog box used to enter a text field into the report design.

Click on Accept and place the text box centered in the Page Header section above the Company field; (don't worry if it is not exactly centered—you can move it later)	The text is placed in the field
Maximize the design window to give yourself more room, and then click on the lower boundary of the Page Header section and drag it down to give more room in the header	When the mouse pointer moves to the boundary, it changes its shape to a double-pointer vertical arrow with a cross line, as shown in figure 9.17
When you see that shape, click and drag down the boundary	

continues

continued

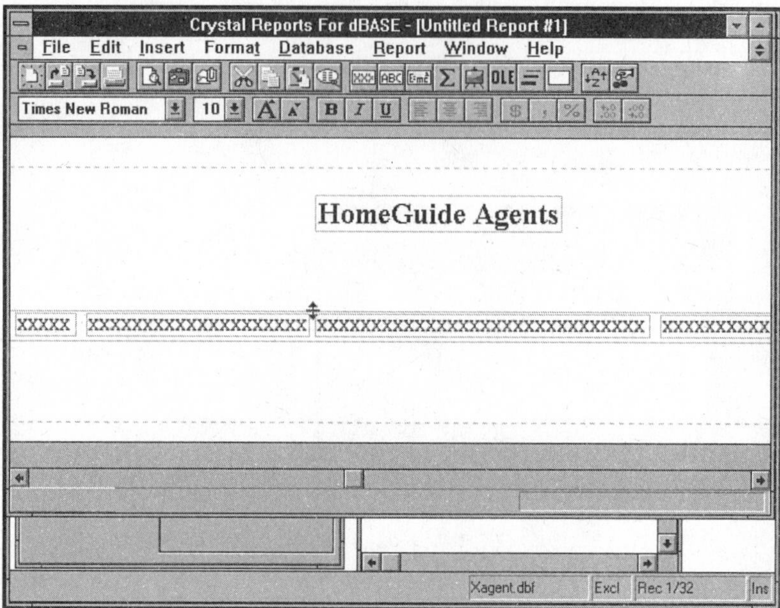

Figure 9.17 The mouse pointer changes shape when it is at a section boundary.

As mentioned earlier, you can press Enter with the insertion point in the Page Header section to give you more room for text.

Notice that the text you entered is displayed in Times New Roman font, 18-point size. This is the default option for the Page Header text, one of the options you can change with the File, Options menu selection, as described earlier. If you don't want all your text changed, you can change the font and size of any single text object after you insert it in the design. Watch the line and letter spacing change after you change the font size.

Now add the column headers that identify the field data; choose Insert, Text Field from the menu bar and enter **Agent ID** in the Edit Text Field dialog box; then click on Accept

Your changes are accepted

Place the text box above the AgentID field skeleton; notice that HomeGuide Agents is also in 18-point font; while the Reduce Font Size button is selected,

click on it until the font size is 10 point (or click on the font size arrow and select 10)

Repeat the preceding steps to add the other field titles: **Agent Last Name, Agency,** and **Office Phone,** in 10-point type

Your design should look like figure 9.18 now (the width of the Company field was reduced somewhat so that it would fit into the design window)

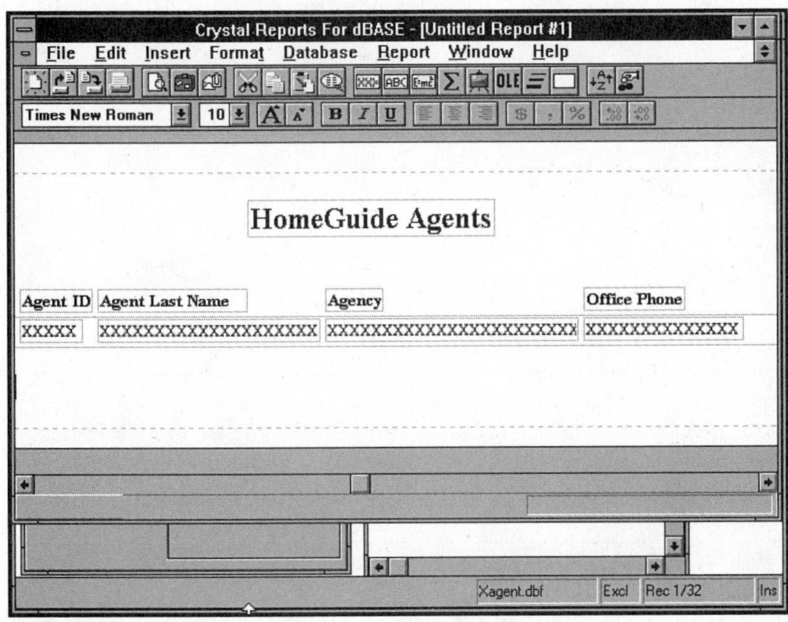

Figure 9.18 The report design with column headers and a title.

Click on the Preview button to preview the data; click and drag the title as necessary to center it over the table data; then click on the Italic button to change the title font style to italic

The title is centered over the data

Next, click on the Line tool button and draw a line under the title

Right-click on the line and choose Change Format from the SpeedMenu

The Line Format dialog box opens

Select a thicker line (3 point) and the color red; then choose OK (see fig. 9.19)

continues

continued

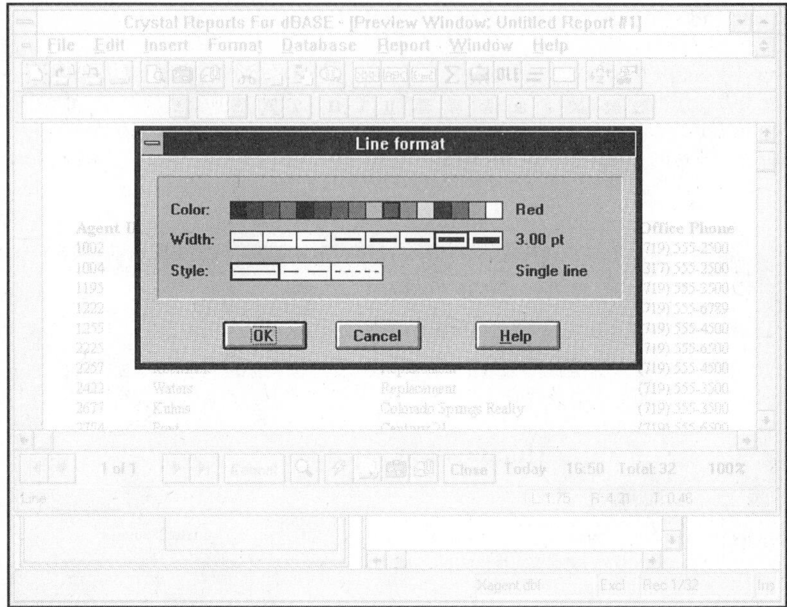

Figure 9.19
Changing a line format.

Notice that you have been making changes to the design while in the preview window rather than the design window. Your design should look like figure 9.20, with a red line under the title text.

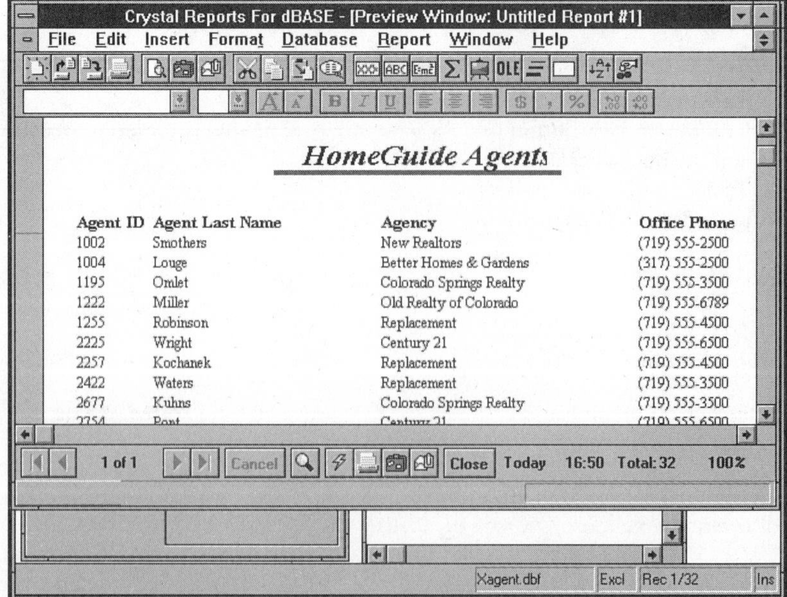

Figure 9.20
The report design with column titles and a line object.

Choose **F**ile, Save **A**s and name the report file **AGTLIST**	Crystal saves the report design with an RPT file extension

A Note from the Author

I always feel better if I save the design as soon as I get to the point where I would not like to have to start over if anything happened to my computer system. That is just about now with respect to the report you are designing in this exercise.

Print your new report by choosing **F**ile, **P**rint or by clicking on the Print button; (be sure that your printer is not still set to print in landscape orientation)	The printed report looks like figure 9.21

HomeGuide Agents

Agent ID	Agent Last Name	Agency	Office Phone
1002	Smothers	New Realtors	(719) 555-2500
1004	Louge	Better Homes & Gardens	(317) 555-2500
1195	Omlet	Colorado Springs Realty	(719) 555-3500
1222	Miller	Old Realty of Colorado	(719) 555-6789
1255	Robinson	Replacement	(719) 555-4500
2225	Wright	Century 21	(719) 555-6500
2257	Kochanek	Replacement	(719) 555-4500
2422	Waters	Replacement	(719) 555-3500
2677	Kuhns	Colorado Springs Realty	(719) 555-3500
2754	Pont	Century 21	(719) 555-6500
3502	Robinson	Replacement	(719) 555-4500
3762	Betker	Colorado Springs Realty	(719) 555-3500
4026	Mashburn	Replacement	(719) 555-4500
4187	Atkinson	Century 21	(719) 555-6500
4528	Brockway	Colorado Springs Realty	(719) 555-3500
4607	Miller	Better Homes & Gardens	(317) 555-2500
5084	Groh	Colorado Springs Realty	(719) 555-3500
5306	Young	Century 21	(719) 555-6500
5528	Brooks	Better Homes & Gardens	(317) 555-2500
5688	Manley	Century 21	(719) 555-6500
6610	Ortiz	Colorado Springs Realty	(719) 555-3500
6769	Rodenbeck	Better Homes & Gardens	(317) 555-2500
7387	Lawson	Century 21	(719) 555-6500
7725	Bogue	Sell Em Realty	(719) 555-4500
7905	Mason	Colorado Springs Realty	(719) 555-3500
8009	Lustig	Century 21	(719) 555-6500
8012	Morris	Better Homes & Gardens	(317) 555-2500
8234	Tidrow	Century 21	(719) 555-6500
8580	Perkins	Colorado Springs Realty	(719) 555-3500
9860	Omura	Century 21	(719) 555-6500
9900	Orkin	Century 21	(719) 555-6500
9947	Flynn	Better Homes & Gardens	(317) 555-2500

Figure 9.21
The printed report of HomeGuide Agents.

continues

continued

Choose Close to return to the design window for the final touches to your report design	The preview window closes
Right-click on the different fields to see the SpeedMenu options available for those field types	

Now add two more fields: the report date and the total number of agents in the list. The date goes in the header and the total goes in the footer.

Choose Insert, Special Field, Date and place the report date field in the upper left corner of the Page Header section	Notice that the field text appears in the default 18-point size
Reduce the font size to 10-point by using the pull-down menu or the SpeedBar button; if you want the report date to be different from the current date, choose Report, Set Print Date, and change the date in the Print Date dialog box	
Select the AgentID field and click on the Summary button (or choose Insert, Summary Field, Grand Total)	The Insert Grand Total dialog box opens
Click on the pull-down arrow, select Count from the menu, and choose OK (see fig. 9.22)	
A new section, Grand Total, is added to your design with a number field in it; drag the new field to the right to make room for some text explaining the total	
Click on the Text tool button and type **Total number of agents:** in the Edit Text Field dialog box. Then click on Accept and place the text object at the left edge of the Grand Total section	

Resize the text object to reduce the space following the characters and drag the total field up next to the text

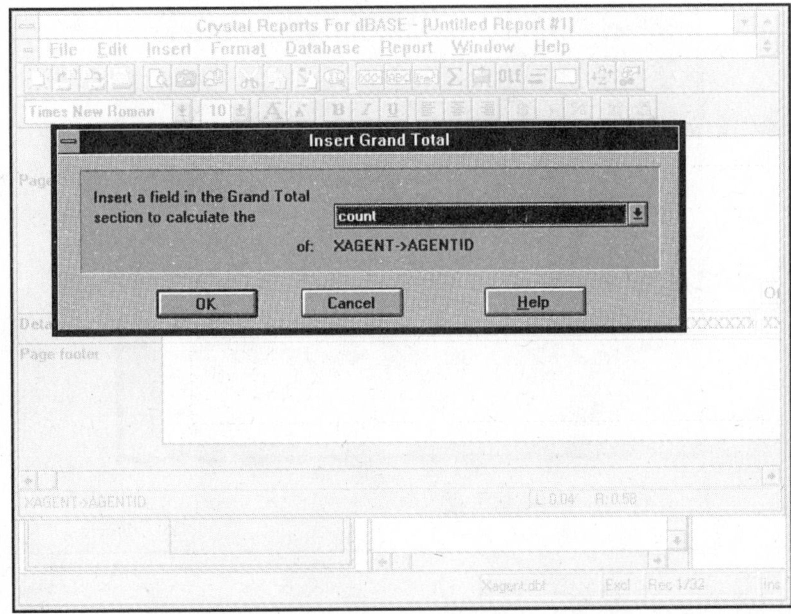

Figure 9.22
Inserting a grand total to count the number of agents.

Before moving on, take a look at the formatting options available for a number field. A count field is by default an integer, but look at the other number-formatting options anyway.

Right-click on the Grand Total number field and choose Change Format	The Format Number dialog box opens, as shown in figure 9.23

continues

continued

Figure 9.23
The Format Number dialog box.

The Format Number options include the customary choices of number of decimal places, rounding protocol, the display of negative values, the specification of the decimal and thousands separators, and the display of leading zeros.

In addition, you have the choice of alignment, suppressing duplicate numbers or zero values, and hiding the number when printing the report. Finally, you can change the currency symbol and its position with respect to the number, and you can limit it to one symbol per page.

Accept the Windows default format for the Grand Total field and choose OK

As a final touch, close up the space between the text and the Grand Total field; left-justify the Grand Total field to eliminate any extra space between it and the text

Select the total field and click on the Left-Align button in the format bar (you also can select the alignment from the Format Number dialog box); then click on the Bold button to make the number match the text

The finished design is shown in figure 9.24

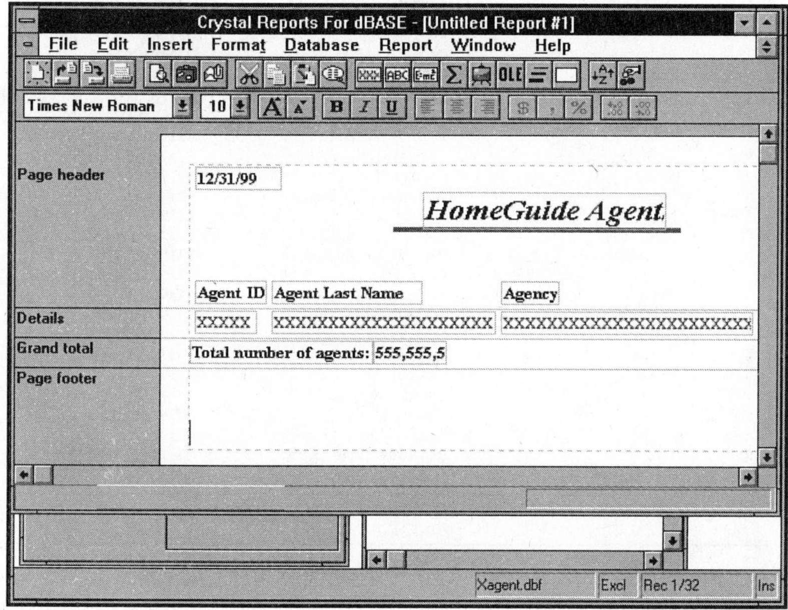

Figure 9.24
The finished Agent List report design.

Print the report

It should look like the report in figure 9.25

Save the finished report, and then choose **W**indow, Close **A**ll

continues

Figure 9.25
The printed finished report of HomeGuide Agents.

Agent ID	gent Last Name	Agency	Office Phone
1002	Smothers	New Realtors	(719) 555-2500
1004	Louge	Better Homes & Gardens	(317) 555-2500
1195	Omlet	Colorado Springs Realty	(719) 555-3500
1222	Miller	Old Realty of Colorado	(719) 555-6789
1255	Robinson	Replacement	(719) 555-4500
2225	Wright	Century 21	(719) 555-6500
2257	Kochanek	Replacement	(719) 555-4500
2422	Waters	Replacement	(719) 555-3500
2677	Kuhns	Colorado Springs Realty	(719) 555-3500
2754	Pont	Century 21	(719) 555-6500
3502	Robinson	Replacement	(719) 555-4500
3762	Betker	Colorado Springs Realty	(719) 555-3500
4026	Mashburn	Replacement	(719) 555-4500
4187	Atkinson	Century 21	(719) 555-6500
4528	Brockway	Colorado Springs Realty	(719) 555-3500
4607	Miller	Better Homes & Gardens	(317) 555-2500
5084	Groh	Colorado Springs Realty	(719) 555-3500
5306	Young	Century 21	(719) 555-6500
5528	Brooks	Better Homes & Gardens	(317) 555-2500
5688	Manley	Century 21	(719) 555-6500
6610	Ortiz	Colorado Springs Realty	(719) 555-3500
6769	Rodenbeck	Better Homes & Gardens	(317) 555-2500
7387	Lawson	Century 21	(719) 555-6500
7725	Bogue	Sell Em Realty	(719) 555-4500
7905	Mason	Colorado Springs Realty	(719) 555-3500
8009	Lustig	Century 21	(719) 555-6500
8012	Morris	Better Homes & Gardens	(317) 555-2500
8234	Tidrow	Century 21	(719) 555-6500
8580	Perkins	Colorado Springs Realty	(719) 555-3500
9860	Omura	Century 21	(719) 555-6500
9900	Orkin	Century 21	(719) 555-6500
9947	Flynn	Better Homes & Gardens	(317) 555-2500
Total number of agents: 32			

Creating a Two-Table Report

In the preceding section, you used most of the basic features of Crystal Reports to design and print a single-table report. In this section, you create a query to link two tables, and then you create a report including data from both tables. The report contains the agent records grouped by agency and you use a formula to concatenate the agent's last names, first names, and middle initials to remove any excess spaces between them. The finished report is shown in figure 9.26.

The first step is to use dBASE to build and save the query to be used as the basis for the report. Then open Crystal Reports to design the report using the fields from the query and group the records by Agency. Follow these steps:

Agents by Agency
December 5, 1994

Agency Code	Agent Code	Agent Name	Home Phone	Office Phone	Mobile Phone
1133	Better Homes & Gardens				
	1004	Louge, Sled	(303) 555-6333	(317) 555-2500	(317) 555-9999
	4607	Miller, Susan	(317) 555-9437	(317) 555-2500	(317) 555-9999
	5528	Brooks, Randolph	(317) 555-9218	(317) 555-2500	(317) 555-9999
	6769	Rodenbeck, Fred	(317) 555-2839	(317) 555-2500	(317) 555-9999
	8012	Morris, Angela	(317) 555-7910	(317) 555-2500	(317) 555-9999
	9947	Flynn, Don	(317) 555-7111	(317) 555-2500	(317) 555-9999
1775	Colorado Springs Realty				
	1195	Omlet, Peggy	(719) 555-1207	(719) 555-3500	(317) 555-9999
	2677	Kuhns, Peter	(317) 555-2020	(719) 555-3500	(317) 555-9999
	3762	Betker, Rosie	(317) 555-5830	(719) 555-3500	(317) 555-9999
	4528	Brockway, Jack	(317) 555-6071	(719) 555-3500	(317) 555-9999
	5084	Groh, Michael	(317) 555-3852	(719) 555-3500	(317) 555-9999
	6610	Ortiz, Herman	(317) 555-7908	(719) 555-3500	(317) 555-9999
	7905	Mason, Gary	(317) 555-8748	(719) 555-3500	(317) 555-9999
	8580	Perkins, Doris	(317) 555-5830	(719) 555-3500	(317) 555-9999
2301	Old Realty of Colorado				
	1222	Miller, Sandra	(719) 555-8820	(719) 555-6789	(317) 555-9999
2398	Sell Em Realty				
	1002	Smothers, Regina	(719) 555-2200	(719) 555-2500	(317) 555-9999
	1255	Robinson, Jack	(719) 555-9805	(719) 555-4500	(317) 555-9999
	2257	Kochanek, Diane	(719) 555-1205	(719) 555-4500	(317) 555-9999
	2422	Waters, Sam	(719) 555-5204	(719) 555-3500	(317) 555-9999
	3502	Robinson, Cheri	(317) 555-2020	(719) 555-4500	(317) 555-9999
	4026	Mashburn, Roy	(317) 555-2340	(719) 555-4500	(317) 555-9999
	7725	Bogue, Robert	(317) 555-9437	(719) 555-4500	(317) 555-9999
2429	Century 21				
	2225	Wright, Tom	(719) 555-1201	(719) 555-6500	(317) 555-9999
	2754	Pont, John	(317) 555-2233	(719) 555-6500	(317) 555-9999
	4187	Atkinson, Jane	(317) 555-7909	(719) 555-6500	(317) 555-9999
	5306	Young, Mary	(317) 555-9218	(719) 555-6500	(317) 555-9999
	5688	Manley, Mary Lynn	(317) 555-2874	(719) 555-6500	(317) 555-9999
	7387	Lawson, Robert	(317) 555-2022	(719) 555-6500	(317) 555-9999
	8009	Lustig, Marianne	(317) 555-5830	(719) 555-6500	(317) 555-9999
	8234	Tidrow, Ron	(317) 555-3260	(719) 555-6500	(317) 555-9999
	9860	Omura, Karen	(317) 555-3091	(719) 555-6500	(317) 555-9999
	9900	Orkin, Herbert	(719) 555-2011	(719) 555-6500	(317) 555-9999

Figure 9.26 The completed Agents by Agency report.

Building and Saving the Query

Return to dBASE and double-click on the <Untitled> icon in the Query panel of the Navigator window; (if you need to review the steps in creating a query, see to Chapter 8, "Querying Your Data")	The Open Table Required dialog box appears
Select the Xagency file name from the Open Table Required dialog box and then choose OK	The file name is selected

continues

continued

In the Query Design window, click on the Add Table button, select the Xagent file from the list in the Open Table required dialog box, and choose OK	The table is added
Draw a line from the Xagency table icon to the Xagent table icon and link the two tables in the Define Relation dialog box using the common AGENCYID field; accept the **O**ne to Many relationship and choose OK	The tables are linked
Check both fields in the Xagency table skeleton and check the AgentID, LastName, FirstName, and all the phone fields in the Xagent table skeleton	
Click on the Order box in the AgencyID field of the Xagency table and choose Ascending order	An up arrow appears in the order box of the Agency ID field

Save the query with the name **AGTRPT.QBE**

You now are ready to begin the report design. Open Crystal Reports to create a new report using the new AGTRPT.QBE file as the basis. The Insert Database Fields dialog box contains all the fields from the query.

Select the AgentID and place it in the Details section of the report design, leaving a margin at the left end (refer to the finished report in fig. 9.26 for spacing)

You want the agent's name to appear next in the report line, with the last name first, followed by a comma and a space, followed by the first name. Because the data fields are a fixed length, placing them in the report design individually leaves trailing spaces between the last and first names. To close up the names, create a formula field to trim the LastName field, and then concatenate the FirstName with the formula.

Click on the Formula tool button (or choose **I**nsert, **F**ormula Field), type **FULLNAME** as the name for the formula, and choose OK	The Expression Builder dialog box opens for you to enter the formula

You can enter the formula by hand or paste elements from the Paste list at the bottom right corner of the box

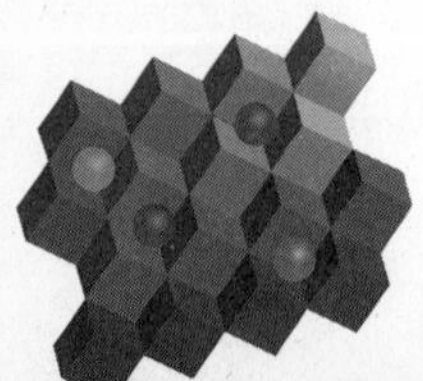

Type the following formula:

RTRIM(XAGENT->LASTNAME)+", "+XAGENT->FIRSTNAME

Choose E<u>v</u>aluate to make sure that the expression is valid

You should see the namein the current Xagent record displayed in the trimmed format below the expression box, as shown in figure 9.27

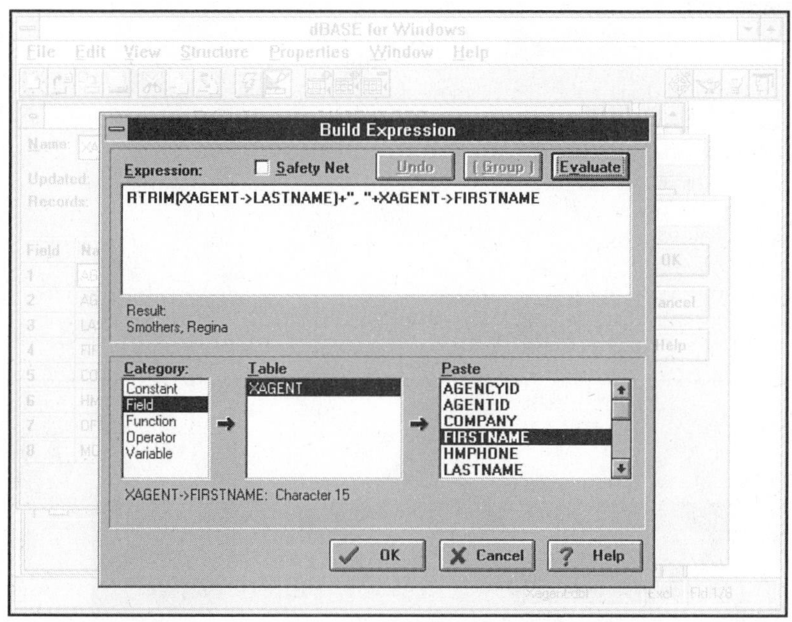

Figure 9.27
Entering a formula in the Build Expression dialog box.

Choose OK to return to the report design window and place the formula field next to the AgentID field in the Details section

Drag the right handle to shorten the field (because you have trimmed the excess spaces, it will not take as much room); right-click on the formula field

You can see the SpeedMenu options that are available

Place the three phone fields in the Details section; You have to scroll the design to the left in order to fit the fields in the design

continues

continued

Now you are ready to add a group section so that the agent records are grouped by agency in the report. When you group data on a specific field, the report designer knows you want to order the groups by the value in the group-by field. Any other sort orders are subsequent to the group sort. That is, the records are ordered within the group in the other sort orders.

Choose Insert, Group Section	The Insert Group Section dialog box opens
Click on the pull-down arrow and choose XAGENCY->AGENCYID from the menu of available fields; the fields already included in the report design are in the top part of the list, and the other fields follow in another list; (you also can change the sort order of the group designator in the Insert Group Section dialog box)	Figure 9.28 shows the dialog box after selecting the field to group by

When you return to the report design, you see that #1 Group has been added with a header and a footer section.

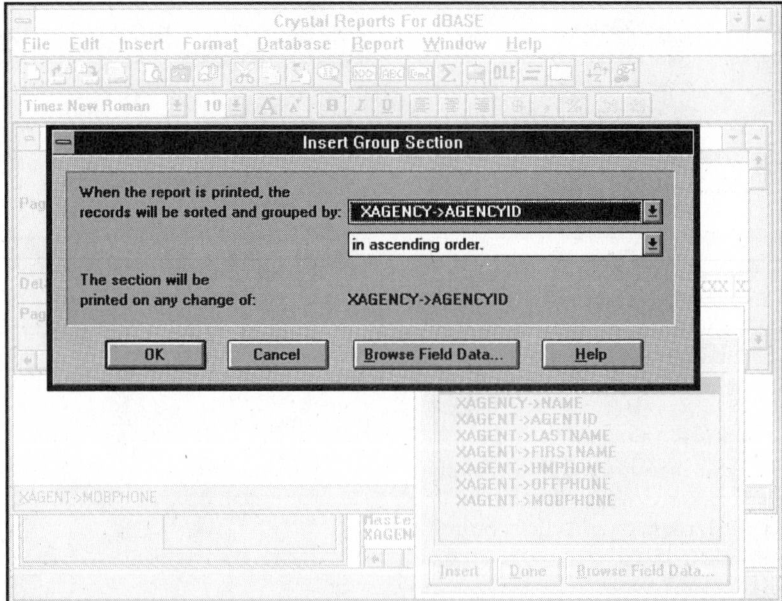

Figure 9.28 Selecting the field to group by in the Insert Group Section dialog box.

Both sections have the same name, so when you have several groups, you can tell which header corresponds to which footer. You can nest as many groups as you need—there is no practical limit.

Select and insert the Xagency fields into the group header section; (notice the automatic 12-point font size in a group header); click on **D**one	The Insert Database Field dialog box closes

Change the font size of both fields to 10 point to match the fields in the Details section.

Add the following text headers in the bottom of the Page Header section directly over the corresponding field object and reduce them to 8-point text.

Agency Code, **Agent Code**, **Agent Name**, **Home Phone**, **Office Phone**, and **Mobile Phone.** Figure 9.29 shows what your design should look like at this point.

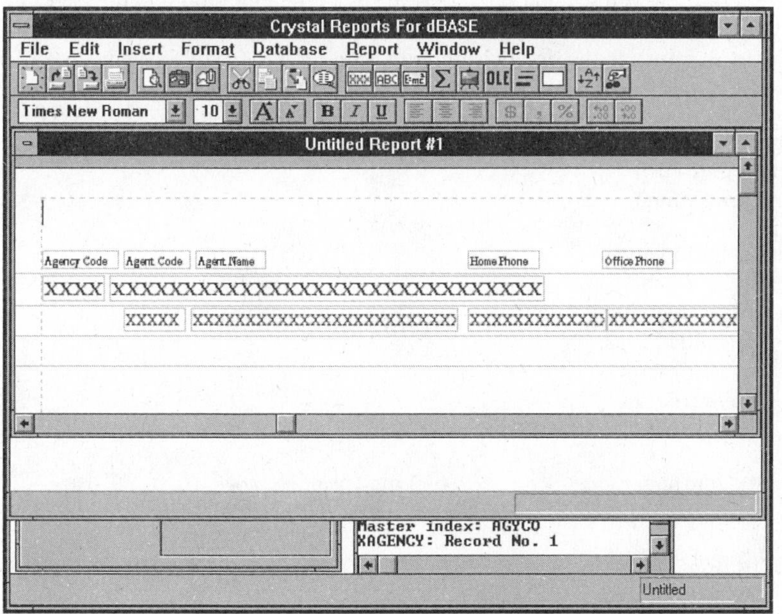

Figure 9.29
The report design with the column headers.

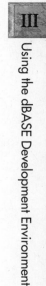

When you are trying to align the field titles with the field data, start at the left end. Most of the fields are left-justified, so aligning the left ends of each pair probably will make the fields look straight. Number fields normally are right-justified, so to line up the title with the field data, left-justify the number or right-align both elements.

continues

continued

Click on the Preview button to see how the report looks with data; If any of the labels or fields look out of place or not symmetrical, drag them around on the design

A Note from the Author

I found that small changes such as resizing and dragging an element to a new position are easily and quickly done in the Preview window. Changing a font size, however, takes more time. If you have any substantial changes to make, it is quicker to return to the design window instead of making those changes in the Preview window.

Looking at the design preview, you see that the report needs a little more room in the page header section and a divider between the column labels and the data. The report also needs a title and a report date, so return to the design window to reposition the existing elements and add some new ones.

Place the insertion point at the end of the field title line in the Page Header section and press Enter

A line is added below the titles

Click on the Line tool button and draw a line all the way across the report design halfway between the column labels and the field objects; (keep drawing as the design scrolls left until you reach the last field, Mobile Phone)

Right-click on the new line and choose Change Format

The Line Format dialog box appears (refer to fig. 9.19)

Choose 1.00 pt (third from the left in the Width options); select a color, too, if you want, and choose OK

This is a good time to save the report design; choose File, Save As. Name the new report **AGTRPT** and choose OK

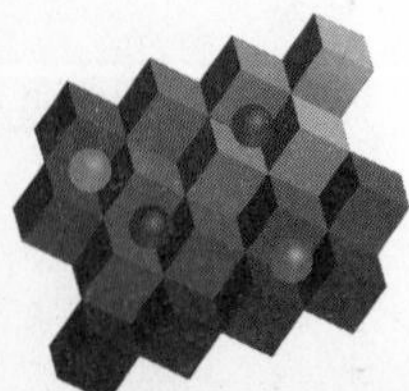

Next, add the report title and the print date; click on the Text tool button and type **Agents by Agency** in the Edit Text Field dialog box; Click on Accept.

The report title and print date are accepted

Insert the new text object in the upper left corner of the Page Header section; leave the font size at 18 points

Choose Insert, Special Field, Date and place the field below the title text field; reduce the font size to 12 points

The final touch is to add wide lines to set off the title and date at the top of the report. To do this, you need to make the Page Header section larger and move some of the objects around to make room for the new lines. Add one blank line above the report title and one blank line below the title.

Click on the Line tool button and draw a line across the entire design above the column labels; right-click on the line and change it to 3-point width

Click and drag down the date and title fields to make room for a new line at the top of the report page

Repeat step before the preceding one to draw a 3-point line above the title

Right-click on the Date field to open the SpeedMenu (see fig. 9.30)

Choose Change Format to display the Format Date dialog box shown in figure 9.31

continues

continued

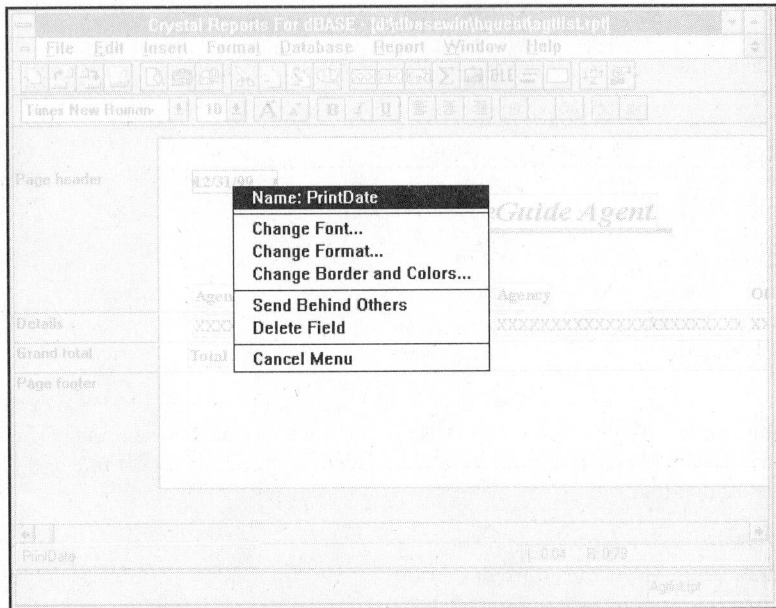

Figure 9.30 The Date field SpeedMenu.

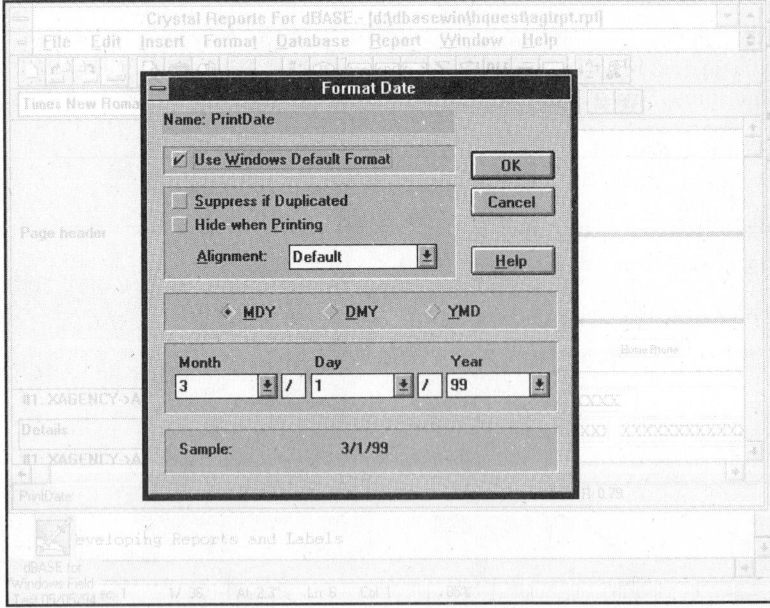

Figure 9.31 The Format Date dialog box.

Click on the Month pull-down arrow and select the whole word for the month; then click on the Year pull-down arrow and select the four-digit year format	
Delete the slash (/) separator in the box between the Month and Day boxes and enter a space instead	
Delete the slash separator between the Day and Year boxes and enter a comma followed by a space; choose OK	The Format Date dialog box closes
Resize the Date field to fit the new format; the finished report design is shown in figure 9.32	

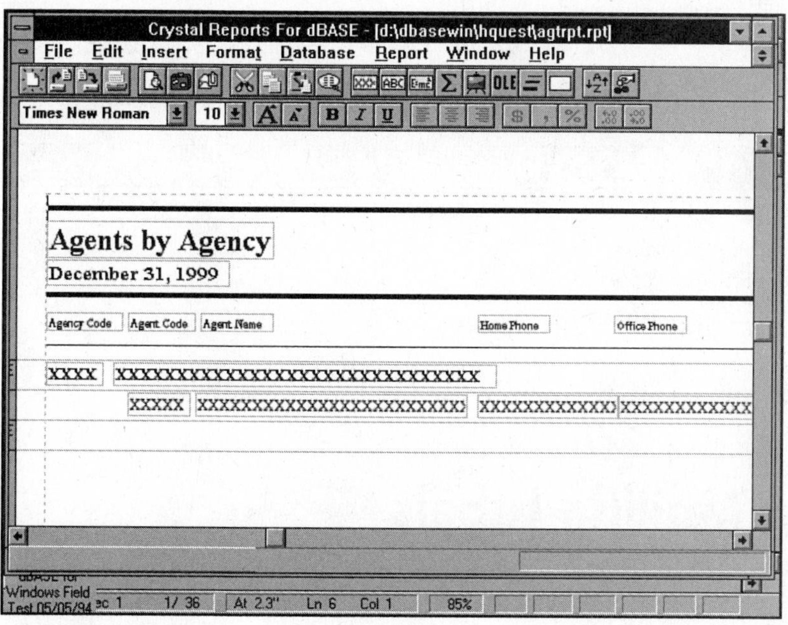

Figure 9.32
The finished report design in the design window.

Preview the report design (see fig. 9.33). Then print the report.

continues

continued

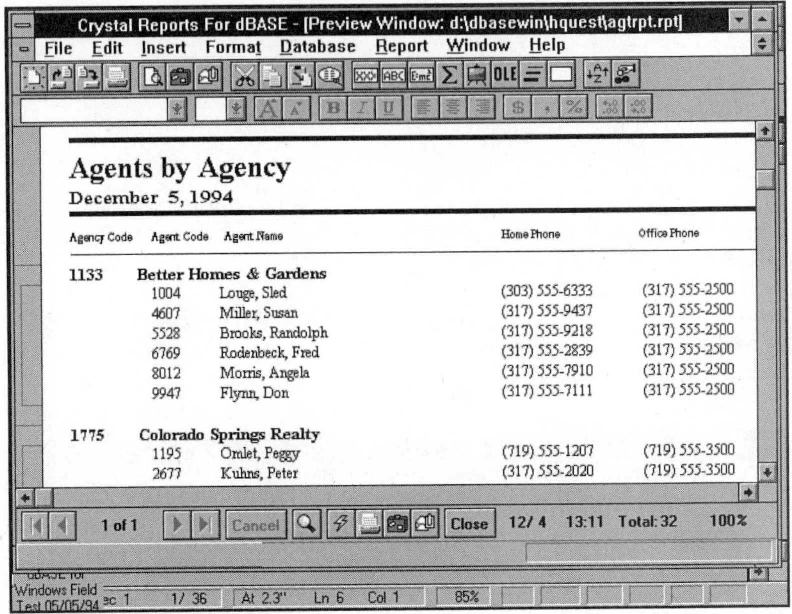

Figure 9.33 Previewing the finished Agents by Agency report.

Choose Close to return to the design window and save the finished report

Choose Window, Close All to end the exercise

Creating Mailing Labels

The term *mailing labels* is much too narrow to describe the types of special documents you can create and print using the Crystal Reports program. You can design a multi-record report to fit almost any size and shape of page your printer can handle. You can design not only address labels, but also labels for disks, file folders, rotary-file cards, postcards, video tapes, and name badges.

In fact, you can design a label report for any item that comes mounted on carrier paper for printing by laser, ink jet, or dot-matrix printers—even circular labels. Some carrier paper is single sheet and some is tractor-feed. Many sizes and layouts of label stock are available commercially, and Crystal Reports has predefined templates for many sizes and layouts. You can define the label size, layout, and paper dimensions you want if they are not included in the Crystal templates.

The major steps in creating a label design follow:

1. Select the size of the carrier paper

2. Specify the size of the individual label and how the labels are laid out on the page

3. Set up the printer to print on the label stock

If you are printing on a laser printer, the label stock is probably on the standard 8 1/2-x-11-inch paper. If you are using a tractor-feed printer, many other paper sizes are available to you. To set the paper size at a different dimension from the default size, choose File, Printer Setup and select a new paper size from the list. If the size you want is not on the list, you must create a user-defined paper size using the Printer section of the Windows Control Panel.

To open the Crystal Report to design a new mailing label, you can use one of the same steps that you use to begin a report design:

- ✔ Choose File, New, Labels from the menu bar

- ✔ Click on the Labels icon in the Navigator window and choose Navigator, New Labels from the menu bar

- ✔ Click on the Labels icon in the Navigator window, and double-click on the <Untitled> icon

- ✔ Click on the New SpeedBar button and choose Labels

- ✔ Type **CREATE LABEL** in the Command window

When you begin to design a new mailing label design, Crystal opens a Mailing Labels dialog box in which you specify the dimensions of the individual labels and their layout on the paper. If you do not choose one of the predefined label templates, you must specify the following:

- ✔ Number of labels across and down the paper

- ✔ Dimensions of a label

- ✔ Gap between labels horizontally and vertically

- ✔ Desired print order: across then down (across the first row, then across the second, and so on) or down then across (down the first column, then down the second, and so on)

All these specifications are made in the first dialog box that Crystal displays after you choose the table or query to use a basis for the labels. The label design window has the same SpeedBar buttons, the same menu and format bar options, and operates much like a regular report. The only difference is that the label design window has only one section: the Details section.

Designing Labels for the Home Buyers

When you send material to your potential property buyers, you want to have professional-looking mailing labels. Crystal has predefined label definitions from which to choose. If you want another label definition, you can create a custom layout.

To create a custom layout, follow the steps in this exercise:

Creating a Custom Layout

Return to the Crystal Reports window

Choose File, New, Labels and select Xbuyer from the Database File dialog box, then choose OK

The Mailing Labels dialog box opens with the default settings shown in figure 9.34

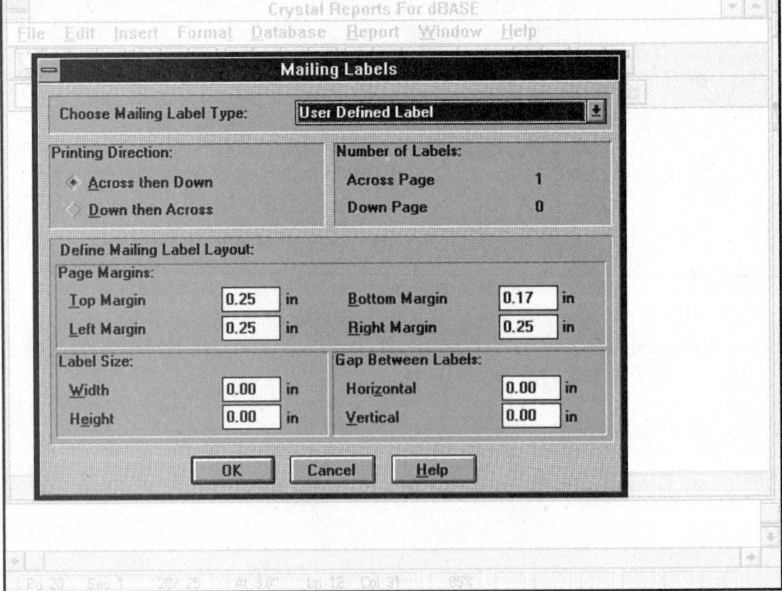

Figure 9.34
The Mailing Labels dialog box.

Click on the Choose Mailing Label Type pull-down arrow and choose Address [Avery 5160]

Notice that when you select a different label type, the layout specifications change to match

Choose OK

The report design window opens for you to insert the database fields (see fig. 9.35)

Place the design elements only in the left-most label frame. The other frames are to illustrate the label size and layout. If you insert a field or other element in one of these frames, you might get some overprinting or other disastrous results.

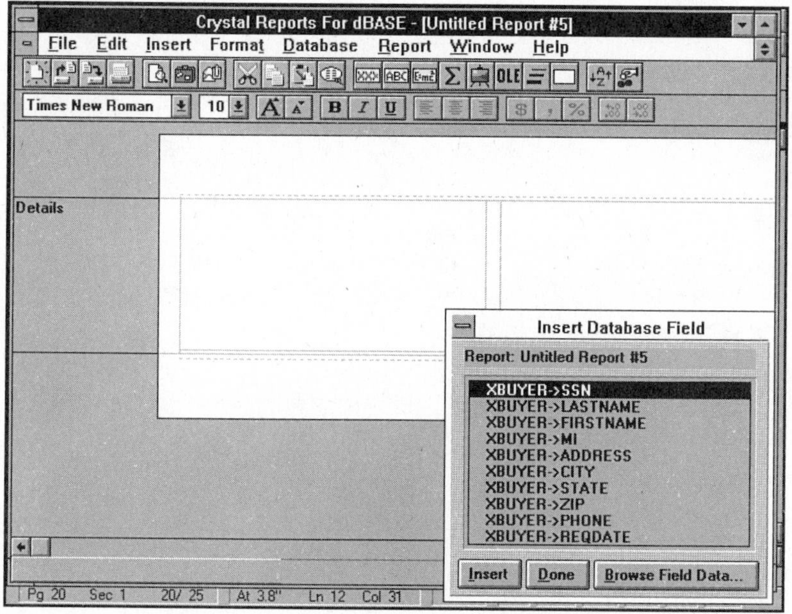

Figure 9.35
The Mailing Labels design window.

The first line contains the buyer's full name with no unnecessary spaces; for this line, you need to create another string-trimming formula

Choose Insert, Formula Field and type **BUYERNAME** as the formula name; choose OK

The Build Expression dialog box opens

Enter the following formula in the expression box (you can enter it manually or paste it from the Paste lists).

RTRIM(XBUYER->FIRSTNAME)+" "+RTRIM(XBUYER->MI)+". " +XBUYER->LASTNAME

continues

continued

Type the entire formula on one line (the expression word-wraps in the box). Don't forget to add a space between each pair of quotation marks.

Choose E<u>v</u>aluate to make sure that the expression is valid and that the words are spaced correctly.

Insert the Address field on the line below the buyer name.

Now you need another formula for the City, State, ZIP line. As before, choose <u>I</u>nsert, <u>F</u>ormula Field and type **CITYSTZIP** as the formula name. Then choose OK.

Type the following formula in the Build Expression dialog box (be sure to type the entire formula on one line):

RTRIM(XBUYER->CITY)+", "+XBUYER->STATE+" "+XBUYER->ZIP

Choose OK and place the Formula field on the line below the Address field in the label design	The Build Expression dialog box closes and you return to the Report Design window
Resize the Formula field to fit the label width	
Click on <u>D</u>one	The Insert Database Field dialog box closes
Preview the label design (see fig. 9.36)	

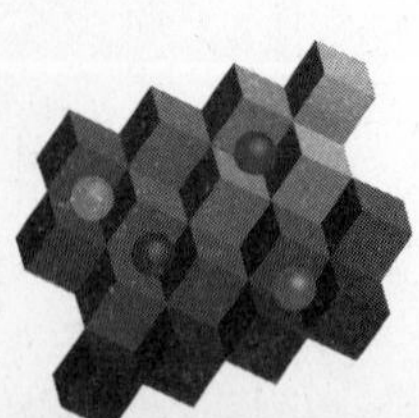

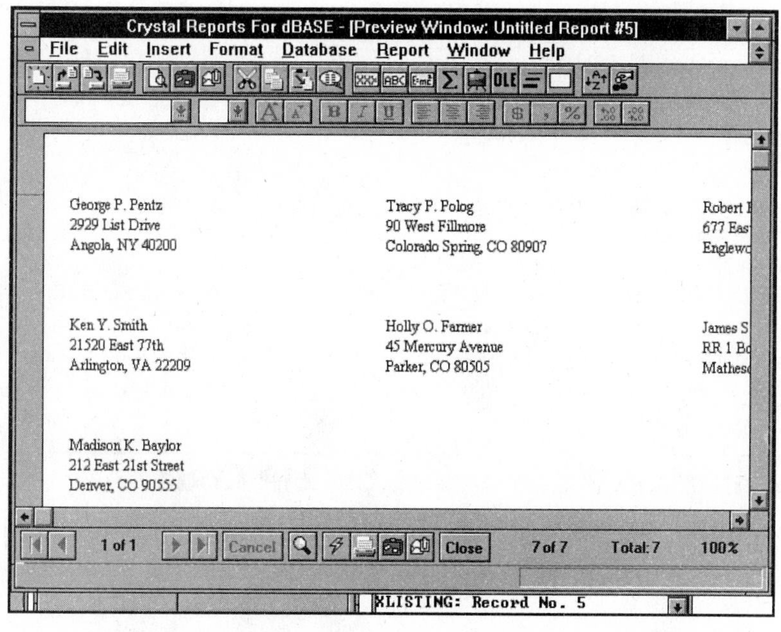

Figure 9.36
A preview of the mailing labels.

If you print a sheet of labels now, the buyer's name begins in the upper left corner of the label. The labels might look better with the printing vertically centered on the labels.

Click on Close — You return to the design window to see the outline of the label

Hold down the Shift key and group-select all three lines; then move the lines down one line in the label frame.

Print the sheet of labels on paper stock.

Save the label file as **BYRMAIL** and keep the label designer open for the next exercise. Crystal saves the file with an RPL extension, and the label file icon appears in the Labels panel of the dBASE Navigator window.

You also can center the text on the labels horizontally. First, resize all the fields until they are the same length. Then, group-select all three lines and click on the Center Align button in the format bar. The text in all three lines should be centered in the label line.

If you are printing on label stock with borders, such as fancy name tags, create a user-defined label layout considering the white space inside the border as the label. The label border then adds to the dimensions of the gap between the labels, horizontally and vertically.

If you have a large mailing list, it often is handy to sort the labels by ZIP code. The Buyer list is not large, but you still can see how to sort the labels. In order to sort on a field in the label design, the field must stand alone and not be part of a formula. To sort the Xbuyer list by ZIP code, then, you must add the ZIP field to the label design. You don't want the ZIP code to print twice, once as part of the formula and again as a separate field, so after you add the field, change the format and choose to hide the field when the labels are printed. To sort the Xbuyer list by ZIP code, follow these steps:

Sorting the Xbuyer List by ZIP Code

Choose **I**nsert, **D**atabase Field and select the ZIP field from the Insert Database Field dialog box	The Insert Database Field dialog box opens
Choose **I**nsert and place the ZIP field on the fourth line	
Click on **D**one	The Insert Database Field dialog box closes
Right-click on the new ZIP field and choose Change Format from the SpeedMenu	
Check the Hide When **P**rinting option and choose OK	The ZIP field on the fourth line now is dim in the label design
Choose **R**eport, Record **S**ort Order to select the sort field from the Record Sort Order dialog box (see fig. 9.37)	
Select XBUYER->ZIP and click on **A**dd	The field name is added to the Sort Fields list as order A
Leave the sort order as Ascending and choose OK	

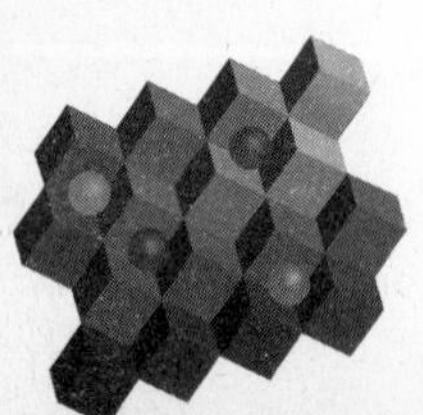

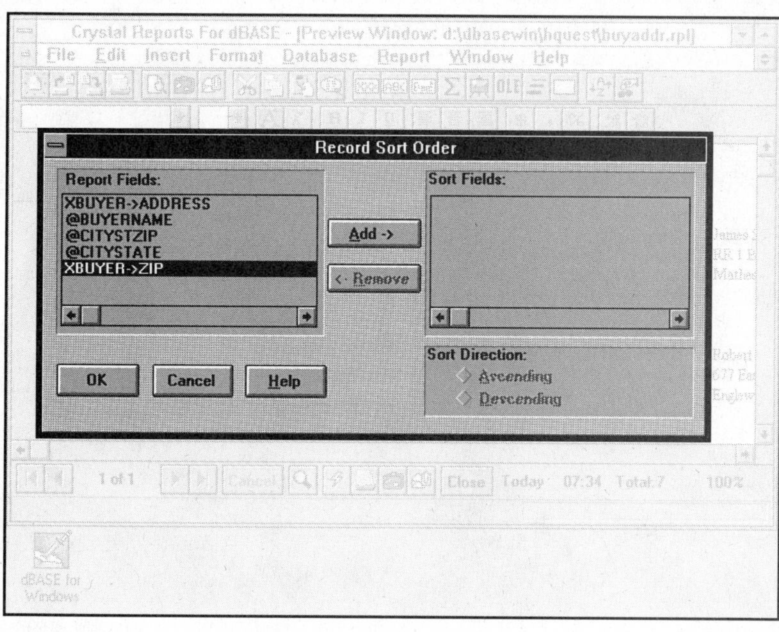

Figure 9.37 The Record Sort Order dialog box.

Preview the label records to see that they are ordered by ZIP code when printed in the default order—across, then down

Print the labels on plain paper (see fig. 9.38)

Return to the design window and save the report design as BUYZIP; choose <u>W</u>indow, C<u>l</u>ose All and exit Crystal to end the exercise

Ken Y. Smith 21520 East 77th Arlington, VA 22209	George P. Pentz 2929 List Drive Angola, NY 40200	James S. Anderson RR 1 Box 222 Matheson, CO 80411
Holly O. Farmer 45 Mercury Avenue Parker, CO 80505	Tracy P. Polog 90 West Fillmore Colorado Spring, CO 80907	Robert K. Graves 677 East Liverdale Drive Englewood, CO 80995
Madison K. Baylor 212 East 21st Street Denver, CO 90555		

Figure 9.38 The Buyer mailing labels sorted by ZIP code.

NRP
NEW RIDERS
PUBLISHING

Part IV

Developing for the Windows Environment

Chapter Snapshot

From its humble beginnings, the dBASE language has evolved into a general-purpose language with dynamic objects, a flexible GUI, and a built-in, high-performance database engine. In this chapter, you learn the following:

You learn about the basic fundamentals of the dBASE language in this chapter. You need not, however, have programming experience. If you have such experience, the early material will be familiar to you. There are separate chapters on object-oriented and event-driven programming.

Understanding the dBASE Language

By Kenneth Chan

The dBASE for Windows language is the heart of dBASE. The form, menu, and query designers generate dBASE code, so there is nothing that they can do that you cannot do as well or better using this language.

The form, menu, and query designers are two-way tools. Unlike many tools that store their designs in special-format files, these two-way tools store their designs directly in dBASE code. This code can be edited manually like any other program, and when the code is reread by the designer, any changes that were made manually in the code will be reflected in the design tool.

Two-way tools make it easier for you to learn the language by letting you see what complete code looks like, and by letting you tweak the code and see the results.

Introducing Programming Concepts

A *program* is a complete set of instructions on how to accomplish a task. As the task varies in complexity, so does the program. Some tasks are very simple and require only that certain things be done in a particular order. Most tasks and programs are more complex and require some decision making to do one thing or another, or to do things in the order desired by the user.

A program or piece of a program is often referred to as *code;* the process of writing programs is called *coding.*

In programming languages, certain words and symbols are reserved because they have special meanings. In dBASE, these words and symbols are analogous to the actions they represent. For example, DEFINE, TIME, and + mean pretty much the same things to dBASE as they do to you. These reserved words are defined as part of the language and can only be used for their designated purposes. Later, when you get to name things, you cannot use these reserved words as names of your own.

Understanding Commands

Commands are the first class of reserved words. *Commands* are the verbs in the language of programming. The command CLEAR clears the Results pane of the Command window. The command QUIT quits dBASE.

Most commands are not this simple. In addition to the command itself, there needs to be a corresponding subject. For example, the ? symbol is used to display information in the Results pane of the Command window. By itself, it displays a blank line. Used in conjunction with an expression, it displays the value of that expression.

Understanding Expressions

If commands are the verbs of programming, then expressions are the nouns. Just as there are many different types of nouns (for example, birds and emotions), there are different types of expressions. Programming languages, including dBASE's, generally utilize both numbers and text, although dBASE also supports other types, such as dates. Although these different types have some things in common, they each have their own unique qualities and capabilities.

Understanding Operators

Each type of expression, or data type, is affected by its own group of operators. For example, the symbol + is a numeric operator that adds two numbers together. dBASE performs any operations required to reduce a complex expression (one with operators in it) into a simple expression, the result of the operation.

Understanding Statements

When you put a command together with any expressions that it needs, you have a program *statement*. A statement, or command line, performs a single action, although that action might be a complex action composed of many smaller steps. Just as the act of tying your shoelaces actually involves dozens of tiny steps that you don't bother thinking about, a single statement may have a number of steps and side effects.

For example, the following statement combines the command verb ? with the complex numeric expression 2 + 2.

```
? 2 + 2
```

The first thing a statement with ? does is start a new line, and so the cursor in the Results pane of the Command window moves down a line. If the cursor is already at the bottom of the window, then the window's contents are scrolled up a line. The cursor is then placed at the beginning of the new line.

dBASE then encounters and calculates the value for the complex expression 2 + 2, which is the simple expression 4. The last step is to display the 4.

A statement is often referred to by its command verb. When referring to the statement ? 2=2, for example, you might refer to it as the ? command (unless of course there are a number of statements with the ? command verb, in which case you would have to be more precise).

Understanding Control Structures

A program is a succession of statements. Normally, these statements are executed once, one after the other. In all but the simplest programs, some statements are repeated, and other statements are not executed at all. These changes to the normal flow of a program are achieved with special statements called *control structures*, because they control the flow of a program.

Getting Started with Programs

The only way to learn programming is to write programs. It can even be said that the best way to learn is to write programs that don't work and fix them. There are two reasons for this. First, in programming, you learn by doing; you cannot be afraid to make mistakes—just keep backups. Second, because programming is such a vast subject, instead of trying to absorb everything at once, concentrate on one thing at a time. When you make a mistake, and you will, you are much more likely to remember the lessons of that mistake then any amount of theory.

This section walks you through the creation of two simple programs. In the process, basic dBASE programming techniques are shown, and a number of terms are introduced. All of the new terminology is explained in more detail later in the chapter.

Creating Your First Program

dBASE programs are stored in ASCII text files with a PRG extension and are often referred to as PRG files. To create a new program, select the Programs pane of the Navigator and double-click on the Untitled icon. This creates a new, empty Untitled program editor window with the cursor at the top left corner. Type in the following, pressing Enter to separate the lines:

```
? "Hello, world!"
? "Today is", date()
```

You do not need to press Enter at the end of the last line of a dBASE program. At this point, your window should look like the one in figure 10.1.

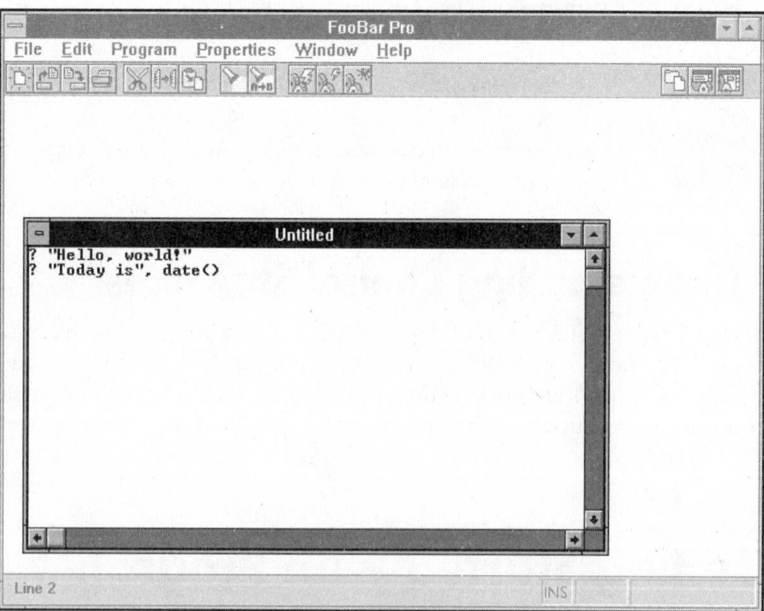

Figure 10.1 Your first program.

To save the program, press Ctrl+W. (You may also close the window by double-clicking the window's control box.) Because the program is untitled, you are asked for a file name.

The file name follows normal Windows file-naming conventions and can be up to eight letters long. Type the name **Hello1** and press Enter.

The file HELLO1.PRG is now saved, and a new program icon labeled Hello1 appears in the Program pane of the File Viewer (see fig. 10.2).

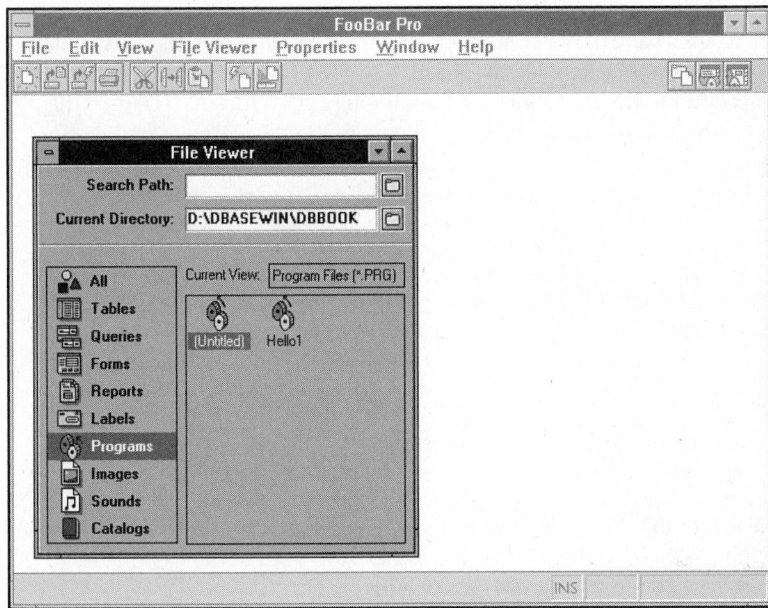

Figure 10.2
Your first program in the File Viewer.

To run the program, double-click on its icon. HELLO1.PRG displays, "Hello, world!" and displays the current date in the Command Results window.

Notice that both commands in HELLO1.PRG start with a ?. There is only one case in which the first word of a command line is not the command itself, and that case is memory variable assignment (often referred to as memvar assignment), which will be covered shortly.

The ? is dBASE's "What is . . ." command. For example, the statement

```
? 2=2
```

can be thought of as "What is 2+2?" dBASE responds with the answer: 4. More precisely, the ? command evaluates and displays the value of any expression in the Results pane of the Command window. It is analogous to the PRINT command in BASIC, writeln in Pascal, and printf() in C. The first thing the ? command does is start a new line.

The next item on the command line is the literal character string, "Hello, world!" A *character string* is one or more characters, and is often referred to as a *text string*, or just *text*.

This character string is *literal* because it is typed into the program with character *delimiters* (usually double quotation marks) that mark its beginning and end. When confronted with a literal character string, the ? command simply displays the text, without the quotation marks, in the Results pane of the Command window.

The second command is similar, but it has two items separated by a comma: first the text "Today is" and then the word DATE(). Again, a new line is started, and the text "Today is" is displayed in the Results pane of the Command window. The word DATE() is a built-in function. When called, a *function* replaces itself with a predetermined value. You can write your own functions, but the DATE() function is a built-in part of dBASE. It returns the current system date, so dBASE displays the current date in the Results pane of the Command window. Items that are separated by commas in the ? command are separated by a space when printed, so there is a space between the text "Today is" and the date.

If you do not get a space between "Today is" and the date, then one of your settings, SET SPACE, has been turned off. It is on by default.

When there are no more commands, the program stops, returning control to wherever it was started from—in this case, back to you, because you started it manually.

This first example was nothing fancy. At its simplest, a program is nothing more than a series of actions that dBASE performs. If you typed these two lines in the Command window, you would have gotten exactly the same results.

Often, when working, you make a decision to do one thing or another. You want your programs to do some of that thinking for you. Your second program does some thinking.

Creating Your Second Program

If you noticed the first time that you double-clicked the Untitled program icon, the words CREATE COMMAND were displayed in the Command window. The CREATE COMMAND command creates PRG files. You can also specify a file name when you CREATE COMMAND. Because you double-clicked on the Untitled program icon, no name was supplied. To edit programs, you can either right double-click on the files icon in the Navigator, or use a variation of the CREATE COMMAND command, the MODIFY COMMAND command.

You can also use the MODIFY COMMAND command to create program files. If you specify a non-existent program to MODIFY, dBASE assumes that you want to CREATE it.

MODIFY COMMAND is often abbreviated as MODI COMM. Many dBASE commands can be abbreviated to the first four letters of each word, as explained later in this chapter. This can save you thousands of keystrokes in the Command window over your lifetime.

To create your second program, type **MODI COMM HELLO2** and press Enter. This opens a new window titled HELLO2. Type in the following (the numbers are only there to help us reference specific lines in the discussion that follows):

```
1.    set talk off
2.    clear
3.    accept "Hello! What's your name? " to cName
4.    do
5.      wait "Do you believe in numerology (Y/N)? " to cBelieve
6.    until cBelieve $ "yYnN"
7.    if cBelieve $ "yY"
8.      nMagic = 0
9.      for nLtr = 1 to len( cName )
10.       cLtr = substr( upper( cName ), nLtr, 1 ))
11.       if isalpha( cLtr )
12.         nMagic = nMagic + asc( cLtr ) - asc( "A" ) + 1
13.       endif
14.     endfor
15.     ? "When you add up the letters in the name", cName
16.     ? "you get the number", nMagic
17.   else
18.     ? "Neither do I."
19.   endif
```

Your program editor window ought to look something like figure 10.3. For clarity, an extra space has been added to the far left of each line in figure 10.3. Notice that line numbers are *not* used in the editor window.

Save the program. Run the program by typing **DO HELLO2** in the command window. Follow the prompts to see what the program does.

dBASE has many settings that affect its operation: TALK is one of these settings, and can be either ON or OFF. For example, when you assign a value to a memory variable (explained shortly), if TALK is ON, the value is displayed in the Results pane of the Command window. TALK controls whether dBASE displays information when certain commands are executed. Normally, when your program is running, you don't want TALK ON because the displayed information messes up *your* desired display. TALK is ON by default to aid interactive users, so the first command, set talk off (as seen in line 1), turns it off. It stays off until you turn it back on.

Figure 10.3
The HELLO2.PRG program in the Program Editor window.

dBASE for Windows Field Test 05/05/94

File Edit Program Properties Window Help

Program Editor (HELLO2.PRG)

```
set talk off
clear
accept "Hello! What's your name? " to cName
do
  wait "Do you believe in numerology (Y/N)? " to cBelieve
until cBelieve $ "yYnN"
if cBelieve $ "yY"
  nMatchgic = 0
  for nLtr = 1 to len( cName )
    cLtr = substr( upper( cName ), nLtr, 1 ))
    if isalpha( cLtr )
      nMagic = nMagic + asc( cLtr ) - asc( "A" ) + 1
    endif
  endfor
  ? "When you add up the letters in the name", cName
  ? "you get the number", nMagic
else
  ? "Neither do I."
endif
```

Another effect of TALK is to slow down your program. If TALK is ON, dBASE will update the Command window and status bar even if the Command window is minimized or the entire dBASE interactive environment has been disabled with the SHELL() function. This has a significantly negative impact on your program's performance. When running applications, always make sure that TALK is OFF.

The CLEAR command (line 2) clears the Command Results window, something you usually want to do at the beginning of a program.

The ACCEPT command (line 3) has two parts. The first is an optional character expression that acts as a prompt, to ask the user a question. The second part, after the word "to," is the name of a memory variable.

A *memory variable* is a named cubbyhole where information is stored. When the program asks for the user's name, it keeps the user's name in the computer's memory. The exact location in memory is identified by the name given after the word "to." Note that the memory variable name does not have quotes around it because it is not text; it is an *identifier.*

The ACCEPT statement in line 3 displays the prompt text ("Hello! What's your name?") and waits for the user to type something. When the user presses Enter, whatever the user enters is stored in the memory variable *cName.* There are rules, but you basically can name the memory variable whatever you want.

You should make the variable name ("cName") meaningful; in this case, the first letter is c to signify that the name consists of characters. The word *Name* is best because it indicates what kind of data is stored in the variable. A complete naming convention is described later in this chapter.

The next command, DO, (in line 4) marks the beginning of a DO . . .UNTIL loop, which ends a few lines down with the UNTIL command in line 6. Everything in between is the *loop body.* The loop body—in this case a single line (line 5)—is indented a few spaces. Indenting is not required, but it helps you to visualize the program's structure.

There is a WAIT command in line 5 of the loop body. The WAIT command behaves much like an ACCEPT command, except that WAIT expects only a single keystroke, and ACCEPT lets users type as much as they want. In this program, the single character captured by the WAIT command is stored in the memory variable *cBelieve.*

The UNTIL statement (line 6) uses the $ character operator (which means "is contained in") to check if the typed character is one of the characters in the string "yYnN." The effect of the DO . . .UNTIL loop is to ask the question "Do you believe" repeatedly until the user responds with a lowercase or uppercase Y or N. After the user does, the UNTIL condition becomes true, and execution proceeds to the next command.

The IF statement uses the same $ operator to see if the user responded with a Y for yes—indicating that he or she believes in numerology. If the condition is true, then the commands after the IF are executed. If the condition is false, all of the commands up to the ELSE in line 17 are ignored. Notice again that all the commands between the IF in line 7 and the ELSE in line 17 are indented to show anyone reading the program that those commands are only executed if the if condition is true.

Line 8 does not start with a command. It starts with an identifier ("nMagic"), which is followed by an = sign. This is a memory variable assignment. In the statement nMagic = 0, the number 0 is assigned to the memory variable *nMagic.* Whenever nMagic is referenced, it will return its value, which is currently set to 0 (zero).

The FOR command in line 9 marks the beginning of a FOR. . .ENDFOR loop (the ENDFOR is in line 14). This loop executes a group of instructions a certain number of times. The loop count is maintained in the *counter* memory variable nLtr. When the loop starts, it is set to 1. The loop counter increases by one every time the loop runs, up to and including the last iteration of the loop, which is equal to LEN(cName). The LEN() function returns the number of characters in a string. This means that this loop executes the same number of times as there are characters in the name that was entered.

The intent of the FOR loop is to execute the same set of instructions for each character in cName. The first statement in the loop (line 10) is a memory variable assignment using the SUBSTR() function. The SUBSTR() function extracts characters (a *substring)* from a string. These characters are not removed from the string. The syntax of the SUBSTR() function is:

```
SUBSTR( <source string>, <starting position>, [ <number of characters
➥to extract> ] )
```

The source string is UPPER(cName), which means that the name the user types in is converted to uppercase before extracting characters. The starting position is the counter memory variable nLtr, which means that the first time the loop is run, the starting position is the first character. The second time the loop is run, the starting position is the second character, and so on. The number of characters to extract is always 1.

For example if the name is "John", the first time through the loop, the character "J" is assigned to cLtr. The second time through, the letter "O" is assigned. Note that this is an uppercase O, since "John" is converted to "JOHN" by the UPPER() function. The third and fourth time, the letters "H" and "N" are assigned.

The ISALPHA() function indicates whether or not a character is a letter of the alphabet. If it is, then the following command yields the position of the letter in the alphabet. The letter's position is determined by where it is situated in the alphabet. For example, A is 1, B is 2, etc.

```
ASC(cLtr) - ASC("A") + 1
```

That number is then added to nMagic, which keeps a running total of all of the letters occurring in cName. If the character is not a letter, (such as a space) the character is skipped. After adding up the position number of all the letters in the name, the total is displayed in the Results pane of the Command window.

If instead the user said they did not believe in numerology, no calculations are done. dBASE executes the ELSE clause beginning in line 17 and simply responds, "Neither do I" (line 18).

Writing Programs

There are a number of things to keep in mind when writing dBASE programs. Some of these things are rules and others are suggestions that make your life easier.

Understanding PRG File Structure

Programs are simple text files. The built-in dBASE program editor is a simple text editor that does not put any formatting codes like margins or fonts into the file. Other suitable text editors are programs like Notepad and the Norton Desktop Editor. There are also a number of professional Windows programmers' editors on the market. Any of these can be used to write PRG files.

You cannot use a word processor like Word or Ami Pro to write PRGs unless you save the file as an ASCII text file, rather than the word processor's native format. Even with ASCII text, a word processor is really not well-suited for writing programs.

Maximum Size

There is no specified limit to the size of a PRG file. There is a limit to the number of procedures that a single file can contain—193 per file.

Line Length

The maximum line length is 4,096 characters, but most commands don't even come close to that. The most likely exception would be a very long REPLACE command. In general, the fewer lines you have, the faster your programs will run. Generally speaking, there is one command per line, except when the commands get too long to follow; when commands are too long, continuation lines are used to continue the command to the following line.

Continuation Lines

Commands get difficult to read long before they reach the maximum line length. They are difficult to edit in your editor—you have to pan left and right to see everything.

To solve this problem, you can break up a single command line into multiple continuation lines. To indicate that the end of a line is not the end of the command, place a semicolon at the end of the line. When dBASE encounters the semicolon, it adds the next line to the current command.

For example, suppose your command looks like this:

```
replace LAST_NAME with cLName, FIRST_NAME with cFName
```

You can break this line up like this:

```
replace ;
  LAST_NAME  with cLName, ;
  FIRST_NAME with cFName
```

Note that breaking up the line enhances readability by lining up the similarly structured clauses of the command. You should only break the line between words and symbols, and never in the middle of a literal character string.

Note that the semicolons at the ends of the line are not counted when determining line length, but the spaces at the beginning of the line are.

Indenting

Every time you begin a control structure, all of the statements inside that structure should be indented. Indenting command lines makes it more obvious that those commands are conditional or part of a loop. You may indent as much as you want; two and four spaces per level are common. You do not have to indent if you don't want to. dBASE does not take indents into account when reading a program.

Comments

As you write your dBASE programs, you will find it useful to leave yourself a "note" within the code from time to time. These notes serve as a way to document the code, explaining how the code works. *Comments* are parts of the PRG that dBASE ignores. They are used as notes to the programmer, both present and future.

Comments are extremely important—for a number of reasons. First, what seems obvious to you may not be obvious to other people who may read your code or have to make modifications to it. Second, what seems obvious to you now might have you completely baffled six months from now. This is especially true of ingenious or peculiar bits of code. Third, comments enable other programmers to learn from your code so that they can write better programs.

There are two kinds of comments: comment lines and end-line comments. A *comment line* is a whole program line that is a comment. Comment lines start with an asterisk (*). You can put any text you want on the comment line. The *end-line comment* is at the end of a command line and begins with a double ampersand (&&). Both types of comments end at the end of the line.

Many programmers create a comment header at the beginning of every PRG they write. The header includes such things as the name of the program, what it is supposed to do, what other programs are required to run it, what date they wrote the program, and other useful information (see fig. 10.4).

You should try to comment your code as you write it; otherwise, after the program is complete and working, you might forget what you did. When commenting, concentrate on the intention of the code and how it interrelates with the overall strategy of the program. For example, the following line is not very helpful, because it is obvious that is what that line does.

```
nCol = nCol + 5     && Add 5 to nCol
```

It would be more useful to say something such as the following:

```
nCol = nCol + 5     && Go to next column
```

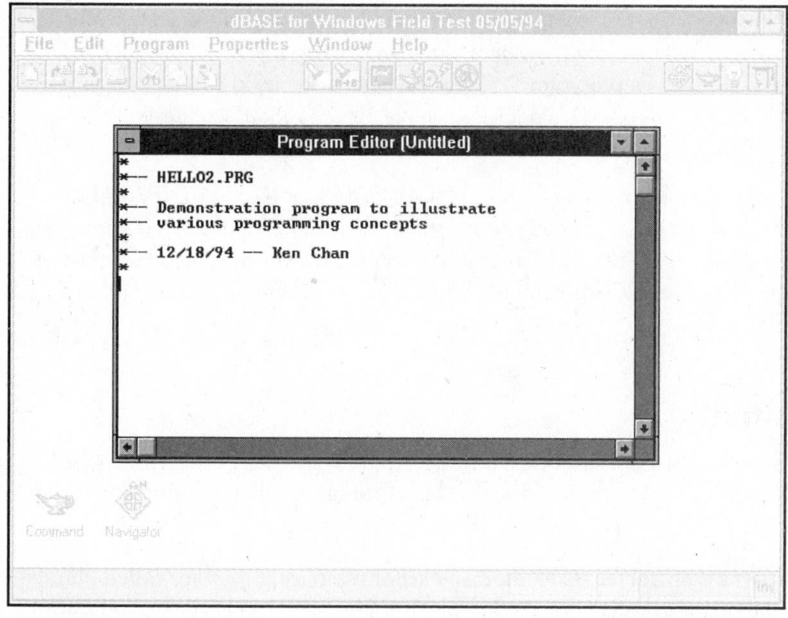

Figure 10.4
An example of a header.

Comment early and comment often. You should comment your code as you write it for two reasons: first, you might forget exactly how the code works, Second, and much more likely, you will get lazy and not comment at all, which is fine—until six months later when you need to read the code and cannot figure it out.

Abbreviating Commands

All dBASE for Windows-compatible commands and functions can be abbreviated to the first four letters of each word. For example MODIFY COMMAND can be abbreviated as MODI COMM.

In the days of dBASE III, the shorter the words were, the faster the programs would run. After the first four letters, dBASE spent its time checking to see if the whole word was not the command word that it thought it was from the first four letters.

With dBASE for Windows, that is no longer true. Programs are compiled before they are run. There is no speed advantage to abbreviating your commands; abbreviations just make your programs easier to read.

Although the word "compile" is often used to mean the conversion of your English-like PRGs into something that dBASE can understand, dBASE does not actually compile programs, it tokenizes them. Tokenizing converts words like MODIFY COMMAND into *tokens*, simple numeric codes that have meaning to dBASE.

This means that whether you type MODI COMM or MODIFY COMMAND, those words are converted into the same token. The PRO file that is generated by dBASE is the result of the tokenization process. The advantage of tokens is that the same PRO file can be used on different systems, such as UNIX and Macintosh.

Case Sensitivity

dBASE is case-insensitive—it does not care if things are in uppercase, lowercase, or any combination of the two. For example, CLEAR, clear, and cLeAr all mean the same thing to dBASE.

The exception to this is character string literals. Part of the reason they are called literals is because they will be interpreted exactly the way they are typed in between quotes, which serve as the string delimiters.

dBASE's case-insensitivity enables you to create your own capitalization rules to make your programs more readable. See the Naming Conventions section later in this chapter for a suggested capitalization scheme.

There are two capitalization "camps" in dBASE. The old school puts reserved words in all caps, with everything else lowercase or mixed caps. For example:

```
If ISALPHA( cltr )
   nmagic = nmagic + ASC( cltr ) - ASC( "A" ) + 1
ENDIF
```

The new school, influenced by the C programming language (in which practically everything is lowercase) and the fact that all caps is really hard on the eyes, puts reserved words in lowercase:

```
if isalpha( cLtr )
   nMagic = nMagic + asc( cLtr ) - asc( "A" ) + 1
```

Pick a style you prefer and stick with it.

Understanding Modular Programming

Most programmers take advantage of *modular programming*, which breaks down a program into its separate tasks, or modules. Modular programming has a number of benefits:

- ✔ The structure of the program is better organized, making it easier to read and follow.
- ✔ Each module can be written and tested separately.
- ✔ Different modules can be written by different programmers.
- ✔ The same module can be reused in different parts of the same program, or in different programs.
- ✔ A module can perform the same operations on different parameters each time.

Suppose you have a data conversion program that merges a couple of large text files generated by a mainframe into a single dBASE file. There are a number of steps involved in processing and sorting the data, as follows:

1. Display a status screen to show the program's progress
2. Import the text files into dBASE format
3. Merge the two files
4. Remove the duplicates
5. Print a report

You could code this as one long program. It might end up being a few hundred lines long. If you comment the program well enough, it will be fairly clear how the program flows and what each part of the program does, as you read through the program, line-by-line and page-by-page. The structure of the program would look like:

```
* DataMerg.prg
*
* Merges payroll files from mainframe into a dBASE table for reporting
*

****************************************
*
*  Display the status screen to show the
*  progress while converting
*
<a few dozen lines of code to paint the screen>
```

```
<and then>

****************************************
*
*  Import the text file into dBASE format
*
<a dozen lines of code to import the file>

<and then>

****************************************
*
*  Merge the payroll files
*
<several dozen lines of code to merge and process the files>

<and then>

****************************************
*
*  Remove the duplicates
*
<a few dozen lines of code to weed out duplicates>

<and finally>

****************************************
*
*  Run the predefined reports
*
<a few dozen lines of code to run the reports>
```

Simply reading through the program skeleton here without the actual working code reveals the problem with writing long programs. To understand what the program does, you have to read through the entire program. You cannot see how the program works at a glance.

The first benefit of modular programming is that it makes your programs better organized and easier to read. This improved organization is achieved with modular programming structures known as procedures.

Procedures

A *procedure* is any logical group of code that accomplishes a task. Each procedure has its own name and can contain any kind of code, except another procedure or other modular programming structure (such as a function, which is explained in the next section). The syntax for a procedure is as follows:

```
PROCEDURE <procedure name>
  <code for procedure>
RETURN
```

In the data conversion program, the individual tasks have already been defined, so it is very simple to divide the one long program into a program with procedures. It would look like:

```
* DataMerg.prg
*
* Merges payroll files from mainframe into a dBASE table for reporting
* with PROCEDUREs!

*
* Begin main procedure
*
do StatScreen       && Display the status screen to show progress
do ImportText       && Import the text file into dBASE
do MergeFiles       && Merge the payroll files
do RemoveDupes      && Remove the duplicates
do RunReports       && Run the predefined reports
RETURN              && end of main procedure

*
* And now the PROCEDURE definitions
*

PROCEDURE StatScreen
****************************************
*
*  Display the status screen to show the
*  progress while converting
*
<a few dozen lines of code to paint the screen>
RETURN && EoP: StatScreen
```

```
PROCEDURE ImportText
****************************************
*
*  Import the text file into dBASE format
*
<a dozen lines of code to import the file>
RETURN && EoP: ImportText

PROCEDURE MergeFiles
****************************************
*
*  Merge the payroll files
*
<several dozen lines of code to merge and process the files>
RETURN && EoP: MergeFiles

PROCEDURE RemoveDupes
****************************************
*
*  Remove the duplicates
*
<a few dozen lines of code to weed out duplicates>
RETURN && Eop: RemoveDupes

PROCEDURE RunReports
****************************************
*
*  Run the predefined reports
*
<a few dozen lines of code to run the reports>
RETURN && EoP: RunReports
```

The first part of the program, before the first PROCEDURE definition, is considered the main procedure. When dBASE runs a program, it starts at the top of the program file and executes statements until one of the following occurs:

- ✔ It reaches the bottom of the program file, that is, there are no more statements to execute

- ✔ It reaches a statement that causes it to stop execution, such as RETURN (QUIT and CANCEL are other such statements)

- ✔ It reaches a modular programming structure, such as a PROCEDURE or FUNCTION, which implies that the main procedure is finished

Do not confuse the concept of the main procedure with any procedure you create that is called Main. You can have both. The former is always the block of code at the beginning of the program file and is referred to as "the main procedure;" the latter is a procedure like any other that happens to be called Main and is referred to as "procedure Main."

In this program, the end of the main procedure is indicated explicitly by a RETURN statement. In this case, it is not required, because the PROCEDUREs that follow indicate the main procedure is finished, but it is always a good idea to indicate the ends of your procedures, just to indicate that that is where they are supposed to finish.

A RETURN statement causes the procedure to stop, just as if there were no more statements to execute, and return to where the procedure was run. For example, if you run the program by double-clicking on its icon in the Navigator, when it is done, control returns back to you. If one program runs another program, when that second program is done, control returns back to the first program, to the statement immediately following the one that ran the second program.

The body of the main procedure is very simple, and very easy to see and understand at a glance. All it does is run each procedure, one after another, with the DO command.

Procedures and functions are two different kinds of *subroutines*. The act of running a subroutine is usually referred to as *calling* the subroutine.

Each DO command calls the procedure by name. You can name your procedure whatever you want, as long as you follow these rules:

- ✔ There is no limit to the number of characters, but dBASE recognizes only the first 32 characters. For example, ThisSureIsAVeryLongProcedureName and ThisSureIsAVeryLongProcedureNameAintIt are the same to dBASE.
- ✔ The name must consist of letters (upper- or lowercase are considered the same), digits, and the underscore (_) character only. The first character cannot be a digit.
- ✔ The name cannot have other punctuation or spaces.
- ✔ The name cannot be the same as a reserved word.

These are the same rules as the ones for identifiers, because a procedure name is a type of identifier. Identifiers are explain later in this chapter.

Obviously you will want to give your procedures meaningful names. But there is no need to go overboard and use all 32 characters all of the time.

When you call a subroutine, dBASE looks for it in several places in a particular order, as detailed in the section "How dBASE Finds Subroutines" below. The order in which the procedures are defined in the program file is unimportant. You can put them in the order in which they are called, in alphabetical order, or any other order that makes sense to you.

You are not limited to calling subroutines from the main procedure. Subroutines can call other subroutines, which in turn can call other subroutines, and so on. This process is called *nesting* subroutines, much like nesting smaller bowls inside larger ones. The number of subroutines you can nest is limited only by available memory.

Subroutines can call themselves, a process known as *recursion*.

An example of nested subroutines could be in the StatScreen procedure. One of the first things you will want to do when displaying your status screen is to clear the screen. But suppose instead of a blank background, you want a slightly fancy background.

You could type the code directly into the StatScreen procedure, but because it is a separate task, it makes more sense to make a separate procedure out of it to reap the benefits of modular programming (call the procedure FancyClear). First, as a separate procedure, it can be written and tested independently. In this particular situation, it is not as much of a benefit, since clearing the screen is the first real thing that the program does. When trying to program a task much later in the program, however, it is very helpful to run and test that module without having to run the rest of the program first. Second, FancyClear can be written by someone else. All you would have to do is include a DO FancyClear statement in the StatScreen procedure. Then you can worry about the rest of StatScreen while someone else writes FancyClear. When FancyClear is ready, you do not have to alter StatScreen, which you may have already debugged and perfected. Third, suppose someone already wrote a really nice FancyClear procedure that you want to use, or maybe you like the one you wrote and want to share it with others. A procedure is the natural way to share bits of code.

You can write and test procedures in a separate PRG file, and then cut and paste them into the actual program file when perfected. Every time you make a change and run the PRG to test the changes, dBASE must recompile the PRG file. As the PRG file gets bigger and bigger with finalized code, this takes longer and longer. You can avoid these delays by testing in a separate PRG file, like a constantly reused TEST.PRG, whenever possible.

Figure 10.5 shows a TEST.PRG file that contains a simple FancyClear procedure.

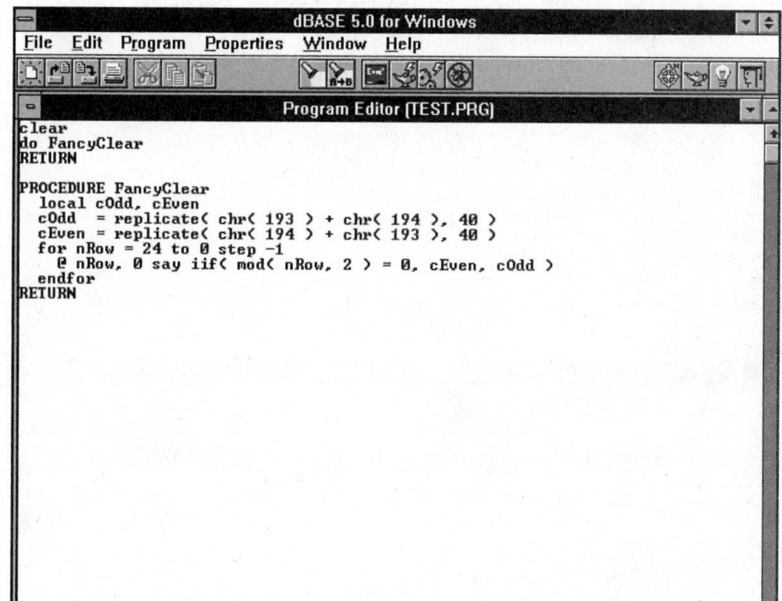

Figure 10.5 The TEST.PRG containing the FancyClear procedure.

After you have developed a FancyClear procedure that you like, you can use it more than once in the same program, or in as many programs as you want. By defining the procedure in one place (see "Procedure Files and Libraries," later in this chapter), if you ever want to make FancyClear even fancier, all you have to do is make the changes once and all of your programs which DO FancyClear will automatically use the newer version.

Functions

Straight out of the box, dBASE contains many functions that return many types of values. You have already seen the DATE() function, which returns the current date. Other examples include the SQRT() function, which returns the square root of a number, and the AT() function, which returns the position of a character inside a string. There are many others. All of these functions are called *built-in functions* because they are built into dBASE.

When dBASE does not have a function to do what you want, you can write your own. These are known as *user-defined functions*, or *UDFs*. For example, dBASE does not include a cube root function. But functions can do much more than simple calculations. In general terms, a function is simply a procedure that returns a value. You can do just about anything inside a function that you can do in a procedure. Although a procedure just does its job, a function does its job and returns a value. Functions have the same naming and calling conventions as procedures. You cannot have a function and a procedure with the same name.

To help differentiate between functions and procedures, when discussing functions outside of code, always use parentheses at the end of the function name, for example DATE() and CUBEROOT(). Also, built-in functions are all caps, and user-defined functions are mixed case.

The syntax for functions is very similar to that of procedures:

```
FUNCTION <function name>
  <code to calculate function value>
RETURN <function value>
```

For example, figure 10.6 shows a CUBEROOT() function and some code to test it:

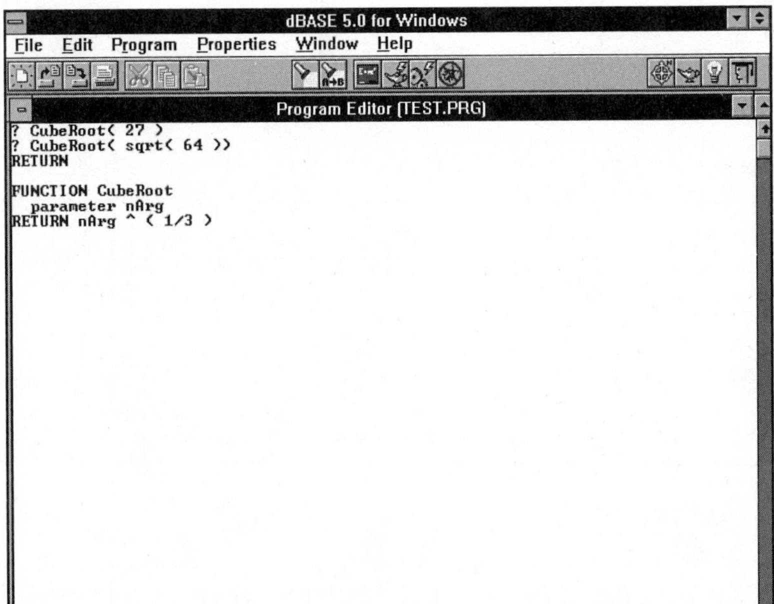

Figure 10.6
The TEST.PRG containing the CUBEROOT() function.

CUBEROOT() is a very simple function. It contains only one statement inside the function, the PARAMETERS statement. When you call the CUBEROOT() function, you have to tell the function what number you want the cube root of by placing it between the parentheses in the function call. This number becomes a *parameter* of the CUBEROOT() function. The act of transferring the value from the caller to the called function is known as *passing* parameters. The PARAMETERS statement assigns the passed value to the named memory variable. In the CUBEROOT() function, the number is assigned to the memory variable nArg. The actual calculation itself is done in the RETURN statement, because it is so simple.

You can pass parameters to both procedures and functions.

Procedure Files and Libraries

There are two places to keep procedures and functions:

- ✔ In the PRG file. The procedures and functions can be defined after the main procedure. This is the place for routines that relate specifically to the task at hand.

- ✔ In a separate procedure file. This file would contain all of your general-purpose routines that are used by different programs. Procedures located in separate files are easily found by dBASE, as explained in the section titled "How dBASE Finds Subroutines" a little later in this chapter.

dBASE provides two levels of procedure files: the library file and procedure files. The library file is meant for your most generic routines, ones that are used throughout your entire application. Customarily, you open the library file with the following command at the beginning of your application and leave it open.

```
SET LIBRARY TO <filename>
```

You can then use procedure files with the following line as needed to use other routines.

```
SET PROCEDURE TO <filename> [ADDITIVE]
```

There is nothing special about a library file itself. What makes it a library file is that it is open with the SET LIBRARY command instead of the SET PROCEDURE command. This places its functions and procedures in a different place in the search order. Also, you can have only one library file open at a time, but as many procedure files open as memory allows.

Keeping too many procedure files open at once hurts your system's performance, because dBASE must search through all open procedure files to look for subroutines. For example, you might use the same set of routines to print. You don't need to keep that procedure file open all the time, only when you print.

If there are any procedure files open, if you use SET PROCEDURE without ADDITIVE, they will be closed and the new file will become the only procedure file. ADDITIVE leaves other procedure files open and is used primarily with forms.

To close a procedure file, use the CLOSE PROCEDURE command. To close a library file, use the SET LIBRARY TO command:

```
CLOSE PROCEDURE <procedure file>
SET LIBRARY TO
```

How dBASE Finds Subroutines

When you call a procedure or function, dBASE looks for it in the following locations in this order:

- ✔ In the currently executing object (PRO) file.
- ✔ Other open PROs, most recently opened first.
- ✔ The SET PROCEDURE files, if there are any active.
- ✔ The SET LIBRARY file, if active.
- ✔ Find and open an object (PRO) file of that name.
- ✔ Find and compile a program (PRG) file of that name.

Using this search order, you can create custom versions of routines with the same name and include them higher in the search order.

Controlling Program Flow

Normally, dBASE executes the commands in the main procedure or a subroutine line-by-line one time, from the beginning to the end. But in many cases, there are some statements that you may or may not want to execute, depending on a particular condition, or some lines that you may want to execute more than once. These two changes to normal program flow are achieved with two kinds of control structures: decision structures and looping structures.

Decision Structures

Decision structures enable you to execute different blocks of code, depending on conditions that exist at the time the program is run.

A *condition* is simply a logical expression (see the Logical section under Data Types, Operator, and Functions below). The condition can be a compound logical expression. For example, "Is today Friday?" is a logical expression. "Is today either Friday or Monday?" is a compound logical expression.

IF . . .ENDIF

The IF . . .ENDIF structure enables you to execute conditionally a section of code. If the condition is true, run the code; if not, do nothing. The syntax for the IF . . .ENDIF structure is:

```
IF <condition>
  <code to run if condition is true>
ENDIF
```

In figure 10.7, addresses are displayed. There are two address line fields. If the second address line is blank, you don't want a blank line displayed, and so the printing of the second address line is executed conditionally upon the contents of the first.

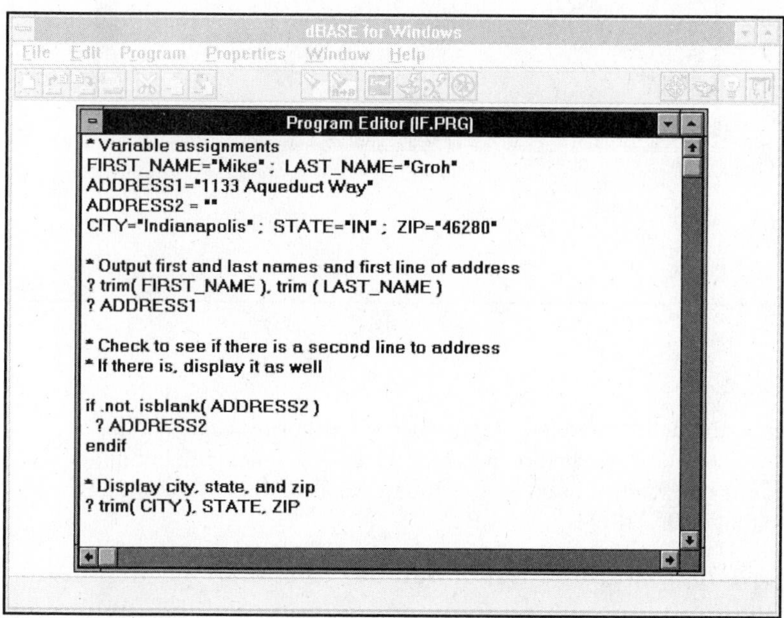

Figure 10.7
A dBASE programming example using the IF. . .ENDIF statement.

IF . . .ELSE . . .ENDIF

The IF . . .ELSE . . .ENDIF structure enables you to do one of two things. If the condition is true, do the first thing. If the condition is false, do the other. The syntax for the IF . . .ELSE . . .ENDIF structure is as follows:

```
IF <condition>
  <code to run if condition is true>
ELSE
  <code to run if condition is not true>
ENDIF
```

As shown in figure 10.8 (depending on whether the user likes fancy graphics), a simple CLEAR or a fancy clear screen procedure is run:

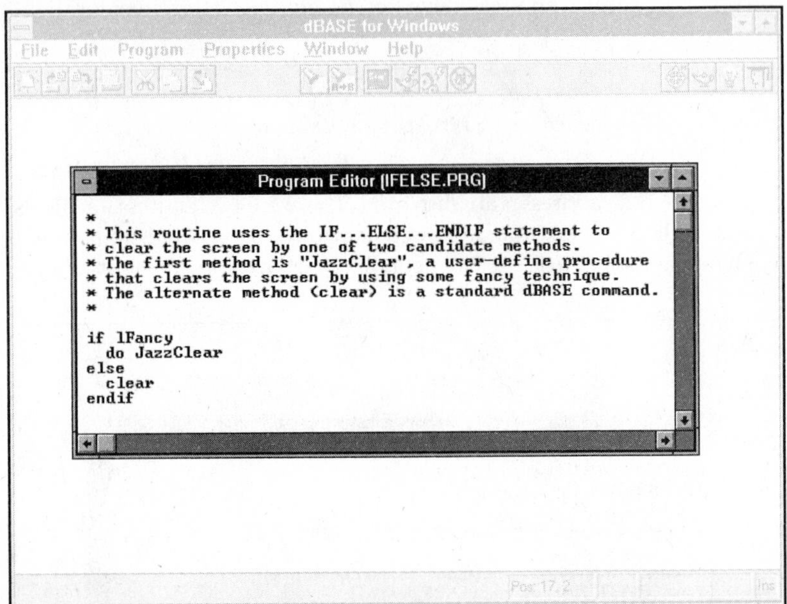
dBASE for Windows
File Edit Program Properties Window Help
Program Editor (IFELSE.PRG)
*
* This routine uses the IF...ELSE...ENDIF statement to
* clear the screen by one of two candidate methods.
* The first method is "JazzClear", a user-define procedure
* that clears the screen by using some fancy technique.
* The alternate method (clear) is a standard dBASE command.
*
if lFancy
do JazzClear
else
clear
endif
Pos 17,2
Ins

Figure 10.8
A programming example using the IF. . .ELSE. . .NDIF statement.

IIF()

When discussing IF, the built-in function IIF(), which stands for *immediate if,* must be explained. IIF() is not a control structure like the IF. . .ENDIF statement, but rather a function that returns one value or another, depending on a condition. The syntax for IIF() is similar to that of IF. . .ELSE. . .ENDIF:

```
IIF(<condition>, <value if true>, <value if false>)
```

There are many cases where IIF() is preferable to IF. For example, although this code is perfectly legal:

```
if ACCT_TYPE = "N"    && Is account new?
  ? "New     "
else
  ? "Renewal"
endif
```

it is much more succinct to use IIF():

```
? iif(ACCT_TYPE = "N", "New     ", "Renewal")
```

This line also runs marginally faster because there are fewer lines of code. Note that within the IF . . .ELSE . . .ENDIF structure, the two actions were the same single ? command, and differed only in the value they were going to print. This is an ideal situation—in which the command is the same, but the expression is different—to use IIF() instead of and IF . . .ENDIF structure.

A couple of things about IIF(): First, it is not required that the two values in the IIF() be of the same data type. Just make sure that the return value can be handled by the routine that includes the IIF() statement. For example, the following is OK:

```
? iif(DATE_START = {}, "Unknown", DATE_START)
```

If the DATE_START is blank, the character string "Unknown" is printed. Otherwise, the date contained in the DATE_START field is printed. The ? command can handle either data type, so no error is generated in either case.

On the other hand, this statement:

```
cDate = dtoc( iif(DATE_START = {}, "Unknown", DATE_START))
```

is not legal. The DTOC() function converts a date into its character string representation. If the DATE_START is blank, the IIF() function will return the character string "Unknown", which DTOC() cannot accept. The proper way to code this would be the following:

```
cDate = iif(DATE_START = {}, "Unknown", dtoc(DATE_START))
```

Here, DTOC() converts the date field DATE_START to a character string, and then the IIF() function will return either the character string "Unknown" or the character string for the date. That character string gets assigned to the memory variable cDate.

Second, The IIF() statement is not appropriate in all situations. For instance, the following use of IIF() is redundant:

```
lLegalAge = iif(AGE >= 21, .t., .f.)
```

Because AGE >= 21 evaluates to a logical expression, either .T. or .F., you can assign it directly to the variable, like this:

```
lLegalAge = (AGE >= 21)
```

The parentheses are not necessary, but they enhance the readability of the code.

DO CASE . . .ENDCASE

The DO CASE . . .ENDCASE structure enables you to run one and only one of a set of different sections of code, depending on a condition. If none of the conditions hold true, the structure can optionally run a different section of code instead. The syntax for the DO CASE . . .ENDCASE structure is as follows:

```
DO CASE
  CASE <condition1>
    <code to execute if condition1 is true>
  CASE <condition2>
    <code to execute if condition1 is false, and
      condition2 is true>
  CASE <condition3>
    <code to execute if condition1 is false,
      condition2 is false, and condition3 is true>
  CASE ...
    ...
  [OTHERWISE]
    [<code to run if none of the condition are true>]
ENDCASE
```

Each condition is tested in turn. Once a condition is true, the code associated with that condition is executed, and processing continues with the command after the ENDCASE statement. None of the conditions following the true condition are evaluated.

If none of the conditions is true, the code in the OTHERWISE section (if present) is executed. If none of the conditions are true and there is no OTHERWISE section, nothing happens.

It is legal to have no code for a particular CASE; if a case is true, it is fine to do nothing. Used in conjunction with the OTHERWISE section, you can specify specific actions for some cases, no actions for other cases, and a different action for each of the other cases.

For example, suppose you run a week-end report on Friday, no report on Sunday, and the same daily report every other day. Your code would look something like figure 10.9.

The CDOW() function in figure 10.9 returns the day of the week for a date. For instance, CDOW({01/28/95}) is Saturday. Because, in this example the argument for CDOW() is DATE() (which returns the current date), CDOW(DATE()) returns today's day of the week.

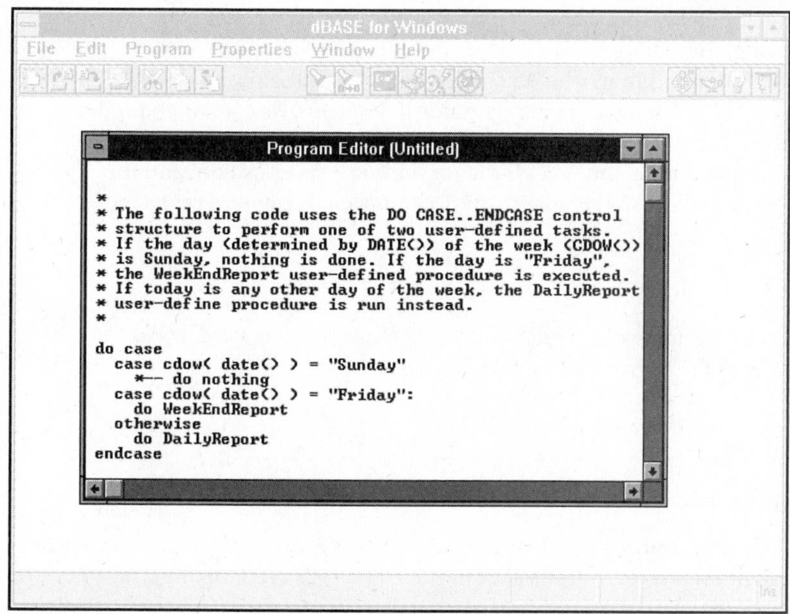

Figure 10.9
A programming example using the DO CASE…ENDCASE statement.

Understanding Looping Structures

Looping structures enable you to execute the same section of code over and over—either indefinitely, a certain number of times, or while a condition is true. This iterated section of code is called the *loop body* or the body of the loop.

DO WHILE . . .ENDDO

The DO WHILE loop repeatedly executes a section of code as long as a condition is true. The condition may be false as the DO WHILE loop begins. The DO WHILE syntax is as follows:

```
DO WHILE <condition>
  <code to execute while condition is true>
ENDDO
```

The condition is tested before each and every iteration of the loop; therefore, it is possible that the loop body will not be executed at all.

For example, this DO WHILE loop removes commas from the character string contained in the variable *cArg*:

```
do while "," $ cArg
  cArg = stuff( cArg, at(",", cArg ), 1, "")
enddo
```

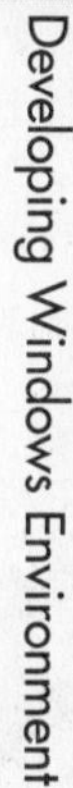

The STUFF() function takes four parameters: a character string to work with, a position number in the string, the number of characters to remove at that position, and a character string to insert at that position. The AT() function returns the position of one string inside another. The $ is a character string operator that means, "is contained in." So the condition for this loop reads, "Do while a comma is contained in the memory variable cArg." While there is a comma, the AT() function finds its exact position, and the STUFF() function removes it (by removing the 1 comma character and replacing it with nothing).

Watch out for endless, or *infinite* loops. Make sure that the condition that controls the loop will allow the loop to exit.

DO . . .UNTIL

The DO . . .UNTIL loop continuously executes a section of code until a condition is true. The condition might even be true at the start of the DO . . .UNTIL loop. Its syntax is:

```
DO
  <code to execute while condition is false>
UNTIL <condition>
```

The condition is tested after each and every iteration of the loop; therefore the loop body always executes at least once.

The difference between DO WHILE and DO . . .UNTIL is twofold: First, DO WHILE checks the condition before the loop, DO . . .UNTIL checks after. Therefore, the loop body contained within the DO WHILE may never be executed. Second, the condition in DO WHILE must remain true for the loop to continue, and the condition must remain false in DO . . .UNTIL.

FOR . . .ENDFOR

The FOR. . .ENDFOR loop executes a section of code a certain number of times. The count is maintained in a memory variable whose value may be used in the loop body. The syntax is as follows:

```
FOR <counter> = <begin> TO <end> [STEP <step>]
  <code>
ENDFOR
```

The *<begin>* and *<end>* values must be numeric. The *<counter>* is set to the *<begin>* value when the FOR statement is first encountered. If the *<step>* value is positive, the *<counter>* is checked to see if it is greater than the *<end>* value. If the *<step>* value is negative, *counter* is checked to see if it is less than the *<end>* value. If *<counter>* is past the *<end>* value, the loop terminates. If the *<start>* value is past the *<end>* value, the loop does not execute at all.

After the execution of the loop body, the value of *<step>* is added to the *counter* value. The STEP parameter is optional. If no STEP is specified, the default step value is 1. FOR. . .ENDFOR loops are useful in accessing the items in an ordered set, such as the elements of an array or the characters in a character string.

SCAN . . .ENDSCAN

SCAN . . .ENDSCAN is a special-purpose DO WHILE loop designed to execute the same block of commands for each record or set of records in a table. Its syntax is as follows:

```
SCAN <scope>
  <code to execute for record in table>
ENDSCAN
```

Scopes are explained in another chapter, but they basically enable you to set a range of records for your actions to affect.

When no scope is specified, SCAN . . .ENDSCAN affects all the records in the currently selected table. When the SCAN command is initially executed, the record pointer is moved to the first record in the table. Each of the commands in the loop body are executed. These commands usually, but are not required to, affect the current record. The one thing commands within the loop body should not do is move the record pointer within the currently selected table. When the ENDSCAN command is executed, a SKIP is implied, moving the record pointer to the next record.

The example in figure 10.10 uses SCAN to move through a table looking for duplicate ID numbers:

In order for the code to work, the table must already be ordered on the ID_NUM field. The GO TOP command moves the record pointer to the first record, and the ID_NUM for that record is stored in the memory variable cID. The SKIP command then moves the record pointer to the second record. The SCAN REST loop processes the rest of the table, including the current record; in other words, from the second record on. The IF command checks if the current record has the same ID_NUM as the previous record, and if so, displays the duplicate ID. The current ID_NUM is then assigned to the memory variable cID, in order to match it against the next record.

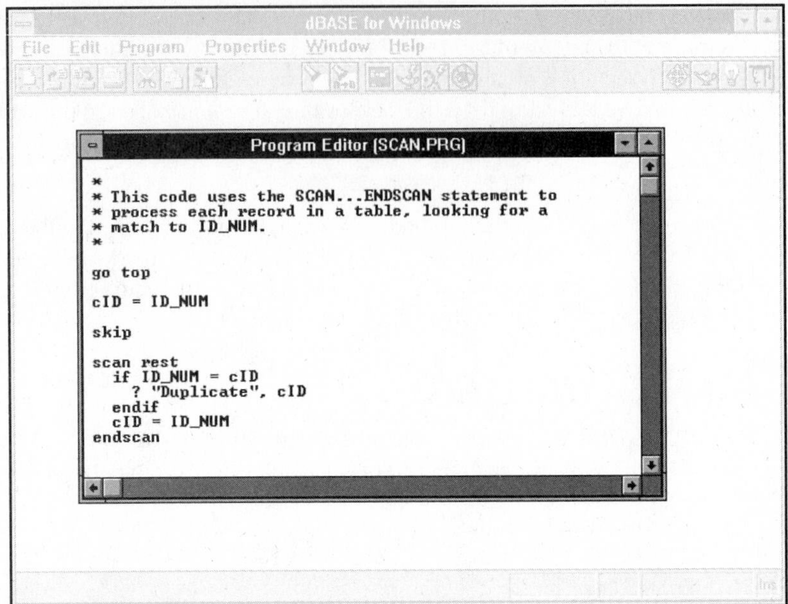
dBASE for Windows
File Edit Program Properties Window Help
Program Editor (SCAN.PRG)
*
* This code uses the SCAN...ENDSCAN statement to
* process each record in a table, looking for a
* match to ID_NUM.
*
go top
cID = ID_NUM
skip
scan rest
if ID_NUM = cID
? "Duplicate", cID
endif
cID = ID_NUM
endscan

Figure 10.10 A programming example using the SCAN...ENDSCAN statement.

LOOP and EXIT

All the looping structures are affected by the two loop override commands, LOOP and EXIT. The LOOP command causes dBASE to skip the rest of the current loop body as if it were not there and to execute the corresponding ENDDO, UNTIL, ENDFOR, or ENDSCAN command.

The EXIT command immediately exits the current loop body, continuing execution with the command following the corresponding ENDDO, UNTIL, ENFOR, or ENDSCAN command.

You should think twice before using the LOOP or EXIT commands because they can make your code hard to follow. If at all possible, try to restructure your loop to avoid having to skip through the loop or prematurely terminate a loop. For example, the following code:

```
do while <condition1>
  <some commands>
  if <condition2>
    loop
  endif
  *— If condition2 is true, skip all these
  <commands to skip if condition2 is true>
enddo
```

Can be restructured as:

```
do while <condition1>
  <some commands>
  if .not. <condition2>
    <commands to skip if condition2 is true>
  endif
enddo
```

Nesting Structures

When one control structure is defined inside another, those structures are considered to be *nested.* All the decision and looping structures can be freely nested, except that you cannot nest two SCAN loops for the same table. The numerology program discussed earlier in this chapter has an IF statement nested within a FOR statement that is itself nested within an IF.

When nesting structures, proper indentation helps keep things clear. It is also helpful to put a comment after the ending structure command to pair it up with the beginning structure command. For instance, the code in figure 10.11 demonstrates effective indenting.

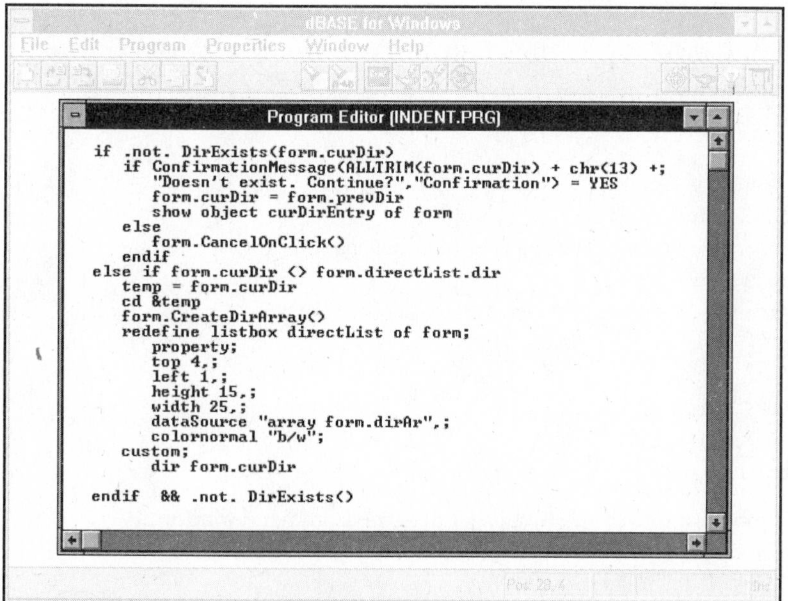

Figure 10.11
An example of effective indenting.

The last line in figure 10.11 includes a comment after the ENDIF to remind you of the condition that initiated the IF loop.

Understanding Subroutines

A *subroutine call* suspends the normal flow of the program. Execution jumps to the beginning of the subroutine, continues in that subroutine, returns when that subroutine ends, and proceeds where it left off.

DO

The DO command calls PROCEDUREs and other PRGs. The syntax is

```
DO <procedure>¦<.PRG> [WITH <parameters>]
```

For example, the following code:

```
? "Start main procedure"
? "Before calling subroutine 1"
do Sub1
? "After calling subroutine 1"
? "Before calling subroutine 2"
do Sub2
? "After calling subroutine 2"
? "End of main procedure"
RETURN

PROCEDURE Sub1
  ? "Subroutine 1"
RETURN

PROCEDURE Sub2
  ? "Subroutine 2"
  ? "Before calling subroutine 3 from subroutine 2"
  do Sub3
  ? "After calling subroutine 3 from subroutine 2"
RETURN

PROCEDURE Sub3
  ? "Subroutine 3"
RETURN
```

results in the following output in the Results pane of the Command window:

```
Start main procedure
Before calling subroutine 1
Subroutine 1
After calling subroutine 1
Before calling subroutine 2
```

```
Subroutine 2
Before calling subroutine 3 from subroutine 2
Subroutine 3
After calling subroutine 3 from subroutine 2
After calling subroutine 2
End of main procedure
```

You can also call procedures, but not PRGs, with the () call operator. See the section "Function Pointers" below.

Function Calls

A function is called by name with the () call operator:

```
<function name>( [<parameters>] )
```

For example, the following code:

```
? "Before calling function"
? "Value returned by function is:"
? Func1()
? "After calling function"
RETURN

FUNCTION Func1
  ? "[Now inside function]"
RETURN "Just a text string"
```

results in the following output in the Results pane of the Command window:

```
Before calling function
Value returned by function is:
[Now inside function]
Just a text string
After calling function
```

Note that evaluating the function Func1() interrupts the normal flow of the program. Only after Func1() is done is the return value printed by the main procedure.

Call Chain

The *call chain* conceptualizes the relative order in which subroutines are called. Caller routines are higher-level than the procedures they call. Figure 10.12 shows a visual representation of the call chain for the DO demonstration code above, sometimes

referred to as the *call stack.* Execution begins at the top, at the desktop level, from the Navigator or the Command window. The main procedure runs directly under the desktop. While the program is running, no other programs can be started from the desktop. Both procedures Sub1 and Sub2 are called from the main procedure, and Sub2 calls the procedure Sub3. Every subroutine call moves down a level, and every time a subroutine finishes, you go back up a level. At any time, the call chain refers to those routines that you went through to get to your current routine. For example, the call chain to procedure Sub3 is:

```
main —> Sub2 —> Sub3
```

The call chain is important when dealing with memory variable scope issues, explained later in this chapter.

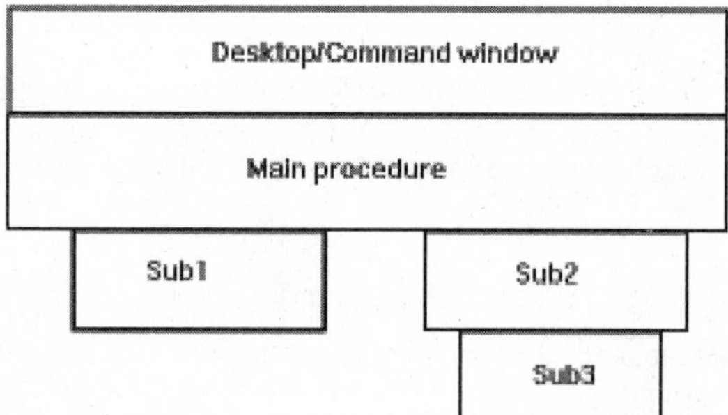

Figure 10.12 A simple call chain.

Understanding Data Types and Memory Variables

There are many different data types. Most of them correspond with data types that you can store in tables, while others are designed specifically for programming. Memory variables are used to store temporary and working values, whereas tables are used to permanently store information.

Identifiers

Identifiers are the names assigned to memory variables, procedures, and other components of your dBASE programs. You are free to name your identifiers whatever you want, as long as you follow these rules:

- ✔ There is no limit to the number of characters, but dBASE recognizes only the first 32 characters. For example, ThisIsUndoubtedlyALongIdentifier and ThisIsUndoubtedlyALongIdentifierAintIt are the same to dBASE.

- ✔ The name must consist of letters (upper- or lowercase are considered the same), digits, and the underscore (_) character only. The first character cannot be a digit.
- ✔ The name cannot have other punctuation or spaces.
- ✔ The name cannot be the same as a reserved word.

Memory Variable Assignment

There are two ways to assign values to memory variables.

By using the following command syntax, you assign the *<value>* to the named memory variable.

```
<identifier> = <value>
```

The *<value>* can be any kind of expression: a literal, or the result of a built-in or user-defined function. For example, these are all valid assignment statements:

```
cText = "Today is"
dToday = date()
nRoot = CubeRoot( 27 )
```

When you assign a value to a memory variable, any previous value in that memory variable, if any, is lost.

You can assign the same value to one or more memory variables with the STORE command. Its syntax is as follows:

```
STORE <value> to <identifier1> [, <identifier2> ...]
```

STORE is usually used to set a number of memory variables to the same value, for example, setting counter variables to zero at the beginning of a routine:

```
store 0 to nLen, nPos, nCnt
```

Data Types, Operators, and Functions

This section lists the different data types, their respective operators, and basic functions for those data types.

Logical

Logical data is the simplest data type. It can have one of only two values: true or false. Logical expressions are used to control decision and looping structures and are the results of comparisons between all data types.

Logical literals can be represented within dBASE programs in two ways. True is either .T. for true or .Y. for yes. False is either .F. for false or .N. for no. The values assigned to logical variables are not case sensitive. Therefore, .T., .t., .Y., and .y. all have positive meanings, while .F., .f., .N., .n. are interpreted as negative values.

Table 10.1 lists the operators that can be used on logical data.

Table 10.1
Logical Operators

Operator	Description
.AND.	Logical AND
.OR.	Logical OR
.NOT.	Logical negation
=	equals
,<>	not equal

The .AND. operator performs a logical .AND. of two logical values. In order for the result to be true, both values must be true. The .OR. operator performs a logical .OR. of two logical values. If either one or both values are true, the result is true. The .NOT. operator inverts the logical value, switching it from .T. to .F. or vice versa. The =, #, and <> operators can be used to determine if two logical values are the same or not.

Consider this code fragment which demonstrates the use of logical operators:

```
nTest = 5
? nTest > 2 .and. nTest > 8         && Displays .F.
? nTest > 2 .or. nTest > 8          && Displays .T.
? nTest > 2 .and. .not. nTest > 8   && Displays .T.
```

Each numeric comparison yields a logical expression, true or false. The first test yields true .AND. false, which is false. The second test evaluates to true .OR. false, which is true. In other words, if nTest is greater than 2 or nTest is greater than 8, or both, the test yields true. In the third test, the .NOT. operator negates the value of the expression nTest > 8, changing it from false to true. This makes the third test true .AND. true, which is true.

All three tests are examples of compound logical expressions, in which a number of logical expression are distilled into a single logical value.

Logical literals need not be used in logical comparisons—such use is redundant. For example, look at the following:

```
if lArg = .T.
```

If the logical memory variable lArg contains .T., then the expression is true. If lArg is .F., the expression is false. In other words, the test = .T. does nothing. The IF can be better expressed as:

```
if lArg
```

But then again, this line:

```
if lArg = .F.
```

can be expressed as the following:

```
if .not. lArg
```

Character

The character data type, also known as *alphanumeric* or *text* data, is the most common type of data. Character data is simple text: letters, numbers, spaces, punctuation, and other characters.

Literal text, usually called *character strings*, are represented in programs by text surrounded by special string *delimiters*. These delimiters mark the beginning and end of the character string and set them apart from the text that represent commands or identifiers. For example:

```
? "clear"
```

Here, the word "clear" is text, not a command.

There are three sets of character delimiters, double quotes (""), single quotes (''), and square brackets ([]). It does not matter which one you use. The main reason to use one over the other is when you want to include some delimiter characters in the string itself, in which case you have to use one of the other delimiters. Some examples include:

```
"This is a plain string"
'This has a double quote " in it, so use single quotes'
[More "double quotes", but using brackets instead]
```

Otherwise, pick one you like (probably not the single quote because the single quote is used as an apostrophe in contractions and possessives) and stick with it.

Unlike character fields, the maximum length of a character memory variable is 32,766 characters. The null or empty string, which should not be confused with the NUL character (ASCII value 0), is represented by delimiters with nothing between them: "" or [].

Table 10.2 lists the operators that work on character data.

Table 10.2
Character Operators

Operator	Description
+	Concatenates
-	Concatenates and groups trailing spaces
=	Equals or begins with
#, <>	Not equal
<	Less than
<=	Less than or equal
>	Greater than
>=	Greater than or equal
$	Is contained in

Concatenate is a fancy word that means to combine two character strings together. For example, "tea" + "cup" gives "teacup". The resulting character string cannot exceed the maximum character string length.

Spaces are treated like any other character. "tea " + "cup " yields "tea cup ". The - concatenator removes all the trailing spaces from the end of the first character string and includes them at the end of the combined string. For example:

```
"Harrison         " - "William Henry    "
```

yields the following:

```
"HarrisonWilliam Henry              "
```

whereas the string:

```
"Harrison         " + "William Henry    "
```

yields the following:

```
"Harrison         William Henry    "
```

Note that the resulting strings are both the same length.

The = operator compares two character strings. The behavior of the = operator depends on the current setting of EXACT. Settings are explained in more detail later in this chapter, but the EXACT setting, which controls string matching, can be either ON or OFF. When SET EXACT is OFF, the default, the = operator behaves like "begins with". For example, when SET EXACT is OFF, the following string is true, because "Smithers" begins with "Smith".

```
"Smithers" = "Smith"
```

Note that all strings can be thought of as beginning with the null string. For example, the following string is also true.

```
"Smithers" = ""
```

In fact, whenever SET EXACT is OFF and a null string is on the right side of the = operator, the comparison always yields true. Therefore, when checking to see if a string is empty, always put the null string on the left side of the = operator, like in the following line:

```
"" = cArg
```

You can also check the length of the string with the LEN() function; an empty string has a length of 0:

```
if len(cArg )= 0    && Is cArg empty?
```

When SET EXACT is ON, the two character strings must match character-for-character, except that trailing blanks in both strings are ignored. So, the following line is false when SET EXACT is ON:

```
"Smithers" = "Smith"
```

But this line is true:

```
"Smithers" = "Smithers"
```

And so are both of the following lines:

```
"Smithers" = "Smithers "

"Smithers " = "Smithers"
```

The # and <> operators are the same. They return the opposite of what an = operator would, with all the same rules regarding SET EXACT. What would have been true with = is false with # and <>; what would have been false with = is true with # and <>.

The <, <=, >, and >= operators compare two strings to see if one string is alphanumerically less than, equal to, and/or greater than the other, respectively. This is not an alphabetic comparison, relying strictly on the characters' position in the alphabet, but an alphanumeric comparison relying on the characters' position in the current language/character character set. The default character set is ASCII.

In ASCII, all uppercase characters have a smaller value than the lowercase characters. Numeric digits have values less than the letters of the alphabet, and spaces are less than both numbers and letters.

It is common practice to convert both strings being compared to either upper- or lowercase before making the comparison to determine their relative order.

The $ operator determines whether a substring is contained in another string. It does not return where in the other string the substring occurs (use the AT() function for that), only whether the substring is found in the string. By definition, for the $ operator, the null string is not contained in any other string, even another null string.

Table 10.3 lists some basic functions that operate on character data.

Table 10.3
Basic Character Functions

Function	Description
UPPER()	Converts string to uppercase
LOWER()	Converts string to lowercase
PROPER()	Converts string to proper noun case
LEN()	Returns length of the string
LEFT()	Returns leftmost part of the string
RIGHT()	Returns rightmost part of the string
SUBSTR()	Returns part of the string
AT()	Returns position of substring in string
TRIM()	Removes trailing spaces from string
LTRIM()	Removes leading spaces from string
STUFF()	Inserts or replaces characters in string
ISBLANK()	Is the string empty or all spaces?
VAL()	Converts string to number

The functions UPPER(), LOWER(), and PROPER() convert the case of all the characters in the character string. UPPER() makes all characters all uppercase while LOWER() makes them all lowercase. PROPER() converts a string to "proper noun" case, meaning the first character of the string and the first character after each space in the string is converted to uppercase, but all the other characters are converted to lowercase.

LEFT(), RIGHT(), and SUBSTR() are substring operations, returning a part or all of a string. LEFT() returns the desired number of characters at the beginning of the string. RIGHT() returns the desired number of characters at the end of the string. SUBSTR() can start anywhere. The desired number of characters to return can be zero, in which case the null string is always returned. For example:

```
? left( "Two words", 2 )       && displays "Tw"
? right( "Two words", 4 )      && displays "ords"
? substr( "Two words", 3, 3 ) && displays "o w"
```

AT() returns the position of a substring in a string, or 0 if the substring is not there.

VAL() converts a string that looks like a number into a number. Otherwise, it returns a 0. For example:

```
? val( "10.24" )           && prints 10.24
? val( ".68 caliber" )     && prints 0.68
? val( "abc" )             && prints 0
```

Numeric

Numeric data represents numbers upon which some mathematical operation, such as counting, totaling, or averaging, needs to be performed. Sometimes data which appears to be numeric (such as ZIP codes and telephone numbers) should be treated as character data.

Numeric literals are represented by digits that are not surrounded by character delimiters in the PRG file. Numbers can start with a digit, a decimal point, or a sign (+ or -) and may be in scientific notation (E format). Numeric literals should not contain commas or other place markers. The following are examples of valid numeric literals:

123

123.45

.25

0.25

-934

-.25

1E10

2.3e6

7.23e-3

-6.43E-20

The E or e is shorthand for "times 10 to the," so 2.3E6 equals 2,300,000. Table 10.4 lists the operators that are used with numeric data, and table 10.5 lists basic numeric functions.

Table 10.4
Numeric Operators

Operator	Description
+	Addition
-	Subtraction
*	Multiplication
/	Division
^, **	Exponentiation
=	Equals or begins with
#, <>	Not equal
<	Less than
<=	Less than or equal
>	Greater than
>=	Greater than or equal

Table 10.5
Basic Numeric Functions

Function	Description
INT()	Round towards zero to nearest integer
FLOOR()	Round down to nearest integer

Function	Description
CEILING()	Round up to nearest integer
STR()	Convert number to character string

INT(), FLOOR(), and CEILING() all round to an integer, but they take different approaches. INT() rounds toward zero, so for positive numbers it rounds down, and for negative numbers, it rounds up. FLOOR() rounds down, and CEILING() rounds up. Compare the following:

```
? int( 2.5 )       && displays 2
? int( -2.5 )      && displays -2
? floor( 2.5 )     && displays 2
? floor( -2.5 )    && displays -3
? ceiling( 2.5 )   && displays 3
? ceiling( -2.5 ) && displays -2
```

Date

dBASE manages dates from 01/01/9999 BC to AD 12/31/9999. Beyond the simple storing and display of data, dBASE supports date math, which enables you do calculate the number of days between dates, or a date that is so many days from another.

Date literals are delimited by curly braces ({}). The date itself is interpreted according to the current date format. There are 11 date options which yield 7 different formats, as listed in table 10.6:

Table 10.6
Date Formats

Option	Format
AMERICAN	MM/DD/YY
ANSI	YY.MM.DD
BRITISH	DD/MM/YY
FRENCH	DD/MM/YY
GERMAN	DD.MM.YY
ITALIAN	DD-MM-YY

continues

Table 10.6, Continued
Date Formats

Option	Format
JAPAN	YY/MM/DD
USA	MM-DD-YY
MDY	MM/DD/YY
DMY	DD/MM/YY
YMD	YY/MM/DD

The default date format is set by the International option of the Windows Control Panel. The default can be changed by setting the DATE parameter in DBASEWIN.INI, and the format can be changed when desired by using the SET DATE command.

Another important setting is the SET CENTURY option. When ON, all dates are displayed with four-digit dates, which include the century. When OFF, only the last two digits of the year are displayed.

The month and the day may have leading zeroes, but they are not required. If the year is one or two digits, it is assumed to be in the current century; three or four digits are taken as is. BC dates are specified by adding the letters BC or bc at the end of the literal. For example, the date literal {12/07/42} is either December 7, 1942 for a MM/DD/YY format, July 12, 1942 for the DD/MM/YY format, or an illegal date for a YY/MM/DD format. The date literal {12/07/42BC} would be the same date, BC.

Note that the separator used in the literal does not have to match the separator used for the format. As long as the separators match (both periods, both hyphens, or both slashes), dBASE properly interprets the data as a date.

Blank dates are represented by a pair of curly braces with nothing in between, {}. Blank dates represent dates that have not been entered. For example, you might be tracking the retirement date of employees. For those employees that have not yet retired, that date is blank.

Table 10.7 lists operators that work on dates.

Table 10.7
Date Operators

Operator	Description
+	Date in the future
-	Date in the past or number of days between dates
=	Equal (same date)
#, <>	Not equal
<	Less than (date is earlier)
<=	Less than or equal
>	Greater than (date is later)
>=	Greater than or equal

When you add a number to a date, the result is the date that is that number of days ahead of the first date. This is one of the few instances when an operator mixes two data types. For example the expression {07/04/95} + 60 yields the date {09/02/95}.

You can also subtract days from a date to get an earlier date. For example, {09/02/95} - 60 is {07/04/95}. If you subtract one date from another, you will get the number of days in between the two dates. For example, {09/02/95} - {07/04/95} is 60.

The normal comparison operators work on dates, determining whether or not two dates are equal to, less than, or greater than each other. In such comparisons, a blank date can be considered a day that will never come, or at least a day that has not come yet. A blank date is greater than all non-blank dates.

This is a change from dBASE for DOS, in which a blank date is neither less than nor greater than all non-blank dates.

Table 10.8 lists some basic functions that operate on character data.

Table 10.8
Basic Date Functions

Function	Description
DAY()	Day portion of date
MONTH()	Month portion of date
YEAR()	Year portion of date
DTOC()	Convert date to character equivalent
CTOD()	Convert character literal to date
DTOS()	Convert date to sortable string

DAY(), MONTH(), and YEAR() return numbers. For the date {07/04/95}, they would return 7, 4, and 1995 respectively.

DTOC() and CTOD() convert back and forth between dates and characters. The date {09/02/95} would become the string "09/02/95" and vice versa.

A perennial problem is how to calculate someone's age. Simple methods subtract the person's birth date from the current date and divide the resulting number of days by 365 (or precisely 365.25). Unfortunately, such methods are not completely accurate. If a toddler is 365 days old, is she one year old or not? That depends on whether she has lived through a February 29th.

In fact, it is impossible to determine someone's age just from the number of days they have been alive.

A completely reliable and reasonably way to determine someone's age is with this expression:

```
floor((val(dtos(<date>)) - val(dtos(<birth date>))) / 10000)
```

The trick here is that DTOS() converts the date to the YYYYMMDD format. Suppose the birth date is August 3, 1967, and today's date is April 21, 1993. DTOS() converts the dates to the following:

April 21, 1993 ==> "19930421"

August 3, 1967 ==> "19670803"

The DTOS() format facilitates simple subtraction. The character strings created by DTOS() are converted to numbers by the VAL() function, and the subtraction is done:

```
  19930421
- 19670803
----------
    259618
```

Dividing the result by 10,000 and rounding down with FLOOR() yields the person's age, 25.

Time

Although date support in dBASE is strong, time support is fairly limited. There is no dedicated time data type. The built-in function TIME() returns a character string with the current time in 24-hour HH:MM:SS format, where HH is hours, MM is minutes, and SS is seconds. By including any parameter in the call to time, for example TIME(1), TIME() returns the hundredths of a second also, in the format HH:MM:SS.hh where hh is hundredths of a second.

The built-in function ELAPSED() returns the number of seconds between two times, and the built-in function SECONDS() returns the number of second since midnight.

Function Pointer

A *function pointer* is a reference to a function or procedure. The name of a user-defined function or procedure is automatically a function pointer to that function. This pointer can be assigned to another identifier, which would become of type function pointer, and can be otherwise treated as a memory variable.

The only operator which works on function pointers is the () call operator, which calls the function or procedure being pointed to. Any parameters that the routine requires are included between the parentheses, as with a normal function call. For example:

```
jMultiply = Double  && point to procedure Double
jMultiply( 4 )      && displays 8
jMultiply = Triple  && point to procedure Triple
jMultiply( 4 )      && displays 12
RETURN

PROCEDURE Double
  parameter nArg
  ? nArg * 2
RETURN

PROCEDURE Triple
  parameter nArg
```

```
   ? nArg * 3
RETURN
```

Function pointers apply only to procedures and functions that dBASE can find, as detailed in "Understanding Subroutines"earlier in this chapter. You cannot use function pointers to point to PRG files.

Actually assigning a function pointer to a memory variable is a fairly advanced programming practice. Suppose that you had many different procedures to process different kinds of data, and the logic to decide which process to use is fairly complicated and done early on, but the actual processing is done much later. You could assign a function pointer to the appropriate process early on, and call that process via the function pointer later, as opposed to running through the same complex logic a second time.

On the other hand, assigning a function pointer to an event property is done all the time with user interface objects, to tell the objects what to do when something happens. See Chapter 12, "Understanding Event-Driven Programming," for details.

Code Block

A *code block* is an anonymous function that is stored in a memory variable. Because the function is stored in a memory variable, you can copy the function and pass it as a parameter to other functions and procedures. This is also a fairly advanced practice. Suppose you have a function which generates and manages new ID numbers, which are stored in a table. For all the different kinds of ID numbers (different lengths, some have letters, some have numbers), the logic to manage them is the same; the method of generating new IDs is the only difference. With code blocks, you can pass a code block to the ID number function which contains the instructions for generating that particular kind of ID number.

There are two types of code blocks: expression code blocks and statement code blocks. Both types of code blocks are executed with the () call operator.

Expression code blocks follow this form:

```
{[¦<parameters>¦] <expression> }
```

Expression code blocks return an expression when executed. Some examples include:

```
k1 = {4 + 5}
? k1()                      && prints 9
k2 = {¦nArg¦ nArg ^ 3 }
? k2(2)                     && prints 8
```

Command code blocks can contain any commands and are of the form:

```
{[¦<parameters>¦]; <statement> [; <statement> ...]}
```

See the following example:

```
k3 = {; ? 4 + 5}
k3()                        && prints 9
```

Code blocks are used extensively in the user interface objects to tell the objects what do when something happens. For short (one to three lines) or one-place-only code, a code block is more convenient than a function pointer.

Array

An *array* is an ordered set of elements, a group of memory variables that are referred to by number. You can use arrays, for example, to store the names of all the months (which would be referred to by the numbers 1 through 12), or all the planets (numbered 1 through 9). If you want to deal with a number of items in a consistent, orderly manner, you can put the items in an array and traverse the array with a FOR. . .ENDFOR loop, much like you would traverse a table with a SCAN . . .ENDSCAN loop.

The first thing you need to do is allocate space for the array. This is done with the DECLARE command. The following line declares a one-dimensional array with 9 elements:

```
declare aPlanets[9]
```

The array identifier can take only one operator, the [] index operator. To reference an array element, the syntax is

```
<array name>[<element number>]
```

The elements are numbered from 1 to the declared size of the array. An array element is treated in all other ways like a memory variable. You can use the AFILL() function to fill the array with a default value. You can also assign values manually:

```
aPlanets[ 1 ] = "Mercury"
aPlanets[ 2 ] = "Venus"
aPlanets[ 3 ] = "Earth"
aPlanets[ 4 ] = "Mars"
```

And so on. An array can have more than one dimension. If a one-dimensional array looks like a row of boxes, then a two-dimensional array looks like the grid of a spreadsheet, a three-dimensional array looks like a cube, and more dimensions are possible but are difficult to visualize. An array can have up to 254 dimensions, but because the total number of elements is limited by memory, you will probably never get that far.

An array can be an array element. In other words, you can have arrays of arrays, in which case, the actual number of dimensions is unlimited. But the total number of elements is still limited by available memory.

Most of the array functions, some of which are listed in table 10.9, work only on one and two-dimensional arrays, which simulate records and tables.

Table 10.9
Basic Array Functions

Function	Description
AFILL()	Fills array with single value
ALEN()	Returns number of elements, row, or columns in an array
ASORT()	Sorts an array

Understanding Operator Precedence

All of the operators for all of the data types have an order of precedence. This order determines which operator is acted upon first when more than one operator is present in an expression.

The order of precedence is:

1. () [] -> . NEW
2. ** ^
3. * /
4. + -
5. = # <> < <= > >=
6. .NOT.
7. .AND. .OR.

Operators at the same level of precedence are performed left to right. You can override the order of precedence by using parentheses. For example:

```
? 2 + 3 * 4          && displays 14
? (2 + 3) * 4        && displays 20
```

Memory Variable Scope

A memory variable's *scope* is defined by two factors: its visibility (which subroutines can see and access it) and its duration (how long it remains in memory). Scoping rules revolve around individual subroutines and the call chain.

PRIVATE

By default, all memory variables created in a program are PRIVATE. This means that the creating subroutine and all subroutines beneath it in the call chain have access to the memory variable. When the creating subroutine ends, the memory variable is thrown away. For example, note the code in figure 10.13.

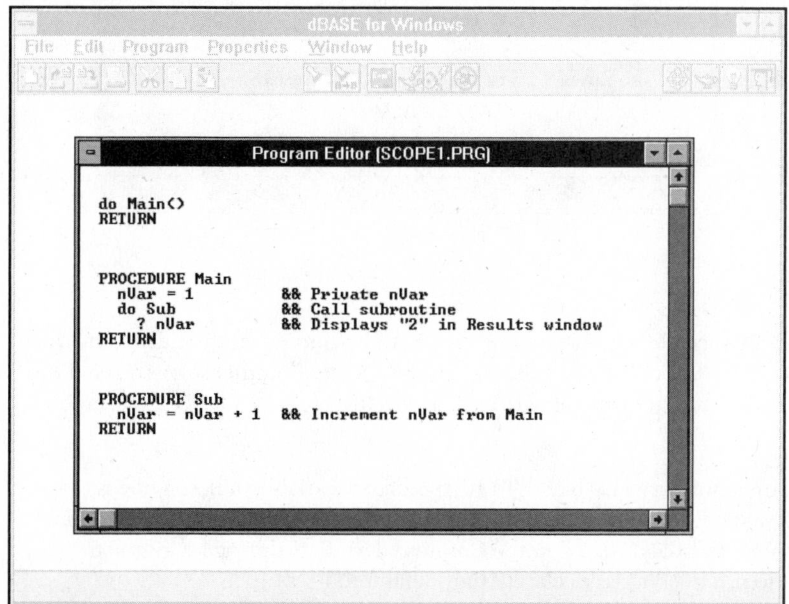
dBASE for Windows
File Edit Program Properties Window Help
Program Editor (SCOPE1.PRG)
do Main()
RETURN
PROCEDURE Main
nVar = 1 && Private nVar
do Sub && Call subroutine
? nVar && Displays "2" in Results window
RETURN
PROCEDURE Sub
nVar = nVar + 1 && Increment nVar from Main
RETURN

Figure 10.13 A simple example of variable scope.

If the lower-level subroutine wants to utilize a memory variable of the same name and not confuse it with the higher-level memory variable, the lower-level subroutine can declare the memory variable as PRIVATE, which hides the higher-level version of the memory variable. Then the subroutine can assign and manipulate its own memory variable of the same name. When the subroutine ends, the higher-level memory variable is unhidden, making it visible to other subroutines. For an example, see figure 10.14.

Note that after Sub1 declares nVar PRIVATE, it cannot increment the nVar declared in Main as Sub2 does; once the PRIVATE statement is executed, nVar is hidden and Sub1 cannot see the nVar that appears in Main. If a memory variable is not to be shared with lower-level subroutines, it is better instead to declare it LOCAL, which will be explained shortly.

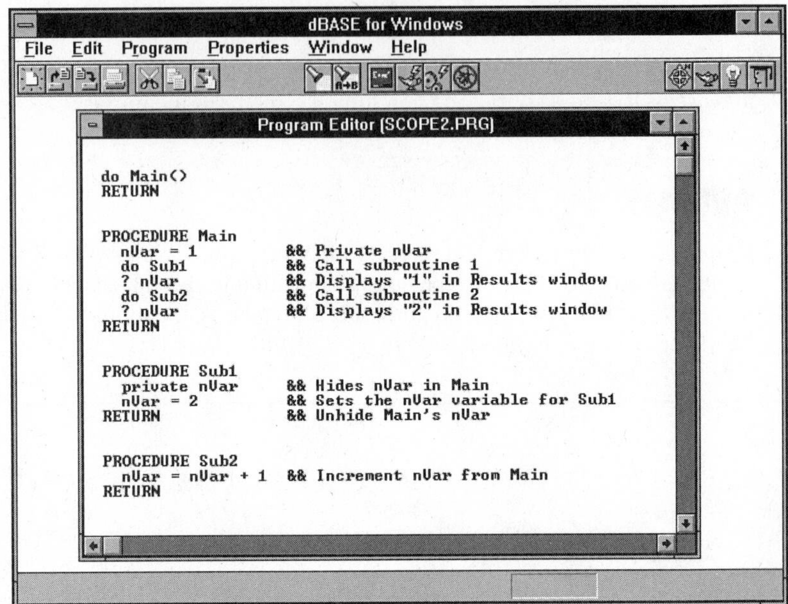
dBASE for Windows
File Edit Program Properties Window Help
Program Editor (SCOPE2.PRG)
do Main()
RETURN
PROCEDURE Main
nVar = 1 && Private nVar
do Sub1 && Call subroutine 1
? nVar && Displays "1" in Results window
do Sub2 && Call subroutine 2
? nVar && Displays "2" in Results window
RETURN
PROCEDURE Sub1
private nVar && Hides nVar in Main
nVar = 2 && Sets the nVar variable for Sub1
RETURN && Unhide Main's nVar
PROCEDURE Sub2
nVar = nVar + 1 && Increment nVar from Main
RETURN

Figure 10.14 nVar has different scope in each procedure.

PUBLIC

A PUBLIC memory variable is visible everywhere, both up and down the call chain. Once declared, it lasts until explicitly RELEASEd or dBASE QUITs. In other words, even if the program finishes and you get control of dBASE again, the memory variable will still be there.

When you declare a memory variable PUBLIC, a memory variable of that name is created with the logical value .F.. You must declare a memory variable PUBLIC before assigning a value to it. Memory variables created in the Command window during an interactive dBASE session do not need to be declared; they default to PUBLIC.

LOCAL

A LOCAL memory variable is visible only in the subroutine that created it and lasts until the subroutine is completed. They are like PRIVATE memory variables, except that there is no danger of the value of a PRIVATE variable being changed by other procedures. To be safe, when writing general-use subroutines, declare all the memory variables you use LOCAL.

STATIC

A STATIC memory variable is a LOCAL memory variable that does not vanish when the subroutine ends. If the subroutine is called again, the memory variable has the same value it had when the subroutine ended before. This is useful for subroutines that are called repeatedly and are used to keep track of internal values.

STATIC memory variables support a special syntax to initialize them to a value the first time they are used. After that, they maintain their value from call to call. For example:

```
do Sub1  && displays 1
do Sub1  && displays 2
do Sub1  && displays 3
RETURN

PROCEDURE Sub1
  static nStatic = 1      && initialize to 1
  ? nStatic               && display current value
  nStatic = nStatic + 1   && increment for next call
RETURN
```

RELEASE

You must explicitly use the RELEASE command to discard PUBLIC and STATIC memory variables.

For example:

```
public c_UserName    && declare a public memory variable
<code for main procedure>
release c_UserName   && clean-up: release public memvar
```

Understanding Naming Conventions

dBASE is not a "strongly typed" language—it does not require you to declare the data type that a memory variable will store. You can also change data types at will, making it easy to write programs but—sometimes hard to read them especially—after you have not looked at the program for months.

One way to help make programs more readable is to choose memory variable names that reflect the contents of the memory variable. Because you usually do not change the type and purpose of a memory variable once it has been assigned, the name should reflect both these properties.

The naming convention used in this book is the standard used by the dBASE Users' Function Library Project (dUFLP or duh-FLOP), a huge free library of procedures, functions, and objects for the dBASE product line. It is available on CompuServe; the only cost is for the download time. The basic naming conventions are repeated here.

To reach the dBASE for Windows forum on CompuServe, type GO DBASEWIN at any ! prompt. Once there, search the file library for the keyword DUFLP for the latest version. The forum is an excellent place to share ideas with other dBASE for Windows users and programmers.

The dUFLP standard is a variant of the "Hungarian notation" convention familiar to many C programmers. The first letter of the memory variable reflects the type of the memory variable, according to table 10.10

Table 10.10
dUFLP Types

Letter	Type
a	Array
c	Character
d	Date
k	Code block
l	Logical
m	Menu
n	Numeric
o	Object

If the memory variable is PUBLIC, the type identifier is followed by an underscore. For example, a PUBLIC user name would be c_UserName, as opposed to just cUserName.

The rest of the identifier is composed of a descriptive name, in mixed upper- and lowercase, with no underscores. Avoid using the type name in the memory variable name; for example dBirthDate is redundant. Some sample memory variable names using dUFLP notation include:

```
cLName                    && character: last name
dBirth                    && date: birthdate
lComplete                 && logical: complete?
nVertPos                  && numeric: vertical position
aRecCopy                  && array: copy of record
```

The dUFLP standard also specifies that all commands be lowercase, except for the words PROCEDURE, FUNCTION, RETURN, CLASS, and ENDCLASS to make programs easier on the eyes. All table and field names are uppercase, which makes those identifiers easy to find and differentiate from memory variables.

Using the Preprocessor

When dBASE compiles a PRG into a PRO file, it first preprocesses the file, producing an intermediate version of the PRG. All preprocessor commands start with the # character.

#DEFINE

The #DEFINE command defines a symbol and, optionally, a value for that symbol. The syntax for #DEFINE is as follows:

```
#DEFINE <symbol name> [<symbol value>]
```

From that point on in the PRG file, that symbol is defined. #DEFINE is used in two ways: as a constant and as a simple flag.

Like the rest of dBASE, the symbol names are case-insensitive. The symbol values are case-sensitive.

DEFINE Constants

A constant is a value that never changes in a program. The INKEY() values are good example of this. Suppose you want to see if the user pressed the Escape key. The INKEY() value for Escape is 27. Your code might look something like this:

```
nKey = inkey(0)          && Wait for keystroke
if nKey = 27                && If user pressed escape
```

Every time you want to test for the Escape key, you have to remember and use the number 27, and then you probably want to comment the line. Using #DEFINE solves this problem by allowing you to assign a meaningful name to the value. Your code would look like the following:

```
#define ESCAPE_KEY 27

nKey = inkey(0)          && Wait for keystroke
if nKey = ESCAPE_KEY
```

This version is self-documenting. The symbol ESCAPE_KEY is defined at the top of the PRG. From then on, in the PRG file, every time dBASE encounters the identifier

ESCAPE_KEY, it replaces it with its value, 27. This is a textual replacement done by the preprocessor at the time the program is compiled. In the example, the following line:

```
if nKey = ESCAPE_KEY
```

is saved in the intermediate version of the PRG as the following:

```
if nKey = 27
```

which is what ends up getting compiled. Note that this is different than using a memory variable like this:

```
nEscapeKey = 27           && Remember key code for Escape

nKey = inkey( 0 )         && Wait for keystroke
if nKey = nEscapeKey
```

A memory variable occupies memory and is changeable. The key code never changes, so there is no reason to waste memory for it.

Another good use for #DEFINE symbols is to replace "magic numbers" inside your code. Suppose you align everything on a particular column number. Instead of repeating the actual number many times in your code, which would make it a hassle to change, define a symbol for that column number and use the symbol instead. Then if you ever want to change the column, simply change the one #DEFINE statement and recompile.

DEFINE Flags

The <*symbol value*>, like the key code 27 above, is optional. If you do not specify a symbol value, the symbol can be used as a flag for conditional compilation.

The symbol __DBASEWIN__ is automatically defined when compiling programs in dBASE for Windows, and can be used for platform-specific code (see example below).

Conditional Compilation

You can detect whether a symbol has been defined with the preprocessor command #IFDEF. Like the control structure IF . . .ELSE . . .ENDIF, the preprocessor commands tell dBASE which block of code to compile into the executable PRO file. The other block(s) are not included at all in the PRO file.

For example, if you have a demonstration version of the program that does not have the printing module, you can conditionally compile the printing procedures only if you create the symbol. See the following example:

```
RETAIL:
     #define RETAIL

     PROCEDURE MainMenu
       ...
     RETURN

     PROCEDURE ViewData
       ...
     RETURN

     #ifdef RETAIL
     PROCEDURE PrintMenu
       ...
     RETURN
     #endif
```

You can also test to see if a symbol is not defined with the #IFNDEF preprocessor command. If demo version had a "where to buy" info screen, you can include that code conditionally with the following:

```
#ifndef RETAIL
PROCEDURE BuyInfo
  ...
RETURN
#endif
```

By changing single #DEFINE, you can switch between two versions of code. When conditional compilation skips a block of code, that code is not included at all in the PRO, unlike compiling the code but simply not calling it. Using conditional compilation results in smaller, leaner programs.

Here is a code fragment that utilizes the __DBASEWIN__ symbol. Conditional compilation is especially important in cross-platform development, since some commands are not recognized on different platforms. For example, suppose you have a banner screen and you want to play a little tune when you start your program. In dBASE for Windows, you would use the PLAY SOUND command, but the PLAY SOUND command is not supported in dBASE for DOS. The code fragment would look like:

```
<code to display banner, which is the same for DOS and Windows>
#ifdef __DBASEWIN__
  play sound TRUMPETS.WAV  && play sound in Windows version
#endif
```

Note that you cannot achieve this with a plain IF . . .ENDIF, since the PLAY SOUND command will not compile in dBASE for DOS.

#INCLUDE

The #INCLUDE preprocessor command reads in the contents of another file into the current file at the location of the #INCLUDE statement. #INCLUDE substitutes the contents of the other file into the spot where the statement is—as if you had typed them there.

The primary use of #INCLUDE is to include header files in a PRG. The primary use of header files is to contain all of your #DEFINEs in a particular group. You only have to type the #DEFINEs once into a header file, and then #INCLUDE that file in all of your PRGs. If there are ever any changes to the #DEFINEs, you only need to change the one header file and recompile your program.

Avoiding Macro Substitution

Macro substitution, also referred to as *¯o substitution* because it involves the & character, is a peculiar capability of the dBASE language. The & character is the macro substitution operator. When an & is encountered immediately before the name of a character memory variable, dBASE substitutes the & and character memory variable name with the contents of that character memory variable and reevaluates the command line. The following example is strange but legal:

```
cText = "se data"
clo&cText.bases
```

cText is a defined character memory variable. The & indicates that cText is to be expanded and substituted. The period (.) after cText marks the end of the character memory variable name. Without the period, it would not be possible to abut text immediately after a ¯o. The period is part of the ¯o and is eliminated.

When the second command is executed, dBASE substitutes the characters in the following command:

```
&cText.
```

with the contents of cText, the characters

```
se data
```

Therefore, the command interprets like the following:

```
close databases
```

This example illustrates the unabashed straightforwardness of ¯o substitution. If dBASE encounters a ¯o substitution—a line with an & followed by something that looks like an identifier—it does not bother figuring out what you are trying to do. Instead, it simply stores the entire line verbatim in the PRO file and defers interpretation of that line until it is executed.

Each and every time that line is encountered, the ¯o substitution is completed and the line is then interpreted. This results in slower programs, because dBASE must check to see if the text after the & is the name of a character memory variable, and, if it is, execute the ¯o substitution, and finally reevaluate the line. Therefore, ¯o substitution should be avoided.

File Indirection

One reason that once was valid was the use of a variable in a file name. For example, take a look at the following command to open a table:

```
use STOCK
```

USE is a command, but STOCK is not, and it is not a memory variable either. It is to be taken as the literal file name. Normally, a character literal is enclosed in delimiters. You would expect the command to be the following:

```
use "STOCK"
```

In which case, using a memory variable for the file name would be such:

```
cFile = "STOCK"
use cFile
```

But that is not how the USE command works. There are a number of examples of this in the dBASE language where an identifier is expected to be a literal. Using ¯o substitution is one way around the problem:

```
cFile = "STOCK"
use &cFile.
```

As discussed, when the ¯o is expanded, this command will look like the first example. But there is a better way. When a command expects a file name literal, you can use a memory variable and parentheses to indicate file indirection (which indirectly indicates the name of a file through a memory variable), like this:

```
cFile = "STOCK"
use (cFile)
```

The difference is that with file indirection, dBASE knows that this is a USE command, expects there to be a memory variable, and also expects that memory variable to contain a file name. On the other hand, with ¯o substitution, dBASE makes no assumptions and handles the command in its normal, inefficient manner for ¯os.

Chapter Snapshot

Object-oriented programming attempts to simplify programming tasks by mimicking the real world through the use of objects. In computer terms, an *object* is an abstract data structure which contains both data and the code to manipulate that data. This chapter covers object-oriented programming in general. The topics include the following:

All of the Windows interface controls in dBASE are objects; an understanding of object-oriented programming is necessary to directly manipulate these controls. The interface objects are covered in detail in Chapter 16.

Understanding Object-Oriented Programming

By Kenneth Chan

Object-oriented programming is shrouded in terminology that obscures the fact that objects are the natural way to create modern event-driven programs. Event-driven programming is discussed in the next chapter.

Object-oriented programming and event-driven programming, abbreviated OOP and EDP respectively, are often mentioned in the same breath—but they are quite different. Although OOP is about combining data and code into objects to make writing programs easier for the programmer, EDP focuses on structuring programs to make them easier for users to use. In doing so, event-driven programs are harder to write. You can write a lot of OOP without getting into EDP, and you can write EDP without using OOP, but OOP makes EDP much easier to manage, so they are a good mix.

Getting Started with Objects

One way to look at objects is to think of them as smart data, or data that knows how to handle itself. For example, BMP and PCX are two bitmapped graphics formats. If you want to display one of these bitmaps without objects, you have to determine what format the bitmap is and then act accordingly. The code would look something like the following:

```
do case
   case cFormat = "BMP"
     do DrawBMP with bBitMap
   case cFormat = "PCX"
     do DrawPCX with bBitMap
   ...
endcase
```

There is no need to use other functions with an object; everything you would want to do with an object it knows how to do itself, because the function to do it is part of the object.

If you want to support a new format, you have to go into that CASE structure and add another case in addition to adding the source code to draw the new format. The code would look something like this CASE structure:

```
bBitMap.Draw()
```

That's it. There is never any need to expand on this simple syntax. Object-oriented programming provides this level of detail and clarity is possible because of the following factors:

- ✔ Objects know about themselves. An *object* is an abstract data type composed of elementary data types such as character strings, numbers, and so forth. In this case, a bitmap object, in addition to knowing the bitmap data itself, would know what format it is in, how wide and tall it is, and whatever data is pertinent to it as a bitmap.
- ✔ Objects know how to handle themselves. An object data type can have its own individualized version of a function. Function calls of an object are then similar to sending messages to an object for it to do something.

  The different flavors of bitmap would each have their own version of the DRAW() function. If new formats are added, those new object types would have their own DRAW() function.

It's really not the same thing to do this with a non-object-oriented function:

```
DRAWBITMAP( bBitMap )
```

because somewhere in DRAWBITMAP() there is probably a CASE structure that determines the format and executes the appropriate code. Adding another format requires tinkering with the function. This is because without objects, the code is separate from the data. With objects, data and code are in the same package.

The hard part of object-oriented programming is the careful engineering of objects and the functions that manipulate them. Objects must be constructed so that they are easy to use and extensible.

Basic Object Terminology

Working with objects requires that you learn new terminology, but it can be kept to a minimum. Unfortunately, the definitions are somewhat circular; however, if you can grasp one of them, you can understand them all.

Object

An object is an instance of a class. If a class is a definition, then an object is an actual thing that follows that definition, much like the difference between a cookie cutter and a cookie. For example, BMP Bitmap is a class, and the actual BMP bitmaps are objects. Car is a very broad class, and the Batmobile and the Love Bug are objects.

Class

The class is the definition of the object; what properties the object contains. Examples of classes include BMP Bitmap and PCX Bitmap, which each define the characteristics that type of bitmap has.

The broad Car class can be further refined into separate PassengerCar and Truck classes, since those two types of objects have different properties.

Properties

A *property* is a characteristic or component of an object and is represented by data of a particular type, even a reference to another object. In the case of bitmaps, a bitmap's width and height are properties of the bitmap, expressed as a number of pixels. For cars, the car's color and number of doors are properties.

Method

A *method* is a property of the type code reference; either a function pointer or code block. Methods represent things that an object knows how to do. For example, a bitmap can DRAW() itself, and a car can DRIVE().

Instantiating Classes

To *instantiate* a class is to create an instance of a class. When you instantiate a class, you create a new object of that class.

Working with Dynamic Objects

Objects in dBASE are dynamic; that is, they can be created, added to, and changed on-the-fly. This is unlike other object-oriented languages like C++, in which you must explicitly declare the structures of your objects through classes before you can work with them. This dynamic nature is very much in the dBASE tradition of doing things, and makes dBASE an excellent environment in which to learn object-oriented programming interactively.

NEW Operator

The NEW operator creates new objects. The syntax of NEW is as follows:

```
NEW <object class>( [<parameters>] )
```

NEW returns an object reference to a newly created object of the class specified in `<object class>`. This object reference is a type of memory variable, and must be assigned to an identifier.

For more information on memvars, see Chapter 10.

The simplest class is the class OBJECT, which is a class with no properties. The following command creates a new property-less object and assigns its reference to the identifier o1:

```
o1 = new object()
```

The class OBJECT is a *stock class*, which means that it is part of dBASE. Most of the stock classes involve the user interface. Later in the chapter, you learn about creating your own classes.

Dot Operator

Much like the -> operator accesses fields of a table, the dot operator accesses the properties of an object. The syntax for the dot operator is:

```
<object reference>.<property>
```

This property reference is treated just like the identifier assigned to a variable. This means you can assign values to the property or retrieve the property value. Like variables, if you assign a value to a property that does not exist, that property will be created in that object.

Because of dBASE's dynamic objects and properties, you should make sure that you spell your property names correctly. Assigning a value to a misspelled property will create that property, leaving you to wonder why that assignment did not seem to take.

For example, the o1 object in the preceding example has no properties. You can create some properties for the object with simple assignment:

```
o1.d1 = date()            && create date property
o1.c1 = "Hello"           && create c1 character property
```

Retrieving property values is just as straightforward:

```
? o1.d1                   && prints the date
? o1.c1                   && prints "Hello"
```

Like memory variables, you can change the property with reassignment:

```
o1.c1 = "Jello"           && reassign c1 property
? o1.c1                   && prints "Jello"
```

Call Operator

If the property of an object is a function pointer or code block, you can use the NORMAL () call operator in conjunction with the dot operator to execute the code. The syntax is a combination of the dot operator and non-object call syntax:

```
<object reference>.<property>( [<parameters>] )
```

This example defines a code block that returns the date one week in the future:

```
o1.k1 = { date() + 7 }    && create code block property
? o1.k1()                 && call k1 code block
```

THIS

The `this` variable is simply a reference pointer back to the object for which it belongs. In general, `this` allows for one part of an object to refer to another part of the object. When `this` is used in a class definition, it refers to the object that will be created or instanciated from the class. In a code block, it refers to the object that code block is a property of. `this` refers to the current object.

Whenever you make a call into an object, the object reference `this`, which points to the object being referenced, is automatically created. You can then use `this` to reference other properties in the same object.

Continuing with the object created in the previous example, the following code returns the date one week from the date in the d1 property, instead of one week from the current date:

```
o1.k1 = { this.d1 + 7 }  && this references current object
? o1.k1()                 && prints d1 in current object + 7
```

`this` is local in scope, which means that it is valid only in the method which is part of the object. In other words, if the function calls another function which is not part of the object, you must pass `this` as a parameter, because there is no `this` defined for that function.

Object References

Although object reference identifiers are much like memory variable identifiers, they differ in one important aspect. When you assign a memory variable to a new identifier, a new memory variable is created, and the contents of the memvar are copied to the new memory variable. For example:

```
c1 = "Yin"                && create memvar
c2 = c1                   && make a copy of memvar
c1 = "Yang"               && change original memvar
? c2                      && prints "Yin"; copy is unchanged
```

When you assign an object reference to a new object reference, only the reference is copied. You then have two identifiers that point to the same object. Any changes made through either reference will change the same object. Therefore, any access through either reference will access the same changed data. For example, continuing with the previously created o1 object:

```
o1.c1 = "Yin"           && set c1 property
o2 = o1                 && copy object reference
o1.c1 = "Yang"          && change c1 property
? o2.c1                 && prints "Yang"; same object
                            && referenced, same property
                            && changed
```

INSPECT()

You can visually inspect all the properties of an object with the INSPECT() function. The syntax for the INSPECT() function is:

```
INSPECT( <object reference> )
```

For example, if you want to inspect the o1 object, the following command

```
inspect( o1 )
```

opens the object inspector (see fig. 11.1).

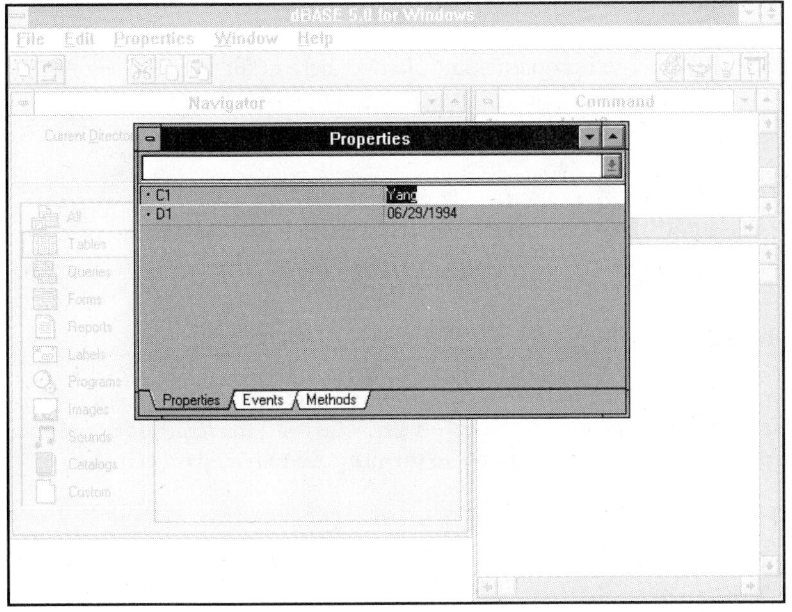

Figure 11.1
The Properties page of the object inspector.

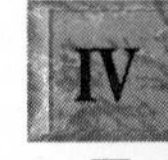

The object inspector has two pages: one for properties and one for events. Events are covered in Chapter 12. Only built-in dBASE user interface objects and objects derived from them have events. Deriving objects and classes is discussed later in this chapter.

Figure 11.2 shows the methods page, which contains the code block defined in the object.

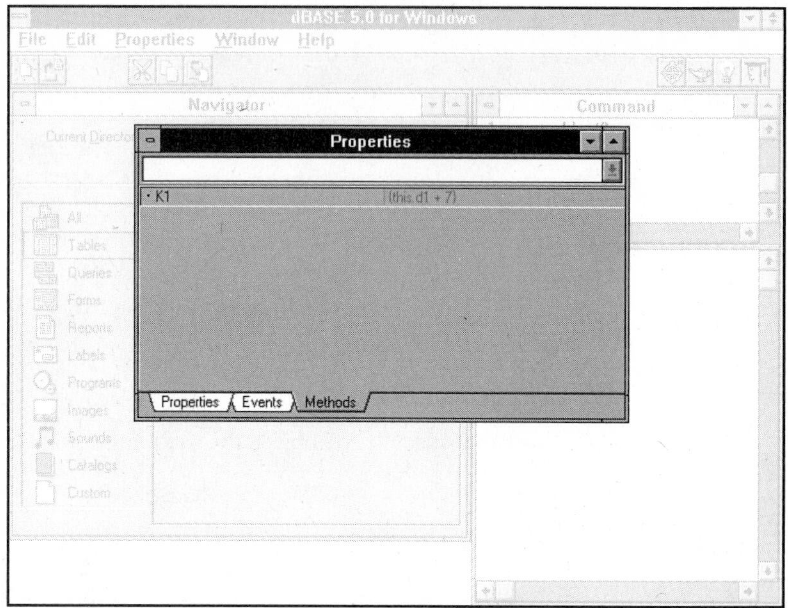

Figure 11.2 The Methods page of the object inspector.

You can highlight any of the listed properties and change them in the entry area at the top of the inspector window.

Object Visibility

Objects can be declared PUBLIC, PRIVATE, LOCAL, or STATIC, just like memory variables, with the same defaults and conditions. Scoping is discussed in Chapter 10.

Object Lifespan

Objects remain in memory as long as there is at least one object reference that points them. Object references are discarded like memory variables, with the RELEASE command. For example, to discard both references to the previously created object:

```
RELEASE o1, o2
```

After all the references to an object are released from memory, the object itself and all its properties are released as well.

Defining Classes

Although you can create a new object that doesn't have properties with the OBJECT class and add properties manually, if you plan to create more than one such object, you should define a new object class. Defining a new object class enables you to automate the process of initializing any new objects, and is the best way to define functions for that class.

The following sections demonstrate classes by building cars and racing them.

CLASS . . .ENDCLASS

The syntax for defining a class is:

```
CLASS <class name>( [<parameters>] )
        [<constructor code>]
        [<member functions>]
ENDCLASS
```

The CLASS . . .ENDCLASS structure is a programming structure and must be in a program file. Like FUNCTIONs and PROCEDUREs, dBASE must be able to find the CLASS definition when you create objects of that class. Follow the guidelines discussed in Chapter 10, in the section "How dBASE Finds Subroutines" to place your class definition. To use classes interactively at the Command window, you must place the class in a PRG file and use the SET PROCEDURE command to make the class available.

Constructors

The class constructor is any and all code between the CLASS statement and the first FUNCTION (if there is any), or the ENDCLASS statement.

The primary task of the constructor is to create and assign properties for any new objects of the class, but just about any code can go in there. The code is executed when the class is called with the NEW operator.

The constructor can test for and use any parameters that are passed to the class. While executing the constructor, the object reference `this` refers to the object created from the class.

The dBASE function PCOUNT() returns the number of parameters passed to a function, procedure, or class constructor.

To design a Car class, consider that a car has many properties, but what the car looks like and how fast it goes are the two of primary interest. To indicate what the car looks like, a character string is in the property cBody. The speed of the car is stored in the property nSpeed. When creating a new Car object, you want to have the option of specifying the car's body style and speed. If you do not specify these properties, you want the constructor to assign some defaults.

To race the cars, you need to keep track of their position. The property nPos, which is initially set to 0, keeps track of the cars' position. A final feature of the constructor is that it draws the car at the starting line when the car is constructed.

GROUND_ROW is a #DEFINEd symbolic constant which indicates the row on-screen which will be used as the "ground" for the cars:

```
class Car( cBody, nSpeed )
   this.cBody  = iif( PCOUNT() < 1, "[##]", cBody )
   this.nSpeed = iif( PCOUNT() < 2, rand() * 2 + 1, nSpeed )
   this.nPos   = 0
    @ GROUND_ROW,this.nPos say this.cBody
  endclass
```

For the properties cBody and nSpeed, the PCOUNT() function determines whether either has been specified in the NEW call; otherwise defaults are used.

Member Functions

A class definition can include functions and procedures designed specifically for that class. These functions are called *member functions* of the class and become methods for the objects of that class.

All the properties in a class are also known as members of the class. Whereas the term "property" is used more commonly with dBASE; the term "member" is used more commonly with C++ The two terms are used somewhat interchangeably, which is the source of some confusion.

A member function definition does two things: first, it defines a function, just like a function definition outside of a class. The object reference `this` is again available and refers to the current object upon which the function is acting.

Second, the definition creates a property whose name is the name of the function and whose value is a function pointer to the function itself.

To move the car, the GO() member function is added to the class definition:

```
function Go
   @ GROUND_ROW,this.nPos say space( len( this.cBody ))
   this.nPos = this.nPos + this.nSpeed
   @ GROUND_ROW,this.nPos say this.cBody
 return ( this.nPos + len( this.cBody ) >= FINISH_COL )
```

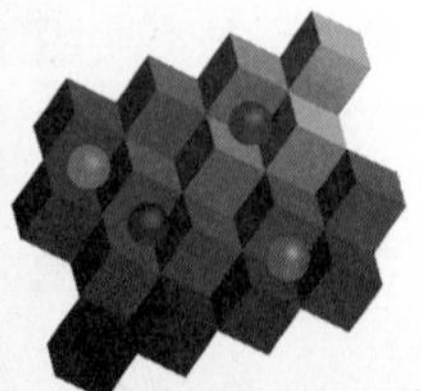

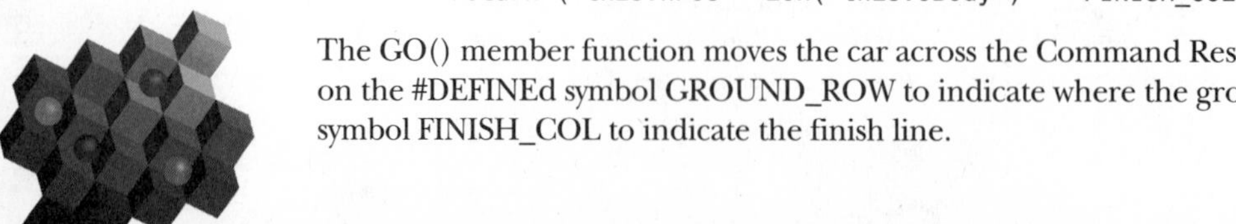

The GO() member function moves the car across the Command Results window. It relies on the #DEFINEd symbol GROUND_ROW to indicate where the ground is, and the symbol FINISH_COL to indicate the finish line.

GO() uses crude animation. It erases the car's previous position, moves the car forward according to its speed, and draws the car in its new position. If the car crosses the finish line, GO() returns .T., otherwise it returns .F.

Now you are ready to race.

The following code can be found in the file named CARS.PRG on the *Inside dBASE for Windows Bonus Disk.*

Objects At The Races

RACES1.PRG looks like this:

```
*-- Row on screen where cars will race
 #define GROUND_ROW 10
 *-- Column of finish line
 #define FINISH_COL 40
 *-- Number of cars in race
 #define NUM_VEHICLES 2
       *-- Clear the screen and draw the ground
 clear
 @ GROUND_ROW + 1, 0 say replicate( chr( 178 ), FINISH_COL )
       *-- Put all the vehicles in an array
 declare aVehicle[ NUM_VEHICLES ]
 *-- The first car is standard issue
 aVehicle[ 1 ] = new Car()
 *-- The second car is a spiffier model
 aVehicle[ 2 ] = new Car( "<==>" )
       *-- Wait for green light
 @ 12, 0
 wait "Press the space bar to start race"
       *-- The race is on
 lFinish = .f.
 do
   for nVehicle = 1 to NUM_VEHICLES
     *-- Move each car
     lFinish = aVehicle[ nVehicle ].Go()
     *-- If a car reaches the finish line the race is over
     if lFinish
       *-- Exit FOR loop; don't bother moving other cars
       exit
```

```
    endif
  next
until lFinish
     class Car( cBody, nSpeed )
  this.cBody  = iif( pcount() < 1, "[##]", cBody )
  this.nSpeed = iif( pcount() < 2, rand() * 2 + 1, nSpeed )
  this.nPos   = 0
  *-- Draw car when constructed
  @ GROUND_ROW,this.nPos say this.cBody
         function Go
    *-- Erase car in current position
    @ GROUND_ROW,this.nPos say space( len( this.cBody ))
    *-- Move car forward
    this.nPos = this.nPos + this.nSpeed
    *-- Draw car in new position
    @ GROUND_ROW,this.nPos say this.cBody
    *-- Has car reached finish line?
  return ( this.nPos + len( this.cBody ) >= FINISH_COL )
     endclass
```

Because the speeds are assigned randomly, when you run RACE1.PRG, sometimes car #1 wins and sometimes car #2 wins. When the speeds are close, it is hard to see what is going on due to the crude animation; car #1 is more likely to win, because it moves first.

After the screen is cleared and the ground is drawn, an array is declared. All the cars are kept in an array so that the program can handle the cars uniformly in sequence.

The first car is a default model. The class constructor creates a new object, assigns a body style, speed, and position, and draws the new car. The object reference to this new car is stored in the first array element. The second car has a custom body style, but is otherwise handled like the first. Its object reference is stored in the second array element. You could define any number of cars this way, but the race might get pretty crowded.

After a key is pressed to start the race, the finished flag is set to false, and the race begins. The race loop is very simple: each car is told to GO() until one of the cars reaches the finish line. The cars are told to go in turn with a FOR loop that traverses the array of cars. After one of the cars reaches the finish line, no other movement is done. The FOR loop is ended, and the DO...UNTIL loop completes. The race is over.

Deriving a Class

Suppose you want to expand the race to include planes. For the purposes of the race, a plane is similar to a car except that a plane has wings and can fly. Because planes are similar to cars in many ways, you can build on the Car class, deriving a new Plane class from the existing Car class, which is then considered the superclass.

CLASS . . .OF . . .ENDCLASS

The syntax for defining a derived class is:

```
CLASS <derived class name>( [<parameters>] ) OF <superclass>( [<param-
eters>] )
        [<constructor code>]
        [<member functions>]
ENDCLASS
```

When creating a new object of the derived class, the parent class constructor is called first with the parent class parameters. Then the constructor in the derived class definition is called with the derived class parameters.

Programming by Difference

The essence of deriving classes is programming by difference. The things the two classes have in common you leave alone; the things that are different you change; and you add the things that the derived class has that the parent class does not contain.

Planes and cars both have a body style. However, because the default body style of a plane is different than that of a car, the constructor code for the cBody property is different. Planes and cars both have certain speed characteristics, or horizontal motion, but planes have the additional characteristic of vertical motion, which is assigned in the nLift property. The actual altitude of the plane is maintained in the nAlt property, and the plane's cruising altitude is in the nCruise property.

The big difference between planes and cars is the way they move. A plane moves up and across until it reaches its cruising altitude, and then moves across only. This means a modified GO() member function. In this race, the planes never land.

The new derived Plane class looks like this:

```
class Plane( nCruise, cBody, nLift, nSpeed ) of Car()
   this.nCruise = nCruise
   this.cBody  = iif( pcount() < 2, "\_=>", cBody )
   this.nLift  = iif( pcount() < 3, rand() * 1 + 0.5, nLift )
   this.nAlt   = GROUND_ROW
   *-- Draw plane when constructed
   @ this.nAlt,this.nPos say this.cBody
           function Go
     *-- Erase plane in current position
     @ this.nAlt,this.nPos say space( len( this.cBody ))
     *-- Move plane forward
     this.nPos = this.nPos + this.nSpeed
     *-- and up to cruising altitude
```

```
    if this.nAlt > this.nCruise
      this.nAlt = this.nAlt - this.nLift
    endif
    *-- Draw plane in new position
    @ this.nAlt,this.nPos say this.cBody
    *-- Has plane reached finish line?
  return ( this.nPos + len( this.cBody ) >= FINISH_COL )
         endclass
```

The constructor code for cBody is different, and the new properties have been added. The unchanged properties nSpeed and nPos are handled in the Car base class constructor.

The drawing of the plane now takes into account the plane's altitude, as does the code to lift the plane up to the cruising altitude.

The Races Revisited

The expanded RACE2.PRG looks like the following code:

```
*-- Row on screen where cars will race
#define GROUND_ROW 10
*-- Column of finish line
#define FINISH_COL 40
*-- Number of vehicles in race
#define NUM_VEHICLES 4
      *-- Clear the screen and draw the ground
clear
@ GROUND_ROW + 1, 0 say replicate( chr( 178 ), FINISH_COL )
      *-- Put all the vehicles in an array
declare aVehicle[ NUM_VEHICLES ]
*-- The first car is standard issue
aVehicle[ 1 ] = new Car()
*-- The second car is a spiffier model
aVehicle[ 2 ] = new Car( "<==>" )
*-- The first plane cruises at row 4
aVehicle[ 3 ] = new Plane( 4 )
*-- The second spiffier plane cruises at row 2
aVehicle[ 4 ] = new Plane( 2, ">>" )
      *-- Wait for green light
@ 12, 0
wait "Press the space bar to start race"
      *-- The race is on
lFinish = .f.
```

```
do
  for nVehicle = 1 to NUM_VEHICLES
    *-- Move each vehicle
    lFinish = aVehicle[ nVehicle ].Go()
    *-- If a vehicle reaches the finish line the race is
    *-- over
    if lFinish
      *-- Exit FOR loop; don't bother moving other vehicles
      exit
    endif
  next
until lFinish
      class Car( cBody, nSpeed )
  this.cBody  = iif( pcount() < 1, "[##]", cBody )
  this.nSpeed = iif( pcount() < 2, rand() * 2 + 1, nSpeed )
  this.nPos   = 0
  *-- Draw car when constructed
  @ GROUND_ROW,this.nPos say this.cBody
        function Go
    *-- Erase car in current position
    @ GROUND_ROW,this.nPos say space( len( this.cBody ))
    *-- Move car forward
    this.nPos = this.nPos + this.nSpeed
    *-- Draw car in new position
    @ GROUND_ROW,this.nPos say this.cBody
    *-- Has car reached finish line?
  return ( this.nPos + len( this.cBody ) >= FINISH_COL )
      endclass
      class Plane( nCruise, cBody, nLift, nSpeed ) of Car()
  this.nCruise = nCruise
  this.cBody  = iif( pcount() < 2, "\_=>", cBody )
  this.nLift  = iif( pcount() < 3, rand() * 1 + 0.5, nLift )
  this.nAlt   = GROUND_ROW
  *-- Draw plane when constructed
  @ this.nAlt,this.nPos say this.cBody
        function Go
    *-- Erase plane in current position
    @ this.nAlt,this.nPos say space( len( this.cBody ))
    *-- Move plane forward
    this.nPos = this.nPos + this.nSpeed
    *-- and up to cruising altitude
    if this.nAlt > this.nCruise
      this.nAlt = this.nAlt - this.nLift
```

```
    endif
    *-- Draw plane in new position
    @ this.nAlt,this.nPos say this.cBody
    *-- Has plane reached finish line?
  return ( this.nPos + len( this.cBody ) >= FINISH_COL ) endclass
```

The only functional differences between RACE1.PRG and RACE2.PRG is that RACE2.PRG has the new derived Plane class, and two planes are created in addition to the cars. The race loop itself is unchanged.

Benefits of Object-Oriented Programming

The three main benefits of object-oriented programming, encapsulation, inheritance, and polymorphism, are seen in the development and expansion the race programs. Like almost everything else in object-oriented programming, these benefits are given big names.

Encapsulation

The first benefit of object-oriented programming is *encapsulation*, which means that data and code are in the same package. The class definition has both the data and the functions that know how to use that data. A properly constructed object has the ability to change, manipulate, and maintain itself. The inner mechanisms are unimportant; the object is a black box to which the program sends messages, and the object responds.

New objects can be introduced into properly structured object-oriented programs simply by introducing new classes.

Inheritance

The second benefit of object-oriented programming is *inheritance*, or the capability of new classes to inherit the properties and methods of other classes. Inheritance makes creating new classes easy and consistent by expanding upon the properties of existing and tested classes.

Polymorphism

The third benefit of object-oriented programming is *polymorphism* (from the Greek, "many forms"), which enables the same name to have different meanings for different things. Polymorphism promotes the use of the same names for similar actions; each object then responds in its own way.

Non-object-oriented programmers are familiar with a kind of polymorphism. The + operator behaves differently for numbers than for characters strings, and is therefore a polymorphic operator. Without polymorphism, you would need a separate add operator and concatenate operator.

But because adding numbers and concatenating strings are both situations in which you put two things together, using a single polymorphic + operator makes your programs easier to read and write.

Chapter Snapshot

Writing true Windows applications requires an understanding of event-driven programming. The familiar controls of Windows programs, such as check boxes, push buttons, and scroll bars, can all be accessed by the mouse or keyboard in any order, and therefore must be able to respond immediately to the user. In this chapter, you learn about the following:

The random order in which Windows applications can be used requires abandoning traditional sequence-driven programming, in which the program blindly moves from one state to another. The new paradigm for Windows applications is *event-driven* programming, in which everything on the screen must be set up at once to enable anything to happen.

Understanding Event-Driven Programming

By Kenneth Chan

Like object-oriented programming, event-driven programming introduces some new terminology and concepts.

An *event* is a single action—usually initiated by the user—such as a keypress. Most events have a *subject.* For example, clicking the mouse is an event. What you click on is the subject of that event.

Different controls respond differently to the same event, and not all things respond to all events. For example, clicking on a check box toggles the check box, but clicking on a push-button presses the push-button. Clicking on a window's title bar usually does nothing (but dragging the title bar moves the window).

Event Handlers

An *event handler* is a procedure or function assigned to a particular event to which a control responds. In addition to the default behavior that a control has in response to an event, you can write your own event handlers. These event handlers are triggered in response to an event, after the default behavior of the event has occurred (for example, clicking on a button causes the button to be "pressed" into the screen). These handlers enable you to do just about anything, such as opening another form when you click a push-button or changing the color of a checkbox when you check it.

dBASE for Windows event handlers have names that usually begin with the word On. For example, the OnClick event handler is called after you click on something on the screen. When you click on a push-button, the push-button appears to be pressed (the default behavior) and then the OnClick event handler is called, if there is one defined for that push-button.

Event-Driven Programming and Objects

Objects are an ideal vehicle for event-driven programming. Because objects are smart about themselves, they can be responsible for their own events in the scheme of the application. The event handler code is encapsulated in each control object.

Each event handler is a property of the object. An event handler property must be either a function pointer or a code block that represents the code to execute when the event occurs.

All the events and their respective handlers are listed in the Events page of the INSPECT() object inspector. If there are no event handlers, the object simply executes the default behavior for the event.

Understanding Windows Interface Issues

Two issues come into play when discussing event-driven programming: *modality* and *focus*. This and the following sections discuss these issues.

Traditional sequence-driven programs operate in modes. Most programs start in a main menu mode. At this point, the program pauses and waits for the user to select from

among a limited set of choices, such as editing old records or printing reports. Each choice leads to a different *mode* of operation.

Another Windows interface issue is focus. *Focus* indicates which object has the attention of Windows, in effect, which object is the focus of the user's actions. When a form opens, for example, on the screen the focus might initially be in the "User ID" field.

Modality

Here's an example of modality: if editing records is selected, the program might go into a get-the-key-number mode in which the user must type in an invoice number or some other identifier. When the program finds the record, it goes into edit mode, in which the user can make changes to the record. The program remains in edit mode until the user completes the transaction or leaves the screen.

Suppose that, halfway through the changes, the user needs to print another record. Because he is in edit mode, his choices are to quickly complete the changes, or to abandon the changes to get out of edit mode. He next must return to the main menu, and then invoke print mode.

This illustrates the weakness of modal programming, in which the program operates as a series of states (or *modes*) each of which provides a limited choice of actions. The opposite of modal programming is *modeless* programming, in which you can do whatever you want, in any order.

The dBASE for Windows interface has many examples of modeless programming. The INSPECT() Object Inspector that was introduced in Chapter 11 is modeless. When the Object Inspector opens up, you can inspect an object, of course. When you are finished inspecting an object, however, you don't have to explicitly close it before going on to another task; you can just ignore it and do something else. The Object Inspector stays open until you want it again.

You can program your dBASE applications the same way. You can, for example, leave the main menu on the screen, but off to one side. If the user wants to print the record that he is in the process of editing, he can simply select the print option from the main menu, print the record, and then continue editing the record. At no time is it necessary to get out of edit mode, close a window, or otherwise interrupt the work flow.

This does not mean that everything should be modeless. Modal dialog boxes are used to present the user with information or an error message that the user must acknowledge before the program continues. A dialog box opened modally will not enable the user to access anything else on the screen, until some input has been accepted.

Because the objects remain on screen and can be called at any time, modeless programs can be implemented only with event-driven programming.

Focus

There are different levels of focus. Among the many applications opened on the desktop, only one has focus. All other tasks are in the background and do not have focus. There may be many windows within an application, only one of which has focus. Within that window, there can be many controls, only one of which has focus.

Windows indicates which control has focus by putting a cursor or dotted box around that control. That control receives all the keyboard events. For example, pressing the space bar toggles a check box or presses a push-button.

Focus is moved among controls in a window by pressing either Tab or Shift+Tab. When Tab is pressed, the current control loses focus, and the next control gains focus. There are also keys for changing focus between windows in an application and between applications on the desktop. In addition to using the keyboard to change focus, the mouse can arbitrarily move the focus to any control, window, or application on the desktop.

Any change of focus generates two events: the loss of focus in the previous object(s), and the gain of focus in the next object(s). For example, clicking on a control in another window causes the following events to occur:

1. The loss of focus in the current control.
2. The loss of focus in the current window.
3. The addition of focus in the window containing the control that was clicked on.
4. The acquisition of focus in the control that was clicked on.

The losing and gaining of focus is represented by two event handlers: OnLostFocus and OnGotFocus.

Adopting an Event-Driven Mind-Set

Event-driven programming is different than traditional sequence-driven programming. In sequence-driven programming, the program execution starts at the top of the program and goes line-by-line to the end. Decision structures, looping structures, and subroutine calls alter the straight top-down execution somewhat, but the essence is still the same. The programmer decides where to go at every turn.

In event-driven programming, program flow is out of the programmer's hands. The user and the system dictate program flow. This can be an unsettling change of mind-set to programmers used to having complete control. But it is the only reasonable way to implement the modern multitasking environments that today's users expect.

Programming Event-Driven Code: The Old Way

A simple example illustrates the different approach required for event-driven programming. The following steps implement a classic sequence-driven menu:

1. Display the menu on screen.
2. Wait for and get the user's choice.
3. Execute the appropriate subroutine.

The following code implements such a menu:

```
#define LEFT_COL 20
#define MENU_WIDTH 15
do
  clear
  *— Display menu
  @  3,LEFT_COL say center( "Main Menu", MENU_WIDTH )
  @  4,LEFT_COL say replicate( "-", MENU_WIDTH )
  @  6,LEFT_COL say "C - Check out"
  @  8,LEFT_COL say "V - View history"
  @ 10,LEFT_COL say "Q - Quit"
  @ 12,LEFT_COL say "Press letter:"
  *— Wait for and get keystroke
  cKey = upper( chr( inkey( 0 )))
  *— Execute appropriate subroutine
  do case
    case cKey = "C"
      do CheckOut
    case cKey = "V"
      do ViewHist
  endcase
until cKey = "Q"
*— Some placeholder code for different options
PROCEDURE CheckOut
  ? "Check Out"
  wait
RETURN
PROCEDURE ViewHist
  ? "History"
  wait
RETURN
```

Programming Event-Driven Code: The New Way

Event-driven code is different. The same menu might look something like the following:

```
#define LEFT_COL 10
#define BTN_WID 20
*— Create form
local f1
f1 = new form( "Main Menu" )
*— Create pushbuttons
define push-button ipCheckOut of f1 ;
  at  6, LEFT_COL ;
  property ;
    Text    "&Check Out",;
    Width   BTN_WID,;
    OnClick CheckOut
define push-button ipViewHist of f1 ;
  at  8, LEFT_COL ;
  property ;
    Text    "&View History",;
    Width   BTN_WID,;
    OnClick ViewHist
define push-button ipQuit of f1 ;
  at 10, LEFT_COL ;
  property ;
    Text    "&Quit",;
    Width   BTN_WID,;
    OnClick {; form.close() }

*— Open the form
f1.open()
*— and let execution drop off into nothingness
RETURN

*— Some placeholder code for different options
PROCEDURE CheckOut
  ? "Check Out"
RETURN
PROCEDURE ViewHist
  ? "History"
RETURN
```

Notice the different approach:

1. Each interface object is created. Here, the three menu choices are represented by three different push buttons.
2. Each push-button is told what to do when it is clicked on.
3. The form containing the pushbuttons is opened.
4. The program ends.

In other words, the program—and therefore programmer—is no longer in control. If this program is run from the Command window, control returns to the Command window, but the form is still open. Clicking on a button causes its OnClick event handler to fire.

Who Is in Charge?

The fact that the program has ended may be the strangest of all. If your program is not running, who is controlling the action? The answer lies in the fact that at the heart of every event-driven interface is a *polling loop*, or polling state. dBASE sits in a polling loop and waits for something to happen. It monitors the mouse, the keyboard, the system timer, and whatever else in the system that might generate an event.

When an event occurs, dBASE gathers the relevant information about the event. For a mouse click, dBASE determines the location of the mouse cursor, and from that, which object was clicked on. Then dBASE sends a message to that object telling it that it has been clicked on and asking it for a response.

dBASE handles the polling and messaging. All you have to do is set up the event handlers so that each object knows what to do when events happen. When dBASE executes an event handler in response to an event, that event handler is in control until it is finished, and then dBASE goes back to polling.

Chapter Snapshot

Part of the appeal of Windows and other graphical user interfaces is the use of a common interface among all applications. This chapter covers the components of a Windows interface used with a dBASE application, including:

Databases in Windows support standard data-entry controls for yes/no questions and multiple-choice fields, and can display graphics and text at the same time. The advantage of using Windows components in your dBASE applications is that users who are familiar with Windows will already know largely how to use your new dBASE application.

Creating the User Interface

By Kenneth Chan

You can do most, if not all, of your user interface design with the Form Designer, as detailed in Chapter 6, "Developing Forms." The Form Designer is a two-way tool, and it generates dBASE code. This means you can learn from and borrow code that is generated by the Form Designer if you decide to code your user interface by hand.

In either case, you need to understand the many properties of dBASE forms and the data-entry controls they contain. These properties control the appearance and behavior of your user interface.

Understanding Windows Interface Concepts

After you have used a few Windows applications, you probably noticed some consistent interface concepts. This section discusses elements of Windows' interface that you need to be familiar with to successfully design your own Windows programs.

It is no accident that almost everything in Windows happens inside a window. The different windows contain your application, the data in your application, and the dialog boxes that the application generates.

Dialog Boxes

A dialog box is a window that pops up in response to some condition, such as a menu choice or error. Dialog boxes are by definition modal; that is, they require you to respond to them before anything else can happen. For example, when you choose **Print**, the Print dialog box appears. You must then either print something or cancel the Print dialog box before you can do anything else in the application.

Multiple Document Interface

The windows that contain your data are modeless; they just sit there and wait for you to interact with them. Many applications enable you to have more than one data window open. For example, you can have two or three documents open in your word processor and work with all of them.

These multiple document windows conform to the Multiple Document Interface, or MDI. These windows are all peers under the control of the application. They do not have to be the same type of window. The directory and file windows in the File Manager are MDI, as are the Navigator and Command windows in dBASE.

Each MDI window has its own title and can be moved and resized. You can press Ctrl+F6 to move from window to window; Ctrl+F4 closes the window, and Alt+Hyphen accesses the window's control box.

Standard Controls

All Windows applications use the same standard controls to represent choices and get data from the user. These standard controls include entryfields, checkboxes, radiobuttons, and pushbuttons.

In the past, dBASE was limited to just entryfields for data entry, and actions such as Save or Delete were initiated with function keys like F2 or F9. These controls required

extensive on-screen hints and user training. Advances in user interface design, first popularized by the Apple Macintosh computer, introduced a richer set of data entry controls, such as radiobuttons for mutually exclusive choices, and pushbuttons that say what they do when you click on them. By using standard Windows controls for data entry, the type of entry desired is visually obvious and consistent across all applications.

Tab Order

Picking a control with the mouse is easy; just click on the one you want. Keyboard navigation relies on the Tab and Shift+Tab keys. The Tab key moves the focus to the next control in the tab order. Repeatedly pressing Tab will move the focus from control to control until the focus moves back to the first control. The Shift+Tab key moves the focus to the previous control in the tab order.

You can set the tab order of the controls so that keyboard users can move through the controls in the most logical order. This order usually corresponds in some degree with the order of the controls on the form.

By default, the tab order follows the order in which controls are created in a form. When using the Form Designer, you can easily reorder the controls so that they will be generated in the proper order.

Selected Entries

When you Tab to a control where you can type a value, the information that already exists in the field is selected. If you type a character, the selected information is deleted and replaced by that character.

When information is selected, you can type new information without having to delete the existing value first. If you want to make changes to the existing value, you can press a cursor key, such as Home or End, to move to where you want to make the changes. When you do this, the value is no longer selected.

Although automatically selecting the contents of a control is standard Windows behavior, it is not what many dBASE users are used to. By default, dBASE disables the behavior, which is controlled by the SelectAll property.

Default Pushbutton

The Tab key moves from control to control; the Enter key signifies an "all done" for dialog boxes. If the focus in not on a pushbutton and you press Enter, the default pushbutton, usually the OK button, is selected.

The Tab and Enter keys make the use of dialog boxes tremendously easy. You simply press Tab to move around in the dialog box from control to control, and then press Enter when you finish, no matter which control happens to be in focus.

The Default property designates the default pushbutton in a form. Be sure to assign it to the most likely or safest pushbutton. For example, when given the option to reformat the hard disk or not, the default pushbutton should be "not."

Hot Keys

In addition to cycling through the controls with the Tab key, individual controls can be chosen by holding down Alt and pressing the appropriate pick key. The appropriate letter for each control is underlined.

The hot key is designated inside the control's Text property and is therefore dependent on the language used for the text label for the control.

For example, in the Print dialog box, the **C**opies field can be accessed by pressing Alt+C; the **S**etup pushbutton can be selected by pressing Alt+S.

If your program has more than a few controls, you may have difficulties designating a unique letter for each control. In general, you do not need to add hot keys for the OK and Cancel buttons, since those are usually represented by the Enter and Esc keys respectively. Concentrate on the options that the user is most likely to change.

Using the DEFINE Syntax

Right out of the box, dBASE contains a number of pre-defined object classes. These are known as *stock classes*. The pre-defined properties of these classes are known as *stock properties*. Interface design in dBASE for Windows is done with the provided stock classes. The controls are objects of the stock classes.

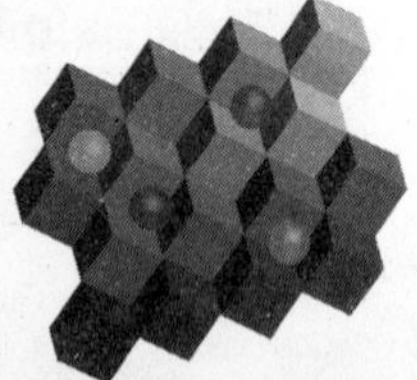

When working with these classes, you can use the NEW syntax as described in Chapter 11, or the more English-like DEFINE syntax. The syntax for the DEFINE command (note that this is a single command) is as follows:

```
DEFINE <class name> <control name> OF <form name>
  [FROM <coordinates> TO <coordinates> ¦ AT <coordinates> ]
  [WITH <parameter list>]
  [PROPERTY <property name> <property value>
         [, <property name> <property value>
         [, ...]]]
  [CUSTOM   <property name> <property value>
         [, <property name> <property value>
         [, ...]]]
```

The <class name> is the name of the stock class. The <control name> is assigned to the Name property of the control, and identifies the control by name. The <form name> is assigned to the Parent property of the control, and identifies which form the control is in. You can have the controls with the same name in different forms.

The <coordinates> values specify where in the form the control is located. The coordinates are either FROM the top left or TO the bottom right, which sets the Top and Left properties and calculates the Height and Width properties. If AT is used, only the Top and Left properties are set and dBASE relies on the default Height and Width for the control.

The <parameter list> is passed to the class constructor. The stock classes have predefined stock properties that control their behavior. You set these stock properties in the PROPERTY clause of the DEFINE command. You can add your own properties to the control objects in the CUSTOM clause.

In the PROPERTY and CUSTOM clauses, the property name and property value are separated by a space, not an equal sign, as they are with property assignment.

For example, the following two sets of commands are equivalent. First the DEFINE syntax:

```
define spinbox inDays of fCheckOut ;
  at 10, 5 ;
  property ;
    rangemin  1, ;
    selectall .t.
```

Now the object syntax:

```
new spinbox( fCheckOut, "inDays" )
fCheckOut.inDays.top       = 10
fCheckOut.inDays.left      = 5
fCheckOut.inDays.rangemin  = 1
fCheckOut.inDays.selectall = .t.
```

You can mix and match. The following code is valid:

```
define spinbox inDays of fCheckOut ;
  at 10, 5 ;
  property ;
    rangemin  1
fCheckOut.inDays.selectall = .t.
```

The use of the PROPERTY clause of the DEFINE command enables dBASE to check the properties you are assigning to make sure that they are stock properties. dBASE will flag any spelling errors you make when compiling the program.

If you use the object syntax, any misspelled property will be created as a new property and assigned the specified value. It will appear as if you made an assignment that "didn't take."

Creating Forms

All the windows you create in dBASE are called forms. A *form* can serve as a data-entry screen, a menu screen, or a dialog box. It can be modal or modeless, MDI or not MDI. All the data-entry controls go into a form.

Table 13.1 lists the stock properties particular to the form class.

Table 13.1
Form Properties

Property	Description
MDI	Whether form is MDI
SysMenu	Whether form has a control box and title bar
Moveable	Whether form is moveable
Sizeable	Whether form is sizeable
Maximize	Allow maximizing of form
Minimize	Allow minimizing of form
WindowState	Current state of form: NORMAL, MINIMIZED, or MAXIMIZED

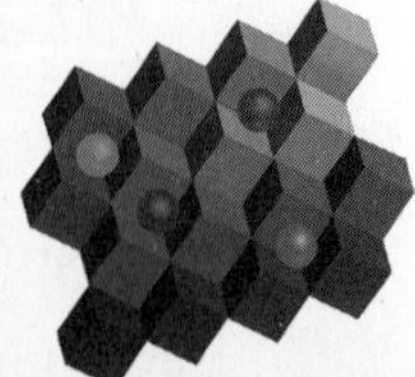

Property	Description
AutoSize	Causes the form to size itself automatically to show all its objects when opened
ScaleFontName	Name of form's scaling font
ScaleFontSize	Size of form's scaling font

MDI Property

If set to .T., the MDI property designates a form as MDI. This has the following effects:

- ✔ The form has a control box and title bar. The form's SysMenu property is set to .T.
- ✔ The form is moveable. The form's Moveable property is set to .T.
- ✔ The form is sizeable. The form's Sizeable property is set to .T.
- ✔ The form can be minimized. The form's Minimize property is set to .F.
- ✔ The form can be maximized. The form's Maximize property is set to .F.
- ✔ Menus created with DEFINE MENU...FORM are displayed in the menu bar of the application window. As each MDI form receives focus, the application window's menu changes.
- ✔ The form cannot be opened with READMODAL().

If the MDI property is set to .F., the effects include:

- ✔ Menus created with DEFINE MENU...FORM are displayed inside the form, under the title bar (if SysMenu is .T.).
- ✔ The form can be opened with READMODAL().

ScaleFont Properties

Together, the ScaleFontName and ScaleFontSize properties designate the font that is the basis of the form's coordinate plane—in other words, how many pixels on-screen is 1 unit. It determines the size and position of both the form and the controls which are contained in it.

Normally, you do not have to change this property.

Using the Right Control

Many different data entry and presentation controls are available. The right one for your work depends on a number of factors.

Each control has unique properties. Table 13.2 summarizes the type of control to use for your type of data.

Table 13.2
Control Usage

Control	Usage
Entryfield	Single fill-in item
Spinbox	Fill-in numeric or date item
Listbox	Select one or more items from a list
Combobox	Fill-in item or select one from a list
Radiobutton	Choose among a small number of choices
Checkbox	Toggle logical value
Browse	Show a table of data
Scrollbar	Choose from a range of values
Text	Display text
Image	Display a bitmap
Box	Draw a box
Pushbutton	Choose an action

Entryfield

The entryfield is the basic data entry control. It accepts a single typed item. Figure 13.1 shows two entryfields: blank and filled in.

The two labels, Name and Address, are not part of the entryfield, but are actually Text controls, which are explained later in this chapter.

Table 13.3 lists properties specific to entryfields.

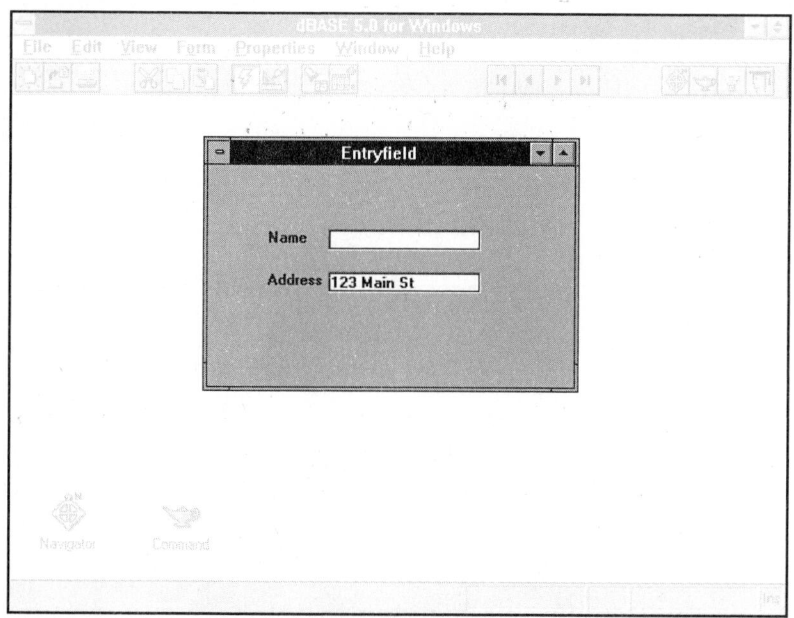

Figure 13.1
Two entryfields, one blank and one filled in.

Table 13.3
Entryfield Properties

Property	Description
Picture	Input mask
Function	Formats text displayed
Valid	Validates entry
ValidRequired	Forced validation even if entry is not changed
ValidErrorMsg	Message to display if validation fails
SelectAll	Determines whether value is selected upon gaining focus

Picture Property

The Picture property specifies an input mask, sometimes referred to as a *picture template.* This is a character string that specifies the type of characters that can be input at each position. For example, a Social Security Number is three digits, a hyphen, two digits, a hyphen, and four digits. In the Picture, digits are represented by the Picture symbol 9. Therefore, the definition for a Social Security Number field would look like:

```
define entryfield ieSSN ;
  property;
    picture "999-99-9999"
```

In addition to the 9, some other popular Picture symbols are listed in table 13.4.

Table 13.4
Basic Picture Symbols

Symbol	Description
9	Restricts entry of character data to numbers and restricts entry of numeric data to numbers and + and - signs
#	Restricts entry to numbers, spaces, periods, and + and - signs
!	Allows any character, but converts letters to uppercase
A	Restricts entry to letters
N	Restricts entry to letters and numbers; no symbols
Y	Restricts entry to Y, y, N, or n and restricts display to Y or N
X	Allows any character

Symbols that are letters can be in upper- or lowercase.

All the Picture symbols are listed in Appendix C. Non-symbol characters, such as the hyphen, are inserted verbatim and are skipped over when editing the entryfield; in other words, they cannot be edited. For the Social Security Number, only the nine digits must be typed; after the third digit, the cursor skips past the first hyphen, and after the fifth digit, the cursor skips past the second hyphen.

Although the Picture string is a character string, a Picture can be used for any type of data. For a numeric memvar, a Picture is required because a numeric memvar has no default width, unlike a numeric field or character memvar. For example, to restrict entry of a numeric memvar to four digits, use the Picture:

```
9999
```

Function Property

The Function property (not to be confused with the FUNCTION command) is a character string containing function symbols. Each symbol represents a particular formatting option. Appendix C lists all the function symbols; the most popular are listed in table 13.5.

Table 13.5
Basic Function Symbols

Symbol	Description
!	Converts letters to uppercase
A	Restricts entry to alphabetic characters
R	Inserts literal characters into display without including them in the field or memvar

The ! Function symbol differs from the ! Picture symbol in that the Function symbol applies to the entire entryfield; the Picture symbol signifies a particular character to be uppercase if that character happens to be a letter (any type of character is allowed with the ! Picture symbol). To force the entry of an uppercase letter, the ! Function must be applied along with an A picture symbol, as in the following example:

```
define entryfield ieMiddleInit ;
  property ;
    function "!", ;
    picture  "A"
```

All the Function symbols can be included in the Picture string by placing them at the front of the string, preceding them with the @ symbol, and leaving a space between the symbol(s) and the picture. For example, a function/picture combination could be achieved with a single picture string:

```
    picture "@! A"
```

Combining the two strings saves a little typing at the expense of readability, but is sometimes necessary when only a Picture string is allowed.

Validation

You can apply any type of validation routine that will return either a .T. or .F. to signify whether the entry is valid. Validation routines are covered in detail in Chapter 18, "Optimizing and Bulletproofing dBASE Applications." The Valid property is a function pointer or code block. If it is a function pointer, the function must return either a .T. or .F.; a code block must evaluate to .T. or .F.

If the validation routine returns .F. you are not allowed to leave the field. To supplement this, you can display a customized message that you store in the ValidErrorMsg property.

The ValidRequired property specifies whether the validation will be run even if the entryfield is not changed. This is only of concern if the value is invalid to begin with—if the value was set or changed without validating it beforehand. If ValidRequired is false (the default), the validation routine will not be run if the field is not changed; an invalid value will be allowed.

Even if ValidRequired is true, the validation check will be made only when you try to move the focus off the entryfield, which of course requires that the entryfield gain focus to begin with. In other words, if the entryfield is never touched, the value will not be checked to see whether it is valid, even if ValidRequired is true.

SelectAll Property

The SelectAll property should be set to true for proper Windows behavior. After an entryfield receives focus, the entire entry is selected (highlighted). If a non-cursor key is pressed, the entire entry will be replaced by that single character and the program will proceed as normal.

However, the default for SelectAll is false. You can leave it at its default if the field will more likely be added onto rather than replaced.

Spinbox

A spinbox is a special-purpose entryfield used to input numeric and date values. The spinbox includes a spinner, which increments and decrements the value by a set amount as long as the mouse is held down. Figure 13.2 shows a spinbox.

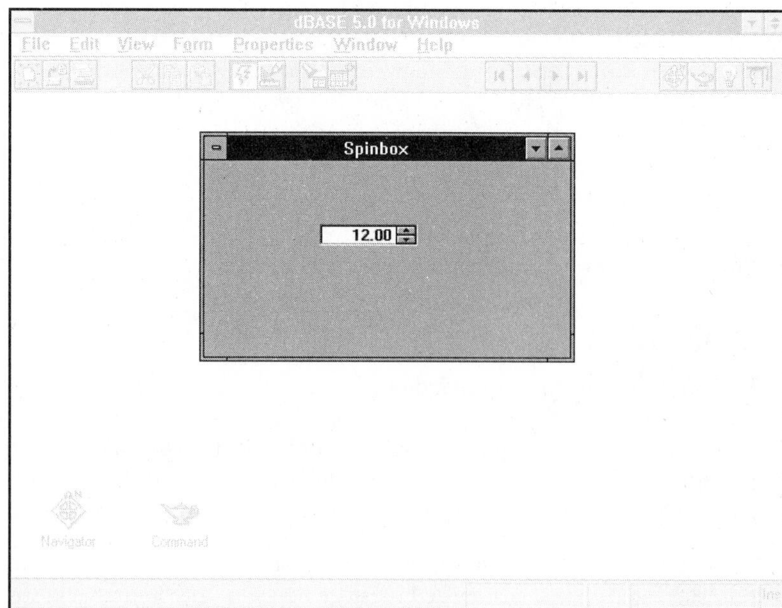

Figure 13.2
A spinbox.

In addition to typing the entry manually, you can click on the spinner to access the desired value. In other words, you can enter a value without taking your hands off the mouse. To do so, press and hold down the mouse button on the spinner; the value will increase or decrease until you lift the mouse button.

The spinbox has all the properties of an entryfield, plus five more, which are listed in table 13.6.

Table 13.6
Spinbox Properties

Property	Description
Step	Amount to change value for each click on the spinner
List	Disable manual entry and force use of spinner
RangeMin	Lower limit for entry
RangeMax	Upper limit for entry
RangeRequired	Forces range check on existing entries

Step Property

The Step property specifies the amount to increment or decrement the value for each click on the spinner. The default is 1—each click causes numbers to go up or down by 1 and dates to go forward or backward 1 day.

By changing the Step value, you can go up or down by 2, 10, 500, or any value you want. If the value is negative, the spinner will be reversed; clicking on the up arrow will decrease the value, and clicking on the down arrow will increase the value.

List Property

You can force the user to click on the spinner to select a value by setting the List property to true. The user will not be able to edit the number or date manually.

For example, used in conjunction with the Step property, this spinbox forces the user to use the spinner, and the values will be increments of 12. Here is an example:

```
define spinbox inEggs ;
  property ;
    step 12, ;
    list .t.
```

Range Checking

You can specify an upper or lower range or both for the entry. If the value is not in the range and you try to leave the entryfield, a message tells you what the range is. You must change the entry so that it falls within that range before you can leave the field.

The RangeMin property specifies the lower boundary for the value; the value must be equal to or greater than the RangeMin. The RangeMax property specifies the upper boundary for the value; the value must be equal to or less than the RangeMax property.

The RangeRequired property functions the same as the ValidRequired property. If it set to true, RangeRequired forces checking even if the entryfield is not changed.

Listbox

A listbox enables you to select one or more of a predefined set of choices. A common use of a listbox is in the Open dialog box: all the existing files appear in a listbox. Figure 13.3 shows such a listbox.

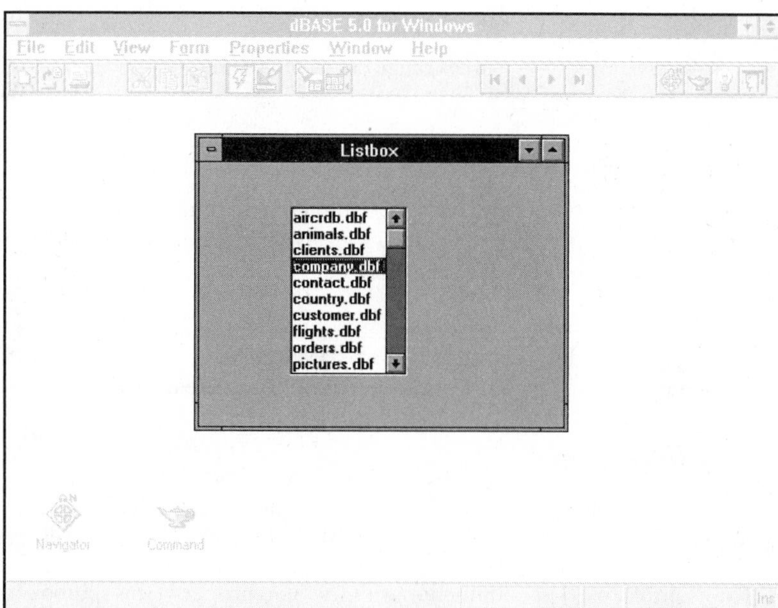

Figure 13.3
A file listbox.

Lists of files are easy to create in dBASE. You can create lists from a field in a table, or from an array. Regardless of a list's origins, only four properties apply specifically to listboxes as described in table 13.7.

Table 13.7
Listbox Properties

Property	Description
DataSource	Contents of the list
CurSel	Currently select listbox prompt
Sorted	Whether the contents are sorted
Multiple	Whether to allow multiple choices

Prompt Property

The Prompt property is a character string that specifies the contents of the listbox. The string must be in one of the following five forms:

1. `"FILE <filename skeleton>"`

   The <filename skeleton> uses standard Windows conventions for wild cards: ? for a single character and * for any group of characters. For example, to list only the DBF files in the current directory, the string would be:

   ```
   "FILE *.DBF"
   ```

2. `"FIELD <field name>"`

   The contents of the listbox are the contents of the field <field name>. The table containing the named field must be open when the listbox is active. Any filters that are active when the listbox is active will be honored.

3. `"STRUCTURE"`

   The prompts in the listbox consist of the field names of the currently selected table.

4. `"ARRAY <array name>"`

   All the elements of the named array are listed. If the array is multi-dimensional, the elements are listed in row-major order.

5. `"TABLES"`

   All the tables in the current SQL database are listed.

CurSel Property

The CurSel property represents the currently selected prompt in the listbox. If the first prompt is selected, CurSel is 1; if the second prompt is selected, CurSel is 2; and so on. In addition to returning the currently selected prompt, you can move the prompt by setting the CurSel property of a listbox to the desired prompt number.

Sorted Property

If the Sorted property is left false (the default), the prompts will appear in natural order: the order in which the files, records, field, elements, or tables appear. If Sorted is set to true, the prompts in the listbox are sorted alphanumerically.

Multiple Choices

You can enable the selection of more than one item by setting the Multiple property to true.

Combobox

A combobox is similar to an entryfield, except it also includes a number of pre-defined values to choose from in a drop-down listbox. You can force the entry to be one of those values, or just provide those values as suggestions. One of these is shown in figure 13.4, with the listbox dropped-down and retracted.

Figure 13.4
A combobox.

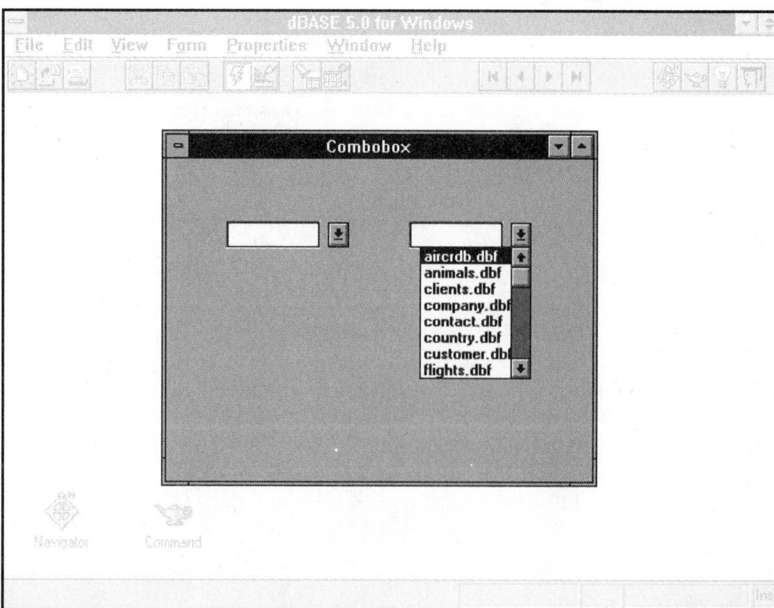

Because a combobox is a combination of entryfield and listbox, it shares some of the properties of both. The important similarities are listed in table 13.8.

Table 13.8
Combobox Properties

Property	Description
DataSource	Contents of the drop-down list
Sorted	Whether the contents of the drop-down list are sorted
Style	The style of the listbox

Style Property

There are three different styles of comboboxes.

Each style is identified by number, which is assigned to the Style property:

0 Simple

The drop-down list is always down. You can type an entry manually in the entry area, or pick from the list. This type is rarely used, since it takes up so much room on-screen.

1 DropDown

The same as Simple, but the drop-down list is up initially. You need to click the arrow on the right of the entrybox to drop the list down. This is the most common style.

2 DropDownList

The same as DropDown, but you must choose from the list; you cannot type an entry manually. This style is recommended whenever you have a long list of choices or the amount of space to display the choices is small. If the number of choices is small and space permits, radiobuttons may be used instead.

Radiobutton

Radiobuttons are used whenever you need to choose one selection from a few choices. If you change the selection, the previously selected item is deselected. Figure 13.5 shows a set of radiobuttons.

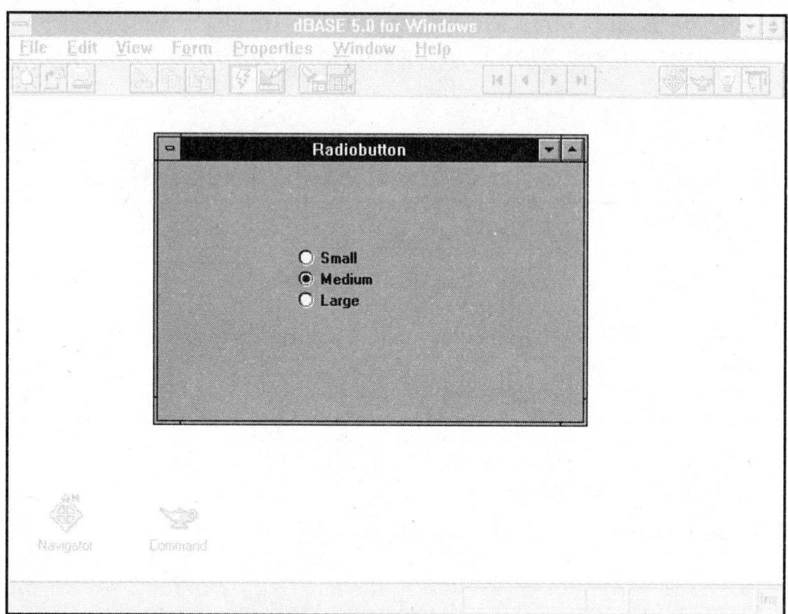

Figure 13.5 A set of radiobuttons.

The term radiobutton comes from older car radios, which had five or six buttons for preset stations. Pushing one button in caused any other button to be pushed back out, which made each station's button mutually exclusive.

Each radiobutton has a text label next to it. Because all the choices are visible simultaneously, you must have enough room to display the choices. Radiobuttons are therefore used when the number of choices is small. Overall they are also somewhat simpler to use, but slightly more complicated to implement. Table 13.9 lists the radiobutton-specific properties.

Table 13.9
Radiobutton Properties

Property	Description
Group	Indicates the start of a new group of pushbuttons
OldStyle	Chooses between the older and newer 3-D style radiobuttons
Text	Text label for radiobutton
TextLeft	Chooses between displaying the text label on the left or right side of the radiobutton

Radiobutton Groups

A form can have more than one group of radiobuttons. In each group only one radiobutton can be chosen.

Each group is assigned a ID number, which is stored in the radiobutton's GroupID property. All the buttons that have the same GroupID are in the same group. By default the ID number is 1. To create new groups, use any number you want.

The first radiobutton in a group has its Group property set to true. All other radiobuttons in the same group have their Group properties set to false. The next radiobutton in the tab order that has its Group property set to true is the first radiobutton in the next group.

OldStyle Property

The OldStyle property determines whether older 2-D style radiobuttons are used in place of the newer 3-D style radiobuttons.

Figure 13.6 shows both styles.

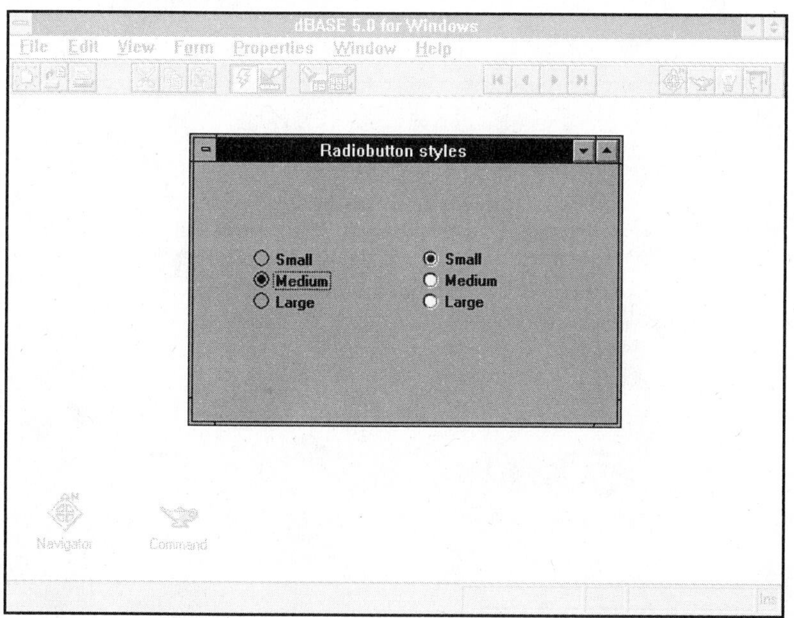

Figure 13.6
Older 2-D style radiobuttons (left) and newer 3-D style radiobuttons (right).

The OldStyle property must be set to .T. for each radiobutton you want to appear in the older 2-D style.

You should pick one style and set all your radiobuttons to that style.

Text Label

The text label for each radiobutton is stored in the Text property. The label is a character string. This text label does double duty. If the radiobutton is selected, the text label is stored in the location pointed to by the radiobutton's DataLink property. DataLink is explained in detail later in this chapter. All radiobuttons in the same group should also have the same DataLink.

Checkbox

A checkbox represents a logical value. Either it is checked or it is not; the value is true or it is false. Figure 13.7 shows a number of checkboxes grouped together to indicate available options on a car:

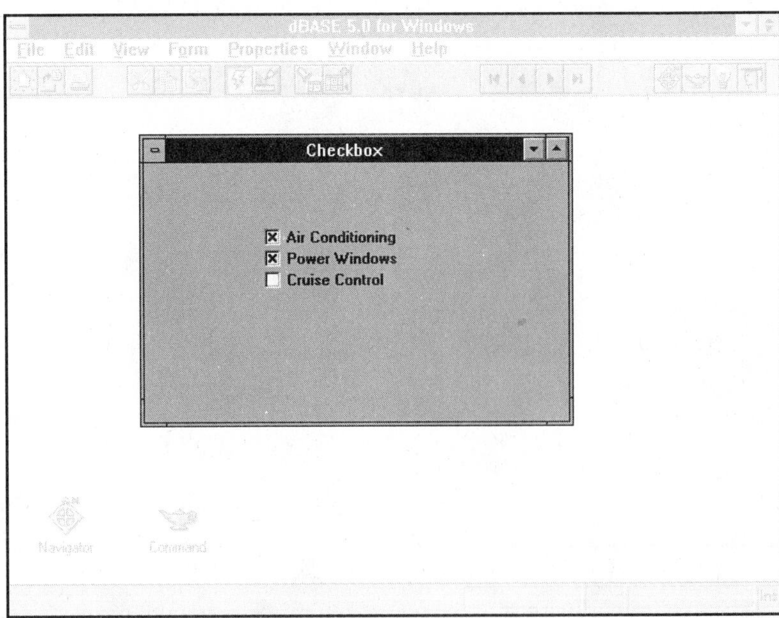

Figure 13.7 Car option checkboxes.

Checkboxes are simple. They only have a few specific properties; table 13.10 lists these properties.

Table 13.10
Checkbox Properties

Property	Description
OldStyle	Chooses between the older and newer 3-D style checkboxes
Text	Text label for checkbox

Both of these properties work the same way as they do with radiobuttons. The different checkbox styles are shown in figure 13.8.

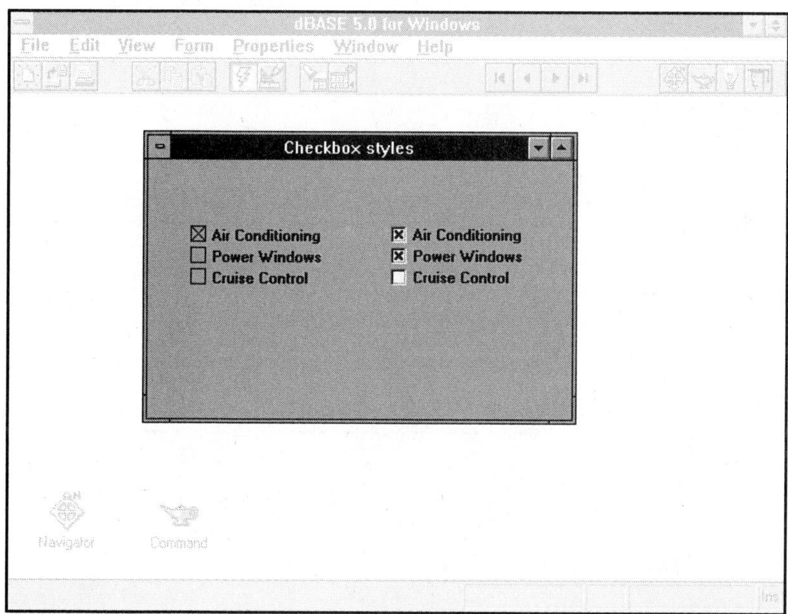

Figure 13.8
Older 2-D style checkboxes (left) and newer 3-D style checkboxes (right).

The text label only serves as a label; the value pointed to by the DataLink property is set to true or false, true if the checkbox is checked, and false if it is unchecked.

Browse

The browse control is the most complicated data entry control. It represents a full-fledged BROWSE inside a form. Many of the options of the BROWSE command have analogous properties in the browse control. Figure 13.9 shows a sample browse control.

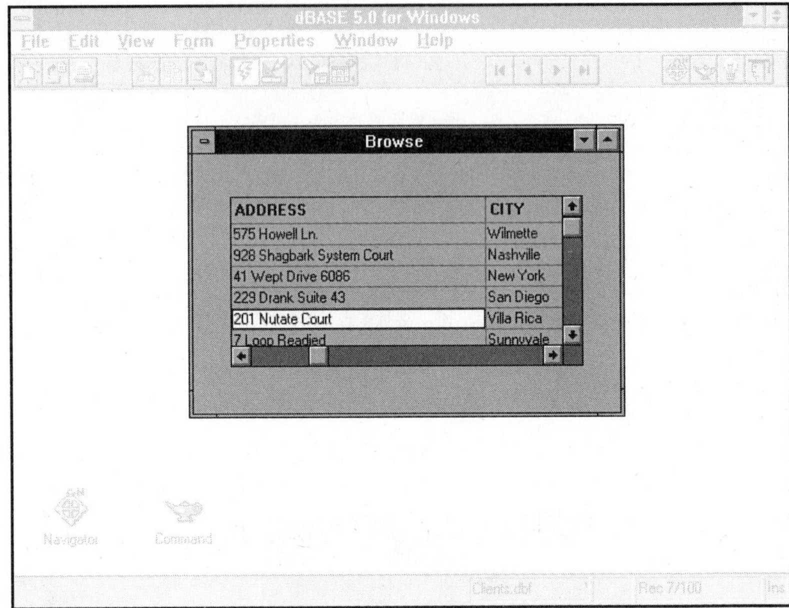

Figure 13.9
A browse control.

Table 13.11 lists the properties of a browse control.

Table 13.11
Browse Properties

Property	Description
Alias	Alias of table being browsed
Fields	List of fields and their field options
Mode	Indicates Browse, Form Edit, or Columnar Edit mode
Append	Allow adding new records to table
Delete	Allow changing of deletion marker
Follow	Follow record if it changes position in the current index order due to a change in the key field(s)
Modify	Allow changes to the data, or make data read-only
Toggle	Allow switching between browse modes

Alias Property

The Alias property is a character string containing the alias of the table being browsed. If the Alias property is left as its default blank character string, the table in the currently selected work area is browsed.

By using the Alias property, you can simultaneously BROWSE different tables in the same form.

Fields Property

The field list is a character string containing the names of the fields to be browsed with options for each field, if desired. The field list is stored in the Fields property. If left blank, the browse will show all the fields in the table.

If used at its simplest, the field list is composed of the field names you want to browse, separated by commas. Its full syntax is as follows:

```
<field 1>[<field option list 1>] ¦
  <calculated field 1>=<exp1>[<calc'd field option list 1>]
[, <field 2>[<field option list 2>] ¦
  <calculated field 2>=<exp2>[<calc'd field option list 2>]
[,...]]
```

The fields are initially displayed in the order they appear in the field list. They can be rearranged manually by the user.

A number of field options can apply to each field, but each set of options only apply to the field they are listed with. Table 13.12 lists the browse field options, many of which are analogous to entryfield properties.

Table 13.12
Browse Field Options

Option	Description
\<column width>	Width of column for field, used only for character fields
\B=<exp1>,<exp2>[\F]	Set a range between <exp1> and <exp2> inclusive, similar to RangeMin and RangeMax
\F	Force range check, even if value was not changed, similar to RangeRequired
\H=<cExp>	Make the column heading <cExp>

continues

Table 13.12, Continued
Browse Field Options

Option	Description
\P=<cExp>	Set the column's Picture/Function to <cExp>
\R	Make column read-only
\V=<lExp>[\F] [\E=<cExp>]	Allow entry only if <lExp> evaluates to true, similar to Valid
\F	Force validation, even if value was not changed, similar to ValidRequired
\E=<cExp>	Error message to display when validation fails, similar to ValidErrorMsg
\W=<lExp>	Allows entry to be edited only when <lExp> evaluates to true, similar to When

Instead of an actual field from a table, each column may display a calculated field. Calculated fields are read-only, and can have the column width and heading options. For example, to display the total charge for a rental car, that portion of the field list would look like:

```
total_rental = FEE * DAYS \20 \H="Total Charge"
```

BROWSE Modes

You can toggle between Browse and Edit modes by pressing the F2 key. The Mode property determines which mode the browse control is initially in, and tracks the changes. Setting the Toggle property to .F. disables the toggle feature.

The Mode property can be one of three numbers, each representing a different mode:

0 Browse

Browse mode uses row-and-column display, and shows multiple records.

1 Form Edit

Form Edit mode displays a single record.

2 Columnar Edit

Columnar Edit mode displays a single record, with one column for the field names and one column for the field values.

Text

A text control is not really a control, but merely informational text used to label entryfields, radiobutton groups, and other screen elements.

The only property of concern is the Text property, which contains the actual text.

Image

The image control displays a bitmap. This DataSource property designates the image itself, and must be in one of the following three forms:

1. "RESOURCE <resource ID> <DLL name>"
2. "FILENAME <filename>"

   Designates a BMP or PCX file
3. "BINARY <binary field>"

   Displays a bitmap stored in the named binary field

Pushbutton

Of all the controls, the pushbutton is the only action control. In other words, selecting a pushbutton actually does something, as opposed to displaying data. Standard pushbuttons are the OK and Cancel buttons, which accept and cancel a dialog box, respectively.

You can also create a menu screen by creating a number of pushbuttons and labeling them properly. Figure 13.10 shows a set of pushbuttons.

Pushbuttons are fairly simple controls. Their properties are listed in table 13.13.

Table 13.13
Pushbutton Properties

Property	Description
Text	Pushbutton label
Default	Indicates the default pushbutton
UpBitMap	Bitmap to display in pushbutton when it is in the up position, but not in focus

continues

Table 13.13, Continued
Pushbutton Properties

Property	Description
FocusBitMap	Bitmap to display in pushbutton when it is in the up position and has focus
DownBitMap	Bitmap to display in pushbutton when it is in the down position
DisabledBitMap	Bitmap to display in pushbutton when it is disabled
OnClick	Code to execute when button is clicked

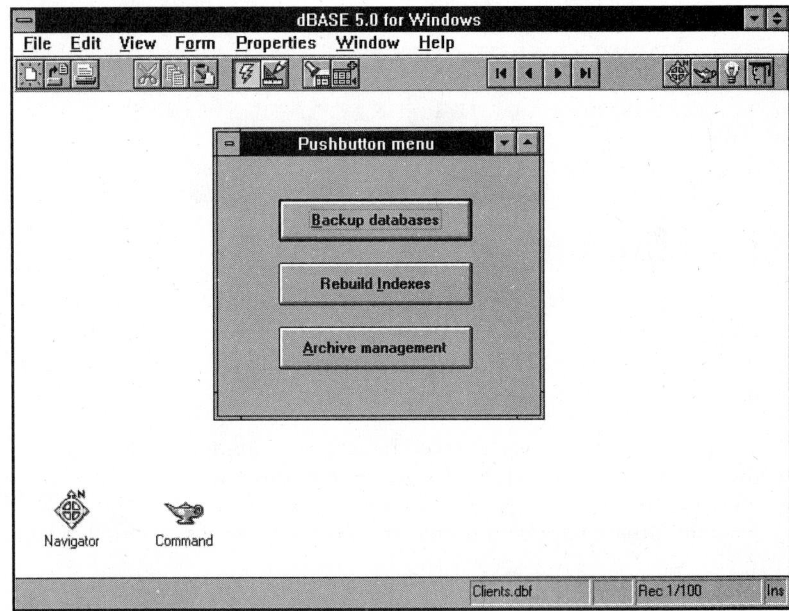

Figure 13.10
A menu screen made up of pushbuttons.

To put a text label in the pushbutton, set the Text property. The text is displayed centered in the pushbutton.

You can designate one pushbutton in your form as the default pushbutton by setting its Default property to true. The default pushbutton is displayed with a highlight around it, indicating that it is the default pushbutton. If a non-pushbutton control has focus and the user presses Enter, the default pushbutton is clicked.

Dialog boxes usually contain an OK pushbutton, which is designated as the default. You may also use the Default property to designate the pushbutton that the user is most likely or is the safest pushbutton to click.

To display a bitmap in the pushbutton, set the four BitMap properties for the different bitmaps to show depending on the button's state. These properties take the same arguments as the BitMap property for image controls.

The OnClick control is a function pointer or code block that is called when the button is clicked.

Common Control Properties

In addition to control-specific properties, all the controls have some properties in common.

Size and Position

The size and position of the controls is determined by the properties listed in table 13.14.

Table 13.14
Size and Position Properties

Property	Description
Height	Height of control
Width	Width of control
Top	Position of top end of control
Left	Position of left side of control

All the dimensions are based on the average height and width of the current active font. The Top and Left properties both default to 0, the top left corner of the form.

Font

The font displayed in the control is determined by the properties listed in table 13.15.

Table 13.15
Font Properties

Property	Description
FontName	Typeface
FontSize	Point size
FontBold	Use bold treatment
FontItalic	Use italic treatment
FontStrikout	Use strikeout treatment
FontUnderline	Use underline treatment

Color

The color of the control is determined by the properties listed in table 13.16.

Table 13.16
Color Properties

Property	Description
ColorNormal	Color of control
ColorHighlight	Color of highlighted text in entryfields, spinboxes, and listboxes

Both color properties are character strings containing dBASE-standard color strings.

Tab Order

The tab order of the controls is set through the Before property. The Before property contains the object reference of the control that the current control comes before in the tab order. In other words, the Before property points to the *next* control in the tab order.

Hot Key

The hot key for a control is designated in its Text property. The hot key letter must be a letter in the control's text label and is preceded by an ampersand. For those controls that

do not have a Text property, create a Text control immediately before it and set the hot there. For example, the following code creates a text label with the hot key "E", followed by a spinbox.

```
define text itEggs ;
  at 11,2 ;
  property ;
    text "&Eggs"
define spinbox isEggs ;
  at 12,2 ;
  property ;
    step 12, ;
    list .t.
```

Pressing Alt+E moves the focus to the spinbox.

Value Property

The actual value of the data-entry control—that is, the state of the checkbox or the text in the entryfield—is stored in the control's Value property.

DataLink Property

All the data-entry controls can be associated with a field or memvar, so that once the value in the control changes, the linked field or memvar changes too.

The DataLink property contains the name of the linked field or memvar.

NEW RIDERS
PUBLISHING

Part V

Developing dBASE for Windows Applications

Chapter Snapshot

This chapter examines the creation of the data entry portion of a modern modeless, event-driven application. Data entry includes adding new records, viewing and editing existing records, and deleting records. The topics covered in this chapter include:

When finished with this chapter, you should have a better understanding of how to plan and initiate your application needs.

Considerations When Programming a dBASE Application

By Kenneth Chan

There is no one right way to create an application. This argument is especially true for dBASE for Windows, which provides many different tools. When you see how an application is built, however, you will at the very least learn some ideas for building your own applications.

For anything but the simplest applications, some planning is required. You do not have to create a rigid planning regimen with dozens of pages of detailed documentation; you only need to think about the various parts of your application and what you want it to do.

Planning the Application

To begin planning your application, identify the reasons why the application is being created. Usually a database application automates some existing process. Two questions should be answered before you proceed:

- ✔ Can the process be automated?
- ✔ Will there be benefits from automating the process, and if so, what are the benefits?

If you have trouble answering the second question, remember that the simplest use of a database is the storage of vast amounts of information. This information is easily retrieved and printed, and is usually grouped or sorted so that you can find information quickly.

As a dBASE developer, you must consider a number of options when you begin an application. Although the dBASE environment provides several dozen different options at the beginning stages of an application, this chapter discusses only those options that are most commonly used.

Setting up DBASEWIN.INI

Whenever a new database session is created, that session uses the settings in the DBASEWIN.INI file. Therefore, it is important that the DBASEWIN.INI file contains the settings you want throughout the application. Changing the settings in DBASEWIN.INI avoids having to manually change settings every time you create a session.

The settings for DBASEWIN.INI can be accessed through the Desktop Properties dialog box, which is also activated by the SET command. Desktop Properties has a number of pages that are accessed by tabs at the bottom of the dialog box, as shown in figure 14.1.

Most of the pages have settings for applications. After you select the desired settings and click on OK, changes are saved to the DBASEWIN.INI file.

Make a backup of the DBASEWIN.INI file in case someone decides to change the settings.

Set Century On

On the Country page of the Desktop Properties shown in figure 14.1 is the Date group, which contains the Century checkbox. You may want to check this option. dBASE assumes that any two-digit year is in the 1900s. As the next millennium approaches, this assumption will be increasingly less accurate.

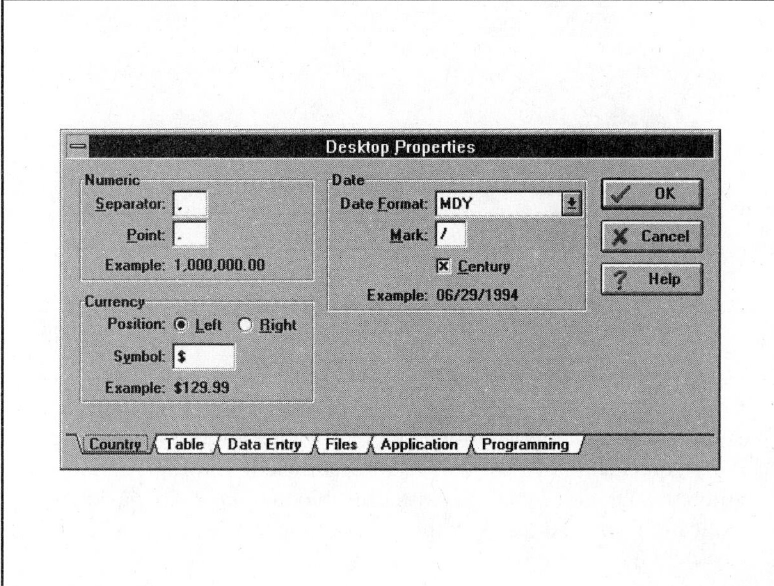

Figure 14.1
The Country page of Desktop Properties.

Although you can change the hundred-year range (for example, all two-digits dates are between 1950 and 2049), eventually dates in databases will span over one hundred years. Two-digit dates will become useless. Therefore, you may want to consider marking the Century checkbox and adopt four-digit years as the standard setting for your databases.

Set Lock Off

On the Table page in figure 14.2, in the Multiuser group, the Lock setting determines whether dBASE automatically performs file and record locks for certain operations. Some operations always perform a lock whether Lock is checked. When you REPLACE fields in a record, for example, the record is always locked.

The locks affected by the Lock setting are primarily table locks on summary operations such as COUNT, SUM, and REPORT FORM (see Appendix B for the complete list). To do these operations, the requested table must have no record or file locks, which reduces the availability of these summary commands.

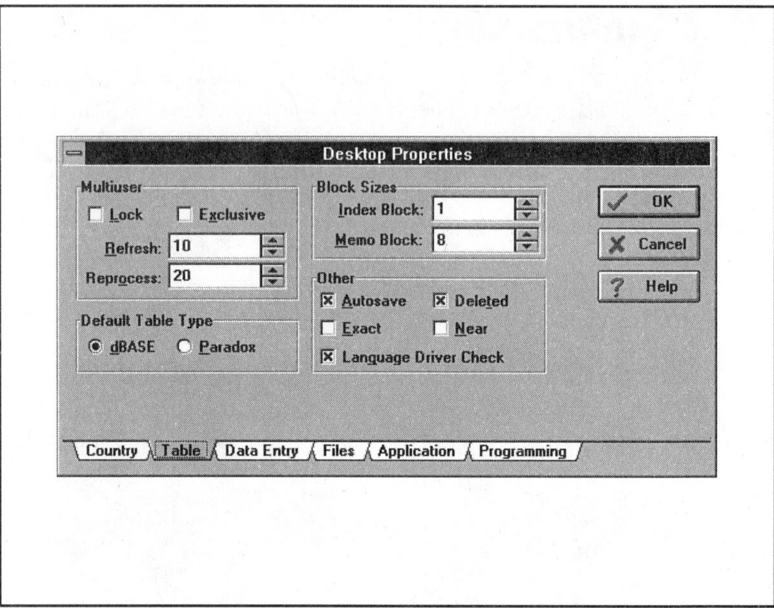

Figure 14.2 The Table page of Desktop Properties.

You can run these summary commands without locking the table, but you may get inaccurate results. These quick-and-dirty results are often sufficient, however, and if you need absolutely accurate results, you can always lock the table manually. To maximize the flexibility of your application, you can uncheck the Lock setting.

Set Exclusive Off

In a multiuser environment, Exclusive should be on only if you are using dBASE interactively, working on your own tables, and you want to avoid having to use all the tables exclusively. In an application environment, Exclusive should always be off.

Set Refresh to 10

The Refresh setting determines the interval in seconds between refreshes when viewing tables. A low Refresh setting of 1 or 2 puts an unnecessary burden on a network. A setting between 5 and 15 gives the user timely updates.

Set Reprocess to 1

Reprocess determines how many times dBASE retries a record or file lock before returning a failure code. Reprocess left at the default 0 causes dBASE to use its standard retry

dialog box. If you want to use your own dialog box, you can set Reprocess to 1. It may not work, however. This puts the locking process directly under the application's control.

Set Autosave On

On the Table page, in the Other group, Autosave determines whether changes are written to disk every time a record is updated. For safety reasons, you can turn it on. Write caching can eliminate some of the waiting associated with writing every change to the disk. For speed concerns in large set operations, you can temporarily turn it off.

Set Deleted On

In a change from dBASE IV, the Deleted setting defaults to on to match Paradox and SQL tables. When Deleted in on, records marked for deletion are not shown or included in any operations.

When a record is to be deleted, it should not only be marked for deletion, but also be blanked and recycled. See Chapter 27, "Networking dBASE for Windows," for a recycling technique, which is also useful in single-user environments.

Set Exact Off

Exact should be unchecked, to allow for partial string matches. When necessary, the exact equal operator == can be used, or Exact can be turned on temporarily.

Set Confirm On

On the Data Entry page (see fig 14.3), under Keyboard, Confirm can be turned on to require users to press Tab or another cursor key to move from one control to another. This is good practice because other Windows programs use this technique.

Set CUA Enter On

In a similar vein, CUA Enter should be on, unless your users are absolutely set on using Enter to move from field to field (dBASE IV used Enter). When CUA Enter is on, Enter clicks the default button and does not move from control to control.

Set Escape Off

During the testing phase, you can leave Escape on, but when you deliver the completed application, make sure it is off so that users cannot interrupt and cancel your application by simply pressing Esc.

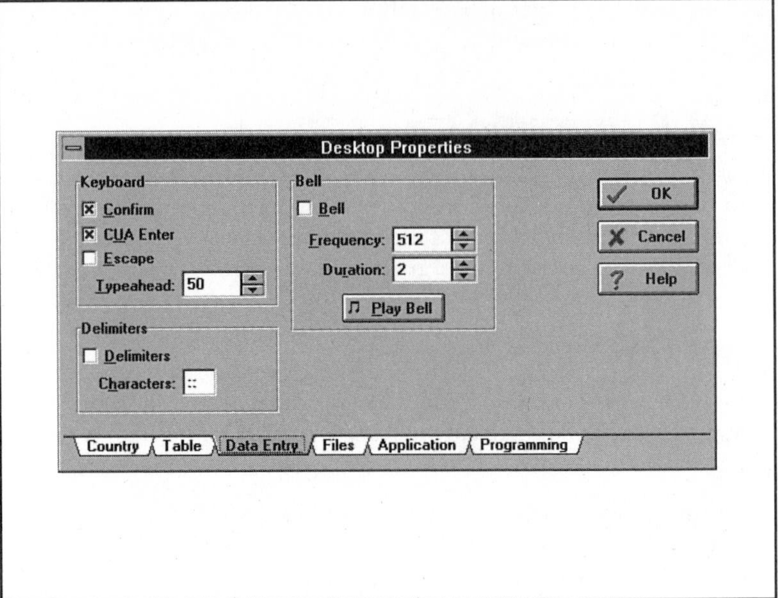

Figure 14.3 The Data Entry page of Desktop Properties.

Set Bell Off

In the Bell group, you should set the Frequency and Duration so that the tone of the bell is to your liking, and then turn the Bell off. The bell goes off more often than it should, and you can always ring the bell manually.

Set Talk Off

On the Programming page (see fig. 14.4), in the Command Output group, the Talk setting should be unchecked. If checked, the results of assignment statements and many other operations are echoed to the Command results window, unnecessarily slowing your application.

Set Safety On

In the Other group, make sure Safety is checked. This safeguards against simple errors, such as accidentally ZAPing a table. When you want to ZAP a table, temporarily turn off the Safety setting using this code:

```
set safety off
zap
set safety on
```

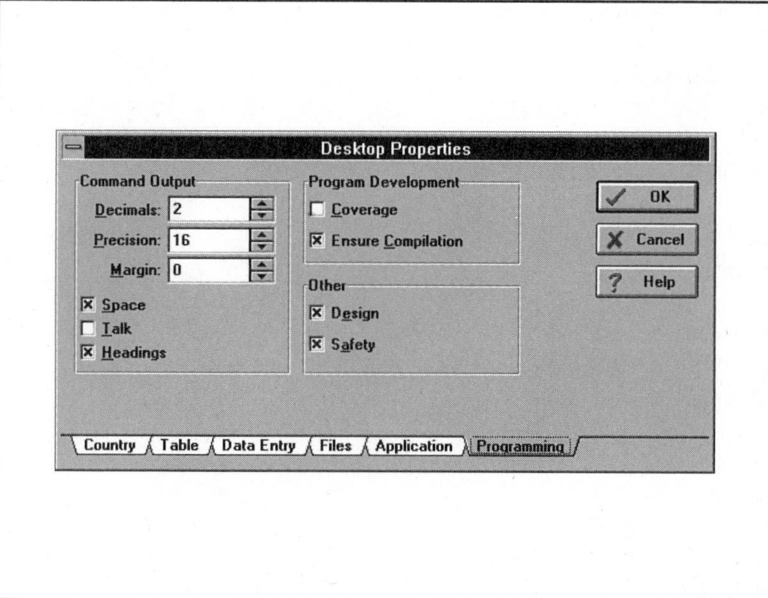

Figure 14.4 The Programming page of Desktop Properties.

Starting the Application

Before you run the application, a number of steps must be taken to set up the working environment, much like the process of booting your computer.

Size the screen

One of the first things your application must do is determine the screen size. In Windows, users can have 640x480, 800x600, 1024x768, and other screen resolutions. All the units that dBASE uses in its forms are dBASE screen units, which vary depending on the screen resolution and default font.

No built-in function exists to determine these units, but some Windows API functions can be called that provide the information:

```
PROCEDURE GetAppUnits
  *-- Get screen width/height in pixels
  extern CINT GetSystemMetrics( CINT ) USER.EXE
  #define SM_CXSCREEN 0
  #define SM_CYSCREEN 1
  _app.XPixels = GetSystemMetrics( SM_CXSCREEN )
  _app.YPixels = GetSystemMetrics( SM_CYSCREEN )
```

```
#define FORM_HEIGHT 4
#define FORM_WIDTH  20
define form fConfig ;
  property ;
    Text      "AutoConfig", ;
    Height    FORM_HEIGHT, ;
    Width     FORM_WIDTH, ;
    MDI       .F., ;
    Sizeable .F., ;
    SysMenu   .F.
fConfig.open()
extern CVOID GetWindowRect( CHANDLE, CPTR ) USER.EXE
#define W_LEFT    1
#define W_TOP     3
#define W_RIGHT   5
#define W_BOT     7
cRect = space( 8 )
GetWindowRect( fConfig.hWnd, cRect )
nWinHeight = ByteVal( cRect, W_BOT,  2 ) - ;
             ByteVal( cRect, W_TOP,  2 )
extern CVOID GetClientRect( CHANDLE, CPTR ) USER.EXE
#define C_WIDTH   5
#define C_HEIGHT  7
cRect = space( 8 )
GetClientRect( fConfig.hWnd, cRect )
nClientWidth  = ByteVal( cRect, C_WIDTH,  2 )
nClientHeight = ByteVal( cRect, C_HEIGHT, 2 )
fConfig.close()
_app.XUnits  = nClientWidth  / FORM_WIDTH
_app.YUnits  = nClientHeight / FORM_HEIGHT
_app.THeight = ( nWinHeight - nClientHeight ) / ;
               _app.YUnits
*-- Calculate screen size in dBASE units
_app.Width   = _app.XPixels / _app.XUnits
_app.Height  = _app.YPixels / _app.YUnits
RETURN
FUNCTION ByteVal( cArg, nPos, nLen )
  if pcount() < 3
    nLen = 1
  endif
  local nRet, nPtr
  nRet = 0
```

```
    for nPtr = nPos to nPos + nLen - 1
      nRet = nRet + asc( substr( cArg, nPtr, 1 )) * ;
             256 ^ ( nPtr - nPos )
    endfor
  RETURN nRet
```

The first step in the code listed here is to get the screen size in pixels. The Windows API function GETSYSTEMMETRICS() performs this function. API functions are first declared using the EXTERN syntax, as described in Appendix A, and then called.

Next, a form of a pre-determined size is created and opened. At this point, the form is a window in Windows, and is assigned a *handle*. This handle is stored as the hWnd property of the form. By using another API function, GETWINDOWRECT(), you receive the size of the resulting window on-screen in pixels.

The size specified when the form is created indicates the size of the inside of the form, and does not include things such as the title bar and resize border. The inside of a form is also referred to as the window's client area; its size is returned by the API function GETCLIENTRECT().

At this point, you have the size of the window in pixels, and the size you defined the form to be. Simple division will get the number of pixels per row and column for dBASE. Dividing those numbers into the screen size gives you the number of rows and columns on-screen.

Where do you store the results? The natural place is to make these values properties of the _app object so that they are always accessible. GETAPPUNITS() creates the following properties of the _app object:

Table 14.1
Measurements Created By GETAPPUNITS()

Property	Description
_app.Width	Width of screen in dBASE units
_app.Height	Height of screen in dBASE units
_app.THeight	Height of all title bars in dBASE units
_app.XUnits	Number of pixels per dBASE column
_app.YUnits	Number of pixels per dBASE row
_app.XPixels	Screen width in pixels
_app.YPixels	Screen height in pixels

THeight is the height of the standard title bar used in all the windows. When specifying the top left location of a form on screen, that includes the title bar, but when specifying the size of the form, it does not. Therefore you need to include the height of the title bar when calculating the position of the form.

The size of the resize borders are not calculated by GETAPPUNITS(). These are generally a handful of pixels and do not influence the positioning of a form a great deal.

Reseed the Randomizer

If you are using the RAND() function to generate pseudo-random numbers in your application, you should reseed the randomizer one time at the beginning of your application. Reseeding the randomizer repeatedly should be avoided because it results in "less random" numbers.

You can use the system clock as the seed value instead of using a predetermined value. This gives you an essentially random seed value. To do this, call the RAND() function with a seed value of -1:

```
rand( -1 ) && Reseed the randomizer
```

The next two chapters detail queries and reports.

Chapter Snapshot

This chapter covers the use of predefined and free-form queries. Specific topics include:

When finished with this chapter, you will be able to create your own queries so that you can better access and manage the data in your tables.

Programming Queries into Applications

By Kenneth Chan

When you have reams and reams of data organized into nicely structured tables, what do you do with that data? You "ask" questions of the data—or in database parlance, you make *queries.*

This chapter helps you make use of simple fill-in queries and predefined queries, and helps you manage free-form queries and utilizing high-performance filters. By using queries, your data becomes even more useful and easy to access than before. You can limit the amount of fields in a particular query, for instance. This chapter takes you through the programming code needed to create your own queries.

Understanding Queries

If you look at the code of any generated QBE file, you see the basic process of creating a query. You must first open all the necessary tables. You then access each table's active index so that the tables can be related and the results will be seen in the proper order. Next, you relate the tables.

If necessary, you can apply a field list so that the fields in separate tables appear to be in one flat file. You also can apply a filter to the tables to get only the records that match the specified criteria.

The Browsing or Editing options show you the results of the query. You can also apply summary operations, such as counting the number of matching records or calculate an average.

Of course, a QBE file is nothing but straight program code you can easily insert into your application. You can generate a stock set of queries interactively and then use the resulting QBE code.

You might, however, want to let the user make queries. You would essentially let the user work with dBASE's built-in interactive query facilities. Unfortunately, those facilities are not always appropriate for end-users; they are complex and potentially dangerous. What is needed is a friendly and safe front-end that the user can interact with, and then the application can build the query code in the background and present the user with the results.

In between a friendly front-end and the actual database is a *fill-in query*, where the structure of the query is the same, but the matching criteria in individual fields varies. For example, finding the orders that different customers made utilizes the same query structure, no matter which customer is being examined. The only difference is the customer name that is used to run the query. Each type of query requires a different approach.

Using Predefined Queries

Use the interactive query facility to build a predefined or "canned" query. You then need to create a form to present the query results. You can make a copy of an existing data entry form and then modify it, or build a form from scratch. The form's View property is then set to the QBE.

To view the query, simply run the form by opening it. dBASE will run the query when it opens the form, and the form will present the results.

Creating Fill-in Queries

A fill-in query starts with a simple form that presents the user with a limited subset of fields. The user can fill in any number of the fields with a value. The query assumes that a record must match all the filled-in fields to be listed.

Now that you have the matching criteria, you can generate a QBE file yourself. Like a PRG, a QBE is a simple text file. You can use SET ALTERNATE to generate a new QBE file containing the instructions for the query. A companion form to the query expects the same-named QBE file. You can run that form, which will run your generated query, and the answer will be generated.

Taking Advantage of High-Performance Filters

dBASE offers high-performance filters, which use indexes to produce query results much faster than other query search methods.

The basic concept of a filter is a logical condition. For example:

```
upper( LAST_NAME ) = "SMITH"
```

You take this condition and apply it to each record in the table. If the condition is true for that table, then that record is shown. A simple filter is slow because the search for matches proceeds sequentially through the table.

For example, if you have a browse with 10 rows, dBASE will attempt to show you 10 matching records to fill the browse. Suppose only 9 matching records are found, and they are all in the first half of the table. After dBASE finds and displays the nine matching records by checking every single record down the line, it will continue to search the rest of the entire table for the tenth record, which it will not find.

High-performance filters take advantage of fields being indexed. dBASE can find matching records in an index quickly, whether or not that index is active.

For the high-performance filter to work, the filter condition must compare an indexed value with an expression. All the comparison operators =, <, and > are supported; the $ operator is not.

The indexed value in the filter expression must match an existing index key expression. In the example expression used for simple filters, that expression can be optimized if there is an index tag with the key expression:

```
upper( LAST_NAME )
```

If there is an index on just plain LAST_NAME, there is no optimization.

Chapter Snapshot

Often the entire reason for using a database application is to produce printed results. Computers are nice, but paper is still the king in most offices. This chapter covers the information you will need to print out a report from dBASE. Specifically, you learn about the following topics:

You learn in this chapter about Crystal Reports for dBASE, a very capable report generator. You learn how to use this very important feature of dBASE, which enables you to preview your report before you print it.

Programming Reports into Applications

By Kenneth Chan

Sometimes reports are straight listings of tables on paper. Other times, you want to print the results of a query. These typical database-oriented reports are best handled by defining a report in a report generator such as Crystal Reports, then simply calling this predefined report from your application.

Sometimes, you need to print something on paper that your report generator cannot handle. In those cases, you must write a custom report in which you have complete control of the content of the output.

In either case, your first hurdle is that your report must be able to print on a wide variety of printers. Luckily, Windows manages most of that for you, and makes switching between printers very simple.

Managing Printers

Windows handles the task of defining printers and ports through the Printer control panel. After the printers are set up, dBASE provides a simple way for the user to choose a printer from within your application.

The CHOOSEPRINTER() function opens dBASE's Print Setup dialog box, as shown in figure 16.1.

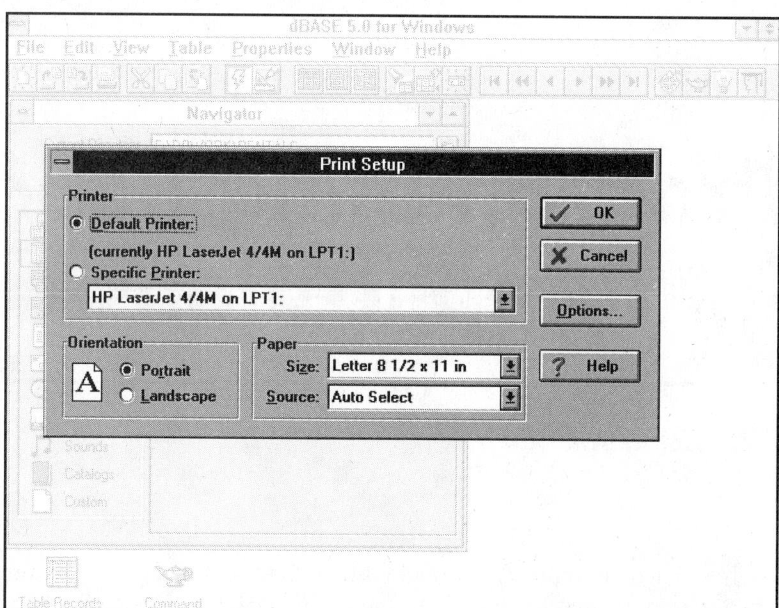

Figure 16.1 The Print Setup dialog box.

CHOOSEPRINTER() returns .T. if the user selects OK, or .F. if the user selects Cancel. If a selection is made, dBASE changes the appropriate settings (namely the _pdriver, _plength, and _porientation system memory variables and the printer destination selected by the SET PRINTER TO command) and that printer becomes the default printer. For details about the printer system memory variables, see the section "Understanding Printer System Memory Variables" later in this chapter.

Using Predefined Reports

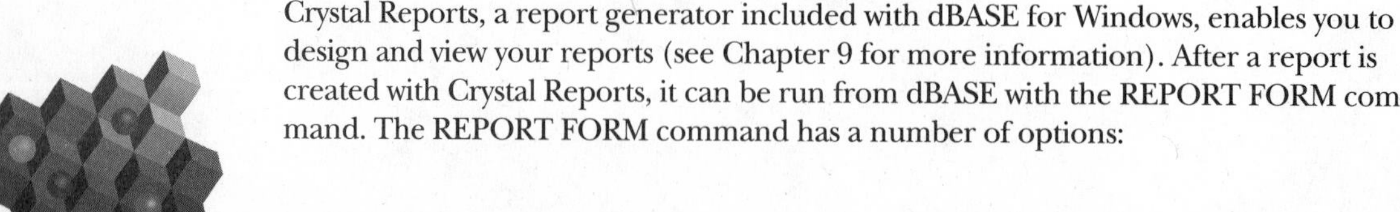

Crystal Reports, a report generator included with dBASE for Windows, enables you to design and view your reports (see Chapter 9 for more information). After a report is created with Crystal Reports, it can be run from dBASE with the REPORT FORM command. The REPORT FORM command has a number of options:

```
REPORT FORM <filename 1> ¦ ? ¦ <filename skeleton>
  [<scope>]
  [FOR <condition 1>]
  [WHILE <condition 2>]
  [HEADING <expC>]
  [NOEJECT]
  [PLAIN]
  [SUMMARY]
  [TO FILE <filename 2> ¦ ?] ¦ [TO PRINTER]
```

The simplest version of the following command:

```
report form <filename>
```

runs the report stored in the file named <filename>. The report is run against the entire currently selected table in its current index order, honoring any filters and relations.

Using either the ? or <filename skeleton> option opens a dialog box that enables the user to select which report to print. This approach is usually not used in a finished application.

The <scope>, FOR, and WHILE conditions limit the records printed by the report. These conditions are in addition to any filters placed on the currently selected table. You have a lot of flexibility to control the records. You can define limits on the table, then add limits when you print the report that are in effect only while you are printing the report.

The HEADING, NOEJECT, PLAIN, and SUMMARY options are used primarily with dBASE IV FRM reports, not with RPT Crystal Reports.

To output the report to the printer instead of to a window, use the TO PRINTER option. This sends the report to the default printer, as chosen by the CHOOSEPRINTER() function. Alternately, you can send the printer output to a file with the TO FILE option. This file will contain the printer control codes for the default Windows printer.

Writing Custom Reports

You can use dBASE's streaming output capabilities (discussed later in this chapter) to send text to the printer. To do so, you need to understand printer system memory variables.

Understanding Printer System Memory Variables

dBASE maintains a number of system memory variables, most of which are printer system memory variables. Printer system memory variables contain settings that control dBASE

IV-style reports. Most of these memory variables are not used by the reports created by Crystal Reports, but they can be used by the application for generating custom reports.

The _pdriver Memory Variable

The _pdriver memory variable contains the name of the printer driver to use. The string has two parts, separated by a comma. The first part is the name of the driver file, and the second part is the name of the printer itself. The value of the _pdriver variable for the LaserJet 4 printer, for example, would be the following:

```
"HPPCL5E,HP LaserJet 4/4M"
```

You can manually assign a value to _pdriver, but it is usually not necessary because the CHOOSEPRINTER() function sets it for you.

The _porientation Memory Variable

The _porientation memory variable can be one of two choices, as listed in table 16.1.

Table 16.1
_porientation Settings

Setting	Description
PORTRAIT	Portrait orientation
LANDSCAPE	Landscape orientation

The _porientation memory variable tells the printer driver which orientation you want the output to be. This system memory variable also is set by the CHOOSEPRINTER() function. Setting _porientation automatically resets the _plength system memory variable, which is discussed next.

The _plength Memory Variable

The _plength memory variable indicates the number of lines in the current page. It is set by the CHOOSEPRINTER() function, and whenever you set the _porientation system memory variable. The setting assumes six lines per inch on a standard 8-1/2×11-inch piece of paper with quarter-inch margins on the top and bottom.

When printing on odd-sized paper, such as checks, you will have to set the _plength manually. _plength is used during printing to detect when the end of the page has been reached.

The _ppitch Memory Variable

The _ppitch memory variable affects the printer font pitch, and can be one of four settings, as listed in table 16.2.

Table 16.2
_ppitch Settings

Setting	Description
PICA	10 characters per inch
ELITE	12 characters per inch
CONDENSED	15-17 characters per inch
DEFAULT	The current setting of the printer

The "PICA" and "ELITE" settings are standard, but the "CONDENSED" setting varies from printer to printer, generally ranging from 15-17 characters per inch. Setting _ppitch to "DEFAULT" means that no pitch selection is made, and that the current setting on the printer is used.

Pitch refers to the number of characters per inch that fit horizontally. This is an older basis of measurement, and is used primarily for monospaced or non-proportional fonts. Font sizes in Windows are usually expressed in points, which refer to the height of the font.

There is no printer system memory variable that controls point size. Point sizes are defined in the [Fonts] settings in the DBASEWIN.INI file, and selected through the STYLE option of the streaming output commands, both of which are explained later.

The _peject Memory Variable

The _peject memory variable can be one of the four settings listed in table 16.3.

Table 16.3
_peject Settings

Setting	Description
BEFORE	Ejects page before the start of the print job
AFTER	Ejects page after the end of the print job

continues

Table 16.3, Continued
_peject Settings

Setting	Description
BOTH	Ejects page both before and after print job
NONE	Does not eject pages

You should pay particular attention to the _peject memory variable when using laser printers, because they hold a page until it is full of text or has been ejected. If a report does not end with a page eject, then the last page of the report stays in the printer until the next print job resets the printer or ejects a page.

There are two ways to eject a page: with form or line feeds (both discussed in the following section).

The _padvance Memory Variable

There are two basic ways to advance paper in a printer, a form feed and a line feed. A *form feed* tells the printer to eject the current page and load a new page, whereas a *line feed* signals the printer to move forward (down the page) by one line.

On page printers (such as laser printers and inkjets), you easily can move the printing to any position on the page, not just down one line. But dBASE does not have any commands to utilize this feature.

The _padvance memory variable controls how dBASE ejects a page, and can be one of the two settings listed in table 16.4.

Table 16.4
_padvance Settings

Setting	Description
FORMFEED	Ejects page by issuing a form feed
LINEFEED	Ejects page by issuing the required number of line feeds

The "FORMFEED" setting is generally preferred. The "LINEFEED" setting is used only when using odd-sized pages, such as when printing on checks, and requires that _plength be set properly.

Directing Streaming Output to the Printer

The ? and ?? commands are not used in dBASE screen forms. By default, their output goes to the results pane of the Command windows, which is usually not visible during an application. Their output can be directed to a file or the printer, and they support options for fonts, styles, and positioning.

By issuing the SET PRINTER ON command, output from the ? and ?? commands is sent to both the Command results window and the printer. The SET CONSOLE OFF command disables output to the Command results window. Using both these commands thereby directs streaming output to the printer instead of the screen.

Using the ? and ?? Commands

The ? and ?? commands are basically the same command. The only difference is that the ? command prints a carriage return and line feed before outputting text. Their syntax is:

```
? [<exp 1>
    [PICTURE <format expC>]
    [FUNCTION <function expC>]
    [AT <column expN>]
    [STYLE [<fontstyle expN>] [<fontstyle expC>] ]
  [,<exp 2>]
  [,]
```

By itself, the ? command prints a blank line, moving the current print position to the beginning of the next line. A bare ?? prints nothing, and is essentially a do-nothing command.

The ? and ?? commands print the results of any number of expressions, separated by commas. The expressions do not have to be all the same type. The ? and ?? commands can be thought of as the "what is?" command. For example:

```
? 2 + 2
```

can be read as, "What is two plus two?" The result 4 is displayed in the results pane of the Command window.

All text results are printed left-justified, while numeric values are printed right-justified. Numeric values are displayed in a column wide enough to accommodate 10 digits to the left of the decimal point, and as many decimal places as specified by the Decimals setting.

The default Decimals setting is 2. The commas that separate the expressions result in single spaces if the Space is on, the default. For example, the following commands:

```
? "Many", 1234567890
? "Few ", 2
```

result in:

```
Many 1234567890.00
Few            200
```

Each expression can individually have any or all of the four ?/?? options: Picture, Function, At, or Style.

The Picture Option

The Picture option specifies a *picture* that defines the display format of the output. With pictures, you can set the number of columns a number displays in, show asterisks instead of leading zeroes, display characters as uppercase, and other formatting options. All Picture options are listed in Appendix A. For example, you can limit the width of numbers printed with the following picture:

```
? "Some", 123 picture "999"
```

which results in the following:

```
Some 123
```

The Function Option

The Function option specifies a formatting function that should be applied to the expression. All Function options are listed in Appendix A. For example, you can force the output of a string to be uppercase:

```
? cdow( date()) function "!"
```

which results in something such as the following:

```
WEDNESDAY
```

The At Option

You can specify the horizontal position of the expression with the At option. The postion is a specific column number, and that column number is converted into inches through the _ppitch setting. For example, if _ppitch is “ELITE”, which is 12 characters per inch, then column 24 is two inches from the left margin of the page. If _ppitch is “PICA”, which is 10 characters per inch, then column 24 is 2.4 inches from the left margin. The column number does not have to be an integer.

Always set the _ppitch to "PICA", which makes it easy to calculate positions—just multiply the inch measurement by 10. You can use other fonts through the Style option.

The Style Option

The Style option enables you to select both a typeface and a font style. Typefaces are defined in the [Fonts] section of DBASEWIN.INI. Each different typeface and size combination is assigned a *font number*, from 1 to (a theoretical) 32,766, for example:

```
[Fonts]
1=Times New Roman,12,ROMAN
2=Arial,10,SWISS
3=Arial,24,SWISS
```

There are three items for each font: the typeface name, the font size, and the font family.

To determine the appropriate values for any font, you can use the following command:

```
? getfont()
```

The GETFONT() function displays a standard font selection dialog box and returns the corresponding values. You can then create a new font entry in the DBASEWIN.INI file. You must restart dBASE for the [Fonts] changes to take effect.

The Font Style Options are presented in table 16.5.

Table 16.5
Font Style Options

Option	Description
B	Bold
I	Italic
U	Underline

continues

Table 16.5, Continued
Font Style Options

Option	Description
R	Superscript
L	Subscript

If you need to specify only the typeface, you can use the typeface number; for example, the following prints the text in typeface number 1:

```
? "Some text" style 1
```

If you use a font style—with or without a typeface number—make the style option a character string, combining all the options together. For example, the following prints the text in bold italic typeface number 2:

```
? "Some bold italic text" style "2BI"
```

Chapter Snapshot

Problems or "bugs" in software applications can be a headache—not to mention a drain of your time. Luckily, dBASE has several options that enable you to zap bugs in the computer software. In this chapter, you learn the following:

Each of the preceding commands automates a different portion of the software life cycle (develop, test, debug, validate, deliver).

Debugging dBASE Applications

By Chris Bolte

After you have developed your dBASE application, the next step is to test it and find all the errors, or "bugs." Several tools have been added to dBASE for Windows to simplify these tasks. You learn in this chapter how to use the Debugger to track variables, values, and lines and to fix errors.

You also learn about the coverage analyzer to determine how often each block of code is executed. Other dBASE features that can help you out include commands that help create test records in your data tables.

This chapter first outlines the types of problems or bugs you might encounter when using dBASE, then the chapter outlines how you can deal with those problems.

Identifying the Problem

Problems in your code show up in three different categories:

- ✔ The program does not compile.
- ✔ The program compiles but does not run.
- ✔ The program compiles and runs but does not work as designed.

The first two errors, called compile-time and run-time errors, can be detected for you by dBASE for Windows.

Finding Compile-Time Errors

The dBASE Compiler reads the PRG file you have generated and translates it into an object module for dBASE to execute. During this process, the Compiler reads each line of code and checks to see whether it matches the syntax of a valid dBASE command or function. If it does not match, the Compiler generates an error message indicating the line where it thinks the error occurs.

To have the Compiler analyze your program, type the following command in the command window:

```
COMPILE program name
```

The program name can be any dBASE code file (*.PRG, *.WFM, *.MNU, *.RPT, and so on). This command creates the object module, but doesn't run the program.

Another way to invoke the Compiler is to run the program by using the DO command. You can issue this command in the command window, from the menu bar, or from the SpeedMenu.

The Compiler detects such errors as a missing ENDIF, mismatched parentheses, and some spelling errors. When the Compiler detects an error, the Program Alert window appears as shown in figure 17.1.

The Program Alert window shows the error that was detected, the name of the file that was being compiled, the name of the module that was being compiled, and the line where the error occurred. You are given four options:

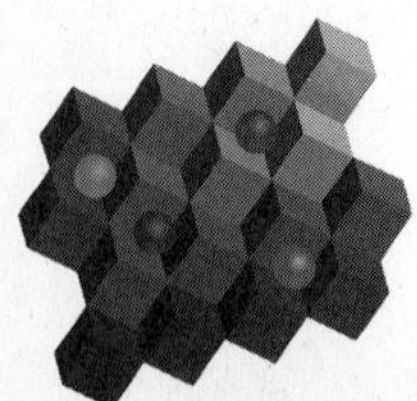

- ✔ Choose Cancel to close the window and cancel the compile.
- ✔ Choose Help to bring up help on the error.
- ✔ Choose Fix to edit the program and fix the error.
- ✔ Choose Ignore to continue compiling to find other errors.

Examine the error message so that you have an idea what dBASE thinks the problem is. If you want to attempt to correct the error, choose Fix, and the Program Editor window appears with your routine loaded and the cursor positioned at the line where the error occurred. Type in any changes needed to correct the error.

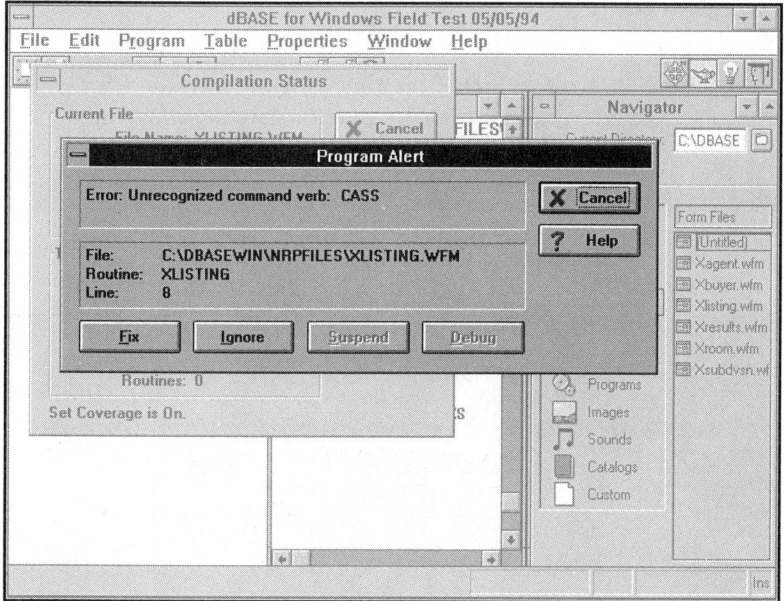

Figure 17.1
The Program Alert window describes the error found.

A dBASE command line that is terminated with the continuation character ';' can't be followed by a blank line.

Select File, Save, and then choose Close. The Compiler starts compiling from where it detected the error and stopped. You can continue to correct all the syntax errors in your program that are found by the Compiler.

Finding Run-Time Errors

After you have corrected all the compile-time errors, you can run your program by using any of the methods previously discussed. Additional errors that were not caught by the Compiler can cause your program to fail to run. While trying to run your program, dBASE detects syntax errors that were not found by the Compiler. It also finds file-access errors and limit errors such as divide-by-zero.

Errors are automatically trapped in dBASE for Windows, so the SET TRAP ON command from dBASE for DOS is not required.

When dBASE detects a run-time error, it displays the same Program Alert window used in the compile-time errors. Note in figure 17.2, however, that you have two additional options now:

- ✔ Choose Suspend to stop program execution temporarily.
- ✔ Choose Debug to start the Debugger with the current program loaded.

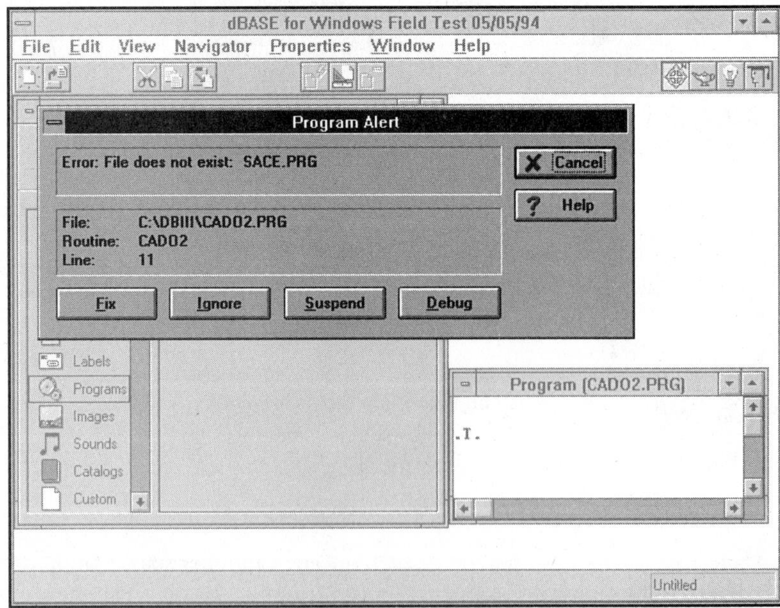

Figure 17.2 dBASE provides additional choices for detected run-time errors.

The Suspend option enables you to use the command window to enter commands and functions. One use for this approach would be to establish values for global variables that are used but not defined in a procedure. The Debugger, which you access with the Debug option, is discussed later in this chapter, in the section called "Using the Debugger." The remaining Program Alert options work the same way they do when you're compiling a program. As with compile-time errors, when you choose Fix, the errors are easy to find because the cursor is on the line where dBASE found the error. You just correct the error, and save and close the file.

Spelling errors in the names of functions and procedures can be detected at run-time. Although the first four characters are sufficient for dBASE to recognize a command or function, if one of the first four letters is mistyped, an error occurs.

Detecting Logic Errors

After you have corrected all the compile-time and run-time errors, you can run your program and validate the user interface and the output. If the screen does not appear the way that you expect, or the output is incorrect, a logic error has occurred in your program. Neither the Compiler nor the dBASE run-time engine can detect logic errors. To determine where these errors occur, dBASE for Windows provides a powerful Debugger. See the next section for details.

Using the Debugger

A powerful Debugger has been added to dBASE for Windows. The Debugger runs as a separate task in its own window under the Windows executive and communicates with the dBASE task running in a separate window. You can start the Debugger directly from the Program Manager, by choosing Debug from a Program Alert window, or by selecting a file and then choosing Debug from the SpeedMenu or the Run menu.

The Debugger displays four windows:

- ✔ The *Module window* displays module code.
- ✔ The *Watch window* displays the values being monitored.
- ✔ The *Break window* displays all breakpoints set.
- ✔ The *Stack window* displays a list of the procedures followed to get to this point.

Loading a Module

When you start the Debugger from the Program Manager, the Debugger starts with no file loaded in the Module window, as shown in figure 17.3. Anytime you are in the Debugger, you can add a module to the Module window.

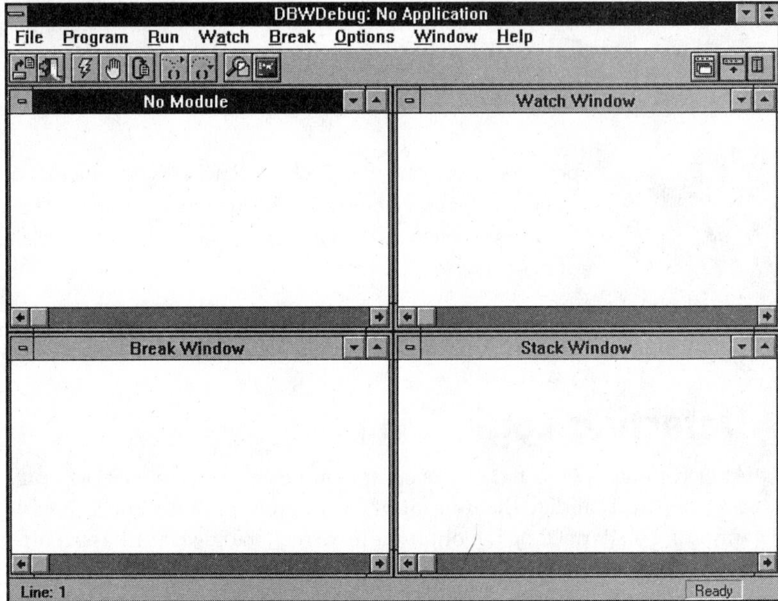

Figure 17.3 The Debugger with no files loaded.

You can load into the Debugger any dBASE code file accessible from your system. Follow these steps to load a file:

Loading a File

Select **F**ile, **O**pen Text File, or choose the Load file from the SpeedMenu	A standard file selection window is presented to enable you to access any drive or directory
Select a file	
Choose OK to load the file	

The Debugger issues a command to start dBASE for Windows, running the module you select. The module is also loaded into the Module window, and the cursor is positioned at the first executable line of code. If you have started the Debugger from dBASE for Windows, you also are in this state when you enter the Debugger. And you can use this

method to open additional routines in the Debugger. Although the Debugger automatically opens any subroutine that is called in your procedure, you might want to view the code before it is called.

Monitoring Values

The best way to detect a logic error in your code is to monitor the values of variables that are used to control loops and conditionals. To monitor a variable, follow the steps in the next exercise.

Monitoring a Variable

Use the mouse or cursor to scroll the highlight line in the Module window down to a variable that you want to monitor	
When the appropriate variable name is highlighted, click the right mouse button to bring up the SpeedMenu	
Select Watch	The Watch query window appears
Confirm the variable name, and then choose OK	

The variable is added to the Watch window with the current value shown in parentheses. All variables start as Variable Undefined. As you step through the code, the value in the Watch window changes.

Setting Breakpoints

To have your program stop at a certain line, scroll down to that line in the Module window. Move the mouse to the left end of the line. When the cursor turns to a stop sign, click to set a breakpoint. The line number is added to the Break window. Click on the line again to clear the breakpoint. Another way to add a line-oriented break is to select Break, Add and insert the routine name and line number in the Add Breakpoint window that appears (see fig. 17.4).

You also can set a breakpoint on a specific condition that is met in your program. Select Break, Add from the menu bar, and the Add Breakpoint window appears. In the Condition box, enter the condition that you want to be true when the program stops, such as

```
(Testvar=14 .or. Testvar=13)
```

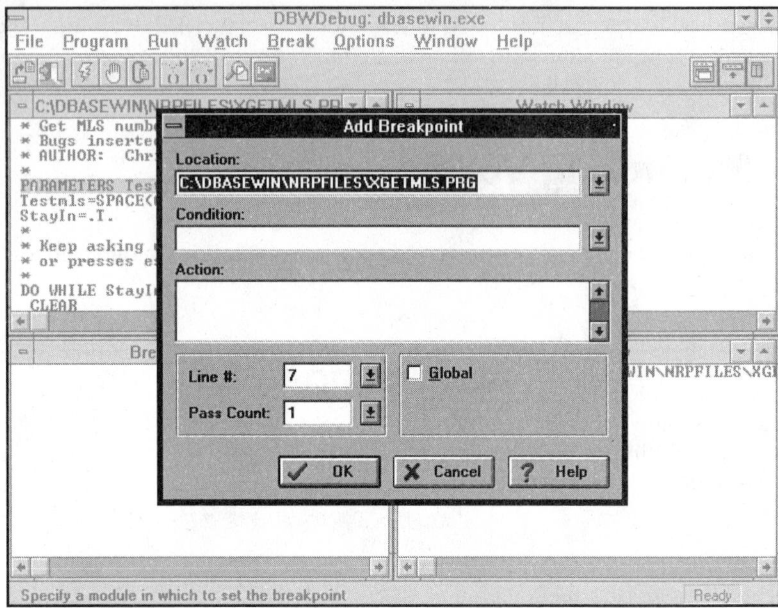

Figure 17.4 The Add Breakpoint window.

Note at the bottom of the window the check box labeled <u>G</u>lobal. If you check this box, the Location field is dimmed, and your break affects all your procedures. You can determine if the break occurs when the condition evaluates to True, or whenever the condition changes.

The Passes field enables you to determine how many times the condition must be met before the break is triggered. This feature is useful for finding errors that seem to occur only after the program has run through several iterations.

The Add Breakpoint window also enables you to perform an action other than simply stopping on a break. In the Action field, you can enter a section of dBASE code that is to be executed whenever the break occurs. An example would be to examine the contents of a data table: BROWSE EQUIPMNT.

Examining the Stack Trace

The Stack window in the Debugger shows the path that dBASE followed to get to your subroutine. Each line and procedure that issued a call is listed in the window. To see quickly the code associated with the line, double-click on the line in the Stack window. The code in the Module window displays the line that you selected and the surrounding lines.

Running a Debug Session

To help illustrate how a debugging session might go, the following routine was created with several minor errors in it:

```
PROCEDURE XGetMLS
* XGetMLS.PRG
* Get MLS number for the HomeGuide system
* Bugs inserted to demonstrate the Debugger
* AUTHOR:  Chris Bolte           DATE:  May 94
*
PARAMETERS Testmls,StayIn
Testmls=SPACE(8)
StayIn=.T.
*
* Keep asking until user doesn't leave blank
* or presses Esc
*
DO WHILE StayIn .AND. (Testmls=SACE(8) .OR. LEN(Testmls)=0)
 CLEAR
 @1,25 SAY "GET MLS NUMBER"
 @7,5 SAY "Enter the MLS number:  "  GET TestMLS PICTURE;
 "99999999"
 READ
 Exitkey=Readkey()
* Check for the Esc key to exit
 IF ExitKEY=11
  StayIn=.F.
 EMDIF
ENDDO
RETURN
```

The following exercise takes you through the procedure you might follow to correct the errors in the program.

Correcting Errors in the Program

The first step in the debugging process is to try to compile the code. Click in the command window, and select Program, Compile. Select the file from the file list

The Compiler starts

continues

continued

In this exercise, the Compiler finds an error in the third to last line, where ENDIF is misspelled as EMDIF. The Program Alert window shown in figure 17.5 appears.

Choose **F**ix to start the Program Editor; Change the *M* to an **N**, select **F**ile, Sa**v**e, and choose **C**lose	Saves the changes

The Compiler finishes compiling and presents a status window, shown in figure 17.6.

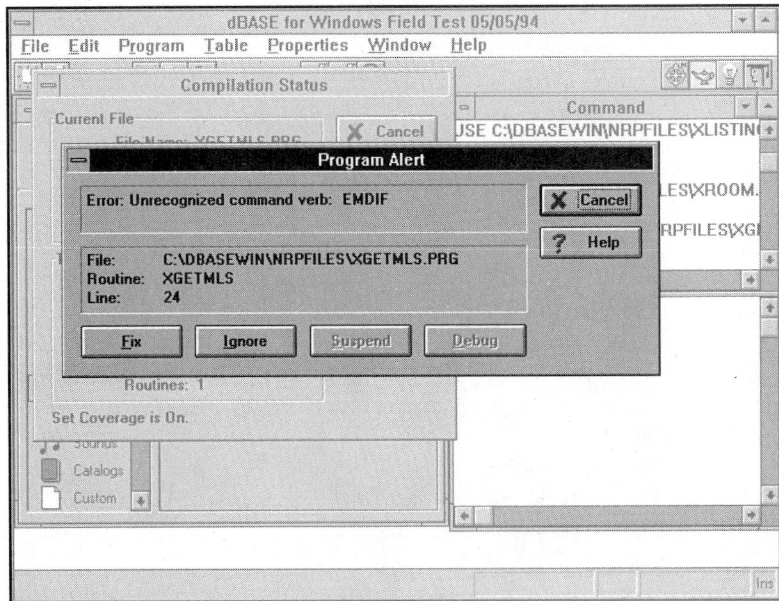

Figure 17.5
Catching compile-time errors.

The next step is to try to run the program by using the DO command.

In the command window, type **DO XGETMLS**	The Program Alert window shown in figure 17.7 appears when dBASE can't find a program called SACE
Choose **F**ix, and add the **P** in the word to make it *SPACE*	
Select **F**ile, Sa**v**e, and choose Close	The data input screen shown in figure 17.8 then appears in the output window

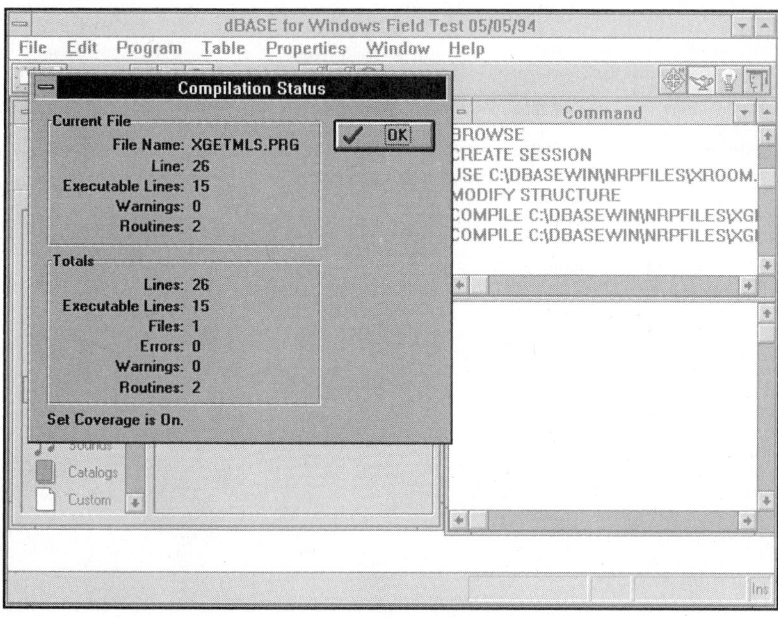

Figure 17.6 Getting compile-time statistics.

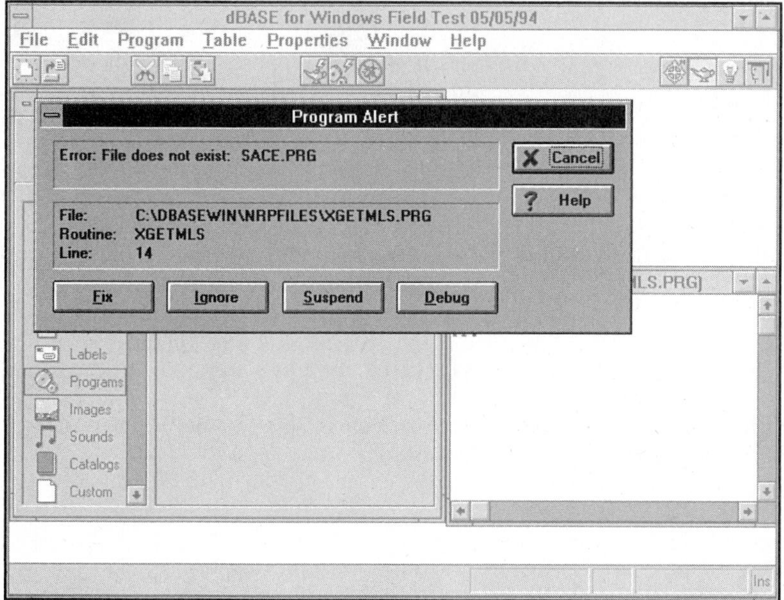

Figure 17.7 Catching run-time errors.

continues

continued

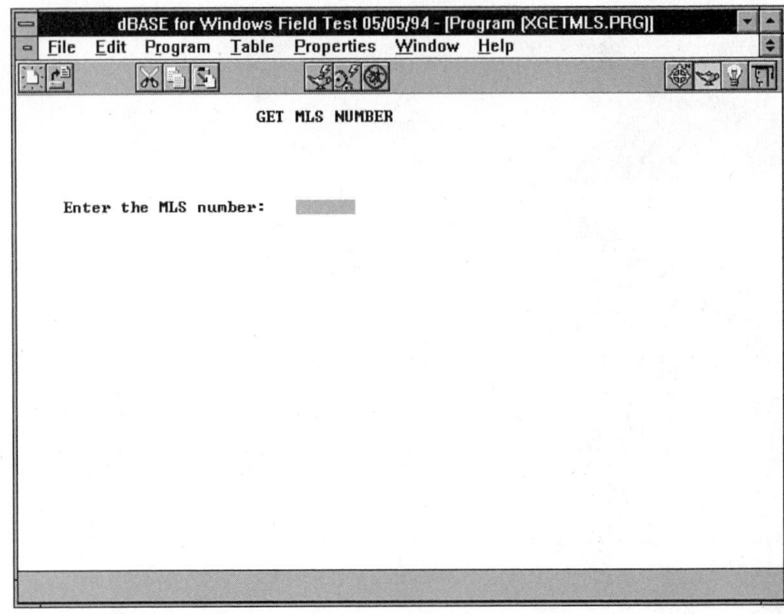

Figure 17.8
Get user input for data.

To test the exit-handling routine, press Esc

The program is supposed to close the screen and exit, but dBASE does not exit

Type **99999999** to exit the routine

Start the Debugger by typing **DEBUG XGETMLS** in the command window

The Debugger is started with XGETMLS loaded in the Module window. As shown in figure 17.9, the first executable line is highlighted, and the Stack window indicates that the program is at line 7 in file XGETMLS.PRG

Add TestMLS, StayIn, and ExitKey to the Watch window by highlighting each one and selecting Watch from the SpeedMenu

Each variable is added to the Watch window, as shown in figure 17.10

Click on the left side of the IF statement to add a line breakpoint

The breakpoint appears in the Break window, as shown in figure 17.11. Notice that the Stack window still shows the next executable line to be line 7, even though you have been scrolling through the code in the Module window

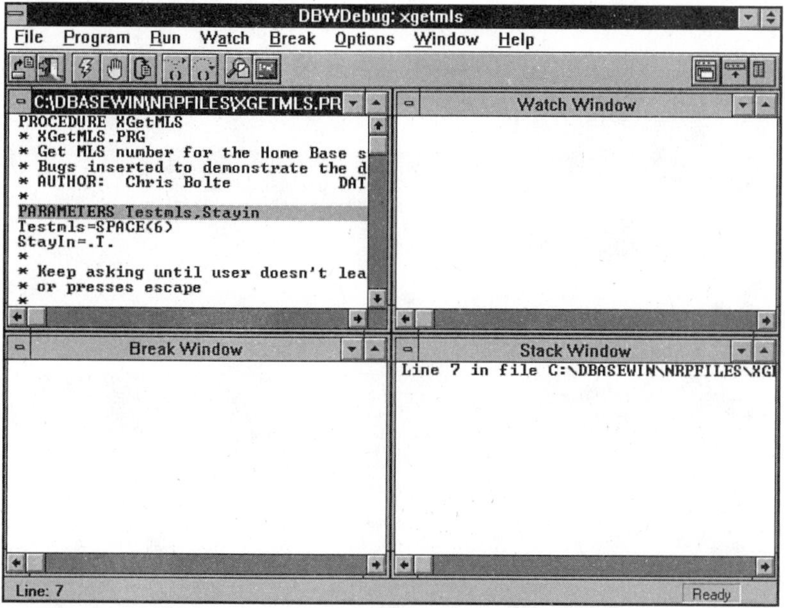

Figure 17.9 Starting the Debugger.

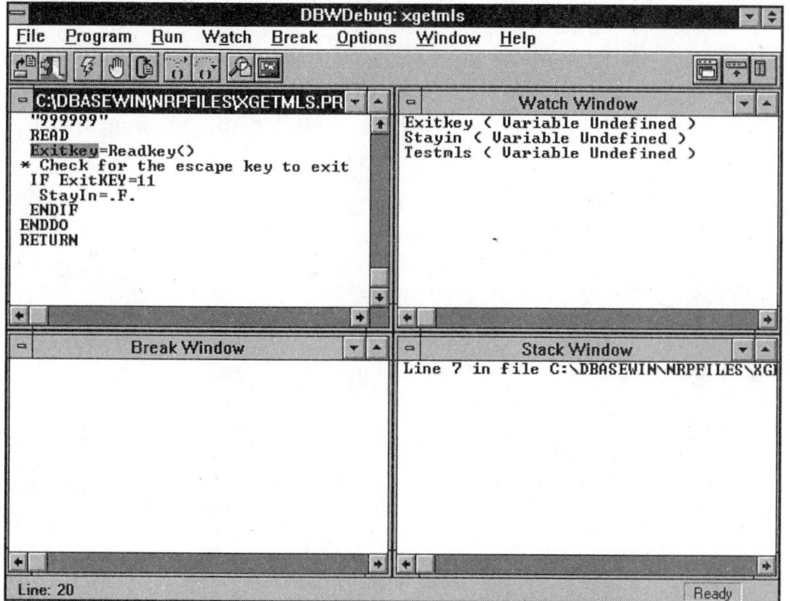

Figure 17.10 Inserting variables to watch.

continues

continued

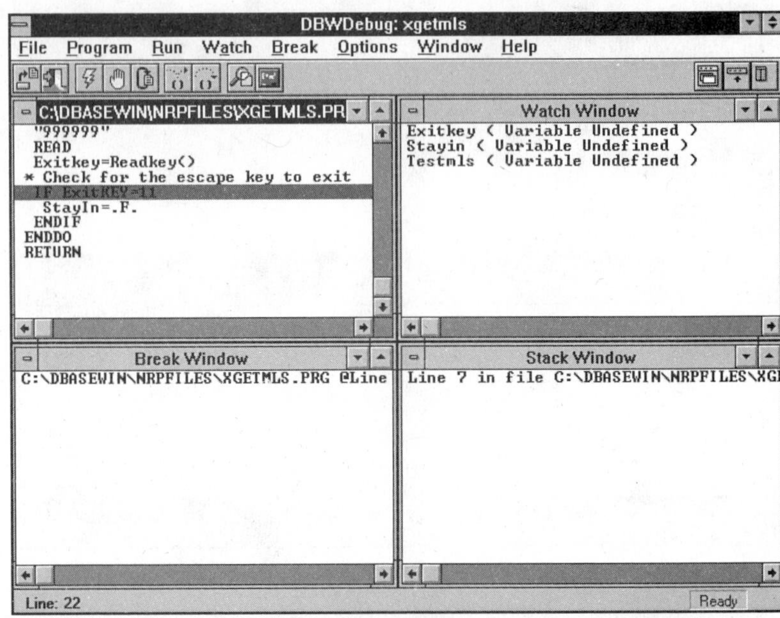

Figure 17.11 Inserting a line breakpoint.

Click on the Run icon to run the program to the breakpoint	The Debugger goes to the background, and the dBASE output window appears with the request for an MLS showing, as in figure 17.8
Press Esc to test the exit handler	The Debugger comes back to the front, with the cursor at the breakpoint

Notice that the values in the Watch window have been updated for all variables. The current value for ExitKey is 12, but the test in your IF statement is for 11.

Use the SpeedMenu to choose Fix	The program editor starts
Change the 11 to **12**, select File, Save, and close the file	
Test the routine once more by typing **DO XGETMLS** in the command window	The routine runs without error

Using the Coverage Analyzer

One of the major problems in the past with code testing was determining whether all branches of the code had been executed. The coverage analysis feature of dBASE for Windows enables you to determine quickly whether blocks are not being executed. The coverage analyzer creates a text file that you can print or edit with any text editor. The analyzer provides summaries of the information in the coverage text file.

Type the following command to have dBASE analyze the contents of the coverage file:

```
DISPLAY program name.COV ALL
```

You get a report that shows how many times each block of code was executed. Blocks of code are identified by line numbers. A block is defined as any section of code set off in a loop or a conditional clause.

Using the Random Data Generator

Random records are helpful for displaying forms and reports with data in the fields. You can create test records for any data table that exists on the disk. The GENERATE command inserts sample information in all character, numeric, and date fields. All existing records are preserved, and the number of new records requested are added at the end of the table. Character fields are filled with varying-length mixed upper- and lowercase character data. Date fields and numeric fields receive random dates and numbers. Memo fields receive an entry, but no data is entered into the memo. Binary fields do not receive data.

The GENERATE <expN> command is new in dBASE for Windows.

To take advantage of this feature, first open the table into which you want to insert test records, by using the USE command or double-clicking on the table in the Navigator. Then, to create the test records, activate the Table Utilities menu by selecting Table, Table Utilities. Choose Generate Records from the menu to bring up a window in which you can enter the number of records to be created. You also can enter the command in the command window as **GENERATE <expN>**.

Chapter Snapshot

This chapter covers both optimizing and bulletproofing, making your applications run faster and safer. Specific points covered are:

There are two facets to making your applications run faster: making the dBASE language run faster, and making the database operations more efficient.

Optimizing and Bulletproofing dBASE Applications

By Kenneth Chan

There is nothing worse in a database application than bad data. Bad data can take a number of forms. The data can be the wrong type—like having letters in Social Security numbers. You can have missing data, or the data can be internally corrupted.

Another major pitfall is a slow application. Of course, users want their applications to be as snappy as possible. More often than not, people are impressed by pure speed—no matter how ingenious or elegant your program may be.

Language Optimizations

Like any programming language, dBASE has a number of do's and don'ts. Several functions work better than others in dBASE, and the following sections detail these functions.

Use IIF() Instead of IF

The IIF() function should be used whenever a value is needed, and the value depends on some condition. For example, the following code:

```
if DATE_DATE < date()
  ? "OVERDUE"
else
  ? "Current"
endif
```

prints "OVERDUE" or "Current", depending on whether the DATE_DUE has passed or not.

Instead of the preceding five-line IF block, a single-line IIF() works faster:

```
? iif( DATE_DUE < date(), "OVERDUE", "Current" )
```

Note that IIF() can only be used where an expression is expected. For example, the following IF block:

```
if cdow( date()) = "Friday"
  report form WEEKEND
else
  report form DAILY
endif
```

prints the week-end report on Fridays.

The following IIF() command is not a legal equivalent:

```
report form iif( cdow( date()) = "FRIDAY", ;
                 "WEEKEND", "DAILY" )
```

because the REPORT FORM command expects a literal name, not an expression. In other words, if the command was the following:

```
report form "WEEKEND"
```

then the IIF() would work. But the command is not, so the IIF() does not apply here.

Use CASE Instead of A Nested IIF()

You can nest IIF()s, but if there are more than a few of them, the command probably executes faster if you use a CASE structure instead.

Avoid ¯o Substitution

¯o substitution causes dBASE to evaluate and recompile an entire command—a relatively slow process. The difference is especially noticeable in a loop, where the command line is reevaluated over and over again.

There are a number of ways to avoid ¯o substitution. When dealing with file names, you can use file name indirection instead. For example, instead of the following:

```
cFile = "CUSTOMER"
use &cFile.
```

with indirection, it would be:

```
cFile = "CUSTOMER"
use ( cFile )
```

Another way to avoid ¯o substitution is with code blocks. With dBASE IV, if you wanted a subroutine to evaluate an expression, you would pass a character string containing the expression, and have the subroutine evaluate the string as an ¯o. See the following code for an example:

```
do PrintThis with "date()"
...
PROCEDURE PrintThis
  parameter cExpr
  ? &cExpr
RETURN
```

With dBASE for Windows, you can use a code block instead:

```
do PrintThis with {date()}
...
PROCEDURE PrintThis
  parameter kExpr
  ? kExpr()
RETURN
```

Use the M-> Alias For Memvars

Whenever you specify a field or memvar name without an alias, dBASE first checks to see if the name is a field name in the current work area. This wastes a little bit of time—more if the current table has a lot of fields.

You can skip this check by prefacing all memvars with the m-> memvar alias; for example: m->cLName instead of just cLName.

Even though naming conventions with capitalization and type prefacing are used for the programmer's benefit, dBASE is case-insensitive. It does not recognize those conventions to determine whether a name is a memvar or a field.

The m-> alias also avoids a bit of ambiguity when using memvar or field names. Especially when writing generic procedures, you are not guaranteed that the name you are using for a memvar is not the name of a field.

If there is both a memvar and field with the same name, without an alias, the field takes precedence.

By using the m-> alias whenever the two can be confused, you can avoid some potentially perplexing problems. For example, instead of just:

```
nRet = nAmt * nTax
```

use:

```
nRet = m->nAmt * m->nTax
```

Note that it is unnecessary to preface nRet with m->, because the = operator works only with memvars, and not with fields.

Call Functions As Seldom As Possible

If you are going to use the same function value repeatedly, you can assign the function value to a memvar once, and use that memvar repeatedly.

Database Optimizations

Database operations invariably involve disk access, which is much slower than internal memory operations. Database optimizations focus on reducing disk access.

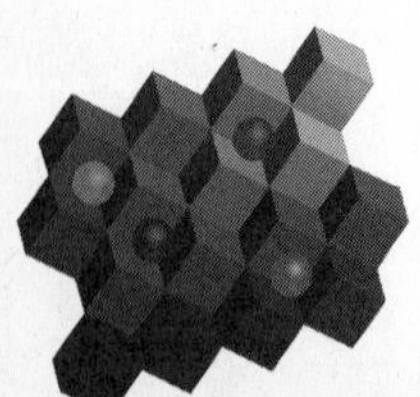

Keep Tables Open

Putting a table in use takes a relatively long time. Closing a table takes a bit of time too. Whenever possible, open a table once at the beginning of the application or module, and leave it open for the entire duration.

Keeping a table open makes it more susceptible to damage due to power loss, rebooting, and similar catastrophes. If these are significant concerns, you may opt for the safety of opening tables only when necessary at the expense of application speed.

Use Scopes Instead of Looping

The use of scopes such as ALL, REST, NEXT <n>, WHILE, and FOR is faster than repeated operations on single records inside a loop, since it is a single set operation.

For example, if everyone with the last name "Smith" gets paid an extra $10, instead of using the following code:

```
seek "Smith"
scan while LAST_NAME = "Smith"
  replace AMT_PAID with AMT_PAID + 10
endscan
```

you can try the following:

```
seek "Smith"
replace while LAST_NAME = "Smith" ;
        AMT_PAID with AMT_PAID + 10
```

Use A Single REPLACE Statement

When replacing values in more than one field, combine all of them into a single REPLACE command. For example, instead of the two commands:

```
replace AMT_PAID with AMT_PAID + 10
replace VAC_DAYS with VAC_DAYS + 5
```

use the following:

```
replace AMT_PAID with AMT_PAID + 10, ;
        VAC_DAYS with VAC_DAYS + 5
```

Avoid Indexes When Possible

When large set operations do not depend on indexes, put the table back in natural order before doing the operation. For example, if you are going to give everyone in the company five extra days of vacation, there is no reason to give it to them in alphabetical order. Turn off any active indexes first:

```
cOrder = order()             && Remember current index
set order to                 && Put in natural order
replace all VAC_DAYS with VAC_DAYS + 5
if .not. isblank( cOrder )  && If there was an active index
  set order to ( cOrder )    && restore it
endif
```

Periodically Rebuild MDX Files

Over time, index trees get unbalanced, resulting in what is known as "MDX-bloat"—the indexes get bigger and take longer to search. You can solve this problem by rebuilding the indexes as part of your regular backup/maintenance routine. (Rebuild the indexes first; there is no need to backup the bloat.)

Instead of a simple REINDEX, you should rebuild the indexes from scratch by first deleting all the tags and then using INDEX ON commands to rebuild each index tag. The ZapTags procedure quickly deletes all the index tags in the currently selected table:

```
PROCEDURE ZapTags
  do while .not. isblank( tag( 1 ))
    delete tag tag( 1 )
  enddo
RETURN
```

The procedure to rebuild all the index tags in your CUSTOMER file might look like the following:

```
use CUSTOMER exclusive   && Must be exclusive to handle tags
do ZapTags
index tag FULL_NAME on upper( LAST_NAME + FIRST_NAME )
index tag ZIP_ADDR  on ZIP_CODE + STREET + ADDR_NUM
use                      && Close table
```

The rebuild-tags routine is an excellent place to document the index tags used in your application, and can be used to rebuild the indexes if they should ever get corrupted. Such a routine should always be included in a distributed application.

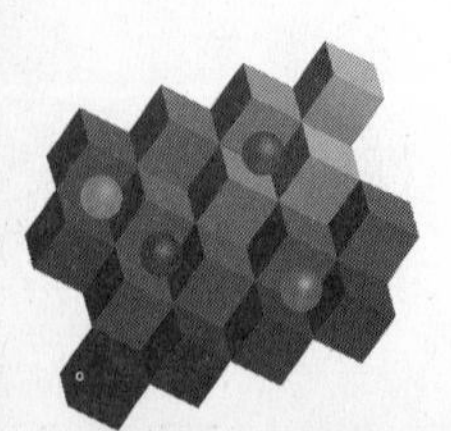

Validating Data

Before a record of data is stored in a table, every effort must be made to ensure that the data is both accurate and complete.

Localized Data

As demonstrated in Chapter 13, data fields can be localized inside the controls of a form. Whenever possible, do not allow the user to edit directly inside the table. Even though the DataLinks make this very easy, avoid it. You can maintain the DataLinks as you browse through the table, but once you switch to edit mode, localize the data inside the form, edit it there, validate it, and then if it is OK, write the data to the table.

Field-level Validation

The first and easiest step to ensure that each field gets the right data is to use the appropriate control. Checkboxes, radiobuttons, combo boxes, and the like present the user with a limited set of predefined choices.

The second line of defense is range checking, and is primarily used with spinboxes for numeric and date values. You can specify a minimum, maximum, or both.

Whenever possible, always specify a range for date fields. Although dBASE automatically ensures that the date is in the proper format—by specifying a minimum and maximum date—you can avoid simple data entry errors.

For example, if you are recording events, the maximum date would be the current date; it cannot be some date in the future. It is easy enough to mis-type a date and be off by a day, month, year, or decade. By specifying the current date as the maximum allowed date, you can eliminate a whole group of potential errors.

The third line of defense is actual field validation. This is done through the VALID property of an entryfield or spinbox. The VALID property must either be a code block or function which returns a logical expression.

One of the most common VALID conditions is that the field must be filled in. This can be checked with the following code block:

```
{.not. isblank( this.Value )}
```

The preceding is a very simple code block. Of course, code blocks can be as complicated as needed, and if appropriate, a separate function can be used for the VALID property.

Record-level Validation

In addition to field-level validation, you should also perform record-level validation before posting a record to a table. The reason is simple: field-level validation only occurs on fields that the user visits.

For example, suppose you have four fields, and they all must be filled in. You have the .NOT. ISBLANK() check on each field. If you open the form, and the user types a value in the first field, and then saves the record, the first field will be checked, but the other fields will not.

Therefore, you need to check the VALID conditions for all your fields before allowing the record to be posted. If all the data fields are localized in the form instead of directly linked to the table, then you control the posting process, which is why you go to the trouble of localizing the data in the first place.

Using Transaction Processing

A transaction is a set of changes to your data that must be treated as a single unit. The classic example is the transfer of $100 from one account to another. This transaction is composed of two changes: the debiting of $100 from one account, and the crediting of $100 to the other account. If, for whatever reason, the credit does not take, the debit must also be canceled—otherwise you have a debit with no corresponding credit.

Transaction processing works by logging all the changes that are made during a transaction. If all the changes take, then the transaction is committed and the log is cleared. If there is an error during the transaction, all the changes are rolled back, based on the information in the transaction log, thereby canceling the entire transaction.

BEGINTRANS()

The BEGINTRANS() function starts a new transaction. From this point on, it logs the actions of the commands (logged during a transaction) in the following list:

APPEND

APPEND BLANK

APPEND MEMO

BLANK

BROWSE

DELETE

EDIT

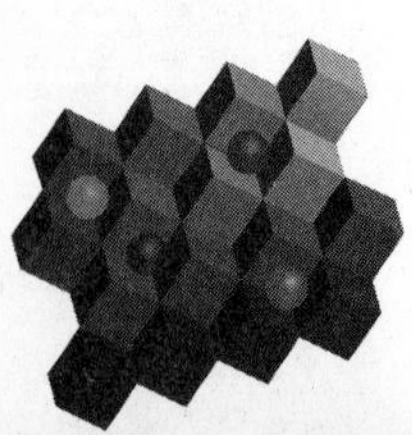

FLOCK()

RECALL

REPLACE

REPLACE MEMO/BINARY/OLE

RLOCK()

The following list of commands are not allowed during a transaction:

BEGINTRANS()

CLEAR ALL

CLOSE ALL/DATABASE/INDEX

CONVERT

CREATE FROM

DELETE TAG

INSERT

MODIFY STRUCTURE

PACK

ZAP

The primary difference between the two is that the commands that are logged change data without changing the structure or status of the table. Also note that you cannot nest transactions. Each session can have only one transaction active at a time.

COMMIT()

After all the changes have been made, the COMMIT() function clears the transaction log, indicating that all the changes are good. It also releases all record and table locks made during the transaction.

COMMIT() returns .T. if the commit was successful. A simple transaction to transfer $100 might look like the following:

```
begintrans()
seek cAcctFrom
replace BALANCE with BALANCE - 100
seek cAcctTo
replace BALANCE with BALANCE + 100
```

```
if .not. commit()
  rollback()
endif
```

ROLLBACK()

If, for whatever reason, the transaction is not successful, the ROLLBACK() function will undo all the changes attempted during the transaction.

Writing An Error Handler

Even with a myriad of safeguards, errors can happen. When they do, your application should handle them as cleanly as possible. This requires an ON ERROR handler, so that the user sees your custom error message instead of the generic dBASE one. You will also want to be able to log this error so that you can track down its cause.

When dBASE encounters an error while running your program, the standard error dialog box appears. Besides providing information which is not that useful to the end-user, that dialog box also gives the user the opportunity to abnormally cancel your application, suspend it, or attempt to fix the problem—none of which you want the user to be able to do.

You can tell dBASE to do something else when it encounters an error with the ON ERROR command. Most often, the ON ERROR command takes the form of:

```
on error do ErrHand with program(), lineno()
```

where ErrHand is the name of your error-handling procedure. There, you can determine the type of error and take the appropriate action.

You will want to get the current values for PROGRAM() and LINENO() when the error handler is called. Using these functions within the error handler will simply return the name and current line number of the error handler procedure, not where the error occurred.

ERROR() and MESSAGE()

The first thing the error handler does is receive the name and line number where the error occurred. Then it needs to determine the error itself. The ERROR() function returns the error code for the last error, and the MESSAGE() function returns the corresponding error message.

The beginning of the procedure ErrHand might look something like the following:

```
PROCEDURE ErrHand
  parameter cProg, nLine
```

```
private nError, cMessage, cWindow, cErrLog
nError   = error()
cMessage = message()
```

RETURN and RETRY

Depending on the error, there are three basic actions you can take:

- ✔ Ignore the error
- ✔ Retry the operation which caused the error
- ✔ Terminate your program

A RETURN command causes execution to return back to the command after the one which caused the error, thereby ignoring the error. Note that this means that the statement which caused the error does not get executed properly.

The RETRY command will retry the command which caused the error. You can attempt some corrective action before retrying.

A CASE structure can be used to determine the appropriate action:

```
do case
  case nError = ERR_FILE_ALREADY_OPEN
    *-- Ignore it
    return
  case nError = ERR_FILE_IN_USE_BY_ANOTHER .or. ;
       nError = ERR_FILE_IN_USE_BY_USERNAME
    *-- Retry operation
    retry
```

Instead of hard-coding the error numbers into the error handler, you can use a header file which #DEFINEs the appropriate symbols.

Error logging

When the error can be neither ignored nor retried, your only other alternative is to terminate your application. Although a simple QUIT will suffice, you may want to log as much information as possible about dBASE's current state to help you determine the cause of the error later. You will also want to display a message to the user that an error has occurred, so that they can remember what they were doing when the error happened and, if necessary, who to contact about the error.

Continuing the CASE structure begun earlier, here is the rest of the ErrHand procedure:

```
otherwise
  define form fErrLog ;
    property ;
      Text    "Fatal Application Error", ;
      Width   40, ;
      Height  15, ;
      MDI     .f.
  if .not. l_ErrHand
    l_ErrHand = .t.
    define text itTitle of fErrLog ;
      property ;
        Text        "A FATAL SYSTEM ERROR HAS " + ;
                    "OCCURRED", ;
        ColorNormal "R+/W", ;
        Top         1, ;
        Left        0, ;
        Width       40, ;
        Alignment   TEXT_ALIGN_TOP_CENTER
    define text itHalt of fErrLog ;
      property ;
        Text        "System operation has been " + ;
                    "halted in", ;
        ColorNormal "N/W", ;
        Top         3, ;
        Left        0, ;
        Width       40, ;
        Alignment   TEXT_ALIGN_TOP_CENTER
    define text itRoutine1 of fErrLog ;
      property ;
        Text        "Routine: ", ;
        ColorNormal "N/W", ;
        Top         4, ;
        Left        0, ;
        Width       10, ;
        Alignment   TEXT_ALIGN_TOP_RIGHT
    define text itLine1 of fErrLog ;
      property ;
        Text        "Line: ", ;
        ColorNormal "N/W", ;
        Top         5, ;
        Left        0, ;
        Width       10, ;
```

```
    Alignment   TEXT_ALIGN_TOP_RIGHT
define text itError1 of fErrLog ;
  property ;
    Text        "Error: ", ;
    ColorNormal "N/W", ;
    Top         6, ;
    Left        0, ;
    Width       10, ;
    Alignment   TEXT_ALIGN_TOP_RIGHT
define text itRoutine2 of fErrLog ;
  property ;
    Text        cProg, ;
    ColorNormal "N/W", ;
    Top         4, ;
    Left        10, ;
    Width       30, ;
    Alignment   TEXT_ALIGN_TOP_LEFT
define text itLine2 of fErrLog ;
  property ;
    Text        ltrim( str( nLine )) + " due to", ;
    ColorNormal "N/W", ;
    Top         5, ;
    Left        10, ;
    Width       30, ;
    Alignment   TEXT_ALIGN_TOP_LEFT
define text itError2 of fErrLog ;
  property ;
    Text        ltrim( str( nError )), ;
    ColorNormal "N/W", ;
    Top         6, ;
    Left        10, ;
    Width       30, ;
    Alignment   TEXT_ALIGN_TOP_LEFT
define text itError3 of fErrLog ;
  property ;
    Text        cMessage, ;
    ColorNormal "N/W", ;
    Top         7, ;
    Left        10, ;
    Width       30, ;
    Alignment   TEXT_ALIGN_TOP_LEFT

define text itWrite1 of fErrLog ;
  property ;
```

```
    Text        "WRITE THIS DOWN ", ;
    ColorNormal "RG+/W", ;
    Top         9, ;
    Left        2, ;
    Width       36, ;
    Alignment   TEXT_ALIGN_TOP_LEFT
define text itWrite2 of fErrLog ;
  property ;
    Text        "while the error is being logged", ;
    ColorNormal "N/W", ;
    Top         9, ;
    Left        nextcol(), ;
    Width       30, ;
    Alignment   TEXT_ALIGN_TOP_LEFT
define text itWrite3 of fErrLog ;
  property ;
    Text        "...", ;
    ColorNormal "N*/W", ;
    Top         9, ;
    Left        nextcol(), ;
    Width       30, ;
    Alignment   TEXT_ALIGN_TOP_LEFT

fErrLog.open()
ErrLog( cProg, nLine, nError, cMessage, cWindow )

fErrLog.Write2.Text = "including what you were " + ;
                      "trying to do and"
define text itWrite4 of fErrLog ;
  property ;
    Text        "the last keys you pressed.", ;
    ColorNormal "N/W", ;
    Top         10, ;
    Left        2, ;
    Width       36, ;
    Alignment   TEXT_ALIGN_TOP_LEFT

define text itTerminate of fErrLog ;
  property ;
    Text        "Notify the System " + ;
                "Administrator as soon as " + ;
                "possible. You must now " + ;
                "terminate this session by " + ;
                "selecting the Terminate button", ;
```

```
            ColorNormal "N/W", ;
            Top         12, ;
            Left        2, ;
            Width       36, ;
            Alignment   TEXT_ALIGN_WRAP_CENTER

        define pushbutton ipTerminate of fErrLog ;
          property ;
            OnClick     {; form.close()}
            Text        "&Terminate", ;
            Top         13, ;
            Left        15, ;
            Height      2, ;
            Width       10

        fErrLog.readmodal()

      endif

      quit

    endcase
  RETURN
```

This first displays a dialog box detailing the error. As the user reads the dialog box, the ERRLOG() function is called, which actually logs the error. Once the error has been logged, a Terminate button appears. When the button is selected, your application quits.

The error logging function simply opens a text file called ERRLOG.DAT and dumps as much useful information as possible:

```
FUNCTION ErrLog
  parameters cProg, nLine, nError, cMessage, cWindow
  private cDate, cTime, cErrLog, cErrNum, nArea
  cDate = date()
  cTime = time()
  set alternate to ERRLOG.DAT additive
  set alternate on
  set console off
  ? "***** ERROR Log:", cDate, cTime
  ? "Routine:", cProg
  ? "   Line:", nLine
  ? "  Error:", nError, cMessage
  ?
  ? "  alias():", alias()
```

```
  ? "    bof():", bof()
  ? "    dbf():", dbf()
  ? "    eof():", eof()
  ? "lastkey():", lastkey()
  ? " memory():", memory()
  ? "  order():", order()
  ? "  recno():", recno()
  ? "   user():", c_UsrNam
  ? "version():", version( 1 )
  ?
  list memory
  list status
  nArea = 1
  do while nArea <= 40
    if "" # alias( nArea )
      ? "Area", str( nArea, 2 ), ;
        "recno():", str( recno( nArea ), 7 )
    endif
    nArea = nArea + 1
  enddo
  ? "----- End error log", date(), time()
  ?
  ?
  set console on
  set alternate off
  close alternate
RETURN ""
```

NRP
NEW RIDERS
PUBLISHING

Part VI

Putting It All Together

Chapter Snapshot

Although DOS and Windows have attempted to make file management easier, the number of tables, forms, queries, and reports in an application can still be overwhelming. To help solve this problem, dBASE uses the concept of a catalog. This chapter assists you in learning the following:

With the information in this chapter, you can better organize your tables, forms, and reports as you work in dBASE.

Working with Projects and Catalogs

By Jim Wetzel

As you work through the application in this book and go on to develop your own projects, you will find that you have a large number of dBASE for Windows files in your working directory—as well as in other drives and directories on your system. You will want to have a way of organizing those files, tables, and records, and the way you do that in dBASE is by using catalogs.

An important part of using dBASE for Windows is understanding exactly what a catalog is. A *catalog* is a mechanism that enables you to group a set of related dBASE files. A catalog is different from a DOS directory in that the files placed in a catalog are not physically moved. The catalog is a special database file, containing file names, paths, and title information that points to the actual files.

Understanding What Catalogs Do

A catalog can point to files from a single directory, or the items in a catalog can point to files that span multiple disks and directories. Later in this chapter you learn more about the Master Catalogs that dBASE maintains as well as User Catalogs that you can create and manage.

To distinguish between the files that exist on your disk and the objects placed in the catalog, the catalog objects are referred to as *items*. Items are pointers to the actual files.

In addition to containing a pointer to the physical file, the catalog can also maintain a description of each file or item contained in the catalog. This feature gives you the ability to expand on the DOS file name restriction of eight characters and a three-character extension, and provide a meaningful description of the file. This description can be as long as 80 characters. Supplementing the description of the items in the catalog, each catalog also has a description associated with the catalog itself.

Keep in mind that in dBASE, the Catalog Viewer window appears as a modified version of the Navigator window and, as such, provides a filtered view of your projects and applications.

dBASE for Windows is compatible with and can use catalogs created in dBASE for DOS.

Creating a New Catalog

As you have seen throughout this book, dBASE usually enables you to do things in a number of different ways. Creating catalogs is no exception. You can create a catalog in the following ways:

- ✔ Use the dBASE command **CREATE CATALOG** <cat name> in the command window.
- ✔ Select File, New, Catalog from the menu.
- ✔ Click on the Create file icon on the SpeedBar, and then select Catalog.
- ✔ Click on the Catalog file type in the Navigator, and then double-click on the Untitled Catalog icon in the file viewer area.

- ✔ Click on the Catalog file type in the Navigator, and then right-click on the Untitled Catalog icon to open a SpeedMenu. Next choose the New Catalog option or use the Shift+F2 hot key.

- ✔ Click on the Catalog file type in the Navigator, and then click on the Untitled Catalog icon and drag the icon to the dBASE desktop or Command window.

Although the topic of creating catalogs is being presented late in this book, starting every project by creating a catalog for that project is a good idea. This approach saves you the trouble of trying to go back later and find all the files related to the project.

Now, if you haven't done so already, start dBASE for Windows, and click on the Catalogs icon at the bottom of the Navigator window. If you still have the DBASEWIN\SAMPLES directory as your current directory, your screen should look similar to the one shown in figure 19.1.

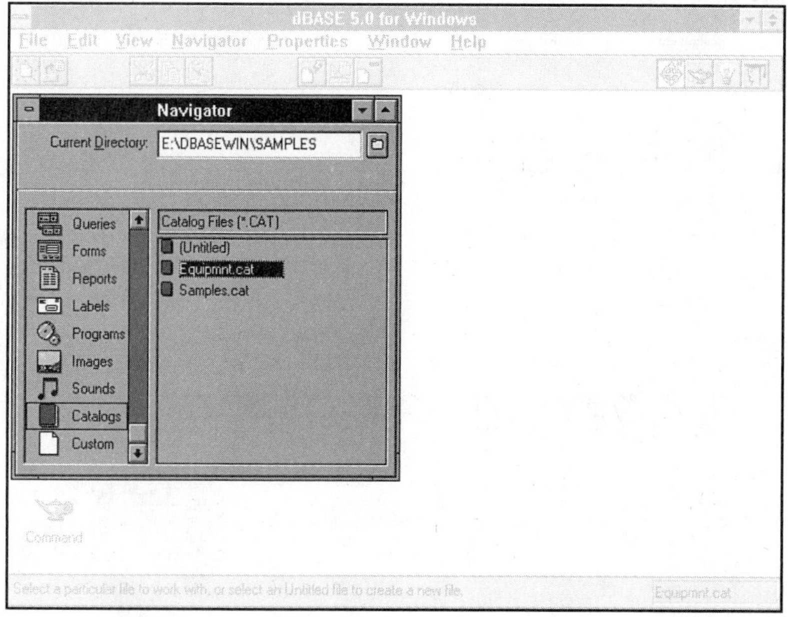

Figure 19.1
The dBASE samples supplied have two catalogs defined.

Now click on the Choose Directory button for the current directory and switch to the directory where you installed the sample Home Search application. In this example it is D:\DATA\HOMESRCH.

Next, right-click on the Untitled icon to bring up the local Catalog menu, and click on New Catalog (see fig. 19.2). The Create Catalog dialog box appears, as shown in figure

19.3. (Remember that all objects in the Navigator have a SpeedMenu for performing common tasks. Most of the Untitled menu items are usually grayed out or not shown because they aren't available until the object is created.)

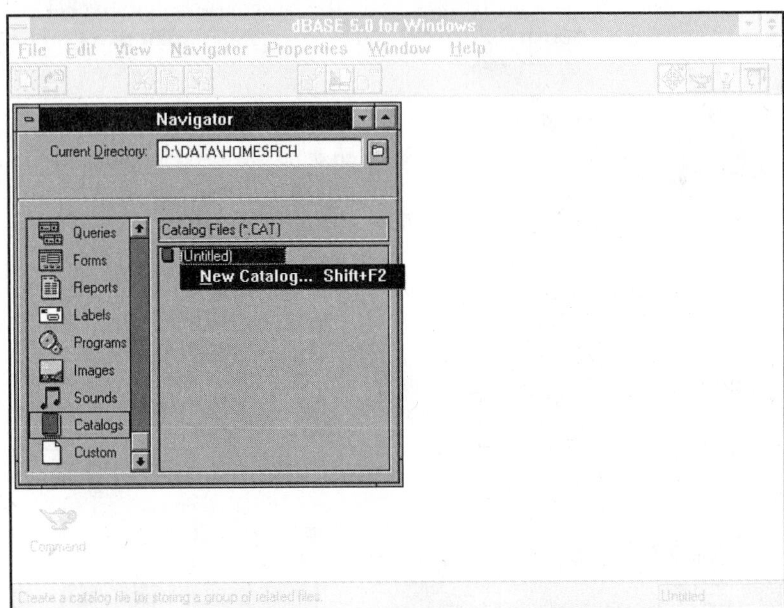

Figure 19.2 Choosing the New Catalog option from the SpeedMenu.

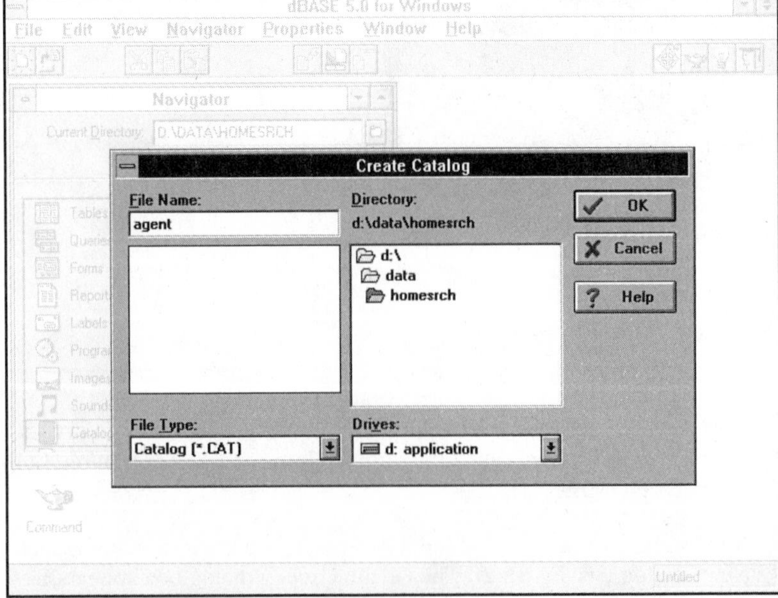

Figure 19.3 The Create Catalog dialog box.

To create the catalog, all you need to do is enter a valid file name and click on the OK button or simply press the Enter key. Suppose, for example, that you want to create an Agent catalog for the Home Search application files that are contained in the HOMESRCH directory that ships with this book. First, type **AGENTS** in the File Name box and press Enter.

Note that you do not have to enter the extension of the file you are saving. Because dBASE knows that you are working with a catalog, the program automatically supplies a CAT extension.

Next, you are prompted with a dialog box for Catalog Description. Enter **Home Search Agent Information** and choose OK or press Enter to accept (see fig. 19.4).

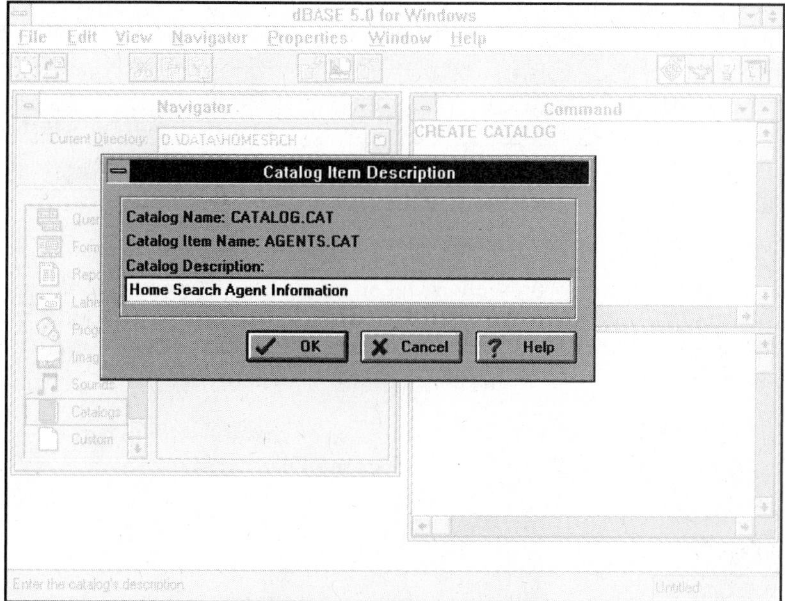

Figure 19.4
The Catalog Item Description.

After you have entered and accepted the catalog description, you see what looks like a modified version of the Navigator on your desktop. Note, if you have the Command window open, dBASE automatically enters the CREATE CATALOG command in the command window for you. Now is a good time to expand your Catalog Viewer to full screen and take a closer look at it. If you click on the Maximize button, your screen should look similar to the one shown in figure 19.5.

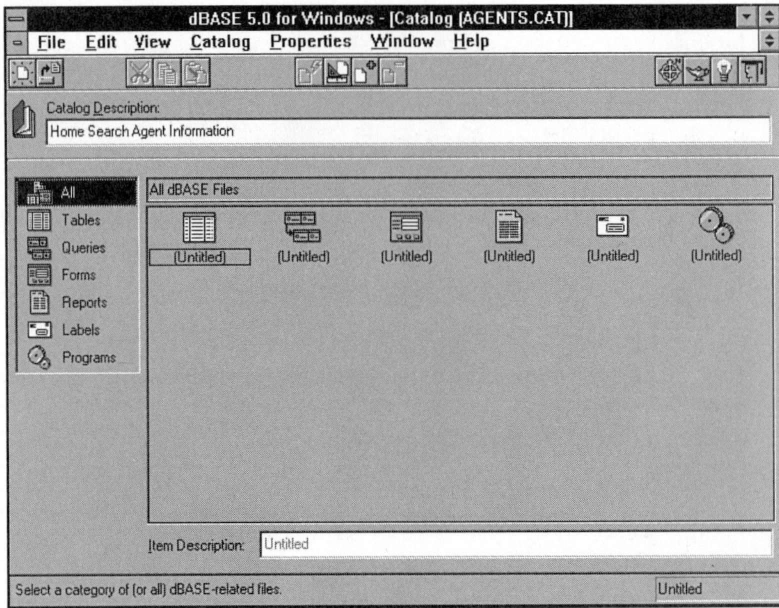

Figure 19.5 The Catalog Viewer.

Catalog Views

When the Catalog window has the focus, the View menu provides an alternate way of highlighting or selecting file types in the Catalog window, and also gives you additional control over the appearance and order of the items in the Catalog window. For the most part, these options are the same as those that appear in the Navigator View menu.

In addition to providing an alternative way of selecting objects that you want to have appear in the Catalog window, the View menu provides several other options.

Associations

The Associations option is a unique view option for the Catalog window. When the Associations option is selected from the View menu, dBASE will display information for Queries, Form, Reports, and Labels that indicate how the files are related (see fig. 19.6). This option is extremely helpful if want to know what reports and forms are associated with a particular query.

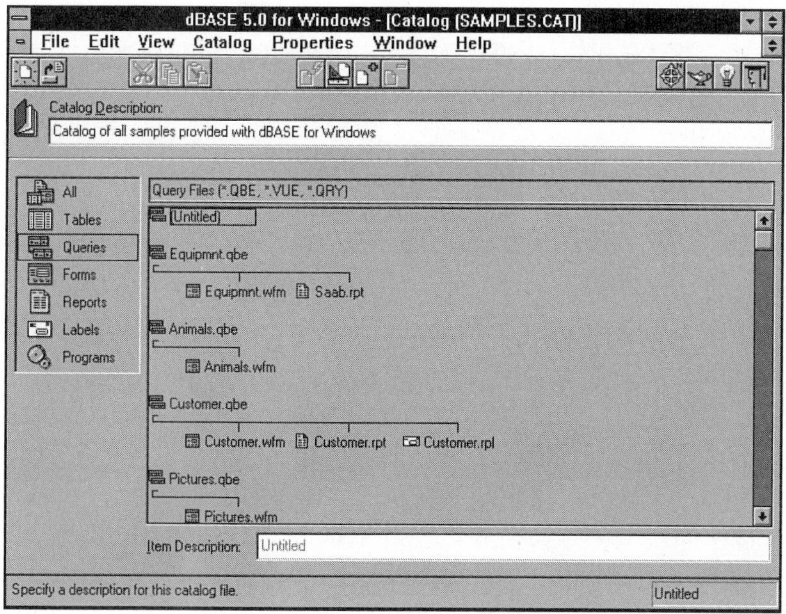

Figure 19.6
Relationships of forms, reports, and labels to their query file.

Sort

While the Catalog window has focus, the Sort option has a submenu that gives you the ability to display dBASE items in one of four ways:

- ✔ **By Name**. All dBASE file items sorted by name regardless of type.
- ✔ **By Type and Extension**. All dBASE file items sorted by name within type (Tables, Queries, Forms, etc.).
- ✔ **By Size**. All dBASE items sorted by file size.
- ✔ **By Date and Time**. All dBASE items sorted by the date and time stamp of the file.

Icons and Details

In addition to the Sort options, you can also specify the size of the dBASE for Windows items icons. The default is small icons, but you can also have dBASE for Windows display large icons. Displaying the large icons is easier on your eyes, but does take up extra screen space that could be used for other purposes. Selecting the large icons will also cause dBASE to use a slightly larger font for the file names and make identification a bit easier when using higher display resolutions.

The last option of the View menu, Details, enables you to display the file details (size, date, and time) along with the small file type icon. The Details option is not available with large icons.

Reviewing dBASE File Types

Before adding entries to your catalog, you might want to review some of the file types that you can store in dBASE catalogs. Valid catalog file types are summarized in table 19.1.

Table 19.1
Summary of Valid Catalog File Types

File Type	Extension	Description
Tables	DBF	dBASE table
	DB	Paradox table
Queries	QRY	Query file (dBASE III+)
	QBE	Query-by-Example source code
	VUE	View file (dBASE III+ queries)
Forms	WFM	Screen form file (dBASE for Windows)
	FMT	Screen form file (dBASE IV/III+)
Reports	FRM	Report file design (dBASE IV/III+)
	FRG	Report file code (dBASE IV)
	RPT	Crystal Reports for dBASE for Windows
	RPC	Crystal Reports for dBASE for Windows
Labels	RPL	Crystal Reports for dBASE for Windows
	LBL	Label file(dBASE IV/III+)
	LBG	Label file(dBASE IV)
Programs	PRG	dBASE programs

Collectively, these file types represent the source code (and tables) of your dBASE application. A number of other files are created during the development of a project, but the source files are the items of which the catalog keeps track.

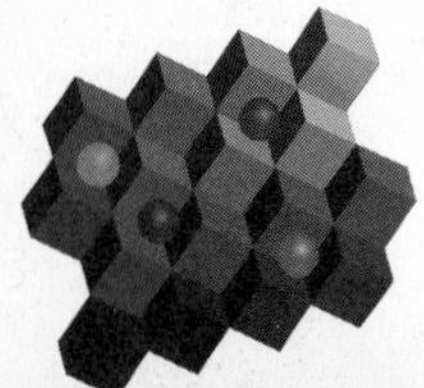

Adding Items to Your Catalog

Now that you know about the various file types associated with the catalog, you are ready to add some items to it.

The first thing you need to do is return the Catalog Viewer back to its normal size by again selecting and clicking on the Maximize button or clicking on the Windows Control Panel, and then clicking on Restore.

Next, you want to move the Catalog Viewer over to the right in the position generally occupied by the Command window and make sure that the Navigator window is visible on the left to prepare for the operations in the next section. At this point, you should have both the Navigator and the Catalog Viewer showing on your screen, enabling you to drag and drop files between each (see fig. 19.7).

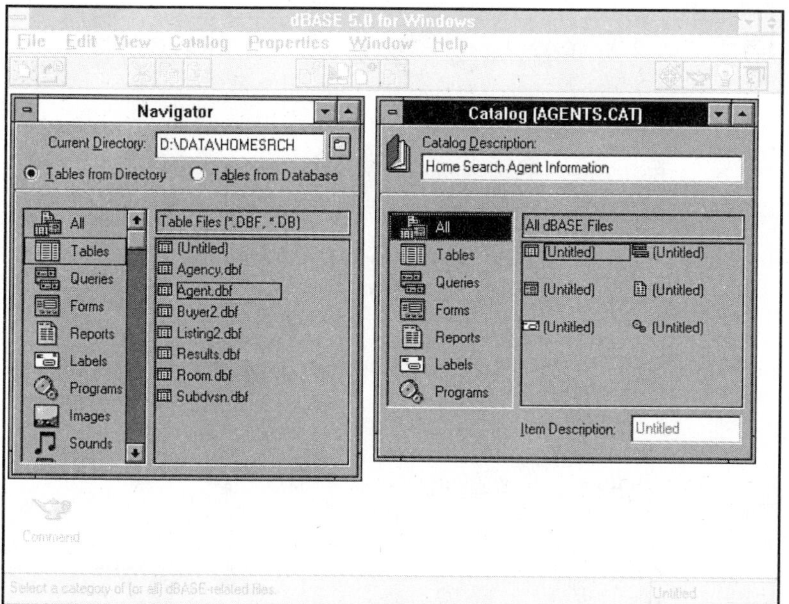

Figure 19.7
The Catalog Viewer next to the Navigator window.

Continuing with the agent information sample, you can now start to add the relevant items to the catalog. The following five primary files make up the basic agent information:

File	Description
AGENT.DBF	Agent Name, Company, and Phone Table
AGENCY.DBF	Agency ID and Company Name Table
AGTRPT.QBE	Query to link agents with agencies
FINAGT.FRM	Find agent form
AGTRPT.RPT	Agents by Agency Report

Dragging and Dropping Existing Objects

Just as dBASE offers a number of ways to create a catalog, so too does it give you several options for adding items to your catalog. The easiest way is to use the drag-and-drop method, which involves the following steps.

Dragging and Dropping Items in a Catalog

Click on the Tables category in the Navigator	Selects the category
Click on the table icon for AGENT.DBF and hold down the left mouse button	Activates the icon
Move the AGENT.DBF icon over to the file view area of the Catalog Viewer	Shows you a visual indication of valid areas where you can drop the item
Release the mouse button to drop the table object	dBASE displays a Catalog Item Description dialog box for you to enter a table description (see fig. 19.8)
Enter **Agent Name and Phone Number File** for the description, and then press Enter or choose OK	The description is entered

You do not have to have the Tables selection highlighted to drop a table item in the Catalog Viewer area. dBASE figures out what type of item you are dropping and stores it in the proper area.

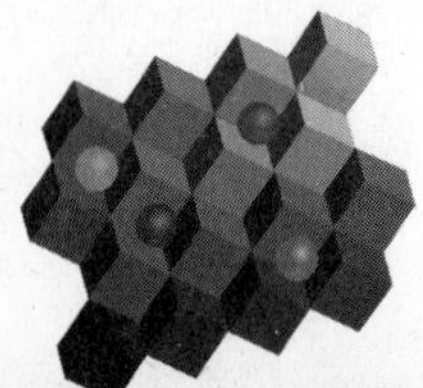

If the Tables category of the Catalog viewer is not active, click on it to show the table in the catalog. You should now see the Agent table object next to the Untitled object. If you click on the Agent object, you can see that the description you entered is also displayed in the Current Item Description area, as shown in figure 19.9.

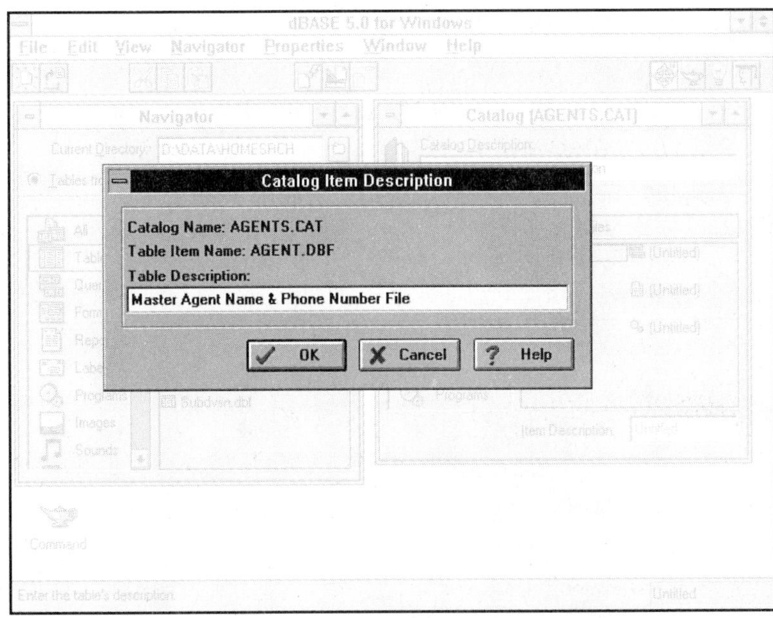

Figure 19.8
The Catalog Item Description dialog box.

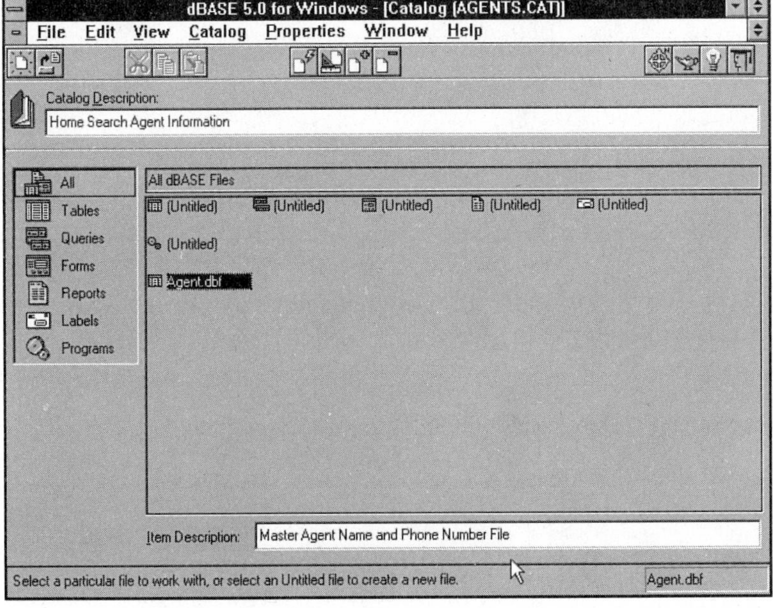

Figure 19.9
A selected item in the Catalog Viewer, with its description in the Current Item Description area.

Using Other Methods of Adding Objects

Other methods for adding items to the catalog include using the SpeedBar Add File or selecting the menu options Catalog, Add Item. And, as in other areas, you can use the Ctrl+A hot key while the Catalog window has the focus.

Either of these two methods brings up an Add Catalog Item dialog box like the one shown in figure 19.10. The default extension in the File Name box is determined by the type of object that was highlighted when you invoked the Add Item option.

Figure 19.10
The Add Catalog Item dialog box.

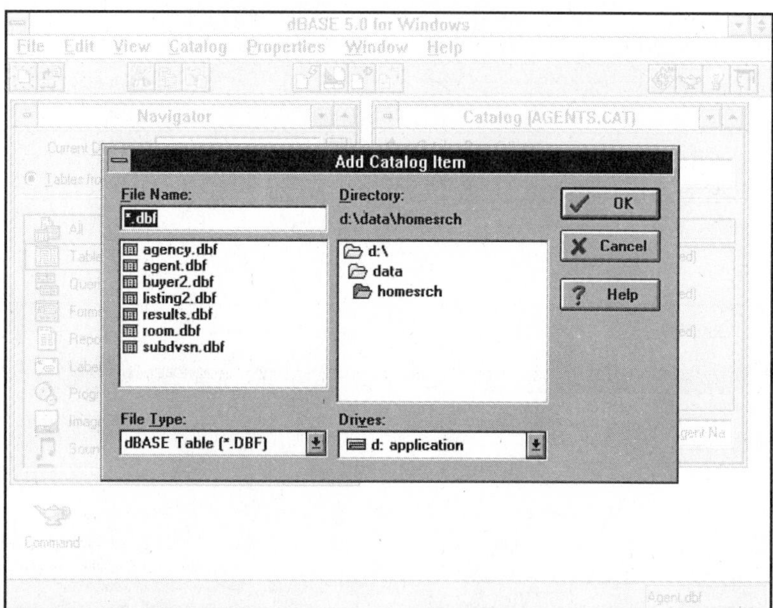

At this point, you can select the item you want to add and double-click on it, or you can click on the item, and then choose OK.

As in the previous example for adding items, at this point dBASE prompts you for an item description, and then adds the item to your catalog.

When you open the Add Catalog File Item dialog box, it defaults to the current directory and selected file type. But you can change the drive by using the Drives selection list, change directories by clicking on the directory you want in the Directories selection window, or change the file type you want to add to the catalog by clicking on the File Types selection list.

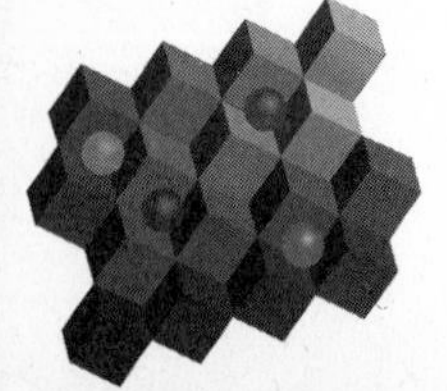

Adding New Items to Catalogs

To add new items to your catalog, you can use the New option of the File menu system just as you do in the Navigator. You can also click on any untitled item with the right mouse button, and a SpeedMenu appears to enable you to create one of those items.

Additionally, if a catalog is active from the results of a SET CATALOG ON or SET CATALOG TO command, all items created are automatically added to that catalog.

Opening a Catalog window from the Navigator also activates a catalog.

Understanding How Added Items Are Used

When adding items to your catalog, you need to be aware of a couple of additional considerations. Because items added to a catalog are only pointers to the real objects or files, you need to understand how these items are used while the catalog is active.

When you drag an object to a catalog, for instance, the object is not moved or copied, but a pointer to that object is created. When adding tables, if a copy of the actual table were placed in the catalog, you would have twice the amount of data. This would cause considerable disk space problems in a very short period.

The same is true for queries, forms, and report objects; however, you might want to consider creating separate copies of these files before adding them to the catalog. This way you can have individual copies and make changes to these items without affecting the other catalogs.

Modifying Entries in Your Catalog

When developing applications, nothing is constant. The same holds true for the catalogs and catalog items you create. As your application progresses, you may need to change the actual catalog object or just the associated descriptions (see fig. 19.11).

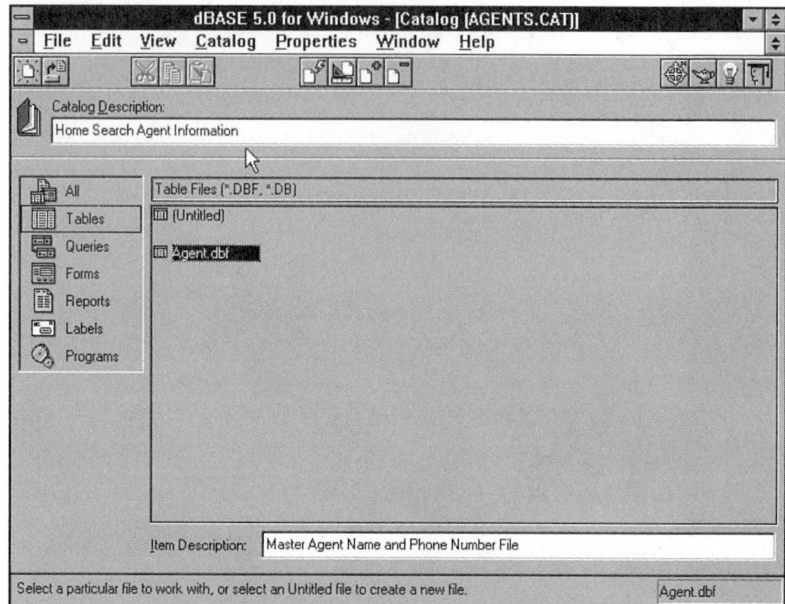

Figure 19.11 The Catalog Description and Item Descriptions are active input areas.

Changing the Catalog and Item Descriptions

As shown in the figure above the Catalog **D**escription and **I**tem Description areas are active input areas. This means that you can click on these areas and type in the desired changes. You can also reach these areas using the designated hot keys.

Changing Other Items

To change or make modifications to the items themselves, all you need to do is click on the object with the right mouse button to display the SpeedMenu, and then select the option you want, just as though you were using the dBASE Navigator (see fig. 19.12).

Removing Items from Your Catalog

As your projects continue you may also need to delete items from the catalog you created. You can remove items from a catalog by using the **D**elete option of the **E**dit menu or the Delete Item on the SpeedBar. Remember, if you delete items from the catalog, you are not deleting the file but merely a pointer to that file. To delete a catalog item, follow the steps in the next exercise.

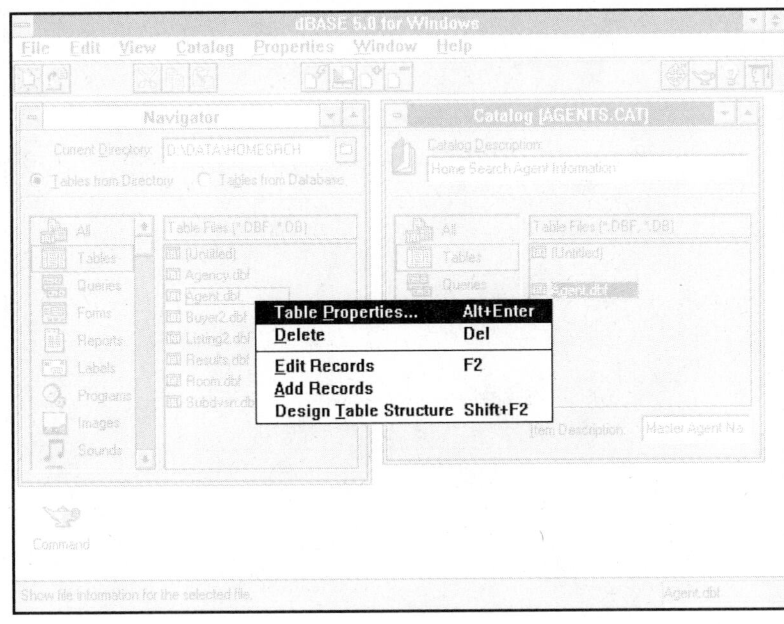

Figure 19.12
The Catalog SpeedMenu options for Tables.

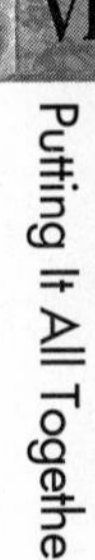

Deleting a Catalog Item

Double-click on a catalog item in the Navigator window	Opens a Catalog
In the Catalog window, click on the file type that contains the item(s) you want to delete or click on All to display all dBASE file types	Selects the file type
Next click on the item you want to delete to highlight it	Selects the item
To use the menu, select **E**dit, **D**elete; or, if you prefer to use the SpeedBar, click on the Delete Document icon. After the catalog item is highlighted you can also use the del key as a hot key to delete the item	Deletes the item

As you delete items from the catalog, dBASE asks for confirmation prior to deleting the item from the catalog (see fig. 19.13). dBASE also asks whether you want to remove the object itself from your disk (see fig. 19.14).

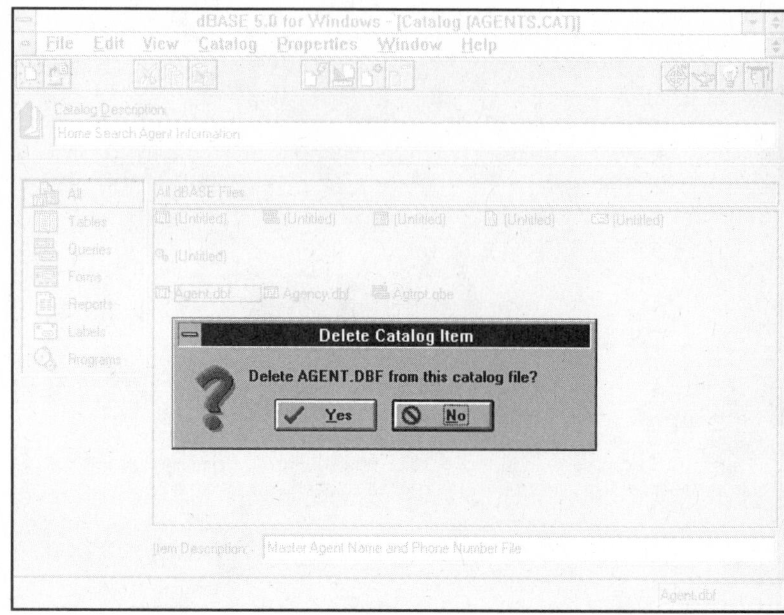

Figure 19.13 Delete Catalog Item confirmation dialog.

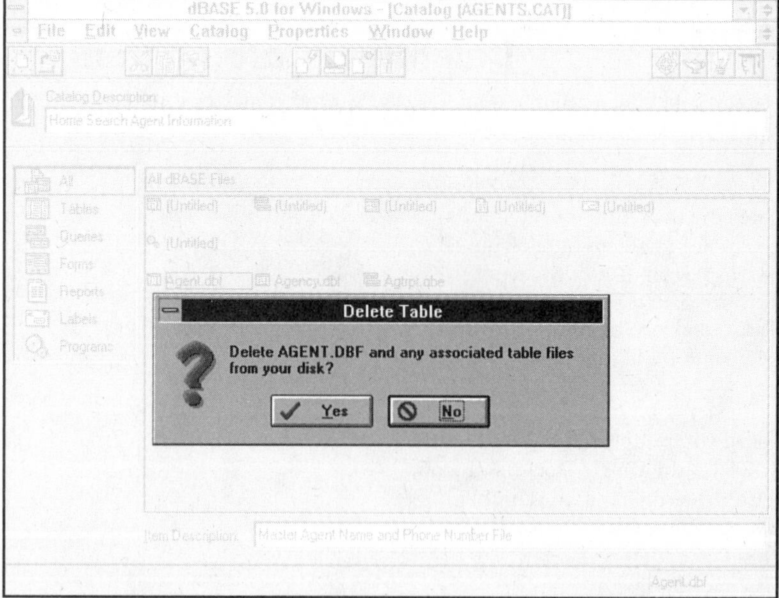

Figure 19.14 The Delete File from disk dialog defaults to No.

Learning More about Catalogs

As you continue to work with catalogs in dBASE, knowing some of the details that go on behind the scenes is sometimes useful. Catalogs come in two varieties: the master catalog, called CATALOG (see fig. 19.15), and the user catalog, identified by the file name you specified when you created the catalog. The following paragraphs give you some additional information about these two types of catalogs.

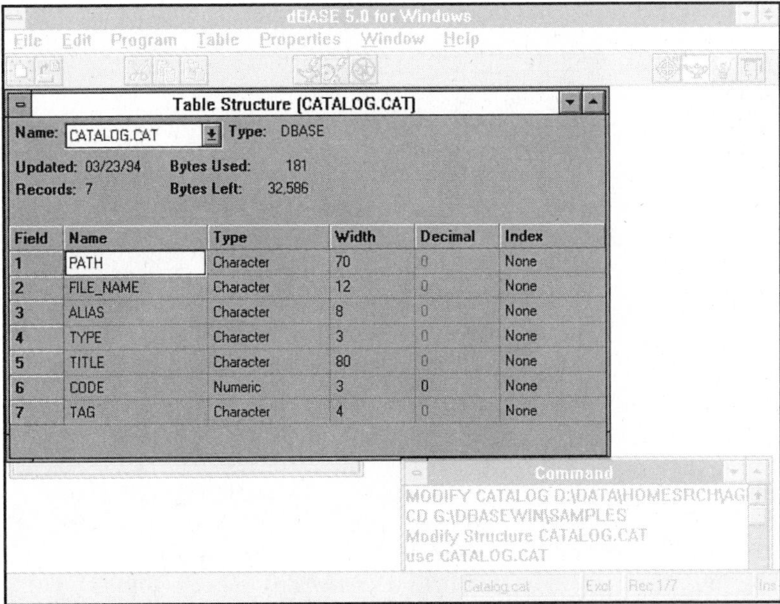

Figure 19.15
The master catalog, a special type of dBASE table.

Working with Master Catalogs

When you created your first catalog, an extra object was created called CATALOG. This object is the *master* catalog and is created the first time you create a catalog in the working directory. This master catalog is a special dBASE file that contains pointers to and descriptions to the user catalogs you create. The information it contains is summarized in table 19.2.

When you are viewing Catalogs in the Navigator, dBASE hides the master catalog from your view but if you use the Windows File Manager you will see a file named CATALOG.CAT in the working directory.

Table 19.2
The Master Catalog

Field	Name	Width	Description
1	PATH	70	File location (full path)
2	FILENAME	12	File name (with extension)
3	ALIAS	08	File name (no extension)
4	TYPE	03	File extension (CAT)
5	TITLE	80	Catalog title
6	CODE	03	Work area code
7	TAG	04	Reserved

Keep in mind the following characteristics of the fields in the master catalog:

The *TYPE* field defaults to the type of the object in the catalog. In this case it is always CAT. You can override the catalog file extension when the catalog is created but this filed will always be CAT. Be forewarned that if you use an extension other than CAT, the catalog will not show up in the Navigator under the Catalog type.

When you create a new catalog or add items to an existing catalog, dBASE by default prompts you for a title. If you do not want to be prompted to title your catalogs (or files), you can use the SET TITLE OFF command from the dBASE command line or in the DBASEWIN.INI settings. If you do, the *TITLE* field (Description) will be blank. The Title option is also available on the Files page of Desktop Properties.

As described in the "Modifying Entries in Your Catalog" section earlier in the chapter you can quickly add or change your descriptions later.

The *CODE* field is used internally by dBASE to track or programs and files associated with various tables.

Working with User Catalogs

Catalogs that you create are called *user catalogs* and they have a format similar to the master catalog—described earlier. Instead of being a pointer to other catalogs like the master catalog, the user catalogs that you create contain pointers to the items or objects in the catalog. Hence, some of the fields are used differently than in the master catalog.

The *ALIAS* field is used only for table items. It defaults to the table name without the extension but can have another name assigned to it as an alias.

The *TYPE* field is expanded to use the full range of valid extensions. But note, as mentioned previously, that if you specify an extension different from the default, the file does not appear in the Navigator window.

The *CODE* field also differs. Program files, like catalogs, have a 0 for the code. Tables have a unique number assigned to them when they are created. This number is incremented for each new database created. Files associated with each database, such as indexes, formats, reports, and forms, are assigned the same number as the database to which they are related.

Chapter Snapshot

Before you finish a dBASE for Windows application and distribute it to your users, you should consider adding a Windows Help system to it. This chapter looks at Windows Help and shows how you can add it to your application. Major topics covered include:

Probably no other enhancement makes your application as usable or professional as an online Help system. After you finish reading this chapter, you will have a thorough understanding of the Windows Help system and how it can assist you in maintaining applications.

Adding Windows Help to Your Applications

By Richard Wagner

A well-designed Windows Help (WinHelp) system integrated with your dBASE for Windows application can save your users considerable time and energy and save you headaches answering support calls. Most users (especially those experienced in the Windows environment) instinctively know to press F1 or click on the Help button when things go awry or when they face uncertainty in performing a task.

Even if you plan to include written documentation along with your database application, you also seriously should consider adding online help. Windows 3.1 features a powerful help system, and nearly all applications running under Windows today take advantage of it. This chapter is intended to help you, as a dBASE developer, design a Help system for your application.

Developing Online Help for Your Applications

As you probably know if you have previous experience in Windows, Windows Help is a hypertext system. It displays a single topic at a time, but has the ability to jump to other topics because of a hypertext link. The user is able to navigate through a Help system, not in any structured order, but in a random manner through jumps, keyword searches, and so on.

A Help file is generated by creating topic files in Rich Text Format (RTF). After an RTF file is written, you use the DOS-based Windows Help compiler (HC.EXE) to transform the text into a resource file with an HLP extension. This Help file can then be displayed using the Windows Help engine (WINHELP.EXE), which is included with Windows itself. Therefore, three tools are required to create and display a Windows Help system:

- ✔ Word for Windows (or other word processor/text editor) that can read/write RTF text
- ✔ Help Compiler
- ✔ Help Engine

With the preceding tools, the process of creating a Help system has four basic stages:

1. Creating the RTF source document (and any graphic files)
2. Creating the Help project file
3. Compiling the Help project
4. Linking the Help file to your dBASE for Windows application.

Creating a Source Help File

To create a source Help file, you need a word processor or text editor that can create RTF files. The standard word processor to use for this task is Microsoft Word for Windows. Because Microsoft is the developer of both the word processor and the Help compiler, you can be assured of compatibility between the two products.

Probably the best information about how to create Help files is on the Microsoft Developer"s Network CD. The CD-ROM includes the Windows SDK documentation on Help files, the Windows Help compilers, the Windows Help

Project Editor, and the Windows Help Authoring Template (used in conjunction with Word for Windows). The CD is available by subscription from Microsoft by calling (800) 759-5474.

A source Help file consists of individual topics separated by hard page breaks in your document. Topics consist of the Help text, graphics, as well as a variety of special control codes you can define in Word. The primary controls you normally use in a Help file include the following:

- ✔ **Context string.** The *context string* is a unique identifier for each topic in your Help system. It is used for linking a topic to: (a) other topics in the Help system through a jump, or (b) your dBASE for Windows application if you are implementing context-sensitive Help. The context string is defined with a pound sign (#) footnote (see fig. 20.1).
- ✔ **Title.** The *title* of a topic is used in the Topics Found list that results from a keyword search and in the Bookmark menu. The title is defined with a dollar sign ($) footnote (see fig. 20.1).
- ✔ **Keywords.** *Keywords* are used to search for a particular topic in the Search dialog box. Keywords are defined with a "K" (the letter "K") footnote (see fig. 20.1).
- ✔ **Browse sequence number.** A *browse sequence number* is used to define an order in which a user can browse through the topics using browse buttons found on the WinHelp window button bar. A browse sequence number is defined with a plus sign (+) footnote (see fig. 20.1).
- ✔ **Jump.** A *jump* is a word or graphic that is linked to other topics in your Help system. A jump is defined using strikethrough or double-underlined text followed immediately (no spaces) by a context string formatted in hidden text (see fig. 20.1).
- ✔ **Popup link.** A *popup link* is a word that is linked to a popup or lookup window. A popup window is usually used to define a word used in a topic. A popup link is defined using underlined text followed immediately (no spaces) by a context string formatted in hidden text (see the headline in fig. 20.1).
- ✔ **No-wrap section.** A *no-wrap section* is a section of text that does not wrap in the Help window. This setting is useful for tables and examples that should not be reformatted. A no-wrap section is defined in Word for Windows 6 by choosing Format, Paragraph from the menu and checking the Keep Lines Together box on the Text Flow tab of the Paragraph dialog box.
- ✔ **Nonscrolling region.** A *nonscrolling region* is a section of text (or graphics) which is displayed in a fixed location immediately below the button bar of the Help window. This section remains fixed when you scroll through the remaining

part of the topic text. A nonscrolling region is defined in Word for Windows 6 by choosing Format, Paragraph from the menu and checking the Keep with Next box on the Text Flow tab of the Paragraph dialog box.

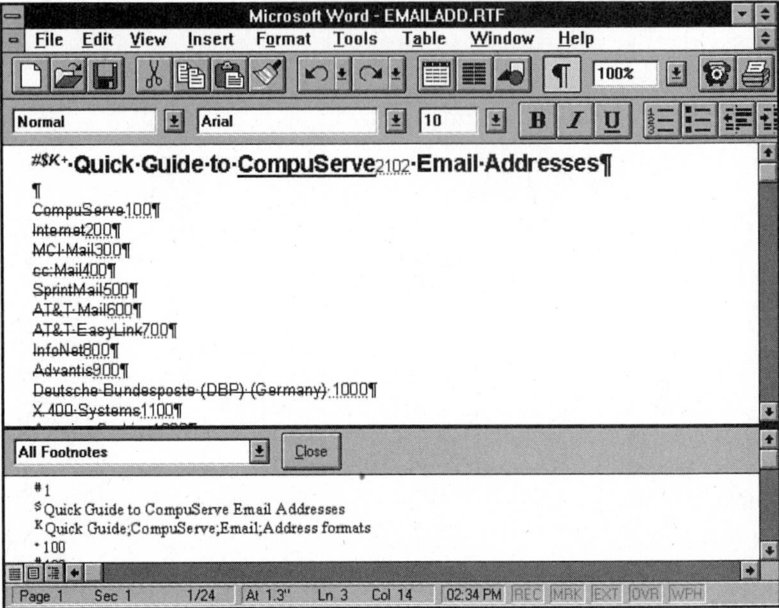

Figure 20.1
The Source Help file.

You also can include graphics in your Help system either by embedding them directly into your source RTF file or by placing the bitmap by reference using the following tag: {bml *filename*}. The bml code specifies the alignment for the graphic: bml (left), bmc (center), or bmr (right). (If you place a bitmap by reference, the filename must be added to the Help project file [Bitmaps] section.)

When you have finished the source Help file, be sure to save it in Rich Text Format.

Creating a Help Project File

The Help project file is a text file containing up to nine sections that look like the sections in a Windows INI file. The Help compiler examines the Help project file to determine what topic and graphics files to compile and how to handle them. Of the nine, four sections are most often used when creating a Help project file:

- ✔ The Files section itemizes the RTF files to be included in the compiling process.
- ✔ The Bitmaps section itemizes the bitmap files to be included (for bitmaps referenced in a Help source file).

- ✔ The Map section enables you to associate context strings with context numbers, which is required when you are creating context-sensitive Help.
- ✔ The Options section enables you to define various options. You do not have to include this section, but if you do, be sure it is the first section of your Help project file. Possible options are described in Table 20.1.

Table 20.1 Help options

Option	Definition
BMROOT	Defines the directory holding bitmap files when placed by reference.
BUILD	Sets the topics to be included in the compiled Help file.
COMPRESS	Sets compression level of the Help file: For 0% compression, use `No`, `False`, or `0`. For 40% compression, use `Medium`. For 50% compression, use `Yes`, `True`, `1`, or `High`.
CONTENTS	Defines the context string of the Contents topic.
COPYRIGHT	Includes a copyright statement in the Help | About dialog box of the Help file.
ERRORLOG	Specifies an output file for error messages generated during the compiling process.
FORCEFONT	Sets all fonts to a single font in the compiled Help file.
ICON	Specifies the icon to be used with the Help file.
LANGUAGE	Sets a different sort order for Scandinavian language Help files.
OPTCDROM	Optimizes a Help file for a CD-ROM when set to Yes.
REPORT	Turns on the display of error messages on screen during the build when set to `Yes`, `True`, `1`, or `On`.
ROOT	Defines the root directory used during the compiling process.
TITLE	Sets the title of the Help window.

continues

Table 20.1, Continued
Help Options

Option	Definition
WARNING	Sets the error message level for the compiler: 1 - report only severe warnings 2 - report intermediate 3 - report all warnings

The other sections are BuildTags, Config, Alias, Windows, and Baggage.

The following list gives a sample Help project file:

```
[Options]
ROOT=D:\IRENT\BUILD
TITLE=Help on IntelliRent
COPYRIGHT=Copyright ©1994 New Riders Publishing
ICON=IRHELP.ICO
ERRORLOG=ERR.TXT
COMPRESS=YES
REPORT=ON
WARNING=3

[Files]
IRENT.RTF

[Map]
Main_Screen                   1000
Data_Entry                    1020
Data_Entry_2                  1030
Data_Entry_3                  1040
Data_Entry_4                  1050
Data_Entry_5                  1060
Results                               1070
UseIR                         1080
UseIR_2                               1090
UseIR_3                               1100
UseIR_4                               1110
UseIR_5                               1120
UseIR_6                               1130
UseIR_7                               1140
```

Compiling the Help Project Using the Help Compiler

The Windows Help Compiler is a DOS program that combines the "raw materials" of Help files into a single finished Help file. The program uses three kinds of raw materials:

- ✔ **Rich Text Format files.** The actual text of the Help file is contained in one or more Rich Text Format (RTF) files.
- ✔ **Graphic files.** Graphics can be either embedded into the RTF files or stored as separate files. Formats supported include: bitmap (BMP), device-independent bitmap (DIB), metafile (WMF), multiple-resolution bitmap (MRB), and segmented-graphics bitmap (SHG).
- ✔ **Help Project file.** The Help Project file is a text file that contains instructions for the Help compiler to use as it makes the Help file. It must have an HPJ extension.

When the Help compiler creates a Help file, it reads the project file to determine what it needs to do. The Help compiler then compiles the RTF files and graphics into a format that the WinHelp engine can display and saves it as a file with an HLP extension.

Several ways exist to get the Help compiler, such as the Windows Software Development Kit (SDK) or Borland language products (such as C++ and Borland Pascal). However, if you do not need documentation, the most cost effective source available is the WINSDK forum on CompuServe (Go WinSDK), where it is provided in the Windows Help library.

To run the Help compiler, you must shell out to DOS and enter the following command line:

```
HC HelpProjectFile
```

For example:

```
HC IRENT.HPJ
```

The Help compiler performs the compiling process and, if successful, generates the HLP file. The HLP file has the same name as your HPJ file.

Integrating Help Files with dBASE for Windows Applications

Before you create a WinHelp system, you need to decide the ways you want to integrate help in your dBASE application. Two main methods are discussed in the sections that follow.

Reference-Style Help

The first, most basic option is to provide *reference-style Help*, in which any calls made from your application to your Help system display the Contents topic in the Help window. You can think of the Contents topic as the table of contents of your Help system, as shown in figure 20.2. Users begin at the Contents topic and navigate through the Help system until they find assistance for the desired command or subject.

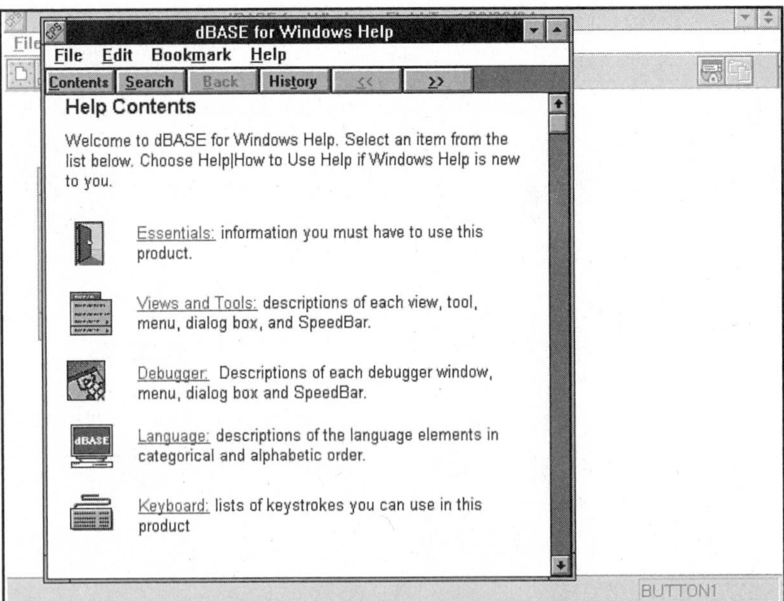

Figure 20.2
The Contents window of a Help file.

Reference-style help is easy to build into your dBASE for Windows application. Use the SET HELP TO command to specify the Help file you would like dBASE to activate. You typically would want to do this when first opening your application. Therefore, place the following code in the OnOpen Event of your form:

```
SET HELP TO IRENT.HLP
```

Because the SET HELP TO command sets the default Help file for dBASE for Windows for the current session, you should reset this setting when you close your application back to the dBASE for Windows Help file. To do that, place the following code in the OnClose Event of your form:

```
SET HELP TO
```

Now that you have specified the Help file to use, you need a means to activate the Help system. The simplest way is to create a Help button (from the Custom tab of the Object Selector) and place it on your form. Place the HELP command in the OnClick Event Editor. The HELP command is used to activate the Help system.

When you run the form and choose the Help button, the WinHelp window appears. If you attach this same method to every Help button you place in your forms, the Contents topic appears consistently no matter where the user accesses Help within your application. Although reference-style help is easy for the developer to implement, the user always has to jump through the Help system to find the desired topic.

Context-Sensitive Help

A much more advanced type of help is known as context-sensitive Help. *Context-sensitive Help* enables users to receive assistance related to the active command or dialog box. For example, place the cursor in the OnClose Event in the Object Inspector and press F1. Notice that Help is shown with the OnClose topic displayed. As this example demonstrates, when you build context sensitivity into your application, you enable the user immediate access to help for the command the user is trying to execute.

Context-sensitive Help matches the command the user is executing with a related topic in the Help system. This matching system is possible because each topic in a Help system is linked to the application. Your job as a developer is to link specific commands or options in your application to corresponding help topics.

The HelpFile and HelpID properties (see fig. 20.3) are the principle means to implement context-sensitive Help in dBASE for Windows.

- ✔ **HelpFile property.** Specifies the name of the HLP file.
- ✔ **HelpID property.** Specifies the keyword used to identify a Help topic.

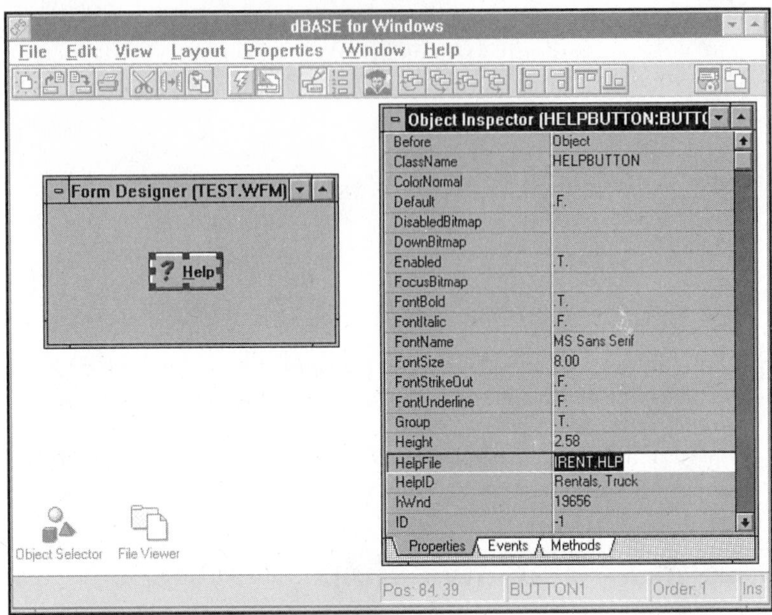

Figure 20.3 The HelpFile and HelpID properties of the Object Inspector.

Typically, each object's HelpID property activates a different topic in the Help system. Context-sensitive help obviously requires a great deal of upfront planning for the developer, but the user is rewarded with a sophisticated, easy-to-use help system.

You can also use the HELP or SET TOPIC commands to specify a specific Help topic as well. If you use an exact keyword as a parameter for either of these commands, the associated topic is displayed. However, if you specify a keyword that does not have an exact match or just the initial characters of a keyword, the Search dialog box is displayed. Users could then use this dialog box to select from a list.

Taking Advantage of Windows Help Authoring Tools

Several tools are available which can help manage the Help development process. This section describes these tools.

- ✔ **Windows Help Project Editor.** The Windows Help Project Editor (WHPE) is a tool that automates the creation of a Help project file.
- ✔ **Windows Help Authoring Template.** The Windows Help Authoring Template (WHAT) is a Word for Windows template that automates the formatting of topic files. Both WHAT and WHPE are designed to work together and are available on the Microsoft Developer's Network CD.

- **RoboHelp.** RoboHelp is a Word for Windows add-on that automates the process of creating Help files. A template provides a specialized menu and floating toolbar that enable easy access to each of the operations necessary to create a Help topic. You have to provide the Help compiler, however, because it is not included with RoboHelp. RoboHelp has a list price of $495 and is available from Blue Sky Software.

- **Doc-To-Help.** Doc-To-Help is another Word for Windows add-on that helps to convert product documentation to Help files. If you have existing documents you want converted, or if you want to produce a written document and Help file, Doc-To-Help is probably your best choice. Doc-To-Help is the only package that includes the Help compiler. Doc-To-Help is available from WexTech Systems for $295.

- **Help Magician.** The Help Magician differs from most of the other tools by providing its own RTF editor. However, it works much the same way as Word for Windows templates offered by other tools. Help Magician is available for $195 from Software Interphase.

- **QD Help.** QD Help provides a "quick and dirty" approach to Help authoring. Using your own ASCII text editor, you insert a set of special commands that QD Help uses to convert your text file to RTF format. One notable utility that comes with QD Help is QDMenu, which examines a Windows EXE file, extracts its menu structure, and writes a file based on the menu structure that can serve as a starting point for creating a Help file. QD Help is shareware and can be downloaded from the Windows SDK forum in CompuServe. Registration is $35.00.

NRP
NEW RIDERS
PUBLISHING

Part VII

Exploring Advanced Concepts

Chapter Snapshot

Migration from one platform or environment to another is never easy and seldom intuitive. dBASE for Windows makes this process far less painful than it might otherwise be. In this chapter, you learn to do the following:

Take the time to learn well the various design surfaces for forms, menus, reports, and so on. After reading this chapter, you will have a thorough background in converting DOS programs to dBASE.

Converting DOS Applications to Windows

By Keith Chuvala

dBASE for Windows offers substantial support for your existing dBASE/DOS code and runs many DOS applications with little or no modification. The results, however, look and work just like your old DOS application. Not very exciting.

An experienced Windows user has expectations about the look and feel of a Windows program; certain behaviors and elements are not only expected, but demanded. The highest calling of a software developer is to meet end-user expectations and solve end-user problems.

With an eye toward living up to this lofty calling, this chapter explores and explains the efficient migration of existing dBASE/DOS applications to fully "Windows-ized" status.

Recognizing the Changes in dBASE/ DOS Commands

Although the support for dBASE/DOS programs in dBASE for Windows is extensive, it is not complete. Some DOS commands are not supported for obvious reasons (usually related to the user interface), and others have been modified or dropped for less obvious reasons.

Table 21.1 lists the commands that have been removed or modified in dBASE. The size of this list might be alarming at first glance, but note that virtually all functionality represented in table 21.1 is available in dBASE for Windows. In many cases the method employed or command involved has changed. And given the wide scope of the dBASE language, this list is actually quite small; more than 99 percent of the dBASE/DOS language has survived intact.

Table 21.1
Commands Changed or No Longer Supported

Command	Comments
SET HISTORY TO SET HISTORY ON/OFF LIST HISTORY DISPLAY HISTORY	The command window makes these obsolete.
BEGIN... END ROLLBACK COMPLETED() ISMARKED() ROLLBACK()	Transaction processing has been revamped.
ACCESS() USER() LIST USERS DISPLAY USERS	Windows now supplies network support.
SAVE MACRO RESTORE MACRO PLAY MACRO	Windows traps keystrokes in a way that makes these commands unusable. You can, however, use the Windows macro recorder.

Command	Comments
LOAD CALL CALL() RELEASE MODULE	You should use DLLs now rather than BINs.
SET SQL	Use SQLEXEC instead.
SET DEBUG SET TRAP SET DBTRAP	The new debugger supersedes these settings.
ASSIST	The Navigator replaces ASSIST.
SET INSTRUCT SET SCOREBOARD SET COLOR TO SET PAUSE SET CLOCK SET HOURS SET HELP TO	These commands have changed or been removed because of user interface issues under Windows.
DGEN() DEXPORT	Template commands are no longer supported.
PROTECT LOGOUT SET ENCRYPTION	Security and data encryption have changed with the advent of client/server support.

Preparing for Migration

As a developer, programmer, weekend hacker, or whatever category of dBASE program writer in which you find yourself, you've undoubtedly come to terms with one of the enduring truths of applications development: good planning makes for easier and more effective development. Migrating your dBASE/DOS applications to Windows earns no exemption to this axiom.

During the planning phase of migration, you should do the following:

- ✔ Take a "dry run" of the application in dBASE for Windows
- ✔ Decide which elements of the program do and don't "fit" in Windows
- ✔ Decide which elements must be redesigned or re-created to work like a Windows program "should"
- ✔ Develop a strategy for moving from a procedural to an event-driven model

Taking a Dry Run

The first step in the migration process is to evaluate what you're starting with. In this chapter, you work with a dBASE program generated by dBASE IV's Applications Generator using the Quick Application feature. A QuickApp has all the basic functionality found in most dBASE programs, with Edit and Browse screens, REPORT and LABEL form output, and essential data management. This sample program is based on SW.DBF, a shareware customer registration data file.

To run the program, set the directory to C:\SW and double-click on SWREG.PRG under the Programs tab in the Navigator. Figure 21.1 shows the program running after you've maximized the command window.

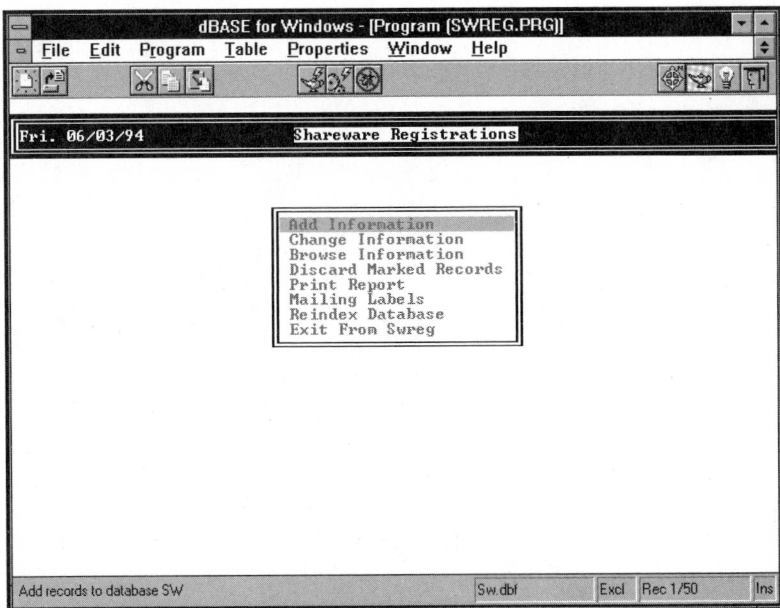

Figure 21.1 Running SWREG.PRG under dBASE for Windows.

You might have trouble getting overly excited about the look of SWREG.PRG when you first bring it into dBASE for Windows, but you need to note that a few "magical" things have happened in the transition:

- ✔ The mouse is fully enabled, regardless of how you implemented or ignored it in dBASE/DOS.
- ✔ The standard Windows Edit menu and dBASE for Windows SpeedBar are activated, indicating that you now have cut-and-paste and other standard Windows capabilities.

Something has been lost from this opening screen, too. The MenuBox procedure generated for any QuickApp displays not only the date, as you can see at the left side of the title box, but also the time, which should but does not appear on the right side.

Unfortunately, SET CLOCK was one of the many DOS victims noted in Table 21.1. Fortunately, the commands that are no longer supported in most cases have little or no bearing on how your application manipulates data. Most of these changes are like SET CLOCK—they affect the user interface only.

More "magic" happens when you look at the Edit screen, shown in figure 21.2. The Edit screen appears when the user selects the Change Information option on SWREG's main menu.

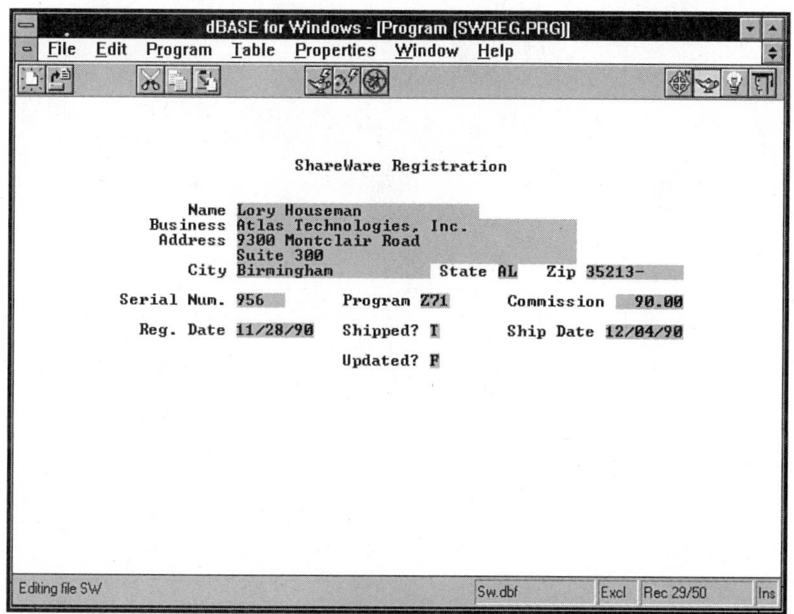

Figure 21.2
The SWREG.PRG Edit screen.

Note how the mouse pointer changes shapes as you move it over an @... GET field. If you're a Windows user, you'll recognize the familiar I-beam cursor right away; it's standard fare in Windows word processing programs and many text-entry fields in a "normal" Windows application. This screen is where you can first play with the Windows editing functions such as Cut, Copy, and Paste.

So far the differences between SWREG running under Windows as opposed to running under DOS have been rather subtle. All pretense of subtlety goes out the, well, "window," however, when you select the Browse Information option from the main menu (see fig. 21.3).

Figure 21.3
The SWREG.PRG Browse screen.

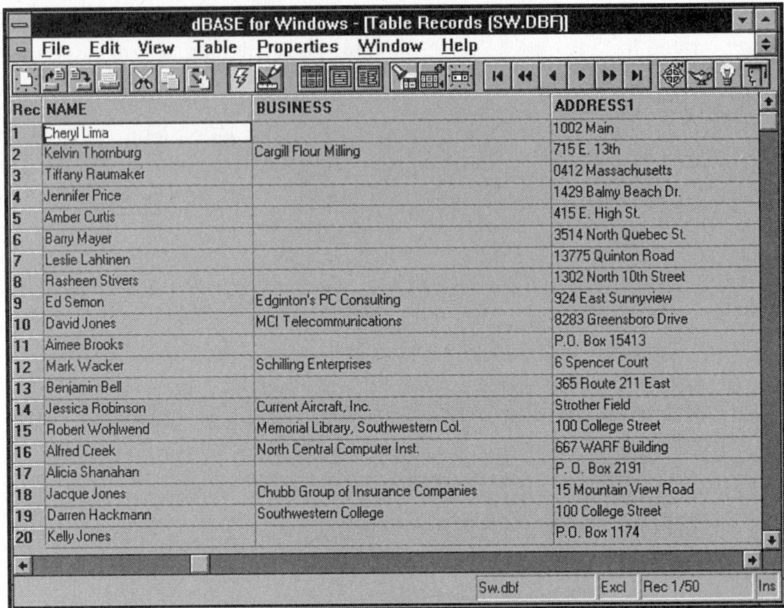

Rec	NAME	BUSINESS	ADDRESS1
1	Cheryl Lima		1002 Main
2	Kelvin Thornburg	Cargill Flour Milling	715 E. 13th
3	Tiffany Raumaker		0412 Massachusetts
4	Jennifer Price		1429 Balmy Beach Dr.
5	Amber Curtis		415 E. High St.
6	Barry Mayer		3514 North Quebec St.
7	Leslie Lahtinen		13775 Quinton Road
8	Rasheen Stivers		1302 North 10th Street
9	Ed Semon	Edginton's PC Consulting	924 East Sunnyview
10	David Jones	MCI Telecommunications	8283 Greensboro Drive
11	Aimee Brooks		P.O. Box 15413
12	Mark Wacker	Schilling Enterprises	6 Spencer Court
13	Benjamin Bell		365 Route 211 East
14	Jessica Robinson	Current Aircraft, Inc.	Strother Field
15	Robert Wohlwend	Memorial Library, Southwestern Col.	100 College Street
16	Alfred Creek	North Central Computer Inst.	667 WARF Building
17	Alicia Shanahan		P. O. Box 2191
18	Jacque Jones	Chubb Group of Insurance Companies	15 Mountain View Road
19	Darren Hackmann	Southwestern College	100 College Street
20	Kelly Jones		P.O. Box 1174

In the Browse screen, all the SpeedBar tools, including the VCR button navigational controls, are at your disposal. Also note that you can resize columns and even rearrange them by using standard mouse dragging techniques.

dBASE/DOS reports and labels offer little excitement, as shown in figure 21.4.

Printing can be problematic when you're moving an application from DOS to Windows. Although DOS programs rely on myriad drivers and somewhat complex interfaces to ensure proper output, Windows applications rely wholly on the Windows printing system. This more centralized approach to printer setup is far easier for the end-user as well as the program.

At the same time, if you are accustomed to sending printer-specific codes to the printer port by using the ??? command or something similar, you need to unlearn this habit. Under Windows, the user and not the programmer should be able to decide which output device is to be used for a given report.

Fortunately, dBASE for Windows handles REPORT FORM and LABEL FORM output well, and unless you've gone to some lengths to accomplish custom output under DOS, the printing situation will be nearly a non-issue in the migration of your applications. dBASE for Windows' new report writer is far superior to the dBASE/DOS one, and you probably want to bring many (if not all) of your old reports up to its standards. Report migration is covered in some detail later in this chapter.

The remaining functions in the SWREG.PRG program work as expected, and no more magic tricks are waiting for you. Now that you know what your baseline is, you're ready to move on to the next step.

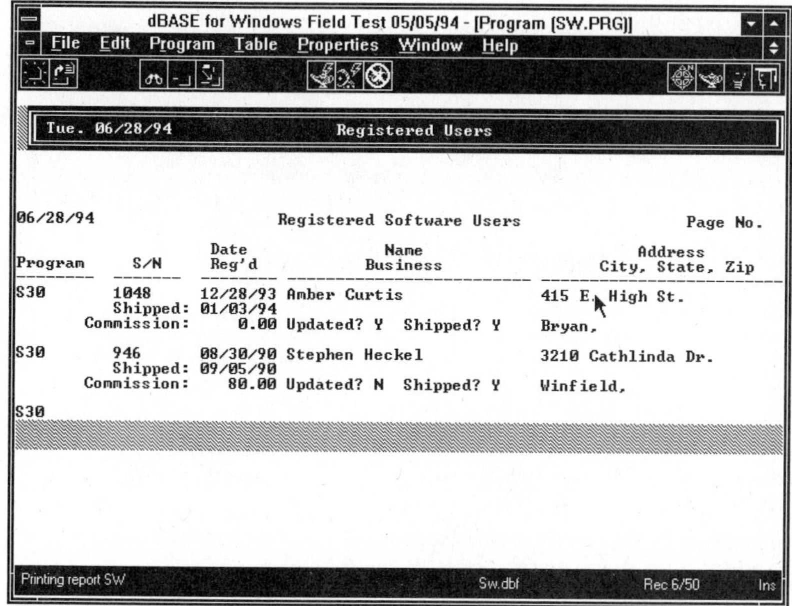

Figure 21.4 Using the SWREG.PRG Report to Screen option.

Deciding Which Program Elements Fit

As the saying goes, you win some, you lose some. So far, the migration process has borne far more wins than losses. You lost SET CLOCK and perhaps one or two other niceties from the DOS version of the program, but you've gained more capable editing and a far superior BROWSE function, and the basic functionality of your DOS program has survived intact.

Is this a Windows program now? Hardly. In the strictest sense, perhaps you could say that you have a real Windows program, because it is running natively under Windows, uses the Windows Clipboard for cut-and-paste operations, and uses the Windows printing system, including the Print Manager and/or any network printers to which you might be attached. But the end-users of your programs won't buy this justification for a minute. A *real* Windows program, after all, has cool pull-down menus with speed keys; dialog boxes with editing controls, push buttons, and cool little pictures; and reports that bear fonts in different sizes. In short, a Windows program is *cool.* The program you just ran under dBASE for Windows is lukewarm at best.

Underneath the menus, dialog boxes, and bitmaps, the code you've written to manipulate data runs unchanged in most cases and needs little if any reworking. You probably need to change how it is invoked, but not what it does.

Aesthetically, this program is a major flop when compared to even the most insignificant "real" Windows application. The data manipulation code you've written remains the same, but little of the user interface survives. The move from character-based dBASE/DOS to graphically oriented dBASE for Windows is just too profound.

The good news is that dBASE for Windows itself assists in migrating your existing user interface (UI) elements to their more acceptable Windows counterparts.

Deciding Which Elements To Redesign or Re-create

Based on your observations thus far, the Browse screen seems to be the only element that looks like it "should" in a Windows program. The following parts, then, you have to rework or rewrite:

- ✔ **The main menu and any submenus.** SWREG.PRG as a QuickApp utilizes a dBASE pop-up. This system works fine but violates most every Windows convention about menu use in existence. Always remember that a primary benefit of using Windows in the first place is consistency of the user interface across all applications, including your dBASE ones.
- ✔ **The Edit screen.** At a minimum you need a Windows dialog box and standard Windows editing controls, including such things as VCR buttons, spin boxes, and check boxes. You have no good reason under Windows to make a user remember the various record and file navigation keys, deal with dBASE/DOS's arcane numeric input, or have to key in T, F, Y, or N for a logical field when a simple click on a check box accomplishes the same purposes more intuitively and with less chance for error. Also, a Windows user expects the Enter key to select a default button to signify that the user is done with a screen, rather than the field-to-field navigation the Enter key accomplishes under the old DOS model.
- ✔ **The reports.** The output you produce now is functional, but it's about as sexy as used sandpaper. A Windows program is expected to produce output that is not only functional, but also attractive.

As you proceed through the migration, other smaller issues make themselves apparent, and you can deal with them as they arise. The important thing is to remain focused at all times on your goal, which is to produce a program that offers at least the same functionality as its DOS predecessor. That new program also will be wrapped in a user interface that is more intuitive, more attractive, and ultimately more satisfying than its DOS ancestor.

Can you make it cute or fun in the process? Definitely. Adding bitmapped pictures, custom controls, and so on is elegant and almost simple in dBASE for Windows, but such additions are best left for the end of the project. First you need to make it work.

Developing a Strategy for Moving to an Event-Driven Model

Perhaps the greatest conceptual leap for the programmer moving from dBASE/DOS to dBASE for Windows is from a procedural model to an event-driven one. Event-driven processing (EDP) is natural under Windows, and if you've ever used a Windows program, you're already acquainted with the EDP model from the end-user's standpoint.

If you're like most dBASE IV programmers, you've already worked with EDP, although you might not have recognized it as such. The dBASE IV Applications Generator produces a mixture of procedural and event-driven code, and many programmers emulate that approach. In fact, dBASE IV leaves little choice but to do just that. Writing entirely procedural programs is possible but not obvious, and writing entirely event-driven programs with the dBASE IV language is nearly impossible.

The following lines are a section of code from SWREG.PRG, edited slightly for space considerations:

```
*— Define the main popup menu for Quickapp
SET BORDER TO DOUBLE
DEFINE POPUP quick FROM 7,27
DEFINE BAR 1 OF quick ;
       PROMPT " Add Information" ;
       MESSAGE "Add records to database SW"
DEFINE BAR 2 OF quick ;
       PROMPT " Browse Information" ;
       MESSAGE "Browse database SW"
DEFINE BAR 3 OF quick ;
       PROMPT " Print Report" ;
       MESSAGE "Run report form SW"
DEFINE BAR 4 OF quick ;
       PROMPT " Exit From Swreg" ;
       MESSAGE "Exit program to dBASE"
ON SELECTION POPUP quick DO Action WITH BAR()

SHOW POPUP quick
DO WHILE gn_barv <> 4
  ACTIVATE POPUP quick
ENDDO
```

```
21 PROCEDURE Action
22 PARAMETERS bar
23 gn_barv = bar
24 DO CASE
25     CASE gn_barv = 1
26         *— Add information
27         SET MESSAGE TO 'Appending records to file SW'
28         APPEND
29     CASE gn_barv = 2
30         *— Browse information
31         SET MESSAGE TO 'Browsing file SW'
32         BROWSE FORMAT
33     CASE gn_barv = 3
34         *— Run report form sw
35         go top
36         REPORT FORM SW.FRG
37     CASE gn_barv = 4
38         DEACTIVATE POPUP
39 ENDCASE
40 RETURN
```

Note that this program never invokes PROCEDURE action directly. No explicit DO ACTION command is included. Instead, ACTION is called only when a selection is made from POPUP Quick. Line 16 establishes this event handling with the ON SELECTION POPUP... command. This design works well, but it can be confusing. Although ACTION is itself called as the result of an event (selecting one of the bars in POPUP Quick), the task performed is ascertained by using conventional procedural program flow, which in this case is handled by a DO CASE construct. In a truly event-driven model, each BAR in POPUP Quick would be tied directly to the code you want executed when that BAR is selected. In dBASE for Windows, this approach is precisely what you use.

You could think of each BAR, and indeed the POPUP itself, as a UI (user interface) object. Note in lines 4 through 6 that when the BAR for "Add Information" is defined, you are creating three items. In line 4 you create the BAR itself (#1 in POPUP Quick). In line 5 you specify a text property, or PROMPT, for this bar ("Add Information"). In line 6 you also specify a MESSAGE property to be associated automatically with this newly created BAR ("Add records to database SW"). What you're doing here is very OOP-like, in that the PROMPT and MESSAGE properties are bound directly to BAR #1. Those properties are automatically used whenever the BAR itself is used. In OOP-speak, this is *encapsulation*, and chances are you've already done quite a bit of it without associating that particular term with the activity.

Encapsulation in a BAR enables you to specify many different properties and events that occur automatically when the BAR, BROWSE, PAD, and so on is used. dBASE for Windows takes this concept much farther. You can specify not only certain properties, but also the functions and/or procedures that should be tied to a particular UI element. Instead of creating a Save button on a form and then using an unwieldy DO WHILE loop to handle the processing and ascertain whether Save was selected, you can associate directly to the Save button the code necessary for saving information. This method makes your code much easier to maintain, and moving elements around on-screen or in the program no longer requires additional changes to a large DO WHILE or DO CASE structure.

How concerned must you be with OOP buzzwords such as encapsulation to accomplish a migration from DOS to Windows? Not very. As you soon see, dBASE for Windows's interactive tools do the vast majority of the code writing for you. You want to become as familiar with the EDP model as possible, however, because making changes to your code and developing new dBASE for Windows programs entails a number of these concepts and techniques. Fortunately, these ideas, which are brand new to dBASE, are not in and of themselves new or proprietary. If you learn event-driven processing and object-oriented programming in dBASE, this learning is invaluable if and when you look at other object-oriented environments and tools.

The order of service for your migration is as follows:

1. Create a new form to replace the DOS FMT file.

2. Create a new report to replace the DOS FRG file.

3. Create a new menu to replace the DOS POPUP.

4. Work on making code itself more event-driven.

The first three of these tasks are rather simple; dBASE for Windows provides outstanding tools to aid in the migration and creation of forms, reports, and menus. Item number 4 takes more work but is certainly within reach of almost any dBASE programmer.

Using the Component Builder

Perhaps the most daunting task in moving from a character-based to a graphics-based user interface is the creation and modification of the screens or dialog boxes to be employed in the new application. The dBASE for Windows Component Builder, CB.PRO, goes to great lengths to minimize the hassle factor in this most important piece of the migration.

CB.PRO is normally installed in the \DBASEWIN\UTILITY directory of the drive on which you installed dBASE for Windows. If you've moved the Component Builder elsewhere, you need to change to the appropriate directory, using the Navigator or the command window. Next, invoke CB with a double-click or by typing **do cb** in the command window (see fig. 21.5).

Note that the Component Builder (CB) looks like a typical Windows application, with menus, graphics, and dialog boxes just like you'd expect to see in a Windows program. Be encouraged, for CB is written completely in dBASE for Windows. It's a fine example of what your own programs can look like.

After you have started CB, change to the directory in which your application is stored (**F**ile, Change **D**irectory) so that newly created files go to the same directory (see fig. 21.6).

Figure 21.5
Starting the Component Builder.

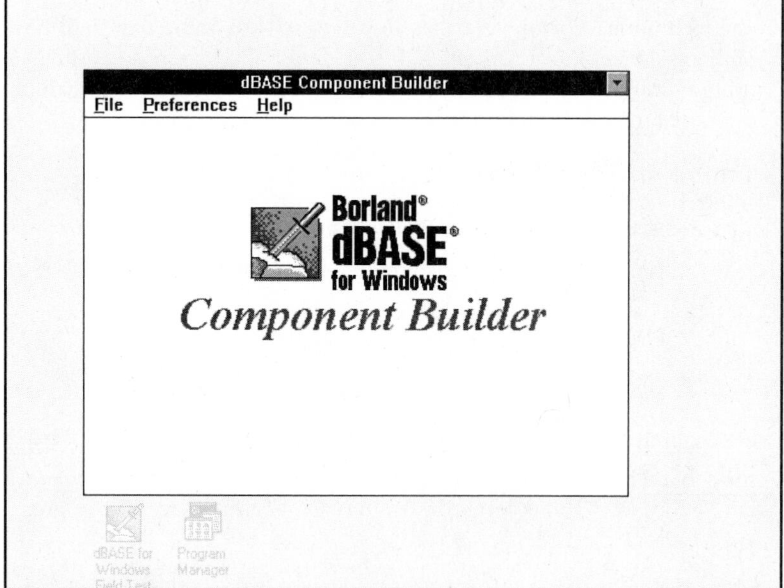

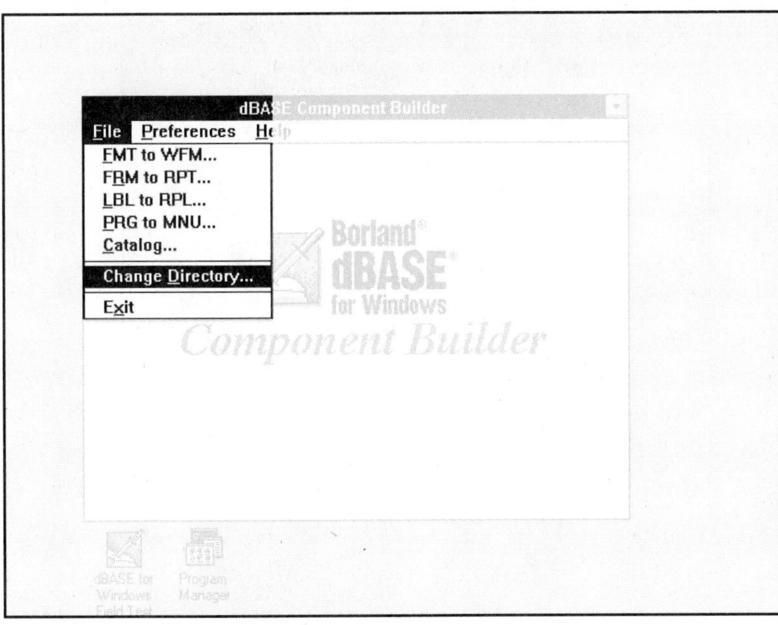

Figure 21.6
Changing to your application directory.

Converting an FMT Screen File

As mentioned previously, your first task in this chapter's example is to work on the input form for the SWREG application. CB takes the existing SW.FMT file and does much of the migration of this code for you. From CB's File menu, select FMT to WFM. Select your project's directory once again as being the source of the FMT file, and select the FMT file with which you want to work (see fig. 21.7).

dBASE for Windows also needs to know which file (DBF) or query (QBE) you plan to use in building your new form. This step is nothing new; in dBASE/DOS you had to use a file before you could properly modify a DOS screen. In the DOS product you could skirt around this link to the data file, but CB is a bit more ornery about this requirement and does not enable you to proceed unless you've specified a file to use. Next, Component Builder prompts you to select the data file to be associated with the form (see fig. 21.8).

After you've selected the FMT and DBF or QBE files, CB goes to work for you. An informational dialog box reports the progress of the conversion (see fig. 21.9), and when the task is completed, you are returned to CB's main window and menu.

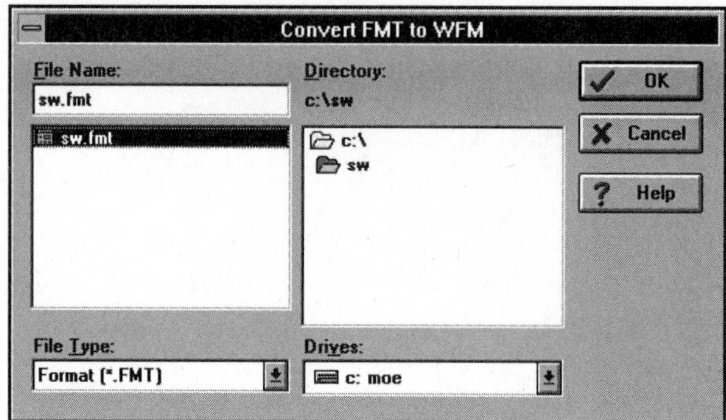

Figure 21.7
Selecting an FMT file for conversion to WFM format.

Instead of continuing the migration, at this point you might want to take a look at what CB has produced for you. Exit CB now, and go back to dBASE for Windows. Edit your new WFM file.

The following is your original SW.FMT file as generated by the dBASE IV screen generator:

```
*******************************************************************************
*— Name.......: SW.FMT
*— Date.......: 4-02-91
*— Version....: dBASE IV, Format 1.1
*— Notes......: Format files use "" as delimiters!
*******************************************************************************

*-- Format file initialization code -----------------------------------
---------

*-- Some of these PRIVATE variables are created based on CodeGen and
may not
*-- be used by your particular .fmt file
PRIVATE lc_talk, lc_cursor, lc_display, lc_status, lc_carry, lc_proc,;
         ln_typeahd, gc_cut
IF SET("TALK") = "ON"
   SET TALK OFF
   lc_talk = "ON"
```

```
ELSE
   lc_talk = "OFF"
ENDIF
lc_cursor = SET("CURSOR")
```

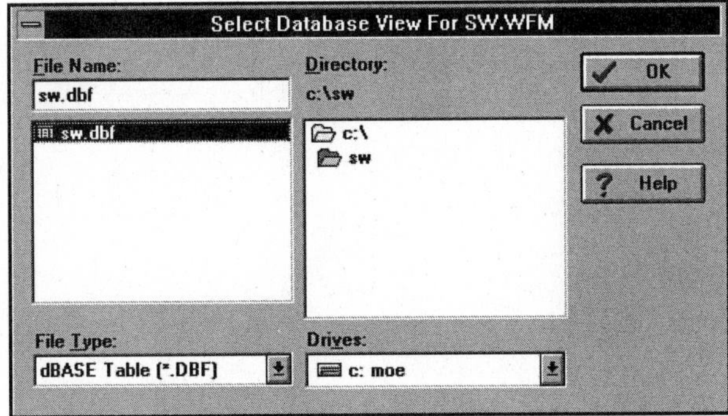

Figure 21.8 Associating a DBF with the form.

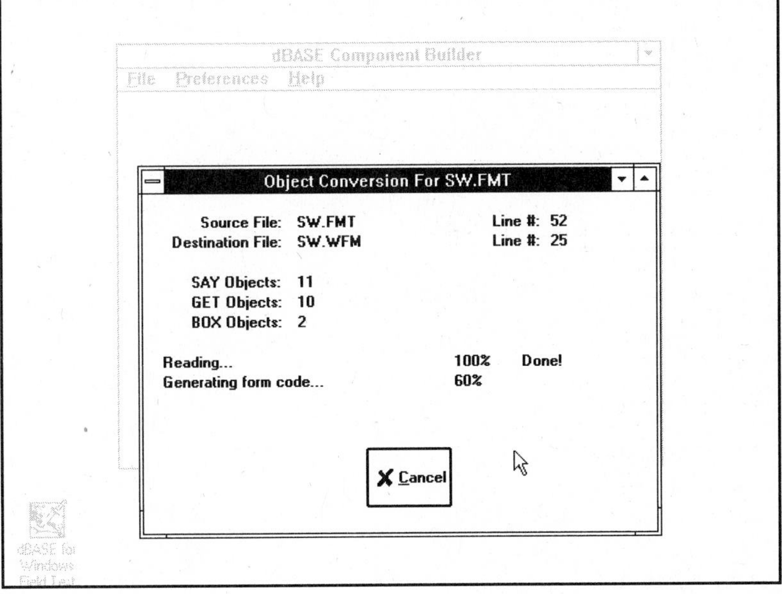

Figure 21.9 FMT to WFM conversion.

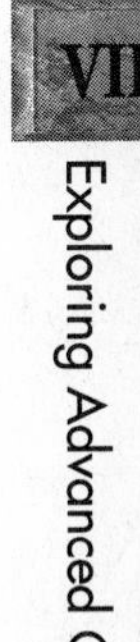

```
SET CURSOR ON

lc_status = SET("STATUS")
*-- SET STATUS was OFF when you went into the Forms Designer.
IF lc_status = "ON"
   SET STATUS OFF
ENDIF
*-- @ SAY GETS Processing. ------------------------------------------
--------
*--  Format Page: 1
@ 3,9 TO 5,70 DOUBLE
@ 4,29 SAY "ShareWare Registration"
@ 6,9 TO 18,70
@ 7,18 SAY "Name"
@ 7,23 GET Name PICTURE "XXXXXXXXXXXXXXXXXXXXXXXXX"
@ 8,14 SAY "Business"
@ 8,23 GET Business PICTURE "XXXXXXXXXXXXXXXXXXXXXXXXXXXXXXXXXXXX"
@ 9,15 SAY "Address"
@ 9,23 GET Address1 PICTURE "XXXXXXXXXXXXXXXXXXXXXXXXXXXXXXXXXXXX"
@ 10,23 GET Address2 PICTURE "XXXXXXXXXXXXXXXXXXXXXXXXXXXXXXXXXXXX"
@ 11,18 SAY "City"
@ 11,23 GET City PICTURE "XXXXXXXXXXXXXXXXXXXX"
@ 11,44 SAY "State"
@ 11,50 GET State PICTURE "!!"
@ 11,55 SAY "Zip"
@ 11,59 GET Zip PICTURE "99999-9999"
@ 13,11 SAY "Serial Num."
@ 13,23 GET Serialno PICTURE "XXXXX"
@ 13,34 SAY "Program"
@ 13,42 GET Program PICTURE "!!!"
@ 13,51 SAY "Commission"
@ 13,62 GET Commission PICTURE "9999.99"
@ 15,13 SAY "Reg. Date"
@ 15,23 GET Regdate
@ 15,34 SAY "Shipped?"
@ 15,43 GET Shipped PICTURE "L"
@ 15,51 SAY "Ship Date"
@ 15,61 GET Shipdate
```

```
@ 17,34 SAY "Updated?"
@ 17,43 GET Updated PICTURE "L"
*-- Format file exit code ---------------------------------------
--------

*-- SET STATUS was OFF when you went into the Forms Designer.
IF lc_status = "ON"  && Entered form with status on
   SET STATUS ON     && Turn STATUS "ON" on the way out
ENDIF
SET CURSOR &lc_cursor.
SET TALK &lc_talk.

RELEASE lc_talk,lc_fields,lc_status
*-- EOP: SW.FMT
```

And the following lines comprise the SW.SFM file produced by the Component Builder:

```
 ***********************************************
***         dBASE Component Builder          ***
***              Form Generation             ***
***                  SW.FMT                  ***
***       Created: 04/30/94 @ 18:59:40       ***
***********************************************

PUBLIC swWFM

swWFM = new sw()
open form swWFM
lVoid = swWFM.setFocus()

CLASS sw of form
   this.Text       = "SW"
   this.View       = "C:\SW\SW.DBF"
   this.Width      = 80.00
   this.Top        = 00.00
   this.Left       = 00.00
   this.Height     = 25.00
   this.Minimize = .F.
   this.Maximize = .F.
```

```
DEFINE RECTANGLE boxObj1 OF THIS;
   Property;
      Text          "",;
      Height        3,;
      Width         62,;
      Top           3,;
      Left          9

DEFINE RECTANGLE boxObj2 OF THIS;
   Property;
      Text          "",;
      Height        13,;
      Width         62,;
      Top           6,;
      Left          9

DEFINE TEXT txtObj1 OF THIS;
   Property;
      Text          "ShareWare Registration",;
      Top           4,;
      Left          29,;
      Width         24

DEFINE TEXT txtObj2 OF THIS;
   Property;
      Text          "Name",;
      Top           7,;
      Left          18,;
      Width          6

DEFINE ENTRYFIELD getObj1 OF THIS;
   Property;
      Width         25,;
      Top           7,;
      Left          23,;
      Picture       "XXXXXXXXXXXXXXXXXXXXXXXXX",;
      DataLink      "Name"

DEFINE TEXT txtObj3 OF THIS;
   Property;
      Text          "Business",;
      Top           8,;
      Left          14,;
      Width         10
```

```
DEFINE ENTRYFIELD getObj2 OF THIS;
   Property;
      Width         35,;
      Top           8,;
      Left          23,;
      Picture       "XXXXXXXXXXXXXXXXXXXXXXXXXXXXXXXXXXX",;
      DataLink      "Business"

DEFINE TEXT txtObj4 OF THIS;
   Property;
      Text          "Address",;
      Top           9,;
      Left          15,;
      Width          9

DEFINE ENTRYFIELD getObj3 OF THIS;
   Property;
      Width         35,;
      Top           9,;
      Left          23,;
      Picture       "XXXXXXXXXXXXXXXXXXXXXXXXXXXXXXXXXXX",;
      DataLink      "Address1"

DEFINE ENTRYFIELD getObj4 OF THIS;
   Property;
      Width         35,;
      Top           10,;
      Left          23,;
      Picture       "XXXXXXXXXXXXXXXXXXXXXXXXXXXXXXXXXXX",;
      DataLink      "Address2"

DEFINE TEXT txtObj5 OF THIS;
   Property;
      Text          "City",;
      Top           11,;
      Left          18,;
      Width          6

DEFINE ENTRYFIELD getObj5 OF THIS;
   Property;
      Width         20,;
      Top           11,;
```

```
        Left          23,;
        Picture       "XXXXXXXXXXXXXXXXXXXX",;
        DataLink      "City"

DEFINE TEXT txtObj6 OF THIS;
    Property;
        Text          "State",;
        Top           11,;
        Left          44,;
        Width          7

DEFINE ENTRYFIELD getObj6 OF THIS;
    Property;
        Width          2,;
        Top           11,;
        Left          50,;
        Picture       "!!",;
        DataLink      "State"

DEFINE TEXT txtObj7 OF THIS;
    Property;
        Text          "Zip",;
        Top           11,;
        Left          55,;
        Width          5

DEFINE ENTRYFIELD getObj7 OF THIS;
    Property;
        Width         10,;
        Top           11,;
        Left          59,;
        Picture       "99999-9999",;
        DataLink      "Zip"

DEFINE TEXT txtObj8 OF THIS;
    Property;
        Text          "Serial Num.",;
        Top           13,;
        Left          11,;
        Width         13
```

```
DEFINE ENTRYFIELD getObj8 OF THIS;
   Property;
      Width          5,;
      Top           13,;
      Left          23,;
      Picture       "XXXXX",;
      DataLink      "Serialno"

DEFINE TEXT txtObj9 OF THIS;
   Property;
      Text          "Program",;
      Top           13,;
      Left          34,;
      Width          9

DEFINE ENTRYFIELD getObj9 OF THIS;
   Property;
      Width          3,;
      Top           13,;
      Left          42,;
      Picture       "!!!",;
      DataLink      "Program"

DEFINE TEXT txtObj10 OF THIS;
   Property;
      Text          "Commission",;
      Top           13,;
      Left          51,;
      Width         12

DEFINE ENTRYFIELD getObj10 OF THIS;
   Property;
      Width          7,;
      Top           13,;
      Left          62,;
      Picture       "9999.99",;
      DataLink      "Commission"

DEFINE TEXT txtObj11 OF THIS;
   Property;
      Text          "Reg. Date",;
```

```
         Top             15,;
         Left            13,;
         Width           11

DEFINE ENTRYFIELD getObj11 OF THIS;
      Property;
      Top             15,;
      Left            23,;
      DataLink        "Regdate"

DEFINE TEXT txtObj12 OF THIS;
      Property;
         Text            "Shipped?",;
         Top             15,;
         Left            34,;
         Width           10

DEFINE CHECKBOX getObj12 OF THIS;
      Property;
         Width           2,;
         Top             15,;
         Left            43,;
         Height          1.50,;
         DataLink        "Shipped"

DEFINE TEXT txtObj13 OF THIS;
      Property;
         Text            "Ship Date",;
         Top             15,;
         Left            51,;
         Width           11

DEFINE ENTRYFIELD getObj13 OF THIS;
      Property;
      Top             15,;
      Left            61,;
      DataLink        "Shipdate"

DEFINE TEXT txtObj14 OF THIS;
      Property;
         Text            "Updated?",;
```

```
            Top             17,;
            Left            34,;
            Width           10

      DEFINE CHECKBOX getObj14 OF THIS;
         Property;
            Width           2,;
            Top             17,;
            Left            43,;
            Height          1.50,;
            DataLink        "Updated"
   ENDCLASS
```

Quite a change, isn't it? All @ SAY...GETs have been changed to TEXT and ENTRYFIELD objects, and the position and other properties of each are bound tightly to the TEXT or ENTRYFIELD itself. Also, the logical field Updated? has been converted not to an ENTRYFIELD but to a CHECKBOX, which as mentioned earlier makes far more sense for a logical field. What exactly does this file look like when run? To find out, go to the Navigator and double-click on SW.WFM. See figure 21.10 for the results.

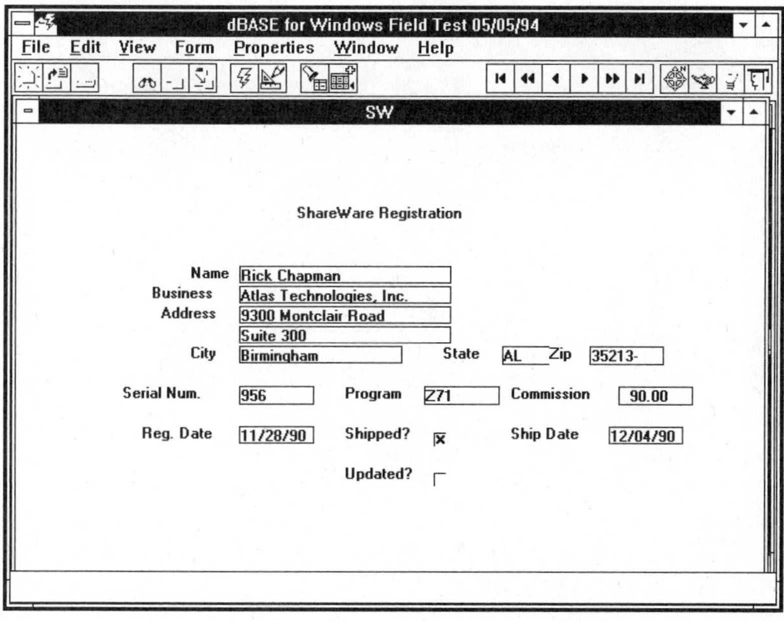

Figure 21.10 SW.WFM as created by the Component Builder.

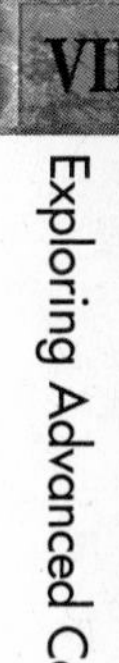

Note that boxes in the DOS form have been converted to take on the stylish "shadowed" look. This screen definitely looks like a Windows entry screen now. CB honored your field text placement, picture clauses, and so forth, to make the WFM version work as much as possible like the FMT one.

You now can use the Forms Designer to add your own additional elements, adjust field spacing or placement, and so on. dBASE for Windows's two-way tools and design surfaces make these adjustments a snap. For this SW.WFM, add two push buttons for record navigation, and an OK button to exit the form. The Previous and Next buttons are from the "custom" control tab, and the OK button is a standard control with this code block attached to the OnClick event property:

```
{; form.release()}
```

See figures 21.11 and 21.12.

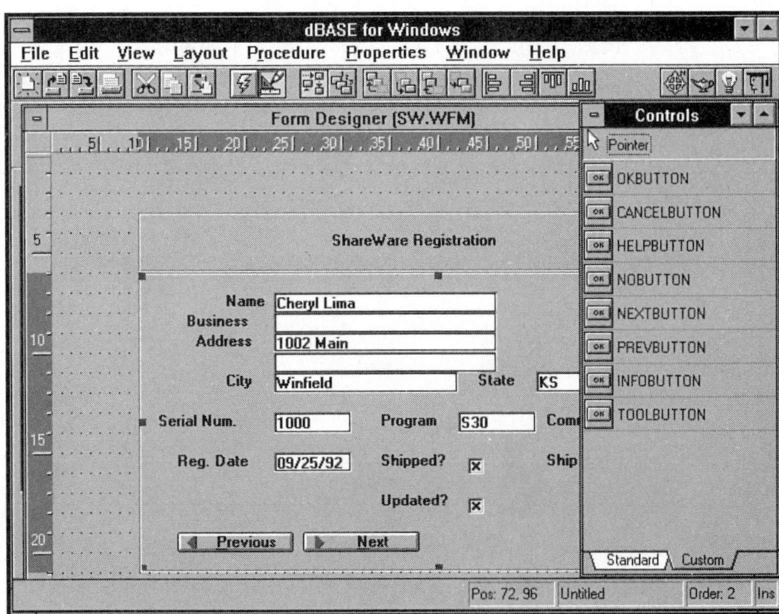

Figure 21.11 Adding Next and Previous custom control buttons.

Note that to accommodate the new buttons, you have to increase the size of the lower box. You can accomplish this task easily by clicking on the box and dragging its bottom size handle down a few notches.

When you invoke this form by clicking on the Run button in the SpeedBar or using any other method, you now have a fully functional form that any Windows user would understand and be able to use. Figure 21.13 shows the end result running under the design surface.

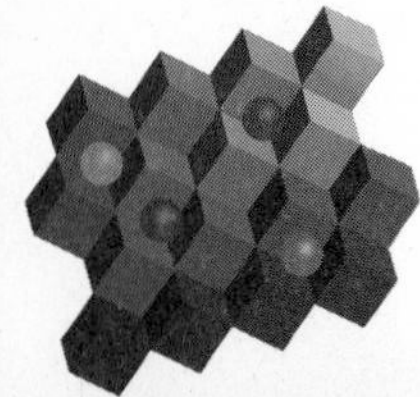

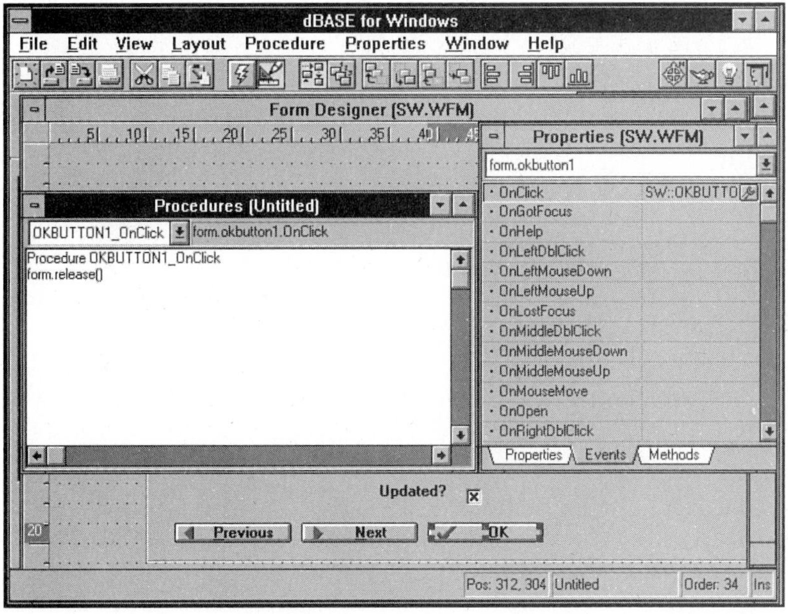

Figure 21.12 Adding an OK button and attaching it to the OnClick event.

Figure 21.13 SW.WFM expanded and with additional buttons added.

You could do much else with this form, but for now you can leave it as is. Note, however, that SW.WFM is not a part of your SWREG application yet; you've merely created the new form. It is not yet "attached" to anything in your application. Later, you tie this form and other new elements you create to the application.

Converting a FRG Report File

Of all the things computer programs do, they are generally rated on input, which you've just covered in converting SW.FMT to SW.WFM, and output. Reports under Windows are expected to be far prettier than their DOS counterparts, even if the information conveyed in those reports is every bit as mundane. In the world of Windows, 12-point Courier is considered passé. dBASE for Windows ships with Crystal Reports for dBASE, a capable report writer with amazing power and flexibility. You need to reconstruct your output into something that can please any Windows user, and Crystal Reports is well up to the task.

As you learned in the last section, converting an FMT to a WFM form is fairly simple and straightforward—as long as you used the dBASE/DOS report generator to write your DOS reports. Converting DOS report program files to Crystal Reports format is also a relatively easy task. Again you rely on CB, the dBASE for Windows Component Builder. CB reads dBASE/DOS FRM files only. If you created your reports by hand and coded them into PRG files, you might be better off writing them from scratch with Crystal Reports, using the CREATE REPORT command.

To begin the conversion, invoke CB as you did earlier, selecting the FRM to RPT option this time (see fig. 21.14).

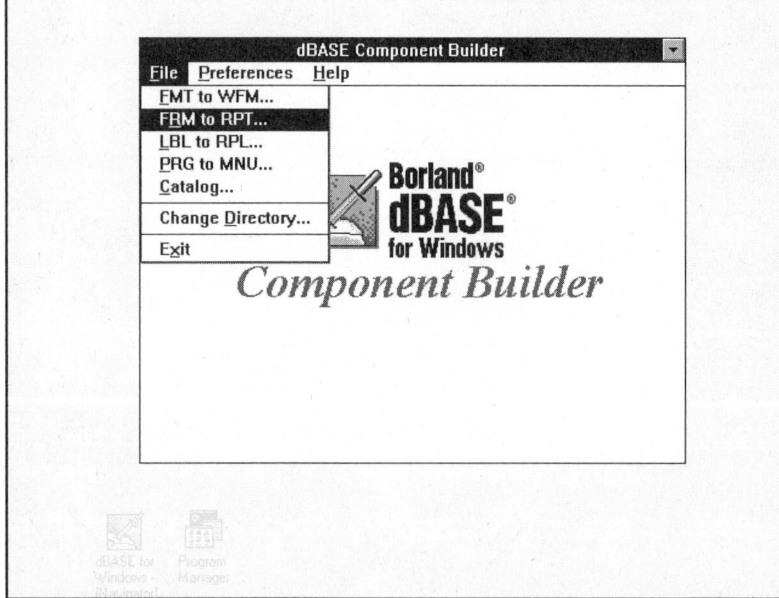

Figure 21.14 Using the Component Builder to convert report (FRM) files.

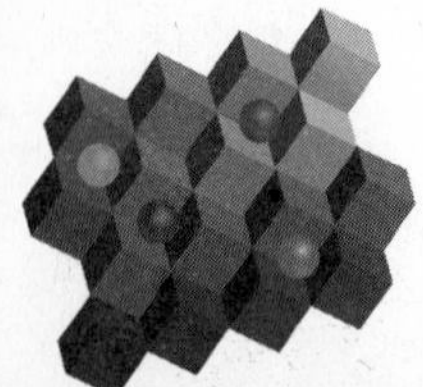

You have to select the FRM file and associated DBF or QBE file just as you did when converting screen files. CB behaves almost exactly as it did with the earlier conversion, working quietly unless problems occur. Figure 21.15 shows the result of the successful conversion of SW.FRM.

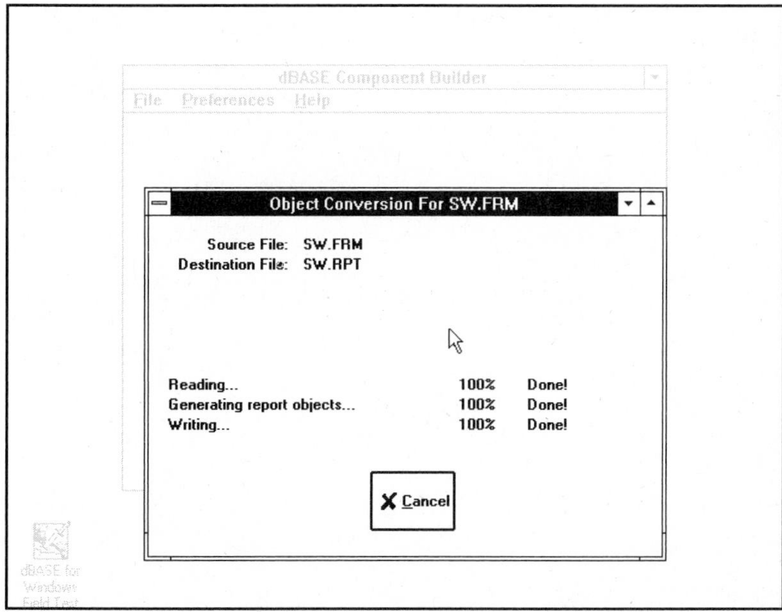

Figure 21.15
FMT to RPT conversion.

You cannot view the source code changes from one format to the next as you could with the screen files. Crystal Reports does not store report format information in source code form but rather in a nonreadable binary form. To see the results of the changes, exit CB, and modify the new report by using the Navigator or command window. Figure 21.16 shows how SW.RPT looks in Crystal Reports.

CB's conversion from FRM to RPT is largely uninspiring when compared to the FMT to WFM conversion, which resulted in some nifty new looks. With reports, making them pretty is up to you as the developer. Fortunately, Crystal Reports makes that task an easy one. The tools to change fonts and sizes, create groups and subgroups, and create new lists, cross tabs, and so forth, are readily available through the menus or the SpeedBar. Figure 21.17 shows SW.RPT jazzed up a bit.

You still use REPORT FORM to invoke new reports created with Crystal Reports, but there the similarities between these new reports and the old FRM DOS ones end. Playing with and learning the vast resources buried in this report writer is to your advantage; it can produce reports that are virtually impossible to generate with the dBASE/DOS report generator.

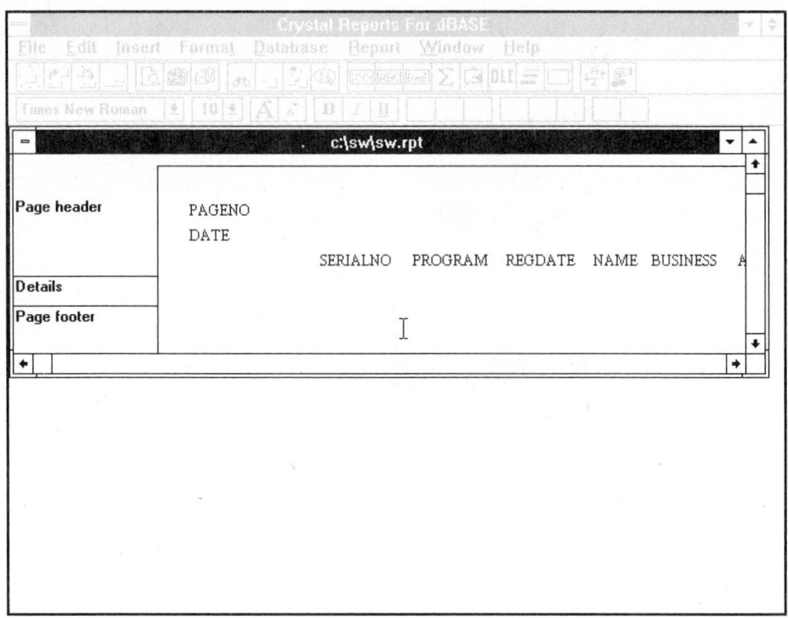

Figure 21.16 The Crystal Reports version of SW.RPT.

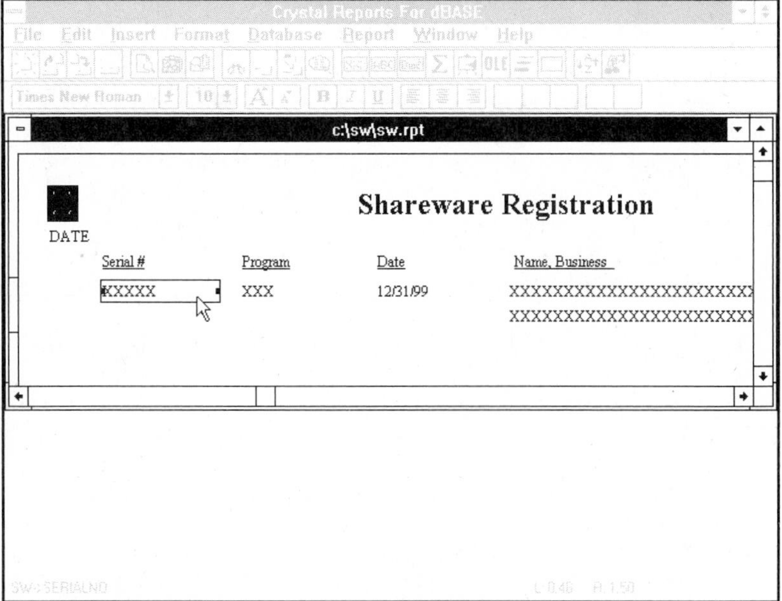

Figure 21.17 SW.RPT with new fonts, sizes, and graphics.

When you run an RPT report on-screen, the report previewer is fully WYSIWYG (see fig. 21.18). Output to a printer, naturally, uses the Windows printing system, enabling you to send your reports to any device Windows supports, either locally or over a network. This capability is a significant leap in friendliness, functionality, and power over your old dBASE/DOS reports. Users eat this stuff up, so use it to your advantage.

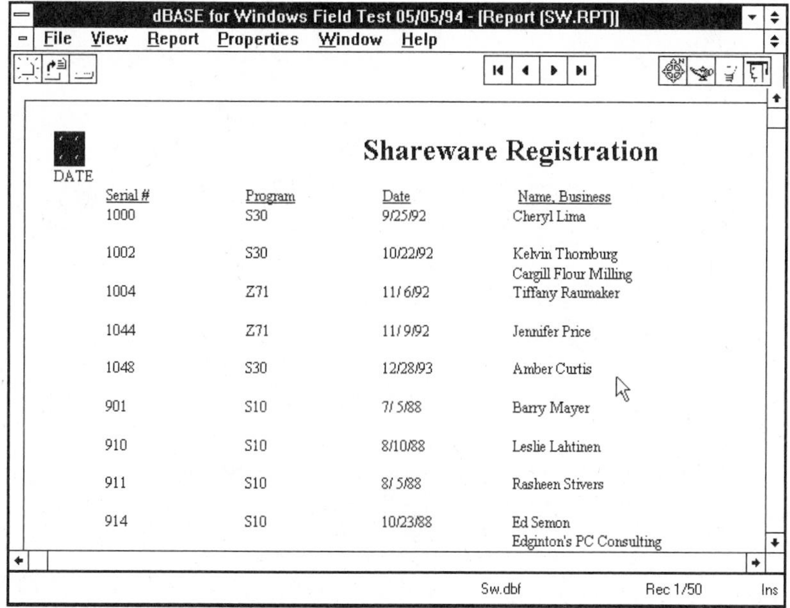

Figure 21.18
Running SW.RPT on-screen.

Converting Menus

You could at this point edit SWREG.PRG to use SW.WFM for appending and editing records, and SW.RPT for reports. Doing so, however, ignores an important part of any Windows program: the main menu. Menus in dBASE for Windows are implemented differently from the way they are in the DOS product, primarily because they are indeed true Windows menus.

Although the previous conversions you've done with the Component Builder have been straightforward and easy to patch into an existing program, menus present a greater challenge. In dBASE/DOS, menus are typically streamlined into procedural code, although as discussed earlier, they do have some event-driven-like properties. In dBASE for Windows, a menu is a true UI object rather than a series of elements grouped via procedural commands.

First, give the Component Builder a crack at helping you out. Launch CB, and select PRG to MNU from the File menu. When you select the program file (assuming that it's a PRG), you get a small editing window in which you highlight the code containing the menu definition (see fig. 21.19). CB then takes this code and produces a MNU file from it.

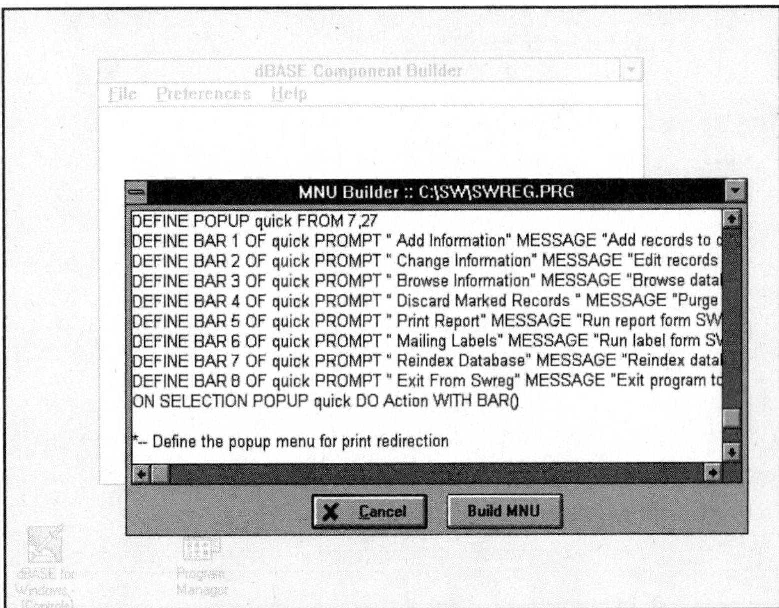

Figure 21.19 Selecting menu code in the Component Builder.

CB prompts you for a menu name (see fig. 21.20). If your DOS application was created with the Applications Generator, and the original menu is stored in an MNU file, do *not* save the converted source to the same file name; give it a new one to preserve the original. Even if you are a conscientious person and always make backups first, this precaution is still a good practice.

The contents of SWMAIN.MNU are different from the menu code you examined earlier:

```
** END HEADER — do not remove this line*
* Generated on 04/30/94
*
Parameter FormObj
SET PROCEDURE TO PROGRAM(1) ADDITIVE
NEW SWMAIN(FormObj,"Root")
CLASS SWMAIN(FormObj,Name) OF MENU(FormObj,Name)
   this.Text = ""
   this.HelpFile = ""
   this.HelpId = ""
```

```
DEFINE MENU FILE OF THIS;
    PROPERTY;
      Text "File",;
      HelpFile "",;
      HelpId ""

      DEFINE MENU PRINT OF THIS.FILE;
          PROPERTY;
            Text "&Print...",;
            HelpFile "",;
            HelpId ""

            DEFINE MENU REPORT OF THIS.FILE.PRINT;
                PROPERTY;
                  Text "&Report",;
                  HelpFile "",;
                  HelpId ""

            DEFINE MENU LABELS OF THIS.FILE.PRINT;
                PROPERTY;
                  Text "&Labels",;
                  HelpFile "",;
                  HelpId ""

      DEFINE MENU EXIT OF THIS.FILE;
          PROPERTY;
            Text "E&xit",;
            HelpFile "",;
            HelpId ""

DEFINE MENU REGISTRANTS OF THIS;
    PROPERTY;
      Text "Registrants",;
      HelpFile "",;
      HelpId ""

      DEFINE MENU APPEND OF THIS.REGISTRANTS;
          PROPERTY;
            Text "&Append",;
            HelpFile "",;
            HelpId ""
```

```
                DEFINE MENU EDIT OF THIS.REGISTRANTS;
                    PROPERTY;
                      Text "&Edit",;
                      HelpFile "",;
                      HelpId ""

                DEFINE MENU BROWSE OF THIS.REGISTRANTS;
                    PROPERTY;
                      Text "&Browse",;
                      HelpFile "",;
                      HelpId ""

          DEFINE MENU UTILITIES OF THIS;
              PROPERTY;
                Text "Utilities",;
                HelpFile "",;
                HelpId ""

                DEFINE MENU REINDEX OF THIS.UTILITIES;
                    PROPERTY;
                      Text "&Reindex",;
                      HelpFile "",;
                      HelpId ""

                DEFINE MENU PACK_FILE OF THIS.UTILITIES;
                    PROPERTY;
                      Text "&Pack File",;
                      HelpFile "",;
                      HelpId ""
ENDCLASS
```

Normally, dealing with menus is easiest in the Menu Designer. The Menu Designer is an easy-to-use facility for creating and modifying Windows-style menus. You may, of course, edit menus as source code if you wish; two-way tools work with menus as they do with other user interface elements. Most developers find that using the Menu Designer is just as fast as, and far easier than, manually editing the source code file. In the command window, enter **modify menu swmain** to invoke the Menu Designer (see fig. 21.21).

The object inspector shows you which events are hooked to which menu elements. As you can see for yourself by doing a little browsing, no events are specified here. The job of hooking the proper functions and/or procedures to the OnClick properties of each menu item is up to you. You also can create new events by clicking on the tool icon associated with the OnClick property, just as you did with the OK button in the SW.WFM form file earlier.

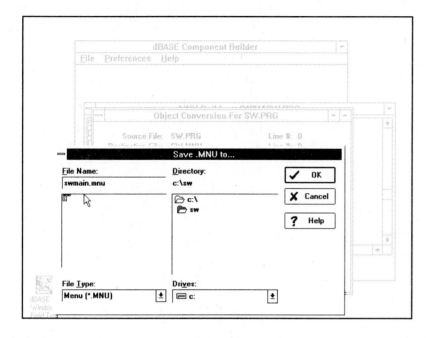

Figure 21.20
Selecting a file name for converted menu code.

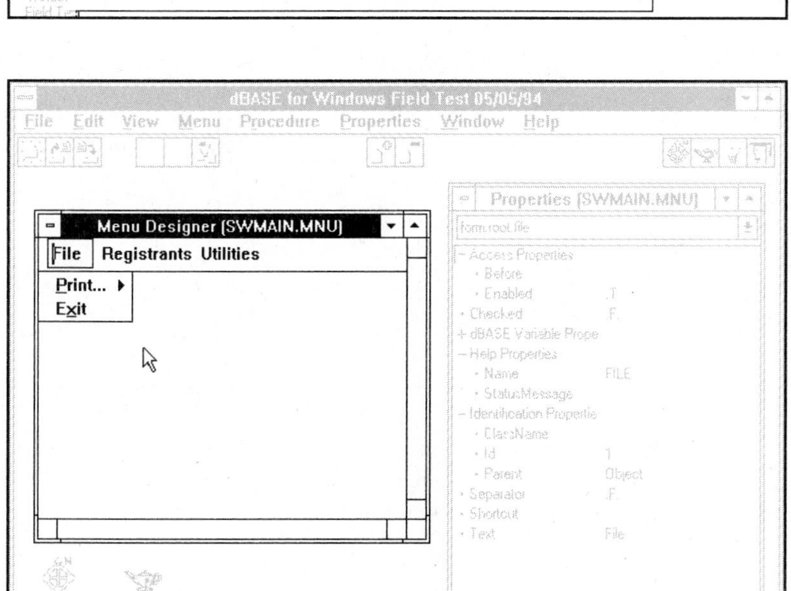

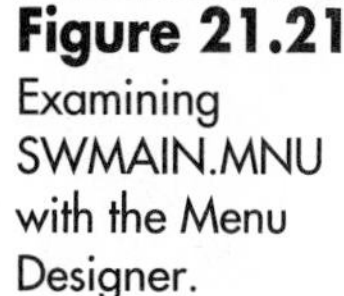

Figure 21.21
Examining SWMAIN.MNU with the Menu Designer.

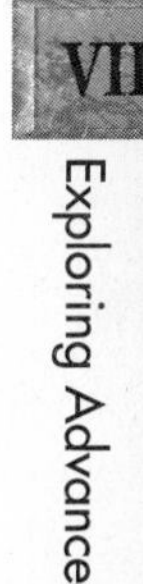

At this point, it is possible to replicate all of the program functionality that the dBASE IV Applications Generator produced for the SWREG.PRG program by simply attaching the desired events to appropriate menu options. For example, figure 21.22 illustrates how REPORT FORM SW can be tied to the File|Print|Report menu option. To do this, you click on the Report menu option in the Menu Designer, click on Events tab in the Property Inspector, and then click on the tool icon for the OnClick event. The Procedures window opens, waiting for you to fill in the contents of Procedure REPORT_OnClick. Typing **report form sw** is all that's required; after you close the Procedures window by selecting Close in its system menu, the code "report form sw" is attached to the Report menu option, and is executed whenever the user selects the Report option from the menu.

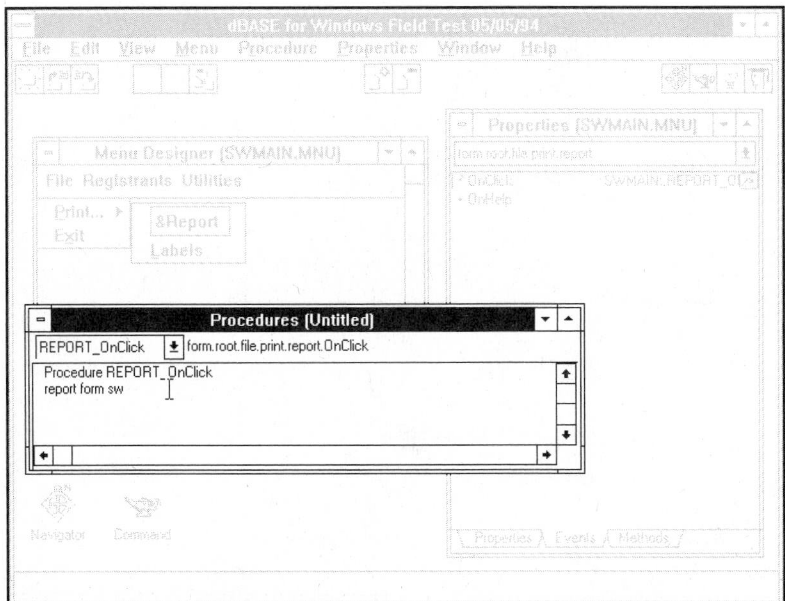

Figure 21.22 Adding code to an OnClick event.

In similar fashion, you could attach data manipulation code as OnClick events for each item. In some cases, the program flow code in your existing applications is thus going to be useless. In many cases, you want to invoke certain procedures and/or functions from your existing code while still keeping the flow of the program directed from this new menu object you've created.

You might have been wondering how to invoke a dBASE for Windows menu. A menu is always attached to a form. Thus far, the only form you've created is the one that CB converted from SW.FMT for you. Generally, you want to create a new form that has little

or nothing on it; then you can attach your application's new MNU file to it for event processing. Figure 21.23 illustrates the "gluing" of a menu to a form.

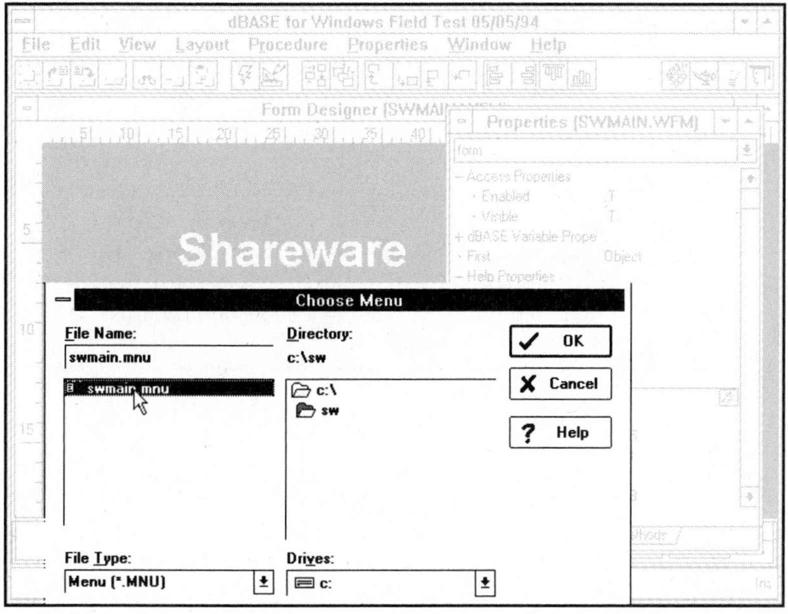

Figure 21.23
Attaching a menu to a form.

To attach the menu to the form, invoke the Forms Designer, click on the form itself to select it, and then click on the Menufile entry on the Properties tab in the Property Inspector. A Choose Menu dialog box appears, enabling you to easily find and specify the menu file you want to use with the form. Select the menu file (SWMAIN.MNU in this example) and click on the OK button. From this point forward, the menu will be attached seamlessly to the form.

You most likely want the menu to attach to the form rather than the dBASE for Windows menu bar when your form is active. To ensure this behavior, change the MDI window property of your form to False (.F.). Also, to force dBASE for Windows itself to a minimized state while your application is running, add the following to the OnOpen event of your main form (see fig. 21.24):

```
_app.framewin.windowstate = 1
```

To have dBASE for Windows go back to its normal state when your application is done, attach the following to the OnClose event of the main form:

```
_app.framewin.windowstate = 0
```

Or to force dBASE for Windows to maximized state, use

```
_app.framewin.windowstate = 2
```

After you've accomplished this "gluing together" of your application components, or objects, you have a product that bears little resemblance to that original DOS-like SWREG.PRG with which you started. Much has happened here in terms of look and feel, but you've done little actual coding. Accomplishing such a migration does indeed require some familiarity with the event model (so that you know to what events to attach code), and understanding dBASE for Windows's object model—at least enough to be able to modify the source code files its design surfaces produce—is very helpful. After you've cleared these learning hurdles, you'll find not only that migration is easier than expected, but also that the end product of that migration is surprisingly stable and useful.

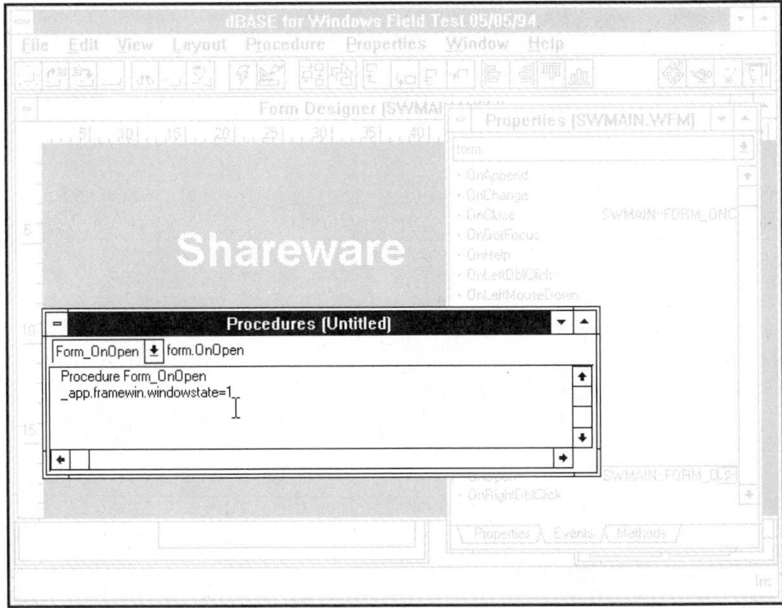

Figure 21.24 Modifying dBASE for Windows's appearance from a form.

Figure 21.25 shows our newly migrated application running. Note that dBASE for Windows itself is minimized, the new menu is active, and SWREG now takes on the look, feel, and behavior of a real Windows application.

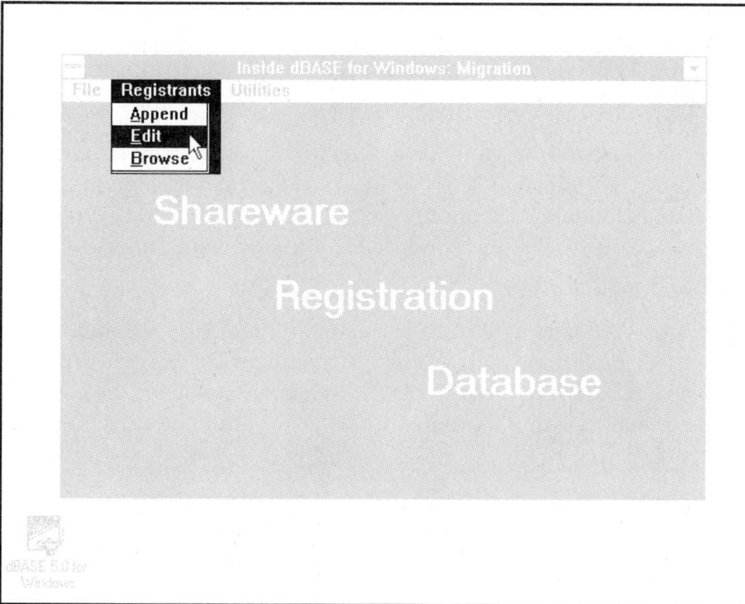

Figure 21.25
SWMAIN.WFM:
A new life for
SWREG.PRG.

Getting Ready To Fly

You've migrated your application; now how do you introduce it to your end-users? Depending on the scope of your project or program, you might decide to do the entire migration before letting the end-users try the program. In other contexts, working the program over a piece at a time and introducing new elements and functionality incrementally would be more appropriate.

A wholesale changeover tends to meet with more confusion on the front end, and because user participation in the end product is minimal, you might encounter some (if only a little) resistance to the new platform. Not so much a matter of problems with learning new keystrokes or a new look and feel, users sometimes feel subordinated by the whole process. This attitude can be a dangerous one for both you and the users.

Ideally, then, you want to have a key end-user or small group of end-users try the product at different stages of migration. You might be a whiz at analyzing the data-entry side of data processing and can predict with great accuracy what will and won't work for your end-users. If you're like most programmers, however, you think too much like a "computer geek" when building your programs, and you can benefit tremendously from the input of your end-users in the migration process. Let them try out the dialog boxes, menus, reporting functions, and so on as you flesh them out; solicit their input on the *process*, and let that direct your programming.

Finally, don't overlook documentation. In terms of user interface, Windows programs tend to require less hand-holding and tutorial-type documentation. But don't forget that the primary function of your program isn't to present a pretty interface, but rather to manipulate database information.

The current trend in the software industry is to move away from printed manuals to on-line help and documentation. Fortunately, Windows has a standardized method for delivering help. If you have help functions built into your existing dBASE/DOS application, they might or might not play well in the Windows environment, and you might consider converting this information into a Windows HLP file.

Don't be intimidated by new OOP and EDP concepts; embrace them, instead, and use them to your advantage. The applications you produce as a result will be of higher quality, your end-users will be happier, and you will gain a greater sense of satisfaction knowing that you can leverage these new tools and this new knowledge to your advantage.

Chapter Snapshot

When working in dBASE, you may find that you have to import data from another program. In such a scenario, you have to deal with conversion issues and much more. This chapter shows you how to deal with those files and covers the following information:

When you are finished with this chapter, you will be familiar with the IMPORT and APPEND FROM commands, and you should be able to work with files that you import from many other database programs.

Importing and Exporting Data

By Kenneth Chan

Although dBASE for Windows supports live access to dBASE, Paradox, and SQL data, sometimes you need to support other data formats. These non-native data formats are usually referred to as *foreign* data files. Occasionally, you might need to read data that has been stored in a different format, or write data in a different format, or both.

Importing is the process of converting an entire foreign file into dBASE format. A new dBASE file can be created, or the foreign data can be added to an existing dBASE table. *Exporting* is the process of writing dBASE data into a new file in another format. In addition to whole-file access, *low-level file functions* can be used to read or write files byte-by-byte or line-by-line.

Importing Structured Data

Two different commands can be used to import data that is stored in another program's data format: IMPORT and APPEND FROM.

The IMPORT command converts a spreadsheet file into dBASE format. IMPORT creates the new dBASE file in the current work area, closing any open file in the process, and puts that file in USE.

Although primarily used to add data from one dBASE table to another, APPEND FROM also supports a number of foreign data formats. APPEND FROM works like IMPORT, except that instead of creating new files, APPEND FROM adds records from the other data file to the end of the currently selected table.

The following sections go into more detail about these two commands.

IMPORT

The IMPORT command supports the spreadsheet formats listed in table 22.1:

Table 22.1
Supported IMPORT Data Formats

Format	Extension	Description
WB1	WB1	Borland Quattro Pro for Windows
WK1	WK1	Lotus 1-2-3 version 2.*x*

The syntax of the IMPORT command is as follows:

```
IMPORT FROM <filename> [TYPE] <format> [Heading]
```

The keyword TYPE is included for readability, but is not necessary. Each format has a default extension associated with that application. If the file you are importing uses a different extension, that extension needs to be specified in the *file name* field. dBASE creates a file with the same name but with a DBF extension in the same directory as the original file.

Databases in spreadsheets usually use column headings at the top of the data as field names. The HEADING keyword causes dBASE to use the first row of cells in the spreadsheet as the field names for the imported table. If there are no column headings in the spreadsheet, do not use the HEADING option; dBASE will create field names in the form FIELD001, FIELD002, etc.

When you import spreadsheet files, the use of the BROWSE command will show that the resulting file looks like the spreadsheet itself (see fig. 22.1).

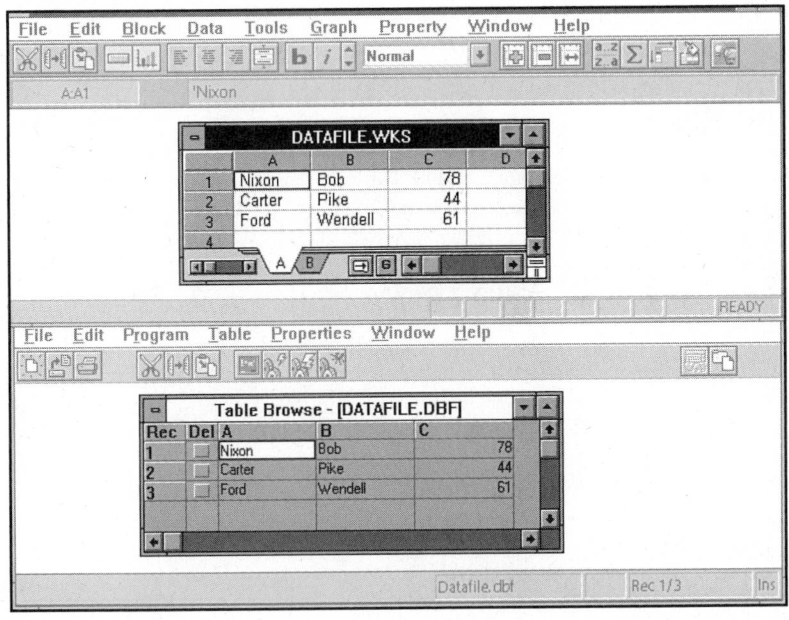

Figure 22.1
A spreadsheet in Quattro Pro and imported into dBASE with the HEADING option.

Because dBASE imports the entire spreadsheet, the spreadsheet should contain only the data itself—plus an optional row for the column headings, as shown in figure 22.1. There should not be any blank rows or text such as titles in the spreadsheet; if there are, these will be imported as data.

When importing, dBASE scans the spreadsheet to determine field types and field lengths. Field types default to character, unless the entire column (not counting the column header) is either numeric or formatted as date, in which case the column is imported as numeric or date. Characters fields in the resulting DBF are wide enough to accommodate the longest cell in the column.

dBASE will import the data from all the pages of a Quattro Pro for Windows spreadsheet.

Different file formats have different specifications and limits on such items as the maximum number of fields per record or number of records per table. dBASE format is fairly generous in this regard, allowing 1,024 fields per record and 1 billion records per table—you should not have trouble with too much data. One restriction that you will probably run into is that field names in dBASE are a maximum of 10 characters. Therefore, many field names may be truncated. If this change causes duplicate field names, the last characters of the conflicting names will be mangled so that they are unique. Another restriction is that dBASE field names do not allow spaces. Any spaces used in foreign field names will be converted to underscores.

APPEND FROM

APPEND FROM supports the data formats listed in Table 22.2:

Table 22.2
Supported APPEND FROM Data Formats

Format	Extension	Description
PARADOX	DB	Borland Paradox for DOS and Windows
DBASE	DBF	Borland dBASE, all versions
DELIMITED	TXT	ASCII Delimited
SDF	TXT	System Data Format

The syntax of APPEND FROM is as follows:

```
APPEND FROM <filename>
[FOR <condition>]
[[TYPE] <format>]
[NOVERIFY]
[POSITION]
[REINDEX]
```

If you forget the name of the file, you can use a single ? or a standard DOS file name skeleton with wildcards for the *<filename>* field to access a dialog box listing the desired file.

If the field types do not match exactly, some conversion occurs. Numeric data appended into a character field converts the numbers into their character equivalents, left justified instead of right justified. Character data that look like numbers append into a numeric field as those numbers.

When appending SDF data, dBASE normally verifies that the data in the SDF file matches the field types in the DBF. If you are sure that they match, you can disable the verification by using the NOVERIFY option, which speeds up the appending.

When you append from databases, dBASE uses the field names to figure out where the data should go. In other words, two files can have their fields in different orders, as long as the field names are the same. You can change this by using the POSITION keyword, which forces APPEND FROM to use the position of the fields, as it does with spreadsheet files. This is useful when data in the other table is in the same order, but the field names are different.

APPEND FROM adds all the records from the other file to the end of the currently selected table. You can limit the records that are added by using a FOR condition. This condition is evaluated for each record as if that record was being added to the table. In other words, you can pretend the record is added first, then the condition is checked. If the test fails, the record is thrown out. Because of this, the FOR condition can only reference fields that exist in the target table; it cannot reference fields that exist only in the source file.

For example, suppose you want to target a certain age group and add the names of people over 50 from the dBASE file NEWCUST.DBF to your main file, CUSTLIST.DBF. There is an AGE field in NEWCUST, but not in CUSTLIST. You cannot use the following command because no AGE field exists in the CUSTLIST table.

```
APPEND FROM NEWCUST for AGE > 50
```

You also cannot use the following command because the NEWCUST file is not actually in USE; you are reading data from the file on disk, not an open table in memory:

```
APPEND FROM NEWCUST for NEWCUST->AGE > 50
```

If you USE NEWCUST IN SELECT() first and then try the same command, it will not work properly; the following occurs:

1. A record from NEWCUST.DBF is read from the file on disk.
2. The AGE field in the current record of open file NEWCUST is checked to see if it is over 50; not the AGE field of the record that was just read from disk.
3. If that AGE happens to be over 50, the record gets appended. If the age is less than 50, it does not get appended.

In other words, either all of the records from NEWCUST get appended or none of them do, depending on whether the AGE of the current record of the open table NEWCUST happens to be over 50.

If you do not want to add an AGE field to CUSTLIST for the sole purpose of solving this APPEND FROM operation, you have a couple of options. One solution is to go to the NEWCUST table, copy the records whose AGE is over 50 to a separate table, and APPEND the new over 50 table.

Another option involves using each record's delete flag. When using APPEND FROM, if SET DELETED is OFF, the source table's delete flags are ignored and all records get appended. If SET DELETED is ON, only those records that are not marked for deletion get appended. In either case, the appended records are not marked for deletion when they get to the target file.

Note that the following command will not work because the .NOT. DELETED() condition parameter applies to the records as if they were appended to CUSTLIST, and as just stated, those delete flags are always false.

```
APPEND FROM NEWCUST for .NOT. DELETED()
```

The previous unsuccessful command appends all the records in NEWCUST, regardless of their delete status.

To use each record's delete flag successfully to append the names of new customers over 50, you need to execute code similar to the following:

```
USE NEWCUST
*-- Mark the ones you do not want to append
delete for .not. AGE > 50
USE CUSTLIST
SET deleted on
APPEND FROM NEWCUST
```

As records are appended, any active indexes will be updated. If there are a number of indexes or a lot of records being added, it might be faster to reindex the entire file after all the records have been added. To do so, include the REINDEX keyword on the APPEND FROM command.

No hard-and-fast rule exists for telling you when to use the REINDEX keyword. You have to compare the amount of time it would take to reindex the whole file—based on the number of index tags and how many records there will be after you append all the records—versus the number of records you are appending. As a rough guide, if you are increasing the number of records by 25 percent or more, you will probably benefit from using the REINDEX keyword.

Structured Text Files

Two plain text formats are supported by APPEND FROM: Delimited and SDF, which are similar in many ways. Both formats default to the file extension TXT. In addition, neither format supports field names; the file is composed of data only. One record's worth of data occupies one line and is terminated by a carriage return and line feed. The two formats differ in how they store the individual fields.

Delimited

Delimited format separates each field in the record with a comma. Each field type is stored a little differently:

- ✔ Character data is enclosed or delimited by double quotation marks.
- ✔ Logical data is a single letter representing the value, either T, t, F, f, Y, y, N, or n.
- ✔ Numeric data is just the number, without delimiters.
- ✔ Dates must be non-delimited numbers in the form YYYYMMDD.

For example, January 17, 1994 would be 19940117. Some short sample records, with last name, first name, birth date, and whether they are members might look like this:

```
"Groggins","Myrtle",19470627,T
"Keach","Trevor",19520313,F
```

The double quotation marks are the standard delimiters. You can use any other single character by specifying WITH <*character*> after the keyword DELIMITED. For example, if single quotation marks were used instead, the command would look like:

```
APPEND FROM MEMBERS type delimited with '
```

The delimiters for character data are only necessary when commas might be part of the character data. Without the delimiters, the commas in the character data would be interpreted as field separators. If you get a data file that has commas separating the fields, but no character delimiters, you may still be able to import the file successfully.

Some formats use a blank space to separate the fields instead of commas. In this case, you can use the option DELIMITED WITH BLANK. Note that this does not mean that character data is enclosed by blank spaces, as the previous DELIMITED WITH <*character*> would lead you to believe.

Because no field names exist, all the fields are appended by position. Make sure the structure of the table you are appending to matches the order of fields in the structure you are appending from. If the field types do not match exactly, some conversion will occur.

SDF

System Data Format (SDF) does not use field delimiters or separators. It relies solely on the width of each field. To illustrate, sample data in SDF is shown below a character counter:

```
12345678901234567890123456789012345678901
Groggins        Myrtle          19470627T
Keach           Trevor          19520313F
```

This file has allocated 16 spaces for both the last name and first name. Any columns not occupied with data are filled with spaces. The date is next (always 8 columns), and the logical field appears right after the date.

One reason SDF is supported in APPEND FROM and not in IMPORT is that IMPORT has no way of deciding where to divide the long line of text. Does the preceding example represent one field or forty? You must have a structure first that matches the SDF file and then you can fill in the rows. The proper structure for such a file would look like this:

```
Structure for database: NAMELIST.DBF
Number of data records:       0
Date of last update   : 02/14/94
Field  Field Name  Type       Width    Dec    Index
    1  LAST_NAME   Character     16              N
    2  FIRST_NAME  Character     16              N
    3  BIRTH_DATE  Date           8              N
    4  MEMBER      Logical        1              N
 ** Total **                     42
```

Exporting Data

The COPY TO command is used to export data into other formats. The COPY TO command creates new files, overwriting any existing file. It cannot be used to add data to existing foreign data files.

The COPY TO command is the opposite of the APPEND FROM command. Although this command is used primarily to copy dBASE data into another dBASE table, it supports all the file formats that APPEND FROM supports, plus one for dBASE III-compatibility, as listed in table 22.3:

Table 22.3
Supported COPY TO Data Formats

Format	Extension	Description
PARADOX	DB	Borland Paradox for DOS and Windows
DBMEMO3	DBF	Borland dBASE III and III Plus
DBASE	DBF	Borland dBASE IV and after

Format	Extension	Description
DELIMITED	TXT	ASCII Delimited
SDF	TXT	System Data Format

The DBMEMO3 format listed in table 22.3 is a special dBASE format in which the memo fields, if there are any, are in dBASE III/III Plus format instead of dBASE IV format.

When copying to another dBASE file, you can specify WITH PRODUCTION to make duplicates of the DBF files' MDX tags as well.

dBASE does not export into spreadsheet formats, but most spreadsheet programs can read dBASE files directly, so this option is not needed.

The syntax of COPY TO is as follows:

```
COPY TO <filename>
 [<scope>]
 [FOR <condition>]
 [WHILE <condition>]
 [FIELDS <field list>]
 [[TYPE] <format>]
 [[WITH] PRODUCTION]
```

The *<scope>*, FOR, and WHILE conditions control the scope of the COPY command, and are explained in Chapter 10, "Understanding the dBASE Language." The *<field list>* designates which fields you want to export and in which order you want to export them. The *<format>* parameter works the same as in the APPEND FROM command.

Understanding Low-Level File Functions

Low-level file functions (LLFFs) offer byte-by-byte and line-by-line access to any type of file. They can be used to augment dBASE's built-in foreign file import/export capabilities, allow direct access to existing files, or create new files in any format imaginable. A few practical applications of LLFFs include:

- ✔ Read the resolution information from PCX file headers to help manage graphics files
- ✔ Convert a fixed-length-record mainframe data file into SDF format
- ✔ Read a mailing list contained in a free-form text file

All LLFFs begin with the letter F. A number have analogs with functions that relate to tables.

Three basic concepts are involved when using LLFFs:

- ✔ File Handle
- ✔ File Access Mode
- ✔ File Pointer

The file handle is how all low-level file operations refer to a particular file. Instead of constantly using the name of the file or a memvar containing the name of the file, the file handle is used.

Before any work can be done with LLFFs, the file must be opened. Existing files are opened with the FOPEN() function. If the file is opened successfully, FOPEN() returns the file handle; otherwise FOPEN() generates an error.

The file handle is actually a number. As files are opened and subsequently closed, the same number can be reused. Therefore, the file handle that you get is only good until you close the file. If you later reopen the same file, the handle may be different.

Even though the file handle is a number, it makes no sense to do any kind of math with file handles. This book places the letter "h" at the beginning of names of memvars that contain file handles.

Opening an Existing File

A file opening command might look like this:

```
hPcx = fopen( "CATS.PCX", "R" )
```

This command opens the file CATS.PCX in Read mode, designated by the second parameter "R." If the file is found and the open is successful, the file handle is stored in the memvar hPcx.

This brings up the second basic concept about low-level file I/O, which is the file access mode. There are three different file access modes:

- ✔ Read
- ✔ Write
- ✔ Append

The file access modes determine what you are allowed to do to the file, under two considerations. First, if you are only reading the file, opening in Read mode will prevent you from accidentally writing to the file. Second, only one person at a time can open a file for writing or appending with low-level file functions. Any simultaneous access, such as on a network, can only be done in Read mode.

Read mode can be combined with either Write or Append. Table 22.4 lists the different file access modes:

Table 22.4
Low-Level File Function Access Modes

Designator	File Access Mode
"R"	Read only
"W"	Write only
"A"	Append only
"RW" or "WR"	Read and Write
"RA" or "AR"	Append and Write

You can open a file using FOPEN() without specifying a file access mode, in which case it defaults to read only.

The difference between Write and Append modes brings up the third basic concept about LLFFs: the file pointer. The file pointer is much like a DBF's record pointer: each opened file has its own file pointer, and it indicates where the next read/write will take place.

When you open a file to read or write or both, the file pointer is initially placed at the beginning of the file. On the other hand, if a file is opened for appending (with or without read), the file pointer is placed at the end of the file, right after the last byte. Other than this initial difference, Write and Append modes are the same.

After the file pointer is placed in its starting position when the file is opened, it can be moved anywhere in the file. The file pointer is a number that represents the byte offset in the file, as illustrated in figure 22.2.

The first byte in a file is at offset zero; the last byte is at offset (*file length* - 1). Offset (*file length*) designates the position at the end of the file, where the next byte would go if you were adding data to a file. This is the starting file pointer position when a file is opened in Append mode.

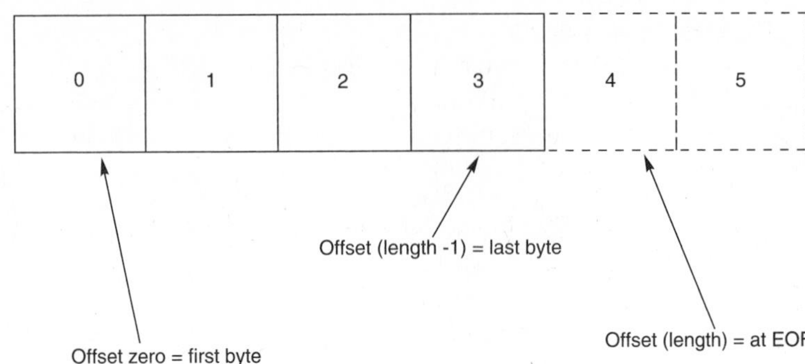

Figure 22.2 How a file pointer relates to a four-byte file.

Moving the File Pointer

The direct way to move the file pointer is with the FSEEK() function. For example, the following command moves the file pointer to the fourth byte (offset 3) of the file referenced by the file handle hPcx.:

```
FSEEK( hPcx, 3, 0 )
```

The third parameter in the FSEEK() function determines how the second parameter is interpreted, as listed in table 22.5:

Table 22.5
FSEEK() Offset Designators

3rd parameter	What 2nd parameter means
0 (default)	Offset from the beginning of the file
1	Offset from the current position
2	Offset from the end of the file

For example, the following command moves the file pointer 5 bytes back from its current position:

```
FSEEK( hPcx, -5, 1 )
```

The following command moves the file pointer to the last byte of the file:

```
FSEEK( hPcx, -1, 2 )
```

Finally, the next command moves the file pointer to the end of the file:

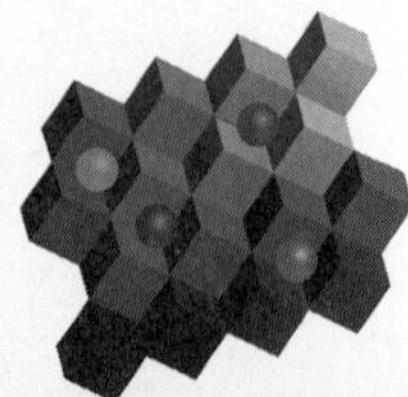

```
FSEEK( hPcx, 0, 2 )
```

The third parameter is optional. If left out, the default is 0, offset from the beginning of the file.

FSEEK() returns the resulting file pointer position as the offset from the beginning of the file. Usually this is of no value because you just told the file pointer where to go, but it is sometimes useful. Using FSEEK() in the last example, which moved the file pointer to the end of the file would be set to the current size of the file, as in the following:

nLen = fseek(hPcx, 0, 2)

Reading From a File

Once the file pointer is in the desired position, you can read from or write to the file. The basic reading function is FREAD(), which will read the designated number of bytes from the file, starting at the current file pointer position. For example, the following command will read two bytes from the file referenced by the file handle hPcx, starting at the current file pointer position.

```
cBytes = fread( hPcx, 2 )
```

When working with foreign file formats, it is necessary to know the structure of the file. Table 22.6 lists some of the basic structure of a PCX file.

Table 22.6
PCX Resolution Information

Offset	Bytes	Value
3	1	Number of bits per pixel per plane
12	2	Horizontal resolution
14	2	Vertical resolution
65	1	Number of color planes

This information will give you the size and color resolution of the PCX file. The following commands will read the information from the PCX file (the memvar cFile contains the name of the file to open):

```
*-- Open the file
hPcx = fopen( cFile, "R" )
*-- Position the file pointer
```

```
fseek( hPcx, 3 )
*-- Read the number of bits per pixel per color plane
nBPP = asc( fread( hPcx, 1 ))
*-- Read the number of color planes
fseek( nPcx, 66 )
nPln = asc( fread( hPcx, 1 ))
*-- Read the horizontal resolution
fseek( nPcx, 12 )
nHRes = asc( fread( nPcx, 1 ))_+ asc( fread( nPcx, 1 )) * 256
*-- Read the vertical resolution
nVRes = asc( fread( nPcx, 1 )) + asc( fread( nPcx, 1 )) * 256
```

Note that since FREAD() returns character data, the ASC() function must be used to convert it to numeric.

As the FREAD() command reads data, it moves the file pointer forward the same number of bytes. For example, when reading the horizontal and vertical resolution, once the file pointer is positioned at the first byte of the horizontal resolution, four consecutive FREAD()s read the four consecutive bytes that make up the horizontal and vertical resolution (two bytes each).

Handling Little-Endian Values

You may be wondering why the horizontal and vertical resolutions were both read one byte at a time instead of two. The answer lies in how different data formats store numeric data.

One way is to store numbers as their character representation. This is how dBASE does it. For example, when storing the number 123 in a DBF, it stores the characters "1," "2," and "3." If you view the file with a generic file viewer, you will see the text "123" where the number is stored.

Another way to store numbers is to store the numeric value themselves. A single byte can store a value from 0 to 255. If you view the file where the value 123 is stored, you will see the ASCII representation of the value 123: the character "{".

When storing values that won't fit in a single byte, the value is broken down into multiples of powers of 256, just like familiar decimal numbers are represented by multiples of powers of 10. For example, the number 640 is:

```
6 x  102 = 600
4 x  101 =  40
```

```
0 x  100 = +  0
                    640
```

in base 10 and

```
2 x 2561 =       512
128 x 2560 = +128
                        640
```

in base 256. Therefore the value 640 would be stored as two bytes, 2 and 128, or 02h and 80h in hexadecimal (as designated by the h suffix).

Multi-byte numbers are stored in little-endian format, which means that the multiples for the smallest powers are stored first. Therefore the number 640 would be stored as follows in the file:

```
80 02
```

The following command reads the first value, 80h (128), then the second value 02h (2), multiplies the second value by 256, and adds them together (128 + 512 = 640):

```
nHRes = asc( fread( nPcx, 1 )) + asc( fread( nPcx, 1 )) * 256
```

It is easier to read one byte at a time, do the required math, and have FREAD() move the file pointer forward than it would be to read both bytes at the same time and then have to divide that character string up to do the same math.

Creating New Files

The FOPEN() function can open existing files, and the FCREATE() function creates new files. Like FOPEN(), FCREATE() takes a file path/name and file access mode as its parameters. Because these files are new, FCREATE() defaults to read/write access.

When a new file is created, FCREATE() returns the file handle for the newly created 0-byte file. Note that FCREATE() will overwrite any existing file without warning, even when SET SAFETY is ON.

Writing to a File

Writing data to a file works a lot like reading data. Data is written starting at the current file pointer and moving the file pointer forward. Any existing data is overwritten with the new data. You cannot insert data into a file with LLFFs as you would insert text into a document with your word processor.

If you wish to insert data into a file with LLFFs, you have two options: first, you can copy the entire file and include the inserted data at the appropriate location. Second, you can shift the contents of the file forward by reading chunks of the file and writing them the appropriate number of bytes forward, starting at the end of the file and working backwards to the point where you want to insert data, and then insert the data. Neither option is very efficient.

The basic file writing function is FWRITE(), which will write a character string into a file; either the whole string or a certain number of bytes. For example, the following command writes the entire character string c1 into the file referenced by the file handle hFile, starting at the byte pointed to by the file pointer:

```
fwrite( hFile, c1 )
```

After the data is written, the file pointer will point to the byte immediately after the last byte written, so that consecutive instances of FWRITE() will write data contiguously. The following command writes the first 12 bytes of c1 or all of c1, whichever is less, to the file:

```
fwrite( hFile, c1, 12 )
```

In both cases, FWRITE() will return the number of bytes written, which you are usually not interested in, especially if you just told it how many bytes to write.

One thing you can do with the value FWRITE () returns is to check it to see if it is greater than zero. If FWRITE() fails to write the data for whatever reason, such as a disk error, it will return 0 for the number of bytes written. You can use this information in code similar to this:

```
if fwrite( hFile, c1 ) = 0
  ? "*** Ack! Error writing to file!"
  *-- Handle error
```

However, whatever causes FWRITE() to fail will often generate an error of its own. For example, if you remove a disk before the data is written to the disk, you will receive a disk error before FWRITE() returns 0, indicating that no data was written. You will want to have error handlers to try and remedy the situation (in this case, put the disk back in) before things fall through to the error handler for FWRITE().

Closing a File

After you finish reading or writing the file or both, you need to close the file with the FCLOSE() function. All file handles are closed using a CLEAR ALL or CLOSE ALL command or when QUIT is used to exit dBASE. However, you should always close a file when you are done with it. There is a limit to the number of files you can have open at one time, and an open file is more susceptible to damage.

FCLOSE() takes the file handle as a parameter and returns .T. or .F., depending on whether it was successful closing the file.

Moving to the End of File and Beyond

You are free to move the file pointer to any positive offset, even past the end of the file. You can tell if you are past the last byte of data with the FEOF() function, which works a lot like the EOF() function for DBFs. The only argument for FEOF() is the required file handle. It is used a lot in DO WHILE loops to process an entire file. For example, the code listed here will print an entire file in uppercase:

```
hFile = fopen( cFile, "R" )
do while .not. feof( hFile )
  ?? upper( fread( hFile, 1 ))
enddo
```

There is no equivalent to a SCAN loop for LLFFs, partly because it is not needed. There is no need to "skip" the file pointer forward in the loop because the FREAD() command moves the file pointer forward as it reads.

If you move the file pointer past the end of the file and try to read there, as in this example, you will always receive a null string:

```
*-- Go way too far
fseek( hFile, 1234567890 )
? len( fread( hFile, 1 ))
*-- will print 0
```

On the other hand, if you move the file pointer past the end of the file and write something there, the file will immediately grow in size to accommodate the new data written. For example, starting with a small 10-byte file called A10BYTE.FIL, these commands will make it 1,000 bytes long:

```
hFile = fopen( "A10BYTE.FIL", "W" )
*-- Move to 1000th byte (offset 999)
fseek( hFile, 999 )
*-- Write something there
fwrite( hFile, "X" )
```

Note that the data between the 10th and 1,000th byte will be whatever happened to be on the disk when the disk space was allocated for the larger file—most likely bits and pieces of deleted files.

If you ever want to grab all the free space on a disk (to test an out-of-disk-space error handler, for example), all you need to do is add these lines of code:

```
hBig = fcreate( "DISKSPAC.HOG" )
fseek( hBig, diskspace() - 1 )
fwrite( hBig, "X" )
fclose( hBig )
```

Truncating a File

In addition to extending a file, you can use FWRITE() to truncate a file, chopping it off at a particular byte. Whenever you write zero bytes to a file, either by writing a null string or explicitly specifying zero bytes to write, everything from the file pointer on is discarded and its position becomes the end of the file.

Continuing with the previous example, you can return A10BYTE.FIL to its original size with the following commands:

```
*-- Move to offset 10 (11th byte)
fseek( hFile, 10 )
*-- Discard 11th byte and on
fwrite( hFile, "" )
*-- leaving 10 bytes
```

Removing the EOF Marker

An EOF character is sometimes used to indicate the end of a file. dBASE does this for a number of the files that it creates. In those cases, the EOF character is considered to be a marker, and not part of the data.

However, this is fairly antiquated thinking. Most programs rely solely on the file length. If there is an EOF at the end of the file, that is considered to be part of the data.

To demonstrate the concepts introduced so far, here is a simple procedure that removes the EOF marker (ASCII 26) from the end of a file, if it is there.

```
PROCEDURE RemoveEOF
   parameter cFile
   *-- Init memvars
   private hFile
   hFile = 0
   *-- Make sure file exists
   if file( cFile )
```

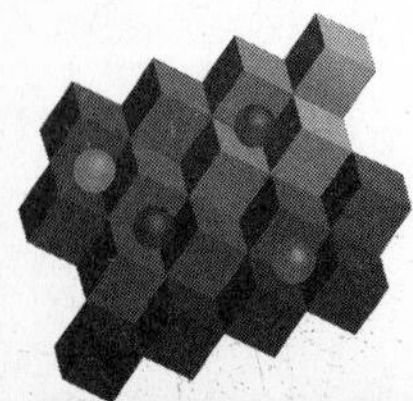

```
          hFile = fopen( cFile, "RW" )
          *-- If successful file open
          if hFile > 0
            *-- Goto last byte
            fseek( hFile, -1, 2 )
                 *-- If it's an EOF
                 if fread( hFile, 1 ) = chr( 26 )
                   *-- Reposition pointer
              fseek( hFile, -1, 2 )
              *-- Truncate file
              fwrite( hFile, "" )
            endif
            *-- Close file
            fclose( hFile )
          endif
        endif
      RETURN
```

The process of removing an EOF involves the following steps:

Removing an EOF

Take a file name as its parameter, and assign it to the memvar cFile	Assigns the file to the cFile
Declare a couple of memvars PRIVATE and initialize them (this is always a good practice with a generic procedure)	Initializes the files
Invoke the function FILE() (which is not an LLFF)	Makes sure the file exists
If the file exists, open the file for read/write access, assigning the file handle to the memvar hFile	Assigns the file handle

A file handle is a non-zero number. If FOPEN() had failed but the error was ignored, hFile would still contain the initializing value zero, in which case you do not want to run the rest of the code.

Using offset type 2 (bytes from EOF), go to the last byte of the file	Goes to the end of the file
Read the last byte	Checks to see if it is an EOF character

continues

continued

If it is, reposition the file pointer, because the FREAD() function moved the file pointer forward	Repositions the pointer
Write a null string at the position where the EOF is	Truncates the null string
Whether there was an EOF, close the file	

This RemoveEOF procedure will come up again at the end of this chapter.

Reading and Writing Text Files

Two LLFFs are designed specifically for reading and writing simple text files: FGETS() and FPUTS(). The "S" in both functions can be thought of as "string." In this case a string is a line of text terminated by an end-of-line indicator, or the end-of-file, whichever comes first.

The standard end-of-line indicator is a carriage return/line feed combination, CHR(13) + CHR(10). With both functions, you can specify any other one or two-byte end-of-line indicator. In any case, the indicator is not included in the string returned by FGETS() and is automatically included in the string written by FPUTS().

For example, suppose a text file started with these lines:

```
alpha
beta
gamma
```

Each line ends with a carriage return/line feed combination. If you open this file and read the first few lines:

```
hGreek = fopen( "GREEK.TXT" )
cLine1 = fgets( hGreek )
cLine2 = fgets( hGreek )
```

the memvar cLine1 will contain the character string "alpha" and cLine2 will contain the character string "beta." This makes sense because when you are reading lines of text, you are not interested in the end-of-line indicator.

Similarly, if you want to write lines of text with the following commands, you do not have to go to the extra trouble of sending the carriage return and line feed for every line; FPUTS() handles that for you:

```
hGreek2 = fcreate( "GREEK2.TXT" )
fputs( hGreek2, cLine1 )
fputs( hGreek2, cLine2 )
```

Converting Fixed-Length-Record Files to SDF

When working with files from mainframes, you may run into a format that looks like, but is not quite, an SDF-type file. As described earlier in this chapter, System Data Format (SDF) files rely solely on the width of each field and do not use field delimiters or separators. In this format, the records are of fixed length, but there is no carriage return and line combination at the end of each record; all the records are contiguous. You can parse this file manually with FREAD(), but it is often easier to convert the file into SDF and let APPEND FROM handle it.

Converting mainframe files to SDF is easy with the following code:

```
hFile = fopen( "MAINFRAM.FIL" )
hSDF  = fcreate( "SDF.TXT" )
do while .not. feof( hFile )
  fputs( hSDF, fread( hFile, 80 ))
enddo
fclose( hFile )
fclose( hSDF )
```

FREAD() reads the fixed length record (in this example, it is an 80-character record), and FPUTS() immediately turns around and writes that record with a carriage return and line feed after it. The reverse technique, reading with FGETS() and writing with FWRITE() can be used to reverse the conversion.

Importing a Mailing List

Suppose you have a text file with a bunch of names and addresses that you want to convert into a DBF to use as a mailing list. The text looks like this:

```
SOURCE: XYZ

DATE: 02/23/86

Larry Appleton

Chicago Sentinel-Recorder

123 Lazenby

Chicago IL 60018

---------------------------------
```

SOURCE: PDQ

DATE: 08/11/77

Chrissy Snow

401 Alta Av Apt 203

Santa Monica CA 90402

```
-------------------------------------
```

Each item ends with a line of all hyphens. You are not interested in the Source code, but you do want to track the Date in addition to the name and address. Looking through the list, each item has one line for the name, one or two address lines, and a line each for the city, state, and zip.

In this situation, the FREAD() function is fairly useless, because it always reads in a fixed number of bytes, and the lines in the file vary in length. FGETS() is therefore the right function, enabling you to read each line and handle it appropriately.

The major difficulty is with the address, which can be either one or two lines. You can read the name and the first line of the address easily enough, but how do know whether the next line is the second line of the address or the line with the city in it? A number of procedures are possible, but the best involves realizing that the city line is always the last line, the one before the all-hyphens line. You can keep reading until you hit the all-hyphens line and use the line before that as the city line.

The following is the code that takes advantage of this arrangement and imports the file:

```
hLst = fopen( "ADDRLIST.TXT" )
do while .not. feof( hLst )
  *-- Read the source/data line
  cTxt = fgets( hLst )
  *-- Extract the date
  d1 = ctod( substr( cTxt, at( "DATE:", cTxt ) + 6 ))
  *-- Read the name
  cName = fgets( hLst )
  *-- Read the first address line
  cAddr1 = fgets( hLst )
  *-- Assume the next line is the city line
  cCity = fgets( hLst )
  *-- Read the line after that
  cTxt = fgets( hLst )
  *-- If it's the all-hyphens line
  if cTxt = "--------"
    *-- assumption was correct
```

```
        *-- Assign null string to cAddr2
        cAddr2 = ""         else
        *-- otherwise what was assumed to be the city line was
        *-- actually the 2nd address line
        cAddr2 = cCity
        *-- and this line is the city line
        cCity = cTxt
        *-- Now read the all-hyphens line to get it out of the way
        cTxt = fgets( hLst )
      endif
      *-- Extract ZIP from end of city line
      nPos = rat( " ", cCity ) + 1
      cZip = substr( cCity, nPos )
      *-- Extract state
      nPos = rat( " ", cCity, 2 ) + 1
      cState = substr( cCity, nState, 2 )
      *-- Truncate city memvar to include just the city
      cCity = left( cCity, nPos - 1 )
      *-- Add record
      append blank
      replace DATE  with d1, ;
              NAME  with cName, ;
              ADDR1 with cAddr1, ;
              ADDR2 with cAddr2, ;
              CITY  with cCity, ;
              STATE with cState, ;
              ZIP   with cZip
    enddo
    fclose( hLst )
```

Removing Duplicates

After importing a file into dBASE format, there may be duplicates that you want to remove. For example, after importing a file that records sales, the same customer may show up many times when you only want the name once.

Removing duplicates is a three step process:

1. Put the records in order so that all the duplicates are grouped together.
2. Mark the first occurrence of each name or item you want to keep.
3. Remove the rest or copy the first occurrences to another file.

Before beginning any operation like removing duplicates, that can adversely affect your entire table, always make a backup.

Grouping the Records

Grouping the records simply involves creating an index on the fields unique among the copied records. For example, with names you can index on LAST_NAME + FIRST_NAME. Of course, some people have the same last name and first name, and sometimes even the same middle name or initial. If possible, it is better to use some more specific identifying field, as long as every record has an entry for this field.

For example, social security number is a good field, as is any customer ID number used by the system from which you are importing data. If those are not available, the phone number is a good field, and so is the address.

If you use the address, many times it is stored in a single field. Unless you break up that field into separate components (the number, the direction, the street name, the street type, etc.—a fairly complex process) you cannot use the whole field because the same address can often be written a number of different ways, as shown in the following lines:

205 Sunset

205 W Sunset

205 W Sunset Bl

205 West Sunset Boulevard

All these addresses may refer to the same place. What does not change is the house number, in this case 205. Unless the number of names is huge, it is extremely unlikely that two people have the same last name and first name, and live in two different places that have the same house number. If you have a ZIP code, that makes it even more specific. Of course, one exception to this is a Jr. and Sr. living in the same house, but if all you have is a simple name and address you cannot know this information.

You can get the house number from the address by simply taking the VAL() of the address. VAL() will attempt to interpret the string as a number, stopping at the first non-numeric character. If the string starts with a non-numeric character, VAL() returns zero. You then use STR() to turn the extracted number back into a fixed-length string, which will be concatenated to the name and ZIP code.

After importing the data file, the INDEX command to put the records in order might look like this:

```
index on LAST_NAME + FIRST_NAME + ZIP + str( val( ADDRESS ),5) tag DUP_CHECK
```

The table is now in order. You can begin marking the duplicates.

Marking the Duplicates

You can either mark the first occurrence of each name or item or mark the duplicate occurrences, depending on how you want to handle the marked records. You can consider the marked records to be the good records and copy them elsewhere, or consider the marked records to be the bad records, and delete them. The latter is used here.

The delete flag serves as a perfect record marker. All records have a delete flag, there is no need to add an extra field, and there are built-in functions that support the delete flag. The data was just imported, so all the delete flags should be clear.

The code to mark the duplicates is as follows:

```
*-- Force mismatch for first record
cKey = "#"
*-- Do a single pass through the table
scan
  *-- See if current record does not match the previous
 if LAST_NAME + FIRST_NAME + ZIP + str( val( ADDRESS ), 5 ) # cKey
   *-- If not a match, it is first occurrence of new name
   *-- Store key value to match with next record
cKey = LAST_NAME + FIRST_NAME + ZIP + str( val( ADDRESS ), 5 )
   else
 *-- Mark the duplicate record for deletion
     delete
   endif
 endscan
```

After this bit of code is run, all the duplicates will be marked for deletion.

Removing the Duplicates

Now that all the duplicates are marked for deletion, you can use the PACK command to permanently remove them from the table. You probably do not need the index tag anymore either, so if you remove that first, you can save some time on the PACK; otherwise dBASE will spend time to reindex the DUP_CHECK tag after PACKing.

```
delete tag DUP_CHECK
pack
```

On the other hand, you can copy the unique names to another file. If for some reason you wanted the names to be in alphabetical order (generally unnecessary because you can create an index for the resulting file), you can leave the DUP_CHECK index in place as you COPY the file:

```
copy to UNIQNAME for .not. deleted()
```

Normalizing a Flat File

Sometimes a name will appear in a file more than once, not because it is a duplicate name, but because other information in the record makes the record unique. For example, suppose you have rental information which not only includes the name of the person, but the date of the rental and what they rented as well. This information is stored in a single file. Every time there is a rental, all the name and address information is repeated. This is an example of a *flat file* database. Getting the information into dBASE format is one thing, but converting the flat file into a normalized database of tables is another. Once the file is in dBASE format, converting the flat file into a normalized database of tables is a separate and more complicated matter.

Normalizing a flat file is a lot like removing duplicates. The steps are as follows:

1. Create the separate tables that will contain the normalized data.

2. Put the file in order so that all the records are grouped properly.

3. On a single pass through the flat file, create entries in the normalized tables.

Creating the Normalized Tables

The normalized tables should simply divide the flat file records into their logical components. In the case of names and rentals, you would have one file with names, and another file with rental dates and what was rented.

To connect the two tables you need a common key field. In this example, a customer ID field will link the two tables. If the imported file has a unique ID for each name, then you can use that, but if not, you can generate one as you process the flat file.

In essence, the single file shown in figure 22.3 would be converted into two files (shown in fig. 22.4) with the ID fields linking the two (shown in fig. 22.5).

If you plan to merge this data into your main normalized tables, be sure to use compatible field structures, especially compatible ID fields; make them the same type and length.

LAST_NAME	FIRST_NAME	DATE	MODEL
Groggins	Myrtle	02/14/89	Escort
Groggins	Myrtle	06/28/92	Escort
Groggins	Myrtle	07/05/93	Rabbit
Keach	Trevor	01/13/86	Tempo
Keach	Trevor	04/05/91	Bentley
Keach	Trevor	08/15/92	Auburn

Figure 22.3
A flat file before normalization.

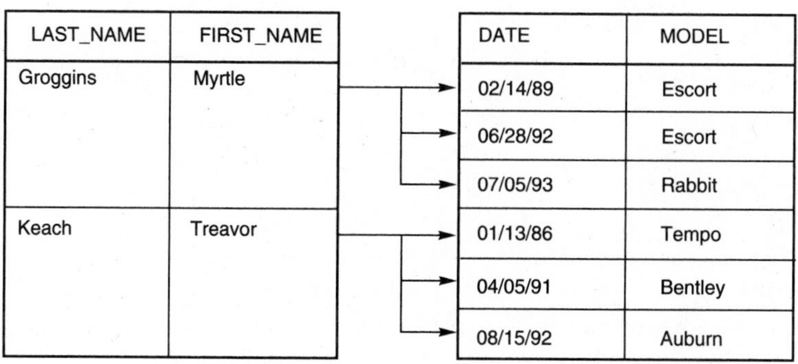

Figure 22.4
The flat file normalized.

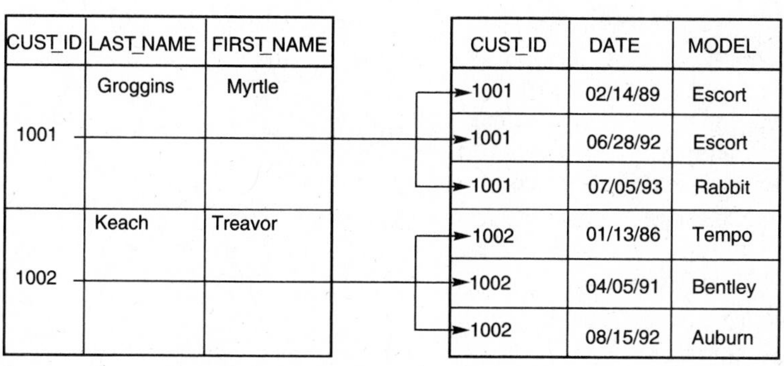

Figure 22.5
The normalized files linked by ID field.

Grouping the Records

As with removing duplicates, the records must be ordered such that the records are grouped according to the relation tree. The same index expression that was used for the duplicates will serve in this case:

```
index on LAST_NAME + FIRST_NAME + ZIP + str( val( ADDRESS), 5) tag NORMALIZE
```

It is not necessary to include the date in the index expression because that table is the last table in the relation chain. Nothing depends on it being in order.

Splitting the Table

Splitting the flat file FLATFILE.DBF into the normalized tables NAMES.DBF and DATES.DBF involves some nested loops. The code is similar to that used to mark the duplicates:

```
*-- Start with an arbitrary ID value
cID  = "1000"
*-- Force mismatch for first record
cKey = "#"
*-- Do a single pass through the flat file
select FLATFILE
scan
  *-- See if current record does not match the previous
  if LAST_NAME + FIRST_NAME + ZIP + str( val( ADDRESS ), 5 )  # cKey
    *-- If not a match, it is first occurrence of new name
    *-- Increment the ID value
    cID = transform( val( ID ) + 1, "@L 9999" )
    *-- Add the new name to NAMES
    select NAMES
    append blank
    replace CUST_ID    with cID, ;
            LAST_NAME  with FLATFILE->LAST_NAME, ;
            FIRST_NAME with FLATFILE->FIRST_NAME, ;
            ADDRESS    with FLATFILE->ADDRESS, ;
            CITY       with FLATFILE->CITY, ;
            STATE      with FLATFILE->STATE, ;
            ZIP        with FLATFILE->ZIP
    select FLATFILE
    *-- Store key value to match with next record
    cKey = LAST_NAME + FIRST_NAME + ZIP + str( val( ADDRESS ), 5 )
  endif
  *-- Each record in FLATFILE always adds a new date
```

```
        select DATES
        append blank
        replace CUST_ID with cID, ;
                DATE    with FLATFILE->DATE, ;
                MODEL   with FLATFILE->MODEL
        select FLATFILE
      endscan
```

This basic technique can be extended to any number of related files.

Redirecting Streaming Output

Creating a new file does not have to be an entirely structured affair. Streaming output from the ? and ?? commands can go into a file. The ALTERNATE file designates where output from the ? and ?? commands goes to, in addition to the screen. If you do not want to see the output on the screen, you can SET CONSOLE OFF.

The first step is to designate the output file. This is done with the command:

```
SET ALTERNATE TO <filename>
```

If that named file already exists, you will overwrite that file, with a warning if SET SAFETY is ON. Instead of overwriting, you can append data to the file by adding the ADDITIVE keyword to the command.

Once the ALTERNATE file has been designated, you activate it with the command:

```
SET ALTERNATE ON
```

From then on, all output from ? and ?? will go into the file. If SET CONSOLE is ON, the output will go to the screen as well. If SET CONSOLE is OFF, the output will go only to the ALTERNATE file. You can temporarily deactivate the ALTERNATE file with the command

```
SET ALTERNATE OFF
```

By mixing the SET ALTERNATE and SET CONSOLE commands, you can direct the streaming output from the ? and ?? commands to the screen, the ALTERNATE file, or both (or neither for that matter).

With SET ALTERNATE, you may have some trouble getting the output to start at the first column of the first line. If you start your output with the ? command, you get a blank line; if you start with the ?? command, you may not start in the first column. The trick is essentially to combine the two:

continues

```
set alternate to WHATEVER.TXT
set console off
?
set alternate on
?? "The first line"
?  "The second line"
```

You stop the redirection of the output with a SET ALTERNATE OFF command and close the ALTERNATE file with the CLOSE ALTERNATE or SET ALTERNATE TO command:

```
? "Last line"
 set alternate off
 set alternate to
```

It is easier to use SET ALTERNATE to generate a text file if you only have to create one text file at a time. There is no need to deal with file handles or use the word FWRITE() or FPUTS() a number of times.

Removing the EOF Marker

One thing that happens to files created by SET ALTERNATE is that when they are closed, dBASE puts an EOF marker on the end. For a text file, the presence of an EOF marker probably does not make much difference, but for a data file, the EOF marker may create problems. In that case, after the file is closed, you should run it through the RemoveEOF procedure that was discussed earlier.

Chapter Snapshot

This chapter examines graphical and multimedia data and shows how you can use dBASE to store and manipulate that data. By reading this chapter, you learn about the following:

You also learn that the requirements involved with storing and working with these types of multimedia data are high. Nevertheless, if you are working on an application which needs to utilize the multimedia capabilities of Windows, then dBASE can be an ideal development tool for you.

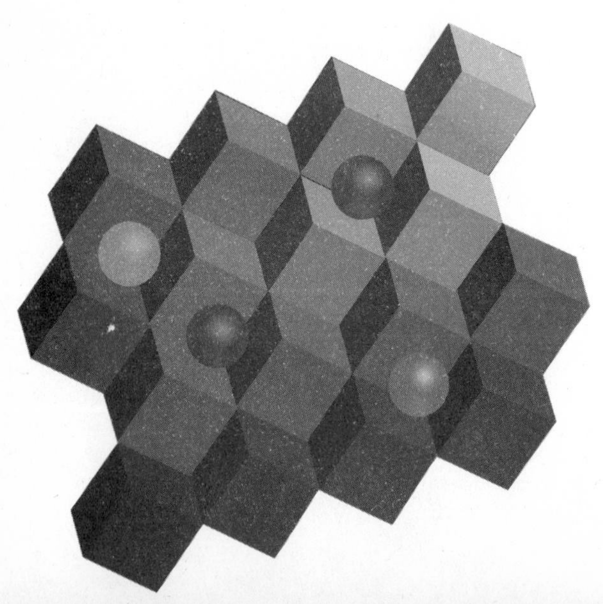

Working with Graphical and Multimedia Data

By Richard Wagner

Until the emergence of Windows databases such as dBASE and Paradox, the terms *graphical* and *multimedia* were alien concepts in the PC database environment. That scenario has changed radically as businesses utilize these types of nontextual data. Reasons for the increased popularity include the following:

- ✔ Widespread use of Windows
- ✔ More powerful processors (DX2, DX4, and Pentium chips)
- ✔ Affordable double- and triple-speed CD-ROM drives
- ✔ Decreasing costs of large-capacity hard drives
- ✔ Sophisticated means of storing graphical data in databases

This chapter examines various issues surrounding graphical and multimedia data and helps determine the best means to store and utilize this data in your dBASE applications.

Working with Graphical and Multimedia Data

When working with graphical and multimedia data, you need to be aware of hardware and software considerations. Using a dBASE table as a storehouse for employee photographs, video presentations, and audio memos can seem like a good idea, but you should remember that this application comes at a considerable cost. Storing these types of data requires massive amounts of storage space and places a strain on a PC's random-access memory (RAM) and processor.

If you want to take the 256-color images of houses in the HomeGuide database, for example, and replace them with 24-bit images, think about this: a single uncompressed 24-bit graphic could easily take up 500 KB of disk space. The storage capacity for 1,000 such images could easily reach 500 MB of disk space. As you explore options of working with graphical and multimedia data, several issues surface:

- ✔ **Quality.** What level of data quality needs to be captured? For an image, does it have to be 24-bit, or could it be just a 16- or 256-color bitmap? For an audio clip, does it need to be of audio CD quality, or can you get by with AM radio quality? For a video, can the video be displayed in a relatively small window, or does it need to be as large as possible?

- ✔ **Compression.** Whether you are working with graphical, audio, or video data, should file compression be used? If compression is to be used, how can you store the data into the dBASE table?

- ✔ **Field types.** When you work with graphical and multimedia data, you also need to determine the best field type in which to store the data. Should you use binary or object linking and embedding (OLE) field types? Table 23.1 lists some of the advantages and disadvantages for both types.

Table 23.1
Comparing Binary and OLE Fields

Capability	Binary	OLE
Provides support for PCX and BMP	Yes	Yes (using Paintbrush as the OLE server)
Provides support for WAV (waveform sound) files	Yes	Yes (using the Sound Recorder as the OLE server)

Capability	Binary	OLE
Provides support for AVI (full-motion video) files	Partial (AVI files can be stored, but not displayed)	Yes (using the Windows Media Player as the OLE Server
Provides support for compressed image files (JPG and GIF)	Partial (compressed files can be stored but not displayed)	Yes (using image processing software which can function as an OLE server)
Enables editing of the data once stored in the table	No	Yes
Enables data to be physically stored (or embedded) in the table	Yes	Yes
Enables data to be linked to a separate file	No	Yes
Enables any type of data to be stored	Yes	No (data must originate from an OLE server)

Working with Graphical Data

dBASE enables you to store graphical data in your databases and display it through the Image Viewer while in a Browse window or through an Image control (and OLE control) on a form. However, before you learn about storing and displaying graphical data in dBASE, you need first to understand the different graphics types that exist, as well as how they can best be used within dBASE.

Understanding Windows Graphics Types

Two types of Windows graphics that you can work with are bitmap and vector graphics. Each of these types is designed for some uses but not others. Vector and bitmap graphics are explained in the following two sections.

Bitmap Graphics

A bitmap graphic is the most widely used graphic type in the Windows environment. A *bitmap* is a pattern of dots that, when combined, form an image on screen or on the printer. Each dot is known as a *pixel.* You can create bitmapped graphics using paint programs, such as Windows Paintbrush, or by scanning a real world image with a scanner.

The quality of bitmap images can be remarkable because you can work with 16 on up to 16.8 million colors. The downfall of bitmapped images is the loss of quality that you get when you try to resize or scale them. Many refer to this loss of quality as the "jaggies" (for the jagged edges).

To create and work with bitmapped images, you need a paint program. Three levels of paint programs are available, depending upon your needs:

- ✔ **Basic (8-bit) Paint.** The basic paint tool is an 8-bit paint program. It is designed to work with black-and-white, indexed 4-bit (16-color), and indexed 8-bit (256-color) graphics. Windows Paintbrush is an example of a basic paint program.
- ✔ **True Color (24-bit) Paint.** Far superior to a basic paint program, a 24-bit paint program can work with 24-bit images and includes a wider assortment of painting tools. Examples of 24-bit paint programs include CA-CricketPaint and Fractal Design Painter.
- ✔ **Image Processing.** Image-editing programs are similar to 24-bit paint programs, but also include gamma correction, resampling, and 4-color separation abilities. Image-editing software is sometimes referred to as an electronic darkroom. Aldus PhotoStyler or PhotoShop is an example of an image-processing application.

Vector Graphics

In contrast with bitmaps, vector (or object-oriented) graphics are not made up of a series of pixels, but of shapes, such as circles, lines, arcs, and squares. These objects can be scaled to any size you want because they are generated from mathematical definitions each time you resize or modify them. No "jaggies" are present on the large object. Vector graphics are ideal for technical drawings and line art because you can pay attention to detail in drawing programs far more easily than in paint programs.

Vector graphics are always created within a drawing or illustration program, such as CorelDRAW!, Arts & Letters, Micrografx Draw, and Aldus Freehand. Drawing programs usually have a distinct set of tools compared to paint programs, which are designed to create and manipulate objects, not pixels.

Bitmap versus Vector: Which To Use?

The appropriate graphic type to use can be determined by examining the purpose for which you are going to be working with it in dBASE. If you plan to store detailed technical drawings or work with scanned photographs, the choice seems more obvious. However, other choices can be more subtle. Table 23.2 provides a brief summary of some of the capabilities of bitmap and vector graphics.

Table 23.2
Choosing the Graphic

Category	Bitmap	Vector
dBASE binary field support	Yes	No
dBASE OLE field support	Yes*	Yes*
Full-color (24-bit) images	Yes	No
Scanned photographs or image manipulation	Yes	No
Custom blending	Yes	No
Pixel level editing	Yes	No
Manipulation of shapes	No	Yes
Technical drawing	No	Yes
Text manipulation and special effects	No	Yes
Clip art	No	Yes

* Graphics software must be an OLE server to provide OLE support.

In general, dBASE provides only direct support for bitmap graphics through its binary field type. However, there are no limitations on how you can utilize graphical data, thanks to the OLE field. (This option, however, does force you to use graphics software that provides OLE server support.)

Understanding Graphic File Formats

In addition to the type of graphic, at least two dozen common graphic file formats exist that you can work with under Windows—although dBASE provides direct support for just two of these formats. These bitmap formats include BMP and PCX:

- ✔ **BMP.** BMP (Bitmap) is the standard graphic file format for Windows. It is supported by nearly all Windows applications, but rarely supported outside of Windows. Windows Paintbrush saves bitmaps in BMP format by default, and graphics displayed as wallpaper on the Windows Desktop must be in BMP format. BMP files support black-and-white, 4-bit, 8-bit, and 24-bit image types.

- ✔ **PCX.** PCX (PC Paintbrush) is probably the standard graphics format for the entire PC platform (Windows and DOS). PCX was one of the first graphics formats available for the PC and was the native format for Zsoft Paintbrush. PCX is probably supported by more Windows and DOS applications than any other format. PCX format supports black-and-white, 4-bit, and 8-bit image types.

Because dBASE provides support for just BMP and PCX format, you might need to convert vector graphics and unsupported bitmap formats (such as TIF) to PCX or BMP format to store them into a binary field.

- ✔ **Converting Between Bitmap Formats.** A bitmap-to-bitmap conversion is probably the easiest file conversion and can be accomplished by using Paintbrush or a popular utility such as Paint Shop Pro. Additionally, most paint programs enable you to import and export bitmaps in a variety of formats. One shareware utility you might want to consider getting is Paint Shop Pro. It can be one of the most economical ways to convert DIB, GIF, IMG, JAS, MAC, MSP, PIC, RAS, RLE, TGA, TIF, and WPG formats to BMP or PCX.
- ✔ **Converting Vector to Bitmap Formats.** Many drawing programs will save a vector graphic in a bitmapped format. If your drawing program does not, you can display the vector graphic onscreen and capture the image with screen capture software or by pressing Print Screen to copy the screen image to the Clipboard. After you import the screen shot into a paint program, you can crop the image as needed.

If you are planning to do many graphics conversions or are trying to convert between lesser-used formats, you should consider getting HiJaak for Windows, a powerful conversion utility available commercially.

Understanding Graphics File Compression

If you plan to work with large numbers of images, you need to consider graphics file compression. This is because both BMP and PCX formats are relatively inefficient and can require 10 times as much space as a compressed image. Two compression formats are popular:

- ✔ **GIF.** GIF (Graphics Interchange Format) is a standard format used to store graphics on CompuServe and other bulletin board systems (BBSs). The format was designed to create the smallest file size in order to minimize the time spent transferring files to and from CompuServe and other online services. GIF is more of a utility format because most applications do not support GIF. However, GIF can be converted into other bitmap formats easily through commercial and shareware paint programs. Both PC and Mac platforms support GIF. There are two GIF file versions—87a and 89a. GIF format supports black-and-white, 4-bit, and 8-bit image types.
- ✔ **JPG.** JPG (Joint Photographic Experts Group) is a new format designed to provide extremely high compression ratios (up to 100:1). The JPG compression

scheme achieves these remarkable ratios by leaving some of the data out during the compression process. However, you can usually use JPG format for images without any noticeable loss of quality of the image. JPG is especially applicable to storing 24-bit color photographic images, which can take up a considerable amount of storage space.

Because dBASE provides no direct support for either GIF or JPG, you have essentially two options if you want to use compressed graphics in your database. First, you can use an OLE field to store data and then select a graphics or image processing software package that provides OLE server support. Each graphic could be stored as an OLE object in your dBASE table.

Be sure to test the file size differences to determine whether it is more advantageous to link or embed your OLE data.

Second, you can store the graphic in a binary field in its compressed format. However, in doing so, dBASE will be unable to display the image in its Image Viewer because it cannot interpret GIF or JPG formats. You would then need to program your own means of viewing the data contained in your table.

Adding a Graphic to a dBASE Table

To add a PCX or BMP file to a binary field of a dBASE table, double-click an empty binary field in a Browse window to display the Empty Binary Field dialog box (see fig. 23.1). Select the Image Viewer option and then choose OK.

In the Image Viewer window, choose File, Insert from File to display the Choose Image dialog box. Use the dialog box to select a graphics file, then choose OK. As you return to the Image Viewer window, the graphic will be displayed.

You can also place images using an OLE field rather than a binary field. To do this, open the OLE viewer by double-clicking an OLE field. Choose Edit, Insert Object from the menu (or right-click and choose Insert Object from the Inspector menu). In the Insert New Object dialog box shown, select Paintbrush Picture, or another OLE graphic from the list, and choose OK. If you select Paintbrush Picture, Paintbrush will open and enable you to create an image that you can embed into your table. When you are finished, choose the Update command from the File menu. These changes are now saved in your table.

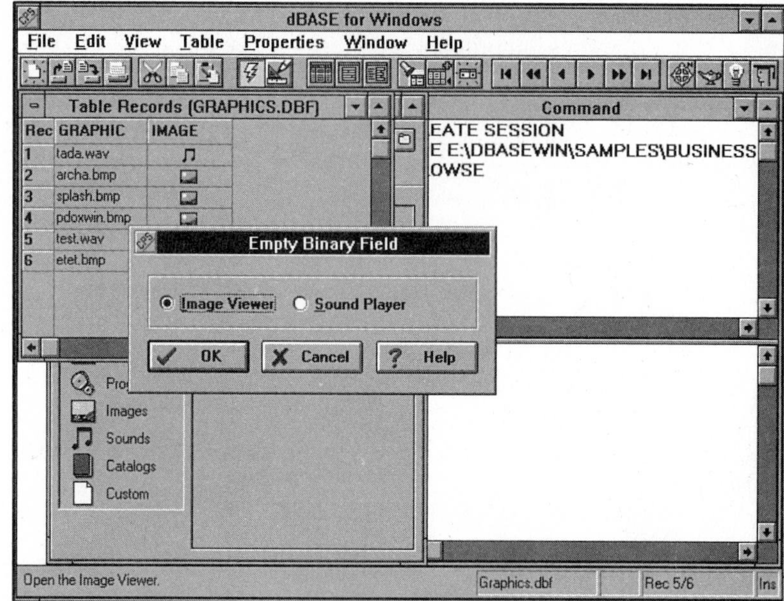

Figure 23.1
The Empty Binary Field dialog box.

Displaying a Graphic in a Browse Window and a Form

To display an image stored in a dBASE table, double-click on the binary field in a Browse window. To view a graphic stored as an OLE object, double-click the OLE field in a Browse window to display the OLE Viewer window.

You can also display a graphic on a form using the Image control from the Controls palette. After you create a form, place an Image control on the form.

Next, you need to link the image to either a file, a database table, or a resource file. To do this, select Image control and display the Data Source property in the Properties Inspector. Click the Tool button to display the Choose Bitmap dialog box (see fig. 23.2).

In the Location box, select the desired source of the image:

- ✔ **Resource.** This option enables you to select bitmaps from a dBASE resource file. The images contained in this file are designed for icons on custom SpeedBars, buttons, and so on. Clicking the Tool button beside the Bitmap list displays a dialog box for you to select an image.

- **Filename.** If you want to display a PCX or BMP file on your form, select the Filename option. Then in the Bitmap box, enter a file name or click the Tool button to locate a file on your hard disk.

- **Binary.** If you would like to display a graphic stored in a binary field, select Binary from the Location list. In the Bitmap box, enter the desired table and field name using the following syntax:

```
tableName->fieldName
```

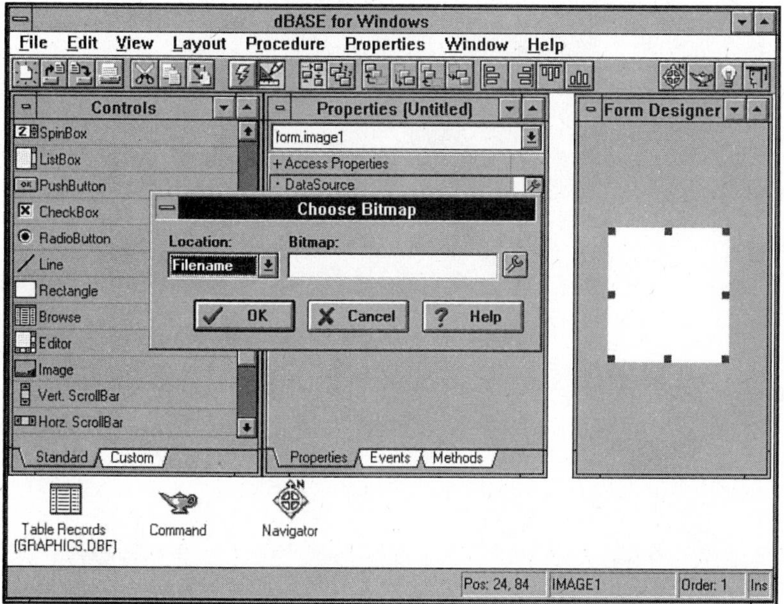

Figure 23.2
The Choose Bitmap dialog box.

Another alternative is to click on the Tool button to select the table and field from the Choose Fields dialog box.

When you run the form, the Image control will display the image (see fig. 23.3).

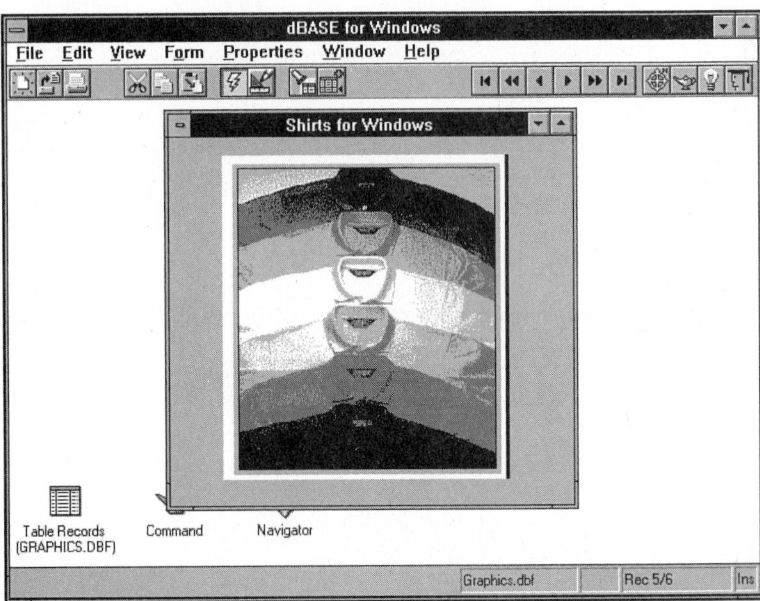

Figure 23.3 Displaying an image on a form.

Creating and Working with Graphics

The Navigator includes an Images category to display all BMP and PCX files in the default directory or database (see fig. 23.4). However, be sure to note that these are separate files and are not necessarily contained in your dBASE tables.

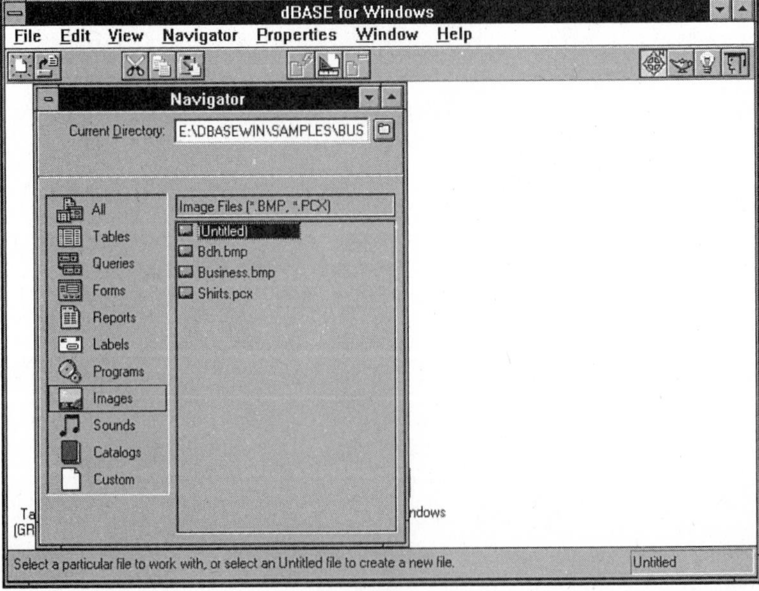

Figure 23.4 The Images category displayed in the Navigator.

To create a new image file, select the Images category from the Navigator window and double-click on the (Untitled) item. Paintbrush is displayed. Use Paintbrush to create an image, and then select File, Save to save the graphic in BMP or PCX format.

To view an image shown in the Navigator, right-click the image file name and choose the Display Image option from the Inspector menu (or press F2).

Working with Multimedia Data

Multimedia is one word that database developers have traditionally stayed far away from, but Windows databases have changed that. In fact, multimedia is now becoming very important to many database developers and corporations. *Multimedia* can be defined as the blending of different kinds of media, such as full-motion video, digital sound, and still 24-bit images, in the computer environment. While combining these types of media is not inherently useful, proper application can provide an ultimate means of bringing the real world into your database environment. Multimedia has an unlimited potential of application within a database. The next sections look at how you can utilize both audio and video data in dBASE.

Working with Audio Data

Multimedia audio has traditionally been dominated by games and other recreational activities. The business uses of audio are becoming increasingly important, however. With multimedia audio, you can attach a sound file to an Excel spreadsheet to explain the rationale for proposed changes to another coworker, or e-mail a voice message to a client by attaching a sound file to the message.

dBASE provides the capability to place sound data into either a binary field or an OLE field. Using the binary field, the file format of the sound files must be in WAV (or waveform) format—the standard Windows sound format.

A sound is recorded digitally and stored in a WAV file through a technique known as sampling. With *sampling*, a sound is sampled at a given frequency (or number of times per second). The higher the sampling frequency, the truer the sound reproduction will be, but the more space it will take to store that sound data. Consequently, WAV files with quality sound can grow very large.

If you are capturing sound data, sampling is a critical decision. An 8-bit mono sample (AM radio quality) takes just .6 MB per minute, while a 16-bit stereo sample (audio CD equivalent) requires 10.6 MB per minute. Be sure to choose the appropriate sampling level for your specific application.

There are other waveform file formats besides the Windows WAV type, such as SND, VOC, and MOD. However, to use them in dBASE binary fields, you first need to convert them to the WAV file format. There are both shareware and commercial utilities available to perform this task.

Adding Sound to a dBASE Table

To add a WAV file to a binary field of a dBASE table, double-click on an empty binary field in a Browse window to display the Empty Binary Field dialog box (see fig. 23.1). Select the Sound Player option, then click on OK

The Sound Player window is displayed. From the File menu, choose Insert from File to display the Choose Sound dialog box. Use the dialog box to select a WAV file and click OK. As you return to Sound Player window, click on the Play button to play the WAV file.

On the other hand, you can add sound data to an OLE field rather than a binary field. To do this, open the OLE Viewer by double-clicking an OLE field. Choose Edit, Insert Object from the menu (or right-click and choose Insert Object from the Inspector menu). In the Insert New Object dialog box shown, select Sound from the list and click on OK. The Sound Recorder will open and enable you to create a sound file which you can embed into your table. When you are finished, choose the Update command from the File menu. These changes are now saved in your table.

Playing Sound from a dBASE Table

If you have a sound board or sound driver, you can play a sound stored in a table by double-clicking the binary field in a Browse window. In the Sound Player window, click the Play button. (You can also play a sound stored as an OLE object by double-clicking it in the OLE Viewer window.)

Even if you do not have a sound card, you can still play WAV files over your standard PC speaker using a special sound driver available from Microsoft. You can find that sound driver on CompuServe in the Zenith forum (GO ZENITH) under the filename SPEAK.EXE.

Creating and Working with WAV Files

The Navigator includes a Sound category to display all WAV files in a given directory or database. However, just as with image files described above, these are separate files and are not contained in your dBASE tables.

To create a new sound file, select the Sound category and double-click on the (Untitled) item in the Navigator window. The Sound Recorder is displayed. The Sound Recorder is a multimedia Windows applet that enables you to record, edit, and play sound files (see

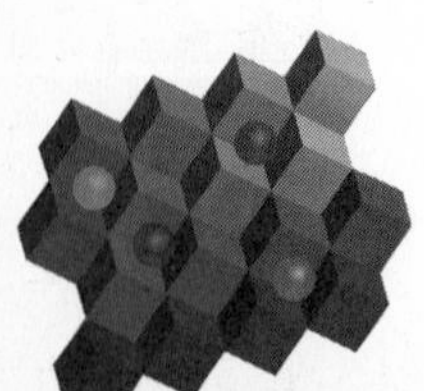

fig. 23.5). You can think of the Sound Recorder as similar to a tape deck. The buttons displayed on the bottom of the window enable you to rewind, fast forward, play, stop, and record sounds.

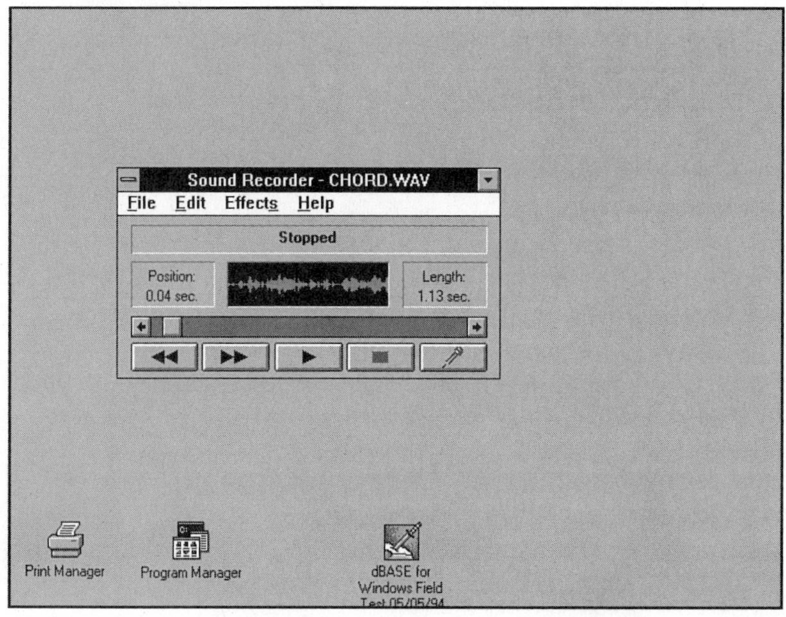

Figure 23.5
The Sound Recorder.

The Sound Recorder is also an OLE server, so any WAV file you work with in the Sound Recorder can be inserted into your table using an OLE field. If you would like to link this WAV file to your table, you can choose **E**dit, **C**opy from the Sound Recorder menu and choose **E**dit, Paste Lin**k** from the OLE Viewer in a dBASE Browse window.

If you have the appropriate hardware, you can record a WAV file using the Sound Recorder and then use **F**ile, **S**ave to save the data to a file. Or, if you would like to modify an existing WAV file, use either **F**ile, **O**pen or **E**dit, **I**nsert File. Use the Sound Recorder controls to modify the WAV file as desired.

Working with Video Data

The capability to view and edit full-motion video (such as viewing a clip from the movie *Casablanca*) still seems like a novelty to many. The capability to capture video data into a database can be extremely powerful and useful, however. For example, a natural extension to HomeGuide would be the addition of a video tour of each house listed in the database. Such an extension would be more than just a novelty; it would be a great help to a prospective home buyer to see a tour of the house before actually visiting it.

If you are working with video in Windows, you are probably working with Microsoft Video for Windows AVI format or QuickTime, which are the two major video file format standards under Windows. The single biggest factor when working with video data is the massive storage requirements required for a video file. For example, a 42-second video clip (which, in fact, would be a really short tour of a house) requires 6 MB of space. Obviously, a database storing just 100 video clips could easily reach 600 MB of space.

If you must use a large number of video clips in your database, you should consider placing these files on a CD-ROM. The costs for creating a custom CD-ROM disk for your files can be less than the cost of a new hard disk for storing video files.

To store video data in your table, you will typically use an OLE field. Place the video clip in the Clipboard by using the Media Player applet or other video utility and then choose Edit, Paste from the OLE Viewer in a dBASE Browse window to embed the video. You also can choose Edit, Paste Link to link the video to your table. Figure 23.6 shows a video clip being displayed on a dBASE form.

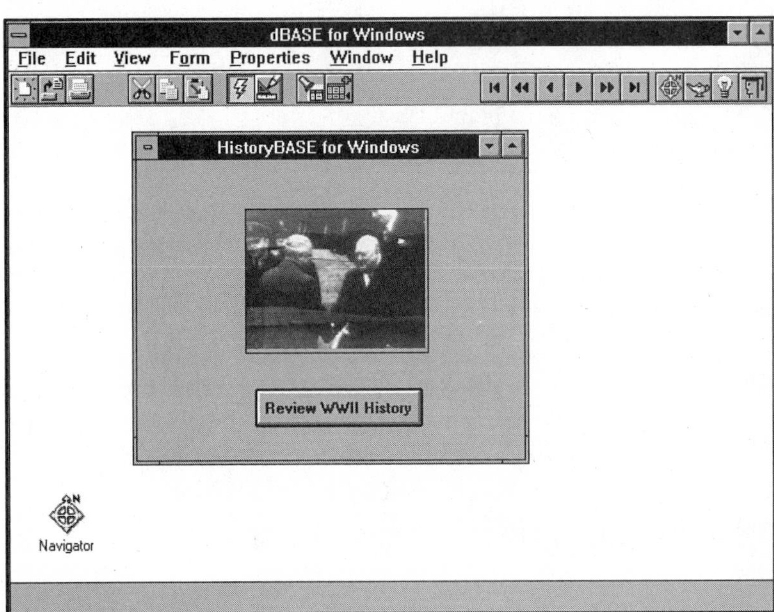

Figure 23.6 A video can be played from a dBASE form.

For more information on linking and embedding OLE objects, read Chapter 24.

Chapter Snapshot

This chapter examines dBASE's ability to integrate with other Windows applications through dynamic data exchange (DDE) and object linking and embedding (OLE). By reading this chapter, you can learn the basic concepts of DDE and OLE, as well as how to do the following:

Through the concepts used in this chapter, you learn how easy it can be to integrate data from different programs.

Integrating dBASE Applications with OLE and DDE

By Richard Wagner

Data becomes more powerful as it is shared. Although this statement can refer to concurrent database access, the statement is equally valid when it applies to using the same data between applications on your Windows desktop. Historically, one of the biggest drawbacks to a DOS-based system has been its "program-centric" view of a computer system. A database management system kept data, but actually porting it to other applications proved difficult. As a result, exchanging data between DOS applications was done in a limited fashion.

In contrast, one of the most powerful aspects of the Windows environment is the capability Windows applications have to communicate and exchange data with each other. Although you can use the traditional cut, copy, and paste method to transfer data, Windows 3.1 offers two technologies that are much more powerful—dynamic data exchange (DDE) and object linking and embedding (OLE). DDE and OLE can be used to integrate dBASE with other Windows applications, such as Word for Windows, Quattro Pro for Windows, Ami Pro, and Excel. The result is that rather than using multiple applications to control multiple sources of data, you can use a single application to maintain source data while allowing multiple applications to access that same information.

Your dBASE directory (such as C:\DBASEWIN) must be in the PATH statement of your AUTOEXEC.BAT file to successfully use DDE and OLE.

Examining Dynamic Data Exchange

DDE is a method you can use to transfer data or instructions between Windows applications without requiring user interaction. To use DDE, you have to establish a *conversation* between a *client* (one who sends or receives data from another application) and a *server* (one who responds to the client application request and provides the requested information). Think of a DDE conversation as a phone call. You initiate the conversation, and if the intended receiver is available, you can begin a conversation and exchange ideas. When you are finished talking, you end the conversation by hanging up the receiver. Obviously, many possible options can occur while the phone call is in process, but DDE is nothing more complicated than a phone call metaphor.

Windows provides two ways to use DDE: interactively or through a programming language. Interactive DDE is based on the Clipboard copy-and-paste metaphor, and DDE programming is based on establishing conversations in user-written code from an application's programming or macro language.

Interactive DDE Links

Some applications provide DDE capabilities that are accessible from their menus. This feature enables you to interactively copy data from one application and paste it into a second application. This once common capability is being superseded, however, with most interactive use of linking now being done through OLE. dBASE provides OLE linking support, but not support for interactive DDE links.

DDE Programming Conversations

Although some think of DDE solely in terms of the Clipboard metaphor, there also exists a far more powerful way to use DDE. Many Windows applications or development platforms have either a programming or a macro language which enables you to establish DDE conversations between two applications. DDE conversations managed by a programming language of the DDE client can be called DDE programming.

In a program, a DDE conversation is created by writing code that initiates a conversation with a server, pokes data to or receives data from the server application, and terminates the DDE conversation. Because of the nature of this type of conversation, a DDE programming conversion usually is considered a *cold link*, or a one-time exchange of data (although you also can program hot links). In addition, because a DDE programming conversation can be coded in a program, no user interaction is required.

DDE programming is a very underrated capability of Windows 3.1. DDE programming can be used to create seamless solutions to the labor-intensive tasks you find yourself doing routinely. Some tasks that require working with several different applications can be controlled by the client application (such as dBASE) with DDE. The result is the user may never have to leave the client application to perform those processes in other applications. This lowers the learning curve with new applications and increases the efficiency of your work.

DDE Protocol: Following the Rules

For applications to converse using DDE, there must be a strict protocol defining how the conversation can be conducted. DDE protocol ensures that two applications are in sync to carry out the conversation. Otherwise, some aspect of the conversation could fail, losing the link between the two applications and potentially the data as well. If you find your DDE conversation cannot be established or are having problems with it, most likely you are not adhering to protocol correctly. Before looking further at the protocol, take a close look at the actors taking part in this conversation:

- ✔ **Client.** A *client* application initiates a DDE conversation with another application. It asks the server application to send data or to receive data or asks the server to perform a command. The client is typically in charge of a conversation and terminates the conversation when it is finished.

- ✔ **Server.** A *server* application responds to the request of the client application. Upon a poke, a server accepts data from the client and places it in the appropriate location. Upon a request for data, a server finds the data the client desires and sends it back to client. (If the server cannot find the data, it informs the client of that as well.) Upon a request to perform an action, the server carries out the command if possible.

Since most major Windows applications (including dBASE) can function both as a client and a server, how you use them depends on your needs. The ideal DDE client application is simply the one you spend the most amount of time in for a given task. The ideal DDE server is one that stores or works with data or can access remote data. Examples include e-mail, fax, and communications software; spreadsheet or database applications; and database front-ends to connect you to remote (for example, SQL server) data. You also could use a DDE server to perform an entire function automatically behind-the-scenes, such as using a word processor as a report generator from within dBASE.

Although each conversation involves a single client and single server, you can have multiple DDE conversations going on simultaneously. A client can have concurrent conversations with two or more servers. Or, if an application can function both as a client and server, it could be utilized as both in two different conversations. There is one caveat: a conversation always occurs between two application windows. Thus, to hold multiple conversations with the same application requires that you have multiple instances of the application opened at once.

Inside DDE Conversations

In a DDE conversation, a client establishes three levels of identification with the server to communicate with it:

- ✔ **Application.** At the top level is the application name of the server. Each DDE server has an assigned application name to which it responds. A server's application name usually is the name of the EXE file (minus the extension). If not, a client cannot start a DDE server if the server is not running when the client attempts to begin a conversation.

dBASEs default application name is dBASEWin, although you can programmatically change it to anything you like using the DDEServiceName property (as discussed later in the chapter).

- ✔ **Topic.** At the second level is the topic. The topic identifies the range of information with which the conversation is going to deal. A common example of a topic most DDE servers use is an open document. DDE protocol requires that a conversation be confined to a single topic; thus, a conversation cannot work with more than one document in the DDE server. Although you can access data from multiple documents, you need to define a new conversation for each new document. Within a particular topic, there may be several data elements exchanged during the conversation.

- ✔ **Item.** At the bottom level is the item. The item identifies the exact data element the client wants to deal with. The client then either requests that data element or pokes data to that data element. An item is typically a reference to a value, such as a cell address (A1B2) or block coordinates (A1B1...A10B1) in a spreadsheet, a field or bookmark in a word processor document, a field in a database application, or a defined variable in a communications program. Data is usually exchanged through a standard Clipboard format (for example, Text) or through a specially registered Clipboard format.

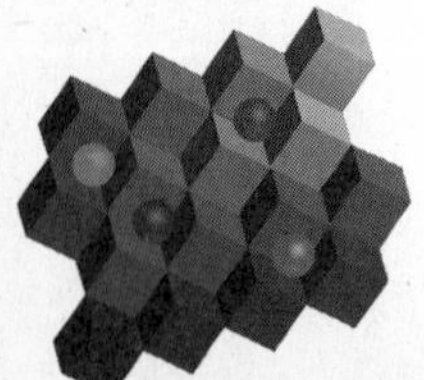

Keep in mind that the application name, topic, and items are always defined by the server. Although a client is in control of a DDE conversation, it is always doing so within the boundaries set forth by the server.

Although topics are specific to an application, a standard topic most servers (though not dBASE) support is called System. The System topic can be used by the client to query the server and to retrieve information which may be relevant to a conversation. Depending on the server, you may be able to receive a list of the available topics and items available under those topics. Table 24.1 lists the items typically available under the System topic.

Table 24.1
Items Typically Available Under the System Topic

Item Name	Purpose
SysItems	A tab-delimited list of names of the items available under the System topic
Formats	A tab-delimited list of Clipboard formats the server supports
Topics	A tab-delimited list of topics currently available to the client
Status	Current status of the DDE server (usually "Ready" or "Busy")

Most developers of Windows applications that have both client and server capabilities stress the software's capabilities as a DDE client, but virtually ignore how it can be used as a DDE server. As a result, you may find trying to find out a software program's application name, set of topics, and set of items to be the most frustrating factor in working with DDE programming. Software documentation often fails to provide this in a clear and concise manner, or even neglects to mention it altogether.

Understanding DDE Messages

Windows provides several application programming interface (API) messages for implementing DDE. Although the low-level programming specifics of these DDE messages is usually of no concern to even an advanced developer, understanding what these messages do is important. Your DDE conversations in some way will be through these messages whether you realize it or not. The DDE messages supported by dBASE can be divided into three groups:

- **System.** The System group includes INITIATE(), TERMINATE(), RECONNECT(), ADVISE(), and UNADVISE(). These commands focus on some aspect of communicating between the client and server.
- **Data.** The Data group contains Poke() and Peek(). These commands are primarily concerned with the actual exchange of data between the client and server application.
- **Task.** The Task group contains just a single command, Execute(). This message enables you to perform native commands of the server application from within a client application.

The following are the basic DDE messages supported by dBASE:

- **Advise().** The ADVISE() message is used by dBASE to ask a server to inform it whenever the value of a data item changes. The ADVISE() message tells the server automatically to send the data back to dBASE.
- **Execute().** The EXECUTE() message is used by dBASE to post a command the server is to execute, making it an ideal way of accessing another application's script or macro language. The command must follow a strict syntax defined by the server and is usually delimited by brackets. In many respects, EXECUTE() is the most powerful of all DDE messages because you can take full control over the server application. EXECUTE() is not concerned with data; in fact, a data item is not utilized in an EXECUTE() command.
- **Initiate().** The INITIATE() message is sent by dBASE to a server application to establish a DDE conversation.
- **Peek().** The PEEK() message is used by dBASE to retrieve the value of a data item in the server application.
- **Poke().** The POKE() message is used by dBASE to send a value to a data item in the server application. POKE() overwrites any existing value held by the item.
- **Reconnect().** The RECONNECT() message is used by dBASE to reestablish a DDE conversation which had been severed by a TERMINATE() message.
- **Terminate().** The TERMINATE() message is sent by dBASE to the server application to end the conversation immediately.
- **Unadvise().** An UNADVISE() message is sent by dBASE to the server whenever it no longer needs a data item updated.

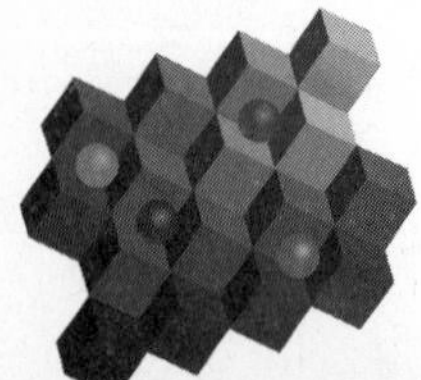

Using dBASE as a DDE Client

dBASE can be used to obtain data from or poke data to other Windows applications, as well as to control them remotely. Suppose, for example, you work with two applications on your desktop—dBASE and Word for Windows. dBASE is used for database interaction, and Word is used for word processing. However, without ever leaving dBASE, you would like to be able to generate a form letter in Word using data from a dBASE table. To perform this action, you need to set up both Word and dBASE.

In Word, set up a pre-formatted letter. To do this, insert a letterhead and the body of the letter into the document, leaving blanks where the address information is to be placed. The document looks like that shown in figure 24.1.

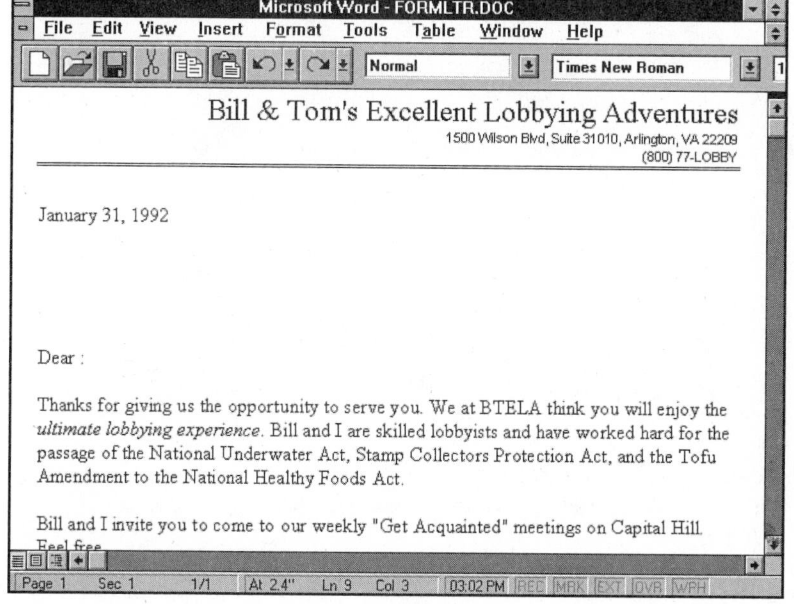

Figure 24.1
Leave blanks where dBASE data is to be poked.

Before dBASE can poke the data into the document, you first need to define DDE items in your Word document. In Word, a bookmark (invisible place holders marking a specific location in a document) serves as a DDE item.

To define a bookmark in Word, go to the line where the name of the company is to be inserted and choose **B**ookmark from the **E**dit menu. In the Bookmark dialog box shown in figure 24.2, type **Name** to name the bookmark, then click on Add. Move the cursor down to the next line and create a bookmark named Address at that location. Continue this process for the remaining address fields—City, State, and ZipCode, except place them all on the same line. Separate City and State bookmarks with a comma and a space, and State and Zip Code with a single space. Add a final bookmark called DearName and insert it just after the "Dear" greeting. Save the document as FORMLTR.DOC and close the document.

Figure 24.2 Entering bookmarks in a Word document.

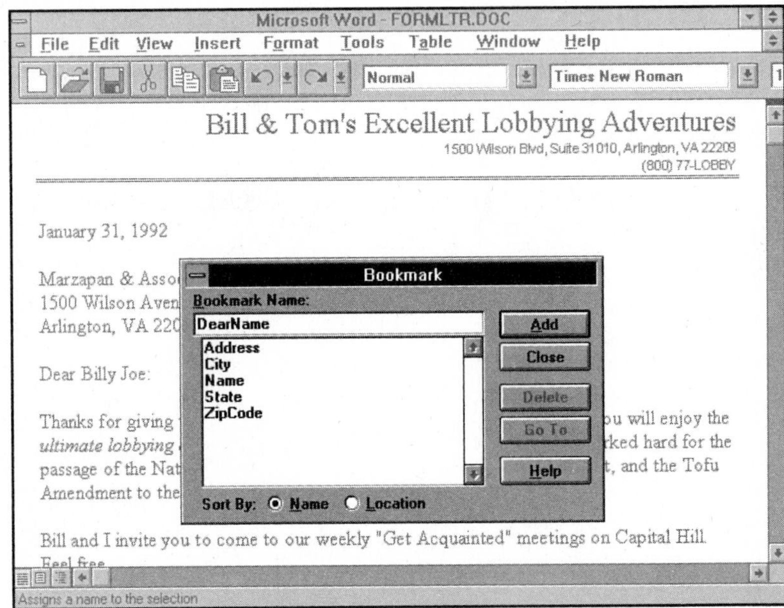

Now that you have set Word up as a DDE server, you can write a dBASE routine to poke address data to Word and ask Word to print a copy of the document to the default printer.

The first step is to create a DDELink object using the following code:

```
PUBLIC ddeLinkObj
ddeLinkObj = new DDELink()
```

Next, initiate the conversation with Word by using INITIATE() with Word's DDE server and document name as the parameters:

```
ddeLinkObj.Initiate("WINWORD", "d:\winword6\formltr.doc")
```

After the conversation is established, you need to poke the data to Word. Use POKE() to define the current item and the value of that item, as shown in the following code:

```
ddeLinkObj.Poke("Name", Marzapan & Associates)
ddeLinkObj.Poke("Address", 1500 Wilson Avenue)
ddeLinkObj.Poke("City", Arlington)
ddeLinkObj.Poke("State", VA)
ddeLinkObj.Poke("ZipCode", 22020)
ddeLinkObj.Poke("DearName", Billy Joe)
```

As this code executes, the data is sent to Word and inserted into the form letter. The next step is to print and close the FORMLTR.DOC file using EXECUTE(). The EXECUTE() method sends the DDE server instructions to perform a specific command(s), the syntax of which is based on a server's script or macro language. The following code sends instructions to Word to print the active document and then close it up:

```
ddeLinkObj.Execute("[FilePrint]")
ddeLinkObj.Execute("[FileClose 2]")
```

Now that all of the tasks have been completed, you can end the conversation with Word by using the TERMINATE() method, as shown in the following code:

```
ddeLinkObj.Terminate()
```

You now have completed the routine. It should look like the following:

```
PUBLIC ddeLinkObj
ddeLinkObj = new DDELink()
ddeLinkObj.Initiate("WINWORD", "d:\winword6\formltr.doc")
ddeLinkObj.Poke("Name", Marzapan & Associates)
ddeLinkObj.Poke("Address", 1500 Wilson Avenue)
ddeLinkObj.Poke("City", Arlington)
ddeLinkObj.Poke("State", VA)
ddeLinkObj.Poke("ZipCode", 22020)
ddeLinkObj.Poke("DearName", Billy Joe)
ddeLinkObj.Execute("[FilePrint]")
ddeLinkObj.Execute("[FileClose 2]")
ddeLinkObj.Terminate()
```

You could attach this code to a push button on a form, so that when clicked, dBASE sends the data to Word to insert it into the form letter document, as shown in figure 24.3.

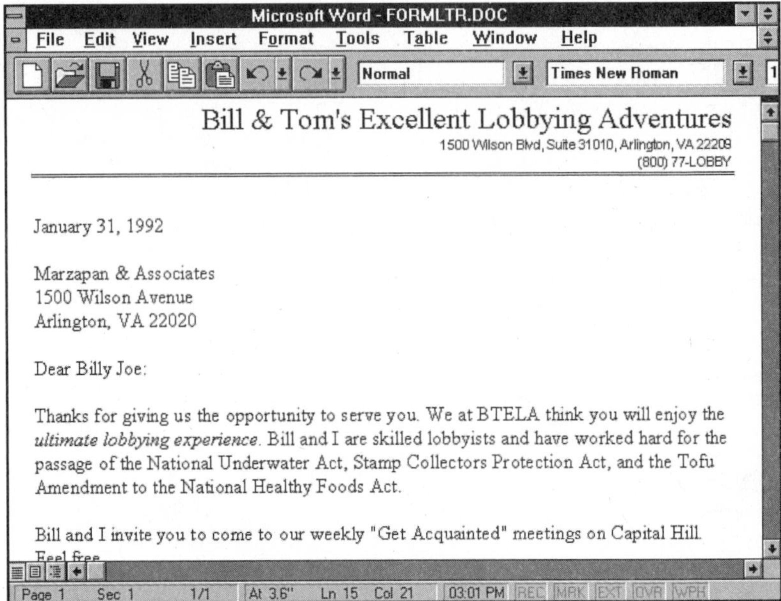

Figure 24.3 Address information poked into the Word document.

Using dBASE as a DDE Server

Not only can dBASE receive data from other Windows applications, other DDE-compliant applications can request data from and poke data to dBASE documents as well as send commands to a dBASE session. However, unlike normal Windows applications which have a given set of topics they respond to, dBASE enables you to create your own DDE server, thus giving you almost unlimited potential in your applications.

To create your own DDE server program, you need to define the manner in which you are going to communicate with the DDE client. dBASE does one thing for you: it defines a default server name (`dBASEWin`). However, you can change this by using the DDEServiceName property, as shown in the following example:

```
_app.DDEServiceName = WinFish
```

Second, you need to create a topic the client application can use to establish a conversation. In dBASE, this is done by creating a DDETopic object. Using the NEW operator, the syntax would look like:

```
PUBLIC ddeSrvObj
ddeSrvObj = NEW DDETopic(Fish)
```

This DDETopic object must reside in memory before a conversation can be established. Thus, you would need to include this in an initialization program before the client attempts a conversation.

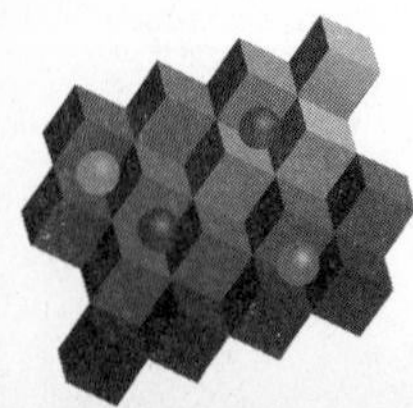

Third, you need to define what your program should do in response to requests or commands from the client application. Use the following properties to do just that:

- ✔ **OnPeek.** Runs a subroutine when a DDE client requests the value of an item from dBASE.
- ✔ **OnPoke.** Runs a subroutine when a DDE client sends a value of an item to dBASE.
- ✔ **OnExecute.** Runs a subroutine when a DDE client sends a command to dBASE.
- ✔ **OnAdvise.** Runs a subroutine when a DDE client requests a hot link with dBASE.
- ✔ **OnUnadvise.** Runs a subroutine when a DDE client requests to terminate a hot link with dBASE.

Your DDE server program need not provide support for all of these DDE commands, only the ones relevant to your application.

Introducing Object Linking and Embedding

The phrase "Information At Your Fingertips" is now well known in the PC community. It was introduced by Bill Gates, chairman of Microsoft, at the 1990 COMDEX and is Microsoft's strategy in personal computing. The idea behind "Information At your Fingertips" is that personal computers will become more "personal" and easier to use in the 1990s. Perhaps no technology demonstrates this new ease of use more than object linking and embedding (OLE). As you discover in the following sections, OLE can transform how you work in ways the Clipboard and dynamic data exchange (DDE) cannot. It makes it easier to focus on the task at hand rather than the tool used to perform the task.

OLE (pronounced *OLAY*) combines some of the features of the Clipboard and DDE, and adds a host of new capabilities to form the highest level of integration in the Windows environment. *Object linking and embedding (OLE)* is a Windows communications protocol that enables one application to use the services of other applications by placing information from the source application into the receiving application's document. As with DDE, the application receiving the data is called the *client application* and the source of the data is known as the *server application.*

OLE is much more powerful than the Clipboard method of data exchange. Using traditional cut, copy, and paste, no linkage exists between the application that creates the data and the application that receives it. OLE, however, enables the information being inserted into the receiving application to maintain a link to the original application. While you read about OLE, consider its advantages;

- ✔ **OLE is task-oriented.** OLE enables users to focus on the task rather than the application required to perform the task.
- ✔ **OLE is document-centered.** OLE is designed to change the traditional application-centered view of computing most people have today. When you create a compound document, you can integrate data from a variety of applications. The focus, however, remains on the document, not the source application.
- ✔ **OLE is dynamic form of data exchange.** Like DDE warm and hot links, a linked OLE object can be updated dynamically.
- ✔ **OLE decentralizes your desktop.** With OLE, each application can specialize in the things it does best. An application is not required to be a "mega-app"—a word processor, spreadsheet, drawing program, and presentation package all rolled up into one. Rather, OLE enables the drawing tool to concentrate what it does best (drawing), the spreadsheet to concentrate on what it does best (crunch numbers), and so on.
- ✔ **OLE is flexible.** An OLE client does not care which objects are embedded or linked in a document, or what an object's native format is or will be. As a result, a compound document is assured of compatibility with a future version of a server application.

A World of Objects

As you work with OLE, you first must understand the term object, which is really the center of attention in OLE. An *OLE object* is a data element that can be displayed or manipulated by the user. An object can be a spreadsheet file, a word processing document, an audio or video clip, or a bitmapped image.

OLE objects are placed in a document known as a compound document (or container document). A *compound document* is maintained by the client application and can receive objects from one or more server applications. The server provides data in the form of an object to the client and enables these objects to be played or edited (or both) in the server application when the server is requested. A server application must be installed on a user's system, although a server document (where the OLE object originated) can be located on a local area network.

All objects are not the same. When you double-click on an object, the type of object it is determines what it can do. For instance, you can "play" or "edit" a video clip, but you would only "edit" an embedded spreadsheet. The actions an object can perform are called *verbs*. In the video clip example, double-clicking on the object causes it to play; this

is its *primary verb.* A server can also perform other actions called *secondary verbs.* These usually are accessed through a menu item. Some objects have a single verb; others have more than one.

Linking and Embedding Objects

As an OLE object is placed into a compound document, it is either embedded or linked to the compound document.

Embedded object. When you *embed* an object into an application document, you physically store the object's data in the receiving application so that it becomes a part of the document. The data contained in the object includes: (1) data the client uses to display the object; (2) data to associate the object with the application that created it; and (3) native data passed to the server application to edit the object. An embedded object can be placed through a Clipboard copy-and-paste process or through the Edit, Insert Object command from the client application's menu.

Linked object. When you *link* an object, the actual data remains separate from the client document, but it is updated automatically when you view it in your compound document. A pointer to that data is stored in the compound document, and a representation of that object is displayed. The actual object data remains in its original location. You can continue to work with a linked object in the server application (the application that created the object), apart from the client application. A linked object is independent of the compound document; an embedded object exists only within the confines of the compound document. A linked object must be copied and pasted through the Clipboard.

The key difference between an embedded and linked object is how it is stored. An embedded object does not exist outside of a compound document, but a linked object does. As a result, a linked object requires much less storage space because the data is contained in an external file.

The difference between linked and embedded objects, however, should be seamless for the user because double-clicking on a linked or embedded object invokes the source application to play or edit the object.

Object linking excels in a networked environment because it enables a single source document to be represented in many compound documents throughout the network. The use of embedded objects would be a nightmare.

To illustrate the benefits of linking objects, suppose that you embed a video clip in a dBASE table and e-mail the table to 10 persons in your workgroup. The video clip is rather lengthy and takes up 5 MB of space. Because the object is embedded, the dBASE table requires over 5 MB of space. Thus, as you send that message to 10 persons, the network now has 50 MB of space devoted to that single 5 MB video clip.

If you store the video clip file on a networked drive and link it to a dBASE OLE field, each member of your workgroup can access that same linked object, and the linked object required just over 5 MB of space. On the other hand, if your object is small, it is probably easier from a file management point-of-view to simply embed the object in the table.

dBASE does provide OLE support, although with some definite limitations. First, it functions only as an OLE client, not an OLE server. Second, the initial release of dBASE for Windows does not support OLE 2, just OLE 1.0.

Using dBASE as an OLE Client

dBASE implements OLE technology in two ways. You can embed OLE objects into a table by using the OLE field type and display them using the OLE Viewer. Second, you can place OLE controls on a form to display OLE objects while running forms.

OLE Objects in Tables

You can use an OLE field in a table to embed data of another application into your dBASE database. Suppose, for example, you have hundreds of Word for Windows documents and would like to manage them by creating a database. You could store such information as DOS file name, title, author, and keywords, and embed each Word document as an OLE object in the database table.

To embed the documents, open the OLE Viewer by double-clicking on an OLE field. Choose Edit, Insert Object from the menu (or right-click and choose Insert Object from the Inspector menu). In the Insert New Object dialog box shown in figure 24.4, choose the type of OLE object you want to embed from the list and click OK. The OLE server application launches and enables you to create a document you can embed.

When you are finished, instead of saving the OLE document, you update it by choosing the Update command from the File menu. These changes are now saved in the OLE object in your table.

You also can embed an OLE object by first copying the object to the Clipboard and then choosing Edit, Paste while the OLE Viewer window is displayed.

Using this example, you could query documents based on keywords or title and double-click on the field to edit them as needed. A simple flat-file table could now serve as a powerful document management system (see fig. 24.5).

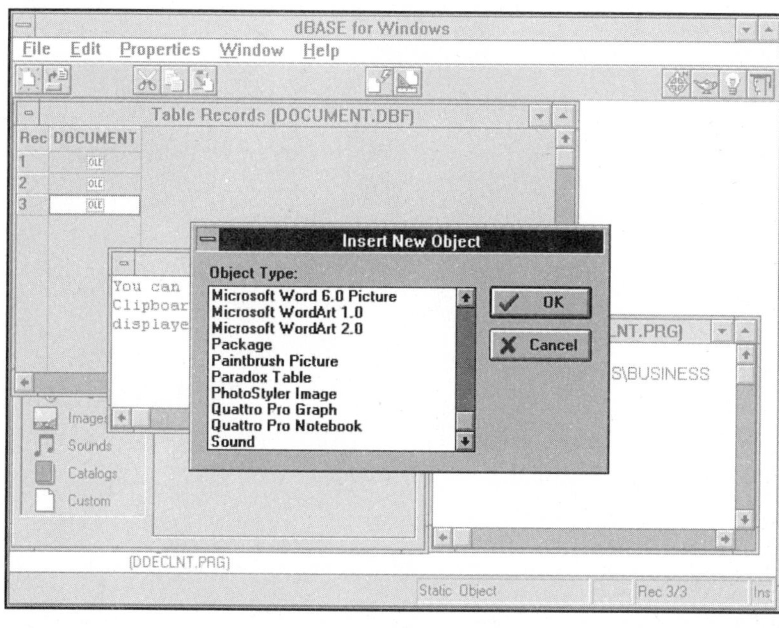

Figure 24.4
The Insert New Object dialog box.

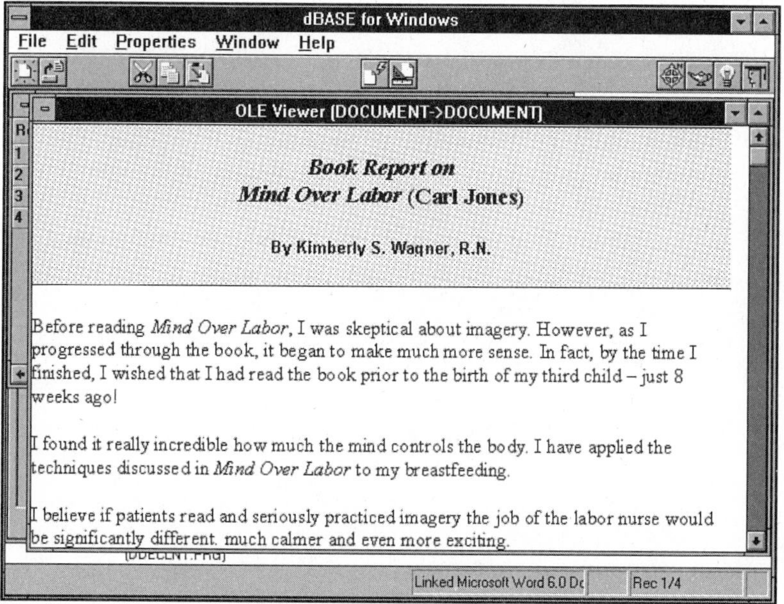

Figure 24.5
A simple document management system.

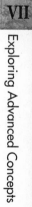

If, for example, you wanted to query your DOCUMENT table for documents which had "FY1992" as a keyword, you could set up a query as shown in figure 24.6.

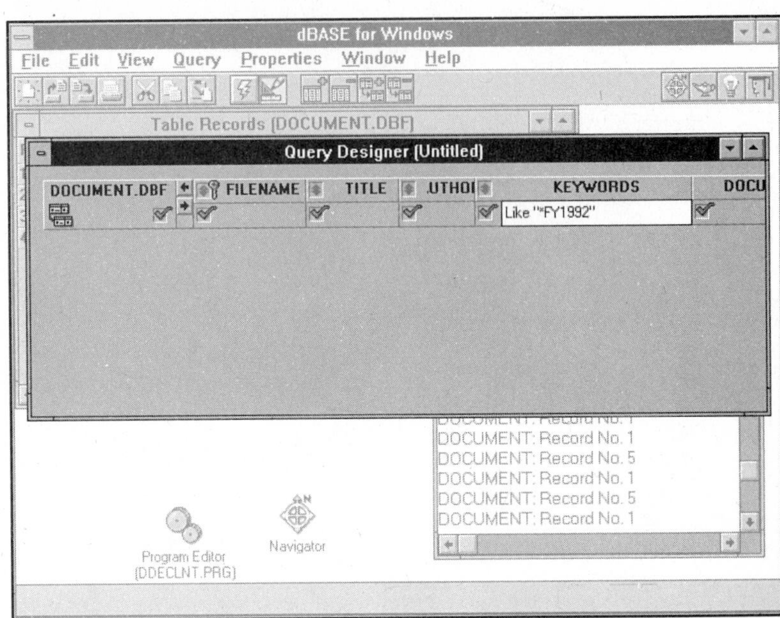

Figure 24.6 Querying the DOCUMENT table.

You are now free to view each Word OLE document by double-clicking on the OLE icon in the Browse window (see fig. 24.7). The OLE object is displayed in the OLE Viewer (see fig. 24.8). If you would like to edit the document, double-click on the document anywhere in the OLE Viewer window. This action invokes Word and displays the embedded document (see fig. 24.9).

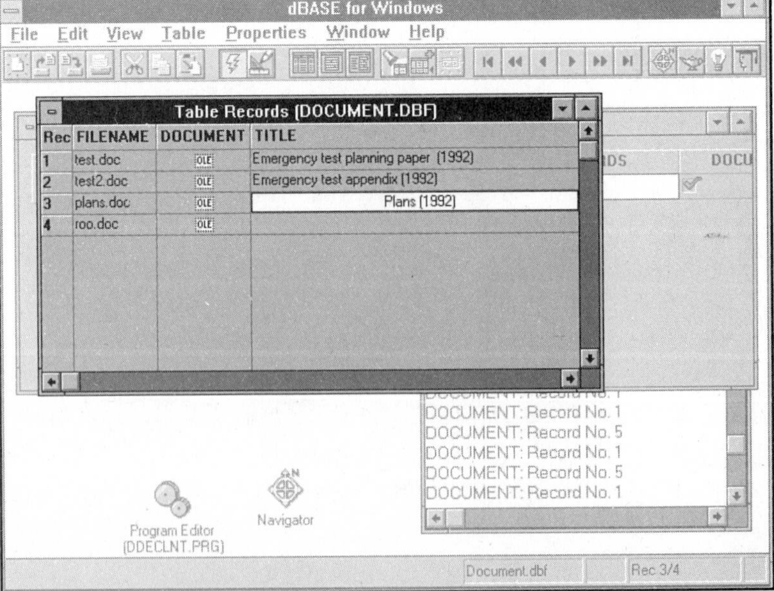

Figure 24.7 Browse window showing an OLE object.

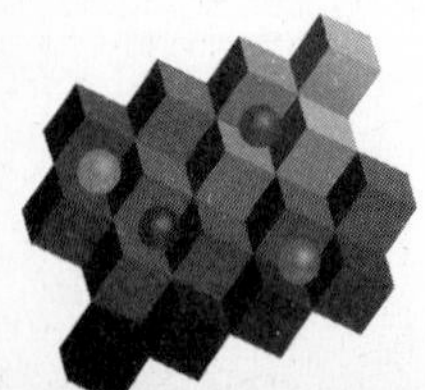

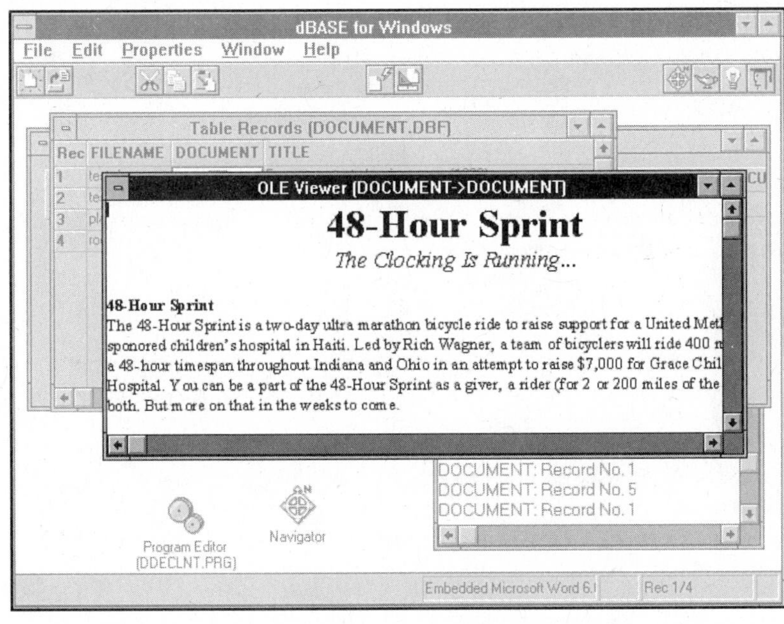

Figure 24.8 The OLE Viewer enables you to look at an OLE object.

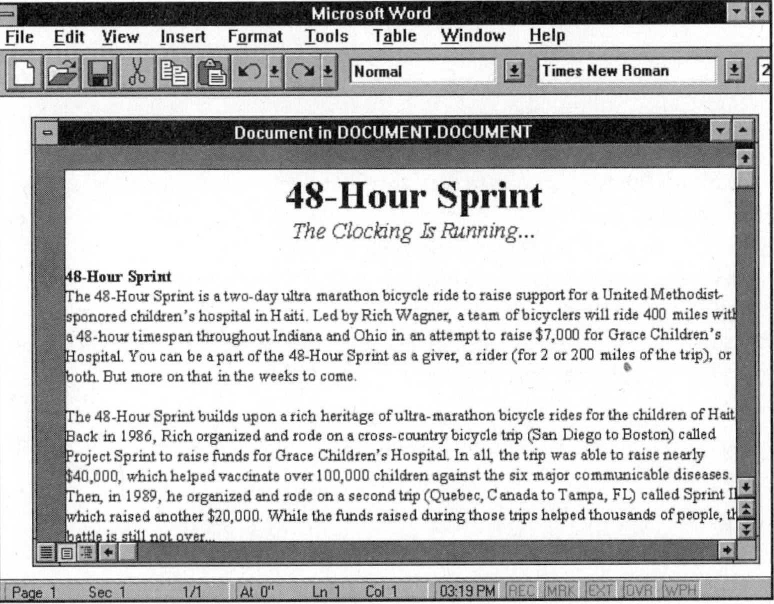

Figure 24.9 Editing an OLE document in Word.

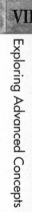

Also, as you move from record to record, the OLE Viewer updates its contents automatically.

Although the preceding example demonstrates embedding objects, you also can link OLE objects to your table. To link an OLE object, first use the server application to copy the object to the Clipboard and then choose **E**dit, **P**aste Link while the dBASE OLE Viewer window is displayed.

Each time you display a linked OLE object in the OLE Viewer window, dBASE attempts to update the contents of the object.

When you have a link established with an OLE object, you can modify those links using the Edit, Links command from the menu. In the Links dialog box shown in figure 24.10, you can choose a number of options to modify the link:

- **Update method.** You can choose either an automatic or a manual updating method. When you create an OLE link, you set up a permanent link between the two applications. The data link is a channel the server uses to inform the client whenever the data in the source document changes. It is permanent because the server continues to inform the client until the link is deleted. A permanent link can be either hot or warm. A *hot* (or automatic) *link* automatically updates the receiving document when the data in the source changes. In a *warm* (or manual) *link* the server notifies the client that a change has been made, but the client must specifically make a request to the server for the data to be updated. Even if the linked data in the source document has changed, a warm link does not update the receiving document until the user asks for it.

Given that a hot link is easier to use (since all updates are performed instantly) why not simply use a hot link all of the time? The reason is that hot links take up system resources. Thus, if you have a sizable number of hot links open at the same time, your system performance may be adversely affected. Warm links, on the other hand, are not persistent and do not put a continuous strain on Windows. Because OLE links do require system memory, the actual number of links possible for a document is limited.

- **Update Now.** Updates the contents of the OLE Viewer to emulate the original document in the OLE server.

- **Cancel Link.** Converts the linked object to an embedded object by terminating the link.

- **Change Link.** Enables you specify a new path for the server document. This option is useful when you have moved a file and want to reestablish links with it.

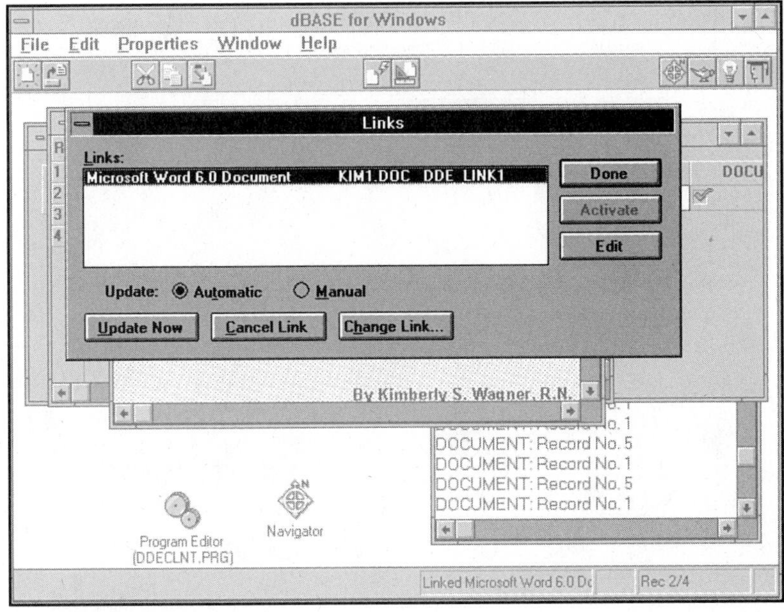

Figure 24.10
The Links dialog box.

Click on Done when you are finished with the dialog box, or click on Edit to activate the server application and modify the OLE object.

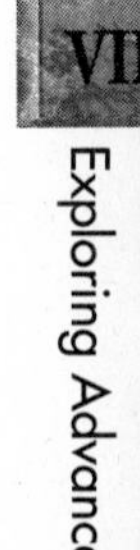

OLE Objects on Forms

You also can work with OLE objects in forms. Suppose you wanted to create a Document Viewer, for example, to display the Word OLE objects you placed in the table in the last section. After creating a form, add an OLE control to the form by using the OLE control from the Controls palette.

Next, link the OLE control to the table containing the OLE objects. To do this, choose the OLE control and display the Data Linkage Properties in the Properties Inspector. In the DataLink property, enter the desired table and field name using the following syntax:

```
tableName->fieldName
```

Alternatively, click the Tool button to choose the table and field from the Choose Fields dialog box.

When you run the form, the OLE control displays the OLE object that is contained in the current record (see fig. 24.11) of the linked table. You can double-click on the control to activate the server and edit the OLE object.

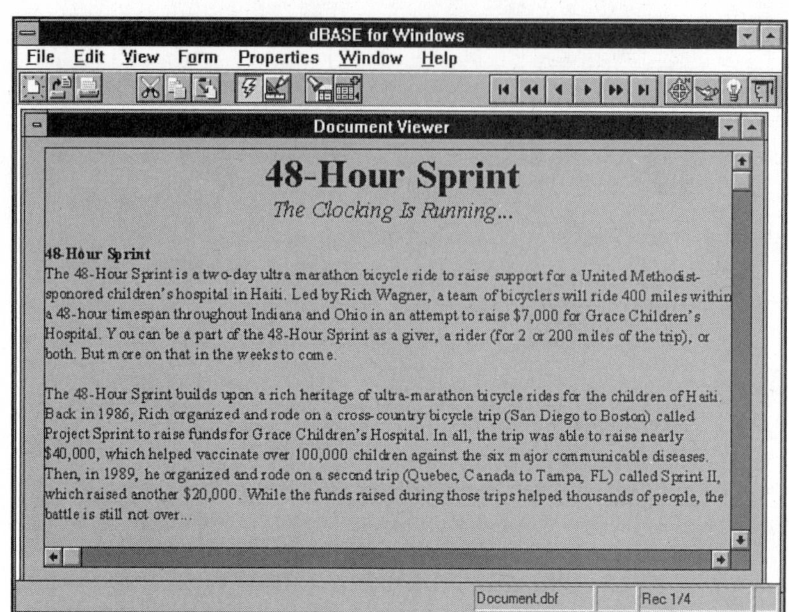

Figure 24.11 The Document Viewer form using OLE.

Chapter Snapshot

In addition to the internal functions of dBASE for Windows, you can take advantage of other functions that help you perform certain tasks in dBASE. This chapter shows you how to use those functions. You learn about the following:

In this chapter, you learn how to expand the power of dBASE, enabling you to simplify tasks and expand others by using external functions and DLLs.

Linking dBASE Applications with DLLs

By Jay Parsons

In this chapter, you learn how to use Dynamic Link Libraries (DLLs) to expand the power of dBASE for Windows. DLLs are files of executable code that dBASE can call upon to perform *external functions*—functions that go beyond the ones built in to the dBASE for Windows product.

You already have at least two types of such libraries: the DLLs that are part of Windows and the BWCC.DLL file distributed with dBASE for Windows. The Windows DLLs, known as the Windows API or Windows Application Programming Interface, are particularly important.

Using the Windows API

The Windows API is the code that Windows itself uses to perform the tasks associated with its distinctive user interface, such as building, moving, sizing and repainting windows. You too can use this code to give your dBASE programs the Windows "look and feel" without extensive programming.

Letting Windows Do Your Work

If you remember dBASE III+, you remember programming fragments such as the following:

```
@ 4,15 TO 8,64 DOUBLE
cAns = " "
@ 6,24 SAY "Do you want to continue? Y/N: " ;
GET cAns PICTURE "Y"
READ
```

The preceding programming code worked, except that the user may have puzzled over what "Y/N" meant. If you tried to help by spelling out "Yes/No" in the SAY clause, the user might not have been sure how to answer in one character. You had to bear the entire burden of calculating the correct numbers for the corners of the box and placing the text in it neatly.

In dBASE IV, designing the interface became easier with the "@M" function, allowing scrolling among the options and support for screen windows and the mouse. Designing and placing the window, text and pushbuttons—and providing code to deal with the creative ways uncertain users might make the selection—were still left to the programmer.

In dBASE for Windows, you can let Windows do it all. You learn later in the chapter about the prototypes, also called declarations, of external functions that dBASE for Windows requires. The prototypes for the Windows API functions are available in a *header file*, WINAPI.H, shipped as part of dBASE for Windows. You can provide the prototypes to your program by including WINAPI.H in your program with the #include directive. The following is the code for a boxed message, followed by the result in figure 25.1:

```
#include <Winapi.h>
nAns = MessageBox(_app.framewin.hwnd , ;
"Do you want to continue?", ;
"First API Window", MB_OKCANCEL)
```

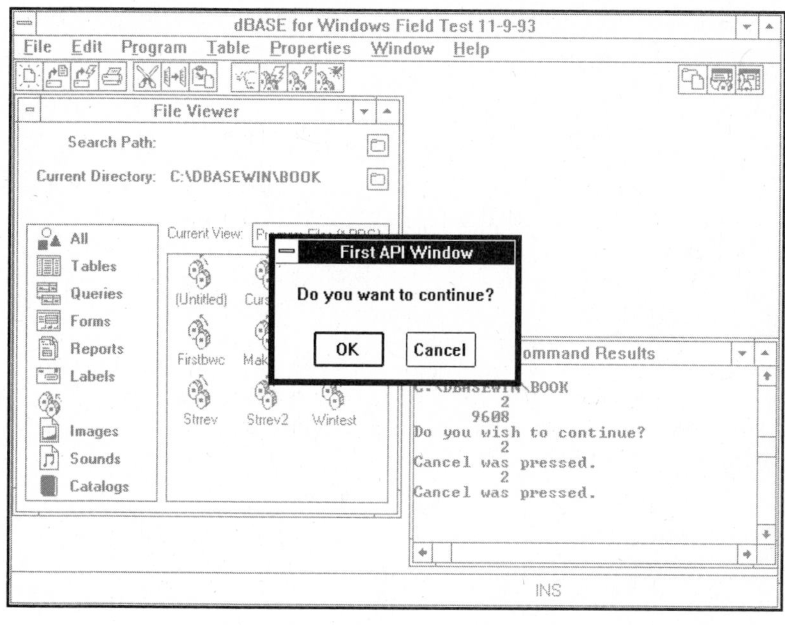

Figure 25.1
The Windows API message box.

Use the File Viewer to select the Program icons. Double right-click on the "Untitled" program icon to edit a new program, and then type in the two logical lines of code above. The second line is too long to fit on a physical line of this book, and too long to see easily in the Editor Window. You can type it as a continuous line without the semicolons, or break it into shorter physical lines—including a semicolon at the break of each physical line as done in the preceding code. Choose File, Save As, then type the name **FIRSTAPI.PRG** (or another name of your choice) as the new name of the program. Or, copy **FIRSTAPI.PRG** from the *Inside dBASE for Windows Bonus Disk.*

You can load the short programs described in this chapter from the *Inside dBASE for Windows Bonus Disk.* You will become comfortable with DLLs and external functions more quickly, however, if you type them into the program editor yourself.

Type **SET TALK ON** in the Command window if you previously set TALK off. Double-click on the FirstAPI program icon. Move the resulting window around the screen. Make a selection and see the value of your selection—1 for OK or 2 for Cancel—reported in the Command Results window. A complete program would use the value of "nAns" to determine the subsequent flow of the program.

You have now—with only one line of code (aside from the #include line)—created a window with a title, "First API Window", a border, a prompt "Do you want to continue?," and "Yes" and "No" pushbuttons. The window is automatically sized, is centered on the screen, can be moved, requires the user to make a selection of "Yes" or "No," and reports the selection for the use of the program. That is a powerful line of code.

Finding and Calling Windows Functions

To call any DLL function, you must let dBASE know what DLL file the function is in. The files of the Windows API are on your hard disk as part of the Windows product. The file WINAPI.H includes, for each function, a prototype including the name of the file in which that function is located. By using the #INCLUDE directive to include WINAPI.H in the dBASE program, you tell dBASE all it needs to know about the API functions.

Without the WINAPI.H file, you will find it difficult to locate the Windows API functions or to describe them to dBASE. Some of the API DLL files, such as USER.EXE and KRN1386.EXE, don't even have the usual DLL extension making them easy to recognize, and there is no simple way to find which functions are where or how they are used.

WINAPI.H includes prototypes but no description of what the Windows API functions do. You might have to purchase the Windows Software Developer's Kit from Microsoft—or a compiler language product for Windows such as BC++ or Turbo Pascal from Borland—to learn enough about the various functions of the Windows API to use them effectively in your programs.

Calling a function of the API can be identical to calling any other DLL function, as long as the following items are known:

- ✔ The required API function
- ✔ The number and kind of arguments it takes
- ✔ The type of value it returns
- ✔ The name of the DLL in which it resides

Calling an API function is actually simpler—in two ways:

- ✔ You need not concern yourself with the path to whatever directory the Windows API files are in, because Windows has already loaded them into memory on starting its run; and
- ✔ You need not load or release the DLL since Windows needs it always loaded.

Prototyping External Functions

Any code that dBASE for Windows calls that is not written in dBASE or part of the dBASE product is an external function. Such functions must be declared (or prototyped) before dBASE can use them. The *declaration* or *prototype* is a line of code, either in the dBASE program that will call the external function or in a header file included in the dBASE program by #INCLUDE, that tells dBASE five things:

- ✔ The name of the external function
- ✔ The DLL file the function is stored in
- ✔ The kind of parameters the function takes
- ✔ The kind of result the function returns
- ✔ The calling convention the function uses

The name of the external function serves two purposes. At compile time, it enables dBASE to match the program code calling the function to the function prototype, and thereby to identify programming errors such as calling with the wrong number or type of arguments. At runtime, it tells dBASE not to look for the function code in the program file or in a file opened with SET PROCEDURE TO. This and the other information dBASE needs about the external function come from an EXTERN statement.

Using the Extern Statement

Each external function must be declared in an EXTERN statement of the following syntax:

```
EXTERN [ CDECL ] <returntype> ;
<functionname>( [<parameter type list>] ) <filespec>
```

The EXTERN statement can be in the program or in a header file included in the program file by #INCLUDE, but either the statement or the #INCLUDE directive must appear earlier in the program file than any other use of the function name.

If the same name must be used for two external functions in the same dBASE program, use #UNDEFINE <functionname> to reverse the effect of the EXTERN statement when you are through with the first function. This makes <functionname> available for the EXTERN statement needed for the second.

The EXTERN statement must include the function name and the name of the DLL in which it resides on disk. Windows loads its API functions before dBASE starts running, so there is no need to give the path name as well as the file name for them. For other DLLs, the EXTERN statement must include the full file specification, including the path if not in the current path, so Windows can find the file to load it. For all DLLs, include the DLL or other file-name extension as part of the file specification.

Declaring Returned Values and Parameters

The return type tells dBASE the type of value the function returns. The return type can be numeric, characters, or none. The names of the types hint at the C language, which with C++ is a popular choice for much of Windows programming—including writing DLLs.

Table 25.1 gives the dBASE names of the return types, the type of value each describes, and the names used in C and the Windows API for values of the same type.

Table 25.1
External Function Return Types

Return Type	Significance	Type(s) in C <and the API>
CDOUBLE	The function returns a floating-point value, a dBASE "float" type	double
CLONG	The function returns a value held in four bytes representing an integer in the range 0–4,294,967,295	long <DWORD, COLORREF>
CPTR	The function returns four bytes containing the address in memory of data of unspecified type	far *
CSTRING	The function returns four bytes containing the address in memory of a null-terminated character string	char far * <LPSTR,LPCSTR>
CVOID	The function returns no value	void

Return Type	Significance	Type(s) in C <and the API>
CWORD	The function returns a value held in two bytes, one word, representing an integer in the range 0–65,535	int <UINT, WORD, BOOL, HANDLE, handle types HWND, HCURSOR, etc>

You must tell dBASE the type of value the function returns so that dBASE can deal with it correctly. If you tell dBASE through the EXTERN statement that an external function returns a CSTRING, dBASE expects to receive a four-byte value, which it will use as the address of a character string.

If you tell dBASE that the function returns a CSTRING but it actually returns a CLONG, dBASE attempts to convert the four-byte value it receives from the function into a memory address; later uses of that value cause it to look in that nonsensical or even nonexistent memory address for a character string not there—with unhappy results. You must make sure that the parameter and return types specified in the EXTERN statement match those required by the code of the external function.

If the function returns no meaningful value, include CVOID as the return type. dBASE then flags any attempt to make use of a value returned from the function as a programming error.

If the function requires parameters, their types must be specified within the parentheses—separated by commas—in the order in which the arguments will be included in the call to the function. The types are the same as the return types shown in table 25.1, except that CVOID is not used in a parameter list.

Using the CDECL and Pascal Models

The CDECL model is unusual. It is provided to facilitate calling functions that take variable numbers of arguments, as some C library functions but very few DLL functions do. Most functions in DLLs use the default, or *Pascal*, model. Declaring a function as CDECL if it is of the usual Pascal type, or vice versa, will cause serious errors that might cause Windows to terminate the dBASE process; if that happens, you lose all your work not yet saved. Any DLL function you use should be assumed to use the Pascal model if not otherwise specified by its supplier.

Grouping Declarations in Header Files

You have seen that WINAPI.H contains declarations for all the Windows API functions. It also defines the constants you see later in this chapter. It is easier and safer to include the header file in your program file by #include than to worry about writing the correct EXTERN statement for each external function into each of your programs.

If you write or otherwise acquire a DLL or group of DLLs that you use often, write your own header file with the appropriate EXTERN statements for all the functions. This limits your effort for each program to inserting the appropriate #include directives.

dBASE attempts to load the DLL based on the file specification in the EXTERN statement. You must either include the path name in the file specification in the EXTERN statement or be sure to have all DLLs available in the dBASE path that will be current when the EXTERN statement is executed.

If the paths can vary among systems on which the DLL is used, writing a header file is complicated by the need to customize the EXTERN statements in the header file for the path in use on the particular system.

One way to deal with this is to write your EXTERN statements with an identifier such as DLLPATH as the path name portion of each file specification. Then, include a #DEFINE DLLPATH <actual pathname> directive in your program just ahead of the #INCLUDE directive. The required syntax for a DLL called MyDll.dll that will be used from C:\dbasewin\special looks like the following:

In the header file:

```
EXTERN [CDECL] <function name>(<parameter type list>) DLLPATH
+ "MyDll.dll"
```

In the program file:

```
#define DLLPATH "c:\dbasewin\special\"
```

Calling External Functions

On the *Inside dBASE for Windows Bonus Disk* is a DLL file called IDFWDLL.DLL. That file contains a function called STRREV() that reverses the characters of a string. Enter the following program in the editor screen:

```
EXTERN CWORD strrev(CSTRING) Idfwdll.dll
Mystring = "Inside dBASE for Windows"
? strrev(Mystring)
? Mystring
```

Save the program as STRREV.PRG and run it. You should see in the Command Results window the number of characters in the string (in this case 24) followed by the reversed string.

You are familiar by now with the parts of the EXTERN statement. The CWORD after EXTERN says the STRREV() function returns an integer in the range 0–65,535. As written, the STRREV() function code returns the length of the string being reversed. The CSTRING in the parentheses tells dBASE that the argument to the function should be a null-terminated string. dBASE passes its address in memory to the function code.

The first "?" line of the program tells dBASE to call the external STRREV() function and print the returned value. The last line tells dBASE to print the original string. It is now reversed. Because dBASE passes the address of the original string to the function, the function operates directly on the original string—not on a copy.

Using DLLs for Speed and Memory Conservation

Writing a function as simple as STRREV() is not difficult in dBASE and can make program maintenance easier. Two independent reasons to use DLLs are speed and conservation of memory. The *Inside dBASE for Windows Bonus Disk* contains a dBASE-language function to reverse a string, DSTRREV.PRG, as well as the assembly source code of STRREV() as included in IDFWDLL.DLL.

If you copy DSTRREV.PRG into your current directory and SET PROCEDURE TO DSTRREV, or simply copy DSTRREV.PRG into the STRREV.PRG program in the editor window, you can call each from a loop executing 1,000 times and time the results. The DLL code is considerably faster as well as being compact—the assembly routine itself, aside from the overhead of the DLL, occupies only 48 bytes of memory.

If you know assembly language, you will see from the source code STRREV.ASM that it and the dBASE function DSTRREV.PRG do not use the same algorithm. The assembly code swaps the two characters at either end and works toward the middle, while the dBASE function backs up through the string adding each character to an originally empty string. You might want to try writing a dBASE function using the assembler algorithm or another method to see whether it is faster than DSTRREV.PRG.

Ignoring the Returned Value

The value returned by STRREV() is the length of the string being reversed. Since the length of a string does not change by reversing it, the length would not be of interest except for one fact: the length of the string is not explicitly passed to the function as an argument. The code of the function relies on dBASE to pass it the address of a null-terminated string. It counts the characters from the starting address to the null to determine the length.

You can see the type of character string dBASE and DLLs use referred to as an ASCIIZ string, from the ASCII character set and Z to indicate the string of characters is terminated by a zero, or chr(0), value. The ending chr(0) is used to mark the end of the string; it must be present and takes up a byte of memory but is not considered part of the string length or contents of the string. Such a character string cannot contain a chr(0) except as a terminating character.

dBASE allows calling functions, whether external or built in, without using the return value. You might want to remove the "?" from the start of the line calling the STRREV() function and run the program again. There should be no difference except that the "24" is not printed. Add the "?" back and put different strings in Mystring to see them reverse and to measure their lengths.

Passing Arguments by Value

Change the function-calling line in the original program to the following:

```
? strrev((Mystring))
```

with an extra pair of parentheses around the argument. When you now run the program, the string is not reversed. As with other functions, placing the argument within an additional set of parentheses causes dBASE to evaluate it and to send the result (in this case a copy of the string) to the function. The original string is left unchanged. Since this STRREV() function does not return the address of the reversed string but only its length, there is no way to find and use the reversed copy.

Change the same line to the following:

```
? STRREV(("Hello"))
```

Then run the program. Much the same thing occurs. You can see from the "5" that the function has been called with a five-character string, but there is no way to find or use the reversed copy. Somewhere in dBASE's string memory space is the reversed "Hello," but it is not associated with any memory variable and is effectively lost forever.

Obeying the Rules of External Functions

The rules for using external functions are the same as for functions built-in to dBASE or for user-defined functions. A call to any function of any type, built-in, user-defined or external, can contain nested calls to other functions of any of the types. The only restriction (aside from the limit on depth of nesting) is that the return type of the inner

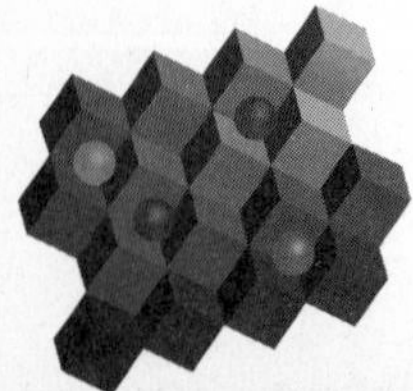

function must be of the correct type for the argument of the outer one. This restriction is satisfied if the return type of the inner function is used in an expression of the correct type which is the argument to the outer function.

Arguments can be expressions, as you learned by putting extra parentheses around "Mystring." You shortly see another use of an expression using a function as an argument in FIRSTBWC.PRG below, in which the last argument to MESSAGEBOX() and BWCCMESSAGEBOX() is an expression using the BITOR() function.

Calling BWCC.DLL

Load FIRSTAPI.PRG (from the *Inside dBASE for Windows Bonus Disk*, if you did not save it earlier) into the program editor and change it to read as follows:

```
#include <Winapi.h>
EXTERN CWORD BWCCMessageBox(CWORD, CSTRING, CSTRING, ;
CWORD) \windows\system\bwcc.dll
nHandle = _app.framewin.hwnd
cPrompt = "Do you want to continue?"
nAns = MessageBox(nHandle, cPrompt, ;
"Second API Window", bitor(MB_OKCANCEL, MB_ICONSTOP))
? iif(nans = IDOK, "OK", iif(nans = IDCANCEL, "Cancel", ;
"Neither")) + " was pressed."
nAns = BWCCMessageBox(nHandle, cPrompt, ;
"First BWCC Window", bitor(MB_OKCANCEL, MB_ICONSTOP))
? iif(nans = IDOK, "OK", iif(nans = IDCANCEL, "Cancel", ;
"Neither")) + " was pressed."
```

Save the new file as FIRSTBWC.PRG. As an alternative, use FIRSTBWC.PRG from the disk.

The API MESSAGEBOX() function and BWCCMESSAGEBOX() each take four parameters and return a value. The types of each of these parameters and return value are described in an EXTERN statement or prototype. For the API function, the EXTERN statement is in WINAPI.H and you included it in your program by including that file with #include. For the BWCC function, the necessary EXTERN statement is written into the program.

The first parameter to each function is a CWORD type called a *handle* that tells Windows what window "owns" the window created. Windows needs this in order to display or hide the message box—depending on whether the parent window is open or closed.

Because the message box created by either function is owned by the main window of dBASE, the handle is the same for each, _app.framewin.hwnd. _app is an object that refers to the currently-running instance of dBASE. You can inspect its properties and those of its framewin property to see the numeric value of this handle.

You also can avoid typing the handle name twice. Once in the call to each function, the value of the handle is saved to nHandle, and that variable is supplied as the argument to the functions.

The second parameter is a character string—the prompt: `Do you want to continue?` This is again the same for each function and likewise stored to a memory variable to save retyping.

The third parameter, another character string, is the title. The windows created by the two functions have different titles, so you can see which is which. The titles are passed literally in quotation marks as the third argument.

The fourth argument has changed from the MB_OKCANCEL of FIRSTAPI.PRG by the addition of MB_ICONSTOP, which adds a stop icon to the attributes of the window, and by the BITOR() function to connect the two elements of the argument. You will learn more about all of these soon.

Run the program and observe the differences. The API message box is like that shown in figure 25.1 except for the addition of a red stop sign. The BWCC message box is shown following in figure 25.2. The windows are slightly different in appearance, the stop icons are different, the API using a stop sign and BWCC a red hand, and the BWCC version has a checkmark and X on the pushbuttons.

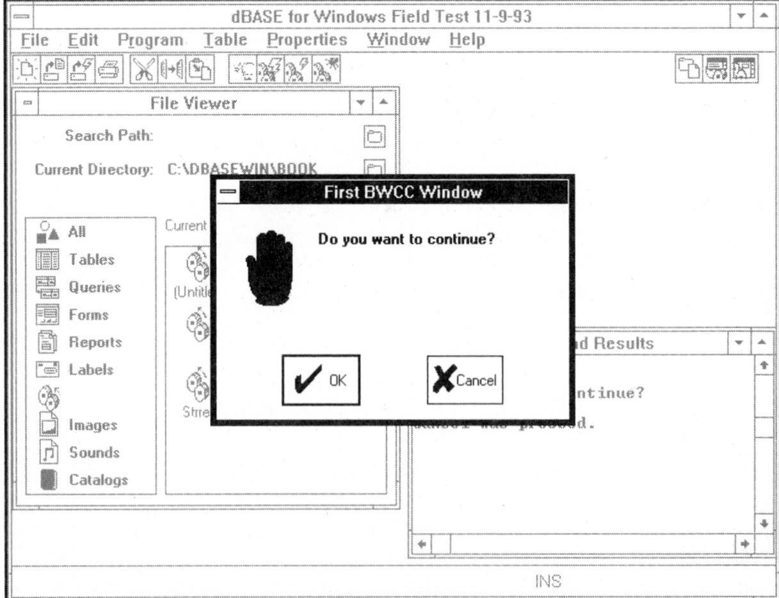

Figure 25.2
The BWCC message box.

Manipulating Bits within Arguments

Windows compresses arguments when possible to minimize stack usage and maximize speed. The final CWORD argument to MESSAGEBOX() and its BWCCMESSAGEBOX() counterpart compresses a number of numeric values describing the type of the window into a "bit map" 16 bits, or one word, long. dBASE uses the BITOR() function to combine the separate values into a single word. The called DLL function then separates them again, a very quick operation in compiled code, to use the values appropriately.

The values MB_ICONSTOP and MB_OKCANCEL are numeric constants found in WINAPI.H. The values of some of the WINAPI.H constants relating to message boxes are shown in table 25.2 in various numeric bases:

Table 25.2
Some Windows API MessageBox Constant Values

Constant	Decimal	Hexadecimal	Binary
MB_OK	0	0x00	0000 0000
MB_OKCANCEL	1	0x01	0000 0001
MB_ABORTRETRYIGNORE	2	0x02	0000 0010
MB_YESNOCANCEL	3	0x03	0000 0011
MB_YESNO	4	0x04	0000 0100
MB_RETRYCANCEL	5	0x05	0000 0101
MB_ICONSTOP	16	0x10	0001 0000
MB_ICONQUESTION	32	0x20	0010 0000
MB_ICONEXCLAMATION	48	0x30	0011 0000
MB_ICONINFORMATION	64	0x40	0100 0000

The value of BITOR(1,16)is 17. You can substitute the number 17 as the fourth argument to MESSAGEBOX() and BWCCMESSAGEBOX() and they will work exactly the same way. Try it if you want. The difficulty is that, if you are trying to maintain your code several months from now, you might well wonder what that magic number 17 means. The expression "BITOR(MB_OKCANCEL, MB_ICONSTOP)" is not likely to make any list of memorable phrases, but at least the expression gives you a limited sense of what it does.

As you see from looking at table 25.2, the API tries to prevent trouble by having different groups of options affect different groups of bits of the resulting value. The first six entries, specifying the pushbuttons, affect the lowest four bits. The next four, specifying the icon if any, affect the next four.

The BITOR() function performs a bitwise or on the bits of two values, in this case 1 and 16. The definition of the or operation on a single bit of two operands is that the result is 1 (if either the bit of the first operand is 1 or the corresponding bit of the second operand is 1, otherwise 0). This operation amounts to writing the values one above the other in binary form and placing a 1 below each column in which at least one 1 appears, as shown in table 25.3.

Table 25.3
Binary OR of 1 and 16

Decimal value	Binary value
1	0000 0001
16	0001 0000
BITOR(1,16)	0001 0001 = 17

dBASE also includes BITAND() and BIXOR() functions to perform bitwise AND and XOR operations. The AND operation yields a 1 if, but only if, the bits of both operands are 1; the XOR operation yields a 1 if one, but only one, of the bits of the two operands is 1. The result of performing these operations on any combination of two bits appears in table 25.4.

Table 25.4
Results of Bitwise OR, AND, and XOR Operations

First	Second	——Result——		
bit	bit	OR	AND	XOR
0	0	0	0	0
0	1	1	0	1
1	0	1	0	1
1	1	1	1	0

The BITAND() and BITXOR() functions have much less frequent application with DLLs than BITOR(), which should always be used instead of the addition operator to combine Windows API and similar constants into a single argument. The bitwise functions cannot

affect a bit larger or smaller than the highest or lowest "1" bit in the operands, while adding two numbers can cause the sum to overflow into higher-order bits intended for something entirely different. Even if no overflow occurs, the result of addition is often different from that of the BITOR() operation—BITOR(1,3) is 3, not 4—and will give an unintended result.

dBASE also includes the functions BITLSHIFT(), BITRSHIFT(), and BITSET() to assist in manipulating these constants. The first two "shift" a value left or right respectively by the number of bits specified, filling the vacated bits with 0. This helps in combining and separating certain constants. For example, some Windows API functions take a color value, a CLONG or COLORREF, of 32 bits. The lowest 8 bits carry the red value, the next the green, the next the blue, and the highest 8 bits are unused. Rather than trying to multiply or divide by 2^{16} to isolate the blue value, it is convenient to shift the combined value 16 bits right. This sends the red and green portions out of the picture and puts the blue part in the lowest 8 bits where it can be dealt with as a value between 0 and 255, expressing the strength of the blue component.

BITSET() is used to test a single bit of a value. It returns .T. if the bit is set, else .F.. This is easier to code and to understand than calculating the value of 2 to the power of the bit position and using BITAND() to accomplish much the same thing.

Do not confuse the BITAND() and BITOR() functions with the logical .AND. and .OR. operators in dBASE. The former operate on numeric expressions and return numeric values; the latter operate on logical or relational expressions with the value .T. or .F. only and resolve to logical values.

Supplying Arguments within Range

dBASE expects most CWORD and CLONG values to be bit maps of several Windows API or other constants. Such constants are always positive integers, and so normally are CWORDs and CLONGs. Sixteen bits can be used to store a binary integer in one of two common ways:

- ✔ The number can be stored as an unsigned integer in the range 0–65,535. In this case the binary value 0111 1111 1111 1111 represents 32,767, the value 1000 0000 0000 0000 produced by adding 1 to it represents 32,768, and so on until 1111 1111 1111 1111, which represents 65,535.
- ✔ The number can be stored as a signed integer with the leftmost or high-value bit reserved for the sign, 1 meaning minus. The values 0 to 32,767 are the same as for unsigned integers, but now 1000 0000 0000 0000 means -32,768. The count continues upward from there to 1111 1111 1111 1111, which now means -1.

You can specify -1 as a CWORD argument to an external function, or 100,000—which is too large to be stored in 16 bits. What actually gets passed to the function is the modulus of the value to the base 65,536, 65,535 for -1 and 34,474 for 100,000. The function will return the appropriate result for an argument of 65,535 or 34,474, as the case might be, but such a result may well be incorrect for the actual argument.

The easy way to stay out of trouble is to use CWORD and CLONG values only for Windows API and similar constants, combined as needed using BITOR()or for values that you know—by testing the result if the value is the result of an expression—will be a positive integer less than 2^{15} for a CWORD or 2^{31} for a CLONG. DLLs that accept numbers for general-purpose arithmetic should and usually do take and return CDOUBLE values, or float types, which create no ambiguities or overflows whatever the sign or magnitude.

You might, in using some DLLs, encounter a situation such as the dBASE IV limit on report pages. The authors of dBASE IV knew page numbers had to be positive integers and stored the number as, in effect, a signed CWORD. This put a limit of 32,767, 2^{15} -1, on the highest page number that could be stored. This limit in turn caused problems with long reports, particularly those that started each report with the page number following the last page number used for the previous report. If you do encounter odd results when using a DLL that uses or returns a CWORD or CLONG, consider the following scenarios:

- ✔ If the CWORD or CLONG is being used to hold API or similar bitmapped constants, be sure any combinations of them have been created using the BITOR() function, not by addition or other operations on them.
- ✔ If the CWORD or CLONG is used to hold an ordinary numeric value, be sure the value of the argument is within the acceptable range.

A similar problem can arise with CPTR and CSTRING types. If you declare a parameter type as CSTRING, be sure that argument is a string of bytes none of which are nulls, but which are terminated by a null byte. This happens automatically if the argument is a dBASE character string or character-type field or memory variable. If the argument is actually something different such as a picture, its address should be passed only to a function looking for a CPTR. A DLL function, such as STRREV() discussed above, might rely on the terminating null for its own purposes.

Extending the Functionality of dBASE

DLLs are important because dBASE cannot reasonably include all the functions that someone, somewhere, would like. The language would grow too big to learn and the product too big even for your newest hard disk. You have seen that the DLLs of the Windows API allow you to use the functionality of Windows in your dBASE programs. Other DLLs are, or will probably soon be, available to assist you in other areas.

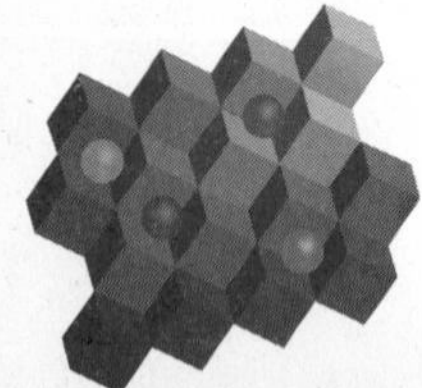

Using BWCC.DLL

BWCC.DLL, which you used above, is a dynamic link library distributed by Borland International with dBASE and its other language products for Windows. In effect, it is an alternate version of the Windows API. Its functions do much the same things as the Windows API functions, but with results slightly different in appearance. You can freely substitute calls to BWCC.DLL functions for those to the corresponding functions of the Windows API. Use whichever version you prefer.

BWCC.DLL, when furnished with Borland's C-language products, comes with a header file, BWCC.H, that serves the same purpose as WINAPI.H. Look in your directories in which dBASE installed files to see if BWCC.H is there. It is usually found in the subdirectory systems of your main Windows directory.

If the file is there and you do not have another Borland language product installed, add a line. Include <BWCC.H> to the FirstBWC program above as the second line and remove the EXTERN logical line. If you have other Borland language products loaded, check whether the copy of BWCC.H you found uses the dBASE terms listed in the first column of table 25.1 for the types of arguments and values returned. If it uses the C or API terms, such as UINT or HWND, listed in the third column of table 25.1, you cannot include its prototypes in a dBASE program unless you convert all such terms to their dBASE equivalents.

Moving Up from BINS

Using external functions to extend dBASE has a long and distinguished history. Many of the abilities now built in to dBASE for Windows began under dBASE for DOS as BIN files—files of binary code that dBASE for DOS, beginning with dBASE III, could execute with the LOAD and CALL commands and later the CALL() function. Turning the cursor off and on again, turning the mouse cursor off and on, changing the tone of the "beep," and finding the DOS version in use are a few examples of extensions first added to dBASE as .BINs.

The LOAD/CALL and CALL() syntaxes have not been carried to dBASE for Windows. If your applications do make use of them, you will have to change them. This is one of the few areas of incompatibility between dBASE for DOS and dBASE for Windows, and of course it is not really a language incompatibility at all—just one relating to the use of other programming languages to extend dBASE.

Most existing BINs cannot be directly linked into DLLs and used from dBASE. The method in which parameters are passed and values returned is quite different, and the method by which the code returns control to dBASE is often different. The code of some

BINs can be very quickly converted to DLL code; you will probably see such DLLs offered on the market soon to fill any gaps in dBASE for Windows that had been filled by BINs under DOS.

Some BINs should not be converted to Windows. In order to gain device independence, Windows manages the hardware, including memory, the screen and the printer. Calling code that attempts to manage these devices directly might cause conflicts with Windows and severe problems.

If you intend to convert a BIN, you will probably spot and be able to change any operations directly performed by the BIN that violate the Windows rules. It is more difficult to be sure that any function linked in from a library intended for DOS programs obeys the rules. You must eliminate all such code (however deeply hidden) and substitute appropriate CALLs to the Windows API system services, or to other Windows-compliant code, to make your code run properly.

Using Third-Party DLLs

Third parties might well offer DLLs that solve the needs of particular groups of dBASE users and programmers. Some programs you might already own or can acquire inexpensively contain DLLs that can help you in dBASE.

For example, Quattro Pro for Windows contains a wealth of financial and statistical functions going far beyond those built in to dBASE. If you are programming a mortgage-management application for a bank or real-estate firm, or dealing with complex statistics, you might find these functions useful.

There are two difficulties in using Quattro Pro functions. First, the documentation required to prototype the functions properly dBASE-style is not readily available. One essential is the file QPROWIN.H, from the Quattro Pro for Windows Developer Toolkit, but it alone does not describe the location by DLL file or precise parameter types of the various functions available. Second, many Quattro Pro functions employ "callbacks" to other functions. Making sure the code needed by the callback is available to the Quattro Pro function while running outside the Quattro Pro environment is complex.

Loading and Releasing Libraries

Windows loads DLLs into memory when needed. Since they take up memory, it might speed performance to release them when no longer needed. In addition, some DLLs contain initialization code that must be executed at some point before the functions of the DLL can be called, and others contain exit code needed to clean up.

Conserving Memory

The main reason for the DLL system is conservation of memory. There is a technical discussion under "Static and Dynamic Linking" in the next section. The essence is that DLL code can be in use by many programs at the same time. This is obviously true of the Windows API, which is used by all or almost all Windows applications as well as by Windows itself.

Because Windows can have more than one instance of dBASE running at the same time even on a single-user system, it is possible that functions in DLLs called only by dBASE can be in use by several instances. When a DLL is needed, Windows checks to see whether it is already in memory. The Windows API will be in memory at all times. Other DLLs might or might not be. If the DLL is not in memory, Windows loads it and sets its user count to 1. If it is already in memory, Windows increments the user count. When an application indicates it has finished using the DLL, Windows decrements the user count. When the count reaches 0, Windows knows it is free to unload that DLL from memory.

Using the LOAD DLL and RELEASE DLL Commands

dBASE provides the LOAD DLL and RELEASE DLL commands to assist with managing the memory used by DLLs. The LOAD DLL command can be used to load a DLL into memory before it is needed, so that any initialization code it contains can be run at a more convenient time than when one of its functions is called. Similarly, RELEASE DLL can be used to tell Windows that a DLL can be unloaded if not in use by Windows itself or other applications.

The LOAD DLL and RELEASE DLL commands are not tremendously useful. If LOAD DLL could be used to give the path name to the DLL file, eliminating the need to deal with the path in the EXTERN statements for its functions which will often be in a header file, it would have more of a purpose. As it is, the EXTERN statements must specify the path. If they are included in the program with an #include directive in its usual place at the start of the program, the DLL will be loaded at once anyway, and there is nothing left for the LOAD DLL command to do. The RELEASE DLL command, its correlative, is similarly unhelpful and does nothing at present.

Using LOADLIBRARY() and FREELIBRARY()

The Windows API provides functions, LOADLIBRARY() and FREELIBRARY(), that do what LOAD DLL and RELEASE DLL are supposed to do. These are somewhat more useful, because DLLs need not contain only functions. DLLs might contain resources such as cursors, bitmaps and icons. To access and load these resources, it is necessary to obtain a handle to the DLL, and that handle can be obtained only from the LOADLIBRARY() function. LOAD DLL does not return a handle or other value. The syntax of LOADLIBRARY() and FREELIBRARY() might be illustrated as follows:

```
#include <winapi.h>
nLibHandle = LoadLibrary(<DLL filespec>)
* code using the library or its resources here
FreeLibrary(nLibHandle)
```

After using LOADLIBRARY(), and assuming the library contains a resource, one of the API functions LOADACCELERATORS(), LOADBITMAP(), LOADCURSOR(), LOADICON(), LOADMENU(), LOADRESOURCE(), or LOADSTRING() can be used to load the resource into memory for use.

Understanding How DLLs Work

The remainder of this chapter discusses DLLs from the inside. It is for you if you are interested in the technicalities or in learning how to write DLL code of your own, but is not essential to your use of DLLS from dBASE.

Static and Dynamic Linking

The ability of DLLs to conserve memory arises from dynamic linking of their routines. This contrasts with the static linking used for executable code for DOS.

Large programs written for DOS are usually written in compiled languages such as C, C++, and Pascal. The programmer writes each program module in the required language using a text editor, either stand alone or included in a compiler product. Many of the operations any program needs, such as writing to the screen, are not directly supported by the language but are accomplished by including in the program a call to a function in the libraries furnished with the product. The function supplies the code to do the job.

After the module is written, the compiler turns it into object code, a file with an OBJ extension. This code contains, among other things, the names of the external library functions the module calls upon.

A separate utility, the linker, then collects the various modules of the program. It places them in a single file with an EXE extension, adds the code of the various library functions called from the program modules, and turns the calls of named functions and modules into calls to the appropriate addresses within the EXE where their code might be found.

The result of this static linking is that the resulting EXE file contains a copy, even if only one copy, of the code of each library function it uses. When the EXE file is run from DOS, it is loaded into memory in its entirety. This works well in DOS since only one program runs at a time. When it finishes, the memory it occupied is available to the next program.

Several processes can run under Windows at once. Having each process load its own copy of code that all or many of the processes use would waste memory. Consequently,

Windows uses DLLs. The code from each DLL file is loaded when any function is needed and the same code is shared by all processes that use it.

The whole file is dropped from memory when none of its functions are needed. This takes more memory than if the functions were loaded separately as needed, but it is a compromise that balances the use of memory against the overhead and frequent disk accesses that would be required to load each function only as needed.

DLL Initialization and Exit Routines

A DLL is a special type of EXE file, often with a different extension such as DLL. It must include the usual EXE header. A DLL also includes a table of its functions and other resources. A DLL normally includes a stub routine that runs if its name is mistakenly typed at the DOS prompt, usually printing "This program must be run under Microsoft Windows" on the screen and quitting.

Each DLL must include an initialization routine called LIBMAIN() that Windows calls when the DLL is loaded. In most cases, this routine need do nothing but unlock the data segment if locked. (See "LibM.c" on the included disk.) Each DLL must contain a Windows Exit Procedure called "WEP", which usually does nothing at all and is included automatically if the DLL is created, as the one on the disk was, using Borland C++ 4.0. This code is called by Windows when the DLL is unloaded to allow it to perform any needed cleanup.

Usage of the Stack and Registers

The functions within a DLL are standard executable code created from modules in any language that can be assembled or compiled into standard OBJ files. The languages most used are probably C, C++, Pascal and Assembler. On the call of an external Pascal-convention function, dBASE pushes the following onto the stack:

1. The arguments, in the order given in the program, left to right. Each argument is pushed as follows:

    ✔ CPTR or CSTRING, two words containing the segment, then offset, of the address.

    ✔ CWORD, one word containing the number in binary.

    ✔ CLONG, two words, high word first, containing the number in binary.

    ✔ CDOUBLE, four words, highest order first, containing the number in IEEE eight-byte floating point format. This comprises, from high bit to low, 1 sign bit, 11 bits of exponent biased 0x3FF and 52 bits of mantissa with the initial "1" omitted as understood.

2. The return address, two words containing the segment then offset of the address.

The call of a CDECL function works the same way except that the arguments are pushed right-to-left. If CDECL is used, the code of the called function should not remove the arguments from the stack. dBASE will do it. The primary use of CDECL is to facilitate writing and calling functions that can accept variable numbers of arguments. The left-most argument, last pushed on the stack, gives the number of arguments to the function code so it will know how many to process; it returns with a simple "retf."

The requirements of a DLL function used with dBASE include the following:

- ✔ The function must preserve the bp, p, and sp registers as well as all segment registers. Changing the ds or es register seems to do no serious harm, but it does cause dBASE to issue an error message. The bx, cx, si, and di registers are fair game and need not be preserved. The ax and dx registers can be changed but on return should contain the return value, if any, of the function if not a CDOUBLE. A CWORD is returned in ax, other types in dx and ax with dx holding the high, or segment, portion. When you are using any language other than assembler to create a DLL, the preservation of the needed registers occurs automatically.

- ✔ The function should expect two words on the stack giving the return address, and it should return by a "far return" or "retf" instruction. All addresses of data should also normally be far, except for temporary data created on the stack.

- ✔ The stack should be assumed to be fairly small, 1,000 bytes or less. By default, all instances of DLL functions share a single data segment, which should be used read-only if the function can yield time to Windows and risk that its data be overwritten by another instance. The stack can be used for a small amount of temporary data, or multiple data segments can be specified to the linker.

- ✔ If the function is called by the standard Pascal convention, it must (in the retf instruction) adjust the stack to remove all passed arguments.

- ✔ The function code must behave properly under Windows, refraining from direct manipulation of the hardware.

- ✔ The name of the function must be exported to the linker either by a statement in the source code, if the language supports it, or by an appropriate directive in a module definition or similar file.

Languages and Tools Needed To Write DLLs

You can write DLLs in any language for which you have an assembler or compiler that can create standard OBJ code modules. You will also need a linker capable of creating a Windows-compliant DLL target from OBJ code.

It is simplest to make use of a product such as Borland's C++ 4.0 that includes a compiler, assembler, linker and Integrated Development Environment with a means of creating module definition files and project files to tie the rest together.

The source assembly code of the STRREV() function and the module definition file used to create Idfwdll.dll are on the accompanying disk along with Libm.c, a rudimentary LIBMAIN() function, and Idfw.ide, a BC++ project file. You can use these to begin the process of learning how to write DLLs.

Chapter Snapshot

You can use dBASE for Windows to work with Paradox for Windows tables, as well as with tables in the dBASE native format. Much of the time, you can ignore the differences entirely and perform the same actions on a Paradox table that you would on a dBASE table. There are, nevertheless, important differences. This chapter discusses the following:

After you finish reading the chapter, you will be able to use Paradox tables in dBASE easily and effectively.

Accessing Paradox Data

By Jay Parsons

You can access Paradox data from dBASE for Windows almost as easily as accessing dBASE data. Much of the time, you can ignore any differences and treat Paradox tables as if they were dBASE tables. This chapter deals with the few differences and restrictions between Paradox and dBASE tables. After you learn these differences, or if you simply refer to this chapter after you encounter a problem using Paradox tables, you should have no difficulty using Paradox tables.

A friend has given HomeGuide the list of people who attended the recent dinner and auction of the local chapter of Furs and Feathers, an organization of hunters of game birds and animals. The list is a Paradox table, DINNER94.DB. HomeGuide agents consider the list a good source of prospects to purchase either land suitable for hunting or homes near hunting areas. Company workers can double-click on the Paradox tables Navigator icon to browse its data—just as they can with a dBASE table, as shown in figure 26.1.

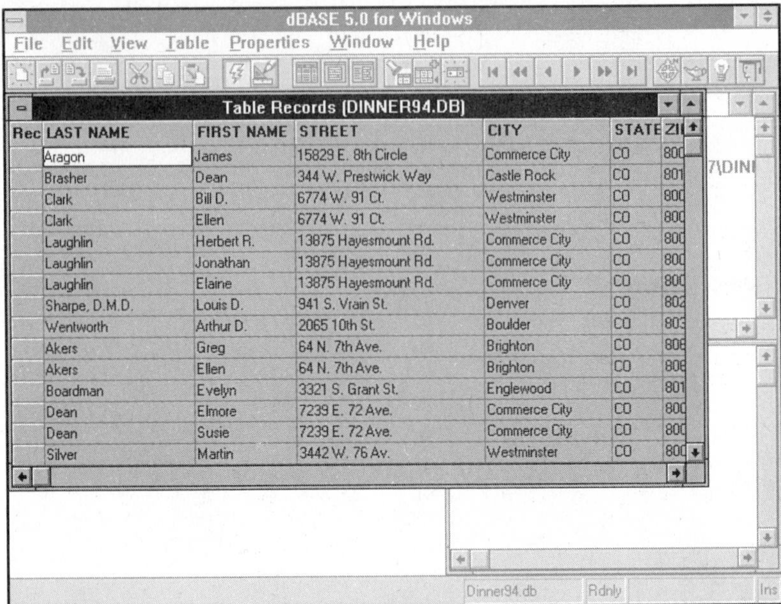

Figure 26.1 Browsing a Paradox table.

Using Paradox Tables and Indexes

You can use a Paradox table just like a dBASE table—subject to the differences noted later in this chapter. You can display, sort, index, modify the data or the table structure, print the data, or do almost everything you could do with a dBASE table using the same commands. The structures of Paradox and dBASE tables are not the same, so you must first be sure that dBASE knows which type of table you are using.

File Extensions, TYPE and DBTYPE

Paradox tables normally have the file extension DB, and dBASE tables normally have the extension DBF. dBASE does not require these extensions.

dBASE uses three clues to determine which type of table to create or open. The clues are the DBTYPE setting, the TYPE option of certain commands, and the file extension.

The DBTYPE setting governs the default table type. You can change it by typing **SET DBTYPE TO DBASE** or **SET DBASE TO PARADOX** in the command window, or by selecting the dBASE or Paradox radio button for the Default Table Type setting on the Table page of the Desktop Properties dialog box, as shown in figure 26.2.

The DBTYPE setting controls what table dBASE creates or tries to open in default of either a file extension or the TYPE option in the command. Commands that require dBASE to create a table include the CREATE command, the COPY...TO command (if the

target file does not exist), and others. You can issue these commands in the Command window by using the SpeedBar icons, or by double right-clicking on the Untitled table icon.

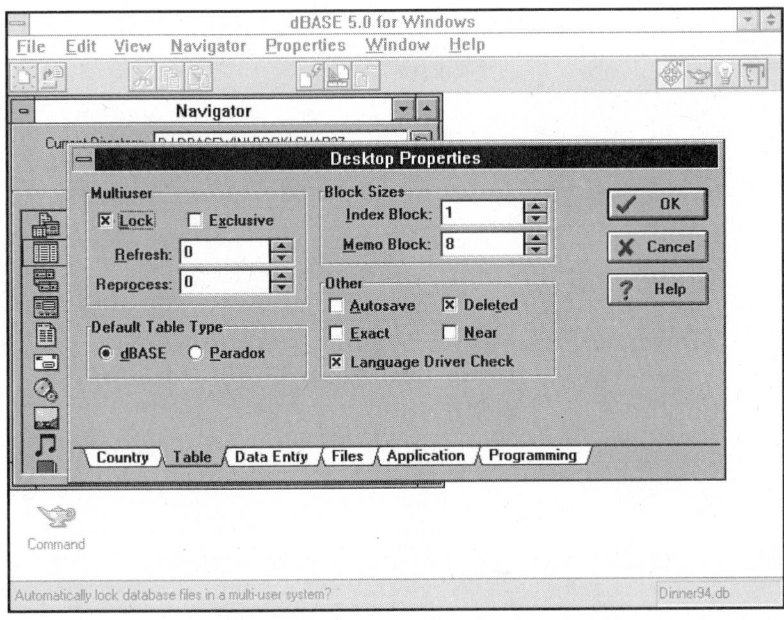

Figure 26.2
Setting the default table type.

You can use similar alternatives to tell dBASE to open a table. Regardless of how the command is issued, the effects of the DBTYPE setting and the file extension are the same. You cannot include the TYPE option in a command, except by typing the command in the command window.

If you give dBASE a command that requires it to create a table—without specifying either TYPE of a file extension—dBASE will create (if possible) a table of the type specified by the DBTYPE setting, with the extension used by default for that type (DBF for dBASE or DB for Paradox). If you tell dBASE to open a table and do not supply a file extension, the program supplies the default extension for the type specified by DBTYPE. An error occurs if dBASE cannot find or open a table with that name and extension. After dBASE finds a file of the specified name and extension, however, it can open it as a dBASE or Paradox table, whichever the file may be—regardless of the DBTYPE setting. The extension may even be the default extension for a table of the other type—DB for a dBASE table or DBF for a Paradox table.

When you tell dBASE to create a table and include a file extension of either DBF or DB, dBASE uses the extension as a clue and creates a table of the type appropriate for the extension, regardless of the DBTYPE setting. If you include a different file extension, dBASE uses the DBTYPE setting to determine which type of table to create.

You can override the table type specified by DBTYPE by including the TYPE option in a command to create or open a table. If you omit the file extension, dBASE supplies the default extension for a table of the TYPE specified. For example, **USE BUSINESS.DB TYPE DBASE** opens BUSINESS.DB as a dBASE table, if it is one, regardless of the file extension or the setting of DBTYPE. If BUSINESS.DB is actually a Paradox table or some other type of file entirely, an error occurs. Similarly, **CREATE CUSTOMER.NEW TYPE PARADOX** creates a Paradox table called CUSTOMER.NEW.

The keyword TYPE is optional. You can include it for readability or leave it out, following the name of the table directly with DBASE or PARADOX to signify the type.

When using your mouse to work with tables of both types, you might want to set DBTYPE as your primary means of specifying the type of table, because you will not usually enter the TYPE option, or, in some cases, the file extension. With or without setting DBTYPE, you can right double-click on the Untitled table icon in the Navigator to create a new file of the type you want. A small list box near the top of the structure design window enables you to choose the type, as shown in figure 26.3. After you begin entering data, you can no longer change the type.

Figure 26.3
Designing a Paradox table.

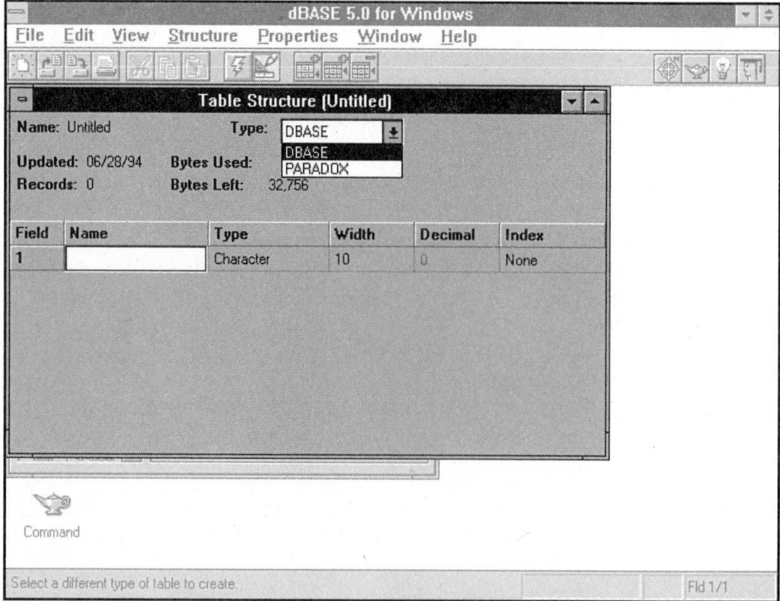

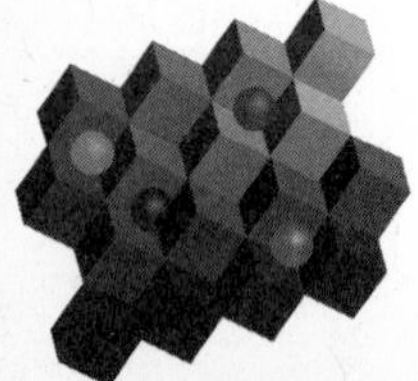

dBASE and Paradox tables that have the same name but different extensions can coexist in the same directory. The following command sequence works to create a dBASE table named DINNER94.DBF, assuming that the Paradox table DINNER94.DB exists and that DBTYPE retains its default setting of dBASE:

```
USE DINNER94 TYPE PARADOX
COPY TO DINNER94
```

The WITH PRODUCTION option of the COPY command does not cause an error, but does not index the target file. The significant differences between the structure of dBASE and Paradox indexes make attempting to copy the production index from one form to another futile. You must re-create the indexes you need for the new table type, using the rules of its language.

Paradox Indexes

Paradox indexes act like tags in a production MDX file. All indexes are always open when the table is open (whether or not they are maintained indexes within Paradox.) You can change which is the master index with SET ORDER TO, but you must name the Paradox index in the command. You cannot refer to it by number like a dBASE tag. Using the SET INDEX command to specify an index for a Paradox table creates an error.

Paradox tables often have a primary index key. Paradox uses this key to enforce referential integrity and does not allow duplicate values in the key field. To set the order to the primary key (if one exists), use SET ORDER TO PRIMARY. You cannot create a primary index on DINNER94.DB without adding a field, because all existing fields have duplicate values.

You can create a Paradox primary index on any field with unique values in a Paradox table, using INDEX ON <*fieldname*> TAG PRIMARY. DISPLAY STATUS or other dBASE commands show the resulting index as UNIQUE, and the UNIQUE() function always returns .T. (True). However, the resulting index is not identical to a dBASE index created with the UNIQUE option of the INDEX command.

First, a Paradox primary index must be on a single field of the table. Its key cannot be a combination of fields such as Last_Name + First_Name like in dBASE, nor an expression such as upper(Last_Name). These restrictions are not accidents. Paradox wants you to use primary keys that are sure to be unique. Names are not ideal for this purpose; Paradox wants you to use Social Security numbers or other arbitrary identifiers unique to the individual to which the record relates.

Second, a Paradox primary index does not allow duplicate entries in the primary key field. In dBASE, a UNIQUE index excludes duplicates from views and reports, but it does not prevent adding duplicates to the file. Paradox prohibits adding duplicates. One effect of this restriction is that you cannot use APPEND BLANK to add several records at once to a Paradox table with a primary index. The duplicate blank values in the key field of the blank records would violate the Paradox design. You can use APPEND AUTOMEM as one workaround; it simultaneously adds the record and fills it from the automem variables.

You can create several indexes for the same Paradox table. The primary index key must be a single field. Each secondary index key must be one or more fields, separated by commas in the INDEX command. To index DINNER94.DB by the DONATION and TABLE fields, you might use the following command:

```
INDEX ON DONATION, TABLE TAG FATCATS
```

Paradox calls an index on multiple fields a *composite* index. It is not required, as with a dBASE index, that the parts of the index expression be converted to character strings. The only two dBASE commands you can use to search a composite index are SET KEY TO and SEEK. In either case, you must again separate the keys with a comma if you are seeking a combination of both, as in the following example:

```
SEEK 500.00,1
```

The FIND command and the search functions such as SEEK(), KEYMATCH(), and LOOKUP() cannot accept composite-key arguments. You can use them to search a composite index for the first key, such as Donation in the above example, but not for the combination of both Donation and Table.

Paradox indexes cannot be unique, conditional, or descending. Attempting to use the FOR and DESCENDING options of the INDEX command on a Paradox table—or the FOR() and DESCENDING() functions on a Paradox index—will result in return errors. The UNIQUE() function creates no error but is useless, because it always returns .T. for primary indexes and .F. for others. SET UNIQUE creates no error but does nothing when used on a Paradox index.

Understanding Paradox's Differences from dBASE

Because of the differences between Paradox and dBASE tables, special means are required to use Paradox tables within dBASE. You know how to specify which type of table to create or use and how to index a Paradox table to find what you need, but you must take account of other differences as well.

Field Names Can Include Spaces

Paradox field names can be up to 25 characters long and contain spaces, slashes, and other characters that dBASE does not allow. dBASE allows only 10 characters in a field name, limited to alphabetic characters (one of which must begin the name), digits, and underscores.

The field name "Gave for Auction/Remarks" in DINNER94.DB is not legal in dBASE. It is too long and contains illegal characters, two spaces and a slash. To refer to such a Paradox field, surround the name with colons as delimiters:

```
LIST :Gave for Auction/Remarks:
```

You can use the colons as field name delimiters wherever a list of one or more field names is required:

```
INDEX ON :Last name:,First Name: TAG NAME
```

You do not need to delimit field names that are acceptable in dBASE, but doing so does no harm.

If you copy a Paradox table to a dBASE table, dBASE truncates all field names longer than 10 characters. dBASE replaces all characters not allowed in dBASE field names with the underscore, "_", except for the first character in a field name; dBASE replaces this with an X if it is not alphabetic. Figure 26.4 shows the field names of DINNER94.DB originally; figure 26.5 shows them as copied into the dBASE file DINNER94.DBF by the COPY... TO command.

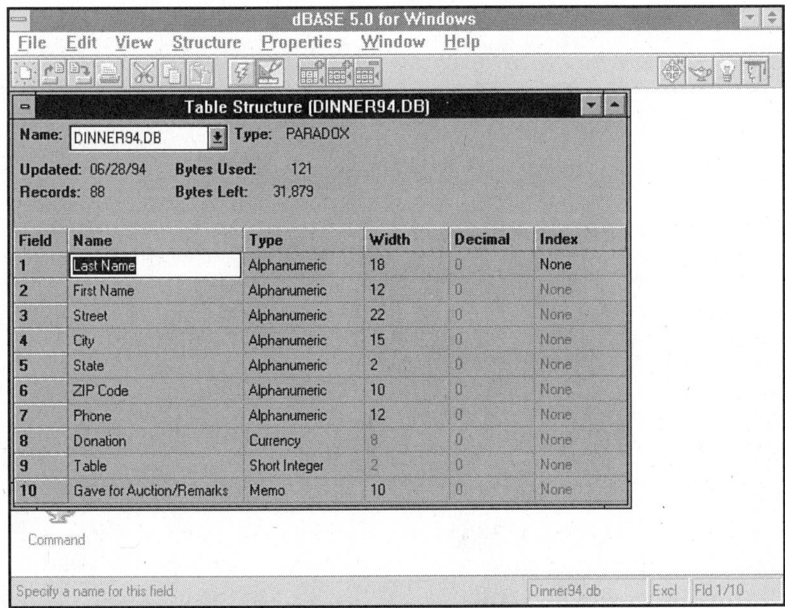

Figure 26.4
The field names of DINNER94.DB.

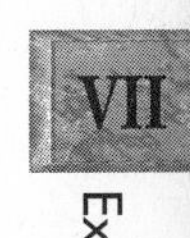

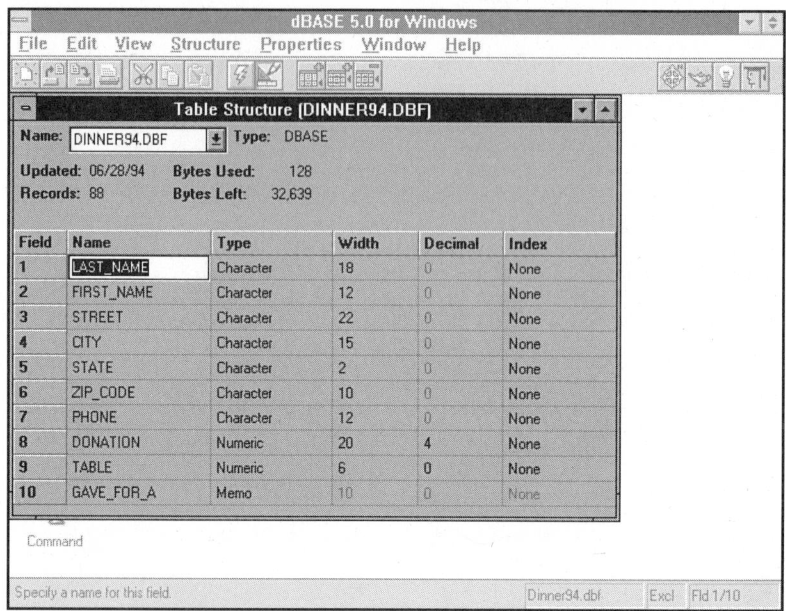

Figure 26.5
The field names of DINNER94.DBF.

Every dBASE field name is a valid Paradox field name, so no such conversion is needed when copying a dBASE table to a Paradox table.

Figure 26.4 illustrates that Paradox, unlike dBASE, does not force field names to uppercase.

Field Types Are Different

The major problem of converting dBASE tables to Paradox, and vice versa, is that the field types are not the same. Figure 26.6 shows the structure-design screen of a Paradox table with the field-type listbox open showing the field types.

To convert data between the two types, dBASE must make some compromises. Table 26.1 shows the eight dBASE field types, the 19 Paradox field types, and the dBASE field types again—in each case—as they convert into field types of the other table type, left to right. Except for the first six types listed, the conversions are one-way only. The distinct nature of a field is lost in the conversions shown later in the table, so conversion back to a table of the original type does not restore the original field type in those cases.

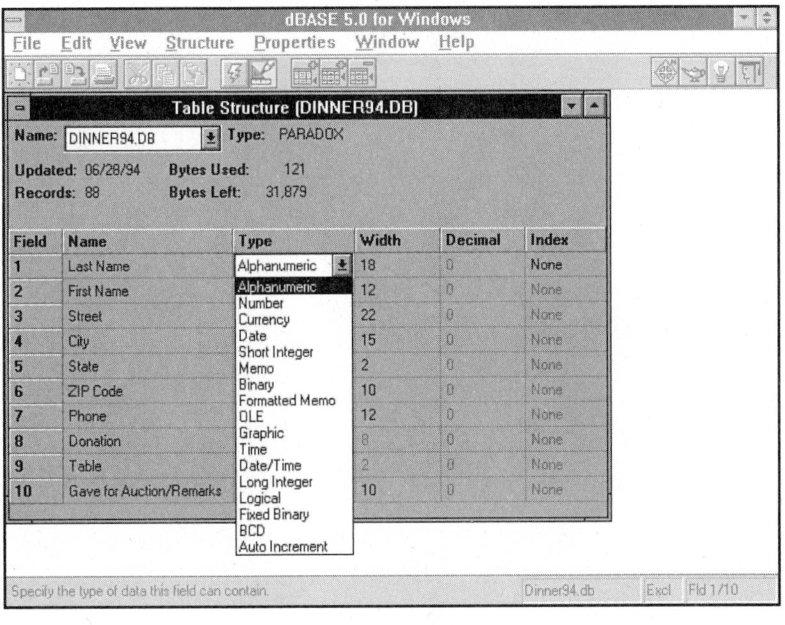

Figure 26.6
The Paradox field type list box.

Table 26.1
dBASE to Paradox and back—Field type conversions

dBASE type	Converts to Paradox	Converts to dBASE
Character	Alpha	Character
Numeric	Numeric	Numeric
Memo	Memo	Memo
Logical	Logical	Logical
Date	Date	Date
Binary	Binary	Binary
Float	Numeric	
OLE	Binary OLE	OLE
[no equivalent]	Money	Numeric
	Short	Numeric

continues

Table 26.1, Continued
dBASE to Paradox and back—Field type conversions

dBASE type	Converts to Paradox	Converts to dBASE
	FmtMemo	Memo
	Graphic	Binary
	Time	Character (length 11)
	Timestamp	Numeric (length 30)
	Long	Numeric (length 11)
	BCD	Character
	Bytes	Causes IDAPI error
	Auto increment	Numeric (length 11)

Paradox Records Have No Numbers

As part of its scheme to enforce proper methods of data access, Paradox hides the record numbers of its table data from the user. You cannot issue GO TO 14 as you can in dBASE, because no record 14 exists in a Paradox table. dBASE provides bookmarks and the BOOKMARK() function. These enable you to mark your place in Paradox tables so you can leave a record and return to it.

After you have found a record of interest in a Paradox table, you can use BOOKMARK() or RECNO() to mark it. Both function identically and return a bookmark value when used on a Paradox table. BOOKMARK() also returns a bookmark value when used on a dBASE table; as you know, RECNO() returns a record number for a dBASE table. You can assign the value returned by BOOKMARK() to a named variable, but you cannot print or see it.

You can compare bookmarks with "=", "<", and similar relational operators, and you can return to the record marked by a bookmark with GO <*name of bookmark variable*>. You can use SKIP to move forward or back in the table from a bookmarked record. If you save the BOOKMARK() of the second record to a bookmark variable, the variables are compared in the order you expect—a skip forward moves you to a record with a larger bookmark than that of the first record. However, you cannot subtract the bookmarks from each other nor can you assign numeric values by which to manipulate them.

```
USE DINNER94.DB
LOCATE FOR :Last Name: = "Akers"
bMark1 = BOOKMARK()
? bMark1                              Bookmark
```

```
SKIP 5
? BOOKMARK() > bmark1                .T.
GO bmark1
? :Last Name                         Akers
```

The hiding of record numbers means the first column (which is the record number) of a browse view of a Paradox table is always blank, as shown in figure 26.1. DISPLAY and LIST do not show record numbers for a Paradox table, regardless of the OFF option of the DISPLAY and LIST commands. GO, GOTO, SET RELATION TO, and the RECORD keyword designating a scope accept bookmark variables, while LOCK() and RLOCK() accept a list of bookmarks.

You can APPEND to a Paradox table, but not INSERT or INSERT BEFORE. If no index is active, INSERT or INSERT BEFORE causes an error. If an index is active, these commands act like APPEND.

Index Keys Cannot Be Expressions

You have seen that Paradox indexes must be on fields or composites of fields. Expressions such as upper(Name) are not allowed. In HomeGuide's DINNER94.DB table, this means that you cannot index the Last Name field into a telephone-directory order. The name of Dr. della Russo will come out last using a standard ASCII sort order because "d" follows "Z" in the ASCII chart. If you must work around this limitation, add a field to your Paradox table holding the uppercase equivalent of each name.

Field Contents Must Be Valid

You know how to create validity checks for your dBASE table data using the Valid property of user input objects such as EntryFields. Paradox tables support built-in validity checks, stored in files of the same name as the table with a VAL extension. dBASE opens the VAL file when it opens the table. When you enter data into such a table, dBASE enforces the Paradox rules. If your entry fails the validity check, dBASE returns an error.

You must use Paradox to create or modify Paradox validity checks. dBASE cannot change them.

Deletion Occurs at Once

In dBASE, you are accustomed to deleting records and having them available for recall until you PACK the table. Paradox deletes records at once. For Paradox tables, the RECALL and PACK commands return an error; DELETED() is always .F., and SET DELETED has no effect.

Do not use the deleted flag in dBASE for Windows to select useful records from a browse view, the way some dBASE for DOS users do. This seems a convenient way to select an arbitrary group of records, which can then, for example, be copied to another table by copying FOR DELETED(). If you use any Paradox tables, you will try this method, sooner or later, and the records you mark will be deleted at once. You will not be able to RECALL them and might create significant problems for yourself in restoring your data.

Chapter Snapshot

In the past few years an incredible number of local area networks (LANs) have appeared in businesses all over the country. In most of these business environments, each employee has a PC on his or her desk. Simultaneous access to the same data is a possibility, and often a necessity.

This chapter covers the following:

Networking dBASE for Windows

By Kenneth Chan

Many database applications started out as simple single-user applications, but like PCs, database applications have also adapted to the increasing popularity of LANs. Simultaneous access, data integrity, and other LAN-related issues are now part of databases. dBASE for Windows incorporates all the capabilities of networked applications and makes it easy to move from a single-user to a networked environment.

Understanding Networking Concepts

On a network, all shared data is stored in a central file server. Access to the server is controlled through user accounts and passwords that you use to log in to the file server. Users are assigned different access levels that determine which files, programs, and services they can see and use.

On most networks, if a user has access to a data file, other users can view the same file at the same time. The data is simply read off the disk in the file server and displayed at the user's workstation. The complexities in networked databases really begin when more than one person tries to write to the same data file.

Simultaneous Access

Suppose user Fred is looking at a record on-screen. The phone rings, and Fred's attention is diverted. User Wilma brings up the same record on another workstation, makes changes to the record, and saves them. When Fred gets off the phone, he too makes his own changes to the record, oblivious to Wilma's changes, and saves those too. Now Fred's version of the record has overwritten Wilma's. As far as Fred is concerned, everything is fine and dandy, but, what happened to the changes Wilma made?

Record Refresh

One thing that might have helped in Fred and Wilma's situation would have been *record refresh.* In this case, when Fred returned to the data-entry screen, he would have noticed two things:

- ✔ Fred would have been notified that someone had changed the record during the time it had been sitting on-screen.
- ✔ The data on-screen would have been refreshed to reflect the changes that Wilma made.

dBASE has an adjustable automatic refresh. Every few seconds, dBASE will check to see if changes have been made to a record, and if so, dBASE will refresh the data. The automatic refresh only operates on the interactive editing surfaces such as BROWSE and EDIT, which many programs do not use. Another method for managing records must be used for dBASE programs.

Record Locking

Suppose Fred had already started to make his own changes when the phone rang. He would not want Wilma's changes to overwrite his changes. In fact, Fred probably would not want Wilma to make any changes at all.

To prevent any possible problems, Fred can put a *lock* on the record he is editing. No other user can change Fred's record while the lock exists. Every time someone (like Fred) edits a record, dBASE automatically puts a lock on that record. Only one person can have a lock on a record at a time. Anyone else who attempts to lock the same record will fail, and if they cannot lock the record, they cannot edit it. After the first person finishes editing the record, dBASE removes the lock—allowing others to lock and edit the record.

File Locking

Later, Wilma wants to run a summary report. For the results to be accurate, no one else can make changes while the report is running. To ensure exclusive access, Wilma attempts to lock the entire file. She will succeed only if no one else has any individual record locks.

Once the file has been locked, no one else can lock the file or any records in the file.

Understanding Locking Concepts

The two kinds of locks—record and file—can be used in different ways.

Active Record Locking

With *active record locking*, you grab and hold the record while you are working on it. Active record locks are automatic when you BROWSE or EDIT a table interactively.

One potential problem with active record locking is the duration of the lock. If a user takes a long time to edit a record or takes a coffee break in the middle of editing a record, the record stays locked for the entire time. No one else can lock that record or the file.

Passive Record Locking

Passive record locking addresses the problem with active locks by using an extra field to indicate that the record is in use. All access to the table must be through programs that know about and understand the extra field.

Active record locks are still used when writing to the record and the in-use field, but the records stay locked only long enough for the actual operation.

Automatic Record Locking

Records are locked automatically when you begin to edit a record while you BROWSE or EDIT a table interactively.

Manual Record Locking with RLOCK()

The RLOCK() function manually locks one or more records. RLOCK() returns .T. or .F. to indicate success or failure. Most often, you lock the current record in the current work area by calling it with no parameters:

```
if rlock()
  *-- Lock was successful
else
  *-- Lock was not successful
endif
```

You can also lock the current record in another work area by specifying that work area's alias, as shown in this example:

```
if rlock( "RENTALS" )
```

More than one record can be locked by using a character string that contains the record numbers to be locked separated by commas:

```
if rlock( "1,3,5" )
```

This expression can be combined with an alias to lock more than one record in another work area. In this case, the alias becomes the second parameter. However this record number string is not used very often.

You can lock up to 100 records per table. After that, all subsequent record lock attempts will fail.

Automatic Table/File Locking

The SET LOCK command determines whether certain operations will automatically lock the entire file. For example, if you want to CALCULATE an average for a numeric field in a table, you usually want to lock the file so that no one can change any of the numbers while you are doing the calculation.

On the other hand, it is often difficult to get a file lock because it requires that no one else have any record locks on the table, which generally means that no one else is working on the table. Other users may not even be editing the field or fields that you are interested in, but there is no way to tell. How much deviation would such changes create anyway?

If you can accept a ballpark figure then you probably do not want to bother with the automatic file lock, in which case you can SET LOCK OFF. See the entry for SET LOCK in Appendix A .

Manual File Locking With FLOCK()

The FLOCK() command locks an entire table. It attempts to lock the table in the current work area unless an alias is specified, and it returns .T. or .F. to indicate success or failure.

Unlocking Records and Files

The UNLOCK command releases all record and file locks in the current work area. You should release your locks as soon as possible so that other users can access the data.

Controlling Network Settings

Two settings are of particular interest in network environments:

- ✔ **SET REFRESH.** Specifies how often to update the data on-screen from the table stored on disk. As an example, the following command causes dBASE to update the screen every five seconds:

  ```
  set refresh to 5
  ```

  Settings lower than 5 are not recommended because they burden the network and server by constantly refreshing the screen for little if any reason. When SET REFRESH is 0 (the default), no screen refresh takes place.

  SET REFRESH only affects data that is directly linked to tables, not memvars. Programs that rely on memvars must use other refresh methods, as described later in this chapter.

- ✔ **SET REPROCESS.** Controls how many times dBASE retries a record or file lock before returning a failure code. By default, SET REPROCESS is set to 0, which produces a dialog box when a lock attempt is unsuccessful (see fig. 27.1).

This generic dialog box may not be suitable for your application. You may want to provide more information, or accept the failure to lock a record or file and do something else. In that case, you can SET REPROCESS TO 1. If it locks, it locks; if it does not, it does not. Then you can handle the results yourself.

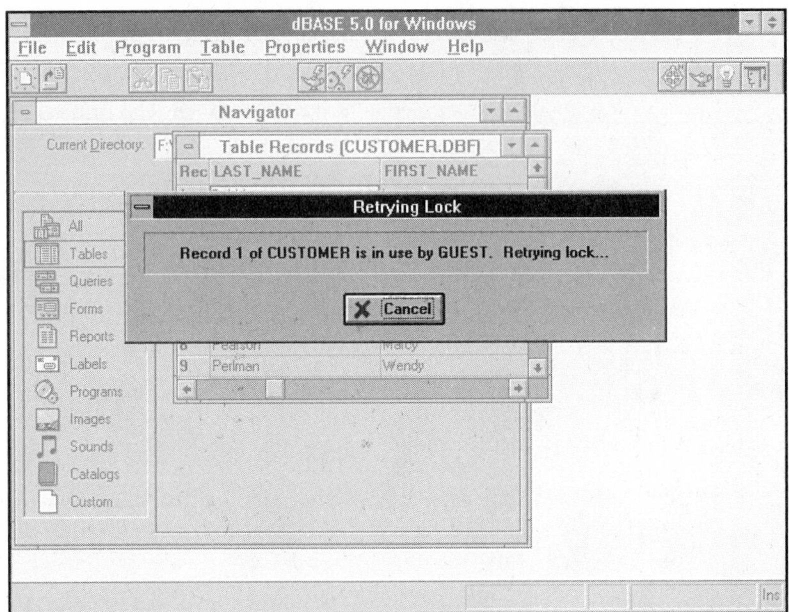

Figure 27.1
The standard retry lock dialog box.

Making Tables Network-Aware

When using DBFs on a network, you often will want to convert them so that you have access to locking information.

CONVERT is a one-time operation that adds a special field named _DBASELOCK to the structure of a table. It becomes the last field of each record, and contains information about locks on that record. It is not accessed directly, but rather through the LKSYS() and CHANGE() functions.

_DBASELOCK contains date, time, and user name information about record locks, and maintains an internal count that is incremented every time the record is updated. It is therefore added for two reasons:

- ✔ _DBASELOCK enables dBASE's automatic record locking. A DBF that has not been CONVERTed cannot be locked automatically.
- ✔ _DBASELOCK provides information about the current and last lock, which is useful in many ways.

If a table has not been CONVERTed, dBASE has no place to store record lock information. The Fred and Wilma example used earlier helps explain this:

1. Fred moves to a particular record and views it.

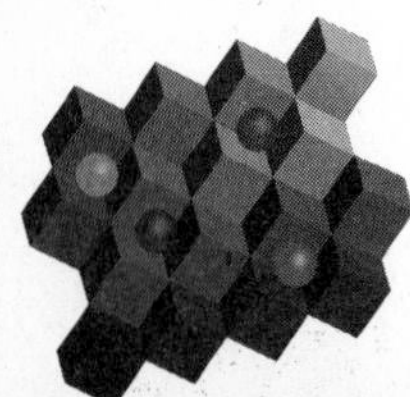

2. Wilma goes to that same record and edits it, while Fred is still looking at it.

3. Fred then decides to change that record.

At this point, without the record lock information that would be in the _DBASELOCK field, dBASE does not know if that record has been changed since Fred first brought it on-screen. Although it is possible to actually compare each field in the record to see if there have been any changes, that may not be enough; Fred may want to know if Wilma edited the record, even if she did not make any changes to the field values.

Therefore, dBASE assumes the worst, and informs Fred with the message:

```
Record may have changed
```

Even if the record had changed, Fred would not know who did it, or when. Worse yet, Fred gets this message on every single record he edits.

Fred can avoid this message if he manually locks each record before he edits it. This informs dBASE that Fred knows that the record may have changed, so dBASE does not display the "Record may have changed" message. It is a nuisance, nonetheless.

CONVERTing the file solves this problem because dBASE can detect whether the record has been changed.

LKSYS()

LKSYS() returns the date, time, and user name of the last lock recorded in the _DBASELOCK field. If the record is currently locked, then that same information reflects the current lock. LKSYS() requires a single numeric code to determine what to return, as listed in table 27.1.

Table 27.1
LKSYS() codes

Code	Returns
0	Time when lock was placed
1	Date when lock was placed
2	Login name of user who locked the record
3	Time of last update or lock
4	Date of last update or lock
5	Login name of user who last updated or locked the record

You can make your programs more self-documenting by using preprocessor symbols for the various LKSYS() codes:

```
#define LKSYS_CURRENT_TIME 0

#define LKSYS_CURRENT_DATE 1

#define LKSYS_CURRENT_NAME 2

#define LKSYS_LAST_TIME   3

#define LKSYS_LAST_DATE   4

#define LKSYS_LAST_NAME   5
```

Store these #DEFINEs in a separate LKSYS.H file or as part of a more generic header file and use #INCLUDE to include the file in your programs.

LKSYS() will return information about the current lock (codes 0, 1, and 2) only after a failed file or record lock attempt. In other words, LKSYS() is used to find out why the lock failed. If you have already locked the record and want to know when that happened, use the codes for the last lock (codes 3, 4, and 5). The following code fragment attempts a record lock and if unsuccessful, tells the user who has locked the record:

```
if rlock()
  *-- Code to execute if lock successful
else
  AlertDialog( "Record lock failed", ;
    "This record is being edited by " + ;
    lksys( LKSYS_CURRENT_NAME ) + ;
    " who locked the record at " + ;
    lksys( LKSYS_CURRENT_TIME ) )
endif
```

LKSYS() does not return any locking information from Paradox tables.

CHANGE()

Whenever you move to a record, the internal counter in the _DBASELOCK field is stored in memory. CHANGE() works by comparing this stored value with the current value in the _DBASELOCK field. If the values are different, then the record has been updated, and CHANGE() returns .T.; otherwise it returns .F..

In some extremely defensive programming situations, tables are never kept open. To work on a record, the table is opened, the record is copied to memory variables, and the table is immediately closed. This process minimizes the vulnerability of the table on disk. In these situations, CHANGE() is useless because the internal counter is always being updated. As a substitute, you can record the values from LKSYS() when you first access the record and compare the values later. This LastLock() UDF returns the last lock information in a single character string:

```
FUNCTION LastLock
  local cRet
  if network()
    cRet = dtos( lksys( LKSYS_LAST_DATE )) + ;
           lksys( LKSYS_LAST_TIME ) + ;
           lksys( LKSYS_LAST_NAME )
  else
    cRet = ""
  endif
RETURN cRet
```

Managing Deleted Records

In a single-user environment, after a set of records has been marked for deletion, the PACK command can be used to remove these records from the table. On a network, however, PACK occasionally is unavailable because it requires exclusive USE of the table. If a networked application is running around the clock, there may be no time to kick everyone off the system just to remove some deleted records, especially from large tables, which take longer to PACK. Another problem with the use of PACK on a network is that it is inherently unsafe.

The Problem with PACK

Picture for a moment: the World Trade Center building that has an observation deck on its roof. Suppose, on the 12th floor of this 100-plus-floor building, the brokerage firm Dewey, Cheatem, & Howe is vacating the premises.

After the office personnel remove their personal belongings, a construction crew comes by with a very large crane. The crane grabs onto the top of the building, scaring all the tourists looking out the windows, and then the construction crew snips out the girders at the 12th floor of the building and gently lowers the rest of the building down, crushing and obliterating the 12th floor. (Of course, Velcro was applied to the floor and ceiling of the former 12th floor to form an unbreakable seal.)

The former 13th floor is now the 12th floor, the 100th floor is now the 99th floor, and so on. The building directory in the lobby and all the stationery and business cards will have to be changed because everyone who was on floor 13 or higher is one floor lower.

Of course, this example is lunacy. This is also what happens when you PACK a table (except for the Velcro part). If you have 100 records and only delete record 12, and then PACK, all the records after record 12 get moved forward one. The record numbers have now changed, which requires all the table's indexes to be rebuilt. For 100 records, this would be no problem, but for 100,000 records you would have a long wait ahead of you.

Worse yet, the PACK command performs an in-place copy, unlike the MODIFY STRUCTURE command, which renames the original file and copies the changed records into a new file. If a power failure or a similar problem occurs while PACKing, you may end up with a mangled table and no backup.

The Solution to PACK

A safer way to handle deleted records is to recycle them. Recycling requires that you do not rely on the physical order of records in your table—no properly designed application should rely on such an unreliable characteristic, except for the simplest of tables.

A table should have a master index that controls the order of its records, regardless of physical location or record number. Such an index is also required to implement record recycling.

When you want to physically delete a record, you need to do two things to it: BLANK it and DELETE it. Blanking the record with the BLANK command wipes out all the information for security reasons and makes it obvious that the record is available for re-use. Deleting the record with the DELETE command marks the record for deletion, which is another indication that the record is available. More importantly, as long as SET DELETED is ON (the default), the blank record will not show up in any BROWSEs, REPORTs, and so on.

This deletion can be automated with the following procedure, which deletes the current record in the designated work area:

```
PROCEDURE DelRec( cAlias )
  *-- Remember the current workarea
  local cOldAlias
  cOldAlias = alias()
  if pcount() >= 1
    *-- Go to specified workarea, if there was one
    select( cAlias )
  endif
  *-- Delete the record
  blank
  delete
  *-- Go back to old workarea
  select( cOldAlias )
RETURN
```

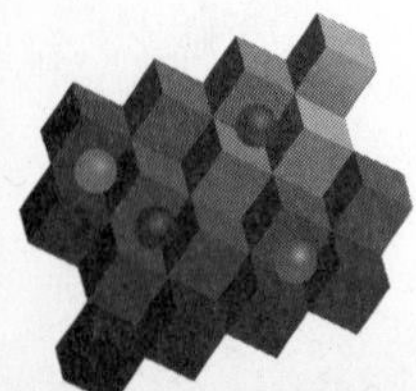

The record in question should be locked before calling DelRec.

Now whenever you need a record, you call NewRec, which looks for an available deleted record. If it doesn't find one, NewRec creates one.

```
PROCEDURE NewRec( cAlias )
  *-- Remember the current workarea
  local cOldAlias
  cOldAlias = alias()
  if pcount() >= 1
    *-- Go to specified workarea, if there was one
  endif
  set deleted off
  *-- Look for available deleted record
  if seek( " " ) .and. deleted() .and. rlock()
    *-- Found one that no one was using, undelete it
    recall
  else
    *-- Did not find one, so create a new one
    append blank
  endif
  set deleted on
  *-- Go back to old workarea
  select( cOldAlias )
RETURN
```

NewRec locks the record it finds so that no one else will grab it. (A record created by APPEND BLANK is automatically locked.) NewRec requires that the table have an active index. It looks for a blank record by SEEKing a blank space. Because most indexes have character expressions for keys, and the entire record was blanked when it was deleted, it is likely that whatever index you have active at the time will suffice. The instances where you would have to change indexes before calling NewRec are with non-character index expressions and those key values that legitimately start with a space.

Generating Key Values

A perennial problem with databases is the automatic generation of unique key values: ID numbers, invoice numbers, and the like. On single-user systems, there are a number of ways to approach this, but on multi-user systems, most of these techniques do not work because any number of people can be vying for a unique key value at the same time.

One method that works equally well for single and multi-user situations is the use of a table of key values. Each user accesses the table, generates a new key value, and updates the table for the next person who will use the table.

Creating the Key Table

One key table contains the key values for all of your other tables. Therefore the key table—KEYS.DBF is a good name for it—has three fields:

- ✔ The name of the table
- ✔ The name of the key field, mostly for identification purposes, but also in case the table has more than one key field
- ✔ A field for the last value of the key field, big enough to accommodate the biggest key field you have

A sample structure is as follows:

Field	Field Name	Type	Length	Dec	Index
1	DBF_NAME	CHARACTER	8		N
2	FIELD_NAME	CHARACTER	10		N
3	SEQ_KEY	CHARACTER	10		N
		Total	28		

KEYS.DBF needs an index to find the desired key field quickly:

```
index on upper( DBF_NAME + FIELD_NAME ) tag DBF_FIELD
```

Note that with this composite key, as long as your table has only one key field, you only need to SEEK for the DBF name as long as SET EXACT is OFF (the default).

The next step is to populate the table.

Accessing the Key Table

All access to KEYS.DBF is done through a single function, NEXTKEY(). To do its work, NextKey() needs to know two things: which key value you want, and how to generate the new key value. Which key value you want is identified by a simple character string containing the name of the DBF, and the field name if necessary.

How to generate the new key value is a bit more complex. Different keys have different formats. Some are simple numbers, others have letters or symbols embedded, and so on. dBASE for Windows has a natural solution for this: a codeblock containing the instructions to increment the key value is also passed to NEXTKEY(). NEXTKEY() looks like this:

```
FUNCTION NextKey( cDbfField, kGenKey )
  *-- Remember the current workarea
  local cOldAlias, cKeyVal
  cOldAlias = alias()
  *-- Select the key table
  select KEYS
  *-- Find the desired key
  if seek( cDbfField )
    *-- Get exclusive access
    do while .not. rlock()
    enddo
    *-- Generate the new key
    cKeyVal = kGenKey( SEQ_KEY )
    *-- Update the key table
    replace SEQ_KEY with cKeyVal
    *-- and unlock the key record
    unlock
  else
    *-- If the key record is not found, something
    *-- is horribly wrong. Generate an error and
    *-- shut down the application.
    AlertDialog( "Really bad news!", ;
      "An error has occurred while trying to " + ;
      "generate a key value for " + cDbfField + ;
      ". The application cannot continue and " + ;
      "must shut down." )
    quit
  endif
  *-- Go back to old workarea
  select( cOldAlias )
RETURN cKeyVal
```

Note that NEXTKEY() simply selects the KEYS.DBF table, which means that it must be opened with the DBF_FIELD index active somewhere. This would be done early in the application, and it will be left open throughout the entire application because constantly opening and closing it would take too much time.

Continuing with the example from the IntelliRent application, the CUST_ID in CUSTOMER.DBF is a simple six-digit number, so the utilization would look like:

```
m->CUST_ID = NextKey( "CUSTOMER", ;
             {|cKey| str( val( cKey ) + 1, 6 ) }
```

Because the first customer is assigned the number 100001 as a matter of convention, the STR() function will convert that to a string with six digits with no problems. If the number had started with 000001, then TRANSFORM() would be used to include the leading zeroes.

Part VIII

Appendixes

dBASE Command and Function Reference

This appendix lists the commands and functions of the dBASE for Windows language. Commands and functions are syntactically different but are often operationally interchangeable in dBASE for Windows. For example, both OPEN FORM, a command, and READMODAL(), a function, serve to open a form.

Commands and Functions by Purpose

In the first section of this reference, commands and functions are arranged according to the purpose for which you use them. A number of commands and functions appear in more than one category.

dBASE Operations

The first group of commands and functions includes those you need to perform essential system tasks and those used to manage data tables on the local system.

Using the Essentials

HELP	Invokes the on-line help system.
QUIT	Terminates dBASE session and returns to operating system.
SET	Changes numerous settings affecting the way dBASE works.
SET()	Returns an ON|OFF setting or a setting that takes no ON|OFF.
SETTO() (new)	Returns the value to which a setting that can be ON or OFF is set.
VERSION()	Returns the version of dBASE in use.

Designing and Using Local Tables and Indexes

AFIELDS() (new)	Copies table structure to an array.
ALIAS()	Returns alias of a table.
CATALOG()	Returns the name of the active catalog.
COPY	Copies a table or its structure.
CLOSE	Closes all tables or other files.
CREATE	Creates a table.
DBF()	Returns name of the current table.
DESCENDING()	Returns whether index is descending.
FDECIMAL()	Returns the number of decimals in a field.

FIELD()	Returns the name of a field.
FLDCOUNT()	Returns the number of fields in a table.
FLDLIST()	Returns the SET FIELDS list.
FLENGTH() (new)	Returns the length of a field.
FOR()	Returns the condition of a conditional index.
INDEX	Creates an index to a table.
JOIN	Makes one table from two others.
KEY()	Returns the key expression of an index.
LUPDATE()	Returns last date a table was changed.
MDX()	Returns name of the active MDX file.
MODIFY STRUCTURE	Changes structure of a table.
NDX()	Returns name of the active NDX file.
ORDER()	Returns name of the controlling index.
RECCOUNT()	Returns number of records in a table.
RECNO()	Returns the number of the record.
RECSIZE()	Returns the size of a record.
REINDEX	Rebuilds one or more indexes.
RELATION() (new)	Returns an expression used to set a relation.
SELECT	Selects a table work area.
SELECT()	Returns the number of an unused work area.
SORT	Sorts the contents of one table into another table.
TAG()	Returns the tag name from its number.
TAGCOUNT()	Returns the number of tags in active indexes.
TAGNO()	Returns the number of a tag from its name.
TARGET() (new)	Returns the name of the child table of a relation.
TYPE()	Returns the data type of a field.

UNIQUE()	Returns whether index keys are unique.
USE	Opens a table.
WORKAREA() (new)	Returns number of a work area.

Navigating Within Tables

BOF()	Returns whether record pointer is at beginning of table.
BOOKMARK()	Returns bookmark for a record.
CONTINUE	Continues a search begun by LOCATE.
EMPTY() (new)	Returns whether a field is blank.
EOF()	Returns whether record pointer is at end of table.
FIND	Searches an index for a value.
FOUND()	Returns whether a search suceeded.
GO|GOTO	Moves to a specified record.
ISBLANK()	Returns whether a field, variable or expression is blank. Same as EMPTY().
LOCATE	Commences serial search in a table.
LOOKUP()	Obtains value of one field based on another.
SEEK	Searches an index for an expression.
SEEK()	Like SEEK, but returns whether successful.
SKIP	Moves by a specified number of records.

Changing Table Data

APPEND	Adds records to a table.
BLANK	Replaces fields of a table with blank values.
BROWSE	Edits a table in spreadsheet-like format.
CHANGE	Same as EDIT, edits a single record.
DELETE	Removes or marks a record for removal.
DELETED()	Returns whether record marked for deletion.

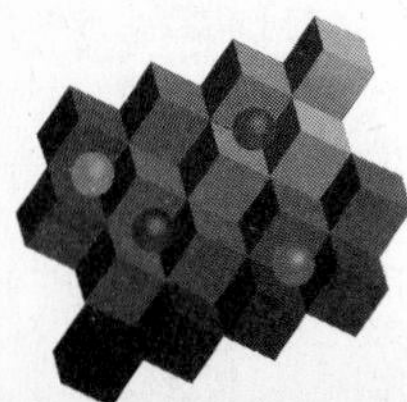

EDIT	Enables edit of one record at a time.
INSERT	Inserts a record into a table.
KEYMATCH()	Returns whether key is a duplicate.
PACK	Permanently removes records in a dBASE table previously marked for deletion.
RECALL	Recalls records marked for deletion.
REPLACE	Changes the values of one or more fields.
UPDATE	Changes the values of fields of all records based on values from another table.
ZAP	Removes all data from a table.

Input and Output Commands

A second major group of dBASE commands and functions contains those you use to obtain input from the user, to print results, and to save and restore data between disk and memory.

Obtaining User Input

@	Obtains input to dBASE IV-style entry field.
ACCEPT	Obtains character data from user.
GETCOLOR() (new)	Opens the Color dialog box.
GETEXPR() (new)	Opens the Expression Builder dialog box.
GETFILE() (new)	Opens the File dialog box.
GETFONT() (new)	Opens the Font dialog box.
INKEY()	Obtains and evaluates a keypress.
INPUT	Obtains data of any type from the user.
KEYBOARD	Simulates keypresses by user.
LASTKEY()	Returns ASCII value of key used to exit a dBASE IV full-screen command.
MCOL()	Returns the mouse column.

MDOWN() (new)	Returns whether the mouse button is down.
MROW()	Returns the mouse row.
NEXTKEY()	Returns next key from the type-ahead buffer.
PUTFILE() (new)	Creates a custom File dialog.
READ	Activates dBASE-IV style @ . . . GET fields.
READKEY()	Returns key used to exit dBASE IV full-screen editing command and reports whether field was changed.

Printing and Displaying Data

@	Performs dBASE IV-style output, primarily to the results pane of the Command window.
?	Performs streaming output to the display, printer or a file on a new line.
??	Same as ? but does not start a new line.
???	Performs streaming output bypassing printer driver.
CLEAR	Clears the results pane of the Command window.
DISPLAY	Shows records of a table in columnar table form, stopping when window is full.
DOWNSCROLL (new)	Scrolls the contents of a window down.
EJECT	Ejects a page from the printer.
ENDPRINTJOB	Ends a PRINTJOB structure.
LABEL FORM	Prints mailing labels.
LENNUM() (new)	Returns printing length of a number.
LIST	Like DISPLAY but does not stop.
PCOL()	Returns the printing column position.
PRINTJOB	Starts a program printing structure.
PRINTSTATUS()	Reports whether a printer has been assigned.
PROW()	Returns the row position.

REPORT FORM	Prints a report.
TYPE	Displays contents of a text file.
UPSCROLL (new)	Scrolls the contents of a window up.

Saving and Restoring Data

CLEAR	Clears memory and definitions.
FLUSH	Saves buffered data to disk.
RELEASE	Releases specified definitions.
RESTORE	Loads variables from disk.
STORE	Saves data to variables.

Screen and Form Commands

A third group contains the commands and functions you will use to create, manage, and release screens, menus, forms, and other parts of the visual user interface.

Using Screens, Forms, and Controls

ACTIVATE	Makes a dBASE IV-style window or control visible and gives it focus.
BAR()	Returns the number of the selected bar.
BARCOUNT()	Returns number of bars in the active popup.
BARPROMPT()	Returns the prompt of the specified bar.
CLASS	Defines a class of objects.
COL()	Returns the display column.
DEACTIVATE	Closes a dBASE IV-style window or control.
DEFINE	Creates a dBASE IV or new-style object.
INSPECT() (new)	Opens the Object Inspection dialog box.
LISTCOUNT() (new)	Returns the number of list box items.
LISTSELECTED() (new)	Returns the name of a selected list box item.
MENU()	Returns the name of the active menu.

MOVE WINDOW	Moves a window.
NEXTCOL() (new)	Returns next column available for an object.
OPEN FORM (new)	Makes a form visible and gives it focus.
PAD()	Returns the name of the selected pad.
PADPROMPT()	Returns the prompt of the specified pad.
POPUP()	Returns the name of the active popup.
PROMPT()	Returns the prompt of the last selection.
READMODAL() (new)	Opens a form as a modal form.
REDEFINE	Redefines an object.
ROW()	Returns the display row.
SHOW	Causes object to display without giving it focus.
UPDATED() (new)	Returns whether any GET fields have changed.
VARREAD()	Returns the name of the active GET field.
WINDOW()	Returns the name of the active window.

Programming Commands

You will use the next group of commands and functions to create and modify programs within your programs. The items beginning with the pound sign "#" in the first section below are the preprocessor directives you may include in your programs to affect the compilation.

Creating and Modifying Programs

#define	Defines a term, value, or inline function.
#else	Allows compilation if preceding condition is false.
#if	Allows compilation when true.
#ifdef	Allows compilation when defined.
#ifndef	Allows compilation when not defined.
#include	Directs inclusion of a file in compilation.

#pragma	Introduces a compiler directive.
#undef	Reverses effect of #define of an item.
*	Introduces a line of program notes.
&&	Adds notes at the end of a program line.
CERROR()	Returns zero if no compilation error occurs.
COMPILE	Compiles a program so that it can be run.
CREATE	Creates a new program, format, or other file.
DEBUG	Invokes the debugger.
GENERATE (new)	Fills a table with random data for testing.
MODIFY	Changes an existing program, format, or other file.
NOTE	Introduces program notes. Same as *.
RESOURCE() (new)	Returns a resource from an external file.

Calling Functions, Procedures, and Programs

DO	Executes a function, procedure, or program.
EXTERN	Prototypes an external function.
FUNCTION	Defines a user-defined function.
LOAD DLL (new)	Establishes link to external Dynamic Link Library file.
LOCAL (new)	Makes variables invisible outside routine.
PARAMETERS	Declares parameters of a routine.
PCOUNT()	Returns the number of parameters passed.
PRIVATE	Makes variables invisible from higher-level routines.
PROCEDURE	Defines a procedure.
PUBLIC	Makes variables global.
RELEASE	Releases variables, objects or DLLs.
RESTORE	Loads variables from a file.

SAVE	Saves variables to a file.
SHELL() (new)	Hides dBASE while a program is running.
STATIC (new)	Makes private and local variables retain their values while invisible.

Controlling the Flow of Execution

CANCEL	Cancels all running programs.
CASE	States one of the choices in a DO CASE structure.
DO . . . UNTIL (new)	Creates a loop until a condition is met.
DO CASE	Creates a multiple-choice control structure.
DO WHILE	Creates a loop while a condition is not met.
ENDCASE	Ends a DO CASE structure.
ENDFOR (new)	Ends a FOR structure.
ENDIF	Ends an IF structure.
ENDPRINTJOB	Ends a PRINTJOB structure.
ENDSCAN	Ends a SCAN structure.
ENDTEXT	Ends a TEXT block.
ERROR()	Returns the number of the last error.
EXIT	Breaks out of the innermost loop.
FOR (new)	Creates a loop executed a fixed number of times.
IF	Provides a choice of execution paths.
IIF()	Chooses between two values.
LINENO()	Returns the current line number.
LOOP	Repeats a loop from the top.
MESSAGE()	Returns the message of the last error.
NEXT	Same as ENDFOR, ends a FOR loop. (The keyword NEXT is also used as one of the scope options.)

ON	Interrupts execution on an event.
PROGRAM()	Returns the name of the current routine.
RESUME	Resumes execution of suspended program.
RETRY	Retries a line that caused an error.
RETURN	Returns from a routine.
SCAN	Commences pass through records of a table.
SLEEP (new)	Creates timed suspension of activity.
SUSPEND	Suspends a running program.
TEXT	Starts a text block.
UNTIL (new)	States the condition that will end execution of a DO . . . UNTIL loop.
WAIT	Suspends activity pending user action.

Mathematical Operations

You will use the next group of commands and functions to perform mathematic operations on your data.

Using Basic Arithmetic

ABS()	Absolute value of a number.
AVERAGE	Averages the values in a field over the records of a table.
CALCULATE	Performs various calculations on one or more fields over the records of a table.
CEILING()	Closest integer not smaller than a number.
COUNT	Counts records of a table that meet a condition.
FLOOR()	Closest integer not larger than a number.
INT()	Integer part of a number.
MAX()	Maximum of two values.
MIN()	Minimum of two values.

MOD()	Remainder of integer division.
ROUND()	Rounds a number to specified decimal places.
SIGN()	Returns the sign of a number.
SUM	Adds the values in a field over the records of a table.
TOTAL	Creates a table subtotalling numeric fields of another by values in field.

Using Binary and Hexadecimal Numbers

BITAND() (new)	Performs bitwise AND.
BITLSHIFT() (new)	Shifts bits left.
BITOR() (new)	Performs bitwise OR.
BITRSHIFT() (new)	Shifts bits right.
BITSET() (new)	Tests a bit.
BITXOR() (new)	Performs bitwise XOR.
HTOI() (new)	Converts hexadecimal string to integer.
ITOH() (new)	Converts integer to hexadecimal string.

Using Higher Mathematics and Finance

ACOS()	Returns the angle given its cosine.
ASIN()	Returns the angle given its sine.
ATAN()	Returns the angle given its tangent.
ATN2()	Returns the angle given its sine and cosine.
COS()	Cosine of an angle.
DTOR()	Converts degrees to radians.
EXP()	Natural antilogarithm of a number.
FV()	Future value of a series of investments.
LOG()	Natural logarithm of a number.
LOG10()	Base-10 logarithm of a number.

PAYMENT()	Periodic payment needed to amortize a loan.
PI()	Ratio of circumference of circle to its diameter.
PV()	Present value of a series of payments.
RANDOM()	Returns pseudorandom number.
RTOD()	Converts radians to degrees.
SIN()	Sine of an angle.
SQRT()	Square root of a number.
TAN()	Tangent of an angle.

Miscellaneous Data Operations

You will use the commands and functions in the next group to perform other operations on your data, including manipulation of character strings, the types data may take on, dates, times, and arrays.

Manipulating Character Data

ANSI() (new)	Converts to ANSI characters from OEM.
AT()	Returns position of one string in another.
CENTER()	Centers a string.
CHARSET() (new)	Returns name of character set in use.
DIFFERENCE()	Tests similarity of sounds of two strings.
ISLOWER()	Returns whether character is lowercase.
ISUPPER()	Returns whether character is uppercase.
LEFT()	Returns leftmost characters.
LEN()	Returns length of a string.
LIKE()	Returns whether string matches a pattern.
LOWER()	Converts to lowercase.
LTRIM()	Removes leading spaces.
MEMLINES()	Number of lines in a memo field.

MLINE()	Number of a line in a memo field.
OEM() (new)	Converts to OEM characters from ANSI.
PROPER()	Capitalizes first letter only of each word.
RAT()	Reverse AT(); position of one string in another starting at the right end.
REPLICATE()	Returns a string of copies of a character.
RIGHT()	Rightmost portion of a string.
RTRIM()	Removes trailing spaces; same as TRIM().
SOUNDEX()	Returns a code based on sound.
SPACE()	Creates a string of spaces.
STUFF()	Replaces characters in a string.
SUBSTR()	Returns a portion of a string.
TRIM()	Removes trailing spaces.
UPPER()	Converts to uppercase.

Obtaining and Converting Data Types

ASC()	Returns ASCII numeric value of a character.
BINTYPE() (new)	Returns type of data in binary field.
CHR()	Returns character value of an ASCII number.
EMPTY()	Returns whether an expression is blank. Treats a zero numeric field or expression as blank.
FLOAT()	Converts type "N" number to type F.
ISALPHA()	Returns whether character is alphabetic.
ISBLANK()	Returns whether a field, variable or expression is blank. Same as EMPTY() except that ISBLANK() distinguishes between blank and zero values for numeric fields and expressions.
STR()	Converts a number to a character string.
TRANSFORM()	Converts a value to a formatted string.

TYPE()	Returns data type of an expression.
VAL()	Converts characters to numeric value.

Using the Date and Time

CDOW()	Returns name of the day of the week.
CMONTH()	Returns name of the month.
CTOD()	Converts characters to date.
DATE()	Returns the system date.
DAY()	Returns number of the day of the month.
DMY()	Formats date as characters, day first.
DOW()	Returns day of the week as a number.
DTOC()	Converts date to characters for display.
DTOS()	Converts date to characters for indexing.
ELAPSED() (new)	Measures seconds between two times.
MDY()	Formats date as characters, month first.
MONTH()	Returns number of the month.
SECONDS() (new)	Returns seconds since midnight.
TIME()	Returns system time.
YEAR()	Returns number of the year.

Managing Arrays

ACOPY() (new)	Copies elements of an array.
ADEL() (new)	Deletes values from a row or column of array.
ADIR() (new)	Records directory information in array.
AELEMENT() (new)	Converts row and column to element number.
AFIELDS() (new)	Copies table structure to an array.
AFILL() (new)	Fills one or more elements of an array with a value.

AGROW() (new)	Adds a row or column to an array.
AINS() (new)	Inserts a row or column in an array.
ALEN() (new)	Returns rows, columns or elements of array.
ARESIZE() (new)	Resizes an array.
ASCAN() (new)	Searches array for a value.
ASORT() (new)	Sorts an array
ASUBSCRIPT() (new)	Converts element number to row or column subscript.
DECLARE	Creates an array.

The Outside World

The final group contains the commands you need to deal with the system hardware, the operating system, non-dBASE local files, and external systems including networks and remote databases.

Knowing and Using the System Hardware

CHOOSEPRINTER() (new)	Opens the Printer dialog box.
DISKSPACE()	Returns the amount of free disk space.
FKLABEL()	Returns the name of a programmable key.
FKMAX()	Returns the number of programmable keys.
ISCOLOR()	Returns whether the system display adapter supports color.
ISMOUSE()	Returns whether a mouse is installed.
MEMORY()	Returns the amount of system memory.
NETWORK()	Returns whether on a network.
PLAY SOUND (new)	Plays a sound file on a system equipped for sound.
VALIDDRIVE() (new)	Returns whether the specified drive exists and can be read.

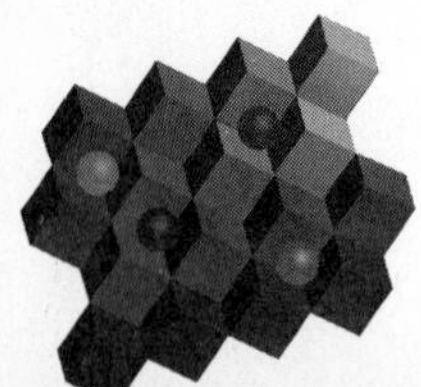

Using the Operating System

!	Calls the operating system command interpreter to run an external program.
DOS	Exits temporarily to the operating system.
GETENV()	Obtains a setting from the operating system environment.
OS()	Returns the name of the operating system.
QUIT	Terminates dBASE and returns to operating system.
RUN	Calls the operating system, same as !.
RUN()	Runs a command or Windows application.

Using Files and Directories

ADIR() (new)	Records directory information in array.
CD	Changes the directory to that specified.
COPY	Copies a file.
CREATE	Creates a file.
DIR	Lists contents of a directory.
DIRECTORY	Same as DIR.
ERASE	Erases a file.
FILE()	Returns whether a file exists.
FUNIQUE() (new)	Returns a file name not in use.
GETDIR() (new)	Opens the Directory dialog box.
HOME()	Returns the name of the path to the directory that contains the dBASE system files.
MD	Makes a new directory.
RENAME	Renames a file.
TYPE	Displays contents of a text file.

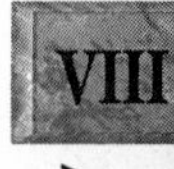

Using Files at Low Level

FCLOSE()	Closes a file.
FCREATE()	Creates and opens a file.
FDATE()	Returns the system date of a file.
FEOF()	Returns whether at end of a file.
FERROR()	Returns an error number.
FFLUSH()	Flushes buffer to disk.
FGETS()	Reads a line from a file.
FOPEN()	Opens an existing file.
FPUTS()	Writes a line to a file.
FREAD()	Reads bytes from a file.
FSEEK()	Moves file pointer.
FSIZE()	Returns system size of a file.
FTIME()	Returns system time of a file.
FWRITE()	Writes bytes to a file.

Networking

CHANGE()	Returns whether record has been changed.
CONVERT	Converts table for multiuser use.
FLOCK()	Attempts to lock a table.
ID()	Returns ID of user.
LKSYS()	Returns information on locked record.
LOCK()	Same as RLOCK(), attempts to lock records.
REFRESH	Reloads table data from disk to buffer.
RLOCK()	Attempts to lock one or more records.
UNLOCK	Unlocks a table or all its records.

Reaching Out for Data

BEGINTRANS() (new)	Begins a transaction using server data.
COMMIT() (new)	Ends a transaction using server data.
DATABASE() (new)	Returns the name of the current database.
DBERROR() (new)	Returns the number of a database error.
DBMESSAGE() (new)	Returns the message of a database error.
ISTABLE() (new)	Reports whether a table exists in database.
OPEN DATABASE (new)	Opens a database, usually on a server.
ROLLBACK()	Ends a transaction without saving it.
SQLERROR() (new)	Returns the number of a server error.
SQLEXEC() (new)	Executes an SQL command.
SQLMESSAGE() (new)	Returns a server error message.

Commands and Functions in Alphabetical Order

This section presents the dBASE for Windows commands and built-in functions in alphabetical (ASCII sorting) order. Each is followed by a syntax paradigm which describes its syntax, with an explanation and often by one or more examples.

Symbols and Abbreviations Used in Syntax Paradigms

The following syntax paradigms are often written on more than one line for clarity. If dBASE statements of the described syntax occupy more than one physical line, each physical line before the last must end with a semicolon. Semicolons are NOT included in the syntax paradigms at the end of each printed line.

Key words to be included literally are printed in UPPERCASE.

Square brackets "[]" are used for three purposes. If they follow the name of an array, you should include them literally to delimit the index expression or expressions that identify the element of the array. dBASE permits the use of square brackets in place of quotation marks as string delimiters, but this reference does not use them as such. In other contexts, square brackets delimit clauses whose inclusion is optional to the syntax. When used with a variable type followed by an equal sign before the syntax paradigm of a function, the included matter is not strictly part of the syntax at all, but indicates the type of value the function returns.

Parentheses following the name of a function are to be included literally and delimit the parameter list to the function.

The vertical bar "|" is a metasymbol, not part of the syntax. It is used to separate alternatives and indicates that any one might be included in the statement. The set of alternatives may be delimited by square brackets [ ] indicating that it is acceptable to include none of the alternatives.

Curly braces "{}" are not part of the syntax. They are included to group elements to make it clear which elements are part of a particular optional or alternative selection, or in certain syntax paradigms involving arrays, to delimit those square braces that are part of the required syntax rather than delimiters of optional parameters.

Angle brackets "<>" are used, (with one exception, see #include) to delimit placeholders indicating that you must include an element of the type signified by the placeholder in the statement. If the placeholder is further delimited by square brackets, inclusion of an element of the signified type is optional.

Placeholders in all lowercase are primarily used to identify the nature of the item to be included. Three placeholders in all lowercase are used to indicate omitted material, as follows:

<etc> — Indicates that the preceding syntactical element might be repeated one or more times, usually limited only by the limit on the length of statements.

<more> — Indicates that the syntax expression itself has been left incomplete with one or more elements omitted. The omitted elements are described later in the entry for the command or function.

<code> — Indicates that code statements of undefined type and number are included between the enclosing statements.

Placeholders in mixed case are used to identify the type of element that must be included in the statement. If the first letter is uppercase, the syntax requires the name of an item of that type, such as <File> for a file. Inclusion of "List" within the angle brackets implies that the syntax allows one or more than one item of the type, separated by commas if there are more than one.

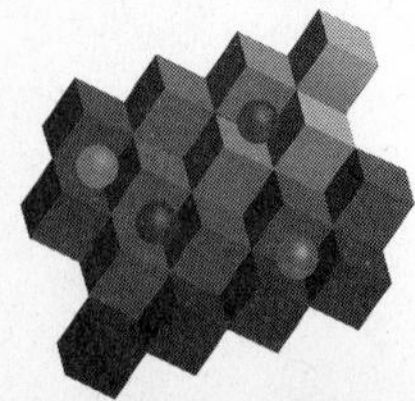

If the first letter is lowercase, it identifies the data type of the element, as listed in table A.1. The data type of a literal is the type of data the characters represent. The data type of an expression is the type of the result of the expression. The data type of a field or variable is the type of data held in the field or variable.

Table A.1
Initial Letters of Mixed-Case Syntax Placeholders

Initial letter	Signifies the element
d	date type
f	float type
k	a bookmark
l	logical type
m	memo type
n	numeric type
x	any of several or all types

Unless otherwise stated, the "n" type in the syntax paradigms includes the "f" type, and commands and functions that both use and return numeric or float types return values of the same type, "n" or "f", as the parameter.

The following three letters of each element might be one of the combinations in table A.2.

Table A.2
Letters 2-4 of Mixed-Case Syntax Placeholders

Letters	Signify
Ltr	element must be included literally
Exp	element must be an expression
Fld	element must name a field of an active table
Var	element must name a defined memory variable.

Where an element is required literally, it must be in one of the forms listed below, as appropriate to its data type:

- ✔ If character type, a string of one or more characters without delimiters or a ¯o expanding to such a character string
- ✔ If date type, a date in curly braces such as {01/01/94}
- ✔ If numeric or float type, a number in standard (-5) or scientific (23.65E-15) notation
- ✔ If logical type, .T. or .F.

Where an expression of a certain type is required, it must (unless otherwise stated in the explanation) be one of the following:

- ✔ If character type, a string delimited by single or double quotation marks or square brackets containing zero or more characters, including the curly-brace-delimited special characters listed under the ??? command
- ✔ If date, numeric, float or logical type, a literal of the required type
- ✔ For any type, the name of a field of an active file, or of a defined memory variable, of the required type.
- ✔ For any type, an expression of any complexity (except as limited by the expression evaluator) resolving to a value of the required type.

Wherever a command or function accepts a numeric expression, but requires an integer, such as space(<nExp>), any fractional part of the result of the numeric expression will be disregarded.

Any additional characters in a placeholder are descriptive of its nature or function and have no syntactical significance.

Three terms that appear frequently in syntax paradigms are shorthand references:

<scope> means a scoping expression limiting the records of a table which the command will process, among the following:

RECORD <number>	The numbered single record.
NEXT <number>	The indicated number of records, beginning with the current record, in natural or indexed order.
ALL	All records in the table.
REST	All records in the table from the current record to the end.

<skeleton> means a file or field skeleton, a name, and extension in the case of a file skeleton, that may contain one or more of the DOS wild-card characters "?" and "*". The question mark substitutes for any single character and the asterisk for any one or more characters. A file skeleton is treated as two parts, the name and the extension, with an asterisk in one part affecting that part only.

<workarea> means a work area in which a table is active. A work area can be specified by an expression which resolves to the work area number, from 1 to 225, to one of the letters A-J or to the alias of the table. If given literally, the letter or alias must be delimited with quotation marks or brackets.

For the first two examples of syntax paradigms, assume cLastname = "Smith". No other variables are defined. There is no key field with the value "cLastname".

Syntax:

```
FIND {<xLtr>|"<xLtr>"}
```

Examples:

```
find Smith            && is OK, a literal
find "Smith"          && also OK; "<xLtr>" works
find cLastname        && .not. found()
find &cLastname       && is OK, &macro is a literal
```

Syntax:

```
SEEK <xExp>
```

Examples:

```
seek Smith            && variable not found error
seek "Smith"          && OK, this is an expression
seek cLastname        && variable is an expression
seek &cLastname       && variable not found error
```

The first syntax paradigm indicates that FIND must be followed by one but only one of two elements, a literal value or a literal in quotation marks. The second shows that SEEK must be followed by an expression resolving to any data type. Here is an additional example of a syntax paradigm:

Syntax:

```
@ <nExpRow>, <nExpCol>
[[SAY <xExp> [<more>]]
 [GET {<xVar>|<xFld>} [<more>]]
 [COLOR [<standard>[,<enhanced>]]]|
<more>]
```

The "@" sign must be followed by two expressions resolving to numeric values, separated by a comma. They represent the row and column. Details such as limitations on these values by range will be explained later in the description of the command or function. The key word SAY followed by an expression of any type might, but need not, follow, and if included, might be followed by options not listed. The key word GET might, but need not, follow. If included, it must be followed by the name of an existing memory variable or field of an active table of any type, and might be followed by options not listed. With or without SAY or GET, a COLOR clause might follow.

If, but only if, none of SAY, GET, or COLOR is included, other options not listed can be included.

Examples:

```
cName = space(10)
@ 5,10 SAY "Enter a name: " GET cName
read
@ row(), col() + 1
```

KEYBOARD "{Ctrl+Y}{13}"

An example of a function paradigm follows:

Syntax:

```
[fVar =] acos(<nExp[r]>)
```

This indicates that ACOS() takes a single parameter, a numeric expression. It returns a float-type value.

The dBASE Commands and Functions

!

Calls the DOS command interpreter.

Syntax:

```
! <command> [<parameter>[ <etc.>]]
```

The ! command invokes the DOS command interpreter to perform a single DOS command. <command> is the path, if necessary, and name of a DOS command, either an internal command such as rmdir or the name of a COM, EXE or BAT file.

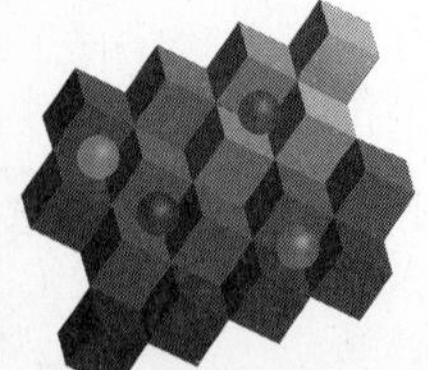

The optional one or more parameters are passed through to DOS as the command line tail, delimited by spaces, not commas. If you do not need to see the output of the DOS program, append >NUL to the end of the parameter list.

If you want to see the output but do not want a pause waiting for a keystroke when the DOS command is finished, issue KEYBOARD chr(13) before the ! command.

Example:

```
keyboard chr(13)
! copy *.DBF A: >NUL
```

The example copies all .dbf files to the disk in drive A: and returns with no pause or screen printing.

See DOS, RUN, RUN().

# #

New; begins one of the preprocessor directives listed:

#define

#else

#endif

#if

#ifdef

#ifndef

#include

#pragma

#undef

#define <defined term> [<value>] is used to create the defined status of <defined term> and optionally to give it a value. This can be for later use in conditional preprocessor constructs, or simply to eliminate hard-coding of constants. By convention, defined constants use all capital letters:

Syntax:

```
#define <defined term> [<value>]
```

Example:

```
#define PO_MAXWEIGHT 70
#define PO_MAXSIZE 108
```

```
     [<code>]
if Mailable(65,12,24,36)
     ? "This package may be mailed"
else
     ? "This package must be sent UPS"
endif

FUNCTION Mailable
      parameters nWeight,n1, n2, n3
      private nLong, nWide, nHigh
      if nWeight > PO_MAXWEIGHT
           RETURN .F.
      endif
      nLong = max(n1,n2)
      nWide = min(n1,n2)
      nHigh = min(nLong,n3)
      nLong = max(nLong,n3)
RETURN nLong + 2*(nWide + nHigh) <= PO_MAXSIZE
```

#else, #endif, #if, #ifdef and #ifndef are used to create preprocessor structures:

Syntax:

```
{#if <lExp1>|#ifdef <xLtr>|#ifndef <xLtr>}
<code>
[#else <code>]
#endif
```

The code, which can be dBASE code or other preprocessor directives, will be included (or not) in the compiled program accordingly. #if, #else and #endif have the same meanings as IF, ELSE, and ENDIF in dBASE, respectively. Unlike IF, ELSE, and ENDIF which cause a decision at runtime which program code to execute, these directives tell the preprocessor which code to compile into the compiled program.

The logical expressions used with #if must be of the form <identifier> = <value>, where the identifer has been defined and given a value in a #define statement. The preprocessor does simple text substitution. It cannot evaluate dBASE expressions such as OS() or ISCOLOR() to determine which code to compile. You might want to achieve a similar result, since omitting large blocks of irrelevant code from your compiled programs makes them smaller and faster. You must define an identifier and give it different values for each version you will compile:

Example:

```
#define OS 1
     [<code>]
```

```
#if OS = 2
     <code for OS/2>
#else
     <code for DOS>
#endif
```

The example compiles a version for DOS. By changing the #define statement in the program, you can cause compilation of an alternate version for OS/2.

#ifdef causes the statements between it and the closing #endif, or the #else if any, to be compiled only if the <xLtr> identifier has been defined with #define.

Syntax:

```
#ifdef <xLtr>
```

Example:

```
#ifdef MYAPI
     #include "Myapi.h"
#else
     #include "Winapi.h"
#endif
```

#ifndef is the opposite of #ifdef. It causes compilation if <xLtr> has not been defined, or if it has been undefined by the #undefine directive.

Example:

```
#ifndef WINDOWS_H
#define WINDOWS_H
     <code>
#endif
```

The foregoing example illustrates the code that appears in almost all header files to prevent including the file twice, which the compiler dislikes. The entire body of code in the file is within the #if . . . #endif structure.

#include is followed by a file name and causes the contents of the file—usually a header file containing declarations of external functions, definitions of constants, or both—to be included in the program before compilation. See the example above under #ifdef. The file name can be delimited by quotation marks as in the examples above or by angle brackets as <Myapi.h>. If quotation marks are used, dBASE looks for the file in the current directory, then in the include directory or directories specified in dBASEWIN.INI. If angle brackets are used, dBASE looks only in the specified include directory or directories.

#pragma introduces a compiler directive. At present, there is only one such compiler directive:

```
#pragma coverage (ON|OFF)
```

If you include this directive in a program with the on option, it notifies the compiler to create a coverage file whenever the program is run. This may be easier than remembering to SET COVERAGE ON before running the program. In the less likely event that you have SET COVERAGE ON by default, you can include the #pragma directive with the OFF option in your program to prevent creation of a coverage file.

See EXTERN, SET COVERAGE.

&&

Introduces comments and directs the compiler to ignore the remainder of the line.

Syntax:

```
[<statement>] && [<comment>] {[;
     <comment line>]}[<etc.>]
```

If the line ends with a semicolon, the compiler ignores the next line, and so on for all consecutive lines through the first line that does not end with a semicolon. If you need to include a string with two ampersands like that returned by SET("ATTRIBUTES") literally in a program, use chr(38)+chr(38) in place of &&.

Example:

```
set near off       &&     We want the closest;
                          match to the name
seek InputName
```

*

Introduces a line containing comments only.

Syntax:

```
* [<comment>][;
    <comment line>][<etc.>]
```

The asterisk directs the compiler to ignore the entire line and all consecutive lines through the first line that does not end with a semicolon. It is an alternative syntax to NOTE.

Example:

```
*******************************************
*     Program:  Primes.prg
*     Date:     01/03/94
*     Purpose:  This program calculates
*               prime numbers.
*******************************************
```

See &&, NOTE.

?

Causes output of a carriage return and line feed, followed by an optional expression list, to the current output streams.

Syntax:

```
? [<xExpList>][,]
where each expression is of the form:
<expression> [PICTURE <cExpPicture>]
[FUNCTION <cExpFunction>]
[STYLE [<appearance>][<font number>]]
[AT <nExp>]
```

This command is the principal way to print anything to the screen, printer, or alternate streams. The status of each stream is set by SET CONSOLE, SET PRINTER and SET ALTERNATE, respectively. Output will be sent to the screen if SET CONSOLE is ON, to the printer (or file or device specified by SET PRINTER TO) if SET PRINTER is ON and to the ALTERNATE file if SET ALTERNATE is on.

The expression list might be any number of expressions, delimited by commas, limited only by the maximum length of a statement.

The optional clauses must follow the expression to which they relate and precede the comma introducing a subsequent expression, but the optional clauses can be in any order among themselves.

If the ? or ?? command ends with a comma, only the first line will print. Subsequent lines of vertically-stretched expressions will be held and printed only when another ? command, a ?? command without a final comma, or an ENDPRINTJOB is executed. If an ON PAGE or ON ESCAPE occurs while portions of expressions are being held, any ? or ?? within the ON PAGE or ON ESCAPE routine will be ignored by the portions previously held. They will be output only after the ON PAGE or ON ESCAPE routine finishes, so that they will print after the page is turned or the ON ESCAPE warning has finished printing.

The optional clauses affect output as follows:

PICTURE <*c*ExpPicture>

The PICTURE clause formats the output. The most basic form is PICTURE with a clause containing a number of "X" characters such as "XXXX", which specifies that four characters only will be printed. If the data requires more, character fields will be truncated at the right and numeric data will display an overflow. The dollar sign and special symbols such as "DB" required by the function codes must have places provided in the picture template, if there is one.

The length of the picture template can exceed the field length, in which case the data will be left-justified (right-justified if numeric) except as affected by the alignment functions described below. Non-memo fields will be truncated if the length of the field exceeds the PICTURE length, regardless of whether the V function causes wrapping of the output to a shorter column width.

The following function and template codes can be used with the picture clause. If functions are used in a picture clause, the symbol "@" must immediately precede the first function code, any other function codes must follow it without spaces between them, and a space must follow the last function code but precede any template codes in the picture clause.

The function codes apply to the entire expression; the template codes only apply to the single position in the template in which the code appears.

Function codes:

!	Converts all lowercase letters to uppercase. When used with @ . . . GET, allows input of any character but converts as indicated.
$	For numeric data only (type N or F), displays it in currency format such as $nnnn.nn, without commas. The CURRENCY, POINT and SEPARATOR settings will affect the currency format displayed.
(	For numeric data only, encloses negative numbers in parentheses.
;	For character data only, causes text to wrap where a semicolon is encountered in the text. The semicolon in the text is not displayed.
A	For character data only, when used with @ . . . GET restricts input to alphabetic characters only.
B	For numeric data only, left-aligns it.

C	For numeric data only, displays CR after a positive number.
D	For dates only, displays date in current SET DATE format.
E	For dates only, displays date in European date format.
H	For memo data only, causes it to wrap, if wrap is .T., using the _lmargin and _rmargin settings.
I	For character data only, centers text.
J	For character data only, right-aligns text.
L	For numeric data only, displays leading zeroes.
M	When used with @ . . . GET, allows list of choices.
R	When used with character data, displays literal characters in the template. When used with @ . . . GET, does not save them to the field.
S<n>	Limits horizontal display width to <n> characters and scrolls characters within that width. <n> must be a positive integer.
T	Trims leading and trailing blanks before any alignment function (B, I, or J) is applied.
V<n>	Restricts display to a vertical column <n> characters wide. Text will wrap. Without the V function, memo fields will appear in the width set by SET MEMOWIDTH. V0 causes memo fields to display as seen in the editor and has no effect on nonmemo data. Stretching one expression vertically causes the next expression to print on the first line, starting by default in the column to the right of column <n> of the stretched expression.
X	For numeric data only, displays DB after a negative number.
Z	For numeric data only, displays zero as blank string. This affects display only and does not BLANK the field. See BLANK, ISBLANK().
^	For numeric data only, displays number in scientific notation.

Template codes:

!	Converts a lowercase letter to uppercase. When used with @ . . . GET, allows input of any character but converts as indicated.

#	When used with @ . . . GET, restricts input to digit, space, sign or SET POINT character.
*	For numeric data only, displays asterisk in place of a leading zero.
,	For numeric data only, marks thousands. The SET SEPARATOR character appears.
.	For numeric data only, marks decimal point. The SET POINT character appears.
9	When used with @ . . . GET, restricts input to digit, or sign for numeric data.
A	When used with @ . . . GET, restricts input to alphabetic character only.
L	When used with @ . . . GET, restricts input to T, F, Y or N. You may enter any of these in lower case. dBASE converts Y, y, T, and t to T, and N, n, F, and f to F.
N	When used with @ . . . GET, restricts input to alphabetic character, digit or underscore.
X	When used with @ . . . GET, allows input of any character. Otherwise, allows output of any character.
Y	When used with @ . . . GET, allows input of Y, y, N, or n. Converts y and n to uppercase.

FUNCTION <cExpFunction>

You can place any function codes allowed in a PICTURE clause in a FUNCTION clause instead, without the introductory @. Use a separate FUNCTION clause for the M function because the list of choices should follow the M and clutter a PICTURE clause. In addition, most of the PICTURE template options are irrelevant to, and the ! template symbol is overridden by, the M function. In other cases, using a FUNCTION clause instead of including any desired functions in the PICTURE clause is optional.

```
STYLE [<appearance>][<font number>]
```

The STYLE clause selects an appearance, font, or both for the output of the printer stream only. The font numbers can be 1 through 32,766 and correspond to the fonts and printer codes set in DBASEWIN.INI under [Fonts]. Appearances are one or more of the following:

B	Bold
I	Italic
L	Lowered/subscript
R	Raised/superscript
U	Underline

AT <nExp>

The AT clause specifies the column, from 0 to 255, at which output of the expression will start. You may include a fraction in the value of <nExp>. If the AT clause is omitted, the expression's output will start at the current print position. You may use the AT clause to create overstrike effects, for the printer stream only, by specifying a number less than the column of the current print position, setting _wrap to .F., and issuing the ?? command.

Example:

```
?     Salesrep picture "!XXXX",;
      Sales picture "@$ 999,999.99" at 8,;
      Notes function "V20" AT 20,;
      Lastsale function "D" AT 42
```

Assuming Salesrep is a character field, Sales is numeric, Notes is a memo field, and Lastsale is a date, the above will print the first 5 characters only of Salesrep, with the first character in uppercase and the others as held in the field. Assuming U.S. settings for CURRENCY, SEPARATOR, and POINT, Sales will print in a 10-character-wide field starting at column 8, with commas and with a dollar sign preceding the first digit. If the value is equal to or greater than $100,000, the dollar sign will not fit and will not print. If the value is equal to or greater than $1,000,000, a numeric overflow occurs and the value will print as asterisks. The value will be right-aligned in the field. Notes will be printed 20 columns wide extending down the page as required. The Lastsale date will be printed in SET DATE format on the first line starting at column 42. If an ON PAGE or ON ESCAPE occurs before the memo field Notes has finished printing, printing of Notes is suspended until any printing required by the ON PAGE or ON ESCAPE routines finishes.

See: ??, @.

??

Causes output of an expression list to the current output stream(s).

Syntax:

```
Same as ?
```

The ?? command is the same as ? except that no carriage return-line feed combination is output before the expression list. If the optional AT clause is omitted, the first expression will be printed on the same line as, and immediately following, whatever expression was last printed with a ? or ?? command.

See ?.

???

Causes output to the current printer stream bypassing the printer driver.

Syntax:

```
??? <cExp>
```

This command should not be used in dBASE to send data to a physical printer, because it might conflict with the Windows driver for the printer. The command is useful with SET PRINTER TO directed to a file to write a binary file, since unlike FWRITE(), it can write a series of nulls, chr(0), with a single statement.

<cExp> can contain the chr(<n>) value for any character except the left curly brace, where <n> is the ASCII decimal value of the character. <cExp> can as always contain several character expressions separated by + signs.

Each character expression can be of the CHR() form or can be an expression in quotation marks containing one or more instances of the following:

- ✔ Any printing character except the double quotation marks and the left curly brace.
- ✔ Any character delimited by curly braces, including {{} to specify the left curly brace.
- ✔ Any expression of the form {CTRL+#} where # is the capital letter whose order in the English alphabet equals the CHR() value to be output: "{CTRL+A}" = chr(1), "{CTRL+B}" = chr(2), and so forth.
- ✔ Any of the following:

{NULL}	= chr(0)
{CTRL+@}	= chr(0)
{BELL}	= chr(7)
{TAB}	= chr(9)

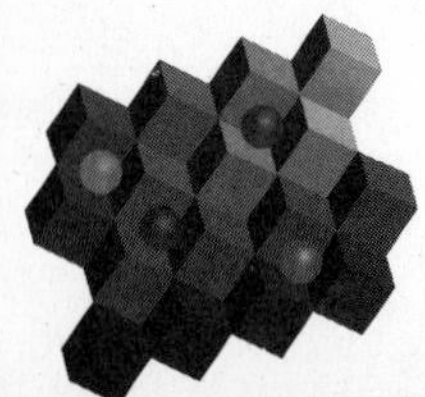

{LINEFEED} = chr(10)

{RETURN} = chr(13)

{ESC} = chr(27)

{ESCAPE} = chr(27)

{CTRL+[} = chr(27)

{CTRL+\} = chr(28)

{CTRL+]} = chr(29)

{CTRL+^} = chr(30)

{CTRL+_} = chr(31)

{DEL} = chr(127)

{DELETE} = chr(127)

Example:

```
(This creates an empty two-field .dbf table)
* describe fields of a two-field table
cFile = "Newfile.dbf"
nFields = 2
declare aFields[nFields, 4]
* field 1
aFields[1, 1] = "LASTNAME"        &&    name
aFields[1, 2] = "C"               &&    type
aFields[1, 3] = 12                &&    length
aFields[1, 4] = 0                 &&    decimals
* field 2
aFields[2, 1] = "SALARY"          &&    name
aFields[2, 2] = "N"               &&    type
aFields[2, 3] = 6                 &&    length
aFields[2, 4] = 0                 &&    decimals
* obtain memo flag, total field length
ndBFtype = 3               && dBASE III or IV file
nFldslen = 0
nMdx = 0
for nF = 1 to nFields
     if aFields[ nF, 2 ] = "M"
          ndBFtype = 139     && 1000 1011 in binary
     endif
     nFldslen = nFldslen + aFields[nF, 3]
```

```
next
* send output to a file
set printer to file &cFile.
??? chr(ndBFtype)
* file change date, today's date YMD
cYear = chr(year(date()) - 1900)
cMo   = chr(month(date()))
cDay  = chr(day(date()))
??? cYear+cMo+cDay
* number of records, none yet
* four different ways to send chr(0)
??? "{0}{NULL}{CTRL+@}" + chr(0)
* number of bytes in the header
nHeadbytes = 32 + (nFields * 32) + 1
nHeadLo = bitand(nHeadbytes, 255)
nHeadHi = bitrshift(nHeadbytes, 8)
??? chr(nHeadLo)+chr(nHeadHi)
* number of bytes in the record
nRecoLen = 1 + nFldslen
nRecLo = bitand(nRecoLen, 255)
nRecHi = bitrshift(nRecoLen, 8)
??? chr(nRecLo)+chr(nRecHi)
* 20 bytes not needed:
* 2 reserved, incomplete transaction flag,
* encryption flag, 12 more reserved for multiuser
* environment, production mdx flag, 3 more bytes
* of which one is the code page flag
for n = 1 to 20
     ??? chr(0)
next
*** field descriptors
for nF = 1 to nFields
     ??? aFields[nF, 1]
     * fill name to 11 chars with nulls
     for n = len(aFields[nF, 1]) to 10
          ??? chr(0)
     next
     * type and four reserved bytes
     ??? aFields[nF, 2]
     ??? chr(0) + chr(0) + chr(0) + chr(0)
     * length and decimals
     ??? chr(aFields[nF, 3])
     ??? chr(aFields[nF, 4])
```

```
        * 14 reserved bytes
        for n = 1 to 14
             ??? chr( 0 )
        next
   next
   * header terminator
   ??? "{RETURN}"
   set printer to
```

Directs full screen input and output.

Syntax:

```
@ <nExpRow>, <nExpCol>
[[SAY <xExp> [<more>]]
 [GET <xVar>|<xFld> [<more>]]
 [COLOR <ColorStandard>][,<ColorEnhanced]]|
<more>]
```

The @ command is the principal command used for screen forms and printing in dBASE III+ and for screen forms in dBASE IV. Its various options position the cursor, clear a portion of the screen, display output, accept input, draw boxes, and scroll the screen contents.

@ <nExpRow>,<nExpCol> positions the next output to the row given by <nExpRow> and the column given by <nExpCol>. Without more, it blanks the remainder of the row. To reposition output without blanking a line, use @ <nExpRow>,<nExpCol> SAY "".

The range of values of nExpCol is 0 to 79, and of nExpRow 0 to one less than the maximum number of rows indicated by the SET (DISPLAY) setting. Unless the Command Results window is maximized, the position specified might be beyond the right edge or bottom edge of the window, or both, making any text invisible. Using the scrollbars of the command window in an attempt to view the text is ineffective, as the position and any text remain fixed with respect to the upper left corner of the window.

@ <nExpRow>,<nExpCol> SAY <xExp> displays the value of the expression at the indicated row and column.

Syntax:

```
@ <more> SAY <xEpr>
[PICTURE <cExp>][FUNCTION <function list>]
[<more>]
[COLOR [<ColorStandard>][,<ColorEnhanced>]]
```

The PICTURE and FUNCTION clauses are identical to those described in connection with ?, except that V, H, and ; cannot be used with @. As indicated under ?, many of the PICTURE and FUNCTION options are applicable only to the GET option of @, not to the SAY portion.

The COLOR option is explained under GET.

@ <nExpRow>,<nExpCol> GET <xVar>|<xFld> displays an entry field. One or more GET fields can be active; a READ statement causes the cursor to move to the first, then to the others in turn, allowing input assigned to the variable <xVar> or to the field <xFld> as specified. <xVar> can be any type. <xFld> can be character, numeric, float, date, or logical, but not memo, binary, or OLE. A variable must be defined before it appears in a GET statement and a field must be in an active table. If the field is not in the current table, its name must be preceded by an alias.

Syntax:

```
@ <more> [<more>] GET <xVar>|<xFld>
[[OPEN] WINDOW <Window>]
[PICTURE <cExp1>][FUNCTION <function list>]
[RANGE [REQUIRED][<xExpLow>],[<xExpHigh>]]
[VALID [REQUIRED] <lExp1> [ERROR <cExp2>]]
[WHEN <lExp2>][DEFAULT <xExp>]
[MESSAGE <cExp3>]
[COLOR [<ColorStandard>][,<ColorEnhanced>]]
```

The PICTURE and FUNCTION options to @ . . . GET are given under the previous description of ? . As with @ . . . SAY, V,H and ; cannot be used.

[[OPEN] WINDOW <Window>] opens or uses a predefined edit window for memo fields.

[RANGE[REQUIRED] [<xExpLow>] , [<xExpHigh>]] sets a range of acceptable input. It is inapplicable where the GET field or variable is of logical type. Either the low limit or the high limit can be included without the other, but the comma is required. The REQUIRED option insists that the input be completed, not aborted by {Esc}.

[VALID[REQUIRED]<lExp> [ERROR cExp]] is like RANGE but accepts input only if the <lExp> condition is true. Otherwise, it displays the ERROR message. As with RANGE, the REQUIRED option forces the user to complete input. The VALID option is commonly used with the name of a user-defined function returning a logical value as <lExp>. This causes the function to be called after the user attempts input. It can perform validity checks of considerable complexity and accept or reject the input by returning .T. or .F.

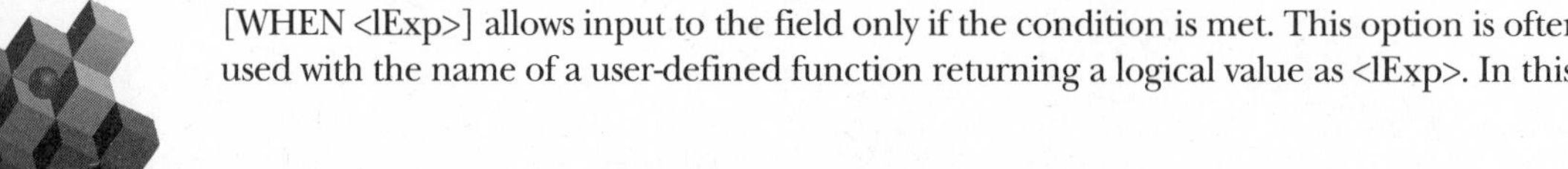

[WHEN <lExp>] allows input to the field only if the condition is met. This option is often used with the name of a user-defined function returning a logical value as <lExp>. In this

case, the function will be called before the user attempts input to the variable or field and might allow or disallow such input by returning .T. or .F.

[DEFAULT <xExp>], in a format file only, sets the default value of the GET variable or field.

[MESSAGE <cExp>] displays a message, on the bottom screen line or as specified by SET MESSAGE, when the cursor is placed on the GET field.

[COLOR [<standard>][,<enhanced>]] sets the colors for output of standard (SAY) and enhanced (GET) data. There can be only one COLOR clause following either or both of the SAY and GET clauses. The colors <standard> and <enhanced> are expressed as dBASE color codes such as W+/B for bright white on blue.

Example:

```
@ 4,15 GET m->Cust ;
PICTURE replicate("!", 10) ;
MESSAGE "Fill in the new Customer ID" ;
WHEN lIDNeeded ;
VALID .NOT. keymatch( m->Cust ) ;
     ERROR "That ID is a duplicate"
```

The above example will obtain input of a customer ID, rejecting ID numbers already contained in the active table ordered on ID numbers. If lIDNeeded is false, no input will be allowed. Up to 10 of any characters can be entered; letters will be forced to uppercase. The user can abort the edit by the {Esc} key because REQUIRED is omitted after VALID.

The options available with @ <nExpRow>,<nExpCol> when neither the SAY nor the GET option is included follow. The effect of all of them is limited to the Command Results Window or the active window if different.

Syntax:

```
@ <nExpRow1>,<nExpCol1>
  [CLEAR [TO <nExpRow2>,<nExpCol2>]|
   FILL TO <nExpRow2>,<nExpCol2> [COLOR <Color>]|
   TO <nExpRow2,<nExpCol2>
     {SCROLL [UP|DOWN|LEFT|RIGHT]
          [BY <nExpHowMany>][WRAP]}|
     {[DOUBLE|PANEL|<border>]
          [COLOR <Color>]}]
```

@ <nExpRow1>,<nExpCol1> CLEAR clears the Command Results Window from <nExpRow1>,<nExpCol1> to the bottom right corner. If the optional <nExpRow2>,<nExpCol2> are included, the clearing stops at the row and column designated by them.

@ <nExpRow1>,<nExpCol1> FILL TO <nExpRow2>,<nExpCol2> fills the region from <nExpRow1>,<nExpCol1> down and to the right to <nExpRow2>,<nExpCol2> with the colors specified in the COLOR option, preserving any text in the region but showing it in the new colors. If the COLOR option is omitted, it erases the region.

Example:

```
@ 3,6 fill to 14,49 color W+/B
```

@ <nExpRow1>,<nExpCol1> TO <nExpRow2>,<nExpCol2> SCROLL scrolls the contents of the described region in the direction given by [UP|DOWN|LEFT|RIGHT]. If no direction is given, the scroll is upward. If BY [<nExpHowmany>] is included, the scroll is by that number of rows or columns, otherwise by one row or column.

If WRAP is specified, text disappearing off one edge of the defined region appears at the opposite edge. By default, WRAP is off.

@ <nExpRow1>,<nExpCol1> TO <nExpRow2>,<nExpCol2> [DOUBLE|PANEL|<border>] [COLOR <Color>] draws a box on the active window. By default, the box is drawn with a single-line border of the NORMAL foreground color. DOUBLE creates a double-line border and PANEL a solid border, as if chr(219) were used for the border. <border> means a comma-delimited set of up to eight CHR() values, delimited characters or ASCII numbers. The set prescribes the characters to be used for the border in the following order:

Edges:	top, bottom, left, right
Corners:	top left, top right, bottom left, bottom right

Omitted border characters will leave that part of the border at its default value, except that specifying only one character will use it for the entire border. If commas as place-holders are omitted and the border set is of fewer than eight characters, dBASE assumes characters are omitted from the end of the set. See SET BORDER.

Example:

```
@ 2,5 TO 15,50 ,,,,"*","*","*","*" ;
     COLOR RG+/R
```

The above example draws a yellow-on-red single-line box with asterisks at the corners. The color of the interior of the box is undefined; it can be filled like the preceding example.

ABS()

Returns the absolute value of the given number.

Syntax:

```
[nVar=] abs(<nExp>)
```

The ABS() function takes a number and returns it unchanged if the number is zero or positive, otherwise returns the negative of the number.

Example:

```
? abs(-3.2)
       3.2
```

ACCEPT

Asks user for character input. Retained for compatibility and should not ordinarily be used under dBASE for Windows.

Syntax:

```
ACCEPT [<cExpPrompt>] TO <cVar>
```

The memory variable <cVar> need not exist, but will be created as character-type. Input is terminated with {Enter}; if {Enter} is pressed without other input, an empty string "" will be assigned to <cVar>. If SET ESCAPE is ON, pressing {Esc} in response to ACCEPT will cancel the program.

Example:

```
ACCEPT "Enter your last name: " TO cLast
```

See @ . . . GET, INPUT, SET ESCAPE.

ACCESS()

The ACCESS() function is not supported in dBASE for Windows.

ACOPY()

New; copies a number of elements from one array to another.

Syntax:

```
acopy(<ArraySource>,<ArrayDest>[,
<nExpSStart>,<nExpElements>[,<nExpDStart>]])
```

The two required parameters name the source and destination arrays. Without any optional parameters, if the destination array exists and has a sufficient number of elements, the entire source array is copied to the destination array. Copying is done as the elements are held in memory and as their numbers are returned by the AELEMENT() function—column after column of the first row then column after column of the next. If the arrays have different numbers of columns, the copying misaligns the elements.

Inclusion of the optional parameter <nExpSStart> causes the copying to start with the specified element of the source array. By default, copying starts with the first element.

Inclusion of <nExpElements> limits the copying to that number of elements. By default, copying is from the starting element to the end of the source array.

Inclusion of <nExpDStart> causes the first element copied to be copied to the specified element of the destination array. By default, the first element copied is copied to the first element of the target array.

If the destination array does not exist or has too few elements for the copy requested, an error occurs.

ACOS()

Returns a float value representing the angle in radians between 0 and π()/2 whose cosine is the numeric parameter. The parameter must be between -1 and 1 inclusive.

Syntax:

```
[fVar =] acos(nExpr)
```

Examples:

```
? rtod(acos(-.5))
    120.00
? type("acos(1)")
F
```

ACTIVATE

Causes activation of a previously defined menu, popup, or window, or of the entire Command Results window.

Syntax:

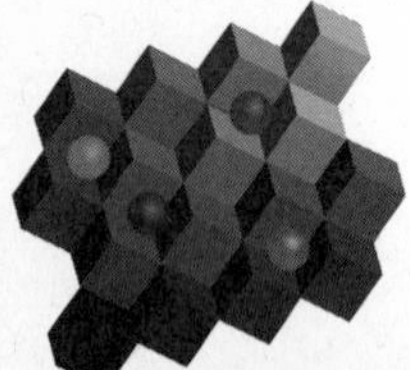

```
ACTIVATE {MENU <Menu> [PAD <Pad> ]}|{POPUP <Popup>}|SCREEN|{WINDOW
{<WindowList>|ALL}}
```

ACTIVATE MENU <Menu> activates the named menu, causing it to appear and allowing movement between its pads and selection of a pad or pad option. The optional PAD <Pad>, if used, places the cursor on the named pad.

ACTIVATE POPUP <Popup> activates the named Popup. The cursor is always placed on the first bar of the popup.

ACTIVATE SCREEN allows access to the full Command Results window for output, while a smaller window remains visible, to allow writing text outside the active window. If you want to restrict output to the smaller window after writing to the larger, issue another ACTIVATE WINDOW command. The ACTIVATE SCREEN option does the same thing you could accomplish by maximizing the Command Results window, defining a window the size of the entire screen and activating it, but with less memory usage and overhead.

ACTIVATE WINDOW {<Window>[,<etc.>]|ALL} allows the defined windows in the list, or all defined windows if the keyword ALL is used, to show in the Command Results window, and directs output to the last window in the list, or the last one defined. ACTIVATE WINDOW opens a window dBASE IV-style. All dBASE IV-style windows appear in the Command Results window.

While a menu, popup, or window is activated, all output is directed to it. This normally forces the user to make a choice, after which the menu, popup or window might or might not be deactivated.

See BAR(), CLEAR, DEACTIVATE, DEFINE, MENU(), ON, POPUP(), PROMPT(), RESTORE, SHOW.

ADEL()

New; deletes a row or column from an array.

Syntax:

```
[nVar =] adel(<Array>, <nExp1>[,<nExp2>])
```

The first parameter names the array. The second gives the number of the row to delete, or column if the third parameter is included and resolves to 2.

Including the third parameter when a row is intended or the array is one-dimensional does no harm if it resolves to 1; otherwise, an error occurs. ADEL() does not resize the array, but it moves all elements beyond the designated row or column up a row or left a column, filling all elements of the last row or column with the value .F. While the major effects of ADEL() are on the array, it does return the number 1.

Example:

```
declare MyArray[2,2]
MyArray[1,1] = "Roses"
MyArray[2,1] = "Red"
MyArray[1,2] = "Violets"
MyArray[2,2] = "Blue"
? adel(MyArray,1,2.5)  && delete #1 column
         1
? MyArray[2,1]
Blue
? MyArray[2,2]
.F.
```

See AGROW(), AINS().

ADIR()

New; stores file-directory information to an array, normally of five columns.

Syntax:

```
[nVar=] adir(<Array>[,<skeleton>[,<cExpAttributes>]])
```

The first parameter names the array. The array must be declared before the call to the function, but its size is immaterial as the function will make it two-dimensional and enlarge it if necessary, and trim off columns beyond the fifth. The optional second parameter resolves to the file skeleton sought, using the standard DOS ? and * wild-card characters. If it is omitted, the function stores all files, except as restricted by the third parameter. The optional third parameter, if supplied, restricts the files stored to those matching the attributes specified.

The function primarily affects the array by filling it with file information. It also returns the number of files found.

The <cExpAttributes> parameter is designed to hold one or more of the letters D, H, S and V, representing Directories, System files, Hidden files and Volume labels. If it is omitted, the function stores all files. If the parameter includes V but none of D, H, or S, in upper, or lowercase, the function stores the volume label in the first element of the array, which can be one- or two-dimensional. It ignores the extension of the second parameter, but if the second parameter specifies one or more characters of a file name, even the characters of the name of the volume, the function will fail to store anything.

If the <cExpAtrributes> parameter contains one or more of the characters H, D, and S, any V is ignored and the function stores all files matching any one or more of the H, D, and S attributes. If the D is included, the files stored include the . and .. directory entries for a subdirectory.

Storage for files other than the volume label is in five columns of the array, as follows:

cFilename nSize xDate cTime cAttributes

nSize is in bytes; it, xDate, and cTime are taken from the directory entry for the file and are the same as the similar items shown by the DOS DIR command. cAttributes includes one or more of the letters A for Archive, D for Directory, H for Hidden, R for Read-only, and S for System. These correspond to the bits of the attribute byte in the disk directory entry except for A. DOS sets the Archive bit to 1 whenever a file is changed and to 0 when it is backed up, to enable backing up only modified files. The dBASE ADIR() function returns the A attribute for all read-write files.

Example:

```
declare MyArray[1]
Attrib = "eve"
Skeleton = "*.db"
? adir(MyArray,Skeleton,Attrib)
         1
? MyArray[1]
MYHARDDISK


? adir(MyArray,Skeleton)
         3
? MyArray[1,1]
CUSTOMER.DB
? MyArray[1,2]
       4096
? MyArray[1,3]
05/19/94
? MyArray[1,4]
08:22:37
? MyArray[1,5]
.A...
```

The ADIR() function will remove extra columns (beyond five) from the array, unless storing a volume label when it removes nothing. It never removes rows from the array. Rows not needed to store files from the most recent call to ADIR() might remain filled with file information from previous calls. You should use the returned value from the function to determine the number of rows of the array that hold file information from the most recent call.

AELEMENT()

New; converts the usual row and column subscripts of an array element to its ordinal offset in the array.

Syntax:

```
[nVar=] Aelement(<Array>,<nExpRow>[,<nExpCol>])
```

The AELEMENT() function returns the row subscript, nExpRow, when called with a one-dimensional array. The third, nExpCol, parameter is the column subscript. It must be supplied when the array is two-dimensional and must be omitted when the array is one-dimensional, or an error occurs.

The function resolves each of the subscript expressions to its integral value, checks for either being out of range and, if both are in range, returns the number equal to (nExpRows - 1) * <number of columns in the array> + nExpCol[**s**]. This is the position number you can reach by counting across the columns, row by row, starting with the first element as #1.

Example:

```
declare MyA[a]rray[5,5]
? aelement(MyArray,4,3)
        18
```

AFIELDS()

New; resembles the COPY TO . . . STRUCTURE EXTENDED command in that it stores information on the structure of the table active in the current work area.

Syntax:

```
[nVar=] afields(<Array>)
```

The two differences are that AFIELDS() stores the information to a declared array and that it omits the fifth column/field stored by the STRUCTURE EXTENDED command, the FIELD_IDX value identifying whether or not the field is an index tag.

The function returns the number of fields (rows in the array) for which information has been stored. The function always stores four columns of information. It will enlarge but not reduce either array dimension, or redimension a one-dimensional array, as needed.

The four columns stored for each field are the field name, a character value, the field type, a letter, and the field length and decimals, both numeric. Fields of Paradox tables are stored in the types to which they would convert if the table were converted to dBASE.

The field type is one of the letters among B, C, D, F, G, L, M, and N, standing respectively for Binary, Character, Date, Float, General(OLE), Logical, Memo, and Numeric.

Example:

```
use ANIMALS
declare FieldArray[1]
? afields( FieldArray )
         5
? FieldArray[5,1]
BMP
? FieldArray[5,2]
B
? type(field(5))
B
```

AFILL()

New; fills one or more consecutive elements of an array with a specified value.

Syntax:

```
[nVar=] afill(<Array>,<xExp>[,<nExpStart>[,nExpCount]])
```

The AFILL() function returns the number of elements filled. The four parameters are the name of the array, the expression of which the value will be filled in, the optional starting element, and the optional count of elements to fill. If nExpStart is omitted, filling starts with the first element. If nExpCount is omitted, filling continues through all remaining elements of the array. The function inserts the value of xExp into each element, starting with nExpStart and proceeding across its row, then through each subsequent row, column by column, until nExpCount elements have been filled. If nExpCount is too large for the dimensions of the array, which occurs when- ever <nExpStart + nExpCount > <number of rows> * <number of columns> + 1, an error occurs.

To fill only certain columns of an array, set nExpStart to the number of the first column to fill, nExpCount to the number of the last column to fill less nExpStart, plus 1, and call the function once for each row of the array, incrementing nExpStart by the number of columns in the array on each iteration.

To calculate the value of nExpStart from its subscripts, use AELEMENT(). The following example fills the interior 16 elements of a 36-element array with "Fudge" and the outside 20 elements with "Chocolate", with the eventual result illustrated by the initials in the comments.

Example:

```
Declare MyArray[6,6]                        && CCCCCC
afill(MyArray,"Chocolate",1,36)             && CFFFFC
nStart = aelement(MyArray,2,2)              && CFFFFC
nCols = 5 - 2 + 1                           && CFFFFC
for nRow = 2 to 5                           && CFFFFC
     afill(MyArray,"Fudge",nStart,nCols)    && CCCCCC
     nStart=nStart+5
next
```

AGROW()

New; adds a row or column to an array.

Syntax:

```
[nVar=] agrow(<Array>,<nExp>)
```

The <nExp> parameter must be 1 to add a row or 2 to add a column.

The AGROW() function adds a row or column to the array, returning the number of elements added. If <nExp> is 1 and the array is one-dimensional, one element is added. The newly-added element, row, or column is filled with the value .F.

Example:

```
declare Myarray[2,2]
Myarray[1,1] = "Here"
Myarray[1,2] = "We"
Myarray[2,1] = "Go"
Myarray[2,2] = "aBerrying"
? agrow( Myarray,2 )
         2
? Myarray[1,3]
.F.
? Myarray[2,2]
See AELEMENT(), AINS().
```

AINS()

New; inserts a row or column of .F. values into an array, moving the following rows down or columns over by one.

Syntax:

```
[nVar=] ains(<Array>,<nExp1>[,<nExp2>])
```

The values

```
declare MyArray[4]
cChars = "My Pop goes weasel hunting every October"
for n = 1 to 4
..... MyArray[n]=substr(cChars, at(" ",cChars,n)+1,n+3)
next
ains(MyArray,3,1)
afill(MyArray,"the ",3,1)
? MyArray[1]+MyArray[2]+MyArray[3]+MyArray[4]
Pop goes the weasel
```

ALEN()

New; returns the number of elements, rows or columns of an array.

Syntax:

```
[nVar=] alen(<Array>[,<nExp>])
```

The first parameter names the array. The second must resolve to 0, 1, or 2, or an error occurs. If the second parameter is 0 or omitted, the function returns the number of elements of the array, which is the number of rows for a one-dimensional array. If the second parameter resolves to 1, the function returns the number of rows. A second parameter of 2 returns the number of columns for a two-dimensional array or 0 for a one-dimensional array.

Example:

```
declare MyArray[4,6]
? alen(MyArray)
        24
? alen(Myarray,1)
        4
? alen(MyArray,2)
        6
```

ALIAS()

Returns the alias name for the specified work area, or the current work area. The work area can be specified by a letter from A through J, by a number from 1 through 225, or by a table name or alias.

Syntax:

```
[cVar=] alias([<workarea>])
```

Example:

```
? alias(2)
Customer
```

ANSI()

New; converts a character string from the OEM character set to the ANSI character set.

Syntax:

```
[cVar=] ansi(<cExp>)
```

The OEM character set is used by DOS and DOS applications, and is the one installed by DOS on your system. There are several OEM character sets, known as *code pages*, designed for different languages. Windows programs use an ANSI character set chosen from the International option of the Windows Control Panel, usually in the Main group of Window icons. They differ primarily in the high-order characters, especially those with CHR() values from 128 through 255. If you have dBASE data saved as OEM characters, you can continue to use your data with an OEM language driver. If you decide to use an ANSI language driver, you will have to use the ANSI() function to convert your data to the characters of the appropriate set. The ANSI() function is the opposite of OEM().

Example:

```
? chr(132),ansi(chr(132))
```

The former expression prints an "a" with two dots (an *umlaut*) over it for use in German and similar languages. The latter prints the Greek letter sigma.

APPEND

Has a new option, AUTOMEM. Append allows adding data to a table.

Syntax:

```
APPEND [AUTOMEM|BLANK|
   {FROM {<File>|?|<skeleton}
    [[TYPE]{SDF|
PARADOX|DBASE|
{DELIMITED [WITH {<cLtrChar>|BLANK}]}]
     [POSITION][REINDEX][FOR <lExpCond1>]}|
   {FROM ARRAY <Array>[REINDEX]
    [FOR <lExpCond2>]}|
   {MEMO <mFld> FROM <File>[OVERWRITE]}]
```

Used alone, APPEND adds a record to the end of the active table and brings up the record for edit. If you terminate the edit by pressing the Esc key while in the first field, the empty record is deleted. If the edit is otherwise terminated, the new record remains.

APPEND AUTOMEM adds a blank record and fills it from the AUTOMEM variables, variables of the same name as the fields of the table. You first must have assigned values to the AUTOMEM variables or the effect will be the same as APPEND BLANK.

APPEND BLANK adds a blank record. This is the standard technique used in programming in dBASE for DOS to extend a table. The command is followed by a REPLACE of the various fields with appropriate values. In dBASE for Windows, APPEND AUTOMEM provides an alternate method of adding a record.

APPEND FROM {<File>|?|<skeleton>} appends records to a table from a file that might, but need not be, a dBASE or Paradox table. If the file appended from is such a table, it must not be open in dBASE. If the ? or <skeleton> options are used, dBASE opens the File dialog box.

The TYPE option tells dBASE how to append non-table files. The word TYPE is optional. The following types are supported:

SDF	System Data File of fixed-length fields, with no delimiters between fields but a CR/LF pair ending each record. The dBASE target table fields must match those of the source file in length. dBASE assumes a TXT extension if none is stated.
PARADOX	Paradox table. Extension DB assumed.
DBASE	dBASE table. Extension DBF assumed.

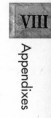

DELIMITED	A text file. Extension TXT assumed. Without more, dBASE expects the file to have its records delimited with commas, its fields separated by CR/LF pairs and all character data enclosed in double quotation marks. The WITH <cLtrChar> option specifies the character given by <cLtrChar> instead of quotation marks as the character-data delimiter. The BLANK option specifies that the fields are separated by single spaces rather than by commas.

When importing from DELIMITED files, dBASE imports data delimited by quotation marks to character fields, dates in YYYYMMDD format to date fields, data consisting of the character T or F to logical fields, and numbers to numeric fields.

The PARADOX and DBASE type keywords are optional. You can specify the file extension in the command, overriding the default extension for which dBASE would otherwise look.

The POSITION option applies to dBASE and Paradox tables. These are normally imported by field name, with only fields whose names match those of the target table added. Each field will be truncated, or contain blanks, as required by the difference between the size of the field in the source table and the size it must adapt itself to in the field of the same name in the target table. The POSITION option tells dBASE to ignore the field names and import the fields in position order. When you use the POSITION option, the data from the second field of the source file will be added to the second field of the target file and be converted to that field's length and type.

REINDEX tells dBASE to postpone reindexing the target table until all records have been appended, and can speed performance. All open indexes are updated in any event, either immediately on the append of each record if REINDEX is not used or when all records have been appended.

The FOR option also applies only to dBASE and Paradox tables. A record is added only if the resulting record in the target table satisfies the condition. The SET DELETED setting and DELETED() state often cause trouble. The rule is that SET DELETED governs which records in the source table will be added, but in the target table no records added will be marked as DELETED() regardless of their state in the source table. Since the resulting record will never be DELETED(), APPEND FROM <tablename> FOR DELETED() does not do what you expect. It adds all records if SET DELETED is off.

To add only the records not marked DELETED() in the source table, SET DELETED ON before appending. To add only the records that are marked DELETED() in the source table, SET DELETED OFF and use COPY TO <filename> FOR DELETED() to copy them to a temporary table. USE the temporary table, RECALL ALL to undelete them and APPEND FROM the temporary table. Similarly, conditions that test states in the source table that cannot apply in the target table will fail to achieve the desired result, such as conditions based on RECNO(), RECCOUNT(), EOF() and the like.

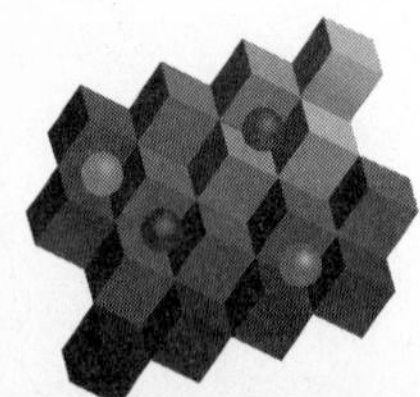

APPEND FROM ARRAY adds one or more records, as many as the rows of the array, and fills the fields of each record left to right from the columns of that row of the array. The filling of fields stops with the last column of the array or the last field of the table, whichever comes first, and will leave empty fields or unused array data if the number of columns does not match the number of fields. A memo field cannot be filled from an array. If a memo field exists as, for example, field 2, the data from column 2 of the array will be used to fill field 3 and so forth. The array must be declared and filled with data before you give the APPEND FROM ARRAY command.

The table is always indexed immediately on the controlling index. If the REINDEX option is omitted, it will also be immediately reindexed on all open noncontrolling indexes. Including the REINDEX option causes reindexing on the noncontrolling indexes to wait until all records are appended, which can speed performance. In a multiuser environment, you can use REINDEX only if the table is opened for exclusive use.

Including the FOR <lExpCond2> option of APPEND FROM ARRAY tests the condition against the new record. If the condition is false, .F., that row of array data is skipped. To test a column of array data, use in the condition the name of the field into which that column's data will go, not the column number itself.

Example:

```
declare NewArray[2,4]
NewArray[1,1]="White Oak"
NewArray[1,2]="temperate"
NewArray[1,3]="moist"
NewArray[1,4]="deciduous"
NewArray[2,1]="Casuarina"
NewArray[2,2]="tropical"
NewArray[2,3]="moist"
NewArray[2,4]="evergreen"
use Trees
display
SPECIES   CLIMATE  HUMIDITY LEAVES    NOTES

append from array NewArray for Climate="tropical"
    1 record added
display
SPECIES   CLIMATE  HUMIDITY LEAVES    NOTES
Casuarina tropical moist    evergreen memo
```

APPEND MEMO reads a file into a named memo field in the current record. If the OVERWRITE option is used, the contents of the file replaces the contents of the memo field. Otherwise, the file contents are appended to the existing contents of the field. If no file extension is specified, dBASE looks for a file with extension TXT.

Example:

```
<continuing the example above>
append memo Notes from CASUARIN.NB overwrite
display
SPECIES    CLIMATE  HUMIDITY LEAVES    NOTES
Casuarina tropical moist    evergreen MEMO
```

The dBASE IV NOORGANIZE option of APPEND is not supported.

See COPY, IMPORT.

ARESIZE()

New; resizes an array to the dimensions given.

Syntax:

```
[nVar=] aresize(<Array>,<nExpNewRows>[,<nExpNewCols>
          [,<nExpRetain>]])
```

The ARESIZE() function adds or subtracts one or more rows or columns to or from an array. The required <nExpNewRows> parameter specifies the new number of rows, or elements of a one-dimensional array. For a two-dimensional array if <nExpCols> is not given, it adds or subtracts rows and fills new rows with .F.

If the <nExpNewCols> parameter is given, it specifies the new number of columns. To change a two-dimensional array to one dimensional, make <nExpNewCols> 0. A <nExpNewCols> value of 1 creates a doubly-subscripted array with only one column, with subscripts such as [1,1] and [2,1].

The <nExpRetain> parameter determines what happens to the values that the array contained before the resize. If <nExpRetain> is omitted or has the value 0 or less, dBASE places the existing values in the new array so they will retain their element numbers as returned by AELEMENT(). Elements from the beginning of one row will become elements at the end of the preceding row as needed to fill the new column or columns, and all succeeding elements will be shifted over accordingly. All elements with AELEMENT() values that did not exist before the resize will be filled with .F. If the resized array had fewer elements than the original array, the values of elements with AELEMENT() values that do not exist in the resized array are lost.

If <nExpRetain> is supplied with a value greater than 0, the existing values will retain the row and column positions they had before the resize. All elements of added rows and columns will be .F.; values of elements in deleted rows or columns will be lost.

ASC()

Returns the ASCII value, in decimal, of the first character of the evaluated parameter, which must be character type.

Syntax:

```
[nVar=] asc(<cExp>)
```

Example:

```
? asc(upper(Lastname))
```

ASCAN()

New; scans the specified elements of an array for a value equal to the result of the given expression.

Syntax:

```
[nVar=] ascan(<Array>,<xExp>[,<nExpStart>[,<nExpCount>]])
```

ASCAN() returns the element number in the array of the match to the value of <xExp> if found, otherwise 0. The optional parameters <nExpStart> and <nExpCount> specify the starting element of the search and the number of elements to search. They default to 1 and all remaining elements respectively. A <nExpCount> value that causes <nExpStart> + <nExpCount> to exceed the number of elements plus 1 creates an error. Searches for character expressions follow the rules established by the SET EXACT setting.

Example:

```
declare MyArray[3]
MyArray[1] = "Income Taxes"
MyArray[2] = {04/15/94}
MyArray[3] = 1350.96
? ascan(MyArray,{12/31/93}+105,1,3)
         2
set exact on
? ascan(MyArray,"I")
         0
set exact off
? ascan(MyArray,"I")
         1
```

ASIN()

Returns a float value representing the angle in radians between -π()/4 and +π()/4 whose sine is the numerical parameter, which must be between -1 and 1 inclusive.

Syntax:

```
[fVar=] asin(nExp[r])
```

Example:

```
? rtod(asin(-.5))
        30.00
```

ASORT()

New; sorts the rows or elements of an array.

Syntax:

```
[nVar=] asort(<Array>[,<nExpStart>,[<nExpCount>[,<nExpDirection>]]])
```

ASORT() returns 1 if successful, or 0. The first and only required parameter is the array name. The three optional parameters are <nExpStart>, the AELEMENT() number of the starting element, <nExpCount>, the number of rows to sort, and <nExpDirection>, the direction of the sort. The defaults for <nExpStart> and <nExpCount> are 1 and all remaining rows respectively. Values for <nExpDirection> are either 0 for ascending, the default, or 1 for descending.

As with other array functions what counts is the integral part of the result of each numeric expression. Expressions resulting in values out of range create errors.

With a one-dimensional array, each row consists of only one element, so ASORT() effectively puts all elements of the sorted range in order. With a two-dimensional array, each row is sorted on the column of the starting element. All columns of each row are moved together to the new row dictated by the result of the sort.

The sort can be based on character (using the current language driver), numeric, date or logical data. In the last case, all .F. values are sorted to come before all .T. values in the default ascending order. If the data in the column being sorted are of different types, a dBASE error occurs.

Example:

```
declare MyArray[3,3]
MyArray[1,1]="Jefferson"
MyArray[1,2]=1801
```

```
MyArray[1,3]=.T.
MyArray[2,1]="Adams"
MyArray[2,2]=1797
MyArray[2,3]=.F.
MyArray[3,1]="Washington"
MyArray[3,2]=1789
MyArray[3,3]=.T.
asort(MyArray,5,2,0)
? MyArray[1,1],MyArray[2,1],MyArray[3,1]
Jefferson  Washington Adams
```

ASSIST

The dBASE IV ASSIST command is not supported.

ASUBSCRIPT()

New; converts element number of an array element into its row or column number.

Syntax:

```
[nVar=] asubscript(<Array>,<nExpElement>,<nExpWhich>)
```

ASUBSCRIPT() returns the row or column number of the element <nExpElement> of the array. If <nExpWhich> evaluates to 1, as it must for a one-dimensional array, the function returns the row number. The row number is the same as nExpElement for a one-dimensional array. If <nExpWhich> evaluates to 2, the function returns the column number for a two dimensional array. Any other values of <nExpWhich>, or values of <nExpElement> beyond the number of elements, cause errors. ASUBSCRIPT() is the inverse of AELEMENT().

The formula used to convert an element to a row of a two-dimensional array is int((<nExpElement>-1)/<number of columns>)+1. To convert an element to a column, the formula is mod((<nExpElement>-1),<number of columns>)+1.

Example:

```
DECLARE MyArray[3,3]
? asubscript(MyArray,8,1)
        3
? asubscript(MyArray,8,2)
        2
```

See AELEMENT().

AT()

Returns the starting position of one character string within another or within a memo field.

Syntax:

```
[nVal=] at(<cExp1>,{<cExp2>|<mFld>}[,<nExp>])
```

The function returns the character position in the character string <cExp2> or the memo field <mFld> of the starting character of the first match to the character string <cExp1>. If the optional <nExp> is included, it counts occurrences of matches; the value returned is the character position of the starting character of the "nExpth" match. If no match, or fewer than <nExp> matches, are found, the function returns 0.

The setting of EXACT has no effect. All matches returned must match all the characters in cExp1. The search is case-sensitive.

Example:

```
Name = "Wilson, Albert W."
LastName = left(Name,at(",",Name)-1)
MidName = substr(Name,at(" ",Name,2)+1)
FirstName = substr(Name,len(LastName+2))
FirstName = left(FirstName,len(FirstName)-len(MidName)-1)
```

ATAN()

Returns a float equal to the number of radians in the angle between -π()/2 and π()/2 whose tangent is the given numeric expression, the inverse tangent or arctangent of the number.

Syntax:

```
[fVar=] atan(<nExpTangent>)
```

Example:

```
? rtod(atan(1))
      45.00
```

ATN2()

Returns a float equal to the number of radians in the angle whose SIN() and COSIN() are the given numeric expressions in the range from -1 to 1. This is the inverse tangent or arctangent of a point.

Syntax:

```
[fVar=] atn2(<nExpSin>,<nExpCosin>)
```

Example:

```
nSin = sin(dtor(60))
nCos = cos(dtor(60))
? rtod(atn2(nSin,nCos))
        60
```

This function differs from ATAN() in taking the sine and cosine as parameters instead of the tangent, which equals sine/cosine. This difference enables the function to return values in all four quadrants between PI() and -PI(). It also avoids divide-by-zero errors that ATAN() can cause. The values for <nExpSin> and <nExpCosin> cannot both be 0 or an overflow occurs.

AVERAGE

Computes the average, or arithmetic mean, of a set of numeric expressions over the defined scope of a file.

Syntax:

```
average [<nExpList>][<scope>][FOR<lExpCond1>]
     [WHILE<lExpCond2>][TO{<nVarList>|<Array>}]
```

If no numeric expressions are listed in <nExpList>, the command averages all numeric and float fields in the designated scope of the table. Otherwise, the expressions listed, which normally involve numeric or float fields of the table, are averaged.

The FOR and WHILE options can be used together without syntax error, but are mutually exclusive in practice. FOR restricts the command to records meeting the condition anywhere in the scope and is used when the table is not indexed on the field(s) of interest. WHILE assumes that the record pointer has been positioned to the first record of interest and that all records of interest are grouped following the first and meeting the same condition.

If the TO option is used with a list of variables, there should be as many variables as the number of expressions or fields being averaged, one to hold each result. If TO is used with an array, the array must be one-dimensional. The averages will be stored to as many array elements as needed, starting with the first.

Be careful with missing and BLANK values. If you are trying to average a set of numeric fields containing salaries, you can safely assume that any 0 values represent missing data. Use average for .not. isblank(Salary), or for Salary>0 which amounts to the same thing, to limit the divisor to the number of fields with positive salary values. If your fields contain numeric fields containing winter temperature observations expressed in degrees Fahrenheit or Celsius, there might well be observed temperatures of 0. If there are blank fields representing missing observations, you have a problem. Neither isblank() nor any other dBASE operation can distinguish the 0 values meaning 0 degrees from those meaning no data. All you can do is take care next time to include a field separate from the temperature field—perhaps a logical field that is set .T. when an observation is recorded—that will enable you to distinguish the absence of data in a record from the value 0.

Example:

```
<assumes a table containing numeric fields Price, Cost>
average Price, Cost, (Price-Cost)/Cost ;
     to m->Price, m->Cost, Markup ;
     for .not. isblank(Cost)
```

BAR()

Returns the number of the bar last selected from a pop-up menu.

Syntax:

```
[nVar=] bar()
```

The function returns 0 if there is no active pop-up menu or if selection was aborted by the Esc key. The function returns the same number used in DEFINE BAR if used, or the number of the line starting with the top line visible in the pop-up window. The BAR() value can be a number larger than the number of lines visible at one time if the user scrolls down to make the selection.

Example:

```
define popup NextMove from 5,10 to 15,23
define bar 1 of NextMove prompt "Buy"
<code>
on selection popup NextMove do NextProc
activate popup NextMove
 . . . .
PROCEDURE NextProc
     do case
          case bar() = 1
               do Buyproc
          <code>
     endcase
RETURN
```

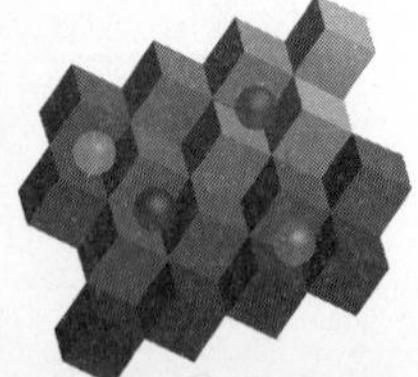

See ACTIVATE POPUP, DEACTIVATE POPUP, DEFINE POPUP, ON POPUP, ON SELECTION POPUP, PROMPT()

BARCOUNT()

Returns the number of bars in the active or a specified pop-up menu.

Syntax:

```
[nVar=] barcount([<cExpPopup>])
```

If the optional <cExpPopup> is provided, it names the pop-up menu for which the function is to return the number of bars. If it is omitted, the function returns the number of bars for the active popup. If there is no popup active or of the name supplied, the function returns 0.

The count returned includes bars defined with SKIP.

See BAR(), DEFINE BAR, SKIP.

BARPROMPT()

Returns the text from a specified bar of a pop-up menu.

Syntax:

```
[cVar=] barprompt(<nExpBar>[,<cExpPopup>])
```

The BARPROMPT() function returns the prompt text from the bar of the given number of the specified popup, or if the optional <cExpPopup> option is omitted, of the active popup. If no such bar or popup exists, it returns an empty string "".

Appendixes

Example:

```
use animals
define popup AniFields prompt fields
on selection popup Anifields do AniProc
activate popup Anifields
  <code>
PROCEDURE AniProc
? "You have chosen the field "+barprompt(bar())
RETURN
```

See also ACTIVATE POPUP, BAR(), DEFINE POPUP, ON SELECTION POPUP.

BEGIN TRANSACTION

Is not supported in dBASE for Windows.

See BEGINTRANS(), COMMIT().

BEGINTRANS()

Initiates a transaction and sets locks.

Syntax:

```
[lVar=] begintrans([<cExpDatabase>])
```

The BEGINTRANS() function begins a transaction, usually but not always involving data on a server. It returns .T. if it is able to set the necessary locks and initiate the transaction, otherwise .F.

If the optional <cExpDatabase> is supplied, it identifies the database on which the transaction is initiated and sets it to the current database. By default, the database specified in SET DATABASE TO is used.

All aspects of a transaction are held until a COMMIT() is issued, at which time the transaction ends and the changes are written to the database. To end a transaction without writing the changes, use ROLLBACK().

You cannot nest transactions, so you cannot call BEGINTRANS() a second time while the transaction initiated by the first call is pending. Beginning a transaction affects the following commands and functions, causing their results to be held until the transaction ends:

@ . . . GET

APPEND {MEMO|BINARY|BLANK|OLE}

BROWSE

DELETE

EDIT|CHANGE

FLOCK()

INSERT

RECALL

REPLACE (including REPLACE {MEMO|BINARY|OLE})

RLOCK()

You cannot use any command that would close open tables or indexes, or the following commands, while a transaction is pending:

BEGINTRANS()

CLEAR ALL

CLOSE {ALL|DATABASES|INDEXES}

CONVERT

CREATE FROM

DELETE TAG

MODIFY STRUCTURE

PACK

ZAP

See COMMIT(), ROLLBACK().

BINTYPE()

New; returns the predefined type number of a binary field.

Syntax:

```
[nVar=] bintype(<Field>)
```

Use BINTYPE() to determine what kind of data is referred to by a binary field. The data for a dBASE binary field is contained in the DBT associated with the table, in the same format as if in a file of the type indicated.

The type numbers for different formats are:

1 to 32,767	available for user definition
32,768	WAV
32,769	BMP
32,769	PCX

32,760	TIF
32,761	GIF
32,762	EPS

You should not use values over 32,762 for your file definitions; these are reserved for future dBASE use, up to 65,535.

The BINTYPE() function returns an error if a non-binary field is specified, or 0 if the specified binary field is empty.

BITAND()

Performs a bitwise AND on the bits of two operands.

Syntax:

```
[nVar=] bitand(<nExp1>,<nExp2>)
```

The BITAND() function compares the bits of the two parameters in binary and returns the number of which the binary equivalent has a 1 bit wherever both parameters have a 1 bit and a 0 bit wherever either parameter has a 0 bit. This is primarily required in assembling and interpreting constants when using external functions and the Windows API, but its use is not so restricted. Both parameters must resolve to integers in the range 0 to 2^{32-1}, 4,294,967,295; any excess or fractional part will be disregarded.

One use of BITAND() is to "mask" a value to ignore bits of no interest by performing a BITAND() using the the value and the sum of the bits of interest if set. The first byte of a dBASE table must contain "011", or 3, in its lowest three bits to avoid a "Not a dBASE table" error. The sum of the lowest three bits if set is 1 + 2 + 4 or 7.

Example:

```
nHandle = fopen("MYTABLE.DBF")
cVar = fread(nHandle,1)
if bitand(asc(cVar),7) # 3
     ? "Not a dBASE table"
endif
```

See BITLSHIFT(), BITOR(), BITRSHIFT(), BITSET(), BITXOR(), HTOI(), ITOH().

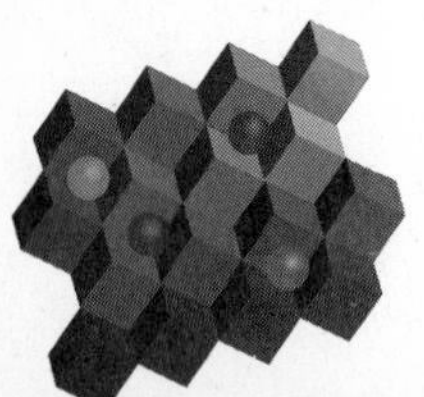

BITLSHIFT()

Returns the numeric value obtained by shifting the given numeric value left by the number of bits specified.

Syntax:

```
[nVar=] bitlshift(<nExp>,<nBits>)
```

The BITLSHIFT() function returns the value equivalent to <nExp> multiplied by $2^{<nBits>}$. It is designed for use with external functions and constants, but is not restricted to such use. The value shifted and the result are restricted to 32 bits, 2^{32}-1, with bits shifted off the high left end of the value being lost. The fractional part of <nExp> is disregarded.

Passing a negative number of <nBits> does not perform a BITRSHIFT(), it returns 0. If a negative value is passed as <nExp>, dBASE converts it to a four-byte signed long integer in binary, shifts that, and returns the result as a signed number, an operation with often meaningless results. Pass positive values only unless you are sure of what you are doing.

Some Windows API functions make use of color values in which the amounts of red, green, and blue, in the range 0-255 each, are packed into four bytes (a byte is eight bits). From high to low, the bytes hold 0 and the blue, green, and red values.

Example:

```
nBlue =  255
nGreen=    0
nRed  =  255
nColor=bitlshift(nBlue,16)+bitlshift(nGreen,8)+nRed
```

See BITAND(), BITOR(), BTRSHIFT(), BITSET(), BITXOR(), HTOI(), ITOH().

BITOR()

Performs a bitwise OR operation on two operands.

Syntax:

```
[nVar=] bitor(<nExp1>,<nExp2>)
```

A BITOR() operation compares the bits of the operands and returns the number of which the binary equivalent has a 1 bit wherever either of the parameters converted to binary has a 1 bit, and a 0 bit wherever both parameters have 0 bits. It is intended for use in combining symbolic constants for use with external functions, but is not so restricted. As with the other bit-manipulation functions, the numeric expressions will be converted to binary and any fractional parts, or bits beyond 32, will be disregarded. Both operands should be 0 or positive.

Example:

```
#include <WINAPI.H>
nAction = MessageBox(_app.framewin.hwnd, ;
          "Do you need help, Boss?", ;
          "You goofed", ;
          bitor( MB_OKCANCEL, MB_ICONQUESTION))
```

The definitions of MB_OKCANCEL and MB_ICONQUESTION, and the EXTERN statement for the MessageBox function, are in WINAPI.H. The example combines the MB_OKCANCEL and MB_ICONQUESTION constants by BITOR() and passes them to Windows. The resulting message box will contain pushbuttons "OK" and "Cancel" and a question mark icon.

BITRSHIFT()

Returns the numeric value given by shifting the given numeric value right by the number of bits specified.

Syntax:

```
[nVar=] bitrshift(<nExp>,<nBits>)
```

The BITRSHIFT() operation is the inverse of BITLSHIFT() and is the equivalent of performing a division of the <nExp> parameter by $2^{<nBits>}$, discarding any remainder. The shift is limited to 32 bits, with any excess of <nExp> being discarded before the shift is performed.

See BITAND(), BITLSHIFT(), BITOR(), BITSET(), BITXOR(), HTOI(), ITOH().

BITSET()

Returns .T. if the specified bit of a numeric expression is set (1), otherwise returns .F.

Syntax:

```
[lVar=] bitset(<nExp>,<nBitno>)
```

The BITSET() function tests a single bit of a numeric expression. The <nBitno> parameter must be an integer from 0 to 31 representing the position of the bit being tested, from 0 on the right to 31 on the left. The position of the bit is the same as the exponent of 2 that will result in the contribution of the bit, if set, to the numeric value, $2^0 = 1$ for bit 0, $2^1 = 2$ for bit 1 and so forth. Note that it is the position of the bit, not its value, that is given in <nBitno>—4 means bit 4, with a value of 2^4 or 16, not bit 2 with a value of 2^2 or 4.

Example:

```
nHandle = fopen("MYTABLE.DBF","R")
cVar = fread(nHandle,1)
if bitset(asc(cVar), 3)
     ? "The table has a .DBT memo file"
else
     ? "The table has no .DBT memo file"
endif
```

The example tests bit 3 of the first byte of the file header of a dBASE table, which is 1 if there is a DBT, 0 if there is not.

See BITAND(), BITLSHIFT(), BITOR(), BITRSHIFT(), BITXOR().

BITXOR()

Performs a bitwise "exclusive or" operation on two numeric operands.

Syntax:

```
[nVar=] bitxor(<nExp1>,<nExp2>)
```

The BITXOR() operation compares the bits of the operands converted to binary and returns the value of which the binary equivalent has a 1 bit where one and only one of the operands has a 1 bit. The returned value has a 0 bit wherever both or neither of the operands has a 1 bit. Like the other bitwise functions, it disregards fractional parts and bits beyond 32 and is intended to operate only on positive numeric values. The BITXOR() function is so named because it returns 1 for each bit in which the first operand or the second operand, but not both, has 1. It is included to round out the set of bitwise functions.

See BITAND(), BITLSHIFT(), BITOR(), BITRSHIFT(), BITSET().

BLANK

Sets one or more fields to an empty condition.

Syntax:

```
BLANK [FIELDS {<FieldList>|{LIKE|EXCEPT}<skeleton>}]
      [REINDEX][<scope>][FOR <lExpCond1>][WHILE <lExpCond2>]
```

The BLANK command returns fields to the state they had when the record was added by APPEND BLANK. This state is not always distinguishable from genuine data. Binary examination reveals that blanked numeric and logical fields contain spaces, unlike fields containing 0 or .F. However, dBASE evaluates blanked numeric and logical fields as 0 or .F. even when you use ISBLANK().

Empty character fields always appear blank and empty date fields as / /. Empty memo fields show up as "memo" in lowercase to full-screen commands such as BROWSE, EDIT and APPEND but as blanks when printed or STOREd. Empty numeric and float fields show as blanks in full-screen commands or to LIST|DISPLAY but as 0 in @ . . . SAY|GET, ? and STORE commands. Empty logical fields show as blanks in full-screen commands and @ . . . SAY|GET, but as .F. otherwise.

BLANK without parameters blanks all fields of the records in scope, except those made invisible by the SET FIELDS setting. The FIELDS option allows specifying a list of visible fields to be blanked, or to be excepted from blanking.

The controlling index is always updated after each record is BLANKed. If you issue REINDEX, updating the non-controlling active indexes is postponed until all records have been blanked. This might speed performance, particularly when large numbers of records are affected.

The FOR and WHILE options allow limiting the BLANK operation to those fields or records within the scope that meet the conditions specified.

Example:

```
blank fields Date, Amount all reindex for ;
 Date<{01/01/1990}
? Date
  / /
? Date <> date()
.F.
? Date = date()
.F.
? Amount
        0
? isblank(Amount)
.T.
? Amount = 0
.T.
```

As the example shows, the result of comparing blank dates to actual dates is always .F. Comparing blank numeric fields or logical fields to other such fields returns results as if the numeric or logical fields contained their default values of 0 or .F., respectively.

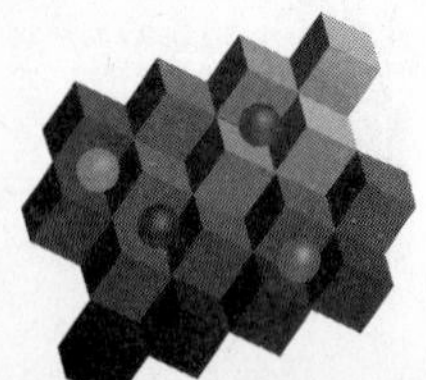

BOF()

Returns .T. when the record pointer is at the beginning of the file.

Syntax:

```
[lVar=] bof([<workarea>])
```

The optional <workarea> can be a work area number, character A-J in quotation marks, table name, or alias name.

The BOF() function is used to detect reaching the top-of-file, often in order to avoid errors from attempting to move the pointer farther up. It returns .F. when not at the top of the file ***or*** when called with no table in use. Although the RECNO() function returns one more than the RECCOUNT() value when the record pointer is at EOF(), it returns 1, not 0, when at BOF().

Example:

```
nKey = inkey(0)
do case
  case nKey = 5                  && up arrow
    if .not. bof()
      skip -1
    else
      ??? chr(7)
    endif
  <code>
endcase
```

BOOKMARK()

New; returns a bookmark for the current record of the current table.

Syntax:

```
kVar=] bookmark()
```

Bookmarks are primarily used for tables that do not have record numbers, although you can use them with dBASE tables. You must assign the BOOKMARK() to a variable to make use of it. The variable is of a special "BookMark" type, "BM" to the TYPE() function. Its value is hidden. If you attempt to print it, dBASE prints "BookMark". If you SKIP to another record or otherwise move the file pointer, save another bookmark for the second record and compare the bookmarks, they will return the relational results you would expect, but you cannot subtract them or otherwise convert them into numbers. You can use them to return to a record with GO or GOTO.

Example:

```
use CUSTOMER.DB type PARADOX
skip 10
kRec1 = bookmark()
? kRec1
BookMark
skip 2
kRec2 = bookmark()
? kRec2 > kRec1
.T.
GOTO kRec1
```

See GO|GOTO, SET DBTYPE, RECNO().

BROWSE

Opens a window showing the current table or view or a portion in spreadsheet-type format for edit, with records in rows and fields in columns.

Syntax:

```
BROWSE [<scope>][FOR <lExpCond1>][WHILE <lExpCond2>]
       [COLOR [<standard>][,[<enhanced>][,[<perimeter>]
               [,<background>]]]]
       [FORMAT][FREEZE <Fld1>][KEY <xExp1>[,<xExp2>][EXCLUDE]]
     ..[LOCK <nExp1>][NOAPPEND][NODELETE][NOEDIT|NOMODIFY]
       [NOFOLLOW][NOINIT][NOORGANIZE][NORMAL][NOTOGGLE][NOWAIT]
       [TITLE <cExp1>][WIDTH <nExp2>][WINDOW <window>]
       [FIELDS {<Fld2>|{<CalcFld> = xExp3>}[<optionlist]}[,<etc.>]]
```

BROWSE displays records in the order set by the controlling index. It displays fields, among those currently in view, in the order set by the view or by the FIELDS option. If no table or view is in use, BROWSE will prompt for a field name.

Used alone, BROWSE does the same thing as a double-click on the Navigator icon for the table or query and is retained for compatibility. Its options provide reasons to issue the command in the Command Window.

The <scope>, FOR and WHILE options perform in standard fashion to restrict the records visible for edit within the BROWSE.

The COLOR option permits you to set the colors for the standard, enhanced, perimeter, and background color areas. You must hold the place of each color area with a comma if you wish to omit its setting but include a setting for a color area later in the list. See SET COLOR TO for more information on colors and color areas.

FORMAT puts the named format file in use for the BROWSE instead of the default spreadsheet-like format.

FREEZE confines the cursor and any editing to the field specified by <Fld1> while allowing the other fields to display.

The KEY option requires that the table be indexed. Its <xExp1> parameter specifies the minimum value of the index key expression. The optional <xExp2> specifies the maximum. You cannot specify a maximum with no minimum. You can achieve the same result by setting <xExp1> to a value less than that of any actual key expression in the table. The optional EXCLUDE parameter directs that records with keys matching <xExp1>, and optionally <xExp2>, exactly be excluded from the BROWSE.

LOCK directs that <nExp1> fields on the left stay visible when you scroll to the right to bring other fields into view. <nExp1> must evaluate to a number from 0 to the number of fields in the BROWSE. This option is useful when the leftmost fields contain a name or other key needed to make sense of the remaining fields. If only ZIP Codes and telephone numbers are in view, it is difficult to be sure which ones go with whom.

NOAPPEND prevents adding new records. Without NOAPPEND, moving the cursor down off the last record brings up an option to APPEND additional records.

NODELETE prevents you from marking records for deletion, or from deleting them if the table is Paradox type.

NOEDIT|NOMODIFY (the keywords are equivalent) makes all fields read-only. You can still add records or mark them for deletion, but otherwise you are limited to examining them without changing them.

NOFOLLOW prevents the records from jumping around to their new order if the key field of an indexed table is edited. In a table indexed on name, for example, changing the spelling of "Felan" to "Phelan" without NOFOLLOW will cause the "F" records you are editing to disappear and the "Ph" records to be shown. This can be annoying when editing the records of a file in sequential order as it causes you to lose your place. Use the NOFOLLOW option in such a case.

NOINIT tells BROWSE to use the table and options from the previous BROWSE.

NOORGANIZE prevents indexing or sorting records and also, like NODELETE, prevents deleting them or marking them for deletion.

NORMAL applies to a BROWSE issued from an active dBASE IV-type window. It directs that the standard dBASE for Windows Table Records window be used for the BROWSE, with any COLOR settings respected. If NORMAL is omitted, the BROWSE appears in the active dBASE IV-type window in the colors of that window.

NOTOGGLE directs that the user may not use F2 to toggle from the BROWSE spreadsheet-like view to an EDIT view of a single record. By default, the user may toggle between the views.

NOWAIT directs that program execution continue even though the user has not closed the BROWSE window. It accomplishes the same thing as, but more than, the NOCLEAR browse option in dBASE IV, as it not only leaves the BROWSE on the screen but leaves it active.

TITLE directs that <cExp> appear as the title of the BROWSE window. By default, dBASE uses "Table Records" and the name of the table in parentheses as the title of a BROWSE window.

WINDOW <window> directs that the BROWSE appear in the specified dBASE IV-type <window>.

WIDTH sets the maximum width for all fields shown. It does not apply to memo or logical fields. Column headings and character data will be truncated. Other data such as numerics and dates that cannot fit in the specified width will not appear at all.

The FIELDS option allows specifying the fields to display, including calculated fields. It is followed by a list of the fields to display, with each field optionally followed by a list of options. Calculated fields are given a name, which appears as the column heading of the BROWSE, and an expression from which the contents of the field displayed are calculated.

Each option in a FIELDS option list must be introduced by a backslash "\". The slash "/" may be substituted if there is only one option for that field. The options are as follows:

\<nExp3>	The column width, <nExp3>, in which the field will be displayed in the BROWSE.
\B = <xExp4>,<xExp5> [,\F]	The range of acceptable data, from <xExp4> to <xExp5>, inclusive. The \F option is like RANGE REQUIRED; if included the cursor cannot leave the field until the value is within the range.
\H = <cExp2>	Header option; <cExp2> will appear at the head of the column in place of the field name.
\P = <cExp3>	Picture option. The field will appear as formatted by the <cExp3> picture clause.
\R	Read only. Prevents edit of the field.
\V = <lExpCond3>	VALID option; disallows entry of values not satisfying [\F] [\E=<cExp4>]<lExpCond3>.The \F VALID is VALID REQUIRED and keeps the cursor in the field until the value satisfies the condition. The \E option specifies that <cExp4>

will appear as an error message while <lExpCond3> is .F.

\W = <lExpCond4> WHEN option; allows edit only if <lExpCond4> is true.

Calculated fields are always read-only, so the \B, \R, \V and \W options do not apply to them. The \P option does nothing. You can format the calculated field by using TRANSFORM() in its defining expression. The column width and \H header options do apply. Although you can give a calculated field any name that qualifies as a field name, you must use the \H option to have two or more words appear as the column heading. Including inapplicable options in the fields list does not create a syntax error, but the options are ignored.

CALCULATE

Performs one of several specified calculations on one or more fields of the designated records of a table or view.

Syntax:

```
CALCULATE [<scope>]<functionList>
  [FOR <lExpCond1>][WHILE <lExpCond2>]
  [TO {<xVarList>}|{ARRAY <Array>}]
```

where each <function> might be one of the following:

AVG(<nExp>)

CNT()

MAX(<nExp>)

MIN(<nExp>)

NPV(<nExpRate>,<nExpFlows>,<nExpInit>)

STD(<nExp>)

SUM(<nExp>)

VAR(<nExp>)

The CALCULATE command produces one or more numeric or floating-point numbers, depending on the calculation, as the results of the calculations. Unless SET TALK is ON or a sufficient xVarList or one-dimensional array to hold the results is supplied with the TO option, the results will be lost.

Consider using ISBLANK() with the CALCULATE command to skip empty records that might distort the calculations.

Where a numeric expression is required for any of the calculation functions, the expressions will normally be the name of a numeric or float field or an expression involving the name of such a field.

References below to "the records" mean all the records of the table or view that are within the specified scope and for which the result of the FOR or WHILE condition, if any, is true.

AVG(<nExp>) returns the arithmetic mean of the values of <nExp> over the records, with the same data type as the expression.

CNT() returns the number of records.

MAX(<nExp>) and MIN(<nExp>) return the maximum or minimum, respectively, result of evaluating <nExp> for each record.

NPV(<nExpRate>,<nExpFlows>[,<nExpInit>]) returns the net present value of a series of cash flows, <nExpFlows>, at the discount rate given by <nExpRate>, assuming an initial investment of <nExpInit>.

In the simplest case, <nExpFlows> identifies a field of the table or view holding a series of signed numeric or float values representing the cash flows (+ meaning to you) expected from an investment. <nExpRate> is the discount rate, such as .06 for six percent, expressed for the same period as the interval between the cash flows. That is, if the cash flows are monthly receipts of rent and you want to calculate the net present value at 6 percent per year, the equivalent you might earn by foregoing the investment and putting your money in the bank instead, the rate should be stated as .06/12 to convert it to a monthly rate.

<nExpInit> is the initial investment, usually a negative number representing an outlay to purchase or create whatever it is you propose to obtain future cash from. If <nExpInit> is included, it is assumed that the first cash flow of <nExpFlows> occurs at the end of one period. If <nExpInit> is omitted, it is assumed that the first of the <nExpFlows> values is the initial investment. When setting up the records of cash flows, be sure to include in the calculation, a record with a cash flow of 0 for each period in which no cash changes hands. Otherwise dBASE assumes later cash comes earlier than it actually will and the calculation will be wrong.

If you want to evaluate an annuity or similar transaction from the point of view of the issuer, the initial investment or cash flow will usually be positive, the amount someone pays you up front, while the later cash flows will be mostly negative, your periodic payments to the annuitant.

NPV() always returns a float-type result.

STD(<nExp>) calculates the population standard deviation of the <nExp> series. The result is the same as SQRT(VAR(<nExp>)) and is always float-type. If you need a sample standard deviation, take the SQRT() of the sample variance determined by the formula below.

SUM(<nExp>) adds the values of <nExp>.

VAR(<nExp>) calculates the population variance of the values of <nExp>, always as a float-type number. As you probably know if you are bold enough to attempt to use this function, this variance is not appropriate to use for a sample, such as a sample of 50 bottles of fruit drink, where the issue is whether the slight short filling of the 50 bottles justifies the conclusion that all bottles taken as a whole are filled short. The formula used by VAR(), where nX is any value of the set, is:

VAR() = (SUM(nX*nX)-SUM(nX) *SUM(nX)/CNT(nX))/CNT(nX)

To obtain a population variance, you can use CALCULATE to obtain the sums and counts, then substitute into the formula above. Test the result against the VAR() result for the same values to be sure you have typed the formula correctly. The results should agree. To amend the formula to calculate a sample variance, simply change the last term of the formula, the second divisor, from CNT(nX) to (CNT(nX)-1).

Examples:

```
CALCULATE AVG(Price),MAX(Price),MIN(Price) ;
  FOR .NOT. isblank( Price ) TO nPavg, nPmax, nPmin
```

The next example assumes 6 Receipts fields hold +2000 each and calculates the value at 7 percent interest of paying $10,000 now to receive $2,000 at the end of each of the next 6 years:

```
CALCULATE NPV(.07,Receipts,-10000) TO nNpv
? transform(nNpv,"@$ 99,999.99)
$-466.92
```

The next example calculates the sample standard deviation of the fruit drink bottles discussed above under VAR():

```
CALCULATE SUM(Ounces),SUM(Ounces*Ounces),CNT() TO nTot, nSqs, nCnt
nDev = sqrt((nSqs - nTot*nTot/nCnt)/(nCnt - 1))
```

CALL, CALL()

The CALL command and CALL() function are not supported by dBASE for Windows. If used they cause dBASE to issue a warning.

CANCEL

Stops the run of the current program and returns control to the Command Window.

Syntax:

```
CANCEL
```

Cancel closes all open program files, but not procedure files or data tables and their associated files. The existence in dBASE of a true debugger makes CANCEL less useful than in dBASE IV, but you may find it helpful to stop execution of a program that you have previously SUSPENDed and that you find requires editing.

See DEBUG, RETURN, SUSPEND.

CASE

Introduces one of the conditions in a DO CASE programming structure.

See DO [CASE].

CATALOG()

Returns the name of the active catalog file, or an empty string if no catalog is active.

Syntax:

```
[cVar=] catalog()
```

The CATALOG() function will return the path as well as the name of the catalog if SET FULLPATH is ON.

CD

New; changes the current directory. The command is the same as the DOS CD or CHDIR command. The "CHDIR" version is not supported by dBASE for Windows.

See SET DIRECTORY TO.

CDOW()

Returns the name of the day of the week of a date.

Syntax:

```
[cVar=] cdow(<dExpDate>)
```

Example:

```
Ocent = set("CENTURY")
set century on
cToday = cdow(date())+", "+mdy(date())
set century iif(Ocent = "OFF",OFF,ON)
? cToday
Wednesday, March 16, 1994
```

CEILING()

Returns the smallest integer equal to or greater than the given numeric expression.

Syntax:

```
[nVar=] ceiling(<nExp>)
```

The value returned will be of the same type as nExp.

Example:

```
<calculates memory paragraphs of 16 bytes required>
nParas = ceiling(nBytes/16)
```

CENTER()

New; centers a string of characters.

Syntax:

```
[cVar=] center({<cExp[?]>|<mFld>}[,<nExpLength>[,<cExpPad>]])
```

The CENTER() function accepts a character expression or memo field and returns it centered. The length of the field in which it is centered is specified by <nExpLength>, default 80.

If the optional <cExpPad> is given, the padding on left and right to fill out the string is the first character of cExpPad. By default, the pad character is a space. If the string is too long for <nExpLength>, it is truncated at both ends to fit. If the number of pad characters or characters to be truncated is odd, the function returns the string or field 1/2 character left of center.

CERROR()

Returns zero if no compilation error occurs, or the number of the last compiler error message.

Syntax:

```
[nVar=] cerror()
```

The CERROR() function always returns 0 when issued in the Command window. Use it in a program that causes compilation of other program, procedure or format files to determine whether the compilation was successful.

See DBERROR(), ERROR().

CHANGE

Alternate syntax for EDIT.

See EDIT

CHANGE()

Returns .T. if a record in a CONVERTed table has been changed since it was read from disk.

Syntax:

```
[lVar=] change([<workarea>])
```

Compares the counter in the memory image of _dbaselock for the record to the same value as stored on disk and returns .T. if they differ, otherwise .F. A second read of the record, using GOTO RECNO() or otherwise moving the table pointer, will return .F. unless the record has been changed again. If an update of a record is attempted in a transaction that is not completed, CHANGE() might return .T. although the record has not been changed. CHANGE() does not work with Paradox tables or SQL databases.

CHARSET()

New; Returns the name of the character set the current or specified table is using.

Syntax:

[cVar=] charset([<workarea>])

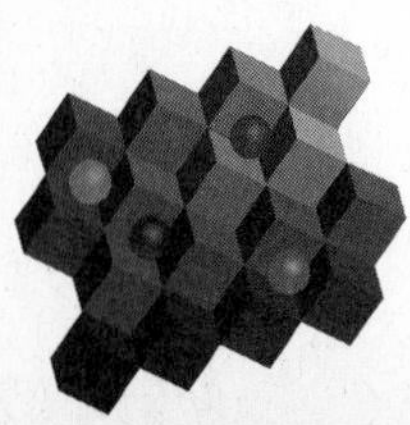

The CHARSET() function normally returns "OEM" or "ANSI" as the character set used by the table that is current, or specified by the optional <workarea> parameter. If you have data that is stored in one character set but the other is in use, you will have to use ANSI() or OEM() to convert the data to the character set in use, or select the other language driver.

See ANSI(), OEM().

CHOOSEPRINTER()

Opens the printer selection dialog box, from which you can specify another printer or change print options.

Syntax:

```
[lVar=] chooseprinter([<cExpTitle>])
```

The function returns .T. if you reset the printer, or .F. if you do not. You can also bring up the printer selection dialog box by choosing **P**rinter, **S**etup from the **F**ile menu, or you can select the printer using the Print Manager from the Windows main group. Your printer will not appear on the list until you install it using the Windows Print Manager.

If you supply it, the optional parameter <cExpTitle> appears as the title of the Printer dialog.

CHR()

Returns character equivalent of a numeric expression.

Syntax:

```
[cVar=] chr(<nExp>)
```

The value of nExp must resolve to an integer from 0 through 255. The character returned by CHR() depends on the current language driver, particularly for nExp values over 127. CHR() is the opposite of ASC().

CHR() can be used to include characters in character expressions. Do not enclose the CHR() expression in the quotation marks used to delimit literal characters or expressions using curly braces. Concatenate CHR() values to delimited characters with plus signs to create character expressions containing both types.

To sound the bell, use ?? chr(7), or use ? (chr(7)+<cExpMessage>) where <cExpMessage> is a message to display.

CHR() can also be used to hold and manipulate an arbitrary byte. The new bit-manipulation and hexadecimal functions, together with the CWORD and similar data types passed to external functions, have greatly reduced the need to use CHR() to manipulate binary values. See, however, the example under ??? of using CHR() to print binary byte values to a file.

In comparing a CHR() value to another character value, the CHR() must be on the right side if its value might be 0. Chr(0) is interpreted as an empty string. Since "=" in character comparisons means "starts with" if SET EXACT is OFF, and all character strings start with an empty string, the comparison chr(0) = <any characters> will return .T.

Example:

```
if .not. file("PRODUCTS.MDX")
  ? chr(7) + "Warning - .MDX file not found!"
  nHandle = 0
  nHandle = fopen("PRODUCTS.DBF","RW")
  if nHandle>0
    if fseek(nHandle,28) = 28
      if fwrite(nHandle,chr(0),1) = 1
        ? ".DBF table patched"
      endif
    endif
    fclose(nHandle)
  endif
endif
```

The example uses CHR() to reset byte 28 of a .DBF table to 0 to allow it to be placed in use although its production MDX file has somehow disappeared.

See ???, ASC().

CLASS

New; commences a CLASS . . . ENDCLASS programming structure declaring a class of objects.

Syntax:

```
CLASS <Class>
     [OF <BaseClass>]
     [<constructor code>]
     [<function code>[,<etc.>]]
ENDCLASS
```

You must give your class a name with <Class>. All other elements are optional. At least at first, you will probably want to declare your class as a subclass of a base class using the OF <BaseClass> option, where <BaseClass> is the name of the base class such as BROWSE, CHECKBOX, etc. Your derived class will then inherit the properties and methods of the base class, so you can build upon them without reinventing them. You are free to develop your own base classes and to derive classes from them as well as to use the defined types dBASE provides.

To declare a variable as a member of a class, precede it with the word "this." including the period.

Example:

```
DO Ciao
RETURN

CLASS Greeting
     this.AM = "Good morning!"
     this.PM = "Good afternoon!"
ENDCLASS

PROCEDURE Ciao
     Hello = new Greeting()
     Hello.AM = "Where's the coffee?"
     ? Hello.AM
     ? Hello.PM
RETURN

<The output of the above program is:>
Where's the coffee?
Good afternoon!
```

A class may include functions as well as data members. These functions can do whatever the class needs to do. If using built-in classes, many of the functions will ordinarily be attached to those properties of the class that can be function-pointer types and will provide the code that reacts to user events such as keypresses and mouse actions. The next example defines a class unrelated to the built-in classes.

Example:

```
#define HAND_SIZE 5
declare aCards[HAND_SIZE]
Myhand = new Deck()
Myhand.Shuffle()
?
```

```
for N = 1 to HAND_SIZE
     aCards[N] = Myhand.Draw()
     ? Myhand.Pips(aCards[N]) + " of " + Myhand.Suit(aCards[N])
endfor
RETURN

CLASS Deck
     * constructor code
     #define DECK_SIZE 52
     DECLARE aDeck[DECK_SIZE]
     for nCard = 1 to DECK_SIZE
          aDeck[nCard] = nCard
     endfor
     *First member function ends constructor

     FUNCTION Shuffle
          this.nDrawn = 0
          for nCard = 1 to DECK_SIZE - 1
               nRand = int(random() * (DECK_SIZE + 1 - nCard)) + nCard
               nTemp = aDeck[nRand]
               aDeck[nRand] = aDeck[nCard]
               aDeck[nCard] = nTemp
               endfor
     RETURN .t.

     FUNCTION Draw
          this.nDrawn = this.nDrawn + 1
     RETURN iif(this.nDrawn > DECK_SIZE, 0, aDeck[this.nDrawn])

     FUNCTION Pips
          parameter nNum
          private cPips
          cPips = "King Ace  DeuceThreeFour Five " ;
               + "Six  SevenEightNine Ten  Jack Queen"
     RETURN trim(substr(cPips, mod(nNum, 13)*5+1, 5))

     FUNCTION Suit
          parameter nNum
          private cSuits
          cSuits = "Clubs   Spades  Hearts  Diamonds"
     RETURN trim(substr(cSuits, mod(nNum, 4)*8+1,8))
ENDCLASS
```

A special kind of code associated with a class is its constructor. It contains the code, if required, to initialize new instances of class members. The constructor is all code in the class up to the start of the first named function or procedure.

CLEAR

Clears the Command Results window or a dBASE IV-mode window, or clears the described types or their values from memory. Has the new options AUTOMEM, KEY and PROGRAM.

Syntax:

```
CLEAR [<cExpChar>|ALL|AUTOMEM|FIELDS|GETS||
       MEMORY|MENUS|POPUPS|PROGRAM|SCREENS|
      ..TYPEAHEAD|WINDOWS]
```

CLEAR alone, or with the optional <cExpChar>, clears the surface of the results pane of the Command window or if a dBASE IV-mode window is active (such windows are always in the results pane) clears that window. If <cExpChar> is given, its first character is used to fill the cleared window. By default, the character is a space " ". See @ and @ . . . CLEAR for methods of clearing a portion of the results pane.

CLEAR ALL closes all tables and their indexes and returns to work area 1. It also closes all format files, releases all memory variables except system memory variables, closes all open windows and forms and releases from memory all defined objects, including forms and their controls and windows, menus, and popups.

CLEAR AUTOMEM creates a set of empty automem variables for the current table. Automem variables exist one per field of the table with the same names. You can use CLEAR AUTOMEM to create a set of automem variables or can employ the AUTOMEM option of USE to have them created when you open the table. You can also use CLEAR AUTOMEM to keep values appropriate to one record from showing up when you change to another.

CLEAR FIELDS acts like SET FIELDS TO for all work areas, canceling all SET FIELDS statements and making all fields available.

CLEAR GETS makes all @ . . . GET fields inactive, preventing their use for editing or entering data.

CLEAR MEMORY clears all memory variables except system memory variables. If you use an existing memory variable to define a user-interface object, CLEAR MEMORY will clear it. This leaves the object visible, but you will not be able to move the cursor to it. It will not appear if you issue a new ACTIVATE WINDOW command.

CLEAR MENUS and CLEAR POPUPS release all dBASE IV-style bar menus and popup menus, respectively, from memory.

CLEAR PROGRAM clears from memory all programs that are not currently executing. It does not affect programs opened by SYSPROC, SET PROCEDURE, or SET LIBRARY or formats opened by SET FORMAT, even if such programs were opened by the current program. It does not affect tables, indexes or other data files. When dBASE loads a program, it also loads all programs and procedures it calls. These stay in memory until you CLEAR MEMORY or until dBASE clears them to free up space it needs. Issue CLEAR PROGRAM to improve performance before doing something that requires significant memory, such as running an external program editor or opening a large number of tables. Do not overuse the command, because requiring dBASE to reload the programs will degrade performance.

CLEAR SCREENS clears from memory all images of the Command Results window saved by the SAVE SCREEN command.

CLEAR TYPEAHEAD clears the keyboard buffer. dBASE stores keypresses in a buffer and processes them in order. CLEAR TYPEAHEAD clears the buffer to assure that the next keypresses acted on will be freshly entered.

CLEAR WINDOWS clears window definitions from memory. You must deactivate windows before clearing them.

CLOSE

Closes all files or all of the indicated type. Now has FORMS as one of the types.

Syntax:

```
CLOSE ALL|ALTERNATE|DATABASES|FORMAT|
        {FORMS <FormList>|{WITH <xExp>}}|INDEXES|PRINTER|PROCEDURE
{<File>|?}
```

CLOSE ALL closes all files open within dBASE including files opened with the low-level file functions and resets the work area to 1. Devices and streams opened by SET DEVICE TO and SET PRINTER TO, but not SET ALTERNATE TO, remain open.

To close any particular type of file, follow the CLOSE command verb with the appropriate option from among those listed.

CLOSE ALTERNATE closes the file opened with SET ALTERNATE TO <File> and is an alternative syntax to SET ALTERNATE TO.

CLOSE DATABASES closes the listed databases or tables, including their related files such as index and format files. If no list is given, it closes all databases, inlcuding all DB and DBF tables and their related files.

CLOSE FORMAT closes format files open in the current work area.

CLOSE FORMS closes the listed form or forms. At least one form must be listed, or the WITH option used. You use the WITH option when attaching CLOSE FORMS to an event of a form you open with READMODAL(). The <xExp> argument specifies the value that the READMODAL() function will return after the form closes.

dBASE first executes the Valid property code of the object with focus. If Valid returns .F., the form does not close. dBASE then executes in order the OnLostFocus code of the object with focus, the OnLostFocus code of the form itself, and the OnClose code of the form, finally removing the form from the screen. The form is not removed from memory and need not be redefined.

CLOSE INDEXES is an alternative syntax to SET INDEX TO. It closes any dBASE index files except the production MDX in the current work area. It has no effect on Paradox or SQL indexes.

CLOSE PRINTER tells the Windows Print Manager to stop saving the printer output and queuing it, and to commence printing it. If used after SET PRINTER TO FILE <cLtrFile>, CLOSE PRINTER closes the file.

CLOSE PROCEDURE closes the specified open procedure or library file. If you supply a question mark instead of a file specification, the File dialog opens to allow you to choose the correct file.

CMONTH()

Returns the name of the month from a date expression.

Syntax:

```
[cVar=] cmonth(<dExp>)
```

Example:

```
? cmonth({03/17/94}+267)
December
```

COL()

Returns a number reflecting the current horizontal position within the current window.

Syntax:

```
[nVar=] col()
```

If the current window is the results pane of the Command window or a window opened by ACTIVATE WINDOW, COL() returns the column of the cursor as a numeric-type value. If the window was opened dBASE for Windows-style with OPEN WINDOW or READMODAL(), COL() returns the column position of the upper left corner of the most recently placed user-interface object as a float-type value.

The measuring unit of the number returned by COL() is the average width of the characters of the default font of the window. If that font is proportional, adding an integer to COL() to position the next object will not necessarily line it up with any particular letter of any text.

Example:

```
? "The space between the arrows-->"
?? "<--is two characters wide" at col()+2
```

COMMIT()

New; ends a transaction and writes the changes.

Syntax:

```
[lVar=] commit([<cExpDatabase>])
```

The COMMIT() function completes a transaction begun by BEGINTRANS(). It writes the data to the database and returns .T. if the write was successful. It releases the locks BEGINTRANS() placed on the data. You will use it primarily in a multi-user environment, where it is possible that tables locked by other users will prevent writing some of the new data involved in the transaction. By using BEGINTRANS() and COMMIT(), you insure that either all or none of the changes to the data will be written. This prevents the corruption that could occur if dBASE wrote changes to less than all of two or more tables containing related data.

If the optional <cExpDatabase> parameter is specified, it identifies the database. You should not ordinarily use this option. If you leave it out, the database specified by SET DATABASE TO, or the current database, is used. You will always want the database to be the same one used in BEGINTRANS(), which will be the case if you omit the parameter. The only situation in which omitting the parameter might lead to trouble occurs if you change the SET DATABASE TO setting in the middle of a transaction—a bizarre thing to attempt. In that case, the database in which the transaction is pending is no longer current and you must specify it as a parameter to COMMIT().

To terminate a transaction without saving the changes, use ROLLBACK().

See BEGINTRANS(), ROLLBACK().

COMPILE

Compiles PRG files into executable PRO dBASE object files.

Syntax:

```
COMPILE (<File>|?|<skeleton>)[ALL]
```

If you issue COMPILE with a filename and omit the extension, dBASE looks for and compiles a PRG file. If you follow COMPILE with ? or <skeleton>, dBASE brings up the File dialog. You can select one file or more, using wildcards.

The ALL option compiles in addition all program and format files called upon by the files whose names or skeletons you gave to COMPILE.

If the compiler encounters a syntax error, it brings up the error dialog box. You can click Cancel to cancel the compilation process, Ignore to cancel compilation of the erroneous file while continuing to compile any other files matching the skeleton, or Fix to edit the file with the error.

COMPLETED()

Is not supported by dBASE for Windows. It always returns .T.

CONTINUE

Continues a search commenced by LOCATE for another record matching the conditions set by LOCATE, in the current work area.

Syntax:

```
CONTINUE
```

CONTINUE continues the serial search started by LOCATE in the current work area. It is possible to use LOCATE in different work areas at the same time. Any of the searches can be carried farther by selecting the appropriate work area and issuing CONTINUE. If the search succeeds, dBASE stops at the matching record. If it fails, it issues an "End of LOCATE scope" message.

CONVERT

Adds a character field _dbaselock to each record of the current table to hold multiuser information.

Syntax:

```
CONVERT [TO <nExp>]
```

The parameter nExp must resolve to 8 through 24 and gives the length of the _dbaselock field. The default value is 16. The first 8 characters of _dbaselock hold three hexadecimal numbers, the first a count of two digits and the second and third three-digit numbers recording the time and date, respectively, that a lock was last placed on the record.

The remaining 0-16 characters of _dbaselock hold the login name, truncated as necessary, of the computer that placed the lock.

Every time the record is updated, dBASE updates the count portion. The CHANGE() function compares the count in the record on disk to its record of the count when the record was read. If the two differ, another user has changed the record since it was read. To reset CHANGE() to .F., GOTO the current record.

You must have exclusive use of a table to convert it. dBASE archives the table before conversion with a CVT extension. You must also SET DELETED OFF before conversion or REINDEX after conversion.

See LKSYS()

COPY

Duplicates files or portions; has new BINARY and TABLE options.

Syntax:

```
COPY {FILE {<FileSource1>|?|<skeleton>} TO {<FileTarget1>|?}}|
     {INDEXES <NDXFileList>[TO {<MDXFile>|?}]}|
     {BINARY <bFld>
           TO {<FileTarget2>|?}[ADDITIVE]}|
     {MEMO <mFld> TO {<FileTarget3>|?}[ADDITIVE]}|
     {STRUCTURE TO {<FileTarget4>|?}
      [[TYPE]{DBASE|PARADOX}][FIELDS <FieldList>]
      [[WITH] PRODUCTION]}|
     {TABLE <FileSource2> TO <FileTarget5>
      [[TYPE]{DBASE|PARADOX}]}|
     {TAG <Tag>[OF <MDXFile>] TO <NDXFile>}|
     {TO {{<FileTarget6>|?}[<more>]}|
      {ARRAY <Array>[<more>]}}
```

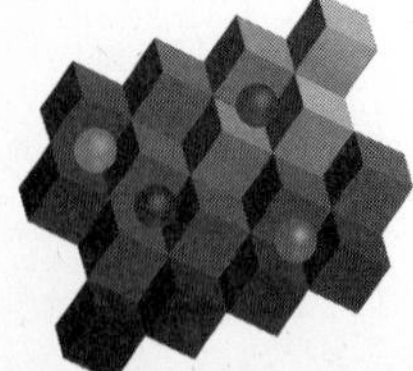

COPY FILE copies one file of any type to another. You must include the extensions for both files, and the drives and paths if different from the current one, except that dBASE can find the source file if it is in the current path. With this and many forms of the COPY command you may issue ? instead of the name of either the source or the target file. You may also issue a skeleton instead of the name of the source file. In all such cases the File dialog opens to allow you to choose the file.

COPY FILE does not copy the DBT or MDX files associated with a table when copying the table. You should ordinarily use COPY TABLE to copy tables. If the source file is of any dBASE type, you must close it within dBASE before copying it.

COPY INDEXES copies the specified dBASE index (NDX) files to become tags in a single dBASE multiple index (MDX) file. The NDX files must be open; see SET INDEX TO. If the TO option is omitted, the tags will be added to the production MDX file for the active table, or such a production MDX will be created and the flag in the DBF table set to show that it exists. By using the TO option you might specify another name for the MDX file to be created or added to or might substiture ? for a filename to bring up the File dialog.

COPY BINARY copies the contents of the named binary field of the current record to a file. If ADDITIVE is included, the field contents will be added to the file. Otherwise, they will overwrite it. The binary field can contain text, an image, sound, or other data. dBASE will add the appropriate file extension such as BMP or WAV for predefined types of data. By default, it adds the TXT extension to target files for binary data of user-defined type. See BINTYPE() for further information about defining binary field data types.

COPY MEMO copies the text of a single memo from the named memo field of the current record to a file. If ADDITIVE is included, the memo will be appended to the file. Otherwise, the memo will overwrite an existing file. If you do not give a file extension, dBASE adds a TXT extension. If SET SAFETY is on, dBASE will warn you if the target file already exists.

COPY STRUCTURE copies the structure of the active table—either dBASE or Paradox—but not the data. You can use ? instead of naming a target file to bring up the File dialog.

You can specify a database as the target or a table of the other type, a Paradox table to receive the structure of a dBASE table, or vice versa. To specify a database table, supply the name of the database, delimited by colons, as a prefix to the table name. If the database is not open, dBASE will open a dialog for you to supply any parameters needed to open it, such as a login name and password. The word TYPE is optional. The FIELDS option allows you to limit the fields copied, as does the SET FIELDS command. By default, all fields are copied. If SET SAFETY is OFF, dBASE will overwrite the target file without warning.

The _dbaselock field of converted files is not copied. If PROTECT is in use, fields to which the user lacks privileges will not be copied. The WITH PRODUCTION option creates a production MDX file for the new table, assuming both tables are DBASE type, but you must have a spare work area available and any aliases or memory variables referred to by any index tags must exist.

COPY TABLE copies a dBASE or Paradox table to another, or to a database table. To specify a database table, supply the name of the database, delimited by colons, as a prefix to the table name. If the database is not open, dBASE will open a dialog for you to supply any parameters needed to open it, such as a login name and password. COPY TABLE copies MDX and other associated files automatically. You should close the source table before copying it.

COPY TAG is the inverse of COPY INDEXES. It copies a single specified tag from an open MDX file to an NDX file. The resulting NDX file will index all records of the table, ignoring any FOR clause applicable to the MDX tag.

COPY TO is the original form of the command and still the workhorse. It copies only dBASE and Paradox tables and their associated memo and index files. Its complete syntax is as follows:

Syntax:

```
COPY TO {{<FileTarget6>|?}|{ARRAY <Array>}}
 [<scope>][FOR <lExpCond1>][WHILE <lExpCond2>]
 [FIELDS <FieldList>]]
```

The following additional COPY TO options apply only when the copy is not to an array:

```
[TYPE]{SDF|
|DBMEMO3|DBASE|PARADOX|
    {DELIMITED [WITH {<cLtrChar>|BLANK}]}}|
 [WITH PRODUCTION]))]
```

You can, as usual, name the target file or use ? to open the File dialog. The <scope>, FOR and WHILE options limit the records of the source file to be copied. By default, all records are copied. The FIELDS option, or the SET FIELDS setting, limits the fields copied. By default, all are copied. You may copy fields from two or more tables to a new one by opening the tables in different work areas and issuing SET FIELDS to select the combination of fields from the source tables to copy. You may also copy to a database table. To specify a database table, supply the name of the database, delimited by colons, as a prefix to the table name. If the database is not open, dBASE will open a dialog for you to supply any parameters needed to open it, such as a login name and password.

COPY TO ARRAY requires that the array be declared before the command is issued. Records of the file are copied to rows of the array and fields to the columns. However, if the array is one-dimensional, the fields of the first record are copied to it, not the first field of several records as you might expect. Memo fields are skipped, with the next field occupying the column of the array following the field before the memo. If the table has more fields or records than will fit in the array, the excess fields or records are not copied.

COPY TO when the copy is to a file, not an array, allows the remaining options listed above. STRUCTURE EXTENDED copies the table structure to a dBASE table of the structure shown in Table A.3:

Table A.3
Structure of a STRUCTURE EXTENDED TABLE

Field name	Field type	Field Length	Decimals	Index
FIELD_NAME	Character	10	0	F
FIELD_TYPE	Character	1	0	F
FIELD_LENGTH	Numeric	3	0	F
FIELD_DEC	Numeric	3	0	F
FIELD_IDX	Logical	1	0	F

Each of the records of the structure extended table describes one of the fields of the original table. This option is most frequently used with CREATE FROM to create a table within a program. Your program might copy the structure of a table and create another table of the same structure, or it might use the usual dBASE commands such as ZAP and REPLACE to create a completely different structure and then create a table from that. The _dbaselock field, if any, is not copied. The FIELD_IDX field reflects only those tags created by checking the Index column of the file structure design view when the file was created or modified. It does not reflect indexes separately created on the field names as keys.

The COPY TO <file> TYPE options allow exporting data from dBASE. The syntax supports copying from a dBASE or Paradox table to another of either type for compatibility, but COPY TABLE is preferred for this use. WITH PRODUCTION requires that the source and target files both be dBASE tables; if they are, it creates a production MDX of the target table with the same tags and options as the production MDX of the source table. All fields referred to in index keys should be copied, and all variables and aliases used in the keys be open, for this to work properly.

The word TYPE is optional. The types of files to which dBASE can copy with this command are:

SDF	System Data Format, a file of fixed length fields. Fields are padded with blanks to the required length. A CR/LF pair separates records, but fields have no delimiters.
DBMEMO3	dBASE III or III+ table with memo fields. dBASE III and III+ files use a slightly different memo structure and cannot use a dBASE for Windows file unless it is exported as this type. If a dBASE for Windows table has no memo fields, dBASE III and III+ can use it directly.

PARADOX	A Paradox table.
DBASE	A dBASE IV or dBASE for Windows table.
DELIMITED	A file of variable-length records with a CR/LF combination separating the records. The character following the WITH option delimits character data, BLANK designating that a blank space delimits such data. By default, a comma is assumed to delimit the data.

See EXPORT.

COS()

Returns the cosine of an angle given in radians.

Syntax:

```
[fVar=] cos(<nExp>)
```

The cosine of an angle is defined in terms of a right triangle of which one of the other angles is the one of interest. Its cosine is equal to the length of the side of the triangle adjacent to it divided by the length of the hypotenuse. Since the side can never be longer than the hypotenuse, the value returned is in the range -1 to 1, and 0 if the angle is itself a right angle. There is no limit on the value of <nExp>. The reciprocal of the cosine of an angle, 1/cos(<nExp>), is the secant of the angle.

See ACOS(), ATAN(), ATN2(), DTOR(), RTOD(), SIN(), TAN().

COUNT

Counts records in the current table, usually those that match given conditions.

Syntax:

```
COUNT [<scope>][FOR <lExpCond1>]
     [WHILE <lExpCond2>][TO <nVar>]
```

The COUNT command counts the records within the current scope that match the given conditions. If SET TALK is OFF and the TO <nVar> option is omitted, the count will neither display nor be stored and will be lost. The COUNT command has largely been superseded by the CNT() option of the CALCULATE command, which can calculate several statistics on a single pass through the file.

CREATE

Creates a file, now including a FORM file or STRUCTURE EXTENDED table.

Syntax:

```
CREATE {<File1>|?}[{[STRUCTURE EXTENDED]
          [[TYPE]{PARADOX|DBASE}]}|
        {FROM {<File2>|?|<skeleton>}
          [[TYPE]{PARADOX|DBASE}]}|
         {{COMMAND|FILE}{<File3|?|<skeleton>}[WINDOW <Window>]}|
         {{APPLICATION|CATALOG|FORM|LABEL|MENU|QUERY|
             REPORT[CROSSTAB]|SCREEN}{<File4>|?|<skeleton>}}|
         {VIEW {<File5>|?}}|
        {VIEW <File6> FROM ENVIRONMENT}|
        SESSION]
```

If you use CREATE alone, followed only by a file name or type, or followed by a ?, the File dialog box and the editor for that type appear. You can accomplish the same thing by right double-clicking on the File Viewer Untitled icon of the required file type. The only operative difference is that if you specify a file name or ? using the CREATE command, you select the file name at once rather than at the end of the edit. The default type is table.

The CREATE options relating to tables support the optional TYPE keyword and the designation of the DBASE or PARADOX table type. You may also create a database table. To specify a database table, supply the name of the database, delimited by colons, as a prefix to the table name. If the database is not open, dBASE will open a dialog for you to supply any parameters needed to open it, such as a login name and password.

CREATE APPLICATION, CREATE FORM, and CREATE SCREEN are equivalent and bring up the Forms Designer.

CREATE QUERY and CREATE VIEW are identical and bring up the Query Designer. CREATE VIEW . . . FROM ENVIRONMENT is different, see below.

CREATE COMMAND or CREATE FILE brings up the text editor to edit a new program or text file. The WINDOW option is included for compatibility with code written for dBASE IV and causes the edit to take place in the previously DEFINEd and ACTIVATEd Window. You should not need this option when creating new code.

CREATE LABEL brings up the Label Designer and CREATE REPORT the Report Designer. The CROSSTAB option of the latter causes the Crosstab dialog to display.

All the CREATE options mentioned above have corresponding MODIFY options, the only difference being that CREATE creates new files and is the same as right double-clicking an Untitled icon, while MODIFY can use an existing file, and is then the same as right double-clicking on a named icon.

The remaining five CREATE options described below have no MODIFY counterparts.

CREATE CATALOG creates a catalog. If SET TITLE is ON, you are prompted for a description. Catalog names are limited to eight characters. dBASE always adds the extension CAT.

CREATE SESSION creates a session. Each session makes all work areas available. You can use a table in more than one session at a time, for reading or writing, but any changes made in one session will affect all sessions. By default, you create a session each time you put a table into use. You cannot close a session or change sessions; each belongs to the tables within it. Each session ends when all tables in it are closed. Creating a new session also restores to their defaults those SET settings that apply separately to each session, as shown in Table A.4.

Table A.4. SET settings that apply on a per-session basis

AUTOSAVE	BLOCKSIZE	CARRY	CENTURY
CONFIRM	CUAENTER	CURRENCY	DATABASE
DATE	DBTYPE	DECIMALS	DEFAULT
DELETED	DELIMITERS	DIRECTORY	EXACT
EXCLUSIVE	FIELDS	FILTER	IBLOCK
INDEX	KEY	LOCK	MARK
MBLOCK	MEMOWIDTH	NEAR	ORDER
PATH	POINT	PRECISION	REFRESH
SAFETY	SEPARATOR	SKIP	TALK
UNIQUE	REPROCESS	RELATION	

CREATE VIEW <File6> FROM ENVIRONMENT creates a dBASE III+ compatible VUE view file form the current environment, saving all active tables, indexes, work areas, relations, field lists, filters, and any active format file.

The CREATE . . . FROM option creates a table from the specified table, which must have been created with the CREATE . . . STRUCTURE EXTENDED or COPY . . . STRUCTURE EXTENDED command. The table created becomes the current table. If the CREATE operation fails, no table will be open in the current work area.

The CREATE . . . STRUCTURE EXTENDED option creates an empty STRUCTURE EXTENDED table. See COPY TO . . . STRUCTURE EXTENDED for the structure of such a table.

CTOD()

Converts a character string to a date.

Syntax:

```
[dVar=] ctod(<cExpDate>)
```

The format of the character string must by default be MM/DD/YY or MM/DD/YYYY. It does not matter whether SET CENTURY is on or off, but a two-digit year will be assumed to be in the twentieth century. The SET DATE and SET MARK settings are given effect and require that the character string be appropriate to the date format in effect. If you pass a character string in the wrong format, or a string in the correct format that represents no real date, to CTOD() by mistake, dBASE will convert to a real date if possible by adding the extra days and months to the months and years. You can create a BC date by adding BC or bc after the numerals of the date and a space. Do not attempt to do date arithmetic with BC dates or any dates predating the current (Gregorian) calendar. dBASE will apply the rules of the current calendar and give an often erroneous result.

Example:

```
SET DATE TO MDY
ddate = ctod("12/25/94")
? ddate, type("ddate"),ddate+7
12/25/94 D 01/01/95
dDate = ctod( "25/12/94" )
? dDate
01/12/96
```


DATABASE()

New; returns the name of the current default database selected with SET DATABASE. If no database is open, returns "".

Syntax:

```
[cVar=] database()
```

DATE()

Returns the current system date.

Syntax:

```
[dVar=] date()
```

Example:

```
? "Today is "
?? date()
```

The date is printed in the format prescribed by SET CENTURY, SET DATE, and SET MARK. By default, the date prints as MM/DD/YY.

DAY()

Returns the number of the day of the month of a date expression.

Syntax:

```
[nVar=] day(<dExp>)
```

Example:

```
Today = {05/28/94}
Nextweek = Today + 7
? day(Nextweek)
         4
```

DBERROR()

Returns the IDAPI number of the last IDAPI error.

Syntax:

```
[nVar=] dberror()
```

The function returns an error number generated by IDAPI in managing a database. To see the error message, use DBMESSAGE().

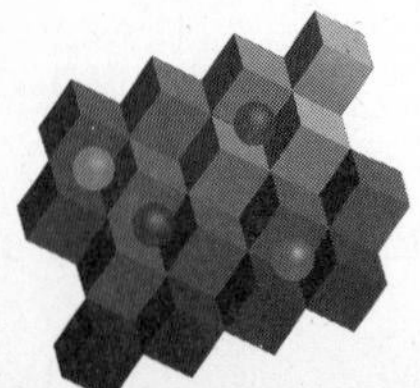

DBF()

Returns the name of the dBASE or Paradox table in use in the current or specified work area.

Syntax:

```
[cVar=] dbf([<workarea>])
```

Example:

```
if "" # dbf()
     select select()
endif
```

DBMESSAGE()

Returns the text of the specified or last IDAPI error message.

Syntax:

```
[cVar=] dbmessage([<nExp>])
```

If you include the <nExp> parameter, the function returns the IDAPI message corresponding to the error number specified, the number returned by DBERROR(). If you omit the parameter, the function returns the last error message.

DEACTIVATE

Removes a menu, popup, or one or more windows from the screen, affecting program flow.

Syntax:

```
DEACTIVATE {MENU|POPUP|WINDOW {<WindowList>|ALL}}
```

DEACTIVATE MENU and DEACTIVATE POPUP remove the active menu or popup, if any, from the screen and return control to the statement following the ACTIVATE MENU or ACTIVATE POPUP that caused it to appear. They cannot be issued outside a program.

DEACTIVATE WINDOW removes the listed window or windows, or all windows with ALL, from the screen and activates the previous window, if any, or the Command window.

The deactivated menu, popup, or window remains in memory and can be reactivated.

DEBUG

Starts the dBASE for Windows debugger.

Syntax:

```
DEBUG [{{<File>|?|<skeleton>}|
     {PROCEDURE <Procedure>}|
     {FUNCTION <Function>}}
     [WITH <ParameterList>]]
```

The dBASE for Windows debugger allows you to execute or step through the code of a program, or of a single procedure or function. You can set watchpoints to show you whether critical values change as and when they should and breakpoints to stop execution when a particular line is reached, as well as observing the flow of execution and the use of the call stack.

The WITH option enables you to pass parameters to the program, procedure, or function you are debugging, if it starts with a PARAMETERS statement. For more information about debugging dBASE applications, see Chapter 17, "Debugging dBASE Applications."

DECLARE

Creates an array in memory.

Syntax:

```
DECLARE
<Array1><nExpDimensionsList1>[,<array2><nExpDimensionsList2>][<etc.>]
```

where each <nExpDimensionsList> is a list, enclosed in square brackets, of numeric expressions separated by commas. Each numeric expression determines the number of elements in one dimension of the array.

DECLARE allocates storage in memory for one or more arrarys each of up to 255 dimensions and fills all elements of the array or arrays with the logical value .F. No reference to an array element is possible until the array has been declared. You can create an array automatically by using some of the array functions, or you can use the NEW operator instead of the DECLARE command. The total size of an array is limited only by available memory. You cannot use most of the array-handling functions to manipulate arrays having more than two dimensions.

Example:

```
? DECLARE FileArray[reccount(), fldcount()]
```

DEFINE

DEFINE has three distinct uses. First, you can use it to create a new object of a defined class. Second, its COLOR option defines a color. Third, its BAR, BOX, MENU, PAD, POPUP and WINDOW options create those dBASE-IV type objects. The three uses of DEFINE are discussed separately below.

The new dBASE for Windows use of DEFINE is to create an object of a defined class and allocate memory storage for it.

Syntax:

```
DEFINE <Class> {<Object>|<nExpOrder>}[OF <Container>]
  {FROM <nExpRow1>,<nExpCol1> TO <nExpRow2>,<nExpCol2>}|
  {AT <nExpRow>,<nExpCol>}
  [PROPERTY <Property1><xExpValue1>[,<etc.>]]
  [CUSTOM <Property2><xExpValue2>[,<etc.>]
  [WITH <ParameterList>]
```

You may use DEFINE, or the NEW operator, to create an object of a custom class you have defined with the CLASS. . . ENDCLASS syntax, or of one of the following 20 standard classes.

BROWSE
: A spreadsheet-like view of the records and fields of a table.

CHECKBOX
: A box allowing a binary selection—one between two states such as Yes|No or ON|OFF.

COMBOBOX
: A control allowing selection of an item either by typing it in or from a list; combines an entryfield and list box.

DDELINK
: A link from dBASE to another application, the DDE server, by which dBASE can send data and instructions to, and request data from, the server.

DDETOPIC
: A class determining how dBASE will respond as DDE server to requests from another application.

EDITOR
: A window with scroll bars for editing a text file or Memo field.

ENTRYFIELD	A control allowing typing-in a selection.
FORM	A screen window containing one or more controls to manage user input and display output.
IMAGE	A rectangular screen area for output of a bitmapped image from a BMP or PCX file or a Memo field.
LINE	A line drawn on a form.
LISTBOX	A control allowing selection from a list. Implements a "picklist."
MENU	A Windows-style menu of a form.
OBJECT	A class without properties you can use as the base class from which to create objects with only those properties you determine.
OLE	A window in which you can edit an object created with an external application by using that application. This applies primarily to graphics, by default created with Paintbrush, and sound files, by default created with the Sound Recorder.
PUSHBUTTON	A control you can select to cause immediate action, usually to terminate use of the containing form.
RADIOBUTTON	A binary control contained in a group from which you can select one and only one of the buttons.
RECTANGLE	A rectangle displayed on a form.
SCROLLBAR	A rectangular control with a movable slider or "thumb" permitting you to increase or decrease a date or numeric value. You should distinguish this class of object, contained within a form and permitting editing of data, from the scrollbars at the foot or right of windows that allow you to see more of the underlying surface. You cannot create the latter type using dBASE except by calling the Windows API.
SPINBOX	A control like a scrollbar without the thumb. A spinbox contains two arrows for increasing or decreasing the date or numeric value.

TEXT	Text displayed within a form. Like an image, line, or rectangle, text has only a pretty face; it cannot receive user input.

Most of the time you will find it easier to use the Forms Designer to design forms and to place objects on them than to write the code. When you use the Forms Designer, dBASE writes the necessary DEFINE statements for you.

In the DEFINE syntax, <Class> is the name of the class of the object, either one of the 20 classes named above or the name you gave your custom class using the CLASS . . . ENDCLASS syntax. You must then name your object, <Object>, or give it a numeric reference <nExpOrder> indicating its order within the form. You will primarily use <nExpOrder> for those radiobuttons and similarly grouped controls that are too numerous to name easily. When you do use the <nExpOrder> option, you must also use the OF <Container> option to identify the containing object, usually a form.

When an object is contained in another, as any object of the other standard classes is contained in a form, use the OF <Container> option to specify the name of the form or other object that contains the one you are defining.

You can use either the FROM . . . TO option or the AT option, but not both, to specify where within the containing form, or within the dBASE main window, the object will appear. Numeric values are given in pairs, horizontal distance then vertical, measured from the upper left corner. Values are given in units of the average character width or height of the default font, and may include fractions for exact placement. You will ordinarily use the AT option for those objects such as text that have their height and width specified by other properties such as the font. Use FROM . . . TO for rectangles and similar objects of arbitrary size, with FROM placing the upper left corner and TO the lower right corner. You do not need either option if you define your object's Top, Left, and if necessary, Width and Height properties, because they will supply the position and size.

The PROPERTY list and CUSTOM list for properties you define give the specifics of the object you are creating—where on the screen it is, how big it is, what it looks like, how it acts on events such as mouse clicks, and much more. You can choose whatever values for the properties of the object you wish. The properties are all part of the DEFINE statement; each physical line except the last must be terminated by a semicolon, as well as each property in the list being separated from others by commas.

The WITH option allows you to include the parameters that dBASE will pass to the object on constructing it. This supposes that the object has a PARAMETERS line as its first line, which is unusual. You can use this option to pass parameters to an object of a custom class that can make use of them.

Example:

```
DEFINE IMAGE EMP_PHOTO OF EMPFORM;
      PROPERTY;
            Top             5.00,;
            Left             30.00,;
            Width             20.00,;
            Height              20.00,;
            Datasource       BINARY EMPS->PHOTO
```

You should whenever possible use the new classes and syntax described previously, not the dBASE IV syntax, in dBASE for Windows. dBASE for Windows provides the older ones so your dBASE IV programs will run, but programs using them will lack the Windows "look and feel."

The second use of DEFINE is in DEFINE COLOR, defining a custom color:

Syntax:

```
DEFINE COLOR <Color><nExpRed>,<nExpGreen>,<nExpBlue>
```

DEFINE COLOR defines a color in terms of the intensity of its red, green, and blue components, each on a scale of 0 to 255 measured in increasing brightness. You will find it easiest to create colors by issuing GETCOLOR() to open the Color dialog. When you have a color you may want to use in future programming, write down its component values so you can use them in the DEFINE COLOR statements you write later.

The third use of DEFINE is to define and allocate storage for dBASE IV-type objects, for compatibility. The syntaxes for the various objects, BAR, BOX, MENU, PAD, POPUP and WINDOW are slightly different and are discussed separately below.

DEFINE BAR creates a single, usually selectable, horizontal bar of a pop-up menu. The term popup in dBASE includes all menus whose selections appear one above the other, including menus that pull down in response to selection from another menu or popup. You cannot use the DEFINE BAR syntax if you have already otherwise defined the bars of the popup by the PROMPT options of the DEFINE POPUP command as FIELD, FILES, or STRUCTURE.

Syntax:

```
DEFINE BAR <nExpLine> OF <Popup>
  PROMPT <cExpPrompt>
  [MESSAGE <cExpMessage>]
  [SKIP [FOR <lExpCond>]]
```

The <nExpLine> expression resolves to the line of the popup you are defining, from 1 to 16,378. The integral value of the result of the expression is used. If the lines you define do not begin with 1 or are not consecutively numbered, blank bars appear. The blank bars will be skipped when the user moves among bars. If you define more bars than will fit, they will scroll. If you define the same bar twice, the latter definition takes effect. Each popup must have at least one bar.

The PROMPT keyword is followed by the text to appear on the bar. It will be truncated if too long and it cannot be made to scroll horizontally.

MESSAGE defines an optional message to appear on the message line, by default the bottom screen line, when the bar is highlighted. Message text for a bar overrides any message prescribed in the DEFINE POPUP command, and must not exceed 79 characters or it will be truncated. If SET STATUS is OFF, the message location is determined by the AT option of SET MESSAGE.

The SKIP option displays the bar, but does not allow selection. The FOR option of SKIP allows you to specify that the bar will be skipped only when the condition is true.

Example:

```
lSummer = month(date())>5.AND.month(date())<10
DEFINE POPUP Soups FROM 3,2 ;
    TO iif(lSummer,13,14),18
DEFINE BAR 1 OF Soups PROMPT "French Onion"
DEFINE BAR 3 OF Soups PROMPT "Chicken Noodle"
DEFINE BAR 2 OF Soups PROMPT "Beef Vegetable"
nBar = 4
IF lSummer
  DEFINE BAR 4 OF Soups PROMPT "Gazpacho"
  nBar = 5
ENDIF
DEFINE BAR nBar OF Soups PROMPT "Chili w/ Beans"
DEFINE BAR nBar+1 OF Soups ;
     PROMPT replicate("-",15) SKIP
DEFINE BAR nBar+2 OF Soups ;
     PROMPT "Fridays only:" SKIP
DEFINE BAR nBar+3 OF Soups ;
     PROMPT "NE Clam Chowder" ;
     SKIP for dow(date()) # 6
DEFINE BAR nBar+4 OF Soups ;
     PROMPT "    No Soup" ;
     MESSAGE "If you do not have soup,"+ ;
             " you may have a salad"
ACTIVATE POPUP Soups
```

Your programming will be easier to read if you arrange the bar definitions in numeric order, but dBASE does not require you to do so. In the example, the “Clam Chowder” selection is visible at all times to entice diners to return on Fridays, but it can be selected only on Fridays. "Gazpacho" is not listed at all except in the summer, and its presence or absence requires using variables to place the later lines and size the popup.

A popup has a border that fills each of the rows and columns listed in the DEFINE POPUP statement. To determine the size required to fit all the data inside the borders, add 1 to the number of bars for the rows and add 1 to the maximum characters per bar for the columns. This gives the number to be added to the FROM number to calculate the TO number in the DEFINE POPUP statement. There are 15 characters in "NE Clam Chowder", and 15 characters + the starting column of 2 + 1 is 18, so the TO column is 18.

Your programs in dBASE for Windows will look more Windows-like if you use the new control classes such as MENU rather than DEFINE POPUP and DEFINE BAR.

See ACTIVATE, DEACTIVATE, ON BAR, ON EXIT BAR, ON EXIT POPUP, SELECTION, ON POP, SET.

DEFINE BOX places a box on the screen.

Syntax:

```
DEFINE BOX FROM <nExpCol1> TO <nExpCol2>
        HEIGHT <nExpHeight>[AT LINE <nExpLine>]
        [SINGLE|DOUBLE|<cExpBorderList>]
```

You should note that DEFINE BOX is unique in that FROM and TO describe columns only, not row and column pairs as with other commands. Additionally, the AT option is used to identify the starting row, whereas in other commands it places the upper left corner of an object.

The remaining option of DEFINE BOX specifies a border of characters, generally using the block and line-segment characters from the upper half of the OEM character set to create a somewhat graphic effect. Such a border looks inappropriate in Windows and will not work at all if the ANSI language driver is in use. SINGLE and DOUBLE use the OEM characters to create a single or double line border. The <cExpBorder> option enables you to specify up to 8 characters to be used for the border. See SET BORDER for details. The NONE and PANEL options of SET BORDER are not available with DEFINE BOX. See the tip above about calculating the size of a box to fit specific contents.

You can use DEFINE BOX and the _box system variable to place a box around streaming output that uses the ? or ?? commands. See the discussion and example under _box in Appendix B, "System Variables Reference."

DEFINE MENU creates a dBASE IV-style menu.

Syntax:

```
DEFINE MENU <Menu> [MESSAGE <cExpMessage>]
```

This command creates an empty dBASE IV- style menu bar.

The MESSAGE option specifies a message. Messages attached to the pads of the menu with DEFINE PAD will override the DEFINE MENU message. Messages will appear on the bottom screen line if SET STATUS is on, otherwise where the AT option of SET MESSAGE places them. Messages longer than 79 characters will be truncated.

DEFINE PAD is like DEFINE BAR but for the horizontally aligned pads of a traditional bar menu. You cannot define a pad unless you DEFINE MENU to define the menu to which it belongs.

Syntax:

```
DEFINE PAD <Pad> OF <Menu>
   PROMPT <cExpPrompt>
   [AT <nExpRow>,<nExpCol>][MESSAGE <cExpMessage>]
   [SKIP [FOR <lExpCond>]]
```

Pads, unlike bars, are named and can be positioned. You can use the AT option to create a vertical menu instead of using DEFINE POPUP and DEFINE BAR if you want to. If you omit the AT option, dBASE places the first pad at the upper left corner of the screen and each additional pad on the same row, row 0, leaving one space after the previous pad prompt. SET SCOREBOARD OFF to prevent the scoreboard from overwriting a menu on row 0. Standard practice in dBASE IV creates a bar menu on row 0 as the main menu of an application, with a pop-up menu pulling down from each of its pads to enable selecting among the principal tasks.

The PROMPT and MESSAGE options and the new PICK and SKIP options are the same as those of DEFINE BAR. The menu is activated by ACTIVATE MENU.

DEFINE POPUP creates a dBASE IV-style pop-up menu.

Syntax:

```
DEFINE POPUP <Pad>
FROM <nExpRow1>,<nExpCol1>
     [TO <nExpRow2><nExpCol2>]
[PROMPT {ARRAY <Array>|
         FIELD <Field>|
         FILES [LIKE <skeleton>]|
         STRUCTURE}]
[MESSAGE <cExpMessage>]
```

The FROM row and column are required. If the TO coordinates are omitted, dBASE makes the popup large enough to fit the data, except as limited by the lower right corner of the screen, less a row if STATUS is ON.

If you use any of the four PROMPT options, you cannot use the DEFINE BAR option. The PROMPT ARRAY option is new in dBASE for Windows. The prompts will be the elements of the named array.

The other prompt options use the values in a named field in the current table, the names of the files in the active catalog or those matching the optional skeleton, or the field names of the table open in the current table. SET FIELDS can limit the field names shown by PROMPT STRUCTURE.

A memo field cannot be used as a prompt with the PROMPT FIELDS option.

The message provided by the MESSAGE option overrides any message set by SET MESSAGE TO while the POPUP is visible, but can itself be overridden, if the DEFINE BAR syntax is used, by the messages attached to the bars.

DEFINE WINDOW creates a dBASE IV-style window. When the window is active, all screen input and output take place within it.

Syntax:

```
DEFINE WINDOW
  {FROM <nExpRow1>,<nExpCol1>
      TO <nExpRow2>,<nExpCol2>}|
  [COLOR <Standard>[,<Enhanced>[,<Frame>]]]
  [DOUBLE|NONE|PANEL|{<cExpBorderList>}]
```

If the new AT option is used to position the window, it will be of the minimum size unless the AUTOSIZE option is included.

The COLOR option enables you to specify a pair of colors, foreground and background, for each of the normal and enhanced text areas and for the window frame.

The final option defaults to a single line border but enables you to specify a double line border, no border, an inverse-video panel, or a border made up of characters. See SET BORDER and DEFINE BOX for details of the character border.

A window created with DEFINE WINDOW is activated by ACTIVATE WINDOW. A form defined using DEFINE FORM or the new keyword is activated by OPEN FORM or READMODAL().

See ACTIVATE, DEACTIVATE, RELEASE, RESTORE, SAVE WINDOW, SET BORDER, SET COLOR, SET MESSAGE, SET SCOREBOARD, SET STATUS.

DELETE

Deletes one or more records or a file, table, or tag. The new TABLE option is an adaptation of DELETE FILE to dBASE and Paradox database tables.

Syntax:

```
DELETE {[<scope>][FOR <lExpCond1>]
           [WHILE <lExpCond2>]}|
       {FILE{<File>|?|<skeleton>}|
       {TABLE {Table>|?|<skeleton>}
           [[TYPE]{DBASE|PARADOX}]}|
       {TAG {<Tag>[OF <MDXFile>|?|<skeleton>]}[,<etc.>]}
```

DELETE without FILE, TABLE, or TAG deletes one or more records from the current table. You can RECALL deleted records in a dBASE table at any time before using the PACK command; DELETE simply marks them for deletion. DELETE removes records from Paradox or SQL tables at once. They cannot be recalled. The default is deletion of the current record only; the <scope> option can specify a number of records up to the entire table. The FOR and WHILE options can limit the deletions to the records meeting the FOR condition or reached before the WHILE condition becomes false.

Example:

```
USE Customer
DELETE ALL FOR Last_Order < date()-365*3
```

DELETE FILE deletes the specified file. Wild cards are not enabled to delete more than one file at a time, but you can use ? or a skeleton option to bring up the File dialog box. You cannot delete an open file.

You should use the DELETE TABLE option to delete a dBASE table. DELETE TABLE deletes the table's associated DBT and production MDX files, while DELETE FILE does not. Do not delete a production MDX file without deleting its DBF, because you will render the DBF table unusable until you reset byte 28 of its header. See the example under CHR() for how to reset the byte.

DELETE TABLE deletes the specified dBASE, Paradox, or database table, its DBT and its production MDX files. You must separately delete any related NDX files or non-production MDX files. You cannot delete an open file, including one opened with the low-level file functions. DELETE TABLE will delete a file with extension DBF whether or not it is a dBASE table. To delete a table in a database defined with IDAPI, give the name of the database delimited by colons before the name of the table. If the database is not open, dBASE will display a dialog prompting you for a login, password, or other input needed to establish a connection to the database.

DELETE TAG deletes the specified tag or tags from the specified MDX files, or by default from the production MDX. The MDX file must be open, but the deleted tag need not be controlling the order of the table. If you delete all the tags, the MDX file is deleted and the DBF table marked to show that it has been deleted. An open catalog is also updated. In a multiuser environment, the table must be in exclusive use to delete tags.

You also can use DELETE TAG to delete secondary indexes of a Paradox table or individual index tags defined for a SQL table. If you issue DELETE TAG with no arguments while a Paradox table is the current one, you will delete its primary index.

DELETED()

Returns .T. for those records of a dBASE table that have been marked for deletion, .F. for others.

Syntax:

```
[lVar=] deleted(<workarea>)
```

The DELETED() function always returns .F. for records of Paradox tables. It also returns .F. if there is no table in use. If SET DELETED is ON, the records marked for deletion will not appear, so such commands as LIST FOR DELETED() will not perform as you might want.

Example:

```
set deleted off
copy to Archive for deleted()
pack
```

If you use Paradox tables, do not use deletion as a method of marking records temporarily. The habit might cause you to mark for deletion Paradox records you intend to copy or otherwise preserve. Marking a Paradox record deletes it immediately, losing the data, rather than simply marking it subject to recall as in dBASE.

DESCENDING()

Returns .T. if the specified tag was created in descending order.

Syntax:

```
[lVar=] descending([[<MDXFile,]<nExpTag>
        [,<workarea>]])
```

By itself, DESCENDING() returns the status of the controlling tag. The second but primary parameter <nExpTag> specifies a tag number, such as that returned by the TAGNO() function. If no MDX is specified, dBASE looks in the production MDX for the specified tag. If a work area is specified, dBASE looks in the specified or production MDX for that workarea. If the tag or specified file cannot be found, an error occurs. If the only index is an NDX file or the table in the workarea is a Paradox table, descending returns .F.

DEXPORT

Is not supported by dBASE for Windows.

DGEN()

Is not supported by dBASE for Windows.

DIFFERENCE()

Determines the difference between two character expressions using their SOUNDEX() codes.

Syntax:

```
[nVar=] difference(<cExp1>|<mFld1>,<cExp2>|<mFld2>)
```

The DIFFERENCE() function resolves the character expressions or Memo fields to literal strings, finds the SOUNDEX() code of each, and computes the difference. It returns an integer from 0 to 4. Four represents two closely matched strings, while 0 occurs only if the two strings have no letters in common that are considered the same by SOUNDEX(). Very short strings that have fewer SOUNDEX() characters than four may return misleadingly high DIFFERENCE() values. This occurs because both their SOUNDEX() values contain one or more zeroes, actually reprepresenting missing characters but considered identical by the function.

Example:

```
use \dbasewin\samples\Customer.db
NewCust = "Howie"
calculate max(difference(NewCust,Name)) to Closest
? Closest
        3
```

```
list Name for difference(NewCust,Name)>2
NAME
Kauai Dive Shoppe
The Depth Charge
The Diving Company
```

See SOUNDEX().

DIR

Displays the tables or files in the current or specified directory.

Syntax:

```
DIR [ON]<Drive>] [[LIKE][<path>]<skeleton>]
```

Any form of the DIR command displays, at the foot of the list the number of files listed, the number of free bytes on the disk and the total number of bytes on the disk.

DIR without more lists the tables in the current directory with extension DBF, including their names, numbers of records, dates last updated and length. If a file with extension DBF is not a dBASE table, dBASE so reports in the list in place of the number of records and update date. If SET DBTYPE is set to Paradox, DIR alone lists no files.

The dBASE DIR command differs from the DOS command in that if you supply a path, only, you must add a backslash at the end to see the tables in that directory. Otherwise, dBASE looks for a table of the name of the last directory.

To list the names of other types of files with their lengths in bytes and dates of last update but not numbers of records, supply DIR with a skeleton appropriate to the drive, path and names or extensions of the files to list. The LIKE and ON keywords do nothing; the drive can as usual be included as the first letter of the skeleton, with a colon to separate it from the path or file portions of the skeleton.

DIRECTORY

Is an alternate form of DIR.

DISKSPACE()

Returns free space on a disk, now with optional drive number.

Syntax:

```
[nVar=] diskspace([<nExpDrive>])
```

The DISKSPACE() function returns the number of free bytes on the default drive, or on the one specified by <nExpDrive>. The result of nExpDrive is interpreted as 1 = Drive A, 2 = Drive B, etc. If you supply 0 or a negative number, dBASE returns the space on the default drive. If you supply a number larger than the number of the last drive you own, dBASE returns 0.

DISPLAY

Displays data from the current table or other information.

The DISPLAY command is the same as LIST, with the same options, except that DISPLAY displays only as many lines as will fill the Command Results window, then prompts the user for input before displaying more. By default, the scope of DISPLAY with no options is one record, while the scope of LIST is the entire table. DISPLAY with a scope of ALL does not pause screen output if SET PRINTER is ON; it prints continuously both to screen and printer.

DISPLAY of a substantial amount of information to the Command Results window causes the earlier information to disappear off the top as later screenfuls are displayed. You cannot stop the display and scroll up or enlarge the Command Results window until the display of all requested information is complete, unless you cancel it. If there is too much information for dBASE's buffer, you will not be able to scroll up to see all of the earlier information. To prevent loss of the output, use the TO PRINT or TO FILE option of LIST instead of using DISPLAY. You might also find it helpful to enlarge the Command Results window before issuing DISPLAY.

The various DISPLAY|LIST options are described under LIST.

See LIST.

You can move the alert box that prompts you for the next screenful out of the way by dragging its title bar before you click one of its pushbuttons. This enables you to see the top few lines of the Command Results window it normally blocks.

DMY()

Converts a date expression into a character expression of the form DD Month YY, or DD Month YYYY if SET CENTURY is ON.

Syntax:

```
[cVar=] dmy(<dExp>)
```

The DMY() function is unaffected by SET DATE. It returns the day as one or two digits, the month spelled out, and the year in two or four digits as specified by SET CENTURY.

Example:

```
cDate = dmy({12/31/99}+1)
? cDate
1 January 00
```

DO

Runs a dBASE program, procedure, or user-defined function. With CASE, WHILE, or UNTIL, commences a program loop structure.

Syntax:

```
DO {{{<File>|?|<skeleton>}|<Procedure>|<UDF>}
    [WITH <ParameterList>]}|
   {CASE|WHILE|{<code> UNTIL}}
```

DO alone executes the specified file, procedure or function. You can use ? or a skeleton to bring up the File dialog from which you can choose a file. Any parameters required by the program, procedure, or function being executed can be passed following the optional WITH.

dBASE ignores the return of a user-defined function executed by DO. You might instead execute such a function by typing its name, or ? followed by its name, into the Command window. Follow the function name with parentheses including the parameter list, or with a pair of parentheses if it takes no parameters.

A procedure or function must reside either in a file of its own name or in an open file—in either case on the search path. dBASE searches as follows:

1. If the call is from within a program, in the current program PRO file. In case a function and procedure with the same name coexist in the file, dBASE executes the one closer to the end of the file.

2. In other PRO files in the calling chain, most recently opened first. This applies only when the call is from a running program that is itself called from another program by DO.

3. In the file specified by SYSPROC = in DBASEWIN.INI.

4. In any files opened with SET PROCEDURE or SET LIBRARY, in the order opened.

5. In a PRO file of the same name in the current path set by SET PATH or SET DIRECTORY, which PRO file dBASE will open.

6. For a PRG file of the same name, which dBASE will compile and run.

An external function cannot be executed by DO from the Command window.

Example:

```
DO MyProc WITH 5, 20
```

If you type this command in the Command window, dBASE will look in the SYSPROC, PROCEDURE, and LIBRARY files, if any, for a procedure or function named MyProc. If it finds none, it will look in the current path for MYPROC.PRO or MYPROC.PRG. If it finds any of them, it will pass the parameters 5 and 20 to the procedure or function and execute its code. If it does not find MyProc, an error occurs.

DO CASE introduces a CASE . . . ENDCASE programming construct.

Syntax:

```
DO CASE
  {CASE <lExpCond>
     <code>}
  [<etc.>]
  [OTHERWISE
     <code>]
ENDCASE
```

dBASE evaluates the CASE <lExpCond> conditions in order until it finds a true one. It then executes the code following that condition and, if execution has not been redirected by a RETURN, CANCEL, or QUIT statement, continues with the statement following ENDCASE. The optional OTHERWISE statement must follow the last CASE and has no condition. It is executed if none of the CASE conditions are true.

C programmers should note that dBASE CASE statements differ from switch/case statements in C. dBASE executes only the first CASE statement with a true condition. C execution "falls through" from one true condition to the next unless a break statement is inserted. In addition, while it is most common for dBASE CASE conditions to test different values of the same field or variable, there is no requirement that they do so.

Example:

```
nHour = val(left(time(),2))
DO CASE
```

```
    CASE nHour >17
      ? "Good evening!"
    CASE nHour >11
      ? "Good afternoon."
    CASE nHour > 8
      ? "Good morning."
    CASE nHour > 6 .AND. dow() = 1
      ? "Did you get the Sunday paper?"
    CASE nHour > 5 .AND. dow() < 6
      ? "Ooh, I hate to get up."
    OTHERWISE
      ? "Good heavens! Go to sleep!"
ENDCASE
```

DO WHILE introduces one of dBASE's four looping constructs—the only one available in dBASE III and III+. (The others are DO . . . UNTIL, discussed just below, FOR . . . ENDFOR|NEXT, and SCAN . . . ENDSCAN.)

Syntax:

```
DO WHILE <lExpCond>
  <code>
  [LOOP]
  [EXIT]
ENDDO
```

If the <lExpCond> condition is true, the code between the DO and the required ENDDO statements is executed repeatedly until it becomes false, when the statement following ENDDO is executed.

dBASE provides the LOOP and EXIT statements to allow you more control of the loop.

LOOP causes execution to return at once to the DO WHILE statement. Any statements below the LOOP statement are ignored. The condition is evaluated and execution continues.

The EXIT statement breaks out of the loop and jumps to the statement following ENDDO without evaluating the condition at all. The presence of the EXIT statement enables you to write a loop with a condition that will never be false, such as DO WHILE .T., relying on an EXIT statement to keep the program from looping endlessly.

Some experts frown on DO WHILE .T., because technically it is always possible to code the loop in a way that makes it unnecessary. In each case, LOOP or EXIT escapes only from the innermost loop in which it occurs. In the example below, the EXIT from the inner loop cannot return processing to the top of the outer loop, so a LOOP command is needed too. RETURN will exit all pending loops in the routine in which it occurs, while CANCEL will exit all loops and program operations at all levels.

Example:

```
#define MAXPRIMES 10000
declare nPrime[MAXPRIMES]
nPrime[1] = 1
nPrime[2] = 2
nPrime[3] = 3
store 3 to nTry, nLastPrime
do while Prime[MAXPRIMES] = .F.
  nTry = nTry + 2
  nRoot = sqrt(nTry)
  nNextPrime = 3
  do while nPrime[nNextPrime] <= nRoot
    if mod(nTry,nPrime[nNextPrime]) = 0
      nNextPrime = 0      && nTry is not prime
      exit
    else
      nNextPrime = nNextPrime + 1
    endif
  enddo
  if nNextPrime = 0
     loop
  endif
  nLastPrime = nLastPrime + 1
  nPrime[nLastPrime] = nTry
enddo
```

DO . . . UNTIL is identical to DO WHILE except the condition follows the WHILE at the end of the loop, and is not evaluated until one pass is complete. Also, the loop ends if the UNTIL condition is true, but ends if a WHILE condition is false.

Syntax:

```
DO
  <code>
  [LOOP]
  [EXIT]
UNTIL <lExpCond>
```

The following example assumes that one of the three called procedures sets the variable lDone to .T. when exit from the loop is appropriate.

Example:

```
lDone = .F.
DO
```

```
        DO GetData
        DO VerifyData
        DO SaveData
    UNTIL lDone
```

DOS

New; interrupts dBASE and shells out to DOS.

Syntax:

```
DOS
```

Issuing the DOS command terminates execution of dBASE and brings up a DOS prompt. You can execute any DOS commands, but in order to avoid memory problems or shortages, do not start another session of Windows or start TSR programs that will remain in memory. Type EXIT at the DOS prompt to return to dBASE when you have finished.

dBASE must find the DOS command interpreter, COMMAND.COM, in order to shell out to it. If this file is not in the root directory of the default disk, its location must be specified by the Comspec environment variable, which you normally set with the "shell" statement in your config.sys file.

By default, the DOS window closes when you return to dBASE. If you want it to stay open in the future, edit the DBASEWIN.PIF file using the Windows PIF Editor in the Main group to disable the "Close Window on Exit" option.

To run a single DOS command or a few such commands, use RUN|! or the RUN() function.

See !, RUN, RUN().

DOW()

Returns a number for the day of the week of a date expression, 1 for Sunday through 7 for Saturday.

Syntax:

```
[nVar=] dow(<dExp>)
```

Among the uses of the DOW() function is finding the date on which a certain day of the week must fall. The United States celebrates Thanksgiving on the fourth Thursday of November, a date that must fall in the range November 22 to November 28. Thanksgiving

is the date in that range with a DOW() of 5; the key date is the date following the last day on which it might occur less the desired DOW() value:

```
FUNCTION Turkey
     parameters year
     private dKeydate
     dKeydate = ctod("11/29/"+str(year,4)) - 5
RETURN dKeydate - dow(dKeydate) + 5
```

See CDOW(), DTOC(), DAY(), and the examples for DEFINE BAR and DO CASE.

DOWNSCROLL

New; scrolls the contents of the results pane of the Command window, the current dBASE IV-type window or the current form down by the specified number of lines.

Syntax:

```
DOWNSCROLL <nExpLines>
```

The DOWNSCROLL command uncovers lines scrolled off the top of a window. It affects the active window if it is the Command Results window, a window created with DEFINE WINDOW and activated with ACTIVATE WINDOW, or a form opened with OPEN FORM or READMODAL(). When the top portion of the surface under the window is visible, the command does nothing more.

You can accomplish the same result by clicking on the up arrow of the vertical scrollbar or dragging its thumb upward. The <nExpLines> parameter must be present. It must resolve to a positive value; the integral part is used.

See UPSCROLL.

DTOC()

Converts a date expression to characters.

Syntax:

```
[cVar=] dtoc(<dExp>)
```

The result of the DTOC() function is by default a character string in the form MM/DD/YY. The order of the parts of the date and the delimiter between the parts are affected by SET DATE and SET MARK and the number of digits shown for the year by SET CENTURY.

Use DTOC() to convert a date to characters that can be printed as part of a character expression concatenated with plus signs, where a date-type value creates an error. Use DTOS(), not DTOC(), to concatenate a date with characters if the result is to be used as an index key, because the sorting order will not be chronological if you use DTOC().

See CTOD(), DTOS(), SET CENTURY, SET DATE.

DTOR()

Converts degrees to radians.

Syntax:

```
[fVar=] dtor(<nExpDegrees>)
```

The DTOR() function converts a numeric value expressed in degrees of arc to radians, the unit required by COS() and similar trigonometric functions. The return of the function is a float-type value. There is no limit on the size of the numeric value. The function multiplies the result of the numeric expression by 180/π().

DTOS()

Converts a date to a string in the form YYYYMMDD.

Syntax:

```
[cVar=] dtos(<dExp>)
```

The DTOS() function returns a character result that is independent of the SET DATE and SET CENTURY expressions. You might concatenate the returned string with other character data to form an index key that sorts chronologically on the date portion.

Example:

```
Use Paychecks
index on dtos(dCheckdate) + cEmp_ID tag PaySummary
```

EDIT

Brings up the data of the current table for edit one record at a time.

Syntax:

```
EDIT
        [<nExpRecord>|<kVarBookmark>]
        [<scope>]
        [FOR <lExpCond1>][WHILE <lExpCond2>]
        COLOR [<Standard>][,[<Enhanced>][,<Border>]]]
        [COLUMNAR][COMPRESS]
        [FIELDS {<Field1>[<options>]|
        <CalcField>=<xExp1>[<options>]}[,<etc>]]
        [FORMAT][FREEZE <Field2>]
        [KEY <xExp2>[,<xExp3>]
        [LOCK <nExp1>]
        [NOAPPEND][NODELETE]
        [NOEDIT|NOMODIFY]
        [NOFOLLOW][NOINIT][NORMAL]
        [NOTOGGLE][NOWAIT]
        [TITLE <cExp>]
        [WIDTH <nExp2>]
        [WINDOW <Window>]
```

EDIT without more brings up the current record of the table active in the current work area. The fields will appear in the order they appear in the table structure arranged across and down a rectangular area, with the title of each field above its data. Edit gives this view focus and enables editing. SET FIELDS TO will affect the fields shown. Pressing F2 will shift to BROWSE mode and allow editing the same fields of the same table in that mode.

EDIT is related to BROWSE. Their options are similar. They function like the properties of objects of the BROWSE and EDITOR classes.

The <nExpRecord>|<kVarBookmark> option enables you to specify the record at which the edit will start. You can give the number of the record for a dBASE table. You can give the name of a variable holding the bookmark of the record for either a dBASE or Paradox table.

The <scope>, FOR, and WHILE options perform their usual jobs enabling you to specify which records to edit.

The COLOR option enables you to specify the colors of your edit window. If you supply fewer than three color codes, by default the first one will govern the standard colors used for the field titles, the second will govern the enhanced colors used for the fields themselves and the third will be used for the window background. You can insert commas as placeholders in the color code string to be sure that the only colors you specify are used for the background, such as ",,N/W".

COLUMNAR causes the fields to appear one above the other in the standard format for EDIT in dBASE IV and earlier dBASE versions. By default, they appear in reading order, left to right across each line from top to bottom, however they best fit in the rectangular window. COLUMNAR has no effect in BROWSE mode.

COMPRESS has no effect in EDIT mode. When you toggle F2 to switch to BROWSE mode, it reduces the number of lines used to display field names, allowing display of an extra record.

The FIELDS option enables you to further restrict the fields to fewer than those specified in SET FIELDS TO, or to add calculated fields. You might supply a list of fields and calculated fields in any order. For calculated fields, you must supply the name of the calculated field and, following an equals operator, the expression it is to evaluate.

The FIELDS option accepts the same options for the fields as BROWSE. See BROWSE for details.

The FORMAT option applies the specifications of a format file opened by SET FORMAT. Any requirements of the format such as PICTURE, RANGE, and VALID clauses will apply to the edit.

FREEZE <Field2> restricts editing to the specified field, although other fields will be visible.

The KEY option restricts the records shown, if an index is active, to those whose keys match the expression <xExp2>, or if the optional <xExp3> is included, to the records whose keys are from <xExp2> to <xExp3> inclusive.

The LOCK option makes the specified number of fields from the beginning of the list of visible fields stay visible at the left end while scrolling among other fields during BROWSE.

NOAPPEND prevents dBASE from asking you whether you want to add more records when you attempt to move off the bottom of an EDIT or BROWSE, and prevents adding records.

NODELETE prevents you from marking records for deletion, or if editing a Paradox table, from deleting them.

NOEDIT and NOMODIFY are equivalent and make all fields and records read-only.

The NOFOLLOW option prevents the display from jumping to its new location when the key field of a record is edited. Use this option if you want to edit all the records of a file in order and you might have to edit a key field; it prevents you from losing your place. Without NOFOLLOW, when you reach the letter K and change Katherine to Catherine you will find yourself in the names beginning with C again.

NOINIT retains the options from the previous EDIT. Use this option if you are editing outside a program to save retyping all the options when reissuing the EDIT command.

NORMAL causes a BROWSE or EDIT within a window to ignore the window and its colors, appearing in full-screen mode. On exit, you are returned to the window.

NOTOGGLE prevents you from using F2 to shift to BROWSE mode.

NOWAIT continues execution of a program after the EDIT window appears from the program, rather than waiting until the EDIT has ended.

The TITLE option specifies a title for the EDIT and BROWSE windows.

The WIDTH <nExp> option specifies the display width for all character fields. <nExp> must evaluate to a positive number; dBASE uses the integral part. You can scroll within the displayed width.

The WINDOW option opens the named window and causes the EDIT or BROWSE to take place within it.

See BROWSE, SET FIELDS, SET FORMAT.

EJECT

Causes the printer to eject a page and advance to the next.

Syntax:

```
EJECT [PAGE]
```

The EJECT command has no effect on the console or alternate streams. EJECT uses the _padvance system variable to determine whether to send a form feed, chr(12), to the printer or to send enough line feeds, chr(10), to finish the page and reach the top of the next. EJECT sets PROW() and PCOL() to 0 for the next page.

Laser printers and some others do not print anything until told the page is complete. Send EJECT to force the printer to print a partial page.

Dot-matrix and other non-laser printers that print a line as soon as received will eject pages improperly if the top-of-form setting of the printer is incorrect. Setting the top of form usually requires aligning the first page by hand, then either pushing a top-of-form button or turning the printer off and on again.

With the PAGE option, EJECT affects the alternate stream as well as the print stream. EJECT PAGE invokes the current ON PAGE handler, if any. You can issue EJECT PAGE before the line that usually invokes it is reached; dBASE will advance the paper as necessary and call the ON PAGE handler. If there is no ON PAGE handler or its line has been passed, dBASE checks that SET PRINTER is ON and that _padvance is FORMFEED. If both are true, it sends a form feed. If _padvance is LINEFEED, or for the printer stream if redirected and for the alternate stream, it issues as many line feeds as indicated by the formula _plength - _plineno.

EJECT PAGE increments _pageno and resets _plineno and _pcolno, as EJECT alone does not.

ELAPSED()

New; measures time between two events.

Syntax:

```
[nVar=] elapsed(<cExpTime1>,<cExpTime2>)
```

The ELAPSED() function returns the number of seconds elapsed between two times, treating the first parameter as the later time. The times must be character expressions in the form HH:MM:SS. You can include hundredths of a second in the time string, such as a string returned by time(0), but ELAPSED() will ignore them. If the first time expression is smaller than the second, ELAPSED() will return a negative number of seconds.

Example:

```
cStart = time()
DO Something
cStop = time()
? elapsed(cStop, cStart)
```

The ELAPSED() function has an unusual number of impediments to effective use. The order of the parameters is counterintuitive. It ignores hundredths of a second, cannot deal with the passage of midnight, and returns the time elapsed as a number of seconds that can be indigestibly large—who knows how long 4523 seconds is? You will probably find the SECONDS() function more useful. To convert a number of seconds into hours, minutes and seconds, here is a formula:

```
Ctime = transform(int(Seconds/3600),"@L 99")+":" ;

+transform(int(Seconds - ; 3600*int(Seconds/3600)/60),"@L
99") ;

+":"+transform(Seconds - 60*int(Seconds/60),"@L 99.99")
```

You should realize, however, that the apparent precision to 1/100 second of times is limited by the fact that the IBM PC family issues a "tick" only approximately 18.2 times per second. Each reported time covers slightly more than 1/20 second, so the difference between the time(0) times recorded at the start and finish of a process can be as much as 0.12 seconds off the correct value.

See SECONDS(), TIME().

ELSE

Introduces the portion of an IF . . . ENDIF construct to be executed when the IF condition is false.

See IF.

ELSEIF

New; introduces a second or subsequent condition in an IF . . . ENDIF programming construct.

See IF.

EMPTY()

Returns .T. if the specified expression is empty, otherwise .F.

Syntax:

```
[lVar=] empty(<xExp>)
```

The expression tested can be a variable, field or other expression of any type. The EMPTY() function is not as useful as the ISBLANK() function. EMPTY() returns .T. if the expression is blank or 0. ISBLANK() distinguishes blank numeric values from 0 values, making it more useful in averaging and similar operations where you wish to exclude missing data.

See BLANK, ISBLANK().

ENDCASE

Ends a DO CASE . . . ENDCASE program structure.

See DO CASE.

ENDDO

Ends a DO WHILE . . . ENDDO program structure.

See DO WHILE.

ENDIF

Ends an IF . . . ENDIF program structure.

See IF.

ENDFOR

Ends a FOR . . . ENDFOR|NEXT program structure.

See FOR.

ENDPRINTJOB

Ends a PRINTJOB . . . ENDPRINTJOB program structure.

See PRINTJOB.

ENDSCAN

Ends a SCAN . . . ENDSCAN program structure.

See SCAN.

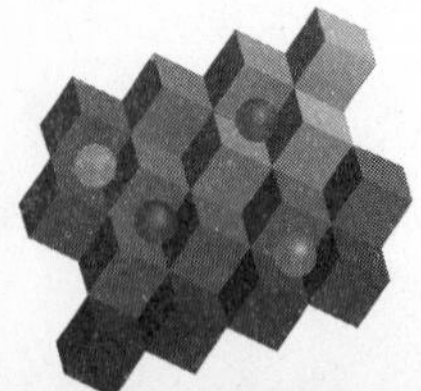

ENDTEXT

Ends a TEXT . . . ENDTEXT program structure.

See TEXT.

END TRANSACTION

Is not supported in dBASE for Windows.

See BEGINTRANS(), COMMIT().

EOF()

Returns .T. if the table pointer is past the last logical record.

Syntax:

```
[lVar=] eof([<workarea>])
```

The optional parameter identifies a work area. The EOF() function returns false if no table is in use in the default or specified work area. EOF() is false if the table pointer is on the last record of the table in its current order, natural or indexed, but is true when the pointer is moved forward from the last record. RECNO() returns one more than RECCOUNT() when EOF() is true and the table is in natural order.

See BOF(), RECCOUNT(), RECNO(), SKIP.

ERASE

Erases a file. ERASE is the equivalent of the DELETE FILE option of DELETE.

See DELETE.

ERROR()

Returns the number of the most recent dBASE error.

Syntax:

```
[nVar=] error()
```

The ERROR() function initially returns 0. After a dBASE error occurs, it returns the number of that error until another error occurs, the program if any completes execution, or a RETRY is executed.

The ERROR() function does not report numbers for DOS errors or system errors, such as those caused by attempting to read from a drive with no diskette in it. The error numbers in dBASE for Windows are not always the same as those in dBASE IV, so if a program written using ERROR() in dBASE IV returns an implausible error number when run under dBASE for Windows, check to be sure the error number has not changed.

To obtain the error message itself, use MESSAGE(). IDAPI errors are returned by different functions, DBERROR() for the number and DBMESSAGE() for the message. Compiler errors can be detected from a program by CERROR().

See CERROR(), DBERROR(), DBMESSAGE(), LINENO(), MESSAGE(), ON ERROR, PROGRAM(), RETRY.

EXIT

Causes termination of a loop program structure and executes the line following the end of the structure.

See DO UNTIL, DO WHILE, FOR, SCAN.

EXP()

Returns the natural antilogarithm of a numeric expression.

Syntax:

```
[fVar=] exp(<nExp>)
```

The EXP() function gives the number resulting from raising *e*, Euler's constant, to the power of <nExp>. The value returned is float-type. This function is the inverse of LOG(). You can see the value of Euler's constant, approximately 2.718, by using SET DECIMALS to a large number of places and issuing ? exp(1).

If you perform calculations using natural logarithms, use EXP() to convert the result back to the number, the antilogarithm. The example makes use of the fact that adding the logarithms of numbers gives the logarithm of the product of the numbers.

Example:

```
x = log(2)
y = log(4)
? exp(x+y)
         8.00
```

EXPORT

Is not supported in dBASE for Windows.

EXTERN

New; registers an external function, specifies its return type and parameter types, and loads the containing file if not loaded.

Syntax:

```
EXTERN [CDECL] <ReturnType>
 <Function>([<ParameterTypeList]) <DLLFile>[FROM
<ExportName>|<ExportOrdinal>]
```

The EXTERN statement tells dBASE that <Function> names an external function and tells dBASE the type of value it returns, the type and number of the parameters it requires, the name and if necessary path of the file containing its code, and its calling convention.

Much of the time, the provider of a DLL will provide a header file, usually with the extension .h, that contains the EXTERN statements needed for the functions within it. dBASE includes the file WINAPI.H containing EXTERN statements for the functions of the Windows API. If you have a header file that contains an EXTERN statement for a function, you should always #include the file instead of writing your own EXTERN statements.

By default, external functions are called using the Pascal convention. The CDECL option specifies the other, C-style, calling convention. The C-style convention is unusual in Windows programming. It will almost certainly cause a serious error to call a function using the wrong convention for the code of the function. Do not use the CDECL option unless you are sure it is required.

The type of value returned by the function is specified by <ReturnType> and the types of the parameters, if any, by the <ParameterTypeList> within the parentheses. The path and name of the file are last as <DLLFile>. You should note that although every file that contains external functions dBASE can call is a DLL, or Dynamic Link Library, not every such file has the file extension .DLL. You must specify the file extension in the EXTERN statement.

dBASE searches for the file in the current directory, the WINDOWS directory, the Windows SYSTEM directory, the directory containing DBASEWIN.EXE and the directories in the current DOS and network paths, so it is often unnecessary to include the path with the file name.

The FROM option is provided in case the creator of a DLL you wish to use has given the functions within it unusable names, such as names that are the same as built-in dBASE functions or user-designed functions in a library you use. Supply as <Function> the name you will use to call the function in dBASE, which must differ from the names of any other functions you might call, and specify as <ExportName> the name the function was given by the creator of the DLL. The <ExportOrdinal> option allows you to designate the function within the DLL by the ordinal number the creator of the DLL gave it. Designating functions by number makes them easier to find and speeds their execution, but is only possible with DLLs created with such calls in mind.

The return value types and parameter types use the same set of special type keywords adapted from the C language:

CDOUBLE	Any numeric value that might involve fractions used in complicated mathematical operations. This is the same as a float-type value and requires eight bytes, 64 bits.
CHANDLE	A Windows handle; an arbitrary 16-bit positive integer.
CINT	A positive integer not greater than 65,535, or zero, expressed in one word of 16 bits.
CLOGICAL	A true (1) or false (0) value held in a word of 16 bits, all but the rightmost being 0.
CLONG	A large positive integer or Windows bitmapped constant. dBASE passes a sequence of four bytes holding the number as a binary integer.
CPTR	A pointer to an object stored somewhere in memory. dBASE passes the address in four bytes, the segment and offset.
CSTRING	A pointer like CPTR to a null-terminated string of characters.
CVAR	A pointer to a dBASE memory variable.

CVOID	Used to indicate that a function returns no value. If a function takes no parameters, leave the parentheses following the function name empty.
CWORD	An integer in the range 0-65,535.

Of the return and parameter types, CPTR cannot be used as a return type. While dBASE can pass to a DLL that presumably knows how to deal with it a pointer to any type of object, dBASE must know the type of any object returned. Also, CVAR can be used only to pass parameters to, or receive results from, external functions that know how to access dBASE memory variables. A system of such functions is installed in the Samples\Extern subdirectory of the dBASE for Windows product.

See LOAD DLL, RELEASE DLL.

FCLOSE()

Closes a low-level file.

Syntax:

```
[lVar=] fclose(<nExpHandle>)
```

The FCLOSE() function closes a file opened with FCREATE() or FOPEN(), using the numeric handle returned by one of those functions. If the numeric expression does not evaluate to the handle of such a file, an error occurs. The FCLOSE() function returns .T. if successful, otherwise .F. CLOSE ALL and CLEAR ALL also close any open low-level files.

Example:

```
nHandle = fopen("MYDBASE.DBF")
if nHandle <= 0
  ? "Cannot open file"
  RETURN
endif
cByte = fread(nHandle, 1)
if "" = cByte
  ? "Cannot read file"
  RETURN
endif
if fseek(nHandle, 0) # 0
  ? "Cannot move file pointer"
  RETURN
endif
```

```
cByte = bitor(bitand(cByte, 248), 3)
if fwrite(nHandle, cByte) # 1
  ? "Cannot write to file"
  RETURN
endif
if .not. fclose(nHandle)
  ? "Cannot close file"
  RETURN
endif
```

The example code, if successful, sets the lowest three bits of the first byte of the file to 011, the signature for a table in dBASE III or later, and can correct some "File is not a dBASE table" errors. Remove the if . . . endif and RETURN statements if using this in the Command window, but check the values returned to be sure the low-level functions are working. **BACK UP YOUR TABLE** before trying to fix it with this technique, and close it with USE before opening it with FOPEN().

See FCREATE(), FERROR(), FGETS(), FOPEN(), FPUTS(), FREAD(), FSEEK() FWRITE().

FCREATE()

Creates a file at low level.

Syntax:

```
[nVar=] fcreate(<cExpFile>,[<cExpPrivilege>])
```

The FCREATE() function calls DOS to create and open a file. The <cExpFile> parameter must resolve to a valid file name and path—if the file is to be created in a different directory or on a different drive. You must include the file extension or the file will have no extension. The optional <cExpPrivilege> parameter must resolve to the letter W for write-only, A for append-only, R for read-only, or a combination of R and either W or A. Append only means the file can be written to, but only by adding at the end. It cannot be overwritten or truncated. By default, dBASE opens the file with RW privileges, allowing reading or writing including overwriting its current contents or truncating it anywhere.

You should save the handle returned by FCREATE() to a variable. If you do not, you will not be able to access the file and will not be able to close it except by CLEAR ALL or CLOSE ALL. If no handle is returned, the attempt to create the file failed. Some failed attempts to FCREATE() a file will cause a dBASE error message for incorrect syntax or because the file is already open or the like. In other cases of failure, the handle returned will be some number other than a positive integer and you can call FERROR() to determine the cause of the problem. Frequent causes are specifying a file that already exists and supplying a nonexistent path.

See FCLOSE().

FDATE()

Returns the operating system date of a file.

Syntax:

```
[dVar=] fdate(<cExpFile>)
```

The FDATE() function returns the date from the directory entry for the file. If the file is open at the time of the call and has been changed since it was opened, this date will not reflect current changes, so close the file before calling FDATE(). The <cExpFile> expression must give the name and extension of the file and can give the full path name. The expression must include the drive and path if the file is not in the current directory or those specified by SET PATH.

The date is returned as a date-type value in whatever format is set by SET CENTURY, SET DATE and SET MARK, by default MM/DD/YY.

See FILE(), FSIZE(), FTIME(), SET CENTURY, SET DATE, SET MARK.

FDECIMAL()

Returns the decimal places in a field of a table.

Syntax:

```
[nVar=] fdecimal(<nExpFieldNo>[,<workarea>])
```

If there is no field in the position within the file structure corresponding to <nExpFieldNo>, or if the field is not numeric, the function returns 0. It also returns 0 if the field exists and is numeric but has 0 decimal places. Use type(Field(<nExpFieldNo>)) to resolve the ambiguity; it will return U if there is no such field and some value other than N or F if the field is not numeric. The position of the field within the file structure you should use for <nExpFieldNo> is its position as if all fields were visible, whether or not SET FIELDS TO has made some fields invisible.

FEOF()

Returns .T. if the file pointer is at the end of a file opened with the low-level file functions.

Syntax:

```
[lVar=] (<nExpHandle>)
```

The <nExpHandle> parameter is the handle of a file opened with FCREATE() or FOPEN(). If result of the expression does not correspond to such a file handle, an error occurs. The function is analogous to the EOF() function for tables.

Example:

```
tempfile ="Mystatus.txt"
oldtalk = set("talk")
set talk off
set alternate to &Tempfile
set alternate on
set console off
list status
set console on
set alternate off
set alternate to
oldexact = set("exact")
set exact off
nHandle = fopen(Tempfile, "R")
if nHandle > 0
  do while .not. feof( nHandle )
    cVar = fgets(nHandle)
    if cVar = "Language Driver"
      ? substr(cVar, at(":", cVar)+2)
      exit
    endif
  enddo
  fclose(nHandle)
endif
erase &tempfile
set exact &oldexact
set talk &oldtalk
return
```

The example program routes the status information displayed by "LIST STATUS" to the file MYSTATUS.TXT using SET ALTERNATE. It then opens MYSTATUS.TXT and reads it line by line until finding the "Language Driver" line, which it prints, or until reaching the end of the file. It finally closes and erases the file.

FERROR()

Returns the operating system error number for a low-level file operation causing a system error.

Syntax:

```
[nVar=] ferror()
```

For a complete list of DOS errors, consult a DOS reference work. Some of the more common ones arising from dBASE low-level file operations are listed below. In some cases, Windows will issue an error message and request a Cancel or Retry before returning control to dBASE.

2	File not found
3	Path not found
4	No more handles (too many files are open)
5	Access denied (such as attempting to write to a file that is marked read-only by the system)
6	Invalid handle
15	Invalid drive specification
19	Disk is write-protected
25	Disk seek error
26	Non-DOS disk
27	Disk sector not found
29	Write error
30	Read error
31	General failure

The FERROR() function returns 0 when the operation succeeded, and also when the request never reached the operating system because dBASE intercepted it. To determine if this has occurred if FERROR() returns 0, use ERROR(). It will hold the dBASE error number if dBASE blocked the request.

FFLUSH()

Flushes the system buffer.

Syntax:

```
[lVar=] fflush(<nExpHandle>)
```

The FFLUSH() function writes the buffer of a low-level file to disk without waiting until the file pointer is moved to a section of the file not in the buffer or the file is closed. Use it for safety if the information is important and the risk of loss significant. The function returns .T. if the write is successful, otherwise .F. For maximum safety, disable any delayed-write feature of your disk-caching program, since such a feature can simply transfer the file buffer to the disk cache buffer rather than actually writing it to disk, while causing the function to return .T.

FGETS()

Reads up to a line from a low-level file.

Syntax:

```
[cVar=] fgets(<nExpHandle>[,<nExpChars>]
    [,<cExpEOL>])
```

The FGETS() function reads and returns a line from the open low-level file whose handle is <nExpHandle>. If the optional <nExpChars> is furnished, dBASE reads only as many characters as <nExpChars>, or to the end of the line, whichever is less. By default, dBASE reads 32,766 characters or to the end of the line.

The FGETS() function returns the line read, except for the end-of-line character or characters. The end-of-line marker is assumed to be the carriage-return line-feed combination, chr(13)+chr(10). You can use the optional <cExpEOL> to specify a different single character or pair as the end-of-line marker. The marker might be the chr(0) null value sometimes used in Europe; dBASE can deal with a single chr(0). However, if the file contains binary information that can include null values that should be kept, use FREAD() to read the file one byte at a time. The FGETS() function will treat every chr(0) as the terminator of the character string whether or not <cExpEOL> designates it as such, and you will lose the rest of the line.

See the example under FEOF().

See FREAD().

FIELD()

Returns the name of the field in the given numbered position in the structure of a table.

Syntax:

```
[cVar=] field(<nExp>[,<workarea>])
```

The FIELD() function returns an empty string if there is no field of the given number, or if no <workarea> is given and no table is open. If <workarea> is given but does not designate a workarea in which a table is open, an error occurs.

SET FIELDS has no effect on field().

Example:

```
use Flights
nY = fldcount()
nTot = 0
scan
      for.nX = 1 to nY
            if type( field( nX ) ) $ "NF"
                  Myfield = field( nX )
                  nTot = nTot + &MyField
            endif
      next
endscan
use
? "The total of all numeric fields in the file is "+transform( nTot,
"99,999,999.99" )
return
```

See FLDCOUNT(), FDECIMAL(), FLENGTH(), TYPE().

FILE()

Returns .T. if the specified file exists, otherwise .F.

Syntax:

```
[lVar=] file(<cExpFile>)
```

Because the syntax of FILE() requires an expression as the parameter, include the name of the file sought in quotation marks or other delimiters. You must include the file extension. You can always include the full path and must do so if the drive is not the current drive or the directory is not in the search path.

You cannot search for a directory as such because FILE() returns .F., but you can on a standalone system and some but not all networks search for the NUL file in the directory you want to test. DOS acts as though a NUL file exists in every directory.

Example:

```
? file("C:\DBASEWIN\SAMPLES")
.F.
? file("C:\DBASEWIN\SAMPLES\NUL")
.T.
```

FIND

Searches for a given key in an indexed table.

Syntax:

```
FIND {<xLtr>|"<xLtr>"}
```

FIND searches the index for the given literal value. If it is found, dBASE moves the file pointer to the first record containing a match of the key sought. SET EXACT governs whether the match must be of all characters (ON) or only of the starting characters (OFF). If a match is found, FOUND() will return .T. and EOF() .F.

If no match is found, behavior depends on SET NEAR. If it is ON, the search stops at the first record with a key greater than the one sought. FOUND() will return .F., but EOF() will be false unless the key sought is greater than the keys of all records in the table. If SET NEAR is OFF, dBASE issues the message "Find not successful" and positions the pointer at EOF().

FIND ignores leading blanks unless the key sought is delimited by quotation marks, single quotation marks, or square brackets. All leading blanks inside the delimiters are considered part of the key sought, and the search will be for a field with the same number of leading blanks.

To use FIND with a memory variable containing the key, use the ¯o. If the value of the memory variable contains leading blanks, enclose the variable name and the & operator in delimiters. If the key starts with delimiters such as quotation marks, include them and it in delimiters of a different type.

Example:

```
use Employees order Last_name
find Johnson
Find not successful
? eof()
```

```
.T.
set near on
find Johnson
? found()
.F.
? eof()
.F.
? Last_Name
Jones
Name = "West"
set near off
set exact on
find Name
Find not successful
find &Name
Find not successful
set exact off
find &Name
? Last_Name
Weston
```

See EOF(), FOUND(), SEEK, SET EXACT, SET NEAR.

FIXED()

Is not supported in dBASE for Windows. It creates no error, but returns the value passed to it unchanged.

FKLABEL()

Returns the label of a function key identified by number.

Syntax:

```
[cVar=] fklabel(<nExp>)
```

Different systems label programmable keys in different ways. The FKLABEL() function enables you to keep your programs portable by telling you what the keys are called by dBASE on different platforms. <nExp> must evaluate to a number from 0 to one less than the number of programmable keys on the platform, FKMAX(), which is 30 for the IBM PC family. The IBM PC keys are, in numeric order, F1 through F10, Ctrl+F1 through Ctrl+F10 and Shift+F1 through Shift+F10. dBASE ignores the F11 and F12 keys present on many enhanced keyboards.

Knowing the names of the programmable keys enables you to use their names in SET FUNCTION and ON KEY LABEL statements. The INKEY() and READKEY() values returned by the programmable keys are listed in Appendix C, "Key Values Reference."

See FKMAX(), ON KEY, SET FUNCTION.

FKMAX()

Returns the number of programmable keys on the keyboard.

Syntax:

```
[nVar=] fkmax()
```

The FKMAX() function gives you the maximum number of keys you can program. You can obtain their names on systems not fully compatible with the IBM PC by using FKLABEL(). dBASE for Windows supports 30 programmable keys on the PC in contrast to 28 supported by dBASE IV. In dBASE for Windows, the F1 key and the Shift+F10 keys can be programmed.

See FKLABEL(), ON KEY, SET FUNCTION.

FLDCOUNT()

Returns the number of fields in the current or specified open table.

Syntax:

```
[nVar=] fldcount([<workarea>])
```

The FLDCOUNT() function returns the number of fields in the structure of the current table, or of the one specified by <workarea>. It disregards any limitation on the visibility of fields imposed by SET FIELDS. If there is no table active in the current or specified work area, it returns 0.

See the example under FIELD().

See FIELD(), LIST STRUCTURE.

FLDLIST()

Returns the field names and calculated field expressions contained in a SET FIELDS list.

Syntax:

```
[cVar=] fldlist([<nExp>])
```

The FLDLIST() function operates on the current SET FIELDS list. If you omit the optional <nExp>, the function returns the entire fields list or the first 254 characters, whichever is shorter. Fields are separated by commas, include the file or alias name, and include /R if read-only.

If you include <nExp>, the function returns the alias and name if an actual field or the name and expression if a calculated field at that position in the list. The function returns an empty string if <nExp> exceeds the number of fields in the list or if the list has been cleared by SET FIELDS TO. SET FIELDS OFF|ON has no effect.

Example:

```
use dbasewin\samples\country
set fields to name, density = population/size
select select()
use dbasewin\samples\flights
set fields to dest
? fldlist(2)
DENSITY = population/size
? fldlist(3)
FLIGHTS->DEST
```

See SET FIELDS.

FLENGTH()

Returns the length of a field of an open table.

Syntax:

```
[nVar=] flength(<nExpFieldNo>[,<workarea>])
```

The FLENGTH() function returns the length of the field at position <nExpFieldNo> in the table structure. If the optional <workarea> is supplied, the function uses the table in that work area; otherwise the current table. If there is no field in the specified position, the function returns 0. For a numeric or float field, the length includes the decimal places and the decimal point. Any limitation on the visibility of the fields imposed by SET FIELDS is ignored.

FLOAT()

Converts a number from BCD N type to floating-point F type.

Syntax:

```
[fVar=] float(<nExp>)
```

The FLOAT() function will return an integer with a decimal point and as many zeroes after it as prescribed by SET DECIMALS. It is not ordinarily necessary to convert a number to float-type to use it in calculations, because if any of the other numbers entering into the calculation are float-type dBASE will automatically promote all the numbers to F type, and the result will be F type. You can increase or decrease the precision of numbers, whether N or F type, used by dBASE for internal calculations by changing SET PRECISION from its default of 16 to any number of digits from 10 to 19, inclusive. You can replace an N type field with an F type value directly; the field will retain its N type.

See SET PRECISION.

FLOCK()

Provides explicit locking of tables, locking being a necessity in a multiuser environment.

Syntax:

```
[lVar=] flock([<workarea>])
```

The FLOCK() function enables you to attempt to lock the current or specified table as a whole. If the optional <workarea> is omitted, dBASE attempts to lock the current table.

This function provides explicit locking in addition to the automatic lock dBASE provides when it performs an operation that can change the table's data. If the lock attempted by dBASE fails, dBASE returns an error. The FLOCK() function returns .T. if the lock succeeds, otherwise .F. You might want to use FLOCK() and test its return value rather than using ON ERROR to trap a failed automatic lock.

If FLOCK() succeeds, the table remains locked until you unlock it with UNLOCK or close it. Others can read a locked table, unlike a table you open with USE EXCLUSIVE, but cannot write to it. Do not FLOCK() a table for longer than you need to on a multiuser system. If you are not performing a REINDEX or updating multiple tables linked on a common key, consider whether you can use LOCK()|RLOCK() instead to lock only the record or records you are changing.

If FLOCK() fails and SET REPROCESS is 0, dBASE prompts you and keeps trying until it succeeds or you tell it to cancel. You can avoid the prompting by changing the value of SET REPROCESS. If FLOCK() is still false after the repeated attempts, you can reissue it.

If you SET RELATION to a parent table and FLOCK() the parent, dBASE attempts to FLOCK() all the child tables.

See LOCK()|RLOCK(), SET RELATION, SET REPROCESS, UNLOCK.

FLOOR()

Returns the largest integer not larger than the parameter passed to the function.

Syntax:

```
[nVar=] floor(<nExp>)
```

The FLOOR() function returns the same value as INT() for a numeric expression that results in a value equal to or larger than 0. For a negative number not an integer, it returns 1 less, the closest integer less than (more negative than) the number.

Example:

```
? floor(23/11)
        2
? floor(2 - 5.5)
       -4
```

See CEILING(), INT().

FLUSH

New; flushes data to disk.

Syntax:

```
FLUSH
```

dBASE normally keeps portions of each table and its associated indexes and memo files in memory buffers until the buffers are full, or until you close the files. The FLUSH command writes the data to disk and releases the memory occupied by the buffers. It safeguards your data against loss if the power fails and makes the memory available for other uses.

Do not issue FLUSH too frequently, because the time dBASE needs to reload the tables, indexes and memos will degrade performance. A good time to use FLUSH is before you or your user goes to lunch, for instance, if the computer is left on.

For maximum safety, disable any delayed-write feature of your disk cache software. If your software caches writes, the dBASE FLUSH command can merely empty dBASE's buffers into those of the cache software without actually writing to disk, which defeats the purpose.

See FFLUSH().

FOPEN()

Opens a file at low level.

Syntax:

```
[nVar=] fopen(<cExpFile>[,<cExpPrivilege>])
```

The FOPEN() command is like FCREATE() except that it fails if the file does not exist, while FCREATE() fails if the file does exist. You must supply the file extension as part of the <cExpFile> expression, and the drive and path if not in the search path. If you omit <cExpPrivilege>, you are asking for read and write access, which might cause a sharing violation if the file is already open. Be sure to close within dBASE any tables before opening them at low level. <cExpPrivilege> can contain R for read privileges, A for append privileges, W for write privileges, or a combination of R and either A or W.

Be sure to save the returned handle to a memory variable, or you will not be able to access or close the file, except by CLOSE ALL or CLEAR ALL.

See FCREATE(), FCLOSE(), FGETS(), FPUTS(), FREAD(), FSEEK(), FWRITE().

FOR

New; introduces a FOR . . . ENDFOR|NEXT programming loop.

Syntax:

```
FOR <nVar> = <nExpStart> TO <nExpEnd>
          [STEP <nExpStep>]
     <code>
     [LOOP]
     [EXIT]
ENDFOR|NEXT
```

The value of <nExpStart> is assigned to <nVar>. The code between the FOR and ENDFOR or NEXT will execute repeatedly until <nVar>, incremented on each pass by the value of <nExpStep>, is greater than <nExpEnd>. The loop ends with <nExpStart> greater than <nExpEnd> by <nExpStep>.

If STEP is omitted, <nVar> will be incremented by 1 on each pass. If the STEP expression is negative, the loop will be executed until <nVar> is less than <nExpEnd>. The starting, ending, and step values can be numeric or float types. None of them can be date, logical, or character type. If the values for the starting, ending, and step values are such that the variable will never reach the ending value, the loop will continue until halted.

ENDFOR and NEXT are equivalent. The LOOP and EXIT commands can be used to repeat or break out of the loop. If the ending or step expressions are variables, changing their values within the loop will not be recognized. The loop will continue to use the old values to determine when to stop. You can vary the value of the <nVar> variable within the loop and have the new value take effect—although doing so is more often hazardous than useful.

A FOR . . . ENDFOR|NEXT loop is useful to perform an action a fixed number of times, when there is no condition inherent in the situation that makes a DO WHILE, DO . . . UNTIL, or SCAN loop more suitable. It is always possible for you to substitute at least one of the other loop constructs, but often with some awkwardness and at a cost in making your code more difficult to understand and maintain.

See DO WHILE, DO . . . UNTIL, SCAN.

FOR()

Returns the expression used as the FOR condition used to create a tag of an MDX file.

Syntax:

```
[cVar=] for([[<MDXFile>,]<nExp>[,<workarea>]])
```

All the parameters are optional. If there are none, FOR() returns the condition applicable to the controlling index. If only one parameter is supplied, it must be <nExp>, the number of the tag. This number is the same one returned by TAGNO(). If no MDX filename is specified by <MDXFile>, it is the number of the tag counting all indexes open in the work area.

NDX files are counted first, one tag each, although if the number of a tag in an NDX file is specified, the function returns an empty string. The production MDX is next, followed by non-production MDX files. The optional work area parameter causes the FOR() function to search the tags in the specified work area.

The FOR() function also returns an empty string if there is no such tag, or the tag does not contain a FOR condition.

Example:

```
DISPLAY STATUS
Currently Selected Table:
```

```
Select area:  1,  Table in USE: D:\BUSINESS\CUSTOMER.DBF
Alias:CUSTOMER
Production MDX file: CUSTOMER.MDX
       Index TAG: NAME  Key: UPPER(Last_Name)
  Master Index TAG: CUST_ID  Key: Cust_ID
      Index TAG: US Key: ZIPCODE  For: Country="USA"
         Index file: CUSTZIPS.NDX  Key:ZipCode
? for(3)
? for("CUSTOMER",3)
Country="USA"
? for()
```

See INDEX, KEY(), TAGNO().

FOUND()

Returns the logical result of a search.

Syntax:

```
[lVar=] found([<workarea>])
```

FOUND() returns .T. if the result of the last CONTINUE, FIND, LOCATE, or SEEK command or LOOKUP() or SEEK() function in the specified work area, or by default the current work area, was successful. It returns .F. if the search was unsuccessful, including when SET NEAR causes the file pointer to point to a record with a key greater than the one sought.

The FOUND() function returns .F. if no search in the work area has occurred or if the file pointer is moved by any other command or function.

FPUTS()

Writes a line to a low-level file, including an end-of-line marker.

Syntax:

```
[nVar=] fputs(<nExpHandle>,<cExpString>
     [,<nExpChars>][,<cExpEOL>])
```

The FPUTS() function writes to the file opened by FCREATE() or FOPEN() whose handle is in <nExpHandle>. It writes the characters in <cExpString>, but if <nExpChars> is supplied, it writes as many as specified by <nExpChars>, with a maximum of 254 and a minimum of 0. After writing the characters, it writes an end-of-line marker to the file, by

default a Carriage Return-Line Feed pair, chr(13)+chr(10). If <cExpEOL> is provided and evaluates to one or two characters, it or they are written as the end-of-line marker.

To write to a low-level file without adding an end-of-line marker, use FWRITE().

FPUTS() returns the number of bytes written, including the end-of-line marker. It returns 0 if the write was unsuccessful.

See FCLOSE(), FCREATE(), FERROR(), FGETS(), FOPEN(), FWRITE().

FREAD()

Reads a string of characters from a low-level file.

Syntax:

```
[cVar=] fread(<nExpHandle>,<nExpChars>)
```

FREAD() reads <nExpChars> characters from the file opened by FOPEN() or FCREATE() of which the handle is given by <nExpHandle>.

FREAD(), unlike FGETS(), pays no attention to what it reads, reading and returning end-of-line markers along with other data. If it reads a null, chr(0), the returned string might be unusable. For greatest control, if you suspect a file otherwise containing text contains nulls, read it one byte at a time.

See FCLOSE(), FCREATE(), FGETS(), FOPEN(), FSEEK().

FSEEK()

Moves the file pointer in a low-level file.

Syntax:

```
[nVar=] fseek(<nExpHandle>,<nExpChars>
          [,<nExpFrom>])
```

The FSEEK() function moves the file pointer in the file opened by FCREATE() or FOPEN() of which the handle is <nExpHandle>. It moves the pointer by <nExpChars>, by default from the beginning of the file. If the optional <nExpFrom> is included and evaluates to 0, 1 or 2, the starting point is taken from it. 0 specifies starting from the start of the file, 1 from the current pointer position and 2 from the end of the file. The <nExpChars> parameter can be a positive or negative integer as large as 2^{31} -1, approximately 2 billion bytes either way, the largest signed values that can be held in four bytes. The FSEEK() function returns the number of bytes of the pointer's new location from the start of the file.

FGETS() and FREAD() position the pointer after what was read, and FPUTS() and FWRITE() position it after what was written. If you want to read then replace one or more bytes, or to read what you have written to verify it, you must reposition the pointer between the read and the write.

See FCLOSE(), FCREATE(), FGETS(), FOPEN(), FPUTS(), FREAD(), FWRITE().

FSIZE()

Returns the file size as reported by the operating system.

Syntax:

```
[nVar=] fsize(<cExpFile>)
```

The FSIZE() function returns the file size as reported by the operating system from its directory entry. You must include the file extension in <cExpFile>, and the drive and path if not in the search path. If the file has been modified but is open, data intended for the disk might not have been written and the system may report an obsolete size. Close the file or FLUSH before calling FSIZE() for accuracy.

See DIR|DIRECTORY, FDATE(), FILE(), FTIME().

FTIME()

Returns the time the file was last changed as reported by the operating system.

Syntax:

```
[cVar=] ftime(<cExpFile>)
```

The FTIME() function returns the time the file was last changed as reported by the operating system from its directory entry. The returned value is a string of the form HH:MM:SS in 24-hour format regardless of SET HOURS. You must include the file extension in <cExpFile>, and the drive and path if not in the search path. If the file has been modified but is open, data intended for the disk might not have been written and the system may report an obsolete time. Close the file or FLUSH before calling FTIME() for accuracy.

See DIR|DIRECTORY, FDATE(), FILE(), FSIZE(), SET HOURS.

FUNCTION

Marks the beginning of a user-defined function in a program or procedure file.

Syntax:

```
FUNCTION <Function>[(<ParameterList>)|
  {PARAMETERS <ParameterList>}]
  [PRIVATE <xVarList>]
     <code>
RETURN <xExp>
```

User-defined functions (UDFs) can be called like built-in functions by placing their name followed by parentheses anywhere an expression of the type returned by the function is legal. Include the arguments corresponding to the parameters within the parentheses.

The name of a user-defined function can be any length, but dBASE uses only the first 32 characters. The first character must be a letter. The other characters can be letters, digits or underscores. Do not give a UDF the same name as a built-in function or of the main program in the file in which it is defined, because dBASE will call the built-in function or the program instead of the UDF.

If the UDF takes parameters, they can be listed within parentheses following the keyword FUNCTION. Alternatively, they can be declared dBASE IV-style in a PARAMETERS statement immediately following the FUNCTION line. The last executable line of a UDF must be RETURN and must be followed by an expression of which the function will return the value.

A UDF can declare variables for use inside the function, but if they happen to have the same names as variables outside the function their values will overwrite those in the same variables outside. To prevent this and enable your function to be callable from other code whatever variables have been declared in the other code, declare all your variables PRIVATE or LOCAL within the function.

It is useless to declare the parameters private; if the UDF changes the parameters' values, the change affects the parameters outside the function anyway. It is good practice to write UDFs to avoid changing the value of the parameters for this reason, unless that is the whole point of the function such as the one following.

Example:

```
FUNCTION Swap(xA, xB)
  private xTemp
  xTemp = xA
  xA = xB
  xB = xTemp
RETURN .T.
```

The previous function swaps its parameters. It will not affect variables named xA, xB or xTemp that might exist outside, but if called by "swap(First,Last)" it will exchange the values of First and Last. If you want to utilize a UDF which you did not write and have not studied and want to be sure it will not change the parameters, enclose each in additional parentheses when calling the UDF. This forces dBASE to evaluate the parameters and pass their values to the function rather than as usual passing their addresses, known as passing by reference. The UDF will not receive the addresses of the originals of the parameters and cannot change them.

Most UDFs return a value without changing the parameter or parameters.

Example:

```
FUNCTION Fahr2Celsius
     parameters nFahrtemp
RETURN (nFahrtemp-32)*5/9
```

UDFs can be placed in the file of the program calling them, following the main code, or can be collected into files of UDFs and procedures opened with SET PROCEDURE or SET LIBRARY.

In dBASE for Windows it is possible to call UDFs like procedures, by DO <Function> [WITH <ParameterList>]. If you do call a UDF this way, the return value is ignored. It is also possible in dBASE for Windows to place the name of a function including a UDF on its own line, followed by parentheses enclosing the parameter list, without preceding the function name by any command verb. dBASE will call the function and ignore the return value.

Even if the return value of the UDF is meaningless as in SWAP(), above, or will never be used, the syntax requires that there be a value returned. Placing a .T. after the RETURN command is the easy way to provide a return value if it does not matter.

See DO, LOCAL, PARAMETERS, PRIVATE, PROCEDURE, PUBLIC, SET PROCEDURE, SET LIBRARY.

FUNIQUE()

Creates a unique file name.

Syntax:

```
[cVar=] funique(<skeleton>)
```

The FUNIQUE() function returns a file name not already used by a file in the same directory. Include the drive and path name if different from the current directory; FUNIQUE() will look there for a match and return a name that does not match any file

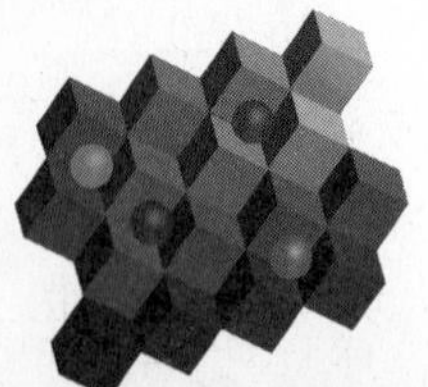

there. Fill the name portion of the skeleton with any letters you want and the ? wild-card character in positions you do not care about; FUNIQUE() will fill those with random digits and keep trying until it finds a name not in use. You will ordinarily want to fill in the extension of the file type for which you need a temporary or other unique name. The FUNIQUE() function may return a name for a DBF table although there is an orphaned MDX or DBT file of the same name in the directory, or vice versa. If this may create a problem, use FILE() to test for the existence of files with the proposed name and each extension you may require.

FV()

Calculates the future value of an investment of equal amounts over a number of consecutive periods at a fixed interest rate.

Syntax:

```
[nVar=] fv(<nExpPayment>,<nExpRate>,<nExpPeriods>)
```

The FV() function returns the amount that will be accumulated over <nExpPeriods> by making a deposit or investment of <nExpPayment> at the end of each period, with interest earned at <nExpRate>. The interest rate should be stated in terms of the periods. If there are 48 monthly payments and the interest rate is 6 percent annually, <nExpRate> should be .06/12, the monthly rate.

Example:

```
? fv(1000, .06, 25)
      54864.51
```

The example calculates the sum accumulated over 25 years of investing 1000 per year at 6 percent interest.

FWRITE()

Writes unformatted data to a low-level file.

Syntax:

```
[nVar=] fwrite(<nExpHandle>,<cExpString>
          [,<nExpChars>])
```

The FWRITE() function is the inverse of FREAD(). It writes data to a file opened by FCREATE() or FOPEN() without concern for line endings. It is the function to use when writing to non-text files. The FWRITE() function writes to the file whose handle is <nExpHandle>. It writes the string of characters <cExpString> or that portion of it that does not exceed <nExpChars> characters if the optional third parameter is passed <nExpChars> must be in the range 0 to 254, inclusive. If you call FWRITE() with <nExpChars> set to 0 and then close the file, you truncate the file at the current file pointer position.

Use FSEEK() if required to position the pointer before writing. FWRITE() cannot insert data into a file, it must overwrite the existing data unless writing at the end of the file. It returns the number of bytes written to the file, or –1 if an error occurs. Use FERROR() to identify the error. Use FPUTS() instead of FWRITE() to write a line of text to a file and include an End-of-Line character or characters.

See FCLOSE(), FCREATE(), FERROR(), FOPEN(), FPUTS(), FREAD(), FSEEK().

GENERATE

New; adds random records to the current table.

Syntax:

```
GENERATE <nExp>
```

The GENERATE command generates the number of records given by <nExp>, fills all their fields with random data and appends them to the current table. The only limits are that no more than 2 billion bytes nor more than 1 million records can be added to the table at once. A <nExp> value less than or equal to zero generates nothing; if you omit the <nExp> parameter dBASE prompts you for a value. The GENERATE command is intended as an aid to testing and debugging your programs.

GETCOLOR()

New; invokes the Color dialog box.

Syntax:

```
[cVar=] getcolor()
```

The GETCOLOR() function brings up the Color dialog box, tool similar to the Color selector in the Windows Control Panel that enables you to choose or design a custom color. The function returns a character string consisting of the values of the red, green, and blue components, on a scale of 0–255, separated by commas. If you cancel the dialog box, the function returns an empty string.

See DEFINE COLOR.

GETDIRECTORY()

New; invokes the Directory dialog box.

Syntax:

```
[cVar=] getdir([<cExpDirectory>])
```

The GETDIRECTORY() function opens the Directory dialog box, enabling you to select a directory—the path to which it returns. It does not itself cause a change to the selected directory. The directory name is returned without an ending backslash, so if you append a file name to it include a backslash between the two.

The optional <cExpDirectory> gives the name of the directory to appear first in the dialog box. If you omit it, dBASE uses the directory selected by the previous use of GETDIRECTORY(), if any, or the current directory.

See CD, DIR|DIRECTORY, SET DIRECTORY.

GETENV()

Returns the contents of a system environment variable.

Syntax:

```
[cVar=] getenv(<cExp>)
```

The GETENV() function returns the setting, as a character string, of an environment variable such as PATH, COMSPEC, PROMPT, DBTMP, or the like from dBASE's copy of the system environment.

If no environment variable <cExp> is found, it returns an empty string. <cExp> is an expression, so the environment variable name, if passed literally, should be in quotation marks.

GETEXPR()

New; invokes the expression builder.

Syntax:

```
[cVar=] getexpr([<cExpExpression>[,<cExpTitle> [,<cExpType>]]]
```

The GETEXPR() function brings up the Expression Builder. Its three parameters are optional, but the first must be given if the second is given and the second must be given if the third is given.

The first parameter is the expression, or initial part of it, to build. If it is omitted, the Expression Builder window is titled "Create an Expression". If it is included the window is titled "Edit an Expression" and <cExpExpression> appears in the window for edit.

The second parameter prescribes an alternate title for the Expression Builder window to display. The third must resolve to one character among the list "CDLNFX," with the character being the initial of the data type to be created, Character, Date, Logical, Numeric, or Float. "X" means the expression can be any type.

You can assign the result of GETEXPR() to a character variable. If you cancel the dialog box, the function returns an empty string. If you exit the dialog box by choosing OK, dBASE returns the expression and inserts it into the environment from which you called the Expression Builder.

GETFILE()

New; invokes the file dialog box.

Syntax:

```
[cVar=] getfile([<cExp1>[,<cExpTitle>
            [,<lExp1>[,<lExp2>]]]])
```

The GETFILE() function opens the File dialog box. Without options, the dialog displays all filenames in the current directory. The first optional parameter is a file skeleton; only files matching it will appear in the dialog. The second prescribes a title for the dialog box in place of the default "Open File". The third parameter, if .T., enables selection of files from directories and drives other than the current one. The fourth determines whether currently-open files appear (.T.) or not (.F.).

The function returns an empty string if the dialog is cancelled. If OK is pressed, the function returns the fully qualified name of the selected file.

The File dialog box appears without the use of GETFILE() whenever you give ? or a skeleton in place of a file name where permitted by a command. The title of the dialog box depends on the context, but the functioning is the same.

GETFONT()

New; opens the Font dialog box.

Syntax:

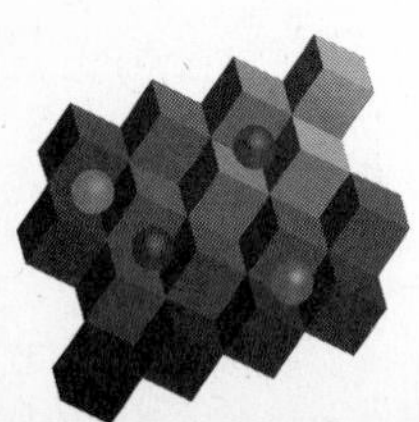

```
[cVar=] getfont()
```

The GETFONT() function opens the Font dialog box, enabling you to choose a font. If the dialog box is cancelled, it returns an empty string. If a selection is made, the function returns the name of the font, its point size and its group in a comma-delimited string, such as "Algerian,10,Decorative" or "Arial,12,Swiss".

GO|GOTO

Moves the record pointer to a specified record or bookmark.

Syntax:

```
GO|GOTO {BOTTOM|TOP|{RECORD <nExp>}|<kBookMark>}
   [IN <workarea>]
```

The GO, or equivalent GOTO, command, enables you to move to the top or bottom of a table, to the record you designate by number, or to the record associated with a bookmark variable. You cannot move to a record number of a Paradox or SQL table. If the optional IN <workarea> clause is omitted, the move is within the current table. The BOTTOM and TOP options will move you to the bottom or top record in logical order if an index is active, otherwise to the bottom or top in natural order. You can move to a deleted record in a dBASE table by its record number even though SET DELETED is ON.

See BOOKMARK(), FIND(), LOCATE(), SEEK(), SKIP.

HELP

Displays help.

Syntax:

```
HELP <cExp>
```

The HELP command brings up the on-line Help system. If the optional <cExp> is included, it brings up help on the first topic starting with the letters of <cExp>, or on the topic most similar in spelling to <cExp>.

The F1 key executes HELP unless reassigned with ON KEY LABEL or SET FUNCTION. During a program, it can bring up context-sensitive help.

See ON KEY, SET FUNCTION, SET HELP.

HOME()

Returns the path to the dBASE system files.

Syntax:

```
[cVar=] home()
```

The HOME() function gives the path to the dBASE for Windows system files, which by default are in C:\DBASEWIN\BIN.

HTOI()

New; converts a character string representing a hexadecimal number to a numeric value.

Syntax:

```
[nVar=] htoi(<cExp>)
```

The HTOI() function converts a character string consisting solely of the digits and the letters A through F, in upper- or lowercase, to the numeric equivalent of the hexadecimal number represented. If the string contains spaces, a leading "0x", a trailing "h", or other characters, an error occurs. There is no limit on the length of <cExp> or the value represented except the standard limits for lengths of strings and numeric values.

Hexadecimal numbers use base 16, with the digits A–F representing 10–15 respectively. They are convenient for many purposes because any byte value, eight bits with a decimal value from 0 to 255, can be represented in two hexadecimal digits, from 00 to FF. F means 15 and base 16 means each place multiplies the value by 16, so F0=16×15, 0F=15, and FF = 16×15+15 or 255. Hexadecimal numbers are used in dBASE to manipulate constants for external functions.

See EXTERN, ITOH().

ID()

Returns the name of the current user on a multi-user system.

Syntax:

```
[cVar=] id()
```

The ID() function returns an empty string on a single-user system or if the user's name is not registered.

See LIST USERS, NETWORK(), USER().

IF

Introduces an IF . . . [ELSEIF]. . . [ELSE]. . . ENDIF program structure.

Syntax:

```
IF <lExpCond1>
   <code>
{[ELSEIF <lExpCond2>
   <code>]}[<etc.>]
[ELSE
   <code>]
ENDIF
```

The IF . . . ENDIF construct is, with the addition of ELSEIF, functionally identical to the DO CASE . . . ENDCASE construct. dBASE evaluates the condition following the IF. If the condition is true, dBASE executes the code immediately following until it reaches an ELSEIF, ELSE or ENDIF, then jumps to the line after ENDIF. If the condition following IF is false, dBASE skips down to the first ELSEIF if any, tests its condition, and does the same things as with IF. If there is no ELSEIF—or if all ELSEIF conditions are false—dBASE executes the code following ELSE if there is an ELSE, otherwise the code following ENDIF. Every IF must be followed by an ENDIF. ELSEIF and ELSE statements are optional and must be between the IF and the ENDIF. There can be at most one ELSE statement. The ELSE statement must follow all ELSEIF statements, of which there can be any number.

Your code will be more readable if you reserve the DO CASE . . . ENDCASE construct for conditions that are alternatives of the same sort—one CASE for roses, one for tulips, one for daisies, and so forth. Use IF . . . ENDIF statements, with few ELSEIF statements, for unrelated conditions.

IF . . . ENDIF and the other looping and branching programming structures, DO WHILE . . . ENDDO, DO . . . UNTIL, SCAN . . . ENDSCAN, DO CASE . . . ENDCASE, and FOR . . . ENDFOR|NEXT, can all be nested within structures of the same or any other type. However, in all cases the delimiting keywords must both be inside, or both outside, the delimiting keywords of any other structure.

Example:

```
if month(date()) > LastComms
     use Sales order SalesRep
     Rep = " "
     scan
          if SalesRep # Rep
               if Rep # " "
                    Do CalcOwed with Rep
```

```
                        endif
                        Rep = SalesRep
                        Comms = 0
                   endif
                   Comms = Comms+Commission
               endscan
               do CalcOwed with Rep
         endif
         LastComms = month(date())
```

If, in the example, the "endscan" switched places with any of the "endif" keywords, the compiler would complain that there was no endscan to match the scan or no endif to match an if. Indentation as above makes the necessary pairing of the keywords easier to see.

See DO, FOR, IIF(), SCAN.

IIF()

Returns one of two values depending on the truth of an expressed condition.

Syntax:

```
[xExp=] iif(<lExpCond>,<xExpTrue>,<xExpFalse>)
```

The IIF() function provides a more compact and often faster alternative to the IF . . . ENDIF structure when one of two values is to be returned. If the condition expression <lExpCond> is true, the function returns the second expression, <xExpTrue>. If the condition expression is false, it returns the third expression, <xExpFalse>. As with other functions, IIF() functions can be nested in order to test multiple conditions. The values returned can be of any type and need not even be of the same type.

Example:

```
? "Dear "+iif(Sex="F","Ms. ","Mr. ") + Last_Name
```

See IF.

IMPORT

Creates dBASE or Paradox tables and copies data from spreadsheets into them.

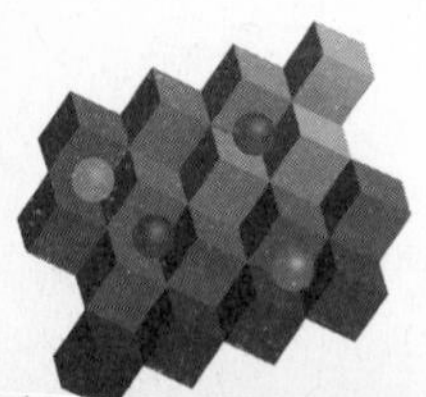

Syntax:

```
IMPORT FROM {<File>|?}
     {[TYPE]WB1|WK1}
     [HEADING]
```

The IMPORT command creates a table of the same name as the source file in the same directory, but with the extension appropriate to its type.

If DBTYPE is set to PARADOX, the created table will be a Paradox table, otherwise a dBASE table. The source file must be a Quattro Pro for Windows spreadsheet, usually with extension WB1, or a Lotus 1-2-3 spreadsheet, usually with extension WK1. dBASE can import a spreadsheet of either type with any extension, but it assumes the extension matches the type if you omit an extension, and the structure of the spreadsheet must match the TYPE option in the IMPORT command. The word TYPE is optional and accomplishes nothing, but you must specify one of the types from which to IMPORT. You cannot omit the type and supply it as the file extension only.

The HEADING option tells dBASE to use the column heading labels from the spreadsheet as field names, converting spaces to underscores, truncating, and mapping characters as necessary to create valid dBASE field names. If HEADING is omitted, the fields will be named FIELD001 and so forth.

INDEX

Indexes a table.

Syntax:

```
INDEX ON {<xExpKey1> TO {<NDXFile>|?|<skeleton1>}[UNIQUE]}|
               {<nExpKey2>}TAG <Tag1>[OF {<MDXFile>|?|<skeleton2>}]
               [FOR <lExpCond>][DESCENDING][UNIQUE]}|
     <FieldList>TAG <Tag2> [PRIMARY]
```

Each key <xExpKey> on which you can index a dBASE table can be a single character, numeric, float or date field, or an expression of any of the same types. The expression describing the key might be 220 characters long, but no key value resulting from evaluating the expression for a record may exceed 100 characters. You can use functions such as UPPER(), DTOS(), STR(), and the like in the key expression to convert values to character type and set the order you want, but do not use TRIM() or other functions that change the length of the key.

You can index a dBASE table to an NDX file containing a single key by specifying the name of the NDX file or ? with the TO keyword, with or without the UNIQUE option. You can alternatively index the table to a named tag of an MDX file with the TAG keyword. If you do not specify the OF option, the production MDX file with the same name as the dBASE table is used. In a multiuser environment, exclusive use of the table is required to create an MDX tag. An NDX file can contain only one index based on a single index expression. An MDX file can contain up to 47 indexes based on separate index expressions and distinguished by tag names.

You can include the OF option and specify another MDX file by name, skeleton, or by ?. Using the ? either for an NDX or MDX brings up the File dialog box, enabling you to choose or enter a file name.

With the TAG option, you can also use any of the FOR, DESCENDING, and UNIQUE options. The UNIQUE option, also available for NDX indexes, includes only the first record of each key value in the index. Creating an index with the UNIQUE option reaches the same result as setting UNIQUE ON before indexing. An index created with the UNIQUE option remains UNIQUE whenever reindexed—whether SET UNIQUE is on or off. If you change a key field of a record not in the index in such a way that it should be included in the index, you must REINDEX to include it. Every REINDEX reevaluates all the keys.

The DESCENDING option puts the index in descending order. The FOR option allows you to state a condition. Only records meeting the condition will be indexed. The condition expression might be 220 characters long but cannot include calculated fields.

If SET SAFETY is ON, dBASE will ask for permission before overwriting a tag or NDX file.

When you create an index, it becomes the controlling index. To change the controlling order, use SET INDEX TO to specify an NDX index or SET ORDER TO to specify a tag of the production or another MDX as the controlling order, or use either one without more to close all indexes but the production MDX and restore the table to natural order.

The <FieldList> options apply to indexing Paradox and SQL tables. You cannot use any of the described INDEX options using TO, TAG, FOR, DESCENDING, or UNIQUE for Paradox tables. You cannot index a Paradox table on an expression or to an NDX or MDX file. You can issue INDEX ON <Field> [PRIMARY] to index it on a field, or INDEX ON <FieldList> to index it on a comma-delimited list of fields. All Paradox indexes are unconditional and in ascending order.

Use the PRIMARY option to create an index on a single field of a Paradox table as the primary key. dBASE will then enforce the Paradox restriction of values you enter into the primary key field of a Paradox table must be unique. Use caution, because if you create a primary index on a field that already contains duplicate values, dBASE will immediately and irrevocably delete the records containing the duplicate key values.

All forms of INDEX ignore SET FILTER and SET DELETED. All records, deleted or not, are included in the index unless excluded by a FOR condition or UNIQUE.

See COPY INDEX, COPY TAG, DELETE TAG, DESCENDING(), FIND, FOR(), KEY(), REINDEX, SEEK, SEEK(), SET DELETED, SET EXCLUSIVE, SET FILTER, SET INDEX, SET ORDER, UNIQUE().

INKEY()

Returns a numeric value associated with the key pressed, or if keys are in the keyboard buffer, with the first key in the buffer.

Syntax:

```
[nVar=] inkey([<nExpSecs>][,<cExpMouse>])
```

The INKEY() function returns an integer characteristic of the key pressed or first in the buffer. The keypress is removed from the buffer or input stream. If the optional <nExpSecs>, which can evaluate to fractions, is included, INKEY() will wait that many seconds for a key. If none is available from the buffer and none is pressed within the time limit, program execution proceeds to the next statement. INKEY(0) waits indefinitely. INKEY() with no parameter does not wait, but returns 0 if no key is ready.

If the second parameter is included and evaluates to M or m, the INKEY() function responds to a mouse click, returning 151, as if it were a keystroke. If the second parameter is omitted or evaluates to something else, mouse clicks are ignored.

INKEY() with no parameter does not return any value for Ctrl+S or the left arrow key unless SET ESCAPE is OFF.

A list of keypress values for INKEY(), LASTKEY(), and READKEY() is in Appendix C.

INPUT

Accepts input to a variable of any type.

Syntax:

```
INPUT [<cExpPrompt>] TO <xVar>
```

The INPUT command enables you to obtain input of noncharacter and character type from the user. The prompt expression is optional. If your program is looking for date input, include in the prompt instructions to the user to enter the date in curly braces. Otherwise, you will have to later use CTOD() to convert the input from characters. Similarly, instruct the user to enter character data in quotation marks. The expression input can be complex. The type of input entered governs what will be stored to the variable <xVar>. The variable will be created if it does not exist.

You must end input by pressing Enter. If you press Enter without other input, dBASE prompts you for input again. If you press Esc and SET ESCAPE is ON during a program, the program terminates.

See @ . . . GET, ACCEPT.

INSERT

Inserts record into a table, has new AUTOMEM option.

Syntax:

```
INSERT [AUTOMEM|BLANK][BEFORE]
```

The INSERT command allows you to add a new record into a table at a specified place, instead of only at the end as with APPEND. With no options and no controlling index, INSERT inserts a blank record after the current record and brings up an edit window to fill it in as with APPEND. The AUTOMEM option fills the record with values from the AUTOMEM variables. It is up to you to create and assign values to the AUTOMEM variables before using INSERT AUTOMEM.

INSERT BLANK inserts a blank record but does not bring up the edit window. The BEFORE option, with or without BLANK or AUTOMEM, causes the insertion to be immediately before the current record.

If the table is indexed or the pointer is already at the end of the table, INSERT behaves like APPEND. Although added to all indexes in its indexed location, the record is physically added at the end of the table, and you are prompted to add more records.

See APPEND.

INSPECT()

New; opens the Object Inspector dialog box.

Syntax:

```
[nVar=] inspect(<Object>)
```

The INSPECT() function invokes the Object Inspector to inspect and edit the properties of the object referred to. The parameter is an object reference. When you create an object, dBASE creates a variable of the same name that refers to it. Place the variable in the parentheses without quotation marks. You can also assign the object reference to a different variable and use that.

INT()

Returns the integral part of a number.

Syntax:

```
[nVar=] int(<nExp>)
```

The INT() function truncates the fractional part of a number. If the integer returned has no fractional part, it is the same as the parameter, otherwise the integer is the next closest number to 0. For a positive number, INT() must be less than or equal to the number. For a negative number, INT() must be greater than or equal to the number.

If you furnish a number with a fractional part to a function or command that requires an integer as an parameter, dBASE truncates it automatically. You do not need to use INT() to assure that the parameter is integral.

Example:

```
Hours = int(Seconds/3600)
```

See CEILING(), FLOOR(), ROUND().

ISALPHA()

Returns .T. if the first character of a string is alphabetic.

Syntax:

```
[lVar] = isalpha(<cExp>|<mFld>)
```

The ISALPHA() function returns .T. if the parameter starts with an alphabetic character, otherwise .F. What is considered alphabetic depends on the language driver. In the United States, the alphabetic characters are A–Z and a–z. If the expression begins with one or more leading spaces, ISALPHA() returns .F.

See ISLOWER(), ISUPPER(), LOWER(), UPPER().

ISBLANK()

Returns .T. if the expression is blank.

Syntax:

```
[lVar=] isblank(<xExp>)
```

The ISBLANK() function tests whether the result of an expression is the same as the value of a blank field of the same type. In the case of a logical expression, this value is .F. Because .F. might be an actual value, you cannot be certain that a .T. returned by ISBLANK() means the value can be disregarded. See BLANK for a discussion of the BLANK values for different types of data.

The ISBLANK() function differs from EMPTY() in distinguishing blank values from 0 values in numeric and float fields.

See BLANK, EMPTY().

ISCOLOR()

Returns .T. if the computer hardware is capable of displaying colors.

Syntax:

```
[lVar=] iscolor()  ??? <nExp>?
```

The ISCOLOR() function returns .T. if the computer reports itself as capable of displaying colors. A monitor cannot report its capabilities to the computer. Many computers with display adapters capable of generating color signals are connected to monitors with only one color of screen phosphor, or to a monochrome LCD display. In such a case ISCOLOR() will return .T. but you will see only one color. You might have to adjust the monitor or set the computer to monochrome mode to make the screen readable.

ISLOWER()

Returns .T. if the first character is lowercase.

Syntax:

```
[lVar=] islower(<cExp>|<mFld>)
```

ISLOWER() returns .T. if the first character of the character expression or memo field is lowercase. Which characters are lowercase depends on the language driver. In the United States, the characters a–z are lowercase. ISLOWER() is .F. if the expression or field is empty or starts with one or more spaces or other nonalphabetic characters.

See ISALPHA(), ISUPPER(), LOWER(), UPPER().

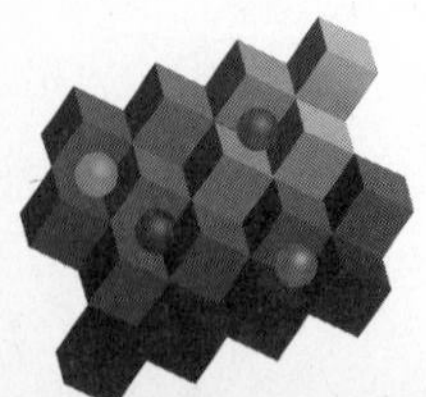

ISMARKED()

Is not supported by dBASE for Windows.

ISMOUSE()

Returns .T. if a mouse driver is installed in the system.

Syntax:

```
[lVar=] ismouse()
```

A mouse driver is software; it is conceivable that a driver could install itself although no physical mouse were present. Most mouse drivers test for the presence of an actual and functioning mouse before installing themselves, so you can rely on a true return from ISMOUSE() as showing that the system has a mouse or equivalent trackball or other pointing device.

Your programs can use the value returned by ISMOUSE() to determine whether the user must use the keyboard to navigate forms and windows, and to supply assistance and alternatives accordingly.

ISTABLE()

New; checks for the existence of a table in a database.

Syntax:

```
[lVar=] istable(<Table>[,<Database>])
```

The ISTABLE() function returns .T. if the current or specified database contains the specified table, otherwise .F. You must specify the path if not in the current path.

ISUPPER()

Returns .T. if the first character is uppercase.

Syntax:

```
[lVar=] isupper(<cExp>|<mFld>)
```

ISUPPER() is .T. if the first character of the character expression or memo field is uppercase. Which characters are uppercase depends on the language driver. In the

United States, the characters A–Z are uppercase. ISUPPER() is .F. if the expression or field is empty or starts with one or more spaces or other nonalphabetic characters.

The terms uppercase and lowercase for alphabetic characters derive from the days when printers composed type by picking metal characters from segmented wooden trays, or cases. The tray holding the capital letters was traditionally above the other.

See ISALPHA(), ISLOWER(), LOWER(), UPPER().

ITOH()

New; converts a number to hexadecimal notation.

Syntax:

```
[cVar=] itoh(<nExp>)
```

The ITOH() function converts a number into a character string of hexadecimal digits. If the number is too large to be held in four bytes (is equal to or larger than 2^{32}, or 4,294,967,296), the function returns the character "0". Any fractional part of the number will be truncated. It might be negative, in which case the function will return an eight-character string giving the hexadecimal digits appropriate to express the number as a "signed long" or "signed CLONG". For most purposes, ITOH() should be used to convert only positive integers less than 2^{32}.

The ITOH() function is primarily used to manipulate constants for external functions.

See EXTERN, HTOI().

JOIN

Joins the records of two tables into a third new table.

Syntax:

```
JOIN WITH <Alias> TO {<File>|?}
   [[TYPE] PARADOX|DBASE][ |
   FOR <lExpCond> [FIELDS <Fieldlist>]
```

The JOIN command starts with the first record of the current table and traverses all the records of the second, WITH table, to determine whether each meets the FOR condition. For each that does, a record is added to the new table. When all records of the second table have been tested, JOIN proceeds to the second record of the first table and tests all

the records of the second table against it, adding a record to the new table for all records that pass the test and so forth. JOIN can provide a test of your hard disk capacity, as the RECCOUNT() of the target table might be the product of the RECCOUNT()s of the source tables.

The JOIN command is rarely used. It is a relic of dBASE II that can create a huge table full of redundant data very slowly. The result is often a poor imitation of the links between two tables that you can quickly and economically create with SET RELATION.

JOIN requires that both tables be active. The JOIN uses the current table and the one identified by its alias in the WITH clause. It creates a third table. You can supply the name of the target table or use ? to bring up the File dialog box. The TYPE keyword is optional; you can specify the target table as of Paradox or dBASE type

The FOR condition is extremely important to make the resulting file meaningful as well as reasonable in size. Usually, it expresses a relation such as Cust_ID between the two tables, which might be one of Customer with their names and addresses and another of Orders to be billed to each.

The FIELDS list gives the fields from each source table, identified as to source by alias or work area, to be added to the target table.

See SET FIELDS, SET RELATION.

KEY()

Returns the key expression used to create the specified index.

Syntax:

```
[cVar=] key([<MDXFile>,]<nExpIndex>[,<workarea>])
```

The required parameter to KEY() is the number of the tag or file holding the key expression. The number of the tag or file is calculated with respect to the list of all open indexes, NDX files first, then the production MDX file, then non-production MDX files, unless you include the first parameter. If you include the first parameter, the MDX file name, the number is the position of the desired tag within that file, which is usually easier to calculate. If the key is controlling, you can use TAGNO() with no parameter to retrieve the number. The optional workarea parameter specifies the workarea of the table and related indexes if not the current work area.

If no index is open, or no tag exists of the number given, KEY() returns an empty string.

See MDX(), NDX(), TAG(), TAGCOUNT(), TAGNO().

KEYBOARD

Stuffs keystrokes into the keyboard buffer.

Syntax:

```
KEYBOARD <cExp> [CLEAR]
```

The keyboard command places the characters from <cExp> in the keyboard buffer, from which dBASE will read them as if typed at the keyboard. <cExp> can contain characters, CHR() values or KEY labels. Chr(0) should not be included.

The CLEAR option clears the keyboard buffer of characters before inserting those supplied by KEYBOARD. The number of keys in the buffer is limited by the SET TYPEAHEAD setting.

You can use KEYBOARD in three principal situations. First, use it when dBASE expects one or more keystrokes to confirm or direct some activity and you want the activity to proceed without user intervention. Place a KEYBOARD command in your program, with the confirming keystrokes, before the command that will cause the request for confirmation. dBASE will receive its confirmation from the KEYBOARD string without user input.

Second, you might want to fill in some portion of a form or other input area based on the content of other input. As an example, you might have a program with entry fields for both Client_ID and Cl_Name, allowing the user to fill in either one that the user knows. The program can then look up whichever of the name or ID the user did not enter and use KEYBOARD to place it in the appropriate entry field. The appearance to the user is as if he or she filled it in and provides visual verification that both the name and ID are present. Even when appearance is not important, KEYBOARD—by providing input to other sections of code that expect user keypresses—can save you from writing two sets of the same code, one for user input and one for program input.

Third, you can use KEYBOARD in a tutorial application to show the user how his or her keystrokes will appear.

You cannot use Enter or Esc in a KEYBOARD command. Use Ctrl+M or {13} for Enter and {27} for Esc. In all cases, put characters and curly-brace-delimited key labels within quotation marks or the other standard character delimiters, the single quotes and square brackets. Put CHR() expressions outside the delimiters, joined with plus signs. Table A.5 gives the supported key labels.

Table A.5
Key labels supported by KEYBOARD

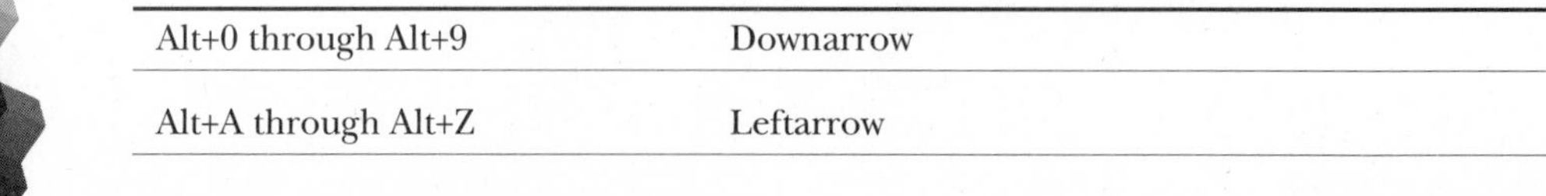

Alt+0 through Alt+9	Downarrow
Alt+A through Alt+Z	Leftarrow

F1 through F10	Rightarrow
Ctrl+F1 through Ctrl+F10	Uparrow
Shift+F1 through Shift+F10	Ctrl+Leftarrow
Backspace	Ctrl+Rightarrow
Backtab	Ctrl+End
Del	Ctrl+Home
End	Ctrl+PgDn
Home	Ctrl+PgUp
Ins	PgUp
Tab	PgDn

See CHR(), CLEAR TYPEAHEAD, SET TYPEAHEAD.

KEYMATCH()

Indicates if a key matching a specified expression is found in an index.

Syntax:

```
[lVar=] keymatch(<xExpKey>[,{<nExpIndexNo>|
[<MDXFile>,]<nExpTag>}[,<workarea>]])
```

The KEYMATCH() function determines if a key in the specified index matches the key expression given. It is primarily used with APPEND to preserve data integrity by reporting the existence of data with the same key and preventing entry of duplicates. The KEYMATCH() function ignores the DELETED, FILTER, and KEY settings to maintain integrity even though you are working with a subset of the table.

If only the key expression <xExpKey> is given, dBASE evaluates the expression for the record to be appended and searches the controlling index for a match, returning .T. if a match is found, otherwise .F. The options to KEYMATCH() enable you to specify the number in index order of the index to search or the tag number, and optionally the work area. If you specify the tag number, you also might specify the MDX containing it.

Example:

```
use Customer order Cust_ID
append from NewCusts for .not. keymatch(Cust_ID)
```

See APPEND, APPEND FROM, FOUND(), SEEK, SEEK(), SET DELETED, SET FILTER, SET KEY, UNIQUE(), USE.

LABEL

Creates labels.

Syntax:

```
LABEL FORM {<File1>|?|<skeleton1>}
  [<scope>][FOR <lExpCond1>][WHILE <lExpCond2>]
  [SAMPLE][TO FILE {<File2>|?|<skeleton2>}|TO PRINTER]
```

The LABEL command prints mailing labels using a label form file. You can give the name of the file literally or give a skeleton or ? to bring up the File dialog box. If you do not include an extension, dBASE looks for the extensions RPL, LBG, and LBL, in order. You can use the scope, FOR, and WHILE options to restrict the labels to a subset of the table.

The SAMPLE option prints a test row of labels so you can verify or adjust the paper alignment and the fit of the labels to your stock. dBASE prompts you to repeat the process as often as you want.

The TO FILE option allows you to print the labels to a file for later use or printing. By default, dBASE assigns a TXT extension to the file. You can give ? or a skeleton instead of the file name to bring up the File dialog box. TO PRINTER sends the labels to the printer. Without either the TO FILE or TO PRINTER options, labels will appear in the Command Results window.

See CREATE|MODIFY LABEL, SET PRINTER.

LASTKEY()

Returns a number representing the key or key combination used to terminate an editing session using @ . . . GET, APPEND, or BROWSE/EDIT.

Syntax:

```
[nVar=] lastkey()
```

The numbers returned by LASTKEY() for different keypresses are listed in Appendix C. LASTKEY() resembles READKEY(), but the key values are not the same, and READKEY() differentiates between edits in which the data was changed and those in which it was not.

LDRIVER()

Returns the name of the language driver in use by a table.

Syntax:

```
[cVar=] ldriver([<workarea>])
```

The LDRIVER() function returns the name of the language driver for the current or specified work area.

See ANSI(), OEM().

LEFT()

Returns the specified number of characters from the left end of a character string or memo field.

Syntax:

```
[cVar=] left({<cExp>|<mFld>},<nExp>)
```

If the specified length <nExp> is longer than the string or memo field, LEFT() returns the string or field as is, without padding it to the specified length. If <nExp> is less than 1, LEFT() returns an empty string. When reading a memo field, LEFT() counts each carriage return/linefeed combination as two characters.

left(<cExp>,<nExp>) is equivalent to substr(<cExp>,1,<nExp>).

Example:

```
Firstword = left(cString, at(" ", cString)-1)
```

The example returns the portion of a string preceding the first space.

See RIGHT(), SUBSTR().

LEN()

Returns the length of a character string or memo field.

Syntax:

```
[nVar=] len(<cExp>|<mFld>)
```

The LEN() function returns the number of characters in a character expression or memo field. It counts each embedded null (chr(0)) character as a single character. In a memo field, it counts each carriage return/linefeed combination as two characters.

To find the length of a particular line of a memo field, use LEN(MLINE(<nExpLineNo>)).

Example:

```
cString = "Hello"+chr(0)+chr(0)+"there"
? cString
Hello
? len(cString)
        12
```

See MEMLINES(), MLINE().

LENNUM()

New; returns the display length of a numeric value.

Syntax:

```
[nVar=] lennum(<nExp>)
```

The LENNUM() function returns the number of character places in which the result of a numeric expression will display, including leading blanks. If it is passed the name of a numeric or float field, it returns the field length.

If a number has 8 or fewer digits and no decimal point, it displays by default in ten places filled with leading blanks. A number with more places or a decimal point, or both, is a floating-point type. It appears in a minimum of ten places to the left of the decimal point, one space for the point and as many decimal places to the right as SET DECIMAL requires.

Large floating-point numbers are displayed with a negative sign if negative but no leading blank if positive. dBASE displays up to 20 digits before the decimal point. It displays the decimal point and as many decimal places as SET DECIMAL requires.

A number that would require more than 20 digits to the left of the decimal point appears in scientific notation. Numbers in scientific notation are always displayed in 20 places. The first place is the sign or leading blank and the second the decimal point. From three to five places at the right end are required for the E, the sign of the exponent and the exponent, expressed as a power of 10 that cannot exceed 308. The remaining places are used for digits of the mantissa to the right of the decimal point.

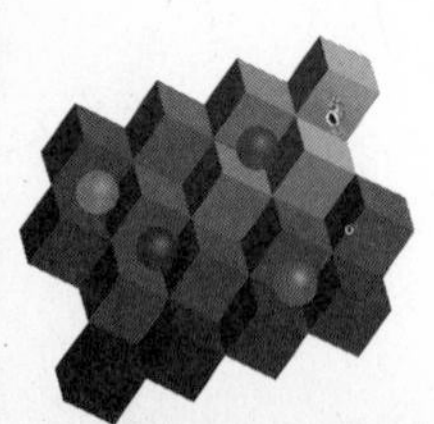

Stop

dBASE will display a large number in as many as 20 or more digits, but not all of them are meaningful. Any digits beyond the number of digits prescribed by SET PRECISION might or might not be accurate or significant.

See SET DECIMALS, SET PRECISION.

LIKE()

Returns .T. if a character string or memo field matches the specified pattern.

Syntax:

```
[lVar=] like(<cExpPattern>,{<cExp>|<mFld>})
```

The <cExpPattern> expression is made up of characters and the wild-card characters * and ?. The question mark represents any single character. The asterisk represents any number of characters including none. The function is case-sensitive. It compares the pattern to the character expression or memo field identified by the second parameter and returns .T. if there is an exact match, otherwise .F.

Do not include spaces in <cExpPattern>. Their inclusion will cause erroneous returns from the function.

Example:

```
? like("*a","Utah")
.F.
? like("*a","California")
.T.
? like("*KK*",upper("bookkeeper"))
.T.
```


LINENO()

Returns the line number of the current line of the currently running program, procedure or user-defined function.

Syntax:

```
[nVar=] lineno()
```

The LINENO() function always returns 0 outside a program. It can be used with ON ERROR and PROGRAM() to identify the line causing an error.

Example:

```
on error do Showline with program(), lineno()
     <code>
PROCEDURE Showline
  parameters cProg, nLine
  ? "Line "+str(nLine)+" of "+cProg+" caused " ;
     + "error "+str(error())
  wait
RETURN
```

In the example, the executing program and line must be determined in the ON ERROR line and used as parameters. If you simply include the PROGRAM() and LINENO() functions in the code of the Showline function, PROGRAM() will return "Showline" and LINENO(), the number of the line in the Showline code.

The dBASE Alert box that appears when a program error occurs will also give you the line number of the error, but not in a form your program itself can readily access.

LIST

Displays the contents of a table in a columnar list; has a new COVERAGE option.

Syntax:

```
LIST [{[FIELDS] <xExpList>][OFF]
      [<scope>][FOR <lExpCond1>][WHILE <lExpCond2>]}|
      {COVERAGE[<File1>|?|<skeleton1>][ALL][SUMMARY]}|
      {FILES [[LIKE]{<File2>|<skeleton2>}][ON <Drive>]}|
      MEMORY|STATUS|{STRUCTURE [IN <workarea>]}]
     [TO {FILE {<File3>|?|<skeleton3>}|PRINTER}]
```

The LIST command, and its close relative DISPLAY, shows the contents of tables and other information. They are the same in all but two respects. First, the default range of DISPLAY is the current record only of the current table, while LIST by default shows the entire table. Second, DISPLAY stops after the results pane of the Command window is full and prompts you to continue. LIST prints the data all at once. The size of the Command window buffer is limited, and you cannot resize the window itself between screenfuls of display. You will often have to LIST or DISPLAY to a file or the printer to avoid having output scroll off and out of the buffer before you can see it. In the remainder of this description, all options that apply to LIST apply as well to DISPLAY.

All varieties of either command share the TO {|FILE|PRINTER} options. By default, the display is to the results pane of the Command window of the screen. The TO PRINTER option sends the output to the printer. The TO FILE option saves it to a disk file. You can name the file or use ? or a skeleton to bring up the File dialog box.

If the display is wider than the screen width, the records wrap. This does not mean records will wrap to fit the visible portion of the results pane of the Command window. They will fill the maximized width of that window whether it is maximized or not, since you can maximize it to see more if you want. Each record will start on a new line in column 0. By default, memo fields are not displayed but represented by the word "memo." "MEMO" will be in uppercase if the memo has contents. Binary fields are represented by the word "BINARY".

Options for the standard LIST operation of showing the records of a table include <scope>, FOR, and WHILE to limit the number of records displayed and the FIELDS option, with the word FIELDS being optional, to limit the fields displayed. If the FIELDS option is given, only the fields and other expressions listed are displayed. The OFF option suppresses display of the record numbers. SET HEADING governs whether the columns will be captioned or not. While expressions included in <xExpList> are normally expressions involving one or more fields of the table, there is no restriction to such expressions. You can use DISPLAY to show the result of a calculation having nothing to do with the current table if you wish.

Example:

```
use animals
list off name, size, weight, bmp for weight<20
NAME              SIZE        WEIGHT         BMP
Angel Fish           2             2         BINARY
Boa                 10             8         BINARY
House Cat           10             5         BINARY
Parrot               5             5         BINARY
Tetras               2             2         BINARY
```

The COVERAGE option of LIST displays the contents of a coverage file created by running a program or procedure with SET COVERAGE ON. By default, the coverage file has the same name as the program or procedure file with a .COV extension. You can name the coverage file or use ? or a skeleton to bring up the File dialog box. The coverage file holds information about the usage of logical blocks of code within the program or procedure covered.

The default information displayed by LIST COVERAGE is the contents of the coverage file for the main program, the total of logical blocks exited and entered and the percentages of logical blocks entered and exited. If you specify the ALL option, coverage files are shown as well for each separate program or procedure file the main program calls, while the totals and percentages are shown as a whole for all blocks in all files combined. If you use the SUMMARY option, the list shows only the logical blocks not entered or exited, the total of the logical blocks entered and exited and the percentages of blocks entered and exited, either for the main program if you omit ALL or for all files combined.

The FILES option of LIST displays the names, sizes, and last update dates of the files specified. By default it displays only DBF files in the current directory. You can give a skeleton with wildcards to indicate the files to include, but not a ? alone. The skeleton might specify a path or drive, or both, or you might specify a drive with the ON option. If you specify a directory only, it must end with a backslash. dBASE interprets a name without a backslash as a file name, and will look for a file in the parent directory of the directory you intended to specify.

The FILES option also shows the number of files listed, the number of bytes used by the listed files, the free space on the disk, and the total disk space.

The HISTORY option of LIST is no longer supported.

LIST MEMORY gives information about variables and memory usage. For memory variables, it lists their names, data types, whether public, private or hidden, and contents. It also shows the number used, the bytes used, and the number still available. It gives the names, types, and current settings of system variables.

LIST STATUS gives the current work area number, the name, alias, language driver, and work area of each table open, the memo and format files open in each work area, and the index files open in each work area with their keys. It identifies the controlling index in each work area and the relations and filters set in each.

LIST STATUS further gives the LDRIVER, PATH, DEFAULT, PRINTER, and DEVICE settings, the numeric settings for MARGIN, DECIMALS, MEMOWIDTH, TYPEAHEAD, and ODOMETER, and the many ON|OFF settings supported by SET commands. It gives the ON KEY, ON ESCAPE, and ON ERROR settings and those of the programmable function keys.

LIST STRUCTURE gives information about the table open in the current work area or in the work area you specify. It gives the name of the table, whether dBASE or Paradox, number of records, and date of last update, and lists the names, types, lengths, and decimals of its fields and whether the index byte of each is set. It shows by a > which fields are in the SET FIELDS list, if any. It shows the number of bytes per record, which for a dBASE table is the sum of the field lengths plus one for the deleted marker.

LISTCOUNT()

New; returns the number of items in a listbox.

Syntax:

```
[nVar=] listcount(<Form>,<ListBox>)
```

Use LISTCOUNT() to determine the number of items in the list of a listbox. The Datasource property can be a file skeleton or other value that leaves the number of items uncertain until the form is opened. You can use LISTCOUNT() to determine the number of items. If the Multiple property of the ListBox was true, more than one of the items may have been selected. You may loop through all the items with LISTSELECTED() to determine which items were selected.

See LISTSELECTED().

LISTSELECTED()

New; returns the prompt of a specified or selected listbox item.

Syntax:

```
[cVar=] listselected(<Form>,<ListBox>[,<nExp>])
```

If you furnish <nExp>, the LISTSELECTED() function returns the name of the prompt for the item at that number in the list, but only if it is selected. The function is primarily useful for finding out which items of a multiple-choice listbox were selected.

To find out the items selected, use LISTCOUNT() to find the number of items and create a loop executing that many times. Within the loop, call LISTSELECTED() with the <nExp> parameter for each item.

If you call the function without <nExp>, the function will return the prompt of the only selected item of a single-choice list box or of the most recently selected item of a multiple choice list box.

See LISTCOUNT().

LKSYS()

Returns information about a locked file.

Syntax:

```
[xVar=] lksys(<nExp>)
```

The numeric parameter of LKSYS() tells it what information to return:

<nExp>	Returns:
0	The time the lock was placed.
1	The date the lock was placed.
2	The name of the user who locked the file.

3	The time of the last update or lock.
4	The date of the last update or lock.
5	The name of the user who last updated or locked the file.

The LKSYS() function returns its information from the _dbaselock field of a table, added with CONVERT. If there is no _dbaselock field, it returns an empty string.

Passing 0, 1, or 2 as an parameter to LKSYS() returns information only after an attempted lock fails. The information is current as of the last lock failure. You can use 3, 4, or 5 as parameters whether or not the file or record is locked; they return information about the last successful lock.

The _dbaselock field requires 8 characters for the count, time, and date information of a lock and may be only 8 characters wide. In this case it returns an empty string when asked for a user name.

Example:

```
do
     if .not. rlock()
          ? "Record locked by "+lksys(2)+" on " ;
            +lksys(1)+" at "+lksys(0)
          WAIT "Try again? Y/N: " TO cRetry
     else
     exit
     endif
until left(cRetry,1) $ "Nn"
```

See CONVERT, FLOCK(), RLOCK().

LOAD

New; initializes a DLL, Dynamic Link Library.

Syntax:

```
LOAD DLL <cLtrDLL>
```

The use of LOAD to load binary code (.BIN) files is no longer supported.

LOAD DLL establishes a link to the specified DLL and calls its initialization code, preparing it to have its functions and resources loaded and used by dBASE.

To utilize the DLL, you can load resources from it or call functions within the DLL. You must prototype functions with EXTERN statements, and can then call them like built-in or user-defined functions.

When you call a DLL function, dBASE looks for the DLL in the current directory, in the \WINDOWS directory, in the \WINDOWS\SYSTEM directory, in the directory containing DBASEWIN.EXE, which is by default \DBASEWIN\BIN, in the current search path, and in any search path mapped in a network. You need not specify the path name in the EXTERN or LOAD DLL statements unless the DLL is in none of these directories.

See EXTERN, UNLOAD DLL.

LOCAL

New; declares memory variables local.

Syntax:

```
LOCAL <xVarList>
```

LOCAL makes memory variables local to the procedure or user-defined function in which they are declared. They cannot be seen from outside that procedure or function, including in procedures or functions called by the procedure or function in which they are declared. This is in contrast with PRIVATE variables, which can be seen from procedures or functions called by the routine in which you declare them but not from routines higher up in the calling chain.

See PRIVATE, PUBLIC.

LOCATE

Searches a table for a given value.

Syntax:

```
LOCATE [<scope>][FOR <lExpCond1>]
          [WHILE <lExpCond2>]
```

The LOCATE command searches the current table, except as limited by the <scope> and WHILE options, for a record that makes the FOR condition true. The use of WHILE with LOCATE is unusual. If a WHILE condition is not true of the current record, the search fails, while if it is true of the current record, the search stops there.

Using the more common FOR condition only, LOCATE starts at the top of the table and tests the condition for each record in the scope, or in the entire table if no scope is specified. If a record is found that satisfies the condition, LOCATE stops with the pointer at that record. If SET TALK is ON, the record number appears. You can use CONTINUE to carry on the search from that point to find another record matching the same condition. If no record that makes the condition true is found, dBASE issues the message "End of LOCATE scope". The FOUND() function returns .T. if a record that satisfies the condition is found, otherwise .F.

LOCATE does not require any index to the table. If an index is active, LOCATE will follow the index order, but it still reads each record of the table rather than simply using the index to find the one record to read. A LOCATE search is much slower than one using FIND, SEEK, or SEEK().

LOCATE is more flexible than FIND, SEEK, or SEEK() because its condition can be based on any field or expresssion, not only the index key field or expression.

See CONTINUE, FIND, SEEK, SEEK().

LOCK()

A synonym for RLOCK().

See RLOCK().

LOG()

Returns the natural logarithm of a number.

Syntax:

```
[fVar=] log(<nExp>)
```

The LOG() function returns the logarithm to the base *e*, Euler's number, of a number. The number <nExp> must be positive. The function returns the power to which *e*, approximately 2.718, must be raised to equal the value of <nExp>. The function is the inverse of EXP(). The value returned is float-type.

Logarithms were extensively used to simplify complex calculations when such calculations were done by hand. They still have numerous uses, but not every day. You might be more interested in logarithms to the base 2, which measure the bits used by binary numbers. To convert a natural logarithm to a base 2 logarithm, divide the natural logarithm by the natural logarithm of 2. In general, to find the base *x* logarithm of *n*, divide LOG(*n*) by LOG(*x*), or LOG10(*n*) by LOG10(*x*) which comes to the same result.

The example obtains the logarithm of 8192 to the base 2, which tells you how many bits (plus one) 8192 requires in binary notation.

Example:

```
? log(8192)/log(2)
        13
```

See EXP(), LOG10().

LOG10()

Returns the base 10 logarithm of a number.

Syntax:

```
[fVar=] log10(<nExp>)
```

The LOG10() function returns as a float the logarithm of a number to the base 10. The integral part of the result, the characteristic, is the number of digits (less 1) it will occupy to the left of the decimal point. The number <nExp> must be positive.

Logarithms base 10 were the principle behind the infamous 10-inch slide rule that tormented generations of engineering and science students until electronic calculators became cheaper. There is no EXP10() function in dBASE comparable to EXP() to find the antilogarithm of a base 10 logarithm. If you need to find a number *n* given LOG10(*n*), convert the logarithm to a natural one by dividing by LOG10(EXP(1)), then use EXP() on the result.

Example:

```
set decimals to 4
nVar = log10(697)
? nVar
        2.8432
? exp(nVar/log10(exp(1)))
      697.0000
```

LOGOUT

Is not supported in dBASE for Windows.

LOOKUP()

Looks up a value in one field in a table and returns the value of another field of the record found.

Syntax:

```
[xVar=] lookup(<ReturnField>,<xExpMatch>,<SearchField>)
```

The LOOKUP() function searches the <SearchField> fields of the records of a table to find a match for <xExpMatch>. If found, it returns the value of <ReturnField> from the record in which the match was found. <ReturnField> might be a field in another table to which SET RELATION has established a link. If the search fails, the ponter is positioned at EOF().

LOOKUP() does not require an index. If there is none, LOOKUP() will perform a sequential search on the table. The search will be much faster if the table is indexed on the <SearchField> field.

In practice, the design of LOOKUP() fits well with an index. It is rarely useful to look up a value in one field as a source of information elsewhere unless the values in the searched field are unique, and this is most likely when the field is designed as the primary key to the table. As the primary key, it will most often be indexed. It can then be used to access information not only from the table in which the search occurs, but in any table to which a relation is set.

Example:

```
Input "Enter the order number " TO Thisord
use Orders order Order_no
use Customer order Cust_ID in select()
set relation to Cust_ID into Customer
if lookup(Customer->Credit, Thisord, Order_no) ;
     < Order_Tot
? Customer->Name +" has a credit limit of " ;
     +Customer->Credit
endif
```

In the example, the order number obtained in somewhat primitive fashion from the user in Thisord is looked up in the Order_no field of Orders, using the controlling index. The example assumes the Orders table contains a Cust_ID field, the ID of the customer placing the order, and an Order_Tot field giving the total money amount of the order.

The relation on Cust_ID moves the pointer in the Customer table to the record of the customer placing the order. The LOOKUP() function returns the Credit field of that customer's record in Customer. The credit limit is lower than the amount of the order, the Order_Tot field in Orders, so a message appears. It makes use of the fact the record pointer in Customer is at the customer's record to obtain the customer's name.

See FIND, LOCATE, SEEK, SEEK().

LOOP

Causes execution to return to the first line of a loop construct.

Syntax:

```
LOOP
```

The LOOP keyword is valid only within one of the loop structures, DO . . . UNTIL, DO WHILE . . . ENDDO, FOR . . . ENDFOR|NEXT, or SCAN . . . ENDSCAN. On reaching the line with the LOOP keyword, execution jumps to the first line of the structure, the line with the DO, FOR, or SCAN, and continues by executing that line, evaluating any condition in it and, continuing accordingly.

Example:

```
scan for balance>1000
    if past_90 > 500
         do Send_Nasty
     elseif past_90 > 0 .and. past_60 > 500
         do Send_Tweak
     endif
     if last_order > 800
         loop
     elseif last_date < date() - 60
         do Send_Query
     endif
     <code>
endscan
```

The example terminates execution of the loop near the middle with LOOP because the remaining conditions and statements are not relevant if the last order was for more than 800.

See DO, EXIT, FOR, SCAN.

LOWER()

Converts uppercase characters in a character expression or memo field to lowercase.

Syntax:

```
[xVar=] lower(<cExp>|<mFld>)
```

The current language driver defines what characters are uppercase and lowercase. In a U.S. language driver, A–Z are uppercase and will be converted by LOWER() to a–z, respectively.

The LOWER() function converts all characters within the expression or memo field to which it is applied, returning the expression or field as converted. It is common to use it with SUBSTR() and similar functions to limit its reach.

Example:

```
replace all message with lower(message)
```

See PROPER(), SUBSTR(), UPPER().

LTRIM()

Trims leading blanks off a character expression or memo field.

Syntax:

```
[xVar=] ltrim(<cExp>|<mFld>)
```

The LTRIM() function is useful to assure that all character fields are left-justified. If they are not, searches on such fields may yield undesired results.

Example:

```
replace all name with ltrim(name)
```

LUPDATE()

Returns the date of last change to a specified table.

Syntax:

```
[dVar=] lupdate([<workarea>])
```

The LUPDATE() function returns the date the current or specified table was last changed. If there is no table open in the work area, it returns a blank date. The date is formatted MM/DD/YY unless otherwise specified by SET CENTURY, SET DATE, and SET MARK.

MAX()

Returns the maximum of two values.

Syntax:

```
[xVar=] max(<xExp1>,<xExp2>)
```

The MAX() function returns the greater of the two values resulting from the expressions passed to it. It returns the greater of two numbers giving effect to signs in the usual fashion, such that -2 is greater than -5. The types of both expressions must be the same except that one may be a type N number and the other a type F number. Memo fields and binary fields cannot be compared by max().

The MAX() of two character expressions is the one that sorts later in the collating order specified by the language driver. With a U.S. language driver, the sort is in ASCII order. The collation is case sensitive with "aardvark" being later and greater than "Zenith" because the uppercase letters all precede the lowercase ones. Of two character strings equal as far as they go, the shorter is the lesser. The digits sort earlier and less than uppercase letters and the space least of all the printing characters, with many punctuation marks early in the order.

Dates sort in chronological order. Between two logical values, .T. is greater than .F. If the two values are equal, MAX() returns one of them.

Example:

```
nTax = max(nRegTax,nAltMinTax)
```

MCOL()

Returns the current column position of the mouse pointer.

Syntax:

```
[nVar=] mcol()
```

The mouse position is returned as an integer, but is measured in terms of the average character width of the default font. This function is retained for compatibility with dBASE IV. Use OnMouseMove, OnLeftMouseDown, and similar properties to manage mouse actions in forms. In general, you will not need to calculate the mouse position because the object will receive a message that the event has occurred only if it occurs while the mouse is over the object.

MD

New; same as DOS MD or MKDIR command. See MKDIR.

MDOWN()

Returns .T. if the left mouse button is down, otherwise .F.

Syntax:

```
[lVar=] mdown()
```

The MDOWN() function reports the status of the primary or "left" mouse button, which may be physically the right button if the buttons have been switched using the Windows Control Panel or may have some entirely different location or configuration on a trackball or other device that acts like a mouse. You may use MROW() and MCOL() to determine where the mouse is at any time. You will find it easier to program using the OnClick and similar event properties of dBASE for Windows objects. Such events trigger only when the mouse is clicked while over the object and free you from the need to determine where it is or to poll for the occurrence of an event.

See MCOL(), MROW().

MDX()

Returns the drive and name of the MDX file in specified position.

Syntax:

```
[cVar=] mdx(<nExp>[,<workarea>])
```

The <nExp> expression is the position of the .MDX file in the list of .MDX files created by one of the commands SET INDEX, SET ORDER or USE . . . ORDER. If there is only one MDX file required by the indexes in use, it is number 1 in the list and <nExp> should be 1. This is not the same as a list of tags or the order of tags as used in the TAGNO() function.

You may specify a work area. If you do not, MDX() returns the MDX name for the current work area. If you do not specify a position number, MDX() returns the name of the MDX in which is the controlling tag. The function returns an empty string if you fail to specify a number and the controlling index is an NDX file, or if there is no MDX in the position specified.

If SET FULLPATH is on, the function returns the fully qualified name, with drive and path.

See NDX(), ORDER(), SET FULLPATH, TAGNO().

MDY()

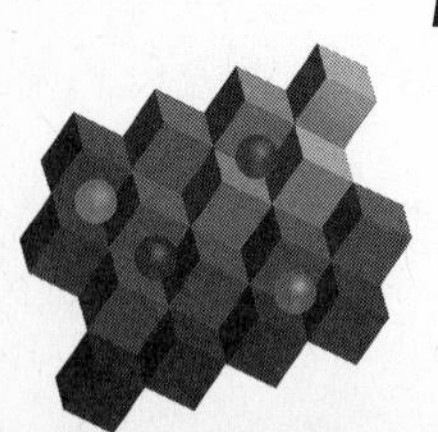

Returns a date formatted as month, day, and year.

Syntax:

```
[cVar=] mdy(<dExp>)
```

The MDY() function formats a date into a form close to but not exactly the form used for most U.S. business correspondence, the month spelled out followed by the day, a comma and the year with the day and year in numbers. The two departures from standard business practice are that the day is shown with a leading zero if it has only one digit and the year is shown in two digits if SET CENTURY is OFF, the default.

Example:

```
? mdy({06/08/94})
June 08, 94
```

You can achieve a more attractive result than MDY() provides:

```
FUNCTION Mymdy
     parameters dDate
RETURN cMonth(dDate) +" "+ltrim(str(day(dDate))) +", " ;
     +str(year(dDate),4)
```

This function returns all digits of the year at all times and suppresses the leading zero of the day.

MEMLINES()

Returns the number of lines in a memo field.

Syntax:

```
[nVar=] memlines(<mFld>[,<nExpChars>])
```

The MEMLINES() function counts memo lines as if word-wrapped in a column as many characters wide as set by the <nExpChars> expression, which can range from 8 to 255, inclusive. If <nExpChars> is omitted, MEMLINES() uses the SET MEMOWIDTH setting, by default 50 characters.

In counting lines, MEMLINES() moves a word that will not fit completely in one line to the beginning of the next line. If the word is too long for any line, MEMLINES() truncates it at the end of a line and moves the excess to the next line.

See MLINE(), SET MEMOWIDTH.

MEMORY()

Returns the amount of free RAM memory.

Syntax:

```
[nVar=] memory([<nExp>])
```

The value of <nExp> is ignored. It is included for dBASE IV compatibility. MEMORY() returns the number of kilobytes of RAM available, which may include memory made available by Windows through a swap file.

MENU()

Returns the name of the current dBASE IV bar menu.

Syntax:

```
[cVar=] menu()
```

The MENU() function returns, in upper case, the name of the current bar menu created with DEFINE MENU. It returns an empty string when no menu is active. This function is included for compatibility. Use INSPECT() to obtain information about forms and their objects.

SEE ACTIVATE MENU, DEFINE MENU.

MESSAGE()

Returns the error message of the most recent dBASE error.

Syntax:

```
[cVar=] message()
```

The MESSAGE() function initially returns an empty string. It will return the error message after an error occurs until the first occurance of another error, issuance of RETRY, or the completion of execution of the program.

See CERROR(), DBERROR(), DBMESSAGE(), ERROR(), SQLERROR(), SQLMESSAGE().

MIN()

Returns the minimum of two values.

Syntax:

```
[xVar=] min(<xExp1>,<xExp2>)
```

The MIN() function returns the lesser of two numeric, character, date, or logical values. It is the inverse of MAX() and returns the value that MAX() does not return.

See MAX().

MKDIR

New; creates a directory.

Syntax:

```
MKDIR <Directory>
```

The <Directory> name may contain a drive or path name or both.

The MKDIR command is equivalent to the DOS MD|MKDIR command and follows the same rules. MD is an alternative syntax in dBASE as in DOS. dBASE for Windows does not support the DOS RD and RMDIR commands to remove directories.

See CD.

MLINE()

Extracts a line from a memo field.

Syntax:

```
[cVar=] mline(<mFld>[,<nExpLine>[,<nExpChars>]])
```

The MLINE() function returns a line of a memo field from the current record. The first parameter gives the name of the memo field. The second optional parameter gives the number of the line of the memo. The default is line 1. The third optional parameter specifies the number of characters per line, from 8 through 255. If it is omitted, the SET MEMOWIDTH setting controls.

The line is returned by wrapping the characters of the memo within lines of the prescribed length until reaching the line requested and filling it. If a word at the end of the line to be returned does not fit, it is moved to the next line and not returned. If a word cannot fit in any line, it is broken at the end of the line and the excess moved to the next line.

See MEMLINES().

MOD()

Returns the remainder of the division of two numbers.

Syntax:

```
[nVar=] mod(<nExp1>,<nExp2>)
```

The MOD() function returns the modulus or remainder of the division of the first number by the second as an N-type integer. The returned value has the sign of the divisor, the second number. If the first number is negative, the function returns the remainder of the first number over the next smaller negative multiple of the second number.

The formula for the modulus is <nExp1>-floor(<nExp1>/<nExp2>)*<nExp2>.

Example:

```
? mod(-6,7)
         1

year = year(date())
isleap = iif(mod(year,100) = 0,mod(year,400), mod(year,4)) = 0

? str(44)+" days is "+str(int(44/7))+" weeks, +str(mod(44,7))+" days"
44 days is 6 weeks 2 days
```

MODIFY

Opens the editor or designer appropriate to the file type.

Syntax:

```
MODIFY {{APPLICATION|FORM|LABEL|MENU|QUERY|REPORT[CROSSTAB]|SCREEN|VIEW}
     [<File1>|?|<skeleton1>]}|
     {{COMMAND|FILE}[<File2>|?|<skeleton2>][WINDOW<Window>]}|
     {STRUCTURE}
```

MODIFY is similar to CREATE. MODIFY must have a file type option after it, while CREATE by default creates a table. MODIFY with a file type option may be issued alone, to bring up a blank editor of the appropriate type, or with a file name, ?, or skeleton. Including a file name, ?, or skeleton brings up the File dialog, from which you can select a new or existing file.

MODIFY COMMAND and MODIFY FILE are identical; they bring up the text editor. The file extension PRG, appropriate for a program (command) file, is assumed.

MODIFY APPLICATION, MODIFY FORM, and MODIFY SCREEN are identical and bring up the Form Designer. File extension WFM is assumed.

MODIFY LABEL brings up the Label Designer. File extension RPL is assumed.

MODIFY MENU opens the Menu Designer. A menu definition file of extension MNU is assumed. You attach the menu to a form by its Menu property.

MODIFY QUERY and MODIFY VIEW are identical and bring up the Query Designer. Extension QBE is assumed.

MODIFY REPORT brings up the Report Designer. File extension RPT is assumed unless you specified the CROSSTAB option, in which case extension RPC is assumed and the Cross-Tab dialog box is displayed.

MODIFY STRUCTURE is the only MODIFY option that deals with tables. It brings up the structure design view of the current table. You can redesign dBASE and Paradox tables, but not SQL tables. If you want to redesign a table with data in it, be sure not to change the field names at the same time you are adding or deleting fields. You can change the field names only or their positions and sizes only, which is what adding or deleting fields does, but not both. If you change both at once, dBASE will not know where or how to copy the data to the modified file and you may lose your data. Finish making a change of one type and close the table before commencing a change of the other type.

See CREATE.

MONTH()

Returns the number of the month of a date.

Syntax:

```
[nVar=] month(<dExp>)
```

The MONTH() function returns the number of the month, 1 for January to 12 for December, of the given date expression.

See CMONTH(), DAY(), DMY(), ISTABLE(), MDY(), YEAR().

MOVE

Moves a window.

Syntax:

```
MOVE WINDOW <Window> {TO <nExpRow>[,<nExpCol>]}|
         {BY <nExpRows>[,<nExpCols>]}
```

The MOVE WINDOW command moves a window, in units related to the font size of the parent window. You may move the window either to an absolute position using TO or relatively using BY.

The rows and columns moved may be positive, to the right and down, or negative. In either case you may leave out the column parameter if you do not want to change the column. To leave the row unchanged, include 0 as the row parameter.

You may move the window whether it is open or closed. If it is open it moves at once. If it is closed it will appear at the new position when ACTIVATE WINDOW is issued.

This command is included for compatibility. Use the Moveable property of forms and their Top, Left, Height, and Width properties to move them.

See ACTIVATE WINDOW.

MROW()

Returns the current row position of the mouse pointer.

Syntax:

```
[nVar=] mrow()
```

The mouse position is returned as an integer, but is measured in terms of the average character height of the default font. This function is retained for compatibility with dBASE IV. Use OnMouseMove, OnLeftMouseDown and similar properties to manage mouse actions in forms. In general, you will not need to calculate the mouse position because the object will receive a message that the event has occurred only if it occurs while the mouse is over the object.

NDX()

Returns the name of an .NDX file.

Syntax:

```
[cVar=] ndx([<nExpPosition>[,<workarea>]])
```

The NDX() function returns the drive and name of the NDX file at the specified position in the list of indexes for the current or specified work area. The positions are those defined in the most recent of the commands SET INDEX, SET ORDER, or USE. If no position is specified, the function uses the controlling index. The function returns an empty string if there is no index or an MDX index in the specified position.

If SET FULLPATH is on, the function returns the path as well as the drive and name.

See MDX(), SET FULLPATH, SET INDEX, SET ORDER, USE.

NETWORK()

Returns .T. if dBASE is running in a network environment.

Syntax:

```
[lVar=] network()
```

The NETWORK() function returns .F. if dBASE is not running on a network, .T. if it is. Use the function to determine whether your code should or should not execute code required only in a multiuser environment.

NEXT

New; ends a FOR . . . ENDFOR|NEXT loop.

NEXT is also used with an entirely different meaning as one of the <scope> keywords. See the discussion of <scope> in the introductory portion of this Appendix.

See FOR.

NEXTCOL()

Returns the next column available for the placement of a UI object.

Syntax:

```
[xVar=] nextcol()
```

The NEXTCOL() function returns a number determined by adding the column position of the user interface object last placed to its width. If the current window has been opened with ACTIVATE WINDOW, the value returned is fixed numeric N type. If you opened the current window with OPEN WINDOW or READMODAL(), the returned value is float-type.

If you attempt to place the cursor or an object at a negative column position, an error occurs.

See COL(), NEXTROW(), ROW().

NEXTKEY()

Returns the INKEY() value of a key in the keyboard buffer.

Syntax:

```
[nVar=] nextkey([<nExp>])
```

The NEXTKEY() function returns the value of the next key in the keyboard buffer, or the key in specified position if the optional <nExp> is included. It does not remove the key from the buffer. It returns 0 if the buffer is empty or contains fewer keys than the value of <nExp>.

See INKEY(), KEYBOARD, SET TYPEAHEAD.

NOTE

Same as *, introduces a comment line to be ignored by the compiler.

Syntax:

```
NOTE [<Comment>]
```

If the line begun by NOTE ends with a semicolon, the compiler will ignore the next line as being part of the note, and so on for each line that ends with a semicolon. The maximum line length is 1,024 characters, so the comment following NOTE may be 1019 characters long, less one if it ends with a semicolon.

See *, &&.

OEM()

New; converts a character expression from the ANSI character set.

Syntax:

```
[cVar=] oem(<cExp>)
```

The OEM() function converts the characters in <cExp> from the ANSI to the OEM character set. dBASE IV and other DOS applications use the Original Equipment Manufacturer (OEM) character set, while Windows uses the American National Standards Institute (ANSI) character set. The sets differ, primarily in the characters with CHR() values above 127. If you use the ANSI set in dBASE for Windows and have any character data with such CHR() values, use OEM() to convert it to the OEM character set before using it in dBASE IV.

The OEM() function is the inverse of ANSI().

See ANSI().

ON

Introduces dBASE IV-style event-driven commands, has the new options ON NETERROR and ON SELECTION FORM.

Syntax:

```
ON {{[EXIT|SELECTION] BAR <nExpBar> OF <Popup>}|
     ERROR|ESCAPE|{KEY [LABEL <Key>]}|
     {[EXIT|SELECTION] MENU <Menu>}|
     MOUSE|NETERROR|
     {[EXIT|SELECTION] PAD <Pad> OF <Menu>}|
     {[EXIT] POPUP <PopUP>}|
     {SELECTION POPUP {<Popup>|ALL}[BLANK]}|
     READERROR}[<Command1>]}|
     {PAGE [AT LINE <nExpLine><Command2>]}|
     {SELECTION FORM <Form>[<FuncPtr>|<codeblockExp>]}
```

The ON command causes a break in normal processing on the happening of an event. There are four categories of events. First is the category of miscellaneous user input actions, ON ESCAPE, ON KEY, and ON MOUSE. Second are error events, ON ERROR, ON READERROR, and now ON NETERROR.

The third category relates to dBASE-IV style menus and popups and includes the ON BAR, ON MENU, ON PAD, and ON POPUP commands with all their options. Finally, ON PAGE and ON SELECTION FORM do not fit in any of the first three categories.

The first three categories, all the ON commands except ON PAGE and ON SELECTION FORM, may be followed by an optional command, shown in the syntax paradigm as <Command1>. This command is the heart of the matter; it directs execution to branch on the happening of the specified event. The command is usually DO followed by the name of a procedure, or in dBASE for Windows a user-defined function, since there is usually more action required than a single command can accomplish. In these categories, if the optional <Command1> is omitted, any previously issued ON command of the same type is disabled.

The first category comprises ON ESCAPE, ON KEY, and ON MOUSE.

ON ESCAPE works only if SET ESCAPE is ON, and is triggered by pressing Esc. If a user-defined window, menu, or popup is active, pressing Esc does not execute the ON ESCAPE command but only deactivates the object. In a program, pressing Esc usually suspends it. If an ON ESCAPE trap is set and SET ESCAPE is ON, pressing Esc causes execution of the ON ESCAPE command, after which the program continues. If both ON ESCAPE and ON KEY traps are triggered at the same time, ON ESCAPE takes precedence.

ON KEY is triggered by pressing a key. It can trap the Esc key only if SET ESCAPE is OFF. The LABEL option of ON KEY may be used to make several key traps active at once, each for the key named. While more than one ON KEY LABEL trap may be active, activating any ON KEY LABEL trap deactivates the ON KEY trap with no label. To deactivate all ON KEY traps, labeled or not, issue ON KEY with no parameters.

Pressing Esc, if SET ESCAPE is ON or if it is trapped by ON KEY, causes immediate action. Any other keypress trapped by ON KEY with or without a label will not interrupt an indexing or similar operation but will take effect when the operation finishes.

To designate a printable key for ON KEY LABEL, follow LABEL with the letter, digit, or other symbol, not in quotation marks or other delimiters. ON KEY LABEL is not case-sensitive. ON KEY LABEL X and ON KEY LABEL x are equivalent. Some keys that could not be trapped with ON KEY in dBASE IV may now be trapped. Table A.6 gives the names to use for nonprinting keys that can be trapped. The names are not case-sensitive, but they are sensitive to embedded spaces or other punctuation and symbols.

Table A.6
Names to Use for On Key Labels for Nonprinting Keys

Backspace
Backtab
Del
End
Enter

Esc
F1 through F10
Home
Ins
Leftarrow, Rightarrow, Uparrow, Downarrow
PgUp, PgDn
Spacebar
Tab
Ctrl-<key> or Ctrl+<key>
Shift-<key> or Shift+<key>
Alt-<key> or Alt+<key>

ON MOUSE is included for compatibility. Use the mouse-related event properties of objects to manage them. Like ON KEY, ON MOUSE will wait for the end of SORT, INDEX, or PACK operations. ON MOUSE works only while SET MOUSE is ON, and is triggered by clicking the mouse only under certain conditions:

- ✔ A @ . . . GET . . . READ combination is active and the user clicks the mouse outside the GET region.
- ✔ A BROWSE or CREATE|MODIFY COMMAND|FILE window is open and the user clicks outside it.
- ✔ A window, menu, or popup is active and the user clicks outside of it.

The second category is ON ERROR, ON NETERROR, and ON READERROR.

ON ERROR responds to dBASE errors with numbers. It will not be triggered by system errors. It will also not be triggered if an error occurs during one of certain dBASE IV full-screen commands that handle errors internally: APPEND, CREATE|MODIFY with APPLICATION, LABEL, REPORT, SCREEN, STRUCTURE or VIEW, or MODIFY with COMMAND or FILE. If ON ERROR and ON ESCAPE or ON KEY traps are triggered at the same time, ON ERROR takes precedence.

The ON ERROR trap is disabled while the procedure called by that particular trap is executing, but you can set another ON ERROR trap inside the procedure. Be careful that the procedure called by the second ON ERROR trap does not reset the first trap, or they may attempt to call each other forever with unhappy results.

ON NETERROR responds to errors specific to multiuser environments. You can use ON ERROR to respond to all errors, or you may use ON NETERROR for multiuser errors. If you do so, ON ERROR will respond only to the errors which ON NETERROR ignores. The ON NETERROR trap is disabled while its called code is executing in the same manner as with ON ERROR.

ON READERROR responds to data input errors including nonexistent dates and data that fails to satisfy a RANGE or VALID clause of @ . . . GET. It supersedes the action that dBASE would otherwise take, or that a user-defined function attached to VALID commands, in such cases.

The third category comprises ON BAR, ON PAD, ON MENU, and ON POPUP. All of these have ON EXIT and ON SELECTION options as well as plain ON.

The ON BAR, ON MENU, ON PAD, and ON POPUP traps are triggered when the user moves to the bar, menu, pad, or popup. The user may move to it with arrow keys, a single click, by pressing the first letter of the prompt (with Alt for menus and pads), or by dragging the mouse cursor in the case of a bar.

The ON EXIT traps for BAR, MENU, PAD, or POPUP are triggered when the user leaves the bar, pad, menu, or popup, as the case may be.

The ON SELECTION traps for BAR, MENU PAD, and POPUP are triggered when the user makes a selection by double-clicking the selection or by pressing Enter when the cursor is on the item.

The ON commands for MENU and POPUP act as defaults. If the particular pad or bar has a trap of its own, that trap will be triggered. If the particular pad or bar does not have its own trap, the corresponding trap for its parent menu or popup is triggered.

The ON SELECTION POPUP command has two additional features, ALL and BLANK. You may use ALL in place of the name of the popup to make the trap applicable to all pop-up menus. The BLANK option hides the popup before executing the command, then redraws it after the command executes.

ON PAGE is used for handling page breaks, typically in reports with headers and footers. The command executed is normally a procedure that prints any footer, ejects the page, and prints the header for the next. ON PAGE is triggered when printing has passed the line specified by the AT clause, by executing ?, or EJECT PAGE.

Issuing ON PAGE with no parameter disables the ON PAGE trap. To calculate the line to use with AT to trigger the ON PAGE handler, use the line that equals the page length less the bottom margin and the footer height, all measured in lines.

dBASE uses _plength to know the page length and will keep track of the position on the page resulting from printing the header and body of the report. You must start the footer

with at least one ? to separate it from the last line of the body. Be sure that the <nExpLine> number is small enough to keep the footer from overflowing to the next page.

Example:

```
_plength = 60           && standard for laser printer
set talk off
on page at line 57 do Pg_brk
set print on
do header
scan
     ? Case_No, Client, Counselor
endscan
eject page
set print off
on page                && disable handler
set talk on
return
PROCEDURE Pg_brk
     do Footer
     eject
     if .not. eof()
          do Header
     endif
RETURN
PROCEDURE Header
     ? "Cases for "+ cmonth(date()-day(date()))
     ?
RETURN
PROCEDURE Footer
     ?                     && feed to line 58
     ? "Page " at 54,str(_pageno,2)      && last line 59
RETURN
```

ON SELECTION FORM uses newer syntax. You must give the name of the form. As with the other ON commands, if you omit the rest of the command it disables any previous ON SELECTION FORM command. In place of the single command you could issue through an ON command of the first three categories, ON SELECTION FORM allows you to include either a function pointer or a codeblock expression.

A *function pointer* is the name of a function or procedure. You do not need the DO to invoke it, just its name following ON SELECTION FORM. If it is a function, do not include parentheses after its name.

A *codeblock expression* is a character variable that contains a codeblock or the codeblock itself enclosed in curly braces. A *codeblock* is a series of dBASE statements each ending with a semicolon. While codeblocks can extend over several lines, your code will be more readable if you restrict codeblocks to very short blocks of one or two statements in curly braces. Use functions or procedures to perform more complex processing.

OPEN

New; OPEN DATABASE establishes connection to a database server. OPEN FORM activates a form.

Syntax:

```
OPEN        {DATABASE <Database>[LOGIN <UserPass>][WITH <cExpOption>]}|
            {FORM {<Form>[ON <Object>]}[,<etc.>]}
```

OPEN DATABASE opens a database defined with the ODAPI configuration utility. With the exception of the STANDARD database consisting of your local dBASE and Paradox tables, you must open a database before you can access its tables. <Database> is the name of the database you want to open. The LOGIN option allows you to give your user name and password in <UserPass> as required by the database server for access. You may add a character string to the command holding whatever options the database may require.

OPEN FORM displays and opens a UI form, giving it the focus and allowing the user to enter data into it through its controls. You may specify a list of forms to open, giving each its name and optionally the ON <Object> option. ON <Object> identifies the object within the form that has the initial focus and will receive the initial user input.

If you specify a list of forms, the first one in the list opens on top of the others and has the focus. When it is closed, the next available form receives the focus. When the last form closes, the execution of the application is completed.

The windows you open dBASE IV-style with ACTIVATE WINDOW can contain only dBASE IV menus and popups. You can provide input through them or through @ . . . SAY . . . GET commands. Only forms defined with DEFINE FORM or the NEW keyword can contain Windows UI objects such as pushbuttons and spinboxes.

When you open a form with OPEN FORM, it is non-modal. It opens, displays on the screen, and is ready for input, but you may ignore it and click on another form or window to give the other form or window the focus. In addition, after dBASE opens the form it will continue with any other processing the program requires.

To open a modal form that requires a response to it before anything else happens, such as the dBASE for Windows Alert boxes, open your form with READMODAL(). Opening a form with READMODAL() stops all other program processing until the form is closed.

See ACTIVATE WINDOW, CLOSE DATABASES, READMODAL().

ORDER()

Returns the name of the controlling index for a table.

Syntax:

```
[cVar=] order([<workarea>])
```

The ORDER() function returns the name of the NDX file containing the controlling index, if any, or the name of the tag of the controlling index in an MDX file. It returns an empty string if there is no controlling index in the specified work area. If you omit the optional work area, dBASE returns the name of the controlling index for the table in the current work area.

Example:

```
cTag = order()
set order to PartName
list all for On_hand < EOQ to print
set order to &cTag
```

See SET ORDER TO, TAG(), TAGNO().

OS()

Returns the name of the operating system.

Syntax:

```
[cVar=] os([<nExp>])
```

The OS() function returns the operating system as a character string consisting of the operating system name, release if applicable, and version number, each separated by a space. You can use this if you create code that can run on several operating systems, so the code can detect on which one it is running and act accordingly. If you include the optional <nExp>, OS() returns the Windows version.

Examples:

```
? os()
DOS version 5.00
? os(0)
Windows version 3.10
```

OTHERWISE

Introduces default case in an ON CASE structure.

See ON CASE.

PACK

Permanently removes all records marked for deletion from the current dBASE table.

Syntax:

```
PACK
```

The PACK command completes dBASE's two-step process of deleting records. DELETE marks each deleted record, and if SET DELETED is on, makes it invisible. RECALL can then restore the deleted records until the PACK command is issued. PACK physically removes the records from the table, after which they cannot be recalled or recovered.

PACK can be used only on the table active in the current work area. PACK has no applicability to Paradox tables. DELETE removes records from Paradox tables at once beyond recall, and issuing either the RECALL or PACK command when a Paradox table is current causes an error.

In a multiuser environment, a table to be packed must be in exclusive use.

dBASE automatically reindexes all open indexes after a table is packed. To update closed indexes, open them and issue REINDEX.

Space in DBT files is not recovered when you PACK the associated table. The memo blocks relating to records removed from the table are simply orphaned with nothing pointing to them. To recover the space used by such memo blocks you must COPY the table. The DBT will be copied, but only the memo blocks relating to records remaining in the table. You may then erase the original table and DBT to conserve disk space.

PACK is probably the most dangerous command in dBASE. PACK operates on the table in place, copying later records down into the places vacated by removed ones, so even a utility file recovery program is unlikely to be able to recover the original data. Use with caution and only after backing up your data.

See DELETE, RECALL, SET DELETED, ZAP.

PAD()

Returns the name of the selected pad of a bar menu.

Syntax:

```
[cVar=] pad()
```

The PAD() function returns the name of the highlighted pad, if any, or the most recently selected pad in a dBASE IV-style menu. It returns an empty string if there is no active bar menu, including after the menu has been deactivated by pressing Esc or the window containing it has been deactivated.

The PAD() function is included for compatibility. Use INSPECT() to receive information about forms and their objects.

See ACTIVATE MENU, DEFINE PAD, PADPROMPT().

PADPROMPT()

Returns the prompt of the specified pad of a dBASE IV-style bar menu.

Syntax:

```
[cVar=] padprompt(<cLtrPad>[,<cLtrMenu>])
```

The PADPROMPT() function with no parameters returns the prompt of the currently highlighted or most recently selected pad of the active menu. You may include <cLtrPad> to specify a different pad, or <cLtrMenu> to specify a different menu. The function returns an empty string if <cLtrMenu> is omitted and there is no active window or the window has no menu. It also returns an empty string if <cLtrMenu> fails to name a menu or <cLtrPad> fails to name a pad on it. PADPROMPT() can return the prompt of a pad from a menu that has not been activated or that has been deactivated, as long as RELEASE or CLEAR MENUS has not removed it from memory.

PADPROMPT() is retained for compatibility. Use INSPECT() to obtain information about forms and objects.

See CLEAR MENUS, DEFINE MENU, DEFINE PAD, PAD(), RELEASE MENU.

PARAMETERS

Introduces the parameters in a procedure or user-defined function dBASE IV-style.

Syntax:

```
PARAMETERS <xVarList>
```

The PARAMETERS keyword, if used, must be the first word in the first line after the PROCEDURE or FUNCTION line defining a procedure or UDF. Follow it with the variable names by which the parameters will be known within the procedure or function.

Each named parameter variable receives a parameter passed to the procedure or function, in order of position, up to the number of parameters passed. The function or procedure can then deal with the values in the variables as required.

As an alternative to using the PARAMETERS keyword, you should give the names of the parameter variables in parentheses following the name of a function or procedure in the FUNCTION or PROCEDURE line defining it This makes the parameter variables local in scope, whereas if you use the PARAMETERS keyword they will be private in scope. A local variable is safer; it cannot be changed by a lower-level routine that uses a variable of the same name.

Example:

```
? FuturVal(10000,.075,10)
_____20610.32
<code>
* Future value of a lump-sum investment
FUNCTION FuturVal
parameters nPrincipal,nRate,nPeriods
RETURN nPrincipal*(1 + nRate)^nPeriods
```

You may pass up to 255 parameters to a program, procedure, or function. You may pass them to a procedure or function by including them in order in the parentheses after its name. You may pass them to a procedure, function, or program executed with DO by including them in the DO line after WITH. You may also pass them to a program executed by a command line such as "win dbasewin myprogram" by including them in the command line after the name of the program. A parameter may be a field, variable, literal, or expression.

See FUNCTION, LOCAL, PRIVATE, PROCEDURE.

PAYMENT()

Returns the level payment required to amortize a loan.

Syntax:

```
[fVar=] payment(<nExpPrincipal>,<nExpRate>,<nExpPeriods>)
```

The PAYMENT() function calculates the amount of the level payment made once at the end of each of <nExpPeriods> periods that will amortize (pay off) a loan of <nExpPrincipal> amount with interest at the rate of <nExpRate> per period. If <nExpPrincipal> is negative, so will the return value be. The return value is a float-type number.

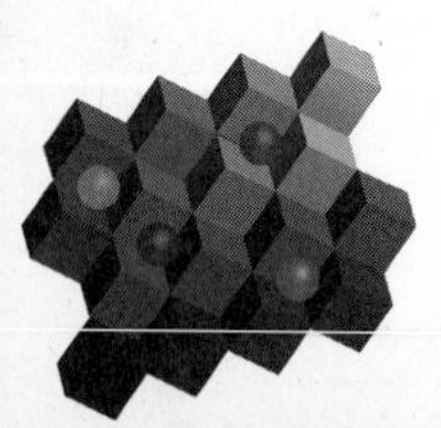

Example:

```
MtgeAmt = 100000
AnnRate = .08
Years   = 30
? payment( MtgeAmt,AnnRate/12,12*Years)
_____733.76
```

PCOL()

Returns the horizontal printing position of the printer.

Syntax:

```
[nVar=] pcol()
```

The PCOL() function returns the column at which the printer will print the next character, starting with the character at the left margin being PCOL()=0. The PCOL() function counts in increments of the value of _ppitch. If you are using a proportional font and know the character widths, you can add or subtract fractional numbers to or from PCOL() in order to align your printing precisely.

You must have SET PRINTER ON or SET DEVICE TO PRINTER in effect to use PCOL().

See PROW().

PCOUNT()

Returns the number of parameters passed to a program, procedure, or UDF.

Syntax:

```
[nVar=] pcount()
```

You can pass fewer parameters to a program, procedure, or UDF than the maximum number it can accept. Inside the code of the program, procedure, or UDF, use PCOUNT() to determine how many parameters were passed.

Example:

```
PROCEDURE MyPack( Workarea)
     local Oldalias
     if pcount() = 1
          Oldalias = alias()
```

```
                select Workarea
                pack
                select &Oldalias
           else
                pack
           endif
      RETURN
```

See FUNCTION, PROCEDURE, PARAMETERS.

PI()

Returns an approximation of the transcendental number π, the ratio of the circumference of a circle to its diameter.

Syntax:

```
[fVar=] pi()
```

The value of π is used in numerous scientific and engineering calculations, not all of them related to circles. The PI() function returns it as a float-type number. You may use SET DECIMALS to control the number of digits displayed. SET DECIMALS does not limit the accuracy of calculations.

See DTOR(), RTOD().

PLAY MACRO

Is not supported by dBASE for Windows.

PLAY SOUND

Reads a sound file and plays the sounds.

Syntax:

```
PLAY SOUND {FILENAME {<File>|?|<skeleton>}}|{BINARY <BinaryFld>}
```

PLAY SOUND plays a sound file or binary field. If the sound is from a file, use the FILENAME option. You may name the file or use ? or a skeleton to bring up the File dialog box. The extension WAV is assumed unless you supply another.

PLAY SOUND BINARY <BinaryFld> plays the sound from the named binary field of the current record of the table active in the current work area.

Sounds may be recorded using the Windows Sound Recorder and other applications. You cannot play sounds on your system unless it has a sound driver or sound adapter board.

POPUP()

Returns the name of the active dBASE IV pop-up menu.

Syntax:

```
[cVar=] popup()
```

The POPUP() function returns the name of the active dBASE IV pop-up menu defined with DEFINE POPUP. The function returns a null string if no popup is active, including after a popup has been deactivated or its window closed.

The POPUP() function is retained for compatibility. Use INSPECT() to obtain information about forms and objects.

See ACTIVATE POPUP, DEACTIVATE POPUP, DEACTIVATE WINDOW, DEFINE POPUP, ON BAR, ON POPUP, ON SELECTION POPUP.

PRINTJOB

Introduces a PRINTJOB . . . ENDPRINTJOB programming structure.

Syntax:

```
PRINTJOB
     <code>
ENDPRINTJOB
```

You can use the PRINTJOB . . . ENDPRINTJOB structure to control a print job using the system variables. Assign values to any system variables you want to change before the PRINTJOB command. You may want to change _pcopies to print more than one copy, _pbpage to start on a page other than 1, _ploffset to move the print to the right on the paper to leave room for punching holes and so forth.

When dBASE executes the PRINTJOB command, it checks _peject and ejects a page if it is set to “BEFORE” or “BOTH”. It also sets _pcolno to 0.

When dBASE executes ENDPRINTJOB, it ejects a page if _peject is “AFTER” or “BOTH” and resets _pcolno to 0.

You should SET PRINTER ON before issuing the PRINTJOB command and OFF after ENDPRINTJOB, and should after ENDPRINTJOB reset any system variables you have changed for that job only.

See ON PAGE, SET PRINTER.

PRINTSTATUS()

Returns .T. if a printer port has been set with SET PRINTER TO.

Syntax:

```
[lVar=] printstatus([<cExpDevice>])
```

The Windows Print Manager performs the actual management of the printer for Windows applications, so you do not need to check the printer status within dBASE. You may use PRINTSTATUS() to check whether a port such as LPT1 or COM1 has been set as the printer port with SET PRINTER TO. The PRINTSTATUS() function will return .F. if you pass it the device name as a parameter and that device has not been set as the printer. If you do not pass it the device name, PRINTSTATUS() checks the default SET PRINTER TO port, returning .F. if no port has been set. The parameter to PRINTSTATUS() must be an expression, so if passing the name of a port such as LPT1 literally, include it in quotation marks or other delimiters. Any port name that the Windows Control Panel recognizes is valid.

PRIVATE

Limits the scope of variables.

Syntax:

```
PRIVATE {<xVarList>|ALL} [LIKE <skeleton1>]
     [EXCEPT <skeleton2>]
```

You can declare variables private using the PRIVATE command. You can list the variables to be made private, can use ALL to make private all variables declared in the procedure or function in which the PRIVATE ALL command appears, or can use LIKE or EXCEPT, or both, with skeletons that fit some variable names but not others.

The PRIVATE command makes variables invisible except in the procedure or function in which they are declared and in any procedures or functions it calls. PRIVATE variables are more visible than LOCAL variables, which cannot be seen from a procedure or function called by the one in which you declare them.

Declaring the variables in procedures and UDFs PRIVATE keeps them from overwriting variables of the same name in the programs that call them. This is particularly important in utility-type procedures and functions that you put in a library and never look at again. You want to be able to write your programs without concerning yourself with what variable names someone might have chosen for variables in the library functions and procedures. If the variable names in the library are all PRIVATE or LOCAL, they cannot interfere with your variables that might happen to have the same names.

If there is a risk that your procedures or functions might call other procedures or functions in which the variables have not been declared PRIVATE, you can protect the variables in your code by declaring them LOCAL. LOCAL variables are protected against interference by variables of the same name both above and below in the calling chain.

If there is a PRIVATE variable active and another variable of the same name in a higher-level routine, DISPLAY or LIST MEMORY run from the lower routine will show the upper-level variable as hidden. The value of the upper-level variable is there and will return when the lower-level routine ends, but is blocked from view by the value of the lower-level private variable.

See LOCAL, PUBLIC.

PROCEDURE

Introduces a procedure in a program file.

Syntax:

```
PROCEDURE <Procedure>[(<ParameterList>)|PARAMETERS<ParameterList>]
<code>
RETURN <ReturnValue>
```

Procedure names can be as long as you want, but dBASE reads only the first 32 characters. The name can contain letters, numbers, and underscores, but must start with a letter or number.

Each procedure can accept up to 255 parameters and must end with a RETURN statement as its last executable statement. You may either list the parameters in parentheses following the procedure name or in the first statement within the procedure, on a separate line, preceded by the PARAMETERS keyword.

In dBASE for Windows procedures can return values. You can call a procedure using the same syntax you use to call a function in order to make use of any value returned.

Procedures should be placed in program files. All procedures and functions should follow the end of the main program if placed in a file with a main program. When it compiles program files, dBASE marks all code that is not part of a named procedure or function as part of a main procedure with the same name as the file in which it is found. You should not name a procedure with the same name as its file if there is a main program in the same file. dBASE will not know which of the two procedures of the same name to call.

You can collect procedures and user-defined functions into special files and activate them with SET PROCEDURE or SET LIBRARY for use by many of your programs. As many as 193 of either procedures or functions of any size can be placed in a single file.

Examples:

```
? Twice( 27 )
        54
<code>
PROCEDURE Twice( Number)
RETURN Number * 2

Result = 0
DO Double WITH 27, Result
? Result
        54
<code>
PROCEDURE Double
PARAMETERS Number, Twiceit
Twiceit = Number * 2
RETURN
```

See FUNCTION, PARAMETERS, RETURN, SET LIBRARY, SET PROCEDURE.

PROGRAM()

Returns the name of the current program, procedure, or user-defined function.

Syntax:

```
[cVar=] program([<nExp>])
```

The PROGRAM() function without <nExp> returns the name of the lowest-level named routine that is executing or suspended. This can be a program, a procedure, or a user-defined function. If no routine is executing or suspended, the function returns an empty string.

The name is returned in uppercase, without the file name, even if the routine named is in a different file from the calling program. You can use PROGRAM() and LINENO() in an ON ERROR routine to determine what line of what routine caused the error.

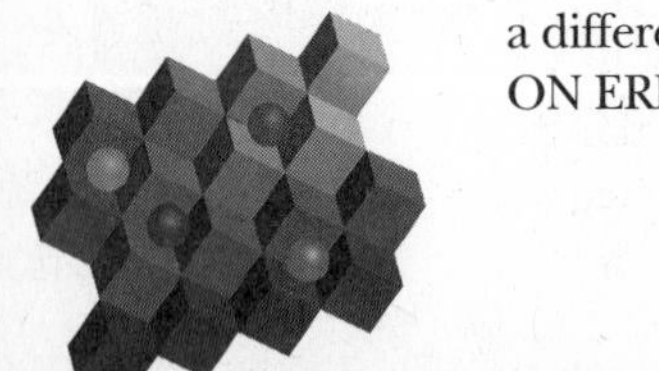

If you include the <nExp> parameter, PROGRAM() returns the fully qualified path, name and extension of the program file containing the lowest-level routine that is executing or suspended.

See LINENO(), ON ERROR.

PROMPT()

Returns the prompt of the currently highlighted or most recently selected option of a pop-up or dBASE IV menu.

Syntax:

```
[cVar=] prompt()
```

The PROMPT() function returns an empty string if the menu or popup most recently highlighted or selected is not in memory or if it was left without making a selection, as by pressing Esc or deactivating its window. Otherwise, the function returns the prompt of the pad or bar currently highlighted or most recently selected, including one from a popup or menu deactivated since the selection. If the popup used the FIELD, FILES, or STRUCTURE prompt option, the value returned is the contents of the field, the fully qualified name of the file in uppercase or the name of the field in uppercase, respectively.

PROMPT() is included for compatibility. Use INSPECT() to learn the properties, including the Text property, of dBASE for Windows objects.

PROPER()

New; returns a character expression or memo field with the first character of each word capitalized.

Syntax:

```
[cVar=] proper(<cExp>|<mFld>)
```

The PROPER() function returns the character string <cExp> or memo field <mFld> with the first letter of each word capitalized and no others. Except for the first character of the string, which it returns in uppercase, it returns each character in uppercase if and only if the character follows a space.

The PROPER() function will do at least 90 percent of the work of putting names into mixed case, but you will still have to go through your list to deal with letters after hyphens, "Mc" and "O'" and to deal with titles and street directions such as "MD" and "SW."

Which characters count as uppercase or lowercase depends on the language driver in use.

See LOWER(), UPPER().

PROTECT

Is not supported by dBASE for Windows.

PROW()

Returns the vertical printing position of the printer.

Syntax:

```
[nVar=] prow()
```

The PROW() function returns the line number of the current printer line on the page, starting with 0. The height of a line is measured according to the font of the parent form. Unless SET PRINTER is ON or SET DEVICE TO is set to PRINTER, PROW() returns 0. If using a proportional font, you may add or subtract fractional numbers to or from the value returned by PROW() to place the next line precisely.

PUBLIC

Declares variables and arrays visible from higher-level routines.

Syntax:

```
PUBLIC <xVarList>|{ARRAY <Array>{[}<nExpRows>[,<nExpCols>]{]}[,<etc.>]}
```

The PUBLIC command makes variables or arrays public or global, so they can be accessed from higher-level routines in the calling chain, as well as the routine in which they are defined and those it calls. If defined in a program, public variables and arrays continue to exist after the program ends and can be accessed from the Command window.

The PUBLIC command can include either a list of variables declared public or a list of arrays. Each array name is followed with its dimensions in brackets. The PUBLIC ARRAY syntax takes the place of giving the array name in a PUBLIC variable list then using DECLARE to dimension the array. In the syntax paradigm above, those brackets enclosed in curly braces must be included literally.

Example:

```
PUBLIC nCount, cString, dDate, fVariance
PUBLIC ARRAY Matrix[9,5], Calendar[6,7]
```

See DECLARE, LOCAL, PRIVATE.

PUTFILE()

New; opens a customized version of the File dialog box.

Syntax:

```
[cVar=] putfile([<cExpTitle>[,<cExpFile>
          [,<cExpExtension>[,<lExpAllTypes>[,<lExpSwitch>]]]]])
```

The PUTFILE() function allows you to give your own title <cExpTitle> to the File dialog box and supply a file name <cExpFile> that appears in its entry field. The third parameter <cExpExtension> is a default extension that will be added to the name you select if you fail to specify an extension.

The <lExpAllTypes> parameter, if .T., the default, specifies that the dialog box will open showing all file types in the directory. If .F., it shows only table file types. <lExpSwitch> is by default .F. Make it .T. if you want the user to be able to switch between the two sets of file types, all and tables only, when within the dialog box.

Each of the earlier parameters must be supplied, or its place held by an empty string and a comma, if you supply any later parameter.

The function returns the fully qualified filename if one is selected, or an empty string.

The directory initially displayed by the PUTFILE() function is the directory last displayed during the last previous use of the function.

PV()

Returns the present value of a series of payments or annuity.

Syntax:

```
[fVar=] pv(<nExpPayment>,<nExpRate>,<nExpPeriods>)
```

The PV() function calculates, as a float-type number, the present cost of a series of future level payments. This is equivalent to the value today of the right to receive a series of level payments in the future, an annuity. The function is the inverse of PAYMENT(). If you use PAYMENT() to calculate the payment needed to amortize a loan of a given amount, plugging that payment and the same interest rate and periods into PV() should yield the amount of the loan, although there will often be a small difference due to rounding the payment.

As with the other financial functions, an annual rate of interest must be divided by the number of payment periods in a year.

Example:

```
? pv(733.76,.08/12,360)
     99999.38
```

The example calculates the present value of the right to receive, or the present cost of the duty to pay, 360 monthly payments of 733.76, at 8 percent annual interest.

See FV(), PAYMENT().

QUIT

Terminates the dBASE for Windows session.

Syntax:

```
QUIT [WITH <nExp>]
```

The QUIT command immediately closes all forms, windows, tables, indexes, and other files including low-level files and program files and terminates the dBASE for Windows session.

It is equivalent to clicking the Close bar of the main dBASE for Windows control menu, except that by using QUIT and including the optional WITH <nExp>, you can pass the value of <nExp>, from 1 through 254, to Windows or another operating system.

To terminate a program normally, use RETURN. To terminate a program abnormally without ending the dBASE session, use CANCEL.

See CANCEL, RETURN.

RANDOM()

Returns a pseudo-random number between 0 and 1.

Syntax:

```
[fVar=] random(<nExp>)
```

The RANDOM() function returns a seemingly random number between 0 and 1 based on the value of <nExp>. Every random-number generator performs mathematical operations on a value, the "seed," to obtain the next random number and the seed for the one after that. If <nExp> is positive, RANDOM() uses it as the seed. Using RANDOM() twice with the same seed will always return the same result. If you omit <nExp> or use 0, RANDOM() uses the previous result of RANDOM() as the seed, or if there is no previous

result a fixed internal seed value. Whatever the seed, the successive numbers generated by RANDOM() with no parameter after the first call appear to be a random series.

If you specify a negative <nExp>, RANDOM() obtains its seed by a calculation involving the system clock. This is very likely to result in a different seed and different series each time, which is what you want for games of chance and most purposes. If you must reproduce the same series of random numbers, use the same positive seed for the first call to RANDOM(). Do not in any case supply any parameter after the first call to RANDOM(), because that will reset the seed and make the series less random.

To convert the returns of RANDOM() to integers in the range 0 through N-1, use int(N*random()). To convert to the range 1 through N, use int(N*random())+1. It is possible (and even likely) that a series of random integers generated with the help of RANDOM() will contain duplicates. If your application requires that the numbers be sequential but randomly arranged, use the technique of the Shuffle function in the example under CLASSES in this Appendix.

Example:

```
random(-1)
?
for n = 1 to 10
     ?? str(int(random()*10),3)  && random digits
endfor
?
  2  5  0  1  5  6  6  4  1  4
```

RAT()

Reverse AT(), finds the last occurrence of one string in another.

Syntax:

```
[nVar=] rat(<cExpSearch>,(<cExp>|<mFld>)[,<nExp>])
```

The RAT() function, like AT(), finds a small string <cExpSearch> within a larger one or memo field. It starts at the right end and works left. Its return is an N-type number representing the character position within the larger string or memo field, measured from the left, at which the match begins. If the third parameter <nExp> is omitted, the function returns the position of the match closest to the right end. If <nExp> is included, the function counts the matches from right to left and returns the position of the match of which the number in the list of matches is <nExp>.

If the small string does not wholly occur within the large one, or occurs fewer than <nExp> times, the function returns 0. The search is case-sensitive and unaffected by SET EXACT.

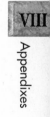

Example:

```
? rat("a","Give me a banana", 3)
        12
```

READ

Activates the @ . . . GET fields in the current window.

Syntax:

```
READ [SAVE]
```

You can use READ to activate @ . . . SAY . . . GET statements in the results pane of the Command window. This is normally done within a program but need not be. You can also use READ to activate GET statements in a window that you have opened in dBASE IV mode with ACTIVATE WINDOW. When a GET statement is active, the cursor is placed within it, and you can edit the contents. READ is included for compatibility; use OPEN FORM and READMODAL() to manage forms in dBASE for Windows.

You can issue several GET statements followed by a single READ. All of the GET fields will be activated at once and you can move from one to the other.

You can include GET statements without a READ in a format file. When you open the format file in a window you have opened with ACTIVATE WINDOW, you can issue not only READ but APPEND, BROWSE FORMAT, CHANGE|EDIT or INSERT to activate them.

You can also place READ commands within a format file, wherever you want a page break. Each one will repaint the window as a new page and activate the GET statements before it and following the previous READ, if any.

READ normally clears the GET statements when editing of them is completed. The SAVE option of READ keeps the GETS open so that the next READ statement will bring the same GETS up for editing again. After a READ SAVE, be sure to issue a CLEAR GETS to keep the GET statements from reappearing indefinitely.

You can nest READ statements, as by having one appear in a procedure or function invoked from another READ by an ON KEY trap or by a WHEN or VALID condition. When the inner READ finishes, control returns to the outer one.

See @ . . . SAY . . . GET, ACTIVATE WINDOW, CLEAR GETS, OPEN FORM, READMODAL(), SET FORMAT, SET WINDOW.

READKEY()

Returns the key used to exit a full-screen command.

Syntax:

```
[nVar=] readkey()
```

The READKEY() function can be issued only in a program, procedure, or function. It returns an integer representing the key used to exit from one of the full-screen commands APPEND, BROWSE, CHANGE|EDIT, INSERT, and READ.

The intergers returned by READKEY() are in the range of 0-36 if the user has not changed the data and the range 256-292 (256 higher in each case) if the user has changed the data, with two exceptions. If the user exits by pressing Ctrl+Q or Esc, the return is always 12 because even if the user does make changes, those changes are not saved. If the user exits with Ctrl+W or Ctrl+End, the return is 270 because any changes are saved, but it is not possible to ascertain from the return of READKEY() alone whether the user made any changes or not.

You can use READKEY() in the VALID clause of a @ . . . SAY . . . GET statement, but it will always return a value below 37 because the exit is not complete at that stage. You can use it to learn which key was pressed, but not whether the user made changes.

See @ . . . SAY . . . GET, LASTKEY().

READMODAL()

New; opens a form as a modal window.

Syntax:

```
[cVar=] readmodal(<Form>[,<Object>[,<lExp>]])
```

Appendixes

The READMODAL() function opens and displays a form as a modal window, which means you must interact with it. You will not be allowed to click on another window to give that window focus before closing the modal window. The READMODAL() window might have child windows with which you can interact, but they must be modal too. The function by default returns the name of the object that has focus when the user closes (*submits*) the form. You can specify a different value to be returned by READMODAL() using the WITH option of CLOSE FORMS.

The first parameter to READMODAL() is the name of the form to open. The second, optional, is the name of the object to receive initial focus. If the second parameter is omitted, the first object placed in the form receives focus. The third parameter is .T., to specify that pressing Esc will close the form, which is the default, or .F.

Execution of the routine that displays the form stops until the form is closed. Execution then proceeds from the line following READMODAL().

The READMODAL() function operates similarly to the ReadModal() method. If you want to open a form as a non-modal window, use OPEN FORM or its Open() method.

See CLOSE FORMS, OPEN FORM.

RECALL

Removes the marks DELETE places on records of dBASE tables to delete them.

Syntax:

```
RECALL [<scope>][FOR <lExpCond1>]
     [WHILE <lExpCond2>]
```

The RECALL command reverses the effects of the DELETE command. DELETE marks records of dBASE tables for deletion, making them invisible when SET DELETED is ON and vulnerable to removal by PACK. RECALL unmarks the records. By default, the scope of RECALL is one record. You can specify the scope and can limit the reach of the command within the scope by the FOR and WHILE options.

RECALL cannot be used on Paradox tables. Attempting to use it causes an error. Paradox tables have no deleted marks. Records deleted are removed at once.

See DELETE, PACK.

RECCOUNT()

Returns the number of records in a table.

Syntax:

```
[nVar=] reccount([<workarea>])
```

The RECCOUNT() function returns the number of records in the current or specified table from the count contained in its header. If no table is in use, it returns 0. The count is independent of any filter set by SET FILTER or any marking of records for deletion and includes all records in the table.

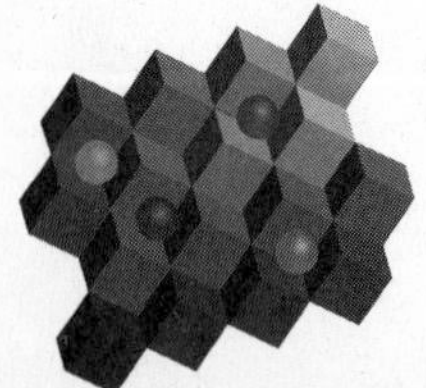

RECNO()

Returns the number of, or a bookmark for, the current record of a table.

Syntax:

```
[nVar=] recno([<workarea>])
```

The RECNO() function returns the number of the current record in the current or specified dBASE table. For a Paradox or SQL table, it returns a bookmark.

The number returned for a dBASE table is the physical position of the record, not its logical position in the controlling order if the table is indexed. RECNO() considers all records without regard to marking for deletion or any filter set by SET FILTER.

If there is no table in the specified work area, RECNO() returns 0. In a dBASE table it will return 1 more than the number of records in the table if EOF() is true. It will never return less than 1 if the table exists even if at BOF() or if there are no records in the table.

See BOF(), BOOKMARK(), EOF().

RECSIZE()

Returns the size of a record in a table.

Syntax:

```
[nVar=] recsize([<workarea>])
```

The RECSIZE() function returns the size in bytes of the current record in the current or specified table. If there is no table open in the work area, it returns 0. The size of a record of a dBASE table is one byte to hold the deleted mark plus the sum of the lengths of its fields. A record of a Paradox table is only as long as the sum of the lengths of its fields.

REDEFINE

New; changes the characteristics of a User Interface object created with DEFINE.

Syntax:

```
REDEFINE <Class> {<Object>|<nExpOrder>}[OF <Container>]
  {FROM <nExpRow1>,<nExpCol1> TO <nExpRow2>,<nExpCol2>}|
  {AT <nExpRow>,<nExpCol>}
  [PROPERTY <Property1><xExpValue1>[,<etc.>]]
  [CUSTOM <Property2><xExpValue2>[,<etc.>]
  [WITH <ParameterList>]
```

REDEFINE is available for each of the 20 predefined classes of User Interface object and for custom classes you define. It uses the same syntax as DEFINE. You can use it to change the characteristics and properties from those previously assigned with DEFINE. You must use DEFINE first to create the object.

See DEFINE.

REFRESH

Refreshes the table buffers.

Syntax:

```
REFRESH [<workarea>]
```

The REFRESH command refreshes the buffers of the current or specified table. It is most often used when using data from a server, since the local copy can in time differ from the copy on the server which has been updated by other users. The command is not limited to use with server data but can be issued for a local dBASE or Paradox table—perhaps one on a multi-user system that was opened and read in shared mode some time ago and might have been changed.

REINDEX

Rebuilds all active indexes in the current work area.

Syntax:

```
REINDEX
```

Use REINDEX to rebuild indexes that were not active when the dBASE IV table was changed. Only the production MDX file and files containing indexes specifically made active by SET INDEX or SET ORDER are updated automatically. When you REINDEX a UNIQUE index, whether created with SET UNIQUE on or the UNIQUE option of INDEX, it remains UNIQUE regardless of the SET UNIQUE setting at the time of the REINDEX. Except for records excluded by UNIQUE, REINDEX includes all records in each index, including deleted ones, regardless of any filters set with SET FILTER.

On a multi-user system, a table must be in exclusive use before you can REINDEX its MDX files.

In theory you should never need to REINDEX a production MDX file or any index that was active when you changed the table. In practice, it cannot hurt and often cures annoying and mysterious problems of data corruption.

See INDEX, SET FILTER, SET INDEX, SET ORDER, SET UNIQUE.

RELATION()

New; returns the expression relating one table to another.

Syntax:

```
[cVar=] relation(<nExp>[,<workarea>])
```

The RELATION() function returns a relation set from the current or specified table to others. The <nExp> parameter gives the number of the relation wanted on a list of all relations set from the specified work area, in order of creation.

The return of the function is simply the relation expression, such as "Cust_ID". The name of the table into which the relation is set is not given. Use TARGET() for that. If no relation is set in the <nExp> position, RELATION() returns an empty string.

RELEASE

Releases variables and other items from memory. Has new options AUTOMEM, DLL, FORMS, OBJECT.

Syntax:

```
RELEASE {<xVarList>|ALL} [LIKE<skeleton1>][EXCEPT <skeleton2>}|
  AUTOMEM|
  DLL <DLLList>|FORMS <FormList>|MENUS <MenuList>|
  OBJECT <Container>.<Object>|
  POPUPS <PopupList|
  SCREENS <ScreenList>|
  WINDOWS <WindowList>
```

Use the RELEASE command to clear listed items from memory, freeing up memory for other uses. The CLEAR command removes all items of a type, which you might not want.

Appendixes

RELEASE without a keyword identifying the type of item releases memory variables. If issued in the Command window with ALL it is equivalent to CLEAR MEMORY and clears all variables except system variables. When issued in a program, function, or procedure, RELEASE does not release public variables wherever declared, or private variables in higher-level routines. It releases only private variables declared in the routine in which you issue it and those at lower levels called by the one in which you issue it. There is ordinarily no need to RELEASE local variables at any level or private ones at a lower level, because they are released automatically when their routines end.

RELEASE when used to release variables accepts LIKE and EXCEPT with skeletons of the variable names as modifiers to a list of variables to release or the ALL option.

RELEASE AUTOMEM releases all variables with the same names as the fields of the current table. You can create AUTOMEM variables with the AUTOMEM option of USE or STORE AUTOMEM, or simply by assigning something to a variable with the same name as the field of the current table. Nothing distinguishes AUTOMEM variables from other variables except the fact their names match those of the fields of the current table. There is no option to release variables with names matching those of a table active in another work area.

The DLL, FORMS, MENUS, OBJECT, POPUPS, SCREENS, and WINDOWS all accept lists of the items of the type to be released. The only nonstandard type is OBJECT. You must use the dot notation <Container>.<Object> with RELEASE OBJECT and can release only one object at a time. You will more often use an object's own Release() method.

See CLEAR, CREATE, DEFINE, LOCAL, PRIVATE, PUBLIC.

RENAME

Renames a file, has new TABLE option.

Syntax:

```
RENAME {{<File1>|?|<skeleton>} TO {<File2>|?}}|
  {TABLE {<File3>|?|<skeleton>) TO {<File4>|?}
   [[TYPE]PARADOX|DBASE]}
```

The RENAME command renames a file. The new name cannot be the same as that of an existing file of the same extension in the same directory. With or without the TABLE option, you can either name the file being renamed or give a ? or skeleton to bring up the File dialog box and choose a file. You can also give a ? and bring up the dialog box to choose the new name. You cannot use the dBASE RENAME command with wild cards to rename more than one file at a time.

The TABLE option renames the associated index and memo files as well as the table itself, which the RENAME command without TABLE does not do. The TYPE option of RENAME TABLE allows you to specify the type of table being renamed. This is necessary only if the table has a nonstandard file extension; it tells dBASE the table type so dBASE knows what associated files to look for and rename. The word TYPE is unnecessary. The RENAME TABLE TYPE option does not enable you to convert a dBASE table to a Paradox table or the reverse, it simply identifies the source table type to aid dBASE in identifying associated files.

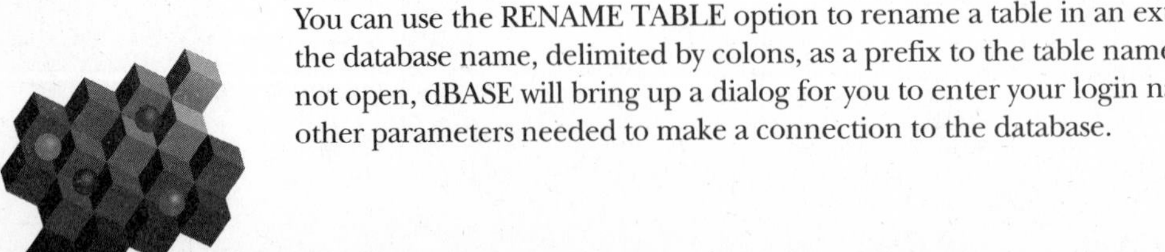

You can use the RENAME TABLE option to rename a table in an external database. Give the database name, delimited by colons, as a prefix to the table name. If the database is not open, dBASE will bring up a dialog for you to enter your login name, password, or other parameters needed to make a connection to the database.

REPLACE

Replaces the contents of fields of the current table. Has new options AUTOMEM, BINARY, MEMO, MEMO . . . FROM, OLE.

Syntax:

```
REPLACE  {{{<Field> WITH <xExp> [ADDITIVE]}[,<etc.>]}|
                         {FROM ARRAY <Array> [FIELDS<FieldList>]}}
                    [<scope>][FOR <lExpCond1>][WHILE
<lExpCond2>][REINDEX]}|
                  AUTOMEM|
          {BINARY <BinField> FROM <File1> [TYPE <BinNumber>]}|
                    {MEMO <mFld> {WITH ARRAY <Array>}|{FROM
<File2>[ADDITIVE]}|
          {OLE <OLEField> FROM <File3>[LINK]}
```

The REPLACE command without the AUTOMEM, BINARY, MEMO, or OLE options replaces the contents of one or more fields of the current table. Following the REPLACE verb is a list of one or more fields to replace, each followed by the expression with which to replace it and the optional keyword ADDITIVE. ADDITIVE is ignored except for memo fields. For memo fields, it specifies that the replacement data be appended to the memo, not overwrite it. Overwriting is the default.

As an alternative to a list of fields and expressions for each, REPLACE can be followed by the FROM ARRAY option. This specifies that the data from the first row of the specified array is to replace the contents of the fields of the current record, with the element from the first column of the array replacing the first field, and so forth. You might use the optional fields list with FROM ARRAY to rearrange the fields. The first field in the list will then be filled from the first column of the array, and so forth. Memo fields will always be skipped. They cannot be filled from an element of an array. If the type of data in an element of an array does not match the type of the field it is to replace, an error occurs, but fields already processed retain their replaced contents. If there are more columns in the array than non-memo fields in the table or fields list—or vice versa—the excess columns go unused or the excess fields remain unchanged, as the case might be.

The default scope of REPLACE is one record. You can use <scope> to specify a different scope and the FOR or WHILE option to limit the records within the scope to be replaced. If you use FROM ARRAY option and a scope of more than one record, data from additional rows of the array will be used to fill the fields in the additional records—one row per record.

REPLACE AUTOMEM replaces the fields of the current record only with the contents of variables of the same name as the fields. If a variable of the same name as a field contains data of a different type, an error occurs. If one or more fields are not matched by variables with the same names, no error occurs, but those fields remain unchanged.

REPLACE BINARY replaces the named binary field of the current record with the file named. If no file extension is given, BMP is assumed. You may use the TYPE <BinNumber> option to tell dBASE the type of binary data as prescribed in the BINTYPE() function, a number up to 32,767 for a type you define or a larger number for a dBASE-defined type. At present only 32,768 for WAV sound files and 32,769 for BMP and PCX graphic files are defined.

REPLACE MEMO has two options, WITH ARRAY and FROM <File>. The WITH array option enables you to place each line proposed for a memo field into an element of an array. You then issue REPLACE MEMO . . . WITH ARRAY. . . , naming the memo field and the array, to have the lines transferred element by element into the memo. Use ADDITIVE to have the lines add to the memo rather than to overwrite it. REPLACE MEMO WITH ARRAY is particularly intended to permit you to edit memos as well as other types of fields with AUTOMEM variables. You cannot use an AUTOMEM variable directly for a memo, but using STORE MEMO TO ARRAY with STORE AUTOMEM you can transfer the memo contents to the array for editing, along with the other data. After editing you can REPLACE AUTOMEM to update the non-memo fields and REPLACE MEMO WITH ARRAY to update the memo field.

The REPLACE MEMO FROM option enables you to replace a memo field with the contents of a file. The file can be a text or other file or an OLE document. If the file is an OLE document, you should use the EMBED or LINK option. EMBED places the document in the memo field while LINK establishes a link from the memo field to the document. There is no ADDITIVE option for REPLACE MEMO FROM.

REPLACE OLE replaces the named OLE field of the current record with data from the OLE document <File3>. By default, the OLE document is embedded in the DBT file. If you use the LINK option, only a reference to the OLE document is stored in the table.

See BINTYPE(), STORE AUTOMEM.

REPLICATE()

Repeats a string or memo field a number of times.

Syntax:

```
[cVar=] replicate((<cExp>|<mFld>),<nExp>)
```

The REPLICATE() function returns the given character expression or memo field repeated <nExp> times. If <nExp> is 0, it returns an empty string. If <nExp> is negative an error occurs. The resulting string cannot exceed the 32,766-character limit on the length of character strings, so <nExp> cannot exceed 32,766 divided by the length of the character expression or memo field being repeated.

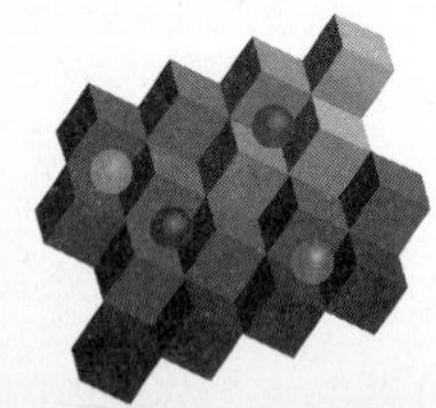

REPLICATE() is often used to fill a PICTURE clause with X, 9, or other template characters.

See @ . . . SAY . . . GET, SPACE().

REPORT FORM

Generates a report.

Syntax:

```
REPORT FORM {<Report>|?|<skeleton1>}
[<scope>][FOR <lExpCond1>][WHILE <lExpCond2>]
[CROSSTAB][HEADING <cExpHeading>][NOEJECT][PLAIN][SUMMARY]
[TO PRINTER|{FILE {<File>|?|<skeleton2>}}]
```

The REPORT FORM command prints a report using a report form you have created. You can give the name of the report form file or use ? or a skeleton to bring up the File dialog box. By default, dBASE assumes the file extensions RPT, FRG and FRM in that order. The report scope by default is all records of the current file; you can use <scope> and the FOR or WHILE option to restrict the records included in the report.

CROSSTAB specifies that the report is a cross-tabulated report, created with the CROSSTAB dialog box.

PLAIN suppresses headers and footers on all but the first page. The HEADING option is effective only if PLAIN is omitted and adds the extra heading specified on the first line of each page.

NOEJECT prevents a page eject before the first page. SUMMARY causes the report to include only groups and subgroups as defined in the report form and to omit the detail lines.

By default, the report prints to the results pane of the Command window or other current window, which is handy for previewing. You can direct the report TO PRINTER or TO FILE, either naming the file or using ? or a skeleton to bring up the File dialog box. The default extension of the save file is TXT.

To use print settings from a print form file with the report, assign the name of the print form file to the _pform system variable.

See CREATE|MODIFY REPORT.

RESET

Is not supported in dBASE for Windows.

RESOURCE()

Returns a resource from a DLL file.

Syntax:

```
[xVar=] resource(<nExpID>,<DLL>)
```

The RESOURCE() function returns a resource from a DLL file. The resource is identified by its ID, an integer specified when the DLL is created. The resource might be a character string from a string table, such as a table of messages or translations of text items, or might be a bitmap, cursor, icon, or other resource.

One of the principal uses of DLL resources is to deal with internationalization. Your program can store all the messages it needs in the language of the user and call upon them at runtime with the RESOURCE() function.

RESTORE

Loads the variables or other items from a specified file into memory, has the new option RESTORE IMAGE that also displays the image.

Syntax:

```
RESTORE {FROM {<File1>|?|<skeleton1>}[ADDITIVE]}|
        {IMAGE FROM {{<File2>|?|<skeleton2>}|
          {BINARY<BinaryField>}}[TIMEOUT <nExp>]
          [TO PRINTER][[TYPE]PCX])}|
        {SCREEN [FROM {<ScreenVar>|
          FILE {<File3>|?|<skeleton3>}}]}|
        {WINDOW {<WindowList>|ALL}
          FROM {File4|?|<skeleton4>}}
```

With each of the variations of the RESTORE command that restores data from a file, you can specify the file name, or use ? or a skeleton to bring up the File dialog box.

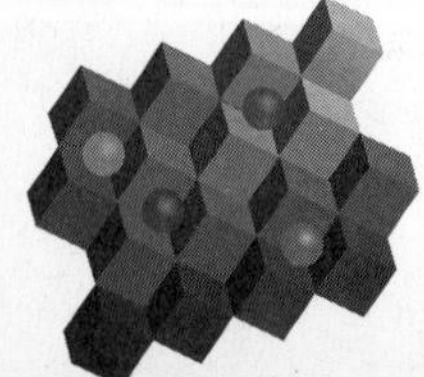

RESTORE without IMAGE, SCREEN, or WINDOW restores memory variables, by default from a file of extension .MEM. If you omit the ADDITIVE option, all variables already in memory except system variables will be cleared. If RESTORE is issued from the Command window, the variables will be public. Variables restored from within a program, procedure, or function are private to it.

RESTORE IMAGE loads a binary image into memory from a file or binary field and displays it. The file is assumed to be a bitmap file of extension BMP, but you can specify a PCX extension with the TYPE option. The word TYPE is unnecessary. TIMEOUT shows the image on the screen for <nExp> seconds, then hides it. By default, the image stays on the screen. TO PRINTER sends the image to the printer as well as to the screen.

RESTORE SCREEN redisplays in the Command Results window the screen contents saved with SAVE SCREEN to a memory variable or file. The storage file is assumed to have the extension SCN. If RESTORE SCREEN is issued without FROM, it restores the Command Results window from the Command Results window buffer.

RESTORE WINDOW restores either ALL the windows or the listed windows from a named file. Its extension is assumed to be WIN. If the window saved included active GETS or UI objects, they are not activated by RESTORE.

RESTORE MACROS is not supported by dBASE for Windows.

See SAVE, SAVE IMAGE, SAVE SCREEN, SAVE WINDOW.

RESUME

Restarts program execution from the point at which it was suspended.

Syntax:

```
RESUME
```

You can press Esc, if SET ESCAPE is ON, to halt a running program and can then SUSPEND it. If an error occurs, you can also choose SUSPEND. While the program is suspended you can examine and change memory variables and the status of tables and indexes. If you change the code of the program, the changes will not take effect until it is recompiled and you run it again. When you have finished doing what you need to while the program is suspended, issue RESUME to continue the program from the point at which it was suspended. You may first want to issue CLEAR so the results of commands you issued while the program was suspended do not get confused with the program output.

See SUSPEND.

RETRY

Re-executes a command that caused an error.

Syntax:

```
RETRY
```

The RETRY command, most useful in a routine called by ON ERROR, repeats the command that caused the error. The usual RETURN from an ON ERROR procedure returns the line following the one that caused the error.

Use RETRY when the nature of the error is known inside the ON ERROR procedure, from ERROR() or otherwise, and it is easily fixed without user intervention. If the command that causes the error is APPEND FROM and the error is that the source file is already open, the error procedure can close the file and issue RETRY. You should provide another course of action if the error is not the one you expect, because the procedure will not then correct the situation. Issuing RETRY will cause a second error and an infinite set of retries and errors, hanging the system.

You cannot set a counter in the ON ERROR procedure to count the retries; variables created in the procedure will be cleared by the RETRY.

See ON ERROR, RETURN.

RETURN

Ends a program, procedure, or user-defined function.

Syntax:

```
RETURN [<xExp>|TO MASTER|TO <Routine>]
```

RETURN is the standard way a routine—a program, procedure, or user-defined function—ends. It returns control to the routine that called it or, if there is none, to the Command window.

A UDF must return a value <xExp> to the higher-level routine. A RETURN causes release of all nonpublic variables declared in the routine. Execution proceeds from the line following the DO line in the calling routine, if the returning routine was called by DO, or to the line containing the call to a UDF by its name alone. If the returning routine was called from an ON SELECTION command, the return is to the active interface object. A return from a routine called with ON ESCAPE, ON ERROR, or ON KEY is to the place in the calling routine where the event occurred that caused the routine to run.

A RETURN to a named routine causes dBASE to examine the calling stack. Return is to the lowest (closest to the returning routine) instance in the stack of the routine named in the RETURN TO statement. dBASE removes intervening routines from the stack and

releases their nonpublic variables. RETURN TO MASTER returns directly to the top routine on the calling stack. dBASE terminates all lower routines and releases their nonpublic variables.

See CANCEL, RETRY.

RIGHT()

Returns the rightmost characters of a character string or memo field.

Syntax:

```
[cVar=] right({<cExp>|<mFld>},<nExp>)
```

The RIGHT() function returns <nExp> characters from the right end of a character expression or memo field. Be sure to TRIM() a character field to remove trailing blanks before using RIGHT() to return the final non-blank characters.

If <nExp> is larger than the character expression or memo field, RIGHT() returns the expression passed but does not pad it to the requested length. If <nExp> is less than or equal to 0, the function returns an empty string.

Example:

```
cSeconds = right(time(), 2)
```

See LEFT(), SUBSTR().

RLOCK()

Locks records of a table.

Syntax:

```
[lVar=] rlock([{<cExpList>|<kBookMarkList>}[,<workarea>]]|[<workarea>])
```

Appendixes

The RLOCK() function locks one or more records of the current table, or the one specified by <workarea>. By default, it locks the current record of the current table. You may include <cExpList>, a list of record numbers in the form "1,2,4,7,19," to lock multiple records. You may substitute a list of bookmarks to lock multiple records of a Paradox or SQL table. If you include both a list and a <workarea>, you must include a comma at the end of the list and before the <workarea>.

RLOCK() locks the named records and all those related to them by SET RELATION to. If the lock is successful, RLOCK() returns .T. Otherwise, it returns .F. and no records are locked.

Records locked are not unlocked until you issue UNLOCK or close the table.

When you are editing an entry field representing a field in a table, pressing Ctrl+O alternately locks and unlocks the record. RLOCK() is equivalent to LOCK(). Try to use RLOCK(); it is easy to confuse LOCK() with FLOCK().

See FLOCK(), UNLOCK.

ROLLBACK

Is not supported in dBASE for Windows. See ROLLBACK().

ROLLBACK()

Has entirely new meaning, ends a transaction begun by BEGINTRANS() without saving the changes.

Syntax:

```
[lVar=] rollback([<cExpDatabase>])
```

Issue ROLLBACK() to end the current transaction begun by BEGINTRANS() without saving the changes. The function returns .T. if the transaction rolls back successfully. To end a transaction and save the changes, use COMMIT().

The optional <cExpDatabase> parameter identifies the database in which the transaction should end. Since only one transaction may be pending at a time and the current database is assumed if you omit the parameter, you should generally omit it.

The dBASE IV use of ROLLBACK() to test the success of a previous ROLLBACK command, and the ROLLBACK command itself, are not supported by dBASE for Windows.

See BEGINTRANS(), COMMIT().

ROUND()

Rounds a number to the given number of decimal places.

Syntax:

```
[nVar=] round(<nExpNumber>,<nExpPlaces>)
```

The ROUND() function examines the digit of the number <nExpNumber> <nExpPlaces>+1 to the right of the decimal point. If that digit is 5 through 9, it adds 1 to the digit to the left of it and performs any needed carrying. It then replaces the digit examined and all to the right of it by 0. If <nExpPlaces> is negative, <nExpNumber> is rounded to that many places to the left of the decimal point. SET DECIMALS controls the digits displayed in the result.

Examples:

```
set decimals to 3
? round(153.74518,2)
       153.750
set decimals to 2
? round(25378.65,-2)
     25400.00
```

If your report adds up a column of dollars-and-cents figures obtained by multiplication and divisions, it may look all right if you SET DECIMALS TO 2, but the total shown may be a few cents different from the sum of the displayed numbers. This results from dBASE holding the numbers internally in precision greater than that of the nearest cent. Use round(<nExp>,2) to remove the fractional cents from each before adding them up to be sure the total will match the sum of the parts.

See CEILING(), FLOOR(), INT(), SET DECIMALS.

ROW()

Returns the current row position in a window.

Syntax:

```
[xVar=] row()
```

The ROW() function is related to COL(). It returns the vertical position of printing in the results pane of the Command [Results] window or one opened with ACTIVATE WINDOW. The return value is type N Attempting to change ROW() by a fractional number operates as if FLOOR() were applied to the number, disregarding the fraction if adding or subtracting one more line than the integral part.

ROW() is included for compatibility. Use the Top property of objects to place them on forms precisely, and PROW() to position printer output.

See COL(), FLOOR(), PROW().

RTOD()

Converts radians to degrees.

Syntax:

```
[fVar=] rtod(<nExp>)
```

The RTOD() function is the inverse of DTOR(). It converts a number of radians to degrees by multiplying by 180 and dividing by PI(). The return value is float-type.

RTOD() is primarily used in trigonometric calculations involving such functions as SIN() and COS() that use radians as their unit of measure.

See ATAN(), ATN2(), COS(), DTOR(), PI(), SIN(), TAN().

RTRIM()

Alternate syntax to TRIM().

See TRIM().

RUN

Executes a single DOS command from within dBASE for Windows.

Syntax:

```
RUN <cLtrDOScommand>
```

Include the DOS command following RUN in the dBASE RUN statement exactly as you would type it at the DOS prompt, with all options and punctuation or lack of it. ! is the equivalent of RUN.

To use DOS for more than a single command, shell out to it with the DOS command.

DOS cannot execute a command unless dBASE loads COMMAND.COM. dBASE uses DBASEWIN.PIF to find COMMAND.COM. DBASEWIN.PIF is in the same directory as the dBASE executable files, by default C:\DBASEWIN\BIN. You cannot edit it using the dBASE or another text editor, but you can using the Windows PIF Editor in the Main group. Use the PIF Editor File menu to specify DBASEWIN.PIF; do not type its name into the first entry field.

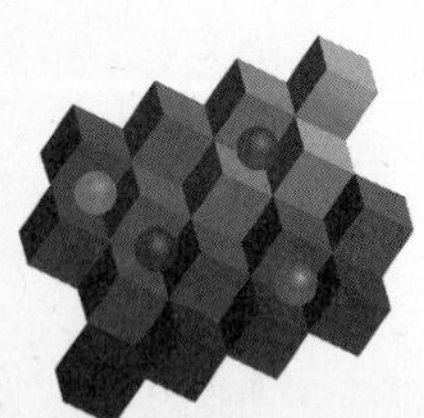

If you cannot see the output of the DOS command because Windows closes its window immediately, use the Windows PIF Editor to edit DBASEWIN.PIF and uncheck the "Close Window on Exit" checkbox.

See !, DOS, RUN().

RUN()

Executes a DOS or Windows command or application.

Syntax:

```
[nVar=] run([<lExp1>,]<cExpDOScommand>[,<lExp2>])
```

The RUN() function executes an external command that may be a DOS or Windows application. The first parameter <lExp1> is .T. for Windows. If it is .F. or omitted, the command is run as a DOS command. <lExp2> does no harm but is ignored. It is included for compatibility with dBASE IV.

DOS cannot execute a command unless dBASE loads COMMAND.COM. dBASE uses DBASEWIN.PIF to find COMMAND.COM. DBASEWIN.PIF is in the same directory as the dBASE executable files, by default C:\DBASEWIN\BIN. You cannot edit it using the dBASE or another text editor, but you can using the Windows PIF Editor in the Main group. Use the PIF Editor File menu to specify DBASEWIN.PIF; do not type its name into the first entry field.

If you cannot see the output of the DOS command because Windows closes its window immediately, use the Windows PIF Editor to edit DBASEWIN.PIF and uncheck the "Close Window on Exit" checkbox.

The RUN() function returns an exit code from DOS commands. The code is 0 if the command was successful. It returns a Windows instance handle from Windows applications—a 16-bit number assigned by Windows—if the function was successful; otherwise, an error code is returned.

See !, DOS, RUN.

SAVE

Stores items from memory to disk and screens to memory.

Syntax:

```
SAVE {TO <File1|?|<skeleton1>[ALL][LIKE<skeleton2>][EXCEPT<skeleton3>]}|
     {SCREEN TO {<ScreenVar>}|{FILE {<File2>|?|<skeleton4>}}|
     {WINDOW {<WindowList>|ALL}[TO {<File3>|?|<skeleton5>}]}
```

SAVE without SCREEN or WINDOW saves memory variables TO the named file. ALL is unnecessary. By default, all variables are saved. The file extension MEM is assumed. You may specify skeletons with LIKE, EXCEPT, or both to limit the variables saved.

SAVE SCREEN saves the contents of the results pane of the Command window. Without more, it saves them to the Command Results window buffer. Use RESTORE SCREEN to redisplay them. There is only one buffer. Each additional SAVE SCREEN will overwrite it. The TO FILE option allows you to save the results pane of the Command window to a file.

The TO <ScreenVar> option allows you to save the Command Results window to a variable, which dBASE assigns type S for screen. By default the variable is private and will be released at the end of the routine creating it. You may declare the variable STATIC, PUBLIC, or LOCAL before using it.

SAVE WINDOW saves the listed dBASE IV- type windows, or ALL windows, to a file. The extension WIN is assumed. This option is included for compatibility. dBASE for Windows forms and objects are saved as program code in .PRG or .WFM files.

SAVE MACROS is not supported by dBASE for Windows.

See RESTORE.

SCAN

Introduces a SCAN . . . ENDSCAN program structure.

Syntax:

```
SCAN [<scope>][FOR <lExpCond1>][WHILE <lExpCond2>]
  <code>
  [LOOP]
  [EXIT]
ENDSCAN
```

The SCAN loop processes the records of the current table, in natural order or the order imposed by the controlling index. By default, it processes the entire table starting at the top. You may use <scope> or the FOR or WHILE options to limit the records scanned. If the scope NEXT or the WHILE option is used, scanning begins at the current record.

LOOP returns to the beginning code of the structure, but does not affect the record pointer. Processing continues with the next record. EXIT terminates the loop and passes control to the statement following ENDSCAN. Unless sooner terminated by the end of the scope, failure of the WHILE condition or EXIT, processing continues to the end of the table, then continues with the statement following ENDSCAN.

SCAN is preferred to DO . . . WHILE or DO . . . UNTIL for processing all or many records of a table. The SCAN structure manages the record pointer. If you use DO, you must include SKIP, which makes processing slightly slower and, more important, is easy to forget or misplace.

Example:

```
use Customer
scan
      replace all past_90 with past_90 + past_60, ;
           past_60 with past_30, ;
           past_30 with current, current with 0
endscan
```

See DO.

SECONDS()

New; returns the number of seconds since midnight.

Syntax:

```
[nVar=] seconds()
```

The SECONDS() function returns the seconds since midnight by the system clock as a number including seconds and hundredths. Its return is more convenient to deal with than TIME(0) because it is numeric, and more accurate than TIME() because it reports hundredths of a second.

Use SECONDS() instead of ELAPSED() if comparing short time periods. If you work past midnight, add 86400, the number of seconds in a day, to the a.m. time before subtracting the p.m. time. Be aware that times returned by the system clock of the IBM PC family are accurate only to 6/100 of a second, so a comparison of two times may be as much as 12/100 of a second off the correct figure.

See ELAPSED(), TIME().

SEEK

SEEK searches an indexed table.

Syntax:

```
SEEK <xExp>
```

The SEEK command searches the index of an indexed table for the first occurrence of a key equal to the value of the expression sought. The search expression is normally a memory variable but can be any expression of the same type as the index key, character, numeric, or date. If the search succeeds, FOUND() is .T., EOF() is .F. and the record pointer points to the record containing the matching key.

If the search fails, FOUND() is .F. If SET NEAR is ON, the record pointer will be at the first record with a key greater than the expression sought and EOF() will be false, unless the expression sought is greater than all keys in the table. If SET NEAR is OFF and the search fails, the record point is at EOF() and EOF() returns true.

SET EXACT governs character searches. If it is OFF, the first record of which the key starts with the expression sought is considered a match.

See EOF(), FIND, FOUND(), SEEK(), SET EXACT, SET NEAR.

SEEK()

Searches an indexed table and returns the result.

Syntax:

```
[lVar=] seek(<xExp>[,<workarea>])
```

The SEEK() function is an empowered version of SEEK. Like the SEEK command, it searches the index of an indexed table to find the first key matching the value of a given expression. Like SEEK, it leaves the record pointer pointing to the record if the search succeeds and to EOF() if not.

The SEEK() function can perform a search in a specified work area instead of the current one only, and it returns the result of its search, .T. for successful and .F. for not, as SEEK cannot except with a separate call to FOUND().

If SET NEAR is ON and no match is found, SEEK() returns .F., the record pointer will be at the first record with a key greater than the expression sought and EOF() will be false, unless the expression sought is greater than all keys in the table. If SET NEAR is OFF and the search fails, the record point is at EOF() and EOF() returns true.

SET EXACT governs character searches. If it is OFF, the first record of which the key starts with the expression sought is considered a match.

See EOF(), FIND, FOUND(), SEEK, SET EXACT, SET NEAR.

SELECT

Makes an alias or work area current.

Syntax:

```
SELECT <workarea>
```

Use the SELECT command to choose which work area will be current among those in which tables are active. You may supply the work area as a number from 1 to 225, as a character expression from "A" through "J" with or without the quotation marks, or as an alias with or without quotation marks.

If a variable holds the number, letter or alias of a work area, you can supply the variable as a parameter to SELECT either by preceding its name with the ¯o operator or by enclosing its name in parentheses to force evaluation.

Examples:

```
use CHICKENS alias Chickens
select select()
use EGGS alias Eggs
set relation to Chick_ID into Chickens
Parent = "Chickens"
select (Parent)  && or select &Parent
```

SELECT()

Returns the number of an available work area or of the work area associated with a specified alias.

Syntax:

```
[nVar=] select([<workarea>])
```

You may use SELECT() with an alias name to obtain the work area number associated with that alias, but you should rarely do so. The use of work area letters is obsolete—at least in programming—as there are only 10 letters available, far too few for the default of 225 work areas allowed dBASE for Windows. The use of work area numbers is also discouraged. Like all "magic numbers" in programs, hard-coded work area numbers convey little information to the reader. It is very easy to forget which area holds which table and to mix them up, usually with unhappy results.

Whenever possible, use SELECT SELECT() to obtain an additional work area. Whenever you open a table, give it an alias and use the alias, not the work area number or letter, to refer to the table when necessary. If you do not know the work area number associated with a table, you will not be tempted to use it and will eliminate the chance of using it incorrectly.

See SELECT.

SET

Sets or toggles one of numerous environmental and other settings and conditions, has numerous new options.

Syntax:

```
SET [<Setting>] <more>
```

SET without <more> opens the dBASE Desktop Properties Inspector from the Properties Menu, allowing you to change many of the settings you can also change with the SET command followed by additional keywords. The various SET commands are described separately below. If the syntax has few options, it is stated only as part of the command listing. Between ON and OFF and similar settings, the default is listed in uppercase.

The words (session based) following a SET command mean that the setting operates separately for each session. When you create a new session, these settings are restored to their defaults for the new session. You can set any of these settings one way in one session and another way in another simultaneously. As you change among sessions, dBASE changes the settings to those you selected for the active session.

SET ALTERNATE controls the alternate stream.

Syntax:

```
SET ALTERNATE {on|OFF}|{TO <File>|?|<skeleton>
     [ADDITIVE]}
```

SET ALTERNATE ON|OFF toggles the alternate stream on and off. You must first define an alternate stream with SET ALTERNATE TO, giving the name of the file to receive the alternate output or ? or a skeleton to bring up the File dialog. The default extension is TXT.

After issuing SET ALTERNATE TO . . . , issue SET ALTERNATE ON to start the alternate stream. The alternate stream copies all output that goes to the results pane of the Command window into the designated file as well. SET ALTERNATE OFF to stop copying the output, and SET ALTERNATE TO or CLOSE ALTERNATE to close the file. Either SET ALTERNATE TO or CLOSE ALTERNATE will SET ALTERNATE OFF as well.

You can change the default settings of SET ALTERNATE in DBASEWIN.INI. To make on the default, change the ALTERNATE parameter in the [OnOffCommandSettings] section. To set a default alternate file name, specify it as the ALTERNATE parameter in the [CommandSettings] section.

SET AUTOSAVE ON|OFF (session based). ON saves each change of a record to the disk. The default of OFF causes dBASE to buffer the records until the buffer is filled. You can change the default by setting it on, or by changing the AUTOSAVE parameter in DBASEWIN.INI.

SET BELL controls the chr(7) sound.

Syntax:

```
SET BELL {ON|OFF}|
     {TO [<nExpFrequency>,<nExpDuration>]}
```

SET BELL TO with a frequency and duration specifies that frequency in Hertz and that frequency in ticks for the tone issued by chr(7). The frequency must be an integer from 19 to 10,000, the duration an integer from 1 to 19. There are approximately 18.2 ticks per second. The default is 512 hertz for 2 ticks. SET BELL TO resets the bell to the settings in DBASEWIN.INI. To change those, change the [OnOffCommandSettings] BELL parameter to on or off, and the [CommandSettings] BELL parameters to the desired frequency and duration.

SET BELL ON|OFF toggles whether the same sound as produced by chr(7) is produced (ON) when you reach the end of a field or variable when entering data, or when you enter invalid data.

SET BLOCKSIZE TO <nExp> (session based) changes the default block size of new DBT and MDX files. The range is from 1 to 63, the blocksize being 512 bytes times the number, with 1 the default. You may use SET IBLOCK and SET MBLOCK to set the index and memo sizes separately. To change the size of memo field blocks of an existing DBT file, set the new size and use COPY TABLE to copy the table and the associated DBT file to new files. You can change the default by changing the BLOCKSIZE parameter in DBASEWIN.INI.

SET BORDER creates borders using characters, not graphics.

Syntax:

```
SET BORDER TO [SINGLE|DOUBLE|PANEL|
      NONE|<BorderList>]
```

SET BORDER TO sets the default border as set in DBASEWIN.INI, by default SINGLE. The SINGLE and DOUBLE options create borders of single and double lines. PANEL creates a border of solid block characters one column wide and one row high. NONE omits any border.

<BorderList> is a string of from one to eight identifiers delimited by commas. If you specify only one identifier, the entire border is drawn with that one. Any identifier may be omitted if its place is held by a comma. The portion of the border corresponding to the omitted identifier will be drawn using its previous setting. If at least one but fewer than seven commas are in the list, the final portions of the list will be considered omitted. The eight parts of the border represented by the identifier positions are, in order:

Top, bottom, left and right edges

Top left, top right, bottom left and bottom right corners;

The identifier specified for each part of the border may be a decimal value for any character in the installed character set, a chr() function, a character string or a memory variable.

The border style applies, unless overridden in the definitions of the items, to boxes drawn with @ . . . TO, to popup menus and to windows opened with ACTIVATE WINDOW.

SET CARRY (session based) causes the contents of one record to fill the next edited.

Syntax:

```
SET CARRY {ON|OFF}|{TO <fieldlist> [ADDITIVE]}
```

SET CARRY ON|OFF causes records added with APPEND, BROWSE, EDIT or INSERT to appear filled with the values from the preceding record instead of blank. The TO option allows you to specify a field list for the carry; other fields will be left blank. ADDITIVE makes the new field list add to the existing list of fields rather than overwriting it. SET CARRY TO with no fields list restores the default with all fields carried.

SET CATALOG manages a catalog table.

Syntax:

```
SET CATALOG {ON|OFF}|{TO {<File>|?|<skeleton>}}
```

SET CATALOG TO opens a catalog file, with extension CAT. You may use ? or a skeleton to open the File dialog box to select the file. SET CATALOG TO also issues SET CATALOG ON. You need only SET CATALOG ON to update DBASEWIN.INI, or you can edit the CATALOG parameter in it manually.

When SET CATALOG is ON, new tables and associated files, index, query, report, label, and format files you use or create are added to the catalog. A catalog is a dBASE table open in a hidden work area that you can open AGAIN in a standard work area to edit. Or, you can close it with SET CATALOG OFF before editing. SET CATALOG TO without more closes the catalog. When SET TITLE and SET CATALOG are both ON, dBASE opens a Catalog Item Description dialog box when adding a new file to the catalog. To avoid this dialog, SET TITLE OFF.

SET CENTURY ON|OFF (session based) sets the display of the century. OFF displays the year in two digits, ON in four. dBASE obtains the default from the International option of the Windows Control Panel, unless that setting is overridden by the CENTURY parameter in DBASEWIN.INI. Changing the setting automatically updates DBASEWIN.INI. When you enter a date using only two digits for the year, dBASE assumes it is in the twentieth century whether or not SET CENTURY is ON.

SET CLOCK is not supported in dBASE for Windows.

SET COLOR controls the colors for specified screen areas and objects.

Syntax:

```
SET COLOR {OF {NORMAL|HIGHLIGHT|MESSAGES|TITLES|
     BOX|INFORMATION|FIELDS} TO <Color1>}|
{TO <Standard>[,<Enhanced>
     [,<Perimeter>[,<Background>]]]}
```

SET COLOR OF prescribes colors for areas of the screen, depending on what the area is used for. It is included for compatibility. Use the ColorNormal and ColorHighlight properties of dBASE for Windows objects to set their colors.

SET COLOR TO sets colors for a particular screen or window. In case of conflict, dBASE uses the command more recently issued.

SET COLOR ON|OFF is not supported by dBASE for Windows, but it causes no error and does change the otherwise meaningless setting that set("COLOR") returns.

By default, the colors used for dBASE for Windows are those set by the Colors applet of the Windows Control Panel.

The SET COLOR OF areas are:

Normal	Standard text, such as @ . . . SAY statements
Highlight	Highlighted bar menu and popup items, highlighted BROWSE fields and all EDIT fields
Messages	Unselected items on bar and popup menus and messages defined with DEFINE PAD, DEFINE POPUP, or @ . . . SAY . . . GET

Titles	Field headings displayed by AVERAGE, CALCULATE, DISPLAY, LIST, or SUM
Box	Borders of boxes and popups
Information	Menu pick characters
Fields	@ . . . GET entry fields

The <Color1> setting used with SET COLOR OF may be two colors separated by a slash, the foreground and background colors. Omission of a color designates that color as black. SET COLOR OF . . . TO with no color parameter restores that screen area to its default colors.

SET COLOR TO prescribes up to four colors for dBASE IV-style screens or windows. Colors omitted from the beginning of the list must have their places marked by commas. The four colors are the standard, enhanced, perimeter, and background colors. The standard color is used for normal text such as ? and @ . . . SAY output. The enhanced color is used for highlighted areas such as highlighted BROWSE cells and @ . . . GET entry fields. The perimeter color is ignored, although the syntax is retained for dBASE IV compatibility. The background color is used for the background on monochrome or other systems that have a uniform background. It may now include an intensity or blinking attribute as well as a color.

The dBASE IV colors and their codes are:

For color display adapters:

Black	N
Blue	B
Green	G
Cyan	BG
Red	R
Magenta	RB
Brown	RG
White	W
Blank	X

For monochrome display adapters:

Black	N
White	W
Blank	X

Attribute codes for both types of adapters are * or + for high intensity, with monochrome adapters also supporting I for inverse and U for underline.

Attribute codes may be used in combination with any color code.

The SET COLOR OF and SET COLOR TO settings do not affect forms, or windows opened like forms with OPEN FORM or READMODAL().

SET CONFIRM ON|OFF (session based) controls what happens when you fill a dBASE IV -type entry field. If SET CONFIRM is OFF, the default, the cursor moves to the next field at once. If SET CONFIRM is ON, it stays in the first field until you press Enter. The CONFIRM parameter in DBASEWIN.INI can change the default.

SET CONSOLE ON|OFF must be issued in a program. It controls display of program output, OFF suppressing the display. It has no effect on error messages, @ . . . SAY. . . GETS or input to the Command window.

SET COVERAGE ON|OFF determines whether dBASE creates and updates a coverage file, extension COV. The COVERAGE parameter in DBASEWIN.INI changes the default, but you also change it just by using the setting. A coverage file accumulates information about how often each logical block of code executes, allowing you to spot sections that have not executed at all in order to test them. You must compile your program with SET COVERAGE ON, or include the #pragma COVERAGE(ON) in your program before compiling it, to be able to create a coverage file for it. You may SET COVERAGE ON from the Command window to have all files compiled with coverage ON and coverage files created for all programs when run.

SET CUAENTER ON|OFF (session based) changes the behavior of the Enter key from Windows mode (ON) to dBASE for DOS mode (OFF). In Windows mode, pressing Enter in a form accepts the objects in the form as set and submits the form, whereas in dBASE for DOS it moves the cursor to the next object. To make Enter behave in dBASE for Windows as it did in dBASE for DOS, set CUAENTER off. Change the default by changing the CUAENTER setting, or by editing the CUAENTER parameter in DBASEWIN.INI.

SET CURRENCY (session based) changes the symbol used for currency.

Syntax:

```
SET CURRENCY LEFT|right|{TO <cExp>}
```

SET CURRENCY TO sets the currency symbol, such as the ($) dollar sign in the United States, to the character or characters given as <cExp>. There is no limit on the length of <cExp>, but dBASE recognizes only the first nine characters. There may be no digits in <cExp>. SET CURRENCY LEFT|RIGHT specifies whether the symbol is to the left or right of the amount. The currency symbol displays in place of the $ PICTURE or FUNCTION symbol. If your currency requires a long symbol on the left, allow enough space in the template that it will be able to display. Without formatting, only as many characters as can fit to the left of the digits left of the decimal point and within 10 spaces will display. If your currency symbol is longer than a single character, use $ in a FUNCTION clause or with @ in a PICTURE clause, rather than using multiple $$$ signs as a template. The latter form causes the first character of the currency symbol to be repeated.

The default is set by the International option of the Windows Control Panel, subject to override by the CURRENCY parameters in DBASEWIN.INI. You can change those parameters by changing the SET CURRENCY settings. To edit them manually, you will find the CURRENCY parameter governing LEFT|RIGHt in the [OnOffCommandSettings] section of DBASEWIN.INI. The symbol itself is controlled by the CURRENCY parameter in the [CommandSettings] section.

SET CURSOR ON|OFF determines whether the text cursor displays or not. You can change the default using the CURSOR parameter in DBASEWIN.INI. SET CURSOR does not affect the display of the mouse pointer if you have a mouse or other pointing device.

SET DATABASE TO [<cExpDatabase>] (session based) sets the default database location for tables used in commands. The <cExpDatabase> expression may name any database opened with OPEN DATABASE. Issue SET DATABASE TO with no parameter to restore the default operation of accessing tables in the current directory and path.

SET DATE (session based) sets the date format.

Syntax:

```
SET DATE {[TO] <cLtrFormat>}|{TO <cExpDate>}
```

SET DATE <cLtrFormat> changes the format for display of dates. <cLtrFormat> must be among the options shown in the left column on Table A.7. SET DATE TO <cExpDate> changes the system date. Oddly, the date in <cExpDate> must be characters, such as "07/02/94," not expressed in date format with curly braces or CTOD(). You may use a DTOC() expression or the name of a memory variable holding a character value. The characters in <cExpDate> must express the date in the current format. You must express the year in four digits (if not within the twentieth century).

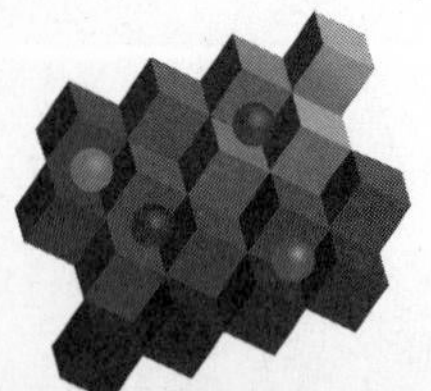

Table A.7
dBASE SET DATE Formats

Format name	Format picture
AMERICAN|MDY	mm/dd/yy
ANSI	yy.mm.dd
BRITISH|FRENCH|DMY	dd/mm/yy
GERMAN	dd.mm.yy
ITALIAN	dd-mm-yy
JAPAN|YMD	yy/mm/dd
USA	mm-dd-yy

See SET CENTURY, SET MARK.

SET DBTRAP is not supported in dBASE for Windows.

SET DBTYPE TO paradox|[DBASE] (session based) specifies the default type of table, either Paradox or dBASE.

The default changes when you use SET DBTYPE, or may be changed using the DBTYPE parameter in DBASEWIN.INI. The type for an individual table may be specified by giving its extension, if DBF for dBASE or DB for Paradox, or by the TYPE option of USE.

See USE.

SET DEBUG is not supported in dBASE for Windows.

SET DECIMALS TO <nExp> (session based) sets the number of decimal places displayed, from 0 to 18, for numeric and float values. dBASE rounds the displayed value to the last place displayed. This does not limit the accuracy of calculations or cause any rounding or truncation of numbers internally or as stored on disk. Changing the setting updates DBASEWIN.INI with a new default value, or you may change its DECIMALS parameter from the default of 2.

SET DEFAULT TO [<Drive>[:]] (session based) sets the default drive. By default, it is the current DOS drive. SET DEFAULT TO with no drive letter restores the default.

SET DELETED ON|OFF (session based) determines whether records marked for deletion in a dBASE table will be processed (OFF) or skipped (ON). Even if SET DELETED is ON you may see a record marked for deletion by using GO|GOTO with its record number. INDEX, REINDEX, and the counting of records for RECCOUNT() or the NEXT or RECORD scope options are unaffected by SET DELETE ON. The default value of SET DELETED is updated in DBASEWIN.INI when you change the setting, or you may edit the DELETED parameter in DBASEWIN.INI.

SET DELIMITERS (session based) manages the delimitation of entry fields.

Syntax:

```
SET DELIMITERS {ON|OFF|TO {<cExp>|DEFAULT}}
```

You do not normally need delimiter characters to delimit entry fields, because the contrast of the screen makes it easy to see where such fields begin and end. If you have SET INTENSITY OFF, or have a display hard to read in low light, you may want to SET DELIMITERS ON. Using the setting changes the default, or you may use the DELIMITERS parameters in the [OnOffCommandSettings] and [CommandSettings] sections of DBASEWIN.INI.

Use SET DELIMITERS TO to prescribe one or two delimiter characters. If you give two, dBASE uses the first as the left delimiter and the second as the right delimiter. It uses a single character at both ends. SET DELIMITERS TO DEFAULT restores the default delimiter, a colon ":".

The DELIMITERS setting affects @ . . . SAY . . . GET, APPEND, EDIT|CHANGE, DEFINE ENTRYFIELD, and INSERT. It is unrelated to the record delimiters specified with the DELIMITED WITH options of APPEND FROM and COPY TO.

SET DESIGN ON|OFF controls accessibility of the CREATE and MODIFY commands. To prevent users from creating or changing tables and other files, SET DESIGN OFF. If issued within a routine, the command is only effective until the routine ends. Change the setting or use the DESIGN parameter of DBASEWIN.INI to change the default.

SET DEVELOPMENT ON|OFF controls automatic compilation. If SET DEVELOPMENT is ON, dBASE recompiles each program, procedure or format file when you open it for execution after making changes. The DEVELOPMENT parameter of DBASEWIN.INI controls the default. Set it OFF in the DBASEWIN.INI you distribute with compiled code, manually or by unchecking the "Ensure Compilation" box on the Programming tabcard of the Desktop Properties inspector. Your customer's or client's system will run slightly faster because dBASE will not need to check time stamps before running a compiled program.

SET DEVICE directs the output of @ . . . SAY . . . GET commands.

Syntax:

```
SET DEVICE TO {SCREEN|PRINTER|FILE {<File>|?|<skeleton>}}
```

The SET DEVICE command directs @ . . . SAY . . . GET output to the results pane of the Command window, the default, or to the printer or a file. With the FILE option you can name the file or use ? or a skeleton to bring up the File dialog. The default file extension is TXT. The PRINTER and FILE options send only the @ . . . SAY output, not the @ . . . GET output, to the printer or file. SET DEVICE TO PRINTER is different from SET PRINTER ON, which sends keystrokes and streaming output created with ?|?? to the printer as well as @ . . . SAY output. Neither SET PRINTER ON nor SET DEVICE TO can redirect full-screen commands such as BROWSE, EDIT|CHANGE, or CREATE|MODIFY COMMAND anywhere but to the screen.

The default of SCREEN can be changed using the DBASEWIN.INI DEVICE parameter.

SET DIRECTORY TO <Path> (session based) changes the directory. With no path specified, it sets the directory to the one from which you loaded dBASE. This is a slight difference from the CD command, which issued alone returns the path of the current directory. You can include a drive letter and colon in the SET DIRECTORY path. If you start the path with "\" dBASE starts from the root directory, without "\" it starts from the current directory. You can use ".." to specify the parent of another directory. Changing the DIRECTORY setting will update DBASEWIN.INI, or you may update its DIRECTORY parameter manually. By default of either, dBASE will start in the directory specified as the Working Directory in the dBASE icon in the Program Manager, and if that is not specified either, in the HOME() directory, the one containing the dBASE executable files.

Example:

```
cd
C:\DBASEWIN\SAMPLES
set directory to ..\bin
C:\DBASEWIN\BIN
```

SET DISPLAY TO {MONO|COLOR|EGA25|EGA43|MONO43|VGA25|VGA43|VGA50} switches among display modes. You cannot use a display mode unless your video adapter hardware supports it. You will see all modes in monochrome if your monitor has only one color of phosphor or an LCD display.

The supported modes are:

MONO	25-line monochrome display adapter display
COLOR	25-line color graphics adapter display
EGA25	25-line enhanced graphics adapter color display
EGA43	43-line enhanced graphics adapter color display
MONO43	43-line enhanced monochrome display
VGA25	25-line video graphics array color display
VGA43	43-line video graphics array color display
VGA50	50-line video graphics array color display

The first two modes are the ones offered with the IBM PC model 1 in the early 1980s and are rarely seen today. The VGA adapters found on most PC-compatible systems today can support the next two and often the last two, subject to the limitations of some monitors. The most common dBASE for Windows display mode is EGA25.

You do not need to SET DISPLAY for applications running only in Windows. Use it to resize the display and the results pane of the Command window for dBASE IV applications

The default for SET DISPLAY is set by the Windows video driver. You can override it with the DISPLAY parameter of DBASEWIN.INI.

SET ECHO ON|OFF opens the debugger. SET ECHO ON is retained for compatibility. It can be issued from a program or from the Command window. If issued from a program it loads the program into the debugger and starts it. If issued from the Command window, it starts the debugger with no program. You can load a program from within the debugger. The preferred way to debug a program is to use the DEBUG command.

See DEBUG.

SET EDITOR TO <cExp> changes the text and program editor to your preference. The default is the dBASE internal editor.

The <cExp> expression gives the command that starts your editor, usually the name of its EXE file or a Windows PIF file. If the name is included literally in <cExp>, delimit it with quotation marks. SET EDITOR TO alone resets the editor to the default. The selected editor appears when you enter a file for edit.

You can set up a Windows PIF file for your favorite editor to include information about whether it should appear in a window, use extended memory and the like. If you set up a PIF file, supply its name and extension as <cExp> in the SET EDITOR command.

The default editor for both text files and memo fields is the dBASE internal editor. You will change the default for text files by using SET EDITOR, or may change the TEDIT parameter of DBASEWIN.INI.

SET ENCRYPTION is not supported in dBASE for Windows.

SET ERROR TO [<cExp1>[,<cExp2>]] specifies optional text to precede and follow dBASE error messages. Each of <cExp1> and <cExp2> can specify up to 33 characters. The <cExp1> string will precede error messages. The <cExp2> string will follow them. SET ERROR TO with no options resets the default, "ERROR:" preceding a message and a blank space following it. You can set the default by the ERROR parameter in DBASEWIN.INI, specifying it as "ERROR = <cExp1>[,<cExp2>]".

SET ESCAPE ON|OFF controls the effect of pressing Esc. If SET ESCAPE is ON, pressing Esc will interrupt an executing program or INDEX, COPY or PACK operation. If SET ESCAPE is OFF, pressing Esc will have no effect on programs or those operations, but it

will take effect to interrupt commands that wait for keyboard input such as ACCEPT, BROWSE, EDIT, INPUT, and READ.

If SET ESCAPE is OFF, you will not be able to stop a program that enters an endless loop or other condition causing it to run forever except by rebooting your computer. Rebooting in the middle of a dBASE session can cause data loss and corruption, so leave SET ESCAPE ON when possible when you are testing programs.

You can change the default using the ESCAPE parameter in DBASEWIN.INI.

SET EXACT ON|OFF (session based) changes the rules for comparison of character strings. If SET EXACT is on, the strings must match exactly to be considered equal.

If SET EXACT is OFF, a string is considered a match if it starts with the key string. An expression in the form <cExp1> = <cExp2> is treated as if the "=" meant "starts with." If <cExp1> starts with all the characters (if any) in <cExp2>, the comparison returns .T. <cExp1> may be longer. Similarly, a search for an expression <cExp2> in the character fields of a table will stop with the first record of which the field starts with all the characters of <cExp2>.

With SET EXACT OFF, to test for an empty string, you must put the empty string on the left of an equality or other relational operator. Every character string starts with the empty string, so <cExp1> = "" is always true. However, a search for "" in character fields always returns false.

Using most non-United States language drivers, SET EXACT OFF treats characters as equal if their primary weights are equal, while SET EXACT ON requires their secondary weights to be equal for a match as well. This means that in German "u" and "ü" are equal if, but only if, SET EXACT is OFF.

You change the default by using the setting, or may edit the EXACT parameter in DBASEWIN.INI.

SET EXCLUSIVE ON|OFF (session based) determines whether tables are opened by default in exclusive mode (ON) or shared mode (OFF). In exclusive mode, no other user can view or otherwise access the tables you open or their indexes. You will get an error if you attempt to access tables that another user is using in exclusive mode.

You can override the SET EXCLUSIVE setting when opening a table by specifying SHARED or EXCLUSIVE in the USE statement. An existing index file opens in the same mode as its table, but a new NDX index you create with the INDEX command is always EXCLUSIVE. To make it shared, close it with SET INDEX TO and open it again with USE . . . INDEX . . . SHARED, or SET EXCLUSIVE OFF, then reopen it. A new MDX index or tag cannot be created unless the table is open exclusive.

The following commands require that the table be open in exclusive mode: CONVERT, COPY INDEXES, DELETE TAG, INDEX . . . TAG, INSERT, MODIFY STRUCTURE, PACK, REINDEX, and ZIP.

You can change the default by using the setting, or may edit with the EXCLUSIVE parameter in dBASEWIN.INI.

SET FIELDS (session based) determines what fields of one or more open tables are visible.

Syntax:

```
SET FIELDS on|OFF|{TO {FieldList|{ALL
     [LIKE <skeleton1>][EXCEPT <skeleton2>]}}}
```

SET FIELDS TO with a field list creates or adds to the list of fields visible. The list might contain fields, with aliases if needed, from all open work areas, calculated fields with their expressions and read-only fields designated by /R after the field name. The ALL and LIKE and EXCEPT <skeleton> options allow you to add groups of fields to the list. You can specify both skeletons at once if you want.

SET FIELDS TO with a list or the ALL or LIKE options sets FIELDS ON. While SET FIELDS is ON, all and only the fields in the list are visible. SET FIELDS TO with no list or options sets FIELDS OFF and restores the default condition of all fields in the current table being visible.

SET FIELDS ON|OFF toggles the status of the fields list. SET FIELDS ON if there is no list makes no fields visible.

If SET FIELDS is ON, the following commands can access only the fields in the list: APPEND, AVERAGE, BLANK, BROWSE, CALCULATE, CHANGE|EDIT, CREATE|MODIFY VIEW, COPY, DISPLAY|LIST, EXPORT, JOIN, SET CARRY, SUM, and TOTAL.

The commands INDEX, LOCATE, SET FILTER, and SET RELATION are not affected by SET FIELDS being ON.

The FIELDS parameter in DBASEWIN.INI can change the default of SET FIELDS ON|OFF.

SET FILTER (session based) controls the visibility of records of the current table.

Syntax:

```
SET FILTER TO [<lCondition>]|
     [FILE {<File>|?|<skeleton>}]
```

You can use the FILE option to specify a query file that specifies the filter condition, or supply ? or a skeleton to bring up the File dialog. The default extension for a query file is QRY. You cannot use a dBASE IV or dBASE for Windows QBE file with the SET FILTER command. Alternatively, you can specify the filter condition in the command.

SET FILTER TO with no options cancels the current filter and makes all records visible.

Filters are not activated until the record pointer is moved, such as with GO|GOTO or SKIP. Even with a filter active, commands such as GO|GOTO that access records by number can move the pointer to records that do not meet the filter condition.

Using filters to BROWSE long files of which relatively few records meet the condition can be slow, because dBASE must evaluate each record as the movement of the record pointer makes it eligible for display. You will often find it quicker to INDEX the table FOR the condition of the filter; access using an index is very fast.

SET FORMAT TO [<File>|?|<skeleton>] opens or closes the specified format file in the current work area. Format files can contain any of the @ commands and READ commands; other commands in such a file have no effect. Opening a format file causes the commands in it to be activated in the results pane of the Command Results window or in a dBASE IV-style window opened with ACTIVATE WINDOW. If there are no READS in the format file to activate it, after the window is activated you can activate them with one of the commands BROWSE, EDIT|CHANGE, INSERT, or READ. Any FIELDS option of EDIT|CHANGE is overridden by the FIELDS specification in the format file. You cannot use a format file with a form opened dBASE for Windows-style with OPEN FORM or READMODAL().

You can specify the format file by name or give ? or a skeleton to open the File dialog. The default format for a compiled format file is FMO. If dBASE fails to find an FMO file it searches for an FMT file, compiles it and opens it. SET FORMAT TO with no parameters, or the equivalent CLOSE FORMAT, closes the format file and terminates its effect.

SET FULLPATH ON|OFF specifies whether functions that return filenames return them fully-qualified, with the full path (ON) or by the filename and extension alone (OFF). SET FULLPATH ON if you are using files in several directories at once; set it off otherwise. The functions affected are CATALOG(), DBF(), MDX(), and NDX(). Using the setting changes the default, which is contained in the FULLPATH parameter of DBASEWIN.INI.

SET FUNCTION <Key> TO <cExp> assigns an expression to a programmable function key.

The programmable keys on the IBM PC family are the function keys F1-F10 and the same keys with either Ctrl or Shift, but not both. Designate any of the keys by its number from 0 through 29, in the order mentioned above. You can designate the unshifted function keys by F1, etc., with or without quotation marks. To designate a shifted function key, prepend Ctrl or Shift followed by a plus sign or hyphen and include the whole in quotation marks, such as "Shift+F5" or "Ctrl+F2". The <cExp> expression can be any statement, expression or function you want to transmit to dBASE, or a list of statements separated by semicolons. End the expression or list with a semicolon if you want to simulate keypress of Enter at the end of it, causing a command to execute at once.

SET FUNCTION <Key> TO with no expression resets the function key to its default expression. Only the unshifted keys have default functions, as shown in table A.8. You cannot program F10; you can program F2 but your setting will be ignored in the browse window.

Table A.8
Default Function Key Settings

Key	Expression
F1	help;
F2	<shifts between BROWSE and EDIT>
F3	list;
F4	dir;
F5	display structure;
F6	display status;
F7	display memory;
F8	display;
F9	append;
F10	<accesses menu>

SET HEADINGS ON|OFF controls the display of field names above the columns of output of AVERAGE, DISPLAY, LIST, and SUM. If SET HEADINGS is ON, the field names are displayed. Changing the setting changes the default, which is the HEADINGS parameter in DBASEWIN.INI.

SET HELP TO <File>|?|<skeleton> determines which help file, extension HLP, dBASE for Windows uses. You can specify the name or use ? or a skeleton to open the File dialog box. When the help file is in the dBASE home directory, dBASE opens it automatically. SET HELP closes any open help file before opening the one you specify.

SET HISTORY is not supported in dBASE for Windows.

SET HOURS is not supported in dBASE for Windows.

SET IBLOCK TO <nExp> (session based) is new. It sets the block size for new MDX files. <nExp> must be a number from 1 to 63. The block size is 512 bytes*<nExp>, but the minimum is 1024 bytes as though 2 were the minimum value of <nExp>. Setting a large block size can make index searches faster. dBASE only reads one block at a time.

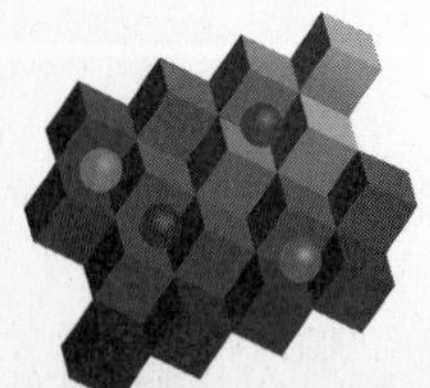

Enlarging the block means it can hold more keys and dBASE is more likely to find the key to the record it needs without repeated reads. However, a large block size wastes disk space, can be useless for the other indexes in the same MDX file, and can actually worsen the situation if several tables are linked by SET RELATION. If files are linked, performance is best if the relevant index blocks for all the tables are in memory at once. If the IBLOCK size of one file is so large it forces the relevant block of another out of memory, dBASE will have to load the blocks of the indexes for the various tables one after another and performance will slow down.

The INDEXBYTES setting governs how much memory is devoted to caching index blocks.

You can change the default setting for IBLOCK using the IBLOCK parameter in DBASEWIN.INI. The setting of IBLOCK in DBASEWIN.INI will be overridden by SET BLOCKSIZE, but that in turn will be overridden by SET IBLOCK.

See SET BLOCKSIZE, SET MBLOCK.

SET INDEX (session based) activates indexes for the current table.

Syntax:

```
SET INDEX TO [<FileList>|?|<skeleton1]
     [ORDER <File1>|{[TAG]<Tag>[OF {<File2>|?|<skeleton2}]}]
```

SET INDEX can be used with or without a list of index files. If used with a list, it opens the indexes in those files, whether NDX or MDX. You can specify ? or a skeleton to bring up the File dialog box. If you omit the list and the File dialog, only the production MDX file will be open.

You can optionally specify the controlling index with the ORDER option, either as a file of type NDX or as a tag. If the controlling index is a tag not in the production MDX, use the OF option to give its filename or bring up the File dialog to select it. The word TAG is unnecessary.

The indexes opened with SET INDEX are kept by dBASE in a list that places all NDX files first, in the order listed in SET INDEX, the tags of the production MDX next in the order listed in that file, and finally indexes in other MDX files, with the tags of each file in their order within it and the files in the order listed. The order of the index list remains until you issue another USE . . . INDEX or SET INDEX command for the same work area, and is used by such functions as KEY(), NDX(), and TAG() to identify the indexes.

SET INDEX TO without more closes all indexes for the current table except the production MDX.

SET INSTRUCT is not supported in dBASE for Windows.

SET INTENSITY ON|OFF determines whether dBASE displays GET entry fields in enhanced colors. The enhanced colors are those you set with SET COLOR OF for FIELDS or with SET COLOR TO for the enhanced colors of a window. If none are set, dBASE displays enhanced colors in reverse video (monochrome displays). If SET INTENSITY is OFF, all fields are displayed in standard colors. To change the default of SET INTENSITY, change the INTENSITY parameter in DBASEWIN.INI. SET INTENSITY is included for compatibility. Use the ColorNormal and ColorHighlight properties of dBASE for Windows objects to set their colors

SET KEY now has two distinct forms. The new one is an alternative syntax for ON KEY LABEL. The other, known to dBASE IV users as SET KEY and having to do with limiting records visible in an indexed table, is now called SET KEY TO.

SET KEY {<cExp>|<nExp>} TO [<Program>|<Procedure>]} runs the specified program or procedure when the key specified by <cExp> or <nExp> is pressed. It is an alternative syntax to ON KEY LABEL. Use SET KEY <cExp>|<nExp> TO with no program or procedure name to cancel the setting. The <nExp> expression is the inkey() value for the key; use <cExp> to name a function key.

SET KEY TO (session based) limits the records processed in the current or specified indexed table to those whose keys match given values.

Syntax:

```
SET KEY TO [<xExpList1>|{RANGE <xExp2>[,]|,<xExp3>|
              {<xExp2>,<xExp3>}}|[LOW <xExpList2>[,]]
              [HIGH [,]<xExpList3>][EXCLUDE][IN <workarea>]]
```

The SET KEY syntax enables you to specify an expression the key must match. Taking the last options first, you may specify the work area affected. By default, the command affects the current work area. The EXCLUDE option specifies that records whose keys match a given limiting value for the key will be excluded. In its absence, such records are included.

The mention of a list in <xExpList1>, and the HIGH and LOW keywords, are applicable to Paradox and SQL tables with conposite indexes on a list of fields. In such a case you can give a comma-delimited list for the expression to match using <xExpList1>. Specify LOW with an expression to match or exceed, or HIGH with an expression to match or be less than, or both. With HIGH or LOW the commas have no significance.

For a dBASE table, you may specify a single expression as <xExpList1>. Only those records whose keys match the expression will be processed. Alternately, use RANGE. It may be followed by limiting expressions in one of three forms:

RANGE <xExp2>[,]	<xExp2> is the minimum key value processed.
RANGE ,<xExp3>	<xExp3> is the maximum key value processed.
RANGE <xExp2>,<xExp3>	<xExp2> is the minimum and <xExp3> the maximum.

SET KEY TO without <more> restores all records to visibility.

SET KEY follows the SET EXACT rules for matching character data. All expressions in the command must be of the same type as the data. If SET KEY is ON and a filter is set, only those records that pass both tests are visible.

SET LDCHECK ON|OFF is new. If OFF, it disables language-driver checking. If ON, dBASE will check for language compatibility of tables and be able to catch differences in character sets and sorting rules. Such differences might cause searches and queries to return incorrect results as well as garbling some characters. You can change the default with the LDCHECK parameter in DBASEWIN.INI.

SET LIBRARY TO [<File>|?|<skeleton>] opens a procedure file as a library file.

You can give the filename or use ? or a skeleton to open the File dialog box. A library file is like a procedure file opened with SET PROCEDURE, but later on the search path. There can be only one library file open at a time. Put your utility procedures and functions in your SET LIBRARY file. Put procedures and functions relevant to a particular application in the files you open with SET PROCEDURE, or in the files containing your programs. If you do this, any conflicts between routines of the same name will cause the routine from the program or PROCEDURE file to be executed. This frees you from concerning yourself with what names the library routines use when you are writing an application. If you use a name for one of your routines, the fact there may be a different routine of the same name in the library file will not keep your routine from executing.

SET LIBRARY TO without options closes the open library file.

SET LOCK ON|OFF (session based) determines whether dBASE attempts to lock a shared table when you access it for operations that only read it.

If you are doing a CALCULATE or similar operation on a table, it might or might not matter that other users can change the data in the middle of your operation's pass through the table. Use SET LOCK OFF to allow other users to read and change the data while you are reading it, or the default SET LOCK ON to preserve the file unchanged while you are using it. The default SET LOCK ON might inconvenience other users. You can change the default by using the command or by editing the LOCK parameter of DBASEWIN.INI.

The commands that automatically lock tables only when SET LOCK is ON are AVERAGE, CALCULATE, COUNT, EXPORT, GRAPH FORM, INDEX, LABEL FORM, REPORT FORM, and SUM, plus, if the table or its associated files are the source or one of the source files, COPY in all its variations, JOIN, SORT and TOTAL.

SET MARGIN TO <nExp> sets the left margin to a number, which can include a fraction, from 0 to 254. The value set becomes the printer's column 0 position. SET MARGIN resets _ploffset but not _lmargin. You can change the default margin from its default value of 0 with the MARGIN parameter in DBASEWIN.INI.

SET MARK TO <cExp> (session based) sets the character used to separate the month, day, and year in dates to the first character in <cExp>. The SET DATE setting also changes the date separator. To have SET MARK effective, issue SET DATE first, then SET MARK.

The default date separator is set in the International option of the Windows Control Panel. You can override that with the MARK parameter in DBASEWIN.INI, which changes when you SET MARK.

SET MBLOCK TO <nExp> (session based) sets the block size of new memo (DBT) files. The range of <nExp> is 1 to 511; the block size is 64*<nExp> with a default of 8, or 512 bytes. You can change the default with the MBLOCK parameter in DBASEWIN.INI or by using SET MBLOCK.

The MBLOCK setting overrides any SET BLOCKSIZE setting as to DBT files. The two settings are similar, but MBLOCK enables you to set one size for DBT files while you set another for MDX files with IBLOCK. SET BLOCKSIZE requires that both settings be the same. In addition, SET MBLOCK allows memo sizes as small as 64 bytes, allowing significant space saving if your memos are mostly very small.

SET MEMOWIDTH TO <nExp> (session based) allows you to set the memo field display and output width to any number from 8 to 255. You can set the default with MEMOWIDTH in DBASEWIN.INI. Memos can be displayed by the commands ?|??, DISPLAY, and LIST. SET MEMOWIDTH affects such display. It does not affect the display of memos in the text editor, which if _wrap is true, is controlled by _lmargin and _rmargin.

When _wrap is true, the @V vertical stretch picture function causes memo fields to be displayed in a vertical column, with _pcolno incremented by the @V value. If the @V value is 0, the memo will wrap within the SET MEMOWIDTH width.

SET MESSAGE TO <cExp> displays the message <cExp> in the status bar when SET STATUS is ON or when a READ is issued after a GET. The message can be 80 characters long. SET MESSAGE TO with no message restores the message set in DBASEWIN.INI. The message set by SET MESSAGE will be overridden by any message set as the StatusMessage property of an object or by the MESSAGE option of a dBASE IV-style bar, menu, pad, or popup.

SET MOUSE ON|OFF removes (OFF) the mouse cursor from the screen. While the cursor is hidden, dBASE ignores mouse actions. SET MOUSE ON restores the cursor and the functionality of the mouse. This command is included for compatibility with dBASE IV.

SET NEAR ON|OFF (session based) controls where the record pointer stays after a failed search in the index of a table. If SET NEAR is on, the search stops at the first record with a key greater than the key sought. If the key is descending, the search will stop at the first record with a key less than the key sought. The record pointer will be at EOF() only if all keys in the table are less (ascending search) than the key sought. If SET NEAR is OFF, the failure to find an exact match will cause the record pointer to be set to EOF().

You can change the default by using the command or with the NEAR parameter in DBASEWIN.INI. Whichever way SET NEAR is set, FOUND() will return false if no exact match (or match to all the characters of the key sought if SET EXACT is OFF) is found.

SET ODOMETER TO <nExp> determines how often dBASE updates the displayed record counter if SET TALK is ON during the operations APPEND, AVERAGE, COPY, COUNT, DELETE, GENERATE, and SUM. SET ODOMETER TO with no expression resets the odometer to the current default. SET ODOMETER TO 0 causes an error.

SET ORDER TO (session based) specifies the controlling index of a table.

Syntax:

```
SET ORDER TO [<nExpPosition>|{<NDXFile>[NOSAVE]}|
{[TAG]<Tag> [OF {MDXFile|?}][NOSAVE]}]
```

The <nExpPosition> option of SET ORDER TO is preserved for compatibility with dBASE III PLUS and can be used only if no MDX file is open. The TAG option, with the word TAG being optional, can be used with an NDX file named as <FileNDX> or with the name of a tag from an MDX file, and optionally its name or a ? to open the File dialog box if the MDX file is not the production MDX file. SET ORDER TO without specifying an index, or with <nExpPosition> equal to 0, causes a dBASE table to appear as if unindexed, in natural, or in record-number order. SET ORDER TO with no index or 0 causes a Paradox table to appear in primary index order. The NOSAVE option directs that a temporary index be deleted after the indexed table closes. If you change your mind, issue SET ORDER to the index again, without the NOSAVE, before closing the table.

SET PATH TO <Path> (session based) specifies the search route that dBASE follows to find files not in the current directory. dBASE searches the path in the order that directories occur within the path. The path can, but need not, start at the root directory. SET PATH TO with no path removes the path list. Using the command changes the default setting, which is the PATH parameter in DBASEWIN.INI.

SET PAUSE is not supported in dBASE for Windows.

SET PCOL TO <nExp> is new. It sets the horizontal position of the printer to the value of <nExp>, from 0 to 32,767 inclusive. It sets the value that PCOL() returns. When you send control strings to your printer, PCOL() does not realize they do not print. It adds 1 to PCOL() for each character sent to the printer. This will cause PCOL() to disagree with the actual print position. You can fix the discrepancy by issuing SET PCOL to reduce the value of PCOL() by the number of nonprinting characters sent to the printer. The PCOL() value is used in @ . . . SAY commands redirected to the printer with SET DEVICE TO PRINTER. dBASE resets the PCOL() value to 0 when printing moves to a new line.

See SET PROW, PCOL(), PROW().

SET POINT TO <cExp> (session based) changes the character used as the decimal separator to the first character of <cExp>. In international usage, the comma is used to separate the integral parts of numbers from decimal fractions. The character specified in <cExp> cannot be a letter, digit, or space. dBASE uses the decimal point as the separator internally, so if you are entering a literal value you must use the period as the separator—regardless of SET POINT.

The default POINT character is set by the International option of the Windows Control Panel. To change it, use the command or edit the POINT parameter in DBASEWIN.INI. SET POINT TO resets the POINT character to that set in DBASEWIN.INI, or if none to that set by the Windows Control Panel.

See SET SEPARATOR.

SET PRECISION TO <nExp> (session based) sets the number of digits dBASE uses internally in mathematical operations on type N numbers. The range of <nExp> is from 10 to 19, the default 16.

To change the default PRECISION, change the setting or edit the PRECISION parameter in DBASEWIN.INI.

SET PRINTER controls whether output to the results pane of the Command window is copied to the printer stream.

Syntax:

```
SET PRINTER ON|OFF|
     {TO [{[FILE] {<File>|?|<skeleton>}}|<Device>]}
```

SET PRINTER TO with a FILE or device option directs the print stream to that file, default extension PRT, or to the specified device. You can give the name of the file or use ? to bring up the File dialog box. The keyword FILE is unnecessary. The device is a printer port. Set up printers and their ports with the Windows Print Manager. Unlike some SET commands, setting PRINTER TO a destination does not itself SET PRINTER ON. You must SET PRINTER ON separately.

The default for SET PRINTER TO is the default printer specified with the Windows Print Manager. To change the default of SET PRINTER OFF, use the PRINTER parameter in the [OnOffCommandSettings] section of DBASEWIN.INI. SET PRINTER TO with no option directs the stream to the default dBASE printer.

SET PRINTER ON|OFF switches the stream of ?|?? output to the specified printer, file, or device ON or OFF. To direct @ . . . SAY lines to a printer or file, use SET DEVICE TO PRINTER|FILE.

SET PROCEDURE opens a file as a procedure file.

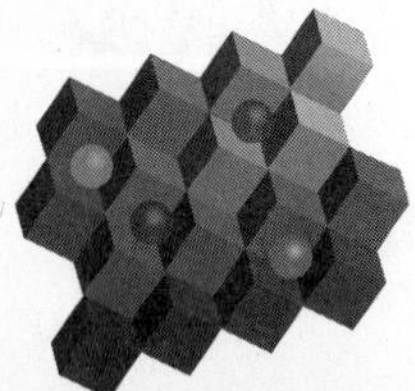

Syntax:

```
SET PROCEDURE TO {<File>|?|<skeleton>}[ADDITIVE]
```

A file opened with SET PROCEDURE must consist of from 1 to 193 procedures or user-defined functions. Opening it with SET PROCEDURE makes the procedures and functions available for call from any program. The dBASE search path looks for SET PROCEDURE files before library file opened with SET LIBRARY TO, so you should put application-specific routines in a SET PROCEDURE file and general utility ones in a SET LIBRARY file. That way, the routine you wrote for your application will always be executed—even if a routine in the library file happens to have the same name.

The ADDITIVE option of SET PROCEDURE TO opens the specified file without closing procedure files previously opened. By default, opening one procedure file closes all others. SET PROCEDURE TO with no options closes all procedure files. To make the procedures and UDFs in your program file available to others, include the line SET PROCEDURE TO PROGRAM(1) ADDITIVE.

See SET LIBRARY.

SET PROW TO <nExp> is new. It sets the vertical printer print position to <nExp>, which must be between 0 and 32,767 inclusive. This sets the value that PROW() returns and accordingly changes the reference of any printer-directed @. . . SAY commands that call for output @ PROW() plus or minus any number.

See PCOL(), PROW(), SET PCOL.

SET REFRESH TO <nExp> (session based) sets the interval after which dBASE refreshes the workstation screen with table information from the server. <nExp> represents seconds and must be from 1 to 3,600, one hour. The default is 0, meaning dBASE does not refresh the worksheet tables. You can change the default interactively or with the REFRESH parameter of DBASEWIN.INI.

Specify a REFRESH interval if you want to see changes made by other users while you are doing a BROWSE or EDIT|CHANGE to edit a shared table. The refresh operation will take some time, and your screen cannot be refreshed until the other user releases any lock on the table or on the records you are viewing.

SET RELATION (session based) links tables.

Syntax:

```
SET RELATION TO [{<xExp>|<xExpList>} INTO <Alias>
          [CONSTRAIN][INTEGRITY[CASCADE|RESTRICTED]]][,<etc.>][ADDITIVE]
```

SET RELATION establishes links between the current table as parent table and other tables as child tables. The child tables must all be open in different work areas. The <xExp> expression is usually a field name of the parent table that is also a field of the child table. The linked table must be indexed on the linking expression, and that index must be the controlling one. It is also possible, for dBASE tables only, to have <xExp> be a numerical expression identifying the record of the child table to link to each record of the parent table. This expression is usually recno(), linking each record of the child table to the same record of the parent table. If a numeric expression identifies the record of the child table to be linked to each record of the parent table, the child table need not be indexed.

Paradox and SQL tables that are indexed on lists of fields can use the list <xExpList> that specifies the index to set the link.

The CONSTRAIN and INTEGRITY options apply only to dBASE tables. CONSTRAIN limits processing of records in the child table to those that match a key value of the parent table. INTEGRITY specifies that when records are added to the child table by APPEND, APPEND BLANK, BROWSE, EDIT, or INSERT, their key fields are set to match key values of the parent table. If you add new records to the parent table, the key must be unique. The matching key fields in the child table are read-only. If you delete records of the parent table or change the value of a key field, a dialog box opens for you to choose whether or not to delete all records of the child table with key values matching the parent key value deleted or changed. This is called performing a cascade delete.

In a program, you will not want the dialog box to appear. Specify the CASCADE option of INTEGRITY to have dBASE perform a cascade delete if the matching key value in the parent table is deleted or changed. Specify the RESTRICTED option to prevent deleting or changing parent records if their keys match those of child records.

If you SET KEY TO on the child table to restrict visibility of child records to those that match a key value of the parent table, this is functionally similar to using CONSTRAIN. dBASE returns an error if you try to use SET KEY TO and CONSTRAIN at once.

The ADDITIVE option adds the relations specified to other relations in effect. By default, the SET RELATION statement closes all preexisting relations from the parent table into others. SET RELATION TO with no options closes all relations from the parent table.

Once a relation is created, moving the table pointer in the parent table moves it in the child table as well. If no record in the child table matches the linking expression, the child table pointer is set at EOF(). The child table pointer does not honor SET NEAR, but a relation will if SET EXACT is OFF moves the child pointer to the first record that starts with the linking expression.

A relation is one-way. You can navigate and access the child tables by using the parent table and identifying child fields by alias, but you cannot select and move through the child table and have the parent table follow. You can cascade relations from parent to child and from child to grandchild, and can set multiple relations from a parent to many children, but you cannot set a direct or indirect cyclic relation that makes the parent the child of one of its own descendants.

Example:

```
use Customer order Cust_ID
select select()
use Orders order Order_ID
set relation to Cust_ID into Customer
select select()
use LineItem order Order_ID
set relation to Order_ID into Orders
set printer on
ThisOrder = space(5)
scan
    if Order_ID # ThisOrder
         if Thisorder > space(5)
              do Ship_tot
              eject
         endif
         ThisOrder = Order_ID
         Order_Tot = 0
         select Orders
         ? Customer->Name
         ? Customer->Street
         ? Customer->City +", " ;
              + Customer->State +" " '
              + Customer->Zipcode
         ?
         ? mdy(date()) at 55
         ?
         ? Order_ID at 30, Ship_Date at 55
         ?
    endif
    select Lineitem
    ? Item-Desc, Quantity at 40, Price at 48 ;
         PICTURE "999.99", ;
      Quantity + Price at 57 PICTURE "9,999.99"
    Order_Tot = Order_Tot + Quantity * Price
endscan
do Ship_tot
eject
set printer off
```

In the previous example, the parent-child terminology used with SET RELATION is contrary to the normal way of expressing the logical relation among tables. The Customer table is normally considered the parent of the Orders table. There might be many orders from a single customer but only one customer to each order. Similarly, Orders is the parent of Line_Item. Nevertheless, an invoicing routine uses SET RELATION the other way, from LineItem to Orders to Customer.

This is not uncommon. You will often want a relation to go from the many to the one. You need a relation to find for each of several orders the one record that holds the correct customer name. If you want to see all the orders for a particular customer, you do not need to set a relation. Instead, index the orders on Cust_ID and SET KEY to <CustomerName>.

See SET ORDER, SET SKIP.

SET REPROCESS TO <nExp> (session based) sets the number of times dBASE will try to lock a record or table before producing an error message. <nExp> can be from -1 to 32,000. A <nExp> value of -1 tells dBASE to try forever without prompting you to retry or cancel. A value of 0 is the default and causes dBASE to prompt you at once to retry or cancel if the attempted lock fails.

SET REPROCESS affects not only the explicit locking commands you issue, FLOCK() and RLOCK()|LOCK(), but also all commands that attempt automatically to lock a file or record. You can change the default value by changing the setting or by using the REPROCESS parameter in DBASEWIN.INI.

SET SAFETY ON|OFF (session based) determines whether dBASE asks you for confirmation before overwriting files or using ZAP to erase the data of a table. You can change the default by changing the setting or with the SAFETY parameter in DBASEWIN.INI. SET TALK OFF has no effect on SET SAFETY warnings, but SET CONSOLE OFF will suppress them.

SET SAFETY affects the following commands:

All commands with a "TO FILE" option in effect.

COPY in all forms except TO ARRAY.

CREATE|MODIFY commands of all varieties.

INDEX, JOIN, SAVE, SORT, TOTAL, UPDATE, ZAP and SET ALTERNATE TO.

SET SCOREBOARD is not supported in dBASE for Windows.

SET SEPARATOR TO <cExp> (session based) sets the character used to separate thousands in numbers to the first character of <cExp>. The character cannot be a number or letter. The comma is used as separator in the United States with the period as the SET POINT character separating the integral part of a number from its decimal fraction. In much of the world, the uses of the period and comma are reversed. The default separator is set in the International option of the Windows control panel, but you

can override it by changing the setting or with the SEPARATOR parameter of DBASEWIN.INI. Since most numbers are displayed by dBASE without separators, SET SEPARATOR affects only the "," PICTURE template character and the display of byte totals for files.

SET SKIP TO [<workarea>[,<etc.>]] (session based) determines how the record pointer is advanced through tables linked with SET RELATION. SET SKIP TO with no alias list cancels previous SKIP settings.

Use SET SKIP when you set a relation from a logical parent table to one of its child tables, a one-to-many relation, and you want to process all the child records using a command such as LIST. If you include the work area of the child in the SET SKIP list, all of its records matching the parent key will be processed before the key is moved in the parent table. Include multiple work areas in the SKIP list in order of the relations to have the grandchild table processed first, then the child and last the parent. SKIP processes the last work area first.

The example under SET RELATION demonstrates setting relations from grandchild to child to parent in order to process all records of the grandchild and child tables. SET SKIP allows you to do somewhat the same thing with the relations running in the opposite but more natural order, from parent to child to grandchild. However, since the current table using SET SKIP is the grandparent table, you cannot use SET SKIP if you must issue commands addressed to each record of the grandchild table. In the SET RELATION example, a ? command directed the printing of each record of the grandchild Line Item table while calculating its price extension, and another command added the line total to the running total.

See SET RELATION.

SET SPACE ON|OFF determines whether dBASE prints a space between expressions when using a single ?|?? to print several expressions separated by commas. You will normally format the line yourself using the AT option of ?|?? to position the expressions, but you will probably want SPACE ON, the default, to separate items printed in quick-and-dirty fashion while you are working. You can change the default using the SPACE parameter in DBASEWIN.INI.

SET SQL is not supported in dBASE for Windows.

SET STATUS is not supported in dBASE for Windows.

SET STEP ON|OFF now starts the Debugger. SET STEP ON originally put programs into single-step mode to assist in debugging them. The command SET STEP ON might still be found deep in some programs where it was placed to help debug a section. Since the Debugger now allows more sophisticated control of single-stepping and other debugging operations, SET STEP ON in a program loads the program into the Debugger and starts it. It is not clear why you would want to type SET STEP ON into the Command window when "Debug" is equivalent and six keystrokes shorter, but either one will start the Debugger with no file loaded. SET STEP OFF does nothing, but also causes no error.

SET TALK ON|OFF (session based) determines whether the results of certain dBASE commands are displayed in the results pane of the Command window. With SET TALK ON, dBASE prints the results of many commands to the results pane of the Command window. Such results include the values assigned to memory variables, the record number being processed, the results of commands such as APPEND FROM, COPY, and PACK, and the results of commands that perform mathematical operations on files such as AVERAGE, CALCULATE, COUNT, and SUM.

The output of SET TALK can be annoying. It will be annoying if SET TALK is ON while a program is running. However, if you SET TALK OFF and run APPEND FROM, COPY, or PACK, you can be left in doubt whether the command succeeded or what exactly it did. If you run one of AVERAGE, CALCULATE COUNT, and SUM without its TO clause, the result will neither be displayed nor saved and will be lost. You can change the default with the TALK parameter in DBASEWIN.INI or by changing the setting.

SET TIME TO <cExp> is new. It resets your system clock. You can specify the time as HH, HH:MM, or HH:MM:SS, using colons or periods to separate the hours, minutes and seconds. You should use 24-hour time and enclose your time expression in quotation marks.

SET TITLE ON|OFF controls display of the catalog file title prompt. When SET CATALOG is ON, files you create are automatically added to the catalog. If SET TITLE is ON, you are prompted to supply a title to accompany the file's title in the catalog. If SET TITLE is OFF, the prompt does not appear. You can change the default by changing the setting or with the TITLE parameter in DBASEWIN.INI.

SET TOPIC TO [<cExp>] is new. It sets the topic that dBASE will display information about if you press F1 or issue the HELP command while in the Command Window. If you give <cExp> as the complete name of a topic, dBASE will display the help screen for that topic. If you give <cExp> as the initial letters of some help topic, dBASE opens a search dialog box with the first topic starting with <cExp> highlighted. If the cursor is in a dBASE panel such as a BROWSE panel, pressing F1 brings up help on BROWSE rather than on the SET TOPIC subject. SET TOPIC TO with no expression causes the help system to display the first topic. You can substitute your own help database for the standard one using SET HELP.

SET TRAP is not supported by dBASE for Windows.

SET TYPEAHEAD TO <nExp> sets the size of the typeahead buffer to <nExp> characters, from 0 to 1600. The default is 50 characters. It may be changed with the TYPEAHEAD parameter in DBASEWIN.INI.

The type-ahead buffer stores keystrokes until dBASE is ready for input, such as when it finishes indexing a table and returns focus to the Command window. dBASE then removes them from the buffer and acts on them. If you fill the typeahead buffer and press another key, the system beeps and the keypress is lost. You might want to increase the size of the buffer to facilitate typing while dBASE is busy or to allow placing larger commands in the buffer with KEYBOARD.

On some occasions you might want to CLEAR TYPEAHEAD and SET TYPEAHEAD TO 0 to assure that input comes directly from the keyboard in real time.

SET UNIQUE ON|OFF (session based) controls whether indexes thereafter created will contain duplicate keys. If an index is created when SET UNIQUE is ON, it contains only a single key of each value. An index created while SET UNIQUE is OFF normally contains a key for each record, but you can use the UNIQUE option of INDEX to accomplish the same thing as if SET UNIQUE were ON. After a UNIQUE index has been created, either by the UNIQUE option of SET INDEX or by using SET UNIQUE ON, it remains UNIQUE indefinitely—regardless of the SET UNIQUE setting and in spite of additions, deletions and rebuilds with REINDEX. You change the default of SET UNIQUE by setting it, or you can edit the UNIQUE parameter in DBASEWIN.INI.

SET VIEW TO <File>|?|<skeleton> opens a previously defined view file. You can supply the file name or use ? or a skeleton to open the File dialog box. The default for VIEW is the current working environment. You can change the default using the VIEW parameter in DBASEWIN.INI. A view includes the open tables and index files, relations, the field list, filters and the format file. To create a new view, use CREATE QUERY or CREATE VIEW.

SET WINDOW OF MEMO TO <Window> specifies a window to use for the edit of a memo field. Use this command to set up a previously defined window for the edit of memo fields you edit in the course of an APPEND, BROWSE, CHANGE|EDIT, or READ command. If you specify a window with the WINDOW clause of the @ . . .GET command that causes edit of a memo field, that window takes precedence over the one set with SET WINDOW. If you SET MEMO OF WINDOW TO without naming a window, dBASE clears any window previously defined with the command.

SET WP TO <cExp> changes the memo editor to your preference. The default is the dBASE internal editor. You can change the default by changing the setting or with the WP parameter in DBASEWIN.INI.

The <cExp> expression gives the command that starts your editor, usually the name of its EXE file or a Windows PIF file. If the name is included literally in <cExp>, delimit it with quotation marks. SET WP TO alone resets the editor to the default. The selected editor appears when you enter a memo field for edit.

You can set up a Windows PIF file for your favorite editor to include information about whether it should appear in a window, use extended memory and the like. If you set up a PIF file, supply its name and extension as <cExp> in the SET WP TO command.

SET()

Returns the status of environmental and other settings made with SET.

Syntax:

```
[xVar=] set(<cExp>)
```

Use SET() near the beginning of your programs and utility routines to learn and store to memory variables the settings it changes. You can then restore them from the stored variables. The <cExp> passed to SET() is usually the keyword following SET in the SET command of interest. Put the keyword, such as "PRINTER" or "MARK", in quotation marks, because dBASE requires an expression, not simply a literal word.

If a SET command has only ON|OFF settings, the return of SET() for that command is either ON or OFF. If a SET command has both ON|OFF and TO settings such as SET ALTERNATE and SET CATALOG, SET() returns ON or OFF and SETTO() returns the TO setting. For a SET command that has only a TO setting such as SET IBLOCK or SET MARK, both SET() and SETTO() return the TO setting.

Certain SET() commands are exceptions and are listed below.

SET("ATTRIBUTES") returns the colors for eight color areas in a string. Each of the colors is returned as two codes separated by a slash comprising the codes for first the foreground then the background of the color area. The code for the foreground or background of an area can be any of the colors listed under SET COLOR TO, including one or more intensity or blink attributes. The codes for the various areas are comma-delimited, with no extra spaces, in the order of the areas listed in SET COLOR OF, with one exception. For compatibility, the codes for the perimeter, which do nothing in dBASE for Windows, are inserted as the third code pair, after NORMAL and HIGHLIGHT, and followed not by a comma but by a space, two ampersands "&&" and another space, after which the codes for MESSAGES, TITLES, BOX, INFORMATION and FIELDS follow delimited by commas. If you want to create your own literal attributes string for use in setting all color areas at once, you must specify the ampersands as {38}{38} or as CHR() functions. If you do not, dBASE will interpret the ampersands as the && comment command and will stop there when compiling the line.

SET() with the name of a function key as <cExp> returns the character expression to which that key is set.

SET("CURRENCY") returns RIGHT or LEFT; SETTO("CURRENCY") returns the currency symbol.

SET("PROCEDURE") returns the name of only the first one loaded if several procedure files are loaded.

SET("TIME") is not supported. Use TIME() to obtain the time.

SETTO()

New; returns the TO setting of those SET commands that have both a TO keyword and an ON|OFF or similar setting.

Syntax:

```
[xVar=] setto(<cExp>)
```

See SET().

SHELL()

New; temporarily hides dBASE.

Syntax:

```
[lVar=] shell(<lExp>)
```

You can issue (.F.) within a program to hide dBASE. The name of the current form—if it is a top level form not an MDI form—appears in the Windows task list as though the application were stand-alone (rather than running under dBASE for Windows). You cannot use the SpeedBar or Command window. You will return to the dBASE environment when you close the form to end the application, and can return by having the program issue (.T.).

If the form is MDI, SHELL(.F.) causes its menu to become the menu of the dBASE for Windows main window. You remain in dBASE and can access the SpeedBar. A click in the Command window will close the form.

Calling SHELL() with a parameter that evaluates to false from the Command window causes a mildly startling and useless exit to Windows and immediate return to dBASE. Using SHELL() in a program is equivalent to changing the Visible property of the dBASE main window, _app.FrameWin.Visible, to .T. or .F. as passed in the parameter to SHELL().

SHOW

Displays but does not activate menus and popups and, as a new option, user interface objects.

Syntax:

```
SHOW {MENU <Menu>[PAD <Pad>]}|POPUP <Popup>|{OBJECT <Object> OF <Con-
tainer>}
```

The SHOW command makes the specified menu, popup or object appear on the screen without activating it to receive input. You can use SHOW to check the appearance of these items while designing them. The PAD option of SHOW MENU designates the pad that SHOW will highlight. If the PAD option is omitted, the first pad is highlighted.

Use the SHOW OBJECT option to refresh the screen appearance of an object to reflect changes you have made to its properties.

SIGN()

Returns the value of the sign of a numeric expression.

Syntax:

```
[nVar=] sign(<nExp>)
```

SIGN() returns 1 if <nExp> is positive, -1 if it is negative and 0 if it is zero. The return of SIGN() is not affected by the possibility that SET DECIMALS TO 0 might be in effect and cause numbers between -1 and 1 to display as 0.

SIN()

Returns the sine of an angle as a float-type number.

Syntax:

```
[fVar=] sin(<nExp>)
```

The parameter to SIN() is an angle measured in radians. The sine of an angle is defined in terms of a right triangle in which the given angle is one of the other angles. The sine is the ratio between the length of the side opposite the given angle and the hypotenuse. SIN() returns 0 when the angle is 0 or a multiple of PI() radians, 180 degrees. The reciprocal of the sine of an angle, 1/sin(<nExp>), is known as the cosecant of the angle.

See ATAN(), ATN2(), COS(), DTOR(), RTOD(), TAN().

SKIP

Moves the record pointer in the current or specified work area by the given number of records.

Syntax:

```
SKIP [<nExp>][IN <workarea>]
```

SKIP enables you to move a record pointer in a table by a given number of records. The IN clause enables you to specify a work area other than the current one. If the IN clause is omitted, the current work area is used. The value of <nExp> can be 0, which does nothing—positive or negative. If negative, the skip is backwards toward the top of the table. SKIP moves the record pointer with respect to the logical order of records in the controlling index, so if an index is active the record number of a record moved to by SKIP might differ from the sum of the previous record number and the SKIP distance.

If you SKIP more records than are in the table in the direction of the SKIP, SKIP takes you to the record past the last record if the skip is positive or to the first record if the skip is negative. EOF() or BOF() will return true, respectively. An additional SKIP in the same direction causes an error.

SLEEP

New; pauses execution for a specified time.

Syntax:

```
SLEEP <nExpSeconds>|
     {UNTIL <cExpTime>[,<cExpDate>]}
```

SLEEP will cause a pause during which dBASE does nothing even if issued in the Command window. It is most used in programs. You can use it, for example, to keep the user from clearing a message by a keypress or mouse action before he or she has had time to read it. If SET ESCAPE is ON, pressing Esc will stop the program and the pause. IF SET ESCAPE is OFF, there is no way to resume processing, although you can shift to another task or quit dBASE entirely.

The pause interval can be specified as <nExpSeconds>, a number evaluating to between 1 and 65,535, inclusive, the latter being about 18 hours. Alternatively, you can give a time and optional date for execution to resume. If the time, or time and date, have passed, execution does not pause.

A time should be stated as "HH:MM:SS" and a date as "MM/DD/YY" or whatever the current SET DATE format is, in both cases as character expressions delimited with quotation marks. You can use any single character except a digit in place of the colons or slashes as separators in the time and date strings. Stating the year in four digits is optional whether or not SET CENTURY is ON.

SORT

Copies the current table into sorted order.

Syntax:

```
SORT TO {<File|?}
[<scope>][FOR <lExpCond1>][WHILE <lExpCond2>]
[[TYPE]{DBASE|PARADOX}]
ON {<Field> [{/{A|D}[C]}|/C]]}[,<etc.>]
[ASCENDING|DESCENDING]
```

You should rarely use the SORT command. For most purposes, indexing the table into the order you need accomplishes as much as sorting the file and more quickly. By doing so, you also save disk space, support fast searches with FIND, SEEK, and SEEK(), and can order the file by an expression rather than only a field list.

SORT copies the current table to a new table. You can give its name or use ? to bring up the File dialog box. By default SORT copies the entire table. You might limit the records copied with the scope clause or FOR or WHILE conditions. If you do not specify the type of the target table, dBASE will create it of the default type specified by DBTYPE. You can specify a table in a database as the target by giving the database name, delimited by colons, as a prefix to the table name. If the database is not open, dBASE will open a dialog prompting you for your login name, password, or other parameters needed to establish a connection to the database.

The SORT can be on as many fields as listed. The fields sorted on may be any type except binary, memo, or OLE. Each field can be sorted ascending, the default, or descending with /D. An ascending sort can, but need not, be specified by /A. You can use /C to make the sort case-insensitive, as for names (if you do not want di Carolis or van Dyke to appear after Ziegler). If you use the C option with /A or /D, express both as /AC or /DC. You may use the DESCENDING keyword to specify that all fields listed in the SORT command except those with /A specified should be sorted descending. The ASCENDING keyword does nothing but aid readability, as by default all fields listed without /D specified will be sorted ascending.

SORT cannot accept an expression as a sort key. If a list of fields is given, the sort will be primarily on the first field, then on the second, etc. If you want a table of dividends received to be grouped by security ticker symbol then by date, sort on Ticker, Date. If you instead want the list in date order primarily, and within each date by ticker symbol, sort on Date, Ticker.

See COPY, INDEX.

SOUNDEX()

Returns a four-character string that encodes the approximate sound of the given character expression or memo field.

Syntax:

```
[cVar=] soundex(<cExp>|<mFld>)
```

The SOUNDEX() function helps you find duplicates that KEYMATCH() and other functions and commands miss because one of them is misspelled. SOUNDEX() returns a code consisting of the first letter of the given expression or field and three digits. It uses only as many characters of the expression or memo field as create three digits following the initial character according to its rules, which disregard several letters. If the expression or field is an empty string or the first nonblank character is nonalphabetic, SOUNDEX() returns "0000". It returns "0" for the first digit or space (other than a leading space) encountered and all following characters.

The SOUNDEX() function is language-driver specific. Using a U.S. language driver it behaves as follows:

1. It ignores leading spaces.
2. It ignores case.
3. It converts the first nonblank character to uppercase and makes it the first character in the return code.
4. It converts each remaining alphabetic character as follows and adds the digit to the return code:

a) B, F, P, and V	1
b) C, G, J, K, Q, S, X, and Z	2
c) D and T	3
d) L	4
e) M and N	5
f) R	6

5. It removes any character following another that yields the same digit.
6. After the first nonblank character, it removes all occurrences of the letters A, E, I, O,U, Y, H, and W.
7. It pads the string to three digits with "0" as needed and truncates any digits over three.

SOUNDEX() is a blunt instrument. If you index on the SOUNDEX() values of words not all that are likely to be spelling variations of the same word will be close together. The SOUNDEX() code of "Katherine" is as close to "Saturnalia" as it is to "Catherine," because SOUNDEX() ignores the similarity of sound of the first letters. The SOUNDEX() function will return "circle" and "crackle" with the same C624 code, but the two forms are unlikely to be spelling variations of the same word.

SPACE()

Returns a string of spaces.

Syntax:

```
[cVar=] space(<nExp>)
```

The SPACE() function does the same thing as REPLICATE() with a space " " as its first parameter, returns a string of <nExp> spaces. If <nExp> is 0 it returns an empty string, if less an error. The maximum value for <nExp> is the maximum length of a string, 32,766.

Example:

```
FUNCTION RightAlign
     parameters cString, nWidth
RETURN space(nWidth - len(cString))+cString
```

SQL

Is unsupported in dBASE for Windows.

SQLERROR()

New; returns the number of the last error returned by a server.

Syntax:

```
[nVar] = SQLERROR()
```

Use SQLMESSAGE() to obtain the message itself.

See DBERROR(), ERROR(), SQLMESSAGE().

SQLEXEC()

New; executes a statement from the SQL language.

Syntax:

```
[nVar=]    sqlexec( <cExpStatement>
           [,<cExpAnswerTable>])
```

The SQLEXEC() function executes a SQL statement <cExpStatement> on the database specified by SET DATABASE. The database can be a server database or local. If SET DATABASE is not set, the statement operates on the active local dBASE or Paradox table. If the optional <cExpAnswerTable> is provided, the designated local table, either dBASE or Paradox as set by SET DBTYPE, is created as the answer table.

The <cExpStatement> must be a valid statment under the rules of the server and must be enclosed in quotation marks. Embedded characters strings and SQL or IDAPI reserved words must also be delimited, usually in single quotes. For local dBASE and Paradox tables, use the ANSI-compliant Borland Interbase database server dialect.

The SQLEXEC() function returns zero if successful, or an ERROR() error code. You may also use the DBERROR() function to investigate IDAPI errors and SQLERROR() to investigate server errors.

The example shows using SQLEXEC() to import information from a sybase table using SQL into a local dBASE table SALESREPS.

Example:

```
set dbtype to dbase
open database sybase1
set database to sybase1
errcode = sqlexec("SELECT Name, HireDate FROM Employee WHERE Department
= Sales","SALESREPS")
if errcode = 0
     set database to
     use SALESREPS
endif
```

Servers can enforce rules such as case sensitivity of column names. Put the SQLEXEC() parameters all on a single long dBASE line to avoid problems with semicolons being sent to the server.

See DBERROR(), ERROR(), OPEN DATABASE, SET DATABASE, SQLERROR().

SQLMESSAGE()

New; returns the message associated with the last server error.

Syntax:

```
SQLMESSAGE()
```

Use SQLMESSAGE() to obtain the message associated with a SQLERROR() number.

See SQLERROR().

SQRT()

Returns the square root of a number.

Syntax:

```
[fVar=] sqrt(<nExp>)
```

The SQRT() function returns, as a float-type number, the square root of <nExp>, which must be 0 or positive. Attempting to take the square root of a negative number returns an error.

Example:

```
FUNCTION Hypotenuse
  parameters nSide1,nSide2
  if nSide1<0 .or. nSide2<0
    RETURN -1
  else
    RETURN sqrt(nSide1*nSide1+nSide2*nSide2)
  endif
```

STATIC

New; declares local variables that retain their values when invisible.

Syntax:

```
STATIC {<xVar> [ = <xExp>][, <etc>]
```

A variable declared STATIC is local in scope. It cannot be accessed or changed from outside the routine in which it is declared, either from a higher-level routine or from a lower-level one. However, unlike other local variables it is not cleared from memory on return from the routine. Its value is retained. If the routine is called again, it has the value it had on the previous exit from the routine. When declared, you can give a STATIC variable a value in the STATIC declaration. If you do not, dBASE creates it with the value .F.

Example:

```
FUNCTION Tries
     static Trycount = 0
    Trycount = Trycount + 1
RETURN Trycount
```

STORE

Stores one or more values in memory, now with AUTOMEM and MEMO options.

Syntax:

```
STORE {<xExp> TO <xVarlist>}|AUTOMEM|{MEMO <mFld>
TO <Array>}
```

The STORE command without AUTOMEM or MEMO stores the value of an expression to one or more variables listed in the statement. The variables can be array elements. If you name an array as a target of STORE but do not identify one or more subscripted elements of the array, dBASE clears the array, creates a non-array variable of the same name, and stores the value to that.

STORE AUTOMEM stores the value of every field of the current table to a variable of the same name and type, simplifying changing table data. dBASE will create the AUTOMEM variables if they do not exist.

STORE MEMO saves the named memo field to a named array, one line per element. In this form, unlike the general form of STORE, no subscripts are given with the name of the array. The array must be declared before STORE MEMO is issued and must be one-dimensional. The memo will be broken into lines of up to the number of characters in MEMOWIDTH. Be sure the array is large enough to hold all the lines. No error will occur if the memo overfills the array, but the excess memo lines will be lost.

The use of "=" to assign a single value to a single variable, using the syntax

```
<xVar> = <xExp>
```

is considered an alternative syntax to STORE. The variable can be an array element or simple variable.

STR()

Converts a number to a character string.

Syntax:

```
[cVar=] str(<nExpValue>[,<nExpLength>
      [,<nExpDecimals>[,<cExpPad>]]])
```

The STR() function converts the numeric expression <nExpValue> to a character string and returns the character string. The optional <nExpLength> specifies the length of the string to return, including sign, decimal point, and decimal places. The valid range is 1 to 20, inclusive, with a default of 10. If the number is too large to fit, dBASE truncates one or more decimal places specified by <nExpDecimals>. If the integral part of the number is still too large, dBASE converts it to a string of asterisks.

<nExpDecimals> specifies how many decimal places are to be included in <nExpLength> if they fit. The default is 0.

The last option, <cExpPad>, specifies a character to use to pad the left of the returned string if the number as converted does not fill <nExpLength> character places. The default for it is a space.

You can use the STR() function whenever you need to manipulate numeric data as characters. Two examples are printing numeric expressions within a longer character expression and creating indexes on keys that combine character and numeric values.

STUFF()

Replaces characters in a string.

Syntax:

```
[cVar=] stuff(<cExp1>|<mFld>,<nExp1>,
                <nExp2>,<cExp2>)
```

The STUFF() function is very useful, but the syntax is hard to remember. It enables you to rebuild a string by adding or subtracting characters at any position within it.

The first parameter, <cExp1>|<mFld>, is the string or memo field to be stuffed. <nExp1> is the first character position of the substitution. <nExp2> is the number of characters to be removed from the string <cExp1> starting at <nExp1>. <cExp2> is a character expression to be inserted at <nExp1>.

Whether the resulting string is longer than the original string depends on whether the length of <cExp2> is greater than <nExp2>. If <cExp2> is longer, more characters will be inserted than removed and the string will be lengthened, and vice versa.

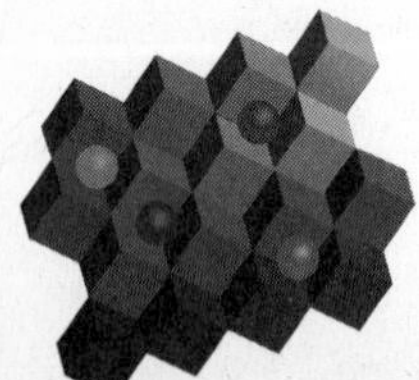

Example:

```
FUNCTION NoDblSpace
     parameters cString1
     private nAt,cString2
     nAt=2
     cString2 = cString1
     do while nAt <= len(cString2)
          if substr(cString2,nAt-1,2) = space(2)
               cString2 = stuff(cString2,nAt,1,"")
          else
               nAt = nAt + 1
          endif
     enddo
RETURN cString2
```

The example function removes each space from the string if the space is preceded by another space. The STUFF() function takes out 1 character and replaces it with an empty string, no characters, thereby shortening the string by the space removed.

SUBSTR()

Returns a specified number of contiguous characters from a string.

Syntax:

```
[cVar=] substr(<cExp>|<mFld>,<nExpStart>
          [,<nExpLength>])
```

The SUBSTR() function returns <nExpLength> characters starting at position <nExpStart> of the character string or memo field <cExp>|<mFld>. <nExpStart> must be positive. If <nExpLength> is omitted, or extends beyond the end of the string, the remainder of the string from <nExpStart> on is returned. The example function converts a numeric digit to its English name.

Example:

```
FUNCTION Dig2Char
     parameters nExp
     cDigits = "Zero One  Two  Three Four Five Six  Seven Eight Nine "
RETURN trim(substr(cDigits, mod(nExp,10)*5+1,5))
```

SUM

Sums numeric fields over the records of a table.

Syntax:

```
SUM <nExpList>
    [<scope>][FOR <lExpCond1>][WHILE <lExpcond2>]
    [TO {<nVarList>|ARRAY <Array>}]
```

The SUM command sums the listed numeric or float fields of a table over all records of the table, except as limited by the <scope> clause and the FOR and WHILE conditions. It optionally saves the results to the specified list of variables or to an existing one-dimensional array.

The positions of the fields in the field list match the positions of the variables in the variable list, or array elements in the array, to which they will be stored. If you omit the variable list or array, the sums will be printed in the results pane of the Command window only. If SET TALK is OFF, they will not be printed and will be lost unless saved to variables or an array.

SUSPEND

Suspends execution of a program.

You can issue SUSPEND from within a program or as one of your choices when an error occurs.

SUSPEND halts the program from running, but keeps its tables and other files and variables intact so you can inspect them and see why it is not behaving as you want. To resume execution, type RESUME. To cancel, type CANCEL.

If you type DO <Program> to restart a program that has been suspended, you start a new instance of it from the beginning. You can eventually run out of memory because both copies of the program are loaded. You can examine and change tables, their status, and variables while a program is suspended. Changes will take effect when you RESUME. You can also examine and change the program code, but changes to it will not take effect when you RESUME. You must recompile the program as changed and start it again after compiling it.

See RESUME.

TAG()

Returns the name of an index or index tag.

Syntax:

```
[cVar=] tag([<MDXFile>,]<nExp>[,<workarea>])
```

The TAG() function returns the name of the index or tag corresponding to the position in the index list for the current or specified work area given by <nExp>. If you give the optional <MDXFile> parameter, <nExp> is interpreted as the number of the tag within that MDX file, in the order in which it is listed within the file. If you omit the <MDXFile> parameter, <nExp> signifies the number in the index list consisting of all NDX indexes, in the order opened, the tags of the production MDX file in the order listed within it, then the tags of each other MDX file. Other MDX files appear in the list in order of opening, and the tags of each in the order listed within the file. If no index or tag exists in position <nExp>, the function returns an empty string.

See MDX(), NDX(), TAGCOUNT(), TAGNO().

TAGCOUNT()

Returns the number of indexes in a work area or MDX file.

Syntax:

```
[nVar=] tagcount([<MDXFile>[,<workarea>])
```

The TAGCOUNT() function with no parameters returns the number of indexes and index tags active in the current work area. You can specify a different work area. If you specify an MDX file, the function returns the number of tags within that file. If there is no such MDX file or no indexes open in the specified work area, the function returns 0.

See MDX(), NDX(), TAG(), TAGNO().

TAGNO()

Returns the positional number of an index or tag.

Syntax:

```
[nVar=] tagno([<Tag>[,<MDXFile>[,<workarea>]]])
```

The TAGNO() function is the complement of TAG(). The TAG() function returns the name of an index or tag given its number in the index list; TAGNO() gives the number in the list given the name.

You can specify a different work area. If you do not, the function uses the current work area. If you specify an MDX file, the number returned is that of the tag within that file. Otherwise, the number returned is with respect to the entire index list for the work area, NDX indexes first in order of opening, tags of the production MDX file, and tags of other MDX files in order of opening.

If you do not specify a tag, TAGNO() returns the number of the tag of the controlling index, or 0 if the table is in natural order.

If the specified index, tag, or MDX file does not exist, the function returns an error.

TAN()

Returns the tangent of an angle measured in radians.

Syntax:

```
[fVar=] tan(<nExp>)
```

The TAN() function returns the tangent of an angle. State the size of the angle, <nExp>, in radians, using DTOR() to convert from degrees if necessary. The function returns a floating-point number unless the result is undefined. The tangent of an angle is the ratio of the opposite side of a right triangle to the adjacent side. If the angle is 90 degrees or 270 degrees, PI()/2 or 3*PI()/2 in radians, the tangent is infinite and the return of the function is undefined.

When the tangent is undefined dBASE returns a value of type U that prints as a string of asterisks. The value can be compared to a number and is larger than any number. You cannot test for the presence of an overflow as though the asterisks were part of a character string. Use the type U to check for an infinite value. The reciprocal of the tangent of an angle, 1/TAN(<nExp>), is known as the cotangent of the angle.

Example:

```
? "The height of trees needed to shade 20 feet of your patio deck"
? " when the sun is 65 degrees above the horizon is "
?? str(20*tan(dtor(65)),4,1) + " feet."
```

See ATAN(), ATN2(), COS() DTOR(), RTOD(), SIN().

TARGET()

New; returns the name of a child table linked with SET RELATION.

Syntax:

```
[cVar=] target(<nExp>[,<workarea>])
```

The TARGET() function returns the name of a table into which a relation has been set from the current or specified table. <nExp> gives the number of the relation in the list of relations set from the specified parent table. The optional <workarea> identifies the work area of the parent table if not the current work area. If there is no relation set corresponding to the number given for the work area, the function returns an empty string.

The RELATION() function gives the expression on which the tables are related.

See RELATION()

TEXT

Introduces a TEXT . . . ENDTEXT program block.

Syntax:

```
TEXT
     <one or more lines of text>
ENDTEXT
```

The TEXT . . . ENDTEXT commands delimit a block of text. dBASE will output the lines between TEXT and ENDTEXT exactly as included in the program. dBASE does not do any interpretation of the text and will not expand ¯os within it. You can use TEXT . . . ENDTEXT to display text in the results pane of the Command window or in a dBASE IV-type window, and you can redirect the text with SET ALTERNATE or SET PRINTER. Overlong lines will wrap only if directed to a dBASE IV-type window. If the length of the text is too great for all the lines to fit in the window, they will scroll.

TIME()

Returns the system time.

Syntax:

```
[cVar=] time([<xExp>])
```

The TIME() function returns the system time. If an expression of any type and value is included as a parameter, the time will be returned as a string in the form "HH:MM:SS.SS", otherwise as a string of the form "HH:MM:SS" with the decimal point and the hundredths of a second omitted.

In passing an expression as a parameter you can be as creative as you want, but the number 0 works as well as any. Do not pass alphabetic characters within the parentheses unless they are delimited with quotation marks, because literal characters are not an expression. They will be interpreted as the name of a memory variable or field, and if no such variable or field exists an error occurs.

The system clock of the IBM PC family operates at 1,193,180 Hertz and issues a tick after a countdown of 65,536 cycles, or approximately 18.2 ticks per second. DOS converts the fractions of a second to hundredths, but you should be aware that the time is accurate only to the last tick, and might be as much as 6/100 second in error.

TOTAL

Sums the numeric fields of a table to a second table.

Syntax:

```
TOTAL ON <xExpKey> TO {<File>|?}
  [[TYPE] DBASE|PARADOX]
  [<scope>][FOR <lExpCond1>][WHILE <lExpCond2>]
  [FIELDS <Fieldlist>]
```

The TOTAL command creates a target table with one record for each unique value of the key field or expression in the current table. It totals type N or F fields of the current table for each value of the key field or expression and copies the totals to the corresponding fields of the corresponding record of the target. The source table must be indexed or sorted on the key field or expression.

You can give the name of the target table or use ? to bring up the File dialog. You can indicate the type of table if not the default type set by DBTYPE. You can also specify a table in a database by prefixing the name of the table with the database name delimited by colons. If the database is not open, dBASE opens a dialog box prompting you for your login name, password or other parameters needed to make the connection.

The <scope>, FOR, and WHILE options allow you to restrict the records included in the totals. The FIELDS list lists the numeric or float-type fields of the original table to be totaled. By default, all numeric or float fields are totaled.

The structure of the target table is the same as that of the source table except that fields of the source table that are memo, binary or OLE, or fields made invisible by the use of

SET FIELDS TO before you issue the TOTAL command, are not copied. All other fields are included. Non-numeric fields and numeric fields excluded from a FIELDS list within the TOTAL command will not be totalled, but will contain data from the corresponding field of the first record of the source table that matched the key value.

Before using TOTAL to summarize the records of a large table you may have to modify its structure to increase the field widths of its numeric and float fields. You will be safe if you add as many places as in the digital representation of the maximum number of records to be totalled to a single record of the target table. That is, if you think no more than 30 records match any single key value, you need as many extra places as in the number 30, or two. If you fail to provide sufficient width in the numeric and float fields to hold the totals, the totals will print to the target table as a useless row of asterisks.

Example:

```
use Orders order Cust_ID
set fields to Cust_ID, Order_Tot, Order_Date
total on Cust_ID to Cust_Order fields Order_Tot ;
     for date() - Order_Date < 180
use Cust_Order
list off fields Cust_ID, Order_Tot

CUST_ID   ORDER_TOT
          A01215            3601.24
          A01222             335.96
          A01458           12187.00
     <more>
```

See AVERAGE, CALCULATE, SUM.

TRANSFORM()

Formats data to a character string.

Syntax:

```
[cVar=] transform(<xExp>,<cExpPicture>)
```

The TRANSFORM() function accepts an expression of any type but memo, binary or OLE and a picture expression defining the format to return. It returns a character string converting the value of the expression to the required format. The <cExpPicture> expression uses the same function and template symbols as @ . . . SAY. The word PICTURE is omitted.

Example:

```
? "TMP"+transform(int(rand()*10000),"@L 9999")
TMP0346
```

TRIM()

Strips trailing blanks from a character string.

Syntax:

```
[cVar=] trim(<cExp>)
```

The TRIM() function returns <cExp> with all trailing spaces removed. Use TRIM() to remove the blanks dBASE uses as padding in table fields, among other uses. RTRIM() is an alternative syntax. Use LTRIM() to remove leading spaces.

Example:

```
Name = trim(First)+" " ;
     +iif(Mid_Init # " ", Mid_Init +". ", "") ;
     +trim(Last)
```

See LEFT(), LTRIM(), RIGHT().

TYPE

Displays a text file.

Syntax:

```
TYPE {<File1>|?|<skeleton1>}[MORE][NUMBER]
[TO {FILE {<File2>|?|<skeleton2>}}|PRINTER]
```

You can use ? or a skeleton to call up the File dialog box instead of specifying either the first, source, file, or the optional target file to which it will be written. By default, dBASE gives the target file a TXT extension.

When dBASE copies the file, it adds two lines at the top, a blank line, and the fully-qualified name and date of the source file. These two lines are never numbered.

The MORE option directs dBASE to pause the output to the results pane of the Command window. It has no effect on the optional output to file or printer.

The NUMBER option causes dBASE to number all lines of output except the first two.

TYPE()

Returns type of an expression.

Syntax:

```
[cVar=] type(<cExpExpression>)
```

The TYPE() function evaluates the expression given by the character expression <cExpExpression> and returns an uppercase letter identifying the type of data of the result:

A = array

B = binary

BM = bookmark

C = character, including Paradox alphanumeric fields

CB = code block

D = date

F = float, including Paradox numeric and currency fields

FP = function pointer

L = logical

M = memo

N = numeric

O = object

S = screen save variable

U = undefined

The syntax of TYPE() is unusual. Its parameter is a character expression that results in an expression, and it is the second expression of which TYPE() returns the type.

The name of a field or variable is a character expression only if it holds character data. Otherwise, it is an expression of the type of data it contains. Accordingly, you cannot give a variable or field name as the parameter to TYPE() to find out what type of data it contains unless you enclose the name in quotation marks or other delimiters. If you do enclose a variable name or field name in quotation marks, the function returns U if no such variable or field exists.

An exception exists when one variable holds the name of another. In this case you can give the name of the first variable as a parameter to TYPE(). It will return the type of data held in the second variable, the one of which the name is held in the first. You can go a step farther, if you want, and create a ¯o to hold the name of the variable holding the name of the variable holding the data of which you want to know the type.

Examples:

```
? type("2+2")
N                   && 2+2 is a numeric expression
? type("3<2=(1<0)")
L                   && 3<2 = (1<0) is a logical expression
nPrice = 1000
cPriceVar = "nPrice"
cMacro = "cPriceVar"
? type("nPrice")
N
? type(cPriceVar)
N
? type(&cMacro)
N
? Type(cMacro)
C                   && "nPrice" in quotes is a character expression
```

If the example continued with type(nPrice), that statement would result in a dBASE error, "Data type mismatch. Expecting: Character", because nPrice is not a character expression. It is a numeric expression.

UNIQUE()

Returns .T. if the specified index is unique, or .F.

Syntax:

```
[lVar=] unique([[<MDXFile>,]
          <nExpPosition>[,<workarea>]])
```

You can call UNIQUE() with a work area. Otherwise, it returns information about an index in the current work area. The index is identified by the number <nExpPosition>. If you give the name of an MDX file, <nExpPosition> is the position of the tag in that file. If you do not give an MDX file name, <nExpPosition> is the position of the tag or index in the list of all indexes active in the work area, starting with NDX indexes in the order opened, then taking the tags of the production MDX in order of their positions within it and finally the tags in order of position within each other MDX file, taking the files in the order opened. If you call UNIQUE() with no parameters, it reports on the controlling index in the current work area.

The UNIQUE() function returns .T. if the index is unique and .F. if it is not. It will be .T. if it was created with the UNIQUE option of INDEX or if SET UNIQUE was ON when it was created, whatever the SET UNIQUE setting at any later time. The function returns .F. if the index is not unique, if there is no MDX file of the name given, if there is no index of the number given or if no number was given and there is no controlling index.

UNLOCK

Unlocks the given table or all records in it.

Syntax:

```
UNLOCK [ALL|{IN <workarea>}]
```

The UNLOCK command unlocks an entire table if it was locked with FLOCK(), or unlocks all the records in it that were locked with RLOCK()|LOCK(). You can specify a work area if the table to be unlocked is not in the current work area. If the ALL option is included, all tables or records in all work areas are unlocked.

When the parent table of a relation is unlocked, so is each child table. dBASE automatically unlocks the table and all of its records when you terminate an edit or close the edit window.

UNTIL

Ends a DO UNTIL loop. See DO.

UPDATE

Replaces data in one table based on data in another.

Appendixes

Syntax:

```
UPDATE ON <xExpKey> FROM <workarea>
{REPLACE <Field> WITH <xExp>}[,<etc.>]
[RANDOM][REINDEX]
```

The UPDATE command enables you to change data in one table to incorporate information from another. The table updated must be the current one and must be indexed on the key expression. The source table must be active in another work area. The effect of the update is given by a list of one or more fields and expressions. The data of each field in the list will be replaced with the expression specified for that field.

There are no explicit scope, FOR, or WHILE conditions allowed for an UPDATE. If you need to exclude one or more fields from being updated under some condition, create a WITH expression for that field that uses IIF(). The IIF() clause should state the condition for update and provide the name of the field itself as the replacement if the condition fails.

The RANDOM option allows the source table to be unindexed. If RANDOM is omitted, the source and target tables must be indexed on the same key expression. REINDEX defers reindexing of the noncontrolling indexes of the target table until after all records are replaced.

You should use UPDATE sparingly if using it to merge transaction information into a table that includes only balances or similar summaries of the transactions. If the table from which the UPDATE is performed remains active, there is a risk that the information in it and in the updated table will disagree for some reason, creating inconsistencies that can be difficult to resolve. On the other hand, if you remove the table from which the UPDATE was performed from use prematurely, you can make corrections more difficult.

As an example, you should not normally update customer balances from an invoice table and remove the invoice table when the invoices are mailed. Doing so makes it unnecessarily difficult to adjust questioned invoices. Keep the invoices active until such time as the experience of the business indicates they will no longer be questioned, or until paid, and perform the update only then.

Example:

```
use ZIPCODES order Zipcode alias Zips
select select()
use PROSPECTS order Zipcode
update on Zipcode from Zips ;
    replace State with Zips->State, ;
    City with Zips->City
```

See REPLACE.

UPDATED()

New; returns .T. if any of the GET fields in a window have been changed.

Syntax:

```
[lVar=] updated()
```

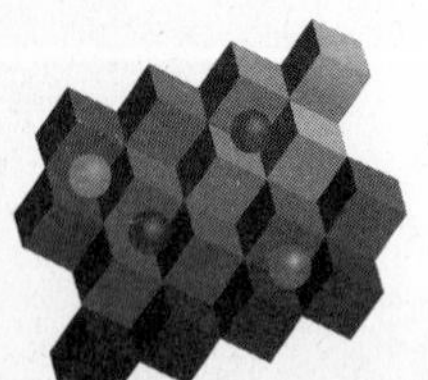

If there are no GET entry fields in the current window, including the results pane of the Command window, if the GETs have not been activated or if none of them have been changed since activated, UPDATED() returns .F. If one or more of the GETs have been changed, it returns .T. This command is included for compatibility with dBASE IV. Use the OnChange and similar properties to manage changed data in forms.

UPPER()

Returns a string with its lowercase characters converted to uppercase.

Syntax:

```
[cVar=] upper(<cExp>|<mFld>)
```

The UPPER() function is the inverse of LOWER(). It capitalizes all the alphabetic characters in the character expression or memo field passed as a parameter and returns the expression or memo field as converted. The current language driver defines which characters are alphabetic, and the uppercase and lowercase versions of each.

See LOWER(), PROPER().

UPSCROLL

Scrolls the current window contents up by a number of lines.

Syntax:

```
UPSCROLL <nExp>
```

The parameter <nExp> gives the number of lines to scroll upward within the window, so you can see later lines. If <nExp> exceeds the number of lines in the window, the scroll stops when the bottom line is visible. UPSCROLL will scroll the results pane of the Command window or the current dBASE IV-style window.

See DOWNSCROLL

USE

Opens a table and optionally its indexes.

Syntax:

```
USE [[<Table>|?|<skeleton1>]
 [[TYPE] PARADOX|DBASE]
 [IN <workarea>]
 [INDEX {<Index>|?|<skeleton2>}[,<etc.>]
```

```
[ORDER [TAG]{<NDXFile>|
   {<Tag>[OF <MDXFile>]}}]
[AGAIN]
[ALIAS <Alias>]
[AUTOMEM]
[EXCLUSIVE|SHARED]
[NOSAVE][NOUPDATE]]
```

USE with no parameters or options closes the table open in the current work area, or in the specified work area if an IN clause is included.

USE otherwise opens a table. You can give its name, or give ? or a skeleton to open the File dialog. You can designate its type, Paradox or dBASE, if it is not the default DBTYPE type. The word TYPE is optional. You may open a table in a database by including the database name, delimited by colons, as a prefix to the table name. If the database is not open, dBASE opens a dialog box to prompt you for your login name, password, or other parameters needed to make the connection.

If you include the IN clause, the table is opened in the specified work area, and whatever work area was current before you issued the command remains current. If you omit the IN clause, the command opens the table in the current work area.

The INDEX option allows you to designate up to 100 indexes for a dBASE table, each of which you can include in the list by name or by ? or skeleton to bring up the File dialog. If the first is an NDX file and you omit the ORDER option, it becomes the controlling index. The ORDER option allows you to specify which NDX file, or which tag and which MDX file it is in if not the production MDX file, will be the controlling index. You also use the ORDER option with Paradox and SQL tables to specify which of their indexes will be controlling. If you fail to specify an ORDER for a Paradox table that has a PRIMARY index, the PRIMARY index will be the master index.

The AGAIN option enables you to open the table for use in one work area while it remains open in another. ALIAS enables you to give the table an alias. By default, the alias for a table not already open is its filename, not including the path or extension. An alias must start with a letter and contain only letters, digits, and underscores. If the filename contains characters that cannot be in an alias, or if the table is opened AGAIN and no new ALIAS specified, dBASE assigns the work area prepended by an underscore as the alias. AUTOMEM initializes and fills as BLANK a memory variable of the same name and type as each field of the table.

EXCLUSIVE prevents other users from using the table while SHARED allows them to access it while it is opened. In a single-user environment, all tables are opened exclusive always.

NOSAVE causes the table, its DBT file, and its production MDX table to be erased when it is closed. If you realize once it is open that you do not want it erased, COPY it WITH PRODUCTION to another table. NOUPDATE makes the table read-only.

See ALIAS(), CATALOG, CLEAR ALL, CLOSE, DBF(), INDEX, SELECT, SELECT(), SET EXCLUSIVE, SET INDEX, SET ORDER.

USER()

Is not supported by dBASE for Windows.

VAL()

Converts a character string to a number.

Syntax:

```
[nVar=] val(<cExp>)
```

The VAL() function converts <cExp> to a number, which can be a float-type. It stops on encountering any character that cannot be part of a number, returning 0 if the first character is ineligible to start a number, otherwise the number formed from the characters up to that character.

Example:

```
? val("-.234E3UX")
      -234.00
? type('val("-.234E3UX")')
F
```

VALIDDRIVE()

New; returns .T. for a valid drive, or .F.

Syntax:

```
[lVar=] validdrive(<cExp>[:])
```

The VALIDDRIVE() function returns .T. if the specified drive is valid and can be read. A drive with no disk in it cannot be read and causes VALIDDRIVE() to return .F. Giving the letter of a CD-ROM drive with no CD in it causes results that depend on the drive. Use VALIDDRIVE() to find out without causing a dBASE or system error whether you must prompt your user to insert a disk or select another drive.

VARREAD()

Returns the name of the variable or field associated with the current @ . . . GET.

Syntax:

```
[cVar=] varread()
```

If a GET is active and has input focus, whether in the results pane of the Command window or a window opened dBASE IV- style, VARREAD() returns its name. If no GET exists or none is activated, VARREAD() returns an empty string. VARREAD() is included for compatibility. Use the Name and other properties of dBASE for Windows objects to manage them.

VERSION()

Returns the dBASE version.

Syntax:

```
[cVar=] version([<nExp>])
```

The VERSION() function returns a character string giving the version of dBASE. If the optional <nExp> numerical expression is included, the version includes the build number and date, which might be important in determining the availability of upgrade releases.

WAIT

Pauses execution until a key is pressed.

Syntax:

```
WAIT [<cExpPrompt>][TO <cVar>]
```

You can use WAIT in a program to pause execution until the user presses a key. If you do not include your own prompt expression <cExpPrompt>, dBASE issues the prompt message "Press a key to continue . . ." If you include the optional TO clause, dBASE stores the keypress character to the memory variable created. It will contain an empty string if the user presses Enter or a key without an ASCII value.

If the user presses Escape and SET ESCAPE is OFF, execution resumes as with any other keypress. If SET ESCAPE is ON, dBASE interrupts execution of the program.

See SET ESCAPE.

WINDOW()

Returns the name of the current dBASE IV-style window.

Syntax:

```
[cVar=] window()
```

The current window is the one with input focus. If not changed by mouse or other action, it is the last window opened, which will be the last one listed in an ACTIVATE WINDOW command that opens several. If no window is open, the function returns an empty string. This command is included for compatibility. Use INSPECT() to obtain information about forms.

WORKAREA()

Returns the number of the current work area.

Syntax:

```
[nVar=] workarea()
```

You can use the WORKAREA() function to save the number of the current work area in order to return to it from other processing. In general, using ALIAS() to obtain the alias of the table active in the current work area accomplishes the same thing with less risk of mixing up the numbers of several work areas.

See ALIAS(), DBF().

YEAR()

Returns the year of a date as a numeric value.

Syntax:

```
[nVar=] year(<dExp>)
```

The YEAR() function returns the year of a date expression as a four-digit number, without regard to the SET CENTURY setting. It returns 0 as the year of a blank date.

ZAP

Removes all data records from the current table.

Syntax:

```
ZAP
```

If SET SAFETY is OFF, ZAP acts at once, so use it with care. ZAP removes all data records from a table, leaving its structure intact but with 0 records. ZAP is faster than DELETE ALL followed by PACK. Records you ZAP cannot be recalled by dBASE.

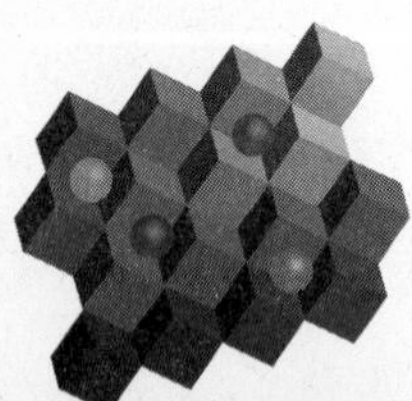

System Variables Reference

By Jay Parsons

System variables first appeared as part of dBASE IV. They serve the same purpose as the SET commands and SET() and SETTO() functions, enabling you to change and obtain the values of various environmental settings.

The use of system variables is somewhat simpler than typing the SET commands or SET() and SETTO() functions, but there is no point-and-shoot facility for changing system variables comparable to the Desktop dialog box you can open from the Properties menu. You may use system variables like any other public variables, except that you cannot release them.

Understanding System Variables

System variables originally controlled printer settings only. There were 25 of these in dBASE IV. dBASE for Windows has introduced five new ones, of which only _porientation has anything to do with printing. Whether or not you prefer the use of system variables to the SET command and SET() and SETTO() functions, you might agree that the somewhat arbitrary division between which items are controlled by SET commands and which by system variables makes learning the language more difficult.

Adding to the confusion, all but two of the system variables are read and write. You can examine their contents to see how things are set, or you may assign new values to change the way dBASE for Windows works.

The new system variables include the following:

- ✔ **_app.** This is an object reference to the dBASE for Windows application and is read-only.
- ✔ **_curobj.** The _curobj variable sets or returns the number of the object with current focus in tabbing order.
- ✔ **_dbwinhome.** This read-only variable holds the name of the directory in which the dBASE system files are located, the same value returned by the HOME() function.
- ✔ **_porientation.** This system variable specifies the direction of printing.
- ✔ **_updated.** This variable allows you to set the value that UPDATED() returns.

Three dBASE IV system variables are not supported by dBASE for Windows: _pecode, _pscode and _pwait. These allowed you to operate a printer without a printer driver. Windows requires that you use a printer driver; the driver manages these tasks.

System Variables in Alphabetical Order

In the syntax paradigms, characters in upper case indicate the default setting. The system variables that accept character values accept either lower or upper case, but convert the value to upper case.

_alignment

Controls justification of ?|?? output.

Syntax:

```
_alignment = "LEFT"¦"center"¦"right"
```

The _alignment variable justifies text printed by the streaming output commands ? and ?? between the margins specified by _lmargin and _rmargin. If _wrap is false, the _alignment setting has no effect because _rmargin has no effect. The "center" option centers each line between the margins, which at first seems useful only to persons using dBASE for Windows to print wedding invitations. It is a convenient way to center titles, page numbers and the like. Similarly, the "right" option allows you to put the date, page number or the like at the right margin without calculating. You may change the alignment within a line. The example prints the report title, date and page number on a single line at the ends and in the center.

Example:

```
_wrap = .T.
                    _alignment = "left"
                    ? "Widget Sales by Region"
                    _alignment = "center"
                    ?? date()
                    _alignment = "right"
                    ?? _pageno
```

_app

New, provides access to the application object.

Syntax:

```
[<oVar> =] _app
```

The _app system variable is a read-only reference to the application object. You may assign the value to a variable or simply use it directly to change the properties of the application. The example changes the title of the dBASE for Windows main window.

Example:

```
_app.framewin.text = "Who Says We're Not" ;
                   +" Having Fun?"
```

_box

Controls the printing of DEFINE BOX boxes.

Syntax:

```
_box = <lExpCond>
```

The _box variable turns on, if .T., or off the printing in streaming output of a box defined with DEFINE BOX. To print a box, use DEFINE BOX to specify its starting and ending column, its height and optionally its border style. You may either specify the line on which it should start printing with the AT LINE option of DEFINE BOX or set _box to false, then set it true when printing reaches the line on which the box should start printing. The height of the box will be as specified, even if you suppress printing of some of the lines. The example prints a box nine lines high with "dashes" for sides because of turning _box on and off for alternate lines. The default of _box is .T.

Example:

```
DEFINE BOX FROM 71 TO 79 HEIGHT 9
            for X = 1 TO 9
                  ?
                  _box = .NOT. _box
                  if X > 3 .and. X < 7
                        ?? substr("PlaceStampHere ", ;
                              5*(X-4)+1,5) at 73
                  endif
            next
```

See DEFINE BOX, _pspacing.

_curobj

New, returns or sets the number in tabbing order of the current object.

Syntax:

```
_curobj = <nExp>
```

The value <nExp> must be from 1 to the number of objects on the current form with TabStop .T.

See CUROBJ().

_dbwinhome

New, returns path to DBASEWIN.EXE.

Syntax:

```
[cVar = ] _dbwinhome
```

The _dbwinhome read-only system variable returns the topmost directory of the dBASE for Windows installation, by default C:\DBASEWIN\. This is slightly different from the HOME() function, which returns the path to the directory in which DBASEWIN.EXE is found, usually C:\DBASEWIN\BIN\.

_indent

Specifies the indentation in characters of each new paragraph.

Syntax:

```
_indent = <nExp>
```

The _indent system variable works only when _wrap is true. When _wrap is true, you should use ?? to print sentences within a paragraph and ? to start each new paragraph. The ? line will be indented. You may specify a negative value for <nExp> to create a hanging indent, but the sum of _lmargin and _indent must be 0 or greater, and less than _rmargin. You may specify a fractional value for precise adjustment. The default for _indent is 0.

See _lmargin, _ppitch, _rmargin, _wrap.

_lmargin

Specifies the left margin in spaces.

Syntax:

```
_lmargin = <nExp>
```

The _lmargin variable is effective only when _wrap is true. It specifies the number of spaces to be output at the beginning of each line before printing expressions with ? and ??. The value of <nExp> must be between 0 and 254 and may include a fraction. The sum of _lmargin and _indent must not be less than 0 and less than _rmargin. The default value of _lmargin is 0.

See _indent, _ppitch, _rmargin, _wrap.

_padvance

Specifies how the printer advances the paper.

Syntax:

```
_padvance = "FORMFEED"¦"linefeeds"
```

If _padvance is set to "FORMFEED", the default, dBASE issues a formfeed, chr(12), to the printer. If _padvance is set to "linefeeds", dBASE sends a number of linefeeds to the printer. The number of linefeeds is _plength – _plineno if the printing is in streaming mode using ? and ?? and one of the following causes the page advance:

- ✔ The EJECT PAGE command with no ON PAGE handler.
- ✔ The EJECT PAGE command when the current line is greater than the ON PAGE line.

- ✔ The program reaches a PRINTJOB or ENDPRINTJOB command that causes a page advance due to the setting of the _peject variable.

In other cases, where EJECT is issued or where SET DEVICE TO PRINT is in use and the @ position is higher than the last, dBASE calculates the number of linefeeds by _plength–mod(prow(),_plength).

You may issue either a linefeed, chr(10), or a formfeed, chr(12), to the printer directly. The _padvance setting will not affect either one.

If you are printing short forms, either continuous forms or forms that take up a fraction of a page, you may set _padvance to "linefeeds" and _plength to the form length in lines. You may then issue an EJECT to position the printing for the next form, bypassing the printer's length setting.

See _plength, _plineno.

_pageno

Sets the page number.

Syntax:

```
_pageno = <nExp>
```

The value of _pageno, by default 1, may be set to any number from 1 to 32,767. dBASE increments the number when printing a report. You may set it to a number greater than 1 when printing the second or later chapter or part of some report that should continue the page numbering scheme from the first part.

The _pageno value determines when _pbpage and _pepage start and stop printing. If you set _pageno to 3, _pbpage to 4 and _pepage to 5, dBASE will skip one page, page 3, then print the next two as 4 and 5. You must set _pageno less than or equal to _pepage for anything to print.

You can use _pageno in a ? or ?? statement to print the current page number.

_pbpage

Specifies the beginning _pageno to be printed.

Syntax:

```
_pbpage = <nExp>
```

The value of _pbpage, by default 1, may be between 1 and 32,767, but must be less than or equal to _pepage. Printing will begin with the page at which _pageno reaches the value of _pepage.

You will find _pbpage most useful when a printer failure or paper jam requires you to reprint a portion of a job. Run the report or program over again from the beginning so it does its calculations and determines how much data will fit on each page, but use _pbpage to suppress printing of the pages you already have in order to save time and paper.

_pcolno

Sets or returns the current printing column.

Syntax:

```
_pcolno = <nExp>
```

The value of _pcolno must be between 0 and 255 and may include a fraction. The default is 0. Use it to place the next expression you are printing with ? and ?? where you want it on the line, as an alternative to using the AT option. _pcolno has no effect on printing with @ . . . SAY.

If you set _wrap to .F., you may set _pcolno to a value less than the current print position to create an overstrike effect.

The _pcolno value affects all streaming output, including output to the console, the SET ALTERNATE file, a file designated by SET PRINTER TO FILE and the TO options of the LIST and DISPLAY commands. Unlike PCOL(), it changes as long as data is being output, even if SET PRINTER is OFF.

_pcopies

Specifies the number of copies of a printjob to print.

Syntax:

```
_pcopies = <nExp>
```

The value of nExp may be from 1 to 32,767. The _pcopies variable works only with PRINTJOB . . . ENDPRINTJOB. If it is set to more than 1, PRINTJOB spools the job to the hard disk, then sends it to the printer <nExp> times. There is no reevaluation of dBASE expressions, so you cannot give different numbers to the different copies within the job.

_pdriver

Specifies the printer driver to use.

Syntax:

```
_pdriver = <cExp>
```

You must install printer drivers using the Windows Print Manager. The value of _pdriver for an installed driver is a character string with two parts separated by a comma, such as "HPPLC,HPLaserJet IIP". The first part is the filename of the Windows driver file. The second is the name given to the printer in WIN.INI. Rather than specifying a different driver by changing the value of _pdriver, you will probably find it easier to use CHOOSEPRINTER() or the Printer Setup option of the File menu to open the Printer dialog box.

The default value of _pdriver is the driver name of the printer you specify as the default printer using the Windows Print Manager. Until you specify a default printer, _pdriver is an empty string.

_peject

Specifies when the printer ejects a page.

Syntax:

```
_peject = "BEFORE"¦"after"¦"both"¦"none"
```

Only the weight of the dead hand of the past explains why "BEFORE" is the default setting of _peject. If you have a PostScript printer or a page printer such as a laser printer, the last page will not print unless you change the setting to "after". Setting it to "both" simply wastes paper by feeding a blank page before starting to print. You will not want to set it to "none" unless you enjoy having to take your printer off line after each job to feed the last page.

The _peject setting works with PRINTJOB . . . ENDPRINTJOB and will not affect printing that does not use those commands.

See EJECT, PRINTJOB.

_pepage

Specifies the last page to print.

Syntax:

```
_pepage = <nExp>
```

Use _pepage with _pageno and _pbpage to print only part of a job, such as to replace pages the dog ate. If the portion you do not need to print following _pepage is long, consider putting code in your program or report that issues the CANCEL command when _pageno is larger than _pepage. This stops the program run when you have printed all you need and saves the time the program or report would require to run to completion.

The value of _pepage may be from 1 to 32,767. The default value is 32,767. The value of _pepage must equal or exceed _pageno and _pbpage for anything to print.

_pform

Specifies a print form file.

Syntax:

```
_pform = <cExp>
```

The default for _pform is an empty string. <cExp> is the name of a print form, PRF, file containing print settings, including the values of all the system variables starting with _p, except _pcolno, _plineno and _pform. When you set _pform to the name of a PRF file, the values from the file are assigned to the system variables and control the printing.

You create a PRF file when you create or modify labels or a report and elect to save the print form settings to a file. Annoyingly, the generated labels and reports do not remember that the settings have been saved. You must set _pform to the name of the saved file to put the settings in effect before you issue a LABEL FORM or REPORT FORM command.

_plength

Sets the output page length.

Syntax:

```
_plength = <nExp>
```

The _plength setting sets the length of a page, in lines. By default it is 66, or 63 if you have a laser printer installed as the default. The value may range from 1 to 32,767. If your reports creep up or down the page, using a continuous-paper printer, or print with extra pages of a few lines using a page printer, suspect the _plength setting. Many laser printers require a _plength of 60 to print properly.

See _padvance.

_plineno

Sets or returns the line number for streaming output.

Syntax:

```
_plineno = <nExp>
```

The <nExp> value, by default 0, may be from 0 to _plength -1, and may contain a fractional part. Like _pcolno, _plineno works on all streaming output. Unlike PROW(), it tracks streaming output even when SET PRINTER is OFF.

See _padvance, _pcolno.

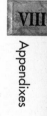

_ploffset

Sets the page left offset.

Syntax:

```
_ploffset = <nExp>
```

By default, the page left offset is 0. You may set _ploffset to a number from 0 to 254, which may include a fraction, or use SET MARGIN which does the same thing.

The _ploffset setting does not affect output to the display or files. It is provided to simplify dealing with paper that is slightly out of alignment in the printer. The _ploffset number and the _lmargin number are added together, _lmargin beginning where _ploffset ends. Other print settings such as _pcolno, _rmargin, and _indent are relative to _lmargin. Changing the _ploffset value does not require attention to any of the others.

Unfortunately, you cannot give _ploffset a negative value to assist in using a standard margin setting on nonstandard paper.

_porientation

New, sets the direction of printing.

Syntax:

```
_porientation = "PORTRAIT"¦"landscape"
```

The _porientation variable is provided for those printers that can print in either of two directions 90 degrees apart. The default is "PORTRAIT", meaning to print on standard letter paper so the reader holds it vertically. The alternative, "landscape", directs that printing be sideways across the long dimension of the paper. If landscape is selected for a printer that does not support landscape printing, the setting stays in portrait mode.

Changing _porientation resets the _plength setting.

_ppitch

Sets or returns the printing pitch.

Syntax:

```
_ppitch = "DEFAULT"¦"pica"¦"elite"¦"condensed"
```

The default setting of _ppitch, "DEFAULT", is in effect when dBASE for Windows starts up, and before it sends any codes to the printer. If you change _ppitch to one of the other values, dBASE sends codes appropriate to the printer driver to change the pitch, or horizontal width of characters, to 10 per inch ("pica"), 12 per inch ("elite"), or approximately 17 per inch ("condensed").

Do not reset _ppitch to "default". dBASE allows you to do so, but sends nothing to the printer. The previous setting remains in effect, but _ppitch now returns "DEFAULT", depriving you of the capability of learning what the current pitch is.

Settings such as _pcolno take account of the current _ppitch setting.

_pquality

Determines whether printing is in letter-quality mode.

Syntax:

```
_pquality = <lExp>
```

The default for _pquality is false, specifying draft-quality printing. The _pquality setting is intended for dot-matrix printers that can print a line either in a single pass or in two passes. The two-pass method looks better but takes longer. The _pquality setting has no effect on PostScript or laser printers.

In particular, if your printer is a page printer with insufficient memory to hold a full page of graphics, you cannot use _pquality to insist that Windows send it the characters as characters of its native font. You must select a printer-based font or Windows will send the commands to build the characters in the selected font dot by dot, overrunning the printer's memory and printing nothing.

_pspacing

Specifies spacing of lines.

Syntax:

```
_pspacing = <nExp>
```

The _pspacing variable may be set to 1, 2 or 3. It disregards any fractional parts of <nExp>. As specified by <nExp>, the result is single, double or triple spacing of all streaming output, including output to the display, ALTERNATE file and the like.

_rmargin

Sets or returns the right margin.

Syntax:

```
_rmargin = <nExp>
```

The value of _rmargin, by default 79, must be a minimum of max(_lmargin, _lmargin+_indent)+1 and a maximum of 255. The _rmargin setting is effective only when _wrap is true.

See _alignment, _indent, _lmargin.

_tabs

Sets tab stops.

Syntax:

```
_tabs = <cExpTabList>
```

The format for <cExpTabList> is a delimited series of ascending numbers separated by commas, such as "5,10,20,49.6,73.2". A tab is set at each number, which may be fractional. Any tab character, chr(9), in the data printed by ? or ?? is expanded to the number of spaces needed to reach the next tab stop.

Although the default value of _tabs is an empty string, dBASE acts as though a tab were set at each multiple of 8.

_updated

New, provides a way to reset UPDATED().

Syntax:

```
_updated = <lExp>
```

The UPDATED() function returns .T. if any of the active GETs have been changed since activated. The _updated system variable gives you a way to reset the value. You are entitled to wonder why the UPDATED() function, a new part of the language with dBASE for Windows, was not discarded when the _updated variable, which accomplishes the same thing with the advantage of allowing you to change it, was created.

_wrap

Enables wrapping of text between margins.

Syntax:

```
_wrap = <lExp>
```

By default, _wrap is false. Set it to true to enable _rmargin and all operations that depend on a fixed width for ?or ?? output, such as _alignment or simply wrapping text within the margins with ??, saving ? to start a new paragraph.

When _wrap is true, streaming output is buffered until the current printing line is completed. You may need to follow your text with ? to flush the buffer.

Keypress Values Reference

By Jay Parsons

The dBASE functions INKEY(), LASTKEY(), and READKEY() return numeric values for keys that are pressed by the user. The reference lists the values in two orders: by name, and by value returned. The INKEY() and LASTKEY() values are the same and are listed together. When the user clicks the mouse to exit a form, however, LASTKEY() returns 26 and :INKEY() returns –100.

READKEY() returns values only for those keys that may be used to exit from full-screen editing commands. The letters, numbers, and other printing characters are omitted. They do not have LASTKEY() or READKEY() values. Their INKEY() values are their ASCII values and are listed in Appendix F.

Like the Shift key, the Ctrl and Alt keys create shift states when the user presses them along with another key such as A. There is no difference between Ctrl+A and Ctrl+a or between Alt+5 and Alt+%. If you press the Shift key as well as Ctrl or Alt and another key, dBASE disregards the Shift key. dBASE also does not recognize key combinations such as Ctrl, Alt, plus another key. Some computers use Ctrl+Alt combinations with other keys to do such things as control keyboard clicking, and as you are aware Ctrl+Alt+Del causes Windows to ask you whether you wish to reboot.

Understanding Keypress Values

The dBASE functions INKEY(), LASTKEY(), and READKEY() return numeric values for keys pressed by the user. This appendix lists the values returned for each nonprinting keypress. This appendix does not include the values returned by INKEY() for standard printing characters with ASCII values such as the letters of the alphabet, digits, and punctuation characters. The INKEY() function returns the ASCII code, as listed in Appendix F, for each printing character.

The LASTKEY() and READKEY() functions are inapplicable to the characters listed in Appendix F. They return values only for the nonprinting keypresses that cause an exit from a full-screen editing command or from an edit of a dBASE for Windows form object.

This appendix lists the returned values in two orders. Table C.1 lists the values by the common name of the keypress, giving the INKEY() and READKEY() values in separate columns. Many of the READKEY() values are listed blank, indicating that there is no READKEY() value applicable to that keypress. The LASTKEY() value is always the same as the INKEY() value, so one column of table C.1 is used for both, but LASTKEY() returns a value only for a key that also has values in the READKEY() columns.

Understanding Keypress Values

The Ctrl and Alt keys, like the Shift keys, create shift states. Pressing any of Ctrl, Alt, or Shift creates no keypress value alone. Each of them modifies the keypress value of another key pressed at the same time. There are four different keypress values associated with any of the standard keys. Pressing A alone creates the lowercase a, of which the ASCII and INKEY() value is 97 as shown in Appendix F. Pressing A and Shift together creates Shift+A or an uppercase A, with an ASCII and INKEY() value of 65. Pressing A and Ctrl together creates Ctrl+A, with an INKEY() value of 1 as shown in table C.1 and, since many Ctrl+character combinations have ASCII values, also as shown in Appendix F. Pressing A and Alt together creates Alt+A, with an INKEY() value of –435 as shown in table C.1. Alt+character combinations have no ASCII values and are not included in Appendix F.

If you press the Shift key as well as either Ctrl or Alt and a third key, the Shift key is disregarded. Pressing Ctrl and Alt together while pressing another key has no meaning to dBASE.

Using Keypresses by Name

In the following table, two values are given for READKEY(). If the data has not been changed, the first value applies. If the data has been changed, the second value, equal to the first plus 256, is returned. If one or more columns are blank for any key, there is no corresponding value.

Differences in keyboards require dBASE to leave some unsupported keypresses that may be possible on your keyboard, and other keys found on all keyboards have no BIOS scan code to permit recognition by dBASE. Pressing keys such as NumLock, ScrollLock, F11 and F12, and other unsupported keys, if any INKEY() value returns at all, returns the value –32,000.

Some key combinations are intercepted by Windows and never reach dBASE. For these, the effect is given in place of an INKEY() value. There is one difference between the value returned by INKEY() and LASTKEY(), as indicated in the last line of table C.1. If you click the mouse, INKEY() returns –100. If the mouse click closed a form, such as a double-click on the form's system menu button, LASTKEY() returns the value 26.

Table C.1
Keypresses by Common Names

Keypress Name	INKEY() LASTKEY() value	READKEY() if no change	READKEY() if change
Alt+0	–452		
Alt+1	–451		
Alt+2	–450		
Alt+3	–449		
Alt+4	–448		
Alt+5	–447		
Alt+6	–446		
Alt+7	–445		
Alt+8	–444		
Alt+9	–443		
Alt+A	–435		
Alt+B	–434		
Alt+C	–433		
Alt+D	–432		
Alt+E	–431		

continues

Table C.1, Continued
Keypresses by Common Names

KeypressINKEY() LASTKEY() Name	value	READKEY() if no change	READKEY() if change
Alt+F	–430		
Alt+G	–429		
Alt+H	–428		
Alt+I	–427		
Alt+J	–426		
Alt+K	–425		
Alt+L	–424		
Alt+M	–423		
Alt+N	–422		
Alt+O	–421		
Alt+P	–420		
Alt+Q	–419		
Alt+R	–418		
Alt+S	–417		
Alt+T	–416		
Alt+U	–415		
Alt+V	–414		
Alt+W	–413		
Alt+X	–412		
Alt+Y	–411		
Alt+Z	–410		
Alt+F1	–30		
Alt+F2	–31		

KeypressINKEY() Name	LASTKEY() value	READKEY() if no change	READKEY() if change
Alt+F3	–32		
Alt+F4	Exits dBASE for Windows		
Alt+F5	–34		
Alt+F6	–35		
Alt+F7	–36		
Alt+F8	–37		
Alt+F9	–38		
Alt+F10	–39		
Alt+Esc	Switches to next application		
Alt+Tab	Switches to last application		
Alt+Enter	–487		
Alt+Del	7		
Alt+grey*	–458		
Alt+grey	–457		
Alt+‘	–404		
Alt+-	–404		
Alt+=	–439		
Alt+[	–409		
Alt+]	–407		
Alt+\	–408		
Alt+;	–441		
Alt+’	–461		

continues

Table C.1, Continued
Keypresses by Common Names

Keypress Name	INKEY() LASTKEY() value	READKEY() if no change	READKEY() if change
Alt+,	–456		
Alt+.	–454		
Alt+/	–453		
Ctrl+0	–404		
Ctrl+1	–404		
Ctrl+2	–404		
Ctrl+3	–404		
Ctrl+4	0		
Ctrl+5	+404		
Ctrl+6	30		
Ctrl+7	–404		
Ctrl+8	–404		
Ctrl+9	–404		
Ctrl+A	1	2	258
Ctrl+B	2		
Ctrl+C	3	7	263
Ctrl+D	4	1	257
Ctrl+E	5	4	260
Ctrl+F	6	3	259
Ctrl+G	7		
Ctrl+H	8	0	256
Ctrl+I	9		
Ctrl+J	10	5	261

Keypress Name	INKEY() LASTKEY() value	READKEY() if no change	READKEY() if change
Ctrl+K	11	4	260
Ctrl+L	12	1	257
Ctrl+M	13	15 16 at beginning of APPEND	271
Ctrl+N	14		
Ctrl+O	15		
Ctrl+P	16		
Ctrl+Q	17	12	
Ctrl+R	18	6	262
Ctrl+S	19	0	256
Ctrl+T	20		
Ctrl+U	21		
Ctrl+V	22		
Ctrl+W	23	270	
Ctrl+X	24	5	261
Ctrl+Y	25		
Ctrl+Z	26		
Ctrl+F1	–10		
Ctrl+F2	–11		
Ctrl+F3	–12		
Ctrl+F4	Closes the active window		
Ctrl+F5	–14		

continues

Table C.1, Continued
Keypresses by Common Names

Keypress Name	INKEY() LASTKEY() value	READKEY() if no change	READKEY() if change
Ctrl+F6	Switches to next window		
Ctrl+F7	–16		
Ctrl+F8	–17		
Ctrl+F9	–18		
Ctrl+F10	–19		
Ctrl+Tab	Switches to next window		
Ctrl+-	–403		
Ctrl+Backspace	–401		
Ctrl+[	27		
Ctrl+]	29		
Ctrl+\	28		
Shift+F1	Invokes Help		
Shift+F2	–21		
Shift+F3	–22		
Shift+F4	Tiles windows		
Shift+F5	Cascades windows		
Shift+F6	–25		
Shift+F7	–26		
Shift+F8	–27		
Shift+F9	–28		
Shift+F10	–29		
F2	–1		

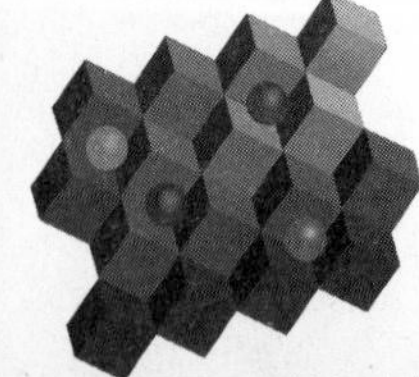

Keypress Name	INKEY() LASTKEY() value	READKEY() if no change	READKEY() if change
F3	–2		
F4	–3		
F5	–4		
F6	–5		
F7	–6		
F8	–7		
F9	–8		
F10	–9		
Shift+Del	–502		
Esc	27	12	
Tab	9		
Backtab	–400		
Backspace	127	256	
Enter	13	15 16 at beginning of APPEND	271
spacebar	2		
Home	26		
Up-arrow	5	4	260
PgUp	18	6	262
left–arrow	19	0	256
right–arrow	4	1	257
End	2		
down–arrow	24	5	261

continues

Table C.1, Continued
Keypresses by Common Names

KeypressINKEY() Name	LASTKEY() value	READKEY() if no change	READKEY() if change
PgDn	3	7	263
Ins	22		
Del	7		
mouse click	–100|26	15	271

Using Keypresses by Returned Value

Table C.2 lists the possible INKEY() values in numeric order with the keypresses causing them. LASTKEY() values are the same except for the mouse click.

Table C.2
Keypresses by Returned INKEY() Value

Returned value	INKEY() keys
–32000	Any of several unsupported keys
–502	Shift+Del
–501	Shift+Right-arrow
–500	Shift+Left-arrow
–461	Alt+'
–458	Alt+grey*
–457	Alt+grey
–456	Alt+,
–454	Alt+.
–453	Alt+/
–452	Alt+0

Returned value	INKEY() keys
–451	Alt+1
–450	Alt+2
–449	Alt+3
–448	Alt+4
–447	Alt+5
–446	Alt+6
–445	Alt+7
–444	Alt+8
–443	Alt+9
–441	Alt+;
–439	Alt+=
–435	Alt+A
–434	Alt+B
–433	Alt+C
–432	Alt+D
–431	Alt+E
–430	Alt+F
–429	Alt+G
–428	Alt+H
–427	Alt+I
–426	Alt+J
–425	Alt+K
–424	Alt+L

continues

Table C.2, Continued
Keypresses by Returned INKEY() Value

Returned value	INKEY() keys
–423	Alt+M
–422	Alt+N
–421	Alt+O
–420	Alt+P
–419	Alt+Q
–418	Alt+R
–417	Alt+S
–416	Alt+T
–415	Alt+U
–414	Alt+V
–413	Alt+W
–412	Alt+X
–411	Alt+Y
–410	Alt+Z
–409	Alt+[
–408	Alt+\
–407	Alt+]
–404	Alt+‘, Alt+—, Ctrl+0 to 3, Ctrl+5, Ctrl+7 to 9
–403	Ctrl+—
–402	Ctrl+Enter
–401	Ctrl+Backspace
–400	Backtab

Returned value	INKEY() keys
–100	mouse click
–39	Alt+F10
–38	Alt+F9
–37	Alt+F8
–36	Alt+F7
–35	Alt+F6
–34	Alt+F5
–33	Alt+F4
–32	Alt+F3
–31	Alt+F2
–30	Alt+F1
–29	Shift+F10
–28	Shift+F9
–27	Shift+F8
–26	Shift+F7
–25	Shift+F6
–24	Shift+F5
–23	Shift+F4
–22	Shift+F3
–21	Shift+F2
–19	Ctrl+F10
–18	Ctrl+F9
–17	Ctrl+F8

continues

Table C.2, Continued
Keypresses by Returned INKEY() Value

Returned value	INKEY() keys
–16	Ctrl+F7
–14	Ctrl+F5
–12	Ctrl+F3
–11	Ctrl+F2
–10	Ctrl+F1
–9	F10
–8	F9
–7	F8
–6	F7
–5	F6
–4	F5
–3	F4
–2	F3
–1	F2
0	Ctrl+4
1	Ctrl+A
2	Ctrl+B, End
3	Ctrl+C, PgDn
4	Ctrl+D, right-arrow
5	Ctrl+E, up-arrow
6	Ctrl+F
7	Ctrl+G, Alt+Del, Ctrl+Del, Del
8	Ctrl+H

Returned value	INKEY() keys
9	Ctrl+I, Tab
10	Ctrl+J
11	Ctrl+K
12	Ctrl+L
13	Ctrl+M, Enter
14	Ctrl+N
15	Ctrl+O
16	Ctrl+P
17	Ctrl+Q
18	Ctrl+R, PgUp
19	Ctrl+S, left-arrow
20	Ctrl+T
21	Ctrl+U
22	Ctrl+V, Ins
23	Ctrl+W
24	Ctrl+X, down-arrow
25	Ctrl+Y
26	Ctrl+Z, Home, LASTKEY() value for mouse click closing form
27	Ctrl+[, Esc
28	Ctrl+\ , F1
29	Ctrl+]
30	Ctrl+6
32	Spacebar
127	Backspace

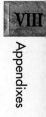

Table C.3 lists the possible READKEY() values in numeric order with the keypresses causing them.

Table C.3
Keypresses by Returned READKEY() Value

Value if no change	Value if change	READKEY() keys
0	256 256	Ctrl+H, Ctrl+S, left-arrow Backspace
1	257	Ctrl+D, Ctrl+L, right-arrow
2	258	Ctrl+A, Ctrl+left-arrow
3	259	Ctrl+F, Ctrl+right-arrow
4	260	Ctrl+E, Ctrl+K, up-arrow
5	261	Ctrl+J, Ctrl+X, down-arrow
6	262	Ctrl+R, PgUp
7	263	Ctrl+C, PgDn
12		Ctrl+Q, Esc
	270	Ctrl+W, Ctrl+End
15	271	Ctrl+M, Enter when completing field
16		Ctrl+M, Enter when at start of a record during APPEND
33	289	Ctrl+Home

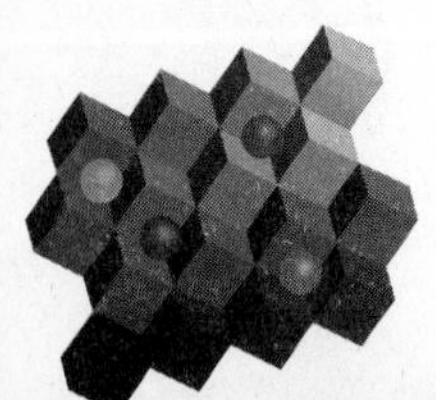

dBASE for Windows Initialization File Specifications

By Jay Parsons

The settings that determine how dBASE for Windows appears at startup, whether ESCAPE, EXACT, and the like are initially ON or OFF and similar issues are in the DBASEWIN.INI file. dBASE for Windows creates DBASEWIN.INI in the same directory as the dBASE for Windows executable files, which by default is C:\DBASEWIN\BIN. DBASEWIN.INI, although different and often larger, serves the purpose that CONFIG.DB served for dBASE for DOS versions.

Structure of DBASEWIN.INI

DBASEWIN.INI is a text file containing several sections. Each section has a title in square brackets, such as [CommandSettings]. Following the title are one or more items setting the options for that section. When you change one of the settings, dBASE writes the change to the file. If you then terminate and restart dBASE for Windows, the changed setting is read from DBASEWIN.INI and takes effect in the new session.

Some of the settings you can make in dBASE for Windows and save in DBASEWIN.INI are normally made as Windows Control Panel international settings. If you change such a setting in dBASE, the changed setting will be saved in DBASEWIN.INI and will override the Control Panel setting whenever you use dBASE. The Control Panel setting will continue to apply to other Windows applications you run.

You can edit DBASEWIN.INI manually—but you should not ordinarily do so. You or your users can make almost all changes to it easily by taking advantage of dBASE's built-in dialog boxes. Because they enable you to make selections (rather than typing), dialog boxes protect you from typing mistakes. Dialog boxes also spare you from memorizing or looking up the syntax of each option.

The Fonts and Install sections, Command and LDriver in the [CommandSettings] section and some items in the [FormDesigner] section cannot be edited except manually. Shareware INI-file editors, such as INIEDIT by Charles Kindel [CompuServe 71551,1455] are available to simplify the task, or you may use any text editor included, by typing **MODIFY COMMAND <path>DBASEWIN.INI** into the Command window, the dBASE for Windows program editor.

If you edit DBASEWIN.INI manually, you can insert comments by using a semicolon to start each line on which comments appear. You can add comment lines above the portions of the file that you need to change regularly explaining the alternatives, to save looking them up each time. You can also add a semicolon at the start of an existing line to inactivate it. You might want to do this to preserve the original setting while making a temporary change or testing a variation. Removing the semicolon restores the original setting.

Use care if editing DBASEWIN.INI manually, because you can easily introduce errors that may be difficult to track down. For example, if you edit the directory item in [CommandSettings] and follow the name of your chosen directory with a backslash, dBASE will not complain, but neither will it honor your selection. It will start up with the directory containing the executable files, by default \DBASEWIN\BIN, as the current directory. As with data in a table, prudence dictates backing up DBASEWIN.INI before making untested changes.

Using Two Or More Configurations

You might want to have two or more different versions of DBASEWIN.INI. One might specify a text editor and contain settings you find convenient for programming, while the other specifies the window sizes and settings you prefer while working with tables. Each version must retain the name DBASEWIN.INI for dBASE to recognize it, so your two versions must be in different directories. The steps to create a second version, in this example for programming, are shown in table D.1.

Table D.1 Creating an Additional DBASEWIN.INI (for Programming)

The Commands You Enter	The Effects of the Commands
MD C:\DBASEWIN\PROGRAMS	Creates a new directory. You can use any name you wish instead of "Programs," can specify a different path, or both.
CD C:\DBASEWIN\PROGRAMS	Moves to the new directory.
COPY ..\BIN\DBASEWIN.INI TO DBASEWIN.INI	Copies the original DBASEWIN.INI to the new directory.
MODIFY COMMAND DBASEWIN.INI	Allows editing of the copy. You can make any changes you want. Among them will often be the "directory" setting in the [CommandSettings] section, specifying the directory that will be current when the new version starts.
Ctrl+Esc	Opens the "Switch to" system menu option to allow switching tasks. You can also open this by clicking on the system menu button and selecting "Switch to."
Select the Program Manager and use the New option of its File menu to create a new dBASE for Windows program group.	Creates a Windows program group for the new configuration of dBASE for Windows.

continues

Table D.1, Continued
Creating an Additional DBASEWIN.INI (for Programming)

The Commands You Enter	The Effects of the Commands
Use the Properties option of the Program Manager File menu to give the new configuration a Description different from that of the original dBASE for Windows group. Leave the Working Directory item set to the directory containing dBASE executable files, usually \DBASEWIN\BIN.	You can also open the Program Item Properties dialog box by Alt+Enter. The new description allows you to distinguish the two dBASE for Windows group icons in the Program Manager window. You may later change the Description of the group icon of the original configuration to something different, such as "dBASE for Windows (Tables)" to make it easier to understand when to select which configuration.
Still in the Program Item Properties dialog box, in the Command Line text add **-cC:\DBASEWIN\PROGRAMS** after DBASEWIN.EXE.	Tells dBASE where to find the new DBASEWIN.INI.

After you have changed DBASEWIN.INI several times, you may wish you had a copy of the standard version to use as a base for different changes. To recreate the standard, remove DBASEWIN.INI from the DBASEWIN\BIN directory. The next time you start dBASE for Windows without a -c parameter on the command line, dBASE will recreate the standard DBASEWIN.INI file in its usual home directory, by default DBASEWIN\BIN. The created copy will lack your name and company from the original DBASEWIN.INI. You can add them to the [Install] section using a text editor.

Sections of DBASEWIN.INI

There may be more than a dozen sections in DBASEWIN.INI. dBASE adds sections, or items to sections, only when you use a dialog box or a SET command to change or reaffirm the relevant setting. The order in which the sections and items appear will

depend on when they were written to the DBASEWIN.INI file. Initially, DBASEWIN.INI contains only the [Fonts] section with four font items, the [CommandSettings] section with the _dbwinhome, directory and procedure items, and the [Install] section with your UserName and Company.

Some of the settings relating to the placement of windows contain four numbers, known as the X1, Y1, X2, and Y2 coordinates of the window. These numbers give the distance in pixels from the upper left corner of the desktop or screen to the corners of the window, in the order:

1. X1, Horizontal distance to the upper left corner
2. Y1, Vertical distance to the upper left corner
3. X2, Horizontal distance to the lower right corner
4. Y2, Vertical distance to the lower right corner

The Windows environment supports two major types of window, MDI (Multiple Document Interface) windows and non-MDI windows. The difference most significant to DBASEWIN.INI is that MDI windows like the Command window are restricted to appear only within the boundaries of a parent window. The parent of the Command window is the dBASE application main window, the dBASE Desktop. You can move the Command window around within the application main window, but you cannot move the Command window outside the Desktop or make it larger than the Desktop.

Non-MDI windows can appear anywhere on the screen. All the dBASE for Windows dialog boxes are non-MDI windows. You can move them outside the dBASE Desktop or make them overlap its borders. Because non-MDI windows can appear anywhere on the screen, their X1, Y1, X2 and Y2 coordinates are given with respect to the upper left corner of the screen. The X1, Y1, X2 and Y2 coordinates of dBASE MDI windows are given with respect to the upper left corner of the dBASE Desktop.

In the tables below listing the settings in the various sections of DBASEWIN.INI, the options are often 1 or 0, on or off or one of a short list of alternatives. In such cases, the default option is given in **boldface**, and in UPPERCASE if alphabetic, instead of being explicitly stated.

[Fonts]

The [Fonts] settings select fonts only for the STYLE options of the ? and ?? commands. They are retained for compatibility with dBASE IV. If you wish to run dBASE IV programs using the STYLE option in dBASE for Windows, you may have to manually edit this section of DBASEWIN.INI to select fonts available in Windows that correspond as closely as possible to the fonts you were using in dBASE IV. Each font is described in Windows format by the name of the typeface in mixed case, the size in points and the typeface family in uppercase, with the elements separated by commas. By default, there are four items in the [Fonts] section:

```
1=Times New Roman,12,ROMAN
2=Arial,10,SWISS
3=Arial,24,SWISS
4=Ariston,24,SCRIPT
```

[CommandSettings]

This section contains a number of settings, listed in table D.2, that are not ON|OFF selections between two alternatives. Except as indicated in the table, they correspond to SET . . . TO commands that may be entered in the Command window. They may also be set by use of the Desktop Properties dialog box. Only the first three, _dbwinhome, directory, and procedure, are present initially. The remainder are listed alphabetically, with the page of the Desktop Properties dialog box on which the dialog box setting for it appears. Many have related ON|OFF settings in the [OnOffCommandSettings] section. Where a setting such as Bell has both ON|OFF options and a value setting, the [CommandSettings] section holds the value setting, the one returned by the SETTO() function, while [OnOffCommandSettings] holds the on|off setting returned by the SET() function.

Table D.2
CommandSettings Settings

Setting	Page	Description
_dbwinhome	None	The dBASE home directory, the parent of the BIN, INCLUDE, and other directories containing executable and other files. By default, this is C:\DBASEWIN. Note that this is not the directory returned by the HOME() function. HOME() returns the directory holding DBASEWIN.EXE, by default C:\DBASEWIN\BIN, followed by a backslash "\". The _dbwinhome value cannot be changed.

Setting	Page	Description
directory	None	The current directory. By default, this is C:\DBASEWIN\SAMPLES. The directory may be changed by the CD command or in the Navigator window as well as by the SET DIRECTORY TO command.
procedure	None	The current procedure file or files. By default, the custom controls file C:\DBASEWIN\SAMPLES\ BUTTONS.CC
BELL	Data Entry	Sets bell frequency in Hertz and duration in ticks (1/18.2 sec). The command is SET BELL TO<frequency>, <duration>. Takes effect only if BELL in [OnOffCommandSettings] is ON.
COMMAND	None	The command dBASE executes on startup. There is neither a dialog box setting nor a SET . . . TO command to change this value; you must change it manually. dBASE interprets the first word following the equals sign as the name of a procedure and the following words as parameters, so the DBASEWIN.INI line COMMAND=Myprog Myval is interpreted as DO MYPROG WITH Myval.
CURRENCY	Country	The currency symbol, by default "$."
DATE	Country	The date format. The default is MDY, displaying as MM/DD/YY.
DBTYPE	Table	The default table type, **DBASE|Paradox**.

continues

Table D.2, Continued
CommandSettings Settings

Setting	Page	Description
DECIMALS	Programming	The number of decimals displayed, from 0 to 18, the default being 2. This setting affects the display of numbers only, not their internal accuracy.
DELIMITERS	Data Entry	The characters used to delimit data entry fields if DELIMITERS in [OnOffCommandSettings] is ON. The default delimiters are colons.
EDITOR	Files	The path and name of the editor used for text files, including programs. By default, this is an empty string and the internal editor is used.
IBLOCK	Table	The block size of new MDX index files, from 1 to 63. The block size will be 512 bytes multiplied by the Iblock value. The default is 1 for compatibility with dBASE IV, but the actual minimum block size is 1,024 bytes.
LDRIVER	None	The current language driver. There is neither a SET LDRIVER TO command nor a dialog box to change this value. You must change it manually, using one of the options described below. By default, the language driver is DB437US0, the driver for American English.
MARGIN	Programming	The printer left margin setting in units of average character width, by default 0.
Mark	Country	The character separating parts of dates, by default the slash, "/".

Setting	Page	Description
MBLOCK	Table	The block size of new DBT memo files, from 1 to 512, default 8. The block size will be 64 bytes multiplied by the Mblock value.
PATH	Files	The file search path. It will be displayed, and may be changed, in the Navigator and Catalog windows if, but only if, SearchPath in the [Navigator] section is set to 1.
POINT	Country	The decimal point symbol, by default the period, ".".
PRECISION	Programming	The precision of type N numbers, from 10 to 20, by default 16.
REFRESH	Table	Seconds after which shared data are updated. The default of 0 means the data are not updated.
REPROCESS	Table	Number of attempts to lock a file or record after one attempt fails. The default of 0 means no retry occurs.
SEPARATOR	Country	The character used to separate thousands from hundreds in numbers, by default the comma, ",".
TYPEAHEAD	Data Entry	The size of the keyboard type-ahead buffer, by default 50 characters.
WP	Files	The path and name of the memo field editor. By default, this is an empty string and the internal editor is used.

Although _dbwinhome is a public system variable that appears in the results pane when you type **DISPLAY MEMORY**, you cannot change it within dBASE. If you manually edit DBASEWIN.INI to remove the _dbwinhome setting or to set it to a nonexistent drive or directory, nothing changes and dBASE continues to report the original value of the _dbwinhome system variable. While at first a variable of this sort that is not read by dBASE and cannot be written seems useless, you can use it for your programs to find their way home.

The LDRIVER setting, if placed in the Settings section of DBASEWIN.INI, overrides the language driver specified in the IDAPI configuration utility. You do not need to concern yourself with language drivers in most cases. However, if you create a table for a European friend using an English language driver, accented characters will be sorted following "z," which is contrary to European practice. Change the driver either in DBASEWIN.INI or in IDAPI.CFG, in the latter case by using the IDAPI configuration utility, before creating the table. Table D.3 lists the available language drivers by the internal driver name, which is the name you must use in DBASEWIN.INI.

Table D.3
Language Drivers

Driver name	Language
DB437DE0	German
DB437ES1	Spanish
DB437FI0	Finnish
DB437FR0	French
DB437IT0	Italian
DB437NL0	Dutch
DB437SV0	Swedish
DB437UK0	British English
DB437US0	American English
DB850CF0	French Canadian
DB850DE0	German
DB850ES0	Spanish
DB850FR0	French
DB850IT1	Italian
DB850PT0	Portuguese
DB850NL0	Dutch
DB850SV1	Swedish
DB850UK0	British English

Driver name	Language
DB850US0	American English
DB860PT0	Portuguese
DB863CF1	French Canadian
DB865DA0	Danish
DB865NO0	Norwegian

The three digits following "DB" (for dBASE) in the name of each driver are the code page. These pages are defined by DOS for international versions. Code page 437 is used for English, 850 by most major Western European languages, 852 by Eastern European languages, 860 by Portuguese, 863 by French Canadian, and 865 for Nordic languages. In general and where possible, use the language driver of which the code page is the one intended for the language.

dBASE will select the driver that matches a table you place in use. You may need to ensure that the underlying DOS code page matches the one in use by dBASE for Windows, so that problems do not arise trying to save and retrieve files whose names contain characters not allowed by the DOS version.

[Install]

The [Install] section contains your UserName and Company as you typed them during the installation procedure. If you made a mistake, you may correct it by manually editing this section. The installation procedure requires you to insert a name. You may use the name of your department if appropriate. If you do not also enter a name for your Company, the copyright window that appears when dBASE for Windows starts will show your company as "Unknown."

[Catalog]

The Catalog settings in table D.4 control the appearance of the Catalog window that appears when you double-click a catalog icon in the Navigator.

Table D.4
Catalog Settings

Setting	Description
Associations	Whether the Associations item in the View menu is checked or not. 1 = checked, 0 = not.
LargeIconXSpacing LargeIconYSpacing SmallIconXSpacing SmallIconYSpacing DetailsIconYSpacing	The horizontal (X) and vertical (Y) spacing between icons, or vertical spacing between detail lines. Whether large icons, small icons or detail lines are displayed is selected from the View menu.
FileSort in the Catalog View menu. The less of the sort	The way in which icons are sorted for display window, selected from the Sort item of the "Untitled" icon always appears first, regard-order. 1 = by name 2 = by type and extension 3 = by size 4 = by date and time last created or changed
IconType	The current type of icons selected from the View menu. 1 = large icons 2 = small icons 3 = detail lines

[CommandWindow]

The CommandWindow settings in table D.5 control the appearance of the Command window. The last two, the PanePosition setting and the fonts, may be changed using the Command Window Properties dialog box. The others are changed by using the standard Windows methods of moving, maximizing, minimizing, opening or closing the window, or in the case of PaneRatio, by dragging and dropping the pane separator.

Table D.5
CommandWindow Settings

Setting	Description
Maximized	Whether the Command window is maximized and fills the entire Desktop. 1 = maximized, 0 = not. A 1 value is ignored if Minimized is also 1, and the window is minimized.

Setting	Description
Minimized	Whether the Command window is minimized to an icon only. 1 = minimized, 0 = not. If both Maximized and Minimized are 0, the window displays in the size specified by the Position setting.
Position	The Command window X1, Y1, X2, and Y2 coordinates effective if Maximized and Minimized are both 0. Since it is an MDI window, the coordinates are relative to the Desktop.
Open	Whether the Command window is open. 1 = open, 0 = closed.
PaneRatio	The percentage of the total Command window occupied by the input pane. The default is 50, giving each of the input and results panes equal halves of the total space.
PanePosition	The orientation of the input and results panes of the Command window. 0 = input pane is above results pane 1 = input pane is below result pane 2 = input pane is left of results pane 3 = input pane is right of results pane
InputPaneFont	The font in use in the input pane. The default is System 16 Bold.
ResultsPaneFont	The font in use in the results pane. The default is Terminal 12.

[ControlsWindow]

The [ControlsWindow] section contains the X1, Y1, X2, and Y2 coordinates of the Controls palette, whether it is Minimized (1 = minimized, 0 = not) and a Control setting. You change these by moving, minimizing or using the Control palette.

[Desktop]

The settings of the [Desktop] section are shown in table D.6. Except as noted in the table, you may change these from the Desktop Properties dialog box.

Table D.6
Desktop Settings

Setting	Page	Description
AddRecordsMode	Files	Whether records are added in form or columnar layout. 0 = Form, 1 = Columnar.
CurrentTab		The current page of the Desktop Properties dialog box. 0 = Country 1 = Table 2 = Data Entry 3 = Files 4 = Application 5 = Programming
EditRecordsMode	Files	Whether records are edited in browse, form or columnar layout. 0 = Browse 1 = Form 2 = Columnar
FormExpert		Which of the Form Expert dialog box radio buttons is pressed by default. 0 = Expert Assistance 1 = Blank Form
OlderFileTypes	Files	Whether the Older File Types checkbox is checked. 1 = checked, 0 = not.
Sessions	Files	Whether the Sessions checkbox is checked. 1 = checked, 0 = not.
SpeedBarPosition		The X1, Yl coordinates of the SpeedBar upper left corner. You change this by setting SpeedBarStyle to one of the floating styles, then moving the SpeedBar.

Setting	Page	Description
SpeedBarStyle		The location and orientation of the SpeedBar. 0 = horizontal, at top 1 = horizontal, at bottom 2 = vertical, at right 3 = vertical, at left 4 = horizontal, floating 5 = vertical, floating
StatusBar	Application	Whether the Status Bar checkbox is checked. 1 = checked, 0 = not.
StatusBarMsgFont	Application	The font used in the Status Bar. The default is MS Sans Serif, 11.

[Dialogs]

The [Dialogs] settings give the X1, Y1, X2, and Y2 coordinates of the dialog boxes listed in table D.7. The names of the dialog boxes are the same as the names of the settings but with spaces between the words. You change these by moving or resizing the dialog box.

Table D.7
Dialog Settings

Setting	Command to Display Dialog Box	Environment
FindRecords	**T**able|**F**ind Records (Ctrl+F)	Table Records view
FindText	**E**dit|**S**earch|**F**ind Text (Ctrl+F)	Command Window, editors
More	displays when Results pane is not tall enough for output	Command window
ReplaceRecords	**T**able|**R**eplace Records (Ctrl+R)	Table Records view
ReplaceText	**E**dit|**S**earch|**R**eplace Text (Ctrl+R)	Command window editors

[FormDesigner]

The [FormDesigner] section contains the Form Designer settings shown in table D.8. Except as noted in the table, you may change them from the Form Designer Properties dialog box.

Table D.8
Form Designer Settings

Name	Description
Controls Window	Whether the Controls palette is displayed when the Form Designer opens. 1 = displayed, 0 = not. This setting must be changed manually.
GridOneCharacter	Whether the grid is in units of a single character or in units of one or more pixels. A character grid is selected by choosing the Coarse grid setting in the Form Form Designer dialog box. Any other grid setting selects pixels. 1 = character, 0 = pixels.
GridPixels	The X, Y spacing of the grid in pixels, if GridOneCharacter is 0. The Fine and Medium grid setting radio buttons in the Form Designer create spacings of X=2, Y=3 and X=5, Y=7, respectively. The Custom radio button activates the spin boxes alllowing various spacings.
MouseRevertToPointer	Whether the mouse cursor reverts to ths standard arrow pointer after a control is placed on the form. If not, the control class remains selected, the mouse cursor remains in the shape of the icon for the control class and each click places another control of that class on the form. 1 = the mouse cursor reverts to a pointer, 0 = not.
ObjectProperties	Whether the Object Properties dialog box is displayed when the Form Designer opens. This must be changed manually. 1 = displayed, 0 = not.

Name	Description
ProcedureEditor	Whether the Procedure Editor is displayed when the Form Designer opens. This must be changed manually. 1 = displayed, 0 = not.
ShowGrid	Whether the grid is visible. 1 = visible, 0 = not.
ShowRuler	Whether the ruler is visible. 1 = visible, 0 = not.
SnapTo	Whether each control will snap to grid intersection when placed on the form. 1 = snaps, 0 = does not.

[MRU_Files]

This section, if it exists, contains two settings and the fully qualified names of up to as many Most Recently Used files as are specified by the MaximumSize setting. The file names are listed at the foot of the File menu.

You can set MaximumSize from the Application page of the Desktop Properties dialog box to any value from 3 to 7, the default being 5. Files are added as used, the name of each being preceded by a letter as in "a=c:\dbasewin\samples\animals.dbf." Any types of editable files selected by name or by icon, including text files, will be given a place in the list, but not index files placed in use, created or reindexed.

Once there are as many file entries as the MaximumSize setting allows, the next one used takes the place and letter in DBASEWIN.INI of the least recently used. The Order setting is always first in the section and might be "Order = bcdea," indicating that file b was most recently used, then c, and so forth. The names listed in the File menu appear in the same order as their letters in the Order setting.

[Navigator]

The Navigator settings control the appearance of the Navigator window at startup.

Table D.9
Navigator Settings

Setting Name	Description
Maximized	Whether the Navigator window is maximized and fills the entire Desktop. 1 = maximized, 0 = not maximized. A 1 value is ignored if Minimized is also 1, and the window is minimized.
Minimized	Whether the Navigator window is minimized to an icon only. 1 = minimized, 0 = not minimized. If both Maximized and Minimized are 0, the window displays in the size specified by the Position setting.
Position	The Navigator window X1, Y1, X2, and Y2 coordinates effective if Maximized and Minimized are both 0. Since it is an MDI window, the coordinates are relative to the Desktop.
Open	Whether the Navigator window is open. 1 = open, 0 = closed.
CustomFilesSkeletonList	The list of current skeletons, including DOS wild-card characters, for the Custom file type. The skeletons may be delimited by commas, semicolons, or spaces. The default is an empty string.
TablesFromDatabase	Whether the "Tables From Database" radio button, which appears only when IDAPI.CFG contains aliases of external databases, is selected. 1 = selected, 0 = not.
SearchPath	Whether the Use Supplemental Search Path check box in the Navigator Properties dialog box is checked. 1 = checked, 0 = not. The path itself is in the [CommandSettings] section.
LargeIconXSpacing LargeIconYSpacing SmallIconXSpacing	The horizontal (X) and vertical (Y) spacing between icons, or vertical spacing between detail lines.

Setting Name	Description
SmallIconXSpacing SmallIconYSpacing DetailsIconYSpcaing	Whether large icons, small icons, or detail lines are displayed is selected from the View menu.
FileSort	The way in which icons are sorted for display in the Navigator, selected from the Sort item of the View menu. The "Untitled" icon always appears first, regardless of the sort order. 1 = by name 2 = by type and extension 3 = by size 4 = by date and time last created or changed
IconType	The current type of icons selected from the View menu. 1 = large icons 2 = small icons 3 = detail lines

[OnOffCommandSettings]

This section contains the toggle settings omitted from the CommandSettings section. Except for CURRENCY, which takes the values LEFT|RIGHT, all values are on or off and each setting may be changed by a command of the form SET <setting> ON|OFF. In every case, the setting is a binary decision between two states only. The options for this section are given in table D.10, with the page of the Desktop Properties dialog box on which they appear. For the numeric or other values applicable when a setting is ON, see the [CommandSettings] section. For further information, see the SET command in Appendix A, the commands and functions reference.

Table D.10
OnOffCommandSettings

Setting	Page	Description
AUTOSAVE	Table	OFF|ON. Determines whether data is saved to disk each time a record changes.

continues

Table D.10, Continued
OnOffCommandSettings

Setting	Page	Description
BELL	Data Entry	ON|OFF. Determines whether the bell sounds. The tone is set in the CommandSettings section.
CENTURY	Country	OFF|ON. Overrides the Windows Control panel setting. Displays year in 4 digits if on, 2 if off.
CONFIRM	Data Entry	OFF, the default, requires Enter, arrow or click to move off a filled field. On moves when the field fills.
COVERAGE	Programming	OFF|ON. If on, a coverage file is created.
CUAENTER	Data Entry	ON|OFF. If ON, specifies that Enter key if pressed in a form performs as specified by Windows. If off, the key performs as in dBASE for DOS.
CURRENCY	Country	LEFT|RIGHT. Determines whether the currency symbol is left or right of the numeric value. The corresponding is SET CURRENCY LEFT|RIGHT.
DELETED	Table	ON|OFF. Determines whether records marked for deletion in dBASE tables are processed by the commands that can process entire tables. When DELETED is ON, records marked for deletion are not processed.
DELIMITERS	Data Entry	OFF|ON. Determines whether the delimiters specified in the CommandSettings section are used.
DESIGN	Programming	ON|OFF. Determines whether CREATE and MODIFY commands may be executed. Developers should turn this off in distributed applications if the users are not allowed to create or modify files.

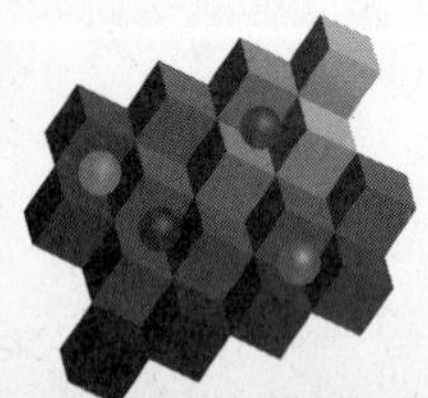

Setting	Page	Description
DEVELOPMENT	Programming	ON|OFF. Determines whether changed programs, etc. are recompiled when opened for execution. In the Desktop Properties dialog box, this is turned ON by checking the "Ensure Compilation" check box.
ESCAPE	Data Entry	ON|OFF. Determines whether pressing Esc interrupts programs.
EXACT	Table	OFF|ON. Determines rules for string comparisons. If OFF, strings will be considered a match if the string found starts with the one sought.
EXCLUSIVE	Database	OFF|ON. Determines whether tables are by default opened exclusive or shared.
FULLPATH	Environment	OFF|ON. If on, functions returning file names also return the path.
HEADINGS	Programming	ON|OFF. Determines whether field names are displayed by AVERAGE, DISPLAY, LIST, and SUM.
LDCHECK	Table	ON|OFF. If ON, a table opened will be checked for the language driver used to create it and that driver used to work with it.
LOCK	Table	Determines whether a shared table you use read-only may be changed by others. ON = no, OFF= yes.
NEAR	Table	OFF|ON. Determines whether record pointer goes to next record after a failed match. By default, it goes to EOF().
SAFETY	Programming	ON|OFF. If ON, requires confirmation before overwriting a file or ZAPping a table.
SPACE	Programming	ON|OFF. If ON, a space is inserted between ?|?? expressions separated by commas.

continues

Table D.10, Continued
OnOffCommandSettings

Setting	Page	Description
TALK	Environment	ON|OFF. Determines whether messages and assignment results are displayed in the Results pane.
TITLE	Environment	ON|OFF. Turns Catalog file title prompt on or off.

[ProgramEditor]

This section, if present, gives the X1, Y1, X2, and Y2 coordinates of the Editor window, as established by moving or resizing it.

[Query]

The only setting here is 1, if complex keys are displayed, 0 if not. The default is 1. This setting is made from the Query Designer Properties dialog box.

Installing dBASE for Windows

By Jay Parsons

The process of installing dBASE for Windows is simple, although providing the hardware it needs can be a significant problem. To install it from floppy disks, start Windows. Place Disk 1 in a floppy disk drive. Assuming the drive is drive A, execute the Program Manager **F**ile **R**un command and enter **A:install** as the command line. (If the disk is in drive B, substitute B for A throughout.)

After a small copyright window appears, the screen changes. A message box in the center asks you what kind of installation you want. A second box asks what directory to install dBASE in, a third asks you for your name and company, and that's it, except you need to be on hand for approximately half an hour to change disks and finally decide whether to install the dBASE group icons or read the README.TXT file, or both.

Hardware Requirements

You can run Windows on a system with an 80286 processor, but you cannot run dBASE. You must have an 80386 processor or better in an IBM-compatible computer.

The most limiting requirement to run dBASE is its appetite for memory. A system with 4 MB (something of a standard for new high-end systems) does not suffice; dBASE requires at least 6 MB. To get adequate performance—without the slowness of Windows as it creates countless swap files—8 MB of RAM is recommended. Additional memory improves performance in many cases.

The entire dBASE product requires at least 21.6 MB of hard disk space, plus 7 or 8 MB more for the sample programs. You can get limited relief, however, by moving some of the documentation files from your hard disk after installation.

You must have an EGA or better (VGA or SVGA) display adapter and a compatible monitor.

Software Requirements

The software needs of dBASE for Windows are less likely to be obstacles to your use of it. You most likely have all the supporting software you need.

You must have DOS, version 3.1 or later. You also must have Windows version 3.1 and run it in Enhanced mode. When a more advanced version of Windows is available, it will also support dBASE for Windows.

dBASE is certified to run on the networks in the following list. This does not mean, however, that dBASE will not run on other networks—simply that there is no assurance that it will run properly on other networks. The certified networks include the following:

- ✔ AT&T Stargroup 2.1a
- ✔ Banyan VINES 5.0
- ✔ DecNet Pathworks 4.1
- ✔ IBM LAN Server 3.0
- ✔ LANtastic 4.1
- ✔ Microsoft LAN MAN 2.1
- ✔ Microsoft Windows for Workgroups
- ✔ Novell NetWare 2.2, 3.11, 3.12, and 4.0

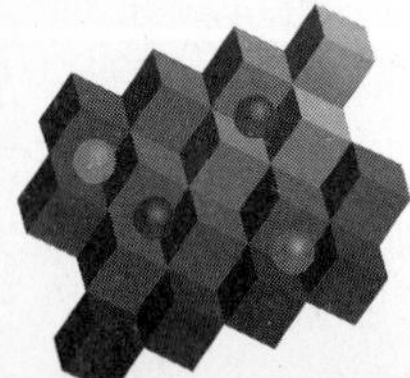

Performing Your Installation

First, make sure you have enough space on your hard disk for the dBASE installation. If necessary, temporarily save other applications on floppy disks or tape to release enough disk space for a complete installation. After the installation is complete, you can move the sample files, documentation files, or both to floppy disks to restore the space for your other applications.

You cannot use the sample or documentation files directly from the original disks on which Borland distributes dBASE. The files are compressed and must be decompressed by the installation procedure.

Insert Disk 1 in the appropriate disk drive, then start Windows and the installation process. If you have not yet started Windows, you can change the current drive to drive A or B (whichever holds dBASE Disk 1), and type **WIN INSTALL**. If Windows is not on the active path set with the DOS PATH command, include the appropriate drive and path before WIN.

If you have already started Windows, use the File, Run command of the Program Manager. In the Run dialog box (see fig. E.1), specify A:INSTALL or B:INSTALL, as appropriate to the floppy drive, as the command line.

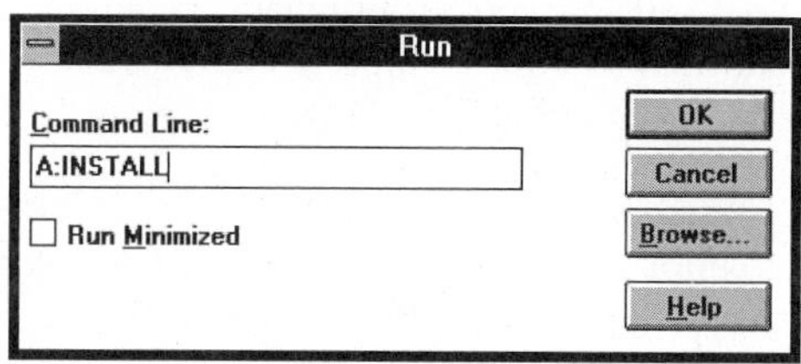

Figure E.1
The Run dialog box.

The first thing you should see is a small copyright notice introducing dBASE for Windows in the middle of your Program Manager Screen. It is followed by the screen clearing and being replaced by a dBASE for Windows screen with a dialog box (see fig. E.2) in the middle. The dialog box asks you to decide among three installation options, Complete, Minimum, or Custom.

If you have sufficient disk space, choose Complete. This will install the entire product. If you must conserve disk space, choose Minimum. This will install only the dBASE system files without the Sample files, Component builder, Tutors, or the Crystal Reports report generator. If you cannot complete the installation without removing files from your hard disk, select Exit to abort the installation. Choose Custom if your disk space is limited and you wish to include some, but not all, of these optional components. Another dialog box asks you to check the components to install.

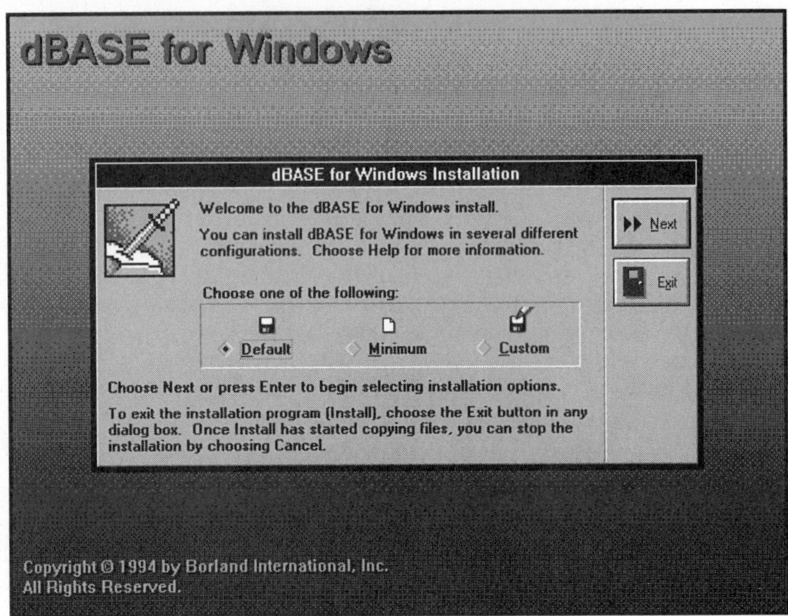

Figure E.2 Selecting the installation option.

You should also choose Custom if you have already installed the system files and are running the installation procedure to add one or more components you omitted previously. In this case, in the next dialog box uncheck the system files and any other components already installed.

When you decide on your installation and click on the Next button or press Enter, another dialog box asks you for the directory in which to install dBASE, as shown in figure E.3. By default, the directory is C:\DBASEWIN. The installation creates several directories. The actual executable files such as DBASEWIN.EXE will be placed in the \BIN subdirectory of the specified directory. By typing over the text, you may change the path to, or the drive or name of, the top-level dBASE for Windows directory.

The installation program then asks for your Name and Company. You need not give a Company, but must give a Name. It need not be your own name—if your employer owns the software it may be appropriate to insert the name of your department. The Name and Company you give appear on the copyright screen, which flashes briefly when you start dBASE. If you enter no Company, the copyright screen displays it as "Unknown."

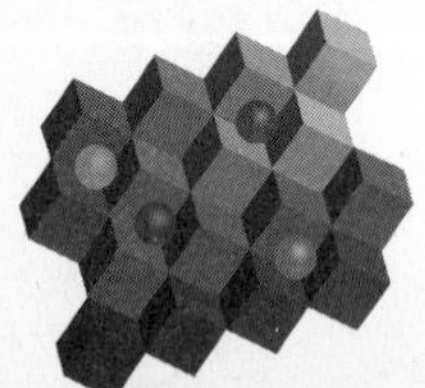

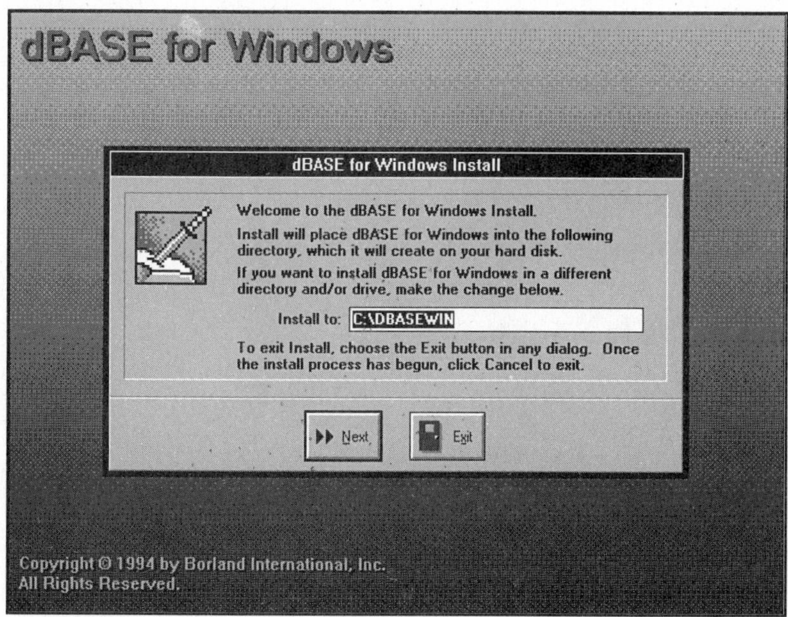

Figure E.3
Specifying the installation path for dBASE.

If you misspell your name or company name, you do not need to abort the install. You can find and change them later during the installation of DBASEWIN.INI, a text file in the DBASEWIN\BIN directory.

After setting your options, the installation process begins. The installation program shows a desert scene with an automobile dashboard. As the installation progresses, you are prompted to insert additional floppies as necessary. The automobile speedometer provides a very rough guide to the percentage of the total installation performed.

You might want to use the speedometer to guess when to go for coffee. If you don't see the automobile dashboard when you return, however, your Windows screen saver has probably become activated.

If you are not certain why your screen looks as it does, press a Shift key. If a screen saver has taken over, you will restore the screen. If not, you will at least not make the situation worse.

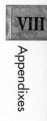

After all files have been copied, the install program prompts you for permission to add the dBASE group and icons to the Program Manager. In most cases, you will want to grant permission by clicking the Next button or by pressing Enter. You can change the group and icons later if you find them unsatisfactory.

If you Skip installing the dBASE group and icons or Exit, you can add the groups and items later using the File, New option of the Windows Program Manager.

Installation Effects

Installing dBASE creates the following directories on your hard drive:

- DBASEWIN\, the top directory, contains README.TXT, which contains documentation that missed the printing date of the manuals, and INSTALL.RPT, a text file that lists the changes the installation program made to WIN.INI and DBASEWIN.INI.
- DBASEWIN\BIN contains the main program files, including the executable file DBASEWIN.EXE, the debugger, the IDAPI configuration utility, the report writer, the DLLs they call, the help file, and the DBASEWIN.INI file.
- DBASEWIN\UTILITY contains conversion utility files.
- DBASEWIN\INCLUDE contains header files for use with dBASE programs. These text files, with the extension H, define constants, external functions of the Windows API, and other items that you might or might not find useful.
- DBASEWIN\SAMPLES holds the sample tables, programs, and related files.
- DBASEWIN\SAMPLES\EXTERN contains dBASE, C++, and related files creating an example system for dBASE to interface with DLLs. The EXTERN statement in dBASE for Windows allows calling DLL functions with simple variables, but the system created here allows calling DLL functions with values that permit the DLL functions to manipulate dBASE variables.
- DBASEWIN\SAMPLES\BUSINESS contains a sample dBASE business application with all forms and programs necessary to examine and process employee data.
- DBASEWIN\SAMPLES\MUSIC contains a sample dBASE music-store application.

In addition, the installation process adds lines to WIN.INI, the Windows configuration file in the WINDOWS directory, telling it where to find the DBASEWIN.INI file and the IDAPI.CFG file.

Successful installation places your name and company in the DBASEWIN.INI file and adds the DBASEWIN.GRP file to PROGMAN.INI. Whether or not installation succeeds, dBASE creates a file, INSTALL.TXT, in the installation directory, by default C:\DBASEWIN. The INSTALL.TXT file says whether or not installation succeeded and summarizes the files created.

Windows Basics for First-Time Users

By Jay Parsons

Using Windows has the great advantage over using DOS in that many actions are available through simple mouse clicks. You will quickly learn how the windows created by Windows and their various controls, including push buttons, check boxes, and spin boxes, work. You will then better understand how an application you create under dBASE for Windows will act, even if you have never used dBASE for Windows before. For more information about control objects, see Chapter 6 "Developing Forms."

Windows for some purposes distinguishes windows by what window, if any, "owns" them. The main dBASE for Windows window is an application window, a main window, and a parent window. The windows that belong to dBASE, such as the Command and Navigator windows, are child windows of the main window.

Table F.1 lists Windows' reserved key combinations. You should avoid use of these key combinations in your dBASE applications.

Table F.1
Windows Reserved Key Combinations

Keystrokes	Effect
Ctrl+Esc	Opens the list of running applications. This is the same as clicking Switch To on the control menu of an application main window.
Alt+Esc	Switches To next application in list. When used after Alt+Tab or Shift+Alt+Tab, returns to the original application.
Alt+Tab	Switches To previous application, the one last used. Holding down Alt while repeatedly pressing Tab cycles forward through all running applications.
Shift+Alt+Tab	Same as Alt+Tab, but cycles backward.
Alt,Spacebar	Opens control menu of an open dialog box, or if none, of the application.
Alt,Hyphen	Opens control menu of the active child window.
Print Screen	Copies screen to Clipboard. Does not work for non-Windows applications running in graphics mode.
Alt+Print Screen	Copies active window to Clipboard.
Alt+F4	Closes the active dialog box, if any, or quits the application.
Ctrl+F4	Closes the active group or child window.
Ctrl+F6	Activates (gives focus to) the next available window. This may be used to cycle among the open windows.

Using The Mouse

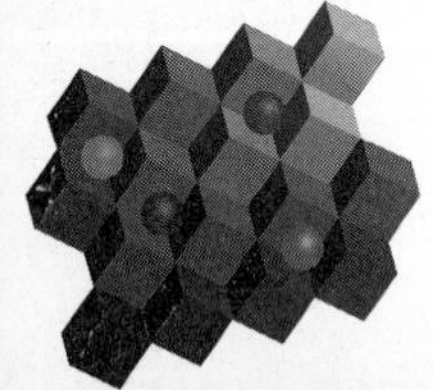

Using Windows and dBASE for Windows without a mouse is possible, although awkward. This book assumes you have a mouse or other pointing device. If you do not have one, you'll want to add one to your system soon. You will quickly save more time than the cost in the first few hours of running Windows and Windows applications. This book uses the term "mouse" to include trackballs and similar pointing devices that work like the mouse.

Windows itself requires only a one-button mouse. On a two- or three-button mouse, the left button is used for almost all mouse actions. You can perform all actions by moving the mouse as required and by a press, a click, a double-click, or a drag-and-drop.

- ✔ A *press* is a press of the mouse button without releasing it.
- ✔ A *click* is a quick press and release of the mouse button.
- ✔ A *double-click* is two clicks in close succession. You may adjust the time interval from the Control Panel.
- ✔ A *drag-and-drop* is the action of moving the mouse to a position, pressing the button, moving the mouse to another position, then releasing the button at the new position.

Almost all mice today have two or three buttons. dBASE for Windows assumes your mouse has at least two buttons. This book refers to actions requiring the second mouse button as if it were the "right" button. Using the left button as the primary button is customary for right-handed users of a standard mouse. Trackballs may have the buttons top and bottom. Left-handed users can reverse the sense of the buttons from the Windows Control Panel to designate the button under the left index finger as the primary button.

Regardless of the design, orientation, and configuration of your pointing device, "click," "double-click," and "drag-and-drop" mean you should use the primary button. "Right-click" and "right double-click" require you to use the other button of a two-button device, or the secondary, usually opposite, button of a three-button device.

dBASE for Windows does not make use of the third mouse button, the "middle" button. Your programs may make use of this button. dBASE supports an "OnMouseMiddleButtonDown" event and similar properties that enable your programs to detect the use of the middle button and to respond as you prescribe. If you are unsure whether all systems on which your programs will run have a three-button mouse, you should provide some other means to perform the middle-button actions. Many programmers decide that providing one more way to perform the same action is not worth the trouble and ignore the middle button.

Understanding the Client Area of a Window

Figure F.1 shows the dBASE for Windows Command window. Each half of the Command window has two principal areas. The interior, or see-through portion of the window, is the *client area.*

Figure F.1
The Command window.

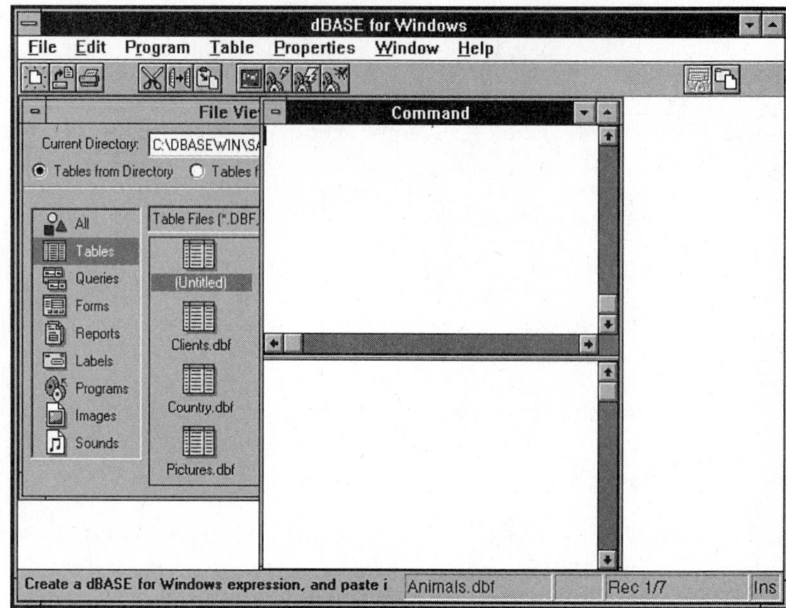

The client area of a window is where the main business of a window takes place. In the Results half of the Command window, the job of the client area is to show the results of the dBASE commands you execute.

Think of the client area of a window as a small framed piece of glass resting on a large sheet of paper. If your image of paper brings up thoughts like "easily ripped" and "difficult to erase," make the underlying sheet pure white Carrera marble. Whatever your choice of mental materials, do imagine two surfaces—the glass and the surface visible through it—because dBASE for Windows can write on either one.

To see the problems that can arise from writing on the wrong surface, click on the Command window to select it. Type **CLEAR**, press Enter, type **@ 1,10 SAY "Glass"**, and then press Enter. Now type **@ 1,10 SAY ""** and press Enter. Finally, type **?? "Paper"** and press Enter. The word `Glass` appears in the Results window. Place the mouse cursor on an arrow button at either end of the Results window's bottom scroll bar. Press the primary mouse button and observe. The scroll bar moves the glass over the paper. This uncovers the text, `Paper`, written with the ?? command. The text written with the **@ . . . SAY** command stays in the same position relative to the upper left corner of the Results window, as if written on the glass. If you use the **@ . . . SAY . . . GET** command with coordinates that are too low or too far right, the text will be invisible. Scrolling the glass around over the paper will not uncover it. You might fail to realize that the output of **@** is even there, unless you think to maximize the window.

To run your dBASE for DOS applications, maximize the Command window. When writing for dBASE for Windows, do not use @ unless you define and activate a custom window of sufficient size to show the output.

Taking Advantage of the Window Frame

The *frame*, or *non-client area* of a window in Windows jargon, contains the parts you use to manipulate the window itself. You have already used the horizontal scroll bar at the bottom of the Results half of the Command window to move the window over the surface beneath it. You probably noticed that the *thumb*, the little box within the scroll bar, moved in the direction you scrolled. Its position is a gauge of where the window is with respect to the limits of the surface. If the thumb is at the left edge of the scroll bar, the window is at the left edge of the surface. The vertical scroll bar at the right of the client area works the same way, but moves the window from top to bottom of the surface. To move the window quickly, drag the thumb itself.

Not all windows have scroll bars, but in those that do, the scroll bars always act the same way. You cannot clear the Command half of the Command window directly, but you can scroll vertically downward to present a clear surface. Or, you can scroll upward to see the *history*, the list of commands most recently executed. This is often helpful in figuring out why what happened did.

Scrolling upward in the Command window provides an easy way to repeat one or more commands. Scroll up to uncover the desired command, click at its end to place the cursor there, and press Enter to execute the command again. To reissue a set of commands, mark them as a block with the mouse by dragging over them, and then press Enter (or click the Run icon on the SpeedBar). This is particularly useful if you issue a set of commands and then realize that you forgot to put a table in the correct order, or to adjust some setting, and have to start over.

At the top of a window is its *title bar*, which usually contains the title of the window. When the window gets or loses the focus, the title bar background changes color. When you click on the Command window to give it focus, a cursor appears in its client area to provide an additional cue that what you type will go to that window.

The title bar has other uses. To move the window as a whole around the screen, place the mouse cursor (usually an arrow) somewhere on the title bar and drag the title bar to where you want it. When you release the mouse button, the window stays at its new location.

The three square boxes at the ends of the title bar are also controls. The one with a "—" in it at the left end is the control menu button. Clicking the control menu button normally shows a menu containing options for the entire window. Figure F.2 shows the control menu for the dBASE for Windows main window.

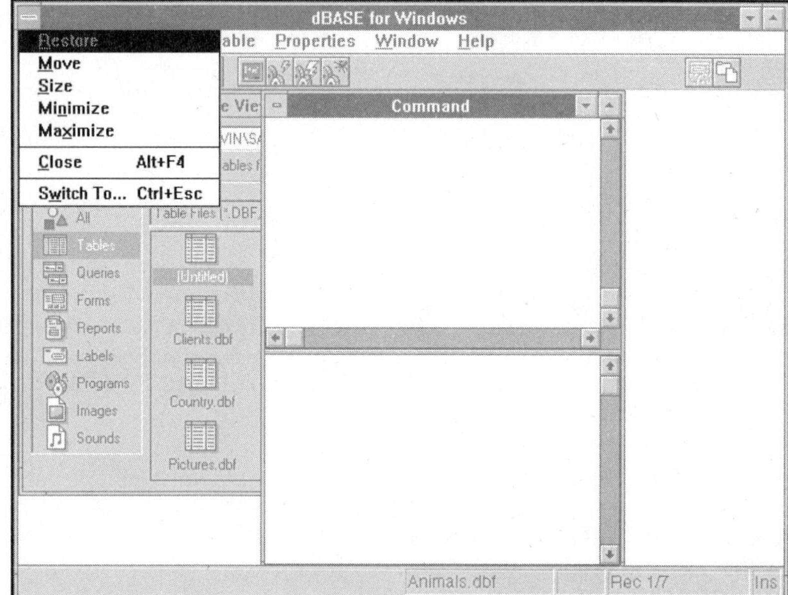

Figure F.2 The control menu of the dBASE main window.

The following are the control menu options available for an application's main window:

- ✔ **Restore.** This option returns the window to its previous size and position when neither maximized nor minimized.
- ✔ **Move.** This option changes the cursor to a four-headed arrow. You can then use the arrow keys to move the window as a whole. Press Enter to end the move at the new position.
- ✔ **Size.** This option is similar to Move, except that the top left corner of the window remains anchored. The lower right corner moves to change the window size.
- ✔ **Minimize.** This option makes the window invisible and substitutes an icon representing the application at the lower left of the screen.
- ✔ **Maximize.** This option expands the window to fill the entire screen.
- ✔ **Close.** This option closes the window and terminates the application.

- ✔ **Switch To.** This option enables you to leave dBASE for Windows or whatever application you are executing and run another of the currently open applications.
- ✔ A control menu may contain the paths and names of files recently used, to facilitate reopening them for additional work. Clicking on a displayed file name selects and opens it.

Double-clicking the control menu box is the same as choosing Close from the control menu. The boxes at upper right do the same thing as choosing Minimize, Maximize, or Restore from the control menu. Clicking the box with a single downward-pointing triangular arrow minimizes the window to an icon. Clicking the box with a single upward-pointing triangular arrow maximizes the window. A maximized main window normally fills the entire screen. A maximized child window is limited to a portion of the main window, usually either the client area or, as in dBASE for Windows, the client area plus the SpeedBar. When you maximize a window, the Maximize box changes to triangles pointing both up and down. Clicking the box when it has this appearance is equivalent to choosing Restore.

The control menu of a child window does not contain the Switch To option. It usually contains the Move option and may contain any of the others.

Application Sessions

You should carefully distinguish between the Minimize and Close options. A minimized application remains in memory, and if it is doing something such as printing a report or indexing a large file, continues to do it. When you double-click the minimized icon or use Switch To from another application to return to the minimized application, its windows reappear as they were before it was minimized and you can continue your work.

If you close the main window of an application, the application terminates, and Windows releases it from memory. If you then restart the application from its group icon, you start a new session from the default directory with all files closed and all default settings in effect.

If you think you have resumed a minimized session but find your files closed and settings and variables gone, look for a minimized icon. You might have started a new session by mistake. To avoid losing your work, you should close the new session and resume the former session.

You can use the frame of a window to resize the window. You have learned how to resize a window by selecting the Size option from the system menu and using the arrow keys. It is usually more convenient to use the mouse to move a side or corner of the window directly. Move the mouse to any side or corner of the frame. Adjust its position slightly if necessary until the arrow cursor changes to a small arrow with two heads.

Then, drag the side or corner to another position, while the other sides remain fixed, and drop it where you wish. The window does not change until you drop the part you are moving. An outline showing where the new sides of the frame will be as you move the mouse helps you judge where to drop your dragged side or corner.

Windows Utilities

In addition to customizing the way the mouse works, the Windows Control Panel can be used to change your default screen colors and other settings. As with any other task, you can use it in the middle of a dBASE for Windows session.

The File Manager and the Clipboard are two other Windows utilities you frequently will wish to use from within dBASE.

The File Manager is in some ways more flexible than the dBASE Navigator. It is not restricted to dBASE-related files and enables you to select several files at once for copying, moving, or deleting.

The Clipboard enables you to move data within or between Windows applications, or, within limits, to and from non-Windows applications. When you use the Cut, Copy, and Paste controls on the dBASE for Windows SpeedBar, you are using the Windows Clipboard. You also can use the Clipboard to paste data, such as a bitmap, from dBASE into another application, or vice versa. To move data from dBASE, use Cut or Copy to move the data to the Clipboard, and then start the other application and use Paste to insert the data into it.

The block of data moved by the Clipboard is *static.* The application to which it is moved obtains a copy. The source application may change the original and the target application may change the copy without either being aware of the other. You will learn about more sophisticated ways of exchanging data, Dynamic Data Exchange (DDE) and Object Linking and Embedding (OLE), in Chapter 24, "Integrating dBASE Applications with OLE and DDE."

Using these techniques, an object from one application used by another reflects the changes made to it in its original application since it was lent to the other.

Installing and Using the Bonus Disk

By Michael Groh

The 1.44 MB 3.5-inch disk included with *Inside dBASE 5 for Windows* contains all of the sample files described in this book. You are free to install these files on your computer, make any modifications to the documents, databases, and other materials as you wish. It is New Riders Publishing's intention that you continue learning about dBASE for Windows by implementing modifications to the materials included on this disk.

Before beginning the installation, please make sure adequate disk space is available. These files require about 2 MB of hard disk space to install properly. As you use these files, new files may be made and old files may be expanded. Please ensure adequate disk space is available for *Inside dBASE 5 for Windows Bonus Disk* files.

The disk includes a Windows setup program much like other Windows applications you may have installed. To run the installation program, perform the following steps:

- ✔ Open File Manager or Program Manager and select Run . . . from the File menu (open the file menu by pressing the F key while holding down the Alt key).
- ✔ Enter A:INSTALL in the Command line input field in the Run dialog box. If your 3.5-inch floppy disk is designated as B:, you should enter B:INSTALL instead of A:INSTALL.

  Alternatively, you could use File Manager to run INSTALL.EXE directly from the floppy disk. If you are unfamiliar with this process, consult your Microsoft Windows documentation to learn how to run applications from File Manager.
- ✔ The installation program will begin running.
- ✔ The first screen of the installation program asks for the path you want to use for the companion files. By default, this path is a directory named INSDBW in the DBASEWIN directory on the C: drive, although you can put the files anywhere.
- ✔ If the specified directory does not exist, the install program will create the target directory.
- ✔ The install program copies files from the floppy disk to the specified directory on the hard disk.

If you encounter problems with any of the sample applications on this disk, please feel free to contact New Riders Publishing through our fax number: (317)581-4670. You can also contact us through the Macmillan Computer Publishing forum on CompuServe (GO PHCP).

Because the sample files included on the bonus disk to *Inside dBASE 5 for Windows* were created by the authors of this book, we regret that we will not be able to provide technical support for these files.

Symbols

B

D

E

F

G

H

I

J

K

L

P

Q

R

S

T

U

V

W

X–Z

Inside dBase 5 for Windows

REGISTRATION CARD

Fill out this card to receive information about future dBASE books and other New Riders titles!

Name ______________________________ **Title** ____________________

Company ____

Address ____

City/State/ZIP ____

I bought this book because: ______________________________

____

I purchased this book from:

☐ A bookstore (Name ______________________)

☐ A software or electronics store (Name ______________)

☐ A mail order (Name of Catalog ___________________)

I purchase this many computer books each year:

☐ 1–5 ☐ 6 or more

I currently use these applications: ________________________

____

____

____

I found these chapters to be the most informative: ____________

____

I found these chapters to be the least informative: ____________

____

Additional comments: ____________________________________

____

☐ I would like to see my name in print! You may use my name and quote me in future New Riders products and promotions. My daytime phone number is: ____________________

New Riders Publishing 201 West 103rd Street • Indianapolis, Indiana 46290 USA

Fold Here

PLACE
STAMP
HERE

New Riders Publishing
201 West 103rd Street
Indianapolis, Indiana 46290
USA

Fold Here

PLACE
STAMP
HERE

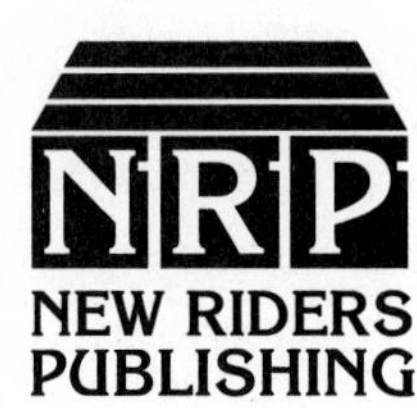

New Riders Publishing
201 West 103rd Street
Indianapolis, Indiana 46290
USA

WINDOWS TITLES

[illegible] [illegible] 13

FORREST HOULETTE, JIM BOYCE, RICH WAGNER, & THE BSU RESEARCH STAFF

The most up-to-date reference for Windows available!

Covers 3.1 and related products

ISBN: 1-56205-125-3

$39.95 USA

[illegible] [illegible] NT

FORREST HOULETTE, RICHARD WAGNER, GEORGE ECKEL, & JOHN STODDARD

A complete tutorial and reference to organize and manage multiple tasks and multiple programs in Windows NT.

Windows NT

ISBN: 1-56205-124-5

$34.95 USA

[illegible] [illegible] [illegible]

JIM BOYCE & ROB TIDROW

This helpful tutorial for Windows provides novice users with what they need to know to gain computer proficiency…and confidence!

Windows 3.1

ISBN: 1-56205-152-0

$18.95 USA

[illegible] [illegible]
APPLICATIONS

ELLEN DANA NAGLER, FORREST HOULETTE, MICHAEL GROH, RICHARD WAGNER, & VALDA HILLEY

This book is a no-nonsense, practical approach for intermediate- and advanced-level Windows users!

Windows 3.1

ISBN: 1-56205-083-4

$34.95 USA

What's on the *Inside dBASE 5 for Windows Bonus Disk*

- ✔ Sample documents: All of the sample documents use throughout *Inside dBASE 5 for Windows*
- ✔ HomeGuide: A complete sample application produced with dBASE 5 for Windows

Installing the *Inside dBASE 5 for Windows Bonus Disk*

The files on the *Inside dBASE 5 for Windows Bonus Disk* are compressed and cannot be used directly off the floppy disk. The files require approximately 2 MB of hard disk space in their expanded, usable form. Installation is quite simple:

1. From File Manager or Program Manager, choose the **R**un option in the **F**ile menu.
2. Enter *<drive>*\INSTALL and press Enter. *<drive>* is the designation of your 3.5" high-density floppy drive and is almost always either A or B.

Follow the on-screen instructions in the installation program. By default, the files will be installed in a subdirectory named C:\DBASEWIN\INSDBW unless you change this name during the install process. Each project described in *Inside dBASE 5 for Windows* has its own subdirectory in the INSDBW directory.